ST. BEDE'S SCHOOL

ASHBY   SCUNTHORPE

FIDES MUNDUM VINCIT

Attainment Prize : Form **First year**

Awarded to **John Byrne**

Date **Nov. 23rd 1970**

R. Doherty

Headmaster

J. P. McGillycuddy

Chairman of the Governors

gggg

The
Guinness
Book
of
Records

Standard Book Number SBN: 900424 02 8
Copyright 1970 by Guinness Superlatives Limited
Standard Book Number SBN: 900424 03 6
Southern African Edition
© 1970 by Guinness Superlatives Limited
World Copyright Reserved
Seventeenth Edition

Note.
In keeping with the standardardization sought by The Booksellers' Association,
The Library Association and The Publishers' Association,
editions have been designated thus:—

Edition	*Published*	
First Edition	October	1955
Second Edition	October	1955
Third Edition	November	1955
Fourth Edition	January	1956
Fifth Edition	October	1956
Sixth Edition	December	1956
Seventh Edition	November	1958
Eighth Edition	November	1960
Ninth Edition	April	1961
Tenth Edition	November	1962
Eleventh Edition	November	1964
Twelfth Edition	November	1965
Thirteenth Edition	October	1966
Fourteenth Edition	October	1967
Fifteenth Edition	October	1968
Sixteenth Edition	October	1969
Seventeenth Edition	October	1970

Note.
No back numbers are now available. Orders for current editions published overseas
will willingly be passed on to the publishers concerned. The date indicates the first year
an edition was established in the country concerned.

Guinness Book of World Records 1956 Casebound U.S.A.
Guinness Book of World Records 1962 Paperback U.S.A.
Le Livre des Extrêmes 1962 Casebound French
Guinness Das Buch Der Rekorde 1967 Paperback German
Guinness Korega Sekai Ichi 1968 Paper (2 vols.) Japanese
Guinness Rekord bog Først og Størst Sidst og Mindst 1970 Casebound Danish
Guinness Rekord bok Først og Størst Sist og Minst 1970 Casebound Norwegian
Enciclopedia Guinness de Superlativos Mundiales 1968 Paperback Spanish
Il Guinness dei Primati 1968 Italian
Guinness Ennätysten Kirja 1968 Casebound Finnish
Guinness Rekord bok Först och Störst 1968 Casebound Swedish
Het Groot Guinness Rekord Boek 1970 Casebound Dutch
Guinnessova kniha rekordu 1971 Paperback Czech

Designed by DENIS WRIGLEY, M.S.I.A.

with illustrations by Denis and Elsie Wrigley

Filmset by Layton-Sun Limited

Printed offset lithography by
Redwood Press Ltd. of Trowbridge,
Wiltshire, England
Made and Printed in Great Britain

 GUINNESS SUPERLATIVES LIMITED, 2 CECIL COURT, LONDON ROAD, ENFIELD, MIDDX.

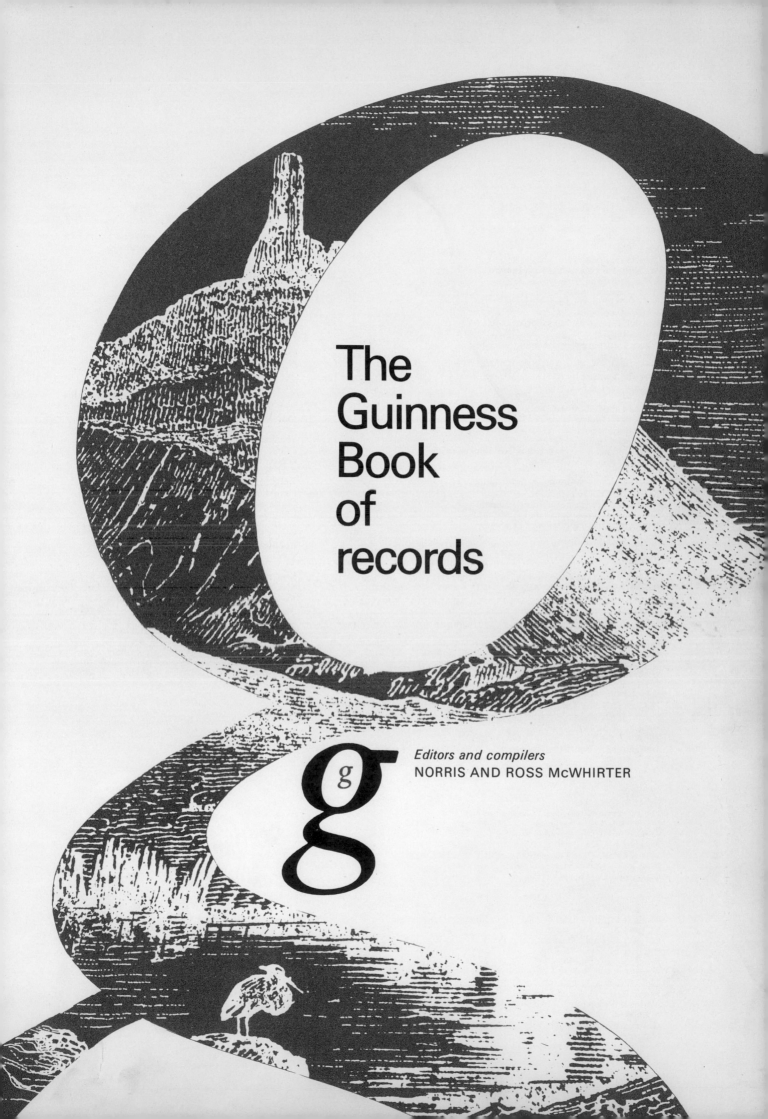

The Guinness Book of records

Editors and compilers
NORRIS AND ROSS McWHIRTER

Acknowledgements

Ian Allen & Co.
The Alpine Club
American Telephone & Telegraph Co.
J. W. Arblaster, Esq., A.I.M.
The Automobile Association
T. Banner, Esq.
James Bond
The Brewers' Society
The British Broadcasting Corporation
British European Airways
British Medical Association
British Museum (Natural History)
British Mycological Society
British Overseas Airways Corporation
British Rail
British Transport Commission
British Travel
British Waterworks Association
A. W. Bulley, Esq.
Burke's Peerage Ltd.
Central Electricity Generating Board
Central Office of Information
Dr. A. J. C. Charig
The Chemical Society
Church Commissioners
Conchological Society of Great Britain and Ireland
County Councils Association
Clerk of Dail Eireann
Department of Employment and Productivity
Eldon Pothole Club
Fédération Aéronautique Internationale
Fédération Internationale de l'Automobile
Fédération Internationale des Hôpitaux
George Fisher, Esq.
Frank L. Forster
Fortune
Dr. Francis C. Fraser
The Fur Trade Information Centre
General Motors Corporation
General Post Office
Geological Survey and Museum
The Gramophone Co. Ltd.
Greater London Council
W. T. Gunston, Esq., Flight International
John I. Haas Inc.
R. Hassell, Esq.
Michael E. R. R. Herridge, Esq.
The Home Office
Imperial War Museum
The Inland Waterways Association
Institut International des Châteaux Historiques
Institute of Strategic Studies
International Association of Volcanology
International Civil Aviation Organization
The Kennel Club
D. G. King-Hele, Esq., F.R.S.
Kline Iron and Steel Company
Frank W. Lane, Esq.
Dr. L. S. B. Leakey
The Library of Congress, Washington, D.C.
Lloyd's Register of Shipping
London Transport Board
J. Lyons & Co. Ltd.
Marconi's Wireless Telegraph Co. Ltd.
Prof. K. G. McWhirter, M.A., M.SC.
Meteorological Office
Metropolitan Police
Ministry of Agriculture, Fisheries and Food
Ministry of Defence
Ministry of Housing and Local Government
Ministry of Labour
Ministry of Public Buildings and Works
Ministry of Social Security
Ministry of Technology
Alan Mitchell, Esq.
The Museums Association
Music Research Bureau
National Aeronautics and Space Administration
National Coal Board
National Geographic Society
National Maritime Museum
National Physical Laboratory

The New York Times
The Patent Office Library
Photo Dealer Magazine
Port of New York Authority
Ransomes and Rapier Ltd.
Registrar General's Annual Report and Statistics Review
Registrar General's Office, Edinburgh
Jean Reville, Esq.
Rolls-Royce Ltd.
Royal Astronomical Society
Royal Botanic Gardens
Royal College of Surgeons of England
Royal Geographic Society
Royal National Life-boat Institution
Royal Norwegian Embassy
Sampson Low, Marston & Co. Ltd.
Dr. Albert Schwartz
B. A. Seaby Ltd.
Cdr. T. R. Shaw, R.N.
Siemens und Halske Aktiengesellschaft
Société Nationale des Chemins de Fer Français
Statutory Publications Office
John W. R. Taylor, Esq.
Time-Life International Inc.
The Treasury
Trinity House
U.N.E.S.C.O.
U.N. Statistical Office
United States Department of Agriculture
United States Department of the Interior
Water & Water Engineering
Gerry L. Wood, Esq., F.Z.S.
World Meteorological Organization
World Record Breakers Association
Zoological Society of London
Zoological Society of Philadelphia
Also to Mrs. Barbara Anderson, Miss Winnie Ashe,
Mrs. Christine Bethlehem, Mrs. Rosemary Bevan,
Mrs. Pamela Croome, Miss Trudy Doyle, Mlle. Béatrice
Frei, Harold C. Harlow, Esq., E. C. Henniker, Esq.,
Mrs. Angela Hoaen, David Hoy, Esq., Mrs. Eileen
Jackson, Mrs. Jane Mayo, G. M. Nutbrown, Esq.,
Mrs. Margaret Orr-Deas, Peter B. Page, Esq.,
John Rivers, Esq., Miss Wendy Shore, Mrs. Judith
Sleath, Mrs. Anne Symonds, Miss Hilary Tippett,
Miss Diana Wilford and, most particularly, to
Mr. Andrew Thomas (Associate Editor 1964–68)

Contents

ACKNOWLEDGEMENTS   8

FOREWORD *by The Rt. Hon. Earl of Iveagh*   10

PREFACE *by Norris and Ross McWhirter*   11

CHAPTER ONE

The human being
1. Dimensions   13
2. Origins   17
3. Longevity   18
4. Reproductivity   19
5. Physiology and Anatomy   22

CHAPTER TWO

Animal and plant kingdoms
1. Mammals   28
2. Birds   36
3. Reptiles   38
4. Amphibians   40
5. Fishes   41
6. Starfishes   42
7. Arachnids   42
8. Crustaceans   42
9. Insects   43
10. Centipedes   44
11. Millipedes   44
12. Segmented Worms   44
13. Molluscs   44
14. Ribbon Worms   45
15. Jelly Fishes   45
16. Sponges   45
17. Extinct Animals   45
18. Protista and Microbes   47
19. The Plant Kingdom   48

CHAPTER THREE

The natural world
1. Natural Phenomena   54
2. Structure and Dimensions   57
3. Weather   63

CHAPTER FOUR

The universe and space

CHAPTER FIVE

The scientific world

CHAPTER SIX

The arts and entertainments
1. Painting   84
2. Language   87
3. The Written Word   90
4. Music   97
5. Theatre   100
6. Gramophone   102
7. Cinema   104
8. Radio Broadcasting   105
9. Television   106

CHAPTER SEVEN

The world's structures
1. Buildings for Working   107
2. Building for Living   109
3. Buildings for Entertainment   111
4. Major Civil Engineering Structures   112
5. Specialized Structures   119

CHAPTER EIGHT

The mechanical world
1. Ships   126
2. Road Vehicles   131
3. Railways   134
4. Aircraft   137
5. Power Producers   142
6. Engineering   144

CHAPTER NINE

The business world
1. Commerce   147
2. Agriculture   158

CHAPTER TEN

Human achievements
1. Endurance and Endeavour   161
2. Honours, Decorations and Awards   178
3. Accidents and Disasters   182

CHAPTER ELEVEN

The human world
1. Political and Social   183
2. Military and Defence   191
3. Judicial   196
4. Economic   207
5. Education   218
6. Religions   220

CHAPTER TWELVE

Sports, games and pastimes   225

All Sports
Angling
Archery
Association Football (see Football)
Athletics (Track and Field)
Australian Rules (see Football)
Badminton
Baseball
Basketball
Beagling (see Fox Hunting)
Billiards
Bobsleigh
Bowling (Ten Pin)
Bowls
Boxing
Bridge (see Contract Bridge)
Bullfighting
Canoeing
Caving
Chess
Contract Bridge
Coursing
Cricket
Croquet
Cross-Country Running
Curling
Cycling
Darts
Diving (see Swimming)
Equestrian Sports
Eton Fives (see Fives)
Fencing
Fishing (see Angling)
Fives
Football (Association)
Football (Australian Rules)
Football (Gaelic)
Football (Rugby League)
Football (Rugby Union)
Fox Hunting
Gaelic Football (see Football)
Gambling
Gliding
Golf
Greyhound Racing
Gymnastics
Handball
Harness Racing (see Trotting)
Hockey
Horse Racing
Hurling
Ice Hockey
Ice Skating
Ice Yachting

Jai Alai (see Pelota Vasca)
Judo (Jiu-Jitsu)
Karate
Lacrosse
Lawn Tennis
Lugeing (see Bobsleigh)
Modern Pentathlon
Motorcycling
Motor Racing
Mountaineering
Netball
Olympic Games
Orienteering
Pelota Vasca (Jai Alai)
Pigeon Racing
Polo
Power Boat Racing
Rackets
Real Tennis (see Tennis)
Rodeo
Roller Skating
Rowing
Royal Tennis (see Tennis)
Rugby Fives (see Fives)
Rugby League (see Football)
Rugby Union (see Football)
Sailing (see Yachting)
Sculling (see Rowing)
Shooting
Show Jumping (see Equestrian Sports)
Skating (Ice) (see Ice Skating)
Skating (Roller) (see Roller Skating)
Ski-ing
Snooker
Speedway
Squash Rackets
Surfing
Swimming
Table Tennis
Tennis (Real or Royal)
Tiddlywinks
Tobogganing (see Bobsleigh)
Track and Field Athletics (see Athletics)
Trampolining
Trotting and Pacing
Tug of War (see Athletics)
Volleyball
Walking
Water Polo
Water Ski-ing
Weightlifting
Wrestling
Yachting

STOP PRESS and INDEX   308

Foreword

By the Rt. Hon. The Earl of Iveagh

When we first brought out this book, some fifteen years ago, we did so in the hope of providing a means for the peaceful settling of arguments about record performances in this record-breaking world in which we live. We realise, of course, that much joy lies in the argument, but how exasperating it can be if there is no final means of finding the answer.

In the event, we have found that the interest aroused by this book has exceeded our wildest expectations. We have now produced nearly 5,000,000 copies, and seven editions in the United States and translations into Czech, Danish, Dutch, French, Finnish, German, Italian, Japanese, Norwegian, Spanish and Swedish are showing the universality of its appeal. Whether the discussion concerns the smallest fish ever caught, the most expensive wine, the greatest weight lifted by a man, the furthest reached in space, the world's most successful racehorse, or—an old bone of contention—the longest river in the world, I can but quote the words used in introducing the first edition, "How much heat these innocent questions can raise: Guinness, in producing this book, hopes that it may assist in resolving many such disputes, and may, we hope, turn heat into light".

Iveagh

Chairman
Arthur Guinness, Son & Co., Ltd.
St. James's Gate Brewery, Dublin
Park Royal Brewery, London

October 1970

Preface

This seventeenth Edition has been completely revised and re-designed. We wish to thank correspondents from most of the countries of the world for raising or settling various editorial points. Strenuous efforts have been made to improve the value of the material presented and these will be continued in future editions.

Norris McWhirter

Editors and compilers

Ross McWhirter

October 1970   Guinness Superlatives Limited, 2 Cecil Court, London Road, Enfield, Middlesex.

g
g

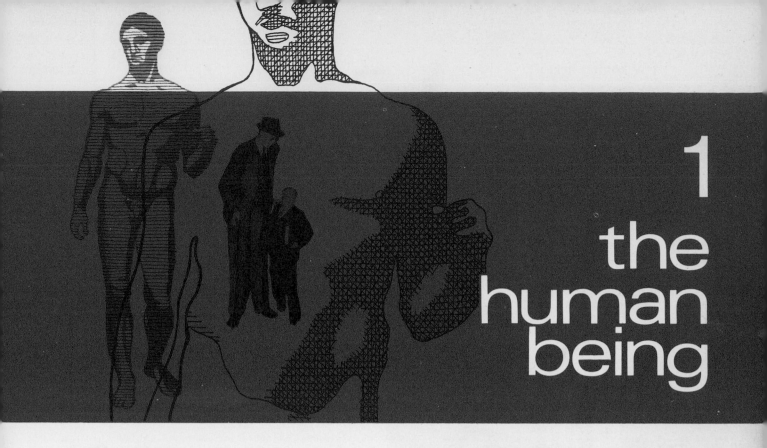

1. Dimensions

The height of human giants is a subject on which accurate information is frequently obscured by exaggeration and commercial dishonesty. The only admissible evidence on the true height of giants is that collected in recent years under impartial medical supervision.

The Biblical claim that Og, the Amorite king of Bashan and Gilead in *c.* 1450 B.C., stood 9 Hebrew cubits (13 feet 2½ inches) is based solely on the length of his basalt sarcophagus or "iron bedstead". The assertion that Goliath of Gath (*c.* 1060 B.C.) stood 6 cubits and a span (9 feet 6½ inches) suggests a confusion of units or some over-zealous exaggeration by the Hebrew chroniclers. The Jewish historian Flavius Josephus (born in A.D. 37 or 38, died after A.D. 93) and some of the manuscripts of the Septuagint (the earliest Greek translation of the Old Testament) attribute to Goliath the more credible height of 4 Greek cubits and a span (6 feet 10 inches).

Extreme mediaeval data, taken from bone measurements, invariably refer to specimens of extinct whale, giant cave bear, mastodon, woolly rhinoceros or other prehistoric non-human remains.

Paul Topinard (1830–1911), a French anthropometrist, stated that the tallest man who ever lived was Daniel Mynheer Cajanus (1714–49) of Finland, standing 283 centimetres (9 feet 3·4 inches). In 1872 his right femur, now in Leyden Museum, in the Netherlands, was measured by Prof. Carl Langer of Germany and indicated a height of 222 centimetres (7 feet 3·4 inches). Pierre Lemolt, a member of the French Academy, reported in 1847 that Ivan Stepanovich Lushkin (1811–44), a drum major in the Russian Imperial Regiment of Guards at Preobrazhenskiy, measured 3 arshin 9¼ vershok (8 feet 3¾ inches) and was "the tallest man that has ever lived in modern days". However, his left femur and tibia, which are now in the Museum of the Academy of Sciences in Leningrad, U.S.S.R., indicate a height of 7 feet 10¼ inches.

Circus giants and others who are exhibited are normally under contract not to be measured and are, almost traditionally, billed by their promoters at heights up to 18 inches in excess of their true heights. There are many notable examples of this, and 23 instances were listed in the *Guinness Book of Records* (14th Edition). The acromegalic giant Eddie Carmel (b. Tel Aviv, Israel, 1938), formerly the "World's Tallest Giant" of Ringling Bros. and Barnum & Bailey's Circus, is allegedly 8 feet 9¼ inches tall (weight 450 lb.), but photographic evidence suggests that his height is *c.* 7 feet 6 inches.

An extreme case of exaggeration concerned Siah Khān ibn Kashmir Khān (born 1913) of Bushehr (Bushire), Iran. Prof. D. H. Fuchs showed photographs of him at a meeting of the Society of Physicians in Vienna, Austria, in January 1935, claiming that he was 320 centimetres (10 feet 6 inches) tall. Later, when Siah Khān entered the Imperial Hospital in Teheran, it was revealed that his actual height was 220 centimetres (7 feet 2·6 inches).

Modern opinion is that the tallest recorded man of whom there is irrefutable evidence was Robert Pershing Wadlow, born on 22 Feb. 1918 in Alton, Illinois, U.S.A. Weighing 8½ lb. at birth, his abnormal growth began almost immediately. His height progressed as follows:

Age in Years	Height ft. ins.		Age in Years	Height ft. ins.		Age in Years	Height ft. ins.	
5	5	4	12	6	10¼	17	8	0½
8	6	0	13	7	1¾	18	8	3¼
9	6	2½	14	7	5	19	8	5½
10	6	5	15	7	8	20	8	6¾
11	6	7	16	7	10½	21	8	8¼

Dr. C. M. Charles, Associate Professor of Anatomy at Washington University's School of Medicine in St. Louis, Missouri, measured Robert Wadlow at 272 centimeteres (8 feet 11·1 inches) in St. Louis on 27 June 1940. Wadlow died 18 days later, on 15 July 1940, in Manistee, Michigan, as a result of cellulitis of the feet aggravated by a poorly fitted brace. He was buried in Oakwood Cemetery, Alton, Illinois in a coffin measuring 10 feet 9 inches in length, 32 inches wide and 30 inches deep. His greatest recorded weight was 491 lb. (35 stone 1 lb.), on his 21st birthday. He weighed 439 lb. (31 stone 5 lb.) at the time of his death. His shoes were size 37AA (18½ inches long) and his hands measured 12¾ inches from the wrist to the tip of the middle finger.

The human being

The tallest human of all-time Robert Wadlow (d. 1940) with his lawyer

The only other men for whom heights of 8 feet or more have been reliably reported are the seven listed below. In each case gigantism was followed by acromegaly, a disease which causes an enlargement of the extremities, especially the hands, feet, jaw and nose, due to renewed activity by the already over-large pituitary gland, which is located at the base of the brain.

John F. Carroll (born 1932) of Buffalo, New York State, U.S.A. (a) 8 feet 7¾ inches (263·5 centimetres).
John William Rogan (1871–1905), a Negro of Gallatin, Tennessee, U.S.A. (b) 8 feet 6 inches (259·1 centimetres).
Don Koehler (born 1926) of Chicago, Illinois, U.S.A. (c) 8 feet 2 inches (248·9 centimetres).
Väinö Myllyrinne (1909–63) of Helsinki, Finland (d) 8 feet 1·2 inches (247 centimetres).
Gabriel Estavão Monjane (born 1944) of Monjacaze, Mozambique (e) 8 feet 1 inch (246·3 centimetres).
Constantine (1872–1902) of Reutlingen, West Germany (f) 8 feet 0·8 inch (246 centimetres).
Sulaimān 'Alī Nashnush (born 1943) of Tripoli, Libya 8 feet 0·4 inch (245 centimetres).

(a) *Severe kypho-scoliosis (two dimensional spinal curvature). The figure represents his height with assumed normal spinal curvature, calculated from a standing height of 8 feet 0 inches, measured on 14 Oct. 1959. His standing height was 7 feet 10 inches in Nov. 1969.*
(b) *Measured in a sitting position. Unable to stand owing to ankylosis (stiffening of the joints through the formation of adhesions) of the knees and hips.*
(c) *He has a twin sister who is 5 feet 9 inches tall.*
(d) *Stood 7 feet 3½ inches at the age of 21 years. Experienced a second phase of growth in his late thirties.*
(e) *Abnormal growth started at the age of 10, following a head injury. He is still growing.*
(f) *Height estimated, as both legs were amputated after they turned gangrenous. He claimed a height of 259 centimetres (8 feet 6 inches).*

A table of the tallest giants of all-time in the 31 countries with men taller than 7 feet 4 inches (223·5 cms.) was listed in the 15th edition of the *Guinness Book of Records* (1968) at page 9.

The claim that Sa'īd Muhammad Ghazi (born 1909) of Alexandria, Egypt (now the United Arab Republic) attained a height of 8 feet 10 inches in February 1941 is now considered unreliable. Photographic evidence suggests his height was more nearly 7 feet 10½ inches, though he may have reached 8 feet at the time of his death.

England The tallest Englishman ever recorded was William Bradley (1788–1820), born in Market Weighton, in the East Riding of Yorkshire. He stood 7 feet 9 inches. John Middleton (1578–1623), the famous Childe of Hale, in Lancashire, was claimed to be 9 feet 3 inches, but the best modern evidence suggests that he was not more than 7 feet 8 inches. James Toller (1795–1819) of St. Neot's near Huntingdon, was alleged to be 8 feet 6 inches but was actually 7 feet 6 inches. Albert Brough (1871–1919), a publican of Nottingham, reached a height of 7 feet 7½ inches. Frederick Kempster (1889–1918) of Bayswater, London, was reported to have measured 8 feet 4½ inches at the time of his death, but photographic evidence suggests that his height was 7 feet 8½ inches. He measured 234 centimetres (7 feet 8·1 inches) in 1913. Henry Daglish, who stood 7 feet 7 inches, died in Upper Stratton, Wiltshire, on 16 March 1951, aged 25. The much-publicized Edward (Ted) Evans (1924–58) of Englefield Green, Surrey, was reputed to be 9 feet 3 inches but actually stood 7 feet 8½ inches. The tallest fully mobile man now living in Great Britain is Christopher Paul Greener (born 21 Nov. 1943 in New Brighton, Cheshire) of Hayes, Kent, who measures 7 feet 4¾ inches. Terence Keenan (born 1942) of Rock Ferry, Birkenhead, Cheshire measures 7 feet 6 inches, but is unable to stand erect owing to a leg condition. His abnormal growth began at the age of 17 when he was only 5 feet 4 inches tall.

Scotland The tallest Scotsman, and the tallest recorded "true" (non-pathological) giant, was Angus MacAskill (1825–63), born on the island of Berneray, in the Sound of Harris, in the Outer Hebrides. He stood 7 feet 9 inches and died in St. Ann's, on Cape Breton Island, Nova Scotia, Canada. Lambert Quételet (1796–1874), a Belgian anthropometrist, considered that a Scotsman named MacQuail, known as "the Scotch Giant", stood 8 feet 3 inches. He served in the famous regiment of giants of Frederick William I (1688–1740), King of Prussia. His skeleton, now in the Staatliche Museum zu Berlin, East Germany, measures 220 centimetres (7 feet 2·6 inches). Sam McDonald (1762–1802) of Lairg in Sutherland, was reputed to be 8 feet tall but actually stood 6 feet 10 inches. The tallest Scotsman now living is George Gracie (born 1938) of Forth, Lanarkshire. He stands 7 feet 3 inches and weighs 28 stone. His brother Hugh (born 1941) is 7 feet 0½ inch.

Wales The tallest Welshman ever recorded was George Auger (1886–1922), born in Cardiff, Glamorganshire. He stood 7 feet 7 inches and died in New York City, N.Y., U.S.A.

Ireland The tallest Irishman was Patrick Cotter O'Brian (1760–1806), born in Kinsale, County Cork. He died at Hotwells, Clifton, Bristol. He said that he was 8 feet 7¾ inches at the age of 26, but his actual living height was 7 feet 10·86 inches, calculated from measurements of his long bones made by Dr. Edward Fawcett, Professor of Anatomy at University College, Bristol, on 3 March 1906, after his coffin had been accidentally exposed.

The tallest Irishman now living is Jim Cully (born 1926) of Tipperary, a former boxer and wrestler. He stands 7 feet 2 inches.

Isle of Man The tallest Manxman ever recorded was Arther Caley (b. 16 Nov. 1829) of Sulby. He was variously credited with heights of 8 feet 2 inches and 8 feet 4 inches, but actually stood 7 feet 6 inches. He died at Clyde, New Jersey, U.S.A. on 12 Feb. 1889 aged 60.

TALLEST GIANTESSES

World Giantesses are, for reasons unknown, much rarer than giants and their heights are less spectacular. The tallest woman in medical history was Wassiliki Calliandji (1882–1904) of Corinth, Greece. She measured 230 centimetres (7 feet 6½ inches) and weighed 120 kilogrammes (18 stone 12½ lb.). The German giantess

Pauline Marianne Wehde (1866–83), long hailed as the tallest woman of all time, was billed at 254 centimetres (8 feet 4 inches) but her true height was estimated to be 224 centimetres (7 feet 4·2 inches). She weighed 160 kilogrammes (25 stone 3 lb.). Anna Swan (1846–88) of Nova Scotia, Canada, was billed at 8 feet 1 inch but actually measured 7 feet 5½ inches. In 1871 she married Martin van Buren Bates (1845–1919) of Whitesburg, Letcher County, Kentucky, U.S.A., who stood 7 feet 2½ inches. The French giantess Emma-Aline Batallaid (1877–95), *alias* "Lady Aama", claimed to be 244 centimetres (8 feet 0 inches) tall but her height at the time of her death was 6 feet 7¾ inches. Ella Ewing (1875–1913) of Gorin, Missouri, U.S.A., was billed at 8 feet 2 inches and reputedly measured 6 feet 9 inches at the age of 10 (*cf.* 6 feet 5 inches for Robert Wadlow at this age). She measured 7 feet 4½ inches at the age of 23 and may have attained 7 feet 6 inches by the time of her death.

The tallest woman living is believed to be Dolores Ann Pullard (born Aug. 1946), a negro girl living in De Quincy, Louisiana, U.S.A. She measured 6 feet 10 inches in March 1961 and grew to 7 feet 5 inches by October 1964. Miss Pullard is now confined to a wheelchair, but a sitting height of 5 feet 9½ inches was recorded for her on 8 Nov. 1967 thus indicating a standing height of about 7 feet 5½ inches. Katja van Dyke, born in 1905 at Roosendaal, in the Netherlands, claims to be 8 feet 4 inches, but is believed to be not more than 6 feet 11 inches. She measured 6 feet 4½ inches at the age of 16.

United Kingdom Britain's tallest ever giantess was probably Ann Hardy (1799–1815) of Rippingale, Lincolnshire, who reached a height of 7 feet 2 inches. She was 6 feet 1 inch and 13 stone at the age of 11. A height of 7 feet 2 inches has also been attributed to Mary Hales (1824–44) of Somerton, Norfolk. She was a sister of Robert Hales (1820–63), the famous "Norfolk Giant", who stood 7 feet 6 inches. Susannah Boyd (1803–31) of Seaford, Sussex, stood 7 feet 1 inch. Information is lacking on an unnamed giantess with a reputed height of 7 feet 5 inches, who died in *c.* 1810, aged 27.

SHORTEST DWARFS
The strictures which apply to giants apply equally to dwarfs, except that exaggeration gives way to understatement. In the same way as 9 feet may be regarded as the limit towards which the tallest giants tend, so 23 inches must be regarded as the limit towards which the shortest mature dwarfs tend (*cf.* the average length of new-born babies is 18 to 20 inches). In the case of child dwarfs the age is often enhanced by their agents or managers.

The shortest type of dwarf is an ateliotic dwarf, known as a midget. In this form of dwarfism the skeleton tends to remain in its infantile state. Midgets seldom grow to more than 40 inches tall. The most famous midget in history was Charles Sherwood Stratton, *alias* "General Tom Thumb", born on 11 Jan. 1832 in Bridgeport, Connecticut, U.S.A. He measured 25 inches at the age of 5 months and grew to only 70 centimetres (27·6 inches) by the age of 13½. He was 30½ inches tall at the age of 18 and 35 inches at 30. He stood 40 inches tall at the time of his death on 15 July 1883.

Another celebrated midget was Józef ("Count") Boruwlaski (born November 1739) of Poland. He measured only 8 inches long at birth, growing to 14 inches at the age of one year. He stood 17 inches at 6 years, 21 inches at 10, 25 inches at 15, 35 inches at 25 and 39 inches at 30. He died near Durham, England, on 5 Sept. 1837, aged 97.

World The shortest mature human of whom there is independent evidence was Pauline Musters ("Princess Pauline"), a Dutch midget. She was born at Ossendrecht on 26 Feb. 1876 and measured 12 inches at birth. At the age of 9 she was 55 centimetres (21·65 inches) tall and weighed only 1½ kilogrammes (3 lb. 5 oz.). She died, at the age of 19, of pneumonia, with meningitis, on 1

March 1895 in New York City, N.Y., U.S.A. Although she was billed at 19 inches, she was measured shortly before her death and was found to be 59 centimetres (23·2 inches) tall. A *post mortem* examination showed her to be exactly 24 inches (her body was slightly elongated after death). Her mature weight varied from 7½ lb. to 9 lb. and her "vital statistics" were 18½–19–17.

The Italian girl Caroline Crachami, born in Palermo, Sicily, in 1815, was only 20·2 inches tall when she died in London in 1824, aged 9. At birth she measured 7 inches long and weighed 1 lb. Her skeleton, measuring 19·8 inches, is now part of the Hunterian collection in the Museum of the Royal College of Surgeons, London.

Male The shortest recorded adult male dwarf was Calvin Phillips, born on 14 Jan. 1791 in Bridgewater, Massachusetts, U.S.A. He weighed 2 lb. at birth and stopped growing at the age of 5. When he was 19 he measured 26½ inches tall and weighed 12 lb. with his clothes on. He died two years later, in April 1812, from progeria, a rare disorder characterised by dwarfism and premature senility.

Another notable case was Max Taborsky, *alias* "Prince Kolibri", born in Vienna, Austria, in January 1863. He measured 35 centimetres (13·8 inches) at birth and stopped growing at the age of 9. When he died, aged 25, in 1888, he stood 69 centimetres (27·2 inches) tall and weighed 5 kilogrammes (11 lb.).

United Kingdom The shortest recorded British dwarfs were Hopkins Hopkins (1737–54) of Llantrisant, Glamorgan, and Miss Edith Barlow (1927–57) of Rotherham, Yorkshire, each 31 inches tall. Hopkins, who died from progeria (see above), weighed 19 lb. at the age of 7 and 13 lb. at the time of his death. Miss Barlow weighed 17 lb. Harold Pyott (1887–1937) of Hemel Hempstead, Hertfordshire, may have been equally short. Although he claimed to be only 23 inches tall, his coffin measured 35 inches.

Ireland The shortest recorded Irish adult dwarf was Mrs. Catharine Kelly (born in August 1756), known as "the Irish fairy", who stood 34 inches tall and weighed 22 lb. She died in Norwich, Norfolk, on 15 Oct. 1785.

Most variable stature By constant practice in muscular manipulation of the vertebrae, the circus performer Clarence E. Willard (1882–1962) of the United States was, in his prime, reputedly able to increase his stature from 5 feet 10 inches to 6 feet 4 inches at will.

RACES
Tallest The tallest race in the world is the Tutsi (also called Batutsi, Watutsi, or Watussi), Nilotic herdsmen of Rwanda and Burundi, Central Africa whose males average 6 feet 1 inch, with a maximum of 7 feet 6 inches. The Tehuelches of Patagonia long regarded as of gigantic stature (*i.e.* 7 to 8 feet) have in fact an average height (males) of 5 feet 10 inches with a maximum of just over 2 metres (6 feet 6¾ inches). A tribe with an average height of more than 6 feet was discovered in the inland region of Passis Manua of New Britain in December 1956. In May 1965 it was reported that the Crahiacoro Indians in the border district of the States of Mato Grosso and Pará, in Brazil, are exceptionally tall—certainly with an average of more than 6 feet. A report in May 1966 specifically attributed great stature to the Krem-Akarore Indians of the Xinga region of the Mato Grosso. In Dec. 1967 the inhabitants of Barbuda, Leeward Islands were reported to have an average height in excess of 6 feet. The tallest people in Europe are the Montenegrins of Yugoslavia, with a male average of 5 feet 10 inches, compared with the men of Sutherland, at 5 feet 9½ inches. In 1912 the average height of the men living in Balmachellan, Kirkcudbrightshire was reported to be 179 centimetres (5 feet 10·4 inches).

A Watusi

Shortest The world's smallest known race is the negrito Onge

The human being

tribe, of whom fewer than 500 survive on Little Andaman Island in the Indian Ocean. Few exceed 4 feet 6 inches. The smallest pygmies are the Mbuti, with an average height of 4 feet 6 inches for men and 4 feet 5 inches for women, with some groups averaging only 4 feet 4 inches for men and 4 feet 1 inch for women. They live in the forests near the river Ituri in the Congo (Kinshasa), Africa. In June 1936 there was a report, not subsequently substantiated, that there was a village of dwarfs numbering about 800 in the Hu bei (Hupeh) province of Central China between Wu han and Lishan in which the men were all less than 4 feet tall and the women slightly taller. The shortest Europeans, apart from those in the mineral-deficient Limousin Hills of France, are those living in the "instep" of southern Italy, with a mean of under 5 feet 2¼ inches.

WEIGHT

Heaviest heavyweights World Men The heaviest recorded human of all time was the 6 ft. 0½ in. tall Robert Earl Hughes (born 4 June 1926) of Monticello, Illinois, U.S.A. An 11¼ lb. baby, he weighed 14½ stone at six years, 27 stone at ten, 39 stone at 13, 49½ stone at 18, 64 stone at 25 and 67½ stone at 27. His greatest recorded weight was 1,069 lb. (76 stone 5 lb.) in February 1958, and he weighed 1,041 lb. (74 stone 5 lb.) at the time of his death. His claimed waist of 122 inches, his chest of 124 inches and his upper arm of 40 inches were also the greatest on record. He died of uraemia (a condition caused by retention of urinary matter in the blood) in a trailer at Bremen, Indiana, on 10 July 1958, aged 32, and was buried in Binville Cemetery, near Mount Sterling, Illinois, U.S.A. His coffin, a converted piano case measuring 7 feet by 4 feet 4 inches and weighing nearly half a ton, had to be lowered by crane.

Johnny Alee (1853–87) of Carbon (now known as Carbonton), North Carolina, U.S.A., is reputed to have weighed 1,132 lb. (80 stone 12 lb.) when he fell through the flooring of his log cabin to die of a heart attack as he was suspended by his armpits. The accuracy of this story has not yet been fully substantiated.

The only other men for whom weights of 800 lb. (57 stone 2 lb.) or more have been reliably reported are the 6 listed below:

	lb.	Stone	lb.
Mills Darden (1798–1857)			
U.S.A. (7 ft. 6 in.)	1,020	72	12
John Hanson Craig (1856–94)			
U.S.A. (6 ft. 5 in.)	907	64	11
Arthur Knorr (1914–60)			
U.S.A. (6 ft 1 in.)	900 (a)	64	4
T. A. Valenzuela (1895–1937)			
Mexico (5 ft. 11 in.)	850	60	10
David Maquire (1904–*fl.* 1935)			
U.S.A. (5 ft 10 in.)	810	57	12
William J. Cobb (b. 1926)			
U.S.A. (6 ft. 0 in.)	802 (b)	57	4

(a) Gained 300 lb. in the last 6 months of his life.
(b) Reduced to 232 lb. (16 stone 8 lb.) by July 1965.

The man now living who is believed to have weighed most is Charles ("Tiny") Kinsey (born *c.* 1923) of Galion, Ohio, U.S.A., who varies from 45 stone to 63 stone, but was reported to be down to 52 stone 11 lb. in August 1964. James Chassé (born 1940) of Vineland, New Jersey, U.S.A. was reported in November 1969 to have reached 750 lb. (53 stone 8 lb.).

Women The heaviest woman ever recorded was a negress whose name was not recorded. She died in Baltimore, Maryland, U.S.A., on 4 Sept. 1888. Her weight was stated to be 850 lb. (60 stone 10 lb.).

A more reliable and better documented case was that of Mrs. Flora Mae (or May) Jackson (*née* King), a 5 ft. 9 in. negress born in 1930 at Sugar Lark, Mississippi, U.S.A. She weighed 10 lb. at birth, 267 lb. (19 stone 1 lb.) at the age of 11, 621 lb. (44 stone 5 lb.) at 25 and 840 lb (60 stone) shortly before her death in Meridian, Florida, on 9 Dec. 1965. She was known in show business as "Baby Flo". In July 1967 an insupportable weight of 59 stone (826 lb.) was attributed to Mrs. Frances Voges of Tampa, who stood only 5 feet 1 inch tall and was thus the closest approach yet to a spherical woman.

Great Britain Men The heaviest recorded man in Great Britain was William Campbell, who was born in Glasgow in 1856 and died on 16 June 1878, when a publican at High Bridge, Newcastle upon Tyne, Northumberland. He was 6 feet 3 inches tall and weighed 53 stone 8 lb., with an 85-inch waist and a 96-inch chest. His coffin weighed 1,500 lb. He was "a man of considerable intelligence and humour". The only other British man with a recorded weight of more than 50 stone (700 lb.) was the celebrated Daniel Lambert (1770–1809) of Leicester. He stood 5 feet 11 inches tall, weighed 52 stone 11 lb. and had a girth of more than 92 inches.

The heaviest man living in Britain today is Arthur Armitage (born a 5 lb. baby on 28 June 1929) of Knottingley, Yorkshire, who scaled 40 stone 1 lb. (561 lb.) in his clothes in February 1970. He is 5 feet 9 inches tall and has vital statistics of 76–80–80.

Women The heaviest recorded woman in Great Britain was Miss Nellie Lambert (born 3 April 1894) of Leicester, who weighed 40 stone 3 lb. at the age of 19 years. She stood 5 feet 3 inches tall, with a waist of 88 inches and 26-inch bicep. She claimed to be a great granddaughter of Daniel Lambert (see above), though he was never married.

The heaviest human of all-time—Robert Hughes when he weighed only 50 stone (700 lb.)

Ireland The heaviest Irishman is reputed to have been Roger Byrne, who was buried in Rosenallis, County Laoighis (Leix), on 14 March 1804. He died in his 54th year and his coffin and its contents weighed 52 stone. Another Irish heavyweight was Lovelace Love (1731–66), born in Brook Hill, County Mayo. He weighed "upward of 40 stone" at the time of his death.

Heaviest twins The heaviest twins in the world are the McCreary twins (born 1948), farmers of Henderson County, North Carolina, U.S.A., who in February 1968 weighed 560 lb. (40 stone) and 640 lb. (45 stone 10 lb.). Their names are Bill and Ben.

Bill and Ben McCreary

Lightest humans The lightest recorded adult was Lucia Zarate (b. San Carlos, Mexico 2 Jan. 1863, d. Oct. 1889), an emaciated Mexican midget of $26\frac{1}{2}$ inches, who weighed $2\frac{1}{8}$ kilogrammes (4·7 lb.) at the age of 17. She "fattened up" to 13 lb. by her 20th birthday. At birth she weighed $2\frac{1}{4}$ lb. The lightest adult reported in the United Kingdom has been Hopkins Hopkins (Shortest dwarfs, see above).

The thinnest recorded adults of normal height are cases of extreme muscular atrophy when the bodyweight may be less than 40 lb. It was recorded that the American exhibitionist Rosa Lee Plemons (born 1873) weighed 27 lb. at the age of 18. Edward C. Hagner (1892–1962), *alias* Eddie Masher, is alleged to have weighed only 48 lb. (3 stone 6 lb.) at a height of 5 feet 7 inches. He was also known as "the Skeleton Dude". In August 1825 the biceps measurement of Claude-Ambroise Seurat (born 10 April 1797, died 6 April 1826) of Troyes, France was 4 inches and the distance between his back and his chest was less than 3 inches. According to one report he stood 5 feet $7\frac{1}{2}$ inches and weighed 78 lb. (5 stone 8 lb.) but in another account was described as 5 feet 4 inches and only 36 lb. (2 stone 8 lb.).

Seurat— the living skeleton (d. 1826)

Slimming The greatest recorded slimming feat was that of William J. Cobb (born 1926), *alias* "Happy Humphrey", a professional wrestler of Macon, Georgia, U.S.A. It was reported in July 1965 that he had reduced from 802 lb. (57 stone 4 lb.) to 232 lb. (16 stone 8 lb.), a loss of 570 lb. (40 stone 10 lb.), in 3 years. His waist measurement declined from 101 inches to 44 inches.

The U.S. circus fat lady Mrs. Celesta Geyer (born 1901), *alias* Dolly Dimples, reduced from 553 lb. to 152 lb. in 1950–51, a loss of 401 lb. in 14 months. Her vital statistics diminished *pari passu* from 79–84–84 to a *svelte* 34–28–36. Her book "How I lost 400 lbs." was not a best-seller because of the difficulty of would-be readers identifying themselves with the dressmaking problems of losing more than 28 stone when 4 ft. 11 ins. tall. In Dec. 1967 she was reportedly down to 110 lb. (7 st. 12 lb.). The speed record for slimming was established by Paul M. Kimelman, 21, of Pittsburgh, Pennsylvania, U.S.A., who from 25 Dec. 1966 to Aug. 1967 went on a crash diet of 300 to 600 calories per day to reduce from 427 lb. ($30\frac{1}{2}$ stone) to 130 lb. (9 st. 4 lb.). In his prime he wore size 56 trousers into one leg of which he can now step easily.

Weight gaining A probable record for gaining weight was set by Arthur Knorr (born 17 May 1914), who died on 7 July 1960, aged 46, in Reseda, California, U.S.A. He gained 300 lb. (21 stone 6 lb.) in the last 6 months of his life and weighed 900 lb. (64 stone 4 lb.) when he died. Miss Doris James of San Francisco, California, U.S.A. is alleged to have gained 325 lb. (23 stone 3 lb.) in the 12 months before her death in August 1965, aged 38, at a weight of 675 lb. (48 stone 3 lb.). She was only 5 feet 2 inches tall.

Man *(Homo sapiens)* is a species in the sub-family Homininae of the family Hominidae of the super-family Hominoidea of the sub-order Simiae (or Anthropoidea) of the order Primates of the infra-class Eutheria of the sub-class Theria of the class Mammalia of the sub-phylum Vertebrata (Craniata) of the phylum Chordata of the sub-kingdom Metazoa of the animal kingdom.

2. Origins

EARLIEST MAN

World The earliest known primates appeared in the Palaeocene period of about 70,000,000 years ago. The sub-order of higher primates, called Simiae (or Anthropoidea), evolved from the catarrhine or old-world sect nearly 30,000,000 years later in the Lower Oligocene period. During the Middle and Upper Oligocene the super-family Hominoidea emerged. This contains three accepted families, *viz* Hominidae (bipedal, ground-dwelling man or near man), Pongidae (brachiating forest apes) and Oreopithecidae, which includes *Apidium* of the Oligocene and *Oreopithecus* of the early Pliocene. Opinion is divided on whether to treat gibbons and their ancestors as a fourth full family (Hylobatidae) or as a sub-family (Hylobatinae) within the Pongidae. Some consider that Proconsulidae should also comprise a family, although others regard the genus *Proconsul,* who lived on the open savannah, as part of another sub-family of the Pongidae.

There is a conflict of evidence on the time during which true but primitive Hominidae were evolving. Fossil evidence indicates that it was some time during the Upper Miocene (about 10,000,000 to 12,000,000 years ago). The characteristics of the Hominidae, such as a large brain, very fully distinguish them from any of the other Hominoidea. Evidence published in August 1969 indicated that *Ramapithecus,* from the north-eastern Indian sub-continent, was not less than 8,000,000 years old and *Australopithecus,* from Eastern Africa possibly 6,000,000 years old.

The earliest known true member of the genus *Homo* was found between 6 Dec. 1960 and 1963 by Dr. Louis Seymour Bazett Leakey (b. 7 Aug. 1903 at Kabete, Kenya) Hon. Director of the Kenya National Museum's Centre for Pre-History and Palaeontology, in Nairobi, and his wife Mary in Bed I in the Olduvai Gorge, Tanganyika (now part of Tanzania). These remains have been determined by stratigraphic, radio-metric and fission-track dating to have existed between 1,750,000 and 2,300,000 years ago. They were first designated *"pre-Zinjanthropus"* but in March 1964 were renamed Handy Man (*Homo habilis*), to differentiate them from the more primitive Nutcracker Man (*Zinjanthropus boisei*), an East African australopithecine who was contemporary with Handy Man throughout Bed I and the greater part of Bed II times. Handy Man was about 4 feet tall.

In August 1965 a fragment of a *humerus* bone from a hominine upper arm was found near Kanapoi, Kenya, by Professor Bryan Patterson, a vertebrate palaeontologist of the Museum of Comparative Zoology at Harvard University, Cambridge, Massachusetts, U.S.A. It was announced in January 1967 that this bone dated from between 2,300,000 and 2,700,000 years ago.

The earliest recorded remains of the species *Homo sapiens,* variously dated from 300,000 to 450,000 years

The earliest dated hominid relic—8 million years old *Ramapithecus* from India

even into their third. The facts are that centenarians surviving beyond their 110th year are of the extremest rarity and the present absolute limit of proven human longevity does not admit of anyone living to celebrate a 114th birthday.

It is highly significant that in Sweden, where alone proper and thorough official investigations follow the death of every allegedly very aged citizen, none has been found to have surpassed 110 years. The most reliably pedigreed large group of people in the world, the British peerage, has, after ten centuries, produced only one peer who reached even his 100th birthday. However, this is possibly not unconnected with the extreme draughtiness of many of their residences.

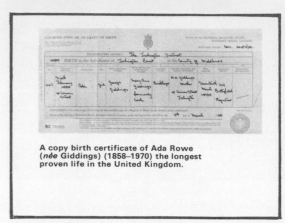

A copy birth certificate of Ada Rowe (*née* Giddings) (1858–1970) the longest proven life in the United Kingdom.

ago in the Middle Pleistocene, were discovered on 24 Aug. 1965 by Dr. Lászlo Vértes in a limestone quarry at Vértesszöllös, about 30 miles west of Budapest, Hungary. The remains, designated *Homo sapiens palaeo-hungaricus,* comprised an almost complete occipital bone, part of a skull with an estimated cranial capacity of nearly 1,400 cubic centimetres (85 cubic inches).

SCALE OF TIME
If the age of the Earth-Moon system (latest estimate at least 4,700 million years) is likened to a single year, Handy Man appeared on the scene at about 8.35 p.m. on 31 December, Britain's earliest known inhabitants arrived at about 11.32 p.m., the Christian era began about 13 seconds before midnight and the life span of a 113-year-old man (see page 19) would be about three-quarters of a second. Present calculations indicate that the Sun's increased heat, as it becomes a "red giant", will make life insupportable on Earth in about 10,000 million years. Meanwhile there may well be colder epicycles. The period of 1,000 million years is sometimes referred to as an aeon.

British Isles The earliest known inhabitants of the British Isles who belonged to the genus *Homo* were Clactonian man (probably fewer than 200 of them), one of whose middens was discovered in Aug. 1969 by Dr. Waechter in the Lower Gravels of the Barnfield Pit at Swanscombe, Kent, together with some of their discarded choppers made of flint cores and blunted flake tools. They probably lived in the Thames valley area during the first third of the Great Interglacial 500,000–475,000 B.C. The oldest human remains ever found in Britain are pieces of a brain case from a specimen of *Homo sapiens fossilis,* believed to be a woman, recovered in June 1935 and March 1936 by Dr. Alvan T. Marston from the Boyn Hill terrace in the Barnfield Pit, near Swanscombe, northern Kent. This find is attributed to Acheulian man, type *III* or *IV*, dating from the warm Hoxnian interglacial period, about 250,000 years ago.

The mandible found in the Red Crag at Foxhall, near Ipswich, in 1863, but subsequently lost in the United States, has been claimed as a Clactonian relic and thus possibly anything up to 100,000 years older than Swanscombe man.

The skulls of *Australopithecus*, a Neanderthal and modern man in silhouette

Scientific research into extreme old age reveals that the correlation between the claimed density of centenarians in a country and its regional illiteracy is 0·83 ±0·03. In late life, very old people often tend to advance their ages at the rate of about 17 years per decade. This was nicely corroborated by a cross analysis of the 1901 and 1911 censuses of England and Wales. Early claims must necessarily be without the elementary corroboration of birth dates. England was among the earliest of all countries to introduce local registers (1538) and official birth registration (1 July 1837), which was made fully compulsory only in 1874. Even in the United States, 45 per cent. of births occurring between 1890 and 1920 were unregistered.

Several celebrated super-centenarians are believed to have been double lives (father and son, brothers with the same names or successive bearers of a title). The most famous example is Christian Jakobsen Dracken-berg allegedly born in Stavanger, Norway on 18 Nov. 1626 and died in Aarhus, Denmark aged seemingly 145 years 326 days on 9 Oct. 1772. A number of instances have been commercially sponsored, while a fourth category of recent claims are those made for political ends, such as the 100 citizens of the Russian Soviet Federative Socialist Republic (population about 132,000,000 at mid-1967) claimed in March 1960 to be between 120 and 156. From data on documented centenarians, actuaries have shown that only one 115-year life can be expected in 2,100 million lives (*cf.* world population was estimated to be 3,600 million at mid-1970).

The height of credulity was reached on 5 May 1933, when a news agency solemnly filed a story from China with a Peking date-line that Li Chung-yun, the "oldest man on Earth", born in 1680, had just died aged 256 years (*sic*). Currently the most extreme case of longevity claimed in the U.S.S.R. is 164 years for Shirali Muslimov of Azerbaijan.

Mythology often requires immense longevity; for example Larak the god-King lived according to Sumerian mythology 28,800 years and Dumuzi even longer. The most extreme biblical claim is that for Methuselah at 969 years (Genesis V, verse 27).

3. Longevity

OLDEST CENTENARIAN
No single subject is more obscured by vanity, deceit, falsehood and deliberate fraud than the extremes of human longevity. Extreme claims are generally made on behalf of the very aged rather than by them.

Many hundreds of claims throughout history have been made for persons living well into their second century and some, insulting to the intelligence, for people living

A rare photograph
of Mrs. Margaret Neve
taken after she was 110
(see Channel Isles, above)

World The greatest authenticated age to which a human has ever lived is 113 years 124 days in the case of Pierre Joubert, a French-Canadian bootmaker. He was born in Charlesbourg, Québec Province, Canada, on 15 July 1701, son of Pierre Joubert (b. 1670) and Magdeleine Boesmier, and died in Québec on 16 Nov. 1814. His longevity was the subject of an investigation in 1870 by Dr. Tache, Official Statistician to the Canadian Government, and the proofs published are irrefutable. The following national records can be taken as authentic:—

	Years	Days		Born		Died	
Canada (a)	113	124	Pierre Joubert	15 July	1701	16 Nov.	1814
United States (b)	112	305	John B. Salling	15 May	1846	16 Mar.	1959
United Kingdom (c)	111	339	Ada Rowe (*née* Giddings)	6 Feb.	1858	11 Jan.	1970
Ireland	111	327	The Hon. Katherine Plunket	22 Nov.	1820	14 Oct.	1932
South Africa (d)	111	151	Johanna Booyson	17 Jan.	1857	16 June	1968
Czechoslovakia	111	+	Marie Bernatkova	22 Oct.	1857	*fl.* Oct.	1968
Channel Islands	110	321	Margaret Ann Neve (*née* Harvey)	18 May	1792	4 April	1903
Yugoslavia	110	150+	Demitrius Philipovitch	9 Mar.	1818	*fl.* Aug.	1928
Japan (e)	110	114	Yoshigiku Ito	3 Aug.	1856	26 Nov.	1966
Netherlands	110	5	Baks Karnebeek (Mrs.)	2 Oct.	1849	7 Oct.	1959
France	109	309	Marie Philoméne Flassayer	13 June	1844	18 April	1954
Italy	109	179	Rosalia Spoto	25 Aug.	1847	20 Feb.	1957
Australia (f)	109	37	James Hull	3 Aug.	1852	9 Sept.	1961
Scotland	109	14	Rachel MacArthur (Mrs.)	26 Nov.	1827	10 Dec.	1936
Norway	109	+	Marie Olsen (Mrs.)	1 May	1850	*fl.* May	1959
Tasmania	109	+	Mary Ann Crow (Mrs.)	2 Feb.	1836		1945
Germany (g)	108	128	Luise Schwatz	27 Sept.	1849	2 Feb.	1958
Portugal	108	+	Maria Luisa Jorge	7 June	1859	*fl.* July	1967
Scotland	107	108	Jane Spier (Mrs.)	23 Nov.	1848	12 Mar.	1956
Finland	107	+	Marie Anderson	3 Jan.	1829		1936
Belgium	106	267	Marie-Joseph Purnode (Mrs.)	17 April	1843	9 Nov.	1949
Austria	106	231	Anna Migschitz	3 Feb.	1850	1 Nov.	1956
Sweden	106	98	Emma Gustaffsson (Mrs.)	18 June	1858	14 Sept.	1964
Isle of Man	105	221	John Kneen	12 Nov.	1852	9 June	1958
Spain (h)	105	217	Maria Cid Cabanes	25 Feb.	1845	30 Nov.	1950

(a) *Mrs. Ellen Carroll died in North River, Newfoundland, Canada on 8 December 1943, reputedly aged 115 years 49 days.*
(b) *Mrs. Betsy Baker (née Russell) was allegedly born 20 August 1842 in Brington, Northamptonshire, and died in Teoumseh, Nebraska, U.S.A. on 24 October 1955, reputedly aged 113 years 65 days. The 67-year old son of Mrs. Tatzumbie Dupea, a Piute Indian at the Good Hope Convalescent Center, Los Angeles claimed that her birthday on 26 July 1969 was not her 112th but her 120th.*
(c) *London-born Miss Isabella Shepeard was allegedly 115 years old when she died at St. Asaph, Flintshire, North Wales, on 20 November 1948, but her actual age was believed to have been 109 years 90 days. Charles Alfred Nunez Arnold died in Liverpool on 15 Sept. 1941 reputedly aged 112 years 66 days based on baptismal evidence.*
(d) *Mrs. Susan Johanna Deporter of Port Elizabeth, South Africa, was reputedly 114 years old when she died on 4 August 1954. Mrs. Sarah Lawrence, Cape Town, South Africa reputedly 112 on 3 March 1968.*
(e) *A man named Nakamura of Kamaishi, northern Japan, was reported to have died on 4 May 1969 aged 116 years 329 days.*
(f) *Reginald Beck of Sydney, New South Wales, Australia was allegedly 111 years old when he died on 13 April 1928.*
(g) *Friedrich Sadowski of Heidelberg reputedly celebrated his 111th birthday on 31 October 1936.*
(h) *Juana Ortega Villarin, Madrid, Spain, allegedly 112 in February 1962.*

The oldest living Britons among an estimated 850 centenarians are Miss Elizabeth Nichol (born 13 May 1861) of Queen's Gate, Kensington, London and Miss Alice Stevenson (born 10 July 1861) of Brambleacres Old People's Home, Worcester Road, Sutton, Surrey. In the face of the above data the claim published in the April 1961 issue of the Soviet Union's *Vestnik Statistiki* ("Statistical Herald") that there were 224 male and 368 female Soviet citizens aged in excess of 120 recorded at the census of 15 Jan. 1959 indicates a reliance on hearsay rather than evidence. Official Soviet insistence on the unrivalled longevity of the country's citizenry is curious in view of the fact that the 592 persons in their unique "over 120" category must have spent at least the first 78 years of their prolonged lives under Tsarism. It has recently been suggested that the extreme ages claimed by some men in Georgia, U.S.S.R., are the result of attempts to avoid military service when they were younger, by assuming the identities of older men.

Most reigns The greatest number of reigns during which any English subject could have lived is ten. A person born on the day (11 April) that Henry VI was deposed in 1471 had to live to only the comparatively modest age of 87 years 7 months and 6 days to see the accession of Elizabeth I on 17 Nov. 1558. Such a person could have been Thomas Carn of London, born 1471 and died 28 Jan. 1578 in his 107th year.

4. Reproductivity

MOTHERHOOD

Most children
World The greatest number of children produced by a mother in an independently attested case is 69 by the first wife of Fyodor Vassilet a peasant of the Moscow Jurisdiction, Russia, who, in 27 confinements, gave birth to 16 pairs of twins, 7 sets of triplets and 4 sets of quadruplets. Most of the children attained their majority. Mme. Vassilet (1816–72) became so renowned that she was presented at the court of Tsar Alexander II.

Great Britain The British record is held by Mrs. Elizabeth Greenhill (*c.* 1615–1681) of Abbot's Langley, Hertfordshire. It is alleged that she gave birth to 39 children (32 daughters and 7 sons), all of whom attained their majority between 1652 and 1690. She was married at 16, had 38 confinements and died at the age of 66. Her descendant Thomas (1681–?1740) became surgeon to the 10th Duke of Norfolk and was the author of the "Art of Embalming" (1705).

Great Britain's champion mothers of today are believed to be Mrs. Margaret McNaught, 48 of Balsall Heath, Birmingham (12 boys and 10 girls, all single births) and Mrs. Mable Constable, 51 of Long Itchington,

The human being

Warwickshire who also has had 22 children including a set of triplets and two sets of twins.

Oldest World Medical literature contains extreme but unauthenticated cases of septuagenarian mothers. The oldest recorded mother of whom there is certain evidence is Mrs. Ruth Alice Kistler (*née* Taylor), formerly Mrs. Shepard, of Portland, Oregon, U.S.A. She was born at Wakefield, Massachusetts, on 11 June 1899 and gave birth to a daughter, Suzan, at Glendale, near Los Angeles, California, on 18 Oct. 1956, when her age was 57 years 129 days. The incidence of quinquagenarian births varies widely with the highest known rate in Albania (nearly 5,500 per million).

Great Britain The oldest British mother reliably recorded is Mrs. Winifred Wilson (*née* Stanley) of Eccles, Lancashire. She was born in Wolverhampton on 11 Nov. 1881 or 1882 and had her tenth child, a daughter Shirley, on 14 Nov. 1936, when aged 54 or 55 years and 3 days. At Southampton on 10 Feb. 1916, Mrs. Elizabeth Pearce gave birth to a son when aged 54 years 40 days. It is believed that live births to quinquagenarian mothers occur only twice in each million births in England and Wales.

Ireland The oldest Irish mother recorded was Mrs. Mary Higgins of Cork, County Cork (born 7 Jan. 1876) who gave birth to a daughter, Patricia, on 17 March 1931 when aged 55 years 69 days.

Descendants In polygamous countries, the number of a person's descendants can become incalculable. The last Sharifian Emperor of Morocco, Moulay Ismail, known as "The Bloodthirsty", was reputed to have fathered a total of 548 sons and 340 daughters.

Capt. Wilson Kettle (born 1860) of Grand Bay, Port aux Basques, Newfoundland, Canada, died on 25 Jan. 1963, aged 102, leaving 11 children by two wives, 65 grandchildren, 201 great-grandchildren and 305 great-great-grandchildren, a total of 582 living descendants. Mrs. Johanna Booyson (see page 19), of Belfast, Transvaal, was estimated to have 600 living descendants in South Africa in January 1968.

Mrs. Sarah Crawshaw (died 25 Dec. 1844) left 397 descendants, according to her gravestone in Stones Methodist Church, Ripponden, Halifax, Yorkshire.

Multiple great grandparents Theoretically a great-great-great-great-grandparent is a possibility, though in practice countries in which young mothers are common generally have a low expectation of life. Mrs. Betty Haley of Hanford, California, who died, aged 94, on 10 Jan. 1956, had two great-great-great-grandchildren among her 256 living descendants, while Hon. General Walter Washington Williams (1855–1959) of Houston, Texas, U.S.A., was reportedly several times a great-great-great-grandfather.

MULTIPLE BIRTHS

World With multiple births, as with giants and centenarians, exaggeration is the rule. Since 1900 one case of nonuplets, five cases of octuplets, 18 cases of septuplets and at least 22 cases of sextuplets have been reported. It was reported on 5 July 1966 that nonuplets had been born in Punjarai, East Pakistan, but it was admitted on 12 July that the report was a hoax. Jamaica is believed to have the highest incidence of multiple births (*i.e.* triplets and upward) at 4 such births per 1,000.

Octuplets The only confirmed case of live-born octuplets was the four boys and four girls born to Señora María Teresa Lopez de Sepulveda, aged 21, in a nursing home in Mexico City, Mexico, between 7 p.m. and 8 p.m. on 10 March 1967. They had an aggregate weight of 9 lb. 10 oz. and ranged between 1 lb. 3 oz. down to 14 oz. All the boys were named José and all the girls Josefina. They all died within 14 hours.

There have been four unconfirmed reports of octuplets since 1900: to Señora Enriquita Ruiba at Tampico, Mexico, in 1921; seven boys and one girl to Mme. Tam Sing at Kwoom Yam Sha, China, in June 1934; a case near Tientsin, China, on 29 Sept. 1947 (one baby died); and still-born babies to Señora Celia Gonzalez at Bahía Blanca, Argentina, on 2 May 1955.

Septuplets There have been five confirmed cases of septuplets since 1900: still-born babies to Britt Louise Ericsson, aged 34, in Uppsala, Sweden, in August 1964; five girls and two boys to Mme. Brigitte Verhaeghe-Denayer in Brussels, Belgium, on 25 March 1966 (all the babies died soon afterwards); four girls and three boys to Mrs. Sandra Cwikielnik in Boston, Massachusetts, U.S.A., on 1 Oct. 1966 (one was born dead and the others died within minutes); a case from Addis Ababa, Ethiopia in March 1969 of seven babies to Mrs. Verema Jusuf of whom two died immediately and a still-born set born in Sweden in 1966.

Sextuplets Among sextuplet births, the case of Mrs. Philip Speichinger provided the earliest irrefutable evidence in the person of a surviving daughter, Marjorie Louise of Mendon, Missouri, U.S.A., born on 9 Aug. 1936. The other five children were still-born. Mrs. Alinicia Parker (*née* Bushnell) was always cited as last survivor of the sextuplets reputedly born on 15 Sept. 1866 to Mrs. James B. Bushnell in Chicago, Illinois, U.S.A. She died, aged 85, in Warsaw, New York State, U.S.A., on 27 March 1952. The birth was registered by Dr. James Edwards but, for obscure reasons, was unrevealed until about 1912. The other children were identified as Lucy (died at 2 months), Laberto (died at 8 months), Norberto (died in 1934), Alberto (died in Albion, N.Y., in *c.* 1940) and Mrs. Alice Elizabeth Hughes (*née* Bushnell) who died in Flagstaff, Arizona, on 2 July 1941. From the sextuplets born to Maria Garcia wife of an Indian farmer in Michoacán State, Mexico, on 7 Sept. 1953, three (one boy and two girls) are reputedly still living. A woman living in a remote village in the Faridpur district of East Pakistan allegedly gave birth to six sons on 11 Nov. 1967.

Mrs. Sheila Ann Thorns (b. 2 Oct. 1938) of Northfield, Birmingham, England, gave birth to sextuplets at the New Birmingham Maternity Hospital on 2 Oct. 1968. In order of birth they were Lynne (2 lb. 6 oz., died 22nd), Ian (2 lb. 13 oz., died 13th), Julie (3 lb. 1 oz.), Susan (2 lb. 11 oz.), Roger (2 lb. 10 oz.) and a girl (died after one hour). A seventh child did not develop beyond the third month of this pregnancy which had been induced by a fertility drug. A second set of British sextuplets were delivered, after use of a fertility drug, of Mrs. Rosemary Letts (*née* Egerton) 23 of Rickmansworth, Hertfordshire by Caesarean section at University College Hospital, London on 15 Dec. 1969. One girl was still-born but the others Cara Dawn (2 lb. 13 oz.), Sharon Marie (2 lb. 9 oz.), Joanne (2 lb. 7 oz.), Gary John (1 lb. 11½ oz.) and Tanya (2 lb. 1 oz.) survived.

Quintuplets The earliest quintuplets in which all survived were: Émilie (died 6 Aug. 1954, aged 20), Yvonne (now in a convent), Cécile (now Mrs. Phillipe Langlois), Marie (later Mrs. Florian Houle died 1 March 1970) and Annette (now Mrs. Germain Allard), born in her seventh pregnancy to Mrs. Oliva Dionne aged 25, near Callander, Ontario, Canada, on 28 May 1934 (aggregate weight 13 lb. 6 oz. with a range of 4 lb. 3 oz. to 3 lb. 1 oz.).

The Dionne quintuplets—born 1934

Quintuplets were recorded in Wells, Somerset on 5 Oct. 1736 where four boys and a girl were all christened. Quins (three boys and two girls) were born to Mrs. Elspet Gordon of Rothes, Morayshire, Scotland in 1858 but all died within 12 hours and at Over Darwen, Lancashire on 24 April 1786 Mrs. Margaret Waddington produced five girls (three still-born) weighing a total of 2 lb. 12 oz.

Quins were born to Mrs. Irene Mary Hanson, 33 of Rayleigh, Essex at the Queen Charlottes Maternity Hospital, Hammersmith, London on 13 Nov. 1969. They are Joanne Lesley (2 lb. 7 oz.), Nicole Jane (2 lb. 13 oz.), Julie Anne (2 lb. 15 oz.), Sarah Louise (3 lb. 7 oz.) and Jacqueline Mary (2 lb. 6½ oz.). A fertility drug was used.

viest quins It was reported that quintuplets weighing 25 lb. were born on 7 June 1953 to Mrs. Lui Saulien of Chekiang province, China. A weight of 25 lb. was also reported for girl quins born to Mrs. Kamalammal in Pondicherry, India, on 30 Dec. 1956. All died shortly afterwards.

uadruplets Heaviest The heaviest quadruplets ever recorded were Brucina Paula (5 lb. 7 oz.), Clifford (5 lb. 0 oz.), Stanford (4 lb. 15 oz.) and Stacey Lynn (4 lb. 7 oz.), totalling 19 lb. 13 oz., born by Caesarean section to Mrs. Ruth Becker, aged 28, between 5.15 a.m. and 5.18 a.m. on 3 Aug. 1962 at the Vancouver General Hospital in Vancouver, British Columbia, Canada.

United Kingdom The earliest recorded quadruplets to have all survived in the United Kingdom were the Miles quads, born at St. Neot's, Huntingdon, on 28 Nov. 1935—Ann (now Mrs Robert Browning), Ernest, Paul and Michael (total weight 13 lb. 15½ oz.). Sarah Coe, one of the quads born to Mrs. Henry Coe of Cambridge on 6–7 Oct. 1766 was reportedly still alive 42 years later in 1808. The other three died at 2, 15 and 20 months respectively. The heaviest set recorded were David John (5 lb. 7 oz.), Thelma Susan (4 lb. 1 oz.), Anthony James (5 lb. 1 oz.) and Beverley Margaret (3 lb. 14 oz.), totalling 18 lb. 7 oz., born on 14 Dec. 1957 to Mrs. Mary Bennett, aged 37, in the East End Maternity Hospital, Stepney, London. The lightest were Yana (3 lb. 8 oz.), Edward (3 lb. 3½ oz.), Lucille (3 lb. 8 oz.) and Christopher (2 lb. 7½ oz.), totalling 12 lb. 11 oz., born to Mrs. Phoebe Meacham (born 1928) of Leigh-on-Sea in Rochford Hospital, Essex, on 3 Jan. 1962.

Ireland The first surviving quadruplets born in Ireland were those born on 23 Jan. 1965 to Mrs. Eileen O'Connell, aged 36, of Pallasgreen, County Limerick, in the Limerick Regional Hospital. On 31 Jan. 1965 they were weighed: Catherine Mary (2 lb. 2 oz.), Gerard Michael (3 lb. 6 oz.), John Paul (3 lb. 11 oz.) and Margaret Anne (3 lb.).

TRIPLETS

Heaviest There is an unconfirmed report of triplets weighing 23 lb., born in Australia in 1946 and one (two boys and a girl) of 26 lb. 6 oz. born to a 21-year-old Iranian woman reported on 18 March 1968. The heaviest recorded triplets born in the United Kingdom, were Robert (7 lb. 5 oz.), Geoffrey (6 lb. 2 oz.) and Paul (8 lb. 6 oz.), born between 8.10 p.m. and 8.25 p.m. on 8 Feb. 1965 to Mrs. Maureen Head, aged 25, of Colwyn Bay, Denbighshire, in the H.M. Stanley Hospital, St. Asaph, Flintshire. They weighed an aggregate of 21 lb. 13 oz.

TWINS

Heaviest The heaviest recorded twins were two boys, the first weighing 17 lb. 8 oz. and the second 18 lb., born in Derbyshire. This was reported in a letter in *The Lancet* of 6 Dec. 1884. A more reliable recent case is that of Jerrald and Jerraldine, weighing 11 lb. each, born at 5.45 a.m. and 7.45 a.m. on 8 Jan. 1941 to Mrs. Beulah Paris (*née* Sehie), aged 34, at her home in Stanford, 4 miles from Louisville, Illinois, U.S.A.

Lightest The lightest recorded birthweight for surviving twins has been 3 lb. 2 oz. in the case of Wendy and Susan, born prematurely on 10 May 1961 to Mrs. Garner in St. Luke's Hospital, Huddersfield, Yorkshire.

Oldest The chances of identical twins both reaching 100 are said to be one in 1,000 million. The oldest recorded twins were Gulbrand and Bernt Morterud, born at Nord Odal, Norway, on 20 Dec. 1858. Bernt died on 1 Aug. 1960 in Chicago, Illinois, U.S.A. age 101, and his brother died at Nord Odal on 12 Jan. 1964, aged 105. Twin sisters, Mrs. Vassilka Dermendjhieva and Mrs. Vassila Yapourdjieva of Sofia, Bulgaria allegedly celebrated their joint 104th birthday on 27 Sept. 1966.

"Siamese" Conjoined twins derived the name "Siamese" from the celebrated Chang and Eng Bunker, born at Maklong, Thailand (Siam), on 11 May 1811. They were joined by a cartilaginous band at the chest and married in April 1843 the Misses Sarah and Adelaide Yates and fathered ten and twelve children respectively. They died within three hours of each other on 17 Jan. 1874, aged 62. There is no genealogical evidence for the existence of the much-publicized Chalkhurst twins, Mary and Aliza, of Biddenden, Kent, allegedly born in c. 1550 (not 1100). Daisy and Violet Hilton, born in Brighton, Sussex on 5 Feb. 1908, were joined at the hip. They died in Charlotte, North Carolina, U.S.A. on 5 Jan. 1969 aged 60.

The original Siamese twins—Chang and Eng Bunker (1811–1874)

The human being

BABIES

LARGEST

World The heaviest normal new-born child recorded in modern times was a boy weighing 11 kilogrammes (24 lb. 4 oz.), born on 3 June 1961 to Mrs. Saadet Cor of Ceyhan, southern Turkey. There is an unconfirmed report of a woman giving birth to a 27 lb. baby in Essonnes, a suburb of Corbeil, central France, in June 1929. A deformed baby weighing 29¼ lb. was born in May 1939 in a hospital at Effingham, Illinois, U.S.A.

United Kingdom The greatest recorded live birth weight in the United Kingdom is 21 lb. for a child born on Christmas Day, 1852. It was reported in a letter to the *British Medical Journal* (1 Feb. 1879) from a doctor in Torpoint, Cornwall. The only other reported birth weight in excess of 20 lb. is 20 lb. 2 oz. for a boy born to a 33-year-old schoolmistress in Crewe, Cheshire, on 12 Nov. 1884. A baby of 33 lb. was reportedly born to a Mrs. Lambert of Wandsworth Road, London *c.* 1930 but its measurements indicate a weight of about 17 lb.

Ireland The heaviest baby recorded in Ireland was Anthony Michael Kinch, weighing 17 lb. 3 oz., who was born on 13 June 1950 to Mrs. Mary Kinch, aged 34, of Bray, County Wicklow

SMALLEST

The lowest birth weight for a surviving infant, of which there is definite evidence, is 10 oz. in the case of Marion Chapman, born on 5 June 1938 in South Shields, County Durham. She was 12¼ inches long. By her first birthday her weight had increased to 13 lb. 14 oz. She was born unattended and was nursed by Dr. D. A. Shearer, who fed her hourly through a fountain pen filler. Her weight on her 21st birthday was 7 stone 8 lb.

A weight of 8 oz. was reported on 20 March 1938 for a baby born prematurely to Mrs. John Womack, after she had been knocked down by a lorry in East Louis, Illinois, U.S.A. The baby was taken alive to St. Mary's Hospital, bur further information is lacking. On 23 Feb. 1952 it was reported that a 6 oz. baby only 6½ inches long lived for 12 hours in a hospital in Indianapolis, Indiana, U.S.A. A twin was still-born.

Longest pregnancy The longest pregnancy reported is one of 389 days for a woman aged 25 in Woking Maternity Hospital, Surrey, England (*Lancet*, 3 Dec. 1954). The baby, weighing 7 lb. 14 oz., was still-born. The average pregnancy is 273 days.

5. Physiology and Anatomy

BONES

Longest The thigh bone or *femur* is the longest of the 206 bones in the human body. It constitutes usually 27½ per cent. of a person's stature, and may be expected to be 19¾ inches long in a 6-foot-tall man. The longest recorded bone was the *femur* of the German giant Constantine, who died in Mons, Belgium, on 30 March 1902, aged 30 (see page 14). It measured 76 centimetres (29·9 inches). The *femur* of Robert Wadlow, the tallest man ever recorded, measured approximately 29½ inches.

Smallest The *stapes* or stirrup bone, one of the three auditory ossicles in the middle ear, is the smallest human bone, measuring from 2·6 to 3·4 millimetres (0·10 to 0·17 of an inch) in length and weighing from 2·0 to 4·3 milligrammes (0·03 to 0·065 of a grain). Sesamoids are not included among human bones.

MUSCLES

Largest Muscles normally account for 40 per cent. of the body weight and the bulkiest of the 639 muscles in the human body is the *gluteus maximus* or buttock muscle, which extends the thigh.

Smallest The smallest muscle is the *stapedius,* which controls the *stapes* (see above), an auditory ossicle in the middle ear, and which is less than 1/20th of an inch long.

Smallest waists Queen Catherine de Medici (1519–89) decreed a waist measurement of 13 inches for ladies of the French court. This was at a time when females were more diminutive. The smallest recorded waist among women of normal stature in the 20th century is a reputed 13 inches in the case of the French actress Mlle. Polaire (1881–1939) and Mrs. Ethel Granger (born 12 April 1905) of Peterborough, who reduced from a natural 22 inches over the period 1929–1939.

Largest chest measurements The largest chest measurements are among endomorphs (those with a tendency toward globularity). In the extreme case of Hughes (see page 16) this was reportedly 124 inches but in the light of his known height and weight a figure of 110 inches would be more supportable. Arthur Armitage, Britain's heaviest man (see page 16), has a chest measurement of 71 inches. Among muscular subjects (mesomorphs), chest measurements above 60 inches are very rare. The largest such chest measurement ever recorded was that of Angus MacAskill (1825–63) of Berneray, Scotland (see page 14), who may well have been the strongest man who ever lived. His chest must have measured 63 inches at his top weight of 37½ stone.

BRAIN

Largest The brain has 10^{10} cells each containing 10^{10} macro-molecules. Each cell has 10^4 interconnections with other cells. After the age of 18 the brain loses some 10^3 cells per day but the macromolecular contingent of each cell is renewed 10^4 times in a normal life span. The brain of an average young adult male weighs 1,410 grammes (3 lb. 1·73 oz.) falling to 1,030 grammes (2 lb. 4·33 oz.). That of the average young adult female weighs 1,271 grammes (2 lb. 12·83 oz.). The heaviest brain ever recorded was that of Ivan Sergeyevich Turgenev (1818–83), the Russian author. His brain weighed 2,012 grammes (4 lb. 6·96 oz.). In January 1891 the *Edinburgh Medical Journal* reported the case of a 75-year-old man in the Royal Edinburgh Asylum whose brain weighed 1,829 grammes (4 lb. 0·5 oz.).

Smallest The brain of a microcephalous idiot may weigh as little as 300 grammes (10·6 oz.).

The inner ear—site of the smallest of the 206 bones in the human body

25-year-old woman Candida de Sousa Barbosa of Rio de Janeiro, Brazil, was believed to be the first ever survivor of the disease in November 1968.

Most notorious carrier
The most notorious of all typhoid carriers has been Mary Mallon, known as Typhoid Mary, of New York City, N.Y., U.S.A. She was the source of the 1903 outbreak, with 1,300 cases. Because of her refusal to leave employment, often under assumed names, involving the handling of food, she was placed under permanent detention from 1915 until her death in 1938.

Touch sensitivity
The extreme sensitivity of the fingers is such that a vibration with a movement of 0·02 of a micron can be detected. On 12 Jan. 1963 the Soviet newspaper *Izvestiya* reported the case of a totally blindfolded girl, Rosa Kulgeshova, who was able to identify colours by touch alone. Later reports suggested that the conditions of the experiment might not have excluded the possibility of collusion.

Most fingers
Voight records a case of someone with 13 fingers on each hand and 12 toes on each foot.

Longest finger nails
The longest recorded finger nails were reported from Shanghai in 1910, in the case of a Chinese priest who took 27 years to achieve nails up to $22\frac{3}{4}$ inches in length. Probably the longest nails now grown are those of Ramesh Sharma of Delhi whose thumb nail attained 9·4 inches after six years. He is a printer—presumably of the single-handed kind. Human nails normally grow from cuticle to cutting length in from 117 to 138 days.

Longest hair
The longest recorded hair was that of Swami Pandarasannadhi, the head of the Thiruvadu Thurai monastery in India. His hair was reported in 1949 to be 26 feet in length.

Longest beard
The longest beard recorded was that of Hans N. Langseth (b. 1846 in Norway) which measured $17\frac{1}{2}$ feet at the time of his death in 1927 after 15 years residence in the United States. The beard was presented to the Smithsonian Institution, Washington, D.C. in 1967. R. Latter of Tunbridge Wells, Kent, who died in 1900 aged 77, reputedly had a beard 16 feet long. The beard of the bearded lady Janice Deveree (born in Bracken County, Kentucky, U.S.A., in 1842) was measured at 14 inches in 1884.

Longest moustache
The longest moustache on record is that of Masuriya Din (born 1908), a Brahmin of the Partabgarh district in Uttar Pradesh, India. It grew to an extended span of 8 feet 6 inches between 1949 and 1962, and costs £13 per annum in upkeep. The longest moustache in Great Britain is that of Mr. John Roy (born 14 Jan. 1910), licensee of the "Cock Inn" at Beazely End, near Braintree, Essex. It attained a span of 41 inches between 1939 and 1967.

Longest necks
The maximum measured extension of the neck by the successive fitting of brass rings, as practised by the Padaung people of Burma, is $15\frac{3}{4}$ inches. From the male viewpoint the practice serves the dual purpose of enhancing the beauty of the female and ensuring fidelity. The neck muscles become so atrophied that the removal of the support of the rings produces asphyxiation.

Commonest illness
The commonest illness in the world is coryza (acute nasopharyngitis) or the common cold. Only 4,720,000 working days were reportedly lost as a result of this illness in Great Britain between mid 1967 and mid 1968, since absences of less than three days are not reported. The greatest reported loss of working time in Britain is from bronchitis, which accounted for 38,580,000, or 11·77 per cent., of the total of 327,570,000 working days lost in the same period.

DISEASE

Commonest
The commonest disease in the world is dental caries or tooth decay. In Great Britain 13 per cent. of people have lost all their teeth before they are 21 years old. During their lifetime few completely escape its effects. Infestation with pinworm (*Enterobius vermicularis*) approaches 100 per cent. in some areas of the world.

Rarest
Medical literature periodically records hitherto undescribed diseases. Of once common diseases, rabies (hydrophobia) was last contracted in Britain in 1922 and last recorded in 1964. Kuru, or laughing sickness, afflicts only the Fore tribe of eastern New Guinea and is 100 per cent. fatal.

Most and least infectious
The most infectious of all diseases is the pneumonic form of plague, with a mortality rate of about 99·99 per cent. Leprosy transmitted by *Mycobacterium leprae* is the least infectious of communicable diseases.

Highest morbidity
Rabies in humans has been regarded as uniformly fatal when associated with the hydrophobia symptom. A

John Roy with his 41-inch span

The human being

Blood groups The preponderance of one blood group varies greatly from one locality to another. On a world basis Group O is the most common (46 per cent.), but in some areas, for example London and Norway, Group A predominates.

The full description of the commonest sub-group in Britain is O MsNs, P+, Rr, Lu(a−), K−, Le(a−b+), Fy(a+b+), Jk(a+b+), which occurs in one in every 270 people.

The rarest blood group on the ABO system, one of nine systems, is AB, which occurs in less than three per cent. of persons in the British Isles. The rarest type in the world is a type of Bombay blood (sub-type A-h) found so far only in a Czechoslovak nurse in 1961 and in a brother and sister in New Jersey, U.S.A. reported in February 1968. The American male has started a blood bank for himself.

Champion blood donor Joseph Elmaleh (born 1915) of Marseilles, France, donated on 22 May 1968 his 597th pint of blood making a total of 74 gallons 5 pints since 1931.

Largest vein The largest vein in the human body is cardiac vein known as the vena cava.

Most alcoholic subject It is recorded that a hard drinker named Vanhorn (1750–1811), born in London, averaged more than four bottles of ruby port per day for the 23 years 1788 to his death aged 61 in 1811. The total of his "empties" was put at 35,688.

The United Kingdom's legal limit for motorists is 80 milligrammes of alcohol per 100 millilitres of blood. The hitherto recorded highest figure in medical literature of 490 mg. per 100 ml. was submerged when a 68-year-old male was carried from his kitchen in Tetbury, Gloucestershire, shortly after midnight on Boxing Day 1968. A figure of 600 mg. per 100 ml. was checked and rechecked by a disbelieving Dr. George Hickey. At the inquest the deceased was described by a close relative as "a fairly heavy drinker".

Longest coma The longest duration of human unconsciousness was 32 years 99 days endured by Karoline Karlsson (born Mönsterås, Sweden in 1862) from 25 Dec. 1875 to 3 April 1908. She died on 6 April 1950 aged 88. The longest recorded coma of any person still living is that of Elaine Esposito (born 3 Dec. 1934) of Tarpon Springs, Florida, U.S.A. She has never stirred since an appendicectomy on 5 Aug. 1941, when she was six, in Chicago, Illinois, U.S.A. She was still living in 1969.

Fastest reflexes The results of experiments carried out in 1943 have shown that the fastest messages transmitted by the nervous system travel at 265 m.p.h. With advancing age impulses are carried 15 per cent. more slowly.

BODY TEMPERATURE

Highest Temperatures of up to 107·6° F (42° C) are induced and maintained in robust subjects undergoing pyrexial therapy. Sustained body temperatures of much over 109° F are normally incompatible with life, although recoveries after readings of 111° F (43·9° C) have been noted. Marathon runners in hot weather attain 105·8° F (41° C).

A temperature of 115° F was recorded in the case of Christopher Legge in the Hospital for Tropical Diseases, London, on 9 Feb. 1934. A subsequent examination of the thermometer disclosed a flaw in the bulb, but it is regarded as certain that the patient sustained a temperature of more than 110° F.

Lowest The lowest body temperature ever recorded for a living person was 60·8° F (16·0° C) in the case of Vickie Mary Davis (born 25 Dec. 1953) of Milwaukee, Wisconsin, when she was admitted to the Evangelical Hospital, Marshalltown, Iowa, U.S.A., on 21 Jan. 1956. The house in which she had been found unconscious on the floor was unheated and the air temperature had dropped to −24° F (−31° C). Her temperature returned to normal (98·4° F or 36·9° C) after 12 hours and may have been as low as 59° F (15·0° C) when she was first found.

Heart stoppage The longest recorded heart stoppage is 3 hours in the case of a Norwegian boy, Roger Arntzen, in April 1962. He was rescued, apparently drowned, after 22 minutes under the waters of the River Nideelv, near Trondheim.

The longest recorded interval in a *post mortem* birth was one of at least 80 minutes in Magnolia, Mississippi, U.S.A. Dr. Robert E. Drake found Fanella Anderson, aged 25, dead in her home at 11.40 p.m. on 15 Oct. 1966 and he delivered her of a son weighing 6 lb. 4 oz. by Caesarean operation in the Beacham Memorial Hospital on 16 Oct. 1966.

Largest stone The largest stone or vesical calculus reported in medical literature was one of 13 lb. 14 oz. (6,294 grammes) removed from an 80-year-old woman by Dr. Humphrey Arthure at Charing Cross Hospital, London, on 29 Dec. 1952.

Earliest influenza An epidemic bearing symptoms akin to influenza was first recorded in 412 B.C. by Hippocrates (c. 460–c. 375 B.C.). The earliest description of an epidemic in Great Britain was in the *Chronicle of Melrose* in 1173, although the term influenza was not introduced until 1743 by John Huxham (1692–1768) of Plymouth, Devonshire.

Hippocrates

Earliest duodenal ulcer The earliest description in medical literature of a duodenal ulcer was made in 1746 by Georg Erhard Hamberger (1696–1755).

Earliest slipped disc The earliest description of a prolapsed intervertebral cartilage was by George S. Middleton and John H. Teacher of Glasgow, Scotland, in 1911.

Pill-taking It is recorded that among hypochondriacs Samuel Jessup (born 1752), a wealthy grazier of Heckington, Lincolnshire, has never had a modern rival. His consumption of pills from 1794 to 1816 was 226,934, with a peak annual total of 51,590 in 1814. He is also recorded as having drunk 40,000 bottles of medicine before death overtook him at the surprisingly advanced age of 65.

Most tattoos Vivian "Sailor Joe" Simmons, a Canadian tattoo artist, had 4,831 tattoos on his body. He died in Toronto on 22 Dec. 1965 aged 77.

Hiccoughing The longest recorded attack of hiccoughs was that afflicting Jack O'Leary of Los Angeles, California, U.S.A. It was estimated that he "hicked" more than 160,000,000 times in an attack which lasted from 13 June 1948 to 1 June 1956, apart from a week's respite in 1951. His weight fell from 9 stone 12 lb. to 5 stone 4 lb. People sent 60,000 suggestions for cures of which only one apparently worked—a prayer to St. Jude, the patron saint of lost causes. The infirmary at Newcastle upon Tyne is recorded to have admitted a young man from Long Witton, Northumberland on 25 March 1769 suffering from hiccoughs which could be heard at a range of more than a mile.

Sneezing The most chronic sneezing fit ever recorded was that of June Clark, aged 17, of Miami, Florida, U.S.A. She started sneezing on 4 Jan. 1966, while recovering from a kidney ailment in the James M. Jackson Memorial Hospital, Miami. The sneezing was stopped by electric "aversion" treatment on 8 June 1966, after 155 days. The highest speed at which expelled particles have been measured to travel is 103·6 m.p.h.

Snoring Loudest Research at the Ear, Nose and Throat Department of St. Mary's Hospital, London, published in November 1968, shows that a rasping snore can attain a loudness of 69 decibels.

Yawning In Lee's case, reported in 1888, a 15-year-old female patient yawned continuously for a period of five weeks.

Swallowing The worst known case of compulsive swallowing was reported in the *Journal of the American Medical Association* in December 1960. The patient, who complained only of swollen ankles, was found to have 258 items in his stomach, including a 3-lb. piece of metal, 26 keys, 3 sets of rosary beads, 16 religious medals, a bracelet, a necklace, 3 pairs of tweezers, 4 nail clippers, 39 nail files, 3 metal chains and 88 assorted coins.

Coin Swallowing The most extreme recorded case of coin swallowing was revealed at Sedgefield General Hospital, County Durham, on 5 Jan. 1958, when it was reported that 366 halfpennies, 26 sixpences, 17 threepences, 11 pennies and four shillings (424 coins valued at £1 17s. 5d.), plus 27 pieces of wire totalling 5 lb. 1 oz., had been extracted from the stomach of a 54-year-old man.

Sword "swallowing" The longest length of sword able to be "swallowed" by a practised exponent, after a heavy meal, is 27 inches. Perhaps the greatest exponent is Alex Linton, born on 25 Oct. 1904 in Boyle, County Roscommon, Ireland. He stands 5 feet 3 inches tall and has "swallowed" four 27-inch blades at one time. He now lives in Sarasota, Florida, U.S.A.

DENTITION

Earliest The first deciduous or milk teeth normally appear in infants at five to eight months, these being the mandibular and maxillary first incisors. There are many records of children born with teeth, the most famous example being Prince Louis Dieudonné, later Louis XIV of France, who was born with two teeth on 5 Sept. 1638. Molars usually appear at 24 months, but in 1956 Bellevue Hospital in New York City, N.Y., U.S.A., reported a molar in a one-month-old baby, Robert R. Clinton.

Most Cases of the growth in late life of a third set of teeth have been recorded several times. A reference to an extreme case in France of a fourth dentition, known as Lison's case, was published in 1896. A triple row of teeth was noted in 1680 by Albertus Hellwigius.

Smallest visible object The resolving power of the human eye is 0·0003 of a radian or an arc of one minute (1/60th of a degree), which corresponds to 100 microns at 10 inches. A micron is a thousandth of a millimetre, hence 100 microns is 0·003937, or less than four thousandths, of an inch. The human eye can, however, detect a bright light source shining through an aperture only 3 to 4 microns across.

Colour sensitivity The unaided human eye, under the best possible viewing conditions, comparing large areas of colour, in good illumination, using both eyes, can distinguish 10,000,000 different colour surfaces. The most accurate photo-

electric spectrophotometers possess a precision probably only one-half to one-third as good as this.

Colour blindness The most extreme form of colour blindness, monochromatic vision, is very rare. The highest recorded rate of red-green colour blindness is in Czechoslovakia and the lowest rate among Fijians and Brazilian Indians.

VOICE

Highest and lowest The highest and lowest recorded notes attained by the human voice before this century were a C in *altissimo* (*c''''*) by Lucrezia Agujari (1743–83), noted by the Austrian composer Wolfgang Amadeus Mozart (1756–91) in Parma, northern Italy, in 1770, and an *A'* (55 cycles per second) by Kaspar Foster (1617–73). Recently singers trained by unorthodox methods have achieved high and low notes far beyond the hitherto accepted extremes. However, notes at the bass extremity of the register tend to lack harmonics and are of little musical value, while the topmost notes must be regarded as almost purely sinusoidal. Frl. Marita Günther, trained by Alfred Wolfsohn, has covered the range of the piano from the lowest note, *A''*, to *c'''''*. Of this range of 7¼ octaves, six octaves are considered to be of musical value. Mr. Roy Hart, also trained by Wolfsohn, has reached notes below the range of the piano. The highest note being sung by a tenor is G in *altissimo* by Louis Lavelle, coached by Mr. S. Pleeth, in *Lovely Mary Donelly*. The lowest note put into song is a D'' by the singer Tom King, of King's Langley, Hertfordshire. The highest note called for in singing was an *f'''''#*, which occurred twice in Zerbinetta's Recitative and Aria in the first (1912) version of the opera *Ariadne auf Naxos* by Richard Strauss (1864–1949). It was transposed down a tone in 1916.

The human being

Greatest range The normal intelligible outdoor range of the male human voice in still air is 200 yards. The *silbo,* the whistled language of the Spanish-speaking Canary Island of La Gomera, is intelligible across the valleys, under ideal conditions, at five miles. There is a recorded case, under freak acoustic conditions, of the human voice being detectable at a distance of $10\frac{1}{2}$ miles across still water at night. It was said that Mills Darden (see page 16) could be heard 6 miles away when he shouted at the top of his voice.

Lowest detectable sound The intensity of noise or sound is measured in terms of power. The power of the quietest sound that can be detected by a person of normal hearing at the most sensitive frequency is $1 \cdot 0 \times 10^{-16}$ of a watt per square centimetre. One tenth of the logarithm (to the base of 10) of the ratio of the power of a noise to this standard provides a unit termed a decibel. Noises above 150 decibels will cause immediate permanent deafness, while a noise of 30 decibels is negligible.

Highest detectable pitch The upper limit of hearing by the human ear has long been regarded as 20,000 Hz (cycles per second), although children with asthma can often detect a sound of 30,000 cycles per second. It was announced in February 1964 that experiments in the U.S.S.R. had conclusively proved that oscillations as high as 200,000 cycles per second can be heard if the oscillator is pressed against the skull.

OPERATIONS

Longest The most protracted operations are those involving brain surgery. Such operations lasting up to 16 hours were reported from the United States as early as 1942.

Oldest subject The greatest recorded age at which a person has been subjected to an operation is 111 years 105 days in the case of James Henry Brett, Jr. (born 25 July 1849, died 10 Feb. 1961) of Houston, Texas, U.S.A. He underwent a hip operation on 7 Nov. 1960. The oldest age established in Britain was the case of Mrs. Harriet Woodhams who had a pin and plate operation for a trochanteric fracture of the left femur on 26 Dec. 1961. This was carried out at St. Helier Hospital, Carshalton, Surrey, when she was 106 years 10 months old.

Heart The first human heart transplant operation was performed on Louis Washkansky, aged 55, at the Groote Schuur Hospital, Cape Town, South Africa, between 1.00 a.m. and 6 a.m. on 3 Dec. 1967 by a team of 30 headed by Prof. Christiaan N. Barnard (born 1924). The donor was Miss Denise Ann Darvall, aged 25. Washkansky died on 21 Dec. 1967. The transplant of the heart of Clive Haupt, a deceased 24-year-old Cape coloured, into Dr. Philip Blaiberg (born 24 May 1909) of Wynberg, Cape Town, was performed at the same hospital between 10.35 a.m. and 4 p.m. on 2 Jan. 1968. Dr. Blaiberg died $19\frac{1}{2}$ months later on 17 Aug. 1969. Britain's longest-surviving heart transplant patient has been Mr. Charles Hendrick who died in Guy's Hospital of a lung infection on 31 Aug. 1969—107 days after his operation.

Dr. Blaiberg

26

Earliest appendicectomy The earliest recorded successful appendix operation was performed in 1736 by Claudius Amyand (1680–1740). He was Serjeant Surgeon to King George II (reigned 1727–60).

Earliest anaesthesia The earliest recorded operation under general anaesthesia was for the removal of a cyst from the neck of James Venable by Dr. Crawford Williamson Long (1815–78), using diethyl ether ($(C_2H_5)_2O$), in Jefferson, Georgia, U.S.A., on 30 March 1842. The earliest use of ether in Great Britain was by Robert Liston (see also below) at the University College Hospital, London on 21 Dec. 1846 for an amputation.

Fastest amputation The shortest time recorded for the amputation of a limb in the pre-anaesthetic era was 33 seconds through a patient's thigh by Robert Liston (1794–1847) of Edinburgh, Scotland. This feat caused his assistant the loss of three fingers from his master's saw.

Surgical instruments The largest surgical instruments are axis-traction obstetric forceps, which measure up to $17\frac{1}{2}$ inches overall. The smallest is Elliot's eye trephine, which has a blade $0 \cdot 078$ of an inch in diameter.

Highest I.Q. On the Terman index for Intelligence Quotients, 150 represents genius level. The indices are sometimes held to be immeasurable above a level of 200 but a figure of 210 has been attributed to Kim Ung-Yong of Seoul, South Korea (born 7 March 1963). He composed poetry and spoke four languages (Korean, English, German and Japanese), and performed integral calculus at the age of 4 years 8 months on television in Tokyo on "The World Surprise Show" on 2 Nov. 1967. Both his parents are University professors and were both born at 11 a.m. on 23 May 1934. Research into past geniuses at Stanford University, California, U.S.A., has produced a figure of "over 200" for John Stuart Mill (1806–73), who began to learn ancient Greek at the age of three. A similar rating has also been attributed to Johann Wolfgang von Goethe (1749–1832) of Frankfurt am Main, West Germany. More than 20 per cent. of the 15,000 members of the international Mensa society have an I.Q. of 161 or above on the Cattell index which is equivalent to 142 on the Terman index.

Human memory Mehmed Ali Halici of Ankara, Turkey on 14 Oct. 1967 recited 6,666 verses of the Koran from memory in six hours. The recitation was followed by six Koran scholars.

Sleeplessness Researches indicate that on the Circadian cycle for the majority peak efficiency is attained between 8 p.m. and 9 p.m. and the low point comes at 4 a.m. The longest recorded period for which a person has voluntarily gone without sleep, while under medical surveillance, is 282 hours 55 minutes (11 days 18 hours 55 mins.) by Mrs. Bertha Van Der Merwe, aged 52, a housewife of Cape Town, South Africa, ending on 13 Dec. 1968.

It was reported that Toimi Artturinpoika Silvo, a 54-year-old port worker of Hamina, Finland, stayed awake for 32 days 12 hours from 1 March to 2 April 1967. He walked 17 miles per day and lost 33 lb. in weight. Mr. Eustace Rushworth Burnett (born 1880) of Hose, Leicestershire, claimed to have lost all desire to sleep in 1907 and that he never again went to bed. He died in January 1965, 58 years later aged 85.

Motionlessness The longest that a man has voluntarily remained motionless is $4\frac{1}{2}$ hours by Private (1st Class) William A. Fuqua of Fort Worth, Texas, U.S.A. He is a male mannequin or "fashioneer" in civil life earning up to $1,300 (£541) per hour for his ability to "freeze". The job is hazardous for it was reported in November 1967 that he was stabbed in the back by a man "proving" to his wife that he was only a dummy.

Fastest talker Few people are able to speak articulately at a sustained speed above 300 words per minute. The fastest broadcaster has been regarded as Jerry Wilmot, the Canadian ice hockey commentator in the post World War II period. Raymond Glendenning (b. Newport, Monmouth, 25 Sept. 1907) of the B.B.C. once spoke 176 words in 30 seconds while commentating on a greyhound race. In public life the highest speed recorded is a 327 words per minute burst in a speech made in December 1961 by John Fitzgerald Kennedy (1917–63), then President of the United States. In October 1965 it was reported that Peter Spiegel, 62, of Essen, West Germany, achieved 908 syllables in one minute at a rally of shorthand writers.

Dr. Charles Hunter of Rochdale, Lancashire, England on 14 Dec. 1968 demonstrated an ability to recite the 262 words of the soliloquy *To Be or Not To Be* from Shakespeare's *Hamlet* (Act III, Scene 1) in 41 secs. or at a rate of 383 words per minute. In March 1968 he covered the first 50 words in 7·2 secs. (a rate of 416·6 words per minute).

Fasting Most humans experience considerable discomfort after an abstinence from food for even 12 hours but this often passes off after 24–28 hours. Records claimed without unremitting medical surveillance are of little value.

The longest period for which anyone has gone without food is 382 days by Angus Barbieri (born 1940) of Tayport, Fife, who lived on tea, coffee, water and soda water in Maryfield Hospital, Dundee, Angus, from June 1965 to July 1966. His weight declined from 33 stone 10 lb. to 12 stone 10 lb.

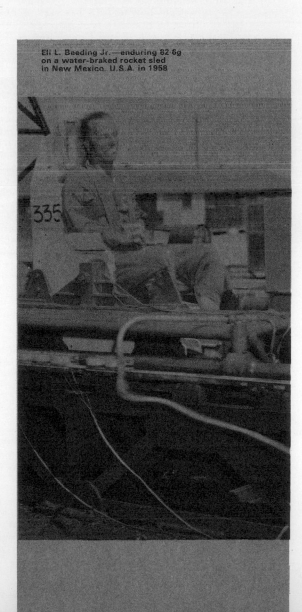

Eli L. Beeding Jr.—enduring 82·6g on a water-braked rocket sled in New Mexico, U.S.A. in 1958

Most voracious fire-eater The hardest blowing fire-eater is Kjell Swing (Sweden), who can produce a flame 6½ feet long.

Hunger strike The longest recorded hunger strike was one of 94 days by John and Peter Crowley, Thomas Donovan, Michael Burke, Michael O'Reilly, Christopher Upton, John Power, Joseph Kenny and Seán Hennessy in Cork Prison, Ireland, from 11 Aug. to 12 Nov. 1920. These nine survivors (Joseph Murphy died on the 76th day) owed their lives to expert medical attention.

Underwater The world record for voluntarily staying under water is 13 minutes 42·5 seconds by Robert Foster, aged 32, an electronics technician of Richmond, California, who stayed under 10 feet of water in the swimming pool of the Bermuda Palms Motel at San Rafael, California, U.S.A., on 15 March 1959. He hyperventilated with oxygen for 30 minutes before his descent. His longest breath-hold without oxygen was 5 mins. 40 secs.

Human salamanders The highest dry-air temperature endured by naked men in U.S. Air Force experiments in 1960 was 400° F, and for heavily clothed men 500° F. Steaks require only 325° F. Temperatures of 140° C (284° F) have been found quite bearable in *Sauna* baths.

g forces The acceleration g, due to gravity, is 32 feet 1·05 inches per second per second at sea-level at the Equator. A *sustained* acceleration of 31 g was withstood for 5 seconds by R. Flanagan Gray, aged 39, at the U.S. Naval Air Development Center in Johnsville, Pennsylvania, in 1959. This makes the bodyweight of a 185 lb. (13 stone 3 lb.) man seem like 5,700 lb. (2·54 tons). The highest value endured in a dry capsule is 25 g. The highest g value endured on a water-braked rocket sled is 82·6 g for 0·04 of a second by Eli L. Beeding Jr. at Holloman Air Force Base, New Mexico, U.S.A., on 16 May 1958. He was put in hospital for 3 days. A man who fell off a 185-foot cliff has survived a *momentary* g of 209 in decelerating from 68 m.p.h. to stationary in 0·015 of a second.

Isolation The longest recorded period for which any volunteer has been able to withstand total deprivation of all sensory stimulation (sight, hearing and touch) is 92 hours, recorded in 1962 at Lancaster Moor Hospital, Lancashire.

Extra sensory perception The highest consistent performer in tests to detect powers of extra-sensory perception is Pavel Stepánek (Czechoslovakia) known in parapsychological circles as "P.S.". His performance on nominating hidden white or green cards from May 1967 to March 1968 departed from a chance probability yielding a Chi^2 value corresponding to $P < 10^{-50}$ or odds of more than 100 octillion to one against the achievement being one of chance. One of the two appointed referees recommended that the results should not be published. The highest published scores in any E.S.P. test were those of a 26-year-old female tested by Prof. Bernard F. Reiss of Hunter College, New York in 1936. In 74 runs of 25 guesses each she scored one with 25 all correct, two with 24 and an average of 18·24 instead of the random 5·00. Such a result would depart from chance probability by a factor $> 10^{700}$.

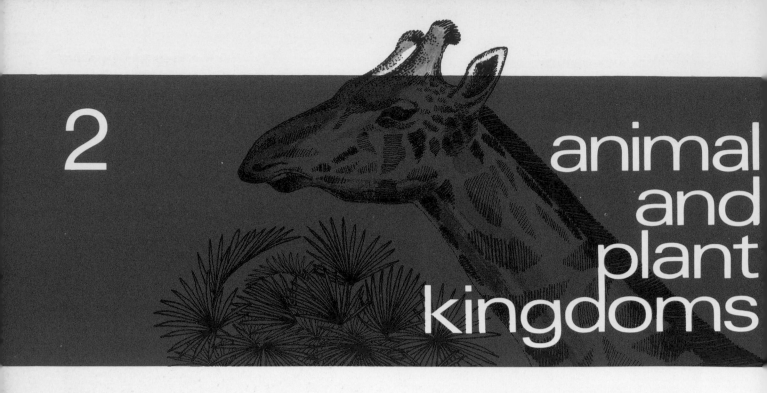

2 animal and plant kingdoms

1. Mammals *(Mammalia)*

Largest and heaviest
The largest animal now living (and probably also unsurpassed in size by any extinct animal) is the blue or sulphur bottom whale (*Balænoptera musculus*), also called Sibbald's rorqual. Practical difficulties and commercial considerations combine to make data on weights very sparse. The highest recorded weight based on the number of cookers filled with blubber, meat and bone at the Prince Olaf flensing station in South Georgia was 163·7 tons for a 96¾-foot female *c.* 1930. This figure, exclusive of blood, indicated a total weight of 174 tons. The longest reliable measurement on record is one of 106 feet for a female taken near the South Shetlands in April 1926. A less reliable claim measuring 118 feet was recorded for a female taken off Victoria Land, Antarctica on 7 Dec. 1927. Applying the cube rule, it seems probable that very long or very corpulent pregnant blue whales must at times have surpassed a weight of 200 tons, though none such has been weighed.

Tallest
If height is confined to land animals, the tallest is the giraffe (*Giraffa camelopardalis*), now found only to the south of the Sahara Desert in Africa. A bull of the Central East African race (*G. camelopardalis tippelskirchi*), measuring 19 feet 3 inches in height from the hoof to the tips of the "horns" has been recorded in Kenya. It weighed nearly 2 tons and was thus 4¾ feet taller than a London double-decker bus. Less credible heights of up to 23 feet have been claimed. The greatest height for a cow is 16 feet 10 inches. A giraffe was first seen in London in 1827.

Longest
The longest animal ever recorded is the jelly fish or coelenterate (*Cyanea arctica*), which inhabits the north-west Atlantic Ocean. One specimen washed up on the coast of Massachusetts, U.S.A. *c.* 1870 had a bell 7½ feet in diameter and tentacles measuring 120 feet, thus giving a theoretical tentacular span of some 245 feet. It weighed about 200 lb.

Smallest
The smallest of all free-living organisms are pleuropneumonia like organisms (P.P.L.O.) of the *Mycoplasma*. One of these, *Mycoplasma laidlawii*, first discovered in sewage in 1936, has a diameter during its early existence of only 100 millimicrons, or 0·000004 of an inch. Examples of the strain known as H.39 have a maximum diameter of 300 millimicrons and weigh an estimated $1·0 \times 10^{-16}$ of a gramme. Thus a 174-ton blue whale would weigh $1·77 \times 10^{23}$ or 177,000 trillion times as much.

Longest lived
Few animals live longer than humans. It would appear that chelonians are the longest lived animals. An age of 129 years has been attributed to a common box turtle (*Terrapene carolina*) from 1806 to 1935 and a span of 152 years, from 1766 to 1918, has been ascribed to a male Marion's tortoise (*Testudo sumerii*) at Port Louis, Mauritius. When the Royal Tongan tortoise, believed to be *Testudo radiata,* named "Tu'malilia" died on 19 May 1966, it was reputed to be over 200 years old, having been presented to the then King of Tonga by Captain James Cook (1728–79) on 22 Oct. 1773.

Fastest
The fastest reliably measured speed of any animal is 106·25 m.p.h. for the spine-tailed swift (*Chaetura caudacuta*) reported from the U.S.S.R. in 1951. In 1934 ground speeds ranging from 171·8 to 219·5 m.p.h. were reported for spine-tailed swifts over a 2-mile course in the Cachar Hills of north-eastern India. Details of these timings were published in March 1942, but the practical difficulties of the experiment indicated a large degree of probable error. This bird is probably the fastest moving living creature and has a blood temperature of 112·5° F. Speeds as high as 185 m.p.h. have been ascribed to peregrine falcons (*Falco peregrinus*) in a stoop, but in recent experiments in which miniature air speedometers were fitted the maximum recorded diving speed was 82 m.p.h. In June 1928 the unacceptable figure of 247 m.p.h. was attributed to frigate birds (genus *Fregata*) in level flight over a 25¼ mile course off the Cardagos Garajos Islands, 250 miles north-east of Mauritius in the Indian Ocean.

Rarest
The best claimant to the title of the world's rarest animal is the pygmy opposum (*Burramys parvus*) which had been thought to be extinct for 20,000 years. On 19 Aug. 1966 a first male was found in the Melbourne University Ski Lodge on Mount Hotham, 130 miles north-east of Melbourne, Australia.

Commonest
It has been estimated that man shares the earth with about 3,000,000,000,000,000,000,000,000,000,000,000 (3,000 quintillion or 3×10^{33}) other living things. Of these, more than 75 per cent. are bacteria, namely 2,200 quintillion (or $2·2 \times 10^{33}$).

Fastest growth
The fastest growth in the Animal Kingdom is that of the blue whale calf (see above). A barely visible ovum weighing a fraction of a milligramme (0·000035 of an ounce) grows to a weight of *c.* 26 tons in 22¾ months,

28

made up of 10¾ months gestation and the first 12 months of age. This is equivalent to an increase of 30,000 million-fold.

Largest eye   The giant squid *Architeuthis sp.* has the largest eye of any living animal. The diameter may exceed 30 centimetres (11·79 inches), compared to 10–12 centimetres (3·93 to 4·71 inches) for the largest blue whales (*Balænoptera musculus*).

The greatest recorded depth to which a whale has dived is 620 fathoms (3,720 feet) by a 47-foot bull sperm whale (*Physeter catodon*) found with his jaw entangled with a submarine cable running between Santa Elena, Ecuador and Chorillos, Peru on 14 Oct. 1955. At this depth the whale withstood a pressure of 1,680 lb. per square inch. Baird's beaked whale (*Berardius bairdii*) and the bottle-nosed whales (genus *Hyperoodon*) may dive even deeper. There is a record of a harpooned northern bottle-nose

The mightiest member of the entire Animal Kingdom—the blue whale

Largest and heaviest World   For details of the blue whale (*Balænoptera musculus*) see page 28. Further information: a female blue whale taken by the *Slava* whaling fleet of the U.S.S.R. in the Antarctic on 17 March 1947 measured 27·6 metres (90 feet 8 inches) in length. Its tongue and heart weighed 4·22 tons and 1,540 lb. respectively.

Blue whales inhabit the colder seas and migrate to warmer waters in winter for breeding. Observations made in the Antarctic in 1946–7 showed that a blue whale can maintain speeds of 20 knots (23 m.p.h.) for 10 to 15 minutes. It has been calculated that a 90-foot blue whale travelling at 20 knots would develop 520 horsepower. The young measure up to 28·6 feet long at birth and weigh up to 3 tons.

It has been estimated that there were about 100,000 blue whales living throughout the oceans in 1935, but that less than 1,000 survived (most of them in the Southern Hemisphere) in 1969. The correct collective noun is a gam or a pod.

British waters   A blue whale allegedly measuring 105 feet in length was stranded on the west coast of Lewis (Outer Hebrides), Scotland *c.* 1870, but the carcase was cut up by the local people before the length could be verified. There was also a report of a female blue whale measuring 101 feet being stranded in the River Humber in September 1750. These measurements, if correct, were probably taken along the curve of the body instead of from the tip of the upper jaw in a straight line to the notch in the flukes. Four blue whales have been stranded on British coasts since 1913. The last occurrence (*c.* 60 ft.) was at Wick, Caithness, Scotland, on 15 Oct. 1923.

whale (*H. ampullatus*) staying underwater for two hours 3 minutes.

Largest on land   The largest living land animal is the African elephant (*Loxodonta africana*). The average adult bull stands 10 feet 6 inches at the shoulder and weighs 5¾ tons. The largest specimen recorded was a bull shot in the Cuando River region of south-western Angola on 13 Nov. 1955. Lying on its side the animal measured 13 feet 2 inches in a straight line from the shoulder to the base of its foot, indicating that its living height was about 12 feet 9 inches. It had an overall length of 33 feet 2 inches, a maximum girth of 19 feet 8 inches and its weight was estimated to be 24,000 lb. (10·7 tons). On 6 March 1959 the mounted specimen was put on display in the Museum of Natural History at the Smithsonian Institution, Washington, D.C., U.S.A. (See also Shooting, Chapter XII.) Another outsize bull elephant known as Zhulamiti ("Taller than the trees") was reported last seen in the tsetse fly corridor in south-eastern Rhodesia in *c.* Jan. 1965. It is reputed to stand over 12 feet at the shoulder.

12′9″

The Scottish
Red Deer

The largest wild mammal in the British Isles, excluding the wild pony, is the Scottish red deer (*Cervus elaphus scoticus*). A full-grown stag stands 4 feet at the withers. The heaviest ever recorded was a stag weighing 476 lb. and standing 4 feet 6 inches, killed at Woburn, Bedfordshire, in 1836. A stag weighing 472 lb. 7 oz. was killed in Warnham Court Park, Sussex, on 7 Sept. 1926. Another stag weighing 472 lb. was killed in the same park in 1952. The wild population in 1968 was estimated at 180,000 to 185,000.

Tallest The tallest mammal is the giraffe (*Giraffa camelopardalis*). For details see page 28.

Smallest The smallest recorded mammal is Savi's white-toothed pygmy shrew (*Suncus etruscus*) which is found along the coasts of the northern Mediterranean and eastwards to Malaysia. It has a body length of only 1½ inches and weighs as little as 2½ grammes (0·09 of an ounce). The smallest mammal found in the British Isles is the pygmy or lesser shrew (*Sorex minutus*), which has a head and body length of 57·8 mm. (2·27 inches) and a tail of 38 mm. (1·49 inches). Mature specimens weigh between 2·4 and 6·1 grammes (0·084 to 0·213 of an ounce). These weights are rivalled by the smallest bats (see page 32).

The smallest marine mammal is probably the sea otter (*Enhydra lutris*), which is found in coastal waters of the North Pacific. It has a maximum length (including tail) of 157 centimetres (62 inches) and weighs up to 39 kilogrammes (85·8 lb.). This size is closely matched by the La Plata dolphin (*Pontoporia blainvillei*), which lives in the estuary of the Rio de la Plata, Argentina. It has a maximum length of 172 centimetres (67·2 inches) and weighs up to 40 kilogrammes (88 lb.).

Rarest The rarest placental mammal in the world is now probably the Javan rhinoceros (*Rhinoceros sondaicus*). In 1964 there were an estimated 56 in the Udjung-Kulon (also called Oedjoeng Kuelon) Reserve of 117 square miles at the tip of western Java, Indonesia, but the number today may be as low as 10. There may also be a few in the Tenasserim area on the Thai-Burmese border. Among sub-species, there are believed to be only 3 or 4 specimens of the Bali tiger (*Panthera tigris balica*), all in western Bali, Indonesia. The last recorded shooting was in 1937. The rarest marine mammal is probably Hose's Sarawak dolphin (*Lagenodephis hosei*), which is known only from a single specimen collected at the mouth of the Lutong River, Baram, Borneo in 1895 in an advanced state of decomposition. The skull is now in the British Museum (Natural History), London.

The rarest British mammal is the pine marten (*Martes martes*), which is found in the highlands of Scotland, particularly in Coille na Glas, Leitire, Ross and Cromarty, and thinly distributed in North Wales and the Scottish border country. The largest specimens measure 34 inches from nose to tail and weigh up to 4 lb. 6 oz.

Fastest The fastest of all land animals is probably the pronghorn antelope (*Antilocapra americana*) of the western United States. Specimens have been observed to travel at 35 m.p.h. for 4 miles, and 53 m.p.h. for 1 mile. On 14 Aug. 1936 at Spanish Lake, in Lake County, Oregon, a hard-pressed buck was timed by a car speedometer at 61 m.p.h. over 200 yards. Speeds of 71, 84 and even 90 m.p.h. have been quoted for the cheetah or hunting leopard (*Acinonyx jubatus*), found on the plains of Africa and southern Asia, but all appear to have been exaggerated. Tests in London in 1939 showed that on an oval greyhound track over 500 yards the cheetah's average speed over three runs was 43·4 m.p.h. (*cf.* 43·26 m.p.h. for the fastest racehorse). In a more recent study (1961) using a series of film sequences the top speed was found to be 56 m.p.h. In Kenya, a cheetah chased by a car reached 50 m.p.h. over 200 yards.

The fastest British land mammal over a sustained distance is the roe deer (*Capreolus capreolus*) which can reach 40 m.p.h. The same speed has been reported for the red fox (*Vulpes vulpes*) over a short distance.

Longest lived No mammal can match the extreme proven age of 113 years attained by Man (*Homo sapiens*) (see page 19). It is probable that the closest approach is over 90 years by the killer whale (*Orcinus orca*). A bull with distinctive markings, known as "Old Tom", was seen from 1839 to 17 Sept. 1930 in Twofold Bay, Eden, New South Wales, Australia.

The longest lived land mammal, excluding Man, is probably the Asiatic elephant (*Elephas maximus*). The greatest age that has been verified with reasonable certainty is an estimated 69 years in the case of a cow named "Jessie", who was taken in 1882 to the Taronga Zoological Park in Sydney, Australia, where she had to be destroyed, because of senile infirmity, on 26 Sept. 1939. Her age on arrival was probably 12 but may have been as high as 20 years. An elephant's age is determined by the persistence of its teeth, which generally wear out around the 50-55th year.

Largest herd The largest herds on record were those of the South African springbok (*Antidorcas marsupialis*) during migration in the 19th century. In 1849 Sir John Fraser of Bloemfontein reported seeing a herd of "Trek-Bokke" that took three days to pass through the settlement of Beaufort West, Cape Province. Another herd seen between Prieska and Bittersprut, Cape Province, in 1888 was estimated to contain 100,000,000 head.

Longest and shortest gestation periods The longest of all mammalian gestation periods is that of the Asiatic elephant (*Elephas maximus*), with an average of 21 to 22 months and a maximum of 760 days (2 years and 30 days)—more than 2½ times that of a human. The duck-billed platypus (*Ornithorhynchus anatinus*) of south-eastern Australia has a gestation period of between 7 and 10 days.

Largest litter The greatest recorded number of young born to a mammal at a single birth is 36, in the case of the common tenrec (*Centetes ecaudatus*), found in Madagascar and the Comoro Islands. The average litter is about 14.

Fastest breeder The streaked tenrec (*Hemicentetes semispinosus*) of Madagascar is weaned after only 5 days, and females are capable of breeding 3–4 weeks after birth.

Heaviest brain The sperm whale (*Physeter catadon*) has the heaviest brain of all living animals. The brain of a 46-foot-long bull weighed 9,200 grammes (20·24 lb.), compared to 8,300 grammes (18·36 lb.) for a 71-foot-long fin whale (*Balænoptera physalus*). The heaviest brain recorded for an elephant (*Loxodonta africana*) is 6,654 grammes (14·6 lb.).

Longest hibernation The common dormouse (*Glis glis*) spends more time in hibernation than any other mammal. The hibernation usually lasts between 5 and 6 months (October to April), but there is a record of an English specimen sleeping for 6 months 23 days without interruption. The common hedgehog (*Erinaceus europaeus*) also exceeds 6 months on occasion, but it is not a continuous sleep.

CARNIVORES

Largest The largest living terrestrial member of the order Carnivora is the Kodiak bear (*Ursus arctos midden-dorffi*) of Alaska. The average adult male has a nose to tail length of 8 feet and weighs about 1,200 lb. In 1894 a weight of 1,656 lb. was recorded for a male shot at English Bay, Kodiak Island, whose *stretched* skin measured 13 feet 6 inches overall. This weight was exceeded by a male in the Cheyenne Mountain Zoological Park, Colorado Springs, Colorado, U.S.A., which scaled 1,670 lb. at the time of its death on 22 Sept. 1955.

The Peninsular brown bear (*Ursus arctos gyas*), also found in Alaska, is almost as large, adult males measuring $7\frac{3}{4}$ feet nose to tail length and weighing about 1,150 lb. A specimen 10 feet long, with an estimated weight of between 1,600 and 1,700 lb. was shot near Cold Bay, Alaska, on 28 May 1948. Another male shot in Clearwater Gap, Alberta, Canada, in November 1949 had a nose to tail measurement of over 9 feet and weighed an estimated 1,600 lb.

Weights in excess of 1,600 lb. have also been reported for the male polar bear (*Thalarctos maritimus*), which has an average nose to tail length of $7\frac{1}{2}$ feet and weighs about 900 lb. In 1960 a polar bear allegedly weighing 2,210 lb. was shot at the polar entrance to Kotzebue Sound, north-west Alaska. In April 1962 the mounted specimen, measuring 11 feet $1\frac{1}{4}$ inches, was put on display at the Seattle World Fair, Washington, U.S.A.

The largest toothed mammal ever recorded is the sperm whale (*Physeter catodon*), also called the cachalot. The average adult bull is 47 feet long and weighs about 33 tons. The largest specimen ever to be measured accurately was a bull 20·7 metres (67 feet 11 inches) long, captured off the Kuril Island in the north-west Pacific by a U.S.S.R. whaler during the summer of 1950. A measurement of 68 feet was credited for a bull killed 60 miles west of Shetland on 25 June 1903 and landed at the Norrona whaling station. The measurement how-ever, was made over the curve of the body and not in a straight line. Nine cachalots have been stranded on British coasts since 1913. In the summer of 1948 a bull with an alleged length of 90 feet was killed off the north-eastern coast of Vancouver Island, British Columbia, Canada, and brought into Nanaimo. Later, however, the length was amended to 56 feet.

Smallest The smallest living carnivore is the least weasel (*Mustela rixosa*) of North America. Its total length (including tail) is up to $22\frac{1}{2}$ centimetres (8·9 inches) and mature specimens weigh between 35 and 70 grammes (from $1\frac{1}{4}$ to $2\frac{1}{2}$ oz.).

Rarest The rarest land carnivore is probably the Mexican grizzly bear (*Ursus nelsoni*), of which no more than 20–30 survive in a small patch of territory about 50 miles north of Chihuahua.

Largest feline The largest of the 36 members of the cat family (Felidae) is the long-haired Siberian tiger (*Panthera tigris longipilis*), also known as the Manchurian, Amar or Mongolian tiger. Specimens have been recorded up to $12\frac{1}{2}$ feet in length (including tail) and 800 lb. in weight. It is now found only in the Khabarovsk and Primorskiy regions of the eastern U.S.S.R.

The average adult male African lion (*Panthera leo*) measures 9 feet overall and weighs about 400 lb. The heaviest specimen found in the wild was one weighing 690 lb., shot near Hectorspruit, in the eastern Transvaal, South Africa in 1936. A weight of 800 lb. has been

A mounted polar bear which weighed $19\frac{3}{4}$ cwt. and measured 11 ft. $1\frac{1}{4}$ ins.

The animal and plant kingdoms

reported for a very corpulent American circus lion. In 1953 an 18-year-old liger (a lion-tigeress hybrid) at the Zoological Gardens of Bloemfontein, South Africa, was weighed at 750 lb.

PINNIPEDS (Seals, Sea-lions and Walruses)

Largest The largest of the 32 known species of pinnipeds is the southern elephant seal (*Mirounga leonina*) which inhabits the sub-Antarctic islands. Adult bulls average 16½ feet in length (snout to tip of tail), 12 feet in girth and weigh 6,000 lb. (2·67 tons). The largest specimen on record was a bull killed in Possession Bay, South Georgia on 28 Feb. 1913 which measured *c.* 22½ feet in length or 21 ft. 4 in. after flensing and weighed nearly 5 tons. There are old records of bulls measuring 25, 27 and even 30 feet, but all lack confirmation. A length of 22 feet has been reported in 1870 for the northern elephant seal (*Mirounga angustirostris*), now restricted to islands off the coast of Mexico and southern California, but the measurement included the hind flippers. The largest seal elephant ever held in captivity is believed to have been "Goliath", a bull of the southern race, exhibited at the Philadelphia Zoological Gardens, Pennsylvania, U.S.A. In the winter of 1933–34, he measured 17 feet in length and weighed an estimated 6,000 lb. The largest among British fauna is the Atlantic or grey seal, the bulls of which have been recorded up to 9 feet in length and 658 lb. in weight.

A bull elephant seal

Smallest The smallest pinniped is the ringed seal (*Pusa hispida*), found on the circumpolar Arctic coasts. Adult animals average 4½ to 4¾ feet in length and weigh 170–200 lb.

Fastest and deepest The highest speed measured for a pinniped is 25 m.p.h. for a California sea lion (*Zalophus californianus*). It was reported in March 1966 that a dive of 600 metres (1,970 feet) had been recorded by a depth gauge attached to a Weddell seal (*Leptonychotes weddelli*). The seal withstood a pressure of 875 lb. per square inch. An hour underwater has been exceeded. Some of this species have been measured to swim under ice for 19 miles, utilizing the layer of air sometimes trapped on the underside of the ice.

Longest lived A ringed seal (*Pusa hispida*) taken on the south-west coast of Baffin Island in 1954 was believed to be at least 43 years old based on a count of dental annuli.

Rarest The Caribbean or West Indies monk seal (*Monachus tropicalis*) was last seen on the beach of Isla Mujueres off the Yucatan Peninsula, Mexico in 1962 and is now believed to be on the verge of extinction. The Japanese sea lion (*Zalophus californianus*), formerly widespread in the Japanese archipelago, probably became extinct in the early 1950's.

BATS

Largest The only flying mammals are bats (order Chiroptera), of which there are about 1,000 living species. That with the greatest wing span is *Pteropus niger*, also called the kalong, a fruit bat found in Indonesia. It has a wing span of up to 170 centimetres (5 feet 7 inches) and weighs up to 900 grammes (31·7 ounces). Some unmeasured specimens of *Pteropus neohibernicus,* another fruit bat found in New Guinea, may possibly reach 6 feet in wing span. The largest bat found in Britain is the noctule or great bat (*Nyctalus noctula*), with a head and body length of 75 to 82 mm. (2·9 to 3·2 inches), with a wing span of up to 387 mm. (15·23 inches) and a weight of up to 40 grammes (1·4 oz.).

Smallest The smallest species of bat is *Pipistrellus nanulus,* found in West Africa. It has a wing span of about 6 inches and a length of 2½ inches, of which one inch is tail. The average weight is about 2½ grammes (0·09 of an ounce). The smallest British bat is the pipistrelle or common bat (*Pipistrellus pipistrellus*), which has a head and body length of 42 mm. (1·6 inches) and a wing span of 200 to 230 mm. (7·8 to 9·1 inches). Mature specimens weigh between 2·6 and 7·5 grammes (0·091 to 0·262 of an ounce).

Fastest The greatest speed attributed to a bat is 32 m.p.h. in the case of a guano bat (*Tadarida mexicana*).

Rarest The rarest of the 13 species native to the British Isles is the mouse-eared bat (*Myotis myotis*). The first specimen to be positively identified (a male) was taken alive at

The mouse-eared bat —Britain's rarest

Girton in Cambridgeshire in 1888 and is now preserved in the University Museum of Zoology at Cambridge. On 18 Feb. 1956 another specimen was found dead in an underground quarry on the Isle of Purbeck, near Swanage, Dorset, where several more have been found subsequently.

Longest lived Some vespertilionid bats (Family Vespertilionidae) banded in the wild have lived for more than 21 years.

PRIMATES

Largest The largest living primate is the eastern lowland gorilla (*Gorilla gorilla manyema*), which inhabits the lowlands in the eastern part of the Upper Congo (Kinshasa) and south-western Uganda. An average adult bull stands 5 feet 9 inches tall, weighs 400 lb. (28½ stone) and has a chest measurement of 60 inches. The greatest reliable height (crown to *heel*) recorded is 196 cms. (6 ft. 5·1 in.) for a bull of the eastern highland race (*Gorilla gorilla beringei*) shot in the Angumu Forest, in the eastern Congo (Kinshasa) in March 1948. It has a chest measurement of 155 cms. (61 inches) and weighed 230 kg. (506 lb.). The heaviest live weight recorded in captivity was for "Mbongo" (born 1926), standing 5 feet 7½ inches tall, who died on 15 March 1942 in the San Diego Zoological Gardens, California, U.S.A. During an attempt to weigh him, shortly before his death, the scales fluctuated from 645 lb. to nearly 670 lb.

Smallest The smallest primate is probably the mouse lemur (*Microcebus murinus*) of Madagascar, with an overall length of up to 28 centimetres (11·0 inches), of which 15 cms. (5·9 inches) is tail. It weighs from 48 to 85 grammes (1·7 to 3·0 oz.).

gest lived The greatest irrefutable age reported for a primate (excluding humans) is *c*. 49 years in the case of the male chimpanzee (*Pantroglodytes*) named "Heine" of Lincoln Park Zoological Gardens, Chicago, Illinois, U.S.A. He arrived there on 10 June 1924 when about 3 years of age.

MONKEYS

Largest The largest monkey is the mandrill (*Mandrillus sphinx*) of equatorial West Africa. Males weigh up to 54 kilogrammes (119 lb.), with a total length of up to 36 inches (tail 3 inches).

The mandrill (*Mandrillus sphinx*) of equatorial West Africa, the largest monkey

The smallest of all monkeys—the pygmy marmoset

Smallest The smallest monkey is the pygmy marmoset (*Cebuella pygmaea*) of southern Colombia, eastern Ecuador, northern Peru and western Brazil. It was discovered in 1823 and has a body length of up to 16 centimetres (6·3 inches) and a tail of between 15 centimetres (5·9 inches) and 20 centimetres (7·9 inches). It weighs from 49 to 70 grammes (1·7 to 2·5 oz.) and rivals the mouse lemur for the title of smallest primate (see above).

Rarest The rarest monkey is the Hairy-eared Dwarf Lemur (*Cheirogaleus trichotis*) of Madagascar, which has only been recorded four times. The last occasion was in 1966 when a live one was found on the east coast near Mananara.

gest lived The greatest reliable age reported for a monkey is 46 years for a male mandrill (*Mandrillus sphinx*) named "George" of London Zoological Gardens, who died on 4 March 1916.

and least intelligent Of sub-human primates, chimpanzees appear to have the most superior intelligence. Lemurs have less learning ability than any monkey or ape and, in some tests, are inferior to dogs and even pigeons.

Largest ## RODENTS
The world's largest rodent is the capybara (*Hydrochoerus hydrocharis*), also called the carpincho or water hog, which is found in tropical South America. It grows up to 4½ feet in length (including short tail) and up to 150 lb. in weight. Britain's largest rodent is now the coypu (*Myocastor coypus*), introduced from Argentina in 1927 by East Anglian nutria fur breeders. Four escaped from Ipswich, Suffolk, in 1937. One was killed

almost immediately, but the others founded a dynasty of wild specimens. Adult males measure up to 36 inches in total length (including tail) and weigh up to 26 lb. in the wild state (40 lb. in captivity).

Smallest The smallest rodent is the Old World harvest mouse (*Micromys minutus*), of which the British form weighs between 4·2 and 10·2 grammes (0·15 to 0·36 of an ounce) and measures up to 13·5 centimetres (5·3 inches) long, including the tail. It was announced in June 1965 than an even smaller rodent had been discovered in the Asian part of the U.S.S.R., but no details are yet available.

Rarest The rarest rodent in the world is believed to be the James Island rice rat (*Oryzomys swarthi*). Four were collected on this island in the Galapagos group in the eastern Pacific Ocean in 1906. The next trace was a skull of a recently dead specimen found in January 1966.

INSECTIVORES
Largest The largest insectivore (insect-eating mammal) is the moon rat (*Echinosorex gymnurus*) also known as the gymnura, found in Thailand, Malaysia, Sumatra and Borneo. It has an overall length of up to 65·5 centimetres (27·8 inches) and weighs up to 1,400 grammes (3·08 lb.).

Smallest The smallest insectivore is Savi's white-toothed shrew (see Smallest mammal, page 30).

ANTELOPES
Largest The largest antelope is the giant or Lord Derby eland (*Taurotragus derbianus*) of West and north-Central Africa which surpasses 2,000 lb. The common eland (*T. oryx pattersonianus*) of East and South Africa has the same shoulder height, of up to 72 inches, but is not quite so massive, although there is one record of a bull being shot in Malawi which weighed 2,078 lb.

Smallest The smallest known antelope, and the smallest ruminant, is the Royal antelope (*Neotragus pygmaeus*) of West Africa, measuring 10 to 12 inches at the shoulder and weighing only 7 to 8 lb. The slenderer Somali dik-dik (*Madoqua swaynei*), which stands 14 inches at the shoulder, weighs only 5 to 6 lb.

Rarest The rarest antelope is probably Jentink's duiker (*Cephalopusjentinki*) which is found only in a restricted area of tropical West Africa. Its total population may be only a few dozen.

DEER
Largest The largest deer is the Alaskan moose (*Alces gigas*). One standing 7 feet 8 inches at the withers, and weighing 1,800 lb., was shot in 1897 in the Yukon Territory, Canada. Unconfirmed measurements of up to 8½ feet at the withers and 2,600 lb. in weight have been claimed. The record antler span is 78½ inches.

Smallest The smallest deer is the mouse deer (*Tragulus javanicus*) or chevrotrain of south-east Asia. It has a shoulder height of up to 33 centimetres (13 inches) and a maximum weight of 4·5 kg. (9·9 lb.).

Rarest The rarest deer in the world is Fea's muntjac (*Muntiacus feae*), which is known only from two specimens collected on the borders of Tenasserim, Burma and Thailand.

TUSKS
Longest The longest recorded elephant tusks are a pair from the eastern Congo (Kinshasa), presented in 1907 to the National Collection of Heads and Horns, kept by the New York Zoological Society in Bronx Park, New York City, N.Y., U.S.A. One measures 11 feet 5½ inches and the other measures 11 feet. Their combined weight is 293 lb. A single tusk of 11 feet 6 inches has been reported, but details are lacking.

Heaviest The heaviest recorded tusks are a pair in the British Museum (Natural History), London. They were first

33

The animal and plant kingdoms

The animal and plant kingdoms

The animal and plant kingdoms

sold in Zanzibar (now part of Tanzania) in 1898, when the Museum acquired one of them. The other was bought by the Museum in 1933. They were measured in 1955, when the first was 10 feet 2½ inches long, weighing 226½ lb., and the second 10 feet 5½ inches long, weighing 214 lb., giving a combined weight of 440½ lb. The heaviest recorded single tusk was one weighing 235 lb., taken from an elephant shot in 1899 on the slopes of Mount Kilimanjaro, in Tanganyika (now part of Tanzania). A tusk with an alleged weight of 117 kilogrammes (258 lb.), from Dahomey, West Africa, was exhibited at the Paris Exposition of 1900.

Longest horns The longest recorded animal horn was one measuring 81¼ inches on the outside curve, with a circumference of 18¼ inches, found on a specimen of domestic Ankole cattle (*Bos taurus*) near Lake Ngami, Botswana (formerly called Bechuanaland).

The longest horns grown by any wild animal are those of the Pamir argali (*Ovis poli*), also called Marco Polo's argali, a wild sheep found in Central Asia. One of these has been measured at 75 inches along the front curve, with a circumference of 16 inches.

The longest recorded anterior horn of a rhinoceros is one of 62¼ inches, found on a female southern race white rhinoceros (*Ceratotherium simum simum*) shot in South Africa. The interior horn measured 22¼ inches. An unconfirmed length of 81 inches has also been once reported.

Blood temperatures The highest mammalian blood temperature is that of the common wolf (*Canis lupus*) with an average of 105° F (40·6° C). The lowest is 73·7° F in the spiny anteater or echidna (*Tachyglossus*), a monotreme found in Australia and New Guinea.

Most valuable furs The highest priced single skins are those of the mink-sable cross breed "mable" or "Kojah" of which 40 selected pelts from the Piampiano Fur Ranch, Zion, Illinois, U.S.A., realized $2,700 (£1,124) in New York City on 26 Feb. 1969. Individual pelts of sea otter (*Enhydra lutris*), known also as Kamchatka beaver, fetched up to $2,700 (then £675) before their 55-year-long protection began in 1912. The extremely rare solid white and solid black chinchilla mutations have not yet been marketed but would probably surpass all other furs in value.

Ambergris The heaviest piece of ambergris on record weighed 1,003 lb. and was recovered from a sperm whale (*Physeter catadon*) on 3 Dec. 1912 by a Norwegian whaling company in Australian waters. The lump was sold in London for £23,000.

MARSUPIALS

Largest The largest marsupials are the great grey kangaroo (*Macropus conguru*) and the red kangaroo (*Macropus rufus*) of Australia. The largest specimen recorded was a great grey kangaroo weighing 200 lb., measuring 8 feet 8 inches from nose to tail, or 9 feet 7 inches along the body curves. The skin is preserved in the Australian Museum, Sydney, New South Wales. A nose to tail measurement of 8 feet 10 inches has been reported for a red kangaroo.

Smallest The smallest known marsupials in the world are the flat-skulled marsupial "mice" (*Planigale ingrami* and *P. tenuirostris*) of Australia. They have a total length of 9·5 centimetres (3¾ inches) and weigh up to 5 grammes (0·18 of an ounce).

Rarest The wolf-like thylacine or Tasmanian tiger (*Thylacinus cnyocephalus*), the largest of the carnivorous marsupials, is now confined to the wildest parts of Tasmania. It is so close to extinction that recent expeditions failed to find any specimens, although there was evidence of their continued existence. The last Tasmanian tiger kept in captivity was taken in a trapper's snare in the Florentine Valley a few miles west of Mountain Field National Park in 1933 and exhibited at Hobart Zoo. It died a few months later. On 2 Jan. 1957 it was reported that one had been kept in sight for two minutes and photographed by a helicopter pilot, Capt. J. Ferguson, on Birthday Bay beach, 35 miles south-west of Queenstown, Tasmania. Experts, who examined the photograph, however, declared that the animal was a dog. In 1965 traces of a lair were found by zoologists in a wrecked ship on the west coast, and in December 1966 it was reported that evidence had been found to prove the existence of a female and pups near Mawbanna.

Longest jump The greatest measured height cleared by a hunted kangaroo is a pile of timber 10 feet 6 inches high. The longest recorded leap was reported in January 1951, when, in the course of a chase, a female red kangaroo (*Macropus rufus*) made a series of bounds which included one of 42 feet. There is an unconfirmed report of a great grey Kangaroo (*Macropus conguru*) jumping nearly 13·5 metres (44·7 feet) on the flat.

DOMESTICATED ANIMALS

HORSES

Oldest The greatest acceptable age for a horse (*Equus caballus*) is 52 years for a draught breed named "Monty", owned by Mrs. Marjorie Cooper of Albury, New South Wales, Australia, which died on 28 Jan. 1970. His jaw is now preserved in the School of Veterinary Science at Melbourne University. In 1919 an age of 54 years was reported for a pony living in France, but further details are lacking.

Largest The heaviest horse ever recorded was "Brooklyn Supreme", a pure-bred Belgian stallion weighing 3,200 lb. and standing 19½ hands (6 feet 6 inches). He died on 6 Sept. 1948, aged 20, in Callender, Iowa, U.S.A. The tallest horse ever recorded was "Dr. Le Gear", a seal brown dapple Percheron gelding standing 21 hands (7 feet 0 inches) and weighing 2,995 lb. (26·74 cwt.). Foaled in 1902, this horse, which measured 16 feet from nose to tail, died in St. Louis, Missouri, U.S.A., in 1919.

The heaviest horse ever recorded in Britain is "Saltmarsh Silver Crest" (born 1955), a Percheron stallion weighing 2,772 lb. (24·75 cwt.), owned by George E. Sneath of Money Bridge, near Pinchbeck, Lincolnshire. The horse stands 18·1 hands (6 feet 1 inch) tall. The tallest horse in Britain is "Wandle Robert", a Shire stallion owned by Young & Co.'s Brewery of Wandsworth, London. He stands 18·3 hands and weighs 1 ton (2,240 lb.).

Britain's heaviest horse—Saltmarsh Silver Crest, aged 14

Heaviest draught The greatest load hauled by a pair of draught horses was 50 logs comprising 36,055 board-feet of timber (=53·8 tons) hauled on the Nester Estate at Ewen, Ontonagon County, Michigan, U.S.A. in 1893.

DOGS

Largest The heaviest breed of domestic dog (*Canis familiaris*) is the St. Bernard. The heaviest example is "Schwarzwald Hof Duke" owned by Dr. A. M. Bruner of Oconomowoc, Wisconsin, U.S.A. He was whelped on 8 Oct.

34

1964 and weighed 283 lb. on 3 April 1968. The largest ever recorded in Britain was one named "Brandy", owned by Miss Gwendoline L. White of Chinnor, Oxfordshire. He weighed 18 stone 7 lb. (259 lb.) on 11 Feb. 1966 and died on 6 March 1966, aged 6½. "Westernisles Ross", known as "Lindwall", a St. Bernard owned by Jean R. Rankin of Glasgow, Scotland, whelped on 1 May 1962, weighed 18 stone 4 lb. (256 lb.) on 28 April 1966, and may have attained 19 stone (266 lb.) by the time of his death on 17 Aug. 1967 aged 5. The heaviest dog now living in Britain is believed to be "Monty", a mastiff owned by Mr. Walter Martin of Wilmington, Sussex, which weighed 17 stone 7 lb. (245 lb.) in Nov. 1967.

Britain's tallest dog —"Marron of Merrowlea", which measures 38 inches at the shoulder

Tallest The world's tallest breed of dog is the Irish wolfhound. The extreme recorded example was "Broadbridge Michael" (born 1926), owned by Mrs. Mary Beynon, then of Sutton-at-Hone, Kent. He stood 39½ inches at the shoulder. The tallest dog now living in Britain is believed to be "Marron of Merrowlea" (born Nov. 1968), a Great Dane owned by Mr. Gordon Jeffrey of Banstead, Surrey, which stands 38 inches at the shoulder.

Smallest The world's smallest breed of dog is the Chihuahua from Mexico. Their *average* weight is 2 to 4 lb., but some specimens weigh only 16 oz. when fully grown. The smallest British breed is the Yorkshire terrier, one of which, named Cody Queen of Dudley, was reported in July 1968 to have weighed only 20 oz. at 16 months. In July 1968 a five-year-old toy poodle owned by Mrs. Sylvia Wise of Bucknall, Staffordshire, called Samson, was reported to weigh only 16 oz.

Fastest The fastest breed of domestic dog is the saluki, also called the Arabian gazelle hound or Persian greyhound. Speeds up to 43 m.p.h. have been claimed but tests in the Netherlands have shown that it is not as fast as the present day greyhound which has attained a measured speed of 41¼ m.p.h.

Oldest Dogs of over 20 are very rare but even 34 years has been accepted by some authorities. The oldest reliably reported dog in the world was "Adjutant", a black labrador gun-dog, who was whelped on 14 Aug. 1936, and died on 20 Nov. 1963, aged 27 years and 3 months, in the care of his lifetime owner, James Hawkes, a gamekeeper at the Revesby Estate, near Boston, Lincolnshire. On 18 Dec. 1937 the death of a collie, aged 27, was reported by its owner, Mrs. Cole of Clerkenwell, London, and in 1951 an Irish terrier aged 28 was reported.

Rarest The rarest dog in the world is the löwchen or lion dog of which only 40 (32 in Germany and four each in Belgium and Great Britain) were alive in early 1969. The breed was a famous lapdog of the nobility of southern Europe during the Renaissance period.

Largest litter The largest recorded litter of puppies is one of 23 thrown on 11 Feb. 1945 by "Lena", a foxhound bitch owned by Commander W. N. Ely of Ambler, Pennsylvania, U.S.A. A litter of 23 has also been reported for a St. Bernard.

Most prolific The dog who has sired the greatest recorded number of puppies is the greyhound "Low Pressure", nicknamed "Timmy", whelped in Sept. 1957 and owned by Mrs. Bruna Amhurst of Regent's Park, London. From Dec. 1961 to the end of July 1969 he had fathered 2,389 registered puppies.

Most popular The breed with the most Kennel Club registrations in 1969 was the Alsation with 16,546. In 1970, Cruft's Dog Show (founded 1886 for terriers only) had an entry of 8,398 including 329 Alsations, compared with the record entry of 10,650 dogs in 1936 before entrants were restricted to prize winners.

Most expensive In January 1956 Miss Mary de Pledge, of Bracknell, Berkshire, England, turned down an offer of £10,500 from an American dog-breeder for her 3½-year-old champion pekingese "Caversham Ku-Ku of Yam".

"Top dog" The greatest altitude attained by any animal is 1,050 miles by the Samoyed husky (Russian, *laika*) bitch fired as a passenger in *Sputnik II* on 3 Nov. 1957. The dog was variously named "Kudryavka" (feminine form of "Curly"), "Limonchik" (diminutive of lemon), "Malyshka", "Zhuchka" or by the breed name "Laika".

Highest and longest jump The canine "high jump" record is held by the British dog "Mikeve", who scaled a wall of 9 feet 6 inches off a springboard in a test in Kensington, London, in 1934. The longest recorded canine long jump was one of 30 feet by a greyhound named "Bang" made in jumping a gate in coursing a hare at Brecon Lodge, Gloucestershire in 1849.

Strongest The greatest load ever shifted by a dog was a sledge weighing 3,142 lb. (1·40 tons), pulled by "Charlie", a husky owned by Larry Clendenon, in a test at Anchor Point, Alaska, U.S.A., on 11 Feb. 1961.

Ratting Mr. James Searle's bull terrier bitch "Jenny Lind" killed 500 rats in 1 hour 30 minutes at "The Beehive" in Liverpool in 1853. Another bull terrier named "Jacko", owned by Mr. Jemmy Shaw, was credited with killing 1,000 rats in 1 hour 40 minutes, but the feat was performed over a period of ten weeks in batches of 100 at a time. The last 100 were accounted for in 5 min. 28 secs. in London on 1 May 1862.

Tracking The greatest tracking feat recorded was performed by the Doberman *Sauer*, trained by Detective-Sergeant Herbert Kruger. In 1925 he tracked a stock thief 100 miles across the Great Karroo, South Africa by scent alone. In Jan. 1969 a German Alsatian bitch was reported to have followed her master 745 miles from Brindisi to Milan, Italy in four months. The owner had left her when he went on a visit.

CATS

Heaviest The heaviest domestic cat (*Felis catus*) ever recorded was a "tiger and white" tom named "Clauz" in San Francisco, California, U.S.A. He weighed 40 lb. in July 1950, when aged 8 years and had a girth of 36 inches. The heaviest recorded in Britain is "Roger", belonging to the Pennock family in Accrington, Lancashire. It was reported on 6 Jan. 1968 that he weighed 38 lb. He was then 7 years old. The average weight is 11 lb.

Oldest According to the American Feline Society a cat living in Hazleton, Pennsylvania, celebrated its 37th birthday on 1 Nov. 1958, but further details are lacking. The oldest cat ever recorded in Britain was the tabby "Puss",

Britain's oldest cats—"Flip" and "Buncle" in their garden at Brighton, Sussex

owned by Mrs. T. Holway of Clayhidon, North Devon. He was 36 on 28 Nov. 1939. A more recent and better documented case was that of the female tabby "Ma" owned by Mrs. Alice St. George Moore of Drewsteignton, Devon. She was put to sleep on 5 Nov. 1957, aged 34.

Largest litter The largest litter ever recorded was one of 12 kittens, born in March 1953 to "Brackledown Beauty", aged 2½, a blue-pointed Siamese cat owned by Mrs. E. F. Morrison of Hastings, Sussex. A litter of 13 has been reported for another Siamese cat, but details are lacking. The usual litter size is between 5 and 9.

Most prolific A cat named "Dusty", aged 17, living in Bonham, Texas, U.S.A., gave birth to her 420th kitten on 12 June 1952.

Greatest fall "Pussycat", owned by Miss Anne Walker of Maida Vale, London, fell 120 feet from the balcony of his owner's 11th-storey flat on 7 March 1965. He landed unhurt.

Most lives "Thumper", a 2½-year-old tabby owned by Mrs. Reg Buckett of Westminster, London was trapped in a lift shaft without food or water for 52 days from 29 March 1964.

Richest and most valuable Dr. William Grier of San Diego, California, U.S.A., died in June 1963, leaving his entire estate of $415,000 (£172,916) to his two 15-year-old cats, "Hellcat" and "Brownie". When the cats died in 1965 the money went to the George Washington University in Washington, D.C., U.S.A. In 1967 Miss Elspeth Sellar of Grafham, Surrey, turned down an offer of 2,000 guineas (£2,100) from an American breeder for her two-year-old champion white Persian tom "Coyun Marcus".

Rarest breed The rarest of the 50 recognized breeds in Britain is the self-red longhair.

Ratting A five-month-old tabby kitten named "Peter" living at Stonehouse railway station, Gloucestershire, killed 400 rats during a four week period in June-July 1938. Many of the kitten's victims seemed almost as large as itself. The greatest mouser on record was a tabby named "Mickey", owned by Shepherd & Sons Ltd. of Burscough, Lancs., which killed more than 22,000 mice during 23 years with the firm. He died in Nov. 1968.

Biggest show There was a record entry of 1,866 cats and kittens for the National Cat Club's 73rd Show at Olympia, London, on 13 Dec. 1969. The largest cat population is that of the U.S.A. with 28 million. Of Great Britain's cat population of 6 million an estimated 100,000 are "employed" by the Civil Service.

RABBITS
The largest breed of rabbit (*Oryctolagus cuniculus*) is the Flemish giant, with an average weight of 14 lb. They measure up to 40 inches long from toe to toe, when fully stretched. The heaviest specimen recorded was a male named "Floppy", who weighed 25 lb. and died in June 1963, aged 8. The smallest breed is the pigmy rabbit (*Sylvilagus idahoensis*) of the south-western United States, which has a total length of 8–11 inches and weighs up to 1 lb.

For auction prices, milk yield and prolificacy records for cattle, sheep and pigs, see under Agriculture.

The smallest bird in the world the bee hummingbird, weighing 18 to the ounce

2. Birds *(Aves)*

LARGEST
Of the 8,600 known living species, the largest is the North African ostrich (*Struthio camelus camelus*) which occurs south of the Atlas Mountains from Upper Senegal and Niger country across to the Sudan and Central Ethiopa. Male examples of this flightless or ratite bird reach 345 lb. in weight and stand 9 feet tall. Ostriches are able to run at a speed of 37 m.p.h.

The heaviest flying bird, or carinate, is the Kori bustard or paauw (*Otis kori*), which has a wing-span of 8 feet or more. Cock birds weighing up to 40 lb. have been shot in South Africa, and one outsized specimen, killed in the Western Transvaal, was estimated to weigh 54 lb. The mute swan (*Cygnus olor*) has an average weight of 28 lb. A single instance has been recorded of one weighing 23 kilogrammes (50·7 lb.). Mute swans are resident in Britain where they have attained 44 lb. A weight of 46·2 lb. has also been reported for the great bustard (*Otis tarda*). The heaviest flying bird of prey is the Andean condor (*Vultur gryphus*), which weighs 20–25 lb. There is also a record of a female harpy eagle (*Harpia harpyja*) caught in Guyana which weighed 27 lb. (average weight 16–17 lb.).

Largest wing-span The wandering albatross (*Diomedea exulans*) of the southern oceans has the largest wing-span of any bird, adult males averaging 10 feet 3 inches with wings tightly stretched. The largest recorded specimen was one measuring 11 feet 10 inches caught by banders in Western Australia in *c.* 1957, but some unmeasured birds may exceed 12 feet. This size is closely matched by the Andean condor (*Vultur gryphus*), which has the greatest wing area of any bird. Adults commonly have a wing-span of 9¾ to 10 feet, and some specimens may reach 11 feet. One example killed in southern Peru in *c.* 1841 was alleged to have had a wing-span of 14 feet 2 inches, but this measurement must be regarded as excessive. In extreme cases the wing-span of the marabou stork (*Leptoptilus crumeniferus*) found in Africa, may also exceed 11 feet (average span 9½ feet), and there is

The wandering albatross, the wing-span of which may exceed 12 feet

The Marabou stork, the wing-span of which may challenge even the albatross

an unconfirmed record of 13 feet 4 inches for a specimen shot in Central Africa. In August 1939 a wing-span of 12 feet was recorded for a mute swan (*Cygnus olor*) named "Guardsman" (died 1945) at the famous swannery at Abbotsbury, near Weymouth, Dorset. The average span is 9 feet.

SMALLEST
World The smallest bird in the world is the male bee hummingbird (*Mellisuga helenae*), also known as Helena's hummingbird or "the fairy hummer", found in Cuba. A fully-grown adult has a wing-span of 1½ inches. The adult male weighs only 2 grammes or 1/18th of an ounce.

This is less than a Sphinx moth. It has an overall length of 55 to 62 millimetres (2·2 to 2·4 inches), the bill and tail accounting for about 40 millimetres (1·6 inches). The adult females measure 57 to 66 millimetres (2·2 to 2·6 inches). The bee hummingbird (*Acestrura bombus*) of Ecuador is about the same size but is slightly heavier.

United Kingdom The smallest resident British bird is the goldcrest (*Regulus regulus*), measuring 3½ inches long and weighing 4½ grammes (0·16 of an ounce). It resembles a small olive warbler and has a bright orange and yellow crown with a black border. The firecrest (*Regulus ignicapillus*) is of almost equal diminutiveness.

MOST ABUNDANT

World The most abundant species of bird is the chicken, the domesticated form of the wild red jungle fowl (*Gallus gallus*) of India and south-east Asia. There are believed to be about 3,000 million in the world. The most abundant wild bird is believed to be the starling (*Sturnus vulgaris*). The most abundant and also the smallest of all sea birds is Wilson's petrel (*Oceanites oceanicus*), being only 7 inches in length. It is found as far south as Antarctica.

The most abundant species *ever* recorded was the passenger pigeon (*Ectopistes migratoria*) of North America. It has been estimated that there were between 5,000,000,000 and 9,000,000,000 of this species before *c*. 1880. Thereafter the birds were killed in vast numbers and the last recorded specimen died on 1 Sept. 1914 in the Zoological Gardens in Cincinnati, Ohio, U.S.A. This bird, a female, was mounted and is now on exhibition in the Smithsonian Institution, Washington, D.C., U.S.A.

United Kingdom The commonest breeding bird in Great Britain and Ireland is the house-sparrow (*Passer domesticus*) estimated in 1959 at *c*. 9,500,000 from Great Britain only. There are single roosts of starlings (*Sturnus vulgaris*) with populations estimated to be between 3,500,000 and 4,500,000 birds. London's population of house-sparrows was estimated to be 300,000 in 1959. It was estimated in 1967 that 250,000 pigeon fanciers owned an average of 40 racing pigeons per loft, making a population of *c*. 10,000,000 in Great Britain.

RAREST

World Perhaps the best claimants to this title would be the ten species last seen in the 19th century but still just possibly extant. They are the New Caledonian lorikeet (*Vini diadema*) (New Caledonia *ante* 1860); the Himalayan mountain quail (*Ophrysia superciliosa*) (eastern Punjab, 1868); Forest Spotted Owlet (*Athene blewitti*) (Central India, *c*. 1872); the Samoan wood rail (*Pareudiastes pacificus*) (Savaii, Samoa, 1873); the Fiji bar-winged rail (*Rallina poecilopterus*) (Ovalau and Viti Levu, 1890); the Kona "finches" (*Psittirostrata flaviceps* and *P. palmeri*) (Kona, Hawaii, 1891 and 1896); the Akepa (*Loxops coccinea*) (Oahu, Hawaii, 1893); the Kona "finch" (*Psittirostrata kona*) (Kona, Hawaii, 1894) and the Mamo (*Drepanis pacifica*) (Hawaii, 1898). The Ivory-billed woodpecker (*Campephilus principalis*) has been confirmed as surviving since 1963. The Maui nukupuu from Hawaii, considered extinct since 1896, was spotted in 1968 but is only a sub-species (*Hemignathus lucidus affinis*).

United Kingdom There are 36 species of birds (8 of them unconfirmed) which have been recorded only once in the British Isles. That which has not recurred for the longest period is the black capped petrel (*Pterodroma hasitata*), one of which was caught on a heath, at Southacre, Swaffham, Norfolk, in March or April 1850. The rarest disclosed and regularly nesting British bird is the osprey (*Pandion haliaetus*) which has enjoyed unremitting protection in Scotland since 1953.

ngest lived The greatest irrefutable age reported for any bird is 68 years in the case of a female European eagle-owl

(*Bubo bubo*) living in 1899. Other records which are regarded as probably reliable include 73 years (1818–91) for a sulphur-crested cockatoo (*Cacatua galerita*), 80 years for a domestic goose (*Anser anser*), 72 years (1797–1869) for an African grey parrot (*Psittacus erithacus*), 70 years (1770–1840) for a mute swan (*Cygnus olor*), and 69 years for a raven (*Corvus corax*). An Egyptian vulture (*Neophron percnopterus*) which died in the menagerie at Schönbrunn, Vienna, Austria, in 1824 was stated to have been 118 years old, but the menagerie was not founded until 1752. On 8 March 1968 the death was reported in the Nottingham Park Aviary of "Cocky", a sulphur-crested cockatoo, aged 114 years, but this record is considered unreliable as several cockatoos named "Cocky" had been kept in this aviary over the years.

Another sulphur-crested cockatoo named "Cocky", owned by Mr. Basil Compton of Bridge Sollers, Hertfordshire, died in October 1969 allegedly aged 125 years.

Fastest flying The fastest flying bird is the spine-tailed swift (*Chaetura caudacuta*), for details see page 28.

The fastest running speed for any bird is 40 m.p.h. for the emu (*Dromiceus novae-hollandiae*).

Of standard game birds, the fastest is the spur-wing goose (*Plectropterus gambiensis*), with a recorded ground speed of 88 m.p.h. in level flight.

Fastest wing beats The fastest recorded wing beat of any bird is 80 beats per second by the male amethystine hummingbird (*Calliphlox amethystina*) of tropical South America. In 1951 wing beats of up to 200 per second were reported for the ruby-throated hummingbird (*Archilochus colubris*) and the rufous hummingbird (*Selasphorus rufus*) of the eastern United States during courtship flights. Large vultures (Vulturidae) only flap their wings about once per second.

Fastest swimmer Gentoo penguins (*Pygoscelis papua*) have been timed at 22½ m.p.h. under water, which is a respectable flying speed for some birds.

Longest flights The longest recorded banded recovery is one of 12,000 miles by a Manx shearwater (*Procellaria puffinus*) which was ringed on Anglesey, Wales in June 1966 and found in New South Wales, Australia, in Dec. 1966. There is also an unconfirmed report of an Arctic Tern (*Sterna paradisaea*) flying 14,000 miles from Arctic U.S.S.R. to Australia in four months. The slender-billed shearwater (*Puffinus tenuirostris*) annually flies 20,000 miles around the Pacific Ocean.

Highest flying The celebrated example of a skein of 17 geese photographed by an astronomer crossing the Sun from Dehra Dun, India, on 17 Sept. 1919, at a height variously estimated at up to 29,500 feet, has been discredited by experts. The highest acceptable altitude is 8,200 metres (26,902 feet) by an alpine chough (*Pyrrhocorax graculus*) on Mount Everest in 1953 but its take-off point may have been as high as 20,000 feet. There is reason to believe migrant birds regularly clear the higher parts of the Himalaya range. On three separate occasions in September 1959 a radar station in Norfolk picked up flocks of small passerine night migrants flying in from Scandinavia at 21,000 feet (3·97 miles). They were probably warblers, chats and fly catchers.

Most acute vision Tests have shown that owls are able to swoop on targets in an illumination of only 0·00000073 of a foot-candle (equivalent to the light from a candle lit 390 yards distant). This acuity is 50 times as great as that of human night vision. In good light and against a contrasting background, a falcon can spot a pigeon at a range of over 3,500 feet.

EGGS

Largest Of living birds, that producing the largest egg is the North African ostrich (*Struthio camelus camelus*). The average egg weighs 3·63 to 3·88 lb., measures 6 to 7 inches in length, 4 to 6 inches in diameter and requires about 40 minutes for boiling. The shell is one-sixteenth of an inch thick and can support the weight of an 18 stone (252 lb.) man. The largest egg laid by any bird on the British list is that of the mute swan (*Cygnus olor*), whose eggs are from 4·3 to 4·9 inches long and between 2·8 and 3·1 inches in diameter.

Smallest The only recorded example of an egg of the bee hummingbird (*Mellisuga helenae*), the world's smallest bird (see page 36), is one measuring 11·4 millimetres (0·45 of an inch) long and 8 millimetres (0·32 of an inch) wide, now in the U.S. National Museum, Washington, D.C., U.S.A. This egg is closely matched in size by the eggs of the green and greyish white Vervain humming-bird (*Mellisuga minima*) of Jamaica, known as "the little doctor bird". Its egg looks like a large pearl and has an average length of 11·5 millimetres (0·45 of an inch) and a diameter of 8·25 millimetres (0·325 of an inch). The smallest eggs laid by any British bird are those of the goldcrest (*Regulus regulus*), which measure from 0·48 to 0·57 of an inch long and between 0·37 and 0·39 of an inch in diameter. The last confirmed nestings were in 1962 and 1965.

Incubation The shortest incubation period is that of the skylark (*Alauda arvensis*) at 11 days and the brown-headed cowbird (*Molothrus ater*) at 11 days, and the longest that of the royal albatross (*Diomedea epomophora*) at up to 81 days. The idlest of cock birds are humming-birds, among whom the hen bird does 100 per cent. of the incubation, whereas the female kiwi (*Apteryx*) leaves this entirely to the male.

The hardest worked avian father— the male Kiwi

Longest feathers The longest feathers are those of the cock birds of the Japanese long-tailed fowls, or onagadori, from Kochi in Shikoku, with tail coverts up to 30 feet in length.

Most feathers In a series of "feather counts" on various species of birds a whistling swan (*Cygnus columbianus*) was found to have 25,216 feathers. A ruby-throated hummingbird (*Archilochus colubris*) had only 940. The common house-sparrow (*Passer domesticus*) has about 3,500 in winter and 3,000 in summer.

Earliest and latest cuckoo It is unlikely that the cuckoo (*Cuculus canorus*) has ever been heard *and* seen in Great Britain earlier than

10 March, on which date one was observed in Devon in 1884 and in Wiltshire in 1938. The two latest dates recorded are 16 Dec. 1912 at Anstey's Cove, Torquay, Devon and 26 Dec. 1897 or 1898 in Cheshire.

Largest turkey The greatest recorded weight for a turkey (*Meleagris gallopavo*) is 70 lb., reported in Dec. 1966 for a stag named "Tom" owned by a breeder in California, U.S.A. Turkeys were first brought to Britain *via* Germany from South America in 1549.

DOMESTICATED BIRDS
The largest caged budgerigar (*Melopsittacus undulatus*) population is that of the United States with 19 million. Britain's population, 7 million in 1956, is now estimated as 4½ million. This small parakeet is wild in Australia.

Longest lived The average budgerigar life-span is 6–8 years. "Bluey," owned by Mrs. Dorothy Riddell, of Findern, near Derby, celebrated its 21st birthday on 10 Jan. 1955.

Most talkative bird A cock budgerigar called "Sparkie Williams", owned by Mrs. M. Williams of Bera Cross, near Bournemouth, Hampshire, had a vocabulary of 531 words, including the words "budgerigar" and "chatterbox". Its last words before its death, on 4 Dec. 1962 aged 8, were reportedly "I love Mama".

3. Reptiles *(Reptilia)*

(Crocodiles, snakes, turtles, tortoises and lizards.)

Largest and heaviest In former times the salt-water or estuarine crocodile (*Crocodylus porosus*) of south-east Asia attained reputed lengths of up to 33 feet. Such a specimen, with a girth of 13 feet 8 inches, was shot in the Bay of Bengal in 1840. It must have weighed about 3 tons and been very aged. Present-day crocodiles do not appear to exceed 22½ feet in length. Strictly carnivorous, they live in tidal waters and have been sighted far out to sea. They will devour anything that they can overcome and will eat human corpses. The largest British reptile, excluding snakes, is the slow worm (*Anguis fragilis*), which has been recorded up to 46 centimetres (18·1 inches) in length.

Smallest The smallest species of reptile is believed to be *Sphaero-dactylus parthenopiom,* a gecko found only on the island of Virgin Gorda, one of the British Virgin Islands, in the West Indies. It is known from 15 specimens, including some gravid females, found between 10 and 16 Aug. 1964. The three largest females measured 18 millimetres (0·71 of an inch) from snout to vent, with a tail of approximately the same length.

Two species of dwarf chameleon, *Evoluticauda tuber-culata* and *Evoluticauda minima,* both found in Madagascar, are each known from only one specimen, each specimen having an overall length of 32 millimetres (1·3 inches). The tails measured 14 and 12 millimetres, respectively, so the specimen of *E. tuberculata* also had a snout-vent length of 18 millimetres. However, chameleons are more bulky than geckos and it is not known if the specimens discovered were fully grown.

It is possible that another gecko, *Sphaerodactylus elasmorhynchus,* may be even smaller. The only speci-men ever discovered was an apparently mature female, with a snout-vent length of 17 millimetres (0·67 of an inch) and a tail of 17 millimetres, found on 15 March 1966 among the roots of a tree in the western part of the Massif de la Hotte in Haiti.

The smallest British reptile is the common or viviparous lizard (*Lacerta vivipara*), with a maximum length of 17·8 centimetres (7 inches).

Fastest The highest measured speed for any reptile on land is

REPTILES

18 m.p.h. by the race-runner lizard (*Cnemidophorus sexlineatus*) in Georgia, U.S.A. The highest speed claimed for any reptile in water is 22 m.p.h. by the leatherback turtle (see below).

Largest lizard The largest of all lizards is the Komodo monitor or Ora (*Varanus komodoensis*), a dragonlike reptile first discovered on the Indonesian island of Komodo in 1912 and now found on Flores. Two specimens more than 11 feet long have been exhibited in zoos in Germany and the Netherlands. Another measuring 10 feet 2 inches long and weighing 365 lb. was reported in 1937. Lengths of up to 13 feet have been quoted.

lest lizard The greatest age recorded for a lizard is more than 54 years for a male slow worm (*Anguis fragilis*) kept in the Zoological Museum of Copenhagen from 1892 until 1946.

CHELONIANS

Largest The largest of all chelonians is the Pacific leatherback turtle (*Dermochelys coriacea schlegelii*). The greatest weight reliably reported is 1,902½ lb. for a specimen captured near San Diego, California, U.S.A. on 20 June 1907 which had an overall length of 9 feet. The largest chelonian found in British waters is the Atlantic leatherback turtle (*Dermochelys coriacea coriacea*). One weighing 997 lb. and measuring more than 7 feet long was caught by a French fishing trawler in the English Channel on 8 May 1958. One described as weighing "nearly a ton" was netted off the Isles of Scilly on 18 June 1916.

The Pacific leatherback turtle

Perhaps the oldest living animal—
the famous Royal Tongan tortoise
"Tu'imalila",
reputedly about 200 years old

The heaviest recorded giant tortoise (*Testudo gigantea*) was one weighing 900 lb., collected in the Aldabra Islands, 270 miles north-east of Madagascar in 1847.

ngest lived The Royal Tongan tortoise named "Tu'imalila", believed to be a specimen of *Testudo radiata,* was reputedly presented to the King of Tonga by Captain James Cook (1728–79) in 1773 and died on 19 May 1966, thus indicating a possible age of about 200 years. The greatest proven age of a continuously observed tortoise is 116 years for a Mediterranean spur-thighed tortoise (*Testudo graeca*) which died in 1957 in Paignton Zoological Gardens, Devonshire. There is a reliable record of a common box turtle (*Terrapene carolina*) which lived for 129 years, from 1806 to 1935. It has been

reported that a male Marion's tortoise (*Testudo sumeirii*) lived at Port Louis, Mauritius, for 152 years, from 1766 to 1918.

Slowest moving Tests on a giant tortoise (*Testudo gigantea*) in Mauritius show that even when hungry and enticed by a cabbage it cannot cover more than 5 yards in a minute (0·17 m.p.h.) on land. Over longer distances its speed is greatly reduced.

SNAKES

Longest The longest (and the heaviest) of all snakes is the anaconda (*Eunectes murinus*) of South America. In 1944 a length of 37½ feet was reliably reported for a specimen killed on the upper Orinoco River in eastern Colombia. It must have weighed nearly 1,000 lb. compared to the normally acceptable limit of 500 lb. Another anaconda killed on the lower Rio Guaviare, in south-eastern Colombia, in Nov. 1956 measured 10 metres 25 centimetres (33 feet 7½ inches) in length. The longest snake ever kept in a zoo was probably "Colossus", a female reticulated or regal python (*Python reticulatus*) who died of tuberculosis on 15 April 1963 in the Highland Park Zoological Gardens, Pittsburgh, Pennsylvania, U.S.A. She measured 28 feet 6 inches on 15 Nov. 1956, when she was growing at the rate of about 10 inches per year. Her girth, before a feed, was measured at 36 inches on 2 March 1955 and she weighed 320 lb. (22 stone 12 lb.) on 12 June 1957. A length of 10 metres (32·8 feet) was reported for a reticulated python killed in the jungles of Celebes, Indonesia, in 1912. An African rock python (*Python sebae*) measuring 9·81 metres (32 feet 2 inches) was killed at Bingerville, Ivory Coast, in 1932. A large standing reward of $5,000 (now £2,083) for any snake over 30 feet is offered by the New York Zoological Society, in Bronx Park, New York City, N.Y., U.S.A. It has not yet been collected.

The longest poisonous snake in the world is the king cobra (*Ophiophagus hannah*), also called the hamadryad. A specimen measuring 18 feet 4 inches long was killed near Bangkok, in Thailand (Siam), in 1924.

The longest British snake is the grass snake (*Natrix natrix*). A female measuring 5 feet 10 inches was seen at Hambledon, Surrey, in 1934–35. It is found throughout southern England, in Wales and in Dumfries-shire, Scotland, but is absent from Ireland.

Heaviest The heaviest snake is the anaconda (*Eunectes murinus*). One 20 ft. 4 in. long specimen shot in Guyana weighed 360 lb., and a weight of 500 lb. has been reported for another that measured 25 feet. The heaviest poisonous snake is the Eastern diamond-backed rattle-snake (*Crotalus adamanteus*), found in the south-eastern United States. A specimen 7 feet 9 inches in length weighed 34 lb. Less reliable measurements of 42 lb. for an 8-foot 9 inch specimen have been reported.

Shortest The shortest known snake is the worm snake (*Leptotyphlops bilineata*), found on the West Indian islands of Martinique, Barbados and St. Lucia. It has a maximum recorded length of 11·9 centimetres (4·7 inches).

Oldest The oldest snake ever recorded was a female anaconda (*Eunectes murinus*) who lived in Switzerland for more than 31 years. She was imported on 18 Aug. 1930 and died on 8 May 1962 in the Zoological Garden, Basel.

Anaconda

Fastest moving The highest measured speed for a snake is that of the black mamba (*Dendroaspis polylepis*). A speed of 7 m.p.h. was recorded on 23 April 1906 near Mbuyani on the Serengeti Plains of Kenya. Stories that mambas can overtake galloping horses (maximum speed 43·26

39

m.p.h.) are wild exaggerations, though a speed of 15 m.p.h. may be possible for short bursts. Some observers maintain that the African grass snake (*Psammophis furcatus*), also called the "lebitsi", can travel faster than the mamba. The British grass snake (*Natrix natrix*) has a maximum speed of 4·2 m.p.h.

Most poisonous Authorities differ on which of the world's 300 poisonous snakes possess the venom which is most toxic. That of the Australian taipan (*Oxyuranus scutellatus*) is perhaps matched by that of the common krait (*Bungarus candidus*) of south-east Asia, and more likely by *Bothrops insularis*, a tree viper found only on the island of Queimada Grande, off south-eastern coast of Brazil. The tiger snake has a minimal lethal dose of only 2 milligrammes (1/14,000th of an ounce). It is believed that the venom of the beaked sea snakes (*Enhydrina schistosa*) found in the tropical and sub-tropical Indo-Pacific waters, may be even more toxic. The longest fangs of any snake are those of the Gaboon viper (*Bitis gabonica*), found in West, Central and South Africa, which measure up to 2 inches in length. A Gaboon viper bit itself to death on 12 Feb. 1963 in the Philadelphia Zoological Gardens, in Philadelphia, Pennsylvania, U.S.A. It was the only one of that species in the Zoo. They measure about 4 feet long and are brown and yellow.

It is estimated that 40,000 people are killed by snakes every year of whom *c*. 25,000 are in India. Burma has the highest mortality rate with 15·4 deaths per 100,000 population per annum.

The only poisonous snake in Great Britain is the adder (*Vipera berus*). Recently recorded deaths have been two in 1941 and one in 1957. The longest specimen recorded was one of 33½ inches, found in St. Leonard's Forest, near Horsham, Sussex, in July 1926.

4. Amphibians (Amphibia)

(Salamanders, toads, frogs, newts, caecilians, etc.)

LARGEST

World The largest species of amphibian is the giant salamander (*Megalobatrachus japonicus*), which is found in Japan and parts of China. The average length is about 36 inches, but one measuring 60 inches was taken in Kweichow (Gui zhou) province, in southern China, in the early 1920s. A captive specimen weighed 40 kilogrammes (88 lb.) when alive and 45 kilogrammes (99 lb.) after death, indicating that its body probably absorbed water from the aquarium after it had died.

The largest newt is the Waltl newt (*Pleurodeles waltl*), found in Morocco and the Iberian peninsula. It grows to a length of 40 centimetres (15¾ inches).

The largest frog is the rare Goliath frog (*Rana* (or *Conraua*) *goliath*), first found in West Africa in 1906. It measures up to 14 inches snout to vent, or 30 inches long with its legs extended. One weighing 3,305 grammes (7 lb. 13 oz.) was caught in the rapids of the River Mbia, Rio Muni, Spanish Guinea on 23 Aug. 1960. This may be matched by a species in central New Guinea, known locally as "agak" or "carn-pnag", first reported in December 1960 which is said to measure 12 to 15 inches long and to weigh more than 6 lb. A giant frog was reported in 1969 in Sumatra.

The giant salamander

40

The largest species of tree frog is *Hyla vasta*, found on the island of Hispaniola (Haiti and the Dominican Republic), in the West Indies. It has a maximum recorded length of 14·3 centimetres (5·6 inches) from snout to vent.

The largest toad is believed to be *Bufo paracnemis*, found in Brazil and northern Argentina. It has a maximum length of 10 inches.

The common toad (Bufo bufo)

Highest The common toad (*Bufo bufo*) is said to have been found at an altitude of 8,000 metres (26,200 feet) in Tibet, and at a depth of 340 metres (1,115 feet) in a mine.

Most poisonous The most active known venom is the batrachotoxin of the kokoi (*Phyllobates latinasus*), an arrow-poison frog of the Chocó in western Colombia, South America. Only about 1/100,000th of a gramme (0·0000004 of an ounce) is enough to kill a man.

Longest frog jump The record for three consecutive leaps is 32 feet 3 inches by a 2 inch long South African sharp-nosed frog (*Rana oxyrhyncha*), recorded by Dr. Walter Rose of the South African Museum on Green Point Common, Cape Town on 16 Jan. 1954. It was named "Leaping Lena" (but later found to be a male). At the annual Calaveras County Jumping Frog Jubilee at Angels Camp, California, U.S.A. in May 1955 another of this species made an unofficial *single* leap of over 15 feet when being retrieved for placement in its container.

Britain The largest British amphibian is the warty or great crested newt (*Triturus cristatus*). Males reach 14·6 centimetres (5·7 inches) in total length and females grow to 16·2 centimetres (6·37 inches). The maximum weight is 10½ grammes (0·37 of an ounce).

SMALLEST

World The smallest species of amphibian is believed to be the arrow-poison frog *Sminthillus limbatus*, a frog found in Cuba. Fully-grown specimens have a maximum recorded length of 13 millimetres (0·51 of an inch).

The smallest tree frog is the least tree frog (*Hyla ocularis*), found in the south-eastern United States. Adults are less than ¾ of an inch long.

The smallest species of toad is *Bufo taitanus beiranus*, first found *c*. 1906 near Beira, Mozambique, Africa. Mature adults have a maximum recorded length of only 24 millimetres (0·94 of an inch).

The smallest species of salamander is *Desmognathus wrighti*, found in the Great Smoky Mountains (in Tennessee and North Carolina), in the U.S.A. Some mature specimens are only 1·4 inches long.

The smallest newt is the striped newt (*Notophthalmus perstriatus*), found in the south-eastern United States. Adults are just over 2 inches long.

Britain The smallest amphibian found in Britain is the palmate newt (*Triturus helveticus*), which measures 7·5 to 9·2 cms. (2·95 to 3·62 inches) in length and weighs up to 2·39 grammes (0·83 of an ounce). The Natterjack or running toad (*Bufo calamita*), which has a maximum length of 8 cms. (3·14 inches) from snout to vent, is shorter but is heavier.

Longest lived A common toad (*Bufo bufo*) lived for 54 years in Copenhagen Zoological Garden, Denmark. A giant salamander (*Megalobatrachus japonicus*) lived for 50 or

52 years in Leyden Zoological Park, in the Netherlands, where it arrived from Japan in 1829 or 1831 and died on 3 June 1881. It was believed to be aged three when it arrived.

5. Fishes *(Pisces, Bradyodonti, Selachii, Marsipoli)*

LARGEST

Sea The largest species of fish is the whale-shark (*Rhinocdon typus* or variously *Rhineodon typus*) first discovered in Table Bay, Cape of Good Hope, South Africa, in April 1828 (length 15 feet). It is not, however, the largest marine animal, since it is smaller than the larger species of whales (mammals). A whale-shark measuring 59 feet long and weighing about 90,000 lb. (42·4 tons) was caught in a bamboo fish-trap at Koh Chik, in the Gulf of Siam, in 1919. Less reliable measurements up to 80 feet have been reported though the average length at maturity is 25 to 35 feet. The plankton-feeding whale-shark, greyish or dark brown with white or yellow spots, is extremely docile and lives in the warmer areas of the Atlantic, Pacific and Indian Oceans.

The largest carnivorous fish (excluding plankton eaters) is the great white shark (*Carcharodon carcharias*), also called the man-eater or the white pointer. A specimen 43 feet long and weighing about 17½ tons was captured after stranding itself in *c.* 1835 at False Bay, near the Cape of Good Hope, South Africa.

The largest fish recorded in the waters of the British Isles was a basking shark (*Cetorhinus maximus*) measuring 40 feet long and 25 feet in girth killed off Mutton Island, Galway Bay, Ireland on 3 May 1935 after becoming entangled in fishermen's nets. It weighed an estimated 14 tons. The largest bony fish found in British waters is the common sun-fish (*Mola mola*) also known as the ocean sun-fish, which grows up to 10 feet long and weighs more than one ton.

The common sturgeon

Freshwater The largest fish which spends its whole life in fresh water is the European catfish or wels (*Silurus glanis*). In September 1918 a specimen weighing 256·7 kg. (564·74 lb.) was caught in the Desna river, six miles from Chernigov, U.S.S.R. Another specimen allegedly weighing 300 kg. (660 lb.) was caught in the Dneiper river, near Kremenchug, U.S.S.R. The Arapaima (*Arapaima gigas*), also called the pirarucu, found in the Amazon and other South American rivers and often claimed to be the largest freshwater fish averages 6½ feet and 150 lb. The largest "authentically recorded" measured 8 feet 1½ inches and weighed 324 lb.

By far the largest of British freshwater fishes is the common sturgeon (*Acipenser sturio*). The heaviest recorded specimen was a female weighing 460 lb. taken in the River Esk, Yorkshire in 1810. Another specimen allegedly weighing "over 500 lb." was caught in the River Severn at Lydney Glos. on 1 June 1937 but further details are lacking. Larger specimens have been taken at sea—notably one weighing 700 lb. and 10 feet 5 inches long netted by the trawler "Ben Urie" off the Orkneys and landed at Aberdeen on 18 Oct. 1956.

SMALLEST

Freshwater The shortest recorded freshwater fish and the shortest of all vertebrates is *Pandaka pygmaea*, an almost transparent goby fish found in streams and lakes in the Philippines. It measures only 9 to 11 mm. (0·35 to 0·43 of an inch) long and weighs only 6 milligrammes (0·0002 of an ounce).

Marine The shortest recorded marine fishes are the Marshall

Islands goby (*Eviota zonura*), measuring 12 to 16 mm., and *Schindleria praematurus* from Samoa, measuring 12 to 19 mm., both in the Pacific Ocean. Mature specimens of the latter, largely transparent and first identified in 1940, have been known to weigh only 2 milligrammes, equivalent to 14,175 to the ounce—the lightest of all vertebrates and the smallest catch possible for any fisherman. The smallest British fish is the scorpion goby (*Gobios scorpoides*) found in the Thames with a maximum length of one inch.

Fastest The Atlantic sailfish (*Istiophorus americanus*) is generally considered to be the fastest species of fish, although the practical difficulties of measurement make data extremely difficult to secure. A figure of 68 m.p.h. (100 yards in 3 secs.) has been cited for one off Florida, U.S.A. The other species of spearfish (family Istiophoridae), including the Pacific sailfish (*Istiophorus greyi*) and the marlins (genus *Makaira*), are believed to be almost equally fast. A maximum of 50 knots (57·6 m.p.h.) has been calculated for a swordfish (*Xiphias gladius*) from a penetration of 22 inches by a bill into hard wood, but 30 to 35 knots (35 to 40 m.p.h.) is the most conceded by some experts. The Mako shark (*Isurus oxyrinchus*) may be even faster, since the flesh of swordfish has been found in the stomachs of captured specimens. Speeds in excess of 35 knots (40 m.p.h.) have also been attributed to the wahoo (*Acanthocybium solandri*) and the tuna (genus *Thunnus*).

Longest lived Aquaria are of too recent origin to be able to establish with certainty which species of fish can fairly be regarded as the longest lived. Early indications are that it is the lake sturgeon (*Acipenser fulvescens*). One aged 82 years was reported in 1954. Another lake sturgeon 81 inches long, and weighing 215 lb., caught on 15 July 1953 in the Lake of the Woods, Kenora, Ontario, Canada, was believed to be 150 years old, based on a growth ring (*annuli*) count in the spiny ray of its pectoral fin. A figure of 150 years has also been attributed to the mirror carp (*Cyprinus carpio*), but the greatest authoritatively accepted age is "more than 50".

Shortest lived The shortest lives of any vertebrate animals are those of the goby fishes (family Gobiidae), which are hatched, grow, reproduce and die in less than a year. The same may also be true of the ice fish (family Chaenichthyidae) of the Antarctic.

Deepest The greatest depth from which living organisms have been recovered is 35,137 feet by the U.S.S.R.'s research vessel *Vityaz* in the Tonga Deep area of the Pacific Ocean in September 1957. Dr. Jacques Piccard sighted a red shrimp one inch long and a flounder-type bottom feeder 12 inches long (tentatively identified as *Chascanopsetta lugubris*) from the bathyscaphe *Trieste* a few feet from its deepest ocean descent (calculated to be 35,802 feet) on 24 Jan. 1960. This sighting has been questioned by some authorities, who still regard 7,500 metres (24,600 feet) as the acceptable known limit for fish, in the case of brotulids of the genus *Bassogigas*.

Most eggs The common sun-fish (*Mola mola*) produces up to 300,000,000 eggs 1/10th of an inch long and 1/20th of an inch in diameter. The cichlids and certain catfish (order Ostariophysi) lay as few as 50.

Largest egg The largest egg of any living animal is that of the whale-shark (*Rhincodon typus*). One measuring 10½ inches long and 6 inches wide was picked up at a depth of 150 feet, 130 miles South of Port Isabel, Texas, U.S.A. in 1955. The egg contained a perfect embryo of a whale-shark 16 inches long.

Most venomous The most venomous fish in the world are the stonefish (*Synanceja verrucosa, S. horrida* and *S. trachynis*) of the tropical Indo-Pacific oceans. Contact with the spines of their fins usually proves fatal.

Most electric The electric eel (*Electrophorus electricus*) measuring up

The animal and plant kingdoms

to 10 feet in length, 90 lb. in weight can discharge a shock of 650 volts at one ampere which is sufficient to stun a man 20 feet distant. It is found in the rivers of Brazil, Colombia and Peru.

6. Starfishes *(Asteroida)*

Largest   The largest recorded starfish is the 19-armed sun starfish (*Solaster sp.*), found on the Pacific coast of North America, which measures up to 3 feet across and weighs several pounds. The largest species found in Britain is the spiny starfish (*Marthasterias glacialis*), which exceptionally measures up to 28 inches but usually 9–12 inches across.

Smallest   The smallest recorded starfish is one of the genus Marginaster, which has a diameter of only half an inch when fully grown. The smallest starfish found in Britain is the cushion starfish (*Asterrina gibbosa*), which has a diameter of about one inch.

7. Arachnids *(Arachnida)*

MOST SOUTHERLY
In 1964 three previously unrecorded species of arachnids were found living in mosses at a height of 5,000 feet on a mountain near the snout of the Robert Scott Glacier, Antarctica, 309 miles from the South Pole. These included *Nano orchestes antarcticus,* a minute pink eight-legged mite 0·01 of an inch long. The temperature was −20° F.

SPIDERS (Order Araneae)

LARGEST
World   The world's largest known spider is the South American "bird-eating" spider (*Theróphosa leblondii*). A male specimen with a leg-span of 10 inches, when fully extended and a body length of 3½ inches, was collected in April 1925 at Montagne la Gabrielle, French Guiana. The heaviest spider ever recorded was a female of the genus *Lasiodora*, collected at Manaos, Brazil, in 1945. It measured 9½ inches across and weighed almost 3 ounces.

Britain   Of the 603 known British species of spider, covering an estimated population of more than 500,000,000,000,000 the longest is the cardinal spider (*Tegenaria parietina*), a species of house spider, among which the males have a leg-span sometimes exceeding 5 inches (length of body 19 mm. or 0·75 of an inch). An outsized specimen of the "Daddy Longlegs" spider (*Pholcus phalangioides*) in England has been measured 6 inches across. The spider *Segestria florentina* has a body measuring up to 23 millimetres (0·92 of an inch) long. The heaviest spider in Britain is *Araneus quadratus* (formerly called *Araneus reaumuri*), an orb-weaver. One specimen captured in Oct. 1943 weighed 1·174 grammes (0·041 of an ounce) and measured 15 millimetres (0·58 of an inch) across the body.

SMALLEST
The smallest known spider in the world is *Microlinpheus bryophilus* (Family Argiopidae) discovered in Lorne, Victoria, Australia in 1932. The adult male has a body length of 0·6 of a millimetre or 1/35th of an inch. The smallest recorded spiders found in Britain are *Saloca diceros,* found among mosses in Dorset and Staffordshire, and *Glyphesis cottonae,* each of which has a body length of 1 mm. (1/25th of an inch).

Largest web   The largest webs are those spun by the female bird-eating golden orb-weaver (*Nephila pipipes*) found in Africa, Asia and Australasia with circumferences up to 12 feet.

42

Most poisonous   The most poisonous spider recorded is the brown recluse spider (*Loxosceles reclusa*), also called the fiddler spider, which is found in the central and southern states of the U.S.A. The bite produces an ulcerating wound which often turns gangrenous. The bite or repeated bites of the female black widow spider (*Latrodectus mactans*) of South America, the Australian red-backed (*Latrodectus hasseltii*) spiders and funnel-web spiders (*Atrax robustus* and *A. formidabilis*) of Australia; and the button spider (*Lactrodectus indistinctus*) can be fatal.

Rarest   The most elusive of all spiders are the primitive burrowing spiders (genus *Liphistius*) found in south-east Asia.

Fastest   The highest speed measured for a spider is 1·73 feet per second (1.17 m.p.h.) in the case of a specimen of *Tegenaria atrica*.

Longest lived   Some of the large bird-eating spiders (*Mygalomorphae*) have been kept in captivity for up to 25 years. The longest lived of British spiders is probably the house spider (*Tegenaria derhamii*) which has been kept in captivity for as long as 7 years.

The house spider

8. Crustaceans *(Crustacea)*

(Crabs, lobsters, shrimps, prawns, crayfish, barnacles, water fleas, fish lice, woodlice, sand hoppers, kril, etc.)

LARGEST
World   The largest of all crustaceans is the scarlet giant Japanese spider crab (*Macrocheira kaempferi*), possessing a body a foot across and legs capable of spanning up to 12½ feet, claw-tip to claw-tip. A specimen spanning 12 feet 1½ inches weighed 14 lb.

The largest species of lobster is the American or North Atlantic lobster (*Homarus americanus*). One weighing 42 lb. was caught in a deep-sea trawl by the smack *Hustler* off the Virginia Capes, Massachusetts, U.S.A. in the autumn of 1934. It is now on exhibition in the Museum of Science, Boston, Massachusetts, U.S.A. Less reliable weights up to 60 lb. have been reported.

Britain   The largest crustacean found in British waters is the common or European lobster (*Homarus gammarus*), with an average length of 13 inches and an average weight of 8 lb. A specimen weighing 14½ lb., caught in Sept. 1969 off St. Anne's Head, is now mounted in the bar of the Amroth Arms, Pembrokeshire, Wales. The largest crab found in British waters is the edible or great crab (*Cancer pagurus*). One weighing 14 lb. measuring 11 inches across was reported in 1895.

The European lobster

The pea crab

Smallest The smallest known crustaceans are water fleas of the genus *Alonella*, which may measure less than 1/100th of an inch long. They are found in British waters. The smallest British crab is the pea crab (*Pinnotheres pisum*), with a shell only 0·25 of an inch long.

Oldest The oldest of all known crustaceans is the *Hutchinsoniella*, similar to the trilobites of 500,000,000 years ago. First found in 1954, it is only 1/100th of an inch in length.

Deepest The marine crab *Ethusina abyssicola* has been taken at a depth of about 14,000 feet.

9. Insects *(Insecta)*

Largest The bulkiest of all insects is *Goliathus regius,* a "Goliath beetle", found in West Africa. It measures up to 5·85 inches in length, 4 inches across the back and weighs up to 3·4 oz. The beetle *Macrodontia cervicornis,* found in South America, is a little longer but less bulky. The longhorn beetle (*Batocera wallacei*) of New Guinea has a body length of 3½ inches but a total length of up to 11 inches, including antennae. The Hercules beetle (*Dynastes hercules*) has a body length of up to 6·56 inches. Some tropical stick-insects (family Phasmidae) have a body length of up to 13 inches and, in the case of the *Palophus titan* from Australia, a wing-span of 10 inches.

The largest British ground insect is the stag beetle (*Lucanus cervus*) found in Hampshire, which has a length of up to 2 inches, including antler-like mandibles. The heaviest ground insect found in Britain is the great silver beetle (*Hydrophilus piceus*), which has an overall length of 1¾ inches. Butterflies and moths (see below) have greater dimensions.

Smallest Several hundred new species of insect are discovered every year, but the smallest of those known are "hairy-winged" beetles of the family Trichopterygidae and the "battledore-wing fairy flies" of the family Mymaridae (parasitic wasps). They measure only 0·2 of a millimetre (0·008 of an inch) in length and the fairy flies have a wing-span of only 1 millimetre (0·04 of an inch). The male bloodsucking banded louse (*Enderleinellus zonatus*), ungorged, and the parasitic wasp *Caraphractus cinctus* may each weigh as little as 0·005 of a milligramme, or 5,670,000 to an ounce. The eggs of the latter each weigh 0·0002 mg., or 141,750,000 to the ounce.

Fastest flying Experiments have proved that widely published statements that the female deer bot-fly could attain a speed of 820 m.p.h. are wildly exaggerated. Acceptable modern experiments have now established that the highest maintainable air-speed of any insect, including the deer bot-fly, is 24 m.p.h., rising to a maximum of 36 m.p.h. for short bursts. A relay of bees (maximum speed 14 m.p.h.) would use only a gallon of nectar in cruising 4,000,000 miles at an average speed of 7 m.p.h.

Longest lived The oldest recorded insect is *Buprestis splendens,* a wood-boring beetle which has been known to live for up to 37 years. Some queen termites (family Termitidae) are, however, believed to live for as long as 40 years.

Loudest The loudest of all insects is the male cicada (family (Cicadidae). At 7,400 pulses per minute its sounding membrane produces a noise (officially described by the United States Department of Agriculture as "Tsh-ee-EEEE-e-ou") detectable more than a quarter of a mile distant. The only British species is *Cicadetta montana,* confined to the New Forest area in Hampshire.

Southernmost The farthest south at which any insect has been found is 77° S. (900 miles from the South Pole) in the case of a springtail (order Collembola).

Largest swarm The greatest recorded swarm of locusts (family Acrididae) was one covering an estimated 2,000 square miles across the Red Sea in 1889. Such a swarm must have contained about 250,000 million insects weighing about 500,000 tons. A swarm of desert locusts (*Schistocerca gregaria*) can consume in 24 hours as much as 4 million elephants.

Fastest wing beat The fastest wing beat of any insect is 57,000 per minute by the midge *Forcipomyia*. In experiments with truncated wings, at a temperature of 98·6° F., the rate increased to 133,080 beats per minute. The muscular contraction-expansion cycle in 0·00045 or 1/2,218th of a second, further represents the fastest muscle movement ever measured.

Most butterflies beat their wings at a rate of 460 to 636 per minute.

Slowest wing beat The slowest wing beat of any insect is 300 per minute by the swallowtail butterfly (*Papilio machaon*).

Largest ant The largest of all ants is the great black ant (*Dinoponera gigantea*), found in the Amazon delta in South America. Females measure up to 1·3 inches overall.

The largest of the 27 species found in Britain is the wood ant (*Formica rufa*), which grows up to 11 millimetres (0·43 of an inch) long. The smallest is the thief ant (*Solenopsis fugax*), with a maximum length of 3 millimetres (0·12 of an inch).

Largest grasshopper The largest of all grasshoppers is *Pseudophyllanax imperialis,* found on the island of New Caledonia, in the south-western Pacific Ocean. It has a wing-span of nearly 10 inches and antennae extending 8 inches.

The largest found in Britain is the great green grasshopper (*Phasgoneura viridissima*), which is up to 3 inches long.

Dragonflies The largest of the 43 species of dragonflies found in Britain is the golden-ringed dragonfly (*Cordulegaster boltonii*), which has been measured at up to 3·3 inches long and may have a wing-span of more than 4 inches. The smallest dragonfly found in Britain is the scarce ischnura (*Ischnura pumilio*), with a body length of 1 inch and a wing-span of 1·3 inches.

Oldest flea A Russian bird flea (Order Siphonaptera) is reported to have lived for 1,487 days or a little more than 4 years.

Longest flea jump The long jump record for a flea is 13 inches by a California rodent flea in 1910. The high jump record is 7 inches. In jumping 130 times its own height a flea subjects itself to a force of 200 g. Siphonapterologists recognize more than 1,300 varieties.

The flea high and long jump records

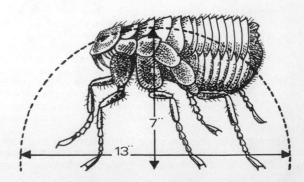

BUTTERFLIES AND MOTHS (Order Lepidoptera)

LARGEST

World The largest known moth is the Hercules Emperor moth (*Coscinoscera hercules*) of Australia and New Guinea. It has a wing area of up to 40·8 square inches and a span of 10 inches. The Indian atlas moth (*Attacus atlas*) and the great owlet moth (*Thysania agrippina*) of Brazil each have a wing-span of fully 12 inches but are less heavily built. The world's largest butterfly is the New Guinea birdwing (*Troides alexandrae*), the female of which has a span of 12 inches.

British The largest of the 21,000 species of insects found in the British Isles is the death's-head hawk moth (*Acherontia atropos*), which has a body length of about 6 centimetres (2·36 inches), an abdomen girth of 4 centimetres (1·57 inches) and a wing-span of up to 13·3 centimetres (5¼ inches). The largest butterfly found in the British Isles is the great monarch butterfly (*Danaus plexippus*), also called the milkweed butterfly, which breeds in the southern United States and Central America. From 1876 to 1968, 215 have been recorded in the United Kingdom. The wing-span of a fully grown specimen may exceed 4 inches. The largest *native* butterfly is the swallowtail (*Papillo machaon*), with a wing-span of 3–3½ inches. This species is now confined to the Norfolk Broads.

SMALLEST

World and Britain The smallest of the estimated 140,000 known species of Lepidoptera is the moth *Nepticula microtheiella*, with a wing-span of 3 millimetres (0·12 of an inch) and a body length of 2 millimetres (0·08 of an inch). It is found in Britain. The smallest known butterfly is the dwarf blue (*Brephidium barberae*) from South Africa. It is 14 millimetres (0·55 of an inch) from wing-tip to wing-tip. The smallest known British butterfly is the small blue (*Cupido minimus*), with a wing-span of 19 to 25 millimetres (0·75 to 1·0 inch).

Rarest The rarest of all butterflies is probably the birdwing *Ornithoptera allottei,* which is found only on Bougainville in the Solomon Islands. A specimen was sold for £750 in Paris on 24 Oct. 1966. A specimen of the Yellow Russian moth (*Rhyacia lucipeta*) taken in Sussex was exhibited in London in November 1968, and a Slender Burnished Brass moth (*Tlusia orichaleea*), whose home is India, was captured in southern England in October 1969. A grey Caradine of Mediterranean origin was first reported in August 1969 from Totteridge, Herts.

Most acute sense of smell The most acute sense of smell exhibited in nature is that of the male silkworm moth (*Bombyx mori*), or in Britain, the Emperor moth, which, according to German experiments in 1961, can detect sex attractant of the female at the almost unbelievable range of 11 kilometres (6.8 miles) upwind. This has been identified as one of the higher alcohols ($C_{16}H_{29}OH$) of which the female carries only $1·0 \times 10^{-13}$ of a gramme.

10. Centipede *(Chilopoda)*

Longest The longest recorded species of centipede is the venomous *Scolopendra gigas,* found on an island in Boca Grande, Venezuela. It has 23 segments (46 legs) and specimens have been measured up to 12 inches long and 1 inch across. The centipede with most segments is a tropical species of the genus *Geophilus,* which has 173 pairs of legs. The longest centipede found in Britain is *Haplophilus subterraneus,* which has between 77 and 83 segments and measures up to 76 millimetres (3 inches) long and 1·4 millimetres (0·055 of an inch) across.

Shortest The shortest recorded centipede is one with only 8 segments and, therefore, 16 legs. The shortest centipede found in Britain is *Lithobius duboscqui,* which has 15

Largest butterfly (c.f. 2s. piece)

segments (30 legs) and measures up to 9·5 millimetres (0·38 of an inch) long and 1 millimetre (0·04 of an inch) across.

11. Millipedes *(Diplopoda)*

Most legs The creatures with the greatest number of legs are millipedes of which there are about 6,500 species. These are distinguished from centipedes by having two instead of one pair of legs on most segments of the body. The largest number of legs reported for a millipede is 784 legs for a species found in Panama in July 1958. Millipedes range in length from 2 millimetres (0·078 of an inch) to 30 centimetres (11·8 inches).

12. Segmented Worms *(Annelida or Annulata)*

Longest earthworm The longest known species of earthworm is probably *Megascolides australis,* first discovered in Gippsland region of eastern Victoria, Australia in 1868. An average specimen measures 4 to 5 feet long and ¾ of an inch thick and weighs nearly a pound. The longest on record measured 11 feet when fully extended. The eggs of this worm measure 2 to 3 inches long and ¾ of an inch in diameter. In Nov. 1967 a specimen of the African earthworm *Microschaetus rappi* measuring 11 feet long, and 21 feet when fully extended, was discovered at Debe Nek, near King William's Town, in the Eastern Cape. The *average* length of this species, however, is believed to be shorter than that of *Megascolides australis.* The longest segmented worm found in Britain is *Lumbricus terrestris,* which measures up to 35 centimetres (13¾ inches) in length.

13. Molluscs *(Mollusca)*

(Squids, octopuses, snails, shellfish, etc.)

Largest squid The heaviest of all invertebrate animals is the Atlantic giant squid (*Architeuthis princeps*), which has been stranded on British shores on occasions. The largest specimen ever recorded was one measuring 55 feet overall (head and body 20 feet, tentacles 35 feet), captured on 2 Nov. 1878, after it had run aground in Tickle Bay, Newfoundland, Canada. Its eyes were 9 inches in diameter. The total weight was calculated to be 8,456 lb. (3·77 tons). Another giant squid washed up at Arnarnaesvick, Iceland, in November or December 1790 and cut up for cod-bait may have been even heavier. It had a head and body length of *c.* 6·60 metres (21 feet 8 inches) and measured 11·88 metres (39 feet) overall (the tentacles had been mutilated). Two other examples stranded on the coast of Labrador, Canada, *c.* 1870 allegedly measured 80 and 90 feet overall, but further details are lacking.

The rare Pacific giant squid (*Architeuthis longimanus*) is much less bulky, but the longest recorded specimen was one measuring 57 feet overall, with a head and body length of 7 feet 9 inches and tentacles of 49 feet 3 inches, found in Lyall Bay, New Zealand, in 1888.

Largest octopus The largest octopus is *Octopus apollyon* of the North Pacific. A specimen caught off the coast of Alaska, U.S.A. had a span of 28 feet and weighed 360 lb. The Pacific octopus (*Octopus hongkongensis*) has been recorded up to 32 feet across, but its body is only about 18 inches long.

Most ancient The longest existing living creature is *Neopilina galatheae,* a deep-sea worm-snail which had been believed extinct for about 320,000,000 years, but which was found at a depth of 11,400 feet off Costa Rica by the Danish research vessel *Galathea* in 1952. Fossils found in New York State, U.S.A., in Newfoundland, Canada, and in Sweden show that this mollusc was also living about 500,000,000 years ago.

SHELLS

Largest The largest of all existing shells is the marine bivalve giant clam (*Tridacna gigas*), found on the Indo-Pacific coral reef. A specimen measuring 43 inches by 29 inches and weighing 579½ lb. (over a quarter of a ton) was collected from the Great Barrier Reef in 1917, and is now in the American Museum of Natural History, Central Park West, New York City, N.Y., U.S.A. The largest British shell is the fan mussel (*Pinna fragilis*), specimens of which, found at Tor Bay, Devon, measured 20 cms. (7·87 inches) in height and 37 cms. (14·56 inches) in length.

Smallest The smallest recorded shells are *Homalogyra atomus* and *H. rota,* marine gastropods found in the Atlantic Ocean. They are only 1/30th of an inch in diameter. The smallest British shell is the land gastropod *Punctum pygmaeum,* which has a height of 0·6 to 0·9 mm. (0·023 to 0·035 of an inch) and a length of 1·2 to 1·5 mm. (0·047 to 0·059 of an inch).

Rarest The most highly prized of all shells in the hands of conchologists is the white-tooth cowrie (*Cypraea leucodon*), measuring 3 inches long and found in deep water off the Cape of Good Hope, South Africa. Two examples are known, one in the British Museum (Natural History), London, and the other at Harvard University, Cambridge, Massachusetts, U.S.A. In 1964 a collector in New York paid $2,000 (£714) for one of the 44 known specimens of the "Glory of the Sea" shell (*Conus gloria-maris*) which he presented to the Academy of Natural Sciences in Philadelphia, Pennsylvania, U.S.A.

Longest lived Some experts regard the giant clam and the freshwater mussel (*Margaritan margaritifera*) as the longest lived shells, at up to 100 years.

SNAILS

Largest The largest recorded species of snail is the sea hare (*Aplysia californica*), which is found in coastal waters off California, U.S.A. The average weight is 7 to 8 lb. but specimens have been recorded up to 16 lb. The largest known land snail is the African giant land snail (*Achatina achatina*), measuring up to 10¾ inches long and weighing up to 1 lb. The largest found in Britain is the Roman or edible snail (*Helix pomatia*), which measures 4 inches long and weighs up to 3 oz.

Speed A snail's pace varies from as slow as 0·00036 m.p.h., or 23 inches per hour, up to 0·0313 m.p.h. (or 55 yards per hour) for the common garden snail (*Helix aspersa*). Tests were carried out at Maryland University, U.S.A.

14. Ribbon Worms (*Nermertina* or *Rhynchopods*)

Longest worm The longest of the 550 recorded species of ribbon worms, also called nemertines (or nemerteans), is the "living fishing-line worm" (*Lineus longissimus*), a highly elastic boot-lace worm found in the North Sea. It has a maximum recorded length of more than 90 feet, making it the longest recorded worm of any variety.

15. Jelly Fishes (*Scyphozoa* or *Scyphomedusia*)

Longest The longest jelly fish is the *Cyanea arctica*. For details see page 28.
The longest coelenterate found in British waters is the "lion's mane" jelly fish (*Cyanea capillata*) or the common sea blubber. It has been recorded up to 3 feet in diameter and 75 feet in length.

16. Sponges (*Parazoa, Porifera* or *Spongida*)

Largest and smallest The largest sponges are the barrel-shaped loggerhead (*Spheciospongia vesparium*), measuring 3½ feet high and 3 feet in diameter, found in the West Indies and Florida, U.S.A., and the Neptune's cup or goblet (*Poterion patera*) of Indonesia, standing up to 4 feet in height. The smallest sponges, fully grown, are 3 millimetres (0·12 of an inch) high. The rarest colouration among the 20,000 known species is blue.

Deepest Sponges have been recovered from depths of up to 18,500 feet (3·5 miles).

17. Extinct Animals

LARGEST
The first dinosaur to be scientifically described was *Megalosaurus bucklandi*, a 20-foot long bipedal theropod, in 1824. The bones of this animal had been discovered before 1818 in a slate quarry at Stonesfield, near Woodstock, Oxfordshire. It stalked across southern England about 130,000,000 years ago. The word "dinosaur" (great lizard) was not used for such reptiles until 1842. The longest recorded dinosaur was *Diplodocus carnegiei,* an attenuated sauropod which wallowed in the swamps of western North America about 150,000,000 years ago. A mounted skeleton in the Carnegie Museum, Pittsburgh, Pennsylvania, U.S.A. measures 87½ feet in length (neck 22 feet, body 15 feet, tail 50½ feet)—nearly the length of three London buses —and stands 11 feet 9 inches at the pelvis (the highest point on the body). This animal weighed an estimated 10·39 tons in life.

The heaviest of all prehistoric animals was the swamp-dwelling *Brachiosaurus*, which lived in East Africa and Colorado, U.S.A., between 135,000,000 and 165,000,000 years ago. This sauropod measured up to 82 feet in length (height at shoulder 21 feet) and weighed up to 77 tons when alive, but isolated bones have been discovered which suggest that some individuals may have weighed as much as 100 tons. It could reach foliage 42 feet above the ground.

Britain's largest prehistoric animal was the sauropod *Cetiosaurus leedsi,* which lived in England about 165,000,000 years ago. It measured up to 60 feet in length and weighed about 10 tons. The bones of this dinosaur were first located in the No. 1 Brickyard of the New Peterborough Brick Co., Peterborough in May 1898 and subsequently in Oxfordshire.

The animal and plant kingdoms

Largest predator The largest theropod was *Tyrannosaurus rex,* which lived about 75,000,000 years ago in what are now the states of Montana and Wyoming (found in 1900) in the U.S.A., and Mongolia. It measured up to 47 feet in overall length, had a bipedal height of up to 18½ feet, a stride of 13 feet and weighed a calculated 6·78 tons. Its 4-foot long skull contained serrated teeth measuring up to 6 inches in length.

Longest tusks The longest tusks of any prehistoric animal were those of the Imperial mammoth (*Archidiskodon imperator*), which lived in North America about 1,500,000 years ago. The longest ever found was one measuring over 16 feet, unearthed in 1933 near Post, Texas, U.S.A. In 1934 this tusk was presented to the American Museum of Natural History in New York City, N.Y., U.S.A.

Heaviest tusks The heaviest single tusk on record is one weighing 330 lb., with a girth of 35 inches, now preserved in the Museo Archeologico, Milan, Italy. It measures 11 feet 9 inches in length. The tallest extinct elephant was the mammoth *Parelephas trogontherii,* which lived about 1,000,000 years ago in central Europe and North America. A fragmentary skeleton found in Mosbach, West Germany, indicates a height of 4·5 metres (14 feet 9 inches) at the shoulder, but measurements up to 15 feet have been reported elsewhere.

Longest horns The prehistoric Giant Deer (*Megaceros giganteus*), erroneously called the Irish elk, which lived in Northern Europe and Northern Asia as recently as 50,000 B.C. stood 7 feet at the shoulder and had greatly palmated antlers measuring up to 14 feet across.

Largest bird The largest prehistoric bird was the elephant bird (*Aepyornis maximus*), also known as the roc bird, which lived in southern Madagascar. It was a flightless bird standing 9 to 10 feet in height and weighing up to 965 lb. It also had the largest eggs of any living creature. One example measures 12¼ inches in length with a diameter of 9⅜ inches, giving a capacity of 2·35 gallons—six times that of an ostrich egg. A more cylindrical egg preserved in the Academie des Sciences, Paris, France, measures 12⅝ inches by 15¾ inches, and probably weighed about 27 lb. with its contents. This bird may have survived until *c.* 1660. The flightless moa *Dinornis giganteus* of South Island, New Zealand, was taller, attaining a height of over 13 feet, but probably weighed about 520 lb.

In may 1962 a single fossilized ankle joint of an enormous flightless bird was found at Gainsville, Florida, U.S.A. The largest actually to fly was probably the condor-like *Teratornis incredibilis,* which lived in North America about 125,000,000 years ago. The remains of one of this species, discovered in Smith Creek Cave, Nevada, in 1952 indicate a wing-span of 5 metres (16 feet 4 inches), and the bird must have weighed at least 50 lb. Another gigantic flying bird named *Osteodontornis,* which lived in what is now the state of California, U.S.A. about 20,000,000 years ago, had a wing-span of 16 feet and was probably even heavier. It was related to the pelicans and storks. The albatross-like *Gigantornis eaglesomei* has been credited with a wing-span of 20 feet on the evidence of a single fossilized breastbone. It flew over what is now Nigeria between 34,000,000 and 58,000,000 years ago.

Southernmost The two southernmost fossil discoveries have been a piece of the jaw of the freshwater amphibian *labyrinthodont* and on 23 Nov. 1969 the skull of the extinct reptile *Lystrosaurus* at Coalsack Bluff some 400 miles from the South Pole.

Largest flying creature The extinct winged reptile *Pteranodon ingens,* which soared over what is now the State of Kansas, U.S.A. about 80,000,000 years ago, probably a dynamic sea-soarer, had a wing-span of up to 27 feet and weighed an estimated 66 lb. Britain's largest extinct flying creature was *Ornithocheirus,* with a wing-span of 10 feet, which flew over the Weald about 100,000,000 years ago.

Most brainless *Stegosaurus* ("plated reptile"), which measured up to 30 feet in length, eight feet in height at the hips and weighed 1¾ tons, had a plum-sized brain weighing only 2½ ounces. It represented 0·004 of one per cent. of its body weight, compared with 0·074 of one per cent. for an elephant and 1·88 per cent. for a human. It roamed widely across the Northern Hemisphere about 150 million years ago, trying to remember where it had been.

Largest mammal The largest prehistoric mammal, and the largest land mammal ever recorded, was *Indricotherium transouralicum* (= *Baluchitherium grangeri*), a long-necked, hornless rhinoceros found in central and western Asia between 20,000,000 and 40,000,000 years ago. It stood up to 17 feet 9 inches at the shoulder (25 feet to the crown of the head), measured 28 feet in length and weighed about 16 tons.

Largest marine reptile The largest marine reptile ever recorded was the short-necked plesiosaur *Kronosaurus,* which swam in the seas around what is now Australia about 100,000,000 years ago. It measured about 50 feet in length, with a skull 9 feet long.

Largest crocodile The largest recorded crocodile was *Phobosuchus* ("horror crocodile"), which lived in the lakes and swamps of what are now the states of Montana and Texas, U.S.A., 75,000,000 years ago. It measured up to 54 feet in length and had a skull 6 feet long. The gavial *Rhamphosuchus,* which lived in northern India about 7,000,000 years ago, was nearly as large, attaining a length of 50 feet.

Largest chelonians The largest prehistoric marine turtle was *Archelon ischyros,* which lived in the shallow seas of North

PROTISTA AND MICROBES

America about 80,000,000 years ago. An almost complete skeleton with a carapace (shell) 6½ feet long was discovered in August 1895 near the south fork of the Cheyenne River in Custer County, South Dakota. The skeleton, which has an overall length of 11 feet 4 inches (16 to 20 feet across the outstretched flippers), is now in the Peabody Museum of Natural History at Yale University, New Haven, Connecticut, U.S.A. This specimen is estimated to have weighed 6,000 lb. (2·7 tons) when it was alive.

The largest prehistoric tortoise was *Colossochelys atlas*, which lived in northern India between 7,000,000 and 12,000,000 years ago. An almost complete skeleton with a carapace 5 feet 5 inches long was discovered in the Siwalik Hills in 1923. It is now in the American Museum of Natural History in New York City, U.S.A. This animal has an overall length of 8 feet and is believed to have weighed about a ton when it was alive.

gest snake The longest prehistoric snake was the python-like *Gigantophis garstini*, which inhabited the United Arab Republic (formerly Egypt) about 50,000,000 years ago. Parts of a spinal column discovered at El Faiyûm indicate a length of about 42 feet.

Largest reptile eggs The largest reptilian eggs so far discovered are those of a *Hypselosaurus priscus* in the valley of the Durance, near Aix-en-Provence, southern France, found in Oct. 1960. The eggs of this 30-foot long sauropod, believed to be 80,000,000 years old, would have had, uncrushed, a length of 12 inches and a diameter of 10 inches.

Largest fish The largest fish ever recorded was the great shark *Carcharodon megalodon*, which lived between 1,000,000 and 25,000,000 years ago. The discovery of 6-inch long fossil teeth near Bakersfield, California, U.S.A. suggest a length of at least 80 feet.

Largest arachnid The largest arachnid ever recorded was *Pterygotus buffaloensis*, a sea scorpion (eurypterid), found off Wales, which lived about 400,000,000 years ago. It grew to a length of 9 feet.

argest insect The largest prehistoric insect was the dragonfly *Meganeura monyi*, which lived between 280,000,000 and 325,000,000 years ago. Fossil remains from Commentry, central France indicate that it had a wing-span reaching up to 70 centimetres (27½ inches).

Largest lled mollusc The Cretaceous fossil ammonite (*Pachydiscus seppenradensis*) which lived about 75,000,000 years ago had a shell measuring up to 8 feet 5 inches in diameter.

Most southerly The most southerly creature yet found is a freshwater salamander-like amphibian *Labrinthodont*, represented by a 2½-inch piece of jawbone found near Beardmore Glacier, Antarctica, 325 miles from the South Pole dating from the early Jurassic of 200,000,000 years ago. This discovery was made in December 1967.

PROTISTA

Protista were first discovered in 1676 by Anton van Leeuwenhoek of Delft (1632–1723), a Dutch microscopist. Among Protista characteristics common to both plants and animals are exhibited. The more plant-like are termed Protophyta (protophytes) and the more animal-like are placed in the phylum Protozoa (protozoans).

Largest The largest protozoans which are known to have existed were the now extinct Nummulites, which each had a diameter of 0·95 of an inch. The largest existing protozoan is *Pelomyxa palustris*, which may attain a length of up to 0·6 of an inch.

Smallest The smallest of all free-living organisms are pleuro-pneumonia-like organisms (P.P.L.O.) of the *Mycoplasma*. For fuller details see page 28. The smallest of all protophytes is *Micromonas pusilla*, with a diameter of less than 2 microns.

Fastest moving The protozoan *Monas stigmatica* has been measured to move a distance equivalent to 40 times its own length in a second. No human can cover even seven times his own length in a second.

Fastest reproduction The protozoan *Glaucoma*, which reproduces by binary fission, divides as frequently as every three hours. Thus in the course of a day it could become a "six greats grandparent" and the progenitor of 510 descendants.

Densest The most densely existing species in the animal kingdom is the sea water dinoflagellate *Gymnodinium breve*, which exists at a density of 240,000,000 per gallon of sea water in certain conditions of salinity and temperature off the coast of Florida, U.S.A.

The meganeura

Earliest of their type			
Type	**Scientific name and year of discovery**	**Location**	**Estimated years before present**
Ape	*Aegyptopitherus zeuxis* (1966)	Fayum, U.A.R.	28,000,000
Primate	tarsier-like	Indonesia	70,000,000
	lemur	Madagascar	70,000,000
Social insect	*Sphecomyrma freyi* (1967)	New Jersey, U.S.A.	100,000,000
Bird	*Archaeopteryx lithographica* (1861)	Bavaria, W. Germany	140,000,000
Mammal	shrew-like (1966)	Thaba-ea-Litau, Lesotho	190,000,000
Reptiles	*Hylonomus, Archerpeton, Protoclepsybrops, Romericus*	all Nova Scotia	290,000,000
Amphibian	*Ishthyostega* (first quadruped)	Greenland	350,000,000
Spider	*Palaeosteniza crassipes*	Aberdeenshire	370,000,000
Insect	*Rhyniella proecursor*	Aberdeenshire	370,000,000
Vertebrates	Agnathans (Jawless fish)	near Leningrad	480,000,000
Mollusc	*Neophilina galatheae* (1952)	off Costa Rica	500,000,000
Crustacean	*Karagassiema* (12 legged)	Sayan Mts., U.S.S.R.	c. 650,000,000

47

The animal and plant kingdoms

BACTERIA

Largest The largest of the bacteria is the sulphur bacterium *Beggiatoa mirabilis,* which is from 16 to 45 microns in width and which may form filaments several milli-metres long.

Highest In April 1967 the U.S. National Aeronautics and Space Administration reported that bacteria had been recently discovered at an altitude of 135,000 feet.

Longest lived The oldest deposits from which living bacteria are claimed to have been extracted are salt layers near Irkutsk, U.S.S.R., dating from about 600,000,000 years ago. The discovery of their survival was made on 26 Feb. 1962 by Dr. H. J. Dombrowski of Freiburg University, West Germany.

Toughest The bacterium *Micrococcus radiodurans* can withstand atomic radiation of 6·5 million röntgens or 10,000 times that fatal to the average man.

VIRUSES

Largest The largest viruses are those of the mantle type (*viz* trachoma and psittacosis), which have a diameter of 0·0004 of a millimetre, equivalent to 400 millimicrons (mμ).

Smallest Of more than 1,000 identified viruses, the smallest are the naniviruses, among which are those causing hepatitis. These measure 25 millimicrons (mμ) in diameter, *viz* 0·000025 of a millimetre. The potato spindle tuber virus consists only of a double helical of RNA without the usual wrapping of a protein coat. In 1966 an RNA virus truncated to only 470 sub units was reported to be viable.

Sub viral infective agents Evidence was announced from the Institute of Research on Animal Diseases at Compton, Berkshire, in January 1967 for the existence of a form of life more basic than both the virus and nucleic acid. It was named SF or Scrapie factor, from the sheep disease. If proven this will become the most fundamental replicating particle known. Its diameter is believed to be not more than 7 millionths of a millimetre. In March 1968 a theory was published that SF is present in an inhibited form in normal tissue and its release does not therefore constitute self-replication.

19. Plant Kingdom *(Plantae)*

Earliest life World If one accepts the definition of life as the ability of an organism to make replicas of itself by taking as building materials the simpler molecules in the medium around it, life probably appeared on Earth about 3,200 million years ago. In April 1969 such a dating was reported for minute spherical bluish fluorescent organisms measuring up to 0·000008 of an inch in diameter found in Swaziland, Southern Africa.

United Kingdom The earliest frond-like impressions found in the United Kingdom are those of *Charnia masoni,* from the Charnwood Forest slate quarry, Leicestershire, which are estimated to be 1,000 million years old.

Earliest flower The oldest fossil of a flowering plant with palm-like imprints was found in Colorado, U.S.A., in 1953 and dated about 65,000,000 years old.

Largest forest World The largest afforested areas in the world are the vast coniferous forests of the northern U.S.S.R., lying mainly between latitude 55° N. and the Arctic Circle. The total wooded areas amount to 2,700,000,000 acres (25 per cent. of the world's forests), of which 38 per cent. is Siberian larch. The U.S.S.R. is 34 per cent. afforested.

Great Britain The largest forest in England is Kielder Forest (72,336

acres), in Northumberland. The largest forest in Wales is the Coed Morgannwg (Forest of Glamorgan) (42,555 acres). Scotland's most extensive forest is the Glen Trool Forest (51,376 acres) in Kirkcudbrightshire. The United Kingdom is 7 per cent. afforested.

PLANT

Rarest Plants thought to be extinct are rediscovered each year and there are thus many plants of which specimens are known in but a single locality. The flecked pink spurred coral-root (*Epipogium aphyllum*) is usually cited as Britain's rarest orchid, having been unrecorded between 1931 and 1953. The rose purple Alpine coltsfoot (*Homogyne alpina*), recorded by Don prior to 1814 in the mountains of Clova, Angus, Scotland, was not again confirmed until 1951. The only known location of the adder's-tongue spearwort (*Ranunculus ophioglossifolius*) in the British Isles is the Badgeworth Nature Reserve, Gloucestershire (see page   ).

Commonest The most widely distributed flowering plant in the world is *Cynodon dactylon,* a toothed grass found as far apart as Canada, Argentina, New Zealand, Japan and South Africa.

Psittacosis virus compared with a red blood corpuscle

Northernmost The yellow poppy (*Papaver radicatum*) and the Arctic willow (*Salix arctica*) survive, the latter in an extremely stunted form, on the northernmost land (83° N.).

Southernmost The most southerly plant life recorded is seven species of lichen found in 1933–34 by the second expedition of Rear-Admiral Richard E. Byrd, U.S. Navy, in latitude 86° 03′ S. in the Queen Maud Mountains, Antarctica. The southernmost recorded flowering plant is the carnation (*Colobanthus crassifolius*), which was found in latitude 67° 15′ S. on Jenny Island, Margaret Bay, Graham Land (Palmer Peninsula), Antarctica.

Deepest roots The greatest recorded depth to which roots have penetrated is a calculated 150 feet in the case of a species of *Acacia,* probably *Acacia giraffae,* in a borehole on Okapanje Farm, about 60 miles east of Windhoek, in South West Africa, reported in 1948.

TREES

World's largest living thing The most massive living thing on Earth is the tallest known California big tree (*Sequoia gigantea*) named the "General Sherman", standing 272 feet 4 inches tall, in the Sequoia National Park, California, U.S.A. It has a base circumference of 101 feet 7 inches. Its mean base diameter is 32 feet 3 inches, with a maximum of 34 feet. The "General Sherman" has been estimated to contain the equivalent of 600,120 board feet of timber, sufficient to make 40 five-roomed bungalows. The foliage is blue-green, and the red-brown tan bark may be up to 24 inches thick in parts. Its total volume was calculated to be 49,660 cubic feet, including bark and top, in 1931. Assuming an average wet weight of 48 lb. per cubic foot, it weighed about 1,065 tons. In addition, the root-system is estimated to weigh about 10 per cent. of the above-ground tree, giving a total weight of about 1,170 tons.

The seed of a "big tree" weighs only 1/6,000th of an ounce. Its growth at maturity may therefore represent an increase in weight of over 250,000 million fold.

Tallest World The world's tallest known species of tree is the coast redwood (*Sequoia sempervirens*), now found only growing indigenously in northern California and a small area of southern Oregon, U.S.A.

48

The world's and Britain's tallest trees compared

The tallest example is now believed to be the Howard Libbey Tree in Redwood Creek Grove, Humboldt County, California announced at 367·8 feet in 1964 but discovered to have an apparently dead top and re-estimated at 366·6 feet on 28 Feb. 1968. The nearby tree announced to a Senate Committee by Dr. Rudolf W. Becking on 18 June 1966 to be 385 feet proved on re-measurement to be no more than 311·3 feet tall. It has a girth of 44 feet. The tallest non-sequoia is a Nobel fir in Gifford Pinchot Park, Washington State, U.S.A., measured in 1964 to be 278 feet tall.

The identity of the tallest tree of all time has never been satisfactorily resolved. In 1872 a mountain ash (*Eucalyptus regnans*) found in Victoria, Australia, measured 435 feet from its roots to the point where the trunk had been broken off by its fall. At this point the trunk's diameter was 3 feet, so the overall height was probably at least 500 feet. Its diameter was 18 feet at 5 feet above the ground. Another specimen, known as the "Baron Tree", was reported to be 464 feet in 1868. Modern opinion tends to the view that the highest accurately measured Australian "big gum" tree is one 346 feet tall felled near Colac, Victoria, in 1890. Claims for a Douglas fir (*Pseudotsuga taxifolia*) of 417 feet with a 77-foot circumference felled in British Columbia in 1940 remain unverified. The tallest specimen now known in the U.S.A. is one of only 221 feet (California, 1966). The most probable claimant was thus a coast redwood of 367 feet 8 inches, felled in 1873 near Guernville, California, U.S.A., thus being one foot taller than the Howard Libbey Tree.

at Britain The tallest tree in Great Britain is a Douglas fir (*Pseudotsuga taxifolia*) at Powis Castle, Montgomeryshire, Wales, measured at 181 feet in 1961. The tallest in England is a Wellingtonia (*Sequoiadendron giganteum*) measured at 165 feet in August 1964 at Endsleigh, Devon. The tallest in Scotland is a European silver fir (*Abies alba*) at Kilbride, Inveraray, Argyllshire. This forked tree once measured 186 feet 6 inches, according

to theodolite readings, but measurements by researchers of the Forestry Commission suggest that its height is now 175 feet and it is now dying back. A growing Grand fir at Ardhinglas Castle, Argyllshire, is expected to yield a figure of 180 feet during 1970.

Ireland The tallest tree in Ireland is a Sitka spruce (*Pitia sitchensis*) 162 feet tall at Shelton Abbey, County Wicklow. The Sitka spruce, planted in 1835, at Carraghmore, now 160 feet tall, will soon surpass the Shelton Abbey specimen.

Greatest girth World The Santa Maria del Tule Tree, in the state of Oaxaca, in Mexico, is a Montezuma cypress (*Taxodium mucronatum*) with a girth of 150 feet at a height of 5 feet above the ground. A figure of 204 feet in circumference was reported for the European chestnut (*Castanea sativa*) known as the "Tree of the 100 Horse" (Castagno di Cento Cavalli) on the edge of Mount Etna, Sicily, Italy in 1770.

Britain's greatest oaks The largest-girthed living British oak is a pollarded *Quercus pedunculata* at Bowthorp, Lincolnshire, with a girth of 39 feet 9 inches in 1965. The largest "maiden" oak is the Majesty Oak at Fredville, Kent, with a girth of 37 feet 5 inches.

OLDEST
The oldest recorded living tree is a bristlecone pine (*Pinus aristata*) designated WPN–114, growing at 10,750 feet above sea-level on the north-east face of Wheeler Peak (13,063 feet) in eastern Nevada, U.S.A. During studies in 1963 and 1964 it was found to be about 4,900 years old. The oldest dated California big tree (*Sequoia gigantea*) is a 3,212-year-old stump felled in 1892, but larger standing specimens are estimated to be between 3,500 and 4,000 years as in the case of the "General Sherman" tree from a ring count from a core drilled in 1931. Dendrochronologists estimate the *potential* life-span of a bristlecone pine at nearly 5,500 years, but that of a "big tree" at perhaps 6,000 years. Ring count dating extends back to 5,150 B.C. by examination of fallen bristlecone pine wood.

Great Britain Of all British trees that with the longest life is the yew (*Taxus baccata*), for which a maximum age well in excess of 1,000 years is usually conceded. The oldest known is the Fortingall Yew near Aberfeldy, Perthshire, part of which still grows. In 1717 this tree was over 50 feet in girth and it cannot be much less than 1,500 years old today.

Earliest The earliest species of tree still surviving is the maidenhair tree (*Ginkgo biloba*) of China, which first appeared about 160,000,000 years ago, during the Jurassic era.

Fastest growing Discounting bamboo, which is not botanically classified as a tree, but as a woody grass, the fastest growing tree

TALLEST TREES IN BRITAIN—BY SPECIES

		ft.			ft.
Alder (Italian)	Westonbirt, Gloucester	90	Larch	Parkhatch, Surrey	146
Alder (Common)	Sandling Park, Kent	85	Lime	Duncombe Park, Yorkshire	154
Ash	Duncombe Park, Yorkshire	148	Metasequoia	Leonardslee, West Sussex	56
Beech	Yester House, East Lothian	142	Monkey Puzzle	Endsleigh, Devon	86
Cedar	Petworth House, Sussex	132	Oak (Sessile)	Whitfield House, Hereford	135
Chestnut (Horse)	Petworth House, Sussex	125*	Oak (red)	West Dean, Sussex	115
Chestnut (Sweet)	Godinton Park, Kent	118*	Pine (Corsican)	Stanage Park, Radnor	147
Cypress (Lawson)	Endsleigh, Devon	120	Plane	Carshalton, Surrey	125
Cypress (Monterey)	Tregothnan, Cornwall	120*	Poplar (Black Italian)	Fairlawne, Kent	140
Douglas Fir	Powis Castle, Montgomery	181	Silver Fir	Kilbride, Inveraray, Argyllshire	c. 180
Elm (Wych)	Fountains Abbey, Yorkshire	125	Spruce (Sitka)	Murthly, Perth	164
Elm (Jersey)	Powderham Castle, Devon	127	Sycamore	Cobham Hall, Kent	110
Grand Fir	Ardhinglas Castle, Argyllshire	175	Tulip-tree	Taplow Court, Buckingham	119
Ginkgo	Linton Park (Maidstone), Kent	90	Walnut	Laverstoke Park, Hampshire	82
Hemlock (Western)	Benmore, Argyllshire	157	Wellingtonia	Endsleigh, Devon	165
Holly	Staverton Thicks, Suffolk	74*	Yew	Midhurst, Sussex	85
Hornbeam	Durdans, Epsom, Surrey	105*			

An asterisk indicates that no taller specimen is recorded in the United States.

The animal and plant kingdoms

is *Eucalyptus saligna,* which has been measured to grow 45 feet in two years in Uganda, central Africa. The youngest recorded age for a tree to reach 100 feet is 7½ years for an Albizzia in Java, Indonesia and for 200 feet is 57 years for a Monterey pine in New Zealand.

Slowest growing The speed of growth of trees depends largely upon conditions, although some species, such as box and yew, are always slow-growing. The extreme is represented by a specimen of Sitka spruce which required 98 years to grow to 11 inches tall, with a diameter of less than one inch, on the Arctic tree-line. The growing of miniature trees or *bonsai* is an oriental cult mentioned as early as c. 1320.

Examples of the art of *bonsai*

Most spreading The greatest area covered by a single clonal growth is that of the wild box huckleberry (*Gaylussacia brachyera*), a mat-forming evergreen shrub first reported in 1796. A colony covering 8 acres was discovered in 1845 near New Bloomfield, Pennsylvania. Another colony, covering about 100 acres, was "discovered" on 18 July 1920 near the Juniata River, Pennsylvania. It has been estimated that this colony began 13,000 years ago.

WOOD
Heaviest The heaviest of all woods is black ironwood (*Olea laurifolia*), also called South African ironwood, with a specific gravity of up to 1·49, and weighing up to 93 lb. per cubic foot.

Lightest The lightest wood is *Aeschynomene hispida,* found in Cuba, which has a specific gravity of 0·044 and a weight of only 2¾ lb. per cubic foot. The wood of the balsa tree (*Ochroma pyramidale*) is of very variable density— between 2½ and 24 lb. per cubic foot. The density of cork is 15 lb. per cubic foot.

BAMBOO
Tallest The tallest recorded species of bamboo is *Dendrocalamas giganteus,* native to southern Burma. It was reported in 1904 that there were specimens with a culm-length of 30 to 35 metres (100 to 115 feet) in the Botanic Gardens at Peradeniya, Ceylon. A growth rate up to 92 centimetres (36 inches) in 24 hours is possible.

Fastest growing Some species of the 45 genera of bamboo have attained growth rates of up to 36 inches per day (0·00002 m.p.h.), on their way to reaching a height of 100 feet in less than three months.

LARGEST BLOOMS
World The mottled orange-brown and white parasitic stinking corpse lily (*Rafflesia arnoldi*) has the largest of all blooms. These attach themselves to the cissus vines of the jungle in south-east Asia and measure up to 3 feet across and ¾ of an inch thick, and attain a weight of 15 lb.

The largest known inflorescence is that of *Puya raimondii,* a rare Bolivian plant with an erect panicle (diameter 8 feet) which emerges to a height of 35 feet. Each of these bears up to 8,000 white blooms (see also Slowest-flowering plant, below).

The word's largest blossoming plant is the giant Chinese wisteria at Sierra Madre, California, U.S.A. It was planted in 1892 and now has branches 500 feet long. It covers nearly an acre, weighs 225 tons and has an estimated 1,500,000 blossoms during its blossoming period of five weeks, when up to 30,000 people pay admission to visit it.

50

Great Britain The largest bloom of any indigenous British flowering plant is that of the wild white water lily (*Nymphaea alba*), which measures 6 inches across. Other species bear much larger inflorescences.

LARGEST LEAVES
The largest leaves of any plant belong to the raffia palm (*Raphia raffia*) of the Mascarene Islands, in the Indian Ocean, and the Amazonian bamboo palm (*R. toedigera*) of South America, whose leaf blades may measure up to 65 feet in length with petioles up to 13 feet.

The largest undivided leaf is that of *Alocasia macrorrhiza,* found in Sabah, East Malaysia. One found in 1966 measured 9 feet 11 inches long and 6 feet 3½ inches wide, and had an area of 34·2 square feet on one side.

The largest leaves to be found in outdoor plants in Great Britain are that of *Gunnera manicata* from Brazil with leaves 6 to 10 feet across on prickly stems 5 to 8 feet long.

Smallest flowering plant The smallest of all flowering plants are duckweeds, seen on the surface of ponds. Of these the rootless *Wolffia punctata* has fronds only 1/50th to 1/35th of an inch long. Another species, *Wolffia arrhiza,* occurs in Great Britain but rarely, if ever, flowers there. The smallest plant regularly flowering in Britain is the chaffweed (*Cetunculus minimus*), a single seed of which weighs 0·00003 of a gramme.

The fastest growing plant and tallest bamboo

Slowest flowering plant The slowest-flowering of all plants is the rare *Puya raimondii,* the largest of all herbs, discovered in Bolivia in 1870. The panicle emerges after about 150 years of the plant's life. It then dies. (See also above under Largest blooms.)

FRUIT
Most and least nutritive An analysis of the 38 commonly eaten fruits shows that the one with by far the highest calorific value is avocado (*Persea drymifolia*), with 1,200 calories per lb. That with the lowest value is rhubarb (*Rheum rhaponticum*), which is 94·9 per cent. water, with 80 calories per lb. The fruit with the highest percentage of invert sugar by weight is plantain or cooking banana (*Musa paradisiaca*), with 25·3 per cent., and that with the lowest is rhubarb, with 0·4 of one per cent. Apple (*Malus pumila*) and quince (*Cydonia oblonga*) are the least proteinous, at 0·3 of one per cent.

RECORD DIMENSIONS AND WEIGHTS FOR FRUIT AND VEGETABLES GROWN IN THE UNITED KINGDOM

Most data subsequent to 1958 comes from the annual *Garden News* Giant Vegetable and Fruit Contest.

Apple	3 lb. 1 oz.	V. Loveridge	Ross-on-Wye, Hereford	1965
Artichoke	8 lb.	A. R. Lawson	Tollerton, Yorkshire	1964
Beetroot	23 lb. 2 oz.	A. Bratton	Ryton, Shropshire	1966
Broad Bean	23⅜ inches	T. Currie	Jedburgh, Roxburghshire	1963
Broccoli	28 lb. 14¾ oz.	J. T. Cooke	Funtington, Sussex	1964
Brussels Sprout	7 lb. 10 oz.	J. Marsh	Whitfield, Kent	1966
Cabbage[1]	69 lb. 8 oz.	P. Hayes	Uttoxeter, Staffordshire	1965
Carrot	7 lb. 2 oz.	R. Clarkson	Preston, Lancashire	1964
Cauliflower	52 lb. 11½ oz.	J. T. Cooke	Funtington, Sussex	1966
Celery	17 lb. 3 oz.	A. Bratton	Ryton, Shropshire	1965
Cucumber	10 lb. 2 oz. (indoor)	W. Hodgson	Birkenhead, Cheshire	1967
	4 lb. 14 oz. (outdoor)	M. Housden	Efford Hill, Hampshire	1966
Gourd	196 lb.	J. Leathes	Herringfleet Hall, Suffolk	1846
Kale	12 ft. tall	B. T. Newton	Mullion, Cornwall	1950
Leek	9 lb. 4 oz.	E. E. Jenkins	Shipston-on-Stour, Warwickshire	1968
Lemon	1 lb. 12 oz. (girth 15 inches)	T. P. Matthews	Iver Heath, Buckinghamshire	1969
Lettuce	16 lb. 2¼ oz.	J. T. Cooke	Funtington, Sussex	1966
Mangold	46 lb.	David Bolland	Spalding, Lincolnshire	1964
Marrow[2]	60 lb.	A. V. Bishop	Snailwell, Cambridgeshire	1963
Mushroom[3]	54" circum.	—	Hasketon, Suffolk	1957
Onion	5 lb. 13 oz.	W. Taylor	Leicester	1965
Parsnip[4]	9 lb. 4 oz. (31" long)	P. C. Richardson	Heighington, Lincolnshire	1962
Pea Pod	10⅛ inches	T. Currie	Jedburgh, Roxburghshire	1964
Pear	1 lb. 12¼ oz.	A. Bratton	Shifnal, Shropshire	1966
Potato[5]	7 lb. 1 oz.	J. H. East	Spalding, Lincolnshire	1963
Pumpkin[6]	161 lb.	A. Chudleigh	Manchester & District H.S. Show	1913
Radish	16 lb. 8 oz.	E. E. Allen	Heston, Middlesex	1966
Red Cabbage	33 lb. 2 oz.	A. Bratton	Ryton, Shropshire	1963
Rhubarb	5 ft. 1⅜ inches	A. C. Setterfield	Englefield, Reading, Berkshire	1968
Runner Bean	33¾ inches	A. Bratton	Ryton, Shropshire	1966
Savoy	38 lb. 8 oz.	W. H. Neil	Retford, Nottinghamshire	1966
Shallot	1 lb. 7 oz.	H. H. May	Inkpen, Berkshire	1962
Strawberry[7]	6 oz.	K. M. Muir	Clacton, Essex	1968
Sugar Beet	15½ lb.	—	Kidderminster, Worcestershire	1958
Swede[8]	32 lb. 8 oz.	R. T. Leeson	Irchester, Northamptonshire	1963
Tomato	3 lb.	B. Austin	Uttoxeter, Staffordshire	1964
Tomato Plant	20 ft. tall 34 lb. fruit	—	Southport, Lancashire	1957
Turnip[9]	33 lb. 8 oz.	R. Speight	Cowplain, Hampshire	1963

[1] *A 75 lb. cabbage has been reported (since 1930) from Bolton, Lancashire. The Swalwell, County Durham cabbage of 1865 grown by R. Collingwood reputedly weighed 123 lb.*

[2] *A 96 lb. marrow has been reported from Suffolk.*

[3] *Same size reported by J. Coombes at Mark, Somerset on 28 July 1965.*

[4] *50 in. long: G. Chesterton near Wyberton, Lincolnshire April 1959.*

[5] *One weighing 18 lb. 4 oz. reported dug up by Thomas Siddal in his garden in Chester on 17 Feb. 1795. A yield of 1,242 lb. 14 oz. from 6 plants reported on 28 Sept. 1969 by J. T. Cooke (see Broccoli above).*

[6] *One weighing 245 lb. grown by M. Jean Giraud of France reported in 1968.*

[7] *The top weight for an un-fasciated berry, also variety Hummi-grundi, was 3 oz.*

[8] *One weighing 39 lb. 8 oz. claimed by E. R. Reay of Gaitsgill Hall, Dalston, Cumberland in 1940 (unratified).*

[9] *A 73 lb. turnip was reported in December 1768.*

ORCHID

Largest The largest of all orchids is *Grammatophyllum speciosum*, native to Malaysia. A specimen recorded in Penang, West Malaysia, in the 19th century had 30 spikes up to 8 feet tall and a diameter of more than 40 feet. The largest orchid flower is that of *Selenipedium caudatum*, found in tropical areas of America. Its petals are up to 18 inches long, giving it a maximum outstretched diameter of 3 feet. The flower is, however, much less bulky than that of the stinking corpse lily (see Largest blooms page 50).

Tallest The tallest of all orchids is the terrestrial tree-orchid (*Angraecum infundibulare*), which grows in the swamps of Uganda to a height of 12 feet.

Smallest The smallest orchid plant is believed to be *Notylia norae,* found in Venezuela. The smallest orchid flower is that of *Bulbophyllum minutissium*, found in Australia.

est priced The highest price ever paid for an orchid is 1,150 guineas (£1,207 10s.), paid by Baron Schröder to Sanders of St. Albans for an *Odontoglossum crispum* (variety *pittianum*) at an auction by Protheroe & Morris of Bow Lane, London, on 22 March 1906.

Longest seaweed Claims made that seaweed off Tierra del Fuego, South America, grows to 600 and even to 1,000 feet in length have gained currency. More recent and more reliable records indicate that the longest species of seaweed is the Pacific giant kelp (*Macrocyctis pyrifera*), which does not exceed 195 feet in length. The longest of the 700 species of seaweed recognized around the coasts of Britain is the brown seaweed *Corda filum* which grows up to a length of 20 feet.

Mosses The smallest of mosses is the pygmy moss (*Ephemerum*), and the longest is the brook moss (*Fontinalis*), which forms streamers up to 3 feet long in flowing water.

FUNGUS

Largest The largest recorded ground fungus was a specimen of the giant puff ball (*Calvatia gigantea*) which was 5 feet 3 inches long, 4 feet 5 inches wide and 9½ inches high. It was discovered in New York State, U.S.A., in 1884.

The largest officially recorded tree fungus was a specimen of *Oxyporus (Fomes) nobilissimus,* measuring 56 inches by 37 inches and weighing at least 300 lb., found by J. Hisey in Washington State, U.S.A., in 1946. The largest recorded in the United Kingdom is an ash fungus

(*Fomes fraxineus*) measuring 50 inches by 15 inches wide, found by the forester A. D. C. LeSueur on a tree at Waddesdon, Buckinghamshire, in 1954.

Largest rose tree
A "Lady Banksia" rose tree at Tombstone, Arizona, U.S.A., has a trunk 40 inches thick, stands 9 feet high and covers an area of 5,380 square feet, supported by 68 posts and several thousand feet of iron piping. This enables 150 people to be seated under the arbour. The original cutting came from Scotland in 1884.

Largest rhododendron
The largest species of rhododendron is the scarlet *Rhododendron arboreum*, examples of which reach a height of 60 feet at Mangalbaré, Nepal.

Largest aspidistra
The aspidistra (*Aspidistra elatior*) was introduced to Britain as a parlour palm from Japan and China in 1822. The height attained by these plants is up to 34 inches, although a plant growing in the shade may have its leaves elongated. A reported height of 42 inches is very much doubted by the Royal Botanic Gardens at Kew, Greater London. A specimen 34 inches tall grown by Leslie Holt of Stoke-on-Trent was reported in August 1968.

Largest vines
The largest recorded grape vine was one planted in 1842 at Carpinteria, California, U.S.A. By 1900 it was yielding more than 9 tons of grapes in some years, and averaging 7 tons per year. It died in 1920. Britain's largest vine is the Great Vine, planted in 1768 at Hampton Court, Greater London. Its girth is 38 inches, with branches up to 110 feet long and an average yield of 1,200 lb.

Tallest hedge
The world's tallest hedge is the Meikleour beech hedge in Perthshire, Scotland. It was planted in 1746 and has now attained a trimmed height of 85 feet. It is 600 yards long.

The tallest yew hedge in the world is in Earl Bathurst's Park, Cirencester, Gloucestershire. It was planted in 1720, runs for 130 yards, reaches 35 feet and takes 30 man-days to trim.

Largest cactus
The largest of all cacti is the saguaro (*Cereus giganteus* or *Carnegieia gigantea*), found in Arizona, New Mexico and California, U.S.A., and Sonora, Mexico. The green fluted column is surmounted by candelabra-like branches rising to a height of 53 feet in the case of a specimen found in 1950 near Madrona, New Mexico. They have waxy white blooms which are followed by edible crimson fruit. A cardon cactus in Baja California, Mexico was reputed to reach 58 feet and a weight of 9 tons.

Most poisonous toadstool
The yellowish-olive death cap (*Amanita phalloides*) is regarded as the world's most poisonous fungus. It is found in England. From six to fifteen hours after tasting, the effects are vomiting, delirium, collapse and death. Among its victims was Cardinal Giulio de' Medici, Pope Clement VII (1478–1534).

The Registrar General's Report states that between 1920 and 1950 there were 39 fatalities from fungus poisoning in the United Kingdom. As the poisonous types are mostly *Amanita* varieties, it is reasonable to assume that the deaths were predominantly due to *Amanita phalloides*. The most recent fatality was probably in 1960.

FERNS

Largest
The largest of all the more than 6,000 species of fern is the tree fern (*Alsophila excelsa*) of Norfolk Island, in the South Pacific, which attains a height of up to 80 feet.

Smallest
The world's smallest ferns are *Hecistopteris pumila*, found in Central America, and *Azolla caroliniana*, which is native to the United States.

SEED

Largest
The largest seed in the world is that of the double coconut or Coco de Mer (*Lodoicea seychellarum*), the single-seeded fruit of which may weigh 40 lb. This grows only in the Seychelles Islands, in the Indian Ocean.

Smallest
The smallest seeds are those of *Epiphytic* orchids, at 35,000,000 to the ounce (*cf.* grass pollens at up to 6,000,000,000 grains per ounce). A single plant of the American ragweed can generate 8,000,000,000 pollen grains in five hours.

Most viable
The most viable of all known seeds are those of the Arctic Lupin (*Lupinus arcticus*) found in frozen silt at Miller Creek in the Yukon, Canada in July 1954. They were germinated in 1966 and dated by the radio carbon method to at least 8,000 B.C. and more probably to 13,000 B.C.

GRASS

Longest
The tallest of the 160 grasses found in Great Britain is the common reed (*Phragmites communis*), which reaches a height of 9 feet 9 inches.

Shortest
The shortest grass native to Great Britain is the very rare sand bent (*Mibora minima*) from Anglesey, which has a maximum growing height of under 6 inches.

Worst weeds
The most intransigent weed is the mat-forming water weed *Salvinia auriculata*, found in Africa. It was detected on the filling of Kariba Lake in May 1959 and within 11 months had choked an area of 77 sq. miles rising by 1963 to 387 sq. miles. The world's worst land weeds are regarded as purple nut sedge, Bermuda grass, barnyard grass, junglerice, goose grass, Johnson grass, Guinea grass, cogon grass and lantana. The most damaging and widespread cereal weeds in Britain are the wild oats *Avena fatua* and *A. ludoviciana*. Their seeds can withstand temperatures of 240° F. for 15 minutes and remain viable.

The tallest of
British grasses

20. Parks, Zoos, Aquaria and Oceanaria

Largest The world's largest park is the Kafue National Park in Zambia, which has an area of 5,336,000 acres (8,650 square miles).

The Lake District National Park has an area of 866 square miles. The largest private park in the United Kingdom is Woburn Park (3,000 acres), near Woburn Abbey, the seat of the Dukes of Bedford.

The largest common in the United Kingdom is Llansaintfread Cwmtoddyr (28,819 acres) in Radnorshire, Wales.

Smallest The world's smallest nature reserve is believed to be the Badgeworth Nature Reserve (346 square yards), near Cheltenham, Gloucestershire. Owned by the Society for the Promotion of Nature Reserves, it is leased to the Gloucestershire Trust for Nature Conservation to protect the sole site in the British Isles of the adder's-tongue spearwort (*Ranunculus ophioglossifolius*).

The smallest park in the world is Mill Ends Park on a safety island on S.W. Front Avenue, Portland, Oregon, U.S.A. It measures 45·8 square inches (*cf.* this page of 96·9 square inches) and was designated in 1948 at the behest of the city journalist Dick Fagan (d. 1969) for snail races and as a colony for leprechauns.

ZOOS

Largest It has been estimated that throughout the world there are some 500 zoos with an estimated annual attendance of 330,000,000. The largest zoological preserve in the world is the Etosha Reserve, South West Africa, with an area which has grown since 1907 to 38,427 square miles and now encloses 150,000 head of game. It is thus larger than Ireland.

Largest collection The largest collection in any zoo is that in the Zoological Gardens of West Berlin, Germany. At 1 Jan. 1970 the zoo had a total of 10,026 specimens from 2,334 species. This total included 1,042 mammals (227 species), 2,747 birds (736 species), 614 reptiles (288 species), 128 amphibians (61 species), 3,245 fishes (791 species) and 2,250 invertebrates (231 species).

Oldest The oldest known zoo is that at Schonnbrunn, Vienna, Austria, built in 1752 by the Holy Roman Emperor Franz Josef for his wife Maria Theresa. The oldest privately owned zoo in the world is that of the Zoological Society of London, founded in 1826. Its collection, housed partly in Regent's Park, London (36 acres) and partly at Whipsnade Park, Bedfordshire (541 acres, opened 1931), is the most comprehensive in the United Kingdom. At the stocktaking on 31 Dec. 1969 there were 2,859 mammals, birds, reptiles and amphibians (from 978 species and sub-species) in Regent's Park, and 2,107 specimens (217 species and sub-species) at Whipsnade, making 4,966 together. In addition, Regent's Park contained 2,500 fishes, 940 marine invertebrates and 600 land invertebrates, all these from 485 species and sub-species, making a total of 9,006 specimens. The record annual attendances are 3,013,571 in 1950 for Regent's Park and 756,758 in 1961 for Whipsnade. The most valuable animal is Chi-Chi, the great panda (*Ailuropoda melanoleuca*) worth £12,000. She was captured in China on 4 July 1957 when aged probably six months.

Largest aquarium The world's largest aquarium is the John G. Shedd Aquarium on 12th Street and Grant Park, Chicago, Illinois, U.S.A., completed in November 1929 at a cost of $3,250,000 (now £1,354,166). The total capacity of its display tanks is 375,000 gallons, with reservoir tanks holding 1,665,000 gallons. Exhibited are 10,000 speci-

Adder's tongue spearwort found in Gloucestershire

mens from 350 species. Salt water is brought in road and rail tankers from Key West, Florida, and a tanker barge from the Gulf of Mexico. The record attendances are 78,658 in a day on 21 May 1931, and 4,689,730 visitors in the single year of 1931.

OCEANARIA

Earliest and largest The world's first oceanarium is Marineland of Florida, opened in 1938 at a site 18 miles south of St. Augustine, Florida, U.S.A. Up to 5,800,000 gallons of sea-water are pumped daily through two major tanks, one rectangular (100 feet long by 40 feet wide by 18 feet deep) containing 375,000 gallons and one circular (233 feet in circumference and 12 feet deep) containing 330,000 gallons. The tanks are seascaped, including coral reefs and even a shipwreck. The salt water tank at the Marineland of the Pacific, Palos Verdes Peninsula, California, U.S.A. is 251½ feet in circumference and 22 feet deep, with a capacity of 530,000 gallons. The total capacity of this whole oceanarium is 1,830,000 gallons.

The London zoo's biggest draw—Chi-Chi

53

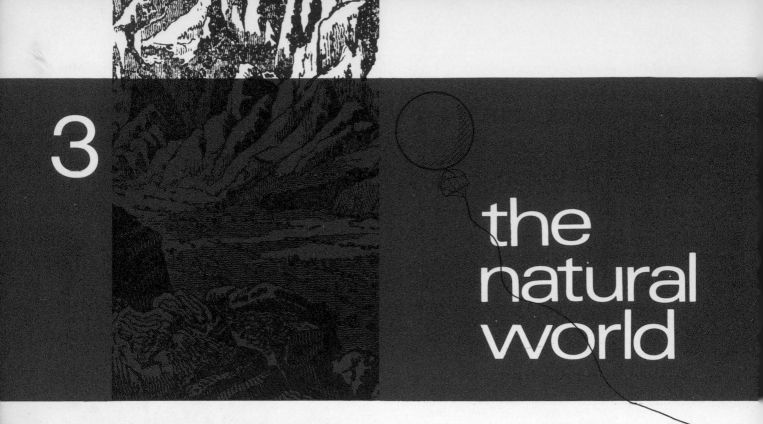

3 the natural world

The Earth is not a true sphere, but flattened at the poles and hence an ellipsoid. The polar diameter of the Earth (7,899·940 miles) is 26·466 miles less than the equatorial diameter (7,926·406 miles). The Earth also has a slight ellipticity of the equator since its long axis (about longitude 0°) is 174 yards greater than the short axis. The greatest departures from the ellipsoid form at sea-level are a protuberance of 62 feet in the neck of the English Channel and a depression of 79 feet to the south-west of Ceylon, in the Indian Ocean. The greatest circumference of the Earth, at the equator, is 24,902·44 miles, compared with 24,860·53 miles at the meridian. The area of the surface is estimated to be 196,951,000 square miles. The period of axial rotation, *i.e.* the true sidereal day, is 23 hours 56 minutes 4·0996 seconds, mean time.

The mass of the Earth is 5,882,000,000,000,000,000,000 tons and its density is 5·517 times that of water. The volume is an estimated 259,902,237,000 cubic miles. It is estimated that the Earth picks up about 2,000 tons of cosmic dust daily. Modern theory is that the Earth has an outer shell or lithosphere about 25 miles thick, then an outer and inner rock layer or mantle extending 1,800 miles deep, beneath which there is an iron-nickel core at an estimated temperature of 3,700° C. and at a pressure of 24,500 tons per square inch or 3,400 kilobars. If the iron-nickel core theory is correct, iron must be by far the most abundant element in the Earth.

1. Natural Phenomena

EARTHQUAKES

Greatest It is estimated that each year there are some 500,000 detectable seismic or micro-seismic disturbances of which 100,000 can be felt and 1,000 cause damage.

The intensity of an earthquake is instrumentally assessed on the Gutenberg-Richter scale. The highest readings yet assigned are magnitudes of 8·9 on three occasions. The first was an earthquake with a submarine epicentre in Lat. 1° N., Long. 81½° W., near the border between Colombia and Ecuador, in South America, on 31 Jan. 1906. The second was a submarine shock about 100 miles from the Sanriku coast of north-eastern Honshū, Japan, on 3 March 1933. These two magnitudes were calculated by C. F. Richter in 1958. The cataclysmic shocks around Lebu, south of Concepción, Chile, on 21–23 May 1960, were originally reported to be 9·2, but

assessments were later moderated. The magnitude of the main shock, at 19 hours 11 minutes 17 seconds G.M.T. on 22 May, was calculated at Strasbourg, France, to be also 8·9. It is possible that the earthquake in Lisbon, Portugal, on 1 Nov. 1755 would have given a reading of between 8¾ and 9 if seismographs, invented in 1853, had been available then. The first of the three shocks was at 9·40 a.m. and lasted for between 6 and 7 minutes. Lakes in Norway were disturbed. The energy of an earthquake of magnitude 8·9 is about $5·6 \times 10^{24}$ ergs, which is equivalent to an explosion of 140 megatons (140,000,000 tons of trinitrotoluene ($C_7H_5O_6N_3$), called T.N.T.).

Worst The greatest loss of life occurred in the earthquake in Shensi Province, China, on 23 Jan. 1556, when an estimated 830,000 people were killed. The greatest material damage was in the earthquake on the Kwanto plain, Japan, at 11·58 a.m. (local time) on 1 Sept. 1923 (magnitude 8·2, epicentre in Lat. 24° 58′ N., Long. 139° 21′ E.). In Sagami Bay the seabottom in one area sank 1,310 feet. The official total of persons killed and missing in the *Shinsai* or great 'quake and the resultant fires was 142,807. In Tōkyō and Yokohama 575,000 dwellings were destroyed. The cost of the damage was estimated at £1,000 million (now more than £3,000 million).

Great Britain The East Anglian or Colchester "twin" earthquake at 9.18 a.m. on 22 April 1884 (epicentres Lat. 51° 48′ N., Long. 0° 53′ E., and Lat. 51° 51′ N., Long. 0° 55′ E.) caused damage estimated at £10,000 to 1,200 buildings and the death of a child at Rowhedge. Langenhoe Church was wrecked. Windows and doors were rattled over an area of 53,000 square miles and the shock was felt in Exeter and Ostend, Belgium. The most marked since 1884 and the worst since instruments have been in use (*i.e.* since 1927) occurred in the Midlands at 3.43 p.m. on 11 Feb. 1957, showing a strength of between five and six. The strongest Scottish tremor occurred at Inverness at 10.45 p.m. on 13 Aug. 1816, and was felt over an area of 50,000 square miles. The strongest Welsh tremor occurred in Swansea at 9.45 a.m. on 27 June 1906 (epicentre Lat. 51° 38′ N., Long. 4° W.). It was felt over an area of 37,800 square miles.

Ireland No earthquake with its epicentre in Ireland has ever been instrumentally measured, though the effects of remoter shocks have been felt. However, there was a shock in August 1734 which damaged 100 dwellings and five churches.

VOLCANOES

The total number of known active volcanoes in the world is 455 with an estimated 80 more submarine. The greatest concentration is in Indonesia, where 77 of its 167 volcanoes have erupted within historic times.

Greatest eruption The total volume of matter discharged in the eruption of Tambora, a volcano on the island of Sumbawa, in Indonesia, 5–7 April 1815, has been estimated at 36·4 cubic miles. The energy of this eruption was $8·4 \times 10^{26}$ ergs. The volcano lost about 4,100 feet in height and a crater seven miles in diameter was formed. This compares with a probable 15 cubic miles ejected by Santoríni and 4·3 cubic miles ejected by Krakatoa (see below). The internal pressure causing the Tambora eruption has been estimated at 46,500,000 lb. per square inch or more than 20,000 tons per square inch.

Greatest explosion The greatest volcanic explosion in historic times was the eruption in *c.* 1470 B.C. of Thíra (Santoríni), a volcanic island in the Aegean Sea. It is highly probable that this explosion destroyed the centres of the Minoan civilization in Crete, about 80 miles away, with a *tsunami* 165 feet high. Evidence was published in December 1967 of an eruption that spewed lava over 100,000 square miles of Oregon, Idaho, Nevada and Northern California about 3,000,000 years ago.

The greatest explosion since then occurred at 9.56 a.m. (local time), or 2.56 a.m. G.M.T., on 27 Aug. 1883, with an eruption of Krakatoa, an island (then 18 square miles) in the Sunda Strait, between Sumatra and Java, in Indonesia. A total of 163 villages were wiped out, and 36,380 people killed, by the wave it caused. Rocks were thrown 34 miles high and dust fell 3,313 miles away 10 days later. The explosion was recorded four hours later on the island of Rodrigues, 2,968 miles away, as "the roar of heavy guns" and was heard over 1/13th part of the surface of the globe. This explosion has been estimated to have had about 26 times the power of the greatest H-bomb test detonation but was still only a fifth part of the Santoríni cataclysm (see above).

HIGHEST

Extinct The highest extinct volcano in the world is Cerro Aconcagua (22,834 feet) on the Argentine side of the Andes. It was first climbed on 14 Jan. 1897 and was the highest climbed anywhere until 12 June 1907.

Dormant The highest dormant volcano is Volcán Llullaillaco (22,058 feet), on the frontier between Chile and Argentina.

Active The highest volcano regarded as active is Volcán Antofalla (20,013 feet), in Argentina, though a more definite claim is made for Volcán Guayatiri or Guallatiri (19,882 feet), in Chile, which erupted in 1959.

Northernmost and southernmost The northernmost volcano is Beeren Berg (7,470 feet) on the island of Jan Mayen (71° 05′ N.) in the Greenland Sea. The island was possibly discovered by Henry Hudson in 1607 or 1608, but definitely visited by Jan Jacobsz May (Netherlands) in 1614. It was annexed by Norway on 8 May 1929. The most southerly known active volcano is Mount Erebus (12,450 feet) on Ross Island (77° 35′ S.), in Antarctica. It was discovered on 28 Jan. 1841 by the expedition of Captain (later Rear-Admiral Sir) James Clark Ross, R.N. (1800–1862), and first climbed at 10 a.m. on 10 March 1908 by a British party of five, led by Professor (later Lieut.-Col. Sir) Tannatt William Edgeworth David (1858–1934).

Largest crater The world's largest *caldera* or volcano crater is that of Mount Aso (5,223 feet) in Kyūshū, Japan, which measures 17 miles north to south, 10 miles east to west and 71 miles in circumference. The longest lava flows known as *pahoehoe* (twisted cord-like solidifications) are 60 miles in length in Iceland.

GEYSERS

World's tallest The Waimangu geyser, in New Zealand, erupted to a height in excess of 1,000 feet in 1909, but has not been active since it erupted violently in 1917. Currently the world's tallest active geyser is the "Giant", discovered in 1870 in what is now the Yellowstone National Park, Wyoming, U.S.A., which erupts at intervals varying from 7 days to 3 months, throwing a spire 200 feet high at a rate of 580,000 gallons per hour. The *Geysir* ("gusher") near Mount Hekla in south-central Iceland, from which all others have been named, spurts, on occasions, to 180 feet.

OCEANS

Largest The area of the Earth covered by the sea is estimated to be 139,000,000 square miles, or 70·6 per cent. of the total surface. The mean depth of the hydrosphere was once estimated to be 12,450 feet, but recent surveys suggest a lower estimate, closer to 12,000 feet. The total weight of the water is estimated to be $1·3 \times 10^{18}$ tons, or 0·022 per cent. of the Earth's total weight. The volume of the oceans is estimated to be 317,000,000 cubic miles compared with only 8,400,000 cubic miles of fresh water.

The largest ocean in the world is the Pacific. Excluding adjacent seas, it represents 45·8 per cent. of the world's oceans and is about 63,800,000 square miles in area. The shortest navigable trans-Pacific distance from Guayaquil, Ecuador to Bangkok, Thailand is 10,905 miles.

Most southerly The most southerly part of the oceans is 85° 34′ S., 154° W., at the snout of the Robert Scott Glacier, 305 miles from the South Pole, in the Pacific sector of Antarctica.

Deepest The deepest part of the ocean was first discovered in 1951 by H.M. Survey Ship *Challenger* in the Marianas Trench in the Pacific Ocean. The depth was measured by sounding and by echo-sounder and published as 5,960 fathoms (35,760 feet). Subsequent visits to the Challenger Deep have resulted in claims by echo-sounder only, culminating in one of 6,033 fathoms (36,198 feet) by the U.S.S.R.'s research ship *Vityaz* in March 1959. A metal object, say a pound ball of steel, dropped into water above this trench would take nearly 63 minutes to fall to the sea-bed 6·85 miles below. The average depth of the Pacific Ocean is 14,000 feet.

Remotest spot from land The world's most distant point from land is a spot in the South Pacific, approximately 48° 30′ S., 125° 30′ W., which is about 1,660 miles from the nearest points of land, namely Pitcairn Island, Ducie Island and Cape Dart, Antarctica. Centred on this spot, therefore, is a circle of water with an area of about 8,657,000 square miles—about 7,000 square miles larger than the U.S.S.R., the worlds largest country (see Chapter X).

Sea temperature The temperature of the water at the surface of the sea varies from −2° C (28·5°F) in the White Sea to 35·6° C (96° F) in the shallow areas of the Persian Gulf in summer. A freak geo-thermal temperature of 56° C (132·8° F) was recorded in February 1965 by the survey ship *Atlantis II* near the bottom of Discovery Deep (7,200 feet) in the Red Sea. The normal sea temperature in the area is 22° C (71·6° F).

The Red Sea

The natural world

Largest sea The largest of the world's seas (as opposed to oceans) is the South China Sea, with an area of 1,148,500 square miles. The Malayan Sea comprising the waters between the Indian Ocean and the South Pacific, south of the Chinese mainland covering 3,144,000 square miles is not now an entity accepted by the International Hydrographic Bureau.

STRAITS
Longest The longest straits in the world are the Malacca Straits between West Malaysia (formerly called Malaya) and Sumatra, in Indonesia, which extend for 485 miles.

Broadest The broadest straits in the world are the Mozambique Straits between Mozambique and Madagascar, which are at one point 245 miles across.

Narrowest The narrowest navigable straits are those between the Aegean island of Euboea and the mainland of Greece. The gap is only 45 yards wide at Chalkis. The Seil Sound, Argyllshire, Scotland, narrows to a point only 20 feet wide where a bridge joins the island of Seil to the mainland and is thus said to span the Atlantic.

Largest gulf The largest gulf in the world is the Gulf of Mexico, with an area of 580,000 square miles and a shoreline of 3,100 miles from Cape Sable, Florida, U.S.A., to Cabo Catoche, Mexico.

Largest bay The largest bay in the world is the Bay of Bengal, with a shoreline of 2,250 miles from south-eastern Ceylon to Pagoda Point, Burma. Its mouth measures 1,075 miles across. Great Britain's largest bay is Cardigan Bay which has a 140 mile long shoreline and measures 72 miles across from the Lleyn Peninsula, Caernarvonshire to St. David's Head, Pembrokeshire in Wales.

Highest seamount The highest known submarine mountain, or seamount, is one discovered in 1953 near the Tonga Trench, between Samoa and New Zealand. It rises 28,500 feet from the sea bed, with its summit 1,200 feet below the surface.

HIGHEST WAVE
The highest officially recorded sea wave was measured by Lt. Frederic Margraff U.S.N. from the U.S.S. *Ramapo* proceeding from Manila, Philippines, to San Diego, California, U.S.A., on the night of 6–7 Feb. 1933, during a 68-knot (78·3 m.p.h.) gale. The wave was computed to be 112 feet from trough to crest. A stereo-photograph of a wave calculated to be 24·9 metres (81·7 feet) high was taken from the U.S.S.R.'s diesel-electric vessel *Ob'* in the South Pacific Ocean, about 600 kilometres (370 miles) south of Macquarie Island, on 2 April 1956. The highest instrumentally measured wave was one calculated to be at least 67 feet high, recorded by the British ship *Weather Reporter* in Lat. 52½° N., Long. 20° W., in the North Atlantic at 9.00 a.m. on 12 Sept. 1961. Its length was 1,150 feet and its period was 15 seconds. It has been calculated on the statistics of the Stationary Random Theory that one wave in more than 300,000 may exceed the average by a factor of 4.

On 9 July 1958 a landslip caused a wave to wash 1,740 feet high along the shore of Lituya Bay, Alaska, U.S.A.

"Tidal" wave The highest recorded seismic sea wave, or *tsunami*, was one of 220 feet which appeared off Valdez, south-west Alaska, after the great Prince William Sound earthquake of 27 March 1964. *Tsunami* (a Japanese word which is singular and plural) have been observed to travel at 490 m.p.h. Between 479 B.C. and 1967 there were 286 instances of devastating *tsunami*.

CURRENT
Greatest The greatest current in the oceans of the world is the Antarctic Circumpolar Current, which was measured in 1969 in the Drake Passage between South America and Antarctica to be flowing at a rate of 9,500 million cubic

56

Tsunami—the Japanese term for a tidal wave now used the world over

feet per second—nearly treble that of the Gulf Stream. Its width ranges from 185 to 620 miles and has a surface flow rate of ¾ of a knot.

Strongest The world's strongest currents are the Saltstraumen in the Saltfjord, near Bodø, Norway, which reach 15·6 knots (18·0 m.p.h.). The flow rate through the 500 foot wide channel surpasses 500,000 cusecs. The fastest current in British territorial waters is 10·7 knots in the Pentland Firth between the Orkney Islands and Caithness.

GREATEST TIDES
World The greatest tides in the world occur in the Bay of Fundy, which separates Nova Scotia, Canada, from the United States' north-easternmost state of Maine and the Canadian province of New Brunswick. Burncoat Head in the Minas Basin, Nova Scotia, has the greatest mean spring range with 47·5 feet, and an extreme range of 53·5 feet.

United Kingdom The place with the greatest mean spring range in Great Britain is Beachley, on the Severn, with a range of 40·7 feet, compared with the British Isles average of 15 feet. Prior to 1933 tides as high as 28·9 feet above and 22·3 feet below datum (total range 51·2 feet) were recorded at Avonmouth though an extreme range of 52·2 feet for Beachley was officially accepted. In 1883 a freak tide of greater range was reported from Chepstow, Monmouthshire.

Ireland The greatest mean spring tidal range in Ireland is 17·3 feet at Mellon, Limerick, on the banks of the River Shannon.

ICEBERGS
Largest The largest iceberg on record was an Antarctic tabular 'berg of over 12,000 square miles (208 miles long and 60 miles wide) sighted 150 miles west of Scott Island, in the South Pacific Ocean, by the U.S.S. *Glacier* on 12 Nov. 1956.

The 200-foot-thick Arctic ice island T.1 (140 square miles) was discovered in 1946, and was still being plotted in 1963.

Most southerly Arctic The most southerly Arctic iceberg was sighted in the Atlantic in 30° 50' N., 45° 06' W., on 2 June 1934. The tallest on record was one calved off North West Greenland with 550 feet above the surface.

The southernmost iceberg reported in British home waters was one sighted 60 miles from Smith's Knoll, on the Dogger Bank, in the North Sea.

Most northerly Antarctic The most northerly Antarctic iceberg was a remnant sighted in the Atlantic by the ship *Dochra* in latitude 26° 30' S., longitude 25° 40' W., on 30 April 1894.

LAND
There is considerable evidence that at one time the Earth's land surface comprised a single primeval continent, now termed Pangaea, and that this split about 150,000,000 years ago, during the Jurassic period, into two super-continents, termed Laurasia (Eurasia Greenland and Northern America) in the north and Gondwanaland (Africa, Arabia, India, South America, Oceania and Antarctica) and named after Gondwana, India.

2. Structure and Dimensions

ROCKS

st—world The greatest recorded age for any reliably dated rock is 3,400 ± 300 million years for G1 granite in Swaziland, southern Africa, according to the rubidium-strontium radio-dating method. A date of 3,300 million years is attributed by the same method to metamorphic rock in the Luiza Basement, Kasai, in the southern Congo (Kinshasa), indicating that this may be even older. Samples taken in 1964 from St. Peter and St. Paul Rocks (0° 56′ N., 29° 22′ W.) in the mid-Atlantic Ocean indicate that they may consist of primordial pieces of the Earth's mantle carried to the surface. These brown hornblende mylonites have been dated at about 4,500 million years old by the rubidium-strontium method. It was announced on 1 April 1966 that the U.S.S.R.'s survey ship *Vityaz* had retrieved a dark greenish iron-silicon-magnesium stone from a depth of 3½ miles off eastern Madagascar. It was believed to be part of the Earth's upper mantle.

The age of the Earth itself was revised in 1964 to at least 4,700 million years by the Isotope Geology Group at the Carnegie Institute in Washington, D.C., U.S.A. In June 1962 Dr. E. Gerling (U.S.S.R.) reported that there were some sub-crustal inclusions in younger rock with ages as high as 6,500 million years at Monchegorsk, south of Murmansk, in Russian Lapland. In view of the dating method used (potassium-argon) this figure has been treated with some suspicion. In March 1967 Dr. V. I. Baranov (U.S.S.R.) concluded that there was some evidence from the isotopic composition of lead which indicated an age of more than 6,000 million years.

Britain The greatest age for any dated rock in the British Isles is 2,460 million years for a potassium felspar from Badcall, Sutherland, Scotland. This figure was calculated by the rubidium-strontium method.

Largest The largest exposed rocky outcrop is the 1,237 foot high Mount Augustus (3,627 feet above sea-level), discovered on 3 June 1858, 200 miles east of Carnarvon, Western Australia. It is an up-faulted monoclinal gritty conglomerate 5 miles long and 2 miles across and thus twice the size of the celebrated monolithic arkose Ayer's Rock (1,100 feet), 250 miles south-west of Alice Springs, in Northern Territory, Australia.

CONTINENTS

argest and smallest Only 29·4 per cent., or an estimated 57,900,000 square miles, of the Earth's surface is land, with a mean height of 2,760 feet above sea-level. The Eurasian land mass is the largest, with an area (including islands) of 21,053,000 square miles.

The smallest is the Australian mainland, with an area of about 2,940,000 square miles, which, together with Tasmania, New Zealand, New Guinea and the Pacific Islands, is described as Oceania. The total area of Oceania is about 3,450,000 square miles, including West Irian (formerly West New Guinea), which is politically in Asia.

d remotest om the sea There is an as yet unpinpointed spot in the Dzoosotoyn Elisen (desert), northern Sinkiang, China, that is more than 1,500 miles from the open sea in any direction. The nearest large town to this point is Wulumuchi (Urumchi) to its south.

The point furthest from the sea in Great Britain is a point near Meriden, Warwickshire, England, which is 72½ miles equidistant from the Severn Bridge, the Dee and Mersey estuaries and the Welland estuary in the Wash. The equivalent point in Scotland is in the Forest of Atholl, Perthshire, 40¼ miles equidistant from the head of Loch Leven, Inverness Firth and the Firth of Tay.

Peninsula The world's largest peninsula is Arabia, with an area of about 1,250,000 square miles.

ISLANDS

Largest Discounting Australia, which is usually regarded as a continental land mass, the largest island in the world is Greenland (part of the Kingdom of Denmark), with an area of about 840,000 square miles. There is some evidence that Greenland is in fact several islands overlayed by an ice-cap.

The mainland of Great Britain (Scotland, England and Wales) is the eighth largest in the world, with an area of 84,186 square miles. It stretches 603½ miles from Dunnet Head in the north to Lizard Point in the south and 287½ miles across from Porthaflod, Pembrokeshire, Wales to Lowestoft, Suffolk. The island of Ireland (32,594 square miles) is the 20th largest island in the world.

LARGEST OFF-SHORE ISLANDS

	Sq. Miles	Name	County	Max. Dimension
Scotland	825·2	Lewis with Harris	Ross and Cromarty, Inverness-shire	61¼ miles
Wales	278·08	Anglesey	Anglesey	23 miles
England	147·34	Isle of Wight	Hampshire	22½ miles
Republic of Ireland	56·83	Achill Island	County Mayo	14½ miles
N. Ireland	5·31	Rathlin Island	County Antrim	4¾ miles

Freshwater The largest island surrounded by fresh water is the Ilha de Marajó (1,553 square miles), in the mouth of the River Amazon, Brazil. The world's largest inland island (*i.e.* land surrounded by rivers) is Ilha do Bananal, Brazil. The largest island in a lake is Manitoulin Island (1,068 square miles) in the Canadian (Ontario) section of Lake Huron. This island itself has on it a lake of 41·09 square miles called Manitou Lake, in which there are several islands. The largest lake island in Great Britain is Inchmurrin in Loch Lomond with an area of 284 acres.

Remotest World The remotest island in the world is Bouvet Øya (formerly Liverpool Island), discovered in the South Atlantic by J. B. C. Bouvet de Lozier on 1 Jan. 1739, and first landed on by Capt. George Norris on 16 Dec. 1825. Its position is 54° 26′ S., 3° 24′ E. This uninhabited Norwegian dependency is about 1,050 miles from the nearest land—the uninhabited Queen Maud Land coast of eastern Antarctica.

The remotest inhabited island in the world is Tristan da Cunha, discovered in the South Atlantic by Tristão da Cunha, a Portuguese admiral, in March 1506. It has an area of 38 square miles (habitable area 12 square miles) and was annexed by the United Kingdom on 14 Aug. 1816. The island's population was 235 in August 1966. The nearest inhabited land is the island of St. Helena, 1,320 miles to the north-east. The nearest continent, Africa, is 1,700 miles away.

British The remotest of the British islets is Rockall, 188 miles west of St. Kilda. This 70 foot high rock measuring 83 feet across was not formally annexed until 1955. The remotest British island which has ever been inhabited is North Rona which is 44 miles from the next nearest land at Cape Wrath and the Butt of Lewis. It was evacuated *c.* 1844. Muckle Flugga, off Unst, in the Shetlands, is the northernmost inhabited.

The western coast of Lewis

The natural world

Newest The world's newest island is the island of Surtsey, south-west of Iceland, which arose from the sea on 15 Nov. 1963 and is now 590 feet high and 0·77 of a square mile in area.

Greatest archipelago The world's greatest archipelago is the 3,500-mile-long crescent of more than 3,000 islands which forms Indonesia.

Northernmost land The most northerly land is Kaffeklubben Øyen (the Coffee Club Island) off the north-east of Greenland, 440 miles from the North Pole, discovered by Dr. Lange Koch in 1921, but determined only in June 1969 to be in latitude 83° 40′ 6″.

Largest atoll The largest atoll in the world is Kwajalein in the Marshall Islands, in the central Pacific Ocean. Its slender 176-mile-long coral reef encloses a lagoon of 1,100 square miles. The atoll with the largest land area is Christmas Island, in the Line Islands, in the central Pacific Ocean. It has an area of 184 square miles. Its two principal settlements, London and Paris, are 4 miles apart.

Longest reef The longest reef in the world is the Great Barrier Reef off Queensland, north-eastern Australia, which is 1,260 geographical miles in length. Between 1959 and 1969 a large section between Cooktown and Townsville was destroyed by the proliferation of the Crown of Thorns starfish *(Acanthaster planci)*.

Kaffeklubben Øyen.

MOUNTAINS

Highest in world An eastern Himalayan peak of 29,028 feet above sea-level on the Tibet-Nepal border (in an area first designated Chu-mu-lang-ma on a map of 1717) was discovered to be the world's highest mountain in 1852 by the Survey Department of the Government of India, from theodolite readings taken in 1849 and 1850. In 1860 its height was computed to be 29,002 feet. The 5½-mile high peak was named Mount Everest after Sir George Everest, C.B. (1790–1866), formerly Surveyor-General of India. After a total loss of 11 lives since the first reconnaissance in 1921, Everest was finally conquered at 11.30 a.m. on 29 May 1953. (For details of ascents, see under Mountaineering in Chapter XII.) The mountain whose summit is farthest from the Earth's centre is the Andean peak of Chimborazo (20,561 feet), 98 miles south of the equator in Ecuador, South America.

The highest insular island in the world is Mt. Sukarno (Carstensz Pyramid) (17,096 feet) in West Irian (formerly New Guinea), Indonesia.

In *The Guinness Book of Records* (seventh edition) a unique table of the highest points in 220 countries and other territories was published. Some additional data and amendments appeared in the 8th, 9th, 10th and 11th editions.

Highest in U.K. and Ireland The highest mountain in the United Kingdom is Ben Nevis (4,406 feet, excluding the 12 foot cairn), 4¼ miles south-east of Fort William, Inverness-shire, Scotland. There is no record of its having been climbed before 1720 and it was not discovered to be higher than Ben Macdhui (4,300 feet) until 1870. In 1830 Bens Macdhui and Nevis were respectively quoted as 4,418 feet and 4,358 feet. There is some evidence that, before being

58

Highest points in the geographical counties of the United Kingdom and the Republic of Ireland

The data given below indicate the highest point of natural land in each geographical county, of which the Ordnance Survey has record. Readings frequently quoted as 4 feet or 2 feet higher than those listed, are accounted for by the addition of the 4-foot-high trigonometric point pillar or the point midway on such a pillar from which readings are actually taken. In a few other cases, heights are exaggerated by the addition of a cairn of stones on the summit, *e.g.* Ben Nevis is sometimes quoted at 4,418 ft.

Numbers in brackets indicate the order of the counties with the highest points.

ENGLAND

Geographical county	Height in feet	Location
Bedfordshire	801	Dunstable Downs
Berkshire	974	Walbury Hill
Buckinghamshire	857	N.E. corner of Alton Wood
Cambridgeshire and Isle of Ely	480	300 yards south of the Hall, Great Shishill
Cheshire	1,908	Black Hill
Cornwall	1,375	Brown Willy
Cumberland (1)	3,210	Scafell Pike
Derbyshire (9)	2,088	Kinder Scout
Devon (10)	2,038	High Willhays
Dorset	908	Pilsdon Pen
Durham, County (6)	2,430	Near Burnhope Seat
Essex	480	In High Wood, nr. Langley
Gloucestershire	1,083	Cleeve Cloud
Hampshire (Inc. Isle of Wight)	937	Pilot Hill, nr. Ashmansworth
Herefordshire (7)	2,306	Black Mountains
Hertfordshire	803	Hastoe
Huntingdon and Peterborough	267	South of Stamford
Kent	824	Westerham (old fort trig. point)
Lancashire (4)	2,635	Old Man of Coniston
Leicestershire	912	Bardon Hill, nr. Coalville
Lincolnshire	550	Normanby-le-Wold
London, Greater	809	33 yds. S.E. of "Westerham Height", (a house) on the Kent-G.L.C. boundary
Monmouthshire (8)	2,228	Chwarel-y-Fan
Norfolk	336	Roman Camp, Sheringham
Northamptonshire	734	Arbury Hill
Northumberland (3)	2,676	The Cheviot
Nottinghamshire	655	S. side of Herrods Hill
Oxfordshire	836	Portobello
Rutland	646	West of Oakham
Shropshire	1,790	Brown Clee Hill
Somerset	1,705	Dunkery Beacon
Staffordshire	1,684	Oliver Hill
Suffolk	420	Rede
Surrey	965	Leith Hill
Sussex	919	Blackdown Hill
Warwickshire	854	Ilmington Downs
Westmorland (2)	3,118	Helvellyn
Wiltshire	964	Milk Hill and Tan Hill
Worcestershire	1,394	Worcestershire Beacon
Yorkshire (5)	2,591	Mickle Fell

SCOTLAND

Geographical county	Height in feet	Location
Aberdeenshire (2)	4,300	Ben Macdhui (shared with Banffshire)
Angus (7)	3,504	Glas Maol
Argyll (6)	3,766	Bidean nam Bian
Ayrshire	2,565	Kirriereoch Hill
Banffshire (2)	4,300	Ben Macdhui (shared with Aberdeenshire)
Berwickshire	1,755	Meikle Says Law (shared with E. Lothian)
Bute	2,868	Goat Fell, Arran
Caithness	2,313	Morven
Clackmannanshire	2,363	Ben Cleugh (Clach) (Ochils)
Dumfries-shire	2,696	White Coomb
Dunbarton (10)	3,092	Ben Vorlich
East Lothian	1,755	Meikle Says Law (shared with Berwickshire)
Fife	1,713	West Lomond
Inverness-shire (1)	4,406	Ben Nevis
Kincardineshire	2,555	Mount Battock (on Angus border)
Kinross-shire	1,630	Innerdowny Hill (Ochils)
Kirkcudbrightshire	2,770	Merrick
Lanarkshire	2,455	Culter Fell
Midlothian	2,137	Blackhope Scar
Moray	2,329	Càrn A'Ghille Chearr
Nairnshire	2,162	Càrn-Glas-Choire
Orkney	1,565	Ward Hill, Hoy
Peebles-shire	2,756	Broad Law (shared with Selkirkshire)
Perthshire (4)	3,984	Ben Lawers
Renfrewshire	1,713	Hill of Stake (on Ayrshire border)
Ross and Cromarty (5)	3,880	Carn Eige (on Inverness-shire border)
Roxburghshire	2,422	Nr. Auchope Cairn (on English border)
Selkirkshire	2,756	Broad Law (shared with Peebles-shire)
Shetland	1,486	Ronas Hill, Northmavine
Stirlingshire (9)	3,192	Ben Lomond
Sutherland (8)	3,273	Ben More Assynt
West Lothian	1,023	The Knock
Wigtownshire	1,051	Craigairie Fell

WALES

Geographical county	Height in feet	Location
Anglesey	720	Myndd Twr
Breconshire (3)	2,906	Pen-y-Fan (Cader Arthur)
Caernarvonshire (1)	3,560	Snowdon (Y Wyddfa)
Cardiganshire	2,468	Plynlimon
Carmarthenshire (6)	2,500+	Carmarthen Fan Foel
Denbighshire (4)	2,713	Moel Sych (shared with Montgomery-shire)
Flintshire	1,820	Moel Fammau
Glamorgan	1,969	Craig-y-Llyn
Merionethshire (2)	2,972	Aran Fawddwy, nr. Bala
Montgomeryshire (4)	2,713	Moel Sych (shared with Denbighshire)
Pembrokeshire	1,760	Prescelly Top
Radnorshire	2,166	In Radnor Forest

NORTHERN IRELAND

Geographical county	Height in feet	Location
Antrim	1,817	Trostàn
Armagh	1,894	Slieve Gullion
Down (1)	2,796	Slieve Donard
Fermanagh	2,188	Cuilcagh
Londonderry	2,240	Sawel Mountain
Tyrone	2,240	Sawel Mountain

REPUBLIC OF IRELAND

Geographical county	Height in feet	Location
Carlow (6)	2,610	Mount Leinster
Cavan	2,188	Cuilcagh
Clare	1,746	Glennagalliagh
Cork	2,321	Knockboy
Donegal	2,466	Errigal
Dublin	2,475	Kippure
Galway	2,395	Benbaun
Kerry (1)	3,414	Carrantuohill
Kildare	1,248	Cupidstown Hill
Kilkenny	1,703	Brandon
Leitrim	2,113	Truskmore
Leix	1,734	Arderin
Limerick (3)	3,018	Galtymore
Longford	916	Cornhill
Louth	1,935	Slieve Foye
Mayo (5)	2,688	Mweelrea
Meath	911	Canbane East
Monaghan	1,255	Slieve Beagh
Offaly	1,734	Arderin
Roscommon	1,284	Corry Mountain
Sligo	2,113	Truskmore
Tipperary (3)	3,018	Galtymore
Waterford (8)	2,609	Knockmealdown
Westmeath	855	Mullaghmeen
Wexford (6)	2,610	Mount Leinster
Wicklow (2)	3,039	Lugnaquillia

59

ground down by the ice-cap, mountains in Loch Bà area of the Island of Mull were 15,000 feet above sea-level.
Highest in England—
Scafell Pike, Cumberland—3,210 feet.
Highest in Wales—
Snowdon (Yr Wyddfa), Caernarvonshire—3,560 feet.
Highest in Ireland—
Carrauntual or Carrauntoohil, Kerry—3,414 feet.
Highest in Northern Ireland—
Slieve Donard, County Down—2,796 feet.
There are 577 peaks and tops over 3,000 feet in the whole British Isles and 165 peaks and 136 tops in Scotland higher than Scafell Pike. The highest mountain off the mainland is Sgùrr Alasdair (3,309 feet) on Skye.

Highest unclimbed Excluding subsidiary summits, the highest separate un-climbed mountain in the world is Gasherbrum III (26,090 feet) in the Karakoram, followed by Kangbachen (25,925 feet) in the Himalaya. These rank, respectively, 15th and 19th in height.

Largest The world's tallest mountain measured from its sub-marine base (3,280 fathoms) in the Hawaiian Trough to peak is Mauna Kea (Mountain White) on the Island of Hawaii, with a combined height of 33,476 feet, of which 13,796 feet are above sea-level. Another mountain whose dimensions, but not height, exceed those of Mount Everest is the Hawaiian peak of Mauna Loa (Mountain Long) at 13,680 feet. The axes of its elliptical base, 15,000 feet below sea-level, have been estimated at 74 miles and 53 miles. It should be noted that Cerro Aconcagua (22,834 feet) is more than 38,800 feet above the 16,000 foot deep abyssal plain or 42,834 feet above the Peru-Chile Trench which is 180 miles distant in the South Pacific.

Greatest ranges The world's greatest land mountain range is the Himalaya-Karakoram, which contains 96 of the world's 108 peaks of over 24,000 feet. The greatest of all mountain ranges is, however, the submarine mid-Atlantic Ridge, which is 10,000 miles long and 500 miles wide, with its highest peak being Mount Pico in the Azores, which rises 23,615 feet from the ocean floor (7,615 feet above sea-level).

Sand dunes The world's highest sand dunes are the Soussusvlei Dunes near the village of Aus, South West Africa, which reach 830 feet. Claims for dunes of 1,000 feet in the Sahara have not been pinpointed.

DEPRESSIONS

Deepest World The deepest depression so far discovered is beneath the Hollick-Kenyon Plateau in Marie Byrd Land, Antarctica, where, at a point 5,900 feet above sea-level, the ice depth is 14,000 feet, hence indicating a bed rock depression 8,100 feet below sea-level.

The deepest exposed depression on land is the shore surrounding the Dead Sea, 1,291 feet below sea-level. The deepest point on the bed of the lake is 2,600 feet below the Mediterranean. The deepest part of the bed of Lake Baykal in Siberia, U.S.S.R., is 4,872 feet below sea-level.

Great Britain The lowest lying area in Great Britain is in the Holme Fen area of the Great Ouse, in northern Huntingdon and Peterborough, at nine feet below sea-level. The deepest depression in England is the bed of part of Windermere, 94 feet below sea-level, and in Scotland the bed of Loch Morar, 987 feet below sea-level.

Largest The largest exposed depression in the world is the Caspian Sea basin in the Azerbaydzhani, Russian, Kazakh and Turkmen Republics of the U.S.S.R. and northern Iran (Persia). It is more than 200,000 square miles, of which 143,550 square miles is lake area. The preponderant land area of the depression is the Prikaspiyskaya Nizmennost', lying around the northern third of the lake and stretching inland for a distance of up to 280 miles.

RIVERS

LONGEST

World The river systems of the world are estimated to contain 55,000 cubic miles of fresh water.

The longest river in the world is the Nile (*Bahr-el-Nil*). It runs 4,145 miles (National Geographic Society survey figure) from its source in Rwanda, the Luvironza branch of the Kagera feeder of the Victoria Nyanza, *via* the White Nile (*Bahr-el-Jebel*) to its delta on the shores of the Mediterranean in the United Arab Republic (formerly Egypt). The U.A.R. Government Irrigation Department's official survey figure is 4,164 miles, of which only 960 miles are navigable.

The Amazon

Recent surveys put the length of the Amazon (Amazonas) at 3,900 miles from Lago Villafro, *via* the Apurimac branch of the Ucayali, to the sea. Its navigable length of 3,750 miles is the greatest of any river. The length of the Mississippi-Missouri-Red Rock complex was assessed at 3,741 miles in 1967. The Mississippi's length may change by as much as 30 miles in a day if the neck of a large meander or loop is worn through. In times past both the Amazon and the Mississippi have been regarded as the world's longest river.

Ireland The longest river in Ireland is the Shannon, which is longer than any river in Great Britain. It rises 258 feet above sea-level, in County Cavan, and flows through a series of loughs to Limerick. It is 240 miles long, including the 56-mile long estuary to Loop Head. The basin area is 6,060 square miles.

Great Britain The longest river in Great Britain is the Severn, which empties into the Bristol Channel and is 220 miles long. Its basin extends over 4,409 square miles. It rises in south-western Montgomeryshire, in Wales and flows through Shropshire, Worcestershire and Gloucestershire. The longest river wholly in England is the Thames, which is 215 miles long to the Nore. Its remotest source is at Seven Springs, Gloucestershire, whence the River Churn joins the other head waters. The source of the Thames proper is Trewsbury Mead, Coate, Cirencester, Gloucestershire. The basin measures 3,841 square miles. The longest river wholly in Wales is the Towy, with a length of 64 miles. It rises in Cardiganshire and flows out into Carmarthen Bay. The longest river in Scotland is the Tay, with Dundee, Angus, on the shore of the estuary. It is 117 miles long from the source of its remotest head-stream, the Tummel, and has the greatest volume of any river in Great Britain, with a flow of up to 49,000 cubic feet per second. Its basin extends over 1,961 square miles.

Greatest flow The greatest flow of any river in the world is that of the Amazon, which discharges an average of 4,200,000 cubic feet of water per second into the Atlantic Ocean, rising to more than 7,000,000 "cusecs" in full flood.

Largest basin and longest tributary The largest river basin in the world is that drained by the Amazon (3,900 miles). It covers about 2,720,000 square miles. It has about 15,000 tributaries and sub-tributaries, of which four are more than 1,000 miles long. These include the Madeira, the longest of all tributaries, with a length of 2,100 miles, which is surpassed by only 14 rivers.

Longest tributary
The longest sub-tributary is the Pilcomayo (1,000 miles long) in South America. It is a tributary of the Paraguay (1,500 miles long), which is itself a tributary of the Paraná (2,500 miles).

Submarine river
In 1952 a submarine river 250 miles wide, known as the Cromwell current, was discovered flowing eastward 300 feet below the surface of the Pacific for 3,500 miles along the equator. Its volume is 1,000 times that of the Mississippi.

Subterranean river
In August 1958 a crypto-river was tracked by radio isotopes flowing under the Nile with a mean annual flow six times greater—560,000 million cubic metres (20 million million cubic feet).

Longest estuary
The world's longest estuary is that of the Ob', in the northern U.S.S.R., at 450 miles.

Largest delta
The world's largest delta is that created by the Ganga (Ganges) and Brahmaputra in East Pakistan and West Bengal, India. It covers an area of 30,000 square miles.

GREATEST RIVER BORES

World
The bore on the Ch'ient'ang'kian (Hang-chou-fe) in eastern China is the most remarkable in the world. At spring tides the wave attains a height of up to 25 feet and a speed of 13 knots. It is heard advancing at a range of 14 miles. The bore on the Hooghly branch of the Ganges travels for 70 miles at more than 15 knots. The annual downstream flood wave on the Mekong sometimes reaches a height of 46 feet. The greatest volume of any tidal bore is that of the Canal do Norte (10 miles wide) in the mouth of the Amazon.

Great Britain
The most notable river bore in the United Kingdom is that on the River Severn, which attained a measured height of 9¼ feet on 15 Oct. 1966 downstream of Stonebench and a speed of 13 m.p.h. It travels 21 miles from Awre to Gloucester.

Fastest rapids
The fastest rapids which have ever been navigated are the Lava Falls on the River Colorado in the United States. At times of flood these attain a speed of 30 m.p.h. (26 knots) with waves boiling up to 12 feet high.

WATERFALLS

Highest
The highest waterfall in the world is the Angel Falls, in Venezuela, on a branch of the River Carrao, an upper tributary of the Caroní, with a total drop of 3,212 feet—the longest single drop is 2,648 feet. It was discovered in 1935 by a United States pilot named Jimmy Angel (died 8 Dec. 1956), who crashed nearby.

Greatest
On the basis of the average annual flow, the greatest waterfall in the world is the Guairá (374 feet high), known also as the Salto dos Sete Quedas, on the Alto Paraná River between Brazil and Paraguay. Although attaining an average height of only 110 feet, its estimated annual average flow over the lip (5,300 yards wide) is 470,000 cubic feet per second. The amount of water this represents can be imagined by supposing that it was pouring into the dome of St. Paul's Cathedral—it would fill it completely in three-fifths of a second. It has a peak flow of 1,750,000 cubic feet per second. The seven cataracts of the Stanley Falls in the Congo (Kinshasa) have an average annual flow of 600,000 cubic feet per second.

Widest
The widest waterfalls in the world are the Khône Falls (50 to 70 feet high) in Laos, with a width of 6·7 miles and a flood flow of 1,500,000 cubic feet per second.

United Kingdom
The tallest waterfall in the United Kingdom is Eas-Coul-Aulin, in the parish of Eddrachillis, Sutherland, Scotland, with a drop of 658 feet. England's highest fall

is Caldron (or Cauldron) Snout, on the Tees, with a fall of 200 feet, in 450 feet of cataracts, but no sheer leap. It is at the junction of Durham, Westmorland and Yorkshire. The highest Welsh waterfall is the Pistyll Rhaiadr (240 feet), on the River Rhaiadr, in southern Denbighshire.

Ireland
The highest falls in Ireland are the Powerscourt Falls (350 feet), on the River Dargle, County Wicklow.

Longest fjords and sea lochs
The world's longest fjord is the Nordvest fjord arm of the Scoresby Sund in eastern Greenland, which extends inland 195 miles from the sea. The longest of Norwegian fjords is the Sogne Fjord, which extends 183 kilometres (113·7 miles) inland from Sygnefest to the head of the Lusterfjord arm at Skjolden. It averages barely 3 miles in width and has a deepest point of 4,085 feet. If measured from Huglo along the Bφmlafjord to the head of the Sφrfjord arm at Odda, the Hardengerfjorden can also be said to extend 183 kilometres (113·7 miles). The longest Danish fjord is the Limfjorden (100 miles long). Scotland's longest sea loch is Loch Fyne, which extends 42 miles inland into Argyllshire.

LAKES AND INLAND SEAS

Largest
The largest inland sea or lake in the world is the Kaspiskoye More (Caspian Sea) in the southern U.S.S.R. and Iran (Persia). It is 760 miles long and its total area is 143,550 square miles. Of the total area some 55,280 square miles (38·6%) is in Iran, where it is named the Darya-ye-Khazar. Its maximum depth is 980 metres (3,215 feet) and its surface is 92 feet below sea-level. Its estimated volume is 21,500 cubic miles of saline water. Since 1930 it has diminished 15,000 square miles in area with a fall of 62 feet, while the shore line has retreated more than 10 miles in some places.

Freshwater
The freshwater lake with the greatest surface area is Lake Superior, one of the Great Lakes of North America. The total area is 31,800 square miles, of which 20,700 square miles are in the United States and 11,100 square miles in Ontario, Canada. It is 600 feet above sea-level. The freshwater lake with the greatest volume is Baykal (see Deepest lake, below) with an estimated volume of 5,750 cubic miles.

Lake in a lake
The largest lake in a lake is Manitou Lake (41·09 square miles) on Manitoulin Island (1,068 square miles) in the Canadian part of Lake Huron.

United Kingdom
The largest lake in the United Kingdom is Lough Neagh (48 feet above sea-level) in Northern Ireland. It is 18 miles long and 11 miles wide and has an area of 147·39 square miles. Its extreme depth is 102 feet.

Great Britain
The largest lake in Great Britain, and the largest inland loch in Scotland is Loch Lomond (23 feet above sea-level), which is 22·64 miles long and has a surface area of 32·81 square miles. It is situated in the counties of

A corner of the world's largest lake,
the Caspian Sea,
which could accommodate both
Great Britain and Ireland

61

The natural world

Stirling and Dunbarton and its greatest depth is 623 feet. The longest lake is Loch Ness which measures 22·75 miles. The largest lake in England is Windermere, in the county of Westmorland. It is 10½ miles long and has a surface area of 5·69 square miles. Its greatest depth is 219 feet in the northern half. The largest natural lake in Wales is Llyn Tegid, with an area of 1·69 square miles, although it should be noted that the largest lake in Wales is that formed by the reservoir at Lake Vyrnwy, where the total surface area is 3·18 square miles.

Republic of Ireland The largest lough in the Republic of Ireland is Lough Corrib in the counties of Mayo and Galway. It measures 27 miles in length and is 7 miles across at its widest point with a total surface area of 41,616 acres (65·0 square miles).

DEEPEST
World The deepest lake in the world is Ozero (Lake) Baykal in central Siberia, U.S.S.R. It is 620 kilometres (385 miles) long and between 20 and 46 miles wide. In 1957 the Olkhon Crevice was measured to be 1,940 metres (6,365 feet) deep and hence 4,872 feet below sea-level.

Great Britain The deepest lake in Great Britain is the 12-mile-long Loch Morar, in Inverness-shire. Its surface is 30 feet above sea-level and its extreme depth 1,017 feet. England's deepest lake is Wast Water (258 feet), in Cumberland.

HIGHEST
World The highest steam-navigated lake in the world is Lago Titicaca (maximum depth 1,214 feet), with an area of about 3,200 square miles (1,850 square miles in Peru, 1,350 square miles in Bolivia), in South America. It is 130 miles long and is situated at 12,506 feet above sea-level. There is a small unnamed lake north of Mount Everest by the Changtse Glacier, Tibet, at an altitude of 20,230 feet above sea-level.

United Kingdom The highest lake in the United Kingdom is the 1·9 acre Lochan Buidhe at 3,600 feet above sea-level in the Cairngorm Mountains, Scotland. England's highest is Broad Crag Tarn (2,746 feet above sea-level) on Scafell, Cumberland, and the highest in Wales is a pool above Llyn y Fign (c. 2,540 feet), 8 miles east of Dolgellan, Merionethshire.

Longest glaciers It is estimated that 6,020,000 square miles, or about 10·4 per cent. of the Earth's land surface, is permanently glaciated. The world's longest known glacier is the Lambert Glacier, discovered by an Australian aircraft crew in Australian Antarctic Territory in 1956–57. It is up to 40 miles wide and, with its upper section, known as the Mellor Glacier, it measures at least 250 miles in length. With the Fisher Glacier limb, the Lambert forms a continuous ice passage about 320 miles long. The longest Himalayan glacier is the Siachen (47 miles) in the Karakoram range, though the Hispar and Biafo combine to form an ice passage 76 miles long.

Greatest avalanches The greatest avalanches, though rarely observed, occur in the Himalaya but no estimates of their volume have been published. It was estimated that 3,500,000 cubic metres (120,000,000 cubic feet) of snow fell in an avalanche in the Italian Alps in 1885. (See also Disasters, end of Chapter XI.)

Largest desert Nearly an eighth of the world's land surface is arid with a rainfall of less than 25 cms. (9·8 inches) per annum. The Sahara Desert in North Africa is the largest in the world. At its greatest length it is 3,200 miles from east to west. From north to south it is between 800 and 1,400 miles. The area covered by the desert is about 3,250,000 square miles. The land level varies from 436 feet below sea-level in the Qattâra Depression, United Arab Republic (formerly Egypt), to the mountain Emi Koussi (11,204 feet) in Chad. The diurnal temperature range in the western Sahara may be more than 80 degrees F. or 45 degrees C.

GORGE
Largest The largest gorge in the world is the Grand Canyon on the Colorado River in north-central Arizona, U.S.A. It extends from Marble Gorge to the Grand Wash Cliffs, over a distance of 217 miles. It varies in width from 4 to 13 miles and is up to 7,000 feet deep.

Deepest The deepest visible canyon in the world is Hell's Canyon, dividing Oregon and Idaho, U.S.A. It plunges 7,900 feet from the Devil Mountain down to the Snake River. The deepest submarine canyon yet discovered is one 25 miles south of Esperance, Western Australia, which is 6,000 feet deep and 20 miles wide.

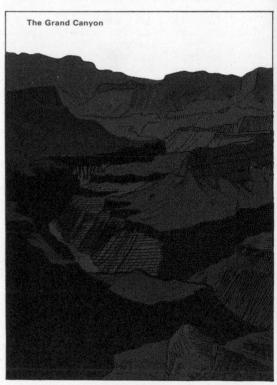

The Grand Canyon

CAVES
Largest The largest known underground chamber in the world is the Big Room of the Carlsbad Caverns (1,320 feet deep) in New Mexico, U.S.A. It is 4,270 feet long and reaches 328 feet in height and 656 feet in width. The largest cavern in Britain is a cavern about 2,500 feet long, discovered on 13 April 1966 under Mynydd-dhu, a hill in Carmarthenshire, Wales. It contains stalagmites 12 feet tall and a waterfall with a drop of 100 feet.

The most extensive cave system in the world is said to be the Flint Ridge Cave system, discovered in 1799 in Kentucky, U.S.A. Its total length is reputed to be more than 150 miles, but it contains only 63·31 miles of actual mapped passageway. The world's longest surveyed cave is the Hölloch in Switzerland, with a measured length of 64·44 miles. The longest cave system in Great Britain is Ogof Ffynnon Dhu, Breconshire in South Wales, in which c. 20·40 miles of passages have so far been surveyed.

DEEPEST CAVES BY COUNTRIES

These depths are subject to continuous revisions.

Feet below Entrance

4,300	Gouffre de la Pierre Saint-Martin, Pyrenees	France/Spain
3,750	Gouffre Berger, Sornin Plateau, Vercors	France
2,906	Spluga della Preta, Lessinische Alps	Italy
2,427	Hölloch, Moutatal, Schwyz	Switzerland
2,329	Gruberhorn höhle, Hoher Göll, Salzburg	Austria
2,099	Sniezna, Tatra	Poland
2,040	Gouffre de Faour Dara	Lebanon
1,770	Abisso Vereo, Istria	Yugoslavia
1,690	Anou Boussouil, Djurdjura	Algeria
>1,300	Provetina, Mount Astraka	Greece
1,214	Cueva-Sima de Ormazaretta, Navarra	Spain
1,184	Neff's Cave, Utah	U.S.A.
1,115	Izvorul Tausoarelor, Rodna	Rumania
1,070	Larshullet, Mo-i-Rana	Norway
800	Ogof Ffynnon Dhu, Breconshire	Wales
653	Oxlow Cavern, Giant's Hole, Derbyshire	England
527	Growling Swallet Cave, Tasmania	Australia
330	Pollnagollum-Poulelva, County Clare	Ireland

LONGEST CAVE SYSTEMS BY COUNTRIES

These surveyed lengths are subject to continuous revision.

Miles

64·44	Hölloch, Schwyz	Switzerland
63·31	Flint Ridge Cave System, Kentucky	U.S.A.
32.74	Sistema Cavernavio de Cuyaguatega	Cuba
*26·10	Eisriesenwelt, Werfen, Salzburg	Austria
22·74	Peschtschera Optimistitscheskaya, Pololien	U.S.S.R.
22·48	Complejo Palomera-Dolencias, Burgos	Spain
c. 20·40	Ogof Ffynnon Dhu, Breconshire	Wales
13·67	Goule de Foussoubie, Ardèche	France
13·67	Baradla Barlang-Jaskyna Domica, Magyarország	Hungary
10·50	Lancaster Hole—Easegill Caverns, Westmorland	England
7·39	Poulnagollum-Poulelva Caves, County Clare	Ireland
>6	Mullamullang Cave	Australia

Longest ice caves, discovered in 1879. Now rank as eighth longest known.

Longest stalactite The longest known stalactite in the world is a wall-supported column extending 195 feet from roof to floor in the Cueva de Nerja, near Málaga, Spain. The rather low tensile strength of calcite (calcium carbonate) precludes very long free-hanging stalactites, but one of 38 feet exists in the Poll an Ionain cave in County Clare, Ireland.

Tallest stalagmite The tallest known stalagmite in the world is La Grande Stalagmite in the Aren Armand cave, Lozère, France, which has attained a height of 98 feet from the cave floor. It was found in September 1897.

SEA CLIFFS
The location of the highest sea cliffs in the world has yet to be established. These may be in north-west Greenland. The highest cliffs in the British Isles are those on the north coast of Achill Island, in County Mayo, Ireland, which are 2,192 feet sheer above the sea at Croaghan. The highest cliffs in the United Kingdom are the 1,300 feet Conachair cliffs on St. Kilda, Scotland (1,397 feet). England's highest cliffs are at Countisbury, North Devon, where they drop 900 feet.

NATURAL BRIDGE
The longest natural bridge in the world is the Landscape Arch in the Arches National Monument, Utah, U.S.A. This natural sandstone arch spans 291 feet and is set about 100 feet above the canyon floor. In one place erosion has narrowed its section to six feet.

Aren Armand cave, Lozère, France

3. Weather

WEATHER RECORDS
The meteorological records given below necessarily relate largely to the last 125 to 145 years, since data before that time are both sparse and unreliable. Reliable registering thermometers were introduced as recently as *c.* 1820.

Palaeo-entomological evidence is that there was a southern European climate in England in *c.* 90,000 B.C., while in *c.* 6,000 B.C. the mean summer temperature reached 67° F, or 6 deg. F higher than the present. The earliest authentic British weather records relate to the period 26–30 Aug. 55 B.C. The earliest reliably known hot summer was in A.D. 664 during our driest ever century and the earliest known severe winter was that of A.D. 763–4. In 1683–84 there was frost in London from November to April. The winter of 1962–63 was the worst recorded in Britain since 1740 (see Longest freeze). Frosts were recorded during August in the period 1668–89.

The world's extremes of temperature have been noted progressively thus:

127·4° F	Ouargla, Algeria	27 Aug. 1884
130° F	Amos, California, U.S.A.	17 Aug. 1885
130° F	Mammoth Tank, California, U.S.A.	17 Aug. 1885
134° F	Death Valley, California, U.S.A.	10 July 1913
136·4° F	Al 'Aziziyah (el-Azizia), Libya*	13 Sept. 1922
136·4° F	San Luis Potosi, Mexico†	11 Aug. 1933

Obtained by the U.S. National Geographic Society but not officially recognized by the Libyan Ministry of Communications.

† A reading of 140° F at Delta, Mexico, in August 1953 is not now accepted because of over-exposure to roof radiation.

A freak heat flash struck Coimbra, Portugal, in September 1933 when the temperature rose to 70° C (158° F) for 120 seconds.

−73° F	Floeberg Bay, Ellesmere Is., Canada		1852
−90·4° F	Verkhoyansk, Siberia, U.S.S.R.	3 Jan.	1885
−90·4° F	Verkhoyansk, Siberia, U.S.S.R.	5 & 7 Feb.	1892
−90·4° F	Oymyakon, Siberia, U.S.S.R.	6 Feb.	1933
−100·4° F	South Pole, Antarctica	11 May	1957
−102·1° F	South Pole, Antarctica	17 Sept.	1957
−109·1° F	Sovietskaya, Antarctica	2 May	1958
−113·3° F	Vostok, Antarctica	15 June	1958
−113·8° F	Sovietskaya, Antarctica	19 June	1958
−117·4° F	Sovietskaya, Antarctica	25 June	1958
−122·4° F	Vostok, Antarctica	7–8 Aug.	1958
−124·1° F	Sovietskaya, Antarctica	9 Aug.	1958
−125·3° F	Vostok, Antarctica	25 Aug.	1958
−126·9° F	Vostok, Antarctica	24 Aug.	1960

Most equable temperature The location with the most equable recorded temperature over a short period is Garapan, on Saipan, in the Mariana Islands, Pacific Ocean. During the nine years from 1927 to 1935, inclusive, the lowest temperature recorded was 19·6° C (67·3° F) on 30 Jan. 1934 and the highest was 31·4° C (88·5° F) on 9 Sept. 1931, giving an

The natural world

Barnaul, U.S.S.R. scene of the barometric record

The most shaded village

WEATHER RECORDS

	World Records	United Kingdom & Ireland
Highest Shade Temperature:	136·4° F, San Luis Potosí, Mexico, 11.8.1933[1]	100·5° F(38° C), Tonbridge, Kent, 22.7.1868
Lowest Screen Temperature:	−126·9° F, Vostok, Antarctica, 24.8.1960[2]	−17° F(−27·2° C), Braemar, Aberdeenshire, Scotland, 11.2.1895[3]
Greatest Rainfall (24 hours):	73·62 in., Cilaos, La Réunion, Indian Ocean, 15–16.3.1952[4]	11·00 in., Martinstown, Dorset, 18–19.7.1955
(Month):	366·14 in., Cherrapunji, Assam, India, July 1861	56·54 in., Llyn Llydau, Snowdon, Caernarvonshire, October 1909
(12 Months):	1,041·78 in., Cherrapunji, Assam, 1.8.1860–31.7.1861	257·0 in., Sprinkling Tarn, Cumberland, in 1954[5]
Greatest Snowfall[6] (12 Months):	1,000·3 in., Paradise Ranger Station (1,550 feet), Mt. Rainier, Washington State, U.S.A., 1955–56 (annual average 575·1 in.)	60 in., Upper Teesdale and Denbighshire Hills, 1947
Maximum Sunshine:	97%+ (over 4,300 hours), eastern Sahara, annual average	77·6% (384·0 hrs.), Eastbourne and Hastings, Sussex, July 1911 (month)
Minimum Sunshine:	Nil at North Pole—for winter stretches of 186 days	6 minutes in a month at Bunhill Row, London, all on 7.12.1890[7]
Barometric Pressure (Highest):	1,079 mb. (31·86 in.), Barnaul, U.S.S.R., 23.1.1900	1,054·7 mb. (31·15 in.), Aberdeen, 31.1.1902
(Lowest):	877 mb. (25·91 in.), about 600 miles north-west of Guam, Pacific Ocean, 24.9.1958	925·5 mb. (27·33 in.), Ochtertyre, near Crieff, Perthshire, 26.1.1884
Highest Surface Wind-speed:[8]	225 m.p.h., Mt. Washington (6,288 ft.), New Hampshire, U.S.A., 24.4.1934 (indicated speed 231 m.p.h.)	144 m.p.h. (125 knots), Coire Cas ski lift (3,525 feet), Cairn Gorm, Inverness-shire, 6.3.1967[9]
Thunder-Days (Year):[10]	322 days, Bogor (formerly Buitenzorg), Java, Indonesia (average, 1916–19)	38 days, Stonyhurst, Lancashire, 1912[11]
Hottest Place (Annual mean):[12]	Lugh Ganane (Lugh Ferrandi), Somalia, 88° F	Penzance, Cornwall, and Isles of Scilly, both 52·7° F (11·5° C), average 1931–60
Coldest Place (Annual mean):	Pole of Cold (78° S., 96° E.), Antarctica, −72° F (16 deg. F lower than the Pole)	Braemar, Aberdeenshire, 43·7° F (6·5° C), average 1931–60
Wettest Place (Annual mean):	Mt. Wai-ʻaleʻale (5,080 ft.), Kauai, Hawaii, U.S.A., 486·1 inches (average, 1920–58). About 335 rainy days per year	Styhead Tarn (1,600 ft.), Cumberland, 172·9 in.
Driest Place (Annual mean):	Calama, in the Desierto de Atacama, Chile (rain never recorded)	Great Wakering, Essex 19·2 in. (1916–1950)
Longest Drought:	c. 400 years, Deiserto de Atacama, Chile	73 days, Mile End, London, 4.3 to 15.5.1893
Most Rainy Days (Year):	Bahía Felix, Chile, 348 days in 1916 (annual average 325 days)	Ballynahinch Castle, Galway, 309 days in 1923
Largest Hailstones:[14]	1·5 lb. (5·4 in. diameter, 17 in. circumference), Potter, Nebraska, U.S.A., 6.7.1928	5 oz., Horsham, Sussex, 5.9.1958
Longest Fogs (Visibility less than 1,000 yards):	Fogs persist for weeks on the Grand Banks, Newfoundland, Canada, and the average is more than 120 days per year.	London, 26.11 to 1.12.1948 (4 days 18 hours) London 5.12 to 9.12.1952 (4 days 18 hours)
Windiest Place:	The Commonwealth Bay, George V Coast, Antarctica, where gales reach 200 m.p.h.	Tiree, Argyllshire (89 ft.), annual average 17·4 m.p.h.

---

[1] *The shade temperature in London on 8 July 1808 may have reached this figure.*
[2] *The coldest inhabited place is the Siberian village of Oymyakon (63° 16′ N., 143° 15′ E.), in the U.S.S.R., where the temperature reached −96° F in 1964.*
[3] *The −23° F at Blackadder, Berwickshire on 4 Dec. 1879, and the −20° F at Grantown-on-Spey on 24 Feb. 1955, were not standard exposures. The −11° F reported from Buxton, Derbyshire on 11 Feb. 1895 was not standard. The lowest official temperature in England is −6° F (−21·1° C) at Bodiam, Sussex on 20 Jan. 1940, at Ambleside, Westmorland on 21 Jan. 1940 and at Houghall, Durham on 5 Jan. 1941 and 4 March 1947.*
[4] *This is equal to 7,435 tons of rain per acre. Elevation 1,200 metres (3,937 feet).*
[5] *The record for Ireland is 154·4 in. near Derriana Lough, County Kerry, in 1948.*
[6] *The record for a single snow storm is 175·4 in. at Thompson Pass, Alaska, on 26–31 Dec. 1955, and, for 24 hours, 76 in. at Silver Lake, Colorado, U.S.A., on 14–15 April 1921. London's earliest recorded snow was on 25 Sept. 1885, and the latest on 27 May 1821. Less reliable reports suggest snow on 12 Sept. 1658 and on 12 June 1791.*
[7] *The south-eastern end of the village of Lochranza, Isle of Arran, Buteshire is in shadow of mountains from 18 Nov. to 8 Feb. each winter.*
[8] *The highest speed yet measured in a tornado is 280 m.p.h. at Wichita Falls, Texas, U.S.A., on 2 April 1958.*
[9] *The figure of 177·2 m.p.h. at R.A.F. Saxa Vord, Unst, in the Shetlands, Scotland, on 16 Feb. 1962, was not recorded with standard equipment. There were gales of great severity on 15 Jan. 1362 and 26 Nov. 1703.*
[10] *At any given moment there are 2,200 thunderstorms in the world, some of which can be heard at a range of 18 miles.*
[11] *The reliable modern record is 32 days at Littleover, Derbyshire, in 1960.*
[12] *In Death Valley, California, U.S.A., maximum temperatures of over 120° F were recorded on 43 consecutive days—6 July to 17 Aug. 1917. At Marble Bar, Western Australia (maximum 121° F), 160 consecutive days with maximum temperatures of over 100° F were recorded—31 Oct. 1923 to 7 April 1924. At Wyndham, Western Australia, the temperature reached 90° F or more on 333 days in 1946.*

[13] *The lowest rainfall recorded in a single year was 9·29 in. at one station in Margate, Kent, in 1921.*
[14] *Much heavier hailstones are sometimes reported. These are usually not single but coalesced stones. An 8½-oz. stone was recorded at Bicester, Oxfordshire, on 11 May 1945.*

Vostok—the coldest place on Earth

extreme range of 11·8 deg. C (21·2 deg. F). Between 1911 and 1966 the Brazilian off-shore island of Fernando de Noronha had a minimum temperature of 18·6° C (65·5° F) on 17 Nov. 1913 and a maximum of 32·0° C (89·6° F) on 2 March 1965, an extreme range of 13·4 deg. C (24·1 deg. F).

idity and scomfort Human discomfort depends not merely on temperature but on the combination of temperature, humidity, radiation and wind-speed. The United States Weather Bureau uses a Temperature-Humidity Index, which equals two-fifths of the sum of the dry and wet bulb thermometer readings plus 15. When the THI reaches 75 in still air, at least half of the people will be uncomfortable while at 79 few, if any, will be comfortable. When the index reaches 86 inside a Federal building in Washington, D.C., everybody may be sent home. A reading of 92 (shade temperature 119° F, relative humidity 22%) was recorded at Yuma, Arizona, U.S.A., on 31 July 1957, but even this must have been surpassed in Death Valley, California, U.S.A.

Greatest peraturе ranges The greatest recorded temperature ranges in the world are around the Siberian "cold pole" in the eastern U.S.S.R. Olekminsk has ranged 189 deg. F from −76° F to 113° F and Verkhoyansk (67° 33′ N., 133° 23′ E.) has ranged 192 deg. F from −94° F (unofficial) to 98° F.

The greatest temperature variation recorded in a day is 100 deg. F (a fall from 44° F to −56° F) at Browning, Montana, U.S.A., on 23–24 Jan. 1916. The most freakish rise was 49 deg. F in 2 minutes at Spearfish, South Dakota, from −4° F at 7.30 a.m. to 45° F at 7.32 a.m. on 22 Jan. 1943. The British record is 50·9 deg. F (34·0° F to 84·9° F) in 9 hours at Rickmansworth, Hertfordshire, on 29 Aug. 1936.

est freeze The longest recorded unremitting freeze (maximum temperature 32° F and below) in the British Isles was one of 34 days at Moor House, Westmorland, from 23 Dec. 1962 to 25 Jan. 1963. This was almost certainly exceeded at the neighbouring Great Dun Fell, where the screen temperature never rose above freezing during the whole of January 1963.

Upper mosphere The lowest temperature ever recorded in the atmosphere is −143° C (−225·4° F) at an altitude of about 50 to 60 miles, during noctilucent cloud research above Kronogård, Sweden, from 27 July to 7 Aug. 1963. A jet stream moving at 408 m.p.h. at 154,200 feet was recorded by Skua rocket above South Uist, Outer Hebrides, Scotland on 13 Dec. 1967.

Deepest ermafrost The greatest recorded depth of permafrost is 1·5 kilometres (4,921 feet) reported in April 1968 in the basin of the River Lena, Siberia, U.S.S.R.

st intense rainfall Difficulties attend rainfall readings for very short periods but the figure of 1·23 inches in one minute at Unionville, Maryland, U.S.A., at 3.23 p.m. on 4 July 1956, is regarded as the most intense recorded in modern times. There was reputedly a cloudburst of "near two foot . . . in less than a quarter of half an hour" at Oxford on the afternoon of 31 May (Old Style) 1682. Since 1860 the most intense rainfall recorded in Britain has been 1·25 inches in 5 minutes at Preston, Lancashire, on 10 Aug. 1893; and 3·15 inches in 30 minutes at Eskdalemuir, Dumfries-shire, on 26 July 1953.

Falsest Swithin's Days The legend that the weather on St. Swithin's Day, celebrated on 15 July since A.D. 912, determines the rainfall for the next 40 days is one which has long persisted. There was a brilliant 13½ hours sunshine in London on 15 July 1924, but 30 of the next 40 days were wet. On 15 July 1913 there was a 15-hour downpour, yet it rained on only nine of the subsequent 40 days in London.

Lightning The visible length of lightning strokes varies greatly. In mountainous regions, when clouds are very low, the flash may be less than 300 feet long. In flat country with very high clouds, a cloud-to-earth flash sometimes measures four miles, though in extreme cases such flashes have been measured at 20 miles. The intensely bright central core of the lightning channel is extremely narrow. Some authorities suggest that its diameter is as little as half an inch. This core is surrounded by a "corona envelope" (glow discharge) which may measure 10 to 20 feet in diameter.

The speed of a lightning discharge varies from 100 to 1,000 miles per second for the downward leader track, and reaches up to 87,000 miles per second (nearly half the speed of light) for the powerful return stroke. In Britain there is an average of six strikes per square mile per annum, and an average of 4,200 per annum over London alone.

Every few million strokes there is a giant discharge, in which the cloud-to-earth and the return lightning strokes flash from the top of the thunder clouds. In these "positive giants" energy of up to 3,000 million joules (3×10^{16} ergs) is sometimes recorded. The temperature reaches about 30,000° C, which is more than five times greater than that of the surface of the Sun.

Highest waterspout The highest waterspout of which there is a reliable record was one observed on 16 May 1898 off Eden, New South Wales, Australia. A theodolite reading from the shore gave its height as 5,014 feet. It was about 10 feet in diameter. A waterspout moved around Tor Bay, Devon on 17 Sept. 1969 which was according to press estimates 1,000 feet in height.

Cloud extremes The highest standard cloud form is cirrus, averaging 27,000 feet and above, but the rare nacreous or mother-of-pearl formation sometimes reaches nearly 80,000 feet. The lowest is stratus, below 3,500 feet. The cloud form with the greatest vertical range is cumulo-nimbus, which has been observed to reach a height of nearly 68,000 feet in the tropics. Noctilucent "clouds", which were observed from Hampshire on 30 June 1950, are believed to pass at a height of over 60 miles.

Best and worst British summers According to Prof. Gordon Manley's survey over the period 1728 to 1969 the best (i.e. driest and hottest) British summer was that of 1949 and the worst (i.e. wettest and coldest) that of 1879.

Most recent White Christmas and Frost Fair London has experienced six "White" Christmas Days since 1900. These have been in 1906, 1917 (slight), 1923 (slight), 1927, 1938 and 1956 (slight). These were more frequent in the 19th century and even more so before the change of calendar in 1752. The last of the nine recorded Frost Fairs held on the frozen river Thames was in December 1813 to 26 Jan. 1814.

The last Thames Frost Fair—1814

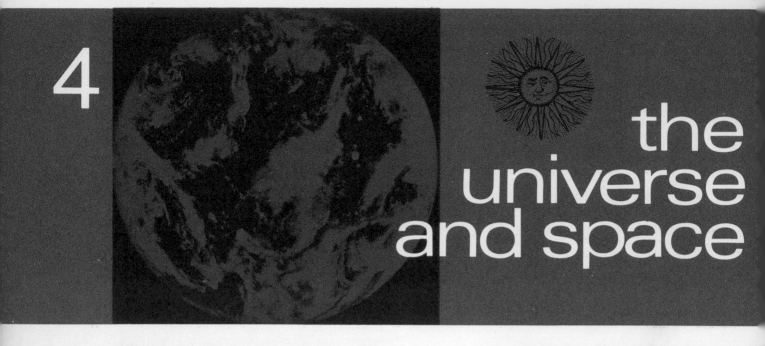

4

the universe and space

The universe is the entirety of space, matter and anti-matter. An appreciation of its magnitude is best grasped by working outward from the Earth, through the Solar System and our own Milky Way galaxy, to the remotest extra-galactic nebulae.

METEOROIDS

Meteor shower Meteoroids are mostly of cometary origin. A meteor is the light phenomenon caused by the entry of a meteoroid into the Earth's atmosphere. The greatest meteor "shower" on record occurred on the night of 16–17 Nov. 1966, when the Leonid meteors (which recur every 33¼ years) were visible between western North America and eastern U.S.S.R. It was calculated that meteors passed over Arizona, U.S.A., at a rate of 2,300 per minute for a period of 20 minutes from 5 a.m. on 17 Nov. 1966.

METEORITES

Largest World When a meteoroid penetrates to the Earth's surface, the remnant is described as a meteorite. The largest known meteorite is one found in 1920 at Hoba West, near Grootfontein in South West Africa. This is a block about 9 feet long by 8 feet broad, weighing 132,000 lb. (59 tons). The largest meteorite exhibited by any museum is the "Tent" meteorite, weighing 68,085 lb. (30·4 tons), found in 1897 near Cape York, on the west coast of Greenland, by the expedition of Commander (later Rear-Admiral) Robert Edwin Peary (1856–1920). It was known to the Eskimos as the Abnighito and is now exhibited in the Hayden Planetarium in New York City, N.Y., U.S.A.

The largest piece of stony meteorite recovered is a piece of the Norton County meteorite which fell in Nebraska, U.S.A. on 18 Feb. 1948. The greatest amount of material recovered from any non-metallic meteorite is from the Allende fall of more than 1 ton in Chihuahua, Mexico on 8 Feb. 1969.

There was a mysterious explosion of about 35 megatons in latitude 60° 55′ N., longitude 101° 57′ E., in the basin of the Podkamennaya Tunguska river, 40 miles north of Vanavara, in Siberia, U.S.S.R., at 00 hours 17 minutes 11 seconds G.M.T. on 30 June 1908. The energy of this explosion was about 10^{24} ergs and the cause has been variously attributed to a meteorite (1927), a comet (1930), a nuclear explosion (1961) and to anti-matter (1965). This devastated an area of about 1,500 square miles and the shock was heard as far as 1,000 kilometres (more than 600 miles) away.

United Kingdom and Ireland The heaviest of the 22 meteorites known to have fallen on the British Isles was one weighing at least 102 lb. (largest piece 17 lb. 6 oz.), which fell at 4.12 p.m. on 24 Dec. 1965 at Barwell, Leicestershire. Scotland's largest recorded meteorite fell in Strathmore, Perthshire, on 3 Dec. 1917. It weighed 22¼ lb. and was the largest of four stones totalling 29 lb. 6 oz. The largest recorded meteorite to fall in Ireland was the Limerick Stone of 65 lb., part of a shower of 106 lb. which fell near Adare, County Limerick, on 10 Sept. 1813. The larger of the two recorded meteorites to land in Wales was one weighing 28 oz., of which a piece weighing 25½ oz. went through the roof of a building in Beddgelert, Caernarvonshire, on 21 Sept. 1949.

Largest craters Aerial surveys in Canada in 1956 and 1957 brought to light a gash, or astrobleme, 8½ miles across near Deep Bay, Saskatchewan, possibly attributable to a very old and very oblique meteorite. There is a possible crater-like formation 275 miles in diameter on the eastern shore of the Hudson Bay, where the Nastapoka Islands are just off the coast.

The largest proven crater is the Coon Butte or Baringer crater, discovered in 1891 near Canyon Diablo, Winslow, northern Arizona, U.S.A. It is 4,150 feet in diameter and now about 575 feet deep, with a parapet rising 130 to 155 feet above the surrounding plain. It has been estimated that an iron-nickel mass with a diameter of 200 to 260 feet, and weighing about 2,000,000 tons, gouged this crater in *c.* 25,000 B.C., with an impact force equivalent to an explosion of 30,000,000 tons of trinitrotoluene ($C_7H_5O_6N_3$), called T.N.T.

Evidence published in 1963 discounts a meteoric origin for the crypto-volcanic Vredefort Ring (diameter 26 miles), to the south-west of Johannesburg, South Africa, and also questions the meteoric origin of the New Quebec (formerly the Chubb) "Crater", first sighted on 20 June 1943 in northern Ungava, Canada. This is now regarded as more likely to be a water-filled vulcanoid.

It is 1,325 feet deep and measures 6·8 miles round its rim.

Tektites The largest tektite of which details have been published has been of 3·2 kilogrammes (7·04 lb.) found *c.* 1932 at Muong Nong, Saravane Province, Laos and now in the Paris Museum. Details of some larger finds are to be published in 1970.

AURORA

frequent Polar lights, known as Aurora Borealis or Northern Lights in the northern hemisphere and Aurora Australis in the southern hemisphere, are caused by electrical solar discharges in the upper atmosphere and occur most frequently in high latitudes. The maximum auroral frequencies, of up to 240 displays per year, have occurred in the Hudson Bay area of northern Canada. The extreme height of auroras has been measured at 1,000 kilometres (620 miles), while the lowest may descend to 45 miles.

hernmost Northern Lights" Displays occur 90 times a year (on average) in the Orkneys, 25 times a year in Edinburgh, seven times a year in London, and once a decade in southern Italy. On 25 Sept. 1909 a display was witnessed as far south as Singapore (1° 25′ N.). The greatest auroral displays over the United Kingdom in recent times occurred on 24–25 Oct. 1870 and 25 Jan. 1938.

THE MOON

The Earth's closest neighbour in space and only natural satellite is the Moon, at a mean distance of 238,856 statute miles centre to centre or 233,813 miles surface to surface. Its closest approach (perigee) and most extreme distance away (apogee) measured surface to surface are 216,420 and 247,667 miles respectively or 221,463 and 252,710 miles measured centre to centre. It has a diameter of 2,159·9 miles. The earliest radar echo from the Moon, which orbits at an average speed of 2,287 m.p.h., was achieved by the United States Army on 10 Jan. 1946.

The first direct hit on the Moon was achieved at 2 minutes 24 seconds after midnight (Moscow time) on 14 Sept. 1959, by the Soviet space probe *Lunik II* near the *Mure Serenitatis*. The first photographic images of the hidden side were collected by the U.S.S.R.'s *Lunik III* from 6.30 a.m. on 7 Oct. 1959, from a range of up to 43,750 miles, and transmitted to the Earth from a distance of 470,000 kilometres (292,000 miles). The first "soft" landing was made by the U.S.S.R.'s *Luna IX*, launched at about 11 a.m. G.M.T. on 31 Jan. 1966. It landed in the area of the Ocean of Storms (*Oceanus Procellarum*) at 18 hours 45 minutes 30 seconds G.M.T. on 3 Feb. 1966.

The Coon Butte Crater, Arizona, U.S.A.

"Blue Moon" Owing to sulphur particles in the upper atmosphere from a forest fire covering 250,000 acres between Mile 103 and Mile 119 on the Alaska Highway in northern British Columbia, Canada, the Moon took on a bluish colour, as seen from Great Britain, on the night of 26 Sept. 1950. The Moon also appeared blue after the Krakatoa eruption of 27 Aug. 1883 (see page 55) and on other occasions.

CRATER

Largest Only 59 per cent. of the Moon's surface is directly visible from the Earth because it is in "captured rotation", *i.e.* the period of revolution is equal to the period of orbit. The largest visible crater is the walled plain Bailly, towards the Moon's South Pole, which is 183 miles across, with walls rising to 14,000 feet. On the averted side the Orientale Basin measures more than 600 miles in diameter.

Deepest The deepest crater is the Newton crater, with a floor estimated to be between 23,000 and 29,000 feet below its rim. The brightest directly visible spot on the Moon is *Aristarchus*.

Highest mountains As there is no water on the Moon, the heights of mountains can be measured only in relation to lower-lying terrain near their bases. The highest lunar mountains were, until 1967, thought to be in the Leibnitz and Doerfel ranges, near the lunar South Pole with a height of some 35,000 feet. On the discovery from Lunar Orbiter spacecraft of evidence that they were merely crater rims, the names have been withdrawn. Currently it is believed that such an elevation would be an exaggerated estimate for any feature of the Moon's surface.

Temperature extremes When the Sun is overhead, the temperature on the lunar equator reaches 243° F. (31 deg. F. above the boiling point of water). By sunset the temperature is 58° F., but after nightfall it sinks to −261° F.

Moon rocks The age attributed to the oldest of the first moon rocks brought back to Earth by the *Apollo XI* crew on 24 July 1969 was breccia aged 4,600 million years.

THE SUN

Distance extremes The Earth's 66,690 m.p.h. orbit of 584,000,000 miles around the Sun is elliptical, hence our distance from the Sun varies. The orbital speed varies between 65,600 m.p.h. (minimum) and 67,800 m.p.h. The average distance of the Sun is 92,956,000 miles (149,600,000 km.). The closest approach (perihelion) is 91,300,000 miles (147,000,000 km.) and the farthest departure (aphelion) is 94,452,000 miles. The Solar System is revolving around the nucleus of the Milky Way at a speed of 481,000 m.p.h. and has a velocity of 42,500 m.p.h. relative to stars in our immediate region such as Vega.

Temperature and dimensions The Sun has an internal temperature of about 35,000,000° C., a core pressure of 500,000,000 tons per square inch and uses up 4,000,000 tons of hydrogen per second, thus providing a luminosity of 3×10^{27} candlepower, or 1,500,000 candlepower per square inch. The Sun has the stellar classification of a "yellow dwarf" and, although its density is only 1·41 times that of water, its mass is 333,430 times as much as that of the Earth. It has a mean diameter of 865,370 miles. The Sun with a mass of $1·961 \times 10^{27}$ tons represents more than 99 per cent. of the total mass of the Solar System.

SUN-SPOT

Largest To be visible to the *protected* naked eye, a Sun-spot must cover about one two-thousandth part of the Sun's hemisphere and thus have an area of about 500,000,000 square miles. The largest recorded Sun-spot occurred in the Sun's southern hemisphere on 8 April 1947. Its area was about 7,000 million square miles, with an extreme longitude of 187,000 miles and an extreme latitude of 90,000 miles. Sun-spots appear darker because they are more than 1,500 deg. C. cooler than the

The universe and space

rest of the Sun's surface temperature of 5,660° C. The largest observed solar prominence was one measuring 70,000 miles across its base and protruding 300,000 miles, observed on 4 June 1946.

Most frequent In October 1957 a smoothed Sun-spot count showed 263, the highest recorded index since records started in 1755 (*cf.* previous record of 239 in May 1778). In 1943 a Sun-spot lasted for 200 days from June to December.

ECLIPSES

Earliest recorded The earliest extrapolated eclipses that have been identified are 1361 B.C. (lunar) and 2136 B.C. (solar). For the Middle East only, lunar eclipses have been extrapolated to 3450 B.C. and solar ones to 4200 B.C. From London there was no total eclipse of the Sun visible for the 575 years from 20 March 1140 to 3 May 1715. The most recent occasion when a line of totality of a solar eclipse crossed Great Britain was on 29 June 1927, and the next instance may just clip the Cornish coast on 11 Aug. 1999. On 30 June 1953 a total eclipse was witnessed in Haroldswick, Unst, Shetland Islands but the line of totality was to the north of territorial waters.

Longest duration The maximum possible duration of an eclipse of the Sun is 7 minutes 58 seconds. This could occur only at the equator, but the longest actually occurring since A.D. 717 was on 20 June 1955 (7 minutes 8 seconds), seen from the Philippines. The longest possible in the British Isles is 5½ minutes. Those of 15 June 885 and 3 May 1715 were both nearly 5 minutes, as will be the eclipse of 2381. An annular eclipse may last for 12 minutes 24 seconds. The longest totality of any lunar eclipse is 104 minutes. This has occurred many times.

Most and least frequent The highest number of eclipses possible in a year is seven, as in 1935, when there were five solar and two lunar eclipses; or four solar and three lunar eclipses, as will occur in 1982. The lowest possible number in a year is two, both of which must be solar, as in 1944 and 1969.

COMETS

Earliest recorded The earliest records of comets date from the 7th century B.C. The speeds of the estimated 2,000,000 comets vary from 700 m.p.h. in outer space to 1,250,000 m.p.h. when near the Sun. The successive appearances of Halley's Comet have been traced to 466 B.C. It was first depicted in the Nuremburg Chronicle of A.D. 684. The first prediction of its return by Edmund Halley (1656–1742) proved true on Christmas Day 1758, 16 years after his death. Its next appearance should be at 9·9 (viz. at 9.30 p.m.) Feb. 1986, 75·81 years after the last, which was on 19 April 1910.

Closest approach On 1 July 1770, Lexell's Comet, travelling at a speed of 23·9 miles per second (relative to the Sun), came within 1,500,000 miles of the Earth. However, the Earth is believed to have passed through the tail of Halley's Comet, most recently on 19 May 1910.

Largest Comets are so tenuous that it has been estimated that even the head of one rarely contains solid matter much more than *c.* 1 kilometre in diameter. In the tail 10,000 cubic miles contain less than a cubic inch of solid matter. These tails, as in the case of the Great Comet of 1843, may trail for 200,000,000 miles.

Shortest period Of all the recorded periodic comets (these are members of the Solar System), the one which most frequently returns is Encke's Comet, first identified in 1786. Its period of 1,206 days (3·3 years) is the shortest established. Not one of its 48 returns (up to May 1967) has been missed by astronomers. Now increasingly faint, it is expected to "die" by 1993. The most frequently observed comets are Schwassmann-Wachmann I, Kopff and Oterma, which can be observed every year between Mars and Jupiter.

Longest period At the other extreme is the comet 1910a, whose path was not accurately determined. It is not expected to return for perhaps 4,000,000 years.

PLANETS

Largest Planets (including the Earth) are bodies which belong to the Solar System and which revolve round the Sun in definite orbits. Jupiter, with an equatorial diameter of 88,700 miles and a polar diameter of 82,790 miles, is the largest of the nine major planets, with a mass 318·354 times, and a volume 1,313 times that of the Earth. It also has the shortest period of rotation on its own equatorial axis, with a "day" of only 9 hours 50 minutes 30·003 seconds.

Smallest Of the major planets, Mercury, whose period of revolution round the Sun is only 87·9686 days, is the smallest, with a diameter of about 2,900 miles and a mass only 0·056 of that of the Earth, that is 330 trillion tons. Mercury has the highest average speed in orbit at 107,030 m.p.h. It rotates on its axis once every 58·65 days.

Hottest The hottest of the major planets is Mercury, which has a maximum surface temperature estimated at over 800° F. on its hot side. This temperature depends, to some extent, upon its distance from the Sun, which varies from 28,566,000 miles to 43,355,000 miles. The surface temperature of Venus is still in conflict but one reading has been 430° C. (806° F.). The planet with a surface temperature closest to Earth's average figure of 59° F. is Mars, with a day-side average of 28° F. (maximum 77° F.) and a night-side minimum of −185° F.

Coldest The coldest planet is, not unnaturally, that which is the remotest from the Sun, namely Pluto, which has an estimated surface temperature of −420° F. (39 deg. F. above absolute zero). Its mean distance from the Sun is 3,664,000,000 miles and its period of revolution is 248·4302 years. Its diameter is about 3,700 miles. Pluto was first recorded by Clyde William Tombaugh (born 4 Feb. 1906) at Lowell Observatory, Flagstaff, Arizona, U.S.A., on 18 Feb. 1930 from photographs taken on 23 and 29 Jan. In March 1969 it was slightly nearer than average.

Nearest The planet whose orbit is closest to the Sun is Mercury, which revolves at a mean distance of 36,000,000 miles. The fellow planet closest to the Earth is Venus, which is, at times, about 25,700,000 miles inside the Earth's orbit, compared with Mars's closest approach of 34,600,000 miles outside the Earth's orbit. Mars, known since 1965 to be cratered, has temperatures ranging from 85° F. to −130° F. but in which infusorians of the *genus* Colpoda *could* survive.

The first object from the Earth to reach another planet

Halley's Comet

was the U.S.S.R.'s *Venus III*, weighing 960 kilogrammes (2,116 lb.), which was launched on 16 Nov. 1965 and impacted on Venus at 6.56 a.m. G.M.T. on 1 March 1966.

Brightest and faintest Viewed from the Earth, by far the brightest of the five planets visible to the naked eye (Uranus at magnitude 5·7 is only marginally visible) is Venus, with a maximum magnitude of −4·4. The faintest is Pluto, with a magnitude of 14.

gest "day" The planet with the longest period of rotation is Venus, which spins on its own axis once every 243·16 days, so its "day" is longer than its "year" (224·7007 days). The shortest "day" is that of Jupiter (see above, Largest).

njunctions The most dramatic recorded conjunction (coming together) of the other seven principal members of the Solar System (Sun, Moon, Mercury, Venus, Mars, Jupiter and Saturn) occurred on 5 Feb. 1962, when 16° covered all seven during an eclipse in the Pacific area. It is possible that the seven-fold conjunction of September 1186 spanned only 12°. The next notable conjunction will take place on 5 May 2000.

SATELLITES
Most Of the nine major planets, all but Mercury, Venus and Pluto have natural satellites. The planet with the most is Jupiter, with four large and eight small moons. The Earth is the only planet with a single satellite. The distance of the Solar System's 32 known satellites from their parent planets varies from the 5,625 miles of *Phobos* from Mars to the 14,812,500 miles of *Hades* (or Satellite IX) from Jupiter.

argest and smallest The largest satellite is Saturn's seventh, *Titan* (diameter 3,550 miles), and the smallest is Mars's outer "moon" *Deimos* (diameter 3·8 miles), discovered on 18 Aug. 1877 by Asaph Hill (U.S.).

Largest Asteroids In the belt which lies between Mars and Jupiter, there are some 45,000 (only 3,100 charted) minor planets or asteroids which are, for the most part, too small to yield to diameter measurement. The largest and first discovered (by Piazzi at Palermo, Sicily on 1 Jan. 1801) of these is *Ceres*, with a diameter of 436 miles. The only one visible to the naked eye is *Vesta*, "discovered" on 29 March 1807 by Dr. Heinrich Wilhelm Olbers, a German amateur astronomer. The closest measured approach to the Earth by an asteroid was 485,000 miles, in the case of *Hermes* on 30 Oct. 1937.

STARS
argest and st massive Of those measured, the star with the greatest diameter is the "red giant" *Epsilon Aurigae B* at 2,500 million miles. This star is so vast that our own Solar System of the Sun and the six planets out as far as Saturn could be accommodated inside it. The *Alpha Herculis* aggregation, consisting of a main star and a double star companion, is enveloped in a cold gas. This system, visible to the naked eye, has a diameter of 170,000 million miles. The fainter component of Plaskett's star discovered by J. S. Plaskett from the Dominion Astrophysical Observatory, Victoria, British Columbia, Canada *c.* 1920 is the most massive star known with a mass *c.* 55 times that of the sun.

Smallest The smallest known star is LP 327-186, a "white dwarf" with a diameter only half that of the Moon, 100 light-years distant and detected in May 1962 from Minneapolis, Minnesota, U.S.A.

Lightest The lightest known star is Strand's star in *Cygnus,* whose mass is only 0·8 of one per cent. of that of the Sun, *viz* about 14,000,000,000,000,000,000,000,000 tons.

Oldest The Sun is estimated to be about 7,500 million years old and our galaxy between 10,000 million and 12,000 million years old. In December 1959 it was computed that the old star cluster NGC 188, on the edge of our galaxy, had burnt 18 per cent. of its hydrogen and may therefore be as much as 24,000 million years old.

Farthest The Solar System, with its Sun, nine major planets, 32 satellites, asteroids and comets, was discovered in 1921 to be about 27,000 light-years from the centre of the lens-shaped Milky Way galaxy (diameter 100,000 light-years) of about 100,000 million stars. The most distant star in our galaxy is therefore about 75,000 light-years distant.

Nearest Excepting the special case of our own Sun, the nearest star is the very faint *Proxima Centauri,* which is 4·3 light-years (25,000,000,000,000 miles) away. The nearest star visible to the naked eye is the southern hemisphere star *Alpha Centauri,* or *Rigil Kentaurus* (4·33 light-years), with a magnitude of 0·1.

Brightest Sirius A (*Alpha Canis Majoris*), also known as the Dog Star, is the brightest star in the heavens, with an apparent magnitude of −1·58. It is in the constellation *Canis Major* and is visible in the winter months of the northern hemisphere, being due south at midnight on the last day of the year. Sirius A is 8·7 light-years away and has a luminosity 26 times as much as that of the Sun. It has a diameter of 1,500,000 miles and a mass of 45,800,000,000,000,000,000,000,000 tons.

Most and least luminous If all stars could be viewed at the same distance, the most luminous would be the apparently faint variable *S. Doradûs,* in the Greater Magellanic Cloud (*Nebecula Major*), which can be 300,000 to 500,000 times brighter than the Sun, and has an absolute magnitude of −8·9. The faintest star detected visually is a very red star 30 light-years distant in *Pisces,* with one two-millionth of the Sun's brightness.

Coolest A 16th magnitude star with a surface temperature of only about 425° C. (800° F.) was detected in *Cygnus* in 1965.

Densest The densest stars are the "white dwarfs". A star with the mass of our Sun but the diameter of our Moon was discovered by W. J. Luyten of Harvard Observatory, U.S.A. in June 1966. The limit of stellar density is at the neutron state, when the atomic particles exist in a state in which there is no space between them. Each cubic inch would then weigh about 1,800 million tons (*sic*). Atoms measure a few Å units in diameter whereas the nuclei are five orders of magnitude smaller and hence have a diameter of 4 ten-trillionths (4×10^{-19}) of a centimetre.

Brightest super-nova Super-novae, or temporary "stars" which flare and then fade, occur perhaps five times in 1,000 years. The brightest "star" ever seen by historic man is believed to be the super-nova close to *Zeta Tauri*, visible by day for 23 days from 4 July 1054. The remains, known as the "Crab" Nebula, now have a diameter of about 30,000,000,000,000 miles and are still expanding at a rate of 700 miles per second. It is about 4,100 light-years away, indicating that the explosion actually occurred in about 3000 B.C.

"Crab" nebula (the arrow indicates fastest pulsar) (see p.70)

The universe and space

Constellations The largest of the 88 constellations is *Hydra* (the Sea Serpent), which covers 1,302·84 square degrees and contains at least 68 stars visible to the naked eye (to 5·5 mag.). The constellation *Centaurus* (Centaur), ranking ninth in area embraces however at least 94 such stars. The smallest constellation is *Equuleus* (Little Horse) with an area of 71·64 square degrees and only 5 stars of 5½ magnitude.

Stellar planets Planetary companions, with a mass of less than 7 per cent. of their parent star, have been found to 61 *Cygni* (1942), Lalande 21185 (1960) and Barnard's Star (Munich 15040) in April 1963. Other near Sun-like stars, which could conceivably have a planetary system, are *Tau Ceti, Epsilon* and *Omicron*-2 *Eridani,* 70 *Ophiuchi* and *Epsilon Indi.* Listening operations ("Project Ozma") on the first two were maintained from 4 April 1960 to March 1961, using an 85-foot radio telescope at Deer Creek Valley, Green Bank, West Virginia, U.S.A. The apparatus was probably insufficiently sensitive for any signal from a distance of 11 light-years.

According to Einstein's Special Theory time dilatation effect (published in 1905), time actually runs more slowly for an object as its speed increases. However time speeds up for an object as it moves away from a body exerting gravitational force. During their mission the crew of the Apollo VIII circum-lunar space flight aged a net 300 microseconds more than earthlings. No formal overtime claim was lodged.

THE UNIVERSE
Outside the Milky Way galaxy, which revolves once every 225,000,000 years, and moves around the centre of the local super-cluster of 2,500 neighbouring galaxies at a speed of 1,350,000 m.p.h., there exist 1,000,000 million other galaxies. These range in size up to 200,000 light-years in diameter. The nearest heavenly body outside our galaxy is the Large Magellanic Cloud near the Southern Cross, at a distance of 160,000 light-years. In 1967 it was determined by the astronomer G. Idlis (U.S.S.R.) that the Magellanic Clouds were detached from the Milky Way by another colliding galaxy, now in *Sagittarius,* about 3,800,000 years ago.

Farthest visible object The remotest heavenly body often visible to the naked eye is the Great Galaxy in *Andromeda* (Mag. 3·47). This is a rotating nebula at spiral form, and its distance from the Earth is about 2,200,000 light-years, or about 13,000,000,000,000,000,000 miles. It is just possible however that, under ideal seeing conditions, Messier 33, the Spiral in Triangulum, (Mag. 5·79) is visible to the naked eye at a distance of 2,300,000 light-years.

Quasars In November 1962 the existence of quasi-stellar radio sources ("quasars" or QSSs) was established. More than 150 had been detected by September 1969. No satisfactory model has yet been constructed to account for the immensely high luminosity of bodies apparently so distant and of such small diameter. The diameter of 3C 446 is only about 90 light-days, but there are measurable alterations in brightness in less than one day. It is believed to be undergoing the most violent explosion yet detected, since it has increased 3·2 magnitudes or 20-fold in less than one year.

The earliest quasar 3C 273?

"Pulsars" The discovery of the first pulsating radio source or "pulsar" CP 1919 was announced from the Mullard Radio Astronomy Observatory, Cambridge, England, on 29 Feb. 1968. The fastest so far discovered is NP 0532 in the Crab Nebula with a pulse of 33 milliseconds. One theory is that it is a rotating neutron star of immense density.

Remotest object The greatest distance yet ascribed to a radio detected and visibly confirmed body is that claimed for a quasar designated 4C 25·5 (red shift of 2·37) identified in 1968 by E. Olsen of the California Institute of Technology, Pasadena, U.S.A., and measured by Dr. Maarten Schmidt (b. Groenegen, Netherlands, 1929) of Mount Wilson and Palomar Observatories, California. Though in January 1967 the Symposium on Relativistic Astrophysics in New York City, U.S.A., concluded that quasars "have no agreed distance from the Earth", a figure of at least 13,000 million light-years has been ascribed to this discovery, based on its estimated speed of recession of 83·8 per cent. of the speed of light, *viz* 156,000 miles per second. PKS 0237—23 announced in March 1967 is the most luminous of observed heavenly bodies. Proponents of the oscillation theory of cosmology believe that the Universe is between 13 and 20,000 million years advanced on the expanding phase of an 80,000 million year expansion-contraction cycle. The number of cycles which may have previously occurred is not discernible.

ROCKETRY AND MISSILES
Earliest experiments The origin of the rocket dates from war rockets propelled by a charcoal-saltpetre-sulphur gunpowder, made by the Chinese as early as *c.* 1100. These early rockets became known in Europe by 1258. The pioneer of military rocketry in Britain was Sir William Congreve, Bt., M.P. (1772–1828), Comptroller of the Royal Laboratory and Inspector of Military Machines, whose "six-pound rocket" was developed to a range of 2,000 yards by 1805 when used by the Royal Navy against Boulogne, France.

The earliest principles of reaction propulsion with the proposal of liquid fuel are usually ascribed to Konstantin Eduardovich Tsiolkovskiy (or Ziolkovsky) (1857–1935), a Russian-born Pole who did his work in 1898 (first published in 1903). However, plans of a three-stage solid fuel rocket and the modern cluster principle were published in *Artis Magnae Artilleriae* by Kazimierz Siemienowicz (Poland) as early as 1650. The first launching of a liquid-fuelled rocket (patented 14 July 1914) was by Dr. Robert Hutchings Goddard (1882–1945) of the United States, at Auburn, Massachusetts, U.S.A., on 16 March 1926, when his rocket reached an altitude of 341 feet and travelled a distance of 184 feet. The U.S.S.R.'s earliest rocket was the OR-1, built in 1929. The earliest British experiments were on Salisbury Plain in 1916 by Archibald Vivian Hill, C.H., O.B.E. (born 26 Sept. 1886), Director of the Anti-Aircraft Experimental Section (Munitions Inventions Dept.). Through the pioneer work of Prof. Hermann Julius Oberth (born 25 June 1894), a Hungarian-born German, and the Society for Space Travel (*Verein für Raumschiffahrt*), founded on 5 June 1927, Germany took the lead in 1931.

Longest ranges The longest range achieved in a ground-to-surface rocket test is 9,000 miles by a U.S. *Atlas,* measuring 85 feet long and weighing 120 tons, fired across the South Atlantic from Cape Canaveral (now Cape Kennedy), Florida, U.S.A., to a point 1,000 miles south-east of the Cape of Good Hope, South Africa, on 20 May 1960. The flight lasted about 53 minutes. The previous record was 7,760 miles by a Soviet rocket in the Pacific on 20 Jan. 1960. On 16 March 1962, Nikita Khrushchyov, then the Soviet Prime Minister, claimed in Moscow that the U.S.S.R. possessed a "global rocket" with a range of about 19,000 miles, *i.e.* more than the Earth's semi-diameter and therefore capable of hitting any target from either direction.

st powerful It has been suggested that the U.S.S.R. Nova class booster which blew up at Tyuratam in the summer (? July) of 1969 had a thrust of 75,000,000 lb. No further details have been released by the U.S.S.R. nor by the U.S. ELINT (Electronic Intelligence Section).

The most powerful rocket that has been publicized is the *Saturn V*, used for the Project Apollo 3-man lunar exploration mission, on which development began in January 1962, at the John F. Kennedy Space Center, Merritt Island, Florida, U.S.A. The 6,218,558 lb. (2,776 ton) rocket is 363 feet 8 inches tall, with a payload of 45,000 lb., and gulps 13·4 tons of propellant per second for 2½ minutes (2,005 tons). Stage I (S-IC) is 138 feet tall and is powered by five Rocketdyne F-1 engines, using liquid oxygen (LOX) and kerosene, each delivering 1,514,000 lb. thrust. Stage II (S-II) is powered by five LOX and liquid hydrogen Rocketdyne J-2 engines with a total thrust of 1,141,453 lb., while Stage III (designated S-IVB) is powered by a single 228,290 lb. thrust J-2 engine. The whole assembly generates 175,600,000 horse-power and weighs up to 6,456,282 lb. (2,882 tons) fully loaded. It was first launched on 9 Nov. 1967.

The most powerful single rocket motor yet tested is the Aerojet-General Corporation SL-1 solid fuel motor with a diameter of 260 inches (21 feet 8 inches) and a length of 80 feet 8 inches. It was first tested on 25 Sept. 1965 at Homestead, Dade County, Florida, U.S.A. It was fired nose down and consumed 750 tons of solid fuel in 2 minutes 10 seconds, developing 3,600,000 lb. static thrust. The Aerojet-General SL-3, a solid fuel motor 70 feet long, with a diameter of 260 inches designed to produce 5,700,000 lb. static thrust was tested at Homestead on 17 June 1967.

United Kingdom The United Kingdom's largest rocket is the Hawker Siddeley *Blue Streak*, standing 69 feet 3 inches tall, weighing 94 tons and powered by twin Rolls-Royce kerosene-LOX RZ 2 engines with a thrust of 137,000 to 150,000 lb. each. The first test flight was at Lake Hart, Woomera, South Australia, on 5 June 1964.

Least powerful The least powerful rocket ever made is the Valveless Subliming Solid Control Rocket, manufactured for a U.S. Navy satellite programme by the Rocket Research Corporation of Seattle, Washington, U.S.A. It has a thrust of only one-millionth of 1 lb.

Ion rockets Speeds of up to 100,000 m.p.h. are envisaged for rockets powered by an ion discharge. It was announced on 13 Jan. 1960 that caesium vapour discharge had been maintained for 50 hours at the Lewis Research Center in Cleveland, Ohio, U.S.A. Ion rockets were first used in flight by the U.S.S.R.'s Mars probe *Zond II*, launched on 30 Nov. 1964.

ARTIFICIAL SATELLITES
The dynamics of artificial satellites were first propounded by Sir Isaac Newton (1642–1727) in his *Philosophiae Naturalis Principia Mathematica* ("Mathematical Principles of Natural Philosophy"), begun in March 1686 and first published in the summer of 1687. The first artificial satellite was successfully put into orbit at an altitude of 142/588 miles and a velocity of more than 17,500 m.p.h. from a site north of the Caspian Sea on the night of 4 Oct. 1957. This spherical satellite, *Sputnik* ("Fellow Traveller") *I*, officially designated "Satellite 1957 Alpha 2", weighed 83·6 kilogrammes (184·3 lb.), with a diameter of 58 centimetres (22·8 inches), and its lifetime is believed to have been 92 days, ending on 4 Jan. 1958. It was designed under the direction of Dr. Sergey Pavlovich Korolyov (1906–1966).

Terrestrial escape velocity (25,022 m.p.h. at the surface but less at altitude) was first achieved by the U.S.S.R.'s solar satellite *Lunik I* (or *Planet X*), fired from Kapustin Yar on 2 Jan. 1959. This is sometimes termed the Second Cosmic velocity.

Solar escape velocity (36,800 m.p.h.) was first achieved in a limited way over the Hollomon Air Base, New Mexico, U.S.A., on 16 Oct. 1957, when aluminium pellets were fired at about 40,000 m.p.h. by a "shaped charge" from an Aerobee rocket at an altitude of 55 miles. The speed necessary for escape from the Milky Way galaxy is 815,000 m.p.h.

Earliest successful manned satellite The first successful manned spaced flight began at 9.07 a.m. (Moscow time), or 6.07 a.m. G.M.T., on 12 April 1961. Flight Major (later Colonel) Yuriy Alekseyevich Gagarin (born 9 March 1934) completed a single orbit of the Earth in 89·34 minutes in the U.S.S.R.'s space vehicle *Vostok* ("East") *I* (10,417 lb.). The take-off was from Baikonur, in western Siberia, and the landing was 108 minutes later near the village of Smelovka, near Engels, in the Saratov region of the U.S.S.R. The maximum speed was 17,560 m.p.h. and the maximum altitude 327 kilometres (203·2 miles). Major Gagarin, invested a Hero of the Soviet Union and awarded the Order of Lenin and the Gold Star Medal, was killed in a jet plane crash near Moscow on 27 March 1968.

First woman in space The first and only woman to orbit the Earth was Junior Lieutenant (now Lt.-Col.) Valentina Vladimirovna Tereshkova, now Mde. Nikolayev (born 6 March 1937), who was launched in *Vostok VI* from Baikonur, U.S.S.R., at 9.30 a.m. G.M.T. on 16 June 1963, and landed at 8.16 a.m. on 19 June, after a flight of 2 days 22 hours 46 minutes, during which she completed over 48 orbits (1,225,000 miles) and came to within 3 miles of *Vostok V*.

PROGRESSIVE ROCKET ALTITUDE RECORDS

Height in Miles	Rocket	Place	Launch Date
0·71 (3,762 ft.)	A 3-inch rocket	near London, England	April 1750
1·24 (6,560 ft.)	Rheinhold Tiling[1] (Germany) solid fuel rocket	Osnabrück, Germany	April 1931
nearly 3	OR-2 liquid fuel (U.S.S.R.)	U.S.S.R.	17 Aug. 1932
8·1	U.S.S.R. "Stratosphere" rocket	U.S.S.R.	1935
52·46	A.4 rocket (Germany)	Peenemünde, Germany	3 Oct. 1942
c. 85	A.4 rocket (Germany)	Heidelager, Poland	early 1944
118	A.4 rocket (Germany)	Heidelager, Poland	mid 1944
244	V-2/W.A.C. Corporal (2-stage) Bumper No. 5 (U.S.A.)	White Sands, N.M., U.S.A.	24 Feb. 1949
250	M.104 *Raketa* (U.S.S.R.)	? Tyuratam, U.S.S.R.	1954
682	Jupiter C (U.S.A.)	Cape Canaveral (now Cape Kennedy), Florida, U.S.A.	20 Sept. 1956
>2,700	Farside No. 5 (4-stage) (U.S.A.)	Eniwetok Atoll	20 Oct. 1957
70,700	Pioneer I-B Lunar Probe (U.S.A.)	Cape Canaveral (now Cape Kennedy), Florida, U.S.A.	11 Oct. 1958
215,300,000*	Lunik I or Planet X (U.S.S.R.)	Kapustin Yar, U.S.S.R.	2 Jan. 1959
242,000,000*	Mars I (U.S.S.R.)	U.S.S.R.	1 Nov. 1962

* *Apogee in solar orbit.*
[1] *There is some evidence that Tiling may shortly after have reached 9,500 m. (5·90 miles) with a solid fuel rocket at Wangerooge, East Friesian Islands, West Germany.*

71

The universe and space

EXTREMES

	Earth Satellites	Earth-Moon Satellites	Solar Satellites or Artificial Planets
Earliest	Sputnik I, 4 Oct. 1957	Lunik III, 4 Oct. 1959	Lunik I, 2 Jan. 1959
Heaviest	Apollo IX, 3 March 1969, 331,000 lb. (147·75 tons)	Apollo X, 22 May 1969, 48½ tons	Jettisoned Apollo VIII, Stage 3, 34,000 lb., 21 Dec. 1968
Lightest	Tetrahedron Research Satellites (TRS), IA and IB, 9 May 1963, each 1·47 lb.	Lunik III, 614 lb.	Pioneer IV, 3 March 1959, 13·0 lb.
Longest First Orbit	1963–39C (Vela II?), 17 Oct. 1963, 106 hours 10 minutes	Luna IV, 29 days 4 hours	Mars I, 1 Nov. 1962, 519 days
Shortest Flight Time	Mercury IV rocket, 13 Sept. 1961, 87·3 minutes	Apollo VIII, 147 hours, 21–27 Dec. 1968	U.S.S.R. Venus Probe, 12 Feb. 1961, 300 days
Longest Expected Lifetime	1964–40A (Vela III?), 17 July 1964, more than 1,000,000 years	Luna IV, unlimited	Unlimited
Shortest Lifetime	Vostok I, 12 April 1961, 108 minutes	Apollo VIII, 147 hours	Unlimited
Nearest First Perigee	1964–16B (Zond I rocket?), 2 April 1964, 76 miles	Lunik III, 25,500 miles	
Furthest First Apogee	Explorer XVIII, called Interplanetary Monitoring Platform (IMP) A, 27 Nov. 1963, 122,793 miles	Luna IV, 400,000 miles	Mars I, 1 Nov. 1962, 242,000,000 miles (maximum)
Lowest Initial Speed	1963–39C (Vela II?), 17 Oct. 1963, 4,410 m.p.h.	Apollo VIII, 24,226 m.p.h.	Mariner IV (Mars Probe), 24,586 m.p.h., 28 Nov. 1964
Highest Initial Speed	Explorer X, 25 March 1961, 24,100 m.p.h.	Lunik III, 24,600 m.p.h.	Mars I, c. 25,600 m.p.h.

The highest and lowest speeds in solar orbit are 89,300 m.p.h. and 47,000 m.p.h. by Mariner II *(27 Aug. 1962)* and Mars I *(see above)*, respectively.
NOTE: *The largest artificial satellite measured by volume has been Echo II (diameter 135 feet), weighing 565 lb., launched into orbit (642/816 miles) from Vandenberg Air Force Base, California, U.S.A., on 25 Jan. 1964. It was an inflated sphere, comprising* a 535 lb. balloon, whose skin was made of Mylar plastic 0·00035 of an inch thick, bonded on both sides by aluminium alloy foil 0·00018 of an inch thick, together with equipment. Echo I was the brightest of artificial satellites (its magnitude was about −1) and it has been claimed that it became the man-made object seen by more people than any other. Its lifetime was from 12 Aug. 1960 to May 1968.*

First admitted fatality Col. Vladimir Mikhailovich Komarov (b. 16 March 1927) was launched in *Soyuz* ("Union") *I* at 00.35 a.m. G.M.T. on 23 April 1967. The spacecraft was in orbit for about 25½ hours but he died during the descent to the ground and was thus the first man undisputedly known to have died during space flight.

First "walk" in space The first person to leave an artificial satellite during orbit was Lt-Col. Aleksey Arkhipovich Leonov (born 30 May 1934), who left the Soviet satellite *Voshkod II* at about 8.30 a.m. G.M.T. on 18 March 1965. Lt.-Col. Leonov was "in space" for about 20 minutes, and for 12 minutes 9 seconds he "floated" at the end of a line 5 metres (16 feet) long. His companion on this flight of over 17 orbits (about 447,000 miles) was Col. Pavel I. Belyayev (1925–1970).

Longest space flight The longest space flight has been that of Lt.-Col. (promoted Colonel) Frank Borman (born 1928), of the U.S. Air Force, and Comdr. (promoted Captain) James A. Lovell, Jr. (born 25 March 1928), of the U.S. Navy, who achieved 206 orbits of the Earth (5,719,446 miles) in *Gemini VII* during a flight of 13 days 18 hours 35 minutes 1 second between 19 hours 30 minutes 4 seconds G.M.T. on 4 Dec. and 2.05 p.m. on 18 Dec. 1965. Lovell has the overall space duration record after his return from his fourth mission, the abortive *Apollo XIII* drama with 713 hours 33 mins. 21 secs.

The first men to land on the Moon from Apollo XI in quarantine

Longest lunar mission The longest duration of any lunar mission was the fourth. *Apollo XII* was absent from Earth for 244 hours 38 minutes on 14–24 Nov. 1969 and was manned by the three U.S. Navy Commanders Charles Conrad, Richard F. Gordon and Alan L. Bean.

Duration record on the Moon The longest stay on the Moon's surface has been 31 hours 32 minutes by Comdrs. Conrad and Bean (see above) in *Intrepid* on the Apollo XII mission on 19–20 Nov. 1969.

Most expensive project The total cost of the U.S. space programme up to and including the lunar mission of *Apollo XIX* has been estimated at $25,241,400,000 (£10,517,250,000).

Accuracy record The most accurate recovery from space was the splashdown of *Gemini IX* on 6 June 1966 only 769 yards from the *U.S.S. Wasp* in the Western Atlantic (27° 52′ N., 75° 0′ 24″ W.).

Captain James A. Lovell U.S.N.

The most accurate splashdown—Gemini IX and U.S.S. Wasp

Apollo XI

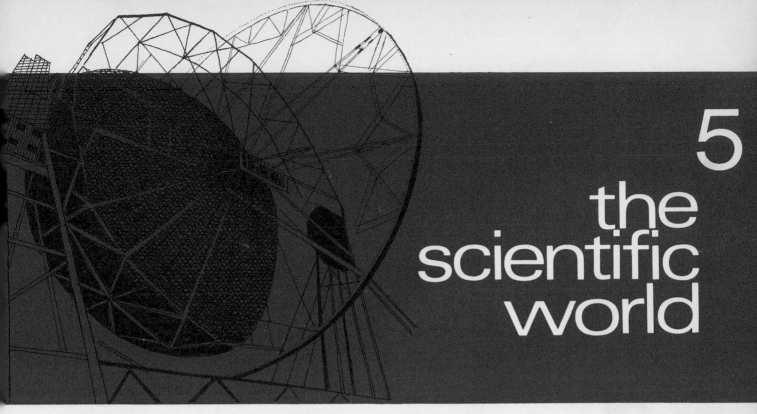

ELEMENTS

All known matter in the Solar System is made up of chemical elements. The total of naturally-occurring elements so far detected is 93, comprising, at ordinary temperature, two liquids, 11 gases and 80 solids. The so-called "fourth state" of matter is plasma, when negatively-charged electrons and positively-charged ions are in flux.

Lightest and heaviest sub-nuclear particles

The number of fundamental sub-nuclear particles catered for by Unitary Symmetry Theory, or SU(3), published in 1964, was 34. The SU(6) system caters for 91 particles, while the later SU(12) system caters for an infinite number, some of which are expected to be produced by higher and higher energies, but with shorter and shorter lifetimes and weaker and weaker interactions. Of SU(3) particles the one with the highest mass is the omega minus, discovered on 24 Feb. 1964 at the Brookhaven National Laboratory, near Upton, Long Island, New York State, U.S.A. It has a mass of $1,686 \pm 8 \text{MeV}/c^2$ and a lifetime of $1 \cdot 85 \times 10^{-10}$ of a second. Of all sub-atomic concepts only the neutrino calls for masslessness. There is experimental proof that the mass, if any, of an electron neutrino cannot be greater than four ten-thousandths of that of an electron, which itself has a rest mass of $9 \cdot 1083 \ (\pm 0 \cdot 0004) \times 10^{-28}$ of a gramme, *i.e.* it has a weight of less than $3 \cdot 64 \times 10^{-31}$ of a gramme. The first neutrino observed in the world's deepest laboratory, 10,492 feet down in the East Rand Proprietary Mine at Boksburg, near Johannesburg, South Africa, was registered at 9.48 p.m. G.M.T. on 23 Feb. 1965.

Fastest particles

A search for the existence of particles, named tachyons (symbol T+ and T−), with a speed *in vacuo* greater than c, the speed of light, was instituted in 1968 by Dr. T. Alvager and Dr. M. Kriesler of Princeton University, U.S.A.

GASES

Lightest

Hydrogen, a colourless gas discovered in 1766 by the Hon. Henry Cavendish (1731–1810), a British millionaire, is less than 1/14th the weight of air, weighing only 0·005611 of one lb. per cubic foot, or 89·88 milligrammes per litre.

Heaviest

The heaviest elemental gas is radon, the colourless isotope Em 222 of the gas emanation, which was discovered in 1900 by Friedrich Ernst Dorn (1848–1916) of Germany, and is 111·5 times as heavy as hydrogen. It is also known as Niton and emanates from radium salts.

Melting and boiling points
Lowest

Of all substances, helium has the lowest boiling point (−268·94° C.). This element, which is at normal temperatures a colourless gas, was discovered in 1868 by Sir Joseph Norman Lockyer, K.C.B. (1836–1920) working with Sir Edward Frankland, K.C.B. (1825–99) and the French astronomer Pierre Jules Cesar Janssen (1824–1907) working independently. Helium was first liquefied in 1908 by Heike Kamerlingh Onnes (1853–1926), a Dutch physicist. Liquid helium, which exists in two forms, can be solidified only under pressure of 26 atmospheres. This was first achieved on 26 July 1926 by W. H. Keesom (b. Netherlands 1876). At this pressure helium will melt at −272° C.

Highest

Of the elements that are gases at normal temperatures, chlorine has the highest melting point (−101·0° C.) and the highest boiling point (−34.1° C.). This yellow-green gas was discovered in 1774 by the German-born Karl Wilhelm Scheele (1742–86) of Sweden.

Commonest

The commonest element in the Universe is hydrogen, which has been calculated to comprise 90 per cent. of all matter and over 99 per cent. of matter in interstellar space.

Rarest

The Earth's atmosphere weighs an estimated 5,187,000,000,000,000 tons, of which nitrogen constitutes 78·09 per cent. by volume in dry air. The heavy hydrogen isotope tritium exists in the atmosphere to an extent of only 5×10^{-23} of one per cent. by volume.

METALS

Lightest

The lightest of all metals is lithium (Li), a metal, light golden brown (*in vacuo*), discovered in 1817 by Johan August Arfvedson (1792–1841) of Sweden. It has a density of 0·5333 of a gramme per cubic centimetre or 33·29 lb. per cubic foot. The isotope Li 6 (7·56 per cent. of naturally-occurring lithium) has a density of only 0·4616 g./cu. cm. compared with 0·5391 for Li 7.

Densest

The densest of all metals and hence the world's most effective paperweight is osmium (Os), a grey-blue metal of the platinum group, discovered in 1804 by Smithson Tennant (1761–1815) of the United Kingdom. It has a density at 20° C. of 22·59 grammes per cubic centimetre or 1,410 lb. per cubic foot. A cubic foot of uranium would weigh 220 lb. less than a cubic foot of osmium. During the period 1955–70 iridium was thought by some inorganic chemists to be the densest metal but has a density of 22·56.

The scientific world

Melting and boiling points
Lowest

Excluding mercury, which is liquid at normal temperatures, caesium (Cs), a silvery-white metal discovered in 1860 by Robert Wilhelm von Bunsen (1811–99) and Gustav Robert Kirchhoff (1824–87) of Germany, has the lowest metallic melting point at 28·6° C. (83·5° F.).

Excluding mercury as above, the metal which vaporises at the lowest temperature is selenium (Se) at 685° C. This greyish solid was discovered in 1818 by Jöns Jakob Berzelius (1779–1848) of Sweden. The metallic element rubidium (Rb) vaporises at 710° C. and caesium (Cs) at 713° C.

Highest

The highest melting point of any pure element is that of tungsten or wolfram (W), a grey metal discovered in 1783 by the Spanish brothers, Juan José d'Elhuyar and Fausto d'Elhuyar (1755–1833). It melts at 3,410° C. ±20 deg. C.

The most refractory substances known are the tantalum carbide ($TaC_{0·88}$), a black solid, and the hafnium carbide ($HfC_{0·95}$), which melt at 4000° C. ±75 deg. C. and 3950° C. ±20 deg. C. respectively.

Expansion

The highest normal linear thermal expansion of a metal is that of caesium which at 20° C., is $9·7 \times 10^{-5}$ of a cm. per cm. per one degree C. The trans-uranic metal plutonium will, however, expand and contract by as much as 8·9 per cent. of its volume when being heated to its melting point of 639·5° C. ±2 deg. C.

The lowest linear expansion is that of the alloy invar, containing 35 per cent. nickel, the remainder being iron, with one per cent. carbon and manganese. This has a linear thermal expansion of 9×10^{-7} of an inch per inch per one degree C. at ordinary temperatures. It was first prepared c. 1930 by Charles Edouard Guillaume (b. Switzerland 1861, d. 1938).

Highest ductility

The most malleable, or ductile, of metals is gold. One ounce (avoirdupois) of gold can be drawn in the form of a continuous wire thread (diameter 2×10^{-4} of an inch) to a length of 43 miles. A cubic inch can be beaten into a leaf five-millionths of an inch thick, so as to cover nearly 1,400 square feet.

Highest tensile strength

The material with the highest known UTS (ultimate tensile strength) is sapphire whisker ($Al_2 O_3$) at $6·2 \times 10^6$ lb. in.[2]. This is equivalent to a whisker of the thickness of a human hair (an as yet unachieved 70 microns) which could support a weight of 621 lb.

Rarest

Of the natural elemental metals, only lutetium (element 71), one of the 15 described as the "rare earths", has not been separated into a metallic purity of greater than 99·5 per cent. Element 43, named technetium (formerly masurium), and element 61, named promethium (formerly illinium), have not yet been detected in a natural state on Earth in amounts which would permit chemical separation. The rarest naturally occurring element is astatine (element 85). It has been calculated that only 0·3 of a gramme exists in the Earth's crust to a depth of 10 miles. The isotope polonium-213 (Po-213) is, however, rarer by a factor of 5×10^{10} which is equivalent to one atom in $3·5 \times 10^{37}$.

The rarest form of matter on Earth has been the few atoms of lawrencium (element 103, symbol Lw) synthesized on 19 Feb. 1961 by Drs. Albert Ghiorso, Torbjorn Sikkeland, Almon E. Larsh and Robert M. Latimer in the University of California's Cyclotron at Berkeley, California, U.S.A. It has a half-life of only 8 seconds.

Commonest

Though ranking behind oxygen (46·60 per cent.) and silicon (27·72 per cent.) in abundance, aluminium is the commonest of all metals constituting 8·13 per cent. by weight of the Earth's crust.

Most magnetic and non-magnetic

The most magnetic material, at ordinary temperatures, known is a cobalt-copper-samerium compound $Co_3 Cu_2 Sm$ with a coercive force of 10,500 oersted. The most non-magnetic alloy yet discovered is 963 parts of copper to 37 parts of nickel.

Newest

The newest artificial trans-uranic element is Element 104 (tentatively named Kurchatovium) with a mass number of 260 and a half-life of 0·3 of a second, synthesized by a team led by Prof. Georgiy Nikolayvitch Flerov at the Laboratory of Intra-Nuclear Reactions in the Joint Institute for Nuclear Research at Dubna, near Moscow, U.S.S.R., and announced in August 1964. There were reports from Dubna, U.S.S.R. that Element 105 had been detected by mass spectograph in Sept. 1967 and Element 106 in 1968 but no details were given. A guarded claim to have detected Element 108 in the Earth's crust was made from Moscow in June 1969.

Dr. Glenn T. Seaborg, Chairman of the United States Atomic Energy Commission, estimated in June 1966 that Elements 106 to 126 would be produced by the year 2000. Attempts to trace Element 110 (eka-platinum) and Element 114 (eka-lead) since November 1968 and Element 111 (eka-gold) since 1969 have been under way at Berkeley, California, U.S.A. Evidence for Element 110 was recorded by the Physics Department of Bristol University, England from emulsion plates in a balloon 25 miles above Palestine, Texas, U.S.A., in September 1968.

Most expensive substance

In October 1968 the U.S. Atomic Energy Commission announced that miniscule amounts of Californium 252 (Element 98) were on sale at $100 for tenth of a microgramme. A fanciful calculation would indicate that the price of an ingot weighing 1 lb. (if such were available) would at this rate be £189,000 million or more than double the entire national wealth of the United Kingdom.

The most expensive stuff

Most and least isotopes The element with the most isotopes is the colourless gas xenon (Xe) with 23 and that with the least is hydrogen with 3. The metallic element with the most is polonium (Po) with 19 and that with the least is beryllium (Be) with 4. Of stable and naturally-occurring isotopes, tin (Sn) has the most with 10.

Longest and shortest half-lives The half-life of a radio-active substance is the period taken for its activity to fall to half of its original value. The highest theoretical figure is 2×10^{18} years for bismuth 209, while the shortest is $2 \cdot 4 \times 10^{-21}$ of a second for helium 5. Radiation has been measured from Neodymium 144 which has a half-life of 5×10^{15} years.

Purest The purest metal yet achieved is the grey-white metal Germanium by the zone refining technique, first mooted in 1939 and published by William G. Pfann of Bell Laboratories, U.S.A. in 1952. By 1967 a purity of 99·99999999 per cent. had been achieved.

Hardest substances In February 1957 it was announced in the United States that, by dint of pressures of 65,000 atmospheres (426 tons per square inch) and temperatures of 1,700° C., a cubic form of boron nitride (BN) ("Borazon") had been produced which matched some diamonds for hardness, with a Mohs value of 10, or 7,000 on the Knoop K100 scale. Prof. Naoto Kawai of Osaka University, Japan announced in June 1967 the production by dint of a pressure of 150 tonnes/cm.² (5,300,000 p.s.i.) of a single crystal of 1 part silica, 1 part magnesium and 4 parts oxygen which was "twice as hard as diamond".

Finest powder The finest powder produced is aluminium dust with an average diameter of 0·03 of a micron and a surface area of 75 square metres (807 square feet) per gramme. It was first marketed in the United States at $30 (then £10 14s.) per ounce in February 1959. Some particles measure only 0·005 of a micron.

SMELLIEST SUBSTANCE
The most pungent of the 17,000 smells so far classified is 4-hydroxy-3-methoxy benzaldehyde or vanillaldehyde. This can be detected in a concentration of 2×10^{-8} of a milligramme per litre of air. Thus $9 \cdot 7 \times 10^{-5}$ (about one ten-thousandth) of an ounce completely volatilized would still be detectable in an enclosed space with a floor the size of a full-sized football pitch (360 feet × 300 feet) and a roof 45 feet high. Only 2·94 ounces would be sufficient to permeate a cubic mile of the atmosphere. The most evil smelling substance must be a matter of opinion but ethyl mercaptan (C_2H_5SH) and butyl seleno-mercaptan (C_4H_9SeH), are powerful claimants, each with a smell reminiscent of a combination of rotting cabbage, garlic, onions and sewer gas.

Most expensive perfume The costliest perfume in the world is "Adoration", manufactured by Nina Omar of Puerto Real, Cadiz, Spain, and distributed in the United States at a retail price of $185 (£77) per half-ounce. Its most expensive ingredient is a very rare aromatic gum from Asia. The biggest and most expensive bottle of perfume sold is the one litre (1·76 pints) size of Chanel No. 5, from France. It retails in Great Britain at £120 per bottle.

Sweetest substance The sweetest naturally-occurring substance is exuded from the red serendipity berry (*Dioscoreophyllum cumminsii*) from Nigeria, which was announced in September 1967 to be 1,500 times as sweet as sucrose.

The chemical 1-n-propoxy-2-amino-4-nitrobenzene was determined by Verkade in 1946 to be 5,600 times as sweet as 1 per cent. sucrose.

Bitterest substance The bitterest known substance is Bitrex, the proprietary name for benzyldiethyl (2:6-xylylcarbamoyl methyl) ammonium benzoate ($C_{28}H_{34}N_2O_3$), first reported from Macfarlan Smith Ltd. of Edinburgh, Scotland. This can be detected in solution at a concentration of one part in 20,000,000 and is thus about 200 times as bitter as quinine sulphate (($C_{22}H_{24}N_2O_2)_2$, H_2SO_4, $2H_2O$).

Strongest acid The strength of acids and alkalis is measured on the pH scale. The pH of a solution is the logarithm to the base 10 of the reciprocal of the hydrogen-ion concentration in gramme ions per litre. The strongest simple acid is perchloric acid ($HClO_4$). Assessed on its power as a hydrogen-ion donor, the most powerful acid is a solution of antimony pentafluoride in fluosulphonic acid ($SbF_5 + FSO_3H$).

Strongest alkali The strength of alkalis is expressed by pH values rising above the neutral 7·0. The strongest bases are caustic soda or sodium hydroxide (NaOH), caustic potash or potassium hydroxide (KOH) and tetramethylammonium hydroxide ($N(CH_3)_4OH$), with pH values of 14 normal solutions. True neutrality, pH 7, occurs in pure water at 22° C.

Most powerful fuel The greatest specific impulse of any rocket propulsion fuel combination is 435 lb. f. sec. per lb. produced by lithium fluoride and hydrogen. This compares with a figure of 300 for liquid oxygen and kerosene.

POISON
Quickest The barbiturate thiopentone, if given as a large intra-cardiac injection, will cause permanent cessation of respiration in one to two seconds.

Most potent Potentially the most poisonous substance yet discovered is the toxin of the bacterium *Pasteurella tularensis*. A *single* organism is believed to be able to institute tularemia variously called alkali disease, Francis disease or deerfly fever, though this is fatal in only 5 to 8 per cent. of cases.

The toxin of the bacterium *Clostridium botulinum* type A is in practice far more virulent. The normal lethal dose for a single adult male, by parenteral injection, would be about 0·12 of a microgramme. Hence 410 grammes (14·19 oz.) would suffice to eliminate the entire human population. *C. botulinum* is not easily disseminated and is not self-propagating. It prevents the release of acetylcholine, thus inducing a block to neuro-muscular transmission, which results in paralysis, asphyxia and death. The only major outbreak of botulism (first described in 1820) in Britain was that at Loch Maree, Ross and Cromarty, in August 1922, when eight persons died. Recent work suggests that a toxin from planktonic dinoflagellates producing "paralytic shellfish poisoning" is comparably lethal.

Historically, more deaths have resulted from the action of *Pasteurella pestis* than from any other organism. Some 140 strains have been identified but about 3,000 organisms are required to cause human fatality from bubonic plague (see Worst pandemic, Accidents and Disasters).

Most powerful nerve gas The nerve gas Sarin or GB, a lethal colourless and odourless gas, has been developed since 1945 in the United States and is reputedly 30 times as toxic as phosgene ($COCl_2$) used in World War I. In the early 1950's substances known as V-agents, notably VX 10 times more toxic than GB, were developed at the Chemical Defence Experimental Establishment, Porton Down, Wiltshire, which are lethal at 1 milligramme per man.

Most powerful drugs The most potent and, to an addict, the most expensive of all naturally-derived drugs is heroin, which is a

The white poppy— the source of heroin

The scientific world

chemically-processed form of opium from the juice of the unripe seed capsules of the white poppy (*Papaver somniferum*). An ounce, which suffices for up to 1,800 hypodermic shots or "fixes", may fetch up to $9,000 (£3,750) in the United States, or a 70,000 per cent. profit over the raw material price in Turkey. The United States had 62,045 narcotics addicts recorded at 31 Dec. 1967, compared with the United Kingdom's 2,782 reported at the end of 1969. In 1969 the figure for New York City was believed to have surpassed the 1967 U.S. national total. The most potent analgesic drug is Etorphine or M-99, announced in June 1963 by Dr. Kenneth W. Bentley (b. 1925) and D. G. Hardy of Reckitt & Sons Ltd. of Hull, Yorkshire, with almost 10,000 times the potency of morphine.

DRINK

The strength of spirituous liquor is gauged by degrees proof. In the United Kingdom proof spirit is that mixture of ethyl alcohol (C_2H_5OH) and water which at 51° F. weighs 12/13ths of an equal measure of distilled water. Such spirit in fact contains 57·06 per cent. alcohol by volume, so that pure or absolute alcohol is 75·254° over proof (O.P.). A "hangover" is due to toxic congenerics such as amyl alcohol ($C_5H_{11}OH$).

Most alcoholic The highest strength spirits which can be produced are raw rum and some Polish vodkas, up to 70° over proof or 97 per cent. alcohol. Royal Navy rum was 40° over proof (79·884 per cent. alcohol) before 1948, but is 4·5° under proof (U.P.) today. The strongest drink sold commercially is Polish White Spirit, produced by the State Spirits Monopoly of Poland. This is 40° O.P. The most powerful aquavit marketed is the Norwegian Vinmonopolet's "Brennevin 60 per cent.", having 60 per cent. alcohol by volume (5° O.P.).

The world's most expensive drink— Tokay Essence

Most expensive alcoholic drink A bottle of Tokay essence of the 'Comet' vintage of 1811, bottled *c.* 1840 for the now extinct princely family of Bretzenheim and imported into Britain *c.* 1925 was auctioned for £220 at Christie's, London on 26 June 1969. It had been walled in during the Hungarian Revolution of 1849.

BEER

Strongest The world's strongest beer is Eku Kulminator Urtyp Hell from West Germany with a gravity of 1,138·06° and an alcohol content by weight of 8·9 per cent. The strongest beer now brewed in the United Kingdom is Gold Label Barley Wine made by Tennant Brothers Ltd. of Sheffield, a subsidiary of Whitbread & Co. Ltd. It has an alcoholic content of 8·6 per cent. by weight (10·6 per cent. by volume). This figure is matched by John Courage's "Russian Stout" which is not brewed at regular intervals, though supplies now exist. The British beer with the highest original gravity is Thomas Hardy Ale brewed by Dorchester Brewery at 1,105°. The strongest lager marketed is Carlsberg Special Brew, with a gravity of 1,081°.

Weakest The weakest liquid ever marketed as beer was a sweet ersatz beer which was brewed in Germany by Sunner, Colne-Kalk, in 1918. It had an original gravity of 1,000·96° and a strength 1/30th that of the weakest beer now obtainable in the United Kingdom.

Most expensive The most expensive beer marketed in the United Kingdom is the German lager Löwenbräu. It is brewed and bottled in Munich and is sold at a price which varies from 4s. 6d. to 8s. per bottle (11·6 fluid oz.), according to the type of bar.

WINE

Most expensive The most expensive wine and the greatest oenological rarity is the Red Bordeaux *Château Lafite Rothschild* of 1806, which has appeared on wine lists at 750 francs (£61) per bottle. A bottle "sacrificed" in 1959 proved eminently drinkable but, not surprisingly, had lost its bouquet. On 16 Jan. 1965 a Jeroboam (equivalent to 8 wine bottles) of *Château Lafite Rothschild* 1925 was sold in Bordeaux, France for £850 (11,300 Francs). The highest price paid at auction for a single bottle is £185 paid by Mr. Maurice C. Driecer of New York, N.Y., U.S.A. for a flagon of Canary Island dry white wine of vintage 1740 at Christie's, London on 4 June 1967.

The highest priced German wine is 1921 *Serringer Vogelsang Riesling Trockenbeerauslese,* which is listed at DM 240 (£21 12s.) from Richard Schwarzwalder of München (Munich), Bavaria as early as 1962.

Largest bottles The largest bottle normally used in the wine and spirit trade is the Jeroboam or double magnum, with a capacity of up to 4 litres (7·04 pints), which is used only for liqueur brandy and champagne. A complete set of Monopole champagne bottles from the ¼ bottle, through the ½ bottle, bottle, magnum, Jeroboam, Rehoboam, Methuselah, Salmanezer and Balthazar, to the Nebuchadnezzar, which has a capacity of 16 litres (28·16 pints), is owned by Miss Denise Joan Wardle of Cleveleys, near Blackpool, Lancashire. In May 1958 a 5-foot-tall sherry bottle with a capacity of 20½ Imperial gallons was blown in Stoke-on-Trent, Staffordshire. This bottle, with the capacity of 131 normal bottles, was named an "Adelaide".

Smallest bottle The smallest and meanest bottles of liquor sold are the "Wee Dram" bottles of Scotch whisky marketed by Aidees of Torquay, Devon. They contain 30 minims or 1/16 of a fluid ounce and retail for 1 shilling.

Most expensive liqueurs The most expensive liqueur in France is *Le Grand Marnier Coronation* at 44 francs (70s. 6d.) per bottle. Owing to excise duties, *Elixir Végétale de la Grande Chartreuse* retails at 101s. per 26 fluid oz. in the United Kingdom.

The scientific world

Ancient *Chartreuse* (before 1903) has been known to fetch more than £15 per litre bottle. An 1878 bottle was sold in 1954 for this price.

expensive spirits
The most expensive spirit is *Grande Fine Champagne Arbellot* 1749 brandy, retailed at Fauchon, Paris, at 667 francs (£55) per bottle. *Courvoisier Grande Fine Champagne Cognac* retails in Britain for £7 14s. a bottle. Five bottles of 1811 *Cognac de Marnier* Napoleon brandy were offered for £1,000 each by A. E. Norman of Pinner, Greater London, on 19 Dec. 1962. In 1968 one was left, at a revised £1,000 5s. 4d. (owing to the increase in spirit duty), in the ownership of Mrs. Norman but withdrawn from offer.

champagne cork flight
The longest distance for a champagne cork to fly from an untreated and unheated bottle is 34 feet recorded at the Mardi Gras at New Orleans, U.S.A. in 1962.

GEMS

Most precious
From 1955 the value of rubies rose, due to a drying up in supplies from Ceylon and Burma. A flawless natural stone of good colour was carat for carat more valuable than emerald, diamond or sapphire and, in some cases have attained a price of £4,000 per carat. The ability to produce very large corundum crystals in the laboratory must now have a bearing on the gem market.

Largest
The largest recorded stone of gem quality was a 520,000 carat (2 cwt. 5 lb.) aquamarine ($Al_2Be_3[Si_6O_{18}]$) found near Marambaia, Brazil, in 1910. It yielded over 200,000 carats of gem quality stones.

Rarest
Only two stones are known of the pale mauve gem Taaffeite ($Be_4Mg_4Al_{16}O_{32}$), first discovered in a cut state in Dublin, Ireland, in November 1945. The larger of the two examples is 0·84 of a carat. There are minerals of which only single examples are known.

Hardest
The hardest of all gems, and the hardest known naturally-occurring substance, is diamond, which is, chemically, pure carbon. Diamond is 90 times as hard as the next hardest mineral, corundum (Al_2O_3), and those from Borneo, in Indonesia, and New South Wales, Australia, have a particular reputation for hardness. Hardnesses are compared on Mohs' scale, on which talc is 1, a finger-nail is $2\frac{1}{2}$, window glass 5, topaz 8, corundum 9 and diamond 10. Diamonds average 7,000 on the Knoop scale, with a peak value of 8,400. This index represents a micro-indentation index based on Kilogrammes per one hundredth of a square millimetre ($kg/(mm^2)^{-2}$).

Densest
The densest of all gem minerals is cassiterite or tinstone (SnO_2), a colourless to yellow stone found in Australia, Bolivia, West Malaysia (formerly called Malaya), Mexico and in Cornwall, England. It has a specific gravity of 6·90, rising to 7·1 in opaque form.

DIAMONDS

The largest diamond ever discovered was a stone of 3,106 metric carats (over $1\frac{1}{4}$ lb.) found by Captain M. F. Wells in the Premier Mine, Pretoria, South Africa, on 26 Jan. 1905. It was named after Mr. (later Sir) Thomas Major Cullinan, D.S.O. (1862–1936), discoverer of the mine in 1902 and chairman of the mining company. It was purchased by the Transvaal government in 1907 and presented to King Edward VII. The Star of Africa No. 1 in the Royal Sceptre, cut from it by Jak Asscher in Amsterdam in 1908, is the largest cut diamond in the world with 74 facets and a weight of 530·2 metric carats.

The rarest coloured diamonds are blue and pink. The largest known are the 44·4 carat vivid blue Hope diamond, probably part of a $112\frac{1}{2}$ carat stone found in the Killur mines, Golconda, India, and purchased in 1642 by Jean Baptiste Tavernier (1605–89); and a 24 carat pink diamond, worth an estimated £450,000, presented to the Queen in 1947 by Dr. John Thoburn Williamson (1907–58), a Canadian geologist. In

November 1958 the Hope diamond was presented to the Smithsonian Institution, Washington, D.C., U.S.A., by Mr. Harry Winston, a jeweller, who had paid a sum variously reported between $700,000 (£289,583) and $1,500,000 (£625,000).

Highest auction price
The highest price ever paid in an auction is $385,000 (then £137,500) for the 213 carat diamond necklace from the late Mrs. John E. Rovensky's collection at the Parke-Bernet Galleries, 980 Madison Avenue, New York City, N.Y., U.S.A., on 23 Jan. 1957. The purchaser was Mr. Julius Furst of New York. The record price for a tiara is £110,000 for the Duke of Westminster's diamond piece sold on 25 June 1959 at the London salerooms of Sotheby & Co. to Mr. Harry Winston of New York City. The auction record for a single diamond is $1,050,000 (£437,500) paid by Cartier, Inc. of Fifth Avenue, New York City at Parke-Bernet Galleries on 23 Oct. 1969 for a flawless 69·42 carat stone set in a platinum ring from the estate of Mrs. Florence Gould Sturgeon. It was acquired one day later by Richard Burton by private treaty for a reported $1,200,000 (£500,000) for his wife Elizabeth Taylor.

The $1,200,000 Cartier diamond given to Elizabeth Taylor

Emeralds
Emerald is green beryl. Hexagonal prisms measuring up to $15\frac{3}{4}$ inches long and $9\frac{3}{4}$ inches in diameter, and weighing up to 125 lb., have been recorded from the Ural mines in the U.S.S.R. An 11,000 carat emerald was reported to have been found by Charles Kempt and J. Botes at Letaba, northern Transvaal, South Africa, on 16 Oct. 1956. The largest cut green beryl crystal is the Austrian Government's 2,680 carat unguent jar carved by Dionysio Miseroni in the 17th century. Of gem quality emeralds, the largest known is the Devonshire stone of 1,350 carats from Muso, Colombia.

Sapphires
Sapphire is blue corundum (Al_2O_3). The largest cut gem sapphire in existence is the "Black Star Sapphire of Queensland", weighing 1,444 carats, carved in 1953–55 from a rough stone of 2,097 carats. It is in the form of a bust of General Dwight David Eisenhower (1890–1969), formerly President of the United States. A carved dark blue sapphire of the head of President Abraham Lincoln (1809–65), weighing 1,318 carats, is also in the custody of the Kazanjian Foundation of Los Angeles, California, U.S.A. It was cut in 1949–51 from a 2,302-carat stone also found at Anakie, Queensland, Australia, in *c.* 1935.

The scientific world

Rubies Ruby is red corundum (Al_2O_3) with chromic oxide impurities. The largest natural gem stone known was a 1,184 carat stone of Burmese origin. In July 1961 a broken red corundum of an original 3,421 carats was reported to have been found in the United States. The largest piece weighed about 750 carats. Laboratory-made ruby prisms for laser technology reach over 12 inches in length.

Pearl Pearls are protective secretory bodies produced by bivalved molluscs. Gem pearls come chiefly from the western Pacific genus *Pinctada* and the fresh water mussel genus *Quadrula*. The largest known natural pearl is the "Pearl of Lao-tze", also called the Pearl of Allah, measuring $9\frac{1}{2}$ inches long and $5\frac{1}{2}$ inches in diameter, and weighing 14 lb. 1 oz. It was discovered in the shell of a giant clam (*Tridacna gigas*), the largest of all bivalves at Palawan, Philippines on 7 May 1934. Since 1936 the pearl has been owned by Wilburn Dowell Cobb of San Francisco, U.S.A. It was valued at $3,500,000 (now £1,458,333) in 1939.

Opal The largest known opal is a yellow-orange one of 220 troy oz. unearthed by a bulldozer at Anda Mooka, South Australia, in January 1970, and valued at $A168,000 (£78,113). The largest gem opal is the 17,700 carat "Olympic Australis" found at Coober Pedy, South Australia in August 1956.

The world's largest gem opal

Crystal The largest crystal ball is the Warner sphere of $106\frac{3}{4}$ lb. and $12\frac{7}{8}$ inches diameter ground from a 1,000 lb. piece of Burmese quartz and now in the U.S. National Museum in Washington, D.C. A single rock crystal weighing 1,728 lb. was placed in the Ural Geological Museum in Sverdlovsk, U.S.S.R. in November 1968. A piezo-quartz crystal weighing 70 tons was reported to have been found in Kazakhstan, U.S.S.R., in September 1958.

Topaz The largest known topaz is a low quality transparent crystal weighing 596 lb., from a pegmatite in the province of Minas Gerais, Brazil. Since 1951 it has been on exhibition in the American Museum of Natural History, New York City, N.Y., U.S.A. The Museum also has a gem topaz of 7,725 carats.

NUGGETS
Gold The largest lump of gold ever found *in situ* was the Holtermann Nugget, weighing 7,560 oz. ($472\frac{1}{2}$ lb.), taken from Hill End, New South Wales, Australia, in 1872. It was interlaced with quartz and had a total weight of 10,080 oz. (630 lb.). A nugget weighing $2,280\frac{1}{4}$ troy oz., named the "Welcome Stranger", was picked up in 1869 at Tarnagulla, near Moliagul, in Victoria, Australia. It yielded 2,248 oz. of pure gold.

Silver The largest silver nugget ever recorded was one of 2,750 lb. troy (2,263 lb. avoirdupois), found in Sonora, Mexico, and appropriated by the Spanish Government before 1821.

Largest slab of marble The largest piece of used marble in the world is the coping stone of the Tomb of the Unknown Soldier in Arlington National Cemetery, Arlington, Virginia, U.S.A. It weighs more than 45 tons and was cut from a 90-ton slab taken from a quarry at Yule, Colorado, U.S.A.

Amber The largest piece of amber ever reported was a piece weighing 23·1 lb. found by a lobster fisherman Eigil Hensen, off the coast of Sweden in October 1969.

Jade The largest piece of gem quality jade recorded is a four-ton boulder of dark green chrome jade found in Noel Creek, British Columbia, Canada by Harry Street in September 1969 and worth $50,000. Local prospectors have taken to tiling their bathrooms with jade.

TELESCOPES

EARLIEST
Although there is evidence that early Arabian scientists understood something of the magnifying power of lenses, their first use to form a telescope has been attributed to Roger Bacon (*c*. 1214–92) in England. The prototype of modern refracting telescopes was that completed by Johannes Lippershey for the Dutch government on 2 Oct. 1608.

LARGEST
Refractor The largest refracting (*i.e.* magnification by lenses) telescope in the world is the 62-foot-long 40-inch telescope completed in 1897 at the Yerkes Observatory, Williams Bay, Wisconsin, and belonging to the University of Chicago, Illinois, U.S.A. The largest in the British Isles is the 28-inch at the Royal Greenwich Observatory completed in 1894.

Reflector The largest operational telescope in the world is the 6 metre (236·2 inch) telescope sited near Zelenchukskaya in the Caucasus Mountains, U.S.S.R., at an altitude of 6,830 feet. The mirror, weighing 70 tons, was completed in Nov. 1967. The overall weight of the 80-foot long assembly is 850 tons. Being the most powerful of all telescopes its range, which includes the location of objects down to the 25th magnitude, represents the limits of the observable Universe.

The largest reflector in the British Isles is the Isaac Newton 98·2-inch reflector at the Royal Greenwich Observatory, Herstmonceux Castle, Sussex. It was built in Newcastle upon Tyne, Northumberland, weighs 92 tons, cost £641,000 and was inaugurated on 1 Dec. 1967.

Radio The world's first fully steerable radio telescope is the Mark I telescope at the University of Manchester Department of Radio Astronomy, Nuffield Radio Astronomy Laboratories, Jodrell Bank, Macclesfield, Cheshire, on which work began in September 1952. The 750-ton 250-foot diameter bowl of steel plates and 180-foot-high supports weigh 2,000 tons. Its cost is believed to have been about £750,000 when it was completed in 1957. The Manchester University Mark V radio telescope at Meifod, Montgomeryshire will have a diameter of 400 feet and is due for completion at a cost of some £5 million in 1975.

The world's largest trainable dish-type radio telescope is the $850,000 (£354,165) installation completed for the United States National Radio Astronomy Observatory at Green Bank, West Virginia, U.S.A., in 1962. It has a diameter of 300 feet. Work started in November 1967 on the £2·35 million, 3,000-ton 328-foot diameter double-swivelling steerable dish for the Max Planck Institute for Radio Astronomy of Bonn in the Effelsberger Valley, West Germany.

The world's largest dish radio telescope is the non-steerable ionospheric assembly built over a natural bowl at Arecibo, Puerto Rico, completed in November 1963 at a cost of about $9,000,000 (£3·75 million). It has a diameter of 1,000 feet and the dish covers 18½ acres.

The most extensive radio telescope in the world is the Cornell University installation, completed in Sept. 1967, at Culgoora, N.S.W., Australia where 96 receivers are on the 6-mile long circumference of a circle covering 1,833 acres. Plans for an assembly of 8 130-foot diameter moveable dishes on a T-track measuring 3,000 yards across and 5,333 yards down were announced by the California Institute of Technology in August 1967. The $16,700,000 (£6,958,333) assembly will be erected in Owens Valley, California, U.S.A.

The British Science Research Council 5 kilometre radio telescope at Lord's Bridge, Cambridgeshire and Isle of Ely to be operated by the Mullard Radio Astronomy Observatory of Cambridge University will utilize 8 mobile 42-foot rail-borne computer-controlled dish aerials, which will be equivalent to a single steerable dish 5 kilometres in diameter. The project, to be operational before the end of 1973, will cost more than £2,100,000.

Observatory Highest The highest altitude observatory in the world is the Mauna Kea Observatory, Hawaii at an altitude of 13,824 feet, opened in 1969. The principal instrument is an 88-inch (224 cm.) telescope.

Solar The world's largest solar telescope is the 480-foot-long McMath telescope at Kitt Peak National Observatory near Tucson, Arizona, U.S.A. It has a focal length of 300 feet and an 80-inch heliostat mirror. It was completed in 1962 and produces an image measuring 33 inches in diameter.

Planetaria The ancestor of the planetarium is the rotatable Gottorp Globe, built by Andreas Busch in Denmark between 1654 and 1664 to the orders of Duke Frederick III of Holstein's court mathematician Olearius. It is 34·6 feet in circumference, weighs nearly 3½ tons and is now preserved in Leningrad, U.S.S.R. The stars were painted on the inside. The earliest optical installation was not until 1923 in the Deutsches Museum, Munich, by Zeiss of Jena, Germany. The world's largest planetarium, with a diameter of 85 feet, is now being completed, at a cost of $1,500,000 (£625,000), on Dangerfield Island, on the Potomac, Washington, D.C., U.S.A.

The United Kingdom's first planetarium was opened at Madame Tussaud's, Marylebone Road, London, on 19 March 1958. Accurate images of 8,900 stars are able to be projected on the 70-foot high copper dome.

The world's largest telescope (left)

The 70 ton mirror of the 236·2 inch telescope (below)

The world's highest observatory in Hawaii (right)

The scientific world

PHOTOGRAPHY

It is estimated that the total expenditure on photography in the United States in 1968 was $3,686,645,000 (£1,536 million) and that 63,130,000 still cameras and 7,700,000 cine cameras were in use. In the United Kingdom the expenditure on amateur photography in 1968 was £95,000,000.

CAMERAS

Earliest The earliest photograph was taken in the summer of 1826 by Joseph Nicéphore Niépce (1765–1833), a French physician and scientist. It showed the courtyard of his country house at Gras, near St. Loup-de-Varennes. It probably took eight hours to expose and was taken on a bitumen-coated polished pewter plate measuring 8 inches by $6\frac{1}{2}$ inches. The earliest photograph taken in England was one of a diamond-paned window in Lacock Abbey, Wiltshire, taken in 1835 by William Henry Fox Talbot (1800–1877), the inventor of the negative-positive process. The world's earliest aerial photograph was taken in 1858 by Gaspard Félix Tournachon (1820–1910), *alias* Nadar, from a balloon near Villacoublay, on the outskirts of Paris, France.

Largest The largest camera ever built was the Anderson Mammoth camera, built in Chicago, Illinois, U.S.A., in 1900. When extended, it measured 9 feet high, 6 feet wide and 20 feet long. Its two lenses were a wide-angle Zeiss with a focal length of 68 inches and a telescope Rapid Rectilinear of 120 inches focal length. Exposures averaged 150 seconds and 15 men were required to work it.

Smallest Apart from cameras built for intra-cardiac surgery and espionage, the smallest camera generally marketed is the Japanese Kiku 16 Model II, which measures $2\frac{3}{8}$ inches $\times$ 1 inch $\times \frac{5}{8}$ of an inch.

Fastest A paper on a camera of highly limited application with a time resolution of $1 \cdot 0 \times 10^{-11}$ of a second has been published by Butslov *et al.* of the U.S.S.R. Academy of Sciences. In June 1969 a camera from the U.S.S.R. was demonstrated at the N.P.L., Teddington, London with "events" moving across image tubes at 167 million m.p.h. or one quarter of the speed of light. Britain's fastest camera is the E.12 image tube camera announced by the Optical Group of the Atomic Weapons Research Establishment at Aldermaston, Berkshire in January 1966, with a rate of 60,000,000 exposures per second. The camera is marketed under the title of TE.12 by Telford Products Ltd., of Greenford, Middlesex, and Imacon by John Hadland (P.I.) Ltd., of Bovingdon, Hertfordshire.

Most expensive The most expensive amateur roll-film camera is the Rolleiflex SL.66 made by Franke und Heidecke of Brunswick, West Germany, with an 80 mm. F/2·8 Planar lens, which retailed for £661 in 1969.

The most expensive miniature camera is the Zeiss Contarex, Pentaprism, Reflex with a built-in photo-electric meter and Zeiss Planar f/1·4 55 mm. lens. With a range of accessories, including two wide-angle and three telephoto lenses, this would cost £1,623 2s. 10d.

Largest print The largest photographic print ever produced was an enlargement of a hand-drawn map of Europe, measuring over 4,000 square feet, made for the British Broadcasting Corporation by the Newbold Wells Organisation Limited of London. In 1964 this company produced the largest colour transparency, a hand-coloured transparency of the London sky-line, measuring 212 feet long by $12\frac{1}{2}$ feet high, for the Vickers stand at the Sydney Exhibition in Australia.

Highest photograph The greatest height from which a man has taken a photograph is 248,400 miles by the crew of Apollo X on 22 May 1969 on the far side of the moon. (See Progressive Human Altitude table.)

X-ray Largest The largest X-ray ever made was of a 17-foot long Mercedes 280 SL car using Agfa-Gevaert Structurix D4 film and a 50-hour exposure in September 1959.

NUMEROLOGY

In dealing with large numbers, scientists use the notation of 10 raised to various powers to eliminate a profusion of noughts. For example, 19,160,000,000,000 miles would be written $1 \cdot 916 \times 10^{13}$ miles. Similarly, a very small number, for example $0 \cdot 0000154324$ of a grain, would be written $1 \cdot 5432 \times 10^{-5}$ of a grain. Of the prefixes used before numbers the smallest is "atto-" from the Danish *atten* for 18, indicating a trillionth part (10^{-18}) of the unit, and the highest is "tera-" (Greek, *teras*=monster), indicating a billion (10^{12}) fold.

NUMBERS

Highest The highest generally accepted named number is the centillion, which is 10 raised to the power 600, or one followed by 600 noughts. Higher numbers are named in linguistic literature the most extreme of which is the milli-millimillillion (10 raised to the power 6,000,000,000) devised by Rudolf Ondrejka. The number Megiston written with symbol ⑩ is a number too great to have any physical meaning. The highest named number outside the decimal notation is the Buddhist *asankhyeya*, which is equal to 10^{140} or 100 tertio-vigintillions (British system) or 100 quinto-quadragintillions (U.S. system).

The number 10^{100} (10,000 sexdecillion) is designated a Googol. This was invented by Dr. Edward Kasner (U.S.) (d. 1955). Ten raised to the power of a Googol is described as a Googolplex. Some conception of the magnitude of such numbers can be gained when it is said that the number of atoms in the observable Universe probably does not exceed 10^{85}. However, it has been said that the theoretical number of patterns of nucleotides (adenine, thymine, guanine and cytosine) in the massive deoxyribonucleic acid (D.N.A.) molecule is 10^{12000}.

The largest number to have become sufficiently well-known in mathematics to have been named after its begetter is the larger of the two Skewes numbers which is 10 to the power 10 to the power 10 to the power 10 to the power 3, obtained by Prof. Stanley Skewes, M.A., Ph.D., now of Cape Town University, South Africa, and published in two papers of 1933 and 1955 concerning the occurrence of prime numbers.

Prime numbers A prime number is any positive integer (excluding 1) having no integral factors other than itself and unity, *e.g.* 2, 3, 5, 7 or 11. The lowest prime number is thus 2. The highest known prime number is $2^{11213}-1$, discovered on 2 June 1963 by Prof. Donald B. Gillies, using the ILLIAC II computer at the University of Illinois, Urbana, Illinois, U.S.A. This number contains 3,376 digits.

Perfect numbers A number is said to be perfect if it is equal to the sum of its divisors other than itself, *e.g.* $1+2+4+7+14=28$. The lowest perfect number is 6 ($1+2+3$). The highest known, and the 23rd so far discovered, is $2^{11212} \times (2^{11213}-1)$, with 6,751 digits.

Most primitive The lowest limit in enumeration among primitive peoples is among the Yancos, an Amazon tribe who cannot count beyond *poettarrarorincoaroac*, which is their word for "three". The Temiar people of West Malaysia (formerly called Malaya) also stop at three. Investigators have reported that the number "four" is expressed by a look of total stupefaction indistinguishable from that for any other number higher than three. It is said that among survivors of the Aimores, naked nomads of Eastern Brazil, there is no apparent word for "two".

Most accurate version of "pi" The greatest number of decimal places to which *pi* (π) has been calculated is 100,265 by Daniel Shanks and

John W. Wrench, Jr., on an IBM 7090 machine in the IBM Data Processing Center, New York City, N.Y., U.S.A., on 29 July 1961. The calculation took 8 hours 43 minutes and the check 4 hours 22 minutes. It was estimated that the same calculation would take 30,000 years for a mathematician with a 10-place electric desk computer. The published value to 100,000 places was 3.141592653589793 . . . (omitting the next 99,975 places) . . . 5493624646.

Earliest measures The earliest known measure of weight is the *beqa* of the Amratian period of Egyptian civilization *c.* 3,800 B.C. found at Naqada, United Arab Republic. The weights are cylindrical with rounded ends from 188·7 to 211·2 grammes and are the basis of the English troy ounce. The unit of length used by the megalithic tomb-builders in Britain *c.* 2300 B.C. appears to have been 2·72±0·003 feet.

TIME MEASURE

Longest The longest measure of time is the *kalpa* in Hindu chronology. It is equivalent to 4,320 million years. In astronomy a cosmic year is the period of rotation of the Milky Way galaxy at the Sun's distance from the centre, *i.e.* about 225,000,000 years. In the Late Cretaceous Period of *c.* 85 million years ago the Earth rotated faster so resulting in 370·3 days per year.

Shortest Owing to variations in the length of a day, which is estimated to be increasing irregularly at the average rate of about two milliseconds per century due to the Moon's tidal drag, the second has been redefined. Instead of being 1/86,400th part of a mean solar day, it has, since 1960, been reckoned as 1/31,556,925·9747th part of the solar (or tropical) year at A.D. 1900, January 0 at 12 hours, Ephemeris time. In 1958 the second of Ephemeris time was computed to be equivalent to 9,192,631,770±20 cycles of the radiation corresponding to the transition of a caesium 133 atom when unperturbed by exterior fields. In a nano-second (1.0×10^{-9} of a second) light travels 11·7 inches.

SMALLEST UNITS

The shortest unit of length is the fermi which is 1.0×10^{-13} of a centimetre. The smallest unit of area is a "shed", used in sub-atomic physics and first mentioned in 1956. It is 1.0×10^{-48} of a square centimetre. A "barn" is equal to 10^{24} "sheds". The reaction of a neutrino occurs over the area of 1×10^{-41} of a square millimetre.

Dr. Enrico Fermi who gave his name to the smallest unit of length (above)

TEMPERATURES

Highest The highest man-made temperatures yet attained are those produced in the centre of a thermonuclear fusion bomb, which are of the order of 300,000,000 to 400,000,000° C. Of controllable temperatures, the highest effective laboratory figure reported is 50,000,000° C. for 2/100ths of a second by Prof. Lev A. Artsimovich at Tokamuk in the U.S.S.R. in 1969. At very low particle densities even higher figures are obtainable. In 1963 a figure of 3,000 million °C. was reportedly achieved in the U.S.S.R. with Ogra injection-mirror equipment.

Lowest The lowest temperature reached is 1×10^{-6} K, achieved by Dr. Nicholas Kurti (b. 1908) at the Clarendon Laboratory, Oxford, in 1959. This temperature was also achieved in the Mullard Cryomagnetic Laboratory, Oxford, in June 1965. Absolute temperatures are defined in terms of ratios and not of differences, so that the temperature of melting ice (273·16° K, 0° C. or 32° F.) is said to be 3.7×10^9 times as high as the lowest temperature ever attained. Absolute zero approximates to −273·16° C. or −459·69° F.

Highest pressures The highest sustained laboratory pressures yet reported are of 5,000,000 atmospheres (32,800 tons per square inch), achieved in the U.S.S.R. and announced in October 1958. Using dynamic methods and impact speeds of up to 18,000 m.p.h., momentary pressures of 75,000,000 atmospheres (490,000 tons per square inch) were reported from the United States in 1958.

Greatest tensile strength The highest tensile strength value reported is one of 3,500,000 lb. per sq. inch (lbf/in^2 or p.s.i.) by Anderegg for a very small glass fibre tested *in vacuo* at −200° C. In February 1967 a load of 3,270,000 p.s.i. was achieved on a thread of tungsten at Kharkov, U.S.S.R. Theoretical considerations indicate that amorphous boron has a maximum cohesive strength of 3,900,000 p.s.i. A boron wire 189·4 miles long could theoretically be suspended without parting.

Highest vacuum The highest (or 'hardest') vacuums obtained in scientific research are of the order of 1.0×10^{-16} of an atmosphere. This compares with an estimated pressure in inter-stellar space of 1.0×10^{-19} of an atmosphere. At sea-level there are 3×10^{19} molecules per cubic centimetre in the atmosphere, but in inter-stellar space there are probably less than 10 per cubic centimetre.

Fastest centrifuge The highest man-made rotary speed ever achieved is 1,500,000 revolutions per second, or 90,000,000 revolutions per minute, on a steel rotor with a diameter of about 1/100th of an inch suspended in a vacuum in an ultra-centrifuge installed in March 1961 in the Rouss Physical Laboratory at the University of Virginia in Charlottesville, Virginia, U.S.A. This work is led by Prof. Jesse W. Beams. The edge of the rotor is travelling at 2,500 m.p.h. and is subject to a stress of 1,000,000,000 g.

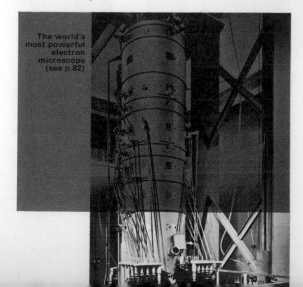

The world's most powerful electron microscope (see p.82)

The scientific world

Most powerful microscopes
Electron microscopes have now reached the point at which individual atoms are distinguishable. In March 1958 the U.S.S.R. announced an electronic point projector with a magnification approaching $\times 2,000,000$, in which individual atoms of barium and molecules of oxygen can be observed. In 1967 a resolution of 1·02 Ångström units diameter was achieved by Dr. K. Yada (Japan) using a Hitachi instrument. In February 1969 it was announced from Pennsylvania State University, U.S.A., that the combination of the field ion microscope invented by their Prof. Erwin W. Müller in 1956 and a spectrometer enabled single atoms to be identified.

Electron microscope
The most powerful electron microscope in the world is the 3,500 kV installation at the National Scientific Research Centre, Toulouse, France which reached testing stage in October 1969. The high voltage generator and accelerator fill a cylinder 15 feet in diameter and 30 feet high. Its six lenses form a column 3 feet by 11 feet and weigh 20 tons.

Highest note
The highest note yet attained is one of 60,000 megahertz (MHz) (60,000 million vibrations per second), generated by a "laser" beam striking a sapphire crystal at the Massachusetts Institute of Technology in Cambridge, Massachusetts, U.S.A., in September 1964. This is 1,000,000 times as high in pitch as the upper limit of human audibility.

Loudest noise
The loudest noise created in a laboratory is 210 decibels or 400,000 acoustic watts reported by N.A.S.A. from Huntsville, Alabama, U.S.A. in October 1965. Holes can be bored in solid material by this means.

Quietest place
The "dead room", measuring 35 feet by 28 feet, in the Bell Telephone System laboratory at Murray Hill, New Jersey, U.S.A., is the most anechoic room in the world, eliminating 99·98 per cent. of reflected sound.

Finest balance
The most accurate balance in the world is the Q01 quartz fibre decimicro balance made by L. Oertling Ltd. of Orpington, Kent, England which has a read-out scale on which one division corresponds to 0·0001 of a milligramme. It can weigh to an accuracy of 0·0002 of a milligramme which is equivalent to little more than one third of the weight of ink on this full stop.

The Q01 balance

Lowest viscosity
The California Institute of Technology, U.S.A., announced on 1 Dec. 1957 that there was no measurable viscosity, *i.e.* perfect flow, in liquid helium II, which exists only at temperatures close to absolute zero (−273·16° C. or −459·69° F.).

Lowest friction
The lowest coefficient of static and dynamic friction of any solid is 0·02, in the case of polytetrafluoroethylene $((C_2F_4)_n)$, called P.T.F.E.—equivalent to wet ice on wet ice. It was first manufactured in quantity by E. I. du Pont de Nemours & Co. Inc. in 1943, and is marketed from the U.S.A. as Teflon. In the United Kingdom it is marketed by I.C.I. as Fluon.

At the University of Virginia (see above, Fastest centrifuge) a 30 lb. rotor magnetically supported has been spun at 1,000 revolutions per second in a vacuum of 10^{-6} mm. of mercury pressure. It loses only one revolution per second per day, thus spinning for years.

Most powerful adhesive
The most powerful adhesive known is epoxy resin, which, after being supercooled to −450° F., can withstand a shearing pull of 8,000 lb. per square inch.

Most powerful electric current
The most powerful electric current generated is that from the Zeus capacitor at the Los Alamos Scientific Laboratory, New Mexico, U.S.A. If fired simultaneously the 4,032 capacitors would produce for a few microseconds twice as much current as that generated elsewhere on Earth.

Most powerful particle accelerator
The world's most powerful particle accelerator is the U.S.S.R. Institute for High Energy Physics' proton synchrotron at Serpukhov, south of Moscow. On 13 Oct. 1967 it was reported to have attained an output of 76 GeV ($7·6 \times 10^{10}$ electron volts). Construction had begun in 1960 and was completed at a cost of nearly £30,000,000.

A minimal output of 200 GeV is expected by 1973 from the 1·24 mile diameter ring at the National Accelerator Laboratory at Weston, Illinois, U.S.A. The plant will cost $250,000,000 or, if 400 GeV is required, $280,000,000 (£116·6 million). A capacity "stretched" to 500 GeV is regarded as feasible.

The building of SLAC, the underground linear accelerator, two miles long, for Stanford University, California, U.S.A. was completed, at a cost of $114,000,000 (£47,500,000), in November 1966. It is believed that it will enable the two intersecting storage rings to yield 20 GeV each in "centre of mass" experiments, producing the equivalent energy of a 1,000 GeV electron hitting a stationary target. The £30 million CERN intersecting storage rings (ISR) project, started in September 1966, using two 28 GeV proton beams, should yield the equivalent of 1,700 GeV in its centre of mass experiments due to run in mid-1971.

World's largest bubble chamber
The largest bubble chamber in the world is at the Argonne National Laboratory, Illinois, U.S.A. It is 12 feet in diameter and contains 5,330 gallons of liquid hydrogen at a temperature of −247° C. The magnet is 18 Kilogauss and the plant went into operation in October 1969 after an expenditure of $18,000,000 (£7½ million).

Strongest magnet
The heaviest magnet in the world is one measuring 200 feet in diameter, with a weight of 36,000 tons, for the 10 GeV synchrophasotron in the Joint Institute for Nuclear Research at Dubna, near Moscow, U.S.S.R. The largest super-conducting magnet is a niobium-zirconium magnet, weighing 15,675 lb., completed in June 1966 by Avco Everett Research Laboratory, Massachusetts, U.S.A. It produces a magnetic field of 40,000 gauss and the windings are super-cooled with 6,000 litres of liquid helium.

Strongest magnetic field
The strongest recorded magnetic fields are ones of more than 1,000,000 gauss, fleetingly produced by declassified atomic bomb technology at the Illinois Institute of Technology, U.S.A. The first megagauss field was announced in March 1967.

The strongest steady magnetic field yet achieved is one of 158,000 gauss in a cylindrical space 1·25 inches in diameter, using 3,000,000 watts of electric power, produced in 1962 in the U.S. Naval Research Laboratory, Washington, D.C., U.S.A.

WIND TUNNELS

World The world's largest wind tunnel is a low-speed tunnel with a closed test section measuring 40 feet by 80 feet, built in 1944 at the Ames Research Center, Moffett Field, California, U.S.A. The tunnel encloses 800 tons of air and cost approximately $7,000,000 (now £2,916,666). The maximum volume of air that can be moved is 60,000,000 cubic feet per minute. The most powerful is the 216,000 h.p. installation at the Arnold Engineering Test Center at Tullahoma, Tennessee, U.S.A. opened in September 1956. The highest Mach number attained with air is Mach 27 at the works of the Boeing Company in Seattle, Washington State, U.S.A. For periods of micro-seconds, shock Mach numbers of the order of 30 have been attained in impulse tubes at Cornell University, Ithaca, New York State, U.S.A.

United Kingdom The largest wind tunnel in the United Kingdom is that at the Royal Aircraft Establishment at Bedford, with a working area of 8 square feet and a compressor absorbing 80,000 h.p. This machine is capable of producing Mach 2·5, which is equivalent to 1,900 m.p.h. at sea level. The shell has a maximum diameter of 47 feet and weighs 5,000 tons.

Finest cut Biological specimens embedded in epoxy resin can be sectioned by a glass knife microtome under ideal conditions to a thickness of 1/875,000th of an inch or 290 Ångström units.

Brightest light The brightest steady artificial light sources are "laser" beams (see below), with a luminosity exceeding the Sun's 800,000 candles per square inch by a factor well in excess of 1,000. In May 1969 the U.S.S.R. Academy of Sciences announced blast waves travelling through a luminous plasma of inert gases heated to 90,000° K. The flare-up for up to 3 micro-seconds shone at 50,000 times the brightness of the Sun *viz.* 40,000 million candles per square inch. Of continuously burning sources, the most powerful is a 200 kW high-pressure xenon arc lamp of 600,000 candle-power, reported from the U.S.S.R. in 1965. The most powerful searchlight ever developed was one produced during the 1939–45 war by the General Electric Company Ltd. at the Hirst Research Centre in Wembley, Greater London. It had a consumption of 600 kW and gave an arc luminance of 300,000 candles per square inch and a maximum beam intensity of 2,700,000,000 candles from its parabolic mirror (diameter 10 feet).

Most durable The average electric light bulb lasts for 750 to 1,000 hours. On 21 Sept. 1908 a stagehand named Barry Burke at the Byers Opera House (now the Palace Theater), Fort Worth, Texas screwed in a new light bulb. The bulb is still burning six years after Burke's death and has been logged by an increasingly mystified Texas Electric Service since 1929. Most Texans believe that the filament escaped from a research laboratory.

"Laser" beams The first illumination of another celestial body was achieved on 9 May 1962, when a beam of light was successfully reflected from the Moon by the use of an optical "maser" (microwave amplification by stimulated emission of radiation) or "laser" (light amplification by stimulated emission of radiation) attached to a 48-in. telescope at Massachusetts Institute of Technology, Cambridge, Massachusetts, U.S.A. The spot was estimated to be 4 miles in diameter on the Moon. A "maser" light flash is focused into a liquid nitrogen-cooled ruby crystal. Its chromium atoms are excited into a high energy state in which they emit a red light which is allowed to escape only in the direction desired. The device was invented in 1958 by Dr. Charles Hard Townes (born 1915) of the U.S.A. Such a flash for 1/2,000th of a second can bore a hole through a diamond by vaporization at 10,000° C., produced by 2×10^{23} photons.

COMPUTERS

World The world's most powerful computer is the Control Data Corporation CDC 7600 first delivered in January 1969. It can perform 36 million operations in one second and has an access time of 27 nano-seconds. It has two internal memory cores of 655,360 and 5,242,880 characters (6 bits per character) supplemented by a Model 817 disc file of 800 million characters. Commercial deliveries have been scheduled from 1972 at a cost of $9 to $15 million (£3¾ to £6¼ million) depending on peripherals.

United Kingdom The largest computer built in the United Kingdom is the £2,500,000 Ferranti "Atlas I". The largest of these was installed in 1964 in the Atlas Computer Laboratory of the Science Research Council, Chilton Didcot, Berkshire. This machine can perform 500,000 arithmetic operations in a second and 25,000,000 48-bit multiplications in two minutes. It has a capacity of 1·2 million characters supplemented by a disc store of 134 million characters. The ICL 1907 computer, manufactured by International Computers Ltd. of London, S.W.6, is capable of 600,000 arithmetic operations per second. The ICL 1906A announced in October 1967 is expected to attain double the capacity of an Atlas by 1970.

The world's largest bubble chamber (see p.82)

The world's largest bubble chamber (see p.82)

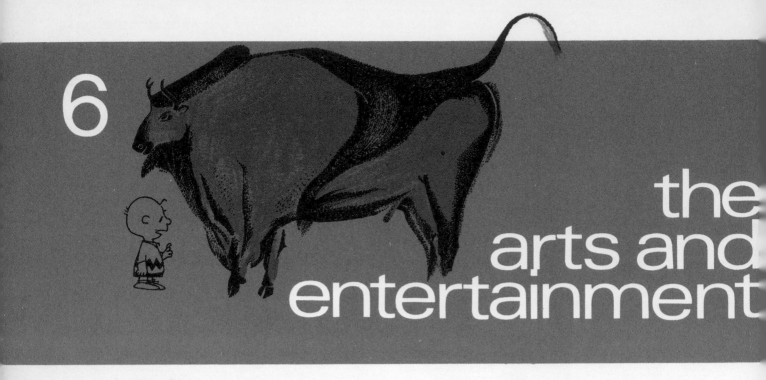

6 the arts and entertainment

1. Painting

Earliest
Specimens of cave art were first discovered in 1834 at Chaffaud, Vienne, France, but the number of stratigraphically dated examples is very limited. The oldest known examples so dated are at La Ferrassie, where black and red pigmented flakes, possibly representing a cervid (a deer-like form), have been ascribed to the period Aurignacian III of *c.* 25,000 B.C. Palaeozoological evidence suggests, however, that the Lascaux cave paintings at Dordogne, France, are pre-Gravettian, i.e. earlier than 65,000 B.C.

The earliest British painting is the representation of a horse's head in Robin Hood Cave, Creswell Crags, Derbyshire. It dates from the Upper Palaeolithic period (*c.* 15,000 to 10,000 B.C.).

LARGEST
World
Panorama of the Mississippi, completed by John Banvard (1815–91) in 1846, showing the river scene for 1,200 miles in a strip probably 5,000 feet long and 12 feet wide, was the largest painting in the world, with an area of more than 1·3 acres. The painting is believed to have been destroyed when the rolls of canvas, stored in a barn at Cold Spring Harbor, Long Island, New York State, U.S.A., caught fire shortly before Banvard's death on 16 May 1891.

The largest painting now in existence is probably *The Battle of Gettysburg,* completed in 1883, after $2\frac{1}{2}$ years of work, by Paul Philippoteaux (France) and 16 assistants. The painting is 410 feet long, 70 feet high and weighs 5·36 tons. It depicts the climax of the Battle of Gettysburg, in southern Pennsylvania, U.S.A. on 3 July 1863. In 1964 the painting was bought by Joe King of Winston-Salem, North Carolina, U.S.A.

The largest "Old Master" is *Il Paradiso*, painted between 1587 and 1590 by Jacopo Robusti, *alias* Tintoretto (1518–94), and his son Domenico on Wall "E" of the Sala del Maggior Consiglio in the Palazzo Ducale (Doge's Palace) in Venice, Italy. The work is 22 metres (72 feet 2 inches) long and 7 metres (22 feet $11\frac{1}{2}$ inches) high and contains more than 100 human figures.

United Kingdom
The largest painting in the United Kingdom is the giant oval *Triumph of Peace and Liberty* by Sir James Thornhill (1676–1734), on the ceiling of the Painted Hall in the Royal Naval College, Greenwich, London. It measures 106 feet by 51 feet and took 20 years (1707–1727) to complete.

Most valuable
It is not possible to state which is the most valuable painting in the world since many very valuable works are permanent museum and gallery acquisitions unlikely ever to come on to the market. Neither can they have an insurance replacement value. Valuations thus tend to be hypothetical. The "Mona Lisa" (*La Gioconda*) by Leonardo da Vinci (1452–1519) in the Louvre, Paris, was assessed for insurance purposes at $100,000,000 (then £35·7 million) for its move for exhibition in Wäshington, D.C., and New York City, N.Y., U.S.A., from 14 Dec. 1962 to 12 March 1963. However, insurance was not concluded because the cost of the closest security precautions was less than that of the premiums. It was painted in *c.* 1503–07 and measures 77×53 cms. or 30.5×20.9 inches. It is believed to portray Mona (short for Madonna) Lisa Gherardini, the wife of Francesco del Gioconda of Florence, who disliked it and refused to pay for it. Francis I, King of France, bought the painting for his bathroom for 4,000 gold florins (now equivalent to £225,000) in 1517. The painting was stolen from the Louvre by the Italian Vicenzo Perruggia (born 1881) on 21 Aug. 1911 but was recovered in Italy in 1913.

HIGHEST PRICE
Old Master
On 6 Feb. 1967 the National Gallery of Art in Washington, D.C., U.S.A., acquired for an undisclosed amount, the oil painting *Ginevra de' Benci*, a portrait of a young Florentine woman, painted in *c.* 1480 by Leonardo da Vinci (1452–1519) of Italy. It was reported on 19 Feb. 1967 that the price was between $5,000,000 and $6,000,000 (then between £1·78 and £2·14 million) paid to Prince Franz Josef II of Liechtenstein. The painting, on poplar wood, measured $15\frac{1}{8}$ inches by $14\frac{1}{2}$ inches and thus possibly realized £9,772 per square inch. Said to portray "sombreness without dejection", it is one of the only nine undisputed Leonardos in existence.

From the unwanted to the uninsurable— the enigmatic *Mona Lisa*

...ion price The highest price ever bid in a public auction for any painting is $2,300,000 (then £821,429) for *Aristotle Contemplating the Bust of Homer,* painted in 1653 by Rembrandt Harmensz (or Harmenszoon) van Rijn (1606–69) of the Netherlands, for a commission of 500 florins from Don Antonio Ruffo of Messina, Italy. The painting was sold by the estate of Mr. and Mrs. Alfred W. Erickson of New York and bought on 15 Nov. 1961 by the Metropolitan Museum of Art, New York, at the Parke-Bernet Galleries, New York City, N.Y., U.S.A. The opening bid received by the auctioneer, Mr. Louis Marion, was $1,000,000. The bidding was concluded in $3\frac{1}{2}$ minutes at the rate of $10,952 per second. At $56\frac{1}{2}$ inches by $53\frac{1}{4}$ inches the cost worked out at just over $764 (then £273) per square inch.

United Kingdom The highest price ever paid at an auction in Europe is 760,000 guineas (£798,000), paid by the Norton Simon Foundation of Los Angeles, California, U.S.A., to Dame Brenda Cook at the salerooms of Christie, Manson & Woods, Ltd., in London, on 19 March 1965, for *A Portrait of the Artist's son Titus* painted by Rembrandt *c.* 1648. The bidding started at 100,000 guineas (£105,000).

...y British artist The highest auction price for any painting by a British artist is £220,000 for *A Cheetah with two Indians* by George Stubbs, R.A. (1724–1806) at Sotheby's on 18 March 1970. It was sold by the Trustees of Sir George Pigot's Will Trust to Thomas Agnew & Sons Ltd. on behalf of an anonymous British client. The painting measures 71×107 inches and was painted *c.* 1765.

Modern painting The highest price paid for a modern painting is $1,550,000 (£645,833) paid by the Norton Simon Foundation of Los Angeles, California, U.S.A. at the Parke-Bernet Galleries, New York City on 9 Oct. 1968 for *Le Pont des Arts* painted by Pierre Auguste Renoir (1841–1919) of France in 1868. Renoir sold the picture to the Paris dealer Durand-Ruel for about £16.

...ng artist The highest price paid for paintings in the lifetime of the artist is $1,950,000 (£812,500) paid for the two

A Cheetah with Two Indians (see above)

canvases *Two Brothers* (1905) and *Seated Harlequin* (1922) by Pablo Diego José Francisco de Paula Juan Nepomuceno Crispín Crispiano de la Santísima Trinidad Ruiz y Picasso (born 25 Oct. 1881) of Spain. This was paid by the Basle City Government to the Staechelin Foundation to enable the Basle Museum of Arts to retain the painting after an offer of $2,560,000 (£1,066,666) had been received from the United States in December 1967. The highest price for a single work at auction for a living artist is the £190,000 paid by the New York dealer David Mann for the blue period Picasso *Mère et enfant de profil* at Sotheby's London, on 26 April 1967. It had been painted in Barcelona, Spain in 1902 and had been first sold to settle a doctor's bill. Picasso's life-time output, a 20,000-piece *oeuvre,* was valued at £100 million in 1966 but a more detailed survey now shows that this valuation could be safely doubled. It has been reported that the limited edition of 50 sets of his "347 Gravures" executed in his studio in Mougins, France between 16 March and 5 Oct. 1968 realized $10 million (£4,166,000) on pre-subscription.

Drawing The highest price ever attached to any drawing is £800,000 for the cartoon *The Virgin and Child with St. John the Baptist and St. Anne,* measuring $54\frac{1}{4}$ inches by $39\frac{1}{4}$ inches, drawn in Milan, probably in 1499–1500, by Leonardo da Vinci (1452–1519) of Italy. On 31 July 1962 the United Kingdom Government announced that it would add £350,000 to the money collected by public subscription (£404,361 by Oct. 1962) and the £50,000 grant from the National Art-Collections Fund to ensure that the work would remain as a national treasure under the trusteeship of the National Gallery, London. Three United States bids of over $4,000,000 (then £1,428,570) were reputed to have been made for the cartoon.

Most prolific painter Antoine Joseph Wiertz (1806–1865) of Belgium painted 131 canvases 50 feet wide and 30 feet high, totalling over 4·5 acres. This is believed to be the greatest area covered by any painter of note.

Largest gallery The world's largest art gallery is the Winter Palace and the neighbouring Hermitage in Leningrad, U.S.S.R. One has to walk 15 miles to visit each of the 322 galleries, which house nearly 3,000,000 works of art and archaeological remains.

Youngest exhibitor at R.A. The youngest ever exhibitor at the Royal Academy of Arts Annual Summer Exhibitions is Lewis Melville ("Gino") Lyons (born 30 April 1962) at their 199th exhibition in 1967 when aged just over 5 years. His picture "Trees and Monkeys" was hung in Gallery IX having been accepted on 7 May 1967. The previous record had been set by Sir Edwin H. Landseer (1802–73) at the age of 13 in 1815.

Upside down duration record The longest period of time for which a modern painting has hung upside down in a public gallery unnoticed is 47 days. This occurred to *Le Bateau,* by Henri Émile Benoît Matisse (1869–1954) of France, in the Museum of Modern Art, New York, between 18 Oct. and 4 Dec. 1961. In this time 116,000 people had passed through the gallery.

MURALS

Earliest The earliest known murals on man-made walls are those at Çatal Hüyük in southern Anatolia, Turkey, dating from *c.* 5850 B.C.

Largest The world's largest mural is *The March of Humanity,* a mural of 54 panels, covering 48,000 square feet, by David Alfaro Siqueiros, which was unveiled in 1968 in the Olimpico Hotel, Mexico City, Mexico. A rainbow mural stretching nearly 300 feet up the sides of the Hilton Rainbow Hotel, Waikiki, Honolulu was completed in 1968.

Largest mobile The largest mobile in the world is one measuring 45 feet by 17 feet and weighing 600 lb., suspended in December 1957 in the main terminal building of the John F. Kennedy International Airport (formerly Idlewild), Long Island, New York State, U.S.A. It was created by Alexander Calder (born 1898), who invented this art form in 1930 as a reaction to sculptures or "stabiles". The heaviest of all mobiles is *Spirale,* weighing 4,000 lb., outside the U.N.E.S.C.O. headquarters in Paris, France. The word "mobile" was coined by Marcel Duchamp in 1932.

Largest mosaic The world's largest mosaic is on the walls of the central library of the Universidad Nacional Autónomao de México, Mexico City. There are four walls, the two largest measuring 12,949 square feet each represent the pre-Hispanic past.

The R.A.'s youngest exhibitor

HIGHEST-PRICED PAINTINGS—PROGRESSIVE RECORDS

Price	Painter, title, sold by and sold to	Dat
£6,500	Correggio's *The Magdalen Reading* (in fact spurious) to Elector Friedrich Augustus II of Saxony.	174
£8,500	Raphael's *The Sistine Madonna* to Elector Friedrich Augustus II of Saxony.	175
£16,000	Van Eyck's *Adoration of the Lamb,* 6 outer panels of Ghent altarpiece by Edward Solby to the Government of Prussia.	182
£24,600*	Murillo's *The Immaculate Conception* by estate of Marshall Soult to the Louvre (against Czar Nicholas I) in Paris.	185
£70,000	Raphael's *Ansidei Madonna* by the 8th Duke of Marlborough to the National Gallery.	188
£100,000	Raphael's *The Colonna Altarpiece* by Sedelmeyer to J. Pierpoint Morgan.	190
£102,880	Van Dyck's *Elena Grimaldi-Cattaneo* (portrait) by Knoedler to Peter Widener (1834–1915).	190
£102,880	Rembrandt's *The Mill* by 6th Marquess of Lansdowne to Peter Widener.	191
£116,500	Raphael's smaller *Panshanger Madonna* by Joseph (later Baron) Duveen (1869–1939) to Peter Widener.	191
£310,400	Leonardo da Vinci's *Benois Madonna* to Czar Nicholas II in Paris.	191
c. £400,000	Vermeer's *Girl's Head* by Prince d'Arenburg to Charles B. Wrightsman (U.S.).	195
£821,429*	Rembrandt's *Aristotle Contemplating the Bust of Homer* by estate of Mr. and Mrs. Alfred Erickson to New York Metropolitan Museum of Art.	196
£1,785,714	Leonardo da Vinci's *Ginevra de' Benci* (portrait) by Prince Franz Josef II of Liechtenstein to National Gallery of Art, Washington, D.C., U.S.A.	196

* Indicates price at auction, otherwise prices were by private treaty.

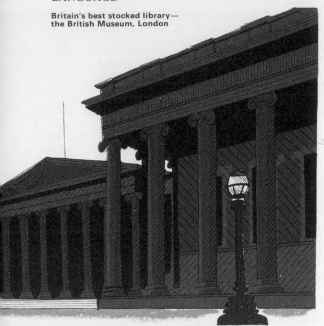

Britain's best stocked library—
the British Museum, London

MUSEUMS

Oldest The oldest museum in the world is the Ashmolean Museum in Oxford, built in 1679.

Largest The largest museum in the world is the American Museum of Natural History on 77th to 81st Streets and Central Park West, New York City, N.Y., U.S.A. Founded in 1874, it comprises 19 interconnected buildings with 23 acres of floor space. The largest museum in the United Kingdom is the British Museum (founded in 1753), which was opened to the public in 1759. The main building in Bloomsbury, London, was built in 1823 and has a total floor area of 17·57 acres.

2. Language

Earliest Anthropologists believe that Handy Man (*Homo habilis*), the earliest known man whose skull survives (see Chapter 1), possessed the physiological capability for speech. The oldest known formally written language is Sumerian, dating from *c*. 3300 B.C. though in July 1967 clay tablets of the Danubian culture discovered 8 months earlier at Tataria, Moros River, Romania were dated to the fourth millennium B.C. The tablets bear symbols of bows and arrows, gates and combs.

Oldest words in English Recent research indicates that several river names in Britain date from pre-Celtic times (*ante* 550 B.C.). These include Ayr, Hayle and Nairn. This ascendant, Indo-Germanic tongue, which was spoken from *c*. 3000 B.C. on the Great Lowland Plain of Europe, now has only fragments left in Old Lithuanian, from which the modern English word *eland* derives. Part of the language brought by the Celts of *c*. 550 B.C. six centuries before the Roman occupation survives in probably not more than 20 words in modern English. Examples include bin, brock, coomb, crag, down/dune, dun, and tor. Of even more extreme antiquity is the word *land* which is traceable to the Old Celtic *landa*, a heath and therefore must have been in use on the continent before the Roman Empire grew powerful in the 6th century B.C.

English became the language of court proceedings in October 1362 and the language for teaching in universities in *c*. 1380. Henry IV (1399–1413) was the first post-Conquest monarch whose mother-tongue was English. The earliest surviving document in English is the proclamation by Henry III, known as the Oxford Provision dated 1258.

Commonest language The language spoken by more people than any other is Northern Chinese, or Mandarin, by an estimated 580,000,000 people at mid-1969. The so-called national language (*guoyu*) is a standardized form of Northern Chinese as spoken in the Peking area. This was alphabetized into *zhuyin zimu* of 39 letters in 1918. In 1958 the *pinyin* system, using a Latin alphabet, was introduced. The next most commonly spoken language and the most widespread is English, by an estimated 320,000,000 in mid-1969. English is spoken by 10 per cent. or more of the population in 29 sovereign countries. Today's world total of languages and dialects still spoken is about 5,000 of which some 845 come from India.

In Great Britain and Ireland there are six indigenous tongues: English, Scots Gaelic, Welsh, Irish Gaelic (Erse), Manx and Romany (Gipsy). Of these English is, of course, predominant, while Manx has almost followed Cornish (last spoken in 1777) into extinction. By 1970 there remained only Mr. Edward (Ned) Maddrell (born in August 1877) of Glen Chass, Port St. Mary, Isle of Man, whose first language, in which he would converse if he had the choice, is Manx. In the Channel Islands, apart from Jersey and Guernsey *patois*, there survive words of Sarkese, in which a prayer book was published in 1812. A movement exists to revive the use of Cornish.

Most complex The following extremes of complexity have been noted: Chippewa, the North American Indian language of Minnesota, U.S.A., has the most verb forms with up to 6,000; Tillamook, the North American Indian language of Oregon, U.S.A., has the most prefixes with 30; Tabassaran, a language in Daghestan, U.S.S.R., uses the most noun cases with 35, while Eskimaux uses 63 forms of the present tense and simple nouns have as many as 252 inflections. In Chinese the K'ang-hsi Dictionary shows 40,000 different characters. The fourth tone of "i" has 84 meanings, varying as widely as "dress", "hiccough" and "licentious". The written language provides 92 different characters for "i⁴".

Rarest and commonest sounds The rarest speech sound is probably the sound written Of even more extreme antiquity is the word *land* which *r* in Czech, which occurs in no other language and is the is the sound is the vowel *a* (as in English father); no language (even Wishram) is known to be without it.

Most and least regular verbs Esperanto was devised in 1887 without irregular verbs. Swahili has a strict 6-class pattern of verbs and no verbs which are irregular to this pattern. According to the more daunting grammars published in West Germany, English has 194 irregular verbs.

Vocabulary The English language contains about 490,000 words plus another 300,000 technical terms, the most in any language, but it is doubtful if any individual uses more than 60,000. "Basic English", devised in 1930 by Charles K. Ogden, consists of 850 words. Written English contains about 10,000 words, while spoken English among the better educated has about 5,000 words.

ALPHABET

Oldest The development of the use of an alphabet in place of pictograms occurred in the Sinaitic world between 2000 and 1700 B.C. This northern Semitic language developed the consonantal system based on phonetic and syllabic principles. Its "O" has remained unchanged and is thereby the oldest of all letters in the 65 alphabets now in use.

Longest and shortest The language with most letters is Cambodian with 74, and Hawaiian has least with 12 (just A, E, H, I, K, L, M, N, O, P, U, W). Amharic has 231 formations from 33 basic syllabic forms, each of which has seven modifications, so this Ethiopian language cannot be described as alphabetic.

Most and least consonants and vowels

The language with most consonants is the Caucasian mountain language Ubyx, with 80 and that with least is Mohawk, an Amerindian language of the Iroquoian family, with only 7 distinct consonantal speech sounds. The language with the most vowels is Sedang, a central Vietnamese language with 55 distinguishable vowel sounds and that with the least is Wishram, the north-western American Indian tongue of the Chinookian family with the single pure vowel *a*.

Largest letter

The largest permanent letter in the world is the giant "W" on the north side of Mount Tenderfoot, behind Western State College in Gunnison, Colorado, U.S.A. The "W" was made with flat stones on 2 May 1923, when it measured 400 feet high and 300 feet wide, with "legs" 16 feet wide. In *c.* 1932 the size of the "W" was increased to 420 feet high and 320 feet wide, making a total area of 25,560 square feet of rock. In sky-writing (normally at *c.* 8,000 feet) a seven letter word may stretch for six miles in length and can be read from 50 miles. The world's earliest example was over Epsom racecourse Surrey on 30 May 1922 when Cyril Turner "spelt out" "London Daily Mail" from an S.E.5A biplane.

Greatest linguist

The most accomplished linguist ever known was Cardinal Giuseppe Caspar Mezzofanti (born 17 Sept. 1774 at Bologna, died 1849), the former chief keeper of the Vatican library in Rome, Italy. He could translate 114 languages and 72 dialects, and spoke 39 languages fluently, 11 others passably and understood 20 others along with 37 dialects. The greatest living linguist is probably Georges Schmidt (b. Strasbourg, France in 1915) of the United Nations Translation Department in New York City, U.S.A. who can speak fluently in 30 languages and can translate 66.

Aristophanes—perpetrator of the 182-letter Greek fricassée (see right)

Longest chemical name

The longest chemical term is that describing trypto-phan synthetase A protein, which has the formula $C_{1289}H_{2051}N_{343}O_{375}S_8$ and the 1,913 letter name: Methionylglutaminylarginyltyrosylglutamylserylleucylphenylalanylalanylglutaminylleucyllysylglutamylarginyllysyglutamylglycylalanylphenylalanylvalylprolylphenylalanylvalylthreonylleucylglycylaspartylprolylglycylisoleucylglutamylglutaminylserylleucyllysylisoleucylaspartylthreonylleucylisoleucylglutamylalanylglycylalanylaspartylalanylleucylglutamylleucylglycylisoleucylprolylphenylalanylserylaspartylprolylleucylalanylaspartylglycylprolylthreonylisoleucylglutaminylasparaginylalanylthreonylleucylarginylalanylphenylalanylalanylalanylglycylvalylthreonylprolylalanylglutaminylcysteinylphenylalanylglutamylmethionylleucylalanylleucylisoleucylarginylglutaminyllysylhistidylprolylthreonylisoleucylprolylisoleucylglycylleucylleucylmethionyltyrosylalanylasparaginylleucylvalylphenylalanylasparaginyllysylglycylisoleucylaspartylglutamylphenylalanyltyrosylalanylglutaminylcysteinylglutamyllysylvalylglycylvalylaspartylserylvalylleucylvalylalanylaspartylvalylprolylvalylglutaminylglutamylserylalanylprolylphenylalanylarginylglutaminylalanylalanylleucylarginylhistidylasparaginylvalylalanylprolylisoleucylphenylalanylisoleucylcysteinylprolylprolylaspartylalanylaspartylaspartylaspartylleucylleucylarginylglutaminylisoleucylalanylseryltyrosylglycylarginylglycyltyrosylthreonyltyrosylleucylleucylserylarginylalanylglycylvalylthreonylglycylalanylglutamylasparaginylarginylalanylalanylleucylprolylleucylasparaginylhistidylleucylvalylalanyllysylleucyllysylglutamyltyrosylasparaginylalanylalanylprolylprolylleucylglutaminylglycylphenylalanylglycylisoleucylserylalanylprolylaspartylglutaminylvalyllysylalanylalanylisoleucylaspartylalanylglycylalanylalanylglycylalanylisoleucylserylglycylserylalanylisoleucylvalyllysylisoleucylisoleucylglutamylglutaminylhistidylasparaginylisoleucylglutamylprolylglutamyllysylmethionylleucylalanylalanylleucyllysylvalylphenylalanylvalylglutaminylprolylmethionyllysylalanylalanylthreonylarginylserine.

Longest words World

The longest word ever to appear in literature occurs in *The Ecclesiazusae,* a comedy by Aristophanes (448–380 B.C.). In the Greek it is 170 letters long but trans-literates into 182 letters in English, thus: lopadotemachoselachogaleokranioleipsanodrimhypotrimmatosilphioparaomelitokatakechyménokichlepikossyphophattoperisteralektryonoptekephalliokigklopeleiolagoiosiraiobaphetraganopterygon. The term describes a fricassee of 17 sweet and sour ingredients.

The longest word in modern use is probably spårvagnsaktiebolagsskensmutsskjutarefackföreningspersonalbeklädnadsmagasinsförrådsförvaltaren, a Swedish word of 94 letters meaning "the manager of the depot for the supply of uniforms to the personnel of the track cleaners' union of the street railway company".

LONGEST WORDS IN VARIOUS LANGUAGES

Serbo-Croatian	Prestolonaslednikovica (22 letters) —wife of an heir apparent.
French	Anticonstitutionellement (24 letters) —anticonstitutionally.
Italian	Precipitevolissimevolmente (26 letters) —as fast as possible.
Russian	Dyerevopererabotyvayoshchiy (27 letters) —timber processing.
Japanese	Ryāgū-no-otohime-no-motoyui-no-kirihanshi (35 letters) —a seaweed, literally of small pieces of the paper hair streamers of the underwater princess.
Dutch	Ryksluchtvaartdienstweerschepenpersoneel (40 letters) —Government aviation department weather ship personnel.
Hungarian	Kikáposztásitottalanitottatokengedelmeskedhetetlensegeskeideseitkert (69 letters) —because of your continued disobedience.

English The longest word in the Oxford English Dictionary is floccipaucinihilipilification (alternatively spelt in hyphenated form with "n" in seventh place), with 29 letters, meaning "the action of estimating as worthless", first used in 1741, and later by Sir Walter Scott (1771–1832). Webster's Third International Dictionary lists among its 450,000 entries pneumononoultramicroscopicsilicovolcanoconiosis (47 letters), the name of a miners' lung disease. It is understood that the inclusion of this entry is largely prompted by the convenience of being able to quote it in reply to unending inquiries as to the longest word in the American version of the English language.

The longest word in an English classic is the nonce word honorificabilitudinitatibus (27 letters), occurring in Act V, scene I of *Love's Labour's Lost* by William Shakespeare (1564–1616), but used with the ending "-tatatibus", making 29 letters, in *The Water Poet* by John Taylor (1580–1653).

In this category may also be placed the 52-letter word used by Dr. Edward Strother (1675–1737) to describe the spa waters at Bristol—aequeosalinocalcalinoceraceoaluminosocupreovitriolic. In his novel *Headlong Hall,* Thomas Love Peacock (1785–1866) described the human physique as "osseocarnisanguineoviscericartilaginonervomedullary"—51 letters.

The longest regularly formed English words are antiinterdenominationalistically (32 letters); antidisestablishmentarianismically (34 letters), used by Mark McShane in his novel *Untimely Ripped,* published in 1963; and praetertranssubstantiationalistically (37 letters). The longest in common use is disproportionableness (21 letters).

Longest palindromic words The longest known palindromic word is *saippuakauppias* (15 letters), the Finnish word for soap-seller. The longest in the English language are *evitative* and *redivider* (each nine letters), while another nine-letter word, *Malayalam,* is a proper noun given to the language of the Malayali people in Kerala, southern India. The nine letter word Rotavator is becoming accepted more widely than a brand name for a horticultural cultivating machine. The contrived chemical term *detartrated* has 11 letters, as does *kinnikinnik* (sometimes written *kinnik-kinnik,* a 12-letter palindrome), the word for the dried leaf and bark mixture which was smoked by the Cree Indians of North America. Some baptismal fonts in Greece and Turkey bear the circular 25 letter inscription ΝΙΨΟΝ ΑΝΟΜΗΜΑΤΑ ΜΗΜΟΝΑΝΟΨΙΝ meaning "wash (my) sins not only (my) face". This appears also at St. Mary's Church, Nottingham. The longest palindromic sentence devised is one of 242 words by Howard Bergeson of Oregon, U.S.A. It begins "Deliver no evil, avid diva . . . and hence predictably ends . . . avid diva, live on reviled."

Most frequently used letters In English the most frequently used letters are in order: e, t, a, i, s, o, n, h, r, d and u. The most frequent initial letters are s, e, p, a, t, b, m, d, r, f and h.

Commonest words In written English the most frequently used words are in order: the, of, and, to, a, in, that, is, I, it, for and as. The most used in conversation is I.

Most accents The French word with most accents is *hétérogénéité,* meaning heterogeneity. An atoll in the Pacific Ocean 320 miles E.S.E. of Tahiti is named Héréhérétué.

Most tongue twisters The most difficult tongue twister in the only anthology of its type *Anthology of British Tongue-Twisters* by Ken Parkin of Teesside, is deemed by the author to be "The sixth sick sheik's sixth sheep's sick"—especially when spoken quickly.

Perhaps the most difficult in the world is the Xhosa (from Natal, South Africa) for "The skunk rolled down and ruptured its larynx" Iqaqa laziqikaqika kwaze kwaqhawaka uqhoqhoqha. The last word contains three "clicks". A European rival is the vowelless *Strch prst skrz krk,* the Czech for "stick a finger in the throat".

Longest abbreviation The longest known abbreviation is S.O.M.K.H.P.B.K.J.C.S.S.D.P.M.W.D.T.B., the initials of the Sharikat Orang-Orang Melayu Kerajaani Hilir Perak Berkerjasama-Serkerjasama Kerama Jimat Chermat Serta Simpanan Dan Pinjam Meminjam Wang Dengan Tanggonan Berhad. This is the Malay name for the Lower Perak Malay Government Servants' Co-operative Thrift and Loan Society Limited, in Telok Anson, Perak State, West Malaysia (formerly Malaya). The abbreviation for this abbreviation is not recorded.

Longest anagrams The longest regular English words which can form anagrams are the 16-letter pair "interlaminations" and "internationalism". The Shakespearean nonce word Honorificabilitudinitatibus (27 letters) yields "Hi ludi, F. Baconis noti, tui ti orbi", which is quoted as an additional proof by some that Bacon wrote Shakespeare.

Shortest holo-alphabetic sentence The shortest English sentence containing all the 26 letters of the alphabet is "Jackdaws love my big sphinx of quartz" with 31 letters.

Longest sentence The longest sentence in classical western literature is one in *Les Misérables* by Victor Marie Hugo (1802–85) which runs to 823 words punctuated by 93 commas, 51 semi-colons and 4 dashes. A sentence of 958 words appears in "Cities of the Plain" by the French author, Marcel Proust (1871–1922), while some authors such as James Joyce (1882–1941) appear to eschew punctuation altogether. The first 40,000 words of *The Gates of Paradise* by George Andrzeyevski (Panther) appear to lack any punctuation.

PLACE-NAMES

Longest World The official name for Bangkok, the capital city of Thailand, consists of the Thai words Krungt'ep ("city of the divine messenger"), plus a long list of Pali titles, as proclaimed at the city's foundation in 1782. A *shortened version* of this name is Krungtepmahanakornbowornratanakosinmahintarayudhayamahadilokpopnoparatanarajthaniburiromudomrajniwesmahasatarnamornpimarnavatarsatitsakatattiyavisanukamprasit (158 letters). The longest place-name now in use in the world is Taumatawhakatangihangakoauauotamatea (turipukakapikimaungahoronuku)pokaiwhenuakitanatahu, the unofficial 85-letter version of the name of a hill (1,002 feet above sea-level) in the Southern Hawke's Bay district of North Island, New Zealand. This Maori name means "the place where Tamatea, the man with the big knee who slid, climbed and swallowed mountains, known as Land-eater, played on his flute to his loved one". The official version has 57 letters (1 to 36 and 65 to 85).

Wales The longest place-name in the United Kingdom is the concocted 58-letter name Llanfairpwllgwyngyllgogerychwyrndrobwllllantysiliogogogoch, which is translated: "St. Mary's Church in a hollow by the white hazel, close to the rapid whirlpool, by the red cave of St. Tysilio". This is the name given to a village in Anglesey, Wales, but the official name consists of only the first 20 letters. The longest genuine Welsh place-name listed in the Ordnance Survey Gazetteer is Lower Llanfihangel-y-Creuddyn (26 letters), a village near Aberystwyth, Cardiganshire.

England The longest single word (unhyphenated) place-name in England is Blakehopeburnhaugh in Northumberland of 18 letters. The hyphenated Sutton-under-Whitestonecliffe, Yorkshire has 27 letters. The longest multiple name is North Leverton with Habbelsthorpe (30 letters), Nottinghamshire, while the longest parish name is Saint Andrew, Holborn above the Bars, with Saint George the Martyr (54 letters), in London.

The arts and entertainments

Scotland The longest single word place-names in Scotland are Claddochknockline, with a population of 18 in 1961, on the island of North Uist, in the Outer Hebrides and the nearby Claddochbaleshare both with 17 letters. The statutory name for Kirkcudbrightshire (18 letters) is however County of Kirkcudbright. The highest point on the Inner Hebridean island of Carna is Cruachan Chàrna Dailachreagain (28 letters).

Ireland The longest place-name in Ireland is Muckanaghederdauhaulia (22 letters), 4 miles from Costello in Carris Bay, County Galway. The name means "soft place between two seas".

Shortest The shortest place-names in the world are the French village of Y (population 143), so named since 1241, in the Somme, and the Norwegian village of Å (pronounced "Aw"). The shortest place-names in Great Britain are the two-lettered villages of Ae (population 199 in 1961) in Dumfriesshire, Oa on the island of Islay off western Scotland. In the Shetland Islands there are skerries called Ve and two stacks called Aa. The island of Iona was originally I. The River E flows into the southern end of Loch Mhór, Inverness-shire, Scotland. The shortest place-name in Ireland is Ta (or Lady's Island) Lough, a sea-inlet off the coast of County Wexford. Tievelough, in County Donegal, is also called Ea. In the United States there are seven two-lettered place-names, including both Ed and Uz in the state of Kentucky.

Earliest The earliest recorded British place-name is Belerion, the Penwith peninsula of Cornwall, referred to as such by Pytheas of Massalia in *c.* 308 B.C. The earliest reference to Britain was as *Pretanic* (implying an earlier *Qrtanic*). The oldest name among England's 41 counties is Kent, first mentioned in its Roman form of Cantium (from the Celtic *canto,* meaning a rim, *i.e.* a coastal district) from the same circumnavigation by Pytheas. The youngest is Lancashire, first recorded in the 12th century. The earliest mention of England is the form *Angelcynn,* which appeared in the Anglo-Saxon Chronicle in A.D. 880.

Commonest The commonest place-name in England and Wales is Newtown or New Town, with 129 entries in the 1961 Census Gazetteer, and Newton with 47. The British place-name most widely used overseas is Richmond, Yorkshire, which has given its name, according to a list compiled by Mr. David Ball, to 43 other villages, towns and cities, including examples in 20 of the 50 states of the U.S.A.

PERSONAL NAMES

Earliest The earliest personal name which has survived is uncertain. Some experts believe that it is En-lil-ti, a word which appears on a Sumerian tablet dating from *c.* 3300 B.C., recovered before 1936 from Jamdat Nasr, 40 miles south-east of Baghdad, Iraq. Other antiquarians regard it purely as the name of a deity, Lord of the air, and claim that the names Lahma and Lahamu, Sumer gods of silt, are older still. N'armer, the father of Men (Menes), the first Egyptian pharaoh, dates from about 2900 B.C. The earliest known name of any resident of Britain is Divitiacus, the Gaulish ruler of the Kent area *c.* 75 B.C.

Longest The longest name used by anyone is Adolph Blaine Charles David Earl Frederick Gerald Hubert Irvin John Kenneth Lloyd Martin Nero Oliver Paul Quincy Randolph Sherman Thomas Uncas Victor William Xerxes Yancy Zeus Wolfeschlegelsteinhausenbergerdorff, Senior, who was born at Bergedorf, near Hamburg, Germany, on 29 Feb. 1904. On printed forms, he uses only his eighth and second Christian names and the first 35 letters of his surname. The full version of the name of 590 letters appeared in the 12th Edition of *The Guinness Book of Records.* He now lives in Philadelphia, Pennsylvania, U.S.A., and has recently shortened his surname to Mr. Wolfe+590, Senior.

90

The longest Christian or given name on record is Napuamahalaonaonekawehiwehionakuahiweanenawawakehoonkakehoaalekeeaonanainananiakeao'Hawaiikawao (93 letters) in the case of Miss Dawn N. Lee so named in Honolulu, Hawaii, U.S.A. in February 1967. The name means "The abundant, beautiful blossoms of the mountains and valleys begin to fill the air with their fragrance throughout the length and breadth of Hawaii".

The longest surname in the United Kingdom was the six-barrelled one borne by the late Major L. S. D. O. F. (Leone Sextus Denys Oswolf Fraudati filius) Tollemache-Tollemache de Orellana Plantagenet Tollemache Tollemache, who was born in 1884 and died of pneumonia in France on 20 Feb. 1917. Of non-repetitious surnames, the most barrelled was that of the Most Noble Sir Richard Plantagenet Campbell Temple-Nugent-Brydges-Chandos-Grenville, G.C.S.I., C.I.E. (1823–99), the 3rd Duke of Buckingham and Chandos and the 10th Lord Kinloss. The longest single English surnames are Featherstonehaugh, usually pronounced "Fanshaw" and Bassingthwaighte both of 17 letters. Fetherstonhaugh (pronounced "Freestonhugh") is used recurringly as a Christian name in one English family.

In Scotland the surname Macghillesheathanaich (21 letters) was first recorded in 1506 on the island of Islay, Argyllshire.

Shortest in Britain There exist among the 42,500,000 names on the Ministry of Social Security index four examples of a one-lettered surname. Their identity has not been disclosed, but they are "E", "J", "M" and "X". Two-letter British surnames include By and On.

Commonest The commonest name in the world is Muhammad, which can be spelt in many ways. The commonest given name in Britain has been John since 1340. Before that in the period 1196–1307 William was the commonest. The commonest names of new-born babies announced in the London *Times* in 1967 were James for boys and Sarah for girls.

The commonest surname in the English-speaking world is Smith. There are 671,550 nationally insured Smiths in Great Britain, of whom 7,081 are plain John Smith and another 22,550 are John (plus one or more given names) Smith. Including uninsured persons, there are over 800,000 Smiths in England and Wales alone, of whom 90,000 are called A. Smith. There were an estimated 1,678,815 Smiths in the United States in 1964.

There are, however, estimated to be 1,600,000 persons in Britain with M', Mc or Mac (Gaelic "son of") as part of their surnames. The commonest of these is Macdonald which accounts for about 55,000 of the Scottish population.

Most contrived name The palm for the most determined attempt to be last in the local telephone directory must be awarded to Mr. Zeke Zzzypt of Chicago, Illinois, U.S.A. He outdid the previous occupant who was a mere Mr. Zyzzy Zzyryzxxy.

THE WRITTEN WORD

Smallest handwriting The smallest writing achieved is a density of 85 letters per square millimetre with an engraving tool on metal by Dr. Anto Leikola of Helsinki, Finland.

In 1968 Mr. C. N. Swift of Edgbaston, Birmingham, England, wrote the Lord's Prayer 25 times on a piece of paper half the size of a standard United Kingdom postage stamp, measuring 22 millimetres (0·87 of an inch) by 18 millimetres (0·71 of an inch) with a density of nearly 37 letters per square millimetre.

TEXTS

Oldest The oldest known written text is the pictograph expression of Sumerian speech, dating from *c.* 3500 B.C. In

A press of the type used by William Caxton for Britain's earliest printed work in 1476

1952 some clay tablets of this writing were unearthed from the Uruk IV level of the Sumerian temple of Inanna (c. 3300 B.C.) at Erech (called Uruk in Sumerian), now Warka, Iraq. The earliest known vellum document dates from the 2nd century A.D.; it contains paragraphs 10 to 32 of Demosthenes' *De Falsa Legatione*. Demosthenes died in the 4th century B.C.

Oldest printed The oldest surviving printed work is a Korean scroll or *sutra* from wooden printed blocks found in the foundations of the Pulguk Sa pagoda, Kyongju, Korea, on 14 Oct. 1966. It has been dated no later than A.D. 704.

anically printed It is generally accepted that the earliest mechanically printed book was the 42-line Gutenberg Bible, printed at Mainz, Germany, in c. 1455 by Johann zum Gensfleisch zur Laden, called "zu Gutenberg" (c. 1398–c. 1468). Recent work on water marks published in 1967 indicates a copy of a surviving printed Latin grammar was made from paper made in c. 1450. The earliest exactly dated printed work is the Psalter completed on 14 Aug. 1457 by Johann Fust (c. 1400–1466) and Peter Schöffer (1425–1502), who had been Gutenberg's chief assistant. The earliest printing in Britain was an Indulgence dated 13 Dec. 1476, issued by Abbot Sant of Abingdon, Berkshire, and printed by William Caxton (c. 1422–1491).

Largest The largest book in the world is *The Little Red Elf*, a story in 64 verses by William P. Wood, who designed, constructed and printed the book. It measures 7 feet 2 inches high and 10 feet across when open. The book is at present on show in a cave at the foot of Beinn Ruadh ("The Red Mountain") beside Loch Eck, Argyllshire, Scotland. The largest art book ever produced was one 210 centimetres (82·7 inches) high and 80 centimetres (31·5 inches) wide, first shown in Amsterdam, in the Netherlands, in May 1963. It contained five "pages", three the work of Karel Appel (born 1921), an abstract painter, and two with poems by Hugo Claus. The price was $5,255 (now £2,177).

Largest blication The largest publication in the world is the 263 volume British Museum Catalogue of Printed Books, 1455–1955, at £1,709 10s. per set. *The National Union Catalog of the United States* is in process of publication for the Library of Congress, Washington, D.C., by Mansell Information/Publishing Ltd. of London, in 610 volumes of 704 pages (429,440 pages) for $9,000 (£3,750) per set. The contract was won as a result of the harnessing of the Williamson Abstractor camera which is handling the 12,000,000 cards.

Smallest The smallest book in the world is a handwritten one— *Poems by Edgar Guest*. It was written in 1942 by Burt Randle. It is less than ⅛ of an inch square and is held by a metal clasp. Edgar Albert Guest (1881–1959) was born in Birmingham, England.

The arts and entertainments

An edition of 150 copies of *The Rubá'iyát of Omar Khayyám* by Edward FitzGerald (1809–83) was published in 1956 in Massachusetts, U.S.A., and weighed a total of 0·34 of an ounce. This book is a collection of *ruba'is,* or quatrains, attributed to Ghiyās-ud-din Abū'l-Fath 'Omar ibn Ibrāhīm al-Khayyāmi (died 1123 or 1132), a Persian mathematician, astronomer and poet.

The smallest book printed in moveable type is *Short Works* by Robert G. Oliphant of Victoria B.C., Canada, with 28 pages $\frac{11}{16} \times \frac{3}{8}$ of an inch (area 0·258 of a square inch) and printed in $5\frac{1}{2}$ point type.

Most valuable The most valuable printed books are the three surviving perfect vellum copies of the Gutenberg Bible, printed in Mainz, Germany, in c. 1455 by Gutenberg (see above). The United States Library of Congress copy, bound in three volumes, was obtained in 1930 from Dr. Otto Vollbehr, who paid about $330,000 (now £137,500) for it. The highest priced newly published book was a single jewel-encrusted parchment edition of lithographs entitled *The Apocalypse,* weighing 226 lb., by Salvador Dali (born 11 May 1904) of Spain, published in Paris by Joseph Foret in March 1961 and priced at 1,000,000 francs (then £72, 339).

Highest priced 20th century book The highest price paid for any book printed in this century in a standard binding and not illustrated with original lithographs is $4,000 (£1,667) paid at the Parke-Bernet Galleries in New York City for one of the first 100 copies of the first edition of *Ulysses* by James Joyce, published in Paris in 1922.

Longest novel The longest important novel ever published is *Les hommes de bonne volonté* by Louis Henri Jean Farigoule (born 26 Aug. 1885), *alias* Jules Romains, of France, in 27 volumes in 1932–46. The English version *Men of Good Will* was published in 14 volumes in 1933–46 as a "novel-cycle". The novel *Tokuga-Wa Ieyasu* by Sohachi Yamaoka has been serialized in Japanese daily newspapers since 1951. When completed it will run to 40 volumes.

ENCYCLOPAEDIA

Most comprehensive The most comprehensive present day encyclopaedia is the *Encyclopaedia Britannica,* first published in Edinburgh, Scotland, in December 1768. A group of booksellers in the United States acquired reprint rights in 1898 and complete ownership in 1899. In 1943 the *Britannica* was given to the University of Chicago, Illinois, U.S.A. The current 24-volume edition contains 28,380 pages, 34,696 articles and 2,247 other entries, 36,674,000 words and 22,670 illustrations. It is now edited in Chicago and in London. There are 10,326 contributors.

Largest The largest encyclopaedia ever compiled was the *Great Standard Encyclopaedia* of Yung-lo of 22,937 manuscripts book (370 still survive), written by 2,000 Chinese scholars in 1403–08.

Top-selling The world's top-selling encyclopaedia is *The World Book Encyclopaedia* published by Field Enterprises Educational Corporation of Chicago, Illinois, U.S.A. Since 1961 the annual average sales have exceeded 450,000 sets per annum.

Largest dictionary The largest dictionary ever published is the 12 volume Royal quarto *The Oxford English Dictionary* of 15,487 pages published between 1884 and 1928 with a first supplement of 963 pages in 1933 with a further 2 volume supplement, edited by R. W. Burchfield, due in 1974. The work contains 414,825 words, 1,827,306 illustrative quotations and 227,779,589 letters and figures.

MANUSCRIPTS

Highest price The highest price ever paid for any manuscript is £100,000, paid in December 1933 by the British Museum, London, to the U.S.S.R. Government for the manuscript Bible *Codex Sinaiticus* originally from the Monastery of St. Catherine on Mt. Sinai, Egypt (now the United Arab Republic). It consists of 390 of the original 730 leaves, measuring 16 inches by 28 inches, of the book, dictated in Greek and written by three scribes in about A.D. 350 and rescued from a waste paper basket in May 1844 by Lobegott Friedrich Konstantin von Tischendorf (1815–74), a German traveller and Biblical critic. The highest price at auction is 1,100,000 New Francs (£94,933 incl. tax) paid by H. P. Krauss, the New York dealer, at the salerooms of Rheims et Laurin, Paris on 24 June 1968 for the late 13th-century North Italian illuminated vellum Manuscript of the Apocrypha.

The highest auction price ever paid for any literary manuscript is £90,000 for the long lost illustrated manuscript of Books 1 to 9 of the translation in 15 parts by William Caxton (*c.* 1422–1491) of the *Metamorphoses* ("Transfigurations") by Publius Ovidius Naso (43 B.C.–A.D. 18), the Roman poet known as Ovid. This manuscript belonged to the collection of Sir Thomas Phillipps and was sold to Mr. L. D. Feldman of the House of El Dieff, in New York City, at the salerooms of Sotheby & Co., London, on 27 June 1966. An export licence was refused and it was announced on 5 Jan. 1967 that the manuscript would stay in Britain, as the result of a loan of $200,000 (then £71,000) from Mr. Eugene Power of Ann Arbor, Michigan, and George Braziller (U.S.A.), a publisher. The manuscript was donated to the library of Magdalene College, Cambridge (which possessed the manuscript of Books 10 to 15), in return for facsimile rights on all 15 Books.

The highest price ever paid for the manuscript of a living author is $18,200 (then £6,500), paid in May 1960 by a New York dealer for the handwritten copy of *A Passage to India* (published in 1924) by E. M. (Edward Morgan) Forster (born 1879) of Britain.

Personal papers The highest price paid for personal papers has been $Can.600,000 (£231,213), announced in April 1968, for those of Earl Russell (1872–1970) by McMaster University, Hamilton, Ontario.

BIBLE

Oldest The oldest known Bible is the Yonan manuscript of the complete New Testament, written in Syriac-Aramaic in about A.D. 350 and presented to the United States Library of Congress in Washington, D.C., on 27 March 1955. The longest of the Dead Sea scrolls is the Temple Scroll measuring 28 feet which first became available for study in June 1967. The earliest Bible printed in English was one edited by Miles Coverdale (*c.* 1488–1569), printed in 1535 at Marberg in Hesse, Germany.

Longest and shortest books The longest book in the Bible is the Book of Psalms, while the longest prose book is the Book of the Prophet Isaiah, with 66 chapters. The shortest is the Third Epistle of John, with 294 words in 14 verses. The Second Epistle of John has only 13 verses but 298 words.

Longest Psalm, verse, sentence and name Of the 150 Psalms, the longest is the 119th, with 176 verses, and the shortest is the 117th, with two verses. The shortest verse in the English language version of the Bible is verse 35 of Chapter XI of the Gospel according to St. John, consisting of the two words "Jesus wept". The longest is verse 9 of Chapter VIII of the Book of Esther, which extends to a 90-word description of the Persian empire. The total number of letters in the Bible is 3,566,480. The total number of words depends on the method of counting hyphenated words, but is usually given as between 773,692 and 773,746. The word "and" appears 46,399 times. The longest name in the Bible is Maher-shalal-hash-baz, the symbolic name of the second son of Isaiah (Isaiah, Chapter VIII, verses 1 and 3).

Bible reading A relay of eight theological students from the University of North Wales, Bangor, read aloud the entire Bible, including the Apocrypha, in 90 hours 55 minutes on 14–18 Feb. 1967. At St. Andrew's Church, Cheadle Hulme, Cheshire, the Revised Standard Version, excluding the Apocrypha, was read in 70½ hours on 5–8 Dec. 1968.

MOST PROLIFIC WRITERS

The most prolific writer for whom a word count has been published was Charles Hamilton, *alias* Frank Richard (1875–1961), the Englishman who created Billy Bunter. At his height in 1908 he wrote the whole of the boys' comics *Gem* (founded 1907) and *Magnet* (founded 1908) and most of two others, totalling 80,000 words a week. His lifetime output was at least 72,000,000 words. He enjoyed the advantages of the use of electric light rather than candlelight and of being unmarried.

The Belgian writer Georges Simenon (born Georges Sim in Liège on 13 Feb. 1903), creator of Inspector Maigret, writes a novel of 200 pages in 11 days and in February 1969 completed his 200th under his own name of which 74 were about Inspector Maigret. He has also written 300 other novels under 19 other pen-names. These are published in 31 countries in 43 languages and have sold more than 300,000,000 copies. He hates adverbs and has had his children's playroom soundproofed. Since 1931 the British novelist John Creasey (born 1908) has, under his own name and 13 *aliases*, written 529 books totalling more than 40,000,000 words. The authoress with the greatest total of published books is Miss Ursula Bloom (Mrs. A. C. G. Robinson), with 420 full-length works, starting in 1922 with *The Great Beginning* and including the best sellers *The Ring Tree* (novel) and *The Rose of Norfolk* (non-fiction).

Short stories The highest established count for published short stories is 3,500 in the case of Michael Hervey (born London, 1914) of Henley, New South Wales, Australia. Aided by his wife Lilyan Brilliant, he has also written 60 detective novels and 80 stage and television plays. The most prolific short story writer in Britain is Herbert Harris (born 1911) of Leatherhead, Surrey, with nearly 3,000 published in Britain and in 28 other countries.

Fastest novelist The world's fastest novelist has been Erle Stanley Gardner (1889–1970) of U.S.A., the mystery writer who created Perry Mason. He dictated up to 10,000 words per day and worked with his staff on as many as seven novels simultaneously. His sales on 140 titles reached 170 million by his death. The British novelist John Creasey (see above) has an output of 15 to 20 novels per annum, with a record of 22. He once wrote two books in a week with a half-day off.

Highest paid writer The highest rate ever offered to a writer was $30,000 (now £12,500) to Ernest Miller Hemingway (1899–1961) for a 2,000-word article on bullfighting by *Sports Illustrated* in January 1960. This was a rate of $15 (£6 5s.) per word. In 1958 a Mrs. Deborah Schneider of Minneapolis, Minnesota, U.S.A., wrote 25 words to complete a sentence in a competition for the best blurb for Plymouth cars. She won from about 1,400,000 entrants the prize of $500 (£208) every month for life. On normal life expectations she will collect $12,000 (£5,000) per word. No known anthology includes Mrs. Schneider's deathless prose.

Top selling author It was announced on 13 March 1953 that 672,058,000 copies of the works of Marshal Iosif Vissarionovich Dzhugashvili, *alias* Stalin (1879–1953), had been sold or distributed in 101 languages.

Among writers of fiction, sales alone of over 300,000,000 have been claimed for Georges Simenon (see above) and for the British authoress Agatha Christie (born Agatha Mary Clarissa Miller), now Lady Mallowan (formerly Mrs. Archibald Christie). Her paperback sales in the United Kingdom alone are 1½ million per annum.

Youngest The youngest recorded commercially-published author is Janet Aitchison who wrote *The Pirate's Tale* when aged 5½ years. It was published as a Puffin Book by Penguin in April 1969 when she was 6½.

POETS LAUREATE

Earliest The earliest official Poet Laureate was John Dryden (1631–1700), appointed in April 1668. It is recorded that Henry I (1100–1135) had a King's versifier named Wale.

John Dryden

Youngest and oldest The youngest Poet Laureate was Laurence Eusden (1688–1730), who received the bays on 24 Dec. 1718, at the age of 30 years and 3 months. The greatest age at which a poet has succeeded is 73 in the case of William Wordsworth (1770–1850) on 6 April 1843. The longest lived Laureate was John Masefield, O.M., who died on 12 May 1967, aged 88 years 11 months. The longest which any poet has worn the laurel is 41 years 322 days, in the case of Alfred (later the 1st Lord) Tennyson (1809–92), who was appointed on 19 Nov. 1850 and died in office on 6 Oct. 1892.

Longest poem The longest poem ever written was the *Mahabharata* which appeared in India in the period *c.* 400 to 150 B.C. It runs to 220,000 lines and nearly 3,000,000 words.

The longest poem ever written in the English language is *Poly-Olbion* or *A Chorographicall Description of Tracts, Rivers, Mountains, Forests, etc.*, written in Alexandrines in 30 books, comprising nearly 100,000 lines, by Michael Drayton (1563–1631) between 1613 and 1622.

Shortest poem The shortest poem published is that of the contemporary concretist poet Aram Saroyan entitled *Blod*. It consists of a single sound written *Blod*.

BEST SELLERS

World The world's best seller is the Bible, portions of which have been translated into 1,280 languages. It has been estimated that between 1800 and 1950 some 1,500,000,000 were printed of which 1,100,000,000 were handled by Bible Societies. The total production of Bibles or parts of the Bible in the United States in the year 1963 alone was reputed to be 50,000,000.

It has been reported that 330,000,000 copies of the red-covered booklet *Quotations from the Works of Mao Ze dong* were sold or distributed between June 1966, when possession became virtually mandatory in China, and March 1967. The name of Mao Tse-tung (born 26 Dec. 1893) means literally "Hair Enrich-East".

Non-fiction The next best selling non-fiction book is *The Common Sense Book of Baby and Child Care* by Dr. Benjamin McLane Spock (born 2 May 1903) of New Haven, Connecticut, U.S.A. It was first published in New York in May 1946 and the total sales were 19,076,822 by December 1965 and probably over 22,000,000 by January 1969. Of perennials, the one with the highest aggregate sale is probably *Le Nouveau Petit Larousse Illustré*, which has sold nearly 20,000,000 copies since 1906. This total has also been attributed to *Baking is Fun*, by Dr. August Otker of Germany, first published in 1890. The top-selling H.M. Stationery Office publication has been The Highway Code with 70,000,000 copies.

The best seller among Government reports has been "The Beveridge Report" (1942) which has sold 280,000 copies.

Fiction The novel with the highest sales has been *Peyton Place* (first published in 1956) by Mrs. Grace de Repentigny Metalious (1924–64) of the United States, with a total of 9,915,785 copies by 31 Dec. 1965. Six million were sold in the first six weeks. In the United Kingdom the highest print order has been 3,000,000 by Penguin Books Ltd. for their paperback edition of *Lady Chatterley's Lover*, by D. H. (David Herbert) Lawrence (1885–1930). The total sales to January 1968 were 3,600,000 copies.

Post-card The top-selling post-card of all time is reputed to be a drawing by Donald Fraser McGill (1875–1962) with the caption: He: "How do you like Kipling?" She: "I don't know, you naughty boy, I've never Kippled". It sold about 6,000,000. Between 1904 and his death McGill sold more than 350,000,000 cards to users and deltiologists (picture post-card collectors).

LARGEST PUBLISHERS

A U.N.E.S.C.O. survey has shown that 22 per cent. of the world's books are in the English language, followed by 17 per cent. in Russian. The most active publishing country in the world is the U.S.S.R., where 1,252,000,000 copies of books *and pamphlets,* comprising 78,204 titles, including more than 30,000 for free distribution, were produced in 1964. The 1967 total of titles was 74,081. Total production of more than 1,500 million copies has been planned for 1970.

The U.K. published a record 31,420 book titles in 1968, of which 22,642 were new titles.

The world's perennial best seller

93

The arts and entertainments

The largest publisher in the world is the United States Government Printing Office in Washington, D.C., U.S.A. The Superintendents of Documents Division dispatches more than 150,000,000 items every year. The annual list of new titles and annuals is about 6,000.

Fastest publishing The shortest interval between the receipt of a manuscript and the publication of a book is 66½ hours, in the case of *The Pope's Journey to the United States—the Historic Record,* a paperback of 160 pages, costing 75 cents (6s. 3d.), written by 51 editors of the strike-bound *New York Times* and published by Bantam Books Inc. of Madison Avenue, New York City, N.Y., U.S.A. It was printed by the W. F. Hall Printing Co. of Chicago, Illinois, U.S.A. The first article reached the publishers at 1.30 p.m. on 4 Oct. 1965 and completed copies came off the printers' presses at 8.00 a.m. on 7 Oct. 1965.

LARGEST PRINTERS

The largest printers in the world are R. R. Donnelly & Co. of Chicago, Illinois, U.S.A. The company founded in 1864, has plants in seven main centres, turning out $200,000,000 (£83,300,000) worth of work per year from 180 presses, 125 composing machines and more than 50 binding lines. Nearly 18,000 tons of inks and 450,000 tons of paper and board are consumed every year.

The largest printing job in the United Kingdom is the annual production by H.M. Stationery Office Press at Harrow, Greater London, of about 13,000,000 telephone directories. The task involves 200 employees, 9,000 tons of paper, and the setting, revising, printing and binding of 20,000 pages at a cost of about £1,000,000.

The print order for the 45th Automobile Association Handbook (1968–69) was 4,600,000 copies. The total print since 1908 has been 48,380,000. It is currently printed by web offset by Petty & Sons of Leeds.

Largest cartoon The largest cartoon ever published was one covering two floors (35 feet by 30 feet) on a building opposite the United Nations Headquarters in New York City, N.Y., U.S.A., depicting the enslavement by the U.S.S.R. of eight Eastern European nations.

Longest lived strip The most durable newspaper comic strip has been the Katzenjammer Kids (Hans and Fritz) first published in the United States in 1897 and currently drawn by Joe Musial. The most read is believed to be "Peanuts" by Charles M. Schultz (born 1922) which since 1950 has grown to be syndicated to 1,000 U.S. newspapers with a total readership of 90,000,000.

LETTERS

Longest Physically the longest letter ever written was one of 3,696 feet 10 inches in length. It was written on an adding machine roll by Miss Terry Finch of Southsea, Hampshire to her boyfriend Sergeant Jerry Sullivan of Texas U.S.A. and posted on 11 June 1969.

To an editor The longest recorded letter to an editor was one of 13,000 words (a third of a modern novel) written to the editor of the *Fishing Gazette* by A.R.I.E.L. and published in 7-point type spread over two issues in 1884.

Shortest The shortest correspondence on record was that between Victor Marie Hugo (1802–85) and his publisher Hurst and Blackett in 1862. The author was on holiday and anxious to know how his new novel *Les Misérables* was selling. He wrote "?". The reply was "!".

AUTOGRAPHS

Earliest Not counting attested crosses in a few charters of the early Norman kings ostensibly affixed by their own hands, the earliest English sovereign whose handwriting is known to have survived is Henry III (1207–72). The earliest signature to have survived is that of Richard II (dated 26 July 1386). The Magna Carta does not bear even the mark of King John (reigned 1199–1216), but carries his seal. In 1932 an attested cross of William I (reigned 1066–87) was sold in London.

Most expensive The highest price ever paid on the open market for a single letter is $51,000 (now £18,214), paid in 1927 for a letter written by the Gloucestershire-born Button Gwinnett (1732–77), one of the three men from Georgia to sign the United States' Declaration of Independence on 4 July 1776. Such an item would probably attract bids of up to $250,000 (£104,163) today.

The highest price ever paid for a letter written by a living person is $3,000 (£1,071) for a four-page letter signed by Mrs. Jacqueline Lee Kennedy (*née* Bouvier), paid in New York City, N.Y., U.S.A., in May 1964.

CROSSWORDS

First The earliest crossword was one with 32 clues invented by Arthur Wynne (born Liverpool, England, died 1945) and published in the *New York World* on 21 Dec. 1913. The first crossword published in a British newspaper was one furnished by C. W. Shepherd in the *Sunday Express* of 2 Nov. 1924.

Largest The largest crossword ever published is one with 3,185 clues across and 3,149 clues down, compiled by Robert M. Stilgenbauer of Los Angeles in 7½ years of spare time between 15 May 1938 and publication in 1949.

Henry III (left) and Richard II (right) (see autographs above)

90

Despite the 125,000 copies distributed not one copy has been returned worked out or even partially worked out.

Slowest In May 1966 *The Times* of London received an announcement from a Fijian woman that she had just succeeded in completing their crossword No. 673 in the issue of 4 April 1932.

dest map The oldest known map is the Turin Papyrus, showing the layout of an Egyptian gold mine, dated about 1320 B.C.

LIBRARIES

Largest The largest library in the world is the United States
World Library of Congress (founded on 24 April 1800), on Capitol Hill, Washington, D.C. On 30 June 1969 it contained more than 59,000,000 items, including 14,846,000 books and pamphlets. The two buildings cover six acres and contain 327 miles of book shelves.

The Lenin State Library in Moscow, U.S.S.R., claims to house more than 20,000,000 books, but this total is understood to include periodicals.

The largest non-statutory library in the world is the New York Public Library (founded 1895) on Fifth Avenue with a floor area of 525,276 square feet. The main part of its collection is in a private research library which has 4,662,326 volumes on 80 miles of shelves, 9,000,000 manuscripts, 120,000 prints, 150,000 gramophone records, and 275,000 maps. There are also 81 tax-supported branch libraries with 3,231,696 books. The central research library is open until the civilized hour of 10 p.m. on every day of the year.

United The largest library in the United Kingdom is that in the
Kingdom British Museum, London. It contains more than 9,000,000 books, about 115,000 manuscripts and 101,000 charters on 158 miles of shelf. There are spaces for 370 readers in the domed Reading Room, built in 1854. The largest public library in the United Kingdom will be the new Birmingham Public Library with a floor area of 230,000 square feet or more than 5¼ acres;

NEWSPAPERS

Most It has been estimated that the total circulation of newspapers throughout the world averaged 320,000,000 copies per day in 1966. The country with the greatest number is the U.S.S.R., with 7,967 in 1966. Their average circulation in 1966 was 110,400,000.

The United States had 1,749 English language daily newspapers at 1 Jan. 1968. They had a combined net paid circulation of 61,397,000 copies per day at 30 Sept. 1966. The peak year for U.S. newspapers was 1910, when there were 2,202. The leading newspaper readers in the world are the people of Sweden, where 515 newspapers were sold for each 1,000 of the population in 1967–68. The U.K. figure was 488.

Oldest The oldest existing newspaper in the world is the Swedish official journal *Post och Inrikes Tidningar*, founded in 1644. It is published by the Royal Swedish Academy of Letters. The oldest existing commercial newspaper is the *Haarlems Dagblad/Oprechte Haarlemsche Courant*, published in Haarlem, in the Netherlands. The *Courant* was first issued as the *Weeckelycke Courante van Europa* on 8 Jan. 1656 and a copy of issue No. 1 survives.

The oldest continuously produced newspaper in the United Kingdom is *Berrow's Worcester Journal* (originally the *Worcester Post Man*), published in Worcester. It was traditionally founded in 1690 and has appeared weekly since June 1709. The oldest newspaper title is that of the *Stamford Mercury* dating back to at least 1714 and traditionally to 1695. The oldest daily newspaper in the United Kingdom is *Lloyd's List*, the shipping intelligence bulletin of Lloyd's, London, established as a weekly in 1726 and as a daily in 1734. The *London Gazette* (originally the *Oxford Gazette*) was first published on 16 Nov. 1665. In November 1845 it became the most expensive daily newspaper ever sold in the United Kingdom, priced at 2s. 8d. per copy. The oldest Sunday newspaper in the United Kingdom is *The Observer*, first issued on 4 Dec. 1791. The 9,327th issue was on 19 Apr. 1970.

Library of Congress on Capitol Hill, Washington D.C.

seating for 1,200 people and an ultimate reference capacity for 1,500,000 volumes on 31 miles of shelving. The oldest public library in Scotland is in Kirkwall, Orkney, founded in 1683.

due books It was reported on 7 Dec. 1968 that a book checked out in 1823 from the University of Cincinnati Medical Library on Febrile Diseases (London, 1805 by Dr. J. Currie) was returned by the borrower's great-grandson Richard Dodd. The fine was calculated as $22,646 (£9,435).

Largest The most massive single issue of a newspaper was the *New York Times* of Sunday 17 Oct. 1965. It comprised 15 sections with a total of 946 pages, including about 1,200,000 lines of advertising. Each copy weighed 7 lb. 14 oz. and sold for 30 cents (2s. 1¾d.).

The largest page size ever used has been 51 inches by 35 inches for *The Constellation*, printed in 1895 by George Roberts as part of the Fourth of July celebrations in New York City, N.Y., U.S.A. The largest page size of any present newspaper is 30 inches by 22 inches

The arts and entertainments

in *The Nantucket Inquirer and Mirror,* published every Friday in Nantucket, on Nantucket Island, Massachusetts, U.S.A.

The smallest recorded page size has been $3\frac{1}{2}$ inches by $4\frac{1}{2}$ inches, as used in *El Telegrama* of Guadalajara, Spain.

HIGHEST CIRCULATION

The first newspaper to achieve a circulation of 1,000,000 was *Le Petit Journal,* published in Paris, France, which reached this figure in 1886, when selling at 5 centimes (now about 0·9 of a penny) per copy.

The claim exercised for the world's highest circulation is that by the *Ashashi Shimbun* of Japan with a 1969 figure of 9,415,500. This however has been achieved by totalling the figures for editions published in various centres with a morning figure of 5,690,500 and an evening figure of 3,725,000. The highest circulation of any single newspaper in the world is that of the Sunday newspaper *The News of the World,* printed in Bouverie Street, London. Single issues have attained a sale of 9,000,000 copies, with an estimated readership of more than 19,000,000. The paper first appeared on 1 Oct. 1843, averaged 12,971 copies per week in its first year and surpassed the million mark in 1905. To provide sufficient pulp for the 1,500 reels used per week, each measuring 5 miles long, more than 780,000 trees have to be felled each year. The latest sales figure is 6,421,089 copies per issue (average for 1 July to 31 Dec. 1969), with an estimated readership of 16,208,000.

The highest circulation of any daily newspaper is that of the U.S.S.R. government organ *Izvestia* (founded in Leningrad on 12 March 1917 as a Menshevik newssheet) with a figure of 8,670,000 in March 1967. The daily tabloid *Pionerskaya Pravda* had an average circulation of 9,181,000 copies per issue in 1966. This is the news organ of the Pioneers, a Communist youth organization founded in 1922.

The highest circulation of any evening newspaper is that of *The Evening News,* established in London in 1881. The average daily net sale reached 1,752,166 in the first six months of 1950. The latest figure is 1,051,861 copies per issue (average for 1 July to 31 Dec. 1969), with an average readership of 2,942,000.

The highest daily net sale of any newspaper in the United Kingdom is that of *The Daily Mirror,* founded in London in 1903. A print of 7,161,704 was sold out on 3 June 1953. The latest sales figure is 5,003,798 (for July–Dec. 1969), with an estimated readership of 14,910,000.

"Earliest" newspaper The first newspaper to be published in the world each day is sometimes said to be the *Fiji Times* because it is closest to the international date-line.

Most read The newspaper which achieves the closest to a saturation circulation is *The Sunday Post,* established in Glasgow in 1914. In 1969 its total estimated readership of 2,931,000 represented more than 80 per cent. of the entire population of Scotland aged 16 and over.

Most smoked newspaper New Guinea's *South Pacific Post,* which circulated only 5,200 copies over about 178,000 square miles, was the most sought after newspaper for smoking and sold for 6d. per lb. for this purpose. Since 1962 the arrival of the *Nu Gini Toktok* has eased the paper shortage.

PERIODICALS

LARGEST CIRCULATION

The largest circulation of any weekly periodical is that of *This Week Magazine,* produced in the United States to circulate with 43 newspapers which find it uneconomical to run their own coloured Sunday magazine section. The circulation was 11,889,211 copies at 31 March 1967. In its 30 basic international editions *The Reader's Digest* (established February 1922) circulates more than 29,000,000 copies monthly, in 14 languages, including a United States edition of 17,500,000 copies (average for July to December 1969) and a United Kingdom edition (established 1939) of 1,500,000 copies (January to December 1969).

The highest circulation of any periodical in the United Kingdom is that of *The Radio Times* (instituted in September 1923). The average weekly sale for 1969 was 3,806,847 copies. The highest sale of any issue was 9,778,062 copies for the Christmas issue of 1955. The materials used include 885 tons of paper, $9\frac{1}{2}$ tons of ink and 355 miles of stapling wire per issue.

ADVERTISING RATES

The highest price asked for advertising space *pro rata* is $98,200 (£35,071) for a four-colour centre-spread in *This Week.* The highest price for a single page is $76,420 (£31,841) for a four-colour back cover in *Life* magazine (circulation 8 million per week).

The colour page rate for the *Radio Times* is £5,800.

The highest expenditure ever incurred on a single advertisement in a periodical is $950,000 (£395,833) by Uniroyal Inc. for a 40-page insert in the May 1968 issue of the U.S. edition of *The Reader's Digest.*

The British record is £30,000 for a 28-page booklet by Morphy-Richards Ltd. in *The Reader's Digest* of October 1964.

Longest editorship On 6 Jan. 1963 Sir Bruce Stirling Ingram, O.B.E., M.C. (1877–1963) celebrated his 63rd completed year as editor of *The Illustrated London News* in 3,272 weekly issues, and died two days later. This span was interrupted only by service in World War I.

The start of musical history, Chinese temple music

1. Music

INSTRUMENTS

Oldest The world's oldest surviving musical notation is a heptonic scale deciphered from a clay tablet by Dr. Duchesne-Guillemin in 1966–67. The tablet has been dated to *c.* 1800 B.C. and was found at a site in Nippur, Sumeria, now Iraq. Musical history is, however, able to be traced back to the 3rd millennium B.C., when the yellow bell (*huang chung*) had a recognized standard musical tone in Chinese temple music. It is possible that either a flute or a mouth bow is the object depicted in a painting from the Magdalenian period (*c.* 18,000 B.C.) in the Trois Frères Caves in the Pyrenees. Rock-gongs probably existed even earlier.

Earliest piano The earliest piano in existence is one built in Florence, Italy, in 1720 by Bartolommeo Cristofori (1655–1731) of Padua, and now preserved in the Kraus Museum of Florence.

Largest organ World The largest and loudest musical instrument ever constructed is the Auditorium Organ in Atlantic City, New Jersey, U.S.A. Completed in 1930, this heroic instrument has two consoles (one with seven manuals and another movable one with five), 1,477 stop controls and 33,112 pipes ranging from $\frac{3}{16}$ of an inch to 64 feet in length. It is powered with blower motors of 365 horse-power, cost $500,000 (now £208,333) and has the volume of 25 brass bands, with a range of seven octaves. The world's largest church organ is that in Passau Cathedral, Germany. It was completed in 1928 by D. F. Steinmeyer & Co. It has 16,000 pipes and five manuals.

United Kingdom The largest organ in the United Kingdom is that installed in Liverpool Cathedral in 1926, with one five-manual and one four-manual console, and 10,936 pipes.

dest stop The loudest organ stop in the world is the Ophicleide stop of the Grand Great in the Solo Organ in the Atlantic City Auditorium (see above). It is operated by a pressure of 100 inches of water ($3\frac{1}{2}$ lb. per square inch) and has a pure trumpet note of ear-splitting volume, more than six times the volume of the loudest locomotive whistles.

Organ marathon The longest organ recital ever sustained was one of 36 hours at All Saints' Church, Hertford, England, by the organist Brian Bromley and his assistant Brian Sawyer from 9 a.m. 7 April to 9 p.m. 8 April 1969.

rmonium marathon The longest recorded non-stop harmonium marathon is 72 hours by Iain Stinson and John Whiteley, both of the Royal Holloway College at Englefield Green, Surrey on 6–9 Feb. 1970.

Brass strument The largest recorded brass instrument is a tuba standing $7\frac{1}{2}$ feet tall, with 39 feet of tubing and a bell 3 feet 4 inches across. This contrabass tuba was constructed for a world tour by the band of John Philip Sousa (1854–1932), the United States composer, in *c.* 1896–98, and is still in use. This instrument is now owned by Mr. Ron Snyder (G.B.).

The greatest number of musicians required to operate a single instrument was the six required to play the gigantic orchestrion, known as the Apollonican, built in 1816 and played until 1840.

Stringed strument The largest stringed instrument ever constructed was a pantaleon with 270 strings stretched over 50 square feet, used by George Noel in 1767.

Largest uble bass The largest bass viol ever constructed was an octo-bass 10 feet tall, built in *c.* 1845 by J. B. Vuillaume (1798–1875) of France. Because the stretch was too great for any musician's finger-span, the stopping was effected by foot levers. It was played in London in 1851.

Most valuable violin The highest recorded auction price for a violin is the £22,000 paid at Sotheby's, London on 7 Nov. 1968 for a 1709 Stradivarius bought by Mr. Jack Morrison. It was sold by Miss Pauline Baring who was given it as a birthday present in 1905 by her mother Marie Hall, the concert violinist. The "Messie" Stradivarius in the Ashmolean Museum at Oxford, England, has been hypothetically valued at £30,000.

The house and workshop of Stradivari in Cremona, Italy

Smallest The smallest fully-functional violin made is one $5\frac{1}{2}$ inches overall, constructed by Mr. T. B. Pollard of Rock Ferry, Birkenhead, Cheshire, England.

Largest drum The largest drum in the world is the Disneyland Big Bass Drum with a diameter of 10 feet 6 inches and a weight of 450 lb. It was built in 1961 by Remo Inc. of North Hollywood, California, U.S.A. and is mounted on wheels and is towed by a tractor.

Longest alphorn The longest Swiss alphorn, which is of wooden construction, is 23 feet $7\frac{7}{8}$ inches long and was completed in 1968.

ORCHESTRAS

Most The greatest number of professional orchestras maintained in one country is 94 in West Germany. The total number of symphony orchestras in the United States, including "community" orchestras, was estimated to be 1,436 in 1969 including 28 major ones.

Largest The vastest "orchestra" ever recorded was that assembled for the Norwegian National Meeting of School Brass Bands at Trondheim in August 1958. The

A facsimile of Stradivari's signature from a violin label

Antonius Stradiuarius Cre

total number of instrumentalists was 12,600. On 17 June 1872, Johann Strauss the younger (1825–99) conducted an orchestra of 2,000, supported by a choir of 20,000, at the World Peace Jubilee in Boston, Massachusetts, U.S.A. The number of violinists was more than 350.

Most highly paid The most highly paid orchestra in the world is the Metropolitan Opera House orchestra, New York City, N.Y., U.S.A. The members receive a basic weekly salary of $225 (£93 15s.).

Greatest attendance The greatest attendance at any classical concert was 90,000 for a presentation by the New York Philharmonic Orchestra, conducted by Leonard Bernstein, at Sheep Meadow in Central Park, New York City, N.Y., U.S.A., on 1 Aug. 1966. It was estimated that the attendance at the Myer Music Bowl, Melbourne, Australia, in March 1967 for a performance by the Seekers was 200,000.

Pop Festival The greatest estimated attendance at a Pop Festival has been 400,000 for the Woodstock Music and Art Fair at Bethel, New York State, U.S.A. on 15–17 Aug. 1969. According to one press estimate "at least 90 per cent." were smoking marijuana. The attendance at the Pop Festival in Hyde Park, London on 18 July 1969 was widely reported as 500,000 but the police estimate was 150,000. This figure was also the estimate for the Bob Dylan Festival on the Isle of Wight on 31 Aug. 1969.

Highest and lowest notes The extremes of orchestral instruments (excluding the organ) range between the piccolo or octave flute, which can reach e^v or 5,274 cycles per second, and the sub-contrabass clarinet, which can reach C_{11} or 16·4 cycles per second. The highest note on a standard pianoforte is c^v (4,186 cycles per second), which is also the violinist's limit. In 1873 a sub Double Bassoon able to reach $B_{111}\#$ or 14·6 cycles per second was constructed but no surviving specimen is known. The extremes for the organ are g^{vi} (the sixth G above middle C) (12,544 cycles per sec.) and C_{111} (8·12 cycles per sec.) obtainable from 64 foot pipes.

EXTREMES - highest & lowest orchestral notes

‹¾ inch Organ pipe (12,544 Hz) g^{vi}

Piccolo or octave flute (5,274 Hz) $f^{\overline{v}}$

Highest piano note (4,186 Hz) $C^{\overline{v}}$

C^I (Middle C, 261.6 Hz)

A_{11} (27.5 Hz) Lowest note on piano

C_{11} (16.4 Hz) Sub contra-bass clarinet

$B^\#_{111}$ (14.6 Hz) Sub double bassoon

C_{111} (8.12 Hz) 64 foot organ pipe

COMPOSERS

Most prolific The most prolific composer of all time was probably Georg Philipp Telemann (1681–1767) of Germany. He composed 12 complete sets of services (one cantata every Sunday) for a year, 78 services for special occasions, 40 operas, 600 to 700 orchestral suites, 44 Passions, plus concertos and chamber music. The most prolific symphonist was Johann Melchior Molter (c. 1695–1765) of Germany who wrote 169. Joseph Haydn (1732–1809) of Austria wrote 104 numbered symphonies some of which are regularly played today.

Most rapid Among composers of the classical period the most prolific was Wolfgang Amadeus Mozart (1756–91) of Austria, who wrote 600 operas, operettas, symphonies, violin sonatas, divertimenti, serenades, motets, concertos for piano and many other instruments, string quartets, other chamber music, masses and litanies, of which only 70 were published before he died, aged 35. His opera *The Clemency of Titus* (1791) was written in 18 days and three symphonic masterpieces, *Symphony No. 39 in E. flat major, Symphony in G minor* and the *Jupiter Symphony in C*, were reputedly written in the space of 42 days in 1788. His overture *Don Giovanni* was written in full score at one sitting in Prague in 1787 and finished on the day of its opening performance.

National anthems The oldest national anthem is the *Kimigayo* of Japan, in which the words date from the 9th century. The anthem of Greece constitutes the first four verses of the Solomos poem, which has 158 verses. The shortest anthems are those of Japan, Jordan and San Marino, each with only four lines. The anthems of Bahrain and Qatar have no words at all.

Longest rendering "God Save the King" was played non-stop 16 or 17 times by a German military band on the platform of Rathenau Railway Station, Brandenburg, on the morning of 9 Feb. 1909. The reason was that King Edward VII was struggling inside the train with the uniform of a German Field-Marshal before he could emerge.

Longest symphony The longest of all orchestral symphonies is No. 3 in D minor by Gustav Mahler (1860–1911) of Austria. This work, composed in 1895, requires a contralto, a women's and a boys' choir and an organ, in addition to a full orchestra. A full performance requires 1 hour 34 minutes, of which the first movement alone takes 45 minutes. The longest traditional instrumental symphony is the No. 8 in C minor, composed in 1884–85 by Anton Bruckner (1824–96) of Austria, and lasting 77 minutes. The Symphony No. 2 (the Gothic, now renumbered as No. 1), composed in 1919–22 by Havergal Brian, has been performed only twice, on 24 June 1961 and 30 Oct. 1966. The total *ensemble* included 55 brass instruments, 31 woodwind, six kettle-drummers playing 22 drums, four vocal soloists, four large mixed choruses, a children's chorus and an organ. The symphony is continuous and required, when played as a recording on 27 Nov. 1967, 100 minutes. Brian has written an even vaster work based on Shelley's "Prometheus Unbound" but the sheer expense of putting it on makes its performance unlikely. He wrote 18 symphonies between 1956, when he was 80 and 1967.

Longest piano composition The longest continuous non-repetitious piece for piano ever composed has been the Opus Clavicembalisticum by Kaikhosru Shapurji Sorabji (born 1892). The composer himself gave it its only public performance on 1 Dec. 1930 in Glasgow, Scotland. The work is in 12 movements with a theme and 49 variations and a Passacaglia with 81 and a playing time of $2\frac{3}{4}$ hours.

The longest piano piece of any kind is *Vexations* by Erik Satie which consists of a 180-note composition which on the composer's orders must be repeated 840 times such that the whole lasts 18 hours 40 minutes. Its first reported public performance in September 1963 in the Pocket Theatre, New York City required a relay of ten pianists. The *New York Times* critic fell asleep at

4 a.m. and the audience dwindled to six masochists. At the conclusion a sado-masochist shouted "Encore".

Longest silence The most protracted silence in a modern composition is one entitled *4 minutes 33 seconds* in a totally silent *opus* by John Cage (U.S.A.). Commenting on this trend among young composers, Igor Fyodorovich Stravinsky (born 1882) said that he now looked forward to their subsequent compositions being "works of major length".

HIGHEST PAID MUSICIANS

Pianist The highest-paid concert pianist was Ignace Jan Paderewski (1860–1941), Prime Minister of Poland from 1919 to 1921, who accumulated a fortune estimated at $5,000,000 (now about £1,800,000), of which $500,000 (£180,000) was earned in a single season in 1922–23. He once received $33,000 (£11,800) for a concert in Madison Square Garden, New York City, the highest fee ever paid for a single performance.

Singers Of great fortunes earned by singers, the highest on record are those of Enrico Caruso (1873–1921), the Italian tenor, whose estate was about $9,000,000 (£3,750,000), and the Italian-Spanish coloratura soprano Amelita Galli-Curci (1889–1963), who received about $3,000,000 (£1,250,000). In 1850, up to $653 (now £272) was paid for a single seat at the concerts given in the United States by Johanna ("Jenny") Maria Lind, later Mrs. Otto Goldschmidt (1820–87), the "Swedish Nightingale". She had a range from g to e^{iii}, of which the middle register is still regarded as unrivalled.

Violinist The Austrian-born Fritz Kreisler (1875–1962) is reputed to have received more than £1,000,000 in his career.

Paderewski   Kreisler

Drummer The most highly paid drummer, or indeed "side man" of any kind, is Bernard ("Buddy") Rich (born 1918) in the band of Harry James, at more than $75,000 (about £27,500) per annum.

OPERA

Longest The longest of commonly performed operas is *Die Meistersinger von Nurnberg* by Wilhelm Richard Wagner (1813–83) of Germany. A normal uncut performance of this opera as performed by the Sadler's Wells company between 24 Aug. and 19 Sept. 1968 entailed 5 hours 15 minutes of music. *William Tell* by Rossini, never now performed uncut, would according to the *tempi* require some 7 or more hours if performed in full.

Aria The longest single aria, in the sense of an operatic solo, is Brünnhilde's immolation scene in Wagner's *Götterdämmerung*. A well-known recording of this has been precisely timed at 14 minutes 46 seconds.

Cadenza The longest recorded cadenza in operatic history occurred in *c.* 1815, when Crevilli, a tenor, sang the two words *felice ognora* ("always happy") as a cadenza for 25 minutes in the Milan Opera House, Italy.

Opera houses Largest The largest opera house in the world is the Metropolitan Opera House, Lincoln Center, New York City, N.Y., U.S.A., completed in September 1966 at a cost of $45,700,000 (£16,320,000). It has a capacity of 3,800 seats in an auditorium 451 feet deep. The stage is 234 feet in width and 146 feet deep. The tallest opera house is one housed in a 42-storey building on Wacker Drive in Chicago, Illinois, U.S.A.

Most tiers The Teatro della Scala (La Scala) in Milan, Italy, shares with the Bolshoi Theatre in Moscow, U.S.S.R., the distinction of having the greatest number of tiers. Each has six, with the topmost in Moscow being termed the Galurka.

BELLS

Heaviest The heaviest bell in the world is the Tsar Kolokol, cast in 1733 in Moscow, U.S.S.R. It weighs 193 tons, measures 22 feet 8 inches in diameter and over 19 feet high, and its greatest thickness is 24 inches. The bell is cracked, and a fragment, weighing about 11 tons, broken from it. The bell has stood on a platform in the Kremlin, in Moscow, since 1836.

The heaviest bell in use is the Mingoon bell, weighing 87 tons, in Mandalay, Burma, which is struck by a teak boom from the outside. The heaviest swinging bell in the world is the Kaiserglock in Cologne Cathedral, Germany, which was recast in 1925 at 25 tons. The heaviest change ringing peal in the world is the 13 bells, weighing 16½ tons, in Liverpool Cathedral of which the tenor alone weighs 82 cwt.

The heaviest bell hung in the United Kingdom is "Great Paul" in St. Paul's Cathedral, London. It was cast in 1881, weighs 16 tons 14 cwt. 2 quarters 19 lb. and has a diameter of 9 feet 6½ inches. "Big Ben", the hour bell in the clock tower of the House of Commons, was cast in 1858 and weighs 13 tons 10 cwt. 3 quarters 15 lb. The heaviest peal is the 13 with a tenor bell weighing 72 cwt. donated by Bishop Grandison (1327–1369).

The heaviest bell ever cast in England and the heaviest tuned bell in the world is the bourdon bell of the Laura Spelman Rockefeller Memorial carillon in Riverside Church, New York City, N.Y., U.S.A. It weighs 18 tons 5 cwt. 1 quarter 18 lb. and is 10 feet 2 inches in diameter.

Oldest The oldest bell in the world is reputed to be that found in the Babylonian Palace of Nimrod in 1849 by Mr. (later Sir) Austen Henry Layard (1817–94). It dates from *c.* 1000 B.C.

The oldest *dated* bell in England is that hung in St. Chad's, Claughton, in the parish of Hornby with Claughton, Lancashire. It weighs about 2½ cwt., is 21¼ inches in diameter and 16½ inches high. Still in perfect condition and in regular use, it is dated 1296. A claim that the church bell at Enborne, Berkshire dates from *c.* A.D. 1260 is accepted by some experts.

CARILLON

Largest The largest carillon in the world is the Laura Spelman Rockefeller Memorial carillon in Riverside Church, New York City, N.Y., U.S.A. It consists of 72 bells with a total weight of 102 tons.

Heaviest The heaviest carillon in the United Kingdom is in St. Nicholas Church, Aberdeen, Scotland. It consists of 48 bells, the total weight of which is 25 tons 8 cwt. 2 quarters 13 lb. The bourdon bell weighs 4 tons 9 cwt. 3 quarters 26 lb. and the carillon comprises four octaves, less the bottom semi-tone.

BELL RINGING

Eight bells have been rung to their full "extent" (a complete "Bob Major" of 40,320 changes) only once without relays. This took place in a bell foundry at Loughborough, Leicestershire, beginning at 6.52 a.m. on 27 July 1963 and ending at 12.50 a.m. on 28 July, after 17 hours 58 minutes. The peal was composed by Kenneth Lewis of Altrincham, Cheshire, and the eight ringers were conducted by Robert B. Smith, aged 25,

The arts and entertainments

of Marple, Cheshire. Theoretically it would take 37 years 355 days to ring 12 bells (maximus) to their full extent of 479,001,600 changes.

SONG

Oldest The oldest known song is *Chadouf*, which has been sung since time immemorial by irrigation workers on the man-powered treadwheel Nile water mills (or *saqiyas*) in Egypt (now the United Arab Republic). The English song *Sumer is icumen in* dates from *c.* 1240.

Top songs of all time The most frequently sung songs in English are *Happy Birthday to You* (based on the original *Good morning to all*), by Mildred and Patty S. Hill of New York (published in 1936 and in copyright until 1996); *For He's a Jolly Good Fellow* (originally the French *Malbrouk*), known at least as early as 1781, and *Auld Lang Syne* (originally the Strathspey *I fee'd a Lad at Michaelmass*), some words of which were written by Robert Burns (1759–96). *Happy Birthday* was sung in space by the Apollo IX astronauts on 8 March 1969.

Top selling sheet music Sales of three non-copyright pieces are known to have exceeded 20,000,000 namely *The Old Folks at Home, Listen to the Mocking Bird* (1855) and *The Blue Danube* (1867). Of copyright material the two top-sellers are *Let Me Call You Sweetheart* (1910, by Whitson Friedman) and *Till We Meet Again* (1918, by Egan Whiting) each with some 6,000,000 by 1967.

Most monotonous The longest song sung on one note is *Ein Ton,* written in 1859 by Peter Cornelius (1824–74) of Germany. The single note (the B above middle C) is repeated 80 times for 30 bars.

Peter Cornelius

Most successful song writers In terms of sales of single records, the most successful of all song writers have been John Lennon and Paul McCartney (see also Gramophone, Fastest sales, p. 104) of the Beatles. Between 1962 and 1 Jan. 1970 they together wrote 30 songs which sold more than 1,000,000 records each.

HYMNS

Earliest There are believed to be more than 500,000 Christian hymns in existence. "Te Deum Laudamus" dates from about the 5th century, but the earliest exactly datable hymn is the French one "Jesus soit en ma teste et mon entendement" from 1490, translated into the well-known "God be in my head" in 1512.

Longest and shortest The longest hymn is "Hora novissima tempora pessima sunt; vigilemus" by Bernard of Cluny (12th century), which runs to 2,966 lines. In English the longest is "The Sands of Time are sinking" by Mrs. Anne Ross Cousin, *née* Cundell (1824–1906), which is in full 152 lines, though only 32 lines in the Methodist Hymn Book. The shortest hymn is the single verse in Long Metre "Be Present at our Table, Lord", anonymous but attributed to "J. Leland".

Most prolific hymnists Mrs. Frances (Fanny) Jan Van Alstyne, *née* Crosby (1820–1915), of the U.S.A., wrote more than 8,000 hymns although she had been blinded at the age of 6 weeks. She is reputed to have knocked off one hymn in 15 minutes. Charles Wesley (1707–88) wrote about 6,000 hymns. In the seventh (1950) edition of *Hymns Ancient and Modern* the works of John Mason Neale (1818–66) appear 56 times.

Longest hymn-in The Cambridge University Student Methodist Society sang through the 984 hymns in the Methodist Hymn Book in 45 hours 42 minutes, and completed 1,000 hymns with 16 more requests in 88 minutes on 7–9 Feb. 1969 in the Wesley Church, Cambridge.

2. Theatre

Origins Theatre in Europe has its origins in Greek drama performed in honour of a god, usually Dionysus. The earliest amphitheatres date from the 5th century B.C. The largest of all known *orchestras* is one at Megalopolis in central Greece, where the auditorium reached a height of 75 feet and had a capacity of 17,000.

Oldest World The oldest indoor theatre in the world is the Teatro Olimpico in Vicenza, Italy. Designed in the Roman style by Andrea di Pietro, *alias* Palladio (1508–80), it was begun three months before his death and finished in 1582 by his pupil Vicenzo Scamozzi (1552–1616). It is preserved today in its original form.

Britain The earliest London theatre was James Burbage's "The Theatre", built in 1576 near Finsbury Fields, London. The oldest theatre still in use in the United Kingdom is the Theatre Royal, Bristol. The foundation stone was laid on 30 Nov. 1764, and the theatre was opened on 30 May 1766 with a "Concert of Music and a Specimen of Rhetorick". Since then it has been more or less continuously in use as a theatre. It is the home of the Bristol Old Vic Company. Actors were legally rogues and vagabonds until the passing of an act (5 Geo. IV C.38) in 1824. The first honour for work on the stage was to Henry Irving (1838–1905) who was knighted in 1895. The earliest Dame was Geneviève Ward made D.B.E. in 1921.

World's largest Theatre, Peking, China

Largest World The world's largest building used for theatre is the National People's Congress Building (*Ren min da hui tang*) on the west side of Tian an men Square, Peking, China. It was completed in 1959 and covers an area of 12·9 acres. The theatre seats 10,000 and is occasionally used as such as in 1964 for the play "The East is Red". The largest regular theatre in the world is Radio City Music Hall in Rockefeller Center, New York City, N.Y., U.S.A. It seats more than 6,200 people and the average annual attendance is more than 8,000,000. The stage is 144 feet wide and 66 feet 6 inches deep, equipped with a revolving turntable 43 feet in diameter and three elevator sections, each 70 feet long.

The greatest seating capacity of any regular theatre in the world is that of the "Chaplin" (formerly the "Blanquita") in Havana, Cuba. It was opened on 30 Dec. 1949 and has 6,500 seats.

United Kingdom The highest capacity theatre is the Odeon, Hammersmith, West London, with 3,485 seats. The largest theatre stage in the United Kingdom is the Opera House in Blackpool, Lancashire. It was opened in July 1939 and has seats for 3,000 people. Behind the 45-foot-wide proscenium arch the stage is 110 feet high, 60 feet deep and 100 feet wide, and there is dressing room accommodation for 200 artists.

Smallest The smallest regularly operated professional theatre in the United Kingdom is the Traverse Theatre (founded in 1963) in Edinburgh, Scotland. It has a capacity of 58. A theatre with only 32 seats operated in 1968 in Tobermory, Isle of Mull, Scotland.

Largest amphitheatre The largest amphitheatre ever built is the Flavian amphitheatre or Colosseum of Rome, Italy, completed in A.D. 80. Covering 5 acres and with a capacity of 87,000, it has a maximum length of 612 feet and maximum width of 515 feet.

Longest runs World The longest run of any show at one theatre anywhere in the world was by the play *The Drunkard*, written by W. H. Smith and "a gentleman". First produced, as a moral lesson, in 1844 by Phineas Taylor Barnum (1810–91), a United States showman, it was not performed commercially again until it was revived on 6 July 1933 at the Theatre Mart in Los Angeles, California, U.S.A. From that date it ran continuously, one show a night, for 7,510 performances, until 3 Sept. 1953. Starting on 7 Sept. 1953, a new musical adaptation of *The Drunkard*, called *The Wayward Way*, started to play alternate nights with the original version. On 17 Oct. 1959 it played its 9,477th and final time. It was seen by more than 3,000,000 people. The producer, Miss Mildred Ilse, was with the play throughout. The Broadway record is 3,213 performances of *Life with Father* at the Empire, which opened on 8 Nov. 1937 and closed at the end of 1947.

The Broadway record for musicals was set by *My Fair Lady,* with 2,717 performances (15 March 1956 to 29 Sept. 1962). It grossed $20,250,000 (£7,230,000) and played to about 3,750,000 people. Abroad and "on the road" it grossed another $46,000,000 (£16,400,000) to 1963. *Hello Dolly* moved to second place with its 2,213th performance on 5 June 1969.

London The longest continuous run of any show at one theatre in the United Kingdom is by *The Mousetrap* by Agatha Mary Clarissa Christie (*née* Miller, now Lady Mallowan) (b. 1890) at the Ambassadors Theatre (capacity 453). This thriller opened on 25 Nov. 1952, and had its 7,000th performance on 1 Oct. 1969. On 19 Aug. 1969 a power cut caused one performance to be missed. So far 111 actors have played its 8 roles. More than 2,600,000 people have seen the play and it has been calculated that, with the United Kingdom's present rate of natural increase, it can be expected to go on indefinitely.

The longest-running musical show ever performed in Britain was *The Black and White Minstrel Show*, a musical variety presentation which opened at the Victoria Palace, London, on 25 May 1962, was performed *twice* nightly and continued until 24 May 1969 reaching 4,354 performances. The total attendance has been estimated at 5,500,000. One chorus girl claims a pedometer strapped to a leg registered $6\frac{1}{2}$ miles in one night. It reopened as *Magic of the Minstrels* on 24 Nov. 1969.

One-man show The longest run of any one-man show has been 213 performances of *Brief Lives* by Roy Dotrice at the Criterion, London from 25 Feb. to 6 Sept. 1969. It also ran 16 nights on Broadway, New York City.

Shortest runs The shortest run on record was that of *The Intimate Revue* at the Duchess Theatre, London, on 11 March 1930. Anything which could go wrong did. With scene changes taking up to 20 minutes apiece, the management scrapped seven scenes to get the finale on before midnight. The run was described as "half a performance". Even this fractional first night was surpassed by *As You Like It* by William Shakespeare (1564–1616) at the Shaftesbury Theatre, London, in 1888. On the opening night the fire curtain was let down, jammed, and did not rise again that night or ever again on this production.

Of the many Broadway shows for which the opening and closing nights coincided the most costly was *Kelly,* a musical costing $700,000 (£291,600) which suffered its double ceremony on 6 Feb. 1965.

Longest play The Oberammergau *Passionsspiel* ("Passion Play"), performed every ten years since 1633, was performed, with 125 speaking parts, 97 times in 1970, each performance occupying $5\frac{1}{2}$ hours or $8\frac{1}{2}$ hours including intervals. The audience for this 36th presentation was 485,000.

Das Passionsspiel

Agatha Christie

The arts and entertainments

Shakespeare The first all amateur company to have staged all 37 of Shakespeare's plays was The Southsea Shakespeare Actors, Hampshire, England, when in October 1966 they presented *Cymbaline*. The director throughout was Mr. K. Edmonds Gateley. Fifteen pupils from Beauchamp Grammar School, Oadby, Leicestershire completed a dramatic reading of all the plays, 154 sonnets and five narrative poems in 85 hours 5 minutes on 20–24 June 1968. The longest is *Richard III*.

Longest title The longest title of any play was that of 122 words on *The Fire of London*, which in full went on for another 118 words and was presented at The Mermaid Theatre, London on 4 Sept. 1966. This 17th century documentary was written by Peter Black, T.V. critic of the *Daily Mail*.

Longest chorus line The world's longest permanent chorus line is that formed by the Rockettes in the Radio City Music Hall, which opened in Dec. 1932 in New York City, U.S.A. The 36 girls dance precision routines across the 144-foot-wide stage. The whole troupe, which won the *Grand Prix* in Paris in July 1937, is 46 strong, but 10 girls are always on alternating vacation or are undergoing repairs. The troupe is sometimes augmented to 64.

Thomas Edison, inventor of the first successful phonograph

3. Gramophone

The gramophone (phonograph) was first described on 30 April 1877 by Charles Cros (1842–88), a French poet and scientist. The first successful machine was constructed by Thomas Alva Edison (1847–1931) of the U.S.A., who gained his first patent on 19 Feb. 1878. It was on 15 Aug. 1877 that he shouted "Mary had a little Lamb". The first practical hand-cranked foil cylinder phonograph was manufactured in the United States by Chichester Bell and Charles Sumner Tainter in 1886.

The country with the greatest number of record players is the United States, with a total of 53,800,000 at mid-1968. A total of more than half a billion dollars (now £209 million) is spent annually on 500,000 juke boxes in the United States.

World sales of records for 1968 have been estimated at 1,141 million. The peak year for record sales in the United States was 1968, when retail receipts totalled $1,124,000,000 (£468·3 million). This compares with $48,000,000 in 1940.

The peak year for value in U.K. sales of records was 1968 with £30,940,000 for 98,345,000 records. In 1964, when there were fewer L.P.'s, sales were 101,257,000 worth £25,602,000 (excluding purchase tax).

OLDEST RECORD

The oldest record in the British Broadcasting Corporation's gramophone library is a record made by Emile Berliner (born Berlin, 1869) of himself reciting the Lord's Prayer. It was made in 1884. Berliner invented the flat disc to replace the cylinder in 1888.

The B.B.C. library, the world's largest, contains over 750,000 records, including 5,250 with no known matrix.

Most successful recording artist On 9 June 1960 the Hollywood Chamber of Commerce presented Harry Lillis (*alias* Bing) Crosby, Jr. (born 2 May 1904 at Tacoma, Washington) with a platinum disc to commemorate his 200,000,000th record sold from 2,600 singles and 125 albums he had recorded. By July 1964 his world sales had reached 250,000,000 and by 1970 were approaching 350,000,000. His first commercial recording was "*I've Got the Girl*" recorded on 10 Oct. 1926 (master number W142785 (Take 3) issued on the Columbia label).

Bing Crosby's unique Platinum Disc

The earliest jazz record made was *Indiana* and *The Dark Town Strutters Ball*, recorded for the Columbia label in New York City, N.Y., U.S.A., on or about 30 Jan. 1917, by the Original Dixieland Jazz Band, led by Dominick (Nick) James La Rocca (1889–1961). This was released on 31 May 1917. The first jazz record to be released was the O.D.J.B.'s *Livery Stable Blues* (recorded 24 Feb.), backed by *The Dixie Jass Band One-Step* (recorded 26 Feb.), released by Victor on 7 March 1917.

GOLDEN DISCS

Earliest The first record to sell a million copies was a performance by Enrico Caruso (born Naples, Italy, 1873, and died 1921) of the aria *Vesti la giubba (On with the Motley)* from the opera *I Pagliacci* by Ruggiero Leoncavallo (1858–1919), the earliest version of which was recorded on 12 Nov. 1902. The first actual golden disc was one sprayed by R.C.A. Victor for presentation to the U.S. trombonist and band-leader Alton 'Glenn' Miller (1904–44) for his *Chattanooga Choo Choo* on 10 Feb. 1942.

Most The singer with the most golden discs claimed is Elvis Aaron Presley (born at Tupelo, Mississippi, U.S.A., 8 Jan. 1935). By 1 Jan. 1970 he had 83 golden discs (75 for singles 1 E.P. and 7 for L.P.s), which marked each sale of each 1,000,000 copies among his best-selling records. His total global sales reached 130,000,000 discs by that date. The only *audited* measure of million-selling records within the U.S., however, is certification by the Record Industry Association of America (R.I.A.A.) introduced in 1958. By this U.S. yardstick Presley has 10 Golden Discs with an additional 9 for million dollar *sales*. The champions for R.I.A.A.

awards are The Beatles with 19 for singles and 15 for L.P.s each of which sold more than 1 million *copies* by 1 Jan. 1970. The Beatles' global total of million sellers was believed to stand at 55 by 1 Jan. 1970.

Youngest The youngest age at which an artist has achieved sales of 1,000,000 copies of a record is 6 years by Osamu Minagawa of Tōkyō, Japan for his single *Kuro Neko No Tango (Black Cat Tango)* released on 5 Oct. 1969.

Fastest sales The singers with the fastest sales are the Beatles. This group from Liverpool, Lancashire, comprises George Harrison, M.B.E. (born 25 Feb. 1943), John Ono (formerly John Winston) Lennon, M.B.E. (born 9 Oct. 1940), James Paul McCartney, M.B.E. (born 18 June 1942) and Richard Starkey, M.B.E., *alias* Ringo Starr (born 7 July 1940). Between February 1963 and January 1970 their sales of single units are claimed to have reached 330,000,000.

Most recorded song Two songs have each been recorded between 900 and 1,000 times in the United States alone—*St. Louis Blues,* written in 1914 by W. C. (William Christopher) Handy (born Memphis, Tennessee 1873 and died 1958), and *Stardust,* written in 1927 by Hoagland ("Hoagy") Carmichael (born Bloomington, Indiana, 22 Nov. 1899).

Biggest sellers The greatest seller of any gramophone record to date is *White Christmas* by Irving Berlin (born Israel Baline, at Tyumen, Russia, 11 May 1888). First recorded in 1941, it sold an estimated 95,000,000 to December 1969. This figure includes Bing Crosby's recording of this song (made for the film *Holiday Inn* in 1942) which, alone, accounted for over 30,000,000 by December 1967. The top-selling "pop" record has been *Rock Around the Clock* by William John Clifton Haley, Jr. (born Detroit, Michigan, March 1927) and the Comets, recorded on 12 April 1954, with collective sales of 22,000,000 by January 1970. The top-selling British record of all-time is *I Want to Hold Your Hand* by the Beatles (see p. 104), with world sales of 11,000,000 to mid-1967, including 5,000,000 in the United States.

Best-sellers' charts Radio Luxembourg's "Top Twenty" Sunday night programme, launched in the autumn of 1948, was the first programme based on current selling strength though best-selling lists had been appearing in *Bill Board,* the Broadway show-business magazine, seven years before this. Based on *New Musical Express* data the longest continuous period for which any record has been in the "Top 30" is 39 weeks by *Stranger on the Shore* by Bernard Stanley ("Mr. Acker") Bilk (born Somerset, England, 28 Nov. 1929) from 25 Nov. 1961 to 18 Aug. 1962. The longest in the "Top 20" was 36 weeks by Frankie Laine (born Frank Paul LoVecchio in Chicago, Illinois, U.S.A., on 30 March 1913) with his *I Believe* (Philips) from 28 March to 28 Nov. 1953. This recording also set records with 35 weeks in the top 10 (4 April to 28 Nov.) and 18 weeks at No. 1 (18 April to 13 June, 27 June to 1 Aug. and 15 Aug. to 29 Aug. 1953). The record for consecutive weeks at No. 1 is 11 by Slim Whitman (born 20 Jan. 1924 at Tampa, Florida, U.S.A.) with his *Rose Marie* from 23 July to 1 Oct. 1955. Only four records have reached the number one position (based on sales, as opposed to sales plus orders) in their week of release—Elvis Presley's *Jailhouse Rock* (released 17 Jan. 1958), *It's Now or Never* (28 Oct. 1960) and *Surrender* (19 May 1961); and *My Old Man's a Dustman* by Andrew (Lonnie) Donegan (born Glasgow, Scotland, 29 April 1931) on 18 March 1960.

Most recordings Ben Selvin (born 1898) of the U.S.A. has made 9,000 recordings as a violinist, band-leader or recording manager from 1919 to 1966.

Greatest monopoly The greatest monopolizing of the sales charts was attained by the Beatles on 31 March 1964. On that date they were No. 1, 2, 3, 4 and 5 in the U.S. charts for the week ending 21 March 1964 with *Twist and Shout,*

Can't Buy Me Love, She Loves You, I Want to Hold Your Hand and *Please Please Me.* They were also No. 1 and 2 on the L.P. charts with *Meet the Beatles* and *Introducing the Beatles.*

Long players The longest stay in the L.P. charts in the U.S.A. has been 490 weeks from late in 1958 to July 1968 by the Columbia album *Johnny's Greatest Hits* (Johnny Mathis). The longest in the U.K. has been *South Pacific* (sound track) with 306 weeks to 18 July 1964.

The best-selling L.P. is the 20th Century Fox album *Sing We now of Christmas,* issued in 1958 and re-entitled *The Little Drummer Boy* in 1963. Its sales were reported to be 13,000,000 by 1 Jan. 1970. The first British L.P. to sell 1,000,000 copies was *With the Beatles* (Parlophone), from November 1963 to January 1964 in the United States and to September 1965 in Britain. The top-selling British L.P. is *Sergeant Pepper's Lonely Hearts Club Band* with more than 7,000,000 to 1 Jan. 1970.

The all-time best-seller among long-playing records of musical film shows is *The Sound of Music* sound track album, released by R.C.A. Victor in U.S.A. on 2 March and in Britain on 9 April 1965, with 13,000,000 to 1 Jan. 1970.

The first classical long-player to sell a million was a performance featuring the pianist Harvey Lavan (Van) Cliburn, Jr. (born in Kilgore, Texas, 12 July 1934) of the *Piano Concerto No. 1* by Pyotr Ilyich Tchaikovsky (1840–93) (more properly rendered Chaykovskiy) of Russia. This recording was made in 1958 and sales reached 1,000,000 by 1961, 2,000,000 by 1965 and about 2,500,000 by January 1968.

Van Cliburn

The longest long-playing record is the 137-disc set of the complete works of William Shakespeare (1564–1616). The recordings, which were made in 1957–1964, cost £260 12s. 6d. per set, and are by the Argo Record Co. Ltd., London, S.W.3. The Vienna Philharmonic's playing of Wagner's "The Ring" covers 19 L.P.s., was eight years in the making, and requires 14½ hours playing time.

Fastest seller The fastest selling record of all time is *John Fitzgerald Kennedy—A Memorial Album* (Premium Albums), an L.P. recorded on 22 Nov. 1963, the day of Mr. Kennedy's assassination, which sold 4,000,000 copies at 99 cents (then 7s.) in six days (7–12 Dec. 1963), thus ironically beating the previous speed record set by the satirical L.P. *The First Family* in 1962–63. The fastest selling British record has been the Beatles' double album *The Beatles* (Parlophone) with "nearly 2 million" in its first week in November 1968.

Advance sales The greatest advance sale was 2,100,000 for *Can't Buy Me Love* by the Beatles, released in the United States on 16 March 1964. The Beatles also equalled their British record of 1,000,000 advance sales, set by *I Want to Hold Your Hand* (Parlophone) on 29 Nov. 1963, with this same record on 20 March 1964. The U.K. record for advance sales of an L.P. is 750,000 for the Parlophone album *Beatles For Sale* on 4 Dec. 1964.

Highest fee The highest fee ever paid to recording artists for a single performance is $189,000 (then £67,500), paid to the Beatles for a performance in the William A. Shea Stadium baseball park, New York City, N.Y., U.S.A., on 23 Aug. 1966.

Auguste and Louis Lumière (see below)

4. Cinema

EARLIEST
The greatest impetus in the development of cinematography came from the inventiveness of Étienne Jules Marey (1830–1903) of France.

The earliest demonstration of a celluloid cinematograph film was given at Lyon (Lyons), France on 22 March 1895 by Auguste Marie Louis Nicolas Lumière (1862–1954) and Louis Jean Lumière (1864–1948), the French brothers. The first public showing was at the Indian Salon of the Hotel Scribe, on the Boulevard des Capucines, in Paris, on 28 Dec. 1895. The 33 patrons were charged 1 franc each and saw ten short films, including *Baby's Breakfast, Lunch Hour at the Lumière Factory* and *The Arrival of a Train*. The same programme was shown on 20 Feb. 1896 at the Polytechnic Institute in Regent Street, London.

The earliest sound-on-film motion picture was demonstrated by Joseph Tykociner of the University of Illinois, U.S.A. in 1922. The event is more usually attributed to Dr. Lee de Forest (1873–1961) in New York City, N.Y., U.S.A., on 13 March 1923. The first all-talking picture was *Lights of New York,* shown at The Strand, New York City on 6 July 1928.

Highest production Japan annually produces most full length films, with 719 films of 1,500 metres (4,921 feet) or more completed

in 1966, compared with 304 films of 3,400 metres (11,155 feet) or more approved by the censor in India in 1964. This compares, however, with Japan's production of 1,000 films in 1928. The average seat price in Japan is 70 yen (1s. 4½d.). In the United Kingdom 71 films of 72 or more minutes duration and 192 short films were registered in the year ending 31 Dec. 1968.

Cinema-going The people of Taiwan go to the cinema more often than those of any other country in the world with an average of 66 attendances per person in 1967. The Soviet Union has the most cinemas in the world, with 140,900 in 1967 including those projecting only 16 mm. film. The number of cinemas in the U.K. declined from 4,542 in 1953 to 1,611 at 31 March 1970. The average weekly admissions declined from 24,700,000 in 1953 to 4,210,000 in 1969.

Cyprus has more cinema seats per total population than any other country in the world, with one cinema seat for every 8 people. Saudi Arabia has no cinemas. Excluding "captive" projectionists, the most persistent voluntary devotee of a film has been Mrs. Myra Franklin (b. 1919) of Cardiff, Wales, who saw *The Sound of Music* more than 900 times.

CINEMAS
Largest World The largest open-air cinema in the world is in the British Sector of West Berlin, Germany. One end of the Olympic Stadium, converted into an amphitheatre, seats 22,000 people.

United Kingdom The United Kingdom's largest cinema is the Odeon Theatre, Hammersmith, London, with 3,485 seats.

Oldest The earliest cinema was the "Electric Theatre", part of a tented circus in Los Angeles, California, U.S.A. It opened on 2 April 1902. The oldest building designed as a cinema is the Biograph Cinema in Wilton Road, Victoria, London. It was opened in 1905 and originally had seating accommodation for 500 patrons. Its present capacity is 700.

Biggest screen The largest cinema screen in the world is one measuring 130 feet by 39 feet (5,070 square feet) built by Andrew Smith Harkness Ltd. of Boreham Wood, Hertfordshire and shipped to South Africa in December 1967.

Most expensive film The most expensive film ever made is the 6 hour 12 min. long *War and Peace,* the U.S.S.R. government adaptation of the masterpiece of Tolstoy produced by Sergei Bondarchuk (born 1921) over the period 1962–67. The total cost has been officially stated to be more than £40,000,000. More than 165,000 uniforms had to be made. The re-creation of the Battle of Borodino involved 12,000 men and 800 horses on a location near Smolensk in 1964. It is reported that in the forthcoming epic "Waterloo" the Red Army is supplying 20,000 extras.

The most expensive musical made has been *Dr. Dolittle* which cost $19,500,000 (£8,125,000) and which had its *première* at the Odeon, Marble Arch, London, W.1, on 12 Dec. 1967.

The highest price ever paid for film rights is $5,500,000 (£1,964,284), paid on 6 Feb. 1962 by Warner Brothers for *My Fair Lady,* which cost $17,000,000 (£6,070,000), thus making it the most expensive musical film then made.

Longest film The longest film ever shown is *The Human Condition,* directed in three parts by Masaki Kobayashi of Japan. It lasts 8 hours 50 minutes, excluding two breaks of 20 minutes each. It was shown in Tōkyō in October 1961 at an admission price of 250 yen (4s. 11d.). The longest non-talking films are *Sleep,* consisting entirely of a man sleeping for eight hours, and *Empire State Building,* showing the building from the one angle for eight hours (8 p.m. to 4 a.m.). The only action in the latter is the lights going on and off. Both films were made by Andy Warhol of New York City, N.Y., U.S.A.

ngest run It was reported in September 1969 that *Me Tarzan You Jane* has been running in one Egyptian cinema since September 1949.

gest title The longest film title is: *Persecution and Assassination of Jean-Paul Marat as performed by the Inmates of the Asylum of Charenton under the direction of the Marquis de Sade,* made by the United Artists.

ghest box ice gross The film which has had the highest gross earnings (amount paid by cinema owners) is *The Sound of Music* (released in February 1965) which reached $112,481,000 (£46,867,000) by September 1969 having cost 20th Century Fox $8,100,000 to produce. The Producer/ Director Robert Wise reportedly received $11¼ million or 10 per cent. of the gross. The most successful black-and-white film has been *The Longest Day*, which cost $10,000,000 (then £3,570,000) to make and grossed $35,000,000 (now £14·58 million) from November 1962 to January 1968.

The fastest-earning film has been *Goldfinger*, the third in the series of films based on stories of James Bond (Agent 007 in the Secret Service) by Ian Lancaster Fleming (1908–64). The film grossed $10,300,000 (£3,678,000) in its first 14 weeks in the United States in 1965.

Highest rnings by an actor The greatest earnings by any film star for one film is expected to be that of Elizabeth Taylor in *Cleopatra*. Her undisputed share of the earnings is $3,000,000 (£1,070,000) and could eventually reach $7,000,000 (£2,500,000).

OSCARS

Walter (Walt) Elias Disney (1901–1966) won more "Oscars"—the awards of the United States Academy of Motion Picture Arts and Sciences, instituted on 16 May 1929 for 1927–28—than any other person. His total was 35 from 1931 to 1969. The only actress to win three Oscars has been Miss Katharine Hepburn, formerly Mrs. Ludlow Ogden Smith (b. 9 Nov. 1909) for the leading roles in *Morning Glory* (1932), *Guess Who's Coming to Dinner* (1968) and *The Lion in Winter* (1969). Oscars are named after Mr. Oscar Pierce of Texas, U.S.A. The films with most awards have been *Ben Hur* (1959) with 11, followed by *West Side Story* (1961) with 10. The film with the highest number of nominations was *All About Eve* (1950) with 14.

Newsreels The world's most durable newsreel commentator has been Bob Danvers Walker, who commentated for Pathé "Gazette" from June 1940 until its demise in February 1970. He is the owner of the car registration numbers TV 1 and RAD 10.

5. Radio Broadcasting

Most stations The country with the greatest number of radio transmitters is the United States, where there were 7,249 authorized transmitting stations in 1969 of which 4,263 were AM (Amplitude modulation) and 2,324 FM (Frequency modulation).

Radio sets There were an estimated 586,000,000 radio sets in use throughout the world at 30 June 1968, equivalent to 169 for each 1,000 people. Of these about 290,000,000 were in the United States (including Puerto Rico and the U.S. Virgin Islands) at 31 Dec. 1968. Of the U.S. total for the end of 1968 74,000,000 were in cars. The equivalent United Kingdom figure is 328 per 1,000 on the basis of 18,177,000 broadcast and broadcast/television licences current on 31 Jan. 1970. Of these only 2,346,000 were for sound only.

Marconi, earliest radio patentee

Origins The earliest description of a radio transmission system was written by Dr. Mahlon Loomis (U.S.A.) (born New York State, 1826) on 21 July 1864 and demonstrated between two kites at Bear's Den, Loudoun County, Virginia in October 1866.

Earliest patent The first patent for a system of communication by means of electro-magnetic waves, numbered No. 12039, was granted on 22 June 1896 to the Italian-Irish Marchese Guglielmo Marconi (1874–1937). The first permanent wireless installation was at The Needles on the Isle of Wight, Hampshire, by Marconi's Wireless Telegraph Co., Ltd., in November 1896.

Earliest broadcast The world's first advertised broadcast was made on 24 Dec. 1906 by Prof. Reginald Aubrey Fessenden (1868–1932) from the 420-foot mast of the National Electric Signalling Company at Brant Rock, Massachusetts, U.S.A. The transmission included the *Largo* by Georg Friedrich Händel (1685–1759) of Germany. Fessenden had achieved the broadcast of highly distorted speech as early as November 1900.

Transatlantic transmissions The earliest transatlantic wireless signals (the letter S in Morse Code) were sent by Marconi from a 10-kilowatt station at Poldhu, Cornwall, and received by Percy Wright Paget and G. S. Kempon at St. John's, Newfoundland, Canada, on 11 Dec. 1901. Human speech was first heard across the Atlantic in November 1915 when a transmission from the U.S. Navy station at Arlington, Virginia was received by U.S. radio-telephone engineers up the Eiffel Tower, Paris.

United Kingdom The first experimental broadcasting transmitter in the United Kingdom was set up at the Marconi Works in Chelmsford, Essex, in December 1919, and broadcast a news service in February 1920. The earliest regular broadcast of entertainment was made from the Marconi transmitter "2 MT" at Writtle, Essex, on 14 Feb. 1922.

Longest The longest B.B.C. broadcast was the reporting of the Coronation of Queen Elizabeth II on 2 June 1953. It began at 10.15 a.m. and finished at 5.30 p.m., after 7 hours 15 minutes. This was well surpassed by Radio Station ELBC, Monrovia, on 23 Nov. 1961 when a transmission of 14 hours 20 minutes was devoted to the coverage of the Queen's visit to Liberia.

The arts and entertainments

Most durable The most durable B.B.C. radio series is *The Week's Good Cause* beginning on 24 Jan. 1926. *Any Questions* was first broadcast on 1 Jan. 1941 and the longest running record programme is *Desert Island Discs* which began on 29 Jan. 1942.

Roy Plumley discussing Desert Island selections with Dame Gladys Cooper

6. Television

Invention The invention of television, the instantaneous viewing of distant objects, was not an act but a process of successive and inter-dependent discoveries. The first commercial cathode ray tube was introduced in 1897 by Karl Ferdinand Braun (1850–1918), but was not linked to "electric vision" until 1907 by Boris Rosing of Russia in St. Petersburg (now Leningrad). The earliest public demonstration of television was given on 26 Jan. 1926 by John Logie Baird (1888–1946) of Scotland, using a development of the mechanical scanning system suggested by Paul Nipkov in 1884. A patent application for the Iconoscope (No. 2,141,059) had been filed on 29 Dec. 1923 by Vladimir Kosma Zworykin (born in Russia on 30 July 1889, became a U.S. citizen in 1924), and a short range transmission of a model windmill had been made on 13 June 1925 by C. Francis Jenkins in Washington, D.C., U.S.A.

Earliest service The world's first public television broadcasting service was opened from Alexandra Palace, London, N.22, on 2 Nov. 1936, when there were about 100 sets in the United Kingdom. A television station at Berlin-Witzleben, Germany, made its first transmission on 4 April 1936.

Most sets In late 1968 the total estimated number of television transmitters in use or under construction was 5,450 serving 217,000,000 sets (63 for each 1,000 of the world population). Of these, about 94,200,000 were estimated to be in use in the United States where 96 per cent. of the population is reached. The number of colour sets in the U.S.A. has grown from 200,000 in 1960 to 20,100,000 in 1969. The number of licences current in the United Kingdom was 15,831,000 on 31 Jan. 1970 of which 226,000 were for colour sets.

Transatlantic transmission The earliest transatlantic transmission by satellite was achieved at 1 a.m. on 11 July 1962, *via* the active satellite *Telstar I* from Andover, Maine, U.S.A., to Pleumeur Bodou, France. The picture was of Mr. Frederick R. Kappel, chairman of the American Telephone and Telegraph Company, which owned the satellite. The first "live" broadcast was made on 23 July 1962. The earliest satellite transmission was one of 2,700 miles from California to Massachusetts, U.S.A., *via* the satellite *Echo I*, on 3 May 1962—the letters M.I.T.

Greatest audience The greatest number of viewers for a televised event is an estimated 600,000,000 for the live and recorded transmissions of man's first lunar landing with the *Apollo XI* mission on 20–21 July 1969. This total was reportedly matched by the viewership of the near-disaster of the *Apollo XIII* space mission of 11–17 April 1970.

Largest T.V. prizes World The greatest amount won by an individual in T.V. prizes was $264,000 (then £94,286) by Teddy Nadler on quiz programmes in the United States up to September 1958. In March 1960 he failed a test to become a census enumerator because of his inability to distinguish between east and west. His comment was, reportedly, "Those maps threw me". In Australia, where T.V. prizes were not subject to income tax, the most successful contestant has been Barry O. Jones, a schoolteacher of Windsor, Victoria, who won $A52,620 (then £21,012 sterling) between June 1960 and June 1966.

United Kingdom The largest T.V. prize won in the U.K. is £5,580 by Bernard Davis, aged 33, on Granada T.V.'s "Twenty-one" quiz programme, reached on 24 Sept. 1958.

Most successful appeal The greatest amount raised by any B.B.C. T.V. or Radio Appeal was £449,950, raised as a result of an appeal on 24 and 25 Aug. 1966 by Clifford Arthur Michelmore (born Cowes, Isle of Wight, 11 Dec. 1919), on behalf of the Disaster Emergency Committee fund for the victims of the earthquake in Eastern Anatolia, Turkey, on 19–20 Aug. 1966.

LARGEST CONTRACT

World The largest T.V. contract ever signed was one for $34,000,000 (£14,166,666) in a three-year no-option contract between Dino Paul Crocetti (b. 7 June 1917) otherwise Dean Martin, and N.B.C. Dean Martin was acclaimed in September 1968 as the top-earning show-business personality of all-time with $5,000,000 (over £2 million) in a year. Television's highest-paid interviewer has been Garry Moore (born Thomas Garrison Morfit on 31 Jan. 1915), who was earning $43,000 (£15,357) a week in 1963, equivalent to $2,236,000 (nearly £800,000) per year. Currently the highest paid performer is Johnny Carson on the N.B.C. "Tonight" show with a weekly salary of more than $30,000 (£10,714) and a clause whereby a $1,000,000 (£357,000) insurance policy will be maintained free of premiums. The advertising revenue from the programme is $7,000 (£2,500) per minute when it is broadcast nation-wide.

United Kingdom The largest contract in British television was one of a reported £9,000,000, inclusive of production expenses, signed by Tom Jones (born Thomas Jones Woodward, 7 June 1939) of Treforest, Glamorgan, Wales in June 1968 with ABC-TV of the United States and ATV in London for 17 one-hour shows per annum from January 1969 to January 1974.

Hourly The world's highest paid television performer based on an hourly rate is Perry Como (born Pierino Como, Canonsburg, Pennsylvania, U.S.A. on 18 May 1912) who began as a barber. In May 1969 he signed a contract with N.B.C. to star in four one-hour video specials at $5,000,000 (£2,083,033) or at the rate of £8,680 11s. per minute. The contract requires him to provide supporting artists.

Longest The longest pre-scheduled telecast on record was "1968—Year Unpredictable" transmitted by WMAQ-TV news from Chicago, Illinois, U.S.A. It lasted 8½ hours from 8 a.m. to 4.30 p.m. on 28 Dec. 1968.

Most durable B.B.C. programme The longest running T.V. programme on B.B.C. is *Panorama* which was first transmitted, introduced by Max Robertson, on 11 Nov. 1953. The News has been featured since 23 March 1938.

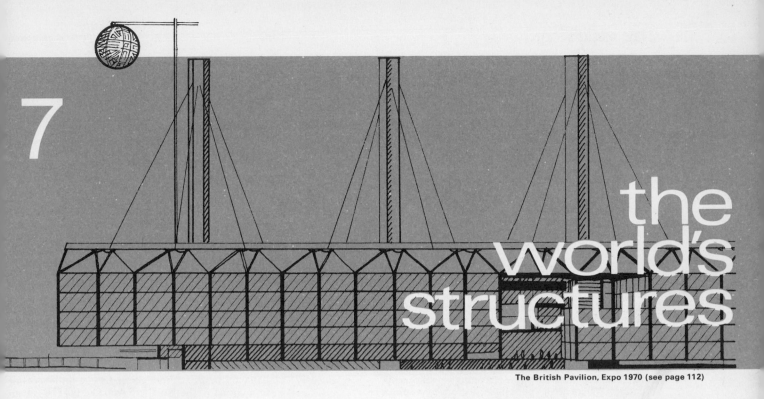

The British Pavilion, Expo 1970 (see page 112)

7 the world's structures

1. Buildings for Working

EARLIEST BUILDINGS

World The earliest evidence of structures yet discovered is that of huts with hearths found in October 1965 at the Terra Amata site in Nice, France and dated by pollen analysis to 300,000 B.C. Excavation carried out between 28 June and 5 July 1966 revealed an oval hut with palisaded walls with axes of 49 feet and 20 feet. There is however evidence of man's ability to make fire in the Abbevillian period c. 500,000 B.C. but no evidence as yet of the earliest hearths being surrounded by structures.

United Kingdom The oldest man-made dwelling discovered in Britain is the mesolithic pit dwelling excavated in September 1950 at Abinger Manor, Surrey, dated before 5,500 B.C. The rock shelter on Oldbury Hill, ¾ mile south-west of Ightham, Kent, is believed to have been occupied by the Mousterian people before the onset of the first phase of the last Ice Age in c. 120,000 B.C. The island of Ireland is not known to have been inhabited before the Larnian Culture of c. 6,000 B.C. and Scotland not before the Obanian Culture of c. 3,000 B.C.

LARGEST BUILDINGS

Manufacturing The most capacious building in the world is the main assembly building at the Boeing Company's works at Everett, Washington State, U.S.A. It has a capacity of 200,000,000 cubic feet. Construction was begun in August 1966 and parts were in use by late 1967. The building, constructed for the manufacture of Boeing 747 jet airliners, has a maximum height of 115 feet and encloses a floor area of 1,565,000 square feet (36·0 acres).

Scientific The most capacious scientific building in the world is the Vehicle Assembly Building (VAB) at Complex 39, the selected site for the final assembly and launching of the Apollo moon spacecraft on the Saturn V rocket, at the John F. Kennedy Space Center (KSC) on Merritt Island, near Cape Kennedy (formerly Cape Canaveral), Florida, U.S.A. It is a steel-framed building measuring 716 feet in length, 518 feet in width and 525 feet high. The building contains four bays, each with its own door 460 feet high. Construction began in April 1963 by the Ursum Consortium. Its floor area is 343,500 square feet (7·87 acres) and its capacity is 129,482,000 cubic feet. The building was "topped out" on 14 April 1965 at a cost of $108,700,000 (£45·3 million).

Administrative The largest ground area covered by any office building is that of the Pentagon, in Arlington County, Virginia, U.S.A. Built to house the U.S. Defense Department's offices, it was completed on 15 Jan. 1943 and cost about $83,000,000 (now £34,583,000). Each of the outermost sides of the Pentagon is 921 feet long and the perimeter of the building is about 1,500 yards. The five storeys of the building enclose a floor area of 6,500,000 square feet. During the day 29,000 people work in the building. The telephone system of the building has over 44,000 telephones connected by 160,000 miles of cable and its 220 staff handle 280,000 calls a day. Two restaurants, six cafeterias and ten snackbars and a staff of 675 form the catering department of the building. The corridors measure 17 miles in length and there are 7,748 windows to be cleaned.

Commercial The largest commercial building in the world is the Merchandise Mart, between Wells Street and Orleans Street, Chicago, Illinois, U.S.A. It was built between August 1928 and January 1931 at a cost of $32,000,000 (now £13·3 million) as a wholesale buying centre with a capacity of 56,000,000 cubic feet and a floor area of 4,023,400 square feet (92·34 acres). It has a river frontage of 577 feet and the rear extends 724 feet along Kinzie Street. The 25 storeys give it an extreme height of 353 feet. The average daily working population is 20,000 and the building consumes up to 201 tons of coal for heating in a day. The air-conditioning equipment has a capacity of 84,000,000 British Thermal Units per hour.

Office The largest commercial office building in the world is the Pan American World Airways (Pan Am) Building above Grand Central Terminal on 43rd and 44th Streets, New York City, N.Y., U.S.A. It contains 2,400,000 square feet of rentable space and 300,000 square feet of public areas. Heating is achieved by 56 acres of the flooring being wired. The air-conditioning plant has a

The world's largest building at Everett, Washington, U.S.A.

107

The world's structures

cooling capacity of 120,000,000 British Thermal Units per hour. The building has 59 storeys, rises 830 feet above street level and cost $100,000,000 (£41·7 million). It was opened on 7 March 1963, after 26 months' work. It is used by 25,000 workers.

Sears Roebuck and Co. announced in December 1969 the start of the construction of a 70 to 100 storey national headquarters building of 4 million square feet west of The Loop in Chicago, Illinois, U.S.A. Completion is expected in 1973 or 1974.

The largest single office in the United Kingdom is that of the West Midlands Gas Board at Solihull, Warwickshire, set up in 1962. It measures 565 feet by 160 feet (2·07 acres) in one open plan room accommodating 1,570 clerical and managerial workers.

TALLEST BUILDINGS

World The tallest inhabited building in the world is the Empire State Building on Fifth Avenue at 34th Street, New York City, N.Y., U.S.A. Standing on two acres of ground, it is 1,472 feet tall to the top of the television tower, which was added between 27 July 1950 and 1 May 1951 to the existing building of 1,250 feet. In its 102 storeys, 940 firms employ 25,000 people. About 1,000 people are constantly employed in day-to-day maintenance, including the cleaning of the 6,500 windows. There are 63 passenger lifts, or, if you prefer to walk, 1,860 steps from top to bottom. Completed on 1 May 1931, it cost £17,000,000 and occupied 7,000,000 man-hours with a peak building force of 4,000. (See footnotes.)

A maximum sway of 2·97 inches was recorded during a gale of 102 m.p.h. on 22 March 1936, though no reading was taken during the 113 m.p.h. hurricane on 14 Oct. 1954. No action is perceptible as the vibration period of 8·25 seconds is too slow to be felt.
Skyscrapers of up to 3,000 feet in height with 400 storeys are now regarded as feasible by the "suspend-arch" principle developed by the U.S. engineer Chelazzi.
The record for climbing the stairs of the Empire State Building was set on 16 Feb. 1932 by five members of the Polish Olympic ski-ing team, led by Stanislaw Skupien, who negotiated the stairs from the 5th to the 102nd floors in 21 minutes.

Work on the 16-acre Port of New York Authority's World Trade Center with twin towers of 110 storeys, standing 1,353 feet tall, was started in August 1966 on Barclay and Liberty Streets, Lower West Side, Manhattan Island, New York City, N.Y., U.S.A. It will not be completed until 1972. The total cost is estimated at $575,000,000 (£239,600,000). Two other buildings of greater height than the Empire State Building are in the planning stage in Chicago, Illinois, U.S.A. They are the Schaumburg Planet Corporation Building of 113 storeys and 1,300 feet (surmounted by a 250-foot antenna making a total height of 1,550 feet), and the Barrington Space Needle of 120 storeys and a height of 1,610 feet projected in Barrington, Illinois.

The government of West Germany has endorsed a feasibility study for a 365-storey tubular skyscraper to house 25,000 people in 8,000 apartments on a site at Münstereifel, 30 miles south-west of Köln (Cologne). The architect, Robert Gabriel, stated in October 1966 that the drawings alone would require three years' work. The height envisaged for the structure is 4,120 feet (0·78 of a mile).

Most storeys The greatest number of storeys planned for any building has been 120 in the 1,253-foot-tall wasp-waisted tower block planned in 1965, at a cost of $23,000,000 (£9,583,000), for Denver, Colorado, and the Barrington Space Needle (see above).

The World Trade Center (see above) will have 110 storeys—eight more than the Empire State Building.

United Kingdom The tallest block in the United Kingdom is the Euston Tower, standing 407 feet tall, completed in 1970, in Euston Road, London. It has 37 storeys and is reputedly worth £38,000,000.

HABITATIONS

Greatest altitude The highest inhabited buildings in the world are those in the Chilean mining village of Aucanquilca, at 17,500 feet above sea-level (see also Chapter XI). During the 1960–61 Himalayan High Altitude Expedition, the "silver hut", a prefabricated laboratory, was inhabited for four months in the Ming Bo Valley at 18,765 feet. In April 1961, however, a 3-room dwelling was discovered at 21,650 feet on Cerro Llullaillaco (22,058 feet), on the Argentine-Chile border, believed to date from the late pre-Columbian period *c*. 1480.

Northernmost The most northerly habitation in the world is the Danish scientific station set up in 1952 in Pearyland, northern Greenland, over 900 miles north of the Arctic Circle. Eskimo hearths dated to before 1,000 B.C. were discovered in Pearyland in 1969. The U.S.S.R. and the United States have maintained research stations on ice floes in the Arctic. The U.S.S.R.'s "North Pole 15" which drifted 1,250 miles passed within 1¼ miles of the North Pole in December 1967.

Southernmost The most southerly permanent human habitation is the United States' Scott-Amundsen I.G.Y. (International Geophysical Year) base 800 yards from the South Pole.

Largest embassy The largest embassy in the world is the U.S.S.R. embassy on Bei Xiao Jie, Peking, China, in the north-eastern corner of the Northern walled city. The whole 45-acre area of the old Orthodox Church mission (established 1728), now known as the *Bei guan*, was handed over to the U.S.S.R. in 1949. The largest in Great Britain is the United States of America Embassy in Grosvenor Square, London. The Chancery Building, completed in 1960, alone has 600 rooms for a staff of 700, on seven floors with a usable floor area of 255,000 square feet.

PLANTS

Atomic The largest atomic plant in the world is the Savannah River Project, near Aitken, South Carolina, U.S.A., extending 27 miles along the river and over a total area of 315 square miles. The plant, comprising 280 permanent buildings, cost $1,400 million (£583 million). Construction was started in February 1951 and by September 1952 the labour force had reached 38,500. The present operating strength is 8,500.

Underground The world's largest underground factory was the Mittelwerk Factory, near Nordhausen in the Kohnstein Hills, south of the Harz Mountains, Germany. It was built with concentration camp labour during World War II and had a floor area of 1,270,000 square feet and an output of 900 V-2 rockets per month.

Tallest chimneys The world's tallest chimney is the stack 1,206 feet tall at the Mitchell plant at Cresap, West Virginia, completed in September 1968. It was built by The M. W. Kellogg Company and the diameter tapers from 95 feet at the base to 37 feet at the top. The tallest chimney in Great Britain is one of 850 feet at Drax Power Station, Yorkshire, begun in 1966 and topped out on 16 May 1969. It was built by Holst & Co. Ltd. of Watford, Hertfordshire.

Cooling towers The largest cooling towers in the United Kingdom are the Ferrybridge "C" power station, Yorkshire, type measuring 375 feet tall and 300 feet across the base. Each of the first 24 of the eventual 38 cost £340,000.

The world's most southerly habitation—800 yards from the South Pole

LARGEST HANGARS

World The world's largest single hangar is Le Hangar N.6 at Orly Airport, Paris, France. It covers an area of 3·85 acres with an opening 300 metres (984 feet 3 inches) long, a depth of 170 feet, a minimum clear height of 15 metres (49 feet) and a maximum of 40 metres (131 feet). The total cost was £2,175,000 and it can house eight Caravelle jet airliners.

The largest group of hangars in the world is at the U.S. Air Force Base near San Antonio, Texas, U.S.A. These, including covered maintenance bays, cover 23 acres.

United Kingdom The largest hangar building in the United Kingdom is the Britannia Assembly Hall at the Bristol Aeroplane Company's works at Filton, Bristol. The overall width of the Hall is 1,054 feet and the overall depth of the centre bay is 420 feet. It encloses a floor area of 7½ acres. The cubic capacity of the Hall is 33,000,000 cubic feet. The building was begun in April 1946 and completed by September 1949.

GRAIN ELEVATOR

The world's largest single-unit grain elevator is that operated by the C-G-F- Grain Company at Wichita, Kansas, U.S.A. Consisting of a triple row of storage tanks, 123 on each side of the central loading tower or "head house", the unit is 2,717 feet long and 100 feet wide. Each tank is 120 feet high, with an inside diameter of 30 feet, giving a total storage capacity of 20,000,000 bushels of wheat. The largest collection of elevators in the world is at Port Arthur, Ontario, Canada, on Lake Superior.

LARGEST GARAGE

The largest garage in the world is that completed in September 1961 for the Austin Motor Works at Longbridge, near Birmingham. It has nine storeys and cost £500,000. It has a capacity of 3,300 cars. The United Kingdom's largest underground garage is Normand Ltd.'s Park Lane Garage, London, W.1, extending over nearly seven acres, 350 yards long by 96 yards wide with a capacity of 1,100 cars. It was opened on 15 Oct. 1962 at a cost of £1,051,915. The air can be changed six times per hour. The East corridor to Marble Arch tube station is 534 yards, or more than three-tenths of a mile, long.

Private garage The largest private garage ever built was one for 100 cars at the Long Island, New York mansion of William Kissam Vanderbilt (1849–1920).

Filling station The largest filling station of 36,000 in the United Kingdom is the Blue Star service station on the M.6 at Charnock Richard, Lancashire. It has 50 petrol pumps supplying five brands and 10 derv pumps (for diesel-engined road vehicles) supplying five brands of diesel fuel and extends over 14 acres.

LARGEST SEWAGE WORKS

World The largest single sewage works in the world is the West-Southwest Treatment Plant, opened in 1940 on a site of 501 acres in Chicago, Illinois, U.S.A. It serves an area containing 2,900,000 people. It treated an average of 735,000,000 gallons of wastes per day in 1965.

United Kingdom The highest average flow in the United Kingdom is that of the G.L.C. (Greater London Council) Beckton Sewage Treatment Works, London, E.6, completed in October 1959. The amount of sewage treated daily varies between 200 million gallons (dry weather) and 650 million gallons (wet weather). It serves an area of 112 square miles and about 3,000,000 people.

LARGEST WAREHOUSES

World The world's largest warehouse will be the Eurostore, now under construction for the Garoner warehousing firm on a 240-acre site near Le Bourget, in north-east Paris, France. The building will provide 5,400,000 square feet (124 acres) of floor-space.

United Kingdom The largest in the United Kingdom is the tobacco warehouse at Stanley Dock, Liverpool, with 11 storeys giving a total floor space of 36 acres, and a frontage of 625 feet.

Glasshouse The largest glasshouses in the United Kingdom are ones 548 feet long and 86½ feet wide, covering 1·09 acres at the Stanley Nurseries, Chichester, Sussex built by Frampton Ferguson Ltd. of Bognor Regis, Sussex.

2. Buildings for Living

EARLIEST BUILDINGS

World The earliest known human structure is a rough circle of sizeable stones, some piled on top of one another, found in 1960 on the very base of the deepest explored layer of the Olduvai Gorge in Tanganyika (now part of Tanzania). This dates from between 1,750,000 and 2,300,000 years ago. (See Chapter I, Earliest man.)

Wooden buildings The oldest wooden building in the world is the Temple of Horyu (Horyu-ji), built at Nara, Japan, in A.D. 708–715. The largest wooden building in the world, the nearby Daibutsuden, built in 1704–11, measures 285·4 feet long, 167·3 feet wide and 153·5 feet tall.

The municipal building occupied by the Department of Education in Wellington, New Zealand built in 1876 has the largest floor area of any wooden building with 101,300 square feet.

CASTLES

EARLIEST

World Castles in the sense of unfortified manor houses existed in all the great early civilizations, including that of ancient Egypt from 3,000 B.C. Fortified castles in the more accepted sense only existed much later. The oldest in the world is that at Gomdan, in the Yemen, which originally had 20 storeys and dates from before A.D. 100.

British Isles The oldest stone castle in the British Isles is Richmond Castle, Yorkshire, built in c. 1075. Iron Age relics from the first century B.C. or A.D. have been found in the lower levels of Dover Castle.

The oldest Irish castle is Ferrycarrig near Wexford dating from c. 1180. The oldest castle in Northern Ireland is Carrickfergus Castle, County Antrim, which dates from before 1210.

LARGEST

World The largest castle in the world is the Qila (Citadel) at Halab (Aleppo) in Syria. It is oval in shape and has a surrounding wall 1,230 feet long and 777 feet wide. It dates, in its present form, from the Humanid dynasty of the 10th century A.D.

The most massive keep in the world is that in the 13th-century château at Coucy-le-Chateau-Auffrique, in the Department of L'Aisne, France. It is 177 feet high, 318 feet in circumference and has walls over 22½ feet in thickness. The walls of Babylon north of Al Hillah, Iraq, built in 600 B.C., were up to 85 feet in thickness. The walls of part of Dover Castle, Kent, measure 20 feet in thickness. The largest Norman keep in Britain is that of Colchester Castle measuring 152½ feet by 111½ feet.

Richmond Castle, Yorkshire

The world's structures

United Kingdom and Ireland The largest castle in the British Isles and the largest inhabited castle in the world is the Royal residence of Windsor Castle at New Windsor, Berkshire. It is primarily of 12th century construction and is in the form of a parallelogram, 1,890 feet by 540 feet. The overall dimensions of Carisbrooke Castle (450 feet by 360 feet), Isle of Wight, if its earthworks are included, are 1,350 feet by 825 feet. The largest castle in Scotland was the now ruined Doune Castle, Perthshire, built *c.* 1425. The most capacious of all Irish castles is Carrickfergus (see p. 109) in Antrim but that with the most extensive fortifications is Trim Castle, County Meath, built in *c.* 1205 with a curtain wall 485 yards long.

Largest palaces
World The largest palace in the world is the Imperial Palace (*Gu gong*) in the centre of Peking (*Bei jing*, the northern capital), China, which covers a rectangle 1,050 yards by 820 yards, an area of 177·9 acres. The outline survives from the construction of the third Ming emperor Yong le of 1307–20, but due to constant re-arrangements most of the intra-mural buildings are 18th century. These consist of 5 halls and 17 palaces of which the last occupied by the last Empress was the Palace of Accumulated Elegance (*Chu xia gong*) until 1924.

The largest residential palace in the world is the Vatican Palace, in the Vatican City, an enclave in Rome, Italy. Covering an area of 13½ acres, it has 1,400 rooms, chapels and halls, of which the oldest date from the 15th century.

United Kingdom The largest palace in the United Kingdom in Royal use is Buckingham Palace, London, so named after its site, bought in 1703 by John Sheffield, the 1st Duke of Buckingham and Normanby (1648–1721). Buckingham House was reconstructed in the Palladian style between 1835 and 1836, following the design of John Nash (1752–1835). The 610-foot-long East Front was built in 1846 and refaced in 1912. The Palace, which stands in 39 acres of garden, has 600 rooms including a ballroom 111 feet long.

The longest ever Royal palace has been Hampton Court Palace, Greater London, acquired by Henry VIII from Cardinal Wolsey in 1525 and greatly enlarged by the King and later by William III, Anne and George I, whose son George II was its last resident monarch.

Largest moat The world's largest moats are those which surround the Imperial Palace in Peking (see above). From plans drawn by French sources it appears to measure 54 yards wide and have a total length of 3,600 yards.

FLATS
Largest The largest block of flats in Britain is Dolphin Square, London, covering a site of 7½ acres. The building occupies the four sides of a square enclosing gardens of about three acres. Dolphin Square contains 1,220 separate and self-contained flats, an underground garage for 300 cars with filling and service station, a swimming pool, eight squash courts, a tennis court and an indoor shopping centre. It cost £1,750,000 to build in 1936 but was sold to Westminster City Council for £4,500,000 in January 1963. Its nine storeys house 3,000 people.

The largest municipal block of flats in Britain is the Quarry Hill development, Leeds, Yorkshire, completed in 1940. The £497,140 building covers 3·65 acres and contains 938 dwellings, comprising 3,188 rooms housing 3,280 people. The Hyde Park development in Sheffield, Yorkshire, comprises 1,322 dwellings and an estimated population of 4,675 persons. It was built between 1959 and 1966.

Tallest The tallest block of flats in the world are Lake Point Towers of 70 storeys, and 645 feet in Chicago, Illinois, U.S.A. The highest in the United Kingdom are at Red Road, Balornock, Glasgow, which have 31 storeys and a height of 265 feet.

HOTELS
Largest
World The world's largest hotel is the Hotel Rossiya in Moscow, U.S.S.R., with 3,200 rooms providing accommodation for 6,000 guests, in three buildings, each of 14 storeys completed in December 1967. The largest hotel in a single building is the Conrad Hilton (formerly the Stevens) on Michigan Avenue, Chicago, Illinois, U.S.A. Its 25 floors contain 2,600 (originally 3,000) guest rooms. It would thus take more than seven years to spend one night in each room of the hotel. The hotel employs about 2,000 people, of whom more than 70 are telephone operators and supervisors, and 72 are lift operators. The laundry of the hotel, with 195 employees, handles 535 tons of flat work each month.

The largest hotel building in the world, on the basis of volume, is the Waldorf Astoria, on Park Avenue, New York City, N.Y., U.S.A. It occupies a complete block of 81,337 square feet (1·87 acres) and reaches a maximum height of 625 feet 7 inches. The Waldorf Astoria has 47 storeys and 1,900 guest rooms and maintains the largest hotel radio receiving system in the world. The Waldorf can accommodate 10,000 people at one time and has a staff of 1,700. The restaurants have catered for parties up to 6,000 at a time. The coffee-makers' daily output reaches 1,000 gallons. The electricity bill is about $360,000 (£150,000) each year.

United Kingdom The greatest capacity of any hotel in the United Kingdom is that of the Regent Palace Hotel, Piccadilly Circus, London (opened on 20 May 1915). It has 1,140 rooms accommodating 1,670 guests. The total staff numbers 1,200. The largest hotel is the Grosvenor House Hotel, Park Lane, London, which was opened in 1929. It is of 8 storeys covering 2½ acres and caters for more than 100,000 visitors per year in 470 rooms. The Great Room is the largest hotel room in Great Britain measuring 181 feet by 131 feet with a height of 23 feet. Banquets for 1,500 are frequently handled.

Tallest The world's tallest hotel is the 34-storey Ukrania in Moscow, U.S.S.R., which, including its tower, is 650 feet tall. The highest hotel rooms in the world are those on the topmost 50th storey of the 509-foot-tall Americana Hotel, opened on 24 Sept. 1962 on 7th Avenue at 52nd Street, New York City, N.Y., U.S.A. Britain's tallest hotel is the 33-storey London Hilton (328 feet tall), completed in Park Lane, London, W.1, in 1962. It was opened on 17 April, 1963.

Most expensive The world's costliest hotel is the Mauna Kea Beach Hotel on Hawaii Island, U.S.A., which was built at a cost of $15,000,000 (£6,250,000) and has only 154 rooms. This implies a construction and amenity cost of more than £40,600 per room.

The most expensive hotel suites in Britain are the luxury suites in the London Hilton, Park Lane, London, W.1. Some suites are 80 guineas (£84) per night.

SPAS
The largest spa in the world measured by number of available hotel rooms is Vichy, Allier, France, with 14,000 rooms. Spas are named after the watering place in the Liège province of Belgium where hydropathy was developed from 1626. The highest French spa is Barèges, Hautes-Pyrénées, at 4,068 feet above sea level.

Housing estate The largest housing estate in the United Kingdom is the 1,670-acre Becontree Estate, on a site of 3,000 acres in Barking and Redbridge, Greater London, built between 1921 and 1929. The total number of homes is 26,822, with an estimated population of nearly 90,000.

Largest house
World The largest private house in the world is the 250-room Biltmore House in Asheville, North Carolina, U.S.A. It is owned by George and William Cecil, grandsons of George Washington Vanderbilt II (1862–1914). The house was built between 1890 and 1895 in an estate of 119,000 acres, at a cost of $4,100,000 (now £1,708,333)

and now valued at $55,000,000 with 12,000 acres. The most expensive private house ever built is La Cuesta Encunada at San Simeon, California, U.S.A. It was built in 1922–39 for William Randolph Hearst (1863–1951), at a total cost of more than $30,000,000 (now £12,500,000). It has more than 100 rooms, a 104-foot-long heated swimming pool, an 83-foot-long assembly hall and a garage for 25 limousines. The house required 60 servants to maintain it.

United Kingdom The largest house in the United Kingdom is Wentworth Woodhouse, near Rotherham, Yorkshire, formerly the seat of the Earls Fitzwilliam. The main part of the house, built over 300 years ago, has more than 240 rooms with over 1,000 windows, and its principal facade is 600 feet long. The Royal residence, Sandringham House, Norfolk, has been reported to have 365 rooms. The largest house in Ireland is Castletown in County Kildare, formerly owned by Lord Carew. Scotland's largest house is Hopetoun House, West Lothian, built between 1696 and 1756 with a west facade 675 feet long.

Palace House, Beaulieu

Stately home most visited The most visited stately home in the United Kingdom is Beaulieu, Hampshire, owned by Lord Montagu of Beaulieu with 533,597 visitors in 1969. The figures for Woburn Abbey, Bedfordshire, owned by the Duke of Bedford, have not been published since 1963 but reached 470,000 as early as 1961.

Smallest The smallest house in Britain is the 19th-century fisherman's cottage on Conway Quay, Caernarvonshire, North Wales. It has a 72-inch frontage, is 122 inches high and has two tiny rooms and a staircase.

Most expensive The most expensive private house in Britain is Ramsbury Manor, Wiltshire, which was bought by an American property dealer as a residence for a price, including the 460-acre grounds, of reportedly £650,000 in May 1965. The house itself, which dates from c. 1660, cost £275,000.

3. Buildings for Entertainment

LARGEST STADIUM

World The world's largest stadium is the Strahov Stadium in Praha (Prague), Czechoslovakia. It was completed in 1934 and can accommodate 240,000 spectators for mass displays of up to 40,000 Sokol gymnasts.

The largest football stadium in the world is the Maracaña Municipal Stadium in Rio de Janeiro, Brazil, where the football ground has a normal capacity of 205,000, of whom 155,000 may be seated. A crowd of 199,854 was accommodated for the World Cup final between Brazil and Uruguay on 16 July 1950. A dry moat, 7 feet wide and over 5 feet deep, protects players from spectators and *vice versa*. The stadium also has facilities for indoor sports, such as boxing, and these provide accommodation for an additional 32,000 spectators.

The largest covered stadium in the world is the Empire Stadium, Wembley, London, opened in April 1923. It was the scene of the 1948 Olympic Games and the final of the 1966 World Cup. In 1962–63 the capacity under cover was increased to 100,000, of whom 45,000 may be seated. The original cost was £1,250,000. The

Azteca Stadium, Mexico City, Mexico, opened in 1968, has a capacity of 107,000 of whom nearly all are under cover.

United Kingdom The highest capacity stadium in the United Kingdom is that at Hampden Park, Glasgow, which accommodated a football crowd of 149,547 on 17 April 1937.

Largest indoor The world's largest indoor stadium is the Harris County Sports Stadium, or Astrodome, in Houston, Texas, U.S.A. opened in April 1965. It has a capacity of 45,000 for baseball and 66,000 (maximum) for boxing. The domed stadium covers 9½ acres and is so large that an 18-storey building could be built under the roof (208 feet high). The total cost was $38,000,000 (£15,830,000). In some conditions of humidity it would rain if the air conditioning equipment, which has a cooling capacity of 79,200,000 British Thermal Units per hour, were turned off (see also Largest dome, p. 121).

Largest roofed stadium Tenders for the construction of a transparent "tent" roof over the Munich Olympic Stadium, West Germany were issued in August 1969 which called for a size of 914,940 square feet in area. It will rest on a steel net supported by masts.

Largest ballroom The largest ballroom in the United Kingdom is the Orchid Ballroom, Purley, Surrey. The room is over 200 feet long and 117 feet wide, and has a total floor area of 23,320 square feet. When laid out for dance championships, the floor of the Earl's Court Exhibition Hall is 256 feet in length. The Empress Ballroom, Blackpool, Lancashire, when used for dances, can accommodate 4,500 couples.

Amusement resort The world's largest amusement resort is Disneyland, in Anaheim, California, U.S.A. It was opened on 18 July 1955 and has an area of 190 acres. The investment has increased from an initial $17,000,000 (£7,083,000) to $95,000,000 (£39,583,000) by 1968. The total attendance surpassed 70,000,000 in 1968. In October 1965 27,443 acres were purchased in Orange and Osceola counties, near Orlando in central Florida, for "Disney World", due to be opened in 1971.

NIGHT CLUBS

Oldest The oldest night club (*boîte de nuit*) is "Le Bal des Anglais" at 6 Rue des Anglais, Paris 5me, France. It was founded in 1843.

Largest The largest night club in the world is that in the Imperial Room of the Concord Hotel in the Catskill Mountains, New York State, U.S.A., with a capacity of 3,000 patrons. In the more classical sense the largest night club in the world is "The Mikado" in the Akasaka district of Tōkyō, Japan, with a seating capacity of 2,000. It is "manned" by 1,250 hostesses, some of whom earn an estimated £4,800 per annum. Long sight is essential to an appreciation of the floor show.

Loftiest The highest night club will be that on the 52nd storey of the Antigone Building, now under construction, in Montparnasse, Paris, at 187 metres (613·5 feet) above street level.

Lowest The lowest night club is the "Minus 206" in Tiberias, Israel, on the shores of the Sea of Galilee. It is 206 metres (676 feet) below sea-level.

PLEASURE BEACH

The largest pleasure beach in the world is Virginia Beach, Virginia, U.S.A. It has 28 miles of beach front on the Atlantic and 10 miles of estuary frontage. The area embraces 255 square miles and 134 hotels and motels.

Longest pleasure pier The longest pleasure pier in the world is Southend Pier at Southend-on-Sea in Essex. It is 1·33 miles in length. It was built in 1889, with final extensions made in 1929. It is decorated with more than 75,000 lamps.

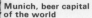
Munich, beer capital of the world

FAIRS

The largest fair ever held was the New York World's Fair, covering 1,216½ acres of Flushing Meadow Park, Queens Borough, Long Island, New York, U.S.A. The fair was open at times between 20 April 1939 and 21 Oct. 1940 and there were 25,817,265 admissions. The attendance of 51,607,037 for the 1964–65 Fair was an all-time record. The one-year record attendance for any fair was 50,306,648 at the Universal and International Exhibition or "Expo 67", which ran from 27 April to 30 Oct. 1967 on a 700-acre site on the Île de Sainte-Hélène and the Île Notre Dame, Montréal, Québec, Canada. Sixty-two nations participated and total costs have been estimated at $750 million. The total loss had been budgeted as $Can. 137,000,000 on an expectation of 35,000,000 visitors but, despite higher attendances, the actual loss incurred a figure of $Can. 250,000,000. The attendance at the Expo 70 at Osaka, Japan opened on an 815-acre site in March 1970 is expected to exceed all previous records.

Big wheel The original Ferris Wheel, named after its constructor, George W. Ferris (1859–96), was erected in 1893 at the Midway, Chicago, Illinois, U.S.A., at a cost of $300,000 (now £125,000). The wheel was 250 feet in diameter, 790 feet in circumference, weighed 1,070 tons, and carried 36 cars each seating 40 people, making a total of 1,440 passengers. The structure was removed in 1904 to St. Louis, Missouri, and was eventually sold as scrap for $1,800 (now £750). In 1897 a Ferris Wheel with a diameter of 300 feet was erected for the Earls Court Exhibition, London. It had ten 1st-class and 30 2nd-class cars.

Fastest switchback The world's fastest gravity switchback is the Bobs in the Belle Vue Amusement Park, Manchester, Lancashire. The cars attain a peak speed of 61 m.p.h. The track is 862 yards 2 inches long and the maximum height is 76 feet.

PUBLIC HOUSES

Largest The largest beer-selling establishment in the world is the Mathäser, Bayerstrasse 5, München (Munich), West Germany, where the daily sale reaches 84,470 pints. It was established in 1829, was demolished in World War II and re-built by 1955 and now seats 5,500 people. The through-put at the Dube beer halls in the Bantu township of Soweto, Johannesburg, South Africa may, however, be higher on some Saturdays when the average consumption of 6,000 gallons (48,000 pints) is far exceeded. The largest public house in the United Kingdom is the Downham Tavern, near Bromley, Kent. Built in 1930 to serve the Downham Estate, it employs 20 permanent staff with an additional 18 to 20 people during rush periods. The two large bars, counter length 45 feet, are able to hold 1,000 customers. During the peak periods, an annexe is opened to accommodate the extra customers and the equivalent of 30,000 bottles of beer per week are served. The total drinking space is 9,271 square feet. It is owned by the Courage Group.

The house with the largest permanently available "drinking space"—11,500 square feet in five bars and lounges—is the Broadway Hotel in Morecambe, Lancashire. It is owned by the Scottish and Newcastle Breweries.

Smallest The smallest pub in the United Kingdom is "The Smith's Arms" in Godmanstone, Dorset, which is only 10 feet wide and 4 feet high at the eaves. It has a licence granted personally by Charles II (reigned 1660–85).

Highest The highest public house in the United Kingdom is the Tan Hill Inn in Yorkshire. It is 1,732 feet above sea-level, on the moorland road between Reeth in Yorkshire and Brough in Westmorland.

Oldest There are various claimants to the title of the United Kingdom's oldest inn. The foremost claimants include "The Angel and Royal" (c. 1450) at Grantham, Lincolnshire, which has cellar masonry dated 1213; the "George" (early 15th century) at Norton St. Philip, Somerset; "The George and Vulture" off Lombard Street, in the City of London, first mentioned in 1175, the oldest inn in Wales the Skirrid Mountain Inn, Llanvihangel Crucorney, Monmouthshire recorded in 1110; and "The Trip to Jerusalem" in Nottingham, with foundations believed to date back to 1070. An origin as early as A.D. 560 has been claimed for Ye Olde Ferry Boat Inn at Holywell, Huntingdonshire. There is some evidence that it ante-dates the local church, built in 980, but the earliest documents are not dated earlier than 1100. There is evidence that the Bingley Arms, Bardsey, near Leeds, Yorkshire, re-built in 1738, existed as the Priest's Inn according to Bardsey Church records dated 953.

Longest name The English pub with the longest name was the 39 letter "The Thirteenth Mounted Cheshire Rifleman Inn" at Stalybridge, Cheshire. The word "Mounted" is now omitted making "The Shoulder of Mutton and Cucumbers Inn" at Yapton, Sussex, a 34 letter candidate.

Shortest name There are three public houses in the United Kingdom with names of only two letters: the "XL", a hotel at Nateby, near Garstang, Lancashire· the "C.B." Hotel, Arkengarthdale, near Richmond, Yorkshire; and the now defunct M.C. Bar, Hawkhill, Dundee.

Longest bars The longest bar with beer pumps is that built in 1938 at the Working Men's Club, Mildura, Victoria, Australia. It has a counter 287 feet in length, served by 32 pumps.

The longest bar in the United Kingdom with beer pumps is the French Bar (198 feet 5½ inches) at Butlin's Holiday Camp, Filey, Yorkshire. It has 20 beer pumps, 12 tills and stillage for 30 barrels, and is operated by 30 barmaids, 20 floor waiters and 20 other hands. The Grand Stand Bar at Galway Racecourse, Ireland completed in 1955, measures 210 feet.

Wine cellar The largest wine cellars in the world are at Paarl, those of the Ko-operative Wijnbouwers Vereeniging (K.W.V.) near Cape Town, in the centre of the wine-growing district of South Africa. They cover an area of 25 acres and have a capacity of 30,000,000 gallons. The largest blending vats have a capacity of 45,700 gallons and are 17 feet high, with a diameter of 26 feet.

4. Major Civil Engineering Structures

TALLEST STRUCTURES

World The tallest structure in the world is a stayed television transmitting tower 2,063 feet tall, between Fargo and Blanchard, North Dakota, U.S.A. It was built at a cost of about $500,000 (£208,000) for Channel 11 of KTHI-TV, owned by the Pembina Broadcasting Company of North Dakota, a subsidiary of the Polaris Corporation from Milwaukee, Wisconsin, U.S.A. The tower was erected in 30 days (2 Oct. to 1 Nov. 1963) by 11 men of the Kline Iron and Steel Company of Columbia, South Carolina, U.S.A., who designed and fabricated it. The cage elevator in the centre rises to 1,948 feet. The tower is built to allow for a sway of up to 13·9 feet in a wind gusting to 120 m.p.h. and is so tall that anyone falling off the top would no longer be accelerating just before hitting the ground.

112

United Kingdom The tallest structure in the United Kingdom is the Independent Television Authority's mast at Belmont, north of Horncastle, Lincolnshire, completed in 1965 to a height of 1,265 feet with 7 feet added by meteorological equipment installed in September 1967. It serves Anglia T.V. and was severely threatened by the icing on 21 March 1969 which two days earlier felled the 1,265-foot Emley Moor mast in Yorkshire.

TALLEST TOWERS

World The tallest self-supporting tower (as opposed to a guyed mast) in the world is the 1,749-foot-tall tower at Ostankino, Greater Moscow, U.S.S.R., topped out in May 1967. It is of reinforced concrete construction and weighs over 22,000 tons. A three-storey restaurant revolves at the 882-foot level and there is a balcony of 1,050 feet. In a high wind the T.V. antennae may sway

up to 26 feet but the restaurant only 3·14 inches. The tower was designed by N. V. Nikitin.

The tallest tower built before the era of television masts is the Eiffel Tower, in Paris, France, designed by Alexandre Gustav Eiffel (1832–1923) for the Paris exhibition and completed on 31 March 1889. It was 300·51 metres (985 feet 11 inches) tall, now extended by a T.V. antenna to 1,052 feet 4 inches, and weighs 6,900 tons. The maximum sway in high winds is 5 inches. The whole iron edifice which has 1,792 steps, took 2 years, 2 months and 2 days to build and cost 7,799,401 francs 31 centimes. The 342nd suicide committed from the tower occurred on 9 Sept. 1965.

The architects André and Jean Polak put forward a design in February 1969 for a tower 2,378·6 feet (725

TALLEST STRUCTURES IN THE WORLD—PROGRESSIVE RECORDS

Height in feet	Structure	Location	Material	Building or Completion Dates
204	Djoser step pyramid (earliest Pyramid)	Saqqâra, Egypt	Tura limestone	c. 2650 B.C.
294	Pyramid of Meidun	Meidun, Egypt	Tura limestone	c. 2600 B.C.
c. 336	Snefru Bent pyramid	Dahshûr, Egypt	Tura limestone	c. 2600 B.C.
342	Snefru North Stone pyramid	Dahshûr, Egypt	Tura limestone	c. 2600 B.C.
480·9[1]	Great Pyramid of Cheops (Khufu)	El Gizeh, Egypt	Tura limestone	c. 2580 B.C.
525[2]	Lincoln Cathedral, Central Tower	Lincoln, England	lead sheathed wood	c. 1307–1548
489[3]	St. Paul's Cathedral	London, England	lead sheathed wood	1315–1561
465	Minster of Notre Dame	Strasbourg, France	vosges sandstone	1420–1439
502[4]	St. Pierre de Beauvais	Beauvais, France	lead sheathed wood	–1568
475	St. Nicholas Church	Hamburg, Germany		1846–1874
485	Rouen Cathedral	Rouen, France	cast iron	1823–1876
513	Köln Cathedral	Cologne, West Germany	stone	–1880
555	Washington Memorial	Washington, D.C., U.S.A.	stone	1848–1884
985·9[5]	La Tour Eiffel	Paris, France	steel	1887–1889
1,046	Chrysler Building	New York City, U.S.A.	steel and concrete	1929–1930
1,250[6]	Empire State Building	New York City, U.S.A.	steel and concrete	1929–1930
1,572	KWTV Television Mast	Oklahoma City, U.S.A.	steel	Nov. 1954
1,610[7]	KSWS Television Mast	Roswell, N. Mexico., U.S.A.	steel	Dec. 1956
1,619	WGAN Television Mast	Portland, Maine, U.S.A.	steel	Sept. 1959
1,676	KFVS Television Mast	Cape Girardeau, Missouri, U.S.A.	steel	June 1960
1,749	WTVM & WRBL TV Mast	Columbus, Georgia, U.S.A.	steel	May 1962
1,749	WBIR-TV Mast	Knoxville, Tennessee, U.S.A.	steel	Sept. 1963
2,063	KTHI-TV Mast	Fargo, North Dakota, U.S.A.	steel	Nov. 1963

[1] *Original height. With loss of pyramidion (topmost stone) height now 449 ft. 6 in.*
[2] *Fell in a storm.*
[3] *Struck by lightning and destroyed in August 1561.*
[4] *Fell April 1573, shortly after completion.*
[5] *Original height. With addition of T.V. antenna in 1957, now 1,052 ft. 4 in.*
[6] *Original height. With addition of T.V. tower on 1 May 1951 now 1,472 ft.*
[7] *Fell in gale in 1960.*

TALLEST TELEVISION AND RADIO MASTS BY COUNTRIES

Country	Structure	Height in feet
United States	KTHI-TV Mast, Fargo, North Dakota	2,063
U.S.S.R.	Ostankino T.V. Tower, Greater Moscow	1,749
Iceland	Loran Mast, Snaefellsnes	1,378
Greenland	Danish Government Navigational Mast, Thule	1,345
West Germany	West Berlin T.V. Tower	1,312
China (mainland)	Peking Radio Mast	1,312
United Kingdom	I.T.A. Mast, Belmont, Lincolnshire	1,272
Australia	Tower Zero, North West Cape, Western Australia	1,271
Netherlands	Zender Lopik (T.V. Mast), near Lopik	1,253
East Germany	East Berlin T.V. Tower	1,185
Pacific Islands	Loran Tower, Tomil, Yap	1,100
Puerto Rico	WAPA-TV Mast, Cayey	1,100
Canada	CHTV Channel 11 Mast, Hamilton, Ontario	1,093
Japan	Tōkyō Television Tower (self-supporting)	1,092
France	Tour Eiffel, Paris	1,052
Finland (10)	Masts at Jyväskylä, Lapua, Kerimäki, Tervola, Eurajoki, Pyhätunturi, Kiiminki, Kuusisto, Sippola and Tiirismaa	1,050
Czechoslovakia	"Jizní Morava" T.V. Mast, Kojál	1,033
Hungary	Lakihegg Mast	1,006
Northern Ireland	I.T.A. Mast, Strabane, County Tyrone	1,000
Scotland (2)	I.T.A. Mast, Black Hill, Lanarkshire, and Durris, Kincardineshire	1,000
Wales	I.T.A. Mast, Brynchain, Caernarvonshire	1,000

PROGRESSIVE RECORD OF WORLD'S LONGEST BRIDGE SPANS

Feet	Location	Type	Completion
121	Martorell, Spain	Stone Arch	219 B.C.
142	Nera River, Lucca, Italy	Stone Arch	14 A.D.
170	Trajan's Bridge, Danube River	Timber Arch	104
251	Trezzo, Italy	Stone Arch	1377
390	Wettingen, Switzerland	Timber Arch	1758
408	Schuylkill Falls, Philadelphia, Pa.	Suspension	1816
449	Union Bridge, Berwick, England	Chain	1820
580	Menai Straits, Wales	Chain	1826
870	Fribourg, Switzerland	Suspension	1834
1,010	Wheeling-Ohio Bridge	Suspension	1849
1,043	Lewiston Bridge, Niagara River	Suspension	1851
1,057	Covington-Cincinnati Bridge (rebuilt 1898)	Suspension	1867
1,268	Clifton Bridge, Niagara Falls	Suspension	1869
1,595½	Brooklyn Bridge, New York City	Suspension	1883
1,706	Forth Bridge, Scotland	Cantilever	1889
1,800	Quebec Bridge, Canada	Cantilever	1917
1,850	Ambassador Bridge, Detroit	Suspension	1929
3,500	George Washington Bridge, New York City	Suspension	1931
4,200	San Francisco Golden Gate	Suspension	1937
4,260	Verrazano-Narrows Bridge, New York City	Suspension	1965

The Mackinac Straits Bridge, Michigan, U.S.A.

metres) in height to be erected at La Défense in Paris.

United Kingdom The tallest tower in the United Kingdom is the Post Office Tower, opened on 8 Oct. 1965 in Maple Street, off Tottenham Court Road, London W.1. It is 580 feet tall to the top of the concrete structure and 620 feet to the top of the lattice mast.* The weight of the tower and its foundations has been estimated at 13,000 tons. Construction of a concrete tower 1,018 feet tall on Emley Moor was begun in November 1969.

The fastest times recorded for racing up the 814 steps to the top observation floor are:—Male: Norman Harrison (Imperial College, London) 4 min. 21·4 secs. Female: Hillary Tanner (Hull University) 7 min. 00·5 sec. both on 6 Feb. 1970. Competitors are limited to students.

5. Bridges

OLDEST

World Arch construction was understood by the Sumerians as early as 3,600 B.C. but the oldest surviving bridge in the world is the slab stone single arch bridge over the River Meles in Smyrna (now Izmir), Turkey, which dates from c. 850 B.C.

Britain The oldest bridge in Britain is the clapper bridge over the River Barle, known as the Tarr Steps, Exmoor, Somerset, built of massive boulder and slab and believed to date from before 500 B.C.

LONGEST

Suspension World The world's longest single span bridge is the Verrazano-Narrows Bridge stretching across the entrance to New York City harbour from Richmond, Staten Island to Brooklyn. Work on the $305,000,000 (then £109 million) project began on 13 Aug. 1959 and the bridge was opened to traffic on 21 Nov. 1964. It measures 6,690 feet between supports and will carry two decks, each of six lanes of traffic. The centre span is 4,260 feet and the tops of the main towers (each 690 feet tall) are 1⅝ inches out of parallel, to allow for the curvature of the Earth. The traffic in the first 12 months was 17,000,000 vehicles, and is expected to rise to 48,000,000 per year on two decks by 1981. The bridge was designed by Othmar H. Ammann (1879–1965), a Swiss-born engineer.

The Mackinac Straits Bridge between Mackinaw City and St. Ignace, Michigan, U.S.A., is the longest suspension bridge in the world measured between supports (8,344 feet) and has an overall length, including viaducts of the bridge proper measured between abutment faces, of 19,203 feet 4 inches. It was completed in November 1957 (opened 28 June 1958) at a cost of $100 million (then £35,700,000) and has a main span of 3,800 feet.

Detailed plans have been published for the building of a $333 million (£138·7 million) suspension bridge with a central span of 1,300 metres (4,265 feet), across the Akashi Straits, west of Kobe, Japan. It will have an overall length of 4,900 metres (16,076 feet or 3·04 miles), including all main and side spans. The distance between the main anchors will be 8,530 feet and the cables will be 126 centimetres (50 inches) in diameter. Even longer main spans are planned for completion in 1976 across the Humber Estuary (4,580 feet), a bridge of 4,600 feet across Tōkyō Bay, Japan, and one of 5,000 feet, with piers 400 feet deep, across the Messina Straits, Italy.

United Kingdom The longest span bridge in the United Kingdom is the Firth of Forth Road Bridge with a main channel span of 3,300 feet and side spans of 1,340 feet each, opened on 4 Sept. 1964. The main towers each stand 512 feet high. It is the sixth longest span in the world and cost £11,000,000 excluding the approaches.

Cantilever World The Quebec Bridge (Pont de Québec) over the St. Lawrence River in Canada has the longest cantilever span of any in the world—1,800 feet between the piers

LONGEST BRIDGE SPANS IN THE WORLD—BY TYPE

Type	feet	metres	Location	Built
Suspension	4,265	1,298·4	Verrazano-Narrows, New York, N.Y., U.S.A.	1964
Cantilever	1,800	548·6	Quebec Railway Bridge, Québec, Canada	1917
Tied Arch (steel)	1,652	503·6	Bayonne (Kill van Kull), New York, N.Y., U.S.A.	1931
Continuous Truss	1,232	375·5	Astarca, Columbia River, Oregon, U.S.A.	1966
Cable-Stayed	1,050	320·0	Knie, Düsseldorf, West Germany	1969
Chain Suspension	1,114	339·5	Florianopolis, Santa Catharina, Brazil	1926
Concrete Arch	1,000	304·8	Gladesville, Sydney, Australia	1964
Plate and Box Girder	856	261·0	Sava I, Belgrade, Yugoslavia	1956

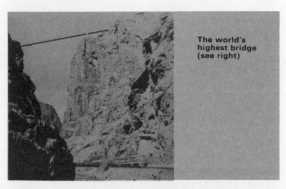

The world's highest bridge (see right)

and 3,239 feet overall. It carries two railway tracks. Begun in 1899, it was finally opened to traffic on 3 Dec. 1917 at a cost of 84 lives, and \$Can. 22,400,000 (£8,400,000).

United Kingdom The longest cantilever bridge in the United Kingdom is the Forth Bridge. Its two main spans are 1,710 feet long. It carries a double railway track over the Firth of Forth 150 feet above the water level. Work commenced in November 1882 and the first test trains crossed on 22 Jan. 1890 after an expenditure of £3 million. Of the 4,500 workers who built it, 57 were killed in various accidents.

Steel arch World The longest steel arch bridge in the world is the Bayonne Bridge over the Kill Van Kull, which has connected Bayonne, New Jersey, to Staten Island, New York, since its completion in November 1931. Its span is 1,652 feet 1 inch—25 inches longer than the Sydney Harbour Bridge, Australia (see below).

United Kingdom The longest steel arch bridge in the United Kingdom is the Runcorn-Widnes bridge from Widnes, Lancashire, to Runcorn, Cheshire, opened on 21 July 1961. It has a span of 1,082 feet and a total length including approaches of 3,489 feet.

Largest The largest steel arch bridge in the world is the Sydney Harbour Bridge in Sydney, New South Wales, Australia. Its main arch span is 1,650 feet long and it carries two electric overhead railway tracks, eight lanes of roadway, a cycleway and a footway, 172 feet above the waters of Sydney Harbour. It took seven years to build and was officially opened on 19 March 1932 at a cost of £A9,500,000 (then £7,600,000). Its total length is 3,770 feet excluding viaducts.

Floating The longest floating bridge in the world is the Hood Canal Bridge near Seattle, Washington State, U.S.A. completed in 1963. Its total length is 9,374 feet and its floating section measures 7,519 feet (1·42 miles). It was built at a cost of \$23,000,000 (£9,583,000).

Railway The longest railway bridge in the world is the Huey P. Long Bridge, New Orleans, Louisiana, U.S.A. with a railway section 22,996 feet (4·35 miles) long. It was completed on 10 Dec. 1935 with a longest span of 790 feet. The longest railway bridge in Britain is the second Tay Bridge (10,780 feet), joining Fife and Angus, opened on 20 June 1887. Of the 85 spans, 74 (length 10,289 feet) are over the waterway.

HIGHEST
The highest suspension bridge in the world is the bridge over the Royal Gorge of the Arkansas River in Colorado, U.S.A. It is 1,053 feet above the water level. It has a main span of 880 feet and was constructed in 6 months, ending on 6 Dec. 1929. The highest railway bridge in the world is the single track span at Fades, outside Clermont-Ferrand, France. It was built in 1901–09 with a span of 472 feet and is 430 feet above the River Sioule. The highest railway bridge in the United Kingdom was the Crumlin Viaduct, Monmouthshire, completed in June 1857 to a height of 200 feet.

WIDEST
The world's widest bridge is the Crawford Street Bridge in Providence, Rhode Island, U.S.A., with a width of 1,147 feet. The River Roch is bridged for a distance of 1,460 feet where the culvert passes through the centre of Rochdale, Lancashire.

Deepest foundations The deepest foundations of any structure are those of the 3,323-foot-span Ponte de Salazar, which was opened on 6 Aug. 1966, at a cost of £30,000,000, across the Rio Tejo (the River Tagus), in Portugal. One of the 625-foot-tall towers extends 240 feet down.

Longest viaduct The world's longest viaduct is the second Lake Ponchartrain Causeway, completed on 23 March 1969, joining Mandeville and Jefferson, Louisiana, U.S.A. It has a length of 126,055 feet (23·87 miles). It cost \$29,900,000 (£12·45 million) and is 228 feet longer than the adjoining First Causeway completed in 1956. The longest railway viaduct in the world is the rock-filled Great Salt Lake Viaduct, carrying the Southern Pacific Railroad 11·85 miles across the Great Salt Lake, Utah, U.S.A. It was opened as a pile and trestle bridge on 8 March 1904, and converted to rock fill in 1955–60.

AQUEDUCTS
Longest Ancient The greatest of ancient aqueducts was the Aqueduct of Carthage in Tunisia, which ran 141 kilometres (87·6 miles) from the springs of Zaghouan to Djebel Djougar. It was built by the Romans during the reign of Publius Aelius Hadrianus (A.D. 117–138). By 1895, 344 arches still survived. Its original capacity has been calculated at 7,000,000 gallons per day. The triple-tiered aqueduct Pont du Gard, built in A.D. 19 near Nîmes, France, is 160 feet high. The tallest of the 14 arches of the Aguas Livres Aqueduct, built in Lisbon, Portugal, in 1748 is 213 feet 3 inches.

Longest Modern The world's longest aqueduct, in the modern sense of a water conduit, is the Colorado River Aqueduct in south-eastern California, U.S.A. The system, complete with aqueduct conduit, tunnels and syphons, is 242 miles long and was completed in 1939. The California Aqueduct (completion due 1972) will be 444 miles long.

United Kingdom The longest aqueduct in the United Kingdom is the Pontcysyllte in Denbighshire, Wales, on the Frankton to Llantisilio branch of the Shropshire Union Canal. It is 1,007 feet long, has 19 arches up to 121 feet high and crosses the valley of the Dee. It was designed by Thomas Telford (1757–1834) of Scotland, and was opened for use in 1803.

115

The world's structures

6. Canals

The Volga-Baltic Canal

EARLIEST
Relics of the oldest canals in the world, dated by archaeologists to 5000 B.C., were discovered near Mandali, Iraq early in 1968.

The first canals in Britain were undoubtedly cut by the Romans. In the Midlands the 11-mile-long Fossdyke Canal between Lincoln and the River Trent at Torksey was built in about A.D. 65 and was scoured in 1122. Part of it is still in use today.

Though Exeter Canal was cut as early as 1564–68, the first wholly artificial major navigation canal in the United Kingdom was the Bridgewater canal, dug in 1759–61. It ran from Worsley to Manchester, Lancashire. Parts of the Sankey Canal from St. Helens to Widnes, Lancashire, were however, dug before the Bridgewater Canal.

LONGEST
World The largest canalized system in the world is the Volga-Baltic Canal opened in April 1965. It runs 1,850 miles from Astrakhan up the Volga, *via* Kuybyshev, Gor'kiy and Lake Ladoga, to Leningrad, U.S.S.R. The longest canal of the ancient world has been the Grand Canal of China from Peking to Hangchou. It was begun in 540 B.C. and not completed until the 13th century by which time it extended for 1,107 miles. Having been allowed by 1950 to silt up to the point that it was in no place more than 6 feet deep, it is reported to have been reconstructed.

The Beloye More (White Sea) Baltic Canal from Belomorsk to Povenets, in the U.S.S.R., is 141 miles long with 19 locks. It was completed with the use of forced labour in 1933 and cannot accommodate ships of more than 16 feet in draught.

The world's longest big ship canal is the still inoperative (since June 1967) Suez Canal in the United Arab Republic, opened on 16 Nov. 1869 by the Khedive, Isma'il Pasha, and officially inaugurated on the following day by a procession of 68 vessels, headed by the French imperial yacht *L'Aigle*, with the Empress Marie Eugénie Ignace Augustine (1826–1920) on board. The canal was planned by the French diplomatist Count Ferdinand de Lesseps (1805–94) and work began on 25 April 1859. It is 100·6 miles in length from Port Said lighthouse to Suez Roads, 60 metres (197 feet) wide and dredged to 34 feet. The original excavation was 97,000,000 cubic yards, which had, by continual dredging, been trebled. It had been intended to dredge to the point that ships drawing 40 feet could transit by 1970.

United Kingdom The longest inland waterway in the United Kingdom is the Grand Union Canal Main Line from Brentford Lock Junction, Middlesex, to Langley Mill, a total distance of 167⅜ miles. The Grand Union System was originally 255 miles long when nine canals, including the Grand Junction, were amalgamated in 1929. The voyage along the whole length of the Grand Union Canal, Main Line, would involve the negotiation of 169 locks.

Seaway The world's longest artificial seaway is the St. Lawrence Seaway (189 miles long) along the New York State-Ontario border from Montreal to Lake Ontario, which enables 80 per cent. of all ocean-going ships, and bulk carriers with a capacity of 26,000 tons, to sail 2,342 miles from the North Atlantic, up the St. Lawrence estuary and across the Great Lakes to Duluth, Minnesota, U.S.A., on Lake Superior (602 feet above sea-level). The project cost $470,000,000 (then £168 million) and was opened on 25 April 1959.

Irrigation The longest irrigation canal in the world is the Karakumskiy Kanal, stretching 546 miles from Haun-Khan to Ashkhabad, Turkmenistan, U.S.S.R. In February 1967 the operative length was reported to have reached 520 miles.

LOCKS
Largest The world's largest locking system is the Miraflores lock system in the Panama Canal, opened on 15 Aug. 1914. The two lower locks are 1,050 feet long, 110 feet wide and have gates 82 feet high, 65 feet long and 7 feet thick, with doors weighing 652 to 696 tons each. The largest liner ever to transit was S.S. *Bremen* (51,730 gross tons), with a length of 899 feet, a beam of 101·9 feet and a draught of 48·2 feet, on 15 Feb. 1939.

The world's largest single lock is that connecting the Schelde with the Kanaaldok system at Zandvliet, west of Antwerp, Belgium. It is 500 metres (1,640 feet) long and 187 feet wide and is an entrance to an impounded sheet of water 18 kilometres (11·2 miles) long.

The largest lock on any canal system in the United Kingdom is the Eastham Large Lock, Eastham, Cheshire, on the Manchester Ship Canal. It can handle craft up to 600 feet long and 80 feet beam.

Deepest The world's deepest lock is the Donzère-Mondragon lock on the River Rhône at Drôme, France. It is 86 feet deep and takes 8 minutes to fill.

Longest flight The world's highest lock elevator is at Arzwiller-Saint Louis in France. The lift was completed in 1969 to replace 17 locks on the Marne-Rhine canal system. It drops 146 feet over a ramp 383·8 feet long on a 41 degree gradient.

The longest flight of locks in the United Kingdom is on the Worcester and Birmingham Canal at Tardebigge, Worcestershire, where a 2½-mile-long flight of 30 consecutive locks raises the canal level 217 feet.

The Gaillard Cut, Panama Canal

rgest cut The Gaillard Cut (known as "the Ditch") on the Panama Canal is 270 feet deep between Gold Hill and Contractor's Hill with a bottom width of 300 feet. In one day in 1911 as many as 333 dirt trains each carrying 357 tons left this site. The total amount of earth excavated for the whole Panama Canal was 8,910,000 tons, which total will be raised by the widening of the Gaillard Cut to 500 feet. In 1968 there were a record 14,807 transits.

7. Dams

Earliest The earliest dam ever built was the Sadd al-Kafara, seven miles south-east of Helwan, United Arab Republic. It was built in the period 2950 to 2750 B.C. and had a length of 348 feet.

Most massive Measured by volume, the largest dam in the world is the Fort Peck Dam, completed in 1940 across the Missouri River in Montana, U.S.A. It contains 125,628,000 cubic yards of earth and rock fill, and is 21,026 feet (3.98 miles) long and up to 251 feet high. It maintains a reservoir with a capacity of 19·1 million acre-feet. Work started in December 1967 on the Tarbela Dam across the River Indus, in the Sind, West Pakistan. The total cost of the 485-foot-tall, 9,000-foot-long construction is expected to reach $815 million (£339·6 million) by completion in 1975 including the $623 million contract awarded to the Impregilo Consortium. The total volume of the dam will be 159,000,000 cubic yards.

Largest concrete The world's largest concrete dam, and the largest concrete structure in the world, is the Grand Coulee Dam on the Columbia River, Washington State, U.S.A. Work on the dam was begun in 1933, it began working on 22 March 1941 and was completed in 1942 at a cost of $56 million. It has a crest length of 4,173 feet and is 550 feet high. It contains 10,585,000 cubic yards of concrete, and weighs about 19,285,000 tons. The hydro-electric power plant (completed in 1951) has a capacity of 1,974,000 kilowatts.

Highest The highest dam in the world is the Grand Dixence in Switzerland, completed in September 1961 at a cost of 1,600 million Swiss francs (£151,000,000). It is 932 feet from base to rim, 2,296 feet long and the total volume of concrete in the dam is 7,792,000 cubic yards. The earth fill Nurek dam on the Vakhsh-Amu Darya river, U.S.S.R. will be 1,017 feet high, have a crest length of 2,280 feet and a volume of 75,900,000 cubic yards. The concrete Ingurskaya dam in western Georgia, U.S.S.R., is planned to have a final height of 988 feet, a crest length of 2,240 feet and a volume of 3,920,000 cubic yards.

Longest The longest river dam in the world is the Hirakud Dam on the Mahanadi River, near Sambalpur, Orissa, India completed in 1956. It consists of a main concrete and masonry dam (3,768 feet), an Earth Dam (11,980 feet), the Left Dyke (five sections of 32,275 feet) and the Right Dyke (35,500 feet), totalling 15·8 miles altogether.

The longest sea dam in the world is the Afsluitdijk stretching 20·195 miles across the mouth of the Zuider Zee in two sections of 1·553 miles (mainland of North Holland to the Isle of Wieringen) and 18·641 miles from Wieringen to Friesland. It has a sea-level width of 293 feet and a height of 24 feet 7 inches.

United Kingdom The most massive (5,630,000 cubic yards), the highest (240 feet) and longest high dam (2,050 feet crest length) in the United Kingdom is the Scammonden Dam, West Riding of Yorkshire, begun in November 1966 and completed in the summer of 1970. This rock fill dam carries the M.62 on its crest and is being built by Sir Alfred McAlpine's. The cost of the project together with the 6½-mile motorway was £8,400,000. There are longer low dams or barrages of the valley cut-off type notably the Hanningfield Dam, Essex, built from July 1952 to August 1956 to a length of 6,850 feet and a height of 64·5 feet. The Llyn Brianne Dam in West Glamorgan, also rock fill, will reach 300 feet in 1972 thus surpassing the concrete Cylwedog Dam (built April 1964–April 1968), Montgomeryshire, of 237 feet as the highest in the United Kingdom.

LARGEST RESERVOIR

The largest man-made is Bratsk Lake on the Angara river, U.S.S.R., with a volume of 137,230,000 acre-feet. The dam was completed in 1964. A volume of 149,000,000 acre-feet has been quoted for Kariba Lake, Zambia-Rhodesia but is now more reliably estimated at 130,000,000 acre-feet.

The completion in 1954 of the Owen Falls Dam near Jinja, Uganda, across the northern exit of the White Nile from the Victoria Nyanza marginally raised the level of that lake by adding 166,000,000 acre-feet, and technically turned it into a reservoir with a surface area of 17,169,920 acres (26,828 square miles).

The most grandiose reservoir project mooted is the Xingu-Araguaia river plan in central Brazil for a reservoir behind a dam at Ilha da Paz with a volume of 780,000 million cubic yards extending over 22,800 square miles. A dam at Óbidos on the Amazon would produce a 744-mile-long back-up and a 68,400-square-mile reservoir at an estimated cost of $3,000 million (£1,250 million).

United Kingdom The largest wholly artificial reservoir in the United Kingdom is the Queen Mary Reservoir, built from August 1914 to June 1925, at Littleton, near Staines, with an available storage capacity of 8,130 million gallons and a water area of 707 acres. The length of the perimeter embankment is 20,766 feet (3·93 miles). Of valley cut-off type reservoirs the most capacious is Llyn Ceyln, North Wales with a capacity of 17,800,000,000 gallons. The capacity of Haweswater, Westmorland, was increased by 18,660 million gallons by the building in 1929–41 of a 1,540-foot-long concrete buttress dam 120 feet high. The natural surface area was trebled to 1,050 acres. The deepest reservoir in Europe is Loch Morar, in Inverness-shire, Scotland, with a maximum depth of 1,017 feet (see also Chapter III).

Largest polder The largest of the five great polders in the old Zuider Zee, Netherlands, will be the 149,000 acre (232·8 square miles) Markerwaard. Work on the 66-mile-long surrounding dyke was begun in 1957. The water area remaining after the erection of the 1927–32 dam is called IJssel Meer, which will have a final area of 487·5 square miles.

Largest levees The most massive earthworks ever carried out are the Mississippi levees begun in 1717 but vastly augmented by the U.S. Federal Government after the disastrous floods of 1927. These extend for 1,732 miles along the main river from Cape Girardeau, Missouri, to the Gulf of Mexico and comprise more than 1,000 million cubic yards of earthworks. Levees on the tributaries comprise an additional 2,000 miles.

The world's highest dam, the Nurek, under construction

The world's structures

PROGRESSIVE WORLD RECORDS

Highest Dams since 1866

Name	River	Location	Year Completed	Feet
Gouffre d'Enfer (Furan)	Le Furan	France	1866	197
Ponthook*	Androscoggen	New Hampshire, U.S.A.	1887	276
Cheeseman	South Platte	Colorado, U.S.A.	1904	236
New Croton	Croton	New York, U.S.A.	1905	297
Buffalo Bill	Shoshone	Wyoming, U.S.A.	1910	326
Arrowrock	Boise	Idaho, U.S.A.	1915	350
Schrah	Aa	Switzerland	1924	364
Diablo	Skagit	Washington, U.S.A.	1929	389
Owyhee	Owyhee	Oregon, U.S.A.	1932	417
Chambon	Romanche	France	1934	446
Hoover	Colorado	Nevada–Arizona, U.S.A.	1936	726
Mauvoisin	Drance de Bagnes	Switzerland	1958	777
Vaiont	Vaiont	Italy	1961	858
Grand Dixence	Dixence	Switzerland	1962	932
Inguri	Inguri	Georgia, U.S.S.R.	—	988
Nurek	Vakhsh	U.S.S.R.	—	1,017

Double-walled masonry earth-filled embankment, 13-foot crest length.

Longest Tunnels

Miles	Yards	Name	Location	Built
	1,015	Euphrates river	Babylon (near Al Hillah), Iraq	2180–2160 B.C.
	1,093	Sámos water supply	Sámos, Aegean Is.	687 B.C.
1	650	Baebelo silver mine	Cazlona, Spain	c. 240 B.C.
3	886	Fucinus Emissarium	Monte Salvino, Celano, Italy	41–51 A.D.
7	800	Noirieu Canal tunnel	St. Quentin, France	–1822
31	880	Rothschönberg	Felberg, Saxony	–1877
33	220	New Croton water tunnel	Croton Dam–Manhattan, New York	–1888
85		West Delaware water supply	Rondout–Hillview, New York	1937–1945

Longest Rail Tunnels

Miles	Yards	Name	Location	Built
3	13	Woodhead No. 1	Cheshire, England	1 Oct. 1838–20 Dec. 1845
3	62	Standedge No. 2	Yorkshire, England	1846–1 Aug. 1849
3	62	Standedge No. 3	Yorkshire, England	April 1868–Oct. 1870
4	1,146	Hoosac	Massachusetts, U.S.A.	1855–1 July 1876
7	1,045	Fréjus (Mont Cenis)	Modane, Fr.-Bardonecchia, It.	18 Aug. 1857–17 Sept. 1871
9	452	St. Gotthard	Göschenen-Airolo, Switz.	13 Sept. 1872–23 May 1882
12	537	Simplon I	Brigue, Switz.-Iselle, It.	1 Aug. 1898–25 Jan. 1906
12	559	Simplon II	Brigue, Switz.-Iselle, It.	1918–16 Oct. 1922

Longest Road Tunnels

Miles	Yards	Name	Location	Built
	1,015	*Euphrates river	Babylon (near Al Hillah), Iraq	2180–2160 B.C.
	1,610	Pausilippo	Naples–Pozzuoli, Italy	36 B.C.
1	189	Vicoforte	Piedmont, Italy	c. 1650
1	382	Castel Hill	Budapest, Hungary	1847
1	628	Col de Rousset	Drôme, France	1867
1	1,724	Dell Colle di Tenda	Limone Piemonte, Italy–Tende, Fr.	1882–89
2	231	*First Mersey Tunnel	Liverpool–Birkenhead, England	1925–34
6	265	*Kanmon	Honshu-Kyushu, Japan	1939–58
7	476	Le Tunnel Routier de Mont Blanc	Pèlerins, Fr.–Entrèves, It.	1959–65
22	1,046	*Seikan Tunnel	Tsugara Strait, Japan	1963–73

Sub-aqueous.

8. Tunnels

LONGEST

Water supply World The world's longest tunnel of any kind is the New York City-West Delaware water supply tunnel begun in 1937 and completed in 1945. It has a diameter of 13 feet 6 inches and runs for 85·0 miles from the Rondout Reservoir into the Hillview Reservoir, in the northern part of Manhattan Island, New York City, N.Y., U.S.A.

United Kingdom The longest water supply tunnel in the United Kingdom is the Thames water tunnel from Hampton-on-Thames to Walthamstow, Greater London, completed in 1960 with a circumference of 26 feet 8 inches and a length of 18·8 miles.

RAILWAY

World The world's longest main-line tunnel is the Simplon II Tunnel, completed after 4 years' work on 16 Oct. 1922. Linking Switzerland and Italy under the Alps, it is 12

miles 559 yards long. Over 60 were killed boring this and the Simplon I (1898–1906), which is 22 yards shorter. Its greatest depth below the surface is 7,005 feet.

Subway tunnel The world's longest continuous vehicular tunnel is the London Transport Board underground railway line from Morden to East Finchley, *via* Bank. In use since 1939, it is 17 miles 528 yards long and the diameter of the tunnel is 12 ft. and the station tunnels 21·2 ft.

United Kingdom The United Kingdom's longest main-line railway tunnel is the Severn Tunnel (4 miles 628 yards), linking Gloucestershire and Monmouthshire, completed with 76,400,000 bricks between 1873 and 1886.

ROAD

World The world's longest road tunnel is the tunnel 7·2 miles long under Mont Blanc (15,771 feet) from Pèlerins, near Chamonix, France, to Entrèves, near Courmayeur in Valle d'Aosta, Italy, on which work began on 6 Jan. 1959. The holing through was achieved on 14 Aug. 1962 and it was opened on 16 July 1965, after an expenditure of £22,800,000. The 29½-foot-high tunnel with its carriage-way of two 12-foot lanes is expected to carry 600,000 vehicles a year. There were 23 deaths during tunnelling.

-aqueous The world's longest sub-aqueous road tunnel is the Kanmon Tunnel, completed in 1958, which runs 6·01 miles from Shimonseki, Honshū, to Kyūshū, Japan. The Seikan Tunnel (22·6 miles), 100 metres (328 feet) beneath the sea-bed of the Tsugara Strait between Tappi Saki, Honshū, and Fukushima, Hokkaidō, Japan, is due to be completed in 1973. Work started on the sub-aqueous section (14 miles) in 1963. On 8 July 1966 the United Kingdom and French governments reached agreement on a Channel Tunnel for electric trains. It would run in two passages, each of 40 miles, 21 miles being sub-aqueous, between Westenhanger, near Dover, Kent, and Sangatte, near Calais. The project, now known as the "Chunnel", was first mooted in 1802. It will cost more than £350,000,000, if proceeded with.

United Kingdom The longest road tunnel in the United Kingdom is the Mersey Tunnel, joining Liverpool, Lancashire, and Birkenhead, Cheshire. It is 2·13 miles long, or 2·87 miles including branch tunnels. Work was begun in December 1925 and it was opened by H.M. King George V on 18 July 1934. The total cost was £7¾ million. The 36-foot-wide 4-lane roadway carries nearly 7½ million vehicles a year. A second Mersey Tunnel was begun in 1966.

Largest The largest diameter road tunnel in the world is that blasted through Yerba Buena Island, San Francisco, California, U.S.A. It is 76 feet wide, 58 feet high and 540 feet long. Up to 35,000,000 vehicles pass through on its two decks every year.

HYDRO-ELECTRIC
The longest hydro-electric tunnel in the world will be the 51·5-mile-long Orange-Fish Rivers Tunnel, South Africa, begun in 1967 at an estimated cost of £250 million. A 30-mile-long tunnel joining the River Arpa with Lake Sevan at an altitude of 6,500 feet in the Armenian Mountains, U.S.S.R. was also reported under construction in 1967.

United Kingdom The longest in the United Kingdom is that at Ben Nevis, Inverness-shire, which has a mean diameter of 15 feet 2 inches and a length of 15 miles. It was begun in June 1926 and was holed through into Loch Treig on 3 Jan. 1930.

BRIDGE-TUNNEL
The world's longest bridge-tunnel system is the Chesapeake Bay Bridge-Tunnel, extending 17·65 miles from the Delmarva Peninsula to Norfolk, Virginia, U.S.A. It cost $200,000,000 (then £71·4 million) and was completed after 42 months and opened to traffic on 15 April 1964. The longest bridged section is Trestle C (4·56 miles long) and the longer tunnel is the Thimble Shoal Channel Tunnel (1·09 miles).

CANAL TUNNELS
Longest World The world's longest canal tunnel is that on the Rove canal between the port of Marseilles, France and the river Rhône, built in 1912–27. It is 4·53 miles long, 72 feet wide and 50 feet high, involving 2¼ million cubic yards of excavation.

Longest U.K. The longest of the 49 canal tunnels in the United Kingdom is the Standedge Tunnel in the West Riding of Yorkshire on the Huddersfield Narrow Canal built from 1794 to 4 April 1811. It measures 3 miles 135 yards in length and was closed on 21 Dec. 1944. The Huddersfield Narrow Canal is also the highest in the United Kingdom, reaching a height at one point of 638 feet above sea-level.

9. Specialised Structures

SEVEN WONDERS OF THE WORLD
The Seven Wonders of the World were first designated by Antipater of Sidon in the 2nd century B.C. They included the Pyramids of Gîza, built by three Fourth Dynasty Egyptian Pharaohs, Hwfw (Khufu or Cheops), Kha-f-Ra (Khafre, Khefren or Chephren) and Menkaure (Mycerinus) near El Gîza (El Gizeh), south-west of El Qâhira (Cairo) in Egypt (now the United Arab Republic). The Great Pyramid ("Horizon of Khufu") was built in c. 2580 B.C. Its original height was 480 feet 11 inches (now, since the loss of its topmost stone or pyramidion, reduced to 449 feet 6 inches) with a base line of 756 feet and thus originally covering slightly more than 13 acres. It has been estimated that a work force of 4,000 required 30 years to manoeuvre into position the 2,300,000 limestone blocks averaging 2½ tons each, totalling about 5,750,000 tons and a volume of 90,700,000 cubic feet.

Of the other six wonders only fragments remain of the Temple of Artemis (Diana) of the Ephesians, built in c. 350 B.C. at Ephesus, Turkey (destroyed by the Goths in A.D. 262), and of the Tomb of King Mausolus of Caria, built at Halicarnassus, now Bodrum, Turkey, in c. 325 B.C. No trace remains of the Hanging Gardens of Semiramis, at Babylon, Iraq (c. 600 B.C.); the 40-foot-tall marble, gold and ivory statue of Zeus (Jupiter), by Phidias (5th century B.C.) at Olympia, Greece (lost in a fire at Istanbul); the 117-foot-tall statue by Charles of Lindus of the figure of the god Helios (Apollo), called the Colossus of Rhodes (sculptured 292–280 B.C., destroyed by an earthquake in 224 B.C.); or the 400-foot-tall lighthouse built by Soscratus of Cnidus during the 3rd century B.C. (destroyed by earthquake in A.D. 1375) on the island of Pharos (Greek, pharos=lighthouse), off the coast of El Iskandarîya (Alexandria), Egypt (now the United Arab Republic).

PYRAMIDS
Largest The largest pyramid, and the largest monument ever constructed, is the Quetzalcóatl at Cholula de Rivadahia, 63 miles south-east of Mexico City, Mexico. It is 177 feet tall and its base covers an area of nearly 25 acres. Its total volume has been estimated at 4,300,000 cubic yards, compared with 3,360,000 cubic yards for the Pyramid of Cheops (see above). The pyramid-building era here was between the 6th and 12th centuries A.D.

The fourth wonder of the world—the Temple of Artemis

The world's structures

The world's tallest totem pole

Oldest The oldest known pyramid is the Djoser step pyramid at Saqqâra, Egypt constructed to a height of 204 feet of Tura limestone in *c.* 2,650 B.C. The oldest New World pyramid is that on the island of La Venta in south-eastern Mexico built by the Olmec people *c.* 800 B.C. It stands 100 feet tall with a base diameter of 420 feet.

TALLEST FLAGSTAFF

World The tallest flagstaff ever erected was that outside the Oregon Building at the 1915 Panama-Pacific International Exposition in San Francisco, California, U.S.A. Trimmed from a Douglas fir, it stood 299 feet 7 inches in height and weighed 45 tons. The tallest unsupported flag pole in the world is a 184-foot-tall pole constructed of metal tubing, weighing 18,000 lb. (8 tons), erected in 1959 at Calipatria, which is situated 184 feet below sea-level in Imperial Valley, California, U.S.A. The pole's diameter tapers from 24 inches to 5 inches.

United Kingdom The tallest flagstaff in the United Kingdom is a 225-foot-tall Douglas fir staff at Kew, London. Cut in Canada, it was shipped across the Atlantic and towed up the River Thames on 7 May 1958, to replace the old 214-foot-tall staff of 1919.

Tallest totem pole The tallest totem pole in the world is one 160 feet tall in McKinleyville, California, U.S.A. It weighs 57,000 lb. (25·4 tons) and was carved from a 500-year-old tree.

MONUMENTS

Tallest The world's tallest monument is the stainless steel Gateway to the West Arch in St. Louis, Missouri, U.S.A., completed on 28 Oct. 1965 to commemorate the westward expansion after the Louisiana Purchase of 1803. It is a sweeping arch spanning 630 feet and rising to a height of 630 feet, and costing $29,000,000 (£12,083,000). It was designed in 1947 by Eero Saarinen (died 1961).

The tallest monumental column in the world is that commemorating the battle of San Jacinto (21 April 1836), on the bank of the San Jacinto river near Houston, Texas, U.S.A. General Sam Houston (1793–1863) and his force of 743 Texan troops killed 630 Mexicans (out of a total force of 1,600) and captured

700 others, for the loss of nine men killed and 30 wounded. Constructed in 1936–39, at a cost of $1,500,000 (now £625,000), the tapering column is 570 feet tall, 47 feet square at the base, and 30 feet square at the observation tower, which is surmounted by a star weighing 196·4 tons. It is built of concrete, faced with buff limestone, and weighs 31,384 tons.

Largest prehistoric Britain's largest monolithic prehistoric monuments are the 28½-acre earthworks and stone circles of Avebury, Wiltshire, rediscovered in 1646. This is believed to be the work of the Beaker people of the later Neolithic period of *c.* 1700 to 1500 B.C. The whole work is 1,200 feet in diameter with a 40-foot ditch around the perimeter. The largest trilithons exist at Stonehenge, to the south of Salisbury Plain, Wiltshire, with single sarsen blocks weighing over 45 tons and requiring over 550 men to drag them up a 9° gradient. The dating of the structure was in 1969 revised to the period *c.* 2400–2200 B.C.

The greatest prehistoric earthwork in Britain is Wansdyke, originally Woden's Dyke, which ran 86 miles from Portishead, Somerset to Inkpen Beacon and Ludgershall, south of Hungerford, Berkshire. It is believed to have been built by the pre-Roman Wessex culture. The most extensive single site earthwork is the Dorset Cursus near Gussage St. Michael, dating from *c.* 1900 B.C. The workings are 6 miles in length, involving an estimated 250,000 cubic yards of excavations. The largest of the Celtic hill-forts is that known as Mew Dun, or Maiden Castle, two miles south-west of Dorchester, Dorset. It covers 115 acres and was abandoned shortly after A.D. 43.

The largest artificial mound in Europe is Silbury Hill, 6 miles west of Marlborough, Wiltshire, which involved the moving of an estimated 670,000 tons of chalk to make a cone 130 feet high with a base of 5½ acres. Prof. Richard Atkinson in charge of the 1968 excavations showed that it is based on an innermost central mound, similar to contemporary round barrows, and may be dated to *c.* 2200 B.C. The largest long barrow in England is that at West Kennet (*c.* 2200 B.C.), near Silbury, measuring 385 feet in length.

Youngest ancient Of all the ancient monuments scheduled in Great Britain, the youngest is Fort Wallington, near Portsmouth, Hampshire. It was begun in 1860, when a French invasion was thought possible, and was not completed until 1870.

OBELISKS

Oldest The longest an obelisk has remained *in situ* is that at Heliopolis (now Masr-el-Gedîda) United Arab Republic (Egypt), erected by Senusret I *c.* 1750 B.C.

Largest The largest standing obelisk in the world is that in the Piazza of St. John in Lateran, Rome, erected in 1588. It came originally from the Circus Maximus (erected A.D. 357) and before that from Heliopolis, Egypt (erected *c.* 1450 B.C.). It is 110 feet in length and weighs 450 tons. The largest obelisk in the United Kingdom is Cleopatra's Needle on the Embankment, London, which is 68 feet 5½ inches tall and weighs 186·36 tons. It was towed down the Thames from Egypt on 20 Jan. 1878.

Largest tomb The largest tomb in the world is that of Emperor Nintoku (died *c.* A.D. 428) south of Osaka, Japan. It measures 1,594 feet long by 1,000 feet wide by 150 feet high.

Ziqqurat The largest surviving ziqqurat (from the verb *zaqaru*, to build high) or stage-tower is the Ziqqurat of Ur (now Muqqayr, Iraq) with a base 200 feet by 150 feet built to at least three storeys of which only the first and part of the second now survive to a height of 60 feet. It was built by the Akkadian King Ur-Nammu (*c.* 2113–2006 B.C.).

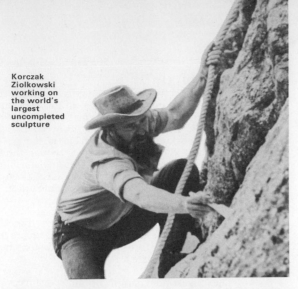

Korczak Ziolkowski working on the world's largest uncompleted sculpture

SCULPTURES

Largest The world's largest sculptures are the mounted figures of Jefferson Davis (1808–89), Gen. Robert Edward Lee (1807–70) and Gen. Thomas Jonathan ("Stonewall") Jackson (1824–63), covering 1·33 acres on the face of Stone Mountain, near Atlanta, Georgia. They are 20 feet higher than the more famous Rushmore sculptures. When completed the world's largest sculpture will be that of the Indian chief Tashunca-uitco, known as Crazy Horse, of the Oglalla tribe of the Dakota or Nadowessioux (Sioux) group. He is believed to have been born in about 1849, and he died at Fort Robinson, Nebraska, on 5 Sept. 1877. The sculpture was begun on 3 June 1948 near Mount Rushmore, South Dakota, U.S.A. A projected 561 feet high and 641 feet long, it will require the removal of 5,000,000 tons of stone and is the life work of one man, Korczak Ziolkowski. The work will take until 1990.

Most expensive The highest price paid for any sculpture is $160,000 (£66,666) for *Reclining Figure* ("Festival Figure") in bronze with a golden patina by Henry Moore O.M., C.H. (b. Castleford, Yorkshire, 30 July 1898) at the Parke-Bernet Galleries, New York City, U.S.A. on 4 April 1968. Three such sculptures were cast in 1951.

Ground figures In the Nazla Desert, south of Lima, Peru there are straight lines (one 5 miles long), geometric shapes and plants and animals drawn on the ground by still unknown persons for an unknown purpose.

Hill figures The largest human hill carving in Britain is the "Long Man" of Wilmington, Sussex, 226 feet in length.

The oldest of all White Horses in Britain is the Uffington White Horse in Berkshire, dating from the late Iron Age (*c.* 150 B.C.) and measuring 374 feet from nose to tail and 120 feet from ear to heel.

TALLEST STATUE
The tallest free-standing statue in the world is that of "Motherland", an enormous female figure on Mamayev Hill, outside Volgograd, U.S.S.R., designed in 1967 by Yevgenyi Vuchetich, to commemorate victory in the Battle of Stalingrad (1942–43). The statue from its base to the tip of the sword clenched in her right hand measures 270 feet.

Near Bamiyan, Afghanistan there are the remains of the recumbent Sakya Buddha, built of plastered rubble, which was "about 1,000 feet" long and is believed to date from the 3rd or 4th century A.D.

The world's tallest statue "Motherland" outside Volgograd, U.S.S.R.

LARGEST DOME
World The world's largest dome is the "Astrodome" of the Harris County Sports Stadium, in Houston, Texas, U.S.A. It has an outside diameter of 710 feet and an inside diameter of 642 feet. (See page 111 for further details.) The largest dome of ancient architecture is that of the Pantheon, built in Rome in A.D. 112, with a diameter of $142\frac{1}{2}$ feet.

Britain The largest dome in Britain is that of the Bell Sports Centre, Perth, Scotland with a diameter of 222 feet, designed by D. B. Cockburn and constructed in Baltic whitewood by Muirhead & Sons Ltd. of Grangemouth, Stirlingshire.

Tallest columns The tallest columns (as opposed to obelisks) in the world are the sixteen 82-foot-tall pillars in the Palace of Labour in Torino (Turin), Italy, for which the architect was Pier Luigi Nervi (born 21 June 1891). They were built of concrete and steel in only 8 days. The tallest load-bearing stone columns in the world are those measuring 69 feet in the Hall of Columns of the Temple of Amun at Al Karnak, the northern part of the ruins of Thebes, the Greek name for the ancient capital of Upper Egypt (now the United Arab Republic). They were built in the 19th dynasty in the reign of Rameses II in *c.* 1270 B.C.

Longest jetty The longest deep water jetty in the world is the Quai Hermann du Pasquier at Le Havre, France, with a length of 5,000 feet. Part of an enclosed basin, it has a constant depth of water of 32 feet on both sides.

Longest pier The world's longest pier is the Dammam Pier at El Hasa, Saudi Arabia, on the Persian Gulf. A rock-filled causeway 4·84 miles long joins the steel trestle pier 1·80 miles long, which joins the Main Pier (744 feet long), giving an overall length of 6·79 miles. The work was begun in July 1948 and completed on 15 March 1950.

The longest pier in Great Britain is the Bee Ness Jetty, completed in 1930, which stretches 8,200 feet along the west bank of the River Medway, 5 to 6 miles below Rochester, at Kingsnorth, Kent.

BREAKWATER
The world's longest breakwater system is that which protects the Ports of Long Beach and Los Angeles, California, U.S.A. The combined length of the four breakwaters is 43,602 feet (8·26 miles) of which the Long Beach section, built between 1941 and February 1949, is the longest at 13,350 feet (2·53 miles). The North breakwater at Tuticorin, Madras Province, Southern India on which construction began in 1968 will extend when complete to 13,589 feet.

The longest breakwater in the United Kingdom is the North Breakwater at Holyhead, Anglesey, which is 9,860 feet (1·87 miles) in length and was completed in 1873.

LARGEST DRY DOCK
The largest dry dock in the world is the Belfast Harbour Commission and Harland and Wolff building dock at Belfast, Northern Ireland. It has been excavated by Wimpey's to a length of 1,825 feet and a width of 305 feet and can accommodate tankers of 1,000,000 gross tons. Work was begun on 26 Jan. 1968 and completed on 30 Nov. 1969 and involved the excavation of 400,000 cubic yards. See also Largest crane.

121

England's oldest working windmill at Outwood, Surrey

LARGEST FLOATING DOCKS
The largest floating docks ever constructed are the United States Navy's advanced base sectional docks (A.B.S.D.). These consist of 10 sectional units giving together an effective keel block length of 827 feet and clear width of 140 feet, with a lifting capacity of 71,000 tons. One designated AFDB 3 at Green Cove Springs, Florida, U.S.A. has a nominal lifting capacity of 80,000 tons.

The largest single-unit floating dock is Admiralty Floating Dock (AFD) 35, which was towed from the Royal Navy's dockyard in Malta to the Cantieri Navali Santa Maria of Genoa, Italy, in May 1965. It has a lifting capacity of 65,000 tons and an overall length of 857 feet 8 inches. It had been towed to Malta from Bombay, India, where it was built in 1947.

LIGHTHOUSES
Brightest The lighthouse with the most powerful light in the world is Créac'h d'Ouessant lighthouse, established in 1638 and last altered in 1939 on l'Île d'Ouessant, Finistère, Brittany, France. It is 163 feet tall and, in times of fog, has a luminous intensity of up to 500,000,000 candelas.

The lights with the greatest visible range are those 1,092 feet above the ground on the Empire State Building, New York City, N.Y., U.S.A. Each of the four-arc mercury bulbs has a rated candlepower of 450,000,000, visible 80 miles away on the ground and 300 miles away from aircraft. They were switched on on 31 March 1956.

The lighthouse in the United Kingdom with the most powerful light is the shorelight Orfordness, Suffolk. It has an intensity of 7,500,000 candelas. The Irish light with the greatest intensity is Aranmore on Rinrawros Point, County Donegal.

Tallest The world's tallest lighthouse is the steel tower 348 feet tall near Yamashita Park in Yokohama, Japan. It has a power of 600,000 candles and a visibility range of 20 miles.

Remotest The most remote Trinity House lighthouse is The Smalls, about 16 sea miles (18·4 statute miles) off the Pembrokeshire coast. The most remote Scottish lighthouse is Sule Skerry, 35 miles off shore and 45 miles north-west of Dunnet Head, Caithness. The most remote Irish light is Blackrock, about 9 miles off the Mayo coast.

Waterwheels The largest waterwheel in the British Isles is the Lady Isabella wheel at Laxey, Isle of Man. It was completed for draining a lead mine in 1854 and has a circumference of 228 feet and a diameter of 72½ feet.

WINDMILLS
The earliest recorded windmills are those used for grinding corn in Iran (Persia) in the 7th century A.D. The earliest known in England was the post-mill at Bury St. Edmunds, Suffolk, recorded in 1191. The oldest working mill in England is the post-mill at Outwood, Surrey, built in 1665, though the Ivinghoe Mill in Pitstone Green Farm, Buckinghamshire, dating from 1627, has been restored. The largest conventional windmill in England is a disused one at Sutton, Norfolk.

Barns The largest barn in Britain is one at Manor Farm, Cholsey, near Wallingford, Berkshire. It is 303 feet in length and 54 feet in breadth (16,362 square feet). The Ipsden Barn, Oxfordshire, is 385½ feet long but 30 feet wide (11,565 square feet).

The longest tithe barn in Britain is one measuring 268 feet long at Wyke Farm, near Sherborne, Dorset.

Largest nudist camp The first nudist camps were established in Germany in 1912. The largest such camp in the world was that at l'Île du Levant, southern France, which had up to 15,000 *adeptes* before it was taken over for defence purposes by the French Navy in 1965. Currently the largest nude sea and sunbathing centre is Montalivet on the west coast of France with up to 10,000 "naturists". The term "nudist camp" went out of favour in the early 'sixties.

LONGEST WALL
World The Great Wall of China, completed during the reign of Shih Huang-ti (246–210 B.C.), is 1,684 miles in length, with a height of from 15 to 39 feet and up to 32 feet thick. Its erection is the most massive construction job ever undertaken by the human race. It runs from Shanhai-kuan, on the Gulf of Pohai, to Chiayukuan in Kansu and was kept in repair up to the 16th century.

Britain The longest of the Roman Walls built in Britain was the 15–20-foot-tall Hadrian's Wall, built in the period A.D. 122–126. It ran across the Tyne-Solway isthmus of 74½ miles from Bowness-on-Solway, Cumberland, to Wallsend-on-Tyne, Northumberland, and was abandoned in A.D. 383.

LONGEST FENCE
The longest fence in the world is the dingo-proof fence enclosing the main sheep areas of Queensland, Australia. The wire fence is 6 feet high, one foot underground and stretches for 3,437 miles.

DOORS
Largest The largest doors in the world are the four in the Vertical Assembly Building near Cape Kennedy, Florida, with a height of 460 feet (see page 107).

The largest doors in the United Kingdom are those to the Britannia Assembly Hall, at Filton, Bristol. The doors are 1,035 feet in length and 67 feet high, divided into three bays each 345 feet across. The largest simple hinged door in Britain is that of Ye Old Bull's Head, Beaumaris, Anglesey, Wales, which is 12 feet wide and 30 feet high.

Oldest The oldest doors in Britain are those of Hadstock Church, Essex, which date from *c.* 1040 and exhibit evidence of Danish workmanship.

LARGEST WINDOWS
The largest sheet of glass ever manufactured was one of 50 square metres (538·2 square feet), or 20 metres (65 feet 7 inches) by 2·5 metres (8 feet 2½ inches), exhibited by the Saint Gobain Company in France at the *Journées Internationales de Miroiterie* in March 1958. The largest windows in the world are the three in the Palace of Industry and Technology at Rond-point de la Défense, Paris, with an extreme width of 218 metres (715·2 feet) and a maximum height of 50 metres (164 feet).

The world's longest stairs

LONGEST STAIRS

The world's longest stairs are reputedly at the Mår power station, Øverland, western Norway. Built of wood, these are 4,101 feet in length, rising in 3,875 steps at an angle of 41 degrees inside the pressure shaft. The length of a very long, now discontinuous, stone stairway in the Rohtang Pass, Manali, Kulu, Northern India, is still under investigation.

TALLEST FIRE ESCAPE

The world's tallest mobile fire escape is a 250-foot-tall turntable ladder built in 1962 by Magirus, a West German firm.

LARGEST MARQUEE

The largest tent ever erected was one covering an area of 188,368 square feet (4·32 acres) put up by the firm of Deuter from Augsburg, West Germany, for the 1958 "Welcome Expo" in Brussels, Belgium.

The largest marquee in Britain is one made by Piggot Brothers in 1951 and used by the Royal Horticultural Society at their annual show (first held in 1913) in the grounds of the Royal Hospital, Chelsea, London. The marquee is 310 feet long × 480 feet wide, and consists of 18¾ miles of 36 inch wide canvas covering a ground area of 148,800 square feet.

LARGEST VATS

The largest vats in the United Kingdom are those used in cider brewing by H. P. Bulmer & Company. Their standard oak vats hold 60,000 gallons and reinforced concrete vats hold up to 100,000 gallons. Largest of all is a lined steel vat with a capacity of 550,000 gallons at Hereford.

The world's largest fermentation vessel is the giant stainless steel container, No. 26M, built by the A.P.V. Co. Ltd. of Crawley, Sussex, for the Guinness Brewery, St. James's Gate, Dublin, Ireland. This has a nominal capacity of 8,000 standard barrels, or 2,304,000 Imperial pints, and dimensions of 63 feet long by 28 feet 9 inches wide by 29 feet 7 inches high.

ADVERTISING SIGNS

Largest The greatest advertising sign ever erected was the electric Citroën sign on the Eiffel Tower, Paris. It was switched on on 4 July 1925, and could be seen 24 miles away. It was in six colours with 250,000 lamps and 56 miles of electric cables. The letter "N" which terminated the name "Citroën" between the second and third levels measured 68 feet 5 inches in height. The whole apparatus was taken down after 11 years in 1936.

The world's largest neon sign was that owned by the Atlantic Coast Line Railroad Company at Port Tampa, Florida, U.S.A. It measured 387 feet 6 inches long and 76 feet high, weighed 175 tons and contained about 4,200 feet of red neon tubing. It was demolished on 19 Feb. 1970. Broadway's largest billboard in New York City is 11,426 square feet in area—equivalent to 107 feet by 107 feet.

The world's largest working sign was that in Times Square at 44 & 45th Streets, New York City, U.S.A., in 1966. It showed two 42½-foot-tall "bottles" of Haig Scotch Whisky and an 80-foot-long "bottle" of Gordon's Gin being "poured" into a frosted glass.

Highest The highest advertising sign in the world is the "R.C.A." on the Radio Corporation of America Building in Rockefeller Plaza, New York City, U.S.A. The top of the 25-foot-tall illuminated letters is 825 feet above street level. The tallest free-standing advertising sign is the 187-foot-high sign of the Stardust Hotel, Las Vegas, Nevada, U.S.A. completed in February 1968.

The highest advertising sign in the United Kingdom was the revolving name board of the contractors "Peter Lind" on the Post Office Tower, London (see Towers). The illuminated letters were 12 feet tall and 563 to 575 feet above the street.

LARGEST GASHOLDER

World The world's largest gasholder is that at Fontaine l'Evêque, Belgium, where disused mines have been adapted to store up to 500 million cubic metres (17,650 million cubic feet) of gas at ordinary pressure. Probably the largest conventional gasholder is that at Wien-Simmering, Vienna, Austria, completed in 1968, with a height of 274 feet 8 inches and a capacity of 10·59 million cubic feet.

United Kingdom The largest gasholder ever constructed in the United Kingdom is the East Greenwich Gas Works No. 2 Holder built in 1891 with an original capacity for 12,200,000 cubic feet. As reconstructed its capacity is 8·9 million cubic feet with a water tank 303 feet in diameter and a full inflated height of 148 feet. The No. 1 holder (capacity 8·6 million cubic feet) has a height of 200 feet. The River Tees Northern Gas Board's 1,186-foot-deep underground storage in use since January 1959 has a capacity of 330,000 cubic feet.

TALLEST FOUNTAIN

World The world's tallest fountain is the "Delacorte Geyser"

123

in Welfare Park, Manhattan, New York City which can attain a height of 600 feet. It was installed in June 1969 at a cost of $350,000 (£145,833) and given to the City by George T. Delacorte, founder of the Dell Publishing Company.

United Kingdom The tallest fountain in the United Kingdom is the Emperor Fountain at Chatsworth, Bakewell, Derbyshire. When first tested on 1 June 1844, it attained the then unprecedented height of 260 feet. Since the war it has not been played to more than 250 feet and rarely beyond 180 feet.

CEMETERIES
The world's largest cemetery is that in Leningrad, U.S.S.R., which contains over 500,000 of the 1,300,000 victims of the German army's siege of 1941–42. The largest cemetery in the United Kingdom is Brookwood Cemetery, Brookwood, Surrey. It is owned by the London Necropolis Co. and is 500 acres in extent with 222,000 interments to 1966.

CREMATORIA
Earliest The oldest crematorium in Britain is one built in 1879 at Woking, Surrey. The first legal cremation took place there on 20 March 1885.

Largest The largest crematorium in Europe is the Golders Green Crematorium, in north London. It extends over 14 acres and currently carries out about 5,500 cremations a year.

10. Borings

DEEPEST
World Man's deepest penetration into the Earth's crust was the test bore-hole made by the Phillips Petroleum Co. with the No. 1 well on their EE University Lease in Pecos County, Texas, U.S.A. After 732 days, the drilling crew reached 25,340 feet (4·80 miles) on 12 Oct. 1958. The well was spudded on 12 Oct. 1956, and plugged and abandoned as a "duster", without producing a drop of oil, on 9 Feb. 1959, having cost more than $3,000,000 (£1,250,000). The highest hole temperature was 351° F. A conception of the depth of this hole can be gained by the realization that it was sufficient in depth to lower the Empire State Building down it 20 times. The bore is however only 3 inches in diameter. The immense weight of drill pipe causes a stretch of up to 20 feet over the unstressed length.

The U.S.S.R. Ministry of Geology announced in March 1966 the start of operations to drill to a depth of 15 kilometres (9·32 miles or 49,213 feet) into the magmatic layer near the Finnish border in Karelia. Completion is scheduled for 1971–72. Early in 1967 it was announced that five other boreholes were to be sunk to a depth of up to 11 miles in "Project Anti-Cosmos". The other sites will be north of the Caspian Sea, in the north of the Russian S.F.S.R., in the outlying Urals, in the Caucasus, and in the Kurile Islands.

It was reported in February 1969 that two of the five super-deep borehole projects in the U.S.S.R. some in the Kola Peninsular and in the Caspian depression at Aral Sor (see Chapter III) have completed their main first-stage to "some 7 to 8 kilometres" (22,966 to 26,247 feet). No formal announcement of having surpassed the 1958 world record of 7·72 km. (25,340 feet) was however made. The other sites will be at Saatly, Azerbaijan (first stage 1970; second stage 1972); and in the Urals and the Kurile Islands.

United Kingdom The deepest oil well in the United Kingdom is the British Petroleum well drilled to a depth of 9,355 feet at Tetney Lock, near Cleethorpes, Lincolnshire, in 1963. A depth of 14,131 feet was attained at an undisclosed site in the North Sea in 1968.

Man's greatest penetration into the Earth—over 2 miles below the ground (see opposite)

OIL FIELDS
Largest The largest oil field in the world is that at Oktyabr'skiy, U.S.S.R., which extends over 1,800 square miles (60 miles by 30 miles). It has been asserted that the Groningen gas field in the Netherlands is the largest yet discovered. It was estimated in 1968 that United Kingdom's segment of the North Sea gas field contains $2·5 \times 10^{13}$ cubic feet of almost pure methane of which the Leman Field (discovered April 1966), operated by the Shell-Esso-Gas Council-Amoco group, accounts for about half.

Greatest gusher The most prolific wildcat recorded is the 1,160-foot-deep Lucas No. 1, at Spindletop, about 3 miles north of Beaumont, Texas, U.S.A., on 10 Jan. 1901. The gusher was heard more than a mile away and yielded 800,000 barrels during the 9 days it was uncapped. The surrounding ground subsequently yielded 142,000,000 barrels.

Greatest flare The greatest gas fire was that which burnt at Gassi Touil in the Algerian Sahara from noon on 13 Nov. 1961 to 9.30 a.m. on 28 April 1962. The pillar of flame rose 450 feet and the smoke 600 feet. It was eventually extinguished by Paul Neal ("Red") Adair, aged 47, of Austin, Texas, U.S.A., using 550 lb. of dynamite. His fee was understood to be about $1,000,000 (then £357,000).

WATER WELLS
The world's deepest water bore is the Stensvad Water Well 11-W1 of 7,320 feet drilled by the Great Northern Drilling Co. Inc. in Rosebud County, Montana, U.S.A. in October-November 1961.

United Kingdom The deepest well in the United Kingdom is a water table well 2,842 feet deep in the Staffordshire coal measures at Smestow. The deepest artesian well in Britain is that at the White Heather Laundry, Stonebridge Park, Willesden, London, N.W.10, bored in 1911 to a depth of 2,225 feet.

MINES
Earliest The earliest known mining operations were in the Ngwenya Hills of the Hhohho District of north-western Swaziland where haematite (iron ore) was mined for body paint *c*. 41,000 B.C.

BORINGS

Deepest World The world's deepest mine is the East Rand Proprietary Mine at Boksburg, Transvaal, South Africa. In November 1959 a depth of 11,246 feet (2·13 miles) below the ground and 5,875 feet below sea-level was first attained. Mining does not now proceed below 10,788 feet where the rock temperature is two degrees cooler at 124° F. The deepest terminal below any vertical mine shaft in the world is No. 3 sub-vertical main shaft on the Western Deep Levels Mine reaching 9,783 feet below the surface. The longest vertical shaft is No. 3 Ventilation Shaft at the mine which measures 9,673 feet in one continuous hole. The longest sub-incline shaft is the Angelo Tertiary at E.R.P.M. (see above) with a length of 6,656 feet (1·26 miles).

United Kingdom The all-time record depth attained is 4,132 feet reached in the Arley Seam of the Parsonage Colliery in February 1949. The record in Scottish coalmines was 3,093 feet in the Michael Colliery, Barncraig, Fife, reached in August 1939. The deepest present mine workings are the Hem Heath Colliery (Moss Seam), Trentham, Staffordshire, England at 3,300 feet. The deepest in Scotland is the Great Seam at Monkton Hall Colliery, Millerhill, Mid-Lothian, at 2,930 feet. The deepest shaft in England was No. 2 shaft at Wolstanton Colliery, Stoke-on-Trent, Staffordshire, at 3,434 feet and the deepest in Scotland was Monkton Hall No. 1, Mid-lothian at 3,054 feet. The deepest Cornish tin mine was Dolcoath mine, near Camborne. The Williams shaft was completed in 1910 to 550 fathoms (3,300 feet) from adit or approximately 3,600 feet from the surface.

GOLDMINES

gest area The largest goldmining area in the world is the Witwatersrand gold field extending 30 miles east and west of Johannesburg, South Africa. Gold was discovered there in 1886 and by 1944 more than 45 per cent. of the world's gold was mined there by 320,000 Bantu and 44,000 Europeans. Currently 74 per cent. of the free world's supply comes from this area.

The largest gold-mine in area is the East Rand Proprietary Mines Ltd., whose 8,785 claims cover 12,100 acres. The largest, measured by volume extracted, is Randfontein Estates Gold Mine Co. Ltd. with 170 million cubic yards—enough to cover Manhattan Island to a depth of 8 feet. The main tunnels if placed end to end would stretch a distance of 2,600 miles.

The largest gold-mine in Britain was Gwynfyngdd, Merionethshire, Wales, where gold was discovered in 1834 and which was worked from 1864 till 1961. Alluvial gold deposits are believed to have been worked in the Wicklow Mountains, Ireland, as early as 1800 B.C.

Richest The richest gold-mine has been Crown Mines with nearly 45 million ounces and still productive. The richest in yield per year was West Driefontein which averaged more than 2½ million ounces per year until disrupted in November 1968 by flooding. The only large mine in South Africa yielding more than one ounce per ton milled is Free State Geduld.

Iron The world's largest iron-mine is at Lebedinsky, U.S.S.R., in the Kursk Magnetic Anomaly which has altogether an estimated 20,000 million tons of rich (45–65 per cent.) ore and 10,000,000 million tons of poorer ore in seams up to 2,000 feet thick. The world's greatest reserves are, however, those of Brazil, estimated to total 58,000 million tons, or 35 per cent. of the world's total surface stock.

Copper Historically the world's most productive copper mine has been the Bingham Canyon Mine (see right) belonging to the Kennecott Copper Corporation with over 9,000,000 short tons in the 65 years 1904–68. Currently the most productive is the Chuquicamata mine of the Anaconda Company 150 miles north of Antofagasta, Chile with 334,578 short tons in 1966.

The world's greatest quarry, Utah, U.S.A.

The world's largest underground copper mine is at El Teniente, 50 miles south-east of Santiago, Chile, with more than 200 miles of underground workings and an annual output of nearly 11,000,000 tons of ore.

Silver, lead and zinc The world's largest lead, zinc and silver mine is the Sullivan Mine at Kimberley, British Columbia, Canada, with 195 miles of tunnels. The mines at Broken Hill, New South Wales, Australia, found in September 1883, produce annually 2,300,000 tons of ore, from which is extracted some 10 per cent. of the world's output of lead. The world's largest zinc smelter is the £15,000,000 Imperial Smelting complex at Avonmouth, England opened in May 1968 with a capacity of 120,000 tons of zinc and 80,000 tons of lead per annum.

Spoil heap The world's largest artificial heap is the sand dump on the Randfontein Estates Gold Mine, South Africa, which comprises 42 million tons of crushed ore and rock waste and has a volume six times that of the Great Pyramid. The largest colliery tip in Great Britain covers 114 acres (maximum height 130 feet) with 18 million tons of slag at Catacre Clough, Lancashire.

QUARRIES
The world's largest excavation is the Bingham Canyon Copper Mine, 30 miles south of Salt Lake City, Utah, U.S.A. From 1906 to mid-1969 the total excavation has been 2,445 million long tons over an area of 2·08 square miles to a depth of 2,280 feet. This is five times the amount of material moved to build the Panama Canal. Three shifts of 900 men work round the clock with 38 electric shovels, 62 locomotives hauling 1,268 wagons and 18 drilling machines for the 28 tons of explosive used daily. The average daily extraction is 96,000 tons of one per cent. ore and 225,000 tons of overburden.

The world's deepest open pit is the Kimberley Open Mine in South Africa, dug over a period of 43 years (1871 to 1914) to a depth of nearly 1,200 feet and with a diameter of about 1,500 feet and a circumference of nearly a mile, covering an area of 36 acres. Three tons (14,504,566 carats) of diamonds were extracted from the 21,000,000 tons of earth dug out. The inflow of water has now made the depth 845 feet to the water surface. The "Big Hole" was dug by pick and shovel.

The largest quarry in Britain is Imperial Chemical Industries Ltd.'s Tunstead Quarry, near Buxton, Derbyshire. The working face is 1½ miles long and 120 feet high.

Largest stone The largest mined slab of quarried stone is one measuring 68 feet by 14 feet by 14 feet, weighing about 1,590 tons, at Ba'labakk (Baalbeck), in the Lebanon. The largest able to be moved from this mine were slabs of 805 tons for the trilithon of the nearby Temple of Jupiter.

The packet ship *Sirius*

the mechanical world

The *United States*—Atlantic Blue Riband holder

1. Ships

EARLIEST BOATS

The earliest known sea-going vessel is a 102-foot-long sailing vessel dated to the Egyptian sixth dynasty from 2420 B.C. Oars found in bogs at Magle Mose, Sjaelland, Denmark, have been dated to *c.* 7000 B.C.

Earliest power The earliest experiments with marine steam engines date from those on the river Seine, France, in 1775. Propulsion was first achieved when in 1783 the Marquis Jouffroy d'Abbans ascended a reach of the river Saône near Lyons, France, in the 180-ton paddle steamer *Pyroscaphe*.

The tug *Charlotte Dundas* was the first successful power-driven vessel. She was a paddle-wheel steamer built in Scotland in 1801–02 by William Symington (1763–1831), using a double-acting condensing engine constructed by James Watt (1736–1819).

The earliest regular steam run was by the *Clermont*, built by Robert Fulton (1765–1815), a U.S. engineer, which maintained a service from New York to Albany from 17 Aug. 1807. The oldest steamer is believed to be the *Skibladner* (206 gross tons), which was built in Motala, Sweden, in 1856 and sank on Lake Mjøsa, Norway, in February 1967 but was raised and refitted for re-commission. Mr. G. H. Pattinson's 40-foot steam launch, raised from Ullswater in 1962, and now on Lake Windermere may date from a year or two earlier.

Turbine The first turbine ship was the *Turbinia*, built in 1894 at Wallsend-on-Tyne, Northumberland, to the design of the Hon. Sir Charles Algernon Parsons, O.M., K.C.B. (1854–1931). The *Turbinia* was 100 feet long and of $44\frac{1}{2}$ tons displacement with machinery consisting of three steam turbines totalling about 2,000 shaft horse-power. At her first public demonstration in 1897 she reached a speed of 34·5 knots (39·7 m.p.h.).

Atlantic crossings Earliest The earliest crossing of the Atlantic by a power vessel, as opposed to an auxiliary engined sailing ship, was a 22-day voyage begun in April 1827, from Rotterdam, Netherlands, to the West Indies by the *Curaçao*. She was a wooden paddle boat of 438 registered tons, built in Dundee, Angus, in 1826 and purchased by the Dutch Government for the West Indian mail service. The earliest Atlantic crossing entirely under steam (with

intervals for desalting the boilers) was by H.M.S. *Rhadamanthus* from Plymouth to Barbados in 1832. The earliest crossing of the Atlantic under continuous steam power was by the condenser-fitted packet ship *Sirius* (703 tons) from Queenstown (now Cóbh), Ireland, to Sandy Hook, N.Y., U.S.A., in 18 days 10 hours on 4–22 April 1838.

Fastest The fastest Atlantic crossing was made by the *United States* (then 51,988, now 38,216 gross tons), flagship of the United States Lines Company. On her maiden voyage between 3 and 8 July 1952 from New York City, N.Y., U.S.A., to Le Havre, France, and Southampton, England, she averaged 35·59 knots, or 40·98 m.p.h., for 3 days 10 hours 40 minutes (6.36 p.m. G.M.T. 3 July to 5.16 a.m. 7 July) on a route of 2,949 nautical miles from the Ambrose Light Vessel to the Bishop Rock Light, Isles of Scilly, Cornwall. During this run, on 6–7 July 1952, she steamed the greatest distance ever covered by any ship in a day's run (24 hours)—868 nautical miles, hence averaging 36·17 knots (41·65 m.p.h.). Her maximum speed is 41·75 knots (48 m.p.h.) on a full power of 240,000 shaft horse-power. The s.h.p. figure was only revealed by the U.S. Defense Department in 1968.

The *United States*, which covered 999·51 statute miles in one day

The fastest crossing of the Atlantic by a British ship is 3 days 15 hours 48 minutes by the Cunard liner *Queen Mary* in September 1946 on a 2,710 mile voyage from Halifax, Nova Scotia, Canada, to Southampton at an average of 30·86 knots (35·54 m.p.h.). On her 2,938 mile crossing from the Ambrose Light to Bishop Rock on 10–14 Aug. 1938, she averaged 31·69 knots (36·49 m.p.h.) for 3 days 20 hours 42 minutes.

Pacific crossing The fastest crossing of the Pacific Ocean (Yokohama, Japan to San Francisco, U.S.A.) is 8 days 35 minutes achieved by the 14,114 ton diesel cargo liner *Italy Maru* in August 1967.

merged The fastest disclosed submerged Atlantic crossing is 6 days 11 hours 55 minutes by the U.S. nuclear-powered submarine *Nautilus*, which travelled 3,150 miles from Portland, Dorset, to New York City, N.Y., U.S.A., arriving on 25 Aug. 1958.

NORTHERNMOST
The farthest north ever attained by a surface vessel is 86° 39′ N. in 47° 55′ E. by the drifting U.S.S.R. ice-breaker *Sedov* on 29 Aug. 1939. She was locked in the Arctic ice floes from 23 Oct. 1937 until freed on 13 Jan. 1940.

SOUTHERNMOST
The farthest south ever reached by a ship was achieved on 3 Jan. 1955, by the Argentine ice-breaker *General San Martin* in establishing the General Belgrano Base, Antarctica, on the shores of the Weddell Sea at 78° S., 39° W., 830 miles from the South Pole.

LARGEST WARSHIP
The warship with the largest dimensions in the world is the 1,101½-foot-long U.S. aircraft carrier *Enterprise* (see p. 128), with a displacement of 85,350 tons, and an overall width of 252 feet. Her maximum draught of 37 feet is, however, doubled by the largest tankers. The *Enterprise* will be overtaken by the U.S.S. *Eisenhower*, a 95,000 ton nuclear aircraft carrier for which $377

million was included in the 1969–70 Defense budget submitted to the U.S. Congress on 31 May 1969. She will have two nuclear engines with fuel cores designed to last 13 years before refuelling. The total cost will be $510,000,000 (£212·5 million).

The world's longest (1,035·2 feet) and largest active liner (66,348 gross tons) is the *France,* owned by the Compagnie Générale Transatlantique. She made her official maiden voyage from Le Havre, France, to New York City, N.Y., U.S.A., on 3 Feb. 1962, and cost £29,000,000.

PASSENGER LINER

LARGEST
The R.M.S. *Queen Elizabeth* (finally 82,998 but formerly 83,673 gross tons), of the Cunard fleet, was the largest passenger vessel in the world and had the largest displacement of any liner in the world. She has an overall length of 1,031 feet and is 118 feet 7 inches in breadth. She was powered by steam turbines which develop 168,000 h.p. Her last passenger voyage ended on 15 Nov. 1968. The *Queen Elizabeth's* normal sea speed was 28½ knots (32·8 m.p.h.). She was sold at Port Everglades, Fort Lauderdale, Florida, U.S.A. as a tourist centre to a United States consortium for $8,600,000 (£3,583,333) on 19 July 1969.

The Cunard S.S. *Mauretania,* holder of the Atlantic Blue Riband from 1909 to 1929

PROGRESSIVE LIST OF WORLD'S LARGEST LINERS

Gross Tonnage	Name	Propulsion	Overall Length in Feet	Dates
1,340	Great Western (U.K.)	Paddle wheels	236	1838–1856
1,862	British Queen (U.K.)	Paddle wheels	275	1839–1844
2,360	President (U.K.)	Paddle wheels	268	1840–1841
3,270	Great Britain (U.K.)	Single screw	322	1845–1937
4,690	Himalaya (U.K.)	Single screw	340	1853–1927
18,914	Great Eastern (U.K.)	Paddles and screw	692	1858–1888
10,650	City of New York (later Harvard, Pittsburgh) (U.S.A.)	Twin screw	528	1888–1923
17,274	Oceanic (U.K.)	Twin screw	705	1899–1914
20,904	Celtic (U.K.)	Twin screw	700	1901–1928
21,227	Cedric (U.K.)	Twin screw	700	1903–1932
23,884	Baltic (U.K.)	Twin screw	726	1904–1933
31,550	Lusitania (U.K.)	4 screws	790	1907–1915
31,938	Mauretania (U.K.)	4 screws	787	1907–1935
45,300	Olympic (U.K.)	Triple screw	892	1911–1935
46,300	Titanic (U.K.)	Triple screw	892	1912–1912
52,022	Imperator (Germany) (later Berengaria [U.K.])	4 screws	919	1913–1938
54,282[2]	Vaterland (Germany) (later Leviathan [U.S.])	4 screws	950	1914–1938
56,621	Bismarck (Germany) (later Majestic [U.K.] and H.M. Troopship Caledonia)	4 screws	954	1922–1939
79,280[3]	Normandie (France) (later U.S.S. Lafayette)	4 screws	1,029	1935–1946
80,774[4]	Queen Mary (U.K.) (later sold to U.S. interests)	4 screws	1,019·5	1936–
83,673[5]	Queen Elizabeth (U.K.) (later sold to U.S. interests)	4 screws	1,031	1940–
66,348	France (France)	4 screws	1,035·2	1961–

[1] *Originally 22,500 tons.*
[2] *Listed as 59,957 gross tons under U.S. registration, 1922–31, but not internationally accepted as such.*

[3] *Gross tonnage later raised by enclosure of open deck space to 83,423 gross tons.*
[4] *Later 81,237 gross tons.*
[5] *Later 82,998 gross tons.*

The mechanical world

BATTLESHIPS

Largest World The largest battleships in the world are now the U.S.S. *Iowa* (completed 22 Feb. 1943) and U.S.S. *Missouri* (completed 11 June 1944), each of which has a full load displacement of 57,950 tons and mounts nine 16-inch and 20 5-inch guns. The U.S.S. *New Jersey* (57,216 tons full load displacement) is, however, longer than either by nine inches, with an overall length of 888 feet. She was, in 1968, the last battleship on active service in the world.

The Japanese battleships *Yamato* (completed on 16 Dec. 1941 and sunk in the Bungo Strait off Kyūshū, Japan, by U.S. planes on 7 April 1945) and *Musashi* (sunk in the Philippine Sea by 11 bombs and 16 torpedoes on 24 Oct. 1944) were the largest battleships ever constructed, each with a full load displacement of 72,809 tons. With an overall length of 863 feet, a beam of 127 feet and a full load draught of 35½ feet, they mounted nine 460 mm. (18·1 inch) guns in three triple turrets. Each gun weighed 162 tons and was 75 feet in length, firing a 3,200 lb. projectile.

Britain Britain's largest ever and last battleship was H.M.S. *Vanguard* with a full load displacement of 51,420 tons, overall length 814 feet, beam 108½ feet, with a maximum draught of 36 feet. She mounted eight 15-inch and 15 5·25-inch guns. A shaft horse-power of 130,000 gave her a sea speed of 29½ knots (34 m.p.h.). The *Vanguard* was laid down in John Brown & Co. Ltd.'s yard at Clydebank, Dunbartonshire, on 20 Oct. 1941, launched on 30 Nov. 1944 and completed on 25 April 1946. She was sold for scrap in August 1960 for £500,000 having cost a total of £14,000,000.

Largest guns The largest guns ever mounted in any of H.M. ships were the 18-inch pieces in the light battle cruiser (later aircraft carrier) H.M.S. *Furious* in 1917. In 1918 they were transferred to the monitors H.M.S. *Lord Clive* and *General Wolfe*. The thickest armour ever carried was in H.M.S. *Inflexible* (completed 1881), measuring 24 inches.

AIRCRAFT CARRIERS

The world's largest aircraft carrier is the atomic-powered U.S.S. *Enterprise*, "launched" on 24 Sept. 1960, commissioned on 25 Nov. 1961 and completed on 20 Dec. 1961, at a cost of $444 million (then £158,500,000). She has a full load displacement of 85,350 tons, an overall length of 1,101½ feet, a flight deck width of 252 feet and a maximum draught of 37 feet. Her 8 water-cooled reactors give 300,000 s.h.p., with a maximum speed in excess of 35 knots (40 m.p.h.). Her complement is 100 aircraft handled on a 4½ acre flight deck and a crew of 4,600.

H.M.S. *Revenge*—Britain's fourth nuclear submarine

Britain's largest ever aircraft carrier is H.M.S. *Ark Royal*, completed on 25 Feb. 1955, with a full load displacement of 50,736 tons (previously 53,340 tons), 845 feet overall, 166 feet wide, maximum draught 36 feet, with a full complement of 2,640 and a capacity of 30 naval jet aircraft and 6 helicopters. Her 152,000 shaft horse-power give her a maximum speed of 31·5 knots (36·27 m.p.h.).

The pilot who has made the greatest number of deck landings is Lt.-Cdr. J. S. Bailey, O.B.E., D.S.C., R.N., who made his 2,000th landing on H.M.S. *Illustrious* on 24 May 1950 and subsequently 282 more. He was killed in a car accident in August 1967.

The cruiser with the greatest fire power is the U.S.S. *Long Beach* (15,947 tons full load). She is nuclear-powered and armed with guided missiles, with a trial speed of 30·5 knots (35·1 m.p.h.). She was completed on 1 Sept. 1961 at a cost of $320 million (then £114 million).

Fastest destroyer The highest speed attained by a destroyer was 45·02 knots (51·84 m.p.h.) by the 3,750 ton French destroyer *Le Terrible* in 1935. She was powered by four Yarrow small tube boilers and two geared turbines giving 100,000 shaft horse-power. She was removed from the active list at the end of 1957.

Fastest warship The world's fastest warship is H.M.C.S. *Bras d'Or* the 180-ton 150·8-foot-long Canadian Navy Hydrofoil commissioned in 1967. On 17 July 1969 outside Halifax harbour, Nova Scotia she attained 61 knots (70·2 m.p.h.).

U.S.S. *New Jersey*,
the world's last active battleship

SHIPS

SUBMARINES

Largest The world's largest submarine is the nuclear-powered ship *Le Redoubtable,* launched for the French navy at Cherbourg, France, on 29 March 1967. She has a submerged displacement of 9,000 tons, a surface displacement of 7,780 tons, a length of 419·9 feet and will be armed with 16 nuclear MSBM (*mer-sol balistique stratégique*) missiles. The largest submarines built for the Royal Navy are the four atomic-powered nuclear missile R class boats with a surface displacement of 7,500 tons and 8,400 tons submerged, a length of 425 feet, a beam of 33 feet and a draught of 30 feet.

Fastest The world's fastest submarines are the 35-knot U.S. Navy's tear-drop hulled nuclear vessels of the *Skipjack* class. They have been listed semi-officially as capable of a speed of 45 knots (51·8 m.p.h.) submerged. In November 1968 the building of attack submarines with submerged speeds in the region of 50 knots was approved for the U.S. Navy.

Deepest The greatest depth recorded by a true submarine was 8,310 feet by the Lockheed *Sea Quest* off California, U.S.A., on 29 Feb. 1968. The 51-foot-long *Aluminaut* launched by the Reynolds Metals Co. on 2 Sept. 1964 is designed for depths of up to 15,000 feet but is prevented from descending below 6,250 feet by prohibitive insurance costs. The U.S. Navy's nuclear-powered NR-1 being built by General Dynamics Inc. will be able to operate at a "very great" but classified depth which is assumed to be lower than the published figure of 20,000 feet for the first 7-man Deep Submergence Search Vehicle DSSV due in service in 1972.

Largest fleet The largest submarine fleet in the world is that of the U.S.S.R. Navy or *Krasni Flot,* which numbers about 375 boats, of which 45 (15 ballistic) are nuclear-powered and missile armed. The U.S. Navy has 41 such submarines in service.

LARGEST TANKERS

The world's largest tankers are the six *Universe* class tankers with a deadweight tonnage of 326,500 tons. Of these the *Universe Portugal* has by a slight margin the highest gross registered tonnage with 149,623 and together with the *Universe Japan* the greatest overall length of 1,135 feet 2 inches. The whole class has a beam of 175 feet 2 inches, a summer draught of 81 feet 5 inches and a capacity of 2·5 million barrels of crude oil and each cost more than $20 million (£8·33 million) from Japanese shipyards. They carry three anchors each of 20·3 tons with seven-tenths of a mile of chain cable weighing 380 tons. The full load displacement of these tankers is believed to be about 400,000 tons. The *Universe Ireland* "launched" on 9 Jan. 1968 completed her maiden voyage to Bantry Bay, Ireland in September 1968.

The first of the largest class of tankers in the world—the *Universe Ireland* at the Bantry Bay, Cork, terminal

The largest ship ever built in Britain —the *Esso Northumbria*

United Kingdom The longest ships in the world of any kind are the Esso class tankers, which have a length of 1,141 feet 1 inch— 106 feet longer than the world's largest-ever liner, *France.* They have a deadweight tonnage of 252,000 tons, a gross registered tonnage of 127,150 and a beam of 170 feet 2 inches. Some idea of this length can be conveyed by the thought that it would take a golfer, standing on the stem, a full-blooded drive and a chip shot to reach the stern. The largest vessels launched in a United Kingdom shipyard are those of this class, the first of which was, on 2 May 1969, the *Esso Northumbria* launched for Esso Petroleum at the yard of Swan Hunter and Tyne Shipbuilders. She is 110 feet longer than the *Queen Elizabeth.*

LARGEST CARGO VESSEL

The largest dry cargo vessel in the world is the *Fuohsan Maru* (63,000 gross tons), built in Japan. She is 849 feet in length and has a beam of 135 feet.

Fastest built During the Second World War "Liberty ships" of prefabricated welded steel construction were built at seven shipyards on the Pacific coast of the United States, under the management of Henry J. Kaiser (1882–1967). The record time for assembly of one ship of 7,200 gross tons (10,500 tons deadweight) was 4 days 15½ hours. In January 1968, 900 Liberty ships were still in service.

LARGEST CABLE SHIP

The world's largest cable-laying ship is the American Telephone & Telegraph Co.'s German-built *Long Lines* (11,200 gross tons), completed by Deutsche Werft of Hamburg in April 1963, at a cost of £6,800,000. She has a fully-laden displacement of 17,000 tons, measures 511 feet 6 inches overall and is powered by twin turbine electric engines.

Largest whale factory The largest whale factory ship is the U.S.S.R.'s *Sovietskaya Ukraina* (32,034 gross tons), with a summer deadweight of 46,000 tons, completed in October 1959. She is 714·6 feet in length and 94 feet 3 inches in the beam.

Most powerful tug The world's largest and most powerful tug is the 17,500 i.h.p. M.T. *Oceanic* (2,046 gross tons). She was built by Bugsier—und Bergungs—Aktiengesellschaft of Hamburg, West Germany and was commissioned in 1969. She is 284 feet 5 inches long, 46 feet 11 inches in the beam, has a speed of 22 knots (25 m.p.h.) and a range of 20,000 miles. She is being followed by an identical twin tug to be named *Arctic.*

Largest car ferry The world's largest car and passenger ferry is the 502-foot-long *Finlandia* (8,100 gross tons), delivered by Wärtsilä Ab. of Helsinki in May 1967, for service between Helsinki and Copenhagen with Finska Angfartygs Ab. She can carry 321 cars and up to 1,200 passengers and achieved a speed of 22 knots (25 m.p.h.) during trials.

Largest hydrofoil The world's largest naval hydrofoil is the 212-foot-long *Plainview* (310 tons full load), launched by the Lockheed Shipbuilding and Construction Co. at Seattle, Washington, U.S.A., on 28 June 1965. She has a service speed of 50 knots (57 m.p.h.). A larger hydrofoil, carrying 150 passengers and 8 cars at 40 knots to ply the Göteborg-Ålborg crossing, came into service in June 1968. It was built by Westermoen Hydrofoil Ltd. of Mandal, Norway.

129

The world's largest icebreaker—the oil tanker,
S.S. *Manhattan*—crashing through the North-west Passage

Most powerful icebreaker	The world's most powerful icebreaker and first atomic-powered ship is the U.S.S.R.'s 44,000 s.h.p. *Lenin* (16,000 gross tons), which was launched at Leningrad on 2 Dec. 1957 and began her maiden voyage on 18 Sept. 1959. She is $439\frac{3}{4}$ feet long, $90\frac{1}{2}$ feet in the beam and has a maximum speed of 18 knots (20·7 m.p.h.). In March 1970 the U.S.S.R. announced the building of a more powerful atomic-powered icebreaker to be named *Arctika*, able to go through ice 7 feet thick at 4 knots.

The largest converted icebreaker is the 1,005-foot-long S.S. *Manhattan* (43,000 s.h.p.), which was converted by the Humble Oil Co. into a 150,000 ton icebreaker with an armoured prow 69 feet 2 inches long. She made a double voyage through the North-west Passage in arctic Canada from 24 Aug. to 12 Nov. 1969.

Largest dredger	The world's largest dredger is one reported to be operating in the lower Lena basin in May 1967, with a rig more than 100 feet tall and a cutting depth of 165 feet. The pontoon is 750 feet long. The largest dredging grabs in the world are those of 635 cubic feet capacity built in 1965 by Priestman Bros. Ltd. of Hull, Yorkshire for the dredging pontoon *Biarritz*.
Wooden ship	The heaviest wooden ship ever built was H.M. Battleship *Lord Clive* at 7,750 tons. She was completed at Pembroke Dock, Wales, on 2 June 1866. She measured 280 feet in length and was sold in 1875.

SAILING SHIPS

Largest	The largest sailing vessel ever built was the *France II* (5,806 gross tons), launched at Bordeaux in 1911. The *France II* was a steel-hulled, five-masted barque (square-rigged on four masts and fore and aft rigged on the aftermost mast). Her hull measured 418 feet overall. Although principally designed as a sailing vessel with a stump topgallant rig, she was also fitted with two steam engines. She was wrecked in 1922.
Largest junks	The largest junk on record was the sea-going *Cheng Ho* of c. 1420, with a displacement of 3,100 tons and a length variously estimated at from 300 feet to 440 feet.

A river junk 361 feet long, with treadmill-operated paddle-wheels, was recorded in A.D. 1161. In c. A.D. 280 a floating fortress 600 feet square, built by Wang Chün on the Yangtze, took part in the Chin-Wu river war. Modern junks do not, even in the case of the Chiangsu traders, exceed 170 feet in length.

Longest day's run under sail	The longest day's run by any sailing ship was one of 465 nautical miles (535·45 statute miles) by the clipper *Champion of the Seas* (2,722 registered tons) of the Liverpool Black Ball Line running before a north-westerly gale in the south Indian Ocean under the command of Capt. Alex. Newlands. The elapsed time between the fixes was 23 hours 17 minutes giving an average of 19·97 knots.

The highest recorded speed by a sailing ship is 22 knots (25·3 m.p.h.) by *Sovereign of the Seas* on a run to Sydney on 18 March 1853. She was built in 1852 by Donald McKay of East Boston, Massachusetts, U.S.A.

Slowest voyage	Perhaps the slowest passage on record was that of the *Red Rock* (1,600 tons), which was posted missing at Lloyd's of London after taking 112 days for 950 miles across the Coral Sea from 20 Feb. to 12 June 1899, at an average speed of less than 0·4 of a knot.

Largest sails	The largest spars ever carried were those in H.M. Battleship *Temeraire*, completed at Chatham, Kent, on 31 Aug. 1877. The fore and main yards measured 11[] feet in length. The mainsail contained 5,100 feet of canvas, weighing 2 tons, and the total sail area was 25,000 square feet. At 8,540 tons the *Temeraire* was the largest brig ever built. The main masts of H.M.S. *Achilles*, *Black Prince* and *Warrior* all measured 17[] feet from truck to deck.
Largest propeller	The heaviest ship's propeller is one of 28 feet in diameter weighing 62 tons. It was built in Kiel, West Germany, in 1967 for a large single-screw tanker. The biggest made in Britain were 32 feet in diameter weighing 57 tons, made in Birkenhead and shipped for fitting to Esso tankers on Tyneside. The first was shipped on 6 Feb. 1969.
Most powerful derricks	The most powerful ship-borne derricks in the world are those mounted in 1966 on the Blue Star Line ship *Australia Star*, with a tested lifting capacity of 330 tons. The 87-foot-long booms each weigh 68 tons and the 76-foot-tall supporting masts each weigh 95 tons. The lifting hooks each weigh 2 tons.
Largest Dracones	The largest Dracones (flexible plastic containers used for bulk transport of liquids) ever built were completed by Frankenstein and Sons (Manchester) Ltd., in July 1962. They are 300 feet in length and can transport 1,200 tons (250,000 gallons) of water.
Deepest anchorage	The deepest anchorage ever achieved is one of 24,600 feet in the mid-Atlantic Romanche Trench by Capt. Jacques-Yves Cousteau's research vessel *Calypso*, with a $5\frac{1}{2}$-mile-long nylon cable, on 29 July 1956.
Largest drilling rig	The world's largest off-shore oil rig is the semi-submersible *Sea Quest* in use in the North Sea with a displacement of 10,000 tons.
Largest wreck	The largest ship ever wrecked has been the Japanese-built, Royal Dutch/Shell owned, 206,600 ton (dead-weight) tanker *Marpessa* after a tank explosion when sailing in ballast from Rotterdam, 50 miles northwest of Dakar, Senegal on 15 Dec. 1969. She was 1,067 feet 5 inches long. The largest vessel ever to be wrecked in British waters has been the 965-foot-long tanker *Torrey Canyon*, of 61,275 tons gross and 118,285 tons deadweight, which struck the Pollard Rock of the Seven Stones Reef between the Isles of Scilly and Land's End, Cornwall, England, at 08.50 on 18 March 1967. The resultant oil pollution from some 30,000 tons of Kuwait crude was "on a scale which had no precedent anywhere in the world". In an attempt to fire the remaining oil, the ship was bombed to virtual destruction on 28–30 March 1967.

130

The world's largest wreck,
the *Marpessa*—206,600 tons

2. Road Vehicles

COACHING

Before the advent of the McAdam road surfaces in *c.* 1815 coaching was slow and hazardous. The zenith was reached on 13 July 1888 when J. Selby, Esq., drove the "Old Times" coach 108 miles from London to Brighton and back with 8 teams and 14 changes in 7 hours 50 minutes to average 13·79 m.p.h. Four-horse carriages could maintain a speed of 21¼ m.p.h. for nearly an hour.

MOTOR CARS

Earliest omobile The earliest automobile of which there is record is a two-foot-long model constructed by Ferdinand Verbiest (died 1687), a Jesuit priest, and described in his *Astronomia Europaea*. His model was possibly inspired either by Giovanni Branca's description of a steam turbine, published in 1629, or by writings on "fire carts" during the Chu dynasty (*c.* 800 B.C.) in the library of the Emperor Khang-hi of China, to whom he was an astronomer during the period *c.* 1665–80.

The earliest mechanically-propelled passenger vehicle was the first of two military steam tractors, completed in Paris in 1769 by Nicolas-Joseph Cugnot (1725–1804). This reached 2¼ m.p.h. Cugnot's second, larger tractor, completed in 1771, today survives in the *Conservatoire Nationale des Arts et Metiers* in Paris. Britain's first successful steam carriage carried four passengers and was built by Richard Trevithick (1771–1833) at Redruth, Cornwall, in 1801, though a 3-wheeled steam locomotive was built by William Murdoch in 1785–6.

The first internal-combustion automobile was that built by Jean Joseph Etienne Lenoir (1822–1900), based on his electrically-ignited two-stroke gas engine (patented in 1860) fitted to a horse brake. In May 1862 it was driven from Rue la Roquette, Paris to Vincennes.

Earliest ol-driven cars The first successful petrol-driven car, the Motorwagen, built by Carl-Friedrich Benz (1844–1929) of Karlsruhe, ran at Mannheim, Germany, in late 1885. It was a 5 cwt. 3-wheeler reaching 8–10 m.p.h. Its single cylinder chain-drive engine (bore 91·4 mm., stroke 160 mm.) delivered 0·85 h.p. at 400 r.p.m. It was patented on 29 Jan. 1886. Its first 1 kilometre road test was reported in the local newspaper, the *Neue Badische Landeszeitung*, of 4 June 1886, under the heading "Miscellaneous". Two were built in 1885 of which one has been preserved in "running order" at the Deutches Museum, Munich since 1959.

The oldest internal-combustion engine car seen on British roads has been the Danish "Hammel". Designed by Albert Hammel, who took out the original patents in 1886, it was completed in 1887. In 1954 it completed the London-to-Brighton run in 12½ hours, averaging 4½ m.p.h. The engine is a twin-cylinder, horizontal water-cooled four-stroke with a capacity of 2,720 c.c., bore and stroke 104·5 mm. × 160 mm., and a compression ratio of 3·5:1.

In Britain F. H. Butler built a petrol-engined 3-wheeled automobile in 1887 but the earliest successful British cars were the 3-wheeled air-cooled 2 h.p. Wolseley built in 1895 by Herbert (the first and last Lord) Austin (1866–1941) and John H. Knight's Surrey-built 3-wheeler of July of the same year. The first car to run on an English road was an 1894 4 h.p. twin-cylinder Panhard-Levassor built in France, driven in June 1895 by the Hon. Evelyn Henry Ellis (1843–1913).

Earliest strations The world's first plates were introduced into New York State, U.S.A., in 1901. Registration plates were introduced in Britain in 1903. The original A1 plate was secured by the 2nd Earl Russell (1865–1931) for his 12 h.p. Napier. This plate, willed in September 1950 to

Mr. Trevor T. Laker of Leicester, was sold in August 1959 for £2,500 in aid of charity. The Rolls-Royce bearing the registration plate RR1 was sold by tender to R. H. Owen Ltd. by the executors of Mr. Sydney Black on 22 July 1968 for £10,800—£3,300 more than the price of the Silver Shadow to which the number plate was affixed.

FASTEST CAR

Jet The highest speed attained by any 4-wheeled automobile is 613·995 m.p.h. over a flying 666·386 yards by the 34-foot 7-inch long 9,000 lb. *Spirit of America—Sonic I*, driven by Norman Craig Breedlove (born 23 March 1938, Los Angeles) on Bonneville Salt Flats, Tooele County, Utah, U.S.A., on 15 Nov. 1965. The car was powered by a General Electric J79 GE-3 jet engine, developing 15,000 lb. static thrust at sea-level.

Wheel-driven The highest speed attained by a wheel-driven car is 429·311 m.p.h. over a flying 666·386 yards by Donald Malcolm Campbell, C.B.E. (1921–67), a British engineer, in the 30-foot-long *Bluebird*, weighing 9,600 lb., on the salt flats at Lake Eyre, South Australia, on 17 July 1964. The car was powered by a Bristol-Siddeley 705 gas-turbine engine developing 4,500 s.h.p. Its peak speed was *c.* 440 m.p.h. It was rebuilt in 1962, after a crash at about 360 m.p.h. on 16 Sept. 1960.

Piston engine The highest speed attained by a piston-engined car is 418·504 m.p.h. over a flying 666·386 yards by Robert Sherman Summers (born 4 April 1937, Omaha, Nebraska) in *Goldenrod* at Bonneville Salt Flats on 12 Nov. 1965. The car, measuring 32 feet long and weighing 5,500 lb., was powered by four fuel-injected Chrysler Hemi engines (total capacity 27,924 c.c.) developing 2,400 b.h.p.

Production The world's fastest and most powerful production car is the Ford Mark IV, with a Ford V8 engine of 6,982 c.c., developing 500 b.h.p. at 6,200 r.p.m. One of these was timed at 213·003 m.p.h. on the Mulsanne straight at Le Mans, France, on 10 June 1967. Only six were built at a cost of more than $600,000 (then £214,286). The fastest obtainable car is the German Porsche 4·5 litre Type 917 launched in March 1969. Its 12 cylinder air-cooled engine develops 520 b.h.p. at 8,000 r.p.m. giving a speed of 200 m.p.h.

A Bugatti Royale

LARGEST

Of cars produced for private road use, the largest has been the Italian Bugatti "Royale", type 41, known in Britain as the "Golden Bugatti", of which only six (not seven) were made, and some survive. First built in 1927, this machine has an 8-cylinder engine of 12·7 litres capacity, and measures over 22 feet in length. The bonnet is over 7 feet long. The longest present-day car is the Aerocar limousine built by Checker Motors Corporation of Kalamazoo, Michigan, U.S.A. This 8-door 12-seat model, announced in July 1965, is 22 feet 5¾ inches long. (For cars not intended for private use, see Largest engines.)

Widest The widest standard production car is the U.S.S.R.'s Zil 114, measuring 6 feet 8·3 inches across. The Rolls-Royce Phantom V and VI are 6 feet 7 inches wide.

The mechanical world

MOST EXPENSIVE

The most expensive car ever built is the U.S. Presidential 1969 Lincoln Continental Executive delivered to the U.S. Secret Service on 14 Oct. 1968. It has an overall length of 21 feet 6·3 inches with a 13-foot 4-inch wheelbase and with the addition of two tons of armour plate weighs 5·35 tons (12,000 lb.). The cost was estimated at $500,000 (£208,000) but it is rented at a nominal $1,200 (£500) per annum. Even if all four tyres were shot out it can travel at 50 m.p.h. on inner rubber-edged steel discs.

The most expensive standard car now available is the 19-foot 10-inch-long 7-seat Rolls-Royce Phantom VI (V8, 6,230 c.c. engine) with coachwork by Park Ward at £13,123 including purchase tax, when introduced in Nov. 1968. The cost of the first series of 25 4·5 litre Porsche Type 917 (see page 131) is £14,000.

Vintage The greatest price paid for any vintage car has been $65,000 (£27,000) for a 1905 Rolls-Royce paid in U.S.A. in January 1969. The greatest collection of vintage cars is the Harrah Collection of some 1,500 in the United States.

Most inexpensive The cheapest car of all-time was the U.S. 1908 Brownicker for children, but designed for road use, which sold for $150 (then £30 17s. 3d.). The Kavan of 1905, also of U.S. manufacture, was listed at $200 (then £41 3s.). The early models of the King Midget cars were sold in kit form for self-assembly for as little as $100 (then £24 16s.) as late as 1948.

Longest production The longest any car has been in production is 42 years (1910–52), including wartime interruptions, in the case of the Jowett "Flat Twin", produced in Britain.

LARGEST ENGINES

Cars are compared on the basis of engine capacity. Distinction is made between those designed for normal road use and machines specially built for track racing and outright speed records.

The largest car ever built is the "Quad Al", constructed in 1965 in California, U.S.A. Intended for drag racing, the car has four-wheel drive and is powered by four V12 Allison V-1710 aircraft engines with a total capacity of 112,088 c.c., developing 12,000 b.h.p. It was first exhibited in January 1966 at the San Mateo Auto Show in California but is unable to move under its own power.

The largest car ever used was the "White Triplex", sponsored by J. H. White of Philadelphia, Pennsylvania, U.S.A. Completed early in 1928, after two years' work, the car weighed about 4 tons and was powered by three Liberty V12 aircraft engines with a total capacity of 81,188 c.c., developing 1,500 b.h.p. at 2,000 r.p.m. It was used to break the world speed record.

The largest racing car was the "Higham Special",

which first raced in 1923 at Brooklands driven by its owner Count Louis Vorow Zborowski, the younger (k. 1924). It was powered by a V12 Liberty aircraft engine with a capacity of 27,059 c.c., developing 400 to 500 b.h.p. at 2,000 r.p.m. Jeffrey G. Parry Thomas renamed the car "Babs" and used it to break the land speed record. The car was wrecked, and Thomas killed, during an attempt on this record at Pendine Sands, Carmarthenshire, Wales, on 3 March 1927.

The highest engine capacity of a production car was 13½ litres (824 cubic inches), in the case of the Pierce-Arrow 6–66 Raceabout of 1912–18, the Peerless 6–60 of 1912–14 and the Fageol of 1918. The largest currently available is the V8 engine of 500·1 cubic inches (8,195 c.c.), developing 400 b.h.p., used in the 1970 Cadillac Fleetwood Eldorado.

Petrol consumption The world record for fuel economy on a closed circuit course was set by D. C. Carlson, J. M. Jones and R. C. Trokey in a highly modified 1959 Fiat sedan (639 c.c. and 1,530 lb.) in the annual Shell Research Laboratory contest at Wood River, Illinois on 5 Oct. 1968. They achieved 244.35 miles per U.S. gallon—equivalent to 293·45 miles on an Imperial gallon.

The best recorded figure in an unmodified 4-wheeled car using pump petrol is 96·59 m.p.g. by a Fiat 500 driven on an out and home course from Cheltenham to Evesham, Gloucestershire, England, by W. (Featherfoot Joe) Dembowski on 1 July 1965.

BUSES

Largest The longest buses in the world are the 60-foot-long articulated 63-seater $64,400 Super Golden Eagles of the Continental Trailways of Dallas, Texas, U.S.A., built by Karl Kassbohrer Fahrzeugwerke of Ulm, West Germany. They have a speed of 70 m.p.h. despite a loaded weight of 20 tons.

Largest trolleybuses The largest trolleybuses in the world are the articulated vehicles put into service in Moscow, U.S.S.R., in May 1959, with a length of 57 feet and a capacity of 200.

Most massive vehicle The most massive vehicle ever constructed is the Marion eight-caterpillar crawler used for conveying *Saturn V* rockets to their launching pads at the John F. Kennedy Space Center, Florida (see Chapter 4, Most powerful rocket). It measures 131 feet 4 inches by 114 feet and cost $12,300,000 (£5,125,000). The loaded train weight is 8,036 tons. Its windscreen wipers with 42-inch blades are the world's largest.

Largest lorry The world's largest lorry is the M-200 Lectra Haul built by Unit Rig and Equipment Co. of Fort Worth, Texas with a capacity of 200 tons. It is powered by a 1,650 h.p. diesel and twin 750 h.p. electric motors. It is 43 feet long and 20 feet high.

The most powerful British-engined prime mover is the Rotinoff Tractor Super Atlantic with a 400 b.h.p.

The bulkiest object ever moved on British roads —a 22,101 cubic foot load

Rolls-Royce engine. In May 1958, one of these hauled the first of 12 atomic power station heat-exchangers at Bradwell, Essex. The gross train weight was 370 tons. The Aveling Barford Sn 35 Dump Truck is fitted with a 450 b.h.p. engine.

Longest vehicle The longest vehicle in the world is the 572-foot-long, 54-wheeled U.S. Army Overland Train Mk. II, built by R. G. Le Tourneau Inc. of Longview, Texas, U.S.A. Its gross weight is 400 tons and it has a top speed of 20 m.p.h. It is driven by a 6-man crew, who control 4 engines with a combined s.h.p. of 4,680, which require a capacity of 6,522 Imperial gallons of fuel. It can carry a 150-ton pay-load at 15 m.p.h. for 400 miles.

Largest bulldozers The world's largest bulldozer is the Le Tourneau Crash Pusher CP-1, measuring 67 feet long and weighing 67 tons. It is driven on 6 tyres 31 feet 5 inches in circumference and 4 feet wide. The most powerful ground clearer is the $196,000 (then £70,000) 125-ton Le Tourneau Electric Tree Crusher built in 1962. It is 74 feet 4 inches long and can clear 4 acres an hour. The largest road grader in the world is the 18·3 ton 28 feet 2 inch long Galion T.700 Grad-o-matic with a 190 h.p. 6-cylinder Cummins diesel engine built in 1960. Mr. Le Tourneau's (1888–1969) autobiography was entitled "Mover of Men and Mountains".

Largest tractor The most powerful tractor in the world is the 142·8 ton K-205 Pacemaker with a 1,260 horse-power rating. It is built by R. G. Le Tourneau, Inc., of Longview, Texas, U.S.A.

Largest taxi fleet The largest taxi fleet was that of New York City, which amounted to 29,000 cabs in October 1929, compared with the 1969 figure of 11,500.

Fastest caravan The world record for towing a caravan in 24 hours is 1,689 miles (average speed 70·395 m.p.h.) by a Ford Zodiac Mk. IV towing a Sprite Major 5-berth caravan, 16 feet long and weighing 14½ cwt., at Monza Autodrome near Milan, Italy, on 15–16 Oct. 1966. The drivers were Ian Mantle, John Risborough and Michael Bowler, all of Great Britain.

LOADS

Heaviest and largest The heaviest road loads moved in the United Kingdom were transformers involving a train weight of 422 tons, carried from Newcastle upon Tyne to Fawley, Southampton, by Robert Wynn & Sons Ltd. of Newport, Monmouthshire, on four occasions starting in February 1967. The longest load moved on British roads was a 170-foot-long distillation column moved 2 miles by Messrs. Pickford from Barry Dock to Sully, Glamorganshire, South Wales, on 29 Nov. 1965. The bulkiest load moved was an air separation unit 93 feet long, 15 feet 3 inches wide and 15 feet 7 inches high for a distance of 14 miles by Robert Wynn & Sons Ltd., from Edmonton, London N.9, to the Royal Victoria Docks for export to Texas, U.S.A. in 1969.

Tallest The tallest load ever conveyed by road comprised two 98-foot-tall cableway towers, each weighing 70 tons, which were taken 25 miles from Ohakuri to Aratiatia, New Zealand, in June 1961. The loads were carried on a 68-wheel trailer, towed by a 230 h.p. Leyland Buffalo tractor, for George Dale and Son Ltd.

The mechanical world

Amphibious vehicle The first Channel crossing by an amphibious vehicle was achieved in 7 hours 33 minutes by Mr. and Mrs. Ben Carlin in an amphibious jeep called "Half-Safe" from Calais, France, to Walmer, England, on 24 Aug. 1951.

Longest skid marks The longest recorded skid marks on a public road have been those 950 feet long left by a Jaguar car involved in an accident on the M.1 near Luton, Bedfordshire, on 30 June 1960. Evidence given in the High Court case *Hurlock v. Inglis and others* indicated a speed "in excess of 100 m.p.h." before the application of the brakes. The skid marks made by the jet-powered *Spirit of America*, driven by Craig Breedlove, after the car went out of control at Bonneville Salt Flats, Utah, U.S.A., on 15 Oct. 1964, were nearly 6 miles long.

Largest tyres The world's largest tyres are mounted on the Le Tourneau twin bucket scraper LT-300. They measure 10 feet 2 inches in diameter, are 5 feet wide and weigh 5,800 lb. (2·59 tons). They are made by the B. F. Goodrich Co. of Miami, Oklahoma, U.S.A.

"L" test Most failures The record for persistence in taking and failing Ministry of Transport's Learners' Test is held by Mrs. Miriam Hargrave, 62, of Wakefield, Yorkshire, who failed her 39th driving test in March 1970. Her husband's comment after eight years was "There will be no more of this unless somebody else pays".

MOTORCYCLES

Earliest The earliest internal combustion-engined motorized bicycle was a wooden-framed machine built in 1885 by Gottlieb Daimler (1834–1900) of Germany. It had a top speed of 12 m.p.h. and developed one-half of one horse-power from its single cylinder 264 c.c. engine at 700 r.p.m. The earliest factory which made motorcycles in quantity was opened in 1894 by J. Hildebrand and A. Wolfmüller at München (Munich), Bavaria, Germany. In its first two years this factory produced over 1,000 machines, each having a water-cooled 1488 c.c. twin-cylinder engine developing about 2·5 b.h.p. at 600 r.p.m.

Fastest road machine The fastest standard motorcycle ever produced is the 4-cylinder 1,177 c.c. N.S.U.-powered Münch 'Mammoth'. This West German machine producing 92 b.h.p. at 6,500 r.p.m. is the most powerful ever produced. It can attain 140 m.p.h. and was priced at £1,000 in the U.K. in April 1969. The Italian 4-cylinder 750 c.c. M.V.-Agusta, due on sale before 1971, is capable of 140 m.p.h. The fastest British road machine is the 66 b.h.p. Dunstall Domiracer-Metisse with a twin-cylinder 745 c.c. Norton engine capable of 131 m.p.h.

Fastest racing machine The fastest racing motorcycle ever has been the 1957 498·6 c.c. 82 b.h.p. Moto Guzzi V8 capable of 178 m.p.h. (see also Motorcycle racing, Chapter 12). Of track machines the fastest British made was the £528 499 c.c. 30M Manx Norton capable of 150 m.p.h.

Largest The largest motorcycle ever put into production was the 1,301 c.c. in-line 4-cylinder Henderson, manufactured in the United States in the period 1926–29.

Most expensive The most expensive motorcycles in current production are the Harley-Davidson FLHB and FLHFB Super Sports Electra Glide machines, made in the U.S.A., with an engine capacity of 1,213 c.c. Extensively used for highway patrol work by State Police Departments, they weigh 661 lb. and sell for £1,320 in the United Kingdom (April 1970).

The most expensive British-made motorcycle in current production is the 745 c.c. Dunstall Norton Commando with a front disc brake. It retailed at £763 in February 1970.

BICYCLES

Earliest Though there were many velocipedes before that time, the term bicycle was first used in 1868. The earliest portrayal of such a vehicle is in a stained glass window, dated 1642, in Stoke Poges Church, Buckinghamshire, depicting a man riding a hobby horse or celeripede.

The first machine propelled by cranks and pedals, with connecting rods, was that invented in 1839 by Kirkpatrick Macmillan (1810–78) of Dumfries. It is now in the Science Museum, South Kensington, London.

Penny-Farthing record The record for riding from London to John o' Groats on Ordinary Bicycles, more commonly known as Penny-Farthings, is 10½ days by Cyril Mundy, 54, and Brian Thompson, 33, on 31 Aug. to 10 Sept. 1969. This performance broke a 96-year-old record set in June 1873.

Longest The longest tandem bicycle ever built is the 21-man vigintipede, measuring 35 feet 4 inches long, completed by Rickman Bros. and Hugh Stevenson Engineering Ltd. of New Milton, Hampshire, England, on 29 July 1968. It weighs 880 lb. and 2 tons laden. The most capacious cycle built is the double banked 28-seat 30-wheeler built in 1968 by the Zug Teachers' College, Switzerland.

Largest tricycle The largest tricycle ever made was one manufactured in 1897 for the Woven-Hose and Rubber Company of Boston, Massachusetts, U.S.A. Its side wheels were 11 feet in diameter and it weighed nearly a ton. It could carry eight riders.

Tallest unicycle The tallest unicycle ever mastered is one 32 feet tall ridden by Steve McPeak of Seattle Pacific College, U.S.A., in 1969. McPeak set a duration record when on 26 Nov. 1968 he completed a 2,000 mile journey from Chicago, Illinois to Las Vegas, Nevada, U.S.A. in 6 weeks on a 13-foot unicycle. He covered 80 miles on some days.

LAWN MOWER

Fastest The inaugural Motor Powered Lawn mower Grand Prix on Mersey Cricket Club ground, Sale, Cheshire, on 6 Oct. 1968 was won by Colin Dunne with 2 minutes 45·28 seconds over the ½-mile course for an average of 10·88 m.p.h.

Pedal cars The record for propelling a pedal car from John o' Groats to Land's End (936 miles) is 166 hours 55 minutes set by Kenneth Budby, Ronald Oldroy, Tony Bradbury, Richard May and Martin Cave on 1–5 Aug. 1968.

3. Railways

EARLIEST

Railed trucks were used for mining as early as 1550 at Leberthal, Alsace and by Ralph Wood from Coombe

Down to Avon in 1731, but the first self-propelled locomotive ever to run on rails was that built by Richard Trevithick (1771–1833) and demonstrated over 9 miles with a 10-ton load and 70 passengers in Penydarren, Glamorganshire, on 21 Feb. 1804. The first railway was the Stockton and Darlington colliery line, County Durham, which ran from Shildon through Darlington to Stockton and opened on 27 Sept. 1825, on which the 7-ton *Locomotion I* (formerly *Active*) could pull 48 tons at a speed of 15 m.p.h. It was built and driven by George Stephenson (1781–1848). The first regular steam passenger run was inaugurated over a one mile section (between Bogshole Farm and South Street) on the 6¼-mile track between Canterbury and Whitstable, Kent, on 3 May 1830 hauled by the engine *Invicta*. The first electric railway was Werner von Siemen's 300-yard-long Berlin electric tramway opened for the Berlin Trades' Exhibition on 31 May 1879.

FASTEST

Electric The world rail speed record is held jointly by two French Railway electric locomotives, the CC7107 and the BB9004. On 28 and 29 March 1955, hauling three carriages of a total weight of 100 tons, they each achieved a speed of 205·6 m.p.h. The runs took place on the 1,500-volt D.C. Bordeaux-Dax line, from Facture to Morceux, and the top speed was maintained by the drivers, H. Braghet and J. Brocca, for 2 kilometres (1·24 miles). The CC7107 weighs 106 tons and has a continuous rating of 4,300 h.p. at 1,500 volts, but developed 12,000 h.p. over the timing stretch. The BB9004 weighs 81 tons and has a continuous rating of 4,000 h.p.

Steam The highest speed ever recorded by a steam locomotive was 126 m.p.h. over 440 yards by the L.N.E.R. 4-6-2 No. 4468 *Mallard* (later numbered 60022), which hauled seven coaches weighing 240 tons gross, near Essendine, down Stoke Bank, between Grantham, Lincolnshire, and Peterborough on 3 July 1938. Driver Duddington was at the controls.

Fastest regular run The fastest point to point schedule in the world is that of the "New Tokaido" service of the Japanese National Railways from Tōkyō to Ōsaka, inaugurated on 1 Nov. 1965. The train covers 320·2 miles in 3 hours 10 minutes, at an average speed of 101·1 m.p.h. and the 212·4 miles between Tōkyō and Nagoya in 120 minutes, to average 106·2 m.p.h. The maximum speed is being raised from 130 to 155 m.p.h. The 72-ton 12-car unit has motors generating 8,160 kW on a single-phase 25,000 volt A.C. system. A peak speed of 159 m.p.h. is eventually expected from the Hikari engine. The fastest regular run on British Rail is over the 65 mile stretch from Rugby to Watford Junction in 47 minutes giving an average of 83·1 m.p.h.

LONGEST NON-STOP

The world's longest daily non-stop run is that of the "Sud Express", which runs for 359·8 miles between Paris and Bordeaux, France. The longest run on British Rail without any advertised stop is the "Motorail Service", which runs from King's Cross, London to Aberdeen, Scotland, a distance of 452¼ miles.

MOST POWERFUL

The world's most powerful compound type steam locomotive was No. 700, a triple articulated or triplex 2-8-8-8-4, the Baldwin Locomotive Co. 6-cylinder engine built in 1916 for the Virginian Railway. It had a tractive force of 166,300 lb. working compound and 199,560 lb. working simple. In 1918 this railway operated a 4-cylinder compound 2-10-10-2 engine, built by the American Locomotive Co., with a starting (*i.e.* working simple) tractive effort of 176,000 lb. Probably the heaviest train ever hauled by a single engine was one of 15,300 tons made up of 250 freight cars stretching 1·6 miles by the Matt H. Shay (No. 5014), a 2-8-8-8-2 engine which ran on the Erie Railroad from May 1914 until 1929.

Trevithick's locomotive of 1804

PERMANENT WAY

The greatest length of unbroken four-lane track in the world is between Castleton and Dunkirk, New York, in the United States, and is 342½ miles in length. The longest stretch of continuous four-lane track in the United Kingdom is between St. Pancras, London, and Glendon North Junction, Northamptonshire, and is 75 miles in length.

Longest straight The longest straight in the world is on the Commonwealth Railways Trans Australian line over the Nullarbor Plain from Mile 496 between Nuringa and Loongana, Western Australia, to Mile 793 between Ooldea and Watson, South Australia, 297 miles dead straight although not level. The longest straight on British Rail is the 18 miles between Selby and Kingston-upon-Hull, Yorkshire.

adhesion is 1:11. This figure is achieved by the Guatemalan State Electric Railway between the River Samala Bridge and Zunil.

The steepest sustained adhesion-worked gradient on a main line in the United Kingdom is the two-mile Lickey incline of 1:37·7 in Worcestershire. From the tunnel bottom to James Street, Liverpool, on the former Mersey Railway, there is a stretch of 1:27; just south of Ilfracombe, Devon, two miles of 1:36; and between Folkestone Junction and Harbour a mile of 1:30.

BUSIEST

The world's most crowded rail system is the Tōkyō service of the Japanese National Railways, which carries about 4,200,000 passengers daily. Professional pushers are employed to squeeze in passengers before

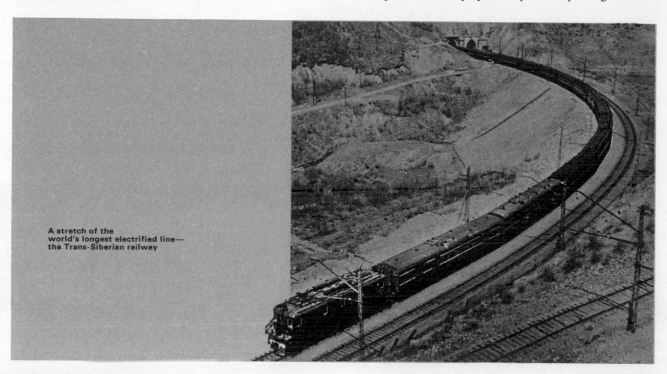

A stretch of the world's longest electrified line—the Trans-Siberian railway

Longest electric line The world's longest stretch of electrified line is the 3,240 miles between Moscow and Irkutsk in Siberia, U.S.S.R., reported completed in late 1960.

Widest The widest gauge in standard use is 5 feet 6 inches. This width is used in India, Pakistan, Ceylon, Spain, Portugal, Argentina and Chile. In 1885 there was a lumber railway in Oregon, U.S.A., with a gauge of 8 feet.

HIGHEST

The highest standard gauge (4 feet 8½ inches) track in the world is on the Central Railway of Peru (owned by the Peruvian Corporation Ltd.) at La Cima, where a branch siding rises to 15,844 feet above sea-level. The highest point on the main line is 15,688 feet in the Galera tunnel.

Great Britain The highest point on the British Rail system is at the pass of Drumochter (or Drumouchter) on the Perth-Inverness border, where the track reaches an altitude of 1,484 feet above sea-level. The highest railway in Britain is the Snowdon Mountain Railway, which rises from Llanberis to 3,493 feet above sea-level, just below the summit of Snowdon (Yr Wyddfa). It has a gauge of 2 feet 7½ inches.

The lowest point on British Rail is in the Severn Tunnel—144 feet below sea-level.

STEEPEST GRADIENTS

The world's steepest standard gauge gradient by

the doors can be closed. Among articles reported lost in the crush in 1964 were 380,353 umbrellas, 256,031 spectacles and hats, 170,189 shoes, and also an assortment of false teeth and artificial eyeballs.

The world's busiest stations are Tōkyō Central, which, in 1969, handled 2,600 trains, and Shinjuku, 2,200,000 passengers daily. The busiest railway junction in Great Britain is Clapham Junction on the Southern Region of British Rail, with over 2,070 trains passing through each 24 hours.

A platform on the world's busiest station—Tōkyō Central

Britain's
largest
rail terminus
— Waterloo
Station,
London

The mechanical world

STATIONS

Largest World
The world's largest railway station is Grand Central Terminal, Park Avenue and 43rd Street, New York City, N.Y., U.S.A., built 1903–13. It covers 48 acres on two levels with 41 tracks on the upper level and 26 on the lower. On average more than 550 trains and 180,000 people per day use it, with a peak of 252,288 on 3 July 1947.

United Kingdom
The largest railway station in extent on the British Rail system is the 17-platform Clapham Junction, London, covering 27¾ acres and with a total face of 11,165 feet. The station with the largest number of platforms is Waterloo, London (24½ acres), with 21 main line and two Waterloo and City Line platforms, with a total face of 15,352 feet. Victoria Station (21¾ acres) with 17 platforms has, however, a total face length of 18,412 feet. The oldest station in Britain is Liverpool Road Station, Manchester, first used on 15 Sept. 1830.

Highest
The highest station in the world on standard gauge railways is Ticlio, at 15,685 feet above sea-level, on the Central Railway of Peru, in South America. The highest passenger station on British Rail is Corrour, Inverness-shire, at an altitude of 1,406 feet above sea-level.

Waiting rooms
The world's largest waiting rooms are those in Peking Station, Changan Boulevard, Peking, China, opened in September 1959, with a capacity of 14,000.

Longest platform
The longest railway platform in the world is the Khargpur platform, south-eastern India, which measures 2,733 feet in length. The State Street Center subway platform staging on "The Loop" in Chicago, Illinois, U.S.A., measures 3,500 feet in length.

The longest platform in the British Rail system is the 1,975-foot-long platform at Colchester, Essex.

Longest freight train
The longest and heaviest freight train on record was one about 4 miles in length consisting of 500 coal cars with three 3,600 h.p. diesels pulling and three more

PROGRESSIVE RAILWAY SPEED RECORDS

Speed m.p.h.	Engine	Place	Date
29·1	The *Rocket* (Stephenson and Booth's 0-2-2)	Liverpool-Manchester	8 Oct. 1829
59	Grand Junction Rly., 2-2-2 *Lucifer*	Madeley Bank, Staffordshire	13 Nov. 1839
c. 85[1]	Atmospheric railway (Frank Elrington)	Dún Laoghaire–Dalkey, Co. Dublin	19 Aug. 1843
62¼	Great Western Rly., 2-2-2 *Ixion*	Twyford-Maidenhead, Berkshire	16 Dec. 1845
74⅓	Great Western Rly., 8 ft. single 4-2-2 *Great Britain*	Wootton Bassett, Wiltshire	11 May 1845
74½	Great Western Rly., 8 ft. single 4-2-2 *Great Western*	Wootton Bassett, Wiltshire	1 June 1846
78	Great Western Rly., 8 ft. single 4-2-2 *Great Britain*	Wootton Bassett, Wiltshire	11 May 1848
81·8	Bristol & Exeter Rly., 9 ft. single 4-2-4 tank No. 41	Wellington Bank, Somerset	June 1854
89·48	Crompton No. 604 engine	Champigny Pont sur Yvonne, France	20 June 1890
98·4[2]	*Philadelphia & Reading Rly., Engine 206*	*Skillmans to Belle Mead, New Jersey*	*July 1890*
102·8[2]	*N.Y. Central & Hudson River Rly. Empire State Express No. 999*	*Grimesville, N.Y., U.S.A.*	*9 May 1893*
112·5[2][3]	*N.Y. Central & Hudson River Rly. Empire State Express No. 999*	*Crittenden West, N.Y., U.S.A.*	*11 May 1893*
90·0	Midland Rly., 7 ft. 9 in. single 4-2-2	Melton Mowbray, Nottingham	Mar. 1897
130[2]	*Burlington Route*	*Siding to Arion, Iowa, U.S.A.*	*Jan. 1899*
101·0	Siemens und Halske Electric	near Berlin	1901
120·0[2][4]	*Savannah, Florida and Western Rly. mail train*	*Screven, Florida, U.S.A.*	*1 Mar. 1901*
124·89	Siemens und Halske Electric	Marienfeld-Zossen, nr. Berlin	6 Oct. 1903
128·43	Siemens und Halske Electric	Marienfeld-Zossen, nr. Berlin	23 Oct. 1903
130·61	Siemens und Halske Electric	Marienfeld-Zossen, nr. Berlin	27 Oct. 1903
99–100[5]	Great Western Rly., 4-4-0 *City of Truro*	Wellington Bank, Somerset	9 May 1904
143·0	Kruckenberg (propeller-driven)	Karstädt-Dergenthin, Germany	21 June 1931
150·9	Co-Co S.N.C.F. No. 7121	Dijon-Beaune, France	21 Feb. 1954
205·6	Co-Co S.N.C.F. No. 7107	Facture-Morceux, France	28 Mar. 1955
205·6	Bo-Bo S.N.C.F. No. 9004	Facture-Morceux, France	29 Mar. 1955
235	*L'Aerotrain* (jet aero engines)	Gometz le Chatel-Limours, France	4 Dec. 1967

[1] *Speed attributed to runaway compressed air train. No independent timings.*
[2] *Not internationally regarded as authentic.*
[3] *Later alleged to be unable to attain 82 m.p.h. on this track when hauling 4 coaches.*

[4] *5 miles in 2½ minutes to a stop, hence fictitious.*
[5] *Previously unauthenticated at 102·3 m.p.h.*

pushing on the Iaeger, West Virginia to Portsmouth, Ohio stretch of 157 miles on the Norfolk and Western Railway on 15 Nov. 1967. The total weight was nearly 42,000 tons.

Greatest load The heaviest single piece of freight ever conveyed by rail was a 1,230,000 lb. (549·2 tons) 106-foot-tall hydro-cracker reactor which was carried from Birmingham, Alabama, to Toledo, Ohio, U.S.A., on 12 Nov. 1965.

The heaviest load carried by British Rail was a 122-foot-long boiler drum, weighing 240 tons, for generating electricity, which was carried from Ettingshall Road, Staffordshire, to Eggbrough, Yorkshire, on 5 June 1965.

Greatest mileage The greatest mileage covered with a weekly roving ticket on British Rail is 8,098 miles between 27 July and 3 Aug. 1969 by Mike Howell and Graham Roberts, who are both blind.

Most expensive freight rate In accordance with British Rail regulations the correct charge for a domestic animal accompanying a passenger was the same as the 2nd class child fare. Thus in travelling from Paddington, London to Plymouth (225¾ miles) a Miss Harries on 7 May 1968 had to pay 30s. 6d. for a budgerigar weighing 1 oz. This was equivalent to more than £238 per ton-mile. The charge was dropped in November 1969.

UNDERGROUND RAILWAYS
The most extensive and oldest (opened 10 Jan. 1863) underground railway system in the world is that of the London Transport Board, with 254 miles of route, of which 67 miles is bored tunnel and 23 miles is "cut and cover". This whole Tube system is operated by a staff of 20,000 serving 277 stations. The 473 trains comprising 3,373 cars carried 655,000,000 passengers in 1968. The record for a day is 2,073,134 on V.E. Day, 8 May 1945. The greatest depth is 192 feet at Hampstead. The record for touring all 277 stations is 15 hours precisely by Leslie R. V. Burwood on 3 Sept. 1968. The record for the Paris Metro's 270 stations (7 closed) is 11 hours 13 minutes by Alan Paul Jenkins (b. 1950) of Bushey, Hertfordshire on 30 Aug. 1967.

The busiest subway in the world is the New York City Transit Authority (opened on 27 Oct. 1904) with a total of 239·87 miles of track and 1,305,854,341 passengers in 1968. The stations are closer set and total 475, while the peak of passengers carried was 2,051,400,973 in 1947. The record for travelling the whole system is 23 hours 16 minutes by Michael Feldman and James Brown on 1 June 1966.

Model railway The record run for a model train was set at Berkeley Square, London, on 2–6 Sept. 1966, when the Hornby engine *Cardiff Castle* ran 153 miles. The run was equivalent, at scale, to 11,600 miles averaging 123·9 m.p.h.

MONORAIL
Highest speed The highest speed ever attained on rails is 3,090 m.p.h. (Mach 4·1) by an unmanned rocket-powered sled on the 6·62-mile-long captive track at the U.S. Air Force Missile Development Center at Holloman, New Mexico, U.S.A., on 19 Feb. 1959. The highest speed reached carrying a chimpanzee is 1,295 m.p.h.

The highest speed attained by a tracked hovercraft is 235 m.p.h. by the jet-powered *L'Aerotrain*, invented by Jean Bertin (see Progressive speed table page 136).

Speeds as high as Mach 0·8 (608 m.p.h.) are planned in 1973 from The Onsoku Kasotai (sonic speed sliding vehicle), a wheelless rocket-powered train running on rollers designed by Prof. H. Ozawa (Japan) and announced in March 1968.

4. Aircraft

Note—The use of the Mach scale for aircraft speeds was introduced by Prof. Acherer of Zürich, Switzerland. The Mach number is the ratio of the velocity of a moving body to the local velocity of sound. This ratio was first employed by Dr. Ernst Mach (1838–1916) of Vienna, Austria in 1887. Thus Mach 1·0 equals 760·98 m.p.h. at sea-level at 15° C. and is assumed, for convenience, to fall to a constant 659·78 m.p.h. in the stratosphere, *i.e.* above 11,000 metres (36,089 feet).

EARLIEST FLIGHTS
World The first controlled and sustained power-driven flight occurred near Kill Devil Hills, Kitty Hawk, North Carolina, U.S.A., at 10.35 a.m. on 17 Dec. 1903, when Orville Wright (1871–1948) flew the 16 h.p. chain-driven *Flyer 1* at an airspeed of 30–35 m.p.h., a ground speed of less than 8 m.p.h. and an altitude of 8–12 feet for 12 seconds, watched by his brother Wilbur (1867–1912) and five coastguards. Both brothers, from Dayton, Ohio, were bachelors because, as Orville put it, they had not the means to "support a wife as well as an aeroplane". The plane is now in the Smithsonian Institution, Washington, D.C.

The first man-carrying powered aeroplane to fly, but not entirely under its own power, was a monoplane with a hot-air engine built by Félix Du Temple de la Croix (1823–90), a French naval officer, and piloted by a young sailor who made a short hop after taking off, probably down an incline, at Brest, France, in *c.* 1874. The first hop by a man-carrying aeroplane entirely under its own power was made when Clément Ader (1841–1925) of France flew in his *Eole* for about 50 metres (164 feet) at Armainvilliers, France, on 9 Oct. 1890.

British Isles The first officially recognised flight in the British Isles was by "Colonel" Samuel Franklin Cody (1861–1913) of the U.S.A., who flew 1,390 feet in his own biplane at Farnborough, Hampshire, on 16 Oct. 1908. Horatio Frederick Phillips (1845–1924) almost certainly covered 500 feet in his "Venetian blind" aeroplane at Streatham, in 1907. The first British citizen to fly was Griffith Brewer (1867–1948), as a passenger of Wilbur Wright, on 8 Oct. 1908.

Two views of the 235 m.p.h. Aerotrain

Louis Blériot

Cross-Channel The earliest cross-Channel flight by an aeroplane was made on 25 July 1909, when Louis Blériot (1872–1936) of France flew his *Blériot XI* monoplane, powered by a 23 h.p. Anzani engine, from Les Baraques, France, to a meadow near Dover Castle, England, in 37 minutes, after taking off at 4.41 a.m.

TRANS-ATLANTIC
The first crossing of the North Atlantic by air was made by Lt.-Cdr. (later Rear Admiral) Albert C. Read (1887–1967) and his crew (Stone, Hinton, Rodd, Rhoads and Breese) in the Curtiss flying boat NC-4 of the U.S. Navy from Trepassy Harbour, Newfoundland, *via* the Azores, to Lisbon, Portugal, on 16 to 27 May 1919. The whole flight of 3,936 miles originating from Rockaway Air Station, Long Island, N.Y. on 8 May required 52 hours 3 minutes flying time for an average of 75·6 m.p.h.

First non-stop The first non-stop trans-Atlantic flight was achieved from 4.13 p.m. G.M.T. on 14 June 1919, from Trepassy Harbour, St. John's, Newfoundland, 1,960 miles to Derrygimla bog near Clifden, County Galway, Ireland, at 8.40 a.m. G.M.T., 15 June, when Capt. John William Alcock, D.S.C. (1892–1919), and Lt. Arthur Whitten-Brown (1886–1948) flew across in a Vickers *Vimy*, powered by two 350 h.p. Rolls-Royce *Eagle VIII* engines. Both men were created K.B.E. on 21 June 1919 when Alcock was aged 26 years 286 days and won the *Daily Mail* prize of £10,000.

First solo The first solo trans-Atlantic flight was achieved by Capt. Charles Augustus Lindbergh (b. 4 Feb. 1902, Detroit) who took off in his 220 h.p. Ryan monoplane "Spirit of St. Louis" at 12.52 p.m. G.M.T. on 20 May 1927 from Roosevelt Field, Long Island, New York State, U.S.A. He landed at 10.21 p.m. G.M.T. on 21 May 1927 at Le Bourget airfield, Paris, France. His flight of 3,610 miles lasted 33 hours 29½ minutes and he won a prize of $25,000 (now £10,400).

A U.S. Army Douglas World Cruiser which made the first aerial circumnavigation in 1924

Fastest The present New York–Paris trans-Atlantic record is 3 hours 19 minutes 41·5 seconds by a General Dynamics/Convair B-58A *Hustler* "Firefly", piloted by Major William R. Payne, U.S.A.F., on 26 May 1961. The 3,669 miles were covered at an average of 1,089 m.p.h. This aircraft was withdrawn from service in January 1970.

The fastest time between New York and London is 4 hours 36 minutes 30·4 seconds by Lt.-Cdr. Brian Davies, 35 and Lt.-Cdr. Peter M. Goddard R.N., 32, of No. 892 Squadron, Royal Navy, on 11 May 1969, flying a McDonnell Douglas F-4K *Phantom II* with Rolls-Royce *Spey* engines. Lt.-Cdr. Goddard was participating in the *Daily Mail* trans-Atlantic air race, which he won (prize of £5,000) with an overall time of 5 hours 11 minutes 22 seconds from the top of the Empire State Building, New York, to the top of the Post Office Tower, London.

Lt.-Cdrs. Goddard and Davies, winners of the *Daily Mail* 1969 New York -London air race

CIRCUMNAVIGATION
Earliest The earliest flight round the world was achieved by two U.S. Army Air Service Douglas amphibian aircraft "Chicago" (Lt. Lowell H. Smith and Sgt. L. L. Arnold) and "New Orleans" (Lt. Erik H. Nelson and Sgt. J. Harding) on 28 Sept. 1924 at Seattle, Washington, U.S.A. The 175-day flight of 26,100 miles began on 24 April 1924 and involved 57 "hops" and a flying time of 351 hours 11 minutes. The earliest solo flight round the world was made from 15 to 22 July 1933 by Wiley Hardeman Post (1899–1935) (U.S.A.) in the Lockheed *Vega* "Winnie Mae" starting and finishing at Floyd Bennett Field, New York City, U.S.A. He flew the 15,596 miles east-about in 7 days 18 hours 49 minutes—in 10 hops with a flying time of 115 hours 36 minutes.

Fastest The fastest circumnavigation of the globe was achieved by three U.S.A.F. B-52 *Stratofortresses,* led by Maj.-Gen. Archie J. Old, Jr., chief of the U.S. 15th Air Force. They took off from Castle Air Force Base, Merced, California, at 1 p.m. on 16 Jan. and flew eastwards, arriving 45 hours 19 minutes later at March Air Force Base, Riverside, California, on 18 Jan. 1957, after a flight of 24,325 miles. The planes averaged 525 m.p.h. and were refuelled four times in flight by KC-97 aerial tankers.

t-engined
Proposals for jet propulsion date back to Captain Marconnet (1909) of France, and to the turbojet proposals of Maxime Guillaume in 1921. The earliest test bed run was that of the British Power Jets Ltd.'s experimental W.U. (Whittle Unit) on 12 April 1937, invented by Flying Officer (now Air Commodore Sir) Frank Whittle (born Coventry, 1 June 1907), who had applied for a patent on jet propulsion in 1930. The first flight by an aeroplane powered by a turbojet engine was made by the Heinkel He 178, piloted by Flug Kapitan Erich Warsitz, at Marienehe, Germany, on 27 Aug. 1939. It was powered by a Heinkel S-3b engine (1,100 lb.s.t.) designed by Dr. Pabst von Ohain and first tested in August 1937.

The first British jet flight occurred when Fl. Lt. P. E. G. "Jerry" Sayer, O.B.E., flew the Gloster-Whittle E.28/39 (wing span 29 feet, length 25 feet 3 inches) fitted with a 860 lb.s.t. Whittle W-1 engine for 17 minutes at Cranwell, Lincolnshire, on 15 May 1941. The second prototype attained 466 m.p.h.

upersonic flight
The first supersonic flight was achieved on 14 Oct. 1947 by Capt. (now Colonel) Charles ("Chuck") E. Yeager, U.S.A.F. (born 13 Feb. 1923), over Edwards Air Force Base, Muroc, California, U.S.A., in a U.S. Bell XS-1 rocket plane ("Glamorous Glennis"), with Mach 1·015 (670 m.p.h.) at an altitude of 42,000 feet.

LARGEST AIRCRAFT

Heaviest
The heaviest aircraft ever built is the Lockheed C-5A *Galaxy*, which first flew from Marietta, Georgia, U.S.A., on 30 June 1968. It measures 245 feet 10¾ inches long, has a wing span of 222 feet 7¼ inches, a gross weight of 341·3 tons and a maximum payload of 118·3 tons. It can cruise at 540 m.p.h. and has a maximum speed of 611 m.p.h. and a range of 6,680 miles with a 100,000 lb. payload. It is powered by four General Electric TF39 turbofan engines, each rated at 41,000 lb. thrust. The Boeing Company is building a supersonic transport (SST) with a maximum weight of 635,000 lb. (283·5 tons), a wing span of 141 feet 8 inches, an overall length of 286 feet and room for 234 tourist passengers. The go-ahead was given by the U.S. Government on 23 Sept. 1969.

Largest wing span
The aircraft with the largest wing span ever constructed was the Hughes H.2 *Hercules* flying boat, which was raised 70 feet into the air in a test run of 1,000 yards, piloted by Howard Hughes, off Long Beach Harbor, California, U.S.A., on 2 Nov. 1947. The eight-engined 190-ton aircraft had a wing span of 320 feet and a length of 219 feet. It never flew again.

Most powerful
The most powerful aircraft ever built was the U.S.A.'s delta-winged North American XB-70A *Valkyrie*. It had a maximum take-off weight of 550,000 lb. (845·5 tons) and was 196 feet long overall, with a wing span of 105 feet. Designed as a bomber but used only for research, it was powered by six General Electric YJ93-3 turbojet engines, which delivered a combined thrust of 186,000 lb. It had its maiden test flight from Palmdale on 21 Sept. 1964 and attained a speed of Mach 3·0 (about 2,000 m.p.h.) on 14 Oct. 1965. It climbed to 74,000 feet. Its last and longest flight was made on 4 Feb. 1969, from Edwards AFB, California, to Wright-Patterson AFB, Ohio, where it is now exhibited in the Air Force Museum, Dayton, Ohio.

Lightest
The lightest aeroplane ever flown was the Beecraft *Wee Bee*, built in 1948 by four Convair employees, at a cost of $200 (then £71), in San Diego, California, U.S.A. It had a wing span of 15 feet, an empty weight of 170 lb. and a loaded weight of 360 lb. It was powered by an 18½ h.p. Navy drone-type engine. The *Gnome*, built by Michael Ward of North Scarle, Lincolnshire and flown in April 1969 weighs 210 lb. or 350 lb. loaded. It has a span of 15 feet 9 inches and is powered by a 1925 Douglas engine with a capacity of some 14 h.p. This aircraft has an imposed maximum ceiling of 10 feet—the lowest of any aircraft.

Smallest
The smallest aeroplane ever flown is the Stits *Skybaby* biplane, designed, built and flown by Ray Stits at Riverside, California, U.S.A., in 1952. It was 9 feet 10 inches long, with a wing span of 7 feet 2 inches, and weighed 452 lb. empty. It was powered by an 85 h.p. Continental C85 engine giving a top speed of 185 m.p.h.

BOMBERS

Heaviest
The world's heaviest bomber is the eight-jet sweptwing Boeing B-52H *Stratofortress*, which has a maximum take-off weight of 488,000 lb. (217·86 tons). It has a wing span of 185 feet and is 157 feet 6¾ inches in length, with a speed of over 650 m.p.h. The B-52 can carry 12 750-lb. bombs under each wing and 84 500-lb. bombs in the fuselage giving a total bomb load of 60,000 lb. or 26·78 tons. The ten-engined Convair B-36J, weighing 183 tons, had a greater wing span, at 230 feet, but is no longer in service. It had a top speed of 435 m.p.h.

Fastest
The world's fastest operational bomber is the French Dassault *Mirage IV*, which can fly at Mach 2·2 (1,450 m.p.h.) at 36,000 feet. The North American XB-70A *Valkyrie* was designed to cruise at a speed of Mach 3 (about 2,000 m.p.h.) but was used only for research (see Most powerful aircraft, left). The fastest Soviet bomber is the Tupolev Tu-22 "Blinder", with an estimated speed of Mach 1·5 (1,000 m.p.h.) at 35,000 feet.

AIRLINERS

Largest World
The highest capacity jet airliner is the Boeing 747, "Jumbo Jet", first flown on 9 Feb. 1969, which has a gross weight of 710,000 lb. (317 tons) (346 tons in later versions) and a capacity of from 362 to 490 passengers with a cruising speed of 595 m.p.h. Its wing span is 195·7 feet and its length 231·3 feet. It entered service on 21 Jan. 1970

United Kingdom
The heaviest airliner built in the United Kingdom is the B.A.C. Super VC10, which first flew on 7 May 1964. It weighs 335,000 lb. (149·5 tons) and is 171·7 feet long, with a wing span of 146·2 feet. The largest ever British aircraft was the prototype Bristol Type 167 *Brabazon*,

The Boeing 747 Jumbo-Jet

which had a maximum take-off weight of 129·4 tons but a wing span of 230 feet and a length of 177 feet. This eight-engined aircraft first flew on 4 Sept. 1949.

Fastest World The world's fastest airliner in service is the Convair CV-990 *Coronado,* one of which flew at 675 m.p.h. at 22,500 feet (Mach 0·97) on 8 May 1961. Its maximum cruising speed is 625 m.p.h. A Douglas DC-8 Series 40, with Rolls-Royce Conway engines, exceeded the speed of sound in a shallow dive on 21 Aug. 1961. Its true air speed was 667 m.p.h. or Mach 1·012 at a height of 40,350 feet. The U.S.S.R.'s Tu-144 supersonic airliner, with a capacity of 121 passengers, first flew on 31 Dec. 1968. Its design speed is Mach 2·35 (1,553 m.p.h. with a ceiling of 65,000 feet and it "went" supersonic on 5 June 1969. The planned speed of the Boeing 2707-300 SST is expected to be Mach 2·7 (1,782 m.p.h.) at 65,000 feet.

Britain The fastest British airliner in service is the three-engined Hawker Siddeley *Trident 1C* which has reached 627 m.p.h. (Mach 0·9) in level flight and 667 m.p.h. (Mach 0·96) in a shallow dive at 24,000 feet. The supersonic BAC/SNIAS *Concorde,* first flown on 2 March 1969, with a capacity of 128 passengers, is expected to cruise at 1,320–1,450 m.p.h. It flew at Mach 1·05 on 10 Oct. 1969.

Longest scheduled flight The longest scheduled non-stop flight is the Buenos Aires, Argentina to Madrid, Spain stage of 6,462 statute miles, by Aerolineas Argentinas and Iberia inaugurated on 7 Aug. 1967. The Boeing 707-320B requires 11½ hours.

HIGHEST SPEED
The official air speed record is 2,070·102 m.p.h. by Col. Robert L. Stephens and Lt.-Col. Daniel André (U.S.A.) in a Lockheed YF-12A near Edwards Air Force Base, California, U.S.A., on 1 May 1965.

The fastest fixed-wing aircraft in the world is the U.S. North American Aviation X-15A-2, which flew for the first time (after conversion) on 28 June 1964 powered by a liquid oxygen and ammonia rocket propulsion system. Ablative materials on the airframe have once enabled a temperature of 3,000° F. to be withstood. The landing speed was 210 knots (241·8 m.p.h.) momentarily. The highest speed attained was 4,534 m.p.h. (Mach 6·72) when piloted by Major William J. Knight, U.S.A.F. (b. 1930), on 3 Oct. 1967. An earlier version piloted by Joseph A. Walker (1920–66), reached 354,200 feet (67·08 miles) also over Edwards Air Base, California, U.S.A., on 22 Aug. 1963. The programme was suspended after the final flight of 24 Oct. 1968.

Fastest jet The world's fastest jet aircraft is the U.S.A.F. Lockheed SR-71 reconnaissance aircraft (a variant of the YF-12A, above) which first flew on 22 Dec. 1964 and is reportedly capable of attaining a speed of 2,200 m.p.h. and an altitude ceiling of close to 100,000 feet. Only 17 were built and 9 had been lost by April 1969.

Fastest biplane The fastest recorded biplane was the Italian Fiat C.R.42B, with a 1,010 h.p. Daimler-Benz DB601A engine, which attained 323 m.p.h. in 1941. Only one was built.

Fastest piston-engined aircraft The fastest piston-engined aeroplane ever built has been a cut-down privately owned Hawker *Sea Fury* which was claimed to have attained 520 m.p.h. in level flight over Texas, U.S.A., in August 1966 piloted by Mike Carroll of Los Angeles. The official record is 482·462 m.p.h. over Edwards AFB, California by Darryl C. Greenmyer, 33 (U.S.) in a Grumman F8F-2 *Bearcat* on 16 Aug. 1969.

Fastest propeller-driven aircraft The Soviet Tu-114 turboprop transport is the world's fastest propeller-driven aeroplane. It has achieved average speeds of more than 545 m.p.h. carrying heavy payloads over measured circuits. It is developed from the Tupolev Tu-20 bomber, known in the West as the "Bear", and has 14,795 horse-power engines.

Largest propeller The largest aircraft propeller ever used was the 22 feet 7½ inches diameter Garuda propeller, fitted to the Linke-Hofmann R II built in Breslau, Germany, which flew in 1919. It was driven by four 260 h.p. Mercédès engines and turned at only 545 r.p.m.

Greatest altitude The official world altitude record by an aircraft which took off from the ground under its own power is 113,892 feet (21·57 miles) by Lt.-Col. Georgiy Mosolov (U.S.S.R.) in a Mikoyan Ye-66A aircraft, powered by one turbojet and one rocket engine, on 28 April 1961. Major R. W. Smith of the U.S. Air Force reached an unofficial record height of 118,860 feet (22·15 miles) in a Lockheed NF-104A over Edwards Air Force Base, California, U.S.A., early in November 1963.

The Lockheed NF104-A which attained an unofficial altitude record of 118,860 feet

DURATION
The flight duration record is 64 days, 22 hours, 19 minutes and 5 seconds, set up by Robert Timm and John Cook in a Cessna 172 light aircraft. They took off from McCarran Airfield, Las Vegas, Nevada, U.S.A., just before 3.53 p.m. local time on 4 Dec. 1958, and landed at the same airfield just before 2.12 p.m. on 7 Feb. 1959. They covered a distance equivalent to six times around the world.

The world's fastest jet aircraft—the 2,200 m.p.h. Lockheed SR-71

AIRCRAFT

AIRPORTS

Largest World
The world's largest airport is the Dulles International Airport, Washington, D.C., U.S.A., which extends over an area of 9,880 acres (15·59 square miles). The largest international airport terminal is that at John F. Kennedy International Airport (opened as Idlewild in July 1948) on Long Island, New York, U.S.A. Terminal City covers an area of 655 acres. Work was started in December 1968 on an 18,000 acre complex at Grapevine between Dallas and Fort Worth, Texas, U.S.A., for completion at a cost of $360 million (£150 million) by 1972. The five terminals will be able to handle 90 jumbo jets simultaneously. The airport under construction between Miami and Naples, Florida, will cover approximately 25,000 acres (39 square miles).

United Kingdom
Fifty-nine airline companies from 49 countries operate scheduled services into London (Heathrow) Airport (2,765 acres), and during 1969 there were a total number of 258,690 air transport movements handled by a staff of over 48,059, employed by the various companies and the British Airports Authority. The total number of passengers, both incoming and outgoing, was 14,224,225 in 1969. The most flights in a day was 928 on 31 July 1969 and the largest number of passengers yet handled in a day was 65,798 on the same day. Aircraft fly to 93 countries.

Busiest
The world's busiest airport is the Chicago International Airport, O'Hare Field, Illinois, U.S.A., with a total of 675,451 movements (632,030 air carrier movements) in 1969. This represents a take-off or landing every 47 seconds.

The busiest landing area is, however, Bien Hoa Air Base, South Vietnam, which handled 857,679 take-offs and landings in 1968. The world's largest "helipad" is An Khe, South Vietnam, which services U.S. Army and Air Force helicopters.

Highest and lowest
The highest airport in the world is El Alto, near La Paz, Bolivia, at 13,358 feet above sea-level. Ladakh airstrip in Kashmir has, however, an altitude of 14,270 feet. The highest landing ever made is 6,080 metres (19,947 feet) on Dhaulagri in the Nepal Himalaya by a high-wing monoplane, named *Yeti,* supplying the 1960 Swiss Expedition. The lowest landing field is El Lisan on the east shore of the Dead Sea, 1,180 feet below sea-level, but the lowest international airport is Schiphol, Amsterdam, at 13 feet below sea-level.

LONGEST RUNWAY

World
The longest runway in the world is one of 7 miles in length (of which 15,000 feet is concreted) at Edwards Air Force Base on the bed of Rogers Dry Lake at Muroc, California, U.S.A. The whole test centre airfield extends over 65 square miles. In an emergency an auxiliary 12-mile strip is available along the bed of the Dry Lake. The world's longest civil airport runway is one of 15,500 feet (2·95 miles) at Salisbury, Rhodesia, completed in 1969.

United Kingdom
The longest runway available normally to civil aircraft in the United Kingdom is Number 1 at London (Heathrow) Airport, measuring 12,799 feet (2·42 miles).

HELICOPTERS

Fastest rotating wing
A Bell YUH-1B Model 533 compound research helicopter, boosted by two auxiliary turbojet engines, attained an unofficial speed record of 316·1 m.p.h. over Arlington, Texas, U.S.A., in April 1969.

Largest
The world's largest helicopter is the Soviet Mi-12 ("Homer"), also known as the V-12, which set up an international record by lifting a payload of 88,636 lb. (39·5 tons) to a height of 6,560 feet on 6 Aug. 1969. It is powered by four 6,500 h.p. turboshaft engines.

Fastest
The world's speed record for a helicopter is 217·77 m.p.h. by a Sud-Aviation S.E.321 Super Frelon, piloted by Jean Boulet and Roland Coffignot (France), over Istrès, France, on 23 July 1963.

Highest
The altitude record for helicopters is 36,027 feet by Jean Boulet in a Sud-Aviation S.E.3150 *Alouette II* at Brétigny-sur-Orge, France, on 13 June 1958.

FLYING BOAT
The fastest flying-boat is the Soviet twin-jet Beriev Be-10 (code name "Mallow"), which set up an official speed record of 566·69 m.p.h. over a measured course on 7 Aug. 1961, piloted by Nikolay Andrievskiy. This aircraft also holds the altitude record for flying-boats, with 49,088 feet, and lifted a record payload of 33,523 lb. (14·96 tons) to 2,000 metres (6,562 feet) on 12 Sept. 1961.

AIRSHIPS
The largest non-rigid airship ever constructed was the U.S. Navy ZPG 3-W. It had a capacity of 1,516,300 cubic feet, was 403·4 feet long and 85·1 feet in diameter, with a crew of 21. It first flew on 21 July 1958, but crashed into the sea in June 1960.

The largest rigid airship ever built was the German *Hindenburg* (LZ129), with a length of 803 feet and a capacity of 7,063,000 cubic feet. She caught fire at Lakehurst, New Jersey, U.S.A., at 7.25 p.m. (E.S.T.) on 6 May 1937.

The largest British airship was the R101 built by the Royal Airship Works, Cardington, Bedfordshire and completed in 1929. She was 777 feet in length and had a capacity of 5,500,000 cubic feet. She crashed near Beauvais, France, killing 48 aboard on 5 Oct. 1930.

The ill-fated R101

Earliest licence
The Royal Aero Club's airship pilot's certificate No. 1 was issued to Ernest T. Willows (d. 1926) who on 4 Nov. 1910 in his flight from Wormwood Scrubs, London to Douai, France, in *Willows III* became the first to make the crossing from England to France.

BALLOONS

Distance record
The record distance travelled is 3,052·7 kilometres (1,896·9 miles) by H. Berliner (Germany) from Bitterfeld, Germany, to Kirgishan in the Ural Mountains, Russia, on 8–10 Feb. 1914. The longest stay aloft is 94½ hours by the *Small World* (Messrs. Timothy and Arnold B. Eiloart and Mr. and Mrs. Colin Mudie), which left Teneriffe on 12 Dec. 1958, and later ditched in the Atlantic after a flight of 1,200 miles.

Largest
The largest balloon ever to fly is the 800-foot-tall balloon built by G. T. Schjeldah for the U.S.A.F., first tested on 18 July 1966. It was used for a Martian re-entry experiment by N.A.S.A. 130,000 feet above Walter AFB, New Mexico, U.S.A. on 30 Aug. 1966. Its capacity is 260 million cubic feet.

Human-powered flight
The earliest successful attempt to fly over half a mile with a human-powered aircraft was made by John C. Wimpenny, who flew 993 yards at an average altitude of 5 feet (maximum 8 feet) and an average speed of

141

19·5 m.p.h. in a pedal-cranked propeller-driven aircraft called "Puffin I" at Hatfield, Herts., on 2 May 1962.

HOVERCRAFT

The inventor of the ACV (air-cushion vehicle) is Sir Christopher Cockerell, C.B.E., F.R.S. (born 4 June 1910), a British engineer who had the idea in 1954, published his Ripplecraft Report 1/55 on 25 Oct. 1955 and patented it on 12 Dec. 1955. The earliest patent relating to an air-cushion craft was taken out in 1877 by John I. Thornycroft (1843–1928) of Chiswick, London. The first flight by a hovercraft was made by the 4-ton Saunders Roe SR-N1 at Cowes on 30 May 1959. With a 1,500-lb. thrust Viper turbojet engine, this craft reached 68 knots in June 1961. The first hovercraft public service was run across the Dee Estuary by the 60-knot 24-passenger Vickers-Armstrong VA-3 between July and September 1962. The largest is the £1,500,000 Westland SR-N4, "Mountbatten", weighing 168 tons, first run on 4 Feb. 1968. It has a top speed of 77 knots powered by 4 Bristol Siddeley Marine Proteus engines with 19 foot propellers. It carries 34 cars and 174 passengers and is 130 feet 2 inches long with a 76-foot 10-inch beam. The longest hovercraft journey was one of 5,000 miles through 8 West African countries between 15 Oct. 1969 and 3 Jan. 1970 by the British Trans-African Hovercraft Expedition. The longest non-stop journey on record is one of 550 miles lasting 33 hours by a Denny Mark II piloted by Sir John Onslow from Poole, Dorset to Fleetwood, Lancashire on 4–5 July 1968.

Model aircraft   The world record for altitude is 22,939 feet by Maynard L. Hill (U.S.A.) on 1 Sept. 1969. The speed record is 203·19 m.p.h. by E. Zanin (Italy) with a Zanin jet in Rome on 26 April 1964. The best British performance is 101·5 m.p.h. by an unsponsored home-built 7·9 c.c. engined model of 32 inch wing span by John Crampton at Dunsfold, Surrey on 20 Oct. 1968.

Britain's fastest model aircraft—the 101·5 m.p.h. 7·9 cc model built by John Crampton (sitting on car wing)

Hypnosis from the air   The first recorded example of hypnosis being performed from the air was when Mr. Henry Blythe hypnotized several people by radio telephone from an aircraft circling 1,500 feet above a marquee at Gloucester, England on 3 Aug. 1963.

5. Power Producers

LARGEST POWER PLANT

World   The world's largest power station is the U.S.S.R.'s hydro-electric station at Krasnoyarsk on the river Yenisey, Siberia, U.S.S.R. with a power of 6,000,000 kW. Its third generator turned in March 1968 and the twelfth will be operative by December 1970. The turbine hall completed in June 1968, is 1,378 feet long. The turbine hall at the Volga-V.I. Lenin Power Plant, Kuybyshev is more than 2,100 feet long.

The largest non-hydro-electric generating plant in the world is the 2,500,000 kW Tennessee Valley Authority installation under construction at Paradise, Kentucky, U.S.A. with an annual consumption of 8,150,000 tons of coal. It cost $189,000,000 (£78,750,000).

The world's largest pumped storage plant is the 900,000 kW plant at Vianden, Luxembourg, completed in 1964.

United Kingdom   The power stations with the greatest installed capacity in the United Kingdom are Ferrybridge "C" near Pontefract, Yorkshire, which reached full power of 2,000 MW in December 1967 and West Burton, which reached the same output in February 1969. A 2,400 MW station is to be completed in Longannet, Fife, Scotland, in 1971. A 3,960 MW station is under construction at Drax, Yorkshire, the first half of which (3 × 660 MW sets) will be completed in 1972.

The largest hydro-electric plant in the United Kingdom is the North of Scotland Hydro-electricity Board's Power Station at Loch Sloy, Dunbartonshire. The installed capacity of this station is 130,450 kW or 175,000 h.p. The Ben Cruachan Pumped Storage Scheme was opened on 15 Oct. 1965 at Loch Awe, Argyll, Scotland. It has a capacity of 400,000 kW and cost £24,000,000.

Biggest black-out   The greatest power failure in history struck seven north-eastern U.S. States and Ontario, Canada, on 9–10 Nov. 1965. About 30,000,000 people in 80,000 square miles were plunged into darkness. Only two were killed. In New York City the power failed at 5.27 p.m. Supplies were eventually restored by 2 a.m. in Brooklyn, 4.20 a.m. in Queens, 6.58 a.m. in Manhattan and 7 a.m. in the Bronx.

THE WORLD'S LARGEST HYDRO-ELECTRIC GENERATING PLANTS
(Progressive List)

Ultimate Kilowattage	First Operational	Location	River
38,400	1898	De Cew Falls No. 1 (old plant)	Welland Canal
132,500	1905	Ontario Power Station	Niagara
403,900	1922	Sir Adam Beck No. 1 (formerly Queenston-Chippawa)	Niagara
1,641,000	1942	Beauharnois, Quebec, Canada	St. Lawrence
1,974,000*	1941	Grand Coulee, Washington State, U.S.A.	Columbia
2,100,000	1955	Volga-V.I. Lenin Station, Kuybyshev, U.S.S.R.	Volga
2,543,000	1958	Volga-22nd Congress Station, Volgograd, U.S.S.R.	Volga
4,500,000	1961	Bratsk, U.S.S.R.	Angara
6,000,000	1967	Krasnoyarsk, U.S.S.R.	Yenisey
6,300,000	—	Sayano-Shushensk, U.S.S.R.	Yenisey
c. 20,000,000	—	Lower Lena, near Verkoyansk, U.S.S.R.	Lena

* Ultimate long-term planned kilowattage will be 9,771,000 kW with the completion of the "Third Powerplant" (capacity 7,200,000 kW).

Scene of
the world's first
sustained
nuclear reaction
—the University
of Chicago
squash court

ATOMIC POWER

Earliest The world's first atomic pile was built in a disused squash court at the University of Chicago, Illinois, U.S.A. It "went critical" on 2 Dec. 1942.

Largest The world's largest atomic power station is the 1,180 MW plant at Wylfa, Anglesey, North Wales, completed in 1970. The Dungeness "B" station in Kent, due to be completed in July 1971, will have a capacity of 1,200 MW followed by Hinkley "B" (1,250 MW) and Heysham, Lancashire (2,500 MW). The largest atomic plant scheduled in the United States is the Sequoyah Nuclear Power Plants Units 1 and 2 each of 1,124 MW due to be completed at Daisy, Tennessee in 1973 and 1974.

LARGEST REACTOR

The largest single atomic reactor in the world will be the 873 MW Westinghouse Electric Corporation pressurized water type reactor being installed at Indian Point No. 2 Station, New York, U.S.A. which became operative in 1969.

TIDAL POWER STATION

The world's first major tidal power station is the *Usine marémotrice de la Rance*, officially opened on 26 Nov. 1966 at the Rance estuary in the Golfe de St. Malo, Britanny, France. It was built in five years, at a cost of 420,000,000 francs (£34,685,000), and has a net annual output of 544,000,000 kWh. The 880-yard barrage contains 24 turbo alternators. This harnessing of the tides has imperceptibly slowed the Earth's rate of revolution. The $1,000 million (£416 million) Passamaquoddy project for the Bay of Fundy in Maine, U.S.A., and New Brunswick, Canada, is not expected to be operative before 1978. The first ever tidal power station was the Dee Hydro Station, Cheshire with a capacity of 635 kW which began producing in October 1913.

LARGEST BOILER

The largest boilers ever designed are those ordered in the United States from The Babcock & Wilcox Company (U.S.A.) with a capacity of 1,330 MW so involving the evaporation of 9,330,000 lb. of steam per hour. The largest boilers now being installed in the United Kingdom are the three 660 MW units for the Drax Power Station (see page 142) designed and constructed by Babcock & Wilcox Ltd.

LARGEST GENERATOR

The largest generator in the world is now a double shaft steam generator with a designed capacity of 800,000 kW, being built since August 1963 at the Elektrosila works, Leningrad, in the U.S.S.R. This is destined for the Lower Lena Hydro-electric works (see p.142). The largest single shaft turbine in the world is a 600,000 kW generator built for the Ohio Power Co. and Buckeye

Power Co. at Brilliant, Ohio, U.S.A. The first 500,000 kW generator in Britain went into service at Ferrybridge, Yorkshire, in 1967. At Drax Power Station, Yorkshire, 660,000 kW generators will be installed by 1972.

LARGEST TURBINES

The largest turbines under construction are those rated at 820,000 h.p. with an overload capacity of 1,000,000 h.p., 32 feet in diameter with a 401-ton runner and a 312½-ton shaft for the Grand Coulee "Third Power-plant" (see page 142).

GAS TURBINE

The largest gas turbine in the world is that installed at the Krasnodar thermal power station in August 1969 with a capacity of 100,000 kW. It was built in Leningrad, U.S.S.R.

LARGEST PUMP TURBINE

The world's largest integral reversible pump-turbine is that made by Allis-Chalmers for the $50,000,000 Taum Sauk installation of the Union Electric Co. in St. Louis, Missouri, U.S.A. It has a rating of 240,000 h.p. as a turbine and a capacity of 1,100,000 gallons per minute as a pump. The Tehachapi Pumping Plant, California will in 1972 pump 18,300,000 gallons per minute over 1,700 feet up.

ELECTRIC MOTOR

Largest This same electrical unit, when used as a motor, is the world's largest, rated at 102,000 h.p. at 106 revolutions per minute. As a generator it is rated at 70,000 kW at 13,800 volts.

Smallest The world's smallest electric motor was completed early in 1965 by William McLellan, aged 35, of Electro-Optical Systems, Inc., of Pasadena, California, U.S.A. It measures 1/64th of an inch in each dimension and has an output of one millionth of one horsepower. The only suggested use so far for this ultra-miniature motor is to run a merry-go-round in a flea circus.

Solar power plant The largest solar furnace in the world is the Laboratoire de l'Energie Solaire, at Mont Louis in the eastern Pyrenees, France. Its parabolic reflector, 150 feet in diameter, is the largest mirror in the world and concentrates the Sun's rays to provide a temperature of 5,432° F. In April 1958 it was announced that Soviet scientists had designed a solar power station for the Ararat Valley, Armenia, U.S.S.R., using 1,300 moving mirrors, totalling 5 acres in area, to provide 2,500,000 kW hours in a year. The U.S. Air Force solar furnace at Cloudcroft, New Mexico, U.S.A., has a parabolic mirror 108 feet in diameter and a flat mirror 154 feet square, yielding temperatures of *c.* 8,500° F.

LARGEST GAS WORKS

The flow of natural gas from the North Sea is diminishing the manufacture of gas by the carbonisation of coal and the reforming process using petroleum derivatives. Britain's largest ever gasworks covering 300 acres at Beckton, Essex, still had in December 1967, a produc-

The Bratsk power station on the Angara River, U.S.S.R.

143

The mechanical world

tion capacity of 700 million cubic feet per day of which 28 per cent. was by carbonisation requiring over 6,000 tons of coal per day.

MOST POWERFUL JET ENGINE
The world's most powerful jet engine is the General Electric GE4/J5 which attained a thrust of 63,200 lb., with after-burning, on 19 Sept. 1968. It may "stretch" to 75,000 lb. The thrust of the Thiokol XLR99-RM-2 rocket motor in each of the three experimental U.S.X-15 aircraft was 56,880 lb. at sea-level, reaching 70,000 lb. at peak altitudes. The Rolls-Royce RB 211-22, first ran on 31 Aug. 1968, for the A-300B Air Bus project and reached 40,600 lb. in April 1969.

6. Engineering

OLDEST MACHINERY
The earliest machinery still in use is the *dâlu*—a water raising instrument known to have been in use in the Sumerian civilization which originated *c.* 3,500 B.C. in Lower Iraq.

The oldest piece of machinery operating in the United Kingdom is the snuff mill driven by a water wheel at Messrs. Wilson & Co.'s Sharrow Mill in Sheffield, Yorkshire. It is known to have been operating in 1797 and more probably since 1730.

LARGEST PRESS
The world's two most powerful production machines are forging presses in the U.S.A. The Loewy closed-die forging press, in a plant leased from the U.S. Air Force by the Wyman-Gordon Company at North Grafton, Massachusetts, U.S.A. weighs 9,469 tons and stands 114 feet 2 inches high, of which 66 feet is sunk below the operating floor. It has a rated capacity of 44,600 tons, and went into operation in October 1955. The other similar press is at the plant of the Aluminium Company of America at Cleveland, Ohio. There has been a report of a press in the U.S.S.R. with a capacity of 70,000 tonnes (68,900 tons), but details are lacking. The most powerful press in Great Britain is the closed-die forging and extruding press installed in 1967 at the Cameron Iron Works, near Edinburgh, Scotland. The press is 92 feet tall (27 feet below ground) and exerts a force of 30,000 tons.

LATHE
The world's largest lathe is the 72-foot-long 385-ton giant lathe built by the Dortmunder Rheinstahl firm of Wagner in 1962. The face plate is 15 feet in diameter and can exert a torque of 289,000 ft. lb. when handling objects weighing up to 200 tons.

EXCAVATOR
The world's largest excavator is the 33,400 h.p. Marion 6360 excavator, weighing 12,500 tons. This vast machine can grab 241 tons in a single bite in a bucket of 85 cubic yards capacity.

DRAGLINE
World The Ural Engineering Works at Ordzhonikdze, U.S.S.R., completed in March 1962, has a dragline known as the ES-25(100) with a boom of 100 metres (328 feet) and a bucket with a capacity of 31·5 cubic yards. The world's largest walking dragline is the Bucyrus-Erie 4250W with an all-up weight of 12,000 tons and a bucket capacity of 220 cubic yards on a 310-foot boom. This machine, the world's largest mobile land machine is now operating on the Central Ohio Coal Company's Muskingum site in Ohio, U.S.A.

United Kingdom The largest dragline excavator in Britain is "Big Geordie", the Bucyrus-Erie 1550W 6250 gross h.p., weighing 3,000 tons and a forward mast 160 feet high. On open cast coal workings at Widdrington, Northumberland in February 1970, it proved able

to strip 100 tons of overburden in 65 seconds with its 65 cubic yard bucket on a 265-foot boom. It is operated by Derek Crouch (Contractors) Ltd.

BLAST FURNACE
The world's largest blast furnace is the No. 3 Blast Furnace at Fuji Stell, Nagoya, Japan, with a volume of 103,295 cubic feet able to produce over 6,900 tons of pig iron per day completed in May 1969. It has a hearth diameter of 38 feet 4½ inches.

Largest forging The largest forging on record is one 53 feet long weighing 396,000 lb. (176·79 tons) forged by Bethlehem Steel for the Tennessee Valley Authority nuclear power plant at Brown Ferry, Alabama, U.S.A. in Nov. 1969.

LONGEST PIPELINES
Oil The longest crude oil pipeline in the world is the Interprovincial Pipe Line Company's installation from Edmonton, Alberta, to Buffalo, New York State, U.S.A., a distance of 1,775 miles. Along the length of the pipe 13 pumping stations maintain a flow of 6,900,000 gallons of oil per day. In Britain the longest pipeline for crude oil is the 245-mile-long British Petroleum–Royal Dutch/Shell line from Merseyside to Greater London opened on 19 March 1969 at a cost of £8½ million.

The eventual length of the Trans-Siberian Pipeline will be 2,319 miles, running from Tuimazy through Ormsk and Novosibirsk to Irkutsk. The first 30-mile section was opened in July 1957.

Natural gas The longest natural gas pipeline in the world is that which runs 1,840 miles from the Rio Grande, southern Texas, to New York, U.S.A., and has a diameter of 30 inches. The Trans-Europe pipeline from the Central Asian fields south of Kuibyshev, U.S.S.R. to near East Berlin will stretch 3,100 miles and have a diameter of 1,420 mm. It is due for completion in 1973. The famous "Big Inch", which has a 24-inch diameter and runs from Longview, Texas, to Linden, New Jersey, U.S.A., is 1,254 miles in length. The Trans-Canada Natural Gas Pipeline, begun in July 1956, will have a length of 2,200 miles, while a system 5,625 miles in length, with a 3,500-mile trunk from northern Russia to Leningrad, is under construction in the U.S.S.R., for completion by 1976.

Largest Cat Cracker The world's largest catalyst cracker is the American Oil Company's installation at the Texas City Refinery, Texas, U.S.A., with a capacity of 3,322,000 gallons per day.

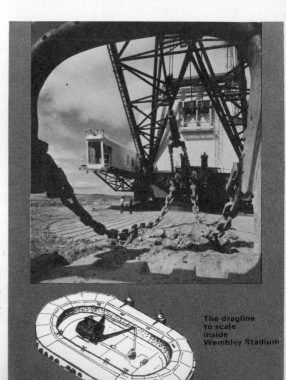

Britain's largest dragline excavator (note size of men)

The dragline to scale inside Wembley Stadium

The mechanical world

Airport, California, U.S.A., comprising two conveyors measuring 450 feet each, and each with a capacity of 7,200 passengers per hour. It was opened on 20 May 1964.

The "travolator", opened in 1960 at the Bank Underground station in the City of London, to replace the 62-year-old "Drain", is 354 feet in length and moves at 180 feet per minute. It has a capacity of 10,000 people per hour.

FASTEST PRINTER
The world's fastest mechanical printer is the I.C.T. line printer, used in conjunction with the I.C.T. 1900 Series computer. It can print the wordage (773,692 words) of the whole Bible in 18 minutes—198 times as fast as the world's fastest typist. Its capacity is 1,350 lines (160 characters per line) per minute of alpha-numeric material or 1,700 lines of numeric material.

TRANSMISSION LINES
Longest The longest span between pylons of any power line in the world is that across the Sogne Fjord, Norway, between Rabnaberg and Flatlaberg. Erected in 1955, by the Whitecross Co. Ltd. of Warrington, England, as part of the high-tension power cable from Refsdal power station at Vik, it has a span of 16,040 feet and a weight of 12 tons. In 1967 two further high tensile steel/aluminium lines 16,006 feet long, and weighing 33 tons, manufactured by Whitecross and B.I.C.C. (see below), were erected here. The longest in Britain are the 5,310 foot lines built by J. L. Eve Co. across the Severn.

Highest The world's highest are those across the Straits of Messina, with towers of 675 feet (Sicily side) and 735 feet (Calabria) and 11,900 feet apart. The highest lines in Britain are those made by British Insulated Callender's Cables Ltd. at West Thurrock, Essex, which cross the Thames estuary suspended from 630-foot-tall towers at a minimum height of 250 feet, with a 130-ton breaking load. They are 4,500 feet in length.

Highest voltages The highest voltages now carried are 765,000 volts A.C. in the United States since 1969. The Swedish A.S.E.A. Company is experimenting with a possible 1,000,000 volt D.C. transmission line.

LONGEST CONVEYOR BELT
The world's longest single flight conveyor belt is one of 5½ miles installed at the N.C.B. power station at Longannet, Fife, Scotland by Cable Belt Ltd. of Camberley, Surrey. Cable Belt Ltd. are also installing a 9-mile-long single-flight conveyor at Cumberland, Tennessee, U.S.A., with a weekly capacity of 140,000 short tons of coal on a 42-inch-wide 800 ft./min. belt.

LONGEST WIRE ROPE
The longest wire rope ever spun in one piece was one measuring 46,653 feet (8·83 miles) long and 3⅛ inches in circumference, with a weight of 28½ tons, manufactured by British Ropes Ltd. of Doncaster, Yorkshire.

CLOCKS
Oldest The earliest mechanical clock, that is one with an escapement, was completed in China in A.D. 725 by I'Hsing and Liang Ling-tsan.

The oldest surviving working clock in the world is one dating from 1386, or possibly earlier, at Salisbury Cathedral, Wiltshire, which was restored in 1956. Earlier dates, ranging back to c. 1335, have been attributed to the weight-driven clock in Wells Cathedral, Somerset, but only the iron frame is original. A model of Giovanni de Dondi's heptagonal astronomical clock of 1348–64 was completed in 1962.

largest nut The largest nuts ever made weigh 26 cwt. (1·3 tons) each and have an inside diameter of 23 inches and an outside diameter of 26 inches. Known as the Pilgrim Nuts, they are manufactured by Moorside Components Ltd. of Oldham, Lancashire, for securing propellers.

TRANSFORMER
The world's largest transformer is one reported from Japan in November 1967 which delivers 680,000 kVA at 275 kV.

HIGHEST ROPEWAY OR TELEPHERIQUE
World The highest and longest aerial ropeway in the world is the Teleferico Mérida (Mérida téléphérique) in Venezuela, from Mérida City (5,379 feet) to the summit of Pico Espejo (15,629 feet), a rise of 10,250 feet. The ropeway is in four sections, involving 3 car changes in the 8 mile ascent in one hour. The fourth span is 10,070 feet in length. The two cars work on the pendulum system—the carrier rope is locked and the cars are hauled by means of three pull ropes powered by a 230 h.p. motor. They have a maximum capacity of 45 persons and travel at 32 feet per second (21·8 m.p.h.). The longest single span ropeway is the 13,500-foot-long span from the Coachella Valley to Mt. San Jacinto (10,821 feet), California, U.S.A., inaugurated on 12 Sept. 1963. The largest cable cars in the world are those at Squaw Valley, California, U.S.A., with a capacity of 121 persons built by Carrosseriewerke A.G. of Aarburg, Switzerland, and first run on 19 Dec. 1968. The breaking strain on the 7,000-foot cable is 279 tons.

Great Britain Britain's longest cabin lift is that at Llandudno, Caernarvonshire, Wales opened in June 1969. It has 42 cabins each with a capacity of 1,000 people per hour and is 5,320 feet in length.

PASSENGER LIFTS
Fastest The fastest domestic passenger lifts in the world are those fitted in the 100-storey, 1,107-foot-tall John Hancock Building in Chicago, Illinois, U.S.A. They operate at a speed of 1,600 feet per minute. Much higher speeds are achieved in the winding cages of mine shafts. A hoisting shaft 6,800 feet deep, owned by Western Deep Levels Ltd. in South Africa, winds at speeds of up to 40·9 m.p.h.

United Kingdom The longest lifts in the United Kingdom are the two 15-passenger cars in the Post Office Tower, Maple Street, London, W.1. They can carry passengers through 540 feet at up to 1,000 feet per minute (11·36 m.p.h.) to the revolving restaurant at the top but are operated at 600 ft./min. Their maximum speed is matched by six of the lifts in the B.P. Building at Moorfields, in the City of London.

FASTEST ESCALATORS
The fastest escalators in the United Kingdom are those at the Leicester Square underground station on the London Transport Board railway. They have a step speed of 180 feet per minute. Escalators were introduced at Earl's Court station in 1911.

The world's longest "moving sidewalk" is the Speedwalk Passenger Conveyor System at San Francisco

145

The mechanical world

Largest World
The world's most massive clock is the Astronomical Clock in Beauvais Cathedral, France, constructed between 1865 and 1868. It contains 90,000 parts and measures 40 feet high, 20 feet wide and 9 feet deep. The Su Sung clock, built in China at Khaifeng in 1088–92, had a 20-ton bronze armillary sphere for 1½ tons of water. It was removed to Peking in 1126 and was last known to be working in its 40-foot-high tower in 1136.

Public clocks
The largest four-faced clock in the world is that on the building of the Allen-Bradley Company of Milwaukee, Wisconsin, U.S.A. Each face has a diameter of 40 feet 3½ inches with a minute hand 20 feet in overall length. The tallest four-faced clock in the world is that of the Williamsburgh Savings Bank in Brooklyn, New York City, N.Y., U.S.A. It is 430 feet above street level.

United Kingdom
The largest clock in the United Kingdom was on the Singer Sewing Machine factory at Clydebank, Dunbartonshire, Scotland. It had four faces, each 26 feet in diameter, the minute hand was 12 feet 9 inches long and the hour hand 8 feet 9 inches. It was built in 1882, re-modelled in 1926 and operated until 5 p.m. on 5 March 1963. The largest clock face constructed in Britain is the Synchronome turret clock (diameter 60 feet) exhibited at Earl's Court, London, in March 1959. The largest clock wheel in the world is the World Time Clock installed at 120 Cheapside, London, E.C.2. It has a diameter of 10 feet and enables the zone times in the major cities of the world to be read off. This was commissioned by J. Henry Schroder Wagg & Co. Ltd., from Martin Burgess.

Most accurate
The most accurate and complicated clock in the world is the Olsen clock, installed in the Copenhagen Town Hall, Denmark. The clock, which has more than 14,000 units, took 10 years to make and the mechanism of the clock functions in 570,000 different ways. The celestial pole motion of the clock will take 25,753 years to complete a full circle and is the slowest moving designed mechanism in the world. The clock is accurate to 0·5 of a second in 300 years.

Most expensive
The highest auction price for any English clock is £15,500 for an ebony bracket clock made by Thomas Tompian (c. 1639–1713) sold at the salerooms of Sotheby & Co., London on 29 April 1968.

WATCHES

Oldest
The oldest watch (portable clock-work time-keeper) is one made of iron by Peter Henlein (or Hele) in Nürnberg (Nuremberg), Bavaria, Germany, in c. 1504 and now in the Memorial Hall, Philadelphia, Pennsylvania, U.S.A. The earliest wrist watches were those of Jacquet-Droz and Leschot of Geneva, Switzerland, dating from 1790.

Most expensive
Excluding watches with jewelled cases, the most expensive standard men's wrist watch is the Swiss Audemars-Piguet 18-carat watch, which costs £576 retail. On 1 June 1964, a record £27,500 was paid for the Duke of Wellington's watch made in Paris in 1807 by Abraham Louis Bréguet, at the salerooms of Sotheby & Co., London, by the dealers Messrs. Ronald Lee for a Portuguese client.

Smallest
The smallest watches in the world are produced by Jaeger Le Coultre of Switzerland. Equipped with a 15-jewelled movement they measure just over half-an-inch long and three-sixteenths of an inch in width. The

The world's largest clock-wheel, 10 feet in diameter —City of London

The world's most powerful crane —in action

movement, with its case, weighs under a quarter of an ounce.

TIME MEASURER

World
The most accurate time-keeping devices are the twin atomic hydrogen masers installed in 1964 in the U.S. Naval Research Laboratory, Washington, D.C. They are based on the frequency of the hydrogen atom's transition period of 1,420,450,751,694 cycles per second. This enables an accuracy to within one second per 1,700,000 years.

United Kingdom
The most accurate time measurer in the United Kingdom is the 14-foot-long rubidium resonance Standard Atomic Clock at the National Physical Laboratory, Teddington, Greater London, devised by Dr. Louis Essen, O.B.E. and Mr. J. V. L. Parry and completed in 1962. It is accurate to within one second in 1,000 years.

Largest radar installations
The largest of the three installations in the U.S. Ballistic Missile Early Warning System (B.M.E.W.S.) is that near Thule, in Greenland, 931 miles from the North Pole, completed in 1960 at a cost of $500,000,000 (now £208·3 million). Its sister stations are one at Clear, Alaska, U.S.A., completed in July 1961, and a $115,000,000 (now £47·9 million) installation at Fylingdales Moor, Yorkshire, completed in June 1963. An installation costing £55 million is being erected at Orfordness, Suffolk.

Smallest tubing
The smallest tubing in the world is made by Accles and Pollock, Ltd. of Oldbury, Worcestershire. It is of pure nickel with an outside diameter of 0·0005 of an inch and was announced on 9 Sept. 1963. The average human hair measures from 0·002 to 0·003 of an inch in diameter. The tubing, which is stainless, can be used for the artificial insemination of bees and for the medical process of "feeding" nerves, and weighs only 5 oz. per 100 miles.

LARGEST CRANE

World
The crane with the world's largest and highest lifting capacity is the Goliath crane installed at Harland and Wolff's shipbuilding dock, Belfast, Northern Ireland, in 1969. The crane spans 460 feet and has a working safe load of 840 tons, but on a test lifted 1,050 tons. It was built to the design of Krupper-Ardelt of Wilhelmshaven, West Germany. A 32-wheeled gantry hydraulic crane with a span of 95 feet with a capacity of 2,000 short tons (1,785·7 tons) is under construction at the Grand Coulee Third Powerplant, Washington, U.S.A. The highest crane reported is a gantry crane at the Bratsk Power Station, Siberia, U.S.S.R., capable of lifting 22 tons to a height of 465 feet.

Hoisting tackle
The greatest weight lifted by hoisting tackle is 700 tons by the Fluor Corporation of Los Angeles, California, U.S.A., in the case of an Isomax reactor 90 feet in length at Shuaiba, Kuwait, on 26 Aug. 1968. The tallest vessel ever erected is a cracking column 270 feet in length by Fluor at Deer Park, Texas, U.S.A., in 2 hours on 24 Oct. 1968.

Floating crane
The world's largest floating cranes are the Foster Parker, *Atlas Number 1* and the *Hercules* derrick barges operated by Brown & Root Inc. of Houston, Texas. These are 350 feet long and 100 feet in the beam and carry a crew of 80 men. The main crane in fixed position at 65 feet radius is capable of hoisting 714 tons.

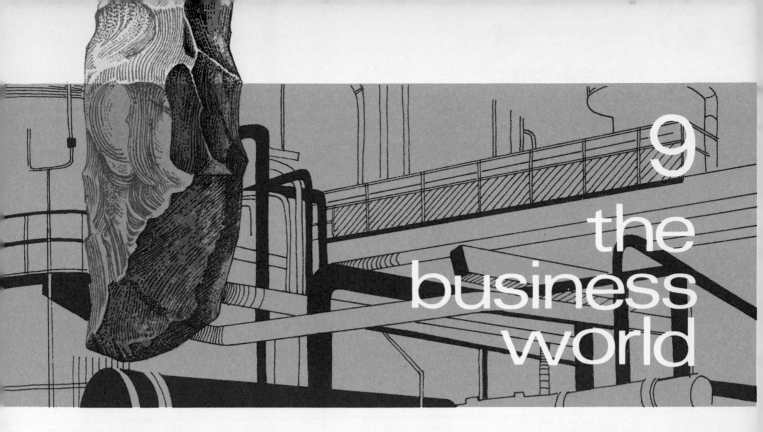

1. Commerce

OLDEST INDUSTRY

Agriculture is often described as "the oldest industry in the world", whereas in fact there is no evidence that it was practised before *c.* 9000 B.C. The oldest industry is believed to be flint knapping, which is allied to the construction of hand axes, which are the earliest human artifacts, dating from between 1,750,000 and 2,300,000 years ago.

OLDEST COMPANY

World The oldest company in the world is believed to be Stora Kopparbergs Bergslags Aktiebolag ("The Great Copper Mountain Mining Corporation") of Falun, Sweden, in which there have been recorded share dealings since 16 June 1288. The earliest trading in share certificates was in those of the Dutch East India Company (*Verenigde Oost Indische Compagnie*) soon after its foundation on 20 March 1602. A share certificate dated 8 Dec. 1606 is in the possession of the Vereniging voor den Effectenhandel, Amsterdam.

Britain The oldest company in Britain is the Faversham Oyster Fishery Co., referred to the Faversham Oyster Fishing Act 1930, has existed "from time immemorial", *i.e.* from before 1189. The Royal Mint has origins going back to A.D. 287. The Whitechapel Bell Foundry of Whitechapel Road, London, E.1, has been in business since 1570. The oldest retail business in Britain is B. Smith, Ltd., in the market place of Thirsk, Yorkshire. Founded in 1580, the company is a firm of drapers, furnishers and caterers. R. Durtnell & Sons, builders, of Brasted, Kent, has been run by the same family since 1591.

GREATEST ASSETS

World The business with the greatest amount in physical assets is the Bell System, which comprises the American Telephone and Telegraph Company, with headquarters at 195 Broadway, New York City, N.Y., U.S.A., and its subsidiaries. The group's total assets on the consolidated balance sheet at 31 Dec. 1969 were valued at $43,903,121,000 (£18,293 million). The plant involved included 92,691,000 telephones. The number of employees was 955,930. The shareholders at 1 Jan. 1970 numbered more than those of any other company, namely 3,062,973. A total of 20,109 attended the Annual Meeting in April 1961, thereby setting a world record. The total of operating revenues and other income in 1969 was $15,683,767,000 (£6,535 million),

from which the net income, after taxes, was $2,198,698,000 (£916 million). The first company to have assets in excess of $1 billion was the United States Steel Corporation with $1,400 million at the time of its creation by merger in 1900.

United Kingdom The enterprise in the United Kingdom with the greatest capital employed is the Electricity Council and the Electricity Boards in England and Wales with £4,501,200,000 in 1969. This ranks third in the western world to Standard Oil and General Motors.

The manufacturing company with the greatest net assets is Imperial Chemical Industries, Ltd., with £1,556,500,000 on 1 Jan. 1970. Its staff and payroll, benefiting from the company's profit-sharing scheme, numbers 145,000. The company, which has 350 U.K. and overseas subsidiaries, was formed on 7 Dec. 1926 by the merger of four concerns—British Dyestuffs Corporation Ltd.; Brunner, Mond & Co. Ltd.; Nobel Industries, Ltd. and United Alkali Co. Ltd. The first chairman was Sir Alfred Moritz Mond (1868–1930), later the 1st Lord Melchett.

The production line of the world's wealthiest company —the Bell System of the U.S. which employs nearly a million people

147

The business world

The net assets of The "Shell" Transport and Trading Co. Ltd., at 31 Dec. 1969, were valued at £1,405,502,442. Of this, £1,398,696,000 represented a 40 per cent. holding of the net assets of the Royal Dutch/Shell Group, which stands at £3,496,740,000. Group companies have 173,000 employees. "Shell" Transport was formed in 1897 by Marcus Samuel (1853–1927), later the 1st Viscount Bearsted.

Greatest sales The first company to surpass the $1 billion (U.S.) mark in annual sales was the United States Steel Corporation in 1917. Now there are more than 120 billion dollar corporations in the world. The list is headed by General Motors (see Motor car manufacturer) with sales in 1969 of $24·29 billion. Measured in terms of sales, there were in 1969, 40 U.S., 6 U.K. and 4 other European industrial companies totalling 50 with figures of more than £1,000 million.

Greatest profit and loss The greatest profit ever made by one company in a year is $2,125,606,440 (now £866 million) by General Motors Corporation of Detroit in 1965. The greatest loss is $143,203,459 (now £59·6 million) by the General Dynamics Corporation in 1961. This, the world's largest private armaments concern, lost $470,000,000 (£195·8 million) overall on its programme to produce Convair 880 and 990 aircraft. The top profit earner in the United Kingdom in 1969 was British Petroleum with £371·2 million and the biggest loss maker Rootes Motors, whose 1969–70 figure is expected to reach £11 million. In July 1970 it became Chrysler (U.K.) Ltd.

Most efficient The major United Kingdom company with highest return on capital employed in 1969 was Lesney Products & Co. The Chairman of this toy-making firm, Mr. P. M. Tapscott, reported a pre-tax profit of £5,567,000 from a capital employed of only £9,715,000.

Biggest work force The biggest employer in the United Kingdom is the Post Office with 412,557 employees in 1969.

ADVERTISING AGENTS

The largest advertising agency in the world is J. Walter Thompson Co. Ltd., which in 1969 had total billings of $736,000,000 (£306·7 million) which were $64 million (£26·7 million) more than the Interpublic Group of Companies, headquartered in New York City.

Biggest advertiser The world's biggest advertiser is Unilever, the Anglo-Dutch group formed in 1937 whose origins go back to 1884. The group has more than 500 companies in more than 60 countries and employs 326,600 people, mainly in the production of foods, detergents and toiletries. The advertising bill for over 1,000 branded products was £159,000,000 in 1969.

Aircraft manufacturer The world's largest aircraft manufacturer is the Boeing Company of Seattle, Washington, U.S.A. The corporation's sales totalled $2,835,000,000 (£1,181 million) in 1969, and it had about 120,500 employees and assets valued at $2,602,444,000 (£1,084 million) at 31 Dec. 1969. Cessna Aircraft Company of Wichita, Kansas, U.S.A., produced 5,887 civil (37 models) and 400 military aircraft in the year ending 31 Dec. 1969, with total sales of $283 million (£117·9 million). The company

The world's largest aircraft manufacturer

148

has produced more than 92,000 aircraft since Clyde Cessna's first was built in 1911.

AIRLINES

Largest The largest airline in the world is the U.S.S.R. State airline "Aeroflot", so named since 1932. This was instituted on 9 Feb. 1923, with the title of Civil Air Fleet of the Council of Ministers of the U.S.S.R., abbreviated to "Dobrolet". It operates nearly 2,000 aircraft over about 300,000 miles of routes, employs 400,000 people and carried 68,000,000 passengers in 1969. The commercial airline carrying the greatest number of passengers in 1969 was United Air Lines of Chicago, Illinois, U.S.A. (formed 1931) with 30,109,000 passengers. The company had 52,207 employees and a fleet of 313 jet planes. The commercial airline serving the greatest mileage of routes is Air France, with 259,000 miles of unduplicated routes in 1970. In 1969 the company carried 5,662,443 passengers. In May 1970 the British European Airways (formed in August 1946) were operating a fleet of 117 aircraft, with 26 on order. BEA employed 22,862 staff and in 1969 carried 8,312,103 passengers.

Oldest The oldest commercial airline is Koninklijke Luchtvaart Maatschappij N.V. (KLM) of the Netherlands, which opened its first scheduled service (Amsterdam-London) on 17 May 1920, having been established in 1919. One of the original constituents of B.O.A.C., Aircraft Transport and Travel Ltd., was founded in 1918 and merged into Imperial Airways in 1924, and one of the holding companies of S.A.S., Det Danske Luftfartselskab, was established on 29 Oct. 1918 but operated a scheduled service only between August 1920 and 1946.

Aluminium producer The world's largest producer of aluminium is Alcan Aluminium Limited, of Montréal, Québec, Canada. With its affiliated companies, the company had an output of 1,692,900 short tons (1,511,500 U.K. tons) and record sales of Can. $1,345,000,000 (£560 million) in 1969. The company's principal subsidiary, the Aluminium Company of Canada, Ltd., owns the world's largest aluminium smelter, at Arvida, Québec, with a capacity of 435,000 short tons (388,400 U.K. tons) per annum.

Bicycle factory The 54-acre plant of Raleigh Industries Ltd. at Nottingham is the largest factory in the world producing complete bicycles. The factory employs 8,330 and makes more than 1,500,000 bicycles, 70,000 motorized two-wheelers and 365,000 wheeled toys a year.

Book shop The world's largest book shop is that of W. & G. Foyle, Ltd., of London, W.C.2. First established in 1904 in a small shop in Islington, the company is now at 119–125 Charing Cross Road. The area on one site is 75,825 sq. ft. The largest single display of books in one room in the world is in the Norrington Room at Blackwell's Bookshop, Broad Street, Oxford. This subterranean adjunct was opened on 16 June 1966 and contains 160,000 volumes on $2\frac{1}{2}$ miles of shelving in 10,000 square feet of selling space.

BREWERY

Largest World The largest single brewing plant in the world is that of Anheuser-Busch, Inc. in St. Louis, Missouri, U.S.A. This plant covers 66 acres and has a capacity of 8,400,000 U.S. barrels. In 1969 the whole company produced 18,712,432 U.S. barrels, equivalent to 13,414,942 Imperial barrels (3,863 million Imperial pints), the greatest annual volume ever produced by a brewing company.

Europe The largest brewery in Europe is the Guinness Brewery at St. James's Gate, Dublin, Ireland, which extends over 58·03 acres. The business was founded in 1759.

United Kingdom The largest brewing company in the United Kingdom is Bass-Charrington Ltd. with 9,357 public houses and

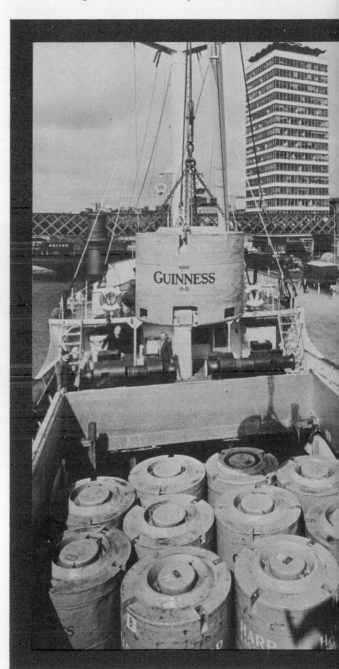

Guinness being exported from Dublin, Ireland

hotels with full on-licences, and 1,419 off-licence premises and 280 hotels. The company has net assets of £324,420,000, a staff of 18,318 plus 38,555 on licensed premises and controls 21 breweries.

Exports The largest exporter of beer, ale and stout in the world is Arthur Guinness, Son & Co. Ltd., of Dublin, Ireland.

The business world

Exports of Guinness from the Republic of Ireland in 1969 were 1,104,700 Imperial barrels, which is equivalent to 1,743,307 half-pint glasses per day.

Brickworks The largest brickworks in the world is the London Brick Company plant at Stewartby, Bedford. The works, established in 1898, now cover 221 acres and produce 15,000,000 bricks and brick equivalent every week.

Building contractors The largest construction company in the United Kingdom is George Wimpey & Co., Ltd. (founded 1880), of London, who undertake building, civil, mechanical, electrical and chemical engineering work. With assets of £87,000,000 and over 35,000 employees, the turnover of work was £203,000,000 in 28 countries in 1969.

Building societies The largest building society in the world is the Halifax Building Society of Halifax, Yorkshire. It was established in 1853 and had total assets of £1,687,142,000 at 31 Jan. 1970. It had 4,000 employees and over 200 branches and 820 agencies. The oldest building society in the world is the Chelmsford and Essex Society, established in July 1845.

An automated control room at the Du Pont de Nemours plant at Waynesboro, Virginia, U.S.A.

Chemical company The world's largest chemical company is E. I. du Pont de Nemours & Co., Inc. (established 1802), of Wilmington, Delaware, U.S.A., with sales of $3,632,000,000 (£1,513 million) in 1969. The company had 118,079 employees and total assets of $3,452,800,000 (£1,438 million) at 1 Jan. 1970.

Chocolate factory The world's largest chocolate factory is that built by Hershey Foods Inc. of Hershey, Pennsylvania, U.S.A., in 1905. In 1969 sales were $315,117,453 (£131,298,000) and the payroll was 7,272 employees.

DEPARTMENT STORES

The largest department store chain, in terms of number of stores, is J. C. Penney Company, Inc., founded in Wyoming, U.S.A., in 1902. The company operates 1,656 stores covering a gross area of 68,000,000 square feet. Its turnover was $3,756,091,636 (£1,565 million) in the 53 weeks ending 31 Jan. 1970, the fifteenth consecutive year of record sales.

United Kingdom The largest department store in the United Kingdom is Harrods Ltd. of Knightsbridge, London, S.W.1 named after Henry Charles Harrod, who opened a grocery in Knightsbridge Village in 1849. It has a total selling floor space of 19 acres, employs 5,300 people and has a total of approximately 10,000,000 transactions a year.

Most profitable The department store with the fastest-moving stock in the world is the Marble Arch store of Marks & Spencer Ltd. at 458 Oxford Street, London, S.W.1. The figure of more than £200-worth of goods per square foot of selling space per year is likely to be revised upwards when the new extension is opened in October 1970.

Distilling plant

Distillery The world's largest distilling company is Distillers Corporation-Seagrams Limited of Canada. Its sales in the year ending 31 July 1969 totalled U.S. $1,342,566,000 (£559 million), of which $1,127,114,000 (£469 million) were from sales by Joseph E. Seagram & Sons, Inc. in the United States. The group employs about 10,000 people, including about 7,500 in the United States.

The largest of all Scotch whisky distilleries is Carsebridge at Alloa, Clackmannanshire, Scotland, owned by Scottish Grain Distillers Limited. This distillery is capable of producing more than 12,000,000 proof gallons per annum. The largest establishment for blending and bottling Scotch whisky is owned by John Walker & Sons Limited at Kilmarnock, Ayrshire, with a potential annual output of 120,000,000 bottles. "Johnnie Walker" is the world's largest-selling brand of Scotch whisky. The world's largest-selling brand of gin is Gordon's.

Games manufacturer The largest company manufacturing games is Parker Bros. Inc. of Salem, Massachusetts, U.S.A. The company's top-selling line is the real estate game "Monopoly", acquired in 1935. More than 50,000,000 sets were sold by April 1970. The daily print of "money" is equivalent to 215,000,000 "dollars", thus exceeding the dollar output of the U.S. Treasury. The most protracted "Monopoly" session was one of 754 hours from 28 July to 29 Aug. 1968 by 21 boys at Hattiesburg, Mississippi, U.S.A. The highest sales of a game in one year is 6,499,584 in the case of Parker's "Instant Insanity".

General merchandise The largest general merchandising firm in the world is Sears, Roebuck and Co. (founded 1886) of Chicago, Illinois, U.S.A. The net sales were $8,862,970,649 (£3,693 million) from 190,000 different items in the year ending 31 Jan. 1970, when the corporation had 826 retail stores and 2,131 catalogue, retail and telephone sales offices and independent catalogue merchants, and total assets valued at $7,079,302,702 (£2,950 million).

Grocery stores The largest grocery chain in the world is The Great Atlantic and Pacific Tea Company, Inc., of New York City, N.Y., U.S.A. At 28 Feb. 1970 the company owned 4,575 stores, including more than 3,000 supermarkets. It operates 27 bakeries, two laundries for the uniforms of its 135,000 employees and a printing plant. The total sales, including subsidiary companies, for the 53 weeks ending 28 Feb. 1970 were $5,753 million (£2,397 million).

Hotelier Hilton form the largest luxury hotel group in the world. Hilton Hotels Corporation operates 39 hotels, with 30,809 rooms, in the continental U.S.A.; Hilton International Co. operates 51 hotels in 33 countries (48 cities), with 16,589 rooms. In 1969, Hilton Hotels Corporation had an operating revenue of more than $210,000,000 (£87·5 million) and 20,000 employees. Hilton International Co. had an operating revenue of $190,785,400 and 20,000 employees. The original corporation was founded by Conrad Nicholson Hilton (born 25 Dec. 1887) who started in 1919 with the Mobley Hotel in Cisco, Texas. Hilton International Co.

began operations in 1949 as a subsidiary of Hilton Hotels Corporation and was spun off from the corporation as a separate company to operate independently in December, 1964. In May, 1967, Hilton International Co. became a wholly-owned subsidiary of Trans World Airlines Inc.

INSURANCE COMPANIES

The company with the highest volume of insurance in force in the world is the Metropolitan Life Insurance Company of 1 Madison Avenue, New York City, N.Y., U.S.A. The company had total assets of $26,829,862,274 at 1 Jan. 1970. The life assurance in force amounted to $157,504,054,069 (£65,627 million), which amount is far greater than the United Kingdom's National Debt. It insured 48,200,000 people.

United Kingdom The largest insurance company in the United Kingdom is the Prudential Assurance Co. Ltd. At 1 Jan. 1970 the total funds were £2,163,268,156 and the total amount assured was £8,053,770,232.

Largest life policy The largest life assurance policy ever written was one of $10,800,000 (£4,500,000) reported on 18 March 1969

market was $10·8 million (£4·5 million) on the *Marpessa* though the loss on the *Andrea Doria* in 1956 was £3·93 million (then $11·0 million). The cost of the repairs to the U.S.S. *Guittaro* the nuclear submarine flooded on 15 May 1969 while fitting out at Mare Island, San Francisco, cost $25 million (£10·42 million). The Cunard liner QE2 was insured (builder's value only) on its sea trials in 1969 for £25·5 million ($61·2 million).

Mineral water The world's largest mineral water firm is Source Perrier, near Nîmes, France with an annual production of more than 1,400,000,000 bottles, of which more than 330,000,000 come from the single spring near Nîmes. The net profits for 1969 were 15,453,817·63 francs (£1,302,000). The French drink 36 litres (63·3 pints) of mineral water per person per year.

Motor car manufacturer The largest manufacturing company in the world is General Motors Corporation of Detroit, Michigan, U.S.A. During its peak year of 1969 world-wide sales totalled $24,295,141,357 (now £10,122 million), including 7,159,526 cars and trucks. Its assets at 31 Dec. 1969

The London headquarters of the Prudential Assurance Co.

taken out by Mr. Michael Davis, 34 from Hollywood, California, U.S.A., chairman of NEBA International Inc., a chain of sandwich stands. His annual premium is $92,200 (£38,000).

Marine insurance The greatest insured value of any ship lost has been the $16·5 million (then £5·89 million) on the *Torrey Canyon*. The greatest loss withstood on the London

were valued at $14,820,094,529 (£6,175 million). Its total 1969 payroll was $6,928,279,079 (£2,886 million) to an average of 793,924 employees. The greatest total of dividends ever paid for one year was $1,509,740,939 (£629 million) by General Motors for 1965.

Production in the United Kingdom in 1969 totalled 1,717,073 cars and 465,720 commercial vehicles. The

The business world

COMMERC

largest manufacturer was the British Leyland Motor Corporation, with 830,874 cars and 186,732 commercial vehicles. The company is the United Kingdom's largest exporter with direct exports valued at £322 million in 1969. The Austin-Morris 1100/1300 was the best-selling car with U.K. sales of 132,857 units representing 13·8 per cent. of that market.

Largest plant The largest single automobile plant in the world is the Volkswagenwerk, Wolfsburg, West Germany, with more than 50,000 employees turning out 5,000 cars daily. The surface area of the factory buildings is 281·95 acres and that of the whole plant 1,730 acres with 40·4 miles of rail sidings.

Oil company refineries The world's largest oil company is the Standard Oil Company (New Jersey), with 145,000 employees and assets valued at $17,537,951,000 (£7,307 million) on 1 Jan. 1970. The world's largest refinery is the Pernis Refinery, Netherlands, operated by the Royal Dutch/ Shell Group with a capacity of 24,000,000 long tons. The largest oil refinery in the United Kingdom is the Esso Refinery at Fawley, Hampshire. Opened in 1921 and much expanded in 1951, it has a capacity of 16,500,000 tons per year. The total investment on the 1,300-acre site is more than £120,000,000.

Paper mills The world's largest paper mill is that established in 1936 by the Union Camp Corporation at Savannah, Georgia, U.S.A., with an output of 903,124 short tons (806,361 long tons). The largest paper mill in the United Kingdom is the Bowater Paper Corporation Ltd.'s Kemsley Mill with an output of 4,600 tons of newsprint and 1,700 tons of fluting medium per week.

Public relations The world's largest public relations firm is Hill and Knowlton, Inc. of 150 East 42nd Street, New York City, N.Y., U.S.A. The firm employs a full-time staff of more than 325 and also maintains offices of wholly-owned subsidiary companies in Brussels, Frankfurt, Geneva, London, Paris, Madrid, Milan, Rome and Tōkyō.

Publishing The world's largest mass media enterprise is the International Publishing Corporation Ltd. of London, with 14 newspapers and 200 periodicals, 29,000 employees and a turnover of £150,000,000 in 1969/70.

Restaurateurs The largest restaurateurs in the United Kingdom ar J. Lyons & Co. Ltd. (incorporated in 1894). Th company has a total of 160 teashops, five Corne Houses, and special restaurants and staff canteens, i which about 280,000,000 meals are served every yea Some of the 35,000 staff produce 40 miles of Swiss ro every day, 12,500,000 pieces of chocolate and suga confectionery every week, 10,000,000 cakes weekly an 30,000,000 portions of ice cream in a peak summer week

BANQUET
Greatest World The greatest banquet ever staged was that by Presiden Loubet, President of France, in the gardens of th Tuileries, Paris, on 22 Sept. 1900. He invited every on of the 22,000 mayors in France and their deputies. Wit the Gallic *penchant* for round numbers, the event ha always been referred to as "le banquet des 100,00 maires".

Great Britain Britain's largest banquet was one catered for by J Lyons & Co. Ltd., at Olympia, London, on 8 Aug. 1925 A total of 8,000 guests were seated at 5 miles of tables served by 1,360 waitresses, supported by 700 cooks an porters. The occasion was a War Memorial fund raising effort by Freemasons. Of the 86,000 glasses an plates used, 3,500 were broken. The world's larges tea party was one for 25,000 on the Gaslight Cok Company's annual sports day at East Ham, Greate London, in 1939, with Lyons again catering.

Shipbuilding In 1969 there were 2,819 ships of more than 100 gros tons, excluding sailing ships and barges, launche throughout the world, excluding the U.S.S.R. an China (mainland). Their total volume was 19,315,29 gross tons, a peacetime record. Japan with 1,072 vessel launched 9,303,453 gross tons (48·2 per cent. of th world total), the greatest tonnage launched in peace time by any single country.

The world's leading shipbuilding firm in 1969 was th Ishi Kawajima Harima Co. of Japan, which launche 59 ships of 1,861,453 gross tons.

Physically the largest shipyard in the United Kingdom is Harland and Wolff Ltd. of Belfast, County Antrim which covers some 250 acres. The largest shipyard i tonnage building is the Swan Hunter Group with 2,071,563 tons in May 1970.

Part of the world's largest restaurant in Peking, China.
It has a capacity of 5,000

ping line The largest shipping group in the world is that owned by the Peninsular and Oriental Steam Navigation Company, London. The company had total net assets of £270,387,000 at 30 Sept. 1969. The company was founded in 1837 by Willcox and Anderson, and among the principal members of the group are 26 shipping and shipowning companies, three transport and forwarding companies and two marine engineering companies. The group's fleet comprises 253 ships, including 198 cargo ships, 24 passenger ships and 6 ferries of 1,640,462 gross tons, 17 tankers and 8 bulk carriers of 1,180,193 deadweight tons.

hoe shop The largest shoe shop in the world is that of Lilley & Skinner, Ltd. at 356/360 Oxford Street, London, W.1. The shop has a floor area of 76,000 square feet, spread over four floors. With a total staff of more than 350 people it offers, in ten departments, a choice of 250,000 pairs of shoes. Every week, on average, over 45,000 people visit this store.

LARGEST SHOPPING CENTRE
The world's largest shopping centre is the Yorkdale Shopping Centre, six miles from the centre of Toronto, Canada. It was built on a 72-acre site with an additional 50 acres for a 6,750 car parking lot. A total of 125 stores and services provide 1,340,000 square feet (30·7 acres) of selling space for 25,000,000 customers per year. It was opened in February 1964 and the enclosed 1,000-foot-long mall is maintained at a temperature of 72° F.

gest shop The world's largest store is R. H. Macy & Co. Inc. at Broadway and 34th Street, New York City, N.Y., U.S.A. It has a floor space of 46·2 acres, and 11,000 employees who handle 400,000 items. Macy's have an average of 150,000 customers a day who make 4,500,000 transactions a year. The sales of the company and its subsidiaries reached a record $758,610,000 (£316,087,000) in 1967. Mr. Rowland Hussey Macy's sales on his first day at his fancy goods store on 6th Avenue, on 27 Oct. 1858, were recorded as $11·06 (now £4 12s. 2d.).

ft drinks The world's top-selling soft drink is Coca-Cola with over 100,000,000 bottles per day in mid-1970 in 135 countries. "Coke" was invented by Dr. John S. Pemberton of Atlanta, Georgia in 1886 and the company was formed in 1892. The fastest bottling line is the plant at Inagi, Tōkyō, Japan, which can fill, crown and pack bottles of Coca-Cola at the rate of 72,000 per hour.

Largest ermarket U.K. The largest supermarket building in the United Kingdom is the Woolco One-Stop Shopping Centre opened in Bournemouth, Hampshire on 29 Oct. 1968. Currently it has an area of 114,000 square feet and parking space for 1,250 cars.

STEEL COMPANY
The world's largest steel company is the United States Steel Company, with sales of $4,825,137,559 (£2,010 million) in 1969. The company had an average of 204,723 employees in 1969, and net assets valued at $5,228,639,713 (£2,179 million) at 31 Dec. 1969.

The Woolco One-Stop Shopping Centre

The largest steelworks in the world —Bethlehem Steel Corporation at Sparrows Point, Maryland, U.S.A.

Largest steelworks The largest steelworks in the world is the Bethlehem Steel Corporation's plant at Sparrows Point, Maryland, U.S.A. with an annual ingot steel capacity of more than 9,000,000 short tons or 8,030,000 long tons.

United Kingdom The largest single British plant is the Margam-Abbey works at Port Talbot, Glamorganshire, of the Steel Company of Wales Division, South Wales Group, British Steel Corporation, which stretch over a distance of 4½ miles, with an area of 2,600 acres. The total number employed at this plant is 16,000 and its capacity is 3,250,000 tons.

Following nationalization in 1967 the British Steel Corporation owns and operates 13 large iron and steel companies and 38 major steel works, which produced some 23,600,000 tons of crude steel in 1968. The Corporation employs 254,000 people and in 1969 reported a profit of £10,421,000 on a turnover of £1,195 million and a capital employed of £1,126,163,000.

Tobacco company The world's largest tobacco company is the British-American Tobacco Company Ltd, (founded 1902), of London. The group's assets were £862,170,000 at 30 Sept. 1969. The 1969 sales were £1,419,670,000. The group has more than 140 factories and nearly 100,000 employees.

Toy manufacturer The world's largest toy manufacturer is Mattel Inc. of Hawthorn, Los Angeles, U.S.A. founded in 1935. Its total sales in 1969 were $240,000,000.

Toy shop World The world's biggest toy store is F.A.O. Schwarz, 745 Fifth Avenue at 58th Street, New York City, N.Y., U.S.A. with 50,000 square feet on three floors. Schwarz have 10 branch stores with a further 100,000 square feet.

United Kingdom Britain's biggest toy shop is that of Hamley Brothers, Ltd., founded in 1760 in Holborn and removed to Regent Street, London, W.1, in 1901. It has selling space of 20,000 square feet on 8 floors and up to 250 employees during the Christmas season.

Fisheries The highest recorded catch of fish was 59,540,000 tons in 1967. The highest proportion of the world catch was that of Peru, with 16·69 per cent. (9,940,000 tons, mostly anchoveta). The United Kingdom's highest figure was 1,187,000 tons in 1948. The world's largest fishmongers are MacFisheries, a subsidiary of Unilever Ltd., with 360 retail outlets as at April 1970.

Landowners The world's largest landowner is the United States Government, with a holding of 765,291,000 acres (1,185,787 square miles), including 529,000 acres outside the U.S. at 30 June 1966. The total cost was $69,357,000,000 (£28,856 million). The United Kingdom's greatest ever private landowner was the 3rd

Duke of Sutherland, George Granville Sutherland-Leveson-Gower, K.G. (1828–92), who owned 1,358,000 acres in 1883. Currently the largest landowner in Great Britain is the Forestry Commission (instituted 1919) with more than 2,890,000 acres. The longest tenure is that by St. Paul's Cathedral of land at Tillingham, Essex, given by King Ethelbert before A.D. 616. Currently the landowner with the largest acreage is the 8th Duke of Buccleuch (born 1894) with 336,000 acres.

LAND VALUES

Highest Currently the most expensive land in the world is that in the City of London. Prime freehold attained £300 per square foot in mid-1969. The 600-foot National Westminster Bank on a 2¼-acre site off Bishopsgate will become the world's highest valued building. At rents of £10 per square foot on 500,000 net square feet and on 18 years purchase, it will, by 1972, be worth £90 million. The value of the whole site of 6½ acres will be £225,000,000. On 1 Feb. 1926 a parcel of land of 1,275 square feet was bought by the One Wall Street Realty Corporation for $1,000 (then £206) per square foot. In February 1964 a woman paid $510 (£212 10s.) for a triangular piece of land measuring 3 inches by 6½ inches by 5¾ inches at a tax lien auction in North Hollywood, California, U.S.A.—equivalent to $365,182,470 (£152·1 million) per acre. The real estate value per square metre of the four topmost French vineyards has not been recently estimated.

Lowest The historic example of low land values is the Alaska Purchase of 30 March 1867, when William Henry Seward (1801–72), the United States Secretary of State, agreed that the U.S. should buy the whole territory from the Russian Government of Czar Alexander II for $7,200,000 (now £3,000,000), equivalent to 1·9 cents per acre. When Peter Minuit (c. 1580–1638) bought Manhattan Island, New York, on 6 May 1626, by paying the Brooklyn Indians (Canarsees) with trinkets and cloth valued at 60 guilders (equivalent to $39 or £16 5s.), he was buying land now worth up to $425 (£177) per square foot for 0·2 of a cent per acre—a capital appreciation of 9,000 million-fold.

Greatest auction The greatest ever auction was that at Anchorage, Alaska on 11 Sept. 1969 for 179 tracts totalling 450,858 acres of the oil-bearing North Slope, Alaska. An all-time record bid of $72,277,133 for a 2,560 acre lease was made by the Amerada Hess Corporation–Getty Oil consortium. This £30,115,472 bid indicated a price of $28,233 (£11,763) per acre. The range of movement of the bidder's eyelash is not recorded.

Highest rent The highest recorded rental is one of 160 shillings per square foot for parts of Woolgate House, near the Guildhall, City of London, in March 1969.

Companies The number of companies on the register in Great Britain at 1 Jan. 1969 was 553,282 of which 16,657 were public and the balance private companies.

Most directorships The world record for directorships was set in September 1959 by Harry O. Jasper, a London real estate financier, with 451. If he had attended all their Annual General Meetings this would have involved him, in normal office hours, in an A.G.M. every 4 hours 33 minutes.

STOCK EXCHANGES

The oldest Stock Exchange in the world is that at Amsterdam, in the Netherlands, founded in 1602. There were 121 throughout the world as of 1 May 1969.

Most markings The highest number of markings received in one day on the London Stock Exchange is 32,655 after the 1959 General Election on 14 Oct. 1959. The record for a year is 4,396,175 "marks" in the year ending 31 March 1960. There were 9,356 securities (gilt-edged 1,228, company 8,128) quoted on 31 March 1969. Their total nominal value was £46,528 million (gilt-edged £25,805 million, company £20,723 million) and their market value was £131,679 million (gilt-edged £18,459 million, company £113,220 million).

The greatest overall daily movement occurred on 24 Feb. 1955, when the market value of United Kingdom Ordinary shares fell by about £200,000,000 or 3·8 per cent.

The highest figure of *The Financial Times* Industrial Ordinary share index (1 July 1935=100) was 521·9 on 19 Sept. 1968. The lowest figure was 49·4 in 1940.

Highest and lowest par values The highest denomination of any share quoted on the London Stock Exchange is £100 for preference shares in Baring Brothers & Co. Ltd., the bankers. The lowest unit of quotation is one penny, in the case of the stock of City of San Paulo Improvements and Freehold Land Co. Ltd. and the capital shares in the Acorn Securities Co., Ltd.

U.S. records The highest index figure on the Dow Jones average (instituted 8 Oct. 1896) of selected industrial stocks at the close of a day's trading was 995·15 on 9 Feb. 1966, when the average of the daily "highs" of the 30 component stocks was 1,001·11. The record trading volume in a day on the New York Stock Exchange of 16,410,030 shares on 29 Oct. 1929, the "Black Tuesday" of the famous "crash" was surpassed when the first 20 million share day (20,410,000) was achieved on 10 April 1968 when the ticker tape fell an unprecedented 47 minutes behind. The trading figure for 13 June 1968 was 21,350,000. The Dow Jones industrial average, which had reached 381·17 on 3 Sept. 1929, plunged 48·31 points in the day, on its way to the Depression's lowest point of 41·22 on 8 July 1932. The total lost in security values was $125,000 million (now £52,083 million). World trade slumped 57 per cent. from 1929 to 1936. The greatest paper loss in a year was $55,925 million (£23,302 million) in 1957. The record daily increase of 28·40 points on 30 Oct. 1929 was beaten on 26 Nov. 1963, when the index increased 32·03 points from 711·49 to 743·52, after three days during which trading had been suspended. The largest deal on record was for a block of 1,153,700 Alcan Aluminium Ltd. shares at $23 per share totalling $26,535,100 (£11,056,291) on the New York Stock Exchange on 31 Oct. 1967.

Largest issue The largest security offering in history was one of $1,200,000,000 (then £428·57 million) in American Telephone and Telegraph Company stock in 1964.

Greatest appreciation It is almost impossible to state categorically which shares have enjoyed the greatest appreciation in value. Spectacular "growth stocks" include the International Business Machines Corporation (IBM), in which 100 shares, costing $5,250 (now £2,187) in July 1932, grew to 13,472 shares with a market value of $4,230,000 (£1,762,500) on 28 March 1969. In addition $233,100 were paid in dividends. The greatest aggregate market value of any corporation is $35·5 billion, assuming a closing price of $314 multiplied by the 113,116,613 shares extant on 28 March 1969. In the United Kingdom an investment of £100 in Drage's Ltd. in 1951 would have been realizable at £108,000 in 1962. The same amount invested in 1947 in the late Mr. Jack Cotton's Mansion House Chambers Co. would have been worth £200,000 in City Centre Properties stock by 1964.

Largest investment house The largest investment company in the world, and also once the world's largest partnership (124 partners, but now 1,082 stockholders), is Merrill Lynch, Pierce, Fenner & Smith, Inc. (founded 6 Jan. 1914) of 70 Pine Street, New York City, N.Y., U.S.A. It has 16,000 employees, 176 offices and 1,090,000 separate accounts, for whom $18,000 million (£5,416 million) in securities is held. The firm is referred to in United States stock exchange circles as "We" or "We, the people" or "The Thundering Herd". The company's assets totalled $2,216,636,670 at 27 Dec. 1968.

est bank The International Bank for Reconstruction and Development (founded 27 Dec. 1945), the United Nations "World Bank" at 1818 H Street N.W., Washington 25, D.C., U.S.A., has an authorized share capital of $24,000 million (£10,000 million). There were 110 members with a subscribed capital of $23,036,400,000 (£9,598 million) at 30 June 1969. The International Monetary Fund in Washington, D.C., U.S.A. has 111 members with total quotas of $21,230,900,000 (£8,846 million) at 30 April 1969. The private bank with the greatest deposits is the Bank of America National Trust and Savings Association, of San Francisco, California, U.S.A., with $22,171,463,000 at 31 Dec. 1969. The largest bank in the United Kingdom is the National Westminster with total assets of £4,103,182,000—a figure second only to the Electricity Council—and 3,600 branches as at 1 Jan. 1970.

gest bank building The largest bank building in the world is the 813-foot-tall Chase Manhattan Building, completed in May 1961 in New York City, N.Y., U.S.A. It has 64 storeys and contains the largest bank vault in the world, measuring 350 feet × 100 feet × 8 feet and weighing 879 tons. Its six doors weigh up to 40 tons apiece but each can be closed by the pressure of a forefinger.

MANUFACTURED ARTICLES
Guinness Superlatives Ltd. has published fine art books in colour on English and Irish Glass; Pottery and Porcelain; Antique Firearms; Edged Weapons and Uniforms, obtainable on order from the publishers or from any good bookshop.

Antique Largest The largest antique ever sold has been London Bridge in March 1968. The sale was made by Mr. Ivan F. Luckin of the Court of Common Council of the Corporation of London to the McCulloch Corporation of Los Angeles, California, U.S.A. for $2,460,000 (£1,029,000). The 10,000 tons of elevational stonework is being re-assembled at Lake Havasu City, Arizona for opening in May 1971.

Armour The highest price paid for a suit of armour is £25,000 for the Pembroke suit of British armour in 1924.

argest bed In Bruges, Belgium, Philip, Duke of Burgundy had a bed 12½ feet wide and 19 feet long erected for the perfunctory *coucher officiel* ceremony with Princess Isabella of Portugal in 1430. The largest bed in Great Britain is the Great Bed of Ware, dating from *c.* 1580, from the Crown Inn, Ware, Hertfordshire, now preserved in the Victoria and Albert Museum, London. It is 10 feet 8½ inches wide, 11 feet 1 inch long and 8 feet 9 inches tall. The largest standard bed currently marketed in the United Kingdom is the London Bedding Centre's "King Size" bed, 7 feet wide by 7 feet long, with 1,600 springs, sold for £170.

CARPETS AND RUGS
Earliest The earliest carpet known is a white bordered black hair pelt from Pazyryk, U.S.S.R. dated to the 5th century B.C. now preserved in Leningrad. The earliest known in Britain were some depicted at the court of Edward IV *c.* 1480.

Largest Of ancient carpets the largest on record was the gold-enriched silk carpet of Hashim (dated A.D. 743) of the Abbasid caliphate in Baghdad, Iraq. It is reputed to have measured 180 feet by 300 feet.

The world's largest carpet now consists of 88,000 square feet (over two acres) of maroon carpeting in the Coliseum exhibition hall, Columbus Circle, New York City, N.Y., U.S.A. This was first used for the International Automobile Show on 28 April 1956.

Most expensive The most magnificent carpet ever made was the Spring carpet of Khusraw made for the audience hall of the Sassanian palace at Ctesiphon, Iraq. It was about 7,000 square feet of silk, gold thread and encrusted with emeralds. It was cut up as booty by a Persian army in A.D. 635 and from the known realization value of the pieces must have had an original value of some £80,000,000.

It was reported in March 1968 that a 16th century Persian silk hunting carpet was sold "recently" to an undisclosed U.S. museum by a member of the Rothschild family for "about $600,000" (£205,000).

Most finely woven The most finely woven carpet known is one with more than 2,490 knots per square inch from a fragment of an Imperial Mughal prayer carpet of the 17th century now in the Altman collections in the Metropolitan Museum of Art, New York City.

CIGARS
Largest The largest cigar ever made is one 170 centimetres (5 feet 7 inches) long and 67 centimetres (26⅜ inches) in circumference, put into the Bünde Tobacco and Cigar Museum, Germany, in 1936. It would theoretically take an estimated 600 hours to smoke. The largest standard cigar in the world is the 9¾-inch-long "Partagas Visible Immensas". The Partagas factory in Havana, Cuba, manufactures special gift cigars 50 centimetres (19.7 inches) long, which retail in Europe for more than £5 each.

Most expensive The world's most expensive regular cigar has been the "Partagas Visible Immensas". This used to be retailed in the United States for $7·50 (62s. 6d.). The most expensive cigars imported into Britain, where the duty is 109s. 8½d. per lb., are the Montecristo 'A', which normally retail for 27s. 0d. each. The peak of cigar smoking was attained in the period 1920–23 with 8,000 million per annum in the United States.

CIGARETTES
Consumption The heaviest smokers in the world are the people of the United States, where about 520,000 million cigarettes (an average of nearly 4,000 per adult) were consumed at a cost of nearly $10,000 million (£4,166 million) in 1969. The peak consumption in the United Kingdom was 2,960 cigarettes per adult in 1969. The peak volume was 243,100,000 lb. in 1961, compared with about 216,000,000 lb. in 1969, when 125,000 million cigarettes were sold.

In the United Kingdom 68·6 per cent. of adult men and 43·2 per cent. of adult women smoke. Nicotine releases acetylcholine in the brain, so reducing tension and increasing resolve. It has thus been described as an anodyne to civilization.

Most expensive The most expensive cigarettes in the world are the gold-tipped "Royal Dragoons", made by Simon Arzt of Cairo, in the United Arab Republic (formerly Egypt). They have been retailed in the United Kingdom for more than a shilling each.

Most popular The world's most popular cigarette is "Winston", a filter cigarette made by the R. J. Reynolds Tobacco Co., which sold 82,000 million of them in 1969. The largest selling British cigarette is W.D. & H.O. Wills' "Embassy Filter", which was introduced in the medium size class

155

in August 1962, with coupons. They are estimated to have attained nearly 24 per cent. of the market in 1968.

Longest and shortest The longest cigarettes ever marketed were "Head Plays", each 11 inches long and sold in packets of five in the United States in about 1930, to save tax. The shortest were "Lilliput" cigarettes, each 1¼ inches long, made in Great Britain in 1956.

Largest collection The world's largest collection of cigarettes is that of Robert E. Kaufman, M.D., of 950 Park Avenue, New York City 28, N.Y., U.S.A. In May 1970 he had 6,300 different kinds of cigarettes from 158 countries. The oldest brand represented is "Lone Jack", made in the U.S.A. in c. 1885. Both the longest and shortest (see above) are represented.

Cigarette packets The world's largest collection of cigarette packets is that of Niels Ventegodt of Copenhagen, Denmark. He had 42,590 different packets from 194 countries by April 1970. The countries supplying the largest numbers were the United Kingdom (5,692) and the United States (3,592). The earliest is the Finnish "Petit Canon" packet for 25, made by Tollander & Klärich in 1860. The rarest is the Latvian 700-year-anniversary (1201–1901) Riga packet, believed to be unique.

Cigarette cards The earliest known and most valuable cigarette card is that bearing the portrait of the Marquess of Lorne published in the United States c. 1879. The only known specimen is in the Metropolitan Museum of Art, New York City. The earliest British example appeared in 1883 in the form of a calendar issued by Allen & Ginter, of Richmond, Virginia, trading from Holborn Viaduct, London. The largest known collection is that of Mr. Edward Wharton-Tigar (b. 1913) of London with a collection of more than 500,000 cigarette and trade cards in about 25,000 sets.

Earliest abstention The earliest recorded case of a man giving up smoking was on 5 April 1679 when Johan Kastu, Sheriff of Turku, Finland wrote in his diary "I quit smoking tobacco". He died one month later.

Finest cloth The finest of all cloths is Shahtoosh (or Shatusa), a brown-grey wool from the throats of Indian goats. It is sold by Neiman-Marcus of Dallas, Texas, U.S.A., at $18·50 (£7 14s. 2d.) per square foot and is both more expensive and finer than Vicuña. A simple hostess gown in Shahtoosh costs up to $5,000 (£2,083).

Largest curtain The world's largest curtain is that covering Jan Styka's painting *The Crucifixion* at Forest Lawn Memorial Park, Glendale, California, U.S.A. It is made of velvet, measures 195 feet wide and 45 feet long and weighs 3,500 lb. (1·56 tons).

The Star of the Order of St. Catherine

The world's most expensive hat

Decoration The highest recorded price at auction for a single decoration is the £2,600 bid at Sotheby's on 15 Oct. 1969 for a breast star of the Order of St. Catherine the Martyr of Russia. The order was founded by Peter the Great on 24 Nov. 1714 and was awarded only to the élite of Russia's aristocracy.

Dinner service The highest price ever paid for a silver dinner service is £207,000 for the Berkeley Louis XV Service of 168 pieces, made by Jacques Roettiers between 1736 and 1738, sold at the salerooms of Sotheby & Co., London, in June 1960.

The most expensive fabric obtainable is an evening wear fabric sequinned with a peacock feather, designed by Mr. Alan Hershman of London costing £105 per yard (36 inches in width) with 194,400 sequins per yard.

Largest firework The most powerful firework obtainable is the Bouquet of Chrysanthemums *hanabi,* marketed by the Marutamaya Ogatsu Fireworks Co. Ltd., of Tōkyō, Japan. It is fired to a height of over 3,000 feet from a 36-inch calibre mortar. Their chrysanthemum and peony flower shells produce a spherical flower with "twice-thrice changing colours", 2,000 feet in diameter.

FLAGS

Oldest The oldest national flag in the world is that of Denmark (a large white cross on a red field), known as the Dannebrog ("Danish Cloth"), dating from 1219, adopted after the Battle of Lindanissa in Estonia, now part of the U.S.S.R. The crest in the centre of the Austrian flag has its origins in the 11th century. The origins of the Iranian flag, with its sword-carrying lion and sun, are obscure but "go beyond the 12th century".

Largest The largest flag in the world is the "Stars and Stripes" displayed annually on the Woodward Avenue side of J. L. Hudson Company's store in Detroit, Michigan, U.S.A. The flag, 104 feet by 235 feet and weighing 1,500 lb., was unfurled on 14 June 1949. The 50 stars are each 5½ feet high and each stripe is 8 feet deep. The largest Union Flag (or Union Jack) was one of 11,720 square feet (144 by 80 feet) used at a military tattoo in the Olympic Stadium, West Berlin in September 1967. The largest flag *flown* from a public building in Britain is a Union Flag measuring 36 feet by 18 feet, flown on occasions from the Victoria Tower of the Palace of Westminster, London.

Float The largest float used in any street carnival is the 200-foot-long dragon *Sun Loon* used in Bendigo, Victoria, Australia. It has 65,000 mirror scales. Six men are needed to carry its head alone.

FURNITURE

Most expensive The highest price ever paid for a single piece of furniture is £63,000 for a Louis XVI marquetry commode by David Rontgen (1743–1807) of Germany, owned by the 6th Earl of Rosebery and sold to a bidder from New York City, N.Y., U.S.A., at the salerooms of Sotheby & Co., London, on 17 April 1964.

Oldest British The oldest surviving piece of British furniture is a three-footed tub with metal bands found at Glastonbury, Somerset, and dating from between 300 and 150 B.C.

Gold The world's highest auction price for a single piece of gold plate is £40,000 for a 20 oz. 4 dwt. George II teapot made by James Ker for the King's Plate horserace for 100 guineas at Leith, Scotland in 1736. The sale was by Christie's of London on 13 Dec. 1967 to a dealer from Boston, Massachusetts, U.S.A.

Hat Most expensive The highest price ever paid for a hat is 165,570 francs (inc. tax) (£14,032) at an auction by Maîtres Liery, Rheims et Laurin on 23 April 1970 for one last worn by Emperor Napoleon I (1769–1821) on 1 Jan. 1815.

Ice cream sundae The most gigantic ice cream sundae made was one comprising 600 lb. of ice cream dripping with 34 quarts of chocolate sauce topped out with 153 ounces of chopped nut valued at $720 (£300). It was produced for a Los Angeles TV Show by Baskin-Robbins Inc., who market a world record 401 flavours.

Jade The highest price paid for jade has been £42,000 for Chinese spinach green screen emblematic of the Four Seasons sold by auction at Christie's, London on 16 July 1963.

Largest jig-saw The largest jig-saw ever made is believed to be one of 10,400 pieces, measuring 15 feet by 10 feet, made in 1954, at the special request of a man in Texas, U.S.A.,

The world's most expensive pistol—a ball butt specimen sold for £5,800

The world's most expensive paperweight sold for £8,500

The world's most expensive ever piece of porcelain

The most bladed knife —1,970 blades

The world's most expensive shoes at £36 5s. 0d. each

The world's longest pipe, a 15-foot specimen preserved in Germany

by Ponda Puzzle Products, Ltd., of St. Leonard's-on-Sea, Sussex.

Longest loaf The longest loaf ever baked was one of 66 feet 1 inch, weighing 84 lb. 5 oz., baked by J. T. Gould of Ohakune, New Zealand, on 27 Sept. 1968.

Matchbox labels The oldest match label is that of John Walker, Stockton-on-Tees, County Durham, England in 1827. Collectors of labels are philliumenists, of bookmatch covers philliberumenists and of matchboxes cumyxaphists. The world's longest and perhaps dullest set is one in the U.S.S.R. comprising 600 variations on interior views of the Moscow Metro.

Longest menu The restaurant with the world's longest menu is Oskar Davidsen's in Copenhagen, Denmark. The menu, which lists 177 dishes, is 3 feet 9½ inches long.

Sheerest nylon The lowest denier nylon yarn ever produced is the 6-denier used for stockings exhibited at the Nylon Fair in London in February 1956. The sheerest stockings normally available are 9 denier. An indication of the thinness is that a hair from the average human head is about 50 denier.

Paperweight The highest price ever paid for a paperweight is £8,500 at Sotheby & Co., London on 16 March 1970 for a Clichy Lily of the Valley weight.

Penknife most blades The penknife with the greatest number of blades is the Year Knife made by the world's oldest firm of cutlers, Joseph Rodgers & Sons Ltd., of Sheffield, England, whose trade mark was granted in 1682. The knife was built in 1822 with 1,822 blades but now has 1,970 to match the year of the Christian era until A.D. 2000 beyond which there will be no further space.

Pipe Most expensive The most expensive smoker's pipe is the "H" standard, top quality straight grained briar pipe retailed by Alfred Dunhill Ltd. of Duke Street, London, S.W.1 at £250.

Longest pipe In the Braunschweig Museum, Germany, there is exhibited an outsize late 19th century pipe, 15 feet in length, the bowl of which can accommodate 3 lb. of tobacco.

Most expensive pistols The highest price ever paid for a pair of pistols is £7,140 for French flintlock pistols with engraved silver mounts, at Christie's on 17 Dec. 1968. They were bought by Mr. Roy Cole (Canada). They date from c. 1800 with lock plates signed by Boutet et fils à Versailles and silver marks probably attributable to Nicholas Boutet. A single wheel-lock ball-butt pistol from the Royal Saxon collection dating from c. 1585 fetched £5,800 at Sotheby's on 23 March 1970. The stock is probably the work of Klaus Hirt of Wasungen.

Porcelain The highest price ever paid for a single piece of porcelain is £46,000 at auction at the salerooms of Sotheby & Co., London on 24 Feb. 1970 for a Chinese *Ju-Yao* (pronounced Rew-Yow) Narcissus bowl of the Northern Sung dynasty of the 11th century. The piece measures 8¾ inches by 2½ inches and is one of only 50 pieces of this type of porcelain known. The highest price for Chinese blue and white is £25,200, for an early 15th century Ming flask auctioned at Christie's of London on 28 Nov. 1966.

Largest rope The largest rope ever made was a coir fibre launching rope with a circumference of 47 inches, made in 1858 for the British liner *Great Eastern* by John and Edwin Wright of Birmingham. It consisted of four strands, each of 3,780 yarns.

Most expensive shoes The most expensive standard shoes obtainable are the shawl-tongued custom golf shoe, Style 5591, made by Brockton Footwear Inc. of Massachusetts, U.S.A., which retail for $174 (£72 10s.) per pair.

Silver The highest price ever paid for a single piece of silver is £45,000 for a Louis XV soup tureen, cover and stand, part of the Service de Paris made for Empress Elizabeth

157

The business world

of Russia in 1758. It was bought on 30 June 1965 at the salerooms of Christie, Manson & Woods Ltd., London.

The highest price for English Silver is £56,000 paid by the London dealer Wartski for the Brownlow James II Tankards at Christie's, London, on 20 Nov. 1968. This pair made in 1686 was in mint condition and weighed nearly 7½ lb. It has been calculated that they appreciated at the rate of 15s. per hour since they were sold by Lord Astor for £17,000 in 1963.

Most expensive snuff The most expensive snuff obtainable in Britain is Fribourg and Treyer's violet scented "Santo Domingo". It sells at 17s. 8d. per oz.

Snuff box The record price for a snuff box is £23,000 for a Louis Quinze box made by Daniel Govaers in 1726 containing miniatures of the king and his queen, realized at Sotheby's, London on 25 Nov. 1968.

Apostle spoons The highest price ever paid for a set of 13 apostle spoons is $30,000 (£10,700), paid by the Clark Institute of Williamstown, Massachusetts, U.S.A. There are only six other complete sets known.

The world's most expensive sword, a 1606 specimen from Saxony bought for £21,000

Sword The highest price recorded for a sword is £21,000 paid at Sotheby's on 23 March 1970 for a swept hilt rapier 48½ inches long made by Israel Schuech in 1606 probably for Elector Christian II or Duke Johann Georg of Saxony. The hilt is inset with pearls and semi-precious stones. It should be noted that prices as high as £60,000 have been rumoured in Japan for important swords by master Japanese swordsmiths.

TAPESTRY

Earliest The earliest known examples of tapestry weaved linen are three pieces from the tomb of Thutmose IV, the Egyptian pharaoh and dated to 1483 to 1411 B.C.

Largest The largest single piece of tapestry ever woven is "Christ in Glory", measuring 74 feet 8 inches by 38 feet, designed by Graham Vivian Sutherland O.M. (born 24 Aug. 1903) for an altar hanging in Coventry Cathedral, Warwickshire. It cost £10,500 and was delivered from Pinton Frères of Felletin, France, on 1 March 1962.

Longest The longest of all ancient tapestries is Queen Matilda of England's famous Bayeux tapestry of embroidery, a hanging 19½ inches wide by 231 feet in length. It depicts events of the period 1064–66 in 72 scenes and was probably worked in Canterbury, Kent, in c. 1086. It was "lost" from 1476 until 1724.

Most expensive The highest price paid for a set of tapestries is £200,000 for four Louis XV pieces at Sotheby & Co., London on 8 Dec. 1967.

Earliest tartan The earliest evidence of tartan is the so-called Falkirk tartan, found stuffed in a jar of coins in Bells Meadow, north of Callendar Park, Scotland. It is of a dark and light brown pattern and dates from c. A.D. 245. The earliest reference to a specific named tartan has been to a Murray tartan in 1618.

158

The world's most expensive vase bought for £27,380

The world's most expensive ever single piece of silver— a Louis XV soup tureen bought for £45,000

Vase Most expensive The highest price ever paid for a vase is 23,000,000 yen (£27,380), obtained by Messrs. Sotheby & Co., at a sale held at the department store of Mitsukoshi in Tōkyō, Japan on 2 Oct. 1969. This was for a 16th century Chinese Kinrade double-gourd green and orange vase 39·4 cms. (15½ inches) tall.

Largest wig The largest wig yet made is that made by Jean Leonard, owner of a salon in Copenhagen, Denmark. It is intended for bridal occasions, made from 24 tresses, measures nearly 8 feet in length and costs £416.

Writing paper The most expensive writing paper in the world is that sold by Cartier Inc. on Fifth Avenue, New York City at $1,904 (£793) per 100 sheets with envelopes. It is of hand made paper from Finland with deckle edges and a "personalized" portrait watermark.

2. Agriculture

Origins It has been estimated that only 21 per cent. of the world's land surface is cultivable and that of this only two-fifths of this is cultivated. The earliest attested evidence of cultivated grain is that from Jarmo, Iraq, dated c. 6750 B.C. The earliest evidence of animal husbandry comes from sheep at Zawi Chemi Shanidar, Iraq, dating from c. 8800 B.C. The order in which animals have been domesticated is: dogs and reindeer (mesolithic period, possibly as early as 18000 B.C.); sheep (c. 9000 B.C.); goats (at Jarmo and Jericho, c. 6500 B.C.); pigs (at Jarmo, c. 6500 B.C.) and cattle (at Banahilk, northern Iraq, before 5000 B.C.).

FARMS
The earliest British farming site yet discovered is one at Staines, Greater London, dating from c. 2500 B.C., found in 1961.

The largest farms in the world are collective farms in the U.S.S.R. These have been reduced in number from 235,500 in 1940 to only 36,000 in 1969 and have been increased in size so that units of over 60,000 acres are not uncommon.

The largest farms in the British Isles are Scottish hill farms in the Grampians. The largest arable farm is that of Elveden, Suffolk, farmed by the Earl of Iveagh. Here 11,356 acres are farmed on an estate of 23,000 acres, the greater part of which was formerly derelict land. This farm is the size of 321 average English farms of 71 acres, and the 1969 production included 783,398 gallons of milk, 3,990 tons of grain and 7,196 tons of sugar beet. The livestock includes 3,031 cattle, 1,647 ewes and 3,388 pigs.

Largest wheat field The world's largest single wheat field was probably one of more than 35,000 acres, sown in 1951 near Lethbridge, Alberta, Canada.

Largest hop field The largest hop field in the world is one of 710 acres at Toppenish, Washington State, U.S.A. It is owned by John I. Haas, Inc., the world's largest hop growers, with hop farms in British Columbia (Canada), California, Idaho, Oregon and Washington, with a total net area of 3,065 acres.

Cattle station The world's largest cattle station was Alexandria Station, Northern Territory, Australia, selected in 1873 by Robert Collins, who rode 1,600 miles to reach it. It has 66 wells, a staff of 90 and originally extended over 7,207,608 acres—more than the area of the English counties of Yorkshire, Devon, Norfolk and Cambridgeshire put together. The present area is 6,500 square miles which is stocked with 58,000 shorthorn cattle. Until 1915 the Victoria River Downs Station, Northern Territory, was over three times larger, with an area of 22,400,000 acres (35,000 square miles).

Sheep station The largest sheep station in the world is Commonwealth Hill, in the north-west of South Australia. It grazes between 70,000 and 90,000 sheep in an area of 3,640 square miles (2,329,006 acres) *i.e.* larger than the combined area of Norfolk and Suffolk.

The largest sheep move on record occurred when 27 horsemen moved a mob of 43,000 sheep 40 miles from Barealdine to Beaconsfield Station, Queensland, Australia, in 1886.

Mushroom farm The largest mushroom farm in the world is the Butler County Mushroom Farm, Inc., founded in 1937 in a disused limestone mine near West Winfield, Pennsylvania, U.S.A. It now has 875 employees working underground, in a maze of galleries 110 miles long, producing about 25,000,000 lb. (11,160 tons) of mushrooms per year.

Turkey farm Europe's largest turkey farm is that of Bernard Matthews, Ltd., at Weston Longville, Norfolk, with up to 300 workers tending 160,000 turkeys.

CROP YIELDS

Wheat Crop yields for highly tended small areas are of little significance. The greatest recorded wheat yield is 169·9 bushels (91 cwt.) per acre from 27·7 acres in 1964 by Yoshino Brothers Farms at Quincy, Washington State, U.S.A. The British record is 71·4 cwt. per acre (variety Viking) on a field of 9·453 acres by J. F. Oliver, near Doncaster, Yorkshire in 1962.

Barley A yield of 69¾ cwt. per acre of variety Pallas was reported in 1962 from a field of 20 acres by Colonel K. C. Lee of Blaco Hill Farm, Mattersey, near Doncaster, Yorkshire.

DIMENSIONS AND PROLIFICACY

Cattle Of heavyweight cattle the heaviest on record was a Hereford-Shorthorn named "Old Ben", owned by Mike and John Murphy of Miami, Indiana, U.S.A. When he died at the age of 8, in February 1910, he had attained a length of 16 feet 2 inches from nose to tail, a girth of 13 feet 8 inches, a height of 6 feet 4 inches at the forequarters and a weight of 4,720 lb. (42·1 cwt.). The stuffed and mounted steer is displayed in Highland Park, Kokomo, Indiana, as proof to all who would otherwise have said "there ain't no such animal". The British record is the 4,480 lb. (40 cwt.) of "The Bradwell Ox" owned by William Spurgin of Bradwell, Essex. He was 15 feet from nose to tail and had a girth of 11 feet.

The highest recorded birthweight for a calf is 225 lb. (16 stone 1 lb.) from a British Friesian cow at Rockhouse Farm, Bishopston, Swansea, Glamorganshire, in 1961.

On 25 April 1964 it was reported that a cow named "Lyubik" had given birth to seven calves at Mogilev, U.S.S.R. A case of five live calves at one birth was reported in 1928 by T. G. Yarwood of Manchester, Lancashire. The life-time prolificacy record is 30 in the case of a cross-bred cow owned by G. Page of Warren Farm, Wilmington, Sussex, which died in November 1957, aged 32. A cross-Hereford calved in 1916 and

owned by A. J. Thomas of West Hook Farm, Marloes, Pembrokeshire, Wales, produced her 30th calf in May 1955 and died in May 1956, aged 40.

Pigs The heaviest pig ever recorded in Britain was one of 12 cwt. 66 lb. (1,410 lb.), bred by Joseph Lawton of Astbury, Cheshire. In 1774 it stood 4 feet 8½ inches in height and was 9 feet 8 inches long. The highest recorded weight for a piglet at weaning (8 weeks) is 81 lb. for a boar, one of nine piglets farrowed on 6 July 1962 by the Landrace gilt "Manorport Ballerina 53rd", *alias* "Mary", and sired by a Large White named "Johnny" at Kettle Lane Farm, West Ashton, Trowbridge, Wiltshire.

The highest recorded number of piglets in one litter is 34, thrown on 25–26 June 1961 by a sow owned by Aksel Egedee of Denmark. In February 1955 a Wessex sow owned by Mrs. E. C. Goodwin of Paul's Farm, Leigh, near Tonbridge, Kent, had a litter of 34, of which 30 were born dead. A litter of 31 piglets (26 survived) was thrown in June 1955 by the sow "Liz", owned by Mr. A. Asplin, of Eye, near Peterborough. In September 1934 a Large White sow, owned by Mr. H. S. Pedlingham, died after having farrowed 385 piglets in 22 litters in 10 years 10 months.

Sheep The highest recorded birthweight for a lamb in Britain is 26 lb., in the case of a lamb delivered on 9 Feb. 1967 by Alan F. Baldry from a ewe belonging to J. L. H. Arkwright of Winkleigh, Devonshire. A case of eight lambs at a birth was reported by D. T. Jones of Priory Farm, Monmouthshire, in June 1956, but none lived.

Egg-laying The highest authenticated rate of egg-laying by a hen is 361 eggs in 364 days by a Black Orpington in an official test at Taranki, New Zealand, in 1930. The U.K. record is 353 eggs in 365 days in a National Laying Test at Milford, Surrey in 1957 by a Rhode Island Red owned by W. Lawson of Welham Grange, Retford, Nottinghamshire. In January 1957 a battery pullet owned by Mr. Thomas Whitwell of Goodies Farm, Firbank, Westmorland, laid 16 eggs in six days.

The largest egg reported is one of 16 ounces, with double yolk and double shell, laid by a white Leghorn at Vineland, New Jersey, U.S.A., on 25 Feb. 1956. The largest in the United Kingdom was one of 8¼ ounces, laid by "Daisy", owned by Peter Quarton, aged 8, at Lodge Farm, Kexby Bridge, near York, in March 1964.

"Manningford Faith Jan Graceful" the highest yielding British cow which gave 145·7 tons of milk during her life

MILK YIELDS

Cows The world lifetime record yield of milk is 334,292 lb. (149·2 tons) at 3·4 per cent. butter fat by the U.S. Holstein cow "College Ormsby Burke" which died at Fort Collins, Colorado in August 1966. The greatest yield of any British cow was that given by the British Friesian "Manningford Faith Jan Graceful", owned by R. and H. Jenkinson of Oxfordshire. This cow yielded 326,451 lb. (145·7 tons) before she died in November 1955, aged 17½ years. The greatest recorded yield for one lactation (365 days) is 45,081 lb. (20·13 tons) by R. A. Pierson's British Friesian "Bridge Birch" in England in 1947–48. The British record for milk yield in a day is 198¼ lb. by R. A. Pierson's British Friesian "Garsdon Minnie" in 1948.

Goats The highest recorded milk yield for any goat is 6,661 pints in 365 days by "Malpas Melba", owned by Mr. J. R. Egerton of Bramford, East Anglia, in 1931.

Milking The hand milking record for cows is 14 lb. 6 oz. in two minutes by Bernard Souza at the Cow Palace, San Francisco, California, U.S.A., in October 1964.

BUTTER FAT
The world record lifetime yield is 12,211 lb. by the U.S. Holstein cow "Minnow Creek Eden Delight" at Orange, Virginia, U.S.A. The British record butter fat yield in a lifetime is 12,144 lb. by the Friesian "Lavenham Wallen 87th" (born 30 Nov. 1946, died 17 Oct. 1967), owned by Mr. John Lindley of Nowers Farm, Wellington, Somerset. The world's lactation (365 days) record is 1,866 lb. by the U.S. Holstein-Friesian "Princess Breezewood R.A. Patsy" while the British record is 1,799 lb. (33,184 lb. milk at 5·42 per cent.) by A. Drexler's British Friesian "Zenda Bountiful" at Manor Farm, Kidlington, Oxfordshire, in the year ending 3 March 1953. This is sufficient to produce 2,116 lb. of butter. The United Kingdom record for butter fat in one day is 9·12 lb. (97 lb. milk at 9·40 per cent.) by Mr. and Mrs. K. McDonald's Jersey cow "Barings Flower".

LIVESTOCK PRICES
The highest nominal value ever placed on a bull is $1,050,000 (then £375,000), implicit in the $350,000 (£125,000) paid on 22 Jan. 1967 for a one-third share in the Aberdeen-Angus bull "Newhouse Jewror Eric", aged 7, by the Embassy Angus Farm of Mississippi, U.S.A.

The highest price ever paid for a bull in Britain is 60,000 guineas (£63,000), paid on 5 Feb. 1963 at Perth, Scotland, by James Dick, co-manager of Black Watch Farms, for "Lindertis Evulse", an Aberdeen-Angus owned by Sir Torquil and Lady Munro of Lindertis, Kirriemuir, Angus, Scotland. This bull failed a fertility test in August 1963.

Cow The highest price ever paid for a cow is Can. $62,000 (£23,890) for the Holstein-Friesian "Oak Ridges Royal Linda" by Mr. E. L. Vesley of Lapeer, Michigan, U.S.A. at the Oak Ridges, Canada dispersal sale on 12 Nov. 1968. In Britain in July 1962 Capt. R. S. de Q. Quincey sold his Hereford cow "Vern Logic" privately to Sir Ellerton Becker for £20,000.

Sheep The highest price ever paid for a sheep is $A27,000 (£12,900) for a two-year-old Collinsville ram by the East Bungaree Pty. Ltd. of Mount Bryan, South Australia at the Perth Ram Sales in September 1969.

The British auction record is £5,000, paid by J. and A. Stoddart for a Scottish Blackface ram lamb owned by Ben Wilson, at Lanark in October 1963.

The highest price ever paid for wool is 1,800 Australian pence ($A15 or £6 19s. 7d.) per lb. for a bale from 120 selected sheep of the Hillcrest Merino stud, bought for Illingworth, Morris & Co. of Shipley, Yorkshire, at an auction at Goulbourn, New South Wales, Australia, on 3 Dec. 1964.

Pig The highest price ever paid for a pig is $10,200 (now £4,250), paid in 1953 for a Hampshire boar "Great Western" by a farm at Byron, Illinois, U.S.A. The U.K. record is 3,300 guineas (£3,465), paid by Malvern Farms for the Swedish Landrace gilt "Bluegate Ally 33rd" owned by Davidson Trust in a draft sale at Reading on 2 March 1955.

Horse The highest price ever given for a farm horse is £9,500, paid for the Clydesdale stallion "Baron of Buchlyvie" by William Dunlop at Ayr, Scotland, in December 1911.

Donkey Perhaps the lowest ever price for livestock was at a sale at Kuruman, Cape Province, South Africa in 1934 where donkeys were sold for less than 4d. each.

Turkey The highest price ever paid for a turkey is $990 (then £353) for a 33 lb. stag bird bought at the Arkansas State Turkey Show at Springdale, Arkansas, U.S.A. on 3 Dec. 1955.

SHEEP SHEARING
The highest recorded speed for sheep shearing in a working day was that of John Ferguson who machine-sheared 567 lambs (average 63 per hour) in 9 hours at Taupo, North Island, New Zealand, in 1969. Godfrey Bowen (New Zealand) sheared a Cheviot ewe in 46 seconds at the Royal Highland Show in Scotland in June 1957. The blade (*i.e.* hand-shearing) record in a 9-hour working day is 350, set in 1899. The female record is held by Mrs. Pamela Warren, aged 21, who machine-sheared 337 Romney Marsh ewes and lambs at Puketutu, near Piopio, North Island, New Zealand on 25 Nov. 1964.

CHEESE
The most active cheese-eaters are the people of France, with an annual average in 1966 of 26·62 lb. per person. The world's biggest producer is the United States with a factory production of 836,400 tons in 1966.

Oldest The oldest and most primitive cheeses are the Arabian *kishk*, made of the dried curd of goat's milk. There are today 450 named cheeses of 18 major varieties, but many are merely named after different towns and differ only in shape or the method of packing. France has 240 varieties.

Most expensive The most expensive of all cheeses is the small goat cheese Crottin de Chavignol, from the Berri area of France, which is marketed in Paris, at times, for 30 francs per kilogramme (22s. 6d. per lb.). Britain's most costly cheeses are Blue Cheshire and Windsor Red both at 8s. per lb.

Largest The largest cheese ever made was a cheddar of 34,591 lb. (15·44 tons), made in 43 hours on 20–22 Jan. 1964 by the Wisconsin Cheese Foundation for exhibition at the New York World's Fair, U.S.A. It was transported in a specially designed refrigerated tractor trailer "Cheese-Mobile" 45 feet long.

Longest sausage The longest sausage ever recorded was one 3,124 feet long, made on 29 June 1966 by 30 butchers in Scunthorpe, Lincolnshire. It was made from 6½ cwt. of pork and 1½ cwt. of cereal and seasoning.

Piggery The world's largest piggery is the Mellersta Sveriges Lantbruks Aktiebolaget at Tornby, Sweden, with an annual production of more than 5,000 pigs.

Cow shed The longest cow shed in Britain is that of the Yorkshire Agricultural Society at Harrogate. It is 456 feet in length with a capacity of 686 cows. The National Agricultural Centre, Kenilworth, Warwickshire, completed in 1967, has, however, capacity for 782 animals.

Foot-and-mouth disease The worst outbreak of foot-and-mouth disease in Great Britain was that from Shropshire on 25 Oct. 1967 to 25 June 1968 in which there were 2,364 outbreaks and 429,632 animals slaughtered at a direct and consequential loss of £150,000,000. The outbreak of 1871, when farms were much smaller, affected 42,531 farms. The disease first appeared in Great Britain at Stratford near London in August 1839.

Ploughing The world championship (instituted 1953) has been staged in 15 countries and won by ploughmen of eight nationalities of which the United Kingdom has been most successful with 6 champions. The only man to take the title three times has been Hugh Barr of Northern Ireland in 1954–55–56. The fastest recorded time for ploughing an acre (minimum 32 right-hand turns and depth 9 inches) is 23 minutes 45 seconds by G. W. Mondon using a five-furrow Bamford plough towed by an International 66 h.p. tractor at Darklake, Roborough, Devon on 27 Sept. 1969.

1. Endurance and Endeavour

LUNAR CONQUEST

Neil Alden Armstrong (born Wapakoneta, Ohio, U.S.A. of Scoto-Irish and German ancestry, on 5 Aug. 1930) command pilot of the Apollo XI mission, became the first man to set foot on the moon on the Sea of Tranquillity at 02.56 and 20 seconds G.M.T. on 21 July 1969. He was followed out of the Lunar Module *Eagle* by Col. Edwin Eugene Aldrin, Jr. (born Montclair, New Jersey, U.S.A. of Swedish, Dutch and British ancestry, on 20 Jan. 1930), while the Command Module *Columbia* piloted by Lt.-Col. Michael Collins (born Rome, Italy, of Irish and pre-Revolutionary American ancestry, on 31 Oct. 1930) orbited above.

Eagle landed at 20.17 hrs. 42 secs. G.M.T. on 20 July and lifted off at 17.54 G.M.T. on 21 July, after a stay of 21 hours 36 minutes. The Apollo XI had blasted off from Cape Kennedy, Florida at 13.32 G.M.T. on 16 July and was a culmination of the U.S. space programme, which, at its peak, employed 376,600 people and attained in the year 1966–67 a peak budget of $5,900,000,000 (£2,460 million).

ALTITUDE

Man   The greatest altitude attained by man was when the crew of the ill-fated Apollo XIII were at apocynthion (*i.e.* their furthest point behind the Moon) 158 miles above its surface and 248,665 miles above the Earth's surface at 1.21 a.m. B.S.T. on 15 April 1970. The crew were Capt. James Arthur Lovell, U.S.N.; Frederick W. Haise and John L. Swigert.

Woman   The greatest altitude attained by a woman is 231 kilometres (143·5 miles) by Jnr. Lt. (now Flt. Major) Valentina Vladimirovna Tereshkova (born 6 March 1937) of the U.S.S.R., during her 48-orbit flight in *Vostok VI* on 16 June 1963. (See also Chapter IV.) The record for an aircraft is 24,336 metres (79,842 feet) by N. Prokhanova (U.S.S.R.) in an E-33 jet, on 22 May 1965.

BALLOONS

Highest manned   The greatest altitude reached in a manned balloon is the unofficial 123,800 feet (23·45 miles) by Nicholas Pianstanida (1933–66) of Bricktown, New Jersey, U.S.A., from Sioux Falls, South Dakota, U.S.A., on 1 Feb. 1966. He landed in a cornfield in Iowa. His intention to improve the free falling parachute record was foiled by a fault in the gondola, which prevented his leaving it. The official record is 113,740 feet by Cdr. Malcolm D. Ross, U.S.N.R. and the late Lt.-Cdr. Victor E. Prather, U.S.N. in an ascent from the deck of U.S.S. *Antietam* on 4 May 1961, over the Gulf of Mexico.

Highest unmanned   The greatest altitude attained by an unmanned balloon is 2,647 miles by the 100-foot-diameter U.S. *Pageos I* balloon released from a Thor Agena D rocket from Vandenberg Air Force Base, California on 24 June 1966.

SPEED

Man   The fastest speed at which any human has travelled is 24,791 m.p.h. when the Command Module of Apollo X carrying Lt.-Col. Thomas P. Stafford and Cdrs. Eugene Andrew Cernan and John William Young, U.S.N., reached this maximum value at the 400,000-foot (75¾-mile) altitude interface on its trans-Earth return flight on 27 May 1969. It was widely but incorrectly reported that the stricken Apollo XIII attained the highest recorded speed on its return on 17 April 1970. Its maximum value was in fact 24,689·2 m.p.h.

Woman   The highest speed ever attained by a woman is 17,470 m.p.h. by Jnr. Lt. (now Flt. Major) Valentina Vladimirovna Tereshkova (born 6 March 1937) of the U.S.S.R. in *Vostok VI* on 16 June 1963. The highest speed ever achieved in an aeroplane is 1,429·2 m.p.h. by Jacqueline Cochran (U.S.A.), in an F-104G1 "Starfighter" jet over Edwards Air Force Base, California, U.S.A., on 18 May 1964. The first woman in Britain to fly at over 1,000 m.p.h. was Flt. Off. Jean Oakes, who flew at 1,125 m.p.h. in an R.A.F. Lightning Mark 4 on 6 Sept. 1962.

The first man on the moon—Neil Alden Armstrong (U.S.)

The holder of the unofficial balloon altitude record at 23·45 miles the late Nicholas Pianstanida

Human achievements

LAND

Man   The highest speed ever achieved on land is 632 m.p.h. by Lt.-Col. John Paul Stapp (born 1912) on a Northrop experimental rocket sled at the Holloman Air Force Base Development Center, Alamogordo, New Mexico, U.S.A., on 10 Dec. 1954. Running on rails and impelled by nine rockets with a total thrust of 40,000 lb., the top speed was reached within five seconds. In the deceleration, which lasted only 1½ seconds, Stapp survived a force of 40g for 0·2 of a second but his haemorrhaged retinas left him partially blinded for 12 weeks. The normal experimental limit is 12g.

Woman   The highest land speed recorded by a woman is 335·070 m.p.h. by Mrs. Lee Ann Breedlove (*née* Roberts) (born 1937) of Los Angeles, California, U.S.A., driving her husband's *Spirit of America–Sonic I* (see Chapter VIII) over the timing kilometre on the Bonneville Salt Flats, Utah, U.S.A., on 4 Nov. 1965.

WATER

The highest speed ever achieved on water is 328 m.p.h. by Donald Malcolm Campbell, C.B.E. (1921–67) of the U.K., on his last and fatal run in the turbo-jet engined 2¼ ton *Bluebird* K7, on Coniston Water, Lancashire, England, on 4 Jan. 1967.

The official record is 285·213 m.p.h. (average of two 1 mile runs) by Lee Taylor, Jr. (born 1934) of Downey, California, U.S.A., in the hydroplane *Hustler* on Lake Guntersville, Alabama, U.S.A., on 30 June 1967.

The world record for propeller-driven craft is 200·42 m.p.h. by Roy Duby (U.S.A.) in a Rolls-Royce-engined hydroplane on Lake Guntersville, Alabama, U.S.A., on 17 April 1962.

Most travelled man   The man who has almost certainly visited more countries than anyone is J. Hart Rosdail (born 1915) of Elmhurst, Illinois, U.S.A. Since 1934 he has visited 137 of the 145 sovereign countries and 65 of the 81 non-sovereign territories of the world making a total of 202. He estimates his mileage as 992,984 miles to 1 March 1970.

The greatest number of flying hours claimed is more than 40,000 by the light aircraft pilot Max. A. Conrad (b. 1903) of the U.S.A., who began his flying career on 13 March 1928. Capt. Charles Blair (Pan American World Airways) logged 35,000 flying hours and more than 10,000,000 miles including 1,450 Atlantic crossings up to July 1969. Capt. Gordon R. Buxton surpassed 8,000,000 miles in 22,750 flying hours in 38 years to 22 May 1966. He retired as Senior B.O.A.C. captain, aged 60, having passed all medicals.

The most travelled man in space is Capt. James Arthur Lovell, U.S.N. with 717 hours 4 mins. 16 secs. and an estimated mileage of 7,270,000.

Most indefatigable cruise passenger   Mrs. Clara Macbeth, the 98-year-old Manhattan millionairess, having lived on the cruise liner *Caronia* for 17 years with a companion at £165 a day, booked four round trips on the *Queen Elizabeth 2* in July 1969.

Cross-Channel record   The record for travelling the 214 miles between Paris (Arc de Triomphe) and London (Marble Arch) is 40 minutes 44 seconds by Sqn. Ldr. Charles G. Maughan, R.A.F. (born 1924), by motorcycle, helicopter and Hunter jet aircraft on 22 July 1959, so winning the *Daily Mail* award.

Sqn. Ldr. Charles G. Maughan, R.A.F., who holds the Marble Arch, London to Arc de Triomphe, Paris record at 40 mins. 44 secs.

162

Captain James Cook, R.N., F.R.S., the earliest sailor to cross the Antarctic Circle— 17 Jan. 1773

CIRCUMNAVIGATION

Earliest   A true circumnavigation of the world must pass through two points antipodean to each other. Man's earliest circumnavigation of the world was achieved by Juan Sebastián de Elcano (died August 1526) and 17 others in the Spanish ship *Vittoria* on 6 Sept. 1522, De Elcano was a navigator to the Portuguese-born explorer Fernão de Magalhães (Ferdinand Magellan) (c. 1480–1521), who, having sailed westward from the estuary of the Guadalquivir, Spain, on 20 Sept. 1519, with five ships and about 270 men, was killed on Mactan Island in the Philippines, on 27 April 1521. The distance sailed was 30,700 miles. Among the crew was one Englishman, Andrews of Bristol. No woman completed the circle until 243 years later in 1764 when it was discovered that the valet of M. de Commerson aboard the Frenchman *La Boudeuse* was a female.

First solo   The first man to complete a solo circumnavigation was Capt. Joshua Slocum, aged 51, who sailed from Newport, Rhode Island, U.S.A., in his 36-foot oyster boat *Spray* and returned after his 46,000-mile voyage 3 years 2 months and 2 days later at 1 a.m. on 27 June 1898. He was a non-swimmer.

First solo with a single stop-over   The first ever solo circumnavigation with a single port of call was the 274-day voyage from Plymouth *via* Sydney and Cape Horn by Sir Francis C. Chichester, K.B.E. (born Shirwell, Devon 17 Sept. 1901) in his 53-foot 18 ton ketch *Gipsy Moth IV*, ending at 7.56 p.m. G.M.T. on 28 May 1967. The first leg of 14,109 miles from Plymouth to Sydney lasted 107 days, from 27 Aug. to 12 Dec. 1966. He left Sydney on 29 Jan. 1967 arriving home 15,517 miles distant 119 days later.

First non-stop solo   The first ever technically non-stop circumnavigation was achieved in 312 days by Robin Knox-Johnston, C.B.E., aged 30, from 14 June 1968 to 22 April 1969 in his 32-foot ketch *Suhaili* from Falmouth, England. He made some unaided repairs at Otago, New Zealand on 21 Nov. 1968. He covered 28,800 miles.

Fastest solo   Lt.-Cdr. Nigel C. W. Tetley, R.N., in his 40-foot trimaran *Victress* "tied the knot" before sinking off the Azores on 21 May 1969. By 10 May he had sailed 26,000 miles (a multi-hull record, solo or with crew) in 236 days at an average of 110·1 miles per day.

Longest voyage   The longest voyage on record is one of about 38,000 miles by Bernard Moitessier (France) (b. Saigon, Viet-nam, 1926) in his 39-foot 13¼ ton steel sailing boat *Joshua*. He left Plymouth, England on 21 Aug. 1968, reached the Cape via Cape Horn but then redoubled to Tahiti, arriving on 22 June 1969.

Submarine   The first submarine circumnavigation was achieved between 24 Feb. and 25 April 1960, during an 83-day 10-hour 41,519-mile voyage ("Operation Magellan") by the U.S. nuclear submarine *Triton* (Capt. Edward Latimer Beach), beginning at New London, Connecticut, U.S.A., on 16 Feb. 1960 and ending on 10 May 1960. The circumnavigation from St. Paul's Rock, South Atlantic, required 30,708 statute miles at an average of 18 knots. There was one brief surfacing off Montevideo, Uruguay, to transfer a sick member of the 183-man crew. On 3 April 1966 it was announced that a flotilla of U.S.S.R. nuclear submarines, under the command of Vice-Admiral A. I. Sorokin, had completed a submerged circumnavigation covering 40,000 kilometres (24,800 miles).

ATLANTIC CROSSINGS

lest boat The smallest boat ever to cross the Atlantic was the *April Fool*, a 6-foot boat sailed by Hugo Vihlen (U.S.) (born 1932) in 84 days from 29 March 1968 out of Casablanca 4,100 miles to Miami Beach, Florida, U.S.A. Because of the off-setting current the craft had to be brought in the last 23 miles by a U.S. Coastguard cutter.

The smallest boat to sail non-stop across the Atlantic eastwards was the 13-foot 6-inch long sloop *Tinkerbelle*, sailed by Robert Manry, aged 48, of Cleveland, Ohio, U.S.A. from Falmouth, Massachusetts, to Falmouth, Cornwall, in 78 days from 31 May to 17 Aug. 1965.

Rowing The first two men to have rowed the Atlantic were the Norwegians George Harbo (1865–1945) and Frank Samuelsen (1869–1946) who left the Battery, Manhattan Island, New York, U.S.A., on 6 June 1896, and covered 3,075 miles in 56 days, landing at St. Mary's, Isles of Scilly, on 1 Aug. 1896. Their boat, the *Richard K. Fox*, was an 18-foot-long clinker built double ender with a 5-foot beam, and had no mast or sails in its equipment. They stowed five pairs of oars. On 15 July they were picked up, given a meal and new provisions, and climbed back into their boat to complete their journey.

The first Britons to complete a row across the Atlantic were Capt. John Ridgway, M.B.E., aged 27 and Sergeant Charles "Chay" Blyth, B.E.M., aged 26, in the 22-foot dory *English Rose III*. They left Orleans, Cape Cod, Massachusetts on 4 June and arrived at Inishmore, Aran Isles, Ireland after 91 days on 3 Sept. 1966.

The first west-east solo
trans-Atlantic row:
Tom McClean's
Super Silver

The first west-east solo row across the Atlantic was achieved by the paratrooper Tom McClean (b. Dublin 1943), from St. John's, Newfoundland 2,058 miles to Blacksod Bay, County Mayo, Ireland in 70 days 17 hours from 17 May to 27 July 1969 in his 20-foot dory *Super Silver*.

The first east-west crossing was achieved by John Fairfax (U.K.) (born 21 May 1937) in his 22-foot-long rowing boat *Britannia*. He left Las Palmas on 20 Jan. 1969 and arrived at Fort Lauderdale, Florida, U.S.A. on 20 July 1969 after a record 182 days in an open boat.

The record for a solo Britain–U.S.A. crossing is 26 days 20 hours 32 minutes by Geoffrey Williams, aged 25, of Redruth, Cornwall in the 57-foot ketch *Sir Thomas Lipton* (waterline length 42 feet). He sailed 3,700 nautical miles from Plymouth, Devon on 1 June reaching Brenton Reef light tower, near Newport, Rhode Island, U.S.A., 2,860 miles distant on a Great Circle course on 27 June 1968.

Fastest The fastest solo crossing of the Atlantic is 20 days achieved by Bernard Rhodes, 24 of Newby Bridge, Lancashire, England in his 22-foot trimaran *Klis* from Las Palmas to Bridgetown, Barbados, landing on 11 Feb. 1967.

Rounding the Horn The earliest rounding of Cape Horn (Cabo de Hornos), Chile by a yacht was by the 36-foot *Pandora* (G. D. Blythe [G.B.] and Peter Arapakis [Greece], crew) on 16 Jan. 1911.

POLAR CONQUESTS

North Pole The claims of neither of the two U.S. Arctic explorers, Dr. Frederick Albert Cook (1865–1940) nor Civil Engineer Robert Edwin Peary, U.S.N. (1856–1920) in reaching the North Pole is subject to positive proof. Cook, accompanied by the Eskimos, Ah-pellah and Etukishook, two sledges and 26 dogs, struck north from a point 60 miles north of Svartevoeg, on Axel Heiberg Is., Canada, 460 miles from the Pole on 21 March 1908, allegedly reaching Lat. 89° 31′ N. on 19 April and the Pole on 21 April. Peary, accompanied by his negro assistant, Matthew Alexander Henson (1866–1955) and the four Eskimos, Ooqueah, Egingwah, Seegloo, and Ootah (1875–1955), struck north from his Camp Bartlett (Lat. 87° 44′ N.) at 5 a.m. on 2 April 1909. After travelling another 134 miles, he allegedly established his final camp, Camp Jessup, in the proximity of the Pole at 10 a.m. on 6 April and marched a further 42 miles quartering the sea-ice before turning south at 4 p.m. on 7 April. Peary's longest claimed 3-day march for a record 163 geographical miles must be regarded as highly improbable. Cook's comparative maximum claim was for 68 geographical miles in 3 days.

The earliest indisputable attainment of the North Pole over the sea-ice was at 3 p.m. (Central Standard Time) on 19 April 1968 by Ralph Plaisted (U.S.) and three companions after a 42-day trek in four Snowmobiles. Their arrival was independently verified 18 hours later by a U.S. Air Force weather aircraft.

Arctic crossing The first crossing of the Arctic sea-ice was achieved by the British Trans-Arctic Expedition which left Point Barrow, Alaska on 21 Feb. 1968 and arrived at the Seven Island Archipelago just north of Spitzbergen 464 days later on 30 May 1969 after a haul of 3,620 miles. The team was Wally Herbert (leader), 34, Major Ken Hedges, 34, R.A.M.C., Allan Gill, 38, and Dr. Roy Koerner (glaciologist), and 34 huskies.

South Pole The first ship to cross the Antarctic circle (Lat. 66° 30′ S.) was the *Resolution* (462 tons), under Capt. James Cook (1728–79), on 17 Jan. 1773. The first person definitely to sight the Antarctic continent was Edward Bransfield (*c.* 1795–1852), Master of the R.N. ship *Williams* who, on 30 Jan. 1820, discovered "Trinity Land", believed to be the island now called Trinity Island, off the coast of Graham Land (Palmer Peninsula). The crew of the U.S. vessel *Cecilia* (Capt. John Davis) were the first men to land on the continent when they went ashore at Hughes Bay, on the Danco Coast of Graham Land (Palmer Peninsula), at 10 a.m. on 7 Feb. 1821. On 15 June 1960 it was claimed in Moscow, U.S.S.R., that Lt. Mikhail P. Lazarev sighted the Princess Marthaland coast of the mainland two days *before* Bransfield from the masthead of the sloop *Mirny* in Lat. 69° 23′ S., Long. 2° 35′ W. Capt. Fabian Gottlieb von Bellingshausen (1779–1852), it was claimed, also sighted the mainland on the same day

Human achievements

from his *Vostok*. Photostats of correspondence were produced to support these claims.

The South Pole was first reached on 14 Dec. 1911 by a Norwegian party, led by Roald Amundsen (1862–1928), after a 53-day march with dog sledges from the Bay of Whales, to which he had penetrated in the *Fram*. Olav Bjaaland, the first to arrive, was the last survivor, dying in June 1961, aged 88. The others were the late Helmer Hanssen, Sverre Hassel and Oskar Wisting.

Antarctic crossing The first crossing of the Antarctic continent was completed at 1.47 p.m. on 2 March 1958, after a 2,158-mile trek lasting 99 days from 24 Nov. 1957, from Shackleton Base to Scott Base *via* the Pole. The crossing party of twelve was led by Dr. (now Sir) Vivian Ernest Fuchs (born 11 Feb. 1908).

The longest Antarctic sledge journey was one of 3,700 miles from Mirny to Vostok to Sovietskaya, reported by the U.S.S.R. expedition in October–November 1958.

MOUNTAINEERING
The conquest of the highest point on Earth, Mount Everest (29,028 feet) was first achieved at 11.30 a.m. on 29 May 1953, by Edmund Percival Hillary (New Zealand) and the Sherpa Tenzing Norkhay (see Mountaineering, Chapter XII).

The highest mountain summit reached by women is Qungur I (Kongur Tiube Tagh) (*c.* 25,146 feet), climbed in 1961 by Shierab and another (unnamed) Tibetan woman. It is possible that Mme. Claude Kogan (died October 1959, aged 40) reached 25,260 feet on Cho Oyu (26,750 feet) on 19 Oct. 1954. A more conservative estimate is 7,550 metres (24,770 feet).

Greatest ocean descent The record ocean descent was achieved in the Challenger Deep of the Marianas Trench, 250 miles south-west of Guam, in the Pacific Ocean, when the Swiss-built U.S. Navy bathyscaphe *Trieste*, manned by Dr. Jacques Piccard (Switzerland), and Lt. Donald Walsh, U.S.N., reached the ocean bed 35,802 feet (6·78 miles) down, at 1.10 p.m. on 23 Jan. 1960 (but see also Chapter III). The pressure of the water was 16,883 lb. per square inch (1,085·3 tons per square foot), and the temperature 37·4° F. The descent required 4 hours 48 minutes and the ascent 3 hours 17 minutes.

Deep sea diving The world's record depth for a salvage observation chamber is that established by the Admiralty salvage ship *Reclaim* on 28 June 1956. In an observation chamber measuring 7 feet long and 3 feet internal diameter, Senior Com. Boatswain (now Lt.-Cdr.) G. A. M. Wookey, M.B.E., R.N., descended to a depth of 1,060 feet in Oslo Fjord, Norway.

SALVAGING
Deepest The deepest salvaging operation ever carried out was on the wreck of the S.S. *Niagara*, sunk by a mine in 1940, 438 feet down off Bream Head, Whangarei, North Island, New Zealand. All but 6 per cent. of the £2,250,000 of gold in her holds was recovered in 7 weeks. The record recovery was that from the White Star Liner *Laurentic*, which was torpedoed in 114 feet of water off Malin Head, Donegal, Ireland, in 1917, with £5,000,000 of gold ingots in her Second Class baggage room. By 1924, 3,186 of the 3,211 gold bricks had been recovered with immense difficulty.

Largest The largest vessel ever salvaged was the U.S.S. *Lafayette*, formerly the French liner *Normandie* (83,423 tons), which keeled over during fire-fighting operations at the West 49th Street Pier, New York Harbour, U.S.A., on 9 Feb. 1942. She was righted in October 1943, at a cost of $4,500,000 (now £1,875,000), and was broken up at Newark, New Jersey, beginning September 1946.

164

The late Mme. Claude Kogan, who may have climbed to 25,260 feet in 1954

Kitty Baldasare, *née* Geisler, the holder of the women's air breathing diving record

OCEAN DESCENTS—PROGRESSIVE RECORDS

Feet	Vehicle	Divers	Location	Date	
c. 245	Steel Sphere	Ernest Bazin (France)	Belle Île		1865
c. 830	Diving Bell	Balsamello Bella Nautica (Italy)			1889
. 1,650	Hydrostat	Hartman			1911
1,426	Bathysphere	Dr. C. William Beebe and Dr. Otis Barton (U.S.A.)	S.E. Bermuda	11 June	1930
2,200	Bathysphere	Dr. C. W. Beebe and Dr. O. Barton (U.S.A.)	S.E. Bermuda	22 Sept.	1932
2,510	Bathysphere	Dr. C. W. Beebe and Dr. O. Barton (U.S.A.)	S.E. Bermuda	11 Aug.	1934
3,028	Bathysphere	Dr. C. W. Beebe and Dr. O. Barton (U.S.A.)	S.E. Bermuda	15 Aug.	1934
7,850	*Converted U-boat*	*Heinz Sellner (Germany) (unwitnessed)*	*Murmansk*	*Aug.*	*1947*
4,500	Benthoscope	Dr. Otis Barton (U.S.A.)	off Santa Cruz, California	16 Aug.	1949
5,085	Bathyscaphe *F.N.R.S. 3*	Lt.-Cdr. Georges S. Houet and Lt. Pierre-Henri Willm (France)	off Toulon	12 Aug.	1953
6,890	Bathyscaphe *F.N.R.S. 3*	Lt.-Cdr. G. S. Houet and Lt. P.-H. Willm (France)	off Cap Ferrat	14 Aug.	1953
10,335	Bathyscaphe *Trieste*	Prof. Auguste and Dr. Jacques Piccard (Switzerland)	Ponza Is.	30 Sept.	1953
13,287	Bathyscaphe *F.N.R.S. 3*	Lt.-Cdr. G. S. Houet and Eng. Off. P.-H. Willm (France)	off Dakar, Senegal	15 Feb.	1954
18,600	Bathyscaphe *Trieste*	Dr. J. Piccard (Swiss) and Andreas B. Rechnitzer (U.S.A.)	Marianas Trench	14 Nov.	1959
24,000	Bathyscaphe *Trieste*	Dr. J. Piccard (Swiss) and Lt. D. Walsh, U.S.N.	Marianas Trench	7 Jan.	1960
35,802	Bathyscaphe *Trieste*	Dr. J. Piccard (Swiss) and Lt. D. Walsh, U.S.N.	Marianas Trench	23 Jan.	1960

DEEP DIVING—PROGRESSIVE RECORDS

BREATH-HOLDING

Feet	Divers	Location	Date	
c. 50	Mother-of-pearl divers	Mediterranean	c. 3,300 B.C.	
c. 120	Sponge and oyster divers (limit)	various	—	
c. 200	Stotti Georghios (Greece)	Adriatic		1913
198	Jacques Mayol (France)	off Freeport, Grand Bahama	July	1966
212½	P.O. Robert Croft, U.S.N.	Floridian coast, U.S.A.	8 Feb.	1967
#125	Evelyn Patterson (Zambia)	off Freeport, Grand Bahama		1967
217½	P.O. Robert Croft, U.S.N.	off Ft. Lauderdale, U.S.A.	19 Dec.	1967
231	Jacques Mayol (France)	Mediterranean	14 Jan.	1968
240	P.O. Robert Croft, U.S.N.	Floridian coast, U.S.A.	12 Aug.	1968

BREATHING AIR

Feet	Divers	Location	Date	
162[1]	A. Lambert (U.K.)	Grand Canary Is.		1885
190[1]	Greek and Swedish divers	off Patras, Greece		1904
210[1]	Lt. G. C. C. Damant, R.N.	Loch Striven, Scotland		1906
274[2]	Chief Gunner S. J. Drellifsak, U.S.N.	from U.S.S. *Walke*	9 Oct.	1914
304[2]	F. Crilley, W. F. Loughman, F. C. L. Nielson, U.S.N.	off Hawaii		1915
344[2]	Diver Hilton, R.N.	British waters		1932
307	Frederick Dumas (France)	Mediterranean		1947
††400[3]	Hope Root (U.S.A.)	U.S. waters		1953
†400[3]	Lt. Maurice Farques (France)	Mediterranean	ante	1954
350[3]	Jean Clarke-Samazen	off Santa Catalina, U.S.A.	Aug.	1954
#320[3]	Katherine Troutt (Australia)	Sydney Heads, Australia	7 Sept.	1964
355[3]	Hal D. Watts and Herb Johnson (U.S.A.)	off Loo Key, Fla., U.S.A.	4 Sept.	1966
380[3]	Hal D. Watts and Arthur J. Muns (U.S.A.)	off Miami Beach, U.S.A.	3 Sept.	1967
#325[3]	Kitty Giesler	off Freeport, Grand Bahama	31 Oct.	1967
437[3]	John J. Gruener and R. Neal Watson (U.S.A.)	off Freeport, Grand Bahama	14 Oct.	1968

BREATHING GAS MIXTURES

Feet	Divers	Location	Date	
420[4]	M. G. Nohl (U.S.A.)	Lake Michigan, U.S.A.	1 Dec.	1937
440[5]	R. M. Metzger and Claude Conger, U.S.N.	Portsmouth, N.H., U.S.A.	22 June	1941
†528[5]	A. Zetterström (Sweden)	Baltic	7 Aug.	1945
450[4]	P.O.'s Wilfred H. Bollard and W. Soper, R.N.	Loch Fyne, Scotland	26 Aug.	1948
540[4]	P.O. W. H. Bollard, R.N.	Loch Fyne, Scotland	28 Aug.	1948
550	Diver J. E. Johnson	Hauriki Gulf, N.Z.		1949
600[4]	Lt.-Cdr. George A. M. Wookey, M.B.E., R.N.	Oslo Fjord, Norway	13 Oct.	1956
728[6]	Hannes Keller (Switzerland) and Kenneth MacLeish (U.S.A.)	Lake Maggiore, Italy	30 June	1961
*1,000[6]	H. Keller (Switzerland) and Peter Small.†(U.K.)	off Santa Catalina, U.S.A.	3 Dec.	1962
**1,025[4]	U.S. Navy Aquanauts		Feb.	1968
**1,100[4]	Carl Deckman (Int. Underwater Contractors, Inc.)	Murray Hill, N.J., U.S.A.	12 Mar.	1968
**1,197[4]	Ralph W. Brauer (U.S.A.) and Réné Veyrunes (France)	Comex Chamber, France	27 June	1968
**1,500[4]	John Bevan and Peter Sharphouse (U.K.)	Alverstoke, Hampshire	11 Mar.	1970

Female record.
† Died on the ascent.
†† Died on the descent.
* Emerged from a diving bell.
** Simulated chamber dive.

[1] *Surface supplied, helmet.*
[2] *Surface supplied, flexible dress.*
[3] *Scuba (self-contained underwater breathing apparatus).*
[4] *Oxygen-helium.*
[5] *Oxygen-hydrogen.*
[6] *Oxygen-helium plus an additive.*

Human achievements

Most expensive
The most expensive salvage operation ever conducted was that by the U.S. Navy off Palomares, southern Spain, for the recovery of a 2,800 lb. 20 megaton H-bomb, between 17 Jan. and 7 April 1966, at a cost of $30,000,000 (£12·5 million). A fleet of 18 ships and 2,200 men took part. A CURV (Cable-controlled Underwater Research Vehicle) was flown from California and retrieved the bomb, dropped from a crashing B-52 bomber, from a depth of 2,850 feet.

Highest award
The highest salvage award ever paid out was £575,000 to the salvors of the S.S. *Toledo* (4,581 gross tons), stranded off Karachi, West Pakistan, in July 1952.

MINING DEPTHS
Man's deepest penetration made into the ground is in the East Rand Proprietary Mine in Boksburg, Transvaal. In November 1959 a level of 11,246 feet or 2·13 miles below ground level was attained in a pilot winze in the Hercules section. The rock temperature at this depth was 126° F. Incline shafts to a planned depth of 12,000 feet are being worked at Western Deep Levels mine, Klerksdorp, South Africa.

Shaft sinking record
The one month (31 days) world record is 1,251 feet for a standard shaft 26 feet in diameter at Buffelsfontein Mine, Transvaal, South Africa, in March 1962. The British record is 336 feet in 31 days in January 1961 at the No. 2 shaft of Kellingley Colliery, Knottingley, Yorkshire.

ENDURANCE

Running
Mensen Ehrnst (1799–1846) of Norway is reputed to have run from Istanbul, Turkey, to Calcutta, in West Bengal, India, and back in 59 days in 1836, so averaging an improbable 94·2 miles per day. The greatest non-stop run recorded is 121 miles 440 yards in 22 hours 27 minutes by Jared R. Beads, 41, of Westport, Maryland in October 1969. The greatest distance covered in 24 hours is the 162 miles 704 yards of George Littlewood (England) on 25 Nov. 1884. The distance comprised 5 miles 154 yards more than six marathons and would entail more than 649 laps of a quarter-mile track.

Six-day races
The greatest distance covered by a man in six days (*i.e.* the 144 permissible hours between Sundays in Victorian times) was 623¾ miles by George Littlewood (England), who required only 139 hours 1 min. for this feat in December 1888 at the old Madison Square Gardens, New York City, U.S.A.

Longest race
The longest race ever staged was the 1929 Transcontinental Race (3,665 miles) from New York City, N.Y., to Los Angeles, California, U.S.A. The Finnish-born Johnny Salo (killed 6 Oct. 1931) was the winner in 79 days, from 31 March to 17 June. His elapsed time of 525 hours 57 minutes 20 seconds gave a running average of 6·97 m.p.h.

North America coast to coast
Bruce Tulloh (Great Britain), aged 33, the 1962 European 5,000 metre champion, lowered the North-American trans-continental record from Los Angeles to New York (2,876 miles) to 64 days 21 hours 50 minutes (average 43·1 miles per day) from 10 a.m. on 21 April to 11.50 a.m. on 25 June 1969. His weight dropped from 8 st. 4 lb. to 7 st. 12 lb.

Walking
The greatest distance ever walked non-stop is 215 miles 1,670 yards by John Sinclair, 51, of Great Britain, in 47 hours 42 minutes round the perimeter of the Wingfield Aerodrome, Cape Town, South Africa on 21–23 April 1969. The greatest distance achieved in a non-stop walking endurance test held under continuous surveillance in Great Britain is 201 miles 722 yards by Bob Thirtle, 49, of King's Lynn, Norfolk around the perimeter of the R.A.F. station Marham, Norfolk

John Sinclair, holder of the world non-stop walking record at 215 miles 167 yards achieved in 1969

William Willis, German-born American, holder of the record for the longest intentional single-handed voyage on a raft— 7,450 miles

(4 miles 627 yards per lap) in 55 hours 40 minutes or 4–6 April 1969. A claim for 211 miles non-stop by Edward Frederick Westcott from Land's End to Bristol in 54 hours 5 minutes on 21–23 Aug. 1967 is not subject to proof.

The longest officially controlled walking race was that of 3,415 miles from New York to San Francisco, U.S.A. from 3 May to 24 July 1926, won by A. L. Monteverde aged 60, occupying 79 days 10 hours 10 minutes. In 1909 Edward Payson Weston walked 7,495 miles on a Trans-continental and return walk in 181 days.

Hike
The longest recorded hike is one of 18,500 miles through 14 countries from Singapore to London by David Kwan aged 22, which occupied 81 weeks from 4 May 1957, on an average of 32 miles a day.

Longest on a raft
The longest recorded survival alone on a raft is 133 days (4½ months) by Second Steward Poon Lim (born Hong Kong) of the U.K. Merchant Navy, whose ship, the S.S. *Ben Lomond*, was torpedoed in the Atlantic 750 miles off the Azores at 11.45 a.m. on 23 Nov. 1942. He was picked up by a Brazilian fishing boat off Salinas, Brazil, on 5 April 1943 and was able to walk ashore. In July 1943, he was awarded the B.E.M.

Dr. Alain Bombard (France) drifted from Casablanca, Morocco to Barbados on his 15-foot inflatable dinghy *Hérétique* in 64 days in 1952. The seals on his food and water rations were unbroken.

The longest intentional single-handed voyage on a raft was one of 7,450 miles by William Willis (born in Germany, 1893) of the U.S.A., who arrived at Upolu, Western Samoa, on 12 Nov. 1963, accompanied by two cats, on his steel-hulled trimaran raft *Age Unlimited* (32 by 20 feet), after a 130-day voyage across the Pacific Ocean. He had been cast off 50 miles off Callao, Peru, on 5 July 1963.

Swimming
The greatest recorded distance ever swum is 760 miles in 23 days down the Rhine from Switzerland to the Hook of Holland by Klaus Pechstein, 28, of Austria ending on 23 Oct. 1969. Gyorgy Schirilla, 30, of Hungary announced his intention in May 1969 to swim 1,240 miles down the Danube from Budapest to the Black Sea.

The longest duration swim ever achieved was one of 168 continuous hours, ending on 24 Feb. 1941, by the legless Charles Zibbelman, *alias* Zimmy (born 1894) of the U.S.A., in a pool in Honolulu, Hawaii, U.S.A.

The longest duration swim by a woman was 87 hours 27 minutes in a pool by Mrs. Myrtle Huddleston of New York City, N.Y., U.S.A., in 1931.

Cycling
The duration record for cycling on a track is 168 hours (7 days) by Syed Muhammed Nawab, aged 22, of Lucknow, India, in Addis Ababa, Ethiopia, in 1964. The monocycle duration record is 11 hours 21 minutes (83·4 miles) by Raymond Le Grand at Maubeuge, France, on 12 Sept. 1955. The longest cycle tour on record is one of 135,000 miles by Mishreelal Jaiswal (born 1924) of India, through 107 countries from 1950 to 5 April 1964, ending in San Francisco, California, U.S.A. He wore out five machines.

Most divorces and marriages
Mrs. Beverly Nina Avery, then aged 48, a barmaid from Los Angeles, California, U.S.A., set a monog-

amous world record in October 1957 by obtaining her sixteenth divorce from her fourteenth husband, Gabriel Avery. She alleged outside the court that five of the 14 had broken her nose. In Malaya, Abdul Rahman, aged 55, of Kuala Lumpur, married his 23rd wife aged 16 in October 1967 but voluntarily never had more than one wife at a time.

The greatest number of marriages accumulated in the monogamous world is 19 by Glynn de Moss Wolfe (U.S.) (b. 1908) who married for the 19th time since 1930 his 17th wife Gloria, aged 23 on 22 Feb. 1969. The most often marrying millionaire was Thomas F. Manville (1894–1967) who contracted his 13th marriage to his 11th wife Christine Erdlen, aged 20 in New York City, U.S.A. on 11 Jan. 1960 when aged 65. His shortest marriage (to his seventh wife) effectively lasted only 34 minutes. His fortune came from asbestos, none of which he could take with him.

Reports in April 1959 that Francis Van Wie, a conductor on the street-cars of the San Francisco Municipal Railway, California, U.S.A., had married his 18th wife, one Minnie Reardon, were later revised when it was discovered that some of his earlier marriages were undissolved.

Longest engagement The longest engagement on record is one of 67 years between Octavio Guillen, 82 and Adriana Martinez, 82. They finally took the plunge in June 1969 in Mexico City, Mexico.

Longest marriage The longest recorded marriage is one of 86 years between Sir Temulji Bhicaji Nariman and Lady Nariman from 1853 to 1940 resulting from a cousin marriage when both were five. Sir Temulji (born 3 Sept. 1848) died, aged 91 years 11 months, in August 1940 at Bombay.

James Frederick Burgess (born 3 March 1861, died 27 Nov. 1966) and his wife Sarah Ann, née Gregory (born 11 July 1865, died 22 June 1965) were married on 21 June 1883 at St. James's, Bermondsey, London, and celebrated their 82nd anniversary in 1965.

Burgesses, nly British couple to survive an d wedding nniversary

eating out The world champion for eating out is Fred E. Magel of Chicago, Illinois, U.S.A. who since 1928 has dined in more than 32,300 restaurants in 60 nations as a restaurant grader. He asserts the most expensive is Voisins, Park Avenue, New York City, U.S.A. where a solo lunch cost him $26.50 (more than £11) and the one serving the largest helpings is Zehnder's Hotel, Frankenmuth, Michigan, U.S.A. Mr. Magel's favourite dishes are South African rock lobster and mousse of fresh English strawberries.

ty giving The most expensive private party ever thrown was that of Mr. and Mrs. Bradley Martin of Troy, N.Y., U.S.A. staged at the Waldorf Hotel, Manhattan in February 1897. The cost to the host and hostess was estimated to be $369,200 in the days when dollars were made of gold.

stmasters The Guild of Professional Toastmasters (founded 1962) has only 12 members. Its founder, Ivor Spencer, has listened to 21,670 speeches to 7 May 1969, including one in excess of 2 hours by the maudlin victim of a retirement luncheon. Winners of the After Dinner Speaker of the Year Trophy (inst. 1967) have been Lord

Redcliffe-Maud, G.C.B., C.B.E. in 1967 and the Rt. Hon. J. H. Wilson, O.B.E., M.P. in 1968. The Guild also elects the most boring speaker of the year, but for professional reasons, does not publicize the winner's name. Red coats were introduced by the earliest professional William Knight-Smith (d. 1932) c. 1900.

Working week The longest working week (maximum possible 168 hours) is up to 136 hours at times by some housemen and registrars in some of the teaching hospitals in London. This figure has been given in evidence by the Action Group of Junior Hospital Medical Staff.

Working career The longest working career in one job in Britain is believed to belong to Mr. Mark Hicks of Crookham, Hampshire (died July 1966 aged 92). He started work for the Basingstoke Canal Co., aged 10, and was still working as bailiff of the canal four days before his death after 82 years.

Longest pension Miss Millicent Barclay, daughter of Col. William Barclay was born posthumously on 10 July 1872 and became eligible for a Madras Military Fund pension to continue until her marriage. She died unmarried on 26 Oct. 1969 having drawn the pension for every day of her life of 97 years 3 months.

MISCELLANEOUS ENDEAVOURS

Apple picking The greatest recorded performance is 151 U.S. bushels (146·3 Imperial bushels) picked in 8 hours by Ray Craig at Ben Nardie's Fruit Farm, Parke County, Indiana, U.S.A. in October 1967.

Autographs The largest collection of autographed photographs signed by celebrities is one of 1,460 amassed by Peter Clark of London, England to mid-May 1970.

Bag carrying The record time for the annual "World Coal Carrying Championship" over the uphill 1,080 yards course at Ossett cum Gawthorpe, Yorkshire, England with a 112 lb. sack is 4 minutes 42 seconds by R. L. Parsons, 26, of Kendal, Westmorland on 30 March 1970. The non-stop distance record carrying 1 cwt. is 12¼ miles in 3 hours 40 minutes from Perranporth to Cambourne, Cornwall by E. John Rapson on 4 April 1953.

Bag-pipes The longest duration pipe has been one of 50 hours by William Donaldson, Donald Grant, John Lovie and William Wotherspoon of Aberdeen University on 21–23 April 1969. The comment of some local inhabitants after the "lang blaw" was "Thank God there's nae smell".

Ball punching Ron Renaulf (Australia) equalled his own world duration ball punching record of 125 hours 20 minutes at 10.20 p.m. on 31 Dec. 1955, at the Esplanade, Southport, Queensland, Australia.

Barrel-jumping The greatest number of barrels jumped by a skater is 17 (total length 28 feet 8 inches) by Kenneth LeBel at the Grossinger Country Club, New York State, U.S.A., on 9 Jan. 1965.

Bed of nails The duration record for lying on a bed of nails (needle-sharp 6-inch nails 2 inches apart) is 25 hours 9 minutes by Zjane Azzar at Walton Store, Park and George Street, Sydney, Australia on 20–21 Nov. 1969. Much longer durations are claimed by uninvigilated fakirs—the most extreme case being Silki who claimed 111 days in Sao Paulo, Brazil ending on 24 Aug. 1969.

Bed-pushing The longest recorded push of a normally sessile object is of 395·3 miles in the case of a wheeled hospital bed by students of the University of Salford, England in 121 hours 21 minutes on 6–11 Feb. 1970.

Best man The world's champion "best man" is Mr. Wally Gant, a bachelor fishmonger from Wakefield, Yorkshire, who officiated for the 50th time since 1931 in December 1964.

Human achievements

Big wheel riding The endurance record for riding a Big Wheel is 14 days 21 hours by David Trumayne, 22, at Ramsgate, Kent ending on 8 June 1969. He completed 62,207 revolutions.

Blanket making On 11 June 1969 fifty blankets were made from fleece to the finished dyed article in 14 hours 4 minutes by 150 members of Charles Early & Marriott (Witney) Ltd. at Witney, Oxfordshire, England. The first blanket was completed in 8 hours 11 minutes.

Body jump The greatest number of "bodies" cleared in a motor-cycle ramp jump is 34 by Joseph Bayle, 20, on a Triumph 500 c.c. of the Kamakasi Stunt Team at Loughborough on 6 Sept. 1969. The 34th man was their instructor J. A. Tidmarsh.

Bomb defusing The highest reported number of unexploded bombs defused by any individual is 8,000 by Werner Stephan in West Berlin, Germany, in the 12 years from 1945 to 1957. He was killed by a small grenade on the Grunewald blasting site on 17 Aug. 1957.

Bond signing The greatest feat of bond signing was that performed by L. E. Chittenden (died 1902), the Registrar of the United States Treasury. In 48 hours (20–22 March 1863) he signed 12,500 bonds worth $10,000,000 (now £4,166,666), which had to catch a steam packet to England. He suffered years of pain and the bonds were never used.

Boomerang throwing Two types of boomerang are used by the natives of Australia: the return type, aimed against birds and used as a plaything, and the war boomerang. Frank Donellan circled a tree at a range of 140 yards in the longest recorded throw in the Centennial Park, Sydney in 1933. The war type can be thrown to strike an object 250 yards away. This is the farthest that anything can be thrown at ground level.

Brick carrying The record for the annual Narrogin Brick Carrying contest in Western Australia (instituted in 1960) is 21·0 miles by Dennis Blechynden, aged 28, on 23 March 1968. The 7 lb. 12 oz. wire-cut semi-pressed brick has to be carried in a downward position with a nominated ungloved hand. The feminine record is 1·6 miles by Pat McDougall, aged 16, but Jeanette Bartlett of Swindon, Wiltshire carried an 8 lb. 13¾ oz. brick more than 1·49 miles on 4 July 1969.

Bricklaying The world record for bricklaying was established in 1937 by Joseph Raglon of East St. Louis, Illinois, U.S.A., who, supported by assistants, placed 3,472 bricks in 60 minutes of foundation-work—at a rate of nearly 58 a minute.

The record for constructional bricklaying was set when J. E. Bloxham, of Stratford upon Avon, England laid a 13½-foot wall of 5,188 bricks in 7 hours 35 minutes with two assistants on 28th May 1960.

Brick throwing The greatest reported distance for throwing a standard 5 lb. building brick is 135 feet 7 inches by James Cantrell at Stroud, Oklahoma, U.S.A., in the annual contest on 17 July 1965. The British record is 134 feet 4 inches by Tony O'Neill of Stroud, Gloucestershire, on 20 July 1967.

Burial alive The longest recorded burial alive is one of 100 days ending on 17 Sept. 1968 in Skegness by Mrs. Emma Smith of Ravenshead, Nottinghamshire, England. The male record is 78 days by Bill Kearns, 36 of South Hiendley, Yorkshire, from 21 June to 7 Sept. 1969.

Car cramming The greatest number of people cramming into a small car is 46 in a Mini Minor, achieved by students at Queensland University, Australia on 3 March 1970. In March 1969 in Graz, Austria 57 students piled into and on top of a Volkswagen which was then successfully driven for 5 metres. A total of 111 members of Glendale Secondary School, Hamilton, Ontario, Canada piled into and on top of a stationary Volkswagen (no parts touching the ground) in November 1969.

Circuit training The most protracted test was one of 100 hours by Jim Hyde and John Pike of King Alfred Boy's Club Winchester, England on 9–13 Sept. 1969. The work was a mixture of punch bag, weight lifting, medicine ball chest expanders, trampoline, floor exercises, skipping and merely running.

Clapping The duration record for continuous clapping is 14 hours 6 minutes by Nicholas Willey, 18 and Christopher Floyd, 17 of Canford School, Dorset, England on 13–14 Dec. 1968. They sustained an average of 140 claps per minute and an audibility range of at least 100 yards.

Coal shovelling The record for filling a half-ton hopper with coal is 56·6 seconds by D. Coghlan of Reefton, New Zealand on 3 Jan. 1969.

Commuter Most durable Bruno Leuthardt commuted 370 miles each day for the 11 years 1957–67 from Hamburg to teach in the Bodelschwingh School, Dortmund, West Germany. He was late only once due to the 1962 Hamburg floods.

Competition winnings The champion winner of consumer and newspaper reader competitions in the United Kingdom over the 8-year period June 1962 to June 1970 has been Mrs. S. G. Bray of Huddersfield, Yorkshire, with 507 prizes valued in cash and kind at £15,267.

The largest single competition prize awarded in Britain has been £5,100 in cash and at least £2,000 worth of gifts by Mrs. Angela Dawson of Lydney, Gloucestershire in the 1967 *Daily Mirror* "Mrs. Britain" contest.

Callum L. de Villier and Vonny Kuchinski, holders of the world marathon dancing record

DANCING

The largest dance ever staged was that put on by the Houston Livestock Show at the Astro Hall, Texas, U.S.A. on 8 Feb. 1969. The attendance was 16,500

Marathon dancing must be distinguished from dancing mania, which is a pathological condition. The worst outbreak of dancing mania was at Aachen, Germany, in July 1374, when hordes of men and women broke into a frenzied dance in the streets which lasted for hours till injury or complete exhaustion ensued.

The most severe marathon dance staged as a public spectacle in the U.S.A. was one lasting 3,780 hours (22 weeks 3½ days) completed by Callum L. deVillier, 24 and Vonny Kuchinski, 20 at Sommerville, Massachusetts, U.S.A. from 28 Dec. 1932 to 3 June 1933. In the last two weeks the rest allowance was cut from 15 minutes per hour to only 3 minutes while the last 52½ hours were continuous. The prize of $1,000 was equivalent to less than 26½ cents per hour.

Bill Kearns after his 78-day "burial"

Ballet Among the world's greatest ballet dancers, Vatslav Fomich Nijinsky (1890–1950), a Russian-born Pole, was alone in being credited with being able to achieve the *entrechat dix*—crossing and uncrossing the feet 10 times in a single elevation. This is not believed by physical education experts since no high jumper can stay off the ground for more than 1 second and no analysable film exists.

st turns The greatest number of spins called for in classical ballet choreography is the 32 *fouettés en tournant* in "Swan Lake" by Pyotr Ilyich Chaykovskiy (Tschaikovsky) (1840–1893). Miss Rowena Jackson, of New Zealand, achieved 121 such turns at her class in Melbourne, Victoria, Australia, in 1940.

Most curtain calls The greatest recorded number of curtain calls ever received by ballet dancers is 89 by Dame Peggy Arias, D.B.E. *née* Hookham (born Reigate, Surrey, 18 May 1919), *alias* Margot Fonteyn, and Rudolf Nureyev (born in a train near Ufa, U.S.S.R., 1938) after a performance of "Swan Lake" at the Vienna Staatsoper, Austria, in October 1964.

allroom arathon The individual continuous world record for ballroom dancing is 106 hours 5 minutes 10 seconds by Carlos Sandrini in Buenos Aires, Argentina, in September 1955. Three girls worked shifts as his partner.

allroom mpions The world's most successful professional ballroom dancing champions have been Bill Irvine, M.B.E. and Bobby Irvine, M.B.E., who have been undefeated as World Professional Champions since 1960.

arleston The Charleston duration record is 22½ hours by John Giola, aged 23, at the Roseland Ballroom, Broadway, New York City, N.Y., U.S.A., in 1926.

amenco The fastest flamenco dancer ever measured is Solero de Jerez aged 17 who in Brisbane, Australia in Sept. 1967 in an electrifying routine attained 16 heel taps per second or a rate of 1,000 a minute.

Go-go The duration record for go-go dancing is 100 hours (with 5 minute breaks each hour) by Faye Walker of Auckland, New Zealand, on 19–23 July 1966.

Jiving The duration record for non-stop jiving is 40 hours by Gordon Lightfoot and Kathleen Fowler at Penrith, on 22–24 April 1960. Breaks of 3½ minutes per hour were permitted for massage. This time was equalled by Terry Ratcliffe, aged 16, and Christina Woodcroft, aged 17, at Traralgon, Victoria, Australia, from 10.15 p.m. on 28 May to 2.13 p.m. on 30 May 1965.

Limbo The lowest height for a bar under which a clothed limbo dancer has passed is 6½ inches by Teresa Marquis of St. Lucia, West Indies, at the Guinness Distribution Depot, Grosvenor Road, Belfast, Northern Ireland on 15 April 1970. Her vital statistics are 34–24–36.

Twist The duration record for the twist is 100 hours by Mrs. Ra Denny in Christchurch, New Zealand, ending on 24 March 1962.

Most expensive course The world's most expensive dance course has been the "Lifetime Executive Course" of Arthur Murray (born Murray Teichmann, 4 April 1895) in the United States. It came after the Lifetime Course ($7,300) and the $9,000 "Gold Medal Course" and cost $12,000, making a total of $28,300 or now equivalent to £11,791.

Modern The longest recorded dancing marathon (50 minutes per hour) in popular style is one of 54 hours by Miss Gillian Smith at Wigan Technical College, Wigan, Lancashire on March 3–5 1970.

Dance band The most protracted session for a dance band is one of 321 hours (13 days 9 hours) by the Black Brothers of Bonn, West Germany ending on 2 Jan. 1969. Never less than a quartet were in action during the marathon.

Disc-jockey The longest continuous period of acting as a disc-jockey is 267 hours (11 days 3 hours) by David Jones of Ipswich, Suffolk in November 1969. The disc-jockey team record, excluding any L.P.'s, is 240 hours by four DJ's at R.A.F. Linton-on-Ouse, Yorkshire on 17–27 April 1970.

Drumming The world's duration drumming record is 119 hours 35 minutes 30 seconds by Eddie Williams of Manchester (with 5 minute intervals each hour) at Leysdown's Island Hotel, Kent on 23–28 Aug. 1959. Les Allen of Grimsby, Lincolnshire achieved a non-stop record of 109 hours.

Egg and spoon racing David Smith and Peter Dilley of Chigwell, Essex completed a local 20-mile fresh egg and dessert spoon marathon in 5 hours 25 minutes on 27 July 1969.

Egg throwing The longest recorded distance for throwing a fresh egg without breaking is 122 feet by Pat Malloy (thrower) to Graham Manly (catcher) at Blenheim, New Zealand on 23 Feb. 1970.

Face-slapping The face-slapping contest duration record was set in Kiev, U.S.S.R., in 1931, when a draw was declared between Vasiliy Bezbordny and Goniusch after 30 hours.

Fruit machines Using 6d. discs a team of four from the Vale of Pewsey Young Conservatives succeeded in feeding in £1,512 12s. worth of discs (*viz* 60,504) in 48 hours, a lever pulling rate of better than once every 3 seconds.

Grave digging It is recorded that Johann Heinrich Karl Thieme, sexton of Aldenburg, Germany, dug 23,311 graves during a 50-year career. In 1826 his understudy dug *his* grave.

Gun running The record for the Royal Tournament naval gun run competition (instituted 1900, with present rules since 1919) is 2 minutes 50·5 seconds by the Fleet Air Arm Gun Crew at Earl's Court, London in 1969. The barrel alone weighs 8 cwt. The wall is 5 feet high and the chasm 28 feet across. The same team in 1968 achieved an unofficial 2 minutes 47·6 seconds in a practice run at Lee-on-the-Solent, Hampshire.

Hairdressing The world record for non-stop barbering is 48 hours by Joseph Bald of Scotland who performed 268 haircuts in this time in February 1970 at Portobello Town Hall. The world's most expensive men's hairdresser is Tristan of Hollywood, California, U.S.A. who charges any "client" $100 (£41 13s. 4d.) on their first visit. This consists of a "consultation" followed by "remedial grooming".

Handshaking The world record for handshaking was set up by Theodore Roosevelt (1858–1919), President of the U.S.A., who shook hands with 8,513 people at a New Year's Day, White House Presentation in Washington, D.C., U.S.A. on 1 Jan. 1907. Outside public life the record has become meaningless because aspirants merely arrange circular queues and shake the same hands repetitively.

Teresa Marquis of St. Lucia
going under a bar at 6½ inches

169

High diving The highest regularly performed dive is that of professional divers from La Quebrada ("the break in the rocks") at Acapulco, Mexico, a height of 118 feet. The leader of the 25 divers in the exclusive Club de Clavadistas is Raúl Garcia (born 1928). The base rocks, 21 feet out from the take-off, necessitate a leap of 27 feet out. The water is 12 feet deep.

On 18 May 1885, Sarah Ann Henley, aged 24, jumped from the Clifton Suspension Bridge across the Avon, England. Her 250-foot fall was slightly cushioned by her voluminous dress and petticoat acting as a parachute. She landed, bruised and bedraggled, in the mud on the Gloucestershire bank and was carried to hospital by four policemen. On 11 Feb. 1968 Jeffrey Kramer, 24, leapt off the George Washington Bridge 250 feet above the Hudson River, New York City, N.Y. and survived. Of the 367 people who have made suicide dives from the Golden Gate Bridge, San Francisco, California, U.S.A. since 1937, the third to have survived was Claud Layton on 17 July 1969. On 10 July 1921 a stuntman named Terry leapt from a hydroplane into the Ohio River at Louisville. The alleged altitude was 310 feet.

Samuel Scott (U.S.A.) is reputed to have made a dive of 497 feet at Pattison Fall (now Manitou Falls) in Wisconsin, U.S.A., in 1840, but this would have entailed an entry speed of 86 m.p.h. The actual height was probably 165 feet.

Hitch-hiking The hitch-hiking record for the 873 miles from Land's End, Cornwall, to John o' Groats, Caithness, Scotland, is 29½ hours by Ian Crawford of Edinburgh on 4–5 April 1965. The time before the first "hitch" on the first day is excluded. This time was equalled in the reverse direction by Bernard Atkins, aged 18, of Donington, Lincolnshire in 11 lifts on 28 July 1966. The fastest time recorded for the round trip is 77 hours 20 minutes by Christine Elvery, 20 and Gwendolen Sherwin, 20 of which 61 hours 20 minutes was travelling on 24–27 March 1969.

Hoop rolling In 1968 it was reported that Zolilio Diaz (Spain) had rolled a hoop 600 miles from Mieres to Madrid and back in 18 days.

Hopscotch The most protracted game of hopscotch on record has been one of 26 hours and 294 games played by 7 boys and 3 girls of the Withycombe Methodist Association Youth Club, Devon, England on 6–7 March 1970.

House of cards The record verified number of storeys achieved is 13 by Ian Greenwood in Swindon, Wiltshire on 3 July 1969.

Human cannon-ball The record distance for firing a human from a cannon is 155 feet in the case of Miss Victoria Zacchini in the Ringling Bros. and Barnum & Bailey Circus, Madison Square Garden, New York City, U.S.A., in April 1959. Her muzzle velocity was 140 m.p.h. On her retirement the management expect to have considerable difficulty in finding another girl of the same calibre.

Juggling The only juggler in history able to juggle—as opposed to "shower"—10 balls or eight plates was the Italian Enrico Rastelli, who was born in Samara, Russia, on 19 Dec. 1896 and died in Bergamo, Italy, on 13 Dec. 1931.

Kite-flying The greatest reported height attained by kites is 35,530 feet by a train of 19 flown near Portage by 10 Gary, Indiana high school boys. The flight took 7 hours and was assessed by telescopic triangulation.

Knitting The longest recorded knitting marathon is one of 100 hours by Mrs. B. M. Hands in the window of Hay's Store, Christchurch, New Zealand on 11–15 Sept. 1967. Time out allowances were 10 minutes per hour and 30 minutes each 6 hours. The world's most prolific hand-knitter is Mrs. Gwen Matthewman of Featherstone, Yorkshire, with a total in 1969 of 423 garments knitted involving 345 lb. of wool (equivalent to the fleeces of 45 sheep). She has been timed to average 108 stitches per minute in a 30-minute test. The longest scarf knitted was one 438 feet long (minimum width 10 inches) by a team from Castle Vale Comprehensive School, Birmingham reported on 7 Feb. 1970. The longest non-stop figure on record is one of 60 hours by 6 students of West London College, London, W.14 on 13–16 March 1970. The finest recorded knitting is a piece of 2,464 stitches per square inch by Douglas Milne of Mount Florida, Glasgow, Scotland in May 1969.

Knot-tying The non-stop knot-tying marathon record is 76,504 links of a drummer's chain knot in ¾ inch tarred sisal rope in 50½ hours by four members of the 9th Beds (Biggleswade) Scout Troop on 29–31 May 1969.

Lion-taming The greatest number of lions mastered and fed in a cage by an unaided lion-tamer was 40, by "Captain" Alfred Schneider in 1925. Clyde Raymond Beatty (1903–65) handled more than 40 "cats" (mixed lions and tigers) simultaneously. Twenty-one lion-tamers have died of injuries since 1900.

Log rolling The most protracted log rolling contest on record was one in Chequamegon Bay, Ashland, Wisconsin, U.S.A. in 1900, when Allan Stewart dislodged Joe Oliver from a 24-inch diameter log after 3 hours 15 minutes birling

Message in a bottle The longest voyage recorded for a message in a bottle was one of 25,000 miles, from the Pacific to the shore of the island of Sylt in the North Sea on 3 Dec. 1968. The bottle had been dropped on 27 May 1947.

Morse The highest recorded speed at which anyone has received morse code is 75·2 words per minute—over 17 symbols per second. This was achieved by Ted R. McElroy of the United States in a tournament at Asheville, North Carolina, U.S.A. on 2 July 1939.

Needle threading The record number of strands of cotton threaded through a number 13 needle (eye $\frac{11}{16}$ of an inch by $\frac{1}{16}$ of an inch) in 2 hours is 2,827 by Miss Kathleen Berry at the College of Education, Matlock, Derbyshire, on 6 May 1967.

Omelette making The greatest number of two-egg omelettes made in 30 minutes is 77 by Leonard Andrew at West Jesmond School Hall, Newcastle on Tyne, England on 29 Nov. 1969.

Quiz league The largest and oldest (established 1959) Quiz league in the world is the Merseyside Quiz League, England with 82 teams and five major trophies.

PARACHUTING

Earliest descent The earliest demonstration of a quasi-parachute was by Sebastien Lenormand (France), with a conical canopy from an observation tower in Montpellier, France, in 1783. The first successful parachute jump from a balloon was by André-Jacques Garnerin (1769–1823) from 2,230 feet over Monceau Park, Paris, on 22 Oct. 1797. The earliest descent from an aeroplane was that of Captain Albert Berry, U.S. Army, over St. Louis, Missouri, on 1 March 1912. The first free fall from an aircraft was by Leslie L. Irvin (1895–1966) of the U.S.A. on 19 April 1919.

Longest delayed drop Male The longest delayed drop and the greatest altitude for any parachute descent was achieved by U.S. Air Force Captain Joseph W. Kittinger, D.F.C., aged 32, over Tularosa, New Mexico, U.S.A. on 16 Aug. 1960. He stepped out of a balloon at 102,200 feet for a free fall of 84,700 feet (16·04 miles) lasting 4 minutes 38 seconds, during which he reached a speed of 614 m.p.h., despite a stabilizing drogue. He experienced a temperature of —94° F. His 28-foot parachute opened at 17,500 feet and he landed after a total time of 13 minutes 45 seconds. The step by the gondola door was inscribed "This is the highest step in the world".

The British record for a group delayed drop is 39,183 feet (7·43 miles) (from 41,383 feet) by 5 R.A.F. Parachute Jumping Instructors over Boscombe Down, Wiltshire on 16 June 1967. They were Sq.-Ldr. J. Thirtle; Fl.-Sgt. A. K. Kidd and Sgts. L. Hicks, P. P. Keane and K. J. Teesdale.

Female The women's delayed drop record is 46,250 feet (8·76 miles) by O. Komissarova (U.S.S.R.) on 21 Sept. 1965.

Highest escape The greatest altitude from which a successful parachute *escape* has been made from an aircraft is from a Canberra jet bomber by Flt.-Lt. John de Salis, aged 29, of Southampton, and Fg. Off. Patrick Lowe, aged 23, of Potters Bar, Hertfordshire, over Monyash, Derbyshire, on 9 April 1958. Their plane exploded at 56,000 feet (10·60 miles) and they fell free in a temperature of −70° F. to a height of 10,000 feet at which altitude their parachutes were automatically opened. The longest descent recorded was one by Lt.-Col. William H. Rankin, U.S.M.C., from an F8U "Crusader" jet fighter at 47,000 feet on 26 July 1959. His "descent" through a thunderstorm over North Carolina took 40 minutes instead of the expected 11 minutes because of violent upward air currents.

Heaviest load The greatest single load ever dropped by parachute is 50,450 lb. (22·52 tons) of steel plates from a U.S. Air Force C-130 Hercules with 6 'chutes near El Centro, California on 28 Jan. 1970. The largest parachute made is a U.S. Air Force cargo parachute with a 100-foot diameter, reported in September 1964.

Most descents The greatest number of parachute jumps is over 5,000 by Lt.-Col. Ivan Savkin (U.S.S.R.) (born 1913), who reached 5,000 on 12 Aug. 1967. Since 1935 he has spent 27 hours in free fall, 587 hours floating and has dropped 7,800 miles. The British record is believed to have been set by Flt.-Lt. Charles Agate, A.F.C. (born March 1905) of the R.A.F., who totalled 1,601 descents with packed parachutes between 1940 and 1946. The speed record is 81 jumps in 8 hours 22 minutes by Michael Davis, 24, and Richard Bingham, 25, at Columbus, Ohio, U.S.A. on 26 June 1966.

Longest fall without a parachute The greatest altitude from which anyone has bailed out without a parachute and survived is 22,000 feet. This occurred in January 1942, when Lt. (now Lt.-Col.) I. M. Chisov (U.S.S.R.) fell from an Ilyushin 4 which had been severely damaged. He struck the ground a glancing blow on the edge of a snow-covered ravine and slid to the bottom. He suffered a fractured pelvis and severe spinal damage. It is estimated that the human body reaches 99 per cent. of its low level terminal velocity after falling 1,880 feet. This is 117–125 m.p.h. at normal atmospheric pressure in a random posture, but up to 185 m.p.h. in a head down position.

The British record is 18,000 feet by Flt.-Sgt. Nicholas Stephen Alkemade, aged 21, who jumped from a blazing R.A.F. Lancaster bomber over Germany on 23 March 1944. His headlong fall was broken by a fir tree and he landed without a broken bone in an 18-inch snow bank.

Highest The record landing height for parachute jumps is 23,405 feet by 10 U.S.S.R. parachutists onto the summit of Lenina Peak reported in May 1969. Four of the ten were killed.

Most northerly The most northerly parachute jump was made in 87° 30′ N. on the polar ice cap on 31 March 1969 by Ray Munro, 47, of Lancaster, Ontario, Canada. His eyes were frozen shut instantly in the temperature of −39° F.

Piano-playing Heinz Arntz (Germany), aged 67, played the piano non-stop, except for an interval of 2 hours in each 24 hours, for 1,054 hours (43 days 22 hours) from 18 Aug. to 1 Oct. 1966. He began in Düsseldorf, played across the Atlantic aboard the liner *United States* and finished at Long Island Fair, N.Y., U.S.A. The British record is 195 hours 17 minutes (with 5 minute breaks each hour) set by Michael George, 24, of Stockport, Cheshire, ending on 24 July 1969.

The women's world record is 133 hours (5 days 13 hours) by Mrs. Marie Ashton, aged 40, in a theatre at Blyth, Northumberland, on 18–23 Aug. 1958.

Piano smashing The record time for demolishing an upright piano and passing the entire wreckage through a circle 9 inches in diameter is 2 minutes 26 seconds by six men representing Ireland led by Johnny Leydon of Sligo, at Merton, Surrey, England on 7 Sept. 1968.

Pillar box standing The record number of people to pile on top of a pillar box (6 square foot oval top) is 26, all students of the City of London College, Moorgate, in Finsbury Circus, London, E.C.2 on London Weekend T.V. on 21 Sept. 1968.

Pipe smoking The duration record for keeping a pipe (3·3 grammes of tobacco) continuously alight with only an initial match is 253 minutes 28 seconds by Yrjö Pentikäinen of Kuopio, Finland on 15–16 March 1968.

Plate spinning The greatest number of plates spun simultaneously is 40 by Holley Gray, who had previously appeared in a David Frost programme, on the David Nixon T.V. Show in London on 26 Jan. 1969.

Pole-squatting There being no international rules, the "standards of living" atop poles vary widely. The record squat is 211 days 9 hours by Miss Maurie Rose Kirby, aged 17, ending on 4 March 1959, on a 71-foot-tall pole at Indianapolis, Indiana, U.S.A. She staged the test as a protest against being called a juvenile delinquent.

The British record is 32 days 14 hours by John Stokes, aged 32, of Moseley, in a barrel on a 45-foot pole in Birmingham, ending on 27 June 1966. This is claimed as a world record for a barrel.

Modern records do not, however, compare with that of St. Daniel (A.D. 409–493), called Stylites (Greek, *stylos*=pillar), a monk who spent 33 years 3 months on a stone pillar in Syria. This is probably the oldest of all human records.

Pop group The duration record for pop-playing is 102 hours 20 minutes by The Smoke at the Market Hall, Bury St. Edmunds, Suffolk on 13–16 Jan. 1970. The group comprised Steve Vaughan-Williams (no kin) (lead guitar); Ted Chapman (bass guitar); Dave Whybrow (drums) and Taffy Ridgeon (vocals).

Pram pushing The greatest distance covered in pushing a pram in 24 hours is 148 miles by 14 members of Pembroke Round Table, No. 637 from Pembroke Castle to Caernarvon Castle, Wales on 21–22 June 1969.

Clifton Suspension Bridge—
scene of Sarah Henley's leap
(see page 170)

Human achievements

Fastest psychiatrist The world's fastest psychiatrist was Dr. Albert L. Weiner of Erlton, New Jersey, U.S.A., who dealt with up to 50 patients a day in four treatment rooms. He relied heavily on narcoanalysis, muscle relaxants and electro-shock treatments. In December 1961 he was found guilty on 12 counts of manslaughter from using unsterilized needles.

Pub-crawling The world's champion pub-crawler is the abstemious Mr. Barry Cameron-Lunn of New Zealand. In Britain alone he has visited 11,700 pubs up to October 1969. His ration is half a pint per pub and his record in one night is 24.

Riveting The world's record for riveting is 11,209 in 9 hours by J. Moir at the Workman Clark Ltd. shipyard, Belfast, Northern Ireland, in June 1918. His peak hour was his seventh with 1,409, an average of nearly $23\frac{1}{2}$ per minute.

Rocking-chair The longest recorded duration of a "Rockathon" is 123 hours by Ian Knowles, 20 at Aberdeen Students' Charities Campaign, Scotland on 21–25 April 1970.

Rolling pin The record distance for a woman to throw a 2 lb. rolling pin is 138 feet 11 inches by Sheri Salyer at Stroud, Oklahoma on 19 July 1969. The British record is 134 feet 2 inches by Ann Cook at Stroud, Gloucestershire on 20 July 1968.

Longest safari The world's longest safari was one mounted in Africa by Peter Parnwell of Johannesburg, South Africa. It lasted 365 days, embraced 37 African countries and territories and extended over 30,000 miles.

See-saw The duration record for see-sawing is 115 hours 33 minutes by David Blaylock, 18 and Peter Haigh, 15 of Hebden Royd Youth Action Group, Yorkshire on 30 March–4 April 1970. Intervals of up to 5 minutes per hour were permitted. The longest see-saw marathon in which the participants did not leave the see-saw is one of 80 hours by David Turner and David Such of the Twyford & Rushcombe Youth Club on 27–30 Dec. 1969.

Sermon The longest sermon on record was delivered by Clinton Locy of West Richland, Washington, U.S.A., in February 1955. It lasted 48 hours 18 minutes and ranged through texts from every book in the Bible. A congregation of eight was on hand at the close. From 31 May to 10 June 1969 the Dalai Lama, the exiled ruler of Tibet, completed a sermon on Tantric Buddhism for five to seven hours per day to total 60 hours.

Sewing machines The fastest time recorded for sewing down a piece of tape 9 yards long with a treadle machine is 4 minutes 41·4 seconds by Harry Walgate at the Joint Reading Round Table competition, Reading, Berkshire on 19 Nov. 1969.

Shaving The fastest barber on record was Mr. Teddy Wick in a saloon in the King's Road, Chelsea, London who, in November 1887, shaved 77 persons with a cut-throat razor in 59 minutes 53 seconds without a slip.

Sheaf tossing The world's best performance for tossing an 8-lb. sheaf is 56 feet by C. R. Wiltshire of Geelong, Victoria, Australia in 1956. Contests date from 1914.

Fastest shorthand The highest recorded speeds ever attained under championship conditions are: 300 words per minute (99·64 per cent. accuracy) for five minutes and 350 w.p.m. (99·72 per cent. accuracy, that is, two insignificant errors) for two minutes by Nathan Behrin (U.S.A.), in New York in December 1922. Behrin (born 1887) used the Pitman system invented in 1837. Morris I. Kligman of New York currently claims to be the world's fastest shorthand writer at 300 w.p.m. He has taken 50,000 words in five hours and transcribed them in under five hours.

In the British Isles only five shorthand writers have passed the official Pitman tests at 250 w.p.m. for fiv[e] minutes:

Miss Edith Ulrica Pearson of London, on 30 June 1927.
Miss Emily Doris Smith of London, on 22 March 1934.
Miss Beatrice W. Solomon of London, in March 1942.
Mrs. Audrey Boyes (*née* Bell) of Finchley, London, in 1956.

Mr. G. W. Bunbury of Dublin, Ireland, holds th[e] unique distinction of writing at 250 w.p.m. for 1[0] minutes on 23 Jan. 1894.

Shouting The greatest number of wins in the national town criers' contest is eight by Herbert T. Waldron of Grea[t] Torrington, Devon. He won every year from 1957 t[o] 1965, except for 1959. (See also Longest-ranged voice Chapter I.)

Showering The most prolonged continuous shower bath on recor[d] is one of 168 hours by Peter Schell, aged 36, of Munich West Germany ending on 19 Jan. 1968. The feminin[e] record is 97 hours 1 minute by an anonymous co-e[d] from Holmes Hall, East Lansing, Michigan, U.S.A[.] ending on 28 Jan. 1969. She is believed to be the world'[s] only anonymous record-holder.

Singing The longest recorded singing marathon is one of 2[4] hours, with 5 minute intervals each hour, by Bo[b] Anthony, 40 of South Africa at the Lyceum, The Strand London on 6–7 Nov. 1969. His repertoire comprised 273 songs. The longest recorded group marathon wa[s] performed by five students (Martin Field, Dave Owe[n] Roger Saunders, Dave Trethewwy and Clive Ward), o[f] the College of Technology, Brighton who sang the tw[o] line refrain "Lloyd George knew my Father—Fath[er] knew Lloyd George" to the tune of Onward Christia[n] Soldiers for 30 hours from 12.45 p.m. 11th March t[o] 6.45 p.m. 12th March 1970.

Skipping The greatest number of turns ever performed withou[t] a break is variously reported as 32,089 and 32,809 b[y]

Bob Anthony (South Africa), holder of the singing marathon record

J. P. Hughes of Melbourne, Victoria, Australia, i[n] 3 hours 10 minutes on 26 Oct. 1953.

Other records made without a break:

Most turns in one jump	5 by Katsumi Suzuki, Tokyo, early 1968.
Most turns in 1 minute	286 by J. Rogers, Melbourne, 10 Nov. 1937. and T. Lewis, Melbourne, 16 Sept. 1938.
Most turns in 2 hours	22,806 by Tom Morris, Sydney, 21 Nov. 1937.
Double turns	2,001 by K. Brooks, Brisbane, January 1955.
Treble turns	70 by J. Rogers, Melbourne, 17 Sept. 1951.
Duration	1,264 miles by Tom Morris, Brisbane–Cairns. Queensland, 1967

Slinging The greatest distance recorded for a sling-shot is $847\frac{1}{2}$ feet using a 34-inch-long sling and a 10 ounce stone by Vernon H. Morton on Clarkston Golf Course, Idaho, U.S.A. on 12 Sept. 1966.

Spinning The duration record for spinning a clock balance wheel by hand is 5 minutes 26·8 seconds by Philip Ashley, aged 16, of Leigh, Lancashire, on 20 May 1968.

Spitting The greatest distance achieved by any national spitting champion, is 24 feet 10½ inches by George Craft, the eleven-time U.S. champion between 1956 and 1968, in a non-title contest at Raleigh, Mississippi in 1967. Distance is dependent on the quality of salivation, absence of cross wind and the co-ordination of the quick hip and neck snap. His prize was a gold-plated slightly used spitoon or cuspidor. The record for projecting a melon seed is 33 feet 3½ inches by Craig Jones at the "world" championship at Pardeeville, Wisconsin, U.S.A. on 13 Sept. 1969.

French tilt-walkers in action in 1892

Stilt-walking The highest stilts ever successfully mastered were 22 feet from the ankle to the ground by Harry Yelding ("Harry Sloan") of Great Yarmouth, Norfolk. Hop stringers use stilts up to 15 feet. In 1892 M. Garisoain of Bayonne stilt-walked the last 8 kilometres into Biarritz in 42 minutes to average 7·1 m.p.h. In 1891 Sylvain Dornon stilt-walked from Paris to Moscow *via* Vilno in 50 stages for the 1,830 miles. Another source gives his time as 58 days.

Stretcher bearing The longest recorded carry of a stretcher case is one of 14 miles of Lt.-Col. Harold Noor (10 stone) by a team of 8 bearers of the 219 (Wessex) General Hospital R.A.M.C. (V) unit under S/Sgt. J. Petrie near Weston-super-Mare, Somerset, England in October 1968.

Submergence The longest submergence in a frogman's suit is 100 hours 3 minutes by Mrs. Jane Lisle Baldasare, aged 24, at Pensacola, Florida, U.S.A., ending on 24 Jan. 1960. Mrs. Baldasare also holds the feminine underwater distance record at 14 miles. Her ex-husband, Fred Baldasare, aged 38, set the underwater distance record of nearly 50 miles in his France-England Channel crossing of 18 hours 1 minute ending on 11 July 1962.

Switchback riding The world endurance record for rides on a roller coaster is 465 circuits of the John Collins Pleasure Park switchback at Barry Island, Glamorgan by a group of 4 men and 2 girls. The test lasted 31 hours on 15–16 Aug. 1968.

Tailoring The highest speed at which a three-piece man's suit has been made is 84 minutes including measuring and pressing by Wallis and Linnell Ltd. of Kettering, Northamptonshire on 18 Dec. 1969 on the occasion of a retirement presentation to Mr. Ernie Earl after 50 years service.

Talking The world record for non-stop talking is 138 hours (5 days 18 hours) by Victor Villimas of Cleveland, Ohio, U.S.A. in Leeds, Yorkshire, England, from 25–31 Oct. 1967. The longest continuous political speech on record was one of 29 hours 5 minutes by Gerard O'Donnell in Kingston-upon-Hull, Yorkshire, on 23–24 June 1959. The longest recorded lecture was one of 35 hours on "*Some* Aspects of Modern Industry and Commerce in Britain" by Paul Maidment, 33, lecturer at Croydon Technical College, England on 20–21 June 1969. The lecture was divided into 90 minute sessions with 5 minute intervals but was otherwise continuous.

A feminine non-stop talking record was set by Mrs. Alton Clapp of Greenville, North Carolina, U.S.A., in August 1958, with 96 hours 45 minutes 11 seconds. In the U.S.A. such contests have been referred to as "gab fests".

T-bone dive The greatest T-bone dive performed was by Colin Scriven in a Humber Super Snipe at Newark, Nottinghamshire on 27 May 1969, when hitting the 40-foot ramp at 65–70 m.p.h. he cleared the first 12 cars, struck the 13th and somersaulted onto the sixteenth.

Teeth-pulling The man with the "strongest teeth in the world" is John Massis of Belgium, who in 1969 demonstrated the ability to pull a 36-ton train along rails with a bit in his teeth.

TIGHTROPE WALKING
The greatest 19th century tightrope walker was Jean François Gravelet, *alias* Charles Blondin (1824–1897), of France, who made the earliest crossing of the Niagara Falls on a 3-inch rope, 1,100 feet long, 160 feet above the Falls on 30 July 1855. He also made a crossing with Harry Colcord, pick-a-back on 15 Sept. 1860. Though this is difficult to believe, Colcord was his agent.

Endurance The world tightrope endurance record is 214 hours by Henri Rochetain (born 1926) of France on a wire 4,950 feet long, 550 feet above La Seuge river at Le Puy, France, on 13–21 Aug. 1966. The feminine record is 34 hours 15 minutes by Francine Pary, aged 17, on a wire 50 feet high at Toulouse, France, in February 1957.

Longest The longest walk by any funambulist was achieved by Henri Rochetain (b. 1926) of France on a wire 3,790 yards long slung across a gorge at Clermont Ferrand, France on 13 July 1969. He required 3 hours 50 minutes to negotiate the crossing.

High-wire act Highest The highest high-wire act was that of the Germans Alfred and Henry Traber on a 520-foot rope stretched from the Zugspitze (9,738 feet) to the Western Peak, Bavaria, Germany, during July and August 1953.

The highest high-wire act

Human achievements

Tree-climbing The fastest tree-climbing record is one of 36 seconds for a 90-foot pine by Kelly Stanley (Canada) at the Toowoomba Show, Queensland, Australia in 1968.

Tree-sitting The duration record for sitting in a tree is 55 days from 10 a.m. 22 July to 10 a.m. 15 Sept. 1930 by David William Haskell (born 1920) on a 4-foot by 6-foot platform up a backyard walnut tree in Wilmar (now Rosemund), California, U.S.A.

Tunnel of fire The longest tunnel of fire (petrol-soaked hoops of straw) negotiated by a trick motorcyclist is one of 35 feet by Dick Sheppard of Gloucester at Rayleigh, Essex on 21 Sept. 1968.

TYPEWRITING

Fastest The highest recorded speeds attained with a ten-word penalty per error on a manual machine are:

One Minute: 170 words, Margaret Owen (U.S.A.) (Underwood Standard), New York, 21 Oct. 1918.
One Hour: 147 words (net rate per minute), Albert Tangora (U.S.A.) (Underwood Standard), 22 Oct. 1923.

The official hour record on an electric machine is 9,316 words (40 errors) on an I.B.M. machine, giving a net rate of 149 words per minute, by Margaret Hamma, now Mrs. Dilmore (U.S.A.), in Brooklyn, New York City, N.Y., U.S.A. on 20 June 1941.

In an official test in 1946 Stella Pajunas, now Mrs. Garnand, attained a speed of 216 words per minute on an I.B.M. machine.

Slowest Chinese typewriters are so complex that even the most skilled operator cannot select characters from the 1,500 offered at a rate of more than 11 words a minute. The Hoang typewriter produced in 1962 has 5,700 Chinese characters. The keyboard is 2 feet wide and 17 inches high.

Longest The world duration record for typewriting on an electric machine is 150 hours by David J. Carnochan, 22 of the University College London Union from noon on 24 Feb. to 6 p.m. 2 March 1970. His breaks were 70 minutes less than the permitted 5 minutes per hour.

The longest duration typing marathon on a manual machine is 120 hours 15 minutes by Mike Howell, a 23-year-old blind office worker from Greenfield, Oldham, Lancashire on 25–30 Nov. 1969 on an Olympia manual typewriter in Liverpool. In aggregating 561,006 strokes he performed a weight movement of 2,482 tons plus a further 155 tons on moving the carriage for line spacing. On an electric machine the total figure would have been 565 tons.

Most travelled typewriter The world's most travelled typewriter is the Underwood Noiseless portable (rebuilt 1938) of Britain's most famous sportswriter Peter Wilson of the *Daily Mirror*. It has accompanied him in covering 45 sports in 51 countries and 60 trans-Atlantic flights for 35 years (1935–1970).

The sportswriter, Peter Wilson of the "Daily Mirror", with his most-travelled typewriter

174

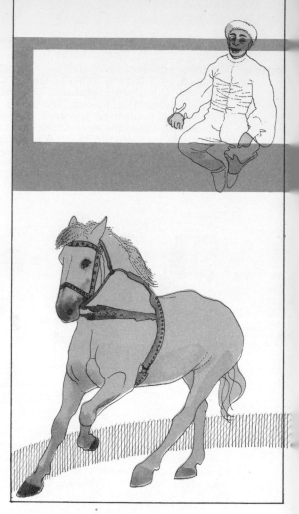

Walking on hands The duration record for walking on hands is 871 miles by Johann Hurlinger, of Austria, who in 55 daily 10-hour stints, averaged 1·58 m.p.h. from Vienna to Paris in 1900.

Whip cracking The longest stock whip ever "cracked" (*i.e.* the end made to travel above the speed of sound—760 m.p.h.) is one of 55 feet by "Saltbush" Bill Mills of Australia.

Wood-cutting The world record for cutting six "shoes" to ascend and sever the top of a 16-foot high 15-inch diameter log is the 1 minute 31 seconds set by the Tasmanian axeman, Doug Youd (born 1938). His brother Roy felled a tree 12 inches in diameter in 1961 in 1 minute 52·3 seconds.

The world record for sawing (hand-bucking) through a 32-inch log is 1 minute 26·4 seconds by Paul M. Searls, aged 46, in Seattle, Washington State, U.S.A. on 5 Nov. 1953. The world record for double-handed sawing through an 18-inch white pine log is 10·2 seconds by Bill Donnelly and Ernie Hogg at Southland, South Island, New Zealand, on 4 Dec. 1955, equalled by N. J. Thorburn and M. Reed at Whangarei, New Zealand, on 3 March 1956. Donnelly and Hogg sawed through a 20-inch white pine log in 12·9 seconds at Invercargill, New Zealand, on 11 Feb. 1956. The 24-inch white pine record is 18·8 seconds by Denis Organ and Graham Sanson at Stratford, North Island, New Zealand on 27 Nov. 1965.

Yo-yo The yo-yo originates from a Filipino jungle fighting weapon recorded in the 16th century weighing 4 lb. with a 20-foot cord. The word means "come-come". The craze was started by Louis Marx (U.S.A.) in 1929. The most difficult modern yo-yo trick is the double-handed cross-over loop the loop. Art Pickles, the 1933–53 world champion once achieved 1,269 consecutive loop the loops. The individual endurance record is 7 hours 31 minutes by Curtis Dorman of the KALL radio station in Salt Lake City, Utah, U.S.A. on 1 April 1960. The group marathon record is 76 hours set by six students with 3 yo-yos at Brierley's Store, Leicester, England on 1–8 March 1969.

CIRCUS RECORDS

The following circus acrobatic feats represent the greatest performed, either for the first time or, if marked with an asterisk, uniquely. A "mechanic" is a safety harness.

Flying Trapeze	Earliest Act	Jules Leotard (France)	Circus Napoleon, Paris	12 Nov. 1859
	Double back somersault	Eddie Silbon	Paris Hippodrome	1879
	Triple back somersault (female)	Lena Jordan (Latvia) to Lew Jordan (U.S.A.)	Sydney, Australia	April 1897
	Triple back somersault (male)	Ernest Clarke to Charles Clarke	Publiones Circus, Cuba	1909
	Triple and a half back somersault	Tony Steele to Lee Strath Marilees	Durango, Mexico	30 Sept. 1962
	Quadruple back somersault (in practice)	*Ernest Clarke to Charles Clarke	Orrin Bros. Circus, Mexico City, Mexico	1915
	Triple back somersault (bar to bar, practice)	Edmund Ramat and Raoul Monbar	Various	1905–10
	Head to head stand on swinging bar (no holding)	*Ed. and Ira Millette (née Wolf)	Various	1910–20
Horse back	Running leaps on and off	*26 by "Poodles" Hanneford	New York	1915
	Three-high column without "mechanic"	*Willy, Baby and Rene Fredianis	Nouveau Cirque, Paris	1908
	Double back somersault mounted	(John or Charles) Frederic Clarke	Various	c. 1905
	Double back somersault from a 2-high to a trailing horse with "mechanic"	Aleksandr Sergey	Moscow Circus	1956
Fixed Bars	Pass from 1st to 3rd bar with a double back somersault	Phil Shevette, Andres Atayde	Woods Gymnasium, New York, European tours	1925–27
	Triple fly-away to ground (male)	Phil Shevette	Folies Bergère, Paris	May 1896
	Triple fly-away to ground (female)	Loretto Twins, Ora and Pauline	Los Angeles	1914
Giant Spring Board	Running forward triple back somersault	John Cornish Worland, (1855–1933) of the U.S.A.	St. Louis, Missouri	1874
Risley (Human Juggling)	Back somersault feet to feet	Richard Risley Carlisle (1814–74) and son (U.S.A.)	Theatre Royal, Edinburgh	Feb. 1844
Acrobatics	Quadruple back somersault to a chair	Sylvester Mezzetti (voltiger) to Butch Mezzetti (catcher)	New York Hippodrome	1915–17
Aerialist	One arm swings 125 (no net) 32 feet up	Vicky Unus (La Toria) (U.S.A.)	Ringling Bros., Barnum & Bailey circuit	Nov. 1962
Teeter Board	Seat to seat triple back somersault	The 5 Draytons		1896
Wire-Juggling	16 hoops (hands and feet)	Ala Naito (Japan) (female)	Madison Square Garden, N.Y.	1937
Low Wire (7 feet)	Feet to feet forward somersault	Con Colleano	Empire Theatre, Johannesburg	1923
		Ala Naito (Japan) (female)	Madison Square Garden, N.Y.	1937
Hire Wire (30–40 feet)	Four high column (with mechanic)	*The Solokhin Brothers (U.S.S.R.)	Moscow Circus	1962
	Three layer, 7 man pyramid	Great Wallendas (Germany)	U.S.A.	1961
Ground Acrobatics	Stationary double back somersault	François Gouleau (France)		1905
	Four high column	The Picchianis (Italy)		1905
	Five high pyramids	The Yacopis (Argentina) with 3 understanders, 3 second layer understanders, 1 middleman, 1 upper middleman and a top mounter	Ringling Bros., Barnum & Bailey circuit	1941

Largest circus
The world's largest permanent circus is Circus Circus, Las Vegas, Nevada, U.S.A. opened on 18 Oct. 1968 at a cost of $15,000,000 (£6,250,000). It covers an area of 129,000 square feet capped by a 90-foot-high tent-shaped flexiglass roof.

WEALTH AND POVERTY

Richest rulers
The Kingdom of Saudi Arabia derived an income of about $500,000,000 (now £208 million) from oil royalties in 1964, but the Royal Family's share was understood to be not more than £25,000,000. The Shaikh of Abu Dhabi, Zaid ibn Sultan Zaid (born 1917), has become extremely wealthy since the Murban oilfield began yielding in 1963, and by 1966 Abu Dhabi was estimated to have an income of $67,000,000 (now £27·9 million) which if divided equally would result in an income of $3,350 per head. Before World War II the income of Maj.-Gen. H. H. Maharajadhiraj Raj Rajeshwar Sawai Shree Yeshwant Rao Holkar Bahadur, G.C.I.E. (1908–61), the Maharaja of Indore, was estimated to be as high as £25,000,000 per annum.

The man with once the highest income in the world was H.H. Shaikh Sir Abdullah as-Salim as-Sabah, G.C.M.G., C.I.E. (1895–1965), the 11th Amir of Kuwait, with an estimated £2,600,000 per week or £135 million a year. The Amir is the Head of State but since 23 Jan. 1963 there has been an elected National Assembly.

Private citizen
According to a survey researched by *Fortune* magazine published in May 1968 the world's two richest private citizens were Jean Paul Getty, 77, and Howard Hughes, 64, with evaluations of $1,338,000,000 (£557·5 million) and $1,373,000,000 (£572 million) respectively. Getty, now resident in Surrey, England, made his first million dollars, "the hardest", in his first 19 months in the oil business in Tulsa, Oklahoma, in June 1916, when aged 22. Getty maintains that "if you can count your millions, you are not a billionaire". More recent estimates suggest that the assets owned and controlled by Mr. Hughes exceed $2 billion (£833 million). The United States' only other possible living dollar billionaire (a "billion" in the U.S.A. is 1,000 million) is Haroldson Lafayette Hunt of Dallas, Texas, owner of the Hunt Oil Company, with an annual income of reputedly $50 million (£20·8 million), of which 27½ per cent. is tax free under the Federal oil depletion allowance.

Human achievements

Billionaires Probably the only other dollar "billionaires" in the United States have been John Davidson Rockefeller, the first (1839–1937), Henry Ford, the first (1863–1947) and Andrew William Mellon (1855–1937). A "billion" dollars is now equivalent to £416,666,666.

The first "billionaire"
John D. Rockefeller
(1839–1937)

Centi-millionaires and millionaires *Fortune* Magazine in May 1968 estimated that there were 153 U.S. Centimillionaires (*i.e.* those with disposable assets of more than $100 million). The fastest centimillionaire has been H. Ross Perot (born 1930), founder and President of Electronic Data Systems, Dallas, Texas in 1962. By 1968 his personal fortune was estimated at $300 million (£126,000,000). By December 1969 it was estimated that the value of his stock holdings might have reached $1,500 million, but he later said he could raise $100 million from his own resources to buy the release of 1,361 U.S. P.o.W.'s in North Vietnam. It was estimated in 1961 that there were 50,000 millionaires in the United States of whom 13,500 came from the State of California. The 1967 total probably surpassed 100,000 of whom 21 succeeded in paying no taxation.

United Kingdom The wealthiest United Kingdom citizen is believed to be Sir John Reeves Ellerman, 2nd baronet (born 21 Dec. 1909), a director of Ellerman Lines Ltd., whose father, Sir John Reeves Ellerman, Bt., C.H. (1862–1933), left £36,684,994, the largest will ever proved in the United Kingdom. His fortune is estimated to be worth about £500 million. The highest death duties ever paid have been £18,000,000 on the estate of Hugh Richard Arthur Grosvenor, G.C.V.O., D.S.O., the 2nd Duke of Westminster (1879–1953), paid between July 1953 and August 1964.

The greatest will proved in Ireland was that of the 1st Earl of Iveagh (1847–1927), who left £13,486,146.

Millionairesses The world's wealthiest woman was probably Princess Wilhelmina Helena Pauline Maria of Orange-Nassau (1880–1962), formerly Queen of the Netherlands (from 1890 to her abdication, 4 Sept. 1948), with a fortune which was estimated at over £200 million.

The largest published estate ever left by a woman was $95,000,000 (then £20,000,000) by the notorious miser Henrietta (Hetty) Howland Green (*née* Robinson) (1835–1916). She had a balance of over $31,400,000 (now £13·08 million) in one bank alone. She was so mean that her son had to have his leg amputated because of the delays in finding a *free* medical clinic. She herself lived off cold porridge because she was too mean to heat it and died of apoplexy in an argument over the virtues of skimmed milk.

The largest amount proved in the will of a woman in the United Kingdom has been the £4,075,550 (duty paid £3,233,454) of Miss Gladys Meryl Yule, daughter of Sir David Yule, Bt. (1858–1928), in August 1957.

Youngest The youngest person ever to accumulate a millionaire estate was the child film actress Shirley Temple (born 23 April 1928), formerly Mrs. John Agar Jr., now Mrs. Charles Black, of the U.S.A. Her accumulated wealth exceeded $1,000,000 (then £209,000) before she was 10 years old.

Earliest The earliest recorded self-made millionairess was Mrs. Annie M. Pope-Turnbo Malone (died 1957), a laundress from St. Louis, Missouri, U.S.A., who in 1905 perfected the permanent straight treatment for those with crinkly hair.

Richest families In May 1968 it was estimated that three members of the Irish-American Mellon family of the U.S.A., from Omagh, County Tyrone: Mrs. Alisa Mellon Bruce (d. 24 Aug. 1969), Paul Mellon and Richard K. Mellon, were each worth between $500 million and $1,000 million (£416·6 million). Another 1968 estimate put the family fortune at more than $3,000 million (about £1,255 million). It has also been tentatively estimated that the combined wealth of the much larger Du Pont family of some 2,100 members may be in excess of this figure.

The largest number of millionaires estates in one family in the British Isles is that of the Wills family of the Imperial Tobacco Company, of whom 14 members have left estates in excess of £1,000,000 since 1910. These totalled £55 million, of which death duties (introduced in 1894) have taken over £27,000,000.

Largest dowry The largest recorded dowry was that of Elena Patiño, daughter of Don Simon Iturbi Patiño (1861–1947), the Bolivian tin millionaire, who in 1929 bestowed £8,000,000 from a fortune at one time estimated to be worth £125,000,000.

SALARIES

Highest World The world's highest salary in 1968 was earned by Mr. Konosuke Matsushita the business executive of Tōkyō, Japan. His total income (including dividends) was £851,991 of which only 80 per cent. was removed in tax. The highest salary in the United States is that of the Chairman of the Board and Chief Executive Officer of the General Motors Corporation, of Detroit, Michigan, U.S.A. James Roche succeeded to this appointment on 30 Oct. 1967. His 1967–68 salary with bonuses was $733,316 (£305,548). In June 1969 he won a Cadillac in a local draw but returned it on the grounds that he was already provided. The record gain from stock options was that of Ralph Cordiner, Chairman of the General Electric Co., who made a paper profit of $1,262,260 (now £525,941) on options exercised in 1957.

United Kingdom

Britain's highest paid business executive was reputed to be Sir William Lyons (born Blackpool 4 Sept. 1901), Chairman and Managing Director of Jaguar Cars Ltd. of Coventry, Warwickshire, who, prior to Jaguar's incorporation in British Motor Holdings in July 1966, is said to have received about £120,000. The highest salary initially disclosed under the 1967 Companies Act was that of Mr. Owen Aisher with £91,722 as Chairman of Marley Tiles Ltd. In 1968 he drew only £77,400 of the £108,600 to which he was entitled. In July 1965 it was reported that Mr. Wilfred Harvey, then Chairman of the British Printing Corporation, was eligible under his commission agreement to have drawn £270,000 in 1964–65. The highest amount paid in a straight salary in 1968 was that of Mr. David Haven Barran (born 23 May 1912), Chairman of Shell Transport and Trading Co. Ltd. at £72,818. His net take home pay from this was less than £12,500.

Highest income

The highest gross income ever achieved in a single year by a private citizen is an estimated $105,000,000 (now £43¾ million) in 1927 by the Chicago gangster Alphonse ("Scarface Al") Capone (1899–1947). This was derived from illegal liquor trading and alky-cookers (illicit stills), gambling establishments, dog tracks, dance halls, "protection" rackets and vice. On his business card Capone described himself as a "Second Hand Furniture Dealer". Henry Ford, the first (1863–1947) earned about £25 million per annum at his peak.

Lowest incomes

The poorest people in the world are the surviving Pintibu (or Bindibu) of whom 42 were found in the Northern Territory of Australia in July 1957. They subsist with water from soak holes and by eating rats. In September 1957 Chinese Government sources admitted that in some areas of the mainland the average annual income of peasants was 42 yuans (£6 18s.) per head. In 1964 China's average income per head was estimated at £25 per annum and the daily calorie intake at 2,200 (see calorific comparative data, Chapter XI).

"Golden Handshake" record

The most golden "golden handshake" was the £83,575 tax-free compensation for loss of office received in 1954 by Sir Charles Blampied Colston, C.B.E., M.C., D.C.M. (born 31 Oct. 1891), Chairman and Managing Director of Hoover Ltd. Since the Finance Act of 1960, which made such payments taxable after the first £5,000, the greatest amount ever paid out is believed to be £124,000, which was announced on 29 June 1964 to have been paid to Philip Gordon Walker (born 9 June 1912), the Managing Director of Albert E. Reed & Co. Ltd. (since renamed the Reed Paper Group) from 1951 until his resignation on 9 July 1963, shortly after the company had been taken over by the International Publishing Corporation. After tax he received an estimated £35,000. The largest leaving present recorded in trade union history was one aggregating a reported £25,000 from branches of the Transport and General Workers' Union to Mr. Frank Cousins in September 1969.

Return of cash

The largest amount of cash ever found and returned to its owners was $240,000 (£85,714) in unmarked $10 (83s. 4d.) and $20 (166s. 8d.) bills found in a street in Los Angeles, California, U.S.A., by Douglas William Johnston, an unemployed negro, in March 1961. He received many letters, of which 25 per cent. suggested that he was insane.

Greatest bequests

The greatest bequests in a life-time of a millionaire were those of the late John Davison Rockefeller (1839–1937), who gave away sums totalling $750,000,000 (now £312·5 million). The greatest benefactions of a British millionaire were those of William Richard Morris, later the Viscount Nuffield, G.B.E., C.H. (1877–1963), which totalled more than £30,000,000 between 1926 and his death on 22 Aug. 1963.

The largest bequest made in the history of philanthropy was the $500,000,000 (£178,570,000) gift, announced on 12 Dec. 1955, to 4,157 educational and other

Owen Aisher, whose £91,722 salary is the highest yet published in Britain

institutions by the Ford Foundation (established 1936) of New York City, N.Y., U.S.A. The assets of the Foundation had a book value of $2,477,984,000 (now £1,032 million) in 1967.

Best dressed Women

The longest reign as the "Best Dressed Woman" was 15 years from 1938 to 1953 by the Duchess of Windsor (born Bessie Wallis Warfield, 19 June 1896, formerly Mrs. Spencer, formerly Mrs. Simpson). In January 1959 the New York Dress Institute put the Duchess and Mrs. William S. "Babe" Paley beyond annual comparison by elevating them to an ageless "Hall of Fame". Also later elevated was Mrs. Jacqueline Bouvier Kennedy-Onassis (born 28 July 1929). Including furs and jewellery, some perennials, such as Mrs. Winston F. C. "Ceezee" Guest, Mrs. Paley and Mrs. Gloria Guinness (née Rubio), are reputed to spend up to $100,000 (£41,666) a year on their wardrobes. Mrs. Henry M. Flagler, the chatelaine of Whitehall, her husband's $300,000 establishment in Palm Beach, Florida, U.S.A. in the era 1902–1914, never wore any dress a second time. Her closets were nonetheless moth proof.

In January 1960 the Institute decided it was politic to list a Top Twelve, not in order of merit, but alphabetically. The youngest winner was Mrs. Amanda Carter Burden, aged 22, a step-daughter of Mr. William Paley (see above), on 13 Jan. 1966. After 1966 rankings were re-established.

GASTRONOMIC RECORDS

Records for eating and drinking by trenchermen do not match those suffering from the rare disease of bulimia (morbid desire to eat) and polydipsia (pathological thirst). Some bulimia patients have to spend 15 hours a day eating, with an extreme consumption of 384 lb. 2 oz. of food in six days by Matthew Daking, aged 12, in 1743 (known as Mortimer's case). Some polydipso-maniacs have been said to be unsatisfied by less than 96 pints of liquid a day.

Jack Keyes, world champion beer drinker

The world's greatest trencherman is Edward Abraham ("Bozo") Miller (born 1909) of Oakland, California, U.S.A. He consumes up to 25,000 calories per day or more than 11 times that recommended. He stands 5 feet 7½ inches tall but weighs from 20 to 21½ stone, with a 57-inch waist. He has been undefeated in eating contests since 1931 (see below). The bargees on the Rhine are reputed to be the world's heaviest eaters with 5,200 calories a day.

Specific records have been claimed as follows:

Baked Beans 40 lb. in 30 minutes by 8 boys from the Coseley Youth Centre, Staffordshire, on 1 Feb. 1970.

Bananas 40 in 39 minutes 40 seconds by Anthony Figg, aged 17, at Eastleigh Technical College, Hampshire, on 26 May 1967. Leslie Jones of Buckley, Flintshire, Wales ate 25 in 4 minutes 23 seconds on 5 Nov. 1968.

Beer Lawrence Hill (b. 1942) of Bolton, Lancashire, drained a 2-pint Yard of Ale in 6 seconds on 17 Dec. 1964. A 3-pint yard was downed in 12·4 seconds by Michael M. Douglas in the Edinburgh University Union on 22 Feb. 1967. Lionel Tuft (b. 1931) of Teddington, Bedfordshire, the 1968 and 1969 winner of the "World Beer Drinking Championship", downed 1 gallon in 7 minutes 33 seconds at the Royal Lancaster Hotel, London on 17 Dec. 1968..
The Oxford University "sconce" record is 12·0 seconds for 2 pints of beer set by the Australian, R. Hawke (University College) in 1955 and Clive Anderson (Magdalen) on 26 Feb. 1967. Two pints in 6·4 seconds in November 1968 and one pint in 2·34 seconds (1/100th second watch) by Brendan Donnison at Ratcliffe, Leicestershire on 7 June 1968.
The world record for 52 oz. (2·6 pints) of beer is 7·9 seconds set by Leo Williams at the University of Queensland, in May 1961, and the record for 2 litres (3·52 Imperial pints) is 11 seconds by J. H. Cochran (Class of 1925, Princeton University, New Jersey, U.S.A.) in Harry's New York Bar, Paris, on 26 June 1932.
The most extreme recorded drinking feat was one recorded in 1810 at Wroxham, Norfolk, England where a man was witnessed to have lowered 54 pints of porter in 55 minutes. This must be regarded as an exaggerated report and the true record is closer to 30·79 pints in 60 minutes by Horst Pretorius (West Germany) aged 36, in June 1968. Jack Keyes, 23, of Londonderry reportedly drank 36 pints in 60 minutes in Blackpool, Lancashire in March 1969.

Beer Upsidedown 3½ pints by Peter Harris at The Anchorage, Plymouth on 17 Jan. 1970. 2 pints by Desmond Bluett, 19 in 4 minutes 50 seconds at Skeffington Arms Hotel, Galway, Ireland on 19 Feb. 1970.

Boiled Eggs 44 in 30 minutes by Georges Grogniet of Belgium on 31 May 1956.

Cheese 16 oz. in 11 minutes 23 seconds by Steve Wheat, 16, at Court School of Dancing, Walthamstow, London on 27 Nov. 1969.

Chicken 27 (2 lb. pullets) by "Bozo" Miller (see above) at Trader Vic's, San Francisco, California, U.S.A., in 1963.

Gherkins 1 lb. in 4 minutes 27 seconds by Robert Harari, 21, at Palmer's Green, London N.13, 6 Nov. 1968.

Goldfish (live) 210 by Charles Winfield, 19, at St. Mary's University, San Antonio, Texas, U.S.A. on 7 Feb. 1969.

Grapes 1 lb. (unpipped) in 126 seconds by Shayne Gould at Court School of Dancing, Walthamstow, London on 27 Nov. 1969.

Haggis 19 oz. haggis in 65 seconds at Waterloo Station, London on 1 Jan. 1967.

Hamburgers 77 at a sitting by Philip Yazdizk (U.S.A.), Chicago, Illinois, U.S.A. on 25 April 1955.

Meat One whole roast ox in 42 days by Johann Ketzler of Munich, Germany in 1880.

Meat Pies 10 8-oz. pies (Steak & Kidney), by John Taylor, 25, at Rugby, Warwickshire in January 1969. Ronald Pattinson, 18, ate 8 "butties" (5 × 3 × ½ inch) in Liverpool in October 1969.

Milk 1 quart in 9·0 seconds, Edward Turner at Cardiff Golf Range Club, 24 Feb. 1970.

Oysters 480 in 60 minutes by Joe Garcia (Australia), in Melbourne, on 5 Feb. 1955. The official record for opening oysters is 100 in 3 minutes 37 seconds in Paris in 1954 by le Champion du Monde des Ecaillers M. Williams Bley.

Pickled Onions 60 in 15 minutes 30 seconds by James Massie, 23, at The Beehive, Carterton, Oxfordshire on 6 Feb. 1970.

Potato Crisps 30 bags in 24 minutes 3·6 seconds, without a drink, by Paul G. Tully of Brisbane University in May 1969.

Prunes 130 in 116 seconds (stoned and soaked), Edward Baxter at St. Edward's Hall, Leek, Staffordshire, 12 Oct. 1968.

Ravioli 324 (first 250 in 70 minutes) by "Bozo" Miller (see above) at Rendezvous Room, Oakland, California, U.S.A. in 1963.

Raw Eggs 24 in 9·4 seconds by Bob Cymberlist of Shane's Health Studios, Belfast, N. Ireland on 2 July 1969. David Taylor at St. Leonards-on-Sea, Sussex ate 16 raw eggs with their shells in 3 minutes 20 seconds on 8 Jan. 1970.

Sausages 25 2-oz. sausages in 4 minutes 37 seconds by Rodney Harrison, 22, at Much Wenlock, Shropshire on 26 May 1969. 30 2-oz. sausages in 10 minutes 11·8 seconds by Walter Cornelius at Peterborough on 8 May 1969.

Spaghetti 100 yards in 1 minute 34 seconds (by 4 people in a 3 ft. diameter circle) at St. Mary's Balham Youth Club, London in October 1967.

Whelks 81 (unshelled) in 15 minutes by William Corfield at the Helyar Arms, East Coker, Somerset on 6 Sept. 1970.

From a medical point of view, record attempts must be regarded as extremely inadvisable.

2. Honours, Decorations and Awards

Eponymous record The largest object to which a human name is attached is the super cluster of galaxies known as Abell 7, after the astronomer Dr. George O. Abell of the University of California, U.S.A. The group of clusters has an estimated linear dimension of 300,000,000 light years and was announced in 1961.

ORDERS AND DECORATIONS

Oldest The earliest of the orders of chivalry is the Venetian order of St. Marc, reputedly founded in A.D. 831. The Castilian order of Calatrava has an established date of foundation in 1158. The prototype of the princely Orders of Chivalry is the Most Noble Order of the Garter founded by King Edward III in c. 1348.

Most titles The most titled person in the world is the 18th Duchess of Alba (Albade Tormes), Doña Maria del Rosario Cagetana Fitz-James Stuart y Silva. She is 8 times a duchess, 15 times a marchioness, 21 times a countess and is 19 times a Spanish grandee.

Rarest British The rarest British medal is the Union of South Africa King's Medal for Bravery in Gold. The unique recipient was Francis C. Drake, aged 14, who rescued a child from a deep well at Parys, in the Orange Free State, on 6 Jan. 1943. However, the Queen's Fire Services Medal for Gallantry (instituted in 1954), which can only be won posthumously, has yet to be awarded.

Of War Medals, only two Naval General Service Medals (1793–1840) were issued with seven bars (the one legged Admiral of the Fleet Sir James Alexander Gordon, G.C.B. [1782–1869] and the one-eyed Rear Admiral Sir John Hindmarsh, K.H. [d. 1860]) and only two Military General Service Medals (1793–1814) with 15 bars (James Talbot of the 45th Foot and Daniel Loochstadt of the 60th Foot).

William Corfield, world champion whelk eater

Commonest Of gallantry decorations, the most unsparingly given was the Military Medal, which was awarded to 115,589 recipients between 1916 and 1919. The most frequently awarded decoration in the 1939–45 war was the Distinguished Flying Cross, which was awarded (including bars) 21,281 times.

Most expensive The highest price paid for any United Kingdom decoration is £1,700 for the Victoria Cross awarded to Lieut. William Rennie for two acts of gallantry on 21 and 25 Sept. 1857 outside Lucknow, India. This was paid on behalf of his regiment, the 3rd Battalion of the Cameroneans (Scottish Rifles) at Sotheby's salerooms, London on 21 Jan. 1969. It was reported on 6 May 1967 when the V.C. of the late Sgt. John Hannah (1921–47) of the R.A.F. was presented to his Squadron (No. 83) by his widow, Janice, that she had refused an offer of £3,000 from New York City, U.S.A.

The Victoria Cross

VICTORIA CROSS

bars
The only three men ever to have been awarded a bar to the Victoria Cross (instituted 1856) are:—

Surg.-Capt. (later Lt.-Col.) Arthur Martin-Leake, V.C.*, V.D., R.A.M.C. (1874–1953) (1902 and bar 1915).
Capt. Noel Godfrey Chavasse, V.C.*, M.C., R.A.M.C. (1884–1917) (1916 and bar posthumously 14 Sept. 1917).
Second Lieut. (later Capt.) Charles Hazlett Upham, V.C.*, N.Z.M.F. (born 1911) (1941 and bar 1942).

Oldest
The greatest age at which a man has won the V.C. is believed to be 69 in the case of Lieut. (later Capt.) William Raynor of the Bengal Veteran Establishment, in defence of the magazine at Delhi, India, on 11 May 1857.

Youngest
The lowest established age for a V.C. is 15 years 3 months for Hospital Apprentice Arthur Fitzgibbon (born at Peteragurh, northern India, 13 May 1845) of the 67th (The Hampshire) Regt. for bravery at the Taku Forts in northern China on 21 Aug. 1860. Later, as an assistant surgeon, he was dismissed for insubordination. The youngest living V.C. is Lance-Corporal Rambahadur Limbu (born Nepal, 1939) of the 10th Princess Mary's Own Gurkha Rifles. The award, announced on 22 April 1966, was for his courage while fighting in the Bau district of Sarawak, East Malaysia, on 21 Nov. 1965.

est lived
The longest lived of all the 1,348 winners of the Victoria Cross was Captain (later General Sir) Lewis Stratford Tollemache Halliday, V.C., K.C.B., of the Royal Marine Light Infantry. He was born on 14 May 1870, won his V.C. in China in 1900, and died on 9 March 1966, aged 95 years 299 days. The oldest living V.C. is Lt.-Col. George Thomas Dorrell, V.C., M.B.E. (born 2 July 1876), who won his decoration as a Sergeant-Major with "L" Battery of the Royal Horse Artillery at Nery, France, on 1 Sept. 1914 having joined the Army on 2 Dec. 1895.

RECORD NUMBER OF BARS (repeat awards) EVER GAZETTED TO BRITISH GALLANTRY DECORATIONS

*=a bar

V.C.*	A first bar has been three times awarded to the Victoria Cross (see above).
D.S.O.***	A third bar has been 16 times awarded to the Distinguished Service Order.
D.S.C.***	A third bar has been uniquely awarded to the Distinguished Service Cross won by Cdr. Norman Eyre Morley, R.N.V.R.
M.C.***	A third bar has been four times awarded to the Military Cross.
D.F.C.**	A second bar has been 54 times awarded to the Distinguished Flying Cross.
A.F.C.**	A second bar has been 13 times awarded to the Air Force Cross.
D.C.M.**	A second bar has been 12 times awarded to the Distinguished Conduct Medal.
C.G.M.*	A first bar has been uniquely awarded to the Conspicuous Gallantry Medal won by C.P.O. A. R. Blore and a second medal to Sea. D. Barry.
G.M.*	A first bar has been 25 times awarded to the George Medal.
K.P.M.**	A second bar has been uniquely awarded to the King's/Queen's Police Medal for Gallantry won by Supt. F. W. O'Gormon.
E.M.*	A first bar has twice been awarded to the Edward Medal in Silver.
D.S.M.***	A third bar has been uniquely awarded to the Distinguished Service Medal won by Petty Officer William Henry Kelly.
M.M.***	A third bar has been uniquely awarded to the Military Medal won by Cpl. Ernest A. Correy.
D.F.M.**	A second bar has been uniquely awarded to the Distinguished Flying Medal won by Flt.-Sgt. (now Group Capt.) Donald Ernest Kingaby, D.S.O., A.F.C.
A.F.M.**	A first bar has been 7 times awarded to the Air Force Medal.
S.G.M.*	A first bar has been uniquely awarded to the Sea Gallantry Medal won by Chief Officer James Whiteley.
B.E.M.*	A first bar has been 4 times awarded to the British Empire Medal for Gallantry (as instituted in 1957).

No bars have yet been awarded to the George Cross (G.C.), the Conspicuous Gallantry Medal (Flying) (C.G.M.). No bars were ever awarded to the Albert Medal in Gold (A.M.), the Albert Medal (A.M.), the Edward Medal (E.M.) or the Empire Gallantry Medal (E.G.M.).

Most mentions in despatches
The record number of "mentions" is 24 by Field Marshal the Rt. Hon. the Earl Roberts, V.C., K.G., K.P., G.C.B., O.M., G.C.S.I., G.C.I.E., V.D. (1832–1914). He was also the only subject with 8 sets of official post-nominal letters.

U.S.S.R.
The U.S.S.R.'s highest award for valour is the Gold Star of a Hero of the Soviet Union. Over 10,000 were awarded in World War II. Among the 109 awards of a second star were those to Marshal Iosif Vissarionovich Dzhugashvili, *alias* Stalin (1879–1953) and Lt.-General Nikita Sergeyevich Khrushchyov (born 17 April 1894). The only war-time triple awards were to Marshal Georgiy Konstantinovich Zhukov, Hon. G.C.B. (born 1896) (subsequently awarded a fourth Gold Star, unique until Mr. Khrushchyov's fourth award) and the leading air aces Guards' Colonel (now Aviation Maj.-Gen.) Aleksandr Ivanovich Polkyrshkin and Aviation Maj.-Gen. Ivan Nikitaevich Kozhedub.

U.S.A.
The highest U.S. decoration is the Congressional Medal of Honor. Five marines received both the Army and Navy Medals of Honor for the same acts in 1918 and 14 officers and men from 1863 to 1915 have received the medal on two occasions.

Most bemedalled
The most bemedalled chest is that of H.I.M. Haile Selassie (born, as Ras Tafari Makonnen, on 23 July 1892), Emperor of Ethiopia, who has over 50 medal ribbons worn in up to 14 rows.

TOP SCORING AIR ACES

World
80 Rittmeister Manfred, Freiherr (Baron) von Richthofen (Germany).
352[2] Major Erich Hartman (Germany).

United Kingdom
73[1] Capt. (acting Major) Edward Mannock, V.C., D.S.O.**, M.C.*.
38[3] Wg.-Cdr. (now Air Vice Marshal) James Edgar Johnson, C.B., C.B.E., D.S.O.**, D.F.C.*.

A compilation of the top air aces of 13 combatant nations in World War I and of 22 nations in World War II was included in the 13th edition of *The Guinness Book of Records*.

[1] *Recent research suggests that Mannock's total may have been lower than that of Major James Thomas Byford McCudden, V.C. D.S.O.*, M.C.*, M.M. (57 victories).*

[2] *A few of these aircraft in this unrivalled total were obsolescent Soviet transport aircraft on the Eastern Front in 1942–45. The German air ace with most victories against the R.A.F. was Oberleutnant Hans-Joachim Marseille (killed 30 Sept. 1942), who, in 388 actions, shot down 158 Allied aircraft, 151 of them over North Africa.*

[3] *The greatest number of successes against flying bombs (V.1's) was by Sqn. Ldr. Joseph Berry, D.F.C.** (born Nottingham, 1920), who brought down 60 in 1944. The most successful R.A.F. fighter pilot was Sqn. Ldr. M. T. St. John Pattle, D.F.C.*, of South Africa, with a known total of at least 40.*

Top jet ace
The greatest number of kills in jet to jet battles is 16 by Capt. Joseph Christopher McConnell, U.S.A.F. (b. 1922) in the Korean war (1950–53). He was killed on 25 Aug. 1954. It is possible that an Israeli ace may have surpassed this total in the period 1967–70 but the identity of pilots is subject to strict security.

Top woman ace
The record score for any woman fighter pilot is 13 by Jnr. Lt. Lila Litvak (U.S.S.R.) in the Eastern Front campaign of 1941–45.

Anti-submarine successes
The highest number of U-boat kills attributed to one ship in the 1939–45 war was 13 to H.M.S. *Starling* (Capt. Frederick J. Walker, C.B., D.S.O.***, R.N.). Captain Walker was in overall command at the sinking of a total of 25 U-boats between 1941 and the time of his death in 1944. The U.S. Destroyer Escort *England* sank six Japanese submarines in the Pacific between 18 and 30 May 1944.

Field Marshal the Rt. Hon. Earl Roberts, V.C., holder of the record number of Mentions in Despatches

179

Human achievements

Most successful U-boat captain The most successful of all World War II submarine commanders was Korvetten-Kapitän (now Kapitän zur See) Otto Kretschmer (b. 1911), captain of the U.23 and later the U.99. He sank one allied destroyer and 44 merchantmen totalling 266,629 gross registered tons in 16 patrols before his capture on 17 March 1941. He is a Knight's Cross of the Iron Cross with Oakleaves and Swords. In World War I Kapitän-Leutnant Lothar von Arnauld de la Periere, in the U.35 and U.139, sank 195 allied ships totalling 458,856 gross tons.

Greatest reception The greatest ticker-tape reception ever given on Broadway, New York City, N.Y., U.S.A., was that for Lt.-Col. (now Col.) John Herschel Glenn, Jr. (born 18 July 1921) on 1 March 1962, after his return from his tri-orbital flight. The New York Street Cleaning Department estimated that 3,474 tons of paper descended. This total compared with 3,249 tons for General of the Army Douglas MacArthur (1880–1964) in 1951 and 1,800 tons for Col. Charles Augustus Lindbergh (born 4 Feb. 1902) in June 1927.

Most statues The world record for raising statues to oneself was set by Generalissimo Dr. Rafael Leónidas Trujillo y Molina (1891–1961), former President of the Dominican Republic. In March 1960 a count showed that there were "over 2,000". The country's highest mountain was named Pico Trujillo (now Pico Duarte). One Province was called Trujillo and another Trujillo Valdez. The capital was named Ciudad Trujillo (Trujillo City) in 1936, but reverted to its old name of Santo Domingo de Guzmán on 23 Nov. 1961. Trujillo was assassinated in a car ambush on 30 May 1961, and 30 May is now celebrated annually as a public holiday. The man to whom most statues have been raised is undoubtedly Vladimir Ilyich Ulyanov, *alias* Lenin (1877–1924), busts of whom have been mass-produced as also in the case of Mao Tse-tung.

NOBEL PRIZES

The Nobel Foundation of £3,200,000 was set up under the will of Alfred Bernhard Nobel (1833–96), the unmarried Swedish chemist and chemical engineer, who invented dynamite in 1866. The Nobel Prizes are presented annually on 10 Dec., the anniversary of Nobel's death and the festival day of the Foundation. Since the first Prizes were awarded in 1901, the highest cash value of the award, in each of the six fields of Physics, Chemistry, Medicine and Physiology, Literature, Peace and Economics was $67,000 (£28,000) in 1968. Only the nationals of 25 countries have shared the three scientific prizes.

MOST AWARDS

By countries The United States has shared in the greatest number of awards (including those made in 1969) with a total of 74, made up of 20 for Physics, 13 for Chemistry, 22 for Medicine-Physiology, 6 for Literature and 13 for Peace.

The United Kingdom has shared in 53 awards, comprising 14 for Physics, 15 for Chemistry, 10 for Medicine-Physiology, 6 for Literature and 8 for Peace.

By classes, the United States holds the records for Medicine-Physiology with 22, for Physics with 20 and for Peace with 13; Germany for Chemistry with 20; and France for Literature with 12. The first Economics Prize (1969) was shared by the Netherlands and Norway.

Individuals Individually the only person to have won two Prizes outright is Dr. Linus Carl Pauling (born 28 Feb. 1901), the Professor of Chemistry since 1931 at the California Institute of Technology, Pasadena, California, U.S.A. He was awarded the Chemistry Prize for 1954 and the Peace Prize for 1962. The only other person to have won two prizes was Madame Marie Curie (1867–1934), who was born in Poland as Marja Sklodowska. She shared the 1903 Physics Prize with her husband Pierre Curie (1859–1906) and Antoine Henri Becquerel (1852–1908), and won the 1911 Chemistry Prize outright. The Peace

Marie Curie— the first double Nobel Prize winner

Prize has been awarded three times to the International Committee of the Red Cross (founded 29 Oct. 1863) of Geneva, Switzerland, namely in 1917, 1944 and in 1963, when it was shared with the International League of Red Cross Societies.

Oldest The oldest prizeman has been Professor Francis Peyton Rous (born Baltimore, Maryland, U.S.A. 5 Oct. 1879) of the Rockefeller Institute in New York City, N.Y., U.S.A. He shared the Medicine Prize in 1966, at the age of 87.

Youngest The youngest laureate has been Professor Sir William Lawrence Bragg, C.H., O.B.E., M.C. (born in Adelaide, South Australia, 31 March 1890), of the U.K., who at the age of 25, shared the 1915 Physics Prize with his father, Sir William Henry Bragg, O.M., K.B.E. (1862–1942), for work on X-rays and crystal structures. Bragg and also Theodore William Richards (1868–1928) of the U.S.A., who won the 1914 Chemistry prize, carried out their prize work when aged 23. The youngest Literature prizeman has been Joseph Rudyard Kipling (1865–1936) at the age of 41 in 1907. The youngest Peace prize-winner has been the Rev. Dr. Martin Luther King, Jr. (1929–68) of the U.S.A., in 1964.

PEERAGE

Most ancient creation The year 1223 has been ascribed to the premier Irish barony of Kingsale (formerly de Courcy), though on the Order of Precedence the date is listed as 1397. The premier English barony, de Ros, was held until her death on 8 Oct. 1956, by a Baroness in her own right and 26th in her line, dating from 1264. It was called out of abeyance on 29 Aug. 1958 in favour of a granddaughter, Mrs. Georgiana Angela Maxwell (born 1933). The earldom of Arundel, a subsidiary title of the Duke of Norfolk, dates from 1139.

Oldest creation The oldest age at which any person has been raised to the peerage is 94 in the case of Sir William Francis Kyffin Taylor, G.B.E., K.C. (born 9 July 1854), who was created Baron Maenan of Ellesmere, County Salop (Shropshire), in 1948, and died, aged 97, on 22 Sept. 1951, when the title became extinct.

The oldest peer: the Rt. Hon. the Lord Goddard, G.C.B., who celebrated his 93rd birthday on 10th April 1970

Human achievements

The most prolific peeress is believed to be Elizabeth (*née* Barnard), who bore 22 children to her husband Lord Chandos of Sudeley (1642–1714).

BARONETS

OLDEST
The greatest age to which a baronet has lived is 101 years 6 months, in the case of Sir Fitzroy Maclean, 10th Bt., K.C.B., who was born on 18 May 1835 and died on 22 Nov. 1936. He was the last survivor of the Charge of the Light Brigade at Balaclava in the Crimea, Russia, on 25 Oct. 1854.

Most and least creations
The largest number of creations this century was 51 in 1919. There were none in 1940 or since 1965.

KNIGHTS
Youngest
The youngest age at which a knighthood has been conferred is 2 years 9 months in the case of Richard, Duke of York, who was born on 17 Aug. 1472 and invested a K.G. on 15 May 1475. He is believed to have been murdered in the Tower of London with his elder brother, ex-King Edward V, probably between July and September 1483.

Order of Merit
The Order of Merit (instituted on 23 June 1902), is limited to 24 members. Up to August 1969 there were only 118 awards plus 9 honorary awards to non-British citizens. The longest lived holder has been the Rt. Hon. Sir William Malcolm Hailey, O.M., G.C.S.I., G.C.M.G., G.C.I.E., the 1st Baron Hailey who died on 1 June 1969 aged 97 years 3 months. The oldest recipient was Admiral of the Fleet the Hon. Sir Henry Keppel, G.C.B., O.M. (1809–1904), who received the Order aged 93 years 2 months on 9 Aug. 1902. Currently the oldest holder is E. M. Forster, O.M. who was born 1 Jan. 1879. The youngest recipient has been H.R.H. the Duke of Edinburgh, K.G., K.T., O.M., G.B.E. who was appointed on his 47th birthday on 10 June 1968.

Most freedoms
The most freedoms conferred upon any citizen of the United Kingdom is 42, in the case of the Rt. Hon. Sir Winston Leonard Spencer Churchill, K.G., O.M., C.H., T.D. (1874–1965).

Most honorary degrees
The greatest number of honorary degrees awarded to any individual is 85, given to Herbert Clark Hoover (1874–1964), former President of the United States (1929–33).

Greatest vote
The largest monetary vote made by Parliament to a subject was the £400,000 given to the 1st Duke of Wellington (1769–1852) on 12 April 1814. He received in all £864,000. The total received by the 1st, 2nd and 3rd Dukes to January 1900 was £1,052,000.

Who's Who
The longest entry in *Who's Who* (founded 1848) was that of the Rt. Hon. Sir Winston Leonard Spencer Churchill, K.G., O.M., C.H., T.D. (1874–1965), who had 211 lines in the 1965 edition. Apart from those who qualify for inclusion by hereditary title, the youngest entry has been Yehudi Menuhin, Hon. K.B.E. (born New York City, U.S.A. 22 April 1916), the concert violinist, who first appeared in the 1932 edition.

"Time" magazine cover
The most frequent subject has been President Johnson with 41 treatments to the end of 1967. The youngest subject for a *Time* (first issued 3 March 1923) cover was Charles Augustus Lindbergh, Jr. (born in June 1930), during the kidnapping case of 1932. The oldest subject was the veteran sports coach Amos Alonzo Stagg (1862–1965) in the issue of 20 Oct. 1958. Summing up his life's work he agreed with the dictum of the Brooklyn baseball manager of 1948 "Lippy" Leo Durocher that "Nice guys come last".

Longest obituary
The obituary of Thomas Edison (11 Feb. 1847– 18 Nov. 1931) occupied 4½ pages in the *New York Times* of the next day.

Oldest peer
The oldest peer ever recorded was the Rt. Hon. Frank Douglas-Pennant, the 5th Baron Penrhyn (born 21 Nov. 1865), who died on 3 Feb. 1967, aged 101 years 74 days. Currently the oldest peer is the Rt. Hon. Rayner Goddard, Baron Goddard of Aldbourne, G.C.B. born 10 April 1877, the Lord Chief Justice of England from 1946 to 1958. The oldest peeress recorded was the Countess Desmond, who was alleged to be 140 when she died in 1604. This claim is patently exaggerated but it is accepted that she may have been 104. Currently the oldest peeress of parliament is the Countess of Kintore, Ethel Sydney Keith-Falconer, Dowager Viscountess Stonehaven, born on 20 Sept. 1874.

Longest and shortest peerages
The peer who has sat longest in the House of Lords was Lt.-Col. Charles Harvey FitzRoy, O.B.E., the 4th Baron Southampton (born 11 May 1867), who succeeded to his father's title on 6 July 1872, took his seat on 23 Jan. 1891, 18 months before Mr. W. E. Gladstone's fourth administration began, and died, aged 91, on 7 Dec. 1958, having held the title for more than 86 years.

The shortest enjoyment of a peerage was the "split second" by which the law assumes that the Hon. Wilfrid Carlyle Stamp (born 28 Oct. 1904), the 2nd Baron Stamp, survived his father, Sir Josiah Charles Stamp, G.C.B., G.B.E., the 1st Baron Stamp, when both were killed as a result of German bombing of London on 16 April 1941. Apart from this legal fiction, the shortest recorded peerage was one of 30 minutes in the case of Sir Charles Brandon, K.B., the 3rd Duke of Suffolk, who died, aged 13 or 14, just after succeeding his brother, the 2nd Duke, when both were suffering a fatal illness, at Buckden, Huntingdonshire, on 14 July 1551.

Highest numbering
The highest succession number borne by any peer is that of the present 35th Baron Kingsale (John de Courcy, born 1941). (See page 180.)

Most creations
The largest number of new hereditary peerages created in any year was the 54 in 1296. The record for all peerages (including life peerages) is 55 in 1964. The greatest number of extinctions in a year was 16 in 1923 and the greatest number of deaths was 44 in 1935.

Longest abeyance
The longest abeyance of any peerage was that of the baronies of Burgh and Strabolgi, which were called out on 9 May 1916, after 547 years in abeyance since 6 April 1369.

Most prolific
The most prolific peer of all time is believed to be Sir Robert Shirley, the 1st Earl Ferrers (1650–1717). By his first wife, Elizabeth (*née* Washington) (died 1693), he had 17 children (10 sons and 7 daughters), and by his second wife Selina (*née* Finch) (died 1762) 10 children (5 sons and 5 daughters), making a total of 27 legitimate children (15 boys and 12 girls). In addition, he fathered 30 illegitimate children. Currently the peer with the largest family is the Rt. Hon. Bryan Walter Guinness, 2nd Baron Moyne, with 6 sons and 5 daughters.

181

WORST IN THE WORLD

Category	Description	Deaths	Date
Pandemic	The Black Death (bubonic plague)	75,000,000	1347–1351
Famine	Influenza	21,640,000	April–Nov. 1918
Flood	Northern China	9,500,000[1]	Feb. 1877–Sept. 1878
	Hwang-ho River, China	900,000	Sept.–Oct. 1887
Earthquake	Shensi Province, China	830,000	23 Jan. 1556
Circular Storm[2]	Haiphong, North Viet-Nam	300,000	8 Oct. 1881
Landslide	Kansu Province, China	200,000	16 Dec. 1920
Conventional Bombing[3]	Tōkyō, Japan	c. 168,000	9–10 Mar. 1945
Atomic Bomb	Hiroshima, Japan	91,223[4]	6 Aug. 1945
Snow Avalanche	Huarás, Peru	c. 5,000[5]	13 Dec. 1941
Marine (single ship)	Wilhelm Gustloff (25,484 tons) off Danzig	4,120	18 Feb. 1945
Panic	Chungking (Zhong qing) China air raid shelter	c. 4,000	c. 8 June 1941
Explosion	Halifax, Nova Scotia, Canada	1,963[6]	6 Dec. 1917
Dam Burst	South Fork Dam, Johnstown, Pennsylvania	2,209	31 May 1889
Fire[7] (single building)	The Theatre, Canton, China	1,670	May 1845
Mining[8]	Honkeiko Colliery, China (coal dust explosion)	1,572	26 April 1942
Crocodiles	Japanese soldiers, Ramree Is., Burma	900	19–20 Feb. 1945
Tornado	South Central States, U.S.A.	689	18 Mar. 1925
Railway	Modane, France	543	12 Dec. 1917
Man-eating Tigress[9]	Champawat district, India, shot by Col. Jim Corbett	436	pre-1945
Hail	Moradabad, Uttar Pradesh, India	246	30 April 1888
Aircraft (Civil)	Maracaibo, Venezuela, D.C.9 jet airliner	155[10]	16 Mar. 1969
Submarine	U.S.S. Thresher off Cape Cod, Massachusetts, U.S.A.	129	10 April 1963
Road[11]	Two trucks crashed into a crowd of dancers, Sotouboua, Togo	>125	6 Dec. 1965
Mountaineering	U.S.S.R. Expedition on Mount Everest	40[12]	Dec. 1952
Fireworks	Hearst Election celebration, Madison Square, New York City, N.Y., U.S.A.	18	1902
Space	Apollo oxygen fire, Cape Kennedy, Fla., U.S.A.	3	27 Jan. 1967

WORST IN THE UNITED KINGDOM

Description	Deaths	Date
The Black Death (bubonic plague)	800,000	1347–1350
Influenza	225,000	Sept.–Nov. 1918
Ireland (famine and typhus)	1,500,000[13]	1846–1851
Severn Estuary	c. 2,000[14]	20 Jan. 1606
City of London	1	6 April 1580
Rowhedge, Essex	1	22 April 1884
"The Channel Storm"	c. 8,000	26 Nov. 1703
Pantglas coal tip No. 7, Aberfan, Glamorganshire	144	21 Oct. 1966
London	1,436	10–11 May 1941
Lewes, Sussex (snowdrifts)	8	27 Dec. 1836
H.M. Troopship Lancastria (16,243 tons) off St. Nazaire	c. 4,000	17 June 1940
Bethnal Green Tube Station (air raid siren)	173	3 Mar. 1943
Chilwell, Notts. (explosives factory)	134	1 July 1918
Bradfield Dam, Dale Dyke, near Sheffield (burst)	238	11 Mar. 1864
New Royal Theatre, Exeter	86[15]	5 Sept. 1887
Universal Colliery, Senghenydd, Caerphilly, Glamorganshire, Wales	439	14 Oct. 1913
Widecombe, Devon	60[16]	21 Oct. 1638
Quintins Hill, Dumfries-shire, Scotland	226[17]	22 May 1915
Avro Tudor V at Sigginston, near Llandow, Glamorgan	81[18]	12 Mar. 1950
H.M.S. Thetis, during trials, Liverpool Bay	99	1 June 1939
R.M. Cadets, run down by bus, Gillingham, Kent	24	4 Dec. 1951
On Ben Nevis, Scotland	5	19 Dec. 1954

1 In 1770 the great Indian famine carried away a proportion of the population estimated as high as one third, hence a figure of tens of millions. It has been estimated that more than 5,000,000 died in the post-World War I famine in the U.S.S.R. The U.S.S.R. government in July 1923 informed Mr. (later President) Herbert Hoover that the A.R.A. (American Relief Administration) had since August 1921 saved 20,000,000 lives from famine and famine diseases.

2 The most damaging hurricane recorded was the billion dollar Betsy (name now retired) in 1965 with an estimated insurance pay-out of $750 million.

3 The number of civilians killed by the bombing of Germany has been put variously as "593,000 and "over 635,000". The death roll in Dresden, Germany on 13–15 Feb. 1945 is believed to have reached 135,000.

4 United States Casualty Commission figure in 1960 was 79,400, while the Hiroshima Peace Memorial Museum gives a figure of 240,000.

5 A total of 10,000 Austrian and Italian troops is reputed to have been lost in the Dolomite valley of Northern Italy on 13 Dec. 1916 in more than 100 avalanches. The total is probably exaggerated though bodies were still being found in 1952.

6 Some sources maintain that the final death roll was over 3,000.

7 84,000 were killed in the U.S. fire raid on Tōkyō, Japan, on 9 March 1945.

8 The worst gold mining disaster in South Africa was 152 killed due to flooding in the Witwatersrand Gold Mining Co. Gold Mine in 1909.

9 In the period 1941–42 c. 1,500 Kenyans were killed by a pride of 22 man-eating lions. Eighteen of these were shot by a hunter named Rushby.

10 Viasa (Venezuelan Air Lines): 84 on board and a toll last reported at 71 on the ground. The highest toll in the air was when a Boeing 727 of All-Nippon Airways, Japan, crashed into Tōkyō Bay on 4 Feb. 1966, killing all 133 aboard (126 passengers and 7 crew).

11 The worst ever years for road deaths in the U.S.A. and the U.K. have been, respectively, 1969 (54,895) and 1941 (9,169). In the U.S.A. in 1968 4,400,000 were injured. The world's highest death rate is said to be in Queensland, Australia but global statistics are not available. The 1969 toll in Japan was 16,258 killed. The greatest pile-up on British roads was on the M.6 near Wigan, Lancashire on 8 Dec. 1969 when 3 were killed and 120 injured in more than 100 vehicles.

12 According to Polish sources, not confirmed by the U.S.S.R.

13 Based on the net rate of natural increase between 1841 and 1851, a supportable case for a loss of population of 3 million can be made out if rates of under-enumeration of 25 per cent. (1841) and 10 per cent. (1851) are accepted. Potato rot (Phytophthora infestans) was first reported on 13 Sept. 1845.

14 Death rolls of 100,000 were reputed in England and Holland in the floods of 1099, 1421 and 1446.

15 In July 1212, 3,000 were killed in the crush, burned or drowned when London Bridge caught fire at both ends. The death roll in the Great Fire of London of 1666 was only 8. History's first "fire storm" occurred in the Quebec Yard, Surrey Docks, London during the 300-pump fire in the Blitz on 7–8 Sept. 1940. Dockland casualties were 306 killed.

16 Killed and injured.

17 Also 226 per Rosebank Cemetery memorial, Leith.

18 The worst crash by a U.K. operated aircraft was that of the B.O.A.C. Boeing 707 which broke up in mid-air near Mount Fuji, Japan, on 5 March 1966. The crew of 11 and all 113 passengers (total 124) were killed. The cause was violent CAT (Clear Air Turbulence).

11 the human world

1. Political and Social

The land area of the Earth is estimated at 57,700,000 square miles (including inland waters), or 29·3 per cent. of the world's surface area. The permanently inhabited continents (*i.e.* excluding Antarctica) and island groups have an estimated area of 52,430,000 square miles, including inland waters.

Largest political division The British Commonwealth of Nations, a free association of 30 independent sovereign states (excluding Fiji) together with their dependencies, covers an area of about 13,700,000 square miles and had an estimated population of 940,000,000 at mid-1970.

COUNTRIES
The total number of separately administered territories in the world is 226, of which 146 are independent countries. Of these 24 sovereign and 65 non-sovereign are insular countries. Only 29 sovereign and 3 non-sovereign countries are entirely without a seaboard. Territorial waters vary between extremes of 3 miles (*e.g.* United Kingdom, Australia, France, Ireland and the U.S.A.) up to 200 miles (*e.g.* Argentina, Ecuador, El Salvador and Panama).

Largest The country with the greatest area is the Union of Soviet Socialist Republics (the Soviet Union), comprising 15 Union (constituent) Republics with a total area of 8,649,550 square miles, or 15·0 per cent. of the world's total land area, and a total coastline (including islands) of 66,090 miles. The country measures 5,580 miles from east to west and 2,790 miles from north to south.

The United Kingdom covers 94,221 square miles (including 1,197 square miles of inland water), or 0·16 per cent. of the total land area of the world. Great Britain is the world's eighth largest island, with an area of 84,186 square miles and a coastline 5,126 miles long, of which Scotland accounts for 2,573 miles, Wales 601 miles and England 1,952 miles.

Smallest The smallest independent country in the world is the State of the Vatican City (Stato della Città del Vaticano), which was made an enclave within the city of Rome, Italy on 11 Feb. 1929. It has an area of 44 hectares (108·7 acres).

The world's smallest republic is Nauru, less than 1 degree south of the equator in the Western Pacific, which became independent on 31 Jan. 1968, has an area of 5,263 acres (8·2 square miles) and a population of 6,056 (Census June 1966).

The smallest colony in the world is Pitcairn Island with an area of 960 acres (1·5 square miles) and a population of 92 (30 June 1966).

FRONTIERS
Most The country with the most frontiers is the U.S.S.R., with 13—Norway, Finland, Poland, Czechoslovakia, Hungary, Romania, Turkey, Iran (Persia), Afghanistan, Mongolia, China (mainland), North Korea and Japan (territorial waters).

Longest The longest continuous frontier in the world is that between Canada and the United States, which (including the Great Lakes boundaries) extends for 3,987 miles (excluding 1,538 miles with Alaska). The frontier which is crossed most frequently is that between the United States and Mexico. It extends for 1,933 miles and there are more than 120,000,000 crossings every year. The Sino-Soviet frontier extends for 4,500 miles with virtually nil crossings.

POPULATIONS
World Estimates of the human population of the world depend largely on the component figure for the population of mainland China (see Largest, page 184). Including the higher assumed figure, the world total at mid-1970 can be estimated to be 3,607 million, giving an average density of 68·7 people per square mile of land (including inland waters). This excludes Antarctica and uninhabited island groups. The daily increase in the world's population was about 180,000 in 1969. It is estimated that about 14,000 were born and about 6,580 died every hour in 1968. The world's population has doubled in the last 63 years and is expected to double again in the next 40 years. It is now estimated that the world's population in the year 2000 will be more than 6,000 million, and possibly closer to 7,000 million. The present

The world's longest continuous frontier— the 3,987-mile U.S.-Canada border

The human world

population "explosion" is of such a magnitude that it has been fancifully calculated that, if it were to continue unabated, there would be one person to each square yard by A.D. 2600, and humanity would weigh more than the Earth itself by A.D. 3700. It is estimated that 74,000,000,000 humans have been born and have died in the last 600,000 years.

WORLD POPULATION—
Progressive mid-year estimates

Date	Millions	Date	Millions
4000 B.C.	85	1965	3,297
A.D. 1	c. 200–300	1966	3,353
1650	c. 500–550	1967	3,420
1750	750	1968	3,483
1800	960	1969	3,551
1850	1,240	1970	3,607
1900	1,650	1975	3,944*
1920	1,862	1980	4,330*
1930	2,070	1985	4,746*
1940	2,295	1990	5,188*
1950	2,517	1995	5,648*
1960	3,005	2000	6,130*
		2050	16,700*
		2070	25,000*

Assessed in 1964, based on an underestimate of 2,998 million for mid-1960, rising to 3,592 million by mid-1970. These estimates will be raised if the higher estimate for China (732 against 722 million) for 31 Dec. 1967 is corroborated.

Largest The country with the largest population in the world is China (mainland only). Owing to the scarcity of available data, estimates vary considerably, but officials of the United Nations have assumed that the total was about 650,000,000 at mid-1960, increasing to 695,000,000 by mid-1965, and will rise to 742,000,000 by mid-1970. If these assumptions are correct, the total at mid-1968 was about 722,000,000. According to the Japanese newspaper *Mainichi,* the Chinese Revolutionary Committee has stated that the Chinese population as of 31 Dec. 1967 was 732 million and hence must have reached over 750,000,000 by mid-1969. Some estimates run considerably higher including the passing of the 800 million mark in late 1968.

Smallest The independent state with the smallest population is the Vatican City or the Holy See (see Smallest country, page 183), with 880 inhabitants at 1 Jan. 1966.

Hong Kong which has spot densities of more than 1 million per square mile

The Principality of Monaco, on the south coast of France, has a population of 23,000 (estimated 1 March 1969) in an area of 369·9 acres, giving a density of 39,800 per square mile.

Of territories with an area of more than 200 square miles, Hong Kong (398¼ square miles) contains 3,988,000 people (estimate, 31 Dec. 1969), giving the territory a density of 10,013 per square mile. The name Hong Kong is the transcription of the local pronunciation of the Peking dialect version of Xiang gang (a port for incense). About 80 per cent. of the population lives in the urban areas of Hong Kong island and Kowloon, on the mainland, and the density there is greater than 200,000 per square mile. At North Point there are 12,400 people living in 6½ acres, giving an unsurpassed spot density of more than 1,200,000 per square mile. In 1959 it was reported that in one house designed for 12 people the number of occupants was 459, including 104 in one room and 4 living on the roof.

Of countries over 1,000 square miles, the most densely populated is the Netherlands, with a population of 12,860,000 (estimate 1 June 1969) on 12,978 square miles of land, giving a density of 990·9 people per square mile. The Indonesian islands of Java and Madura (combined area 51,033 square miles) have a population of 62,993,056 (census of 31 Oct. 1961), giving a density of 1,234 per square mile. The United Kingdom (94,221 square miles) had an estimated home population of 55,534,000 at 30 June 1969, giving a density of 589·4 people per square mile. The projected population figures for 1980 and 2000 are 59,548,000 and 70,339,000. The population density for England alone (50,869 square miles) is 959·8 per square mile.

Sparsest Antarctica became permanently occupied by relays of scientists from October 1956. The population varies seasonally and reaches 1,500 at times.

The least populated territory, apart from Antarctica, is Greenland, with a population of 43,000 (estimate 1 July

BRITISH ISLES—LARGEST AND SMALLEST COUNTIES

	By Area (in acres) Largest		Smallest		By Home Population (estimate, 30 June 1968)* Largest		Smallest	
England	Yorkshire	3,923,359	Rutland	97,273	Lancashire	5,180,090	Rutland	29,680
Wales	Carmarthen	588,472	Flint	163,707	Glamorgan	1,258,320	Radnorshire	18,210
Scotland	Inverness-shire	2,695,094	Clackmannan	34,937	Lanarkshire	1,551,900	Kinross	6,300
Northern Ireland	Tyrone	806,918	Armagh	327,907	Antrim	717,100	Fermanagh	50,100
Republic of Ireland	Cork	1,843,408	Louth	202,806	Dublin	794,047	Longford	28,989

Figures for the Republic of Ireland refer to the mid-1966 inter-censal estimate.
NOTE: *Lanarkshire includes the City of Glasgow (945,000); Antrim includes Belfast County Borough (390,700) and Dublin includes Dublin County Borough (650,153). The largest Welsh town is the City of Cardiff (population 287,460 at 30 June 1968). The English county with the longest coastline is Cornwall (320 miles) and that with the longest in Wales is Pembrokeshire with 183 miles. Westmorland has the shortest coastline with 5½ miles. Of the 91 counties of the United Kingdom all but 28 have a coastline. Fermanagh in Northern Ireland comprises 9·04 per cent. inland water.*

The world's most densely populated territory—Macau, Southern China

Densest The most densely populated territory in the world is the Portuguese province of Macau (or Macao), on the southern coast of China. It has an estimated population of 261,000 (31 Dec. 1967) in an area of 6·2 square miles, giving a density of 42,100 per square mile. At the census of 31 Aug. 1940, Macau had a population of 374,737, giving a density of 60,660 per square mile. The population has, since 1968, increased considerably as a result of the influx of Chinese refugees.

1967) in an area of 840,000 square miles, giving a density of about 0·051 of a person per square mile, or one person to every 19½ square miles. The ice-free area of the island (now believed to be several islands) is only 132,000 square miles.

CITIES

Most populous The most populous city in the world is Tōkyō, the capital of Japan since 1868. The 23 wards (*ku*) of the

184

POLITICAL AND SOCIAL

old City contained 9,037,215 people at July 1969, while Tōkyō-to (Tōkyō Prefecture) had 11,462,230 in its 823·6 square miles at 31 July 1969. The population of this area had surpassed that of Greater London and New York in early 1957 and in January 1962 it became the first urban area in history whose recorded population exceeded 10,000,000. At the census of 1 Oct. 1960, the "Keihin Metropolitan Area" (Tōkyō-Yokohama Metropolitan Area) of 1,081 square miles contained 13,787,766 people. The density in the 23 wards is 39,655 people per square mile.

In December 1964 the population of Shanghai, in China, was unofficially reported to be 10,700,000. The city proper population figure in the 1957 census was 6,900,000.

United Kingdom The largest conurbation in Europe is Greater London (established on 1 April 1965), with an estimated home population of 7,763,820 (30 June 1968) in an area of 396,516 acres (619·5 square miles). The population of the City of London (677 acres) is 4,210 at the same date.

Largest The largest metropolitan census area in the world is that of New York and north-eastern New Jersey, which includes the cities of New York, Jersey City and Newark, N.J., U.S.A. It has a population of 15,981,300 (estimate, 1 July 1966) and an area of 4,409·4 square miles, giving a density of 3,588 per square mile. The area extends to an extreme of 136 miles from Columbus Circle (New York City centre) to Pine Hill in Ulster county. The population for the Standard Metropolitan Statistical Area for New York City was estimated at 11,457,600 in mid-1966.

The world's largest city not built by the sea or on a river is Mexico City (Ciudad de México), the capital of Mexico, with an estimated population of 3,287,334 at 30 June 1966. Greater Mexico City's population was 7.123.000 (mid-1968 estimate).

La Paz, Bolivia, 11,900 feet above sea-level

Highest World The highest capital city in the world, before the domination of Tibet by China, was Lhasa, at an elevation of 12,087 feet above sea-level. La Paz, the administrative and *de facto* capital of Bolivia, stands at an altitude of 11,916 feet above sea-level. The city was founded in 1548 by Capt. Alonso de Mendoza on the site of an Indian village named Chuquiapu. It was originally called Ciudad de Nuestra Señora de La Paz (City of Our Lady of Peace), but in 1825 was renamed La Paz de Ayacucho, its present official name. Sucre, the legal capital of Bolivia, stands at 9,301 feet above sea-level. The new town of Wenchuan, founded in 1955 on the Chinghai-Tibet road, north of the Tangla range, is the highest in the world at 5,100 metres (16,732 feet) above sea-level. The highest village in the world is the Andean mining village of Aucanquilca, in Chile, at 17,500 feet above sea-level.

Great Britain The highest village in England is Flash, in northern Staffordshire, at 1,518 feet above sea-level. The term "flash" money probably relates to the former winter-time counterfeiting activities of the villagers. The highest in Scotland is Wanlockhead, in Dumfries-shire at 1,380 feet above sea-level.

The 9,750-year-old city—Jericho, Jordan

Oldest World The oldest known walled town in the world is Arīhā (Jericho), in Jordan. Radio-carbon dating on specimens from the lowest levels reached by archaeologists indicate habitation there by perhaps 3,000 people as early as 7800 B.C. The village of Zawi Chemi Shanidar, discovered in 1957 in northern Iraq, has been dated to 8910 B.C. The oldest capital city in the world is Dimashq (Damascus), the capital of Syria. It has been continuously inhabited since *c.* 2500 B.C.

Great Britain The oldest town in Great Britain is often cited as Colchester, the old British Camulodunon, headquarters of Belgic chiefs in the 1st century B.C. However, the place called Ictis, referred to by Pytheas in *c.* 308 B.C., has been identified with Marazion, close to St. Michael's Mount, Cornwall.

Largest in area The world's largest town, in area, is Kiruna, in Sweden. Its boundaries have, for fiscal avoidance purposes, been extended to embrace an area of 5,458 square miles. The largest city in the United Kingdom is Greater London.

Smallest hamlet The only hamlet in Great Britain with an official population of one is Gallowhill in the parish of Inveravon, Banffshire, Scotland.

Northernmost The world's northernmost town is Hammerfest (population 6,000) on the island of Kvaløy, in Norway, in 70° 40′ N. The northernmost village is Ny Ålesund (78° 55′ N.), a coal mining settlement on King's Bay, Vest Spitsbergen, in the Norwegian territory of Svalbard, inhabited only during the winter season. The northernmost capital is Reykjavík, the capital of Iceland, in 64° 06′ N. Its population was estimated to be 79,813 at 1 Dec. 1967. The northernmost permanent human occupation is the base at Alert (82° 31′ N.), on Dumb Bell Bay, on the north-east coast of Ellesmere Island, northern Canada.

Southernmost The world's southernmost village is Puerto Williams (population about 350), on the north coast of Isla Navarino, in Tierra del Fuego, Chile, about 680 miles north of Antarctica. Wellington, North Island, New Zealand is the southernmost capital city on 41° 17′ S. The world's southernmost administrative centre is Port Stanley (51° 43′ S.), in the Falkland Islands, off South America.

Most remote from sea The large town most remote from the sea is Wulumuchi (Urumchi) formerly Tihwa, Sinkiang, capital of the Uighur Autonomous Region of China, at a distance of about 1,400 miles from the nearest coastline. Its population was estimated to be 275,000 at 31 Dec. 1957.

EMIGRATION
More people emigrate from the United Kingdom than from any other country. A total of 277,700 emigrated from the U.K. in 1968 (latest available data). The largest number of emigrants in any one year was 360,000 in 1852, mainly from Ireland in the post-famine period.

IMMIGRATION
The country which regularly receives the most immigrants is the United States, with 454,448 in 1968. It has been estimated that, in the period 1820–1968, the U.S.A. has received 44,430,733 immigrants. The peak year for immigration into the United Kingdom was the 12 months from 1 July 1961 to 30 June 1962, when about 430,000 Commonwealth citizens arrived. The number of immigrants in 1968 was 277,700.

MOST TOURISTS
In 1969 Italy received 31,201,699 foreign visitors—

185

more than any other country except Canada, which in 1967 received 40,514,602, of whom more than 61 per cent. entered and left the same day. In 1969 the United Kingdom received 5,800,000 visitors who spent an estimated £359,600,000. Of this total 800,000 came from the Irish Republic.

BIRTH RATE

Highest and lowest Based on the last data available, the highest recorded crude live birth rate is 62 live births per each 1,000 of the population in Guinea (Africans only, based on births reported for the 12 month period preceding the sample survey of 15 Jan. to 31 May 1955). The next highest figure is 56·1 per 1,000 in the Ivory Coast. A rate of 67·0 registered births per 1,000 was recorded in Lagos, the capital of Nigeria, in 1963. The rate for the whole world was 34 per 1,000 in 1960–64.

The lowest of the latest available recorded rates is 12·5 per 1,000 in the Panama Canal Zone; 14·0 in the Isle of Man and 14·6 in Hungary all in 1967.

The 1969 rate in the United Kingdom was 16·6 per 1,000 (16·3 in England and Wales, 17·4 in Scotland and 21·5 in Northern Ireland), while the 1967 rate for the Republic of Ireland was 21·1 registered births per 1,000.

DEATH RATE

Highest and lowest The highest of the latest available recorded death rates is 40 deaths per each 1,000 of the population in Guinea (Africans only, 12 months preceding 1955 sample survey). The next highest figure is 35 per 1,000 in the Upper Volta in the 12 months before the sample survey carried out between 30 Sept. 1960 and 22 April 1961. The rate for the whole world was 16 per 1,000 in 1960–64.

The lowest of the latest available recorded rates is 2·4 deaths per 1,000 in the Panama Canal Zone in 1968 and in Tonga in 1967. The lowest rate in an independent country in 1967 was 5·4 per 1,000 registered in Singapore.

The 1969 rate in the United Kingdom was 11·9 per 1,000 (11·8 in England and Wales, 12·3 in Scotland and 10·8 in Northern Ireland), while the 1967 rate for the Republic of Ireland was 10·8 registered deaths per 1,000. The highest S.M.I. (Standardized Mortality Index where the national average is 100) is in Salford, Lancashire with a figure of 133.

NATURAL INCREASE

The highest of the latest available recorded rates of natural increase is 39·5 per 1,000 in Kuwait (births 45·6, deaths 6·1) in 1964. A rate of 53·5 per 1,000 (registered births 67·0, registered deaths 13·5) was recorded in Lagos, the capital of Nigeria, in 1963. The rate for the whole world was 34−16=18 per 1,000 in 1960–65.

The 1969 rate for the United Kingdom was 4·7 per 1,000 (4·5 in England and Wales, 5·1 in Scotland and 10·7 in Northern Ireland). The figure for the Republic of Ireland was 10·6 per 1,000 in 1965.

There are three territories in which the death rate exceeds the birth rate, and which thus have a rate of natural decrease: West Berlin, Germany, 6·7 per 1,000 (birth rate 11·6, death rate 18·3) in 1967; East Berlin 0·6 per 1,000 and the Isle of Man 3·3 per 1,000 (registered births 14·0, registered deaths 17·3) in 1965. The lowest rate of natural increase in an independent country in 1967 was 1·6 per 1,000 in East Germany (birth rate 14·8, death rate 13·2).

MARRIAGE AGES

The country with the lowest average ages for marriage is India, with 20·0 years for males and 14·5 years for females. At the other extreme is Ireland, with 31·4 for males and 26·5 years for females.

SEX RATIO

The country with the largest recorded feminine surplus is the U.S.S.R., with 1,208·7 females to every 1,000 males at 1 Jan. 1961. The country with the largest recorded woman shortage is Pakistan, with 900·7 to every 1,000 males at 1 Feb. 1961. The ratio in the United Kingdom was 1,052·1 females to every 1,000 males at 30 June 1966, and is expected to be 1,014·2 per 1,000 by A.D. 2000.

INFANT MORTALITY

Based on deaths before one year of age, the lowest of the latest available recorded rates is 8·7 deaths per 1,000 live births in Tonga in 1965, compared with 12·9 per 1,000 in Sweden in 1967.

The highest recorded infant mortality rate recently reported has been 259 per 1,000 live births among the indigenous African population of Zambia (then Northern Rhodesia) in the 12 months preceding the sample survey of 30 June 1950. Among more recent estimates from the very incomplete returns available the highest is an annual average of 146·5 per 1,000 for Sierra Leone in 1967.

The United Kingdom figure for 1969 was 18·4 per 1,000 live births (England and Wales 17·9, Scotland 21·1, Northern Ireland 24·3).

Many countries do not make returns. Among these is Ethiopia, where the infant mortality rate was estimated to be nearly 550 per 1,000 live births in 1969.

LIFE EXPECTATION

There is evidence that life expectation in Britain in the 5th century A.D. was 33 years for males and 27 years for females. In the decade 1890–1900 the expectation of life among the population of India was 23·7 years. The British figure for 1901–1910 was 48·53 years for males and 52·83 years for females.

Based on the latest available data, the highest recorded expectation of life for males at birth is 71·6 years in Sweden, and the highest for females is >76 years in Iceland.

The lowest recorded expectation of life at birth is 27 years for both sexes in the Vallée du Niger area of Mali in 1957 (sample survey, 1957–58).

The latest available figures for England and Wales (1961–63) are 67·9 years for males and 73·9 years for females; for Scotland (1964) 66·67 years for males and 72·79 years for females; for Northern Ireland (1962–64) 67·92 years for males and 72·76 years for females; and for the Republic of Ireland (1960–62) 68·13 years for males and 71·86 years for females.

At the age of 60, the highest recorded expectation of life for males is in Bolivia, with 20·39 years (1949–51). More reliable figures include 18·64 years in Puerto Rico (1959–61), 18·6 years in Iceland (1951–60) and 18·52 years in Norway (1951–55). The highest recorded figure for females is 21·66 years in Ryukyu Islands (1960), 20·67 years in Albania (1960–61) and 20·4 years in Iceland (1951–60).

The figures for England and Wales (1961–63) are 14·9 years for men and 18·9 years for women; for Scotland (1961–63) 14·15 years for men and 17·83 years for women; for Northern Ireland (1961–63) 15·29 years for men and 18·22 years for women; and for the Republic of Ireland (1950–52) 15·40 years for men and 16·83 years for women.

STANDARDS OF LIVING

National incomes The country with the highest income per person in 1969 was Nauru, with nearly $4,000 (£1,666) per head, followed by Kuwait and the U.S.A. The U.S.A. in 1967 leads on the basis of major industrial countries measured by real product per head at 190 (U.K.=100).

COST OF LIVING

The place with the greatest recorded recent increase in the cost of living, based on an index figure of 1958=100, is Seoul, the capital of South Korea, where the cost of living index rose from 0·3 to 273 between 1947 and October 1966. The index of food prices alone rose from 0·3 to 310. The greatest increase since 1958 has been in Djakarta, the capital of Indonesia, where the index figure reached 2,568 (food 3,061) in March 1964, but fell to 2,165 (food 2,317) by June 1964. The Indonesian Minister for Economic Affairs announced on 11 July 1967 that prices were 3,600 times as high as those in 1957.

In the United Kingdom the official index of retail prices (16 Jan. 1962=100) was 139·1 on 19 May 1970—a rise of 6·7 points or 5·1 per cent. in 12 months. When the cost of living rises 7½ per cent. per annum on present tax structure, a £10,000 a year man requires a rise of £1,700 a year to stand still in purchasing power. A man on £20 per week needs an extra 36s. per week to keep pace.

CAPITAL

and least expensive

According to data published by the U.N. Statistical Office in June 1969, the world's most expensive capital city is Riyadh, Yemen (105) and the world's cheapest is Belize, British Honduras (66). These indices compare with the cost of living in New York of 100 in 1968. The figure for London is 70.

HOUSING

For comparison, dwelling units are defined as a structurally separated room or rooms occupied by private households of one or more people and having separate access or a common passageway to the street.

The country with the greatest recorded number of private housing units is India, with 79,193,602 occupied in 1960. These contain 83,523,895 private households.

Great Britain comes fourth among reporting countries, with 18,488,000 dwellings (England 15,773,000, Wales 943,000, Scotland 1,772,000) at December 1969. The 1968 figure for Northern Ireland was 435,000. The Republic of Ireland had 687,304 private households in 1966.

Piped water

Austria reported that 100 per cent. of its dwellings had piped water inside or outside (63·6 per cent. inside) in 1961. This is matched by the urban areas of the Panama Canal Zone, which have 100 per cent. with piped water inside. In England and Wales 98·3 per cent. of dwellings (where an occupier was present) had piped water inside in 1961. In Scotland 98·6 per cent. of dwellings had piped water inside or outside in 1961, while in Northern Ireland 80·7 per cent. of private households had piped water inside in 1961. In the Republic of Ireland 57·2 per cent. of dwellings had piped water inside or outside (51·0 per cent. inside) in 1961.

Baths

The country with the highest recorded proportion of dwellings with a bath is New Zealand, with 97·1 per cent. (1961), compared with 100 per cent. in the urban areas of the Panama Canal Zone (1958).

Subject to the qualifications given above (under "Piped water"), and excluding dwellings with only shower installations, the 1968 United Kingdom figure was 84 per cent.

The world's most productive maternity hospital

Electricity Luxembourg had 99·9 per cent. of its dwellings equipped with electricity in 1960, compared with 100 per cent. in the Cocos (Keeling) Islands in 1960, and 100 per cent. in the urban areas of Hong Kong (1960), the Panama Canal Zone (1958) and Switzerland where in October 1968 Furna, Graubünden, ceased to be the last village without electricity.

PHYSICIANS

The country with the most physicians is the U.S.S.R., with 503,200 in 1966, or one to every 460 persons. In England and Wales there were 24,131 doctors employed by the National Health Service on 30 Sept. 1969.

The country with the highest proportion of physicians is Israel, where there were 6,339 (one for every 410 inhabitants) in 1966. The country with the lowest recorded proportion is Upper Volta, with 65 physicians (one for every 76,230 people) in 1966.

Dentists The country with the most dentists is the United States, where 120,000 were registered members of the American Dental Association in 1969.

Psychiatrists The country with the most psychiatrists is the United States. The registered membership of the American Psychiatric Association was 16,000 in 1969. The membership of the American Psychological Association was 29,000 in 1969.

HOSPITALS

Largest World

The largest medical centre in the world is the District Medical Center in Chicago, Illinois, U.S.A. It covers 478 acres and includes five hospitals, with a total of 5,600 beds, and eight professional schools with more than 3,000 students.

The largest hospital in the world is Danderyd Hospital in northern Stockholm, Sweden. In 1969 it had 12,000 beds.

The largest mental hospital in the world is the Pilgrim State Hospital, on Long Island, New York State, U.S.A., with 12,800 beds. It formerly contained 14,200 beds.

The largest maternity hospital in the world is the Kandang Kerbau Government Maternity Hospital in Singapore. It has 239 midwives, 151 beds for gynaecological cases, 388 maternity beds and an output of 31,255 babies in 1969 compared with the record "birthquake" of 39,856 babies (more than 109 per day) in 1966.

United Kingdom

The largest hospitals of any kind in the United Kingdom are the Rainhill Hospital near Liverpool, and St. Bernard's Hospital, Southall, Middlesex, which each have 2,267 staffed beds for mental patients.

The largest general hospital in the United Kingdom is the St. James Hospital, Leeds, Yorkshire, with 1,350 available staffed beds.

The largest maternity hospital in the United Kingdom is the Mill Road Maternity Hospital, Liverpool, with 214 staffed beds.

The largest children's hospital in the United Kingdom is Queen Mary's Hospital for Children, at Carshalton, Surrey, with 736 staffed beds.

Largest baby-sitting service

The world's largest baby-sitting organization is the Carol Agency (est. 1950), Washington Blvd., Los Angeles, California, U.S.A., with 800 registered "sitters" serving 25,000 families.

ROYALTY

Oldest ruling house

The Emperor of Japan, Hirohito (born 29 April 1901), is the 124th in line from the first Emperor, Jimmu Tenno or Zinmu, whose reign was traditionally from 660 to 581 B.C., but probably from c. 40 to c. 10 B.C. His

Hirohito, Japan's 124th Emperor

Imperial Majesty Muhammad Rizā Shāh Pahlavi of Iran (born 26 Oct. 1919) claims descent from Cyrus the Great (reigned *c.* 559–529 B.C.).

Her Majesty Queen Elizabeth II (born 21 April 1926) represents a dynasty which has ruled since about A.D. 500—that of Eirc of Dalriada (now Lorne, Argyllshire, Scotland), who is believed to be her 48-greats grandfather.

REIGNS

Longest The longest recorded reign of any monarch is that of Pepi II, a Sixth Dynasty Pharaoh of ancient Egypt. His reign began in *c.* 2272 B.C., when he was aged 6, and lasted 91 years. Musoma Kanijo, chief of the Nzega district of western Tanganyika (now part of Tanzania), reputedly reigned for more than 98 years from 1864, when aged 8, until his death on 2 Feb. 1963. The 6th Japanese Emperor Koo-an traditionally reigned for 102 years (from 392 to 290 B.C.), but probably his actual reign was from about A.D. 110 to about A.D. 140. The reign of the 11th Emperor Suinin was traditionally from 29 B.C. to A.D. 71 (99 years), but probably from A.D. 259 to 291. The longest reign in European history was that of King Louis XIV of France, who ascended the throne on 14 May 1643, aged 4 years 8 months, and reigned for 72 years 110 days until his death on 1 Sept. 1715, four days before his 77th birthday.

Currently the longest reigning monarch in the world is King Sobhuza II, K.B.E. (born July 1899, the *Ngwenyama* (Paramount Chief) of Swaziland, under United Kingdom protection, since December 1899, and independent since 6 Sept. 1968. Hirohito (see page 187) has been Emperor of Japan since 25 Dec. 1926.

Shortest The shortest recorded reign was that of the Dauphin Louis Antoine, who was technically King Louis XIX of France for the fifteen minutes between the signature of Charles X (1757–1836) and his own signature to the act of abdication, in favour of Henri V, which was executed at the Château de Rambouillet on 2 Aug. 1830.

BRITISH MONARCHS

Longest reign The longest reign of any King of Great Britain was that of George III, from 25 Oct. 1760 to 29 Jan. 1820 (59 years 96 days) and the longest of a Queen was that of Victoria, from 20 June 1837 to 22 Jan. 1901 (63 years 216 days). James Francis Edward (born 10 June 1688), the Old Pretender, known to his supporters as James III, styled his reign from 16 Sept. 1701 until his death on 1 Jan. 1766, thus lasting over 64 years.

Shortest reign The shortest reign of any post-Conquest King of England was that of Edward V, from 9 April until he was deposed on 25 June 1483 (seventy-seven days). He died probably between July and September 1483. If Sweyn "Forkbeard", the Danish King of England, reigned from "Christmas to Candlemas" in 1013–14, it was for a period of perhaps 40 days but there is, however, doubt as to when, in the autumn of 1013, he in fact acceded. The shortest reign of a Queen was that of Jane, who acceded on 6 July 1553, was proclaimed Queen on 10 July and was deposed on 19 July 1553, after a reign of only 13 days (or nine days from proclamation).

Longest lived Excluding the 8 who suffered violent death, English monarchs have had an average life span of 57 years. The longest lived British monarchs were King George III, who died on 29 Jan. 1820 aged 81 years 239 days, and Queen Victoria, who, at the time of her death on 22 Jan. 1901, had surpassed his age by four days. The oldest monarch at the time of succession was William IV, who became King on 26 June 1830, aged 64 years 10 months.

The oldest member of the Royal Family was H.R.H. Princess Augusta Caroline Charlotte Elizabeth Mary Sophia Louise of Cambridge, C.I., the Grand Duchess of Mecklenburg-Strelitz, the elder daughter of H.R.H. Prince Adolphus Frederick, the 1st Duke of Cambridge, seventh son of King George III. She was born on 18 July 1822 and died, aged 94 years 139 days, on 4 Dec. 1916. The oldest male member of the Royal Family was H.R.H. Prince Arthur William Patrick Albert, the 1st Duke of Connaught and Strathearn, K.G., K.T., K.P., G.M.B., G.C.S.I., G.C.M.G., G.C.I.E., G.C.V.O., G.B.E., V.D., T.D., the third son of Queen Victoria. He was born on 1 May 1850 and died, aged 91 years 260 days, on 16 Jan. 1942.

Youngest The youngest English monarch to accede was Henry VI, who was born on 6 Dec. 1421 and came to the throne on 1 Sept. 1422, aged less than 9 months. Scotland's youngest was Queen Mary, born on 7 or 8 Dec. 1542. She succeeded to the Scottish throne on 14 Dec. 1542, aged 6 or 7 days.

England's youngest Queen was Isabella, daughter of King Charles VI of France. She was born on 9 Nov. 1389 and became the second wife of Richard II at Calais, probably on 4 Nov. 1396, when a few days short of her seventh birthday.

Most children The King with the most legitimate children was Edward I (1239–1307), who had 16 by his two queens, Eleanor of Castille (died 1290) and Margaret of France (1282–1317).

The monarch with the greatest number of illegitimate children was Henry I (1068–1135), who had at least 20 (9 sons, 11 daughters) and possibly 22, by six mistresses, in addition to one (possibly two) sons and a daughter born legitimately.

The largest number of children born to a Queen regnant was nine to Queen Victoria (1819–1901) and the largest number to a Queen consort was 15 to Queen Charlotte Sophia (1744–1818), the wife of George III (1738–1820). Before coming to the throne in 1702, Queen Anne (1665–1714) conceived 18 children, of whom only five were live-born and all of these died in infancy. Prince William, K.G. (1689–1700), the Duke of Gloucester, survived to the age of 11 years 6 days.

Most often married The most often married English King was Henry VIII whose sixth and last wife, Catherine Parr (*c.* 1512–1548), was England's most married Queen. She was first married to the Hon. Sir Edward Burgh (died 1529 or earlier), secondly to John Neville, the 3rd Lord Latimer (died 1542 or 1543), thirdly on 12 July 1543 to Henry VIII, and fourthly and finally on 3 March 1547, five weeks after Henry's death, to Thomas, Lord Seymour of Sudeley, K.G. She died on 7 Sept. 1548, eight days after giving birth to a daughter.

Royal absences The longest absence of a monarch from the country was that of Richard I from his accession on 12 Dec. 1189 until 6 April 1194. George III never once left the country in his reign of over 59 years (1760–1820).

Tallest and shortest England's tallest monarch was Edward IV (reigned 1461–1483), who was between 6 feet 3 inches and 6 feet 4 inches and was regarded as a giant in his time. Charles I (reigned 1625–1649) was, on the evidence of

Edward IV (1461–83),
England's tallest monarch

his armour, barely over 5 feet tall. This compares with the 4 feet 9½ inches of the 12-year-old Edward V. Queen Matilda, wife of William I, who died in 1083, was 4 feet 2 inches.

LEGISLATURES

PARLIAMENTS

Oldest The oldest legislative body is the *Alpingi* (Althing) of Iceland, founded in A.D. 930. This body, which originally comprised 39 local chieftains, was abolished in 1800, but restored by Denmark to a consultative status in 1843 and a legislative status in 1874. The legislative assembly with the oldest continuous history is the Tynwald Court in the Isle of Man, which is believed to have originated more than 1,000 years ago.

Largest The largest legislative assembly in the world is the National People's Congress of China (mainland). The fourth Congress, which met in March 1969, had 3,500 members.

Smallest quorum The House of Lords has the smallest quorum, expressed as a percentage of eligible voters, of any legislative body in the world, namely one-third of one per cent. To transact business there must be three peers present, including the Lord Chancellor or his deputy. The House of Commons quorum of 40 M.P.'s, including the Speaker or his deputy, is nearly 20 times as exacting.

Most paid legislators The most highly paid of all the world's legislators are Senators of the United States, who receive a basic annual salary of $42,500 (£17,708). Of this, up to $3,000 (£1,250) is exempt from taxation. In addition, up to $130,000 (£54,166) per annum is allowed for office help, with a salary limit of $13,345 (£5,560) per assistant per year. Senators also enjoy free travel, telephones, postage, medical care, telegrams (to a limit of $2,000 (£833) per session), flowers and haircuts. They also command very low rates for stationery, filming, speech and radio transcriptions and, in the case of women senators, beauty treatment. When abroad they have access to "counterpart funds".

Longest membership The longest span as a legislator was 83 years by József Madarász (1814–1915). He first attended the Hungarian Parliament in 1832–36 as *ablegatus absentium* (*i.e.* on behalf of an absent deputy). He was a full member in 1848–50 and from 1861 until his death on 31 Jan. 1915.

Filibusters The longest continuous speech in the history of the United States Senate was that of Senator Wayne Morse of Oregon on 24–25 April 1953, when he spoke on the Tidelands Oil Bill for 22 hours 26 minutes without resuming his seat. Interrupted only briefly by the swearing-in of a new senator, Senator Strom Thurmond (South Carolina, Democrat) spoke against the Civil Rights Bill for 24 hours 19 minutes on 28–29 Aug. 1957. The United States national record duration for a filibuster is 28 hours 15 minutes by Texas State Senator Kilmer Corbin of Lubbock at Austin, Texas, on 17–18 May 1955. He was speaking against the financing of water projects by taxation.

Greatest parliamentary petition The greatest petition was supposed to be the Great Chartist Petition of 1848 but of the 5,706,000 "signatures" only 1,975,496 were valid. The all time largest was for the abolition of Entertainment Duty with 3,107,080 signatures presented on 5 June 1951.

ELECTIONS

Largest The largest election ever held was that for the Indian *Lok Sabha* (House of the People) on 15–21 Feb. 1967 (except in certain snow-bound areas of Himachal Pradesh where the election was held in June 1967). About 165,000,000 of the electorate of 250,681,530 chose from 1,979 candidates for 520 seats.

Closest The ultimate in close general elections occurred in Zanzibar (now part of Tanzania) on 18 Jan. 1961, when the Afro-Shirazi Party won by a single seat, after the seat of Chake-Chake on Pemba Island had been gained by a single vote.

Most one-sided North Korea recorded a 100 per cent. turn-out of electors and a 100 per cent. vote for the Workers' Party of Korea in the general election of 8 Oct. 1962. The previous record had been set in the Albanian election of 4 June 1962, when all but seven of the electorate of 889,875 went to the polls—a 99·9992 per cent. turn-out. Of the 889,868 voters, 889,828 voted for the candidates of the Albanian Party of Labour, *i.e.* 99·9955 per cent. of the total poll.

Highest personal majority The highest personal majority was 157,692 from 192,909 votes cast, by H.H. Maharani of Jaipur (born 23 May 1919) in the Indian general election of Feb. 1962.

Communist parties The largest national Communist party outside the Soviet Union (about 12,400,000 members in 1966) and Communist states has been the Partito Communista Italiano (Italian Communist Party), with a membership of 2,300,000 in 1946. The total fell to 1,350,000 by 1965, but rose to 1,575,000 in 1966. The now illegal Partai Komunis Indonesia had about 2,000,000 members in 1964. The membership in mainland China was estimated to be 21,000,000 in 1966. The Communist Party of Great Britain, formed on 31 July 1920 in Cannon Street Station Hotel, London, attained its peak membership of 56,000 in December 1942, compared with 30,607 in June 1969.

Most parties The country with the greatest number of political parties is Italy with 73 registered for the elections of 19 May 1968. These included "Friends of the Moon" with one candidate.

PRIME MINISTERS

Oldest The longest lived Prime Minister of any country is believed to have been Christopher Hornsrud, Prime Minister of Norway from 28 Jan. to 15 Feb. 1928. He was born on 15 Nov. 1859 and died on 13 Dec. 1960, aged 101 years 28 days.

El Hadji Muhammad el Mokri, Grand Vizier of Morocco, died on 16 Sept. 1957, at a reputed age of 116 Muslim (*Hijri*) years, equivalent to 112·5 Gregorian years.

Longest term of office Prof. Dr. António de Oliveira Salazar, (Hon.) G.C.M.G. (1889–1969) was the President of the Council of Ministers (*i.e.* Prime Minister) of Portugal from 5 July 1932 until 27 Sept. 1968—36 years 83 days. He was superceded 11 days after going into a coma.

UNITED KINGDOM

Longest parliament The earliest known use of the term "parliament" in an official English royal document, in the meaning of a summons to the King's council, dates from 19 Dec. 1241.

The Houses of Parliament of the United Kingdom, in the Palace of Westminster, London, had 1,686 members (House of Lords 1,056, House of Commons 630) in July 1969.

The longest English Parliament was the "Pensioners" Parliament of Charles II, which lasted from 8 May 1661 to 24 Jan. 1679, a period of 17 years 8 months and 16 days. The longest United Kingdom Parliament was that of George V, Edward VIII and George VI, lasting from 26 Nov. 1935 to 15 June 1945, a span of 9 years 6 months and 20 days.

Shortest The parliament of Edward I, summoned to Westminster for 30 May 1306, lasted only one day. The parliament of Charles I from 13 April to 5 May 1640 lasted only 22 days. The shortest United Kingdom Parliament was that of George III, lasting from 15 Dec. 1806 to 29 April 1807, a period of only 4 months and 14 days.

189

Longest sittings The longest sitting in the House of Commons was one of $41\frac{1}{2}$ hours from 4 p.m. on 31 Jan. 1881 to 9.30 a.m. on 2 Feb. 1881, on the question of better Protection of Person and Property in Ireland. The longest sitting of the Lords has been 13 hours 32 minutes, from 2.30 p.m. on 2 July 1963 to 4.02 a.m. on 3 July 1963, on the fourth day of the report stage of the London Government Bill.

Most divisions The record number of divisions in the House of Commons is 42 in the single session of 20–21 March 1907.

ELECTORATES

Largest and smallest The largest electorate of all time was the estimated 217,900 for Hendon, Middlesex, now part of Greater London, prior to redistribution in 1941. The largest electorate for any seat on the register in force until February 1971 is 124,215 in Billericay, Essex. The smallest electorate of all time was in Old Sarum (number of houses nil, population nil) in Wiltshire, with eight electors who returned two members in 1821, thus being 54,475 times as well represented as the Hendon electorate of 120 years later. The smallest electorate for any seat on the current register is Ladywood, Birmingham with 18,884 electors.

MAJORITIES

Party The largest party majorities were those of the Liberals, with 307 seats in 1832 and 356 seats in 1906. In 1931 the Coalition of Conservatives, Liberals and National Labour candidates had a majority of 425. The narrowest party majority was that of the Whigs in 1847, with a single seat.

The largest majority on a division was one of 463 (464 votes to 1), on a motion of "no confidence" in the conduct of World War II, on 29 Jan. 1942. Since the war the largest majority has been one of 461 (487 votes to 26) on 10 May 1967, during the debate on the government's application for Britain to join the European Economic Community (the "Common Market").

Largest personal The largest individual majority of any Member of Parliament was the 62,253 of Sir A. Cooper Rawson, M.P. (Conservative) at Brighton in 1931. He polled 75,205 votes against 12,952 votes for his closer opponent, the Labour Candidate Lewis Coleman Cohen, later Lord Cohen of Brighton (1897–1966), from an electorate of 128,779. The largest majority of any woman M.P. was 38,823 in the same General Election by the Countess of Iveagh (née Lady Gwendolen Florence Mary Onslow), C.B.E. (1881–1966), the Conservative member for Southend-on-Sea, Essex, from November 1927 to October 1935.

Narrowest personal The closest result occurred in the General Election of 1886 at Ashton-under-Lyne, Lancashire when the Conservative and Liberal candidates both received 3,049 votes. The Returning Officer, Mr. James Walker, gave his casting vote for John E. W. Addison (Con.), who was duly returned while Alexander B. Rowley (Gladstone-Liberal) was declared unelected. On 13 Oct. 1892 there was a by-election at Cirencester, Gloucestershire, which resulted in an election petition after which the number of votes cast for the Conservative and Liberal were found to have been equal. A new election was ordered.

Two examples of majorities of one have occurred. At Durham in the 1895 General Election, Matthew Fowler (Lib.) with 1,111 votes defeated the Hon. Arthur R. D. Elliott (Liberal-Unionist) (1,110 votes) after a recount.

At Exeter in the General Election of December 1910 a Liberal victory over the Conservatives by 4 votes was reversed on an election petition to a Conservative win by H. E. Duke, K.C. (later the 1st Lord Merrivale) (Unionist) with 4,777 votes to R. H. St. Maur's (Lib.) 4,776 votes.

The smallest majority since "universal" franchise wa one of two votes by Abraham John Flint (born 1903 the National Labour candidate at Ilkeston, Derbyshir on 27 Oct. 1931. He received 17,587 votes, compare with 17,585 for G. H. Oliver, D.C.M. (Labour). Th smallest majority of any current member is that of S Harmer Nicholls who was elected the member fc Peterborough by a majority of three votes, 23,944 vote compared with 23,941 for M. J. Ward (Labour), afte a record seven recounts, on 31 March–1 April 1966. Th counts from the victor's point of view went thus:– −163, −163; −2; +2; +6; −1; +2 and + 3. Eigh counts were also required at Brighton, Kemptown o 16 Oct. 1964 to give Dennis H. Hobden (Labour) majority of 7.

Fewest votes The smallest number of votes received by any candidat in a parliamentary election since "universal" franchis is 23 in the case of Richard Wort (Independer Conservative) in the Kinross and West Perthshir by-election of 7 Nov. 1963.

Most rapid change of fortune In 1874 Hardinge Stanley Giffard (Con.), later the 1s Earl of Halsbury (1823–1921), received one vote a Launceston, Cornwall. On 3 July 1877 he was returne unopposed for the same seat.

Greatest swing The greatest swing, at least since 1832, was that a Dartford, Kent when on 27 March 1920 Labour turne a Coalition majority of 9,370 to a win by 9,048. Thi represented a swing of 38·7 per cent. compared with th swing of 26·8 per cent. at Orpington, Kent on 14 Marc 1962 to the Liberals.

Highest poll The highest poll in any constituency since "universal franchise was 93·42 per cent. in Fermanagh and Sout Tyrone, Northern Ireland, at the General Election o 25 Oct. 1951, when there were 62,799 voters from ar electorate of 67,219. The Anti-Partition candidate Mr. Cahir Healy (born 1877), was elected with a majority of 2,635 votes. The highest poll in any constituency in the 1966 General Election was 87·5 per cent in North Cornwall.

M.P.s Youngest Edmund Waller (1606–1687) was the Member of Parliament for Amersham, Buckinghamshire, in the Parliament of 1621, in which year he was 15. The official returns, however, do not show him as actually having taken his seat until two years later when, in the Parliament of 1623–24, he sat as Member for Ilchester. In 1435 Henry Long (1420–1490) was returned for an Old Sarum seat also at the age of 15. His precise date of birth is unknown. Minors were debarred in law in 1695 and in fact in 1832. Since that time the youngest Member of Parliament has been the Hon. Esmond Cecil Harmsworth (now the 2nd Viscount Rothermere), who was elected for the Isle of Thanet, Kent, on 28 Nov. 1919, when one day short of being 21 years 6 months. The youngest M.P. in 1970 was Miss Bernadette Devlin (born 23 April 1947) who was elected for Mid Ulster on 17 April 1969 and who made her maiden speech the day before her twenty-second birthday.

Oldest The oldest of all members was Samuel Young (born 14 Feb. 1822), Nationalist M.P. for East Cavan (1892–1918), who died on 18 April 1918, aged 96 years 63 days. The oldest "Father of the House" in Parliamentary history was the Rt. Hon. Charles Pelham Villiers (born 3 Jan. 1802), who was the Member for Wolverhampton when he died on 16 Jan. 1898, aged 96. He was a Member of Parliament for 63 years 6 days, having been returned at 16 elections. The oldest member sitting in 1970 was the Rt. Hon. Emanuel Shinwell, C.H. (born 18 Oct. 1884), M.P. (Labour) for the Easington division of Durham since 1950. He was first elected on 15 Nov. 1922 and retired on 29 May 1970 aged 85 years 7 months.

Longest span The longest span of service of any M.P. is 63 years 10 months (October 1900 to September 1964) by the Rt.

190

Hon. Sir Winston Leonard Spencer Churchill, K.G., O.M., C.H., T.D. (1874–1965), with a break only from November 1922 to October 1924. The longest unbroken span was that of C. P. Villiers (see above). The longest span in the Palace of Westminster (both Houses of Parliament) has been 73 years by the 10th Earl of Wemyss, G.C.V.O., who, as Sir Francis Wemyss-Charteris-Douglas, served as M.P. for East Gloucestershire (1841–46) and Haddingtonshire (1847–83) and then took his seat in the House of Lords, dying on 30 June 1914, aged 95 years 330 days.

Earliest M.P.s The first woman to be elected to the House of Commons was Mme. Constance Georgine Markievicz (*née* Gore Booth). She was elected as member (Sinn Fein) for St. Patrick's, Dublin, in December 1918. The first woman to take her seat was the Viscountess Astor, C.H. (1879–1964) (born Nancy Witcher Langhorne at Danville, Virginia, U.S.A.; formerly Mrs. Robert Gould Shaw), who was elected Unionist member for the Sutton Division of Plymouth, Devonshire, on 28 Nov. 1919, and took her seat three days later.

House of Lords The youngest member of the House of Lords is H.R.H. the Prince Charles Philip Arthur George, K.G., the Prince of Wales (born 14 Nov. 1948). All Dukes of Cornwall, of whom Prince Charles is the 24th, are technically eligible to sit, regardless of age—in his case from his succession on 6 Feb. 1952, aged 3. The 20th and 21st holders, later King George IV (born 1762) and King Edward VII (born 1841), were technically entitled to sit from birth.

The oldest member ever was the Rt. Hon. the 5th Baron Penrhyn, who was born on 21 Nov. 1865 and died on 3 Feb. 1967, aged 101 years 74 days. The oldest member now is the Rt. Hon. Lord Goddard, G.C.B., formerly Lord Chief Justice of England (born 1877).

Longest speech The longest recorded continuous speech in the House of Commons was that of Henry Peter Brougham (1778–1868) on 7 Feb. 1828, when he spoke for 6 hours on Law Reform. He ended at 10.40 p.m. and the report of this speech occupied 12 columns of the next day's edition of *The Times*. Brougham, created the 1st Lord Brougham and Vaux on 22 Nov. 1830, also holds the House of Lords record, also with six hours, on 7 Oct. 1831, speaking on the second reading of the Reform Bill.

The longest post-war speech has been one of 2 hours 37 minutes by Malcolm K. Macmillan (born 1913), the Labour member for the Western Isles, on 15–16 March 1961.

PREMIERSHIP

Longest term No United Kingdom Prime Minister has yet matched in duration the continuous term of office of Great Britain's first Prime Minister, the Rt. Hon. Sir Robert Walpole, K.G., later the 1st Earl of Orford (1676–1745), First Lord of the Treasury and Chancellor of the Exchequer from 3 April 1721 to 12 Feb. 1742. The office was not, however, officially recognised until 1905, since when the longest tenure has been that of Herbert Henry Asquith, later the 1st Earl of Oxford and Asquith (1852–1928), with 8 years 243 days from 8 April 1908 to 7 Dec. 1916. This was 7 days longer than the three terms of Sir Winston Churchill, between 1940 and 1955. The Hon. Sir Thomas Playford, G.C.M.G. (born 5 July

1896) was State Premier of South Australia from 5 Nov. 1938 to 10 March 1965.

Shortest term The shortest term as Prime Minister was that of the 1st Duke of Wellington, K.G., G.C.B., G.C.H. (1769–1852), whose third ministry survived only 22 days from 17 Nov. to 9 Dec. 1834.

Most times The only Prime Minister to have accepted office five times was the Rt. Hon. Stanley Baldwin, later the 1st Earl Baldwin of Bewdley (1867–1947). His ministries were those of 22 May 1923 to 22 Jan. 1924, 4 Nov. 1924 to 5 June 1929, 7 June 1935 to 21 Jan. 1936, from then until 12 Dec. 1936 and from then until 28 May 1937.

Oldest The oldest Prime Minister of the United Kingdom has been the Rt. Hon. Sir Winston Leonard Spencer Churchill, K.G., O.M., C.H., T.D. (born 30 Nov. 1874), who surpassed the age of the Rt. Hon. William Ewart Gladstone (1809–98) on 21 April 1963 and died on 24 Jan. 1965, aged 90 years 55 days.

Youngest The youngest of Great Britain's 46 prime ministers has been the Rt. Hon. the Hon. William Pitt (born 28 May 1759), who accepted the King's invitation to be First Lord of the Treasury on 19 Dec. 1783, aged 24 years 205 days. He had previously declined on 27 Feb. 1783, when aged 23 years 270 days.

William Pitt the Younger, who declined the Premiership at 23

CHANCELLORSHIP

Longest and shortest tenures The Rt. Hon. Sir Robert Walpole, K.G., later the 1st Earl of Orford (1676–1745), served 22 years 5 months as Chancellor of the Exchequer, holding office continuously from 12 Oct. 1715 to 12 Feb. 1742, except for the period from 16 April 1717 to 2 April 1721. The briefest tenure of this office was 26 days in the case of the Baron (later the 1st Earl of) Mansfield (1705–93), from 11 Sept. to 6 Oct. 1767.

Most appointments The only man with four terms in this office was the Rt. Hon. William Ewart Gladstone (1809–98) in 1852–55, 1859–66, 1873–74 and 1880–82.

SPEAKERSHIP

Longest Arthur Onslow (1691–1768) was elected Mr. Speaker on 23 Jan. 1728, at the age of 36. He held the position for 33 years 43 days, until 18 March 1761.

2. Military and Defence

WAR

Longest The longest of history's countless wars was the "Hundred Years War" between England and France, which lasted from 1338 to 1453 (115 years), although it may be said that the Holy War, comprising the nine Crusades from the First (1096–1104) to the Ninth (1270–91), extended over 195 years. It has been calculated that in the 3,466 years since 1496 B.C. there have been only 230 years of peace throughout the civilized world.

Last battle on British soil The last pitched land battle in Britain was at Culloden Field, Drummossie Moor, Inverness-shire, on 16 April 1746. The last Clan battle in Scotland was between Clan Mackintosh and Clan MacDonald at Mulroy, Inverness-shire, in 1689. The last battle on English soil was the Battle of Sedgemoor, Somerset, on 6 July 1685, when the forces of James II defeated the supporters of Charles II's illegitimate son, James Scott (formerly called Fitzroy or Crofts), the Duke of Monmouth (1649–85). During the Jacobite rising of 1745–46, there was a skirmish at Clifton Moor, Westmorland, on 18 Dec. 1745, when the British forces under Prince William, the Duke of Cumberland (1721–65), defeated the rebels of Prince Charles Edward Stuart (1720–88).

Shortest war The shortest war on record was that between the United Kingdom and Zanzibar (now part of Tanzania) from 9·02 to 9·40 a.m. on 27 Aug. 1896. The U.K. battle fleet under Rear-Admiral (later Admiral Sir) Harry Holdsworth Rawson (1843–1910) delivered an ultimatum to the self-appointed Sultan Sa'īd Khalid to evacuate his palace and surrender. This was not forthcoming until after 38 minutes of bombardment. Admiral Rawson received the Brilliant Star of Zanzibar (first class) from the new Sultan Hamud ibn Muhammad. It was proposed at one time that elements of the local populace should be compelled to defray the cost of the ammunition used.

Bloodiest war By far the most costly war in terms of human life was World War II (1939–45), in which the total number of fatalities, including battle deaths and civilians of all countries, is estimated to have been 54,800,000.

In the case of the United Kingdom, however, the heaviest casualties occurred in World War I (1914–18), with 765,399 killed out of 5,500,000 engaged (13·9 per cent.), compared with 265,000 out of 5,896,000 engaged (4·49 per cent.) in World War II. The heaviest total for one day was 21,392 fatalities and 35,493 wounded in the First Battle of the Somme on 1 July 1916. The total casualties in the Third Battle of Ypres (Passchendaele), from 31 July to 6 Nov. 1917, were about 575,000 (238,313 British and 337,000 German). The total death roll from World War I was only 17·7 per cent. of that of World War II, *viz.* 9,700,000.

Most costly Although no satisfactory computation has been published, it is certain that the material cost of World War II far transcended that of the rest of history's wars put together. In the case of the United Kingdom the cost of £34,423 million was over five times as great as that of World War I (£6,700 million) and 158·6 times that of the Boer War of 1899–1902 (£217 million). The total cost of World War II to the Soviet Union was estimated semi-officially in May 1959 at 2,500,000,000,000 roubles (£100,000 million).

Bloodiest civil war The bloodiest civil war in history was the T'ai-p'ing ("Peace") rebellion, in which peasant sympathizers of the Southern Ming dynasty fought the Manchu Government troops in China from 1853 to 1864. The rebellion was led by the deranged Hung Hsiu-ch'üan (poisoned himself in June 1864), who imagined himself to be a younger brother of Jesus Christ. His force was named *T'ai-p'ing Tien Kuo* (Heavenly Kingdom of Great Peace). According to the best estimates, the loss of life was between 20,000,000 and 30,000,000, including more than 100,000 killed by Government forces in the sack of Nanking on 19–21 July 1864.

Bloodiest battle The battle with the greatest recorded number of fatalities was the First Battle of the Somme from 1 July to 19 Nov. 1916, with more than 1,030,000—614,105 British and French and *c.* 420,000 (*not* 650,000) German. The gunfire was heard on Hampstead Heath, London. The greatest battle of World War II and the greatest ever conflict of armour was the Battle of Kursk of 5–22 July 1943 on the Eastern front, which involved 1,300,000 Red Army troops with 3,600 tanks, 20,000 guns and 3,130 aircraft in repelling a German Army Group which had 2,500 tanks. The final investment of Berlin by the Red Army in 1945 is, however, said to have involved 3,500,000 men; 52,000 guns and mortars; 7,750 tanks and 11,000 aircraft on both sides.

Ancient Modern historians give no credence to the casualty figures attached to ancient battles, such as the 250,00 reputedly killed at Plataea (Greeks *v.* Persians) in 4 B.C. or the 200,000 allegedly killed in a single day Châlons-sur-Marne, France, in A.D. 451. This view on the grounds that it must have been logistically qui impossible to maintain forces of such a size in the fie at that time.

British soil The bloodiest battle fought on British soil was th Battle of Towton, in Yorkshire, on 29 March 146 when 36,000 Yorkists defeated 40,000 Lancastrian The total loss has been estimated at between 28,000 an 38,000 killed. A figure of 80,000 British dead w attributed by Tacitus to the battle of A.D. 61 betwee Queen Boudicca (Boadicea) of the Iceni and the Roma Governor of Britain Suetonius Paulinus, for the loss 400 Romans in an Army of 10,000. The site of the batt is unknown but may have been near Borough Hil Daventry, Northamptonshire, or more probably nea Hampstead Heath, London. It is improbable that, fc such a small loss, the Romans could have killed mo than 20,000 Britons.

GREATEST INVASION

Seaborne The greatest invasion in military history was the Allie land, air and sea operation against the Normand coasts of France on D-day, 6 June 1944. Thirty-eigh convoys of 745 ships moved in on the first three day supported by 4,066 landing craft, carrying 185,000 me and 20,000 vehicles, and 347 minesweepers. The a assault comprised 18,000 paratroopers from 1,08 aircraft. The 42 available divisions possessed an a support from 13,175 aircraft. Within a month 1,100,00 troops, 200,000 vehicles and 750,000 tons of stores we landed. On D-day 2,132 were killed and 8,592 wounde among the invading force.

Airborne The largest airborne invasion was the Anglo-America assault of three divisions (34,000 men), with 2,80 aircraft and 1,600 gliders, near Arnhem, in the Nether lands, on 17 Sept. 1944.

Last on British soil The last invasion of Great Britain occurred on 12 Feb 1797, when the Irish-American adventurer Genera Tate landed at Carreg Gwastad with 1,400 Frenc troops. They surrendered near Fishguard, Pembroke shire, to Lord Cawdor's force of the Castlemartin Yeomanry and some local inhabitants armed with pitchforks.

Worst sieges The worst siege in history was the 900-day siege o Leningrad, U.S.S.R. by the German Army from 30 Aug 1941 until 27 Jan. 1944. The best estimate is tha between 1·3 and 1·5 million defenders and citizens died The longest siege in military history was that of Centa which was besieged by the Moors under Mulai Ismai for the 26 years 1674 to 1700.

LARGEST ARMED FORCES

Numerically, the country with the largest regular armed force is the United States, with 3,450,000 at mid-1969 compared with the U.S.S.R.'s 3,300,000 at the same date. The Chinese People's Liberation Army, which includes naval and air services, has more than 2,800,00 regulars, but there is also a civilian home guard militia claimed to be 200 million strong but regarded by the Institute for Strategic Studies to have an effective element of not more than 7,000,000.

**Battle of Sedgemoor 1685
(see page 191)**

MILITARY AND DEFENCE

DEFENCE
The estimated level of spending on armaments through-out the world in 1969 was $171,000 million (£71,000 million). This represents £19 per person per annum, or close to 10 per cent. of the world's total production of goods and services. It was estimated in 1969 that there were 15,750,000 full-time military and naval personnel and 30,000,000 armament workers.

The expenditure on "defence" by the government of the United States in the year ending 30 June 1970 was $81,240 million (£33,850 million), or about 9·2 per cent. of the country's gross national product. The forecast for 1970–71 is $79,432 million (£33,097 million).

The U.S.S.R.'s official "defence" budget for 1968–69 was 17,700 million roubles (£8,200 million at the official exchange rate). Almost certainly, this does not include space research costs or the research and development budget for advanced weapons systems. If considered in terms of purchasing power equivalent to U.S. dollars, total military expenditure by the U.S.S.R., including elements not in the official budget, is probably nearer $53,000 million (£22,080 million) per year, or 11·7 per cent. of the country's G.N.P.

At the other extreme is Andorra, whose defence budget, voted on 11 March 1962, amounted to 34s. 10d.

NAVIES
Largest The largest navy in the world is the United States Navy, with a manpower of 761,000 and 302,000 Marines at 30 June 1969. The active strength in 1969 included 15 attack and 7 anti-submarine carriers, 37 *Polaris*-armed and 102 other submarines, 68 guided missile ships (9 cruisers, 29 destroyers and 31 frigates), 225 other anti-submarine and fleet defence destroyers and 157 amphibious assault ships. In addition, there are more than 300 escorts and about 15 cruisers in reserve. The active fleet and reserves include about 250 support ships, and 72 minesweepers.

The strength of the Royal Navy in mid-1969 was 2 aircraft carriers, 2 commando ships, 2 assault ships, 8 destroyers (6 guided missiles), 54 frigates, 6 nuclear and 22 other submarines and 46 minesweepers. The uniformed strength was run down to 88,600 by 1 April 1970 though there are more than 100,000 Navy Department civilians. In 1914 the Royal Navy had 542 warships including 31 battleships with 5 building.

Greatest naval battle The greatest number of ships and aircraft ever involved in a sea-air action was 231 ships and 1,996 aircraft in the Battle of Leyte Gulf, in the Philippines. It raged from 22 to 27 Oct. 1944, with 166 United States and 65 Japanese warships engaged, of which 26 Japanese and 6 U.S. ships were sunk. In addition 1,280 U.S. and 716 Japanese aircraft were engaged. The greatest naval battle of modern times was the Battle of Jutland on 31 May 1916, in which 151 Royal Navy warships were involved against 101 German warships. The Royal Navy lost 14 ships and 6,097 men and the German fleet 11 ships and 2,545 men. The greatest of ancient naval battles was the Battle of Lepanto on 7 Oct. 1571, when an estimated 25,000 Turks were lost in 250 galleys, sunk by the Spanish, Venetian and Papal forces of more than 300 ships in the Gulf of Lepanto, now called Korinthiakós Kólpos, or the Gulf of Kórinthos (Corinth), Greece.

Greatest evacuation The greatest evacuation in military history was that carried out by 1,200 Allied naval and civil craft from the beachhead at Dunkerque (Dunkirk), France, between 27 May and 4 June 1940. A total of 338,226 British and French troops were taken off.

ARMIES
Largest Numerically, the world's largest army is that of China (mainland), with a total strength of about 2,500,000 in mid-1969. The total size of the U.S.S.R.'s army

Members of the eleven-strong world's smallest army in San Marino

(including the ground elements of the Air Defence Command) in mid-1969 was estimated at 2,000,000 men, believed to be organized into about 148 divisions.

Smallest The smallest army in the world is that of San Marino, with a strength of 11, while Costa Rica (since 1948), Iceland, Liechtenstein, Monaco and Nauru have no army at all.

Oldest The oldest army in the world is the 83-strong Swiss Guard in the Vatican City, with a regular foundation dating back to 21 Jan. 1506. Its origins, however, extend back before 1400.

Members of the Swiss Guard in the Vatican City— established 464 years

The human world

Oldest old soldiers The oldest old soldier of all time was probably John B. Salling of the army of the Confederate States of America and the last accepted survivor of the U.S. Civil War (1861–65). He died in Kingsport, Tennessee, U.S.A., on 16 March 1959, aged 112 years 305 days. The oldest Chelsea pensioner, based only on the evidence of his tombstone, was the 111-year-old William Hiseland (born on 6 Aug. 1620 and died on 7 Feb. 1732). The last survivor of the Afghan war of 1878–79 was Alfred Hawker, who died on 10 Dec. 1962, aged 104 years 41 days.

Oldest British Army regiment The oldest regular regiment in the British Army is the Royal Scots, raised in French service in 1633, though the Buffs (Royal East Kent Regiment) can trace back their origin to independent companies in Dutch pay as early as 1572. The Coldstream Guards, raised in 1650, were, however, placed on the establishment of the British Army before the Royal Scots and the Buffs. The oldest armed body in the United Kingdom is the Honourable Artillery Company. Formed from the Finsbury Archers, it received its charter from Henry VIII in 1537, and is now the senior regiment of the Territorial and Army Volunteer Reserve.

TANKS

Earliest The prototype of all tanks was the "Little Willie", built by William Forster & Co. Ltd. of Lincoln, and first tested in September 1915. The tank was first taken into action by the Machine Gun Corps (Heavy Section), which later became the Royal Tank Corps, at the battle of Flers, in France, on 15 Sept. 1916. It was known as the Mark I and was armed with a pair of 6-lb. guns and four machine-guns. It weighed 28 tons and, driven by a motor developing 105 horse-power, moved at two miles per hour.

Heaviest The heaviest tank ever constructed was the German Panzer Kampfwagen Maus II, which weighed 189 tons. By 1945 it had reached only the experimental stage and was not proceeded with.

The heaviest operational tank used by any army was the 81·5-ton 13-man French Char di Rupture 3C of 1923. It carried a 155 mm. howitzer and had two 250 h.p. engines giving a maximum speed of 8 m.p.h. On 7 Nov. 1957, in the annual military parade in Moscow, U.S.S.R., a Soviet tank possibly heavier than the German Jagd Tiger II (71·7 tons), built by Henschel, and certainly heavier than the Stalin III, was displayed.

The heaviest British tank ever built is the 76-ton prototype "Tortoise". With a crew of seven and a designed speed of 12 m.p.h., this tank has a width two inches less than that of the operational 65-ton "Conqueror". The most heavily armed is the 52-ton "Chieftain", put into service in November 1966, with a 120 mm. gun.

GUNS

Earliest Although it cannot be accepted as proved, the best opinion is that the earliest guns were constructed in North Africa, possibly by Arabs, in *c.* 1250. The earliest representation of an English gun is contained in an illustrated manuscript dated 1326 at Oxford. The earliest anti-aircraft gun was an artillery piece on a high angle mounting used in the Franco-Prussian War of 1870 by the French against Prussian balloons.

Largest The remains of the most massive guns ever constructed were found near Frankfurt am Main, Germany, in 1945. They were "Schwerer Gustav" and "Dora", each of which had a barrel 94 feet 9 inches long, with a calibre of 800 millimetres (31·5 inches), and a breech weighing 108 tons. The maximum charge was 2,000 kilogrammes (4,409 lb.) of cordite to fire a shell weighing 4,800 kilogrammes (4·7 tons) a distance of 55 kilometres (34 miles). The maximum projectile was one of 7 tons with a range of 22 miles. Each gun with its carriage weighed 1,323 tons and required a crew of 1,500 men.

During the 1914–18 war the British Army used a gun of 18 inches calibre. The barrel alone weighed 125 tons. In World War II the "Bochebuster", a train-mounted howitzer with a calibre of 18 inches, firing a 2,500 lb. shell to a maximum range of 22,800 yards, was used from 1940 onwards as part of the Kent coast defences.

Greatest range The greatest range ever attained by a gun is by the H.A.R.P. (High Altitude Research Project) gun consisting of two 16-inch calibre barrels in tandem in Barbados. In 1968 a 200 lb. projectile had been fired to a height of 400,000 feet (75¾ miles).

The famous "Big Bertha" guns, which shelled Paris in World War I, were the "Lange Berta" of which seven were built with a calibre of 21 cm. (8·26 inches), a designed range of 79·5 miles and an achieved range of more than 75 miles.

Mortars The largest mortars ever constructed were Mallets mortar (Woolwich Arsenal, London, 1857), and the "Little David" of World War II, made in the U.S.A. Each had a calibre of 36¼ inches (920 mm.), but neither was ever used in action.

The 65-ton Conqueror tank

Largest Cannon The highest calibre cannon ever constructed is the *Tsar Puchka* (King of Cannons), now housed in the Kremlin, Moscow, U.S.S.R. It was built in the 16th century with a bore of 36 inches (915 mm.) and a barrel 17 feet long. It was designed to fire cannon balls weighing 2 tons but was never used. The Turks fired up to seven shots per day from a bombard 26 feet long, with an internal calibre of 42 inches, against the walls of Constantinople (now Istanbul) from 12 April to 29 May 1453. It was dragged by 60 oxen and 200 men and fired a stone cannon ball weighing 1,200 lb.

Military engines The largest military catapults, or onagers, were capable of throwing a missile weighing 60 lb. a distance of 500 yards.

Longest march The longest march in military history was the famous Long March by the Chinese Communists in 1934–35. In 368 days, of which 268 days were of movement, from October to October, their force of 90,000 covered 6,000 miles northward from Kiangsi to Yünnan. They crossed 18 mountain ranges and six major rivers and lost all but 22,000 of their force in continual rear-guard actions against Nationalist Kuo-min-tang (K.M.T.) forces.

Most rapid march The most rapid recorded march by foot-soldiers was one of 62 miles in 26 hours on 28–29 July 1809, by the Light Brigade under Brigadier- (later Major-) General Robert Craufurd (1764–1812), coming to the relief of Lieut.-Gen. Sir Arthur Wellesley, later Field Marshal the 1st Duke of Wellington (1769–1852), after the Battle of Talavera (Talavera de la Reina, Toledo, Spain) in the Peninsular War.

The longest recorded march by a body of 60 without any fall-outs was one of 14 hours 23 minutes by the London Rifle Brigade on 18–19 April 1914. On 8 April 1922, two officers and 27 other ranks of the London Scottish Regiment covered the 53 miles from London to Brighton in 13 hours 59 minutes, each carrying 46 lb. of equipment, but two men failed to finish.

AIR FORCES
The earliest autonomous air force is the Royal Air Force whose origins began with the Royal Flying Corps (created 13 May 1912); the Air Battalion of the Royal Engineers (1 April 1911) and the Corps of Royal Engineers Balloon Section (1878) which was first operational in Bechuanaland (now Botswana) in 1884.

Largest The greatest Air Force of all time was the United States Army Air Force (now called the U.S. Air Force), which had 79,908 aircraft in July 1944 and 2,411,294 personnel in March 1944. The U.S. Air Force had 869,000 personnel and 7,000 first-line combat aircraft in mid-1969. The U.S.S.R. Air Force, with about 500,000 men in mid-1969, had about 3,400 fighter aircraft. In addition, the U.S.S.R.'s Strategic Rocket Forces had about 330,000 operational personnel in mid-1969.

BOMBS
The heaviest conventional bomb ever used operationally was the Royal Air Force's "Grand Slam", weighing 22,000 lb. and measuring 25 feet 5 inches long, dropped on Bielefeld railway viaduct, Germany, on 14 March 1945. In 1949 the United States Air Force tested a bomb weighing 42,000 lb. at Muroc Dry Lake, California, U.S.A.

Atomic The two atom bombs dropped on Japan by the United States in 1945 each had an explosive power equivalent to that of 20,000 tons (20 kilotons) of trinitrotoluene

Planes of the
U.S. Army Air Force,
which once deployed
nearly 80,000 aircraft

An atom bomb of
the "Littleboy" type
dropped on Hiroshima
on 6 Aug. 1945

($C_7H_5O_6N_3$), called T.N.T. The one dropped on Hiroshima, known as "Little Boy", was 10 feet long and weighed 9,000 lb. The most powerful thermo-nuclear device so far tested is one with a power equivalent to 57,000,000 tons of T.N.T., or 57 megatons, detonated by the U.S.S.R. in the Novaya Zemlya area at 8.33 a.m. G.M.T. on 30 Oct. 1961. The shock wave was detected to have circled the world three times, taking 36 hours 27 minutes for the first circuit. Some estimates put the power of this device at between 62 and 90 megatons. On 9 Aug. 1961, Nikita Khrushchyov, then the Chairman of the Council of Ministers of the U.S.S.R., declared that the Soviet Union was capable of constructing a 100-megaton bomb, and announced the possession of one in East Berlin, Germany, on 16 Jan. 1963. It has been estimated that such a bomb would make a crater 19 miles in diameter and would cause serious fires at a range of from 36 to 40 miles. Work started in the U.S.S.R. on atomic bombs in June 1942 although their first chain reaction was not achieved until December 1945 by Dr. Igor Kurchatov. The patent for the fusion or H bomb was filed in the United States on 26 May 1946 by Dr. Janos (John) von Neumann (1903–57), a Hungarian-born mathematician, and Dr. Klaus Emil Julius Fuchs (born in Germany, 1911), the defected physicist.

Largest atomic arsenal It was estimated early in 1970 that the United States possessed 4,250 deliverable thermo-nuclear warheads including 1,054 land-based I.C.B.M.s. The U.S.S.R.'s arsenal was estimated at 1,900 including 1,200 I.C.B.M.s (Inter-Continental Ballistic Missiles).

No official estimate has been published of the potential power of the device known as Doomsday, but this far surpasses any tested weapon. A 50,000 megaton cobalt-salted device has been mooted which could kill the entire human race except those who were deep underground and who stayed there for more than five years.

Largest "conventional" explosion The largest military use of conventional explosive was in tunnels under the German positions on the Messines Ridge, Belgium. These were mined from January 1916 to June 1917 by 6,000 men, under Capt. Cropper (Canadian Army), and packed with more than 500 tons of ammonal. The detonation at 3.10 a.m. on 17 June 1917 was heard in London.

3. Judicial

LEGISLATION AND LITIGATION

STATUTES

Oldest The earliest known judicial code was that of King Urnammu during the third dynasty of Ur, Iraq, in c. 2145 B.C. The oldest British statute in operation is a section of the Statute of Marlborough of 1267, retitled in 1948 "The Distress Act, 1267". Chapter 4 of the Provisions of Merton, 1236, was repealed by the Statute Law Revision Act, 1953.

Longest in the United Kingdom Measured in bulk the longest statute of the United Kingdom is the Income Tax Act, 1952, which runs to 511 pages. However, its 532 sections are surpassed in number by the 748 of the Merchant Shipping Act, 1894.

Of old statutes, 31 George III xiv, the Land Tax Act of 1791, written on parchment, consists of 780 skins forming a roll 1,170 feet long.

Shortest The shortest statute is the Parliament (Qualification of Women) Act, 1918, which runs to 27 operative words— "A woman shall not be disqualified by sex or marriage from being elected to or sitting or voting as a Member of the Common House of Parliament". Section 2 contains a further 14 words giving the short title.

Most It was computed in March 1959 that the total number of laws on Federal and State statute books in the United States was 1,156,644. The Illinois State Legislature only discovered in April 1967 that it had made the sale of cigarettes illegal and punishable by a $100 fine for a second offence in 1907.

Earliest English patent The earliest of all known English patents was that granted by Henry VI in 1449 to Flemish-born John of Utynam for making the coloured glass required for the windows of Eton College. The greatest number of applications for patents filed in the United Kingdom in any one year was 63,614 in 1969.

Most protracted litigation The longest contested law suit ever recorded ended in Poona, India, on 28 April 1966, when Balasaheb Patloji Thorat received a favourable judgment on a suit filed by his ancestor Maloji Thorat 761 years earlier in 1205. The points at issue were rights of presiding over public functions and precedences at religious festivals.

The dispute over the claim of the Prior and Convent of Durham Cathedral to administer the spiritualities of the diocese during a vacancy in the See grew fierce in 1283. It smouldered until 1939, having flared up in 1672, 1890 and 1920. In 1939 the Archbishop of Canterbury exercised his metropolitan rights and appointed the Dean as guardian of spiritualities of Durham "without prejudice to the general issue", then 656 years old.

Longest tish trial The longest trial in the annals of British justice was the Tichborne personation case. The civil trial began on 11 May 1871, lasted 103 days and collapsed on 6 March 1872. The criminal trial went on for 188 days, resulting in a sentence on 28 Feb. 1874 for two counts of perjury (14 years imprisonment and hard labour) on the London-born Arthur Orton, *alias* Thomas Castro (1834–98), who claimed to be Roger Charles Tichborne (1829–54), the elder brother of Sir Alfred Joseph Doughty-Tichborne, 11th Bt. (1839–66). The whole case, during which, miraculously, no juryman fell ill, thus spanned 827 days and cost £55,315. The jury were out for only 30 minutes.

The impeachment of Warren Hastings (1732–1818), which began in 1788, dragged on for seven years until 23 April 1795, but the trial lasted only 149 days. He was appointed a member of the Privy Council in 1814.

Murder The longest murder trial in Britain was that in which Ronald and Reginald Kray (twins), 35, were found guilty of the murder by shooting of George Cornell, 38, at the Blind Beggar public house on 9 June 1966, and by stabbing of Jack "The Hat" McVitie, 38, in Evering Road, Stoke Newington in October 1967. They were sentenced by Mr. Justice Melford Stevenson to imprisonment for not less than 30 years on 5 March 1969 after a 39-day trial at the Old Bailey, London. The costs of the trial were estimated at more than £200,000.

The shortest recorded British murder hearings were *R. v. Murray* on 28 Feb. 1957 and *R. v. Cawley* at Winchester Assizes on 14 Dec. 1959. The proceedings occupied only 30 seconds on each occasion.

Divorce The longest trial of a divorce case in Britain was *Gibbons v. Gibbons and Roman and Halperin*. On 19 March 1962, after 28 days, Mr. Alfred George Boyd Gibbons was granted a decree *nisi* against his wife Dorothy for adultery with Mr. John Halperin of New York City, N.Y., U.S.A.

Longest address The longest address in a British court was in *Globe and Phoenix Gold Mining Co. Ltd. v. Amalgamated Properties of Rhodesia*. Mr. William Henry Upjohn, K.C. (1853–1941) concluded his speech on 22 Sept. 1916, having addressed the court for 45 days.

attended trial The greatest attendance at any trial was at that of Major Jesús Sosa Blanco, aged 51, for an alleged 108 murders. At one point in the 12½-hour trial (5.30 p.m.

to 6 a.m., 22–23 Jan. 1959), 17,000 people were present in the Havana Sports Palace, Cuba.

Highest bail The highest amount ever demanded as bail was $46,500,000 (then £16,608,333) against Antonio De Angelis in a civil damages suit by the Harbor Tank Storage Co. filed in the Superior Court, Jersey City, New Jersey, U.S.A. on 16 Jan. 1964. (See also Greatest swindle, page 206.)

The highest bail figure in a British court is £140,000, granted to Manick Banthia at Uxbridge Court, Middlesex on 14 Oct. 1966. The amount involved £30,000 on his own recognizances, a surety of £50,000 and three of £20,000 each. He was charged with an attempt illegally to export £30,000 from London Airport in 60 Bank envelopes. Two other men, Joe Cohen and Amarendra Goswami also charged, had a combined bail of £170,000.

On 2 June 1959 the original bail fixed at Dublin, Ireland, for Dr. Paul Singer, aged 48, managing director of Shanahan's Stamp Auctions Ltd., was £100,000. This was later reduced to £15,000.

Greatest compensation The greatest Crown compensation for wrongful imprisonment was £10,000, paid on 23 Sept. 1931 to T. Boevey Barrett, who had been wrongfully convicted of alleged frauds in 1921. After serving three years' imprisonment in Accra, Ghana, he was granted a free pardon in 1930.

The greatest compensation paid for wrongful imprisonment in the United Kingdom was £6,000, paid in 1929 to Oscar Slater (*né* Leschziner), who had been arraigned for the murder of Miss Marion Gilchrist, aged 83, in Glasgow on 6 May 1909.

GREATEST DAMAGES
Loss of life The greatest damages awarded as compensation for loss of life were $2,000,000 (£714,285), awarded in 1965 to Mrs. Trese Hollerich, whose husband died when a Boeing 720-B airliner owned by Northwest Airlines crashed on 12 Feb. 1963 near Miami, Florida, U.S.A. In July 1965 the Boeing Company and Northwest Airlines settled the case out of court for $1,225,000 (£437,500).

Breach of contract The greatest damages ever awarded for a breach of contract were £610,392, awarded on 16 July 1930 to the Bank of Portugal against the printers Waterlow & Sons Ltd., of London, arising from their unauthorized

The Kray twins— central figures in the 39 day murder trial at the Old Bailey in 1969 printing of 580,000 five-hundred escudo notes in 1925. This award was upheld in the House of Lords on 28 April 1932. One of the perpetrators, Arthur Virgilio Alves Reis, served 16 years (1930–46) in gaol.

Personal injury The greatest damages ever awarded for personal injury were $1,125,000 (£401,785), awarded on 4 July 1964 to Stanley Miller, aged 17, in a court at Morristown, New Jersey, U.S.A. The award was made against his school for negligence after he became paralyzed as a result of an accident in the school gymnasium in 1962.

The greatest damages ever awarded for personal injury in a British court were £78,398, awarded to Christopher Povey, 19, of Hale, Cheshire for injuries sustained in a gymnasium accident at Rydal School, Colwyn Bay, by Mr. Justice Crichton at Manchester Assizes on 12 Mar. 1969. This figure was later reduced to £62,500 on appeal on 8 Dec. 1969. On 22 April 1969 £74,500 was awarded for road accident damage to Mr. John Rodney de Winton Kitcat of Buntingford, Hertfordshire in 1966 by Mr. Justice Paull with a stay granted in respect of £24,500.

An award of £66,447, subsequently reduced on appeal by £15,000 to £51,447, was made by Mr. Justice Cantley to Mr. William Henry Fletcher (born 1908) of Walton, Liverpool on 15 June 1967 for severe brain damage (and serious physical injuries) sustained in a road accident (in July 1964).

On 5 Feb. 1960, the Dublin High Court awarded £87,402 damages for motor injuries to Mr. Kevin P. McMorrow, aged 38, of County Leitrim, against his driver Mr. Edward Knott. It is understood that, after an appeal, a settlement was made out of court for £50,000.

Breach of promise The largest sum involved in a breach of promise suit in the United Kingdom was £50,000, accepted in 1913 by Miss Daisy Markham, *alias* Mrs. Annie Moss (died on 20 Aug. 1962, aged 76), in settlement against the 6th Marquess of Northampton (born 6 Aug. 1885).

Defamation The greatest damages for defamation ever awarded in the United Kingdom were £117,000, awarded on 21 July 1961 in *The Rubber Improvement Co. Ltd. v. Associated Newspapers Ltd.* for 51 words which appeared in the *Daily Mail* of 23 Dec. 1958. The company was represented by Colin Duncan, M.C. (now a Q.C.) and Mr. (now Sir) Helenus Patrick Joseph Milmo, Q.C. (born 24 Aug. 1908), who has since become a judge. After appeal proceedings by both sides this action was settled out of court for a substantially smaller amount.

Divorce The highest award made to the dispossessed party in a divorce suit was $70,000 (£25,000), awarded to Mr. Demetrus Sophocles Constantinidi against Dr. Henry William Lance for bigamous adultery with his wife Mrs. Julia Constandinidi. She married Dr. Lance after going through a form of divorce in Sioux Falls, South Dakota, U.S.A., on 27 Feb. 1902.

ALIMONY
World The greatest alimony ever paid was $11,550,000 (£4,125,000), paid by Reuben Hollis Fleet, the United States millionaire aircraft manufacturer, to his second wife Dorothy (*née* Mitchell) in 1945, after their separation, following "verbal abuse".

Britain The highest alimony awarded in a British court is £5,000 per annum, but in 1919 the 2nd Duke of Westminster, G.C.V.O., D.S.O. (1879–1953) settled £13,000 per annum upon his first wife, Constance Edwina (*née* Cornwallis-West), C.B.E., later Mrs. Lewis.

HIGHEST SETTLEMENT
Divorce The greatest amount ever paid in a divorce settlement

is $9,500,000 (£3,393,000), paid by Edward J. Hudson to Mrs. Cecil Amelia Blaffer Hudson, aged 43. This award was made on 28 Feb. 1963 at the Domestic Relations Court, Houston, Texas, U.S.A. Mrs. Hudson was, reputedly, already worth $14,000,000 (£5,000,000).

Patent case The greatest settlement ever made in a patent infringement suit is $9,250,000 (£3,303,000), paid in April 1952 by the Ford Motor Company to the Ferguson Tractor Co. for a claim filed in January 1948.

HIGHEST COSTS
The highest costs in English legal history arose from the case of the *Société Rateau v. Rolls-Royce,* an action concerning the alleged infringement of a French patent of 4 Dec. 1939 for an axial flow jet engine. Mr. Justice Lloyd-Jacob held in April 1967 that the patent had not been infringed. Costs were estimated at £325,000.

Income tax Highest reward The greatest amount paid for information concerning a case of income tax delinquency was $79,999·93 (£28,571), paid by the United States Internal Revenue Service to a group of informers. Payments are limited to 10 per cent. of the amount recovered as a direct result of information laid. Informants are often low-income accountants or women scorned. The total of payments in 1965 was $597,731 (then £213,475).

The greatest lien ever imposed by the U.S. Internal Revenue Service was one of $21,261,818 (£7,593,500), filed against the California property of John A. T. Galvin in March 1963, in respect of alleged tax arrears for 1954–57.

WILLS
Shortest The shortest valid will in the world is "Vše zene", the Czech for "All to wife", written and dated 19 Jan. 1967 by Herr Karl Tausch of Langen, Hesse, Germany. The shortest will contested and subsequently admitted to probate in English law was the case of *Thorn v. Dickens* in 1906. It consisted of the three words "All for Mother".

Longest The longest will on record was that of Mrs. Frederica Cook (U.S.A.), in the early part of the century. It consisted of four bound volumes containing 95,940 words.

JUDGE
Oldest World The oldest recorded active judge was Judge Albert R. Alexander (1859–1966) of Plattsburg, Missouri, U.S.A. He was the magistrate and probate judge of Clinton County until his retirement aged 105 years 8 months on 9 July 1965.

Britain The greatest recorded age at which any British judge has sat on a bench was 93 years 9 months in the case of Sir William Francis Kyffin Taylor, G.B.E., K.C. (later Lord Maenan), who was born on 9 July 1854 and retired as presiding judge of the Liverpool Court of Passage in April 1948, having held that position since 1903. The greatest age at which a House of Lords judgment has been given is 92 in the case of the 1st Earl of Halsbury (born 3 Sept. 1823) in 1916.

Youngest The youngest certain age at which any English judge has been appointed is 31, in the case of Sir Francis Buller (born 17 March 1746), who was appointed Second Judge of the County Palatine of Chester on 27 Nov. 1777, and Puisne Judge of the King's Bench on 6 May 1778, aged 32 years 1 month. The Hon. Daines Barrington (*c.* 1727–1800) was appointed Justice of the Counties of Merioneth and Anglesey sometime in 1757 and may have been even younger.

Youngest Q.C. The earliest age at which a barrister has taken silk since 1900 is 33 years 8 months in the case of Mr. (later the Rt. Hon. Sir) Francis Raymond Evershed (1899–1966) in April 1933. He was later Lord Evershed, a Lord of Appeal in Ordinary.

198

est paid lawyer It was estimated that Jerry Giesler (1886–1962), an attorney in Los Angeles, California, U.S.A., averaged $50,000 (£17,850) in fees for each case which he handled during the latter part of his career. Currently, the most highly paid lawyer is generally believed to be Louis Nizer of New York City, N.Y., U.S.A.

CRIME AND PUNISHMENT

GREATEST MASS KILLINGS

China The greatest massacre in human history ever imputed is that of 26,300,000 Chinese during the régime of Mao tse Tung between 1949 and May 1965. This accusation was made by an agency of the U.S.S.R. Government in a radio broadcast on 7 April 1969. The broadcast broke down the total into four periods:— 2·8 million (1949–52); 3·5 million (1953–57); 6·7 million (1958–60); and 13·3 million (1961–May 1965). The highest reported death figures in single monthly announcements on Peking radio were 1,176,000 in the provinces of Anhwei, Chekiang, Kiangsu, and Shantung, and 1,150,000 in the Central South Provinces. Po-ipo, Minister of Finance, is alleged to have stated in the organ *For a lasting peace, for a people's democracy* "in the past three years (1950–1952) we have liquidated more than 2 million bandits". General Jacques Guillermaz, a French diplomat estimated the total

executions between February 1951 and May 1952 at between 1 million and 3 million.

U.S.S.R. The total death roll in the Great Purge, or *Yezhovshchina*, in the U.S.S.R., in 1936–38 has never been published, though evidence of its magnitude may be found in population statistics which show a deficiency of males from before the outbreak of the 1941–45 war. The reign of terror was administered by the *Narodny Kommissariat Vnutrennykh Del* (N.K.V.D.), or People's Commissariat of Internal Affairs, the Soviet security service headed by Nikolay Ivanovich Yezhov (1895–?1939), described by Nikita Khrushchyov in 1956 as "a degenerate". S. V. Utechin, an expert on Soviet affairs, regards estimates of 8,000,000 or 10,000,000 victims as "probably not exaggerations".

Nazi Germany At the S.S. (*Schutzstaffel*) extermination camp (*Vernichtungslager*) called Auschwitz-Birkenau (Oswiecim-Brzezinka), near Oswiecim (Auschwitz), in southern Poland, where a minimum of 900,000 people (Soviet estimate is 4,000,000) were exterminated from 14 June 1940 to 29 Jan. 1945, the greatest number killed in a day was 6,000. The man who operated the release of the "Zyklon B" cyanide pellets into the gas chambers there during this time was Sergeant Mold. The Nazi (*Nationalsozialistiche Deutsche Arbeiter Partei*) Com-

Prisoners in the S.S. extermination camp at Auschwitz in Southern Poland

199

mandant during the period 1940–43 was Rudolf Franz Ferdinand Höss, who was tried in Warsaw from 11 March to 2 April 1947 and hanged, aged 47, at Oswiecim on 15 April 1947. Erich Koch, the war-time *Gauleiter* of East Prussia and *Reichskommissar* for German-occupied Ukraine, was arrested near Hamburg on 24 May 1949, tried in Warsaw from 20 Oct. 1958 to 9 March 1959 and sentenced to death for his responsibility for, or complicity in, the deaths of 4,232,000 people. The death sentence was later commuted to imprisonment.

Obersturmbannführer (Lt.-Col.) Karl Adolf Eichmann (born Solingen, West Germany 19 March 1906) of the S.S. was hanged in a small room inside Ramleh Prison, near Tel Aviv, Israel, at just before midnight (local time) on 31 May 1962, for his complicity in the deaths of 5,700,000 Jews during World War II, under the instruction given in April 1941 by Adolf Hitler (1889–1945) for the "Final Solution" (*Endlösung*), *i.e.* the extermination of European Jewry.

Forced labour No official figures have been published of the death ro in Corrective Labour Camps in the U.S.S.R., firs established in 1918. The total number of such camp was known to be more than 200 in 1946 but in 195 many were converted to less severe Corrective Labou Colonies. An estimate published in the Netherland puts the death roll between 1921 and 1960 at 19,000,00 The camps were administered by the *Cheka* until 192 the O.G.P.U. (1922–34), the N.K.V.D. (1934–1946) the M.V.D. (1946–1953) and the K.G.B. since 195 Daily intake has been limited to only 2,400 calorie since 1961.

Largest criminal organization The largest syndicate of organized crime is the Mafia o La Cosa Nostra, which has infiltrated the executive judiciary and legislature of the United States. It con sists of some 3,000 to 5,000 individuals in 24 "families federated under "The Commission", which has Sicilian-Jewish axis and an estimated annual turnove in vice, gambling, protection rackets and rigged tradin of $30,000 million per annum of which some 25 per cent is profit. The biggest Mafia (means *swank* from Sicilian word for beauty or pride) killing was o 10 Sept. 1931 when the topmost man Salvatore Maranzano, *Il Capo di Tutti Capi*, and 40 allies were liquidated.

Murder rate Highest The country with the highest recorded murder rate i Nicaragua, with 29·3 registered homicides per eacl 100,000 of the population in 1965. It has been estimated that the total number of murders in Colombia during *La Violencia* (1945–62) was about 300,000, giving a rate over a 17-year period of nearly 48 per day. A total o 592 deaths was attributed to one bandit leader, Teófilo ("Sparks") Rojas, aged 27, between 1948 and his death in an ambush near Armenia on 22 Jan. 1963. Some sources attribute 3,500 slayings to him.

Britain In Great Britain the highest annual total of murders since 1900 has been 242 in 1945, and the lowest 124 in 1937 and 125 in 1958.

Lowest The country with the lowest officially recorded rate in the world is Spain, with 42 murders (a rate of 1·35 per each million of the population) in 1963, or one murder every 9 days. In the Indian protectorate of Sikkim, in the Himalayas, murder is, however, practically unknown, while in the Hunza area of Kashmir, in the Karakoram, only one definite case has been recorded since 1900.

MOST PROLIFIC MURDERER

World The greatest number of victims ascribed to anyone has been 610 in the case of Countess Erszébet Báthory (1560–1614) of Hungary. At her trial which began on 2 Jan. 1611 a witness testified to seeing a list of her victims in her own handwriting totalling this number. All were alleged to be young girls from the neighbourhood of her castle at Csejthe where she died on 21 Aug. 1614. She had been walled up in her room for the 3½ years, after being found guilty.

Gille de Rays (Raies or Retz) (1404–40) was reputed to have murdered ritually between 140 and 200 kidnapped children. The best estimates put the total of his victims at about 60. He was hanged and burnt at Nantes, France, on 25 Oct. 1440.

The most prolific murderer known in recent criminal history was Herman Webster Mudgett (born 16 May 1860), better known as H. H. Holmes. It has been estimated that he disposed of some 150 young women "paying guests" in his "Castle" on 63rd Street, Chicago, Illinois, U.S.A. After a suspicious fire on 22 Nov. 1893, the "Castle" was investigated and found to contain secret passages, stairways and a maze of odd rooms, some windowless or padded, containing hidden gas inlets and electric indicators. There was also a hoist, two chutes, a furnace, an acid bath, a dissecting table, a selection of surgical instruments and fragmentary human remains. Holmes was hanged on 7 May 1896, on a charge of murdering his associate, Benjamin F. Pitezel.

Murderess
The greatest total of victims ascribed to a recent murderess is 16, together with a further 12 possible victims, making a total of 28. This was in the case of Bella Poulsdatter Sorensen Gunness *née* Grunt (1859–1908) of La Porte, Indiana, U.S.A. Evidence came to light when her farm was set on fire on 28 April 1908, when she herself was found by a jury to have committed suicide by strychnine poisoning. Her victims, remains of many of whom were dug from her hog-lot, are believed to comprise two husbands, at least eight and possibly 20 would-be suitors lured by "Lonely Hearts" advertisements, three women and three children. A claim that Vera Renczi murdered 35 persons in Romania this century lacks authority.

Britain
The only man to be arraigned on a charge of nine murders was Peter Thomas Anthony Manuel, aged 32, a New York born Lanarkshire woodworker. He was found guilty, on 29 May 1958, after a 16-day trial at Glasgow High Court, of the capital murders of five females and two males. Two other charges were not proceeded with and three other murders were later admitted by him, making a total of twelve. He was hanged at Barlinnie Prison, near Glasgow, at 8 a.m. on 11 July 1958. The total number of murders committed by "Doctor" William Palmer (born 1824) of Rugeley,

Peter Thomas Anthony Manuel, arraigned on a charge of 9 murders

Staffordshire, is not definitely known but was at least 13 and most probably 16, the victims having been poisoned by strychnine or antimony. He was hanged at Stafford on 14 June 1856. Scotland's most prolific known murderer was the Irish-born William Burke (1792–1829), who, in partnership with William Hare, murdered at least 13 derelicts in Edinburgh within 12 months, to sell their corpses. Hare turned King's evidence and Burke was hanged on 28 Jan. 1829.

Gang murders
During the period of open gang warfare in Chicago, Illinois, U.S.A., the peak year was 1926, when there were 76 unsolved killings. The 1,000th gang murder in Chicago since 1919 occurred on 1 Feb. 1967. Only 13 cases have ended in convictions.

Thuggee
It has been estimated that at least 2,000,000 Indians were strangled by Thugs (*burtotes*) during the period of the Thuggee cult, from 1550 until finally suppressed in 1852. It was established at the trial of Buhram that he had strangled at least 931 victims with his yellow and white cloth strip or *ruhmal* in the Oudh district between 1790 and 1830.

"Smelling out"
The greatest "smelling out" recorded in African history occurred before Shaka (1787–1828) and 30,000 Nguni subjects near the River Umhlatuzana, Zululand (now Natal, South Africa) in March 1824. After 9 hours, over 300 were "smelt out" as guilty of smearing the Royal *Kraal* with blood, by 150 witch-finders led by the hideous female *isangoma* Nobela. The victims were declared innocent when Shaka admitted to having done the smearing himself to expose the falsity of the power of his diviners. Nobela poisoned herself with atropine ($C_{17}H_{23}NO_3$), but the other 149 witch-finders were thereupon skewered or clubbed to death.

Suicide
The estimated daily total of suicides throughout the world surpassed 1,000 in 1965. The country with the highest recorded suicide rate is Hungary, with 33·9 per each 100,000 of the population in 1965, or an average of 9·3 suicides each day. The latest available figure for West Berlin, Germany, is 55 per 100,000 in 1966. The country with the lowest recorded rate is the United Arab Republic (formerly called Egypt), with 16 suicides (0·1 per 100,000) registered in Health Bureau localities (about 48 per cent. of the population) in 1963.

In the United Kingdom there were *c.* 5,100 suicides in 1968, or an average of 13·9 per day. In the northern hemisphere April and May tend to be peak months.

CAPITAL PUNISHMENT
Capital punishment was first abolished *de facto* in Liechtenstein in 1798. Capital punishment in the British Isles dates from A.D. 450, but fell into disuse in the 11th century, only to be revived in the Middle Ages, reaching a peak in the reign of Edward VI (1547–1553), when an average of 560 persons were executed annually at Tyburn alone. The most people executed at one hanging was 24 at Tyburn (Marble Arch, London) in 1571. Even into the 19th century, there were 223 capital crimes, though people were, in practice, hanged for only 25 of these.

Between 1830 and 1955 the largest number hanged in a year was 27 (24 men, 3 women) in 1903. The least was 5 in 1854, 1921 and 1930.

In 1956 there were no hangings in England, Wales or Scotland, since when the highest number in any year has been 5. The last hangings were those of Peter Anthony Allen (born 4 April 1943) at Walton Prison, Liverpool, and John Robson Walby (born 1 April 1940), *alias* Gwynne Owen Evans, at Strangeways Gaol, Manchester, both on 13 Aug. 1964. They had been found guilty of the capital murder of John Alan West, aged 53, a laundry van driver, who was stabbed and battered to death at his home in Workington, Cumberland, on 7 April 1964.

The human world

Last public hanging The last public execution in England took place outside Newgate Prison, London, on 25 May 1868, when Michael Barrett was hanged for his part in the Fenian bomb outrage on 13 Dec. 1867, when 12 were killed outside the Clerkenwell House of Detention, London. The earliest non-public execution was of the murderer Thomas Wells on 13 Aug. 1868. The last public hanging in Scotland was that of the murderer Joe Bell in Perth in 1866.

Last from yard-arm The last naval execution at the yard-arm was the hanging of Marine John Dalliger aboard H.M.S. *Leven* in the River Yangtze, China, on 13 July 1860. Dalliger had been found guilty of two attempted murders.

Youngest Although the hanging of persons under 18 was expressly excluded only in the Children's and Young Persons' Act, 1933 (Sec. 33), no person under that age had, in fact, been executed since 1887. Though it has been published widely that a girl of seven was hanged in 1808 and a boy of nine in 1831, the name of neither can be produced. In 1801 Andrew Benning, aged 13, was executed for housebreaking. The youngest persons hanged since 1900 have been 18 years old:— J. H. Clarkson at Leeds on 29 March 1904; Henry Jacoby on 7 Jan. 1922; Bishop in 1925; another case in 1932; James Farrell on 29 March 1949; and Francis Robert George ("Flossie") Forsyth on 10 Nov. 1960.

Oldest The oldest person hanged in the United Kingdom since 1900 was a man of 71 named Charles Frembd (*sic*) at Chelmsford Gaol on 4 Nov. 1914, for the murder of his wife at Leytonstone, Essex. In 1822 John Smith, said to be 80, of Greenwich, London, was hanged for the murder of a woman.

Last public guillotining The last person to be publicly guillotined in France was the murderer Eugen Weidmann before a large crowd at Versailles, near Paris, at 4.50 a.m. on 17 June 1939. Dr. Joseph Ignace Guillotin (1738–1812) died a natural death. He had advocated the use of the machine designed by Dr. Antoine Louis in 1789 in the French constituent assembly.

Most attempts The only man in Britain to survive three attempts to hang him was John Lee at Exeter Gaol, Devonshire, on 23 Feb. 1885. Lee had been found guilty of murdering, on 15 Nov. 1884, Emma Ann Whitehead Keyse of Babbacombe, who had employed him as a footman. The attempts, in which the executioner, James Berry, failed three times to get the trap open, occupied about seven minutes. Sir William Harcourt, the Home Secretary, commuted the sentence to life imprisonment. After release, Lee emigrated to the United States in 1917, was married and lived until 1933. The rope is now owned by Mr. D. A. Dale of Histon, Cambridge. In 1803 it was reported that Joseph Samuels was reprieved in Sydney, Australia after three unsuccessful attempts to hang him in which the rope twice broke.

Slowest The longest delay in carrying out a death sentence in recent history is in the case of Sadamichi Hirasawa (born 1906) of Tōkyō, Japan, who was sentenced to death in January 1950, after a trial lasting 16 months, on charges of poisoning twelve people with potassium cyanide in a Tōkyō bank. In November 1962 he was transferred to a prison at Sendai, in northern Honshū, where he was still awaiting execution in May 1970. The longest stay on "death row" in the United States has been one of more than 14 years by Edgar Labat, aged 44, and Clifton A. Paret, aged 38, in Angola Penitentiary, Louisiana, U.S.A. In March 1953 they were sentenced to death, after being found guilty of rape in 1950. They were released on 5 May 1967, only to be immediately re-arrested on a local jury indictment arising from the original charge.

Caryl Chessman, aged 39 and convicted of 17 felonies, was executed on 2 May 1960 in the gas chamber at the California State Prison, San Quentin, California,

202

U.S.A. In 11 years 10 months and one week on "death row", Chessman had won eight stays.

EXECUTIONER
The longest period of office of a Public Executioner was that of William Calcraft (1800–1879), who was in office

from 1828 to 1871 and officiated at nearly every hanging outside and later inside Newgate Prison, London. The most "suitably qualified" executioner on the Home Office list for the last remaining gallows at Wandsworth Prison, London against possible use for traitors, violent pirates and Royal dockyard arsonists is believed to be Mr. Harry Allen, 52.

BLOODIEST ASSIZES

In the West Country Assizes of 1685 (Winchester to Wells), George Jeffreys, the 1st Baron Jeffreys of Wem (1645–1689), sentenced 330 persons to be hanged, 841 to be transported for periods of ten or more years and larger numbers to be imprisoned and flogged. These sentences followed the Duke of Monmouth's insurrections.

against the sentence failed in 1948, had served 34 years for manslaughter up to 1954, when he was released. He died on 24 Dec. 1956. The longest single period served by a reprieved murderer in Great Britain this century was 40 years 11 months by John Watson Laurie, the Goat Fell or Arran murderer, who was reprieved on the grounds of insanity in November 1889 and who died in Perth Penitentiary on 4 Oct. 1930.

The longest prison sentence ever passed under United Kingdom law was one of three consecutive and two concurrent terms of 14 years, thus totalling 42 years, imposed on 3 May 1961 on George Blake (born, Rotterdam, 11 Nov. 1922 of an Egyptian-born Jewish-British father and a Dutch mother as George Behar), for treachery. Blake, formerly U.K. vice-consul in

Lord Jeffreys of Wem, the notorious 17th century Judge

LONGEST SENTENCES

World The longest recorded prison sentence is one of 6,616 years 6 months and one day awarded to José Crespo Ruiz in a court in Madrid, Spain, on 19 April 1967. The sentence comprised consecutive terms for the sale of each of many non-existent holiday flats on the Costa Brava, "worth" £3,500,000.

Richard Honeck was sentenced to life imprisonment in the United States in 1899, after having murdered his former schoolteacher. It was reported in November 1963 that Honeck, then aged 84, who was in Menard Penitentiary, Chester, Illinois, was due to be paroled after 64 years in prison, during which time he had received one letter (a four-line note from his brother in 1904) and two visitors, a friend in 1904 and a newspaper reporter in 1963. He was released on 20 Dec. 1963.

United Kingdom On 17 May 1939, William Burkitt, three times acquitted of murder by a jury (1915, 1925 and 1939), was sentenced by Mr. Justice Cassells "to be kept in prison for the rest of your natural life". Burkitt, whose appeal

Seoul, South Korea, had been converted to Communism during 34 months' internment there from 2 July 1950 to April 1953. It has been alleged that his betrayals may have cost the lives of up to 42 United Kingdom agents. He was "sprung" from Wormwood Scrubs Prison, London, W.12, on 22 Oct. 1966.

The longest recorded prison sentence imposed on a woman in the United Kingdom was 20 years for Mrs. Lorna Teresa Cohen (née Petra), *alias* Helen Joyce Kroger, for conspiring to commit a breach of Section 1 of the Officials Secrets Act, 1911. The sentence was passed at the Old Bailey, London, on 22 March 1961. She had conspired with her husband to transmit to East Germany United Kingdom defence data collected by Col. Konon Trofimovich Molody, *alias* Gordon Arnold Lonsdale, aged 37, of the U.S.S.R. Committee of State Security (*Komitet Gosudarstvennoi Besopasnosty* or K.G.B.). A remission of sentence was announced by the Foreign Secretary on 24 July 1969.

Broadmoor The longest period for which any person has been

The human world

detained in the Broadmoor hospital for the criminally insane, near Crowthorne, Berkshire, is 76 years in the case of William Giles. He was admitted as an insane arsonist at the age of 11 and died there on 10 March 1962, at the age of 87.

Greatest riot The greatest riot in England was the anti-Roman Catholic London riot of 2–13 June 1780, led by Lord George Gordon (1751–1793). Troops killed at least 285 rioters (some estimates are 700) and 135 were tried. Of these, 59 were sentenced to death, of whom 21 were hanged. A total of 280 troops were killed, making a minimum total of 565 deaths.

Greatest mass arrest The greatest mass arrest in the United Kingdom occurred on 17 Sept. 1961, when 1,314 demonstrators supporting the unilateral nuclear disarmament of the United Kingdom were arrested for wilfully disregarding the directions of the police and thereby obstructing highways leading to Parliament Square, London, by sitting down.

Lynching The worst year in the 20th century for lynchings in the United States has been 1901, with 130 lynchings (105 Negroes, 25 Whites), while the first year with no reported cases was 1952.

The last lynching recorded in Britain was that of Panglam Godolan, a Pakistani and a suspected murderer, in London on 27 Oct. 1958. The last case previous to this was of a kidnapping suspect in Glasgow in 1922.

LONGEST PRISON ESCAPES
The longest recorded escape from prison was that of Leonard T. Fristoe, 77, who escaped from Nevada State Prison, U.S.A., on 15 Dec. 1923 and was turned in by his son on 15 Nov. 1969 at Compton, California. He had had 46 years of freedom under the name Claude R. Willis. He had killed two sheriff's deputies in 1920.

The longest period of freedom achieved by a British gaol breaker is more than $14\frac{1}{2}$ years by Irish-born John Patrick Hannan, who escaped from Verne Open Prison at Portland, Dorset, on 22 Dec. 1955 and was still at large in May 1970. He had served only 1 month of a 21-month term for car-stealing and assaulting two policemen.

Broadmoor The longest escape from Broadmoor was one of 39 years by the Liverpool wife murderer James Kelly, who got away on 28 Jan. 1888, using a pass key made from a corset spring. After an adventurous life in Paris, in New York and at sea he returned in April 1927, to ask for re-admission. After some difficulties this was arranged. He died in 1930.

An aerial view of Broadmoor institution near Crowthorne, Berks.

Greatest gaol break The greatest gaol break in Britain was that from Wandsworth, South London, on 24 June 1961. Eleven men got away, of whom one was immediately recaptured with a broken leg. The other ten were all rounded up within a few days.

ROBBERY

Greatest The greatest robbery on record was that of the German National Gold Reserves by a combine of United States military personnel and German civilians in Bavaria in June 1945. A total of 730 gold bars valued at £3,528,000, together with six sacks of bank notes and 25 boxes of platinum bars and precious stones, disappeared in transit, but none of those responsible has been brought to trial. It has been suggested that this robbery was a Soviet propaganda invention to discredit the United States administration during the early period of quadripartite control. (See, however, Industrial espionage, right.)

Embezzlement In 1959 the Venezuelan Government asked the United States Government for the extradition of Col. Marcos Pérez Jiménez to face charges of embezzling more than $13,000,000 (about £4,600,000) in Government funds during his Presidency. He had been President of Venezuela from 3 Dec. 1952 until being deposed on 23 Jan. 1958, after which he fled the country and went to live in Miami, Florida, where he was finally turned over to the Venezuelan authorities on 16 Aug. 1963 and flown to Venezuela. His fortune has been estimated at $700,000,000 (£250 million).

Bank On 23 March 1962, 150 *plastiqueurs* of the *Organisation de l'Armée Secrète* (O.A.S.) removed by force 23,500,000 francs (£1,703,000) from the Banque d'Algérie in Oran, Algeria, after the collapse of civil order.

The biggest "inside job" was that at the National City Bank of New York, from which the Assistant Manager, Richard Crowe, removed $883,660 (£315,593). He was arrested on 11 April 1949. On 23 Oct. 1969 it was disclosed that $13,193,000 (£5,497,000) of U.S. Treasury bills were inexplicably missing from the Morgan Trust, Wall Street, New York City, U.S.A.

Train The greatest recorded train robbery occurred between about 3.10 a.m. and 3.45 a.m. on 8 Aug. 1963, when a General Post Office mail train from Glasgow, Scotland, was ambushed between Sears Crossing and Bridego Bridge at Mentmore, near Cheddington, Buckinghamshire. The gang escaped with about 120 mailbags containing £2,595,998 worth of bank notes being taken to London for pulping. Only £343,448 had been recovered by 9 Dec. 1966.

Art The greatest recorded art robbery was the theft of eight paintings, valued at £1,500,000, taken during the night of 30–31 Dec. 1966 from the Dulwich College Picture Gallery in London. The haul included three paintings by Peter Paul Rubens (1577–1640), one by Adam Ehlsheimer (1578–1610), three by Rembrandt van Rijn (1606–69) and one by Gerard Dou (1613–75). Three of the paintings were recovered on 2 Jan. 1967 and the remaining five on 4 Jan. 1967.

Jewels The greatest recorded theft of gem stones occurred on 13 Nov. 1969 in Freetown, Sierra Leone, when an armed gang stole diamonds belonging to the Sierra Leone Selection Trust worth £1,500,000. The haul from Carrington & Co. Ltd. of Regent Street, London, on 21 Nov. 1965 was estimated to be £500,000.

Coins The largest numismatic robbery ever made was in the home of Willis H. Du Pont at Coconut Grove, Miami, Florida on 5 Oct. 1967 when $1,500,000's (£625,000) worth of Russian and United States material were removed by five men.

Industrial espionage It has been alleged that a division of the American Cyanamid Company about 1966 lost some papers and vials of micro-organisms through industrial espionage, allegedly organized from Italy, which data had cost them $24,000,000 (then £8·57 million) in research and development. It is arguable that this represents the greatest robbery of all-time.

Greatest kidnapping ransom The greatest ransom ever extracted in a kidnapping case was $600,000 (£214,285), obtained by Carl Austin Hall and Mrs. Bonny Brown Heady for the release of Robert C. Greenlease, Jr., aged 6, who was kidnapped on 28 Sept. 1953 and found dead nine days later. Both kidnappers were executed on 18 Dec. 1953 at Missouri State Prison, Jefferson City, Missouri, U.S.A. Of the ransom money, $301,690 (£107,746) is still missing.

The greatest amount paid for the return of a live child is $250,000 (£89,285) by Herbert King, President of the

The Royal Mail rail compartment from which the greatest recorded train robbery was perpetrated

Gibraltar Finance Corporation of Beverly Hills, California, for the return of his son Kenneth, aged 11, in April 1967. On 13 Oct. 1968 it was reported that a ransom equivalent to £1,250,000 was being demanded by some Sardinian bandits for the return of Giuseppe (Peppino) Ticca, aged 69.

Largest narcotics haul The largest recorded haul of narcotics was made by police in Hong Kong on 7 Feb. 1965, when they seized almost 4,000 lb. of opium and morphine which had been smuggled into Hong Kong aboard a British ship from Bangkok, Thailand. Such an amount would produce about 830 lb. of pure heroin, now marketable at $75,000,000 (£31,250,000).

Greatest bigamists It has been recorded that Mrs. Theresa Vaughan (or Vaughn), aged 24, while on trial in Sheffield, Yorkshire, on 19 Dec. 1922, confessed to 61 bigamous marriages within five years. No confirmation of this case is obtainable from local police records. A male record of 72 has been claimed.

Largest court The largest judicial building in the world is the Johannesburg Central Magistrates' Court, opened in 1941 at the junction of Fox and West Streets, Johannesburg, South Africa. There are 42 court-rooms (8 civil and 34 criminal), with a further seven criminal court-rooms under construction. The court has a panel of 70 magistrates and deals with an average of 2,500 criminal cases every week, excluding petty cases in which guilt has been admitted in writing.

Penal camps The largest penal camp systems in the world were those near Karaganda and Kolyma, in the U.S.S.R., each with a population estimated in 1958 at between 1,200,000 and 1,500,000. The official N.A.T.O. estimate for all Soviet camps was "more than one million" in March 1960. It was estimated in 1966 that the total population of penal camps in China was about 10,000,000.

Devil's Island The largest French penal settlement was that of St. Laurent du Maroni, which comprised the notorious Îles du Diable, Royale and St. Joseph (for incorrigibles) off the coast of French Guiana, in South America. It remained in operation for 99 years from 1854 until the last group of repatriated prisoners, including Théodore Rouselle, who had served 50 years, was returned to Bordeaux on 22 Aug. 1953. It has been estimated that barely 2,000 *bagnard* (ex-convicts) of the 70,000 deportees ever returned. These, however, include the executioner Ladurelle (imprisoned 1921–37), who was murdered in Paris in 1938.

PRISONS
Largest World The largest prison in the world is Kharkov Prison, in the U.S.S.R., which has at times accommodated 40,000 prisoners.

British Isles The largest prison in the United Kingdom is Wormwood Scrubs, West London, with 1,240 cells. The highest prison walls in Great Britain are those of Leicester Prison, measuring 30 feet high.

The largest prison in Scotland is Barlinnie, near Glasgow, with 962 single cells. Ireland's largest prison is Mountjoy Prison, Dublin, with 808 cells.

Smallest The smallest prison in the world is usually cited as that on the island of Sark, in the Channel Islands, which has a capacity of two. In fact the prison on Herm, a neighbouring island, is smaller, with a diameter of 13 feet 6 inches, and must rank with the single person lock-ups such as that at Shenley, Hertfordshire. The smallest prison in England is Oxford Prison (also the oldest, built in c. 1640), with 120 cells. The smallest in Scotland is Penninghame Open Prison, Wigtownshire with accommodation for 63. Ireland's smallest prison is that at Sligo, with 100 cells.

Highest population The highest daily average prison population, including Borstals and detention centres, for England and Wales was the figure for 1 April 1969 to 31 March 1970 of 39,254 (passed 40,000 in June 1970). In Scotland the average prison population was 4,834 and in Northern Ireland 721 in 1969.

Most secure prison After it became a maximum security Federal prison in 1934, no convict was known to have lived to tell of a successful escape from the prison on Alcatraz ("Pelican") Island in San Francisco Bay, California, U.S.A. A total of 23 men attempted it but 12 were recaptured, 5 shot dead, one drowned and 5 presumed drowned. On 16 Dec. 1962, three months before the prison was closed, one man reached the mainland alive, only to be recaptured on the spot.

Largest bribe An alleged bribe of £30,000,000 offered to Shaikh Zaid ibn Sultan of Abu Dhabi, Trucial Oman, by a Saudi Arabian official in August 1955, is the highest on record. The affair concerned oil concessions in the disputed territory of Buraimi on the Persian Gulf.

Greatest forgery The greatest recorded forgery was the German Third Reich government's forging operation, code name "Bernhard", engineered by Herr Naujocks in 1940–41. It involved £150,000,000's worth of £5 notes.

Greatest swindle The greatest swindle ever perpetrated in commercial history was that of Antonio (Tino) De Angelis (born 1915), a 5 ft. 5 in. 290 lb. ex-hog-cutter from New York City, U.S.A. His Allied Crude Vegetable Oil Refining Corporation (formed 19 Nov. 1955) operated from an uncarpeted office adjoining a converted tank farm in Bayonne, New Jersey. The tanks were rigged with false dipping compartments and were interconnected such that sea water could be pumped to substitute for phantom salad oil which served as collateral for warehouse receipts. A deficiency of 927,000 short tons of oil valued at $175,000,000 (then £62·5 million) was discovered.

Europe's greatest swindler was Ivar Kreuger (1882–1932), the Swedish Match king, managing director of *Svenska Tändsticks AB*. His largest deal was a long-term dollar loan of $125,000,000 to Germany in return for a national monopoly supply agreement. After Kreuger shot himself in Paris on 12 March 1932 it was found by auditors that both assets and profits of his company were largely fictitious and that the accounts had been falsified.

Passing bad cheques The record for passing bad cheques was set by Frederick Emerson Peters (1886–1959), who, by dint of some 200 impersonations, netted $250,000 (£89,300) with 28,000 bad cheques. Among his many philanthropies was a silver chalice presented to a cathedral in Washington, D.C., U.S.A., also paid for with a bad cheque.

FINES
A fine equivalent to £9·83 million was imposed on Juan Vila Reyes, president of the Barcelona textile machinery manufacturer Matesa, by the Currency Crime Court, Madrid, Spain on 19 May 1970 for converting export development funds to his own use.

Heaviest The heaviest fine ever imposed in the United Kingdom was one of £277,500, plus £3,717 costs, on I. Hennig & Co. Ltd., the London diamond merchants, at Clerkenwell Magistrates' Court, London, on 14 Dec. 1949. The amount was later reduced on appeal.

Smallest The smallest recorded fine in Britain was one penny, imposed on Philip Cathie of Hove, Sussex, at Marlborough Street, London, on 19 April 1960, for reversing in a Soho one-way street to allow a taxi to pass. On 23 Feb. 1962, the same stipendiary fined George Shrimpton and Hamish Smith one penny for moving a locked car owned by a woman.

Alcatraz Island,
San Francisco Bay,
California—
once the world's
most secure prison

**Rarest
prosecution**

There are a number of crimes in English law for which there have never been prosecutions. Among unique prosecutions are *Rex v. Crook* in 1662 for praemunire and *Rex v. Gregory* for selling honours under the Honours (Prevention of Abuses) Act, 1924, in 1933. Maundy Gregory (d. 1941) was the honours broker of Lloyd George's 1919–20 Coalition Government.

4. Economic

MONETARY AND FINANCE

LARGEST BUDGET

The greatest annual expenditure budgeted by any country has been $200,771 million (£83,654 million) by the United States government (federal expenditure) for the fiscal year ending 30 June 1971.

The highest budgeted revenue in the United States has been $202,102 million (£84,209 million) in 1970–71. The estimated revenue receipts of the U.S.S.R. Government

in 1969 were 139,000 million roubles (*officially* equivalent to $148,800 million or £62,000 million).

In the United States, the greatest surplus was $8,419,469,844 (now £3,006,953,516) in 1947–48, and the greatest deficit was $57,420,430,365 (now £20,507,296,559) in 1942–43.

**United
Kingdom**

The greatest annual budget expenditure of the United Kingdom was £12,822,145,000 in the year ending 31 March 1970. The highest budget revenue was £15,266,559,000 in 1969–70.

The greatest annual surplus achieved was £2,444,414,000 in 1969–70 and the greatest deficit was £2,825 million in 1944–45.

Foreign aid

The total net foreign aid given by the United States government between 1 July 1945 and 31 Dec. 1968 was $116,681 million (£48,617 million), of which $78,189 million (£32,578 million) was non-military. The country which received most U.S. aid in 1968 was India, with $588,000,000 (£245 million). U.S. foreign aid began

207

with $50,000 to Venezuela for earthquake relief in 1812.

TAXATION

Most taxed The major national economy with the highest rate of taxation (central and local taxes, plus social security contribution) is that of Sweden, with 46·6 per cent. of her Gross National Product in 1967. The lowest proportion for any advanced national economy in 1967 was 20·3 per cent. in Japan, which also enjoys the highest economic growth rate. The comparable figure for the United Kingdom in 1967 was 37·7 per cent. but more than 41·0 per cent. in 1969.

There is no income tax paid by residents on Lundy Island.

Highest surtax The country with the most confiscatory marginal rate of income tax is Burma, where the rate is 99 per cent. (equivalent to 19s. 9·6d. in the £) for annual incomes exceeding 300,000 kyats (pronounced chuts) (£22,540). In November 1969 Premier Ne Win proclaimed "the way of true Socialism—the Burmese way". The second highest marginal rate is in the United Kingdom, where the topmost surtax level was 97·5 per cent. (19s. 6d. in the £) in 1950–51 and 96·25 per cent. (19s. 3d. in the £) in 1966–67. A married man with two children earning £5,000 per year in 1938 would in March 1968 have to earn £71,660 to enjoy the same standard of living.

In volume, as opposed to *per caput,* the most taxed country is the United States, where the total of individual income taxes collected in the year ended 30 June 1967 was $69,371,000,000 (£28,904 million), compared with total personal income of $626,400 million (£261,500 million) in 1967.

Least taxed The advanced country with the least "advanced" system of tax collection would appear to be Italy. In August 1963 it was admitted that, from a working population approaching 20,000,000, only 1,194,328 tax returns were filed. No figures for 1966–67 are available.

Highest and lowest rates in United Kingdom Income tax was introduced in Great Britain in 1799 at the standard rate of 2s. in the £. It was discontinued in 1815, only to be re-introduced in 1842 at the rate of 7d. in the £. It was at its lowest at 2d. in the £ in 1875, gradually climbing to 1s. 3d. by 1913. From April 1941 until 1946 the record peak of 10s. in the £ was maintained to assist in the financing of World War II. Death Duties (introduced in 1894) on millionaire estates began at 8 per cent. (1894–1907) and were raised to a peak of 80 per cent. by 1949.

NATIONAL DEBT

The largest national debt of any country in the world is that of the United States, where the gross federal public debt of the Federal Government reached its peak figure of $374,700,000,000 (£156,125 million), equivalent to $1,834 (£764) per person, in January 1970. This amount in dollar bills would make a pile 25,421 miles high, weighing 356,150 tons.

The United Kingdom National Debt, which became a permanent feature of Britain's economy as early as

Lundy Island off the North Devon coast, one of the world's few remaining tax havens

1692, was £33,070 million, or £611 per person, at 31 March 1970. This amount placed in a pile of brand new £1 notes would be 2,032 miles in height.

Gross National Product
The estimated world aggregate of Gross National Products in 1968 exceeded £800,000 million. The country with the largest Gross National Product is the United States, with an estimated $960,000 million (£400,000 million) for 1970. The long awaited "Trillion Dollars" should be attained in 1971. The estimated G.N.P. of the United Kingdom was £38,617 million in 1969.

National wealth
The richest large nation, measured by real Gross National Product per head, has been the U.S.A. since about 1910. The average share G.N.P. in the U.S.A. was $4,700 (£1,958) in 1970. It has been estimated that the value of all physical assets in the U.S.A. in 1966 was $2,460,000,000,000 or $12,443 (£5,184) per head. The comparative figure for the United Kingdom was £84,299 million at 31 Dec. 1961. In addition, the net value of claims on foreigners held by United Kingdom residents was £1,124 million, making the total estimated national wealth £85,423 million.

National Savings
The highest total of National Savings recorded in a year was £573,549,000 (net receipts) in 1945/46. The highest net receipts in a week were £42,423,000 for the week ending 11 May 1946. The total amount invested was £8,615 million on 19 Apr. 1969. The greatest withdrawals in a week were £21,208,000 (including interest) in the week ending 23 Dec. 1967. Mr. Arthur Ellis of Saltergate, Chesterfield between 1958 and 1969 has won one £250, two £100 and 37 £25 premium bond draw prizes.

GOLD RESERVES
The country with the greatest monetary gold reserve is the United States, whose Treasury had $11,882 million (£4,951 million) on hand in January 1970. The United States Bullion Depository at Fort Knox, 30 miles south-west of Louisville, Kentucky, U.S.A. is the principal depository. Gold is stored in standard mint bars of 400 troy ounces (439 oz. avoirdupois), measuring 7 inches by $3\frac{5}{8}$ inches by $1\frac{5}{8}$ inches, and each worth $14,000 (£5,833).

The greatest accumulation of gold in the world is now in the Federal Reserve Bank at 33 Liberty Street, New York City, N.Y., U.S.A. The bank admits to having gold valued at $13,000 million (£5,416 million) owned by foreign central banks and stored 85 feet below street level, in a vault 50 feet by 100 feet behind a steel door weighing 89 tons.

United Kingdom
The highest published figure for the sterling area's gold and convertible currency reserves was $4,190 million (then £860 million) on 31 Aug. 1938, and the lowest of recent times $298,000,000 (then £74 million) on 31 Dec. 1940. The figure was £1,153 million ($2,767 million) at 31 May 1970.

BANK RATE
In 1969 the highest bank rate in the world was that of South Korea at 28 per cent. and the lowest that of Portugal at 2·5 per cent. The lowest that the Bank of England bank rate has ever been is 2 per cent., first from 22 April 1852 to 6 Jan. 1853. The highest ever figure was 10 per cent., first on 9 Nov. 1857, and most recently on 6 Aug. 1914. The highest yearly average was 7·35 per cent. in 1864 (6 per cent. to 9 per cent.). The longest period without a change was the 12 years 13 days from 26 Oct. 1939 to 7 Nov. 1951, during which time the rate stayed at 2 per cent.

PAPER MONEY
Paper money is an invention of the Chinese and, although the date of 119 B.C. has been suggested, the innovation is believed to date from the T'ang dynasty of the 7th century A.D. The world's earliest bank notes

were issued by the Stockholms Banco, Sweden, in July 1661. The oldest surviving note is one for 5 dalers dated 6 Dec. 1662. The oldest surviving printed Bank of England note is one for £555 to bearer, dated 19 Dec. 1699 ($4\frac{1}{2} \times 7\frac{3}{4}$ inches).

Largest and smallest
The largest paper money ever issued was the one kwan note of the Chinese Ming dynasty issue of 1368–99, which measured 9 inches by 13 inches. The smallest bank note ever issued was the 5 cent. note of the Chekiang Provincial Bank (established 1908) in China. It measured 55 millimetres (2·16 inches) by 30 millimetres (1·18 inches).

A U.S. Treasury half billion dollar note

Highest denominations World
The highest denomination of paper currency ever authorized in the world are United States gold certificates for $100,000 (£41,666), bearing the head of former President Thomas Woodrow Wilson (1856–1924), issued by the U.S. Treasury in 1934. There also exists in the U.S. Bureau of Engraving and Printing an example of a U.S. Treasury note for $500,000,000 bearing interest coupons for $15,625 million each 6 months for 14 years at $6\frac{1}{4}$ per cent.

The highest denomination notes in circulation are U.S. Federal Reserve Bank notes for $10,000 (£4,166). They bear the head of Salmon Portland Chase (1808–73). None has been printed since July 1944 and their circulation fell from 4,600 at 31 Dec. 1941 to only 394 at 30 June 1967 but rose to 1,900 by March 1969. On 15 July 1969 the U.S. Treasury announced that no further notes higher than $100 would be issued.

United Kingdom
Two Bank of England notes for £1,000,000 still exist, dated before 1812, but these were used only for internal accounting. Facsimile million pound notes were reproduced by J. Arthur Rank Productions Ltd. to publicize their film *The Million Pound Note* made in 1954. These were dated 20 June 1903. The highest issued denominations were £1,000 notes, first printed in 1725, discontinued in 1943 and withdrawn on 30 April 1945. A total of 63 of these notes were still unaccounted for up to July 1968 after which no data has been issued by the Bank.

The highest denomination notes currently issued by the Bank of England are those for £10, but Scottish banks issue notes up to £100 denomination. The Bank of England intend re-introducing £20 notes (previously issued from 1725–1943) in 1970. The rarest Bank of England £1 or 10 shilling note are those signed by Cyril Patrick Mahon, who was in office for only 4 months from their issue on 22 Nov. 1928 to 26 March 1929.

The lowest ever denomination Bank of England note was for a penny, dated 10 Jan. 1828, which was adapted from a £5 note and doubtless used to adjust an overnight difference. In 1868 it was purchased by the Bank for £1 from the landlord of the "Blue Last", Bell Alley, in the City of London.

Most expensive The highest price paid for a note no longer valid currency is believed to be $3,600 (£1,500), paid in 1900 for the first Ming note (see page 209) ever found.

Highest circulation The highest ever Bank of England note circulation in the United Kingdom was £3,463,000,000 on 19 Dec. 1969—equivalent to a pile of £1 notes 206·9 miles high.

DEVALUATION
Devaluation was practised by Emperor Nero of Rome (A.D. 54–68), who debased his coinage. Since 1945, 112 of the world's 120 currencies have devalued including the pound twice, the rouble 3 times and the Chilean

Pioneer of devaluation, Emperor Nero

currency 46 times (since 1 Jan. 1949). The U.S. dollar has only been devalued once vis-à-vis gold (in 1934).

WORST INFLATION
The world's worst inflation occurred in Hungary in June 1946, when the 1931 gold pengö was valued at 130 trillion ($1·3 \times 10^{20}$) paper pengös. Notes were issued for szazmillio billion (100 trillion or 10^{20}) pengös. Currently the worst inflation is in Brazil, where the cruzeiro depreciated 42 times, in terms of the United States dollar, between 1 Feb. 1957 (64·80 per $) and March 1967 (2,720 per $). A new cruzeiro, equivalent to 1,000 old cruzeiros, was introduced on 8 Feb. 1967. In 1966–67 there was a further 21·2 per cent. inflation.

CHEQUES
Largest World The greatest amount paid by a single cheque in the history of banking was $960,242,000·00 (£342,943,571), paid on 31 Jan. 1961 by the Continental Illinois National Bank and Trust Company of Chicago, Illinois, U.S.A. This bank headed a group which bought the accounts receivable of Sears, Roebuck & Co., to whom the cheque was paid.

United Kingdom The largest cheque drawn in Britain was one for £119,595,645 12s., drawn on 24 Jan. 1961 by Lazard Brothers & Co. Ltd. and payable to the National Provincial Bank, in connection with the takeover of the British Ford Motor Company. The total number of cheques cleared in 1968 was 678 million.

Oldest The oldest surviving English cheque is one drawn on 14 March 1664.

COINS
Oldest World The earliest certainly dated coins are the electrum (alloy of gold and silver) staters of Lydia, in Asia Minor (now Turkey), which were coined in the reign of King Gyges (c. 685–652 B.C.). Primitive uninscribed "spade" money of the Chou dynasty of China is now *believed* to date from c. 770 B.C. Countries without any coins are Paraguay, Laos and Indonesia.

British The earliest coins to circulate in Britain were Gallo-Belgic gold imitations of the Macedonian staters of Philip II (359–336 B.C.). The Bellovaci type has been tentatively dated c. 130 B.C. The earliest date attributed to coins minted in Britain is c. 95 B.C. for the Westerham type gold stater.

Heaviest The Swedish copper 10 daler coins of 1659 attained a weight of up to $43\frac{1}{2}$ lb. Of primitive exchange tokens, the most massive are the holed stone discs, or *Fé*, from the Yap Islands, in the western Pacific Ocean, with diameters of up to 12 feet. A medium-sized one was worth one Yapese wife or an 18-foot canoe.

Smallest The smallest coins in the world were the gold "pin-head" coins used in Colpata, southern India, in c. 1800, which weighed as little as one grain, or 480 to the troy ounce.

HIGHEST DENOMINATION
World The 1654 Indian gold 200 mohur (£500) coin of the Mughal Emperor Khurram Shihāb-ud-dīn Muhammad, Shāh Jahān (reigned 1628–57), is both the highest denomination coin and that of the greatest intrinsic worth ever struck. It weighed 33,600 grains (70 troy oz.) and hence has an intrinsic worth of £875. It had a diameter of $5\frac{3}{8}$ inches. The only known example disappeared in Patna, Bihar, India, in c. 1820, but a plaster-cast of this coin exists in the British Museum, London.

British Gold five-guinea pieces were minted from the reign of Charles II (1660–1685) until 1753 in the reign of George II. A pattern 5 guinea piece of George III dated 1777 also exists.

LOWEST DENOMINATION
The 1 aurar piece of Iceland, had a face value of 0·0114 of a penny in 1969. Quarter farthings (sixteen to the penny) were struck in copper at the Royal Mint, London, in the Imperial coinage for use in Ceylon, in 1839 and 1851–53. The lowest denomination gold coins ever struck are the Kruger gold 3d. pieces struck in South Africa at the behest of Mr. Solly Marks. One is dated 1894 and 215 are dated 1898. They are now worth more than £200 each.

RAREST
British During the period 1526–44 several new coins were introduced, among them the George noble (value 6s. 8d.) and its half. Only a single specimen of the half George noble is known to exist. A unique half sovereign of Edward VI was sold for £620 in October 1956.

Bronze coinage was introduced in Queen Victoria's reign in 1860. There are known to be single examples extant of an Edward VIII 1937 penny, halfpenny and farthing. There is only a single specimen of a penny dated 1954 in private hands. Its insurance value was put at £15,000 by its owners. It was reported on 12 July 1967 that a unique half-crown dated 1952, bearing the head of George VI, had been found by Mr. Horace Burrows of London. It was sold for £1,700 on 7 Sept. 1967 but a second specimen was reported in January 1968. Only two specimens are also known of the English shilling dated 1952.

MOST EXPENSIVE

World The highest price paid in auction for a single coin is an "almost extremely fine" Philip IV Spanish 100 Scudos gold piece of 1633 (Segovia mint) sold by Sotheby's, London for H.H. the Prince de Ligne for £15,500 on 27 June 1968. It is believed that the sole example in private hands of the Canadian silver dollar piece of 1911 was acquired by Mr. John McKay-Clements of Haileybury, Ontario, for a sum of more than Can. $60,000 (£22,700) in June 1965. A private treaty sale of a single undisclosed coin for about $75,000 (£31,250) was reported in 1964. The only complete collection of United States coins, owned by Louis Eliasberg of Baltimore, Maryland, U.S.A., includes the unique 1870 $3 gold piece with a San Francisco mint-mark, which is potentially worth far more. The two U.S. gold $50 pieces of 1877 in the Smithsonian Institution, Washington, D.C., have been valued at $100,000 (£41,666) each as have the seven surviving examples of the U.S. Brasher Doubloon of 1787.

The highest auction price paid for an English coin is £10,500 paid by the London dealer Spink at the salerooms of Messrs. Glendining and Co. on 17 Oct. 1968 for a gold Edward IV London Noble of the Heavy Coinage period (1461–1464). This coin, together with 85 others, was part of the Fishpool Hoard discovered on 22 March 1966. The coins were sold by Mr. Bernard Beeton, a retired lorry driver, one of the 6 people accredited with the discovery, and one of only two who wisely complied with the law in relation to Treasure Trove. The coins fetched a total of £85,000, about one-sixth of the value of the entire hoard (see Treasure Trove).

LEGAL TENDER COINS

Oldest The oldest legal tender Imperial coins in circulation are the now rare silver shillings and sixpences of the reign of George III, dated 1816. All gold coinage of or above the least current weight dated onward from 1838 is legal tender to a limit of £20. The oldest legal tender bronze coinage is that of Queen Victoria dated 1860.

Largest The five-shilling (5s.) piece or crown is the largest of all current United Kingdom coins, with a circumference of 4·84 inches. Silver crowns have been struck for all reigns since Elizabeth I (1558–1603), except that of Edward VIII, although 2,473 crowns dated 1936, and bearing the head of George V, were issued.

viest and highest mination The gold five-pound (£5) piece or quintuple sovereign is both the highest current denomination coin in the United Kingdom and also, at 616·37 grains (1·4066 oz.), the heaviest. The most recent specimens available to the public are dated 1937, of which only 5,501 were minted. The rarest are the six surviving pattern pieces of William IV, dated 1831, of which an example was sold by private treaty for £4,250 in July 1966.

htest and smallest The silver Maundy penny piece is the smallest of the British legal tender coins and, at 7·27 grains (just under 1/60th of an ounce), the lightest. These coins exist for every date since 1822 and are 0·453 of an inch in diameter.

Greatest collection It was estimated in November 1967 that the Lilly coin collection of 1,227 U.S. gold pieces now at the Smithsonian Institution, Washington, D.C., U.S.A.,

had a market value of $5½ million (£2,290,000). The greatest single coin collection ever amassed in Britain was that of Richard Cyrin Lockett (1873–1950) of Liverpool, Lancashire. The collection realized a record of £387,457.

The greatest hoard of gold of unknown ownership ever recovered is one valued at about $3,000,000 (£1,070,000), from the lost $8,000,000 (£2,860,000) carried in 10 ships of a Spanish bullion fleet which was sunk by a hurricane off Florida, U.S.A., on 31 July 1715. The biggest single haul was by the diver Kip Wagner on 30 May 1965.

Largest Treasure Trove The largest hoard of coins ever found in the United Kingdom was the Tutbury hoard, discovered on the bed of the River Dove in Staffordshire in June 1831. It consisted of about 20,000 silver coins of Edward I and Edward II and some of Henry III. The chest is believed to have been deposited in c. 1324–25. The most valuable hoard ever found was one of more than 1,200 gold coins from the reigns of King Richard II to Edward IV, worth more than £500,000, found on 22 March 1966 by John Craughwell, aged 47, at Fishpool, near Mansfield, Nottinghamshire.

Largest mint The largest mint in the world is the U.S. Treasury's mint built in 1965–69 on Independence Mall, Philadelphia, covering 500,000 square feet with an annual capacity on a 3 shift seven day a week production of 8,000 million coins. A single stamping machine can produce coins at a rate of 10,000 per minute.

Greatest hoarders It was estimated in November 1968 that about $22,500 million (£9,375 million) worth of gold is being retained in personal possession throughout the world and that $4,800 million (£2,000 million) of this total is held by the population of France.

Largest pile The tallest column of pennies on record was one 11 feet 10 inches tall containing some 99,600 coins (worth £415) collected for Muscular Dystrophy at the A.B.C. Bowl, North Harrow, London. The pile was pulled over on 27 Feb. 1970. Lower pyramids but of 145,080 pennies (£604 10s.), collected by the licensee Mr. Frank Steele, were "knocked down" in the Coffee House Hotel, Wavertree, Liverpool, for the Royal Wavertree School for Blind Children in January 1969.

TRADE UNIONS

Largest World The world's largest union is the Industrie-Gewerkschaft Metall (Metal Workers' Union) of West Germany, with a membership of 2,070,000 at 1 Jan. 1970. The union with the longest name is probably the F.N.O.M. M.C.F.E.T.M.F., the National Federation of Officers, Machinists, Motormen, Drivers, Firemen and Electricians in Sea and River Transportation of Brazil.

Maundy money—
60 of the 1d. pieces
weigh less than 1 oz.

The human world

Britain The largest trade union in the United Kingdom is the Transport and General Workers' Union, with 1,531,607 members at 1 Jan. 1970. The smallest T.U.C.-affiliated trade union is the Sheffield Wool Shear Workers' Trade Union, whose membership was only 27 on 1 Jan. 1970.

LABOUR DISPUTES

Largest The highest total of trade disputes to occur in any one year was 1,067 in 1920. The disputes involved about 1,600,000 people and a total of 26,500,000 working days were lost. The 1969 figure was 6,799,000 working days.

The most serious single labour dispute in the United Kingdom was the General Strike of 4–12 May 1926, called by the Trades Union Congress in support of the Miners' Federation. During the nine days of the strike 1,580,000 people were involved and 14,500,000 working days were lost.

was 0·9 per cent. on 11 July 1955, when 184,929 persons were registered. The peak figure for the total working population in employment in Great Britain has been 26,290,000 in September 1966. The figure for September 1969 was 25,817,000.

Largest The largest single association in the world is the Blue Cross, the U.S.-based medical insurance organization with a membership at 1 Jan. 1969 of 72,821,784. Benefits paid out exceeded $3·5 billion (£1,487 million). The largest association in the United Kingdom is the Automobile Association, with a membership of 4,091,746 on 18 June 1970.

FOOD CONSUMPTION

Calories Of all countries in the world, based on the latest available data, New Zealand has the largest available total of calories per person. The net supply averaged 3,470 per day in 1966. The United Kingdom average was

A London scene during the General Strike of May 1926

During the year 1926 a total of 2,750,000 people were involved in 323 different labour disputes and the working days lost during the year amounted to 162,300,000, the highest figure ever recorded.

Longest The world's longest recorded strike ended on 4 Jan. 1961, after 33 years. It concerned the employment of barbers' assistants in Copenhagen, Denmark. The longest recorded major strike was that at the plumbing fixtures factory of the Kohler Co. in Sheboygan, Wisconsin, U.S.A., between April 1954 and October 1962. The strike is alleged to have cost the United Automobile Workers' Union about $12,000,000 (£4·3 million) to sustain.

UNEMPLOYMENT

Highest The highest recorded unemployment in Great Britain was on 23 Jan. 1933, when the total of unemployed persons on the Employment Exchange registers was 2,903,065, representing 22·8 per cent. of the insured working population. The highest figure for Wales was 244,579 (39·1 per cent.) on 22 Aug. 1932.

Lowest The lowest recorded peace-time level of unemployment

3,220 per day in 1966–67. The highest calorific value of any foodstuff is that of pure animal fat, with 930 calories per 100 grammes (3·5 oz.). Pure alcohol provides 710 calories per 100 grammes.

Protein New Zealand has the highest recorded consumption of protein per person, an average of 109 grammes (3·84 oz.) per day in 1966. The United Kingdom average was 89 grammes (3·14 oz.) per day in 1966–67.

The lowest *reported* figures are 1,780 calories per day in Somalia in 1961–63 and 34 grammes (1·20 oz.) of protein per day in Gabon in 1961–63.

Cereals The greatest consumers of cereal products—flour, milled rice, etc.—are the people of Turkey, with an average of 492 lb. per person in 1960–61. The United Kingdom average was 180 lb. in 1966–67 and the figure for the Republic of Ireland was 209 lb. in 1966.

Potatoes The greatest eaters of potatoes and root flour are the people of Gabon, who consumed 3·94 lb. per head per day in 1963–5. The United Kingdom average was 9·67 oz. per day in 1966–67. The average for Ireland was 9·45 oz. in 1966.

Sugar The greatest consumers of refined sugar are the people of Costa Rica, with an average of 5·78 oz. per person in 1963. The United Kingdom average was 4·79 oz. per day in 1966–67 and the average in Ireland was 4·75 oz. in 1966.

Meat The greatest meat eaters in the world—figures include offal and poultry—are the people of Argentina, with an average consumption of 10·89 oz. per day per person in 1966. The United Kingdom average was 7·08 oz. per day in 1966–67 and the Irish average was 7·01 oz. per day in 1966.

BEER
Of reporting countries, the nation with the highest beer consumption per person is Czechoslovakia, with 29·2 gallons per person in 1968. In the Northern Territory of Australia, however, the annual intake has been estimated to be as high as 52 gallons per person. A society for the prevention of alcoholism in Darwin had to disband in June 1966 for lack of support. The United Kingdom average was 20·85 gallons, or 166·8 pints, per person in 1968. The January 1970 edition of the U.S.S.R. periodical *Sotsialistichekaya Industria* claimed that the Russians invented beer.

SPIRITS
The freest spirit drinkers are the white population of South Africa, with 1·71 gallons of proof spirit per person per year, and the most abstemious are the people of Belgium, with 2 pints per person. It was estimated in 1969 that 13 per cent. of all males between 20 and 55 years in France were suffering from alcoholism.

Largest dish The largest single dish in the world is roasted camel, prepared occasionally for Bedouin wedding feasts. Cooked eggs are stuffed in fish, the fish stuffed in cooked chickens, the chickens stuffed into a roasted sheep carcass and the sheep stuffed into a whole camel.

Most expensive food The most expensive food is white truffle of Alba which in 1969 fetched £35 per lb. in the market.

Largest cake The largest cake ever baked was a six-sided "birthday" cake weighing 25,000 lb., made in August 1962 by Van de Kemp's Holland Dutch Bakers of Seattle, Washington State, U.S.A., for the Seattle World's Fair (the "Century 21 Exposition"). The cake was 23 feet high, with a circumference of 60 feet. The ingredients included 18,000 eggs, 10,500 lb. of flour, 4,000 lb. of cane sugar, 7,000 lb. of raisins, 2,200 lb. of pecans and 100 lb. of salt.

SPICES
Most expensive The most expensive of all spices is Mediterranean saffron (*Crocus sativus*). It takes 96,000 stigmas and therefore 32,000 flowers to make a pound, which retails for £33 12s. in the United Kingdom.

The world's biggest meat-eaters —the Argentines eat 7,300 tons of meat per day

Mediterranean saffron —source of the most expensive spice

"Hottest" The hottest of all spices is the capsicum hot pepper known as Tabasco, first reported in 1888 by Mr. Edmund McIlhenny on Avery Island, Louisiana, U.S.A.

Rarest condiment The world's most prized condiment is Cà Cuong, a secretion recovered in minute amounts from beetles in North Vietnam. Owing to war conditions, the price rose to $100 (now £41 12s.) per ounce before supplies virtually ceased.

Sweets The biggest sweet eaters in the world are the people of Britain, with 7·6 oz. of confectionery per person per week in early 1970. The figure for Scotland was more than 9 oz. in 1968.

Tea The most expensive tea marketed in the United Kingdom is "Oolong", specially imported for Fortnum and Mason of Piccadilly, London, W.1, where, in 1970, it retails for £4 4s. per lb. It is blended from very young Formosan leaves.

The world's largest tea company is Brooke Bond Liebig Limited (a merger of Brooke Bond Tea Ltd. of London founded 1869 and Liebig's Extract of Meat Co. Ltd. made in May 1968), with a turnover of £208,681,000 in the year ended 30 June 1969. The company has 36,525 acres of mature plantations in India, Ceylon and East Africa, and ranches in Argentina, Paraguay and Rhodesia extending over 2,686,180 acres and employs over 50,000 people.

Coffee The world's greatest coffee drinkers are the people of Sweden, who consume 13 kilogrammes (28·6 lb.) of

The human world

coffee per person per year. This compares with 1·59 kg. (3·5 lb.) for the United Kingdom in 1969.

Oldest tinned food

The oldest tinned food known was roast beef canned by Donkin, Hall and Gamble in 1823 and salvaged from H.M.S. *Fury* in the Northwest Passage, Canada. It was opened on 11 Dec. 1958.

Recipe

The oldest known surviving recipe is one dated 1657 handed down from Bernice Bardolf of the Black Horse Tavern, Barnsley, Yorkshire found buried in September 1969 in the yard of the Alhambra Hotel, Barnsley. Barnsley Bardolf, a variant, is now on the menu.

Fresh water

The world's greatest consumers of fresh water are the people of the United States, whose average daily consumption of over 387,500 million gallons in 1967 is expected to rise to 411,200 million gallons by 1970. By 31 Dec. 1967, 40·6 per cent. was fluoridized.

ENERGY

To express the various forms of available energy (coal, liquid fuels and water power, etc., but omitting vegetable fuels and peat), it is the practice to convert them all into terms of coal. On this basis the world average consumption was the equivalent of 3,633 lb. (32·4 cwt.) of coal, or its energy equivalents, per person in 1967.

The highest consumption in the world is in the United States, with an average of 21,667 lb. per person in 1967. The United Kingdom average was 11,029 lb. (98·5 cwt.) per person. The lowest recorded average for 1967 was 15·4 lb. per person in Burundi.

MASS COMMUNICATIONS

AIRLINES

The country with the busiest airlines system is the United States, where 125,414 million revenue passenger miles were flown on scheduled domestic and regional services in 1969. This was equivalent to an annual trip of 618 miles for every one of the inhabitants of the U.S.A. The United Kingdom airlines flew 168,036,000 miles and carried 132,408,000 passengers in 1969. This is equivalent to an annual flight of 167 miles for every person in the United Kingdom.

MERCHANT SHIPPING

The world total of merchant shipping excluding vessel of less than 100 tons gross, sailing vessels and barge was 50,276 vessels of 211,660,893 tons gross on 1 July 1969. The largest merchant fleet in the world as at mid 1969 was that under the flag of Liberia with 29,215,15 tons gross. Liberian registration overtook the United Kingdom Merchant fleet of 21,716,148 tons gross in 1967. The U.K. figure for mid-1969 was 23,843,79 tons gross but the British Commonwealth was 7,189 ships of 33,158,251 tons gross.

Largest and busiest ports

Physically, the largest port in the world is New York Harbour, N.Y., U.S.A. The port has a navigable waterfront of 755 miles (460 miles in New York State and 295 miles in New Jersey) stretching over 92 square miles. A total of 261 general cargo berths and 130 other piers give a total berthing capacity of 391 ships at one time. The total warehousing floor space is 18,400,000 square feet (422·4 acres). The world's busiest port and largest artificial harbour is the Rotterdam-Europoort in the Netherlands. It handled 32,145 sea-going vessels and about 250,000 barges in 1968. It is able to handle 310 sea-going vessels simultaneously. In 1969 239,200,000 tons of seaborne cargo was handled.

RAILWAYS

The country with the greatest length of railway is the United States, with 210,573 miles of track at 31 Dec. 1966. The greatest density is in Belgium, which has one mile of railway track for every 1·4 square miles of land area, followed by the U.K. (32,475 miles of track), with one mile of railway track for every 2·90 square miles.

Part of the world's largest port— New York Harbour which can berth 391 ships simultaneously

214

The farthest anyone can get from a railway on the mainland island of Great Britain is 54 miles in the case of Cape Wrath, Sutherland, Scotland.

The number of journeys made on British Rail in 1969 was 805,235,000, with an average journey of 22·85 miles, compared with the peak year of 1957, when 1,101 million journeys (average 20·51 miles) were made.

ROADS
The country with the greatest length of road is the United States (50 States), with 3,704,914 miles of graded roads at 1 Jan. 1968. The average speed of cars at off-peak times has risen from 45·0 m.p.h. in 1945 to 58·8 m.p.h. by 1966. There is no speed limit in Nevada.

The country with the greatest number of motor vehicles per mile of road is the United Kingdom, with 217,935 miles of road including 591 miles of Motorway at 31 March 1968 and 14,708,418 vehicles in September 1968. If they were all equally spaced on public roads, there would be a vehicle every 25·0 yards. A total of 17,000,000 vehicles by 1970 and 36,000,000 by 2010 is forecast.

Busiest The highest traffic volume of any point in the world is at the Harbor and Santa Monica Freeways interchange in Los Angeles, California, U.S.A. with a 24-hour average on Fridays of 420,000 vehicles in 1970.

The greatest traffic density at any one point in the United Kingdom is at Hyde Park Corner, London. The average daytime flow in 1968 was 158,508 vehicles every 12 hours. The busiest Thames bridge in 1968 was Putney Bridge, with a 12-hour average of 36,249 vehicles. The greatest reported aggregation of London buses was 38, bumper to bumper, along the Vauxhall Bridge Road on 18 Nov. 1965. Censuses are biennial.

Widest The widest street in the world is the Monumental Axis, running for 1½ miles from the Municipal Plaza to the Plaza of the Three Powers in Brasília, the capital of Brazil. The six-lane boulevard was opened in April 1960 and is 250 metres (273·4 yards) wide. The Bay Bridge Toll Plaza has 34 lanes (17 in each direction) serving the Bay Bridge, San Francisco, California.

Narrowest The world's narrowest street is St. John's Lane in Rome, with a width of 19 inches. The narrowest street in the United Kingdom is Parliament Street, Exeter, Devon, which at one point measures 26 inches across.

Britain's narrowest street

Longest straight road The longest straight road in the United Kingdom was a stretch of 22¾ miles between Bailgate in the City of Lincoln and Broughton village, Lincolnshire. Part of the Roman road Ermine Street, it now comprises sections of Class I (A.15), Class III and unclassified road, with only two slight deviations of less than 50 feet from the true straight line. Part of the road was closed for an airfield, reducing the straight section to 16½ miles.

Longest World The longest motorable road in the world is the Pan-American Highway, which will stretch 13,859 miles from Anchorage, Alaska, to southern Chile. There remains a gap of 450 miles, known as the Darien gap, in Panama and Colombia.

Longest street This title has been accorded to Figueroa Street which stretches 30 miles from Pasadena at Colorado Blvd. to the Pacific Coast Highway, Los Angeles, U.S.A.

Britain The longest designated road in Great Britain is the 404-mile-long A.1 from London to Edinburgh. The longest Roman roads were Watling Street, from Dubrae (Dover) 215 miles through Londinium (London) to Viroconium (Wroxeter), and Fosse Way, which ran 218 miles from Lindum (Lincoln) through Aquae Sulis (Bath) to Isca Dumnoniorum (Exeter). However, a 10-mile section of Fosse Way between Ilchester and Seaton remains indistinct. The oldest roads in Britain are trackways dating from pre-Celtic times (*i.e.* before 550 B.C.). An example is the Ridgeway running across the Berkshire Downs. The commonest street name in Greater London is Park Road, of which there are 43.

Britain's longest road— the 404-mile-long A.1

Longest hill The longest steep hill on any road in the United Kingdom is on the road westwards from Lochcarron toward Applecross in Ross and Cromarty, Scotland. In 6 miles this road rises from sea-level to 2,054 feet, with an average gradient of 1 in 15·4, the steepest part being 1 in 4.

Highest World The highest pass ever used by traffic is the Bódpo La (19,412 feet above sea-level), in western Tibet. It was used in 1929 by a caravan from the Shipki Pass on the trade route to Rudok. The highest carriageable road in the world is one 1,180 kilometres (733·2 miles) long between Tibet and south-western Sinkiang, completed in October 1957, which takes in passes of an altitude up to 18,480 feet above sea-level. Europe's highest pass (excluding the Caucasian passes) is the Col de Restefond (9,193 feet) between Jausiers and Saint-Etienne-de-Tinée, France. It is usually closed between early October and early June. The highest motor road in Europe is the Pico de Veleta in the Sierra Nevada, southern Spain. The shadeless climb of 22·4 miles brings the motorist to 11,384 feet above sea-level.

United Kingdom The highest road in the United Kingdom is the A.6293 tarmac extension at Great Dun Fell, Westmorland (2,780 feet) leading to a Ministry of Defence radar installation. A permit is required to use it. The highest classified road in England is the B.6293 at Killhope Cross (2,056 feet) on the Cumberland-Durham border near Nenthead. The highest classified road in Scotland is the A.93 road over the Grampians through Cairn Well,

215

a pass between Alyth, Perthshire, and Braemar, Aberdeenshire, which reaches about 1,850 feet at a crook called the Devil's Elbow, 9½ miles south of Braemar. The highest classified road in Wales is the Rhondda-Afan Inter-Valley road (A.4107), which reaches 1,750 feet 2½ miles east of Abergwynfi, Glamorganshire.

Longest viaduct The longest elevated road viaduct in Europe is the 9,680-foot-long Chiswick-Langley section of the M.4 motorway in West London. It was completed at a cost of £19,000,000 on 24 March 1965.

Traffic jams The worst traffic jams in the world are in Tōkyō, Japan. Only 9 per cent. of the city area is roadway, compared with London (23 per cent.), Paris (25 per cent.), New York (35 per cent.) and Washington, D.C. (43 per cent.). The longest traffic jam reported in Britain was one of 35 miles in length between Torquay and Yarcombe, Devonshire, on 25 July 1964 and 35 miles on the A.30 between Egham, Surrey and Micheldever, Hampshire on 23 May 1970.

Traffic lights Traffic lights were introduced into Great Britain with a one day trial in Wolverhampton on 11 Feb. 1928. They were first permanently operated in Leeds, Yorkshire on 16 March and in Edinburgh, Scotland on 19 March 1928.

Parking meters The earliest parking meters ever installed were those put in the business district of Oklahoma City, Oklahoma, U.S.A., on 19 July 1935. They were the invention of Carl C. Magee (U.S.A.) and reached London in 1958.

A modern example of a 35-year-old invention

Briefest offence On 7 March 1963 Mr. Charles William Rossiter of Willesden, London, N.W.10, was fined £1 in the West London Court for exceeding a parking limit in Gloucester Road, London, from 3.20 to 3.21 p.m. on 10 Dec. 1962.

Worst driver It was reported that a 75-year-old *male* driver received 10 traffic tickets, drove on the wrong side of the road four times, committed four hit-and-run offences and caused six accidents, all within 20 minutes, in McKinney, Texas, U.S.A., on 15 Oct. 1966.

Milestone Britain's oldest milestone *in situ* is a Roman stone dating from about A.D. 150 on the Stanegate, at Chesterholm, near Badron Mill, Northumberland.

TELEPHONES
There were an estimated 237,900,000 telephones in the world at 1 Jan. 1969. The country with the greatest number was the United States, with 109,256,000 instruments, equivalent to 540·2 for every 1,000 people, compared with the United Kingdom figure of 12,900,000 (third largest in the world to the U.S.A. and Japan), or 232·4 per 1,000 people, at 31 March 1969.

The only one of the world's 146 sovereign countries without telephones is Bhutān. The territory with fewest telephones is Pitcairn Island with 15.

The country with the most telephones per head of population is Monaco, with 609·3 per 1,000 of the population at 1 Jan. 1969. The countries with the least are the Yemen and Rwanda with 0·3 of a telephone per 1,000 people at 1 Jan. 1969.

The greatest total of calls made in any country is in the

United States, with 140,955 million (701·0 calls per person) in 1968.

The lowest recorded figure was the Niger Republic. with 0·8 of a call per person in 1968.

The United Kingdom telephone service connected 8,643,650,000 calls in the year ending 31 March 1969 an average of 155·7 per person.

The city with most telephones is New York City, N.Y., U.S.A., with 5,723,353 (708 per 1,000 people) at 1 Jan. 1969. The town with the highest proportion at 1 Jan. 1969 was Beverly Hills, near Los Angeles, California. U.S.A., with 1,586 per 1,000 people, compared with Washington, D.C., U.S.A., with 981 per 1,000.

Longest call The longest telephone connection on record was one of 550 hours from 28 Nov. to 21 Dec. 1966 between co-eds of Ford Hall (7th floor) and the 7th floor of Moore Hall at Kansas State University.

Longest cable The world's longest submarine telephone cable is the Commonwealth Pacific Cable (COMPAC), which runs for more than 9,000 miles from Australia, *via* Auckland, New Zealand and the Hawaiian Islands to Port Alberni, Canada. It cost about £35,000,000 and was inaugurated on 2 Dec. 1963.

POSTAL SERVICES
The country with the largest mail in the world is the United States, whose population posted 78,367 million letters and packages in 1967 when the U.S. Postal Service employed 715,970 people. The United Kingdom total was 11,300 million letters in the year ending 31 March 1969.

The United States also takes first place in the average number of letters which each person posts during one year. The figure was 371 in 1966. The United Kingdom figure was 203·6 per head in 1968–69. Of all countries the greatest discrepancy between incoming and outgoing mail is for the U.S.A. whence in 1967 only 627 million items were mailed in response to 1,198 million items received from foreign sources.

POSTAGE STAMPS
Earliest The earliest adhesive postage stamps in the world were the "Penny Blacks" of the United Kingdom, bearing the head of Queen Victoria, placed on sale on 1 May for use on 6 May 1840. A total of 64,000,000 were printed. The National Postal Museum possesses a unique full proof sheet of 240 stamps, printed in April 1840, before the corner letters, plate numbers or marginal inscriptions were added.

Largest The largest postage stamps ever issued were the 1913 Express Delivery stamps of China, which measured 9¾ inches by 2¾ inches. The largest standard postage stamps ever issued were the 27 cruzeiro Brazilian commemoratives, measuring 4·1 by 1·85 inches, issued on 12 Sept. 1960.

Smallest The smallest stamps ever issued were the 10 cents and 1 peso of the Colombian State of Bolívar in 1863–66. They measured 8 millimetres (0·31 of an inch) by 9·5 millimetres (0·37 of an inch).

Highest and lowest denomination The highest denomination stamp ever issued was a red and black stamp for £100, issued in Kenya in 1925–27. The highest denomination stamp ever issued in the United Kingdom was the £5 orange Victoria stamp issued on 21 March 1882. Owing to inflations it is difficult to determine the lowest denomination stamp but it was probably the 1946 3,000 pengö Hungarian stamp, worth at one time only $1·6 \times 10^{-14}$d.

Highest price World The highest price ever paid for a single philatelic item is the $380,000 (£158,333) for two 1d. orange "Post

The only £100 stamp ever issued—
that of Kenya in 1925

The highest denomination U.K. stamp,
the £5 orange of 1882

Office" Mauritius stamps of 1847 on a cover bought at H. R. Harmer's Inc., New York City, U.S.A. by Raymond Weill Inc. of New Orleans, Louisiana for an unnamed client from the Liechtenstein-Dale collection on 21 Oct. 1968. The item was discovered in 1897 in an Indian bazaar by a Mr. Charles Williams who paid less than £1 for it.

Most valuable There are a number of stamps of which but a single specimen is known. Of these the most celebrated is the one cent black on magenta issued in British Guiana (now Guyana) in February 1856. It was originally bought for six shillings from L. Vernon Vaughan, a Schoolboy, in 1873. This is the world's most renowned stamp, for which £A16,000 (£12,774 sterling) was paid in 1940, when it was sold by Mrs. Arthur Hind. It was insured for £200,000, when it was displayed in 1965 at the Royal Festival Hall, London. It was sold on 24 March 1970 by auction in New York City, U.S.A. for $280,000 (£116,666) by Erwin Wynberg for a syndicate. It was alleged in October 1938 that Hind had, in 1928, purchased and burned his stamp's twin.

Great Britain The highest price paid for stamps in Britain is £28,000, paid on 1 Oct. 1963 for a 1d. orange-red and a 2d. deep blue of Mauritius on an 1847 envelope. The most valuable philatelic piece of Great Britain is the Buccleuch block of 48 (4×12) unused Plate 2 imperforate 2d. Blues printed on 21 July 1840. These were found in 1945 by Mr. A. Martin at Dalkeith House, Scotland, and were auctioned, along with some minor pieces, by H. R. Harmer Ltd. for £6,300 in June 1946.

There are three unique British stamps. They are an unissued 1860, 1½d. rosy-mauve error, corner-lettered with an O for a C and an Edward-VII 1d. War Office error overprinted "Official", which are both in the Royal Collection; and an unused 9d. straw of 1862 on azure paper, discovered in 1938. The rarest British stamp which is not an error is the King Edward VII 6d. dull purple Inland Revenue Official stamp issued and withdrawn on 14 May 1904. Only 11 or 12 are known and one was sold for £3,500 unused in Feb. 1967.

Commonest British stamp The most frequently reproduced United Kingdom stamp has been the definitive Elizabeth II 3d. violet, issued from 1 Oct. 1953 to 17 May 1965, of which 19,920 million were issued.

Largest collection The greatest private stamp collection ever auctioned was that of Josiah K. Lilly of Indianapolis, Indiana,

U.S.A. By 7 Dec. 1968 the total reached $3,134,127 (£1,305,886). It has been suggested that the collection of Maurice Burrus (died 1959) of Alsace, France, may eventually realize $4,000,000 (£1,566,000).

The largest national collection in the world is that at the British Museum, London, which has had the General Post Office collection on permanent loan since March 1963. The British Royal collection, housed in 400 volumes, is also believed to be worth more than £1,000,000. The largest international collection is that of the Universal Postal Union (founded 1875) in Geneva, Switzerland, which receives 400 copies of each new issue of each member nation.

The world's
most valuable stamp,
the £116,666 1c.
British Guiana

POSTAL ADDRESSES

Highest numbering The practice of numbering houses began in 1463 on the Pont Notre Dame, Paris, France. The highest numbered house in Britain is No. 2,679 Stratford Road, Solihull, Warwickshire, occupied since 1966 by Mr. & Mrs. H. Hughes. The highest numbered house in Scotland is

No. 2,629 London Road, Mount Vernon, Glasgow, which is part of the local police station.

Post Offices The General Post Office's northernmost post office is at Haroldswick, Unst, Shetland Islands and its most southerly is at Samarès, Jersey.

Pillar-boxes Pillar-boxes were introduced into Great Britain at the suggestion of the novelist Anthony Trollope (1815–82). The oldest site on which one is still in service is one dating from 8 Feb. 1853 in Union Street, St. Peter Port, Guernsey though the present box is not the original. The oldest original box in Great Britain is another Victorian example at Barnes Cross, Holwell, near Bishop's Caundle, Dorset, also dating from probably later in 1853.

TELEGRAMS
The country where most telegrams are sent is the U.S.S.R., whose population sent 322,800,000 telegrams in 1967. The United Kingdom total was 15,663,000, including 7,317,000 sent overseas, in the year ending 31 March 1969.

The world's largest telegraph company is the Western Union Telegraph Company of New York City, N.Y., U.S.A. It had 26,269 employees on 1 Jan. 1969, a total of 11,000 telegraphic offices and agencies and 5,734,792 miles of telegraph channels.

The largest British telegraphic undertaking is Cable and Wireless Ltd., which operates 144,000 nautical miles of ocean cables (including 14,000 miles of telephone cable) and about 300,000 miles of radio circuits. It has a fleet of six cable ships, more than 80 overseas stations and 9,322 employees.

INLAND WATERWAYS
The country with the greatest length of inland waterways is Finland. The total length of navigable lakes and rivers is about 50,000 kilometres (31,000 miles). In the United Kingdom the total length of navigable rivers and canals is 3,940 miles.

Longest navigable river The longest navigable natural waterway in the world is the River Amazon, which sea-going vessels can ascend as far as Iquitos, in Peru, about 2,300 miles from the Atlantic seaboard.

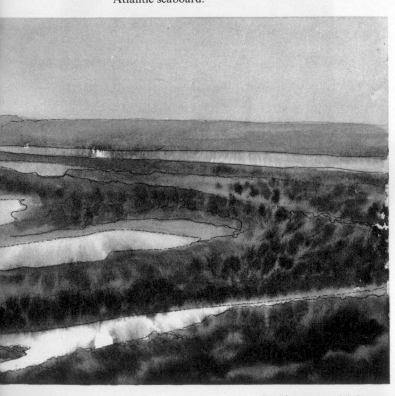

The Amazon—world's longest river recently measured to be 30 miles longer than the Nile

5. Education

ILLITERACY
Literacy is variously defined as "ability to read simple subjects" and "ability to read and write a simple letter". The looseness of definition and the scarcity of data for some countries preclude anything more than approximations, but the extent of illiteracy among adults (15 years old and over) is estimated to have been 39·3 per cent. throughout the world at the opening of the last decade in 1961. In 1969 a United Nations' estimate put the level at 810 million out of 2,335 million adults or 34·7 per cent. The continent with the greatest proportion of illiterates is Africa, where 81·5 per cent. of adults are illiterate. The latest figure available for the Niger Republic is 99·1 per cent. A U.S.S.R. report published in June 1968, affirms that more than 300 million people in China are still "completely illiterate".

UNIVERSITY
Oldest World Probably the oldest educational institution in the world is the University of Karueein, founded in A.D. 859 in Fez, Morocco. The European university with the earliest date of foundation is that of Naples, Italy, founded in 1224 by charter of Frederick II (1194–1250), Holy Roman Emperor.

United Kingdom The oldest university in the United Kingdom is the University of Oxford, which came into being in c. 1167. The oldest college is quoted as University College (1249), though its foundation is less well documented than that of Merton College in 1264. The earliest college at Cambridge University is Peterhouse, founded in 1284. The largest college at either university is Trinity College, Cambridge. It was founded in 1546. The oldest university in Scotland is the University of St. Andrews, Fife. It was established in 1411.

Greatest enrolment The university with the greatest enrolment in the world is the University of Calcutta (founded 1857) in India, with more than 170,000 students (internal and external) and 31 professors in 1964–65. Owing to the inadequacy of the buildings and number of lecturers, the students are handled in three shifts per day. The enrolment at all branches of the State University of New York, U.S.A., was 139,149 in January 1968 and is expected to reach 290,400 by 1974. The University of London had 37,626 internal students in December 1969.

Largest building The largest university building in the world is the M. V. Lomonosov State University on the Lenin Hills, south of Moscow, U.S.S.R. It stands 240 metres (787·4 feet) tall, has 32 storeys and contains 40,000 rooms. It was constructed in 1949–53.

Richest The richest university in the world is Harvard University in Cambridge, Massachusetts, U.S.A. Its endowments had a book value of $621,795,041 (£259 million) in 1968.

PROFESSORS
Youngest The youngest at which anybody has been elected to a chair in a major university is 21 years 10 months, in the case of William Rowan Hamilton (born 4 Aug. 1805), Andrews Professor of Astronomy at the University of Dublin, Trinity College, Dublin, Ireland, on 16 June 1827. He died of alcoholism at the age of 60 on 2 Sept. 1865. In July 1967 Dr. Harvey Friedman, Ph.D., was appointed Assistant Professor of Mathematics at Stanford University, California, U.S.A. aged just 19 years.

Most durable The longest period for which any professorship has been held is 63 years in the case of Thomäs Martyn (1735–1825), Professor of Botany at Cambridge University from 1762 until his death. His father, John Martyn (1699–1768), had occupied the chair from 1733 to 1762.

Senior Wranglers Since 1910 the Wranglers (first class honours students in the Cambridge University mathematical Tripos,

Part of the University College, Oxford reputedly founded in 1249

part 2) have been placed in alphabetical order only. In 1890 Miss P. G. Fawcett of Newnham was placed "above the Senior Wrangler".

SCHOOLS

Largest World
The largest school in the world was the De Witt Clinton High School in the Bronx, New York City, N.Y., U.S.A., where the enrolment attained a peak of 12,000 in 1934. It was founded in 1897 and now has an enrolment of 6,000.

United Kingdom
The school with the most pupils in the United Kingdom in 1968 was the Thomas Bennett School, Crawley, West Sussex with 2,167 pupils at December 1969.

Oldest in Britain
The title of the oldest school in Britain is contested. It is claimed that King's School in Canterbury, Kent, was a foundation of Saint Augustine, some time between his arrival in Kent in A.D. 597 and his death in c. 604.

Oldest old school tie
The practice of wearing distinctive neckties bearing the colours or registered designs of schools, universities, sports clubs, regiments, etc., appears to date from c. 1880. The practice originated in Oxford University, where boater bands were converted into use as "ribbon ties". The earliest definitive evidence stems from an order from Exeter College for college ties, dated 25 June, 1880.

Most expensive World
The most expensive school in the world is the Oxford Academy (established 1906) in Pleasantville, New Jersey, U.S.A. It is a private college-preparatory boarding school for boys with "academic deficiencies". The school has 15 masters and each of the 47 boys is taught individually in each course. The tuition fee for the school year is $8,400 (£3,500).

United Kingdom
The most expensive school in the United Kingdom is Millfield at Street, Somerset, founded by R. J. O. Meyer in 1937. The termly fees for late entrant pupils amount to £1,200 per annum, and £990 for those entering at under 15 years. The most expensive girls' schools in 1969 were St. James's School, West Malvern (founded 1896) Westwood House, Peterborough (1936) and Wycombe Abbey, Buckinghamshire (1896) with annual fees of £660.

Greatest enrolment
Between June 1966 and March 1967 about 110,000,000 Chinese schoolchildren over 9 years were excused

attendance to aid the 22,000,000 Red Guards (*Hung Wei Pings*) in prosecuting the "Great Cultural Revolution".

Most 'O' and 'A' levels
Ruth Felicity Chadwick (b. Birmingham 16 Oct. 1951) now of Lichfield, Staffordshire between summer 1966 and summer 1969 passed 23 G.C.E. examinations (17 'O' and 6 'A' levels). In August 1970 she awaited the results of one further 'O' and one further 'A' level.

Youngest headmaster
The youngest headmaster of a major public school was Henry Montagh Butler (born 2 July 1835), appointed Headmaster of Harrow School on 16 Nov. 1859, when aged 24 years 137 days. His first term in office began in January 1860.

The largest Cambridge College—Trinity

The human world

6. Religions

LARGEST

Religious statistics are necessarily the roughest approximations. The test of adherence to a religion varies widely in rigour, while many individuals, particularly in the East, belong to two or more religions.

Christianity is the world's prevailing religion, with over 925,000,000 adherents in 1968 and probably an additional 150,000,000 Protestants who are not in membership with the Church of their baptism. The total of 175,000,000 practising and 150,000,000 non-practising Protestants is easily outnumbered by the 580,000,000 who have received baptism into the Roman Catholic Church. The largest non-Christian religion is Islām, with about 490,000,000 adherents in 1968.

In the United Kingdom the Anglicans comprise members of the Established Church of England, the Dis-established Church in Wales, the Episcopal Church in Scotland and the Church of Ireland. In 1968 there were 27,700,000 living persons who had been baptized in Anglican churches in the provinces of Canterbury and York. In the same area it is estimated that there were 9,970,000 persons confirmed, of whom nearly 2,000,000 were Easter communicants in 1968. In Scotland the most numerous group is the Church of Scotland (the Presbyterians), which had 1,201,933 members, apart from adherents, at 1 Jan. 1969.

SMALLEST

In New Zealand the 1966 Census revealed 94 religious sects with a single follower each. These included a Millenarian Heretic and an Aesthetic Hedonist. Such followers might alternatively be described as leaders.

Largest clergy The world's largest religious organization is the Roman Catholic Church, with about 580,000,000 members, 418,000 priests and 946,000 nuns in 1964. The total number of cardinals, patriarchs, metropolitans, archbishops, bishops, abbots and superiors is 2,800, of whom 260 are in Italy. There are about 416,000 churches.

Jews The total of world Jewry was estimated to be 13,970,000 in 1968. The highest concentration was in the United States, with 5,720,000, of whom 2,381,000 were in Greater New York. The total in Israel was 2,780,500. The total of British Jewry is 450,000, of whom 280,000 are in Greater London, 28,000 in Manchester and 13,500 in Glasgow. The total in Tōkyō, Japan, is only 250.

Largest Temple The largest religious building ever constructed is Angkor Wat (City Temple), covering 402 acres, in Cambodia, south-east Asia. It was built to the God Vishnu by the Khmer King Suryavarman II in the period 1113–50. Its curtain wall measures 1,400 yards by 1,400 yards and its population, before it was abandoned in 1432, was 80,000.

CATHEDRALS

Largest World The world's largest cathedral is the cathedral church of the Diocese of New York, St. John the Divine, with a floor area of 121,000 square feet and a volume of 16,822,000 cubic feet. The corner stone was laid on 27 Dec. 1892, and the Gothic building was still uncompleted in 1967. In New York it is referred to as

A map showing the prevalence of Christianity which extends over nearly one-third of the world's population

"Saint John the Unfinished". The nave is the longest in the world, 601 feet in length, with a vaulting 124 feet in height.

The cathedral covering the largest area is that of Santa María de la Sede in Sevilla (Seville), Spain. It was built in Spanish Gothic style between 1402 and 1519 and is 414 feet long, 271 feet wide and 100 feet high to the vault of the nave.

United Kingdom The largest cathedral in the British Isles is the Anglican Cathedral of Liverpool. Built in modernized Gothic style, work was begun on 19 July 1904, and when completed will have cost over £3,000,000. The building encloses 100,000 square feet and has an overall length of 671 feet. The Vestry Tower is 331 feet high.

allest in United Kingdom The smallest cathedral in use in the United Kingdom (excluding converted parish churches) is St. Asaph in Flintshire, Wales. It is 182 feet long, 68 feet wide and has a tower 100 feet high. Oxford Cathedral in Christ Church (College) is 155 feet long. The nave of the Cathedral of the Isles on the Isle of Cumbrae, Buteshire measures only 40 × 20 feet. The total floor area is 2,124 square feet.

Longest The longest Gothic church in the United Kingdom is Winchester Cathedral, Hampshire, which is 560 feet long (internal length 526 feet).

st nave The longest nave in the United Kingdom is that of St. Albans Cathedral, Hertfordshire, which is 285 feet long.

CHURCHES

Largest World The largest church in the world is the basilica of St. Peter, built between 1492 and 1612 in the Vatican City, Rome. The length of the church, measured from the apse, is 611 feet 4 inches. The area is 18,110 square yards. The inner diameter of the famous dome is 137 feet 9 inches and its centre is 119 metres (390 feet 5 inches) high. The external height is 457 feet 9 inches.

The elliptical Basilique of St. Pie X at Lourdes, France, completed in 1957 at a cost of £2,000,000 has a capacity of 20,000 under its giant span arches and a length of 659 feet.

The crypt of the underground Civil War Memorial Church in the Guadarrama Mountains, 28 miles from Madrid, Spain, is 853 feet in length. It took 21 years (1937–58) to build, at a reported cost of £140,000,000 and is surmounted by a cross 492 feet tall.

United Kingdom The largest parish church in the United Kingdom is Holy Trinity Parish Church, Kingston-upon-Hull, Yorkshire. The church exterior is 295 feet long and 104 feet wide, and parts of the transept date from 1285. The internal area is 26,384 square feet. The parish church of St. Nicholas at Great Yarmouth, Norfolk, formerly the largest in England, was destroyed by bombing in 1942 but was rededicated in May 1961. Its side aisles are 40 feet wide.

Smallest World The world's smallest church is the Union Church at Wiscasset, Maine, U.S.A., with a floor area of 31½ square feet (7 feet by 4½ feet). Les Vaubelets Church in Guernsey has an area of 16 feet by 12 feet, room for one priest and a congregation of two.

Britain The smallest church in use in England is Bremitham Church, Cowage Farm, Foxley near Malmesbury, Wiltshire which measures 12 feet by 12 feet and is used for service twice a year. The smallest completed English church in regular use is that at Culbone, Somerset, which measures 35 feet by 12 feet. The smallest Welsh chapel is St. Trillo's Chapel, Rhôs-on-Sea (Llandrillo-yn-Rhos), Denbighshire, measuring only 12 feet by 6 feet. The smallest chapel in Scotland is St. Margaret's, Edinburgh, measuring 16½ feet by 10½ feet, giving an area of 173¼ square feet.

St. Asaph—Great Britain's smallest Cathedral

OLDEST

World The oldest known religious structure is Temple XVII, discovered in 1949 at Eridu (Abu Shahraim), in Iraq, dating from the Halaf period (c. 4500 B.C.). The oldest surviving Christian church in the world is Qal'at es Salihige in eastern Syria, dating from A.D. 232. A list of the oldest religious buildings in 43 countries was included in the 11th edition of *The Guinness Book of Records,* at page 117. The oldest wooden church in Great Britain and probably in the world is St. Andrew's, Greensted, near Ongar, Essex dating to A.D. 835 though some of the timbers date to the original building of c. A.D. 650.

United Kingdom The oldest church in the United Kingdom is St. Martin's Church in Canterbury, Kent. It was built in A.D. 560 on the foundations of a 1st century Roman church. The oldest church in Ireland is the Gallerus Oratory, built in c. 750 at Ballyferriter, near Kilmalkedar, County Kerry. Britain's oldest nunnery is St. Peter and Paul Minster, on the Isle of Thanet, Kent. It was founded in c. 748 by the Abbess Eadburga of Bugga.

St. Peter's, Rome, the world's largest Church

The tallest
cathedral spire
in the world
at Ulm, Germany

United Kingdom The highest spire in the United Kingdom is that of the church of St. Mary, called Salisbury Cathedral, Wiltshire. The Lady Chapel was built in the years 1220–25 and the main fabric of the cathedral was finished and consecrated in 1258. The spire was added later, 1334–65, and reaches a height of 404 feet. St. Paul's Cathedral, London, possessed a 489-foot spire built in 1315, but this was struck by lightning in August 1561. The height of the present cross above the dome is 365 feet.

LARGEST SYNAGOGUES

World The largest synagogue in the world is the Temple Emanu-El on Fifth Avenue at 65th Street, New York City, N.Y., U.S.A. The temple, completed in September 1929, has a frontage of 150 feet on Fifth Avenue and 253 feet on 65th Street. The Sanctuary proper can accommodate 2,500 people, and the adjoining Beth-El Chapel seats 350. When all the facilities are in use, more than 6,000 people can be accommodated.

Great Britain The largest synagogue in Great Britain is the Edgware Synagogue, Greater London, completed in 1959, with a capacity of 1,630 seats.

Largest mosque The world's largest mosque is the Jama Masjid (1644–58) in Delhi, India, with an area of more than 10,000 square feet and two 108-foot-tall minarets. The now ruined Bibi-Khanum (1399–1404) at Samarkand, Uzbekistan, U.S.S.R., had an area of 12,940 square feet. The largest mosque will be the Merdeka Mosque in Djakarta, Indonesia, which was begun in 1962. The cupola will be 45 metres (147·6 feet) in diameter and the capacity in excess of 50,000 people.

Tallest Minaret The world's tallest minaret is the Qutb Minar, south of New Delhi, India, built in 1194 to a height of 238 feet.

Tallest pagoda The tallest Chinese temple is the Pagoda of the Six Harmonies, outside Hangchou, which is 334 feet tall.

SAINTS

Most and least rapidly Canonized The shortest interval that has elapsed between the death of a Saint and his canonization was in the case of St. Anthony of Padua, Italy, who died on 13 June 1251 and was canonized 352 days later on 30 May 1252. This was one day faster than St. Peter of Verona (1206–52) canonized on 6 April 1253.

The other extreme is represented by St. Bernard of Thiron, for 20 years Prior of St. Sabinus, who died in 1117 and was made a Saint in 1861—744 years later. The Italian monk and painter, Fra Giovanni da Fiesole (né Guido di Pietro), called Il Beato ("The Blessed") Fra Angelico (c. 1400–1455), is still in the first stage of canonization.

POPES

Longest reign The longest reign of any of the 262 Popes has been that of Pius IX (Giovanni Maria Mastai-Ferretti), who reigned for 31 years 236 days from 16 June 1846 until his death aged 85, on 7 Feb. 1878.

Shortest reign Pope Stephen II was elected on 24 March 752 and died two days later, but he is not included in the Liber pontificalis or the Catalogue of the Popes. The shortest reign of any genuine Pope is that of Giambattista Castagna (1521–90), who was elected Pope Urban VII on 15 Sept. 1590 and died twelve days later on 27 Sept. 1590.

Oldest It is recorded that Pope St. Agatho (reigned 678–681) was elected at the age of 103 and lived to 106, but recent scholars have expressed doubts. The oldest of recent Pontiffs has been Pope Leo XIII (Vincenzo Gioacchino Pecci), who was born on 2 March 1810, elected Pope at the third ballot on 20 Feb. 1878 and died on 20 July 1903, aged 93 years 140 days.

Youngest The youngest of all Popes was Pope Benedict IX

TALLEST SPIRES

World The tallest cathedral spire in the world is that of the Protestant Cathedral of Ulm in Germany. The building is early Gothic and was begun in 1377. The tower, in the centre of the west façade, was not finally completed until 1890 and is 528 feet high. The world's tallest church spire is that of the Chicago Temple of the First Methodist Church on Clark Street, Chicago, Illinois, U.S.A. The building consists of a 22-storey skyscraper (erected in 1924) surmounted by a parsonage at 330 feet, a "Sky Chapel" at 400 feet and a steeple cross at 568 feet above street level.

The election of Pope Gregory X—a process which occupied 31 months

(Theophylact), who had three terms as Pope: in 1032–44; April to May 1045; and 8 Nov. 1047 to 17 July 1048. It would appear that he was aged only 11 or 12 in 1032, though the Catalogue of the Popes admits only to his "extreme youth".

Last non-Italian Cardinalate English Popes
The last non-Italian Pope was the Utrecht-born Cardinal Priest Adrian Dedel (1459–1523) of the Netherlands. He was elected on 9 Jan. 1522, crowned Pope Adrian VI on 31 Aug. 1522 and died on 14 Sept. 1523. The last Pope elected from outside the College of Cardinals was Bartolomeo Prignano (1318–89), Archbishop of Bari, who was elected Pope Urban VI on 8 April 1378. The only Englishman to be elected Pope was Nicholas Breakspear (born at Abbots Langley, near Watford, Hertfordshire, in *c.* 1100), who, as Cardinal Bishop of Albano, was elected Pope Adrian IV on 4 Dec. 1154, and died on 1 Sept. 1159.

Last married
The first 37 Popes had no specific obligation to celibacy. The last married Pope was Adrian II (867–872). Rodrigo Borgia was the father of at least four children before being elected Pope Alexander VI in 1492.

Slowest election
After 31 months without declaring *Habemus Papam* ("We have a Pope"), the cardinals were subjected to a bread and water diet and the removal of the roof of their conclave by the Mayor before electing Teobaldo Visconti (*c.* 1210–76), the Archbishop of Liège, as Pope Gregory X at Viterbo on 1 Sept. 1271. Cardinal Eugenio Maria Guiseppe Giovanni Pacelli (1876–1958), who took the title of Pius XII, was reputedly elected by 61 votes out of 62 at only the third ballot on 2 March 1939, his 63rd birthday.

CARDINALS
Oldest
By March 1970 the Sacred College of Cardinals contained 130 declared members compared with 136 a year earlier. The oldest is Cardinal Bishop Paolo Giobbe of Italy (born 10 Jan. 1880).

Youngest
The youngest Cardinal of all-time was Giovanni de' Medici (born 11 Dec. 1475), later Pope Leo X, who was made a Cardinal Deacon in March 1489, when aged 13 years 3 months. The youngest in 1970 is Cardinal Bishop Stephan Sou Hwan Kim of South Korea (born 6 May 1922). He was named as a cardinal in April 1969 when aged 46.

BISHOPS
Oldest
The oldest serving Bishop (excluding Suffragans and Assistants) in the Church of England at 1 Jan. 1970 was the Rt. Rev. Cyril Easthaugh, M.C. (born 22 Dec. 1897), the 34th Bishop of Peterborough.

The oldest Roman Catholic bishop in recent years was Mgr. Alfonso Carinci (born 9 Nov. 1862), who was titular Archbishop of Seleucia, in Isauria, from 1945 until his death on 6 Dec. 1963, at the age of 101 years 27 days. He had celebrated Mass about 24,800 times. He was the oldest bishop at the first session of the Second Vatican Council (the 21st Oecumenical Council), held in Rome from 11 Oct. to 8 Dec. 1962.

Youngest
The youngest bishop of all time was Hugnes, whose father, the Comte de Vermandois, successfully demanded for him the archbishopric of Reims from the feeble Pope John X (reigned 914–928), when he was only five years old.

The youngest serving bishop (excluding Suffragans and Assistants) in the Church of England at 1 Jan. 1970 was the Rt. Rev. Stuart Yarworth Blanch (born 2 Feb. 1918), the 5th Bishop of Liverpool.

BISHOPRIC
Longest tenure
The longest tenure of any Church of England bishopric is 57 years in the case of the Rt. Rev. Thomas Wilson, who was consecrated Bishop of Sodor and Man on 16 Jan. 1698 and died in office on 7 March 1755. Of English bishoprics the longest tenure, if one excludes

the unsubstantiated case of Aethelwulf, reputedly bishop of Hereford from 937 to 1012, are those of 47 years by Jocelin de Bohun (Salisbury) 1142–1189 and Nathaniel Crew or Crewe (Durham) 1674–1721.

STAINED GLASS

Oldest The oldest stained glass in the world represents the Prophets in a window of the cathedral of Augsburg, Bavaria, Germany, dating from *c.* 1050. The oldest stained glass in the United Kingdom is represented by 12th century fragments in the Tree of Jesse in the north aisle of the nave of York Minster, dated *c.* 1150. An earlier date (*c.* 1080) has been attributed to glass in a window of the church at Compton, Surrey.

Longest incumbency The longest incumbency on record is one of 76 years by the Rev. Bartholomew Edwards, Rector of S Nicholas, Ashill, Norfolk from 1813 to 1889. Th parish of Iden, East Sussex had only two incumben in the 117-year period from 1807 to 1924.

Oldest parish register The oldest parish registers in England are those of S James Garlickhythe and St. Mary Bothaw, two o City of London parishes, dating from 1536. Scotland oldest surviving register is that for Anstruther-Weste Fife, with burial entries from 1549.

Largest crowd The greatest recorded number of human bein assembled with a common purpose was more tha 5,000,000 at the 21-day Hindu festival of Kumbh-Mel

Part of the oldest
stained glass window
in the world in
Augsburg, West Germany

Largest The largest stained glass window is one measuring 300 feet long by 23 feet high at the John F. Kennedy International Airport (formerly Idlewild), Long Island, New York State, U.S.A.

PARISHES

Largest and smallest The latest population figures for parishes in the United Kingdom are from the census of 23 April 1961. The most populous parish was the Parish of Kirkby St. Chad, Liverpool, with 52,177 parishioners. Of the nine parishes uninhabited in 1961, Iham Parish, in the diocese of Chichester, Sussex, has had a nil population since 1931.

which is held every 12 years at the confluence of th Yamuna (formerly called the Jumna), the Ganges an the invisible "Sarasviti" at Allahabad, Uttar Pradesh India, on 21 Jan. 1966. According to the Jacob Formul for estimating the size of crowds, the allowance of are per person varies from 4 square feet (tight) to $9\frac{1}{2}$ squar feet (loose). Thus such a crowd must have occupied a area of more than 700 acres.

Biggest demonstrations A figure of 2·7 million was published from China fo the demonstration against the U.S.S.R. in Shangh on 3–4 April 1969 following the border clashes, and on of 10 million for the May Day celebrations of 196 in Peking.

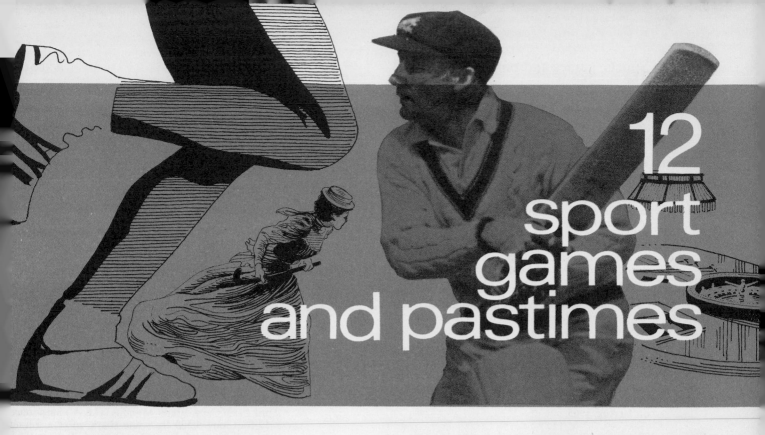

All Sports

Earliest The origins of sport stem from the time when self-preservation ceased to be the all-consuming human preoccupation. Archery was a hunting skill in mesolithic times (before 20,000 B.C.), but did not become an organized sport until c. A.D. 300, among the Genoese. The earliest dated origin for any sport is c. 3000 B.C. for wrestling, depicted on pre-dynastic murals at Ben Hasan, Egypt (now the United Arab Republic), and also from early Sumerian sources at Kyafefe, Iraq.

Fastest The governing body for aviation, *La Fédération Aéronautique Internationale,* records maximum speeds in lunar flight of up to 24,791 m.p.h. However, these achievements, like all air speed records since 1923, have been para-military rather than sporting. In shooting, muzzle velocities of up to 7,100 feet per second (4,840 m.p.h.) are reached in the case of a U.S. Army Ordnance Department standard 0·30 calibre M1903 rifle. The highest speed reached in a non-mechanical sport is in sky-diving, in which a speed of 185 m.p.h. is attained in a head-down free falling position, even in the lower atmosphere. In delayed drops a speed of 614 m.p.h. has been recorded at high rarefied altitudes. The highest projectile speed in any moving ball game is c. 160 m.p.h. in pelota. This compares with 170 m.p.h. (electronically-timed) for a golf ball driven off a tee.

Slowest In wrestling, before the rules were modified towards "brighter wrestling", contestants could be locked in holds for so long that single bouts could last for up to 11 hours. In the extreme case of the 2 hours 41 minutes pull in the regimental tug o' war in Jubbulpore, India, on 12 Aug. 1889, the winning team moved a net distance of 12 feet at an average speed of 0·00084 m.p.h.

Longest The most protracted sporting test was an automobile duration test of 222,618 miles by Appaurchaux and others in a Ford Taunus. This was contested over 142 days in 1963. The distance was equivalent to 8·93 times around the equator.

The most protracted non-mechanical sporting event is the *Tour de France* cycling race. In 1926 this was over 3,569 miles, lasting 29 days. The total damage to the French national economy of this annual event, now reduced to 23 days, is immense. If it is assumed that one-third of the total working population works for only two-thirds of the time during the currency of *Le Tour* this would account for a loss of more than three-quarters of one per cent. of the nation's annual Gross National Product. In 1970 this was more than £40,000 million, so the loss would have been about £300,000,000.

Shortest Of sports with timed events the briefest recognized for official record purposes is the quick draw in shooting in which electronic times down to 0·06 of a second have been returned.

Most expensive The most expensive of all sports is the racing of large yachts—"J" type boats, last built in 1937, and International 12-metre boats. The owning and racing of these is beyond the means of individual millionaires and is confined to multi-millionaires or syndicates.

Largest crowd The greatest number of live spectators for any sporting spectacle is the estimated 1,000,000 (more than 20 per cent. of the population) who line the route of the annual San Sylvestre road race of 8,600 metres (5 miles 605 yards) through the street of São Paulo, Brazil, on New Year's night. However, spread over 23 days, it is estimated that more than 10,000,000 see the annual *Tour de France* along the route (see also above).

The largest crowd travelling to any sporting venue is "more than 400,000" for the annual *Grand Prix d'Endurance* motor race on the Sarthe circuit near Le Mans, France. The record stadium crowd was one of 199,854 for the Brazil v. Uruguay match in the Maracaña Municipal Stadium, Rio de Janeiro, Brazil, on 16 July 1950.

Largest field The largest pitch of any ball game is that of polo, with 12·4 acres, or a maximum length of 300 yards and a width, without side boards, of 200 yards.

Most participants The annual Nijmegen Vierdaagse march in the Netherlands over distances up to 50 kilometres (31 miles 120 yards) attracted 16,667 participants in 1968. The greatest number of competitors in any competitive event on land is for the "Vasa Lopp" Nordic skiing race in Sweden. There were 7,887 entrants on 3 March 1968.

Heaviest sportsmen The heaviest sportsman of all-time was the wrestler William J. Cobb of Macon, Georgia, U.S.A., who in

225

1962 was billed as the 802 lb. (57 st. 4 lb.) "Happy Humphrey". The heaviest player of a ball-game was Bob Pointer, aged 18, the 447 lb. (31 st. 13 lb.) tackle on the 1967 Santa Barbara High School team, California, U.S.A.

Worst disasters The worst sports disaster in recent history was when an estimated 604 were killed after some stands at the Hong Kong Jockey Club racecourse collapsed and caught fire on 26 Feb. 1918. During the reign of Antonius Pius (A.D. 138–161) the upper wooden tiers in the Circus Maximus, Rome collapsed during a gladiatorial combat killing some 1,100 spectators. Britain's worst sports disaster was when 33 were killed after a section of the barriers collapsed at the Bolton Wanderers' Ground at Burnden Park, Bolton, Lancashire, during the Cup tie match against Stoke City on 9 March 1946. The game was played to a finish. At the Scotland v. England international at Ibrox Park, Glasgow, in 1902, part of the terracing collapsed, resulting in 542 casualties with 25 killed.

Youngest world record breaker The youngest age at which any person has broken a world record is 12 years 328 days in the case of Karen Yvette Muir (born 16 Sept. 1952) of Kimberley, South Africa, who broke the women's 110 yards backstroke world record with 1 minute 08·7 seconds at Blackpool on 10 Aug. 1965.

Youngest and oldest internationals The youngest age at which any person has won international honours is 8 years in the case of Miss Joy Foster, the Jamaican singles and mixed doubles table tennis champion in 1958. It would appear that the greatest age at which anyone has actively competed for his country is 73 years in the case of Oscar G. Swahn (Sweden), who won a silver medal for shooting in the Olympic Games at Antwerp in 1920.

Youngest and oldest champions The youngest age at which anyone has successfully participated in a world title event is 12 years in the case of Bernard Malvoire (France), cox of the winning coxed fours in the Olympic regatta at Helsinki in 1952. The youngest individual Olympic winner was Miss Marjorie Gestring (U.S.A.), who took the springboard diving title at the age of 13 years 9 months at the Olympic Games in Berlin in 1936. The greatest age at which anyone has held a world title is 60 years in the case of Pierre Etchbaster, who retired in 1955, after 27 years as undefeated world tennis champion from May 1928.

Longest reign The longest reign as a world champion is 27 years by Pierre Etchbaster (see above).

The longest reign as a British champion is 41 years by

the archer Miss Legh who first won the Championship in 1881 and for the 23rd and final time in 1922.

Greatest earnings The greatest fortune amassed by an individual in sport is an estimated £17,000,000 by the late Sonja Henie of Norway (1912–1969), the triple Olympic figure skating champion (1928–32–36), when later (1936–56) a professional ice skating promoter starring in her own ice shows and 11 films.

Largest trophies The world's largest sporting trophy is the Helms World Trophy for the sportsman of the year which stands 6 feet 2 inches in height on a marble base, which is 21 inches in height, making an overall height of 7 feet 11 inches. It is housed at the Helms Hall, 8760 Venice Boulevard, Los Angeles, California, U.S.A.

Angling

LARGEST CATCHES

The largest fish ever caught on a rod is an officially ratified man-eating great white shark (*Carcharodon carcharias*) weighing 2,664 lb., and measuring 16 feet 10 inches long, caught on a 130 lb. test line by Alf Dean at Denial Bay, near Ceduna, South Australia, on 21 April 1959. Capt. Frank Mundus (U.S.A.) harpooned a 17-foot-long 4,500 lb. white shark, after a 5-hour battle, off Montauk Point, New York, U.S.A., in 1964.

The largest marine animal ever killed by hand harpoon was a blue whale 97 feet in length, killed by Archer Davidson in Twofold Bay, New South Wales, Australia, in 1910. Its tail flukes measured 20 feet across and its jaw bone 23 feet 4 inches. To date this has provided the ultimate in "fishing stories".

SMALLEST CATCH

The smallest full-grown fish ever caught is the *Schindleria praematurus*, weighing 1/14,000 of an ounce (see page 41) found in Samoa, in the Pacific. The smallest mature shark is the rare *Squalidus laticaudus*, found off the Philippines, which measures only 6 inches in length.

Spear fishing The largest fish ever taken underwater was an 804 lb. Giant Black Grouper or Jewfish by Don Pinder of the Miami Triton Club, Florida, U.S.A., in 1955. The British spearfishing record is 89 lb. 0 oz. for an angler fish by J. Brown (Weymouth Association Divers) in 1969.

Casting record The longest surf casting distance ever reported is one of 1,000 feet achieved on a beach in South Africa. The official world record under I.C.F. (International Casting

Karen Yvette Muir (born 1952), who broke a world record 37 days before her 13th birthday

Federation) rules is 161 metres (528 feet 2½ inches) by Walter Kummerow (West Germany).

Longest fight The longest recorded fight with a fish is 32 hours 5 minutes by Donal Heatley (b. 1938) (New Zealand) with a black marlin (estimated length 20 feet and weight 1,500 lb.) off Mayor Island off Tauranga, North Island

on 21–22 Jan. 1968. It towed the 12-ton launch 50 miles before breaking the line.

Rarest fish The burbot, the rarest British fish, is "almost extinct", so it has been agreed that no record for this species should be published, at least until 1974, in the interests of conservation.

WORLD RECORDS (All tackle)

(Sea fish as ratified by the International Game Fish Association to 30 June 1969. Freshwater fish, ratified by *"Field & Stream"*, are marked *)

Species	Weight lb. oz.	Name of Angler	Location	Date
Amberjack	149 0	Peter Simons	Bermuda	21 June 1964
Barracuda	103 4	C. E. Benet	West End, Bahamas	11 Aug. 1932
Bass (Californian Black Sea)	563 8	James D. McAdam	Anacapa Island, California, U.S.A.	20 Aug. 1968
Bass (Giant Sea)	680 0	Lynn Joyner	Fernandina Beach, Florida, U.S.A.	20 May 1961
*Carp†	55 5	Frank J. Ledwein	Clearwater Lake, Minnesota, U.S.A.	10 July 1952
Cod	98 12	Alphonse J. Bielevich	Isel of Shoals, Massachusetts, U.S.A.	8 June 1969
Marlin (Black)	1,560 0	Alfred C. Glassell, Jr.	Cabo Blanco, Peru	4 Aug. 1953
Marlin (Blue)	845 0	Elliot J. Fishman	St. Thomas, Virgin Is.	4 July 1968
Marlin (Pacific Blue)	1,153 0	Greg. D. Perez	Ritidian Point, Guam	21 Aug. 1969
Marlin (Striped)	465 0	James Black	Mayor Island, New Zealand	27 Feb. 1948
Marlin (White)	161 0	L. F. Hooper	Miami Beach, Florida, U.S.A.	20 Mar. 1938
*Pike (Northern)	46 2	Peter Dubuc	Sacandaga Reservoir, New York State, U.S.A.	15 Sept. 1940
Sailfish (Atlantic)	141 1	Tony Burnand	Ivory Coast, Africa	26 Jan. 1961
Sailfish (Pacific)	221 0	C. W. Stewart	Santa Cruz I., Galapagos Is.	12 Feb. 1947
*Salmon (Chinook)††	92 0	H. Wichmann	Skeena River, British Columbia, Canada	19 July 1959
Sawfish	890 8	Jack Wagner	Fort Amador, Canal Zone	26 May 1960
Shark (Blue)	410 0	Richard C. Webster	Rockport, Massachusetts, U.S.A.	1 Sept. 1960
	410 0	Martha C. Webster	Rockport, Massachusetts, U.S.A.	17 Aug. 1967
**Shark (Mako)	1,000 0	B. D. H. Ross	Mayor Island, New Zealand	14 Mar. 1943
Shark (White or Man-eating)	2,664 0	Alfred Dean	Denial Bay, Ceduna, South Australia	21 April 1959
Shark (Porbeagle)	430 0	Desmond Bougourd	South of Jersey, C.I.	29 June 1969
Shark (Thresher)	922 0	W. W. Dowding	Bay of Islands, New Zealand	21 Mar. 1937
Shark (Tiger)	1,780 0	Walter Maxwell	Cherry Grove, South Carolina, U.S.A.	14 June 1964
*Sturgeon (White)	360 0	Willard Cravens	Snake River, Idaho, U.S.A.	24 April 1956
Swordfish	1,182 0	L. E. Marron	Iquique, Chile	7 May 1953
Tarpon	283 0	M. Salazar	Lago de Maracaibo, Venezuela	19 Mar. 1956
*Trout (Lake)#	63 2	Hubert Hammers	Lake Superior	25 May 1952
Tuna (Allison or Yellowfin)	269 8	Henry Nishikawa	Hanalei, Hawaii, U.S.A.	30 May 1962
Tuna (Atlantic Big-eyed)	295 0	Dr. Arsenio Cordeiro	San Miguel, Azores	8 July 1960
Tuna (Pacific Big-eyed)	435 0	Dr. Russel V. A. Lee	Cabo Blanco, Peru	17 April 1957
Tuna (Bluefin)	977 0	Dr. McI. Hodgson	St. Ann Bay, Nova Scotia, Canada	4 Sept. 1950
Wahoo	149 0	John Pirovano	Cat Cay, Bahamas	15 June 1962

† *A carp weighing 83 lb. 8 oz. was taken (not by rod) near Pretoria, South Africa.*
†† *A salmon weighing 126 lb. 8 oz. was taken (not by rod) near Petersburg, Alaska, U.S.A.*
** *A 1,295 lb. specimen was taken by two anglers off Natal, South Africa on 17 March 1939 and a 1,500 lb. specimen harpooned inside Durban Harbour, South Africa in 1933.*

A 102 lb. trout was taken from Lake Athabasca, northern Saskatchewan, Canada, on 8 Aug. 1961.

BRITISH ROD-CAUGHT RECORDS (Sea fish)

(Selected from the complete list of 72 species)

Species	Weight lb. oz.	Name of Angler	Location	Yea
Angler Fish	68 2	H. G. T. Legerton	Canvey Island, Essex	196
Bass	18 2	F. C. Borley	Felixstowe Beach, Suffolk	194
Black Bream	6 1	F. W. Richards	The Skerries, Dartmouth	196
Red Bream	7 8	A. F. Bell	Fowey, Cornwall	192
Brill	16 0	A. H. Fisher	Derby Haven, Isle of Man	195
Bull Huss (Greater Spotted Dogfish)	21 3	J. Holmes	Hat Rock, Cornwall	195
Coalfish	23 8	H. Millais	Land's End, Cornwall	192
Cod	46 0½	R. Baird	Firth of Clyde	197
Conger	84 0	H. A. Kelly	Dungeness, Kent	193
Dab	2 10¾	A. B. Hare	The Skerries, Dartmouth	196
Dogfish (Lesser Spotted)	4 8	J. Beattie	off Ayr Pier, Ayrshire	196
Dogfish (Spur)	16 12½	W. R. Legg	Abbotsbury, Chesil Beach, Dorset	196
Flounder	5 11½	A. G. L. Cobbledick	Fowey, Cornwall	195
Garfish	2 9⅞	A. W. Bodfield	Dartmouth, Devonshire	196
Grey Mullet	10 1	P/O. P. C. Libby	Portland, Dorset	195
Gurnard	11 7¼	C. W. King	Wallasey, Cheshire	195
Gurnard (Red)	3 1	J. A. Tooth	Skerries Bank	196
Haddock	9 4½	Mrs. L. Morley	Mevagissey, Cornwall	196
Hake	25 5½	Herbert W. Steele	Belfast Lough	196
Halibut	161 12	W. E. Knight	Orkney	196
John Dory	10 12	B. Perry	Porthallow, Cornwall	196
Ling	45 0	H. C. Nicholl	Penzance, Cornwall	191
Lumpsucker	6 3¼	F. Harrison	Redcar, Yorkshire	196
Mackerel	5 6½	S. Beasley	N. of Eddystone Lighthouse	196
Megrim	3 10	D. DiCicco	Ullapool, Ross-shire	196
Monkfish	66 0	G. C. Chalk	Shoreham, Sussex	196
Mullet (Red)	3 10	John E. Martel	St. Martin's, Guernsey	196
Plaice	7 15	Ian B. Brodie	Salcombe, Devonshire	196
Pollack	23 8	G. Bartholomew	Newquay, Cornwall	195
Pouting	5 8	R. S. Armstrong	off Berry Head, Devon	196
Ray (Spotted)	9 0	F. Johnstone	Loch Fyne, Argyllshire	196
Ray (Thornback)	38 0	J. Patterson	Rustington, Sussex	193
Scad	3 3	J. B. Thornton	Deal, Kent	193
Allis Shad	3 4½	Bernard H. Sloane	Torquay, Devonshire	196
Twaite Shad	{ 3 2	S. Jenkins	Tor Bay, Devonshire	195
	{ 3 2	T. Hayward	Deal, Kent	194
Shark (Blue)	218 0	N. Sutcliffe	Looe, Cornwall	195
Shark (Mako)	498 8	Ken C. Burgess	Looe, Cornwall	196
Shark (Porbeagle)	430 0	see world record page 227		
Shark (Thresher)	280 0	H. A. Kelly	Dungeness, Kent	193
Skate (Common)	214 0	J. A. E. Olsson	Scapa Flow	1968
Sole	4 1⅞	R. A. Austin	Bordeaux Vale, Guernsey	196
Sting Ray	59 0	J. M. Buckley	Clacton-on-Sea, Essex	195
Three-bearded Rockling	2 13⅛	K. Westaway	Portland Harbour, Dorset	196
Tope	74 11	A. B. Harries	Caldy Island, Pembrokeshire	1964
Tunny	851 0	L. Mitchell-Henry	Whitby, Yorkshire	193
Turbot	29 0	G. M. W. Garnsey	The Manacles, Cornwall	196
Greater Weever	2 4	P. Ainslie	Brighton, Sussex	192
Whiting[1]	6 0	E. H. Tame	Loch Shieldaig, Ross and Cromarty	194
Wrasse (Ballan)	7 2	P. R. F. Collins	River Yealm, Devonshire	196

BRITISH ROD-CAUGHT RECORDS (Freshwater fish)

It will be noted that nine former "records" achieved between 1923 and 1955 have been discarded because they cannot be substantiated under the existing rules. These are noted as being "open to claim" if a specimen comes up to or over the "minimum qualifying standard".

Species	Weight lb. oz.	Name of Angler	Location	Year
Barbel[2]	record open to claim			
Bleak	0 3½	N. D. Sizmur	Walton-on-Thames, Surrey	1963
Bream (Common)	record open to claim			
Bream (Silver)	record open to claim			
Carp	44 0	Richard Walker	Redmire Pool, Herefordshire	1952
Chub	record open to claim			
Crucian Carp	record open to claim			
Dace	record open to claim			
Eel	8 10	A. Dart	Hunstrete Lake	1969
Grayling	record open to claim			
Gudgeon	record open to claim			
Gwyniad (Whitefish)	1 4	J. R. Williams	Llyn Tegid, Merionethshire	1965
Loch Lomond Powan	1 1¼	F. Buller	Loch Lomond	1968
Perch	4 12	S. F. Baker	Oulton Broad, Norfolk	1962
Pike[3]	record open to claim			
Roach	{ 3 14	W. Penney	Lambeth Reservoir, Molesey, Surrey	1938
	{ 3 14	A. Brown	Pit, near Stamford, Lincolnshire	1964
Rudd	4 8	Rev. E. C. Alston	Mere, near Thetford, Norfolk	1933
"Ruffe"	4	B. B. Poyner	River Stour, Warwickshire	1969
Salmon[4]	64 0	Miss G. W. Ballantyne	River Tay	1922
Tench	9 1	John Salisbury	Hemingford Grey, Huntingdonshire	1963
Trout (Brown)[5]	18 2	K. J. Grant	Loch Garry, Inverness-shire	1965
Trout (Rainbow)	8 8	Lt.-Col. L. J. Creagh-Scott	Blagdon, Somerset	1924
Trout (Sea)	record open to claim			

[1] An unratified Whiting of 6 lb. 0½ oz. was claimed by Mr. Lee off the Yorkshire coast in 1966.
[2] A 16 lb. 4 oz. Barbel was caught in the close season by R. Beddington in the R. Avon at Christchurch, Hants. in April 1934.
[3] A Pike of allegedly 52 lb. was recovered when Whittlesea Mere, Cambridgeshire and Isle of Ely, was drained in 1851.
[4] The 8th Earl of Home is recorded as having caught a 69¾ lb. specimen in the R. Tweed in 1730. J. Wallace claimed a 67-pounder at Barjarg, Dumfries-shire in 1812.
[5] In 1866 W. C. Muir is reputed to have caught a 39¼ lb. specimen in Loch Awe, and in 1816 a 36 lb. specimen was reported from the R. Colne, near Watford, Hertfordshire.

IRISH ANGLING RECORDS (as ratified by the Irish Specimen Fish Committee)

Species	Weight lb. oz.		Name of Angler	Location	Date	
SEA FISH						
Angler Fish	71	8	M. Fitzgerald	Cork (Cóbh) Harbour	5 July	1964
Bass	16	0	Major Ashe Windham	Waterville, Kerry	Aug.	1909
Sea Bream (Red)	9	6	P. Maguire	Valentia, Kerry	24 Aug.	1963
Coalfish	24	7	J. E. Hornibrook	Kinsale, Cork	26 Aug.	1967
Cod	42	0	I. L. Stewart	Ballycotton, Cork		1921
Conger	72	0	J. Greene	Valentia, Kerry	June	1914
Dab	1	12½	Ian V. Kerr	Kinsale, Cork	10 Sept.	1963
Dogfish (Greater Spotted)	19	12	Michael Courage	Bray, Co. Wicklow	6 July	1969
Dogfish (Spur)	16	4	C. McIvor	Strangford Lough, Co. Down	20 June	1969
Flounder	4	3	J. L. McMonagle	Killala Bay, Co. Mayo	5 Aug.	1963
Garfish	3	10¼	Evan G. Bazzard	Kinsale, Cork	16 Sept.	1967
Gurnard (Grey)	3	1	Brendan Walsh	Rosslare Bay	21 Sept.	1967
Gurnard (Red)	3	9½	James Prescott	Broadhaven Bay, Co. Mayo	17 July	1968
Gurnard (Tub)	10	2¼	E. Sederholm	Belmullet, Co. Mayo	19 May	1969
Haddock	10	13½	F. A. E. Bull	Kinsale, Cork	15 July	1964
Hake	25	5½	Herbert W. Steele	Belfast Lough	28 April	1962
Halibut	152	12	E. C. Henning	Valentia, Kerry		1926
John Dory	6	9⅝	Kenneth W. Foott	Ballycotton, Cork	9 Aug.	1960
Ling	46	8	Andrew J. C. Bull	Kinsale, Cork	26 July	1965
Mackerel	3	6	J. O'Connell	Valentia, Kerry	24 Sept.	1969
Monkfish	69	0	Mons. Michael Fuchs	Westport, Co. Mayo	1 July	1958
Mullet (Grey)	6	0	N. Fitchett	Ballycotton, Cork	8 Sept.	1965
Plaice	7	0	Ernest Yemen	Portrush, Antrim	28 Sept.	1964
Pollack	19	3	J. N. Hearne	Ballycotton, Cork		1904
Pouting	4	10	W. G. Pales	Ballycotton, Cork		1937
Ray (Blonde)	36	8	D. Minchin	Cork (Cóbh) Harbour	9 Sept.	1964
Ray (Thornback)	37	0	M. J. Fitzgerald	Kinsale, Cork	28 May	1961
Shark (Blue)	206	0	J. L. McMonagle	Achill, Co. Mayo	7 Oct.	1959
Shark (Porbeagle)	365	0	Dr. M. O'Donel Browne	Keem Bay, Achill, Co. Mayo	28 Sept.	1932
Skate (Common)	221	0	T. Tucker	Ballycotton, Cork		1913
Skate (White)	165	0	Jack Stack	Clew Bay, Westport, Co. Mayo	7 Aug.	1966
Sting Ray	46	8	P. Charlton	Rosslare Strand	27 Aug.	1962
Tope	60	12	Crawford McIvor	Strangford Lough, Co. Down	12 Sept.	1968
Turbot	26	8	J. F. Eldridge	Valentia, Kerry		1915
Whiting	4	8½	Eddie Boyle	Kinsale, Cork	4 Aug.	1969
Wrasse (Ballan)	7	6	Anthony J. King	Killybegs, Donegal	26 July	1964
FRESHWATER						
Bream	11	12	A. Pike	River Blackwater, Co. Monaghan	July	1882
Carp	18	12	John Roberts	Abbey Lake	6 June	1958
Dace	1	2	John T. Henry	River Blackwater, Cappoquin	8 Aug.	1966
Eel (River)	5	15	Edmund Hawksworth	River Shannon, Clondra	25 Sept.	1968
Perch	5	8	S. Drum	Lough Erne		1946
Pike	42	0*	M. Watkins	River Barrow	22 Mar.	1964
Roach	2	12½	Anthony Mason	River Blackwater, Cappoquin	24 Sept.	1969
Rudd	3	1	A. E. Biddlecombe	Kilglass Lake	27 June	1959
Rudd-Bream hybrid	5	5	W. Walker	Coosan Lough, Garnafailagh, Athlone	5 June	1963
Salmon	57	0†	M. Maher	River Suir		1874
Tench	7	12	Edmund Hawksworth	River Shannon, Clondra	4 June	1966
Brown Trout (Lake)	26	2††	William Meares	Lough Ennell	15 July	1894
Brown Trout (River)	20	0	Major H. H. Place	River Shannon, Corbally	22 Feb.	1957
Rainbow Trout	8	7	Dr. J. P. C. Purdon	Lough Eyes, Co. Fermanagh	11 Mar.	1968
Sea Trout	12	0	T. Regan	River Dargle, Co. Wicklow	3 Oct.	1958

* A Pike in excess of 92 lb. is reputed to have been landed from the Shannon at Portumna, County Galway, in c. 1796.

† A 58 lb. Salmon was reported from the River Shannon in 1872 while one of 62 lb. was taken in a net on the lower Shannon on 27 March 1925.

†† A 35½ lb. Brown Trout is reputed to have been caught at Turlaghvan, near Tuam, in August 1738. "Pepper's Ghost", the 30 lb. 8 oz. fish caught by J. W. Pepper in Lough Derg in 1860, has now been shown to have been a salmon.

Archery

Earliest references Palaeolithic drawings of archers indicate that bows and arrows are an invention of at least 20,000 years ago. Archery developed as an organized sport at least as early as the 4th century A.D. The oldest archery body in the British Isles is the Royal Company of Archers, the Sovereign's bodyguard for Scotland, dating from 1676, though the Ancient Scorton Arrow meeting in Yorkshire was first staged in 1673. The world governing body is the *Fédération Internationale de Tir à l'Arc* (FITA), founded in 1931.

Flight shooting The longest flight shooting records are achieved in the footbow class. The longest recorded distance is 1,100 yards 1 inch by the professional Harry Drake at Ivanpha Dry Lake, California, U.S.A., on 8 or 9 Oct. 1966. The unlimited bow class (*i.e.* standing stance with bow of any weight) record is 850 yards 8 inches by Don Lamore (U.S.A.) at Lancaster, Pennsylvania, U.S.A., on 22 Aug. 1959.

The British record is 647 yards 1 foot 11 inches by Alan Webster at York on 20 April 1969.

HIGHEST SCORES

World The world records for FITA Rounds (see below) are: men 1,250 points by Jorma Sandelen (Finland) at Varkaus, Finland on 2–3 Sept. 1969, and women 1,208 points by Mrs. Nancy E. Myrick (U.S.A.) at the World Championships at Amersfoort, Netherlands, 23–28 July 1967.

The record for a FITA Double Round is 2,467 points by Jorma Sandelen (Finland) at Varkaus, Finland on 2–3 Sept. 1969. The feminine record is 2,361 points by Mrs. Dorothy Lidstone (Canada) at Valley Forge, Pennsylvania, U.S.A. on 17–18 Aug. 1969.

British York Round (6 dozen at 100 yards, 4 dozen at 80 yards and 2 dozen at 60 yards).
Single Round, 1,097 J. Ian Dixon at Oxford, on 4 July 1968.
Double Round, 2,138 Roy Matthews at Oxford, on 3–4 July 1968.
FITA Round (Men) (3 dozen each at 90, 70, 50 and 30 metres).
Single Round, 1,212 Edward G. Gamble at Narborough, Leicester, on 6 July 1969.
Double Round, 2,305 J. Ian Dixon at Valley Forge, Pennsylvania, U.S.A., on 17–18 Aug. 1969.
FITA ROUND (Women's) (3 dozen each at 70, 60, 50 and 30 metres).
Single Round, 1,154 Mrs. J. E. Hills in Surrey, on 21 July 1968.
Double Round, 2,274 Miss Pauline Edwards at Valley Forge, Pennsylvania, U.S.A., on 17–18 Aug. 1969.
Hereford (Women) (6 dozen at 80 yards, 4 dozen at 60 yards and 2 dozen at 50 yards).
Single Round, 1,077 Miss Lynne A. Thomas at Oxford, on 4 July 1969.
Double Round, 2,122 Miss Lynne A. Thomas at Leeds, on 4–5 Sept. 1969.

Most titles The greatest number of world titles (instituted 1931) ever won by a man is four by H. Deutgen (Sweden) in 1947–48–49–50. The greatest number won by a woman is seven by Mrs. Janina Spychajowa-Kurkowska (Poland) in 1931–32–33–34, 1936, 1939 and 1947.

The greatest number of British Championships is twelve by Horace A. Ford between 1849 and 1867, and 23 by Miss Legh in 1881, 1886–87–88–89–90–91–92, 1895, 1898–99–1900, 1902–03–04–05–06–07–08–09, 1913 and 1921–22.

Athletics

Earliest references Track and field athletics date from the ancient Olympic Games. The earliest accurately known Olympiad dates from 21 or 22 July 776 B.C., at which celebration Coroebus won the foot race. The oldest surviving measurements are a long jump of 23 feet 1½ inches (7·05 metres) by Chionis of Sparta in *c.* 656 B.C. and a discus throw of 100 cubits by Protesilaus.

Fastest runner Robert Lee Hayes (born 20 Dec. 1942) of Jacksonville Florida, U.S.A., was timed at 26·9 m.p.h. at the 75-yard mark of a 100-yard race in May 1964. Wyomia Tyus (U.S.A.) was timed at 23·78 m.p.h. in Kiev, U.S.S.R. on 31 July 1965.

Highest jumper There are several reported instances of high jumpers exceeding the official world record height of 7 feet 5¾ inches. The earliest of these came from unsubstantiated reports of Tutsi tribesmen in Central Africa (see page 15) clearing up to 8 feet 2½ inches, definitely however, from inclined take-offs. The greatest height cleared above an athlete's own head is 16⅞ inches, first achieved by Valeriy Brumel (born 14 April 1942) of the U.S.S.R., standing 6 feet 0⅞ inch tall, when clearing the world record height of 7 feet 5¾ inches in Moscow, U.S.S.R., on 21 July 1963. The same differential was achieved by Ni Chih-chin (also born on 14 April 1942) of China, standing 6 feet 0½ inch tall, when he cleared 7 feet 5⅜ inches in Phnôm Penh, Cambodia, on 30 Nov. 1966. The greatest height cleared by a woman above her own head is 6 inches by Miroslava Rezkova (Czechoslovakia), standing 5 feet 6½ inches when she jumped 6 feet 0½ inch at Povazka Bystrica, Czechoslovakia on 20 July 1969.

Most Olympic gold medals Ray C. Ewry (U.S.A.) won eight individual Olympic gold medals, three in 1900, three in 1904 and two in 1908. Paavo Johannes Nurmi (Finland) won six individual and three team race gold medals between 1920 and 1928. The greatest number of gold medals won in a single celebration is five by Paavo Nurmi (Finland) in 1924 (1,500 metres, 3,000 metres team, 5,000 metres, cross-country team and individual). The most individual wins is four by Alvin C. Kraenzlein (U.S.A.) in 1900 (60 metres, 110 metres and 200 metres hurdles and long jump). The most wins by a woman is four by Francina E. Blankers-Koen (born 26 April 1918) of the Netherlands in 1948 (100 and 200 metres, 80 metres hurdles, and the last stage in the 4 × 100 metres relay), and four by Betty Cuthbert (born 20 April 1938) of Australia in 1956 (100 metres, 200 metres and the last stage in the 4 × 100 metres relay) and 1964 (400 metres).

Most medals The most Olympic medals (of any metal) won by a man is 12 (nine gold and three silver) by Nurmi. The most won by a woman is seven by Shirley de la Hunty (*née* Strickland) of Australia between 1948 and 1956. The United Kingdom record is four by Guy M. Butler in 1920 and 1924 and for women three by Dorothy Hyman, M.B.E., in 1960 and 1964, and Mrs. Mary Denise Toomey (formerly Rand, *née* Bignal), M.B.E., in 1964.

Most national titles The greatest number of national A.A.A. titles won by one athlete is fourteen individual and two relay titles by Emmanuel McDonald Bailey (born Williamsville, Trinidad 8 Dec. 1920), between 1946 and 1953.

The greatest number of consecutive title wins is seven by Denis Horgan (Ireland) in the shot putt (1893–99), Albert A. Cooper (2 miles walk, 1932–1938), Donald Osborne Finlay, D.F.C., A.F.C. (120 yards hurdles, 1932–1938), Harry Whittle (440 yards hurdles, 1947–1953) and Maurice Herriott (3,000 metres steeplechase, 1961–67). The record for consecutive W.A.A.A. titles is eight by Mrs. Judy U. Farr (Trowbridge & District A.C.) (b. 24 Jan. 1942), who won the 1½ mile/2,500 metre walk from 1962–69.

Earliest landmarks The first time 10 seconds ("even time") was bettered for 100 yards under championship conditions was when John Owen recorded 9⅘ seconds in the United States A.A.U. Championships at Analostan Island, Washington, D.C., U.S.A., on 11 Oct. 1890. The first recorded instance of 6 feet being cleared in the high jump was when Marshall Jones Brooks jumped 6 feet 0⅛ inch at Marston, near Oxford, England, on 17 March 1876. The breaking of the "4-minute barrier" in the one mile was first achieved by Dr. Roger Gilbert Bannister, C.B.E. (born Harrow, England 23 March 1929), when he recorded 3 minutes 59·4 seconds on the Iffley Road track, Oxford, at 6.10 p.m. on 6 May 1954.

World record breakers Oldest The greatest age at which anyone has broken a world athletics record in a standard Olympic event is 35 years 255 days in the case of Dana Zátopkova, *née* Ingrova (born 19 Sept. 1922) of Czechoslovakia, who broke the women's javelin record with 182 feet 10 inches (55·73 metres) at Prague, Czechoslovakia, on 1 June 1958. On 20 June 1948 Mikko Hietanen (Finland) (born 22 Sept. 1911) bettered his own world 30,000 metres record with 1 hour 40 minutes 46·4 seconds at Jyväskylä, Finland, when aged 36 years 272 days.

Youngest Doreen Lumley (born Sept. 1921) of New Zealand equalled the world record for the women's 100 yards of 11·0 seconds at Auckland, New Zealand on 11 March 1939, when aged 17 years 6 months.

Eighteen relay events are included on the official schedule of I.A.A.F. world athletes records

WORLD RECORDS—MEN

The complete list of World Records for the 54 scheduled men's events (excluding the 6 walking records, see under WALKING) passed by the International Amateur Athletic Federation as at 30 June 1970. Those marked with an asterisk are awaiting ratification.

RUNNING

Event	Mins. secs.	Name and Nationality	Place	Date
100 yards	9·1	Robert Lee Hayes (U.S.A.)	St. Louis, Missouri, U.S.A.	21 June 1963
	9·1	Harry Winston Jerome (Canada)	Edmonton, Alberta, Canada	15 July 1966
	9·1	James Ray Hines (U.S.A.)	Houston, Texas, U.S.A.	13 May 1967
	9·1	Charles Edward Greene (U.S.A.)	Provo, Utah, U.S.A.	15 June 1967
	9·1	John W. Carlos (U.S.A.)	Fresno, California, U.S.A.	10 May 1969
220 yards (straight)	19·5	Tommie C. Smith (U.S.A.)	San Jose, California, U.S.A.	7 May 1966
220 yards (turn)	20·0	Tommie C. Smith (U.S.A.)	Sacramento, California, U.S.A.	11 June 1966
440 yards	44·7	Curtis Mills (U.S.A.)	Knoxville, Tennessee, U.S.A.	21 June 1969
880 yards	1:44·9	James Ronald Ryun (U.S.A.)	Terre Haute, Indiana, U.S.A.	10 June 1966
1 mile	3:51·1	James Ronald Ryun (U.S.A.)	Bakersfield, California, U.S.A.	23 June 1967
2 miles	8:19·6	Ronald William Clarke, M.B.E. (Australia)	London, England	24 Aug. 1968
3 miles	12:50·4	Ronald William Clarke, M.B.E. (Australia)	Stockholm, Sweden	5 July 1966
6 miles	26:47·0	Ronald William Clarke, M.B.E. (Australia)	Oslo, Norway	14 July 1965
10 miles	46:44·0	Ronald Hill (United Kingdom)	Leicester, England	9 Nov. 1968
15 miles	1H 12:48·2	Ronald Hill (United Kingdom)	Bolton, Lancashire	21 July 1965
100 metres	9·9	James Ray Hines (U.S.A.)	Sacramento, California, U.S.A.	20 June 1968
	9·9	Ronald Ray Smith (U.S.A.)	Sacramento, California, U.S.A.	20 June 1968
	9·9	Charles Edward Greene (U.S.A.)	Sacramento, California, U.S.A.	20 June 1968
	9·9	James Ray Hines (U.S.A.)	Mexico City, Mexico	14 Oct. 1968
200 metres (straight)	19·5	Tommie C. Smith (U.S.A.)	San Jose, California, U.S.A.	7 May 1966
200 metres (turn)	19·8	Tommie C. Smith (U.S.A.)	Mexico City, Mexico	16 Oct. 1968
400 metres	43·8	Lee Edward Evans (U.S.A.)	Mexico City, Mexico	18 Oct. 1968
800 metres	1:44·3	Peter George Snell (New Zealand)	Christchurch, New Zealand	3 Feb. 1962
	1:44·3	Ralph D. Doubell (Australia)	Mexico City, Mexico	15 Oct. 1968
1,000 metres	2:16·2	Jürgen May (East Germany)	Erfurt, East Germany	20 July 1965
	2:16·2	Franz-Josef Kemper (West Germany)	Hanover, West Germany	21 Sept. 1966
1,500 metres	3:33·1	James Ronald Ryun (U.S.A.)	Los Angeles, California, U.S.A.	8 July 1967
2,000 metres	4:56·2	Michel Jazy (France)	St. Maur des Fosses, France	12 Oct. 1966
3,000 metres	7:39·6	Kipchoge Keino (Kenya)	Hälsingborg, Sweden	27 Aug. 1965
5,000 metres	13:16·6	Ronald William Clarke, M.B.E. (Australia)	Stockholm, Sweden	5 July 1966
10,000 metres	27:39·4	Ronald William Clarke, M.B.E. (Australia)	Oslo, Norway	14 July 1965
20,000 metres	58:06·2	Gaston Roelants (Belgium)	Louvain, Belgium	28 Oct. 1966
25,000 metres	1H 15:22·6	Ronald Hill (United Kingdom)	Bolton, Lancashire	21 July 1965
30,000 metres	1H 32:25·4	James Joseph Hogan, *né* Cregan (U.K.)	Walton-on-Thames, Surrey	12 Nov. 1966
1 hour	12 miles 1,478 yards (20,664 metres)	Gaston Roelants (Belgium)	Louvain, Belgium	28 Oct. 1966

HURDLING

120 yards (3′ 6″ hurdles)	13·2	Karl Martin Lauer (West Germany)	Zürich, Switzerland	7 July 195
	13·2	Lee Quency Calhoun (U.S.A.)	Bern, Switzerland	21 Aug. 196
	13·2	Earl Ray McCullouch (U.S.A.)	Minneapolis, Minnesota, U.S.A.	16 July 196
	13·2	Erv. Hall (U.S.A.)	Knoxville, Tennessee, U.S.A.	19 June 196
	13·2*	Willie Davenport (U.S.A.)	Zürich, Switzerland	4 July 196
220 yards (2′ 6″) (straight)	21·9	Donald Augustus Styron (U.S.A.)	Baton Rouge, Louisiana, U.S.A.	2 April 196
440 yards (3′ 0″)	48·8*	Ralph Mann (U.S.A.)	Des Moines, Iowa, U.S.A.	20 June 197
110 metres (3′ 6″)	13·2	Karl Martin Lauer (West Germany)	Zürich, Switzerland	7 July 195
	13·2	Lee Quency Calhoun (U.S.A.)	Bern, Switzerland	21 Aug. 196
	13·2	Earl Ray McCullouch (U.S.A.)	Minneapolis, Minnesota, U.S.A.	16 July 196
	13·2*	Willie Davenport (U.S.A.)	Zürich, Switzerland	4 July 196
200 metres (2′ 6″) (straight)	21·9	Donald Augustus Styron (U.S.A.)	Baton Rouge, Louisiana, U.S.A.	2 April 196
200 metres (2′ 6″) (turn)	22·5	Karl Martin Lauer (West Germany)	Zürich, Switzerland	7 July 195
	22·5	Glenn Ashby Davis (U.S.A.)	Bern, Switzerland	20 Aug. 196
400 metres (3′ 0″)	48·1	David Peter Hemery (United Kingdom)	Mexico City, Mexico	15 Oct. 196
3,000 metres Steeplechase	8:22·2	Vladimir Dudkin (U.S.S.R.)	Kiev, U.S.S.R.	19 Aug. 196

FIELD EVENTS

Event	ft.	ins.	Metres	Name and Nationality	Place	Date
High Jump	7	5¾	2·28	Valeriy Nikolayevich Brumel (U.S.S.R.)	Moscow, U.S.S.R.	21 July 196
Pole Vault	17	10¼	5·44	John Thomas Pennel (U.S.A.)	Sacramento, California, U.S.A.	21 June 196
Long Jump	29	2½	8·90	Robert Beamon (U.S.A.)	Mexico City, Mexico	18 Oct. 196
Triple Jump	57	0¾	17·39	Viktor Saneyev (U.S.S.R.)	Mexico City, Mexico	17 Oct. 196
Shot Putt	71	5½	21·78	James Randel Matson (U.S.A.)	College Station, Texas, U.S.A.	22 April 196
Discus Throw	224	5	68·40	L. Jay Silvester (U.S.A.)	Revo, Nevada, U.S.A.	18 Sept. 196
Hammer Throw	247	8	75·48	Anatoliy Bondarchuk (U.S.S.R.)	Rovno, U.S.S.R.	11 Oct. 196
Javelin Throw	304	1	92·70	Jorma V. P. Kinnunen (Finland)	Tampere, Finland	18 June 196

DECATHLON

8,417 points	William Toomey (U.S.A.)	Los Angeles, California, U.S.A.	10–11 Dec. 196
	(1st day: 100m. 10·3s., Long Jump 25′ 5½″,	(2nd day: 110m. Hurdles 14·8s.,	
	Shot Putt 47′ 2¼″, High Jump 6′ 4″,	Discus 152′ 6″, Pole Vault 14′ 0¼″,	
	400m. 47·1s.)	Javelin 215′ 8″, 1,500 m. 4:39·4s.)	

THE MARATHON

There is no official marathon record because of the varying severity of courses. The best time over 26 miles 385 yards (standardized in 1924) is 2 hours 08 minutes 33·6 seconds (av. 12·24 m.p.h.) by Derek Clayton (born 1942, at Barrow-in-Furness, England) of Australia, at Antwerp, Belgium, on 30 May 1969.
The best time by a British international is 2 hours 10 minutes 30·0 seconds by Ronald Hill of Bolton United Harriers, at Boston, Massachusetts, U.S.A. on 20 April 1970.
The best time by a female is 3 hours 07 minutes 26·2 seconds (av. 8·39 m.p.h.) by Anni Pede (West Germany), aged 27, from Waldmeil to Erdkamp, West Germany, on 16 Sept. 1967.

RELAYS

Event	Mins. secs.	Team	Place	Date
4 × 110 yards (two turns)	38·6	University of Southern California, U.S.A. (Earl Ray McCullouch, Fred Kuller, Orenthal James Simpson, Lennox Miller [Jamaica])	Provo, Utah, U.S.A.	17 June 1967
4 × 220 yards and 4 × 200 metres	1:22·1	San Jose State College, California, U.S.A. (Ken Shackleford, Bob Talmadge, Lee Edward Evans, Tommie Smith)	Fresno, California, U.S.A.	13 May 1967
	1:21·7*	Texas Agricultural & Mechanical College (Donald Rogers, Rocklie Woods, Marvin Mills, Curtis Mills)	Des Moines, U.S.A.	25 April 1970
4 × 440 yards	3:02·8	Trinidad and Tobago (Lennox Yearwood, Kent Bernard, Edwin Roberts, Wendell A. Mottley)	Kingston, Jamaica	13 Aug. 1966
4 × 880 yards	7:14·6	West Germany (Bodo Tummler, Walter Adams, Harald Norpath, Franz-Josef Kemper)	Fulda, West Germany	13 June 1968
4 × 1 mile	16:05·0	Oregon Track Club (U.S.A.) (Roscoe Divine, C. Wade Bell, Arne Kvalheim (Norway), David Wilborn)	Eugene, Oregon, U.S.A.	30 May 1968
4 × 100 metres	38·2	United States National Team (Charles Edward Greene, Melvin Pender, Ronald Ray Smith, James Ray Hines)	Mexico City, Mexico	20 Oct. 1968
4 × 400 metres	2:56·1	United States National Team (Vincent Matthews, Ronald Freeman, G. Lawrence James, Lee Edward Evans)	Mexico City, Mexico	20 Oct. 1968
4 × 800 metres	7:08·6	West Germany "A" Team (Manfred Kinder, Walter Adams, Dieter Bogatzki, Franz-Josef Kemper)	Wiesbaden, West Germany	13 Aug. 1966
4 × 1,500 metres	14:49·0	France "A" Team (Gérard Vervoort, Claude Nicolas, Michel Jazy, Jean Wadoux)	St. Maur des Fosses, France	25 June 1965

* Awaiting ratification

Vladimir Dudkin (U.S.S.R.), the world's fastest steeplechaser

WORLD RECORDS—WOMEN

The complete list of World Records for the 28 scheduled women's events passed by the International Amateur Athletic Federation as at 1 Aug. 1969. Those marked with an asterisk are awaiting ratification.

RUNNING

Event	Mins. secs.	Name and Nationality	Place	Date
100 yards	10·3	Marlene Judith Willard (*née* Mathews) (Australia)	Sydney, N.S.W., Australia	20 Mar. 1958
	10·3	Wyomia Tyus (U.S.A.)	Kingston, Jamaica	17 July 1965
	10·3	Wyomia Tyus (U.S.A.)	Dayton, Ohio, U.S.A.	8 June 1968
	10·3*	Chi Cheng (Taiwan, China)	Dublin, Ireland	29 July 1969
	10·3*	Chi Cheng (Taiwan, China)	Claremont, Maryland, U.S.A.	28 Mar. 1970
220 yards (turn)	22·9	Margaret Ann Burvill (Australia)	Perth, Western Australia	22 Feb. 1964
440 yards	52·4	Judith Florence Pollock (*née* Amoore) (Australia)	Perth, Western Australia	27 Feb. 1965
880 yards	2:02·0	Dixie Isobel Willis (Australia)	Perth, Western Australia	3 Mar. 1962
	2:02·0	Judith Florence Pollock (*née* Amoore) (Australia)	Stockholm, Sweden	5 July 1967
1 mile	4:36·8	Maria Francesca Gommers (Netherlands)	Leicester, England	14 June 1969
60 metres	7·2	Betty Cuthbert (Australia)	Sydney, N.S.W., Australia	21 Feb. 1960
	7·2	Irina Robertovna Bochkaryova (*née* Turova) (U.S.S.R.)	Moscow, U.S.S.R.	28 Aug. 1961
100 metres	11·0	Wyomia Tyus (U.S.A.)	Mexico City, Mexico	15 Oct. 1968
200 metres (turn)	22·5	Irena Kirszenstein (now Szewinska) (Poland)	Mexico City, Mexico	18 Oct. 1968
400 metres†	51·7	Nicole Duclos (France)	Athens, Greece	18 Sept. 1969
	51·7	Colette Besson (France)	Athens, Greece	18 Sept. 1969
800 metres†	2:00·5	Vera Nikolić (Yugoslavia)	Crystal Palace, London	20 July 1968
1,500 metres	4:10·7	Jaroslava Jehličková (Czechoslovakia)	Athens, Greece	20 Sept. 1969

† *Shin Geum Dan (North Korea) has also achieved the following performances: 400 metres, 51·4 secs. at Djakarta, Indonesia, on 13 Nov. 1963, and 51·2 secs. at P'yongyang, North Korea, on 21 Oct. 1964; 800 metres, 1:59·1 at Djakarta, Indonesia, on 12 Nov. 1963, and 1:58·0 at P'yongyang, North Korea, on 5 Sept. 1964;* but the meeting in Indonesia, the Games of the New Emerging Forces (GANEFO), was not recognized by the I.A.A.F., and she was under suspension by the I.A.A.F. at the time of the other performances.

Nadyezhda Chizhova (U.S.S.R.), who dominates the small world of feminine shop putting

HURDLING

Event	Secs.	Name and Nationality	Place	Date
100 metres (2′ 9″)	13·3	Karen Balzer (East Germany)	Warsaw, Poland	20 June 1969
	13·3	Teresa Sukniewicz (Poland)	Warsaw, Poland	20 June 196
	12·8*	Teresa Suknieivicz (Poland)	Warsaw, Poland	20 June 197
200 metres (2′ 6″)	27·1	Maureen R. Caird (Australia)	Sydney, Australia	24 May 1969
	25·8*	Pamela Kilborn (Australia)	Melbourne, Australia	17 Dec. 1969

FIELD EVENTS

Event	ft.	ins	Metres	Name and Nationality	Place	Date
High Jump	6	3¼	1·91	Iolanda Söter (*née* Balas) (Romania)	Sofia, Bulgaria	16 July 1961
Long Jump	22	4½	6·82	Viorica Viscopoleanu (Romania)	Mexico City, Mexico	14 Oct. 1968
Shot Putt	67	0¼	20·43	Nadyezhda Chizhova (U.S.S.R.)	Athens, Greece	16 Sept. 1969
Discus Throw	209	10	63·96	Liesel Westermann (West Germany)	Hamburg, W. Germany	27 Sept. 1969
Javelin Throw	204	8½	62·40	Yelena Yegorovna Gorchakova (U.S.S.R.)	Tōkyō, Japan	16 Oct. 1964

PENTATHLON

5,352 points	Liesl Prokop (Austria)	Vienna, Austria	4–5 Oct. 1969

RELAYS

Event	Mins. Secs.	Team	Place	Date
4 × 110 yards	45·0	United Kingdom National Team (Anita D. Neil, Maureen Dorothy Tranter, Janet Mary Simpson, Lillian Barbara Board)	Portsmouth, England	14 Sept. 1968
4 × 220 yards	1:35·8*	Australia (Marian Hoffman, Jennifer Lamy, Raelene Boyle, Pamela Kilborn)	Brisbane, Australia	9 Nov. 1969
4 × 100 metres	42·8	United States National Team (Barbara Ferrell, Margaret Bailes [*née* Johnson], Mildrette Netter, Wyomia Tyus)	Mexico City, Mexico	20 Oct. 1968
4 × 200 metres	1:38·8	United Kingdom National Team (Maureen Dorothy Tranter, Della P. James, Janet Mary Simpson, Valerie Peat [*née* Wild])	London, England	24 Aug. 1968
4 × 400 metres	3:30·8	United Kingdom National Team (Rosemary Olivia Stirling, Patricia Barbara Lowe, Janet Mary Simpson, Lillian Barbara Board)	Athens, Greece	16 Sept. 1969
	3:30·8	French Team (Bernadette Martin, Nicole Duclos, Eliane Jacq, Colette Besson)	Athens, Greece	16 Sept. 1969
4 × 800 metres	8:33·0	East German National Team (Gertrud Schmidt, Gunhild Hoffmeister, Waltrud Pohland, Barbara Wieck)	Coltus, East Germany	4 Oct. 1969

N.B. Inaugural record for 4 × 440 yards relay has yet to be ratified.

UNITED KINGDOM (NATIONAL) RECORDS—MEN

Event	Mins. Secs.	Name	Place	Date
100 yards	9·4	Peter Frank Radford	Wolverhampton	28 May 1960
220 yards (turn)	20·5	Peter Frank Radford	Wolverhampton	28 May 1960
440 yards	45·9	Robbie Ian Brightwell, M.B.E.	London (White City)	14 July 1962
880 yards	1:47·2	Christopher Sydney Carter	London (White City)	3 June 1968
1 mile	3:55·7	Alan Simpson	London (White City)	30 Aug. 1965
2 miles	8:30·2	Richard George Taylor	Leamington, Warwickshire	17 June 1967
3 miles	13:04·6	Richard George Taylor	London (White City)	13 Aug. 1969
6 miles	27:10·2	Richard George Taylor	London (Crystal Palace)	22 June 1969
10 miles	46:44·0	Ronald Hill	Leicester	9 Nov. 1968
15 miles	1H 12:48·2	Ronald Hill	Bolton, Lancashire	21 July 1965
100 metres	10·2	Emmanuel McDonald Bailey	Belgrade, Yugoslavia	25 Aug. 1951
	10·2	Walter Menzies Campbell	San Jose, California, U.S.A.	20 May 1967
	10·2	Walter Menzies Campbell	Modesto, California, U.S.A.	27 May 1967
200 metres	20·5	Peter Frank Radford	Wolverhampton	28 May 1960
400 metres	45·7	Adrian Peter Metcalfe	Dortmund, West Germany	2 Sept. 1961
	45·7	Robbie Ian Brightwell, M.B.E.	Tōkyō, Japan	18 Oct. 1964
	45·7	Robbie Ian Brightwell, M.B.E.	Tōkyō, Japan	19 Oct. 1964
800 metres	1:46·3	Christopher Sydney Carter	Budapest, Hungary	4 Sept. 1966
1,000 metres	2:18·2	John Peter Boulter	London (Crystal Palace)	6 Sept. 1969
1,500 metres	3:39·1	Alan Simpson	London (White City)	15 Aug. 1964
	3:39·1	Ian Stewart	London (White City)	1 Sept. 1969
2,000 metres	5:08·2	Colin Robinson	Stretford, Lancashire	7 Sept. 1968
3,000 metres	7:47·6	Richard George Taylor	London (Crystal Palace)	6 Sept. 1969
5,000 metres	13:29·0	Richard George Taylor	London (White City)	13 Aug. 1969
10,000 metres	28:06·6	Richard George Taylor	London (Crystal Palace)	22 June 1969
20,000 metres	58:39·0	Ronald Hill	Leicester	9 Nov. 1968
25,000 metres	1H 15:22·6	Ronald Hill	Bolton, Lancashire	21 July 1965
30,000 metres	1H 32:25·4	James Joseph Hogan (*né* Cregan)	Walton-on-Thames, Surrey	12 Nov. 1966
1 hour	12 miles 1,268 yards	Ronald Hill	Leicester	9 Nov. 1968

HURDLING

Event	Secs.	Name	Place	Date
120 yards	13·6	David Peter Hemery	Brno, Czechoslovakia	5 July 1969
110 metres	13·6	David Peter Hemery	Brno, Czechoslovakia	5 July 1969
200 metres (turn)	23·0	Alan Peter Pascoe	Loughborough, Leicestershire	5 June 1969
220 yards (straight)	23·3	Peter Burke Hildreth	Imber Court, Surrey	27 Aug. 1955
220 yards (turn)	23·7	Paul Ashley Laurence Vine	London (White City)	15 July 1955
	23·7	John Michael Walter Hogan	London (White City)	9 May 1964
400 metres	48·1	David Peter Hemery	Mexico City, Mexico	15 Oct. 1968
440 yards	50·2	David Peter Hemery	London (White City)	13 July 1968
3,000 metres Steeplechase	8:30·8	Gerald Stevens	London (White City)	1 Sept. 1969

FIELD EVENTS

Event	ft. ins.	Name	Place	Date
High Jump	6 10	Gordon Albert Miller	London (White City)	18 May 1964
Pole Vault	16 7½	Michael Anthony Bull	Portsmouth, Hampshire	14 Sept. 1968
Long Jump	27 0	Lynn Davies, M.B.E.	Bern, Switzerland	30 June 1968
Triple Jump	54 0	Frederick John Alsop	Tōkyō, Japan	16 Oct. 1964
Shot Putt	64 2	Arthur Rowe	Mansfield, Nottinghamshire	7 Aug. 1961
Discus Throw	189 6	John T. Watts	London (White City)	2 Sept. 1968
	189 6	William Tancred	London (White City)	13 Aug. 1969
Hammer Throw	223 9*	Andrew Howard Payne	Warley, Worcs.	20 June 1970
Javelin Throw	268 9	John Henry Peter FitzSimons	Long Beach, California, U.S.A.	23 Mar. 1969

DECATHLON (1962 Scoring Tables)

7,451 points*	Clive Citrine Olaf Longe	Kassel, West Germany	28–29 June 1969

Doctor Ronald Hill,
Britain's fastest ever
marathon runner

RELAYS

Event	Time	Team	Place	Date
4 × 110 yards	40·0	United Kingdom National Team (Peter Frank Radford, Ronald Jones, David Henry Jones, Thomas Berwyn Jones)	London (White City)	3 Aug. 196
4 × 220 yards and 4 × 200 metres	1:26·0	London Team (David Henry Jones, Brian Andrew Smouha, Peter Frank Radford, David Hugh Segal)	London (White City)	30 Sept. 195
4 × 440 yards	3:06·5	England Team (Martin John Winbolt-Lewis, John Austin Adey, Peter Warden, Timothy Joseph Michael Graham)	Kingston, Jamaica	13 Aug. 196
4 × 880 yards and 4 × 800 metres †	7:20·4	United Kingdom National Team (Malcolm David Rothwell, A. Duncan Middleton, John Peter Boulter, Christopher Sydney Carter)	London (White City)	28 Aug. 196
4 × 1 mile	16:24·8	Northern Counties Team (Stanley George Taylor, John Paul Anderson, Alan Simpson, Brian Hall)	Dublin, Ireland	17 July 196
4 × 100 metres	39·3	United Kingdom National Team (Joseph William Speake, Ronald Jones, Ralph Banthorpe, Barrie Harrison Kelly)	Mexico City, Mexico	19 Oct. 196
4 × 400 metres	3:01·2	United Kingdom National Team (Martin John Winbolt-Lewis, Colin William Ashburner Campbell, David Peter Hemery, John Sherwood)	Mexico City, Mexico	20 Oct. 196
4 × 1,500 metres	15:27·2	United Kingdom National Team (Ralph Henry Dunkley, David Charles Law, Douglas Alastair Gordon Pirie, George William Nankeville)	London (White City)	23 Sept. 195

† A U.K. National Team recorded 7:14·6 for 4 × 880 yards at the Crystal Palace London, on 22 June 1966, but lap times were illegally communicated to the runners

UNITED KINGDOM (NATIONAL) RECORDS—WOMEN

*=awaiting ratification

Event	Mins. Secs.	Name	Place	Date
100 yards	10·6	Heather Joy Young (*née* Armitage)	Cardiff	22 July 1958
	10·6	Dorothy Hyman, M.B.E.	London (White City)	7 July 1962
	10·6	Dorothy Hyman, M.B.E.	London (White City)	4 July 1964
	10·6	Mary Denise Toomey (formerly Rand *née* Bignal), M.B.E.	London (White City)	4 July 1964
	10·6	Daphne Arden (now Slater)	London (White City)	4 July 1964
	10·6	Valerie Peat	Huddersfield	10 Aug. 1968
	10·6	Maureen Dorothy Tranter	Birmingham	7 Sept. 1968
220 yards (turn)	23·6	Daphne Arden (now Slater)	London (White City)	4 July 1964
440 yards	54·1	Deirdre Ann Watkinson	Kingston, Jamaica	8 Aug. 1966
880 yards	2:04·2	Anne Rosemary Smith	London (White City)	2 July 1966
1 mile	4:37·0	Anne Rosemary Smith	Chiswick, Greater London	3 June 1967
100 metres	11·3	Dorothy Hyman, M.B.E.	Budapest, Hungary	2 Oct. 1963
	11·3	Dorothy Hyman, M.B.E.	Budapest, Hungary	3 Oct. 1963
	11·3	Valerie Peat	Mexico City, Mexico	14 Oct. 1968
200 metres	23·2	Dorothy Hyman, M.B.E.	Budapest, Hungary	3 Oct. 1963
400 metres	52·1	Lillian Barbara Board	Mexico City, Mexico	16 Oct. 1968
	52·0*	Marilyn Neufville	London (Crystal Palace)	30 May 1970
800 metres	2:01·1	Ann Elizabeth Packer (now Brightwell), M.B.E.	Tōkyō, Japan	20 Oct. 1964
1,500 metres	4:15·9	Rita Ridley (*née* Lincoln)	Athens, Greece	20 Sept. 1969

HURDLING

Event	Secs.	Name	Place	Date
100 metres	13·5	Christine Perera	London	19 July 1968
200 metres	27·3	Patricia Ann Jones	Stretford, Lancashire	22 July 1967

FIELD EVENTS

Event	ft. ins.	Name	Place	Date
High Jump	5 10½	Linda Hedmark (*née* Knowles)	Skellefteå, Sweden	17 June 1969
Long Jump	22 2¼	Mary Denise Toomey (formerly Rand *née* Bignal), M.B.E.	Tōkyō, Japan	14 Oct. 1964
Shot Putt	53 6¼	Mary Elizabeth Peters	Belfast, Northern Ireland	1 June 1966
Discus Throw	180 7*	Christine Rosemary Payne (*née* Charters)	The Hague, Netherlands	17 May 1970
Javelin Throw	182 5	Susan Mary Platt	London (Chiswick)	15 June 1968

PENTATHLON

Points	Name	Place	Date
5,035 points	Mary Denise Toomey (formerly Rand *née* Bignal), M.B.E. (80m. Hurdles 10·9 secs., Shot Putt 36 ft. 3 ins., High Jump 5 ft. 7¾ ins., Long Jump 21 ft. 6 ins., 200m. 24·2 secs.)	Tōkyō, Japan	16–17 Oct. 1964

RELAYS

Event	Mins. Secs.	Name	Place	Date
4 × 110 yards	45·0	United Kingdom National Team (Anita Doris Neil, Maureen Dorothy Tranter, Janet Mary Simpson, Lillian Barbara Board)	Portsmouth	14 Sept. 1968
4 × 220 yards	1:37·6	London Olympiades A.C. (Della Patricia James, Barbara M. Jones, Lillian Barbara Board, Janet Mary Simpson)	Solihull, Birmingham	10 June 1967
4 × 100 metres	43·7	United Kingdom National Team (Anita Doris Neil, Maureen Dorothy Tranter, Janet Mary Simpson, Lillian Barbara Board)	Mexico City, Mexico	19 Oct. 1968
4 × 200 metres	1:33·8	(for details see World records page 234)		
4 × 400 metres	3:30·8	(for details see World records page 234)		
4 × 800 metres	8:27·0*	Great Britain Team (Sheila Carey [née Taylor], Patricia Barbara Lowe, Rosemary Olivia Stirling, Lillian Barbara Board)	Edinburgh	13 June 1970

Professional records Professional records include: 100 yards, 9·3 seconds by Ken Irvine (Australia) at Dubbo, New South Wales, Australia, on 9 March 1963; Mile, 3 minutes 59·7 seconds from scratch by Harold Downes (Australia) in a handicap race at Bendigo, Victoria, Australia, on 9 March 1963; Shot Putt, 64 feet (19·507 metres) by Arthur Rowe (born 17 Aug. 1936) of Barnsley, Yorkshire, at Keswick, Cumberland, on 6 Aug. 1962.

Shot putt with hands The greatest combined distance for putting the shot is 106 feet 10¼ inches (61 feet 0¾ inch with the right hand and 45 feet 9½ inches left hand) by William Parry O'Brien (born 28 Jan. 1932) of the U.S.A., at Culver City, California, U.S.A., on 17 Aug. 1962.

Longest tug o' war The longest recorded pull is one of 2 hours 41 minutes between "H" Company and "E" Company of the 2nd Battalion of the Sherwood Foresters (Derbyshire Regiment) at Jubbulpore, India, on 12 Aug. 1889. "E" Company won.

The longest recorded pull under A.A.A. Rules (in which lying on the ground or entrenching the feet is not permitted) is one of 8 minutes 18·2 seconds for the first pull between the R.A.S.C. (Feltham) and the Royal Marines (Portsmouth Division) at the Royal Tournament of June 1938.

Three-legged race The fastest recorded time for a 100 yards three-legged race is 11·0 seconds by Harry L. Hillman and Lawson Robertson at Brooklyn, New York City, N.Y., U.S.A., on 24 April 1909.

Greatest caber toss The 230 lb. Braemar Caber, originally 21 feet in length, defied all comers until it was successfully tossed by George Clark at the Braemar Gathering, Aberdeenshire, Scotland, in September 1951.

INTERNATIONALS

Most The greatest number of full Great Britain internationals won by a British male athlete is 51 by Crawford William Fairbrother (born 1 Dec. 1936), the high jumper, from 1957 to mid-1970. The feminine record is 34 full internationals by Suzanne Allday (née Farmer) from 1951 to 1964.

Oldest and youngest Of full Great Britain (outdoor) internationals the oldest have been Harold Whitlock (born 16 Dec. 1903) at the 1952 Olympic Games, aged 48 years 218 days, and Mrs. Dorothy Tyler, (née Odam) (born 19 March 1920) at the 1956 Olympic Games, aged 36 years 269 days. The youngest have been William Land (born 29 Nov. 1914) versus Italy in 1931, aged 16 years 271 days, and Miss Sylvia Needham (born 28 March 1935) versus France in 1950, aged 15 years 166 days.

Blind 100 yards The fastest time recorded for a 100 yards by a blind man is 11·0 seconds by George Bull, aged 19, of Chippenham, Wiltshire, in a race at the Worcester College for the Blind, on 26 Oct. 1954.

Pancake race record The annual Housewives Pancake Race at Olney, Buckinghamshire, was first mentioned in 1445. The record for the winding 415-yard course is 63·0 seconds, set by Miss Janet Bunker, aged 17, on 7 Feb. 1967. The record for the counterpart race at Liberal, Kansas, U.S.A. is 59·1 seconds by Kathleen West, 19, on 10 Feb. 1970.

Standing high jump The best standing high jump is 5 feet 9¼ inches by Johan Christian Evandt (Norway) at Oslo on 4 March 1962.

Caber tossing—one of the events featured in Highland Games

Badminton

Origins The game was devised at the end of the 1860s a[t] Badminton Hall in Gloucestershire, the seat of the Dukes of Beaufort.

International Championships Malaysia have won the International Championship or Thomas Cup (instituted 1948) four times: Malaya (now part of Malaysia) won in 1948–49, 1951–52 and 1954–55, and as Malaysia, by the default of Indonesia in the final in 1966–67.

The inaugural Ladies International Championship or Uber Cup (instituted 1956) was won by the United States, who successfully defended in 1960 and 1963, since when Japan have won and retained the Cup (1966 and 1969).

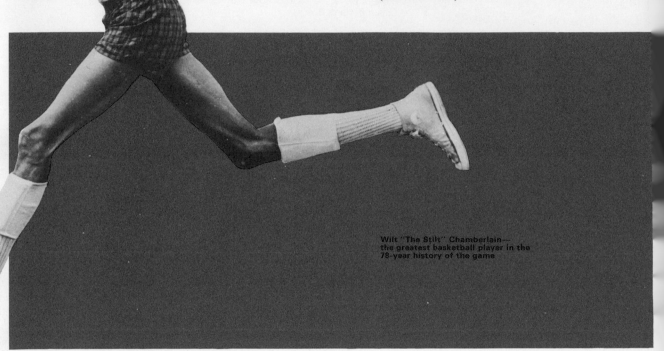

Wilt "The Stilt" Chamberlain—
the greatest basketball player in the
78-year history of the game

Most titles Most wins in the All-England Championships (instituted 1899):—

Event	Times	Holder	Dates
Men's Singles	7	Erland Kops (Denmark)	1958, 1960–63, 1965, 1967
Women's Singles	10	Mrs. G. C. K. Hashman (*née* Judy Devlin) (U.S.A.)	1954, 1957–58, 1960–64, 1966–67

Most titles (*i.e.* including doubles):—

	Times	Holder	Dates
Men	21	G. A. Thomas (later Sir George Thomas, Bt.)	from 1903 to 1928
Women	17	Miss M. Lucas (U.K.)	from 1899 to 1910

Most internationals Most international appearances:—

	Times	Men	Times	Women
England	96	A. D. Jordan, 1951 to 1969	52	Mrs. W. C. E. Rogers (*née* Cooley) 1955 to 1969
Ireland	37	J. J. Fitzgibbon, 1946 to 1962	40	Mrs. E. T. Bryan (*née* O'Sullivan) 1955 to 1969
,,	37	K. Carlisle, 1954 to 1968		
Scotland	33	R. S. McCoig, 1956 to 1969	28	Miss C. E. Dunglison, 1956 to 1967
Wales	16	R. J. Evans, 1928 to 1936	22	Mrs. L. W. Myers, 1928 to 1939
,,	16	C. G. Gooding, 1930 to 1939		

Longest hit Frank Rugani drove a shuttlecock 79 feet 8½ inches in tests at San Jose, California, U.S.A., on 29 Feb. 1964.

Longest games The longest recorded game has been one of 163 hours by 5 students from the Brooklands County Technical College, Weybridge, Surrey maintaining continuous singles on 20–27 March 1970 when 653 games were completed.

Mrs. W. C. E. Rogers—
52 times capped
for England

Baseball

Earliest game
"Baste-Ball" was a pursuit banned at Princeton, New Jersey, U.S.A., as early as 1786. On 4 Feb. 1962, it was claimed in *Nedelya,* the weekly supplement to the Soviet newspaper *Izvestiya,* that "Beizbol" was an old Russian game. The earliest baseball game under the Cartwright rules was at Hoboken, New Jersey, U.S.A., on 19 June 1846, with the New York Nine beating the Knickerbockers 23–1 in 4 innings.

Highest batting average
The highest average in a career is 0·367 by Tyrus Raymond Cobb (1886–1961), the "Georgia Peach" of Augusta, Anniston, Detroit (1905–26) and Philadelphia (1927–28). During his career Ty Cobb made a record 2,244 runs from a record 4,191 hits made during a record 11,429 times at bat in a record 3,033 major league games.

HOME RUNS

Most
The highest number of home runs hit in a career is the 714 by George Herman ("Babe") Ruth (1895–1948) of Baltimore-Providence, Boston, Red Sox (American League), New York Yankees and Boston (National League), between 1914 and 1935. His major league record for home runs in one year is 60 in 154 games between 15 April and 30 Sept. 1927. Roger Maris (born 1935) (New York Yankees) hit 61 homers in a 162-game schedule in 1961. Left-hander Joe Baumann of Roswell, New Mexico, hit 72 homers in the minor league in 1954.

Longest
The longest home run ever measured was one of 618 feet by Roy Edward Carlyle in a minor league game at Emeryville Ball Park, California, U.S.A., on 4 July 1929. In 1919 Babe Ruth hit a 587-foot homer in a Boston Red Sox *v.* New York Giants match at Tampa, Florida, U.S.A. The longest throw (ball weighs between 5 and 5¼ oz.) is 445 feet 10 inches by Glen Gorbaus on 1 Aug. 1957. The longest throw by a woman is 296 feet by Miss Mildred "Babe" Didrikson (later Mrs. George Zaharris) at Jersey City, New Jersey, U.S.A. on 25 July 1931. The fastest time for circling bases is 13·3 seconds by Evar Swanson at Columbus, Ohio, in 1932.

Pitching
The first "perfect game" (no hits, no runs) pitched in a World Series was by Don Larsen (New York Yankees) with 97 pitches (71 in the strike zone) against Brooklyn Dodgers on 8 Oct. 1956.

Highest earnings
The greatest earnings of a baseball player is $1,091,477 (now £454,782) amassed by "Babe" Ruth between 1914 and 1938.

Record attendances and receipts
The World Series record attendance is 420,784 (6 games with total receipts of $2,626,973·44, then £938,205), when the Los Angeles (ex-Brooklyn) Dodgers beat the Chicago White Sox 4–2 on 1–8 Oct. 1959. The single game record is 92,706 for the fifth game (receipts $552,774·77, then £197,420) at the Memorial Coliseum, Los Angeles, California, on 6 Oct. 1959. The record net receipts for a series has been $3,018,113 (then £1,257,547) from a paid attendance of 379,670, who saw the Detroit Tigers beat the St. Louis Cardinals 4–3 on 2–10 Oct. 1968. The highest seating capacity in a baseball stadium is 74,056 in the Cleveland Municipal Stadium, Ohio, U.S.A.

Highest catch
Joe Sprinx (Cleveland Indians) caught a baseball dropped from an airship at 800 feet in July 1931. The force of the ball broke his jaw.

Basketball

Origins
Ollamalitzli was a 16th century Aztec precursor of basketball played in Mexico. If the solid rubber ball was put through a fixed stone ring the player was entitled to the clothing of all the spectators. Modern Basketball was devised by the Canadian-born Dr. James A. Naismith (1861–1939) at the Training School of the International Y.M.C.A. College at Springfield, Massachusetts, U.S.A., in December 1891 and first played on 20 Jan. 1892. The first public contest was on 11 March 1892. The game is now a global activity. The Amateur Basketball Association of England and Wales was founded in 1936.

World Olympic champions
The U.S.A. have won the Olympic title since its inception at Berlin in 1936 (7 times with 54 successive victories) and also the 1954 world title (instituted 1950). Brazil won in 1959 and 1963.

Largest ever gate
The Harlem Globetrotters (U.S.A.) played an exhibition to 75,000 in the Olympic Stadium, West Berlin, Germany, in 1951. The largest indoor basketball stadium is the Astrodome, Houston, Texas, U.S.A., where 52,693 watched a match on 20 Jan. 1968.

Greatest playing record
The Harlem Globetrotters set unapproached attendance and scoring records in their silver jubilee season of 1951–52. They won 333 games and lost 8 before over 3,000,000 spectators. Boston Celtic won 11 A.B.A. titles in the 13-year seasons from 1957 to 1969.

The team was founded by the London-born Abraham M. Saperstein (1903–66) of Chicago, Illinois, U.S.A., and the first game was played at Hinckley, Illinois, on 7 Jan. 1927. In the 39 seasons to 1965 they won 8,434 games and lost 322. They have travelled almost 5,000,000 miles, visited 87 countries on six continents, and have been seen by an estimated 53,000,000 people.

U.S.A. professional records
The greatest number of points scored in a career is 30,000 by Wilton ("Wilt the Stilt") Norman Chamberlain (born 21 Aug. 1936) in the 11 seasons 1959–1970. He stands 7 feet 1 1/10 inches tall.

Most points scored in a season: Chamberlain, now with the Philadelphia 76ers, scored 4,029 points for the Philadelphia Warriors in the 1961–62 season. Most points scored in a single game: Chamberlain scored 100 points against the New York Knickerbockers at Hershey, Pennsylvania, on 2 March 1962. Most points scored by a team: 173, by Boston Celtics, against Minnesota Lakers (139 points) at Boston, Massachusetts, on 28 Feb. 1959. Most points in a match: 316, between the Philadelphia Warriors (169 points) and the New York Knickerbockers (147 points), as above. The longest field goal on record is 84 feet 11 inches by George Linn, aged 20, of Alabama against North Carolina at Tuscaloosa, Alabama, in January 1955.

Non-A.B.A. scoring record
Clarence (Bevo) Francis of Rio Grande College, Rio Grande, Ohio, U.S.A., scored 3,964 points (an average of 101 points per game) in the 1953–54 season. This total includes 150 points scored in one game.

Tallest players
The tallest player of all time was Vasiliy Akhtayev (born 1935) of the U.S.S.R., who played for Kazakhastan in 1956, when measuring 232 centimetres (7 feet 7·3 inches). The tallest woman player is Ulyana Semyonova (born 1950), who plays for T.T.T. Riga, Latvia and stands 6 feet 9½ inches. The tallest international player in the world today is Christopher Greener (see Chapter 1) of L.L.S.K., London whose debut was for England *v.* France on 17 Dec. 1969.

A stand for the ancient Aztec precursor of basketball *Ollamalitzli*

Sports, games and pastimes

Most expensive
In 1969 Ferdinand Lewis Alcindor (born 16 April 1947) signed a five year contract for $1,400,000 (£583,333) with Milwaukee Bucks. Alcindor stands 7 feet 1⅜ inches tall.

Most accurate
The greatest goal shooting demonstration has been by the professional trick specialist Wilfred Hetzel (b. 1912) who once achieved a run of 144 straight baskets from the foul line off one foot.

Longest games marathon record
The longest recorded basketball marathon was of 85 hours by 18 boys of the Kesgrave Youth Club, Suffolk, England with two five-man teams continuously on court on 1–5 Aug. 1969.

Britain
The most A.B.B.A. titles (initiated 1936) have been won by the London Central Y.M.C.A. with eight wins in 1957–58, 1960 and 1962–63–64–67–69. The highest score in a final was 98 points by London Polytechnic *v.* Nottingham Y.M.C.A. in 1954. Four women's titles (instituted 1965) have been won by Malory.
The record score by an England international team is 101–33, when beating Wales at Belfast in 1962.

Billiards

Earliest mention
The earliest recorded mention of billiards was in a poem by Clément Marot (1496–1544) of France, and it was mentioned in England in 1591 by Edmund Spenser (*c.* 1552–99). The first recorded public billiards room in England was the Piazza, Covent Garden, London, in the early part of the 19th century. Rubber cushions were introduced in 1835 and slate beds in 1836.

Highest breaks
Tom Reece (England) made an unfinished break of 499,135, including 249,152 cradle cannons (2 points each), in 85 hours 49 minutes against Joe Chapman at Burroughes' Hall, Soho Square, London, between 3 June and 6 July 1907. This was not recognized because press and public were not continuously present. The highest certified break made by the anchor cannon is 42,746 by W. Cook (England) from 29 May to 7 June 1907. The official world record under the then baulk line rule is 1,784 by Joe Davis, O.B.E. (born 15 April 1901) in the United Kingdom Championship on 29 May 1936. Walter Lindrum (Australia) made an official break of 4,137 in 2 hours 55 minutes against Joe Davis at Thurston's on 19–20 Jan. 1932, before the baulk-line rule was in force. The amateur record is 702 by Robert Marshall *versus* Tom Cleary in the Australian Amateur Championship at Brisbane on 17 Sept. 1953. Davis has an unofficial personal best of 2,502 (mostly pendulum cannons) in a match against Tom Newman in Manchester in 1930.

Fastest century
Walter Lindrum, M.B.E. (1899–1960) of Australia made an unofficial 100 break in 27·5 seconds in Australia on 10 Oct. 1952. His official record is 100 in 46·0 seconds, set in Sydney in 1941.

Most world titles
The greatest number of world championship titles (instituted 1870) won by one player is eight by John Roberts, Jnr. (England) in 1870 (twice), 1871, 1875 (twice), 1877 and 1885 (twice). The greatest number of United Kingdom titles (instituted 1934) won by any player is seven (1934–39 and 1947) by Joe Davis (England), who also won four world titles (1928–30 and 1932) before the series was discontinued in 1934. Willie Hoppe (U.S.A.) won 51 "world" titles in the United States variants of the game between 1906 and 1952.

Most amateur titles
The record for world amateur titles is four by Robert Marshall (Australia) in 1936–38–51–62. The greatest number of British Amateur Championships (instituted

1888) ever won is eight by Sidney H. Fry (1893 to 1925) and A. Leslie Driffield (1952–54, 1957–59, 1962 and 1967).

Bar billiards marathon
The duration record for bar billiards is 72 hours by 5 players from Harrow County Grammar School who scored a total of 772,550 points on 6–9 April 1970.

Bobsleigh

Origins
The oldest known sledge is dated *c.* 6500 B.C. and came from Heinola, southern Finland. The word toboggan comes from the Micmac American Indian word *tobaakan*. The oldest bobsleigh club in the world is St. Moritz Tobogganing Club, home of the Cresta Run, founded in 1887. Modern world championships were inaugurated in 1924. Four-man bobs were included in the first Winter Olympic Games at Chamonix in 1924 and two-man boblets from the third Games at Lake Placid, U.S.A., in 1932.

Cresta Run
The skeleton one-man toboggan dates, in its present form, from 1892. On the 1,327-yard-long Cresta Run at St. Moritz, Switzerland, dating from 1884 speeds of up to 83·8 m.p.h. were reached by Fl. Lt. (now Sqn. Ldr.) Colin Mitchell (Great Britain) in February 1959. The record from the Junction (2,868 feet) is 43·59 seconds by Nino Bibbia (born 9 Sept. 1924) of Italy in 1965. The record from Top (3,981 feet) is 54·67 seconds by Bibbia in 1965.

The greatest number of wins in the Cresta Run Grand National (inst. 1885) is seven by the 1948 Olympic champion Nino Bibbia (Italy) in 1960–61–62–63–64–66–68. The greatest number of wins in the Cresta Run Curzon Cup (inst. in 1910) is eight by Bibbia in 1950–57–58–60–62–63–64–69 who hence won the Double in 1960–62–63–64.

Olympic and World titles
The Olympic four-man bob has been won three times each by the U.S.A. (1928–32–48) and Switzerland (1924–36–56). Only the U.S.A. (1932, 1936) and Italy (1956, 1968) have won the Olympic boblet event twice.

The world four-man bob has been won eight times by Switzerland (1924–36–39–47–54–55–56–57). Italy won the two-man title twelve times (1954–56–57–58–59–60–61–62–63–66–68–69). Eugenio Monti (Italy) has been a member of eleven world championship crews.

LUGEING
In lugeing the rider adopts a sitting, as opposed to a

prone position. It was largely developed by British tourists at Klosters, Switzerland, from 1883. The first European championships were at Reichenberg, East Germany, in 1914 and the first world championships at Oslo, Norway, in 1953. The International Luge Federation was formed in 1957. Lugeing attracts more than 20,000 competitors in Austria.

Most ld titles The most successful rider in the world championships is Thomas Köhler (East Germany), who won the single-seater title in 1962, 1966 and 1967 and shared in the two-seater title in 1967 and 1968 (Olympic). Otrun Enderlein (East Germany) has won thrice (1965, 1966 and 1967).

Highest speed The fastest luge run is at Krynica, Poland, where speeds of more than 80 m.p.h. have been recorded.

Bowling—Ten Pin

Origins The ancient European game of nine-pins was exported to the United States in the early 17th century. In about 1845 the Connecticut and New Haven State Legislatures prohibited the game so a tenth pin was added to evade the ban; but there is some evidence of 10 pins being used in Suffolk about 300 years ago.

In the United States there were 9,378 bowling establishments and 145,000 bowling lanes in 1968–69 and 29,000,000 bowlers. The world's largest bowling centre is a bowling centre in Japan with 250 lanes which is almost complete. The largest in Europe is the Excel Bowl at Nottingham, England, where the game was introduced in 1960, with 48 lanes on two floors (24 on each floor).

Highest scores The highest individual score for three sanctioned games (possible 900) is 886 by Albert (Allie) Brandt of Lockport, New York State, U.S.A., on 25 Oct. 1939. The record for consecutive strikes in sanctioned match play is 29 by Frank Caruana at Buffalo, New York, on 5 March 1924, and 29 by Max Stein at Los Angeles, California, on 8 Oct. 1939. The highest number of santioned 300 games is 22 (till 1969) by Elvin Mesger of Sullivan, Missouri, U.S.A. The maximum 900 for a three-game series has been recorded three times in unsanctioned games—by Leo Bentley at Lorain, Ohio, U.S.A., on 26 March 1931; by Joe Sargent at Rochester, New York State, U.S.A., in 1934; and by Jim Margie in Philadelphia, Pennsylvania, U.S.A., on 4 Feb. 1937. These series must have included at least 36 consecutive strikes.

The United Kingdom record for a three-game series is 771 by David Pond (b. 1948) of Harlow, Essex at Hoddesdon, Hertfordshire on 17 Dec. 1968. The record score for a single game is 300 by Albert Kirkham, aged 34, of Burslem, Staffordshire, on 5 Dec. 1965.

World pionships The world championships were instituted in 1954. The highest pinfall in the individual men's event is 5,708 by David Pond (G.B.) of Harlow, Essex, at Malmö, Sweden, in 1967.

Marathon Bill Halstead (U.S.A.) bowled 1,201 games (knocked down 165,959 pins) scoring 1,948 strikes, lifted 130·3 tons and walked 127·2 miles in 151 hours 25 minutes at Tampa, Florida, U.S.A., on 27 Nov. to 3 Dec. 1966.

SKITTLES
The duration record for knocking down skittles (9-pins) is 53 hours (56,191 pins down) by 9 men at the Plymouth Inn alley Totnes, Devon on 30 June–2 July 1969.

The highest score in 24 hours is 44,144 pins by 8 members of the Buckland Brewer Methodist Youth Club at Bideford, Devon on 27–28 Feb. 1970.

Bowls

Origins Bowls can be traced back to at least the 13th century in England. The Southampton Town Bowling was formed in 1299. After falling into disrepute, the game was rescued by the bowlers of Scotland who, headed by W. W. Mitchell, framed the modern rules in 1848–49.

World title In the inaugural World Championship held in Sydney, Australia in October 1966 the Singles Title was won by David John Bryant (b. 1931) (England) and the team title (Leonard Cup) by Australia.

David Bryant (England)—only lawn bowler to have won all four E.B.A. titles

Most title wins In the annual International Championships (instituted 1903) Scotland have won 23 times to England's 19. The most consecutive wins is five by England from 1958 to 1962 and five by Scotland from 1965 to 1969.

English titles The only man to have won four Singles Titles (instituted 1905) is E. Percy C. Baker (Poole Park, Dorset) in 1932, 1946, 1952 and 1955. He has also shared two pairs wins (1950 and 1962) and a triples win in 1960. The most Pairs Titles (instituted 1912) is four by Worthing, in 1937–38, 1955 and 1957. The Triples Title (instituted 1945) has never been won twice. The Rinks (instituted 1905) have been won three times by Belgrave (Leicester) in 1919, 1922 and 1954. David Bryant skipped Clevedon to the E.B.A. Triple Title in 1966 and so became the only man ever to have won all four titles.

Most internationals The greatest number of international seasons by an English bowler is 21 by R. Kivell (Exonia, Devon) between 1947 and 1969.

Boxing

Earliest references The origins of fist-fighting belong to Greek mythology. The earliest prize-ring code of rules was formulated in England on 16 Aug. 1743 by the champion pugilist Jack Broughton (1704–89), who reigned from 1729 to 1750. Boxing, which had, in 1867, come under the Queensbury Rules formulated for John Sholto Douglas, 8th Marquess of Queensbury, was not established as a legal sport in Britain until after the ruling of Mr. Justice Grantham on 24 April 1901, following the death of Billy Smith.

Longest fight The longest recorded fight with gloves was between Andy Bowen of New Orleans (k. 1894) and Jack Burke in New Orleans, Louisiana, U.S.A., on 6–7 April 1893. The fight lasted 110 rounds and 7 hours 19 minutes from 9.15 p.m. to 4.34 a.m., but was declared a no contest when both men were unable to continue. The longest recorded bare knuckle fight was one of 6 hours 15 minutes between James Kelly and Jack Smith at Melbourne, Australia, on 19 Oct. 1856. The greatest recorded number of rounds is 278 in 4 hours 30 minutes, when Jack Jones beat Patsy Tunney in Cheshire in 1825.

Teddie Barker (left) victor of a 7 second fight

and also the largest fists with a 14¾-inch circumference. The lightest champion was Robert Prometheus Fitzsimmons (1862–1917), who was born at Helston, Cornwall, and, at a weight of 167 lb. (11 stone 13 lb.) won the title by knocking out James J. Corbett in 14 rounds at Carson City, Nevada, U.S.A., on 17 March 1897.

The greatest differential in a world title fight was 86 lb. between Carnera (270 lb. or 19 stone 4 lb.) and Tommy Loughran (184 lb. or 13 stone 2 lb.) of the U.S.A., when the former won on points at Miami, Florida, U.S.A. on 1 March 1934.

Tallest and shortest The tallest world champion was the 6 feet 6¼ inches tall Jess Willard, the Kansas Cowboy (1882–1968) (U.S.A.) who won the title by knocking out Jack Johnson (U.S.A.) in the 26th round at Havana, Cuba, on 5 April 1915. Carnera was 6 feet 5¾ inches. The shortest was Tommy Burns (1881–1955) of Canada, world champion from 23 Feb. 1906 to 26 Dec. 1908, who stood 5 feet 7 inches.

Oldest and youngest The oldest man to win the heavyweight crown was Jersey Joe Walcott (born Arnold Raymond Cream, 31 Jan. 1914 at Merchantville, New Jersey, U.S.A.) who knocked out Ezzard Charles on 18 July 1951 in Pittsburgh, Pennsylvania, when aged 37 years 5 months 18 days. Walcott was the oldest holder at 38 years 7 months 23 days losing his title on 23 Sept. 1952 and in 1953 the oldest challenger. The youngest age at which the world title has been won is 21 years 331 days by Floyd Patterson (born Waco, North Carolina, 4 Jan. 1935) of the U.S.A. After the retirement of Rocky Marciano, Patterson won the vacant title by beating Archie Moore in 5 rounds in Chicago, Illinois, U.S.A., on 30 Nov. 1956. He is also the only man ever to regain the heavyweight championship. He lost to Ingemar Johansson (Sweden) on 26 June 1959 but defeated him on 20 June 1960 at the New York Polo Grounds Stadium.

Earliest title fight The first world heavyweight title fight, with gloves and 3-minute rounds, was that between John Lawrence Sullivan (1858–1918) and "Gentleman" James J. Corbett (1866–1933) in New Orleans, Louisiana, U.S.A., on 7 Sept. 1892. Corbett won in 21 rounds.

Undefeated Only James Joseph (Gene) Tunney (b. Greenwich Village, New York City, 25 May 1898) (1926–1928) and Rocky Marciano (1952–56) *finally* retired as undefeated champions. Cassius Marcellus Clay 7th (later Muhammad Ali Haj) (born Louisville, Kentucky, 17 Jan. 1942) was undefeated in 29 fights during a professional career of 6 years and 5 months when stripped of his heavyweight title on 28 April 1967 for refusing to be inducted into the U.S. services.

WORLD CHAMPIONS (any weight)

Longest and shortest reign Joe Louis's heavyweight duration record of 11 years 8 months stands for all divisions. The shortest reign has been 55 days by the French featherweight Eugène Criqui from 2 June to 26 July 1923. The disputed flyweight champion Emile Pladner (France) reigned only 47 days from 2 March to 18 April 1929, as did the disputed featherweight champion Dave Sullivan from 26 Sept. to 11 Nov. 1898.

Youngest and oldest The youngest age at which any world championship has been claimed is 19 years 6 days by Pedlar Palmer (born 19 Nov. 1876), who won the bantamweight title in London on 26 Nov. 1895. Willie Pep (born William Papaleo, 22 Nov. 1922), of the U.S.A., won the featherweight crown in New York on his 20th birthday, 22 Nov. 1942. After Young Corbett III knocked out Terry McGovern (1880–1918) in two rounds at Hartford, Connecticut, U.S.A., on 28 Nov. 1901, neither was able to get his weight down to nine stone, and the title was claimed by Abe Attell, when aged only 17 years 8 months 6 days. The oldest world champion

Shortest fight There is a distinction between the quickest knock-out and the shortest fight. A knock-out in 10½ seconds (including a 10-second count) occurred on 26 Sept. 1946, when Al Couture struck Ralph Walton while the latter was adjusting a gum shield in his corner at Lewiston, Maine, U.S.A. If the time was accurately taken it is clear that Couture must have been more than half-way across the ring from his own corner at the opening bell. The shortest fight on record appears to be one at Palmerston, New Zealand on 8 July 1952 when Ross Cleverley (R.N.Z.A.F.) floored D. Emerson (Pahiatua) with the first punch and the referee stopped the contest without a count 7 seconds from the bell. Teddie Barker (Swindon) scored a technical knock-out over Bob Roberts (Nigeria) at the first blow in a welterweight fight at Maesteg, Glamorganshire, Wales, on 2 Sept. 1957. The referee, Joe Brimell, stopped the fight without a count 10 seconds from the bell.

The shortest world heavyweight title fight occurred when Tommy Burns (1881–1955) (né Noah Brusso) of Canada knocked out Jem Roche in 1 minute 28 seconds in Dublin, Ireland, on 17 March 1908. The duration of the Clay v. Liston fight at Lewiston, Maine, U.S.A. on 25 May 1965 was 1 minute 57 seconds (including the count) as timed from the video tape recordings, despite a ringside announcement giving a time of 1 minute. The shortest world title fight was when Al McCoy knocked out George Chip in 45 seconds for the middleweight crown in New York on 6 April 1914. The shortest ever British title fight was one of 40 seconds (including the count), when Dave Charnley knocked out David "Darkie" Hughes in a lightweight championship defence in Nottingham on 20 Nov. 1961.

Tallest and heaviest The tallest and heaviest boxer to fight professionally was Gogea Mitu (born 1914) of Romania in 1935. He was 7 feet 4 inches and weighed 23 stone 5 lb. (327 lb.). John Rankin, who won a fight in New Orleans, Louisiana, U.S.A., in November 1967, was reputedly also 7 feet 4 inches.

WORLD HEAVYWEIGHT CHAMPIONS

Longest and shortest reigns The longest reign of any world heavyweight champion is 11 years 8 months and 9 days by Joe Louis (born Joseph Louis Barrow, Lafayette, Alabama, 13 May 1914), from 22 June 1937, when he knocked out James J. Braddock in the eighth round at Chicago, Illinois, U.S.A., until announcing his retirement on 1 March 1949. During his reign Louis made a record 25 defences of his title. The shortest reign was by Primo Carnera (Italy) for 350 days from 29 June 1933 to 14 June 1934. However, if the disputed title claim of Marvin Hart is allowed, his reign from 3 July 1905 to 23 Feb. 1906 was only 235 days.

Heaviest and lightest The heaviest world champion was Primo Carnera (1906–67) of Italy, the "Ambling Alp", who won the title from Jack Sharkey in 6 rounds in New York City, N.Y., U.S.A., on 29 June 1933. He scaled 270 lb. (19 stone 4 lb.), had a chest measurement of 53 inches, the longest reach at 85½ inches (finger tip to finger tip)

242

BOXING

was Archie Moore (U.S.A.) who was recognized as a light-heavyweight champion in June 1961, when he was believed to be between 44 and 47 (born either 13 Dec. 1913 or 1916). Bob Fitzsimmons (1862–1917) had the longest career of any official world title-holder with over 32 years from 1882 to 25 Nov. 1903 when he won his last world title aged 41 years 5 months and 21 days. He was an amateur from 1880 to 1882.

Sugar Ray Robinson (right)

Longest fight The longest world title fight (under Queensbury Rules) was that between the lightweights Joe Gans (1874–1910), of the U.S.A., and Oscar Matthew "Battling" Nelson (1882–1954), the "Durable Dane", at Goldfield, Nevada, U.S.A., on 3 Sept. 1906. It was terminated in the 42nd round when Gans was declared the winner on a foul.

Most captures The only boxer to win a world title five times at one weight is "Sugar" Ray Robinson (born Walker Smith Jr., in Detroit, 3 May 1920) of the U.S.A., who beat Carmen Basilio (U.S.A.) in the Chicago Stadium on 25 March 1958, to regain the world middleweight title for the fourth time. The other title wins were over Jake LaMotta (U.S.A.) in Chicago on 14 Feb. 1951, Randolph Turpin (United Kingdom) in New York on 12 Sept. 1951, Carl "Bobo" Olson (U.S.A.) in Chicago on 9 Dec. 1955, and Gene Fullmer (U.S.A.) in Chicago on 1 May 1957. The record number of title bouts in a career is 33 or 34 (at bantam and featherweight) by George Dixon (1870–1909), *alias* Little Chocolate, of the U.S.A., between 1890 and 1901.

Greatest weight span The only man to hold world titles at three weights *simultaneously* was Henry ("Homicide Hank") Armstrong (born 22 Dec. 1912), now the Rev. Harry Jackson, of the U.S.A., at featherweight, lightweight and welterweight from August to December 1938.

Greatest "tonnage" The greatest "tonnage" recorded in any fight is 601 lb. when Ewart Potgieter (South Africa) at 335 lb. (23 stone 13 lb.) knocked out Bruce Olson (U.S.A.) at 266 lb. (19 stone) at Portland, Oregon, on 2 March 1957. The greatest "tonnage" in a world title fight was 488¾ lb. (34 stone 12¼ lb.) when Carnera (then 259¼ lb.) fought Paolino Uzcuden (229¼ lb.) of Spain in Rome on 22 Oct. 1933.

Most k-downs in title fights Vic Toweel (South Africa) knocked down Danny O'Sullivan of London 14 times in 10 rounds in their world bantamweight fight at Johannesburg on 2 Dec. 1950, before the latter retired.

ALL FIGHTS

Largest purse The greatest purse was $990,445·54 (now £412,685) received by Gene Tunney (U.S.A.) for his fight against Jack Dempsey (born Manassa, Colorado, 24 June 1895) of the U.S.A., at Soldiers Field, Chicago, Illinois, U.S.A., on 22 Sept. 1927.

Greatest receipts The greatest total receipts from any boxing fight is $4,665,420 (then £1,666,221) for the world heavyweight title fight between Floyd Patterson (U.S.A.) and Charles ("Sonny") Liston (U.S.A.) at Comiskey Park, Chicago, Illinois, U.S.A., on 25 Sept. 1962. Patterson was knocked out after 2 minutes 6 seconds of the first round. The highest gate receipts were those for the Tunney-Dempsey fight of 1927 (see above) when 104,943 paid $2,658,660 with a ringside price of $40.

Attendances Highest The greatest paid attendance at any boxing fight has been 120,757 (with a ringside price of $27·50) for the Tunney v. Dempsey world heavyweight title fight at the Sesqui-centennial Stadium, Philadelphia, Pennsylvania, U.S.A., on 23 Sept. 1926. The indoor record is 37,321 at the Clay v. Terrell fight in the Astrodome, Houston, Texas, on 6 Feb. 1967.

The highest non-paying attendance is 135,132 at the Tony Zale v. Billy Prior fight at Juneau Park, Milwaukee, Wisconsin, U.S.A., on 18 Aug. 1941.

Lowest The smallest attendance at a world heavyweight title fight was 2,434 at the Clay v. Liston fight at Lewiston, Maine, U.S.A. on 25 May 1965.

Highest earnings in career The largest known fortune ever made in a fighting career was $4,760,338 (now £1,983,474), amassed by Rocky Marciano (born Rocco Francis Marchegiano at Brockton, Massachusetts, U.S.A., on 1 Sept. 1923) from 39 of his 49 professional bouts (43 knock-outs and 6 on points) between 21 Feb. 1947 and 21 Sept. 1955. He retired, undefeated, on 27 April 1956 and was killed in an air crash in central Ohio, U.S.A. on 31 Aug. 1969. Including earnings for refereeing and promoting, Jack Dempsey has grossed over $10,000,000 (now £4,166,666) to 1967. Floyd Patterson (U.S.A.) received $2,384,737 (then £851,692) for his three fights against Ingemar Johansson (Sweden) on 26 June 1959, 20 June 1960, and 13 March 1961 and possibly grossed $7,500,000 (£3,125,000) as a boxer to the end of 1965. The total known earnings from title fights by Clay (Muhammad Ali Haj) to March 1967 were $3,135,302 (then £1,119,750). His career gross has been estimated at $5½ million (£2,290,000).

Most knock-outs The greatest number of finishes classed by the rules prevailing as "knock-outs" in a career is 136 by Archie Moore (born Archibald Lee Wright, 13 Dec. 1916) of the U.S.A. The record for consecutive K.O.'s is 44, set by Lamar Clark of Utah at Las Vegas, Nevada, U.S.A., on 11 Jan. 1960. He knocked out 6 in one night (5 in the first round) at Bingham, Utah, on 1 Dec. 1958.

Most fights The greatest recorded number of fights in a career is 1,309 by Abraham Hollandersky, *alias* Abe the Newsboy (U.S.A.), in the fourteen years from 1905 to 1918. He filled in the time with 387 wrestling bouts (1905–1916).

Most fights without loss Hal Bagwell of Gloucester, England, was undefeated in 183 consecutive fights, of which only 5 were draws, between 10 Aug. 1938 and 29 Nov. 1948.

Two sporting superlatives—Cassius Clay (left) and Wilt Chamberlain (right)

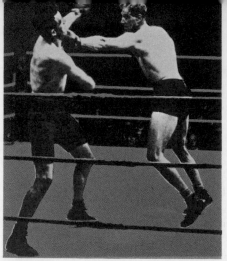

Sports, games and pastimes

Greatest weight difference The greatest weight difference recorded in a major bout is 10 stone (140 lb.) between Bob Fitzsimmons (12 stone 4 lb.) and Ed Dunkhorst (22 stone 4 lb.) at Brooklyn, New York City, N.Y., U.S.A., on 30 April 1900. Fitzsimmons won in two rounds.

Longest career The heavyweight Jem Mace, known as "the gypsy" (born at Beeston, Norwich, 8 April 1831), had a career lasting 35 years from 1855 to 1890, but there were several years in which he had only one fight. He died, aged 78, in Liverpool on 3 March 1910. Walter Edgerton, the "Kentucky Rosebud", knocked out John Henry Johnson, aged 45, in 4 rounds at the Broadway A.C., New York City, N.Y., U.S.A., on 4 Feb. 1916, when aged 63.

British titles The most defences of a British heavyweight title is 13 by "Bombardier" Billy Wells (born 21 Aug. 1889, died 11 June 1967) from 1911 to 1919. The only British boxer to win three Lonsdale Belts outright has been Henry Cooper, the current heavyweight champion.

Father and son British titles won by father and son were at featherweight by "Spider" Jim Kelly (23 Nov. 1938 to 28 June 1939) and "Spider" Billy Kelly (22 Jan. 1955 to 4 Feb. 1956) and at heavyweight by Jack London (1913–63) from 15 Sept. 1944 to 17 July 1945 and Brian London (born Brian Sydney Harper at West Hartlepool 1934) from 3 June 1958 to 12 Jan. 1959.

Most Olympic gold medals The only amateur boxer ever to win three Olympic gold medals is the southpaw László Papp (born 1926 (Hungary), who took the middleweight (1948) and the light-middleweight titles (1952 and 1956). The only man to win two titles in one celebration was O. L. Kirk (U.S.A.), who took both the bantam and featherweight titles at St. Louis, Missouri, U.S.A., in 1904, when the U.S. won all the titles. In 1908 Great Britain won all the titles.

MOST A.B.A. TITLES
The greatest number of A.B.A. titles won by any boxer is 6 by Joseph Steers at middleweight and heavyweight between 1890 and 1893.

Class	Instituted	Wins	Name	Years
Flyweight (8 stone or under)	1920	5	T. Pardoe	1929–33
Bantamweight (8 stone 7lb. or under)	1884	4	W. W. Allen	1911–12, 1914, 1919
Featherweight (9 stone or under)	1888	5	G. R. Baker	1912–14, 1919, 1921
Lightweight (9 stone 7 lb. or under)	1881	4	M. Wells	1904–07
		4	F. Grace	1909, 1913, 1919–20
Light-Welterweight (10 stone or under)	1951	2	D. Stone	1956–57
		2	R. Kane	1958–59
		2	L./Cpl. B. Brazier	1961–62
		2	R. McTaggart	1963, 1965
Welterweight (10 stone 8 lb. or under)	1920	3	N. Gargano	1954–55–56
Light-Middleweight (11 stone 2 lb. or under)	1951	2	B. Wells	1953–54
		2	B. Foster	1952, 1955
		2	S. Pearson	1958–59
		2	T. Imrie	1966, 1969
Middleweight (11 stone 11 lb. or under)	1881	5	R. C. Warnes	1899, 1901, 1903, 1907, 1910
		5	H. W. Mallin	1919–23
		5	F. Mallin	1928–32
Light-Heavyweight (12 stone 10 lb. or under)	1920	4	H. J. Mitchell	1922–25
Heavyweight (any weight)	1881	5	F. Parks	1899, 1901–02, 1905–06

Longest span The greatest span of A.B.A. title-winning performances is that of the heavyweight H. Pat Floyd, who won in 1929 and gained his fourth title 17 years later in 1946.

Bullfighting

The first renowned professional bullfighter was Francisco Romero of Ronda, in Andalusia, Spain, who fought in about 1700. The earliest treatise was *Tauromaquiá o Arte torear* by José Delgado y Galvez. Spain now has some 190 active matadors. Since 1700, 42 major matadors have died in the ring.

Largest stadiums The world's largest bullfighting ring is the Plaza, Mexico City, with a capacity of 48,000. The largest of Spain's 312 bullrings is the Plaza Monumental, Madrid with a capacity of 23,663. The record gate has been $75,000 (now £31,250), taken at the Tijuana Plaza Monumental, Mexico, on 13 May 1962.

Most successful matadors The most successful matador measured by bulls killed was Lagartijo (1841–1900), born Rafael Molina, whose lifetime total was 4,867. The longest career of any 20th century *espada* was that of Juan Belmonte (1892–1962) of Spain who survived 29 seasons from 1909–1937. In 1919 he killed 200 bulls in 109 *corridas* and was gored 50 times. In 1884 Romano set a record by killing 18 bulls in a day in Seville and in 1949 El Litri (Miguel Báes) set a Spanish record with 114 *novilladas* in a season.

Highest paid The highest paid bullfighter in history is El Cordobés (born Manuel Benítez Pérez, probably on 4 May 1936, Palma del Rio, Spain), who became a sterling millionaire in 1966, when he fought 111 *corridas* up to 4 Oct. of that year, latterly receiving a minimum fee of 1 million pesetas (then £6,945) for each half-hour in the ring. On 19 May 1968 he received £9,000 for a *corrida* in Madrid.

Canoeing

Origins The acknowledged pioneer of canoeing as a sport was John Macgregor, a British barrister, in 1865. The Canoe Club was formed on 26 July 1866.

Most Olympic medals Gert Fredriksson of Sweden won the 1,000 metres Kayak singles in 1948, 1952 and 1956, the 10,000 metres Kayak singles in 1948 and 1956 and the 1,000 metres Kayak doubles in 1960. With 6 Olympic titles and 3 others (1,000 metres K.1 in 1950 and 1954 and 500 metres K.1 in 1954) his total of world titles is 9. The Olympic 1,000 metre record of 3 minutes 14·38 seconds represents an average speed of 11·51 m.p.h. and a striking rate of 125 strokes per minute.

British titles The most British Open titles (instituted 1936) ever won is 23, of which 11 were individual, by Alistair Wilson (Ayrshire Kayak Club) with K.1 500 metres 1962–64–65–66; 1,000 metres 1962–64–65–66; 10,000 metres 1963–66–67; K.2 500 metres 1963–68; 1,000 metres 1965; 10,000 metres 1963–66; K.4 1,000 metres 1964–65–66 and K.1 4 × 500 metres Relay 1963–64–65–

66. David Mitchell (Chester S. & C.C.) won his sixth consecutive British slalom title in 1968.

The only United Kingdom canoeists to win world titles have been Paul Farrant (died 18 April 1960) of Chalfont Park Canoe Club, who won the canoe slalom at Geneva, Switzerland, in August 1959, and Alan Emus, who won the canoe sailing at Hayling Island, Hampshire, in August 1961 and on the Boden See (Lake of Constance) in August 1965. Emus also won this event in the European Championship at Stockholm, Sweden, in August 1963.

Trans-Atlantic In 1928 E. Romer (Germany) crossed the North Atlantic in a 19½-foot canvas kayak named *Deutsches Sport*.

Cross-Channel The singles record for canoeing across the English Channel is 3 hours 36 minutes by David Shankland, aged 29, of Cardiff, in a home-made N.C.K.I. named "Jelly Roll", from Shakespeare Bay, Dover, to Cap Gris Nez, France, on 21 June 1965. The doubles record is 3 hours 20 minutes 30 seconds by Capt. William Stanley Crook and the late Ronald Ernest Rhodes in their glass-fibre K.2 "Accord", from St. Margaret's Bay, Dover, to Cap Blanc Nez, France, on 20 Sept. 1961.

Devizes-Westminster The Senior Class record for the annual Devizes-Westminster Challenge Cup race (instituted 1948) over 125 miles with 77 locks is 19 hours 14 minutes 20 seconds by R. Evans and P. Pagnanelli (16 Parachute Brigade C.C.) in a K.2 Glider on 27–28 March 1970 on their third consecutive win. The record for the Junior Class event (held over 4 days) is 18 hours 51 seconds by A. Hunter and J. West (Leander Sea Scouts) on 27–30 March 1970. There are 77 portages and 21 miles of tidal water.

Eskimo rolls The record for Eskimo rolls is 312 in just over 24 minutes by Ellis Whitelock in a K.W.7 slalom kayak at the Waltham Forest Technical College in 1969.

DOWN STREAM CANOEING

River	Miles			Date	
Rhine	820	Sgt. Charles Kavanagh	Chur, Switzerland to Willemstad, Neths.	13 Feb. 1961	17½ days
Murray	1,400	Terry Lees and Tony Summerville	Gundagai to Renmark	17 March–1 May 1967	44 days
Nile	4,000	John Goddard (U.S.), Jean Laporte and André Davy (France)	Kagera to the Delta	Nov. 1953–July 1954	9 months

Caving

PROGRESSIVE WORLD DEPTH RECORDS

Feet	Cave	Cavers	Date
210	Lamb Lair, near West Harptree, Somerset	John Beaumont (explored)	c. 1676
454	Macocha, Moravia	Joseph Nagel	May 1748
742	Grotta di Padriciano, Trieste	Antonio Lindner, Svetina	1839
1,079	Grotta di Trebiciano, Trieste	Antonio Lindner	6 April 1841
1,293	Nidlenloch, Switzerland	—	1909
1,433	Geldloch, Austria		1923
1,476	Abisso Bertarelli, Yugoslavia	R. Battelini, G. Cesca	24 Aug. 1925
1,491	Spluga della Preta, Venezia, Italy	*L. de Battisti	18 Sept. 1927
1,775	Antro di Corchia, Tuscany, Italy	E. Fiorentino Club	1934
1,980	Trou de Glaz, Isère, France	F. Petzl, C. Petit-Didier	4 May 1947
2,389	Gouffre de la Pierre Saint Martin, Basses-Pyrénées, France	*Georges Lépineux	15 Aug. 1953
2,428	Gouffre Berger, Sornin Plateau, Vercors, France	J. Cadoux, G. Garby	11 Sept. 1954
2,963	Gouffre Berger, Sornin Plateau, Vercors, France	*F. Petzl and 6 men	25 Sept. 1954
3,230	Gouffre Berger, Sornin Plateau, Vercors, France	L. Potié, G. Garby et al.	29 July 1955
>3,600	Gouffre Berger, Sornin Plateau, Vercors, France	Jean Cadoux and 2 others	11 Aug. 1956
>3,600	Gouffre Berger, Sornin Plateau, Vercors, France	*Frank Salt and 7 others	23 Aug. 1962
>3,700	Gouffre Berger, Sornin Plateau, Vercors, France	Kenneth Pearce	4 Aug. 1963
>3,700	Gouffre Berger, Sornin Plateau, Vercors, France	Kenneth Pearce	Aug. 1966
3,799	Gouffre de la Pierre Saint Martin, Basses-Pyrénées, France	French team	Aug. 1966
3,872	Gouffre de la Pierre Saint Martin, Basses-Pyrénées, France	C. Quefféléc and 10 others	1968

* Leader

Cheddar Gorge, Somerset

David Lafferty holder of the British troglodyte record

Duration (trogging) The endurance record for staying in a cave is 193 days by Milutin Veljkovic (Yugoslavia) in a cave in northern Yugoslavia reported in May 1970. The British record is 130 days by David Lafferty, aged 27, of London, who stayed in Boulder Chamber, Gough's Cave, Cheddar Gorge, Somerset, from 27 March to 4 Aug. 1966. He was alone until 1 Aug. when he thought it was 7 July.

WORLD'S DEEPEST CAVES

According to the latest available revised measurements, the deepest caves in the world are:—

Feet	Cave	Location
4,300	Gouffre de la Pierre Saint Martin	Basses-Pyrénées, France/Spain
3,750	Gouffre Berger	Sornin Plateau, Vercors, France
3,051	Réseau Trombe	Pyrénées, Haute-Garonne, France
2,906	Spluga della Preta	Lessinische Alps, Italy
2,647	Grotta del Monte Cucco	Perugia, Italy
2,641	Antro di Corchia	Apuanian Alps, Italy

NOTE: *The Provetina Cave, Greece has the world's longest vertical pitch of 1,298 fe The highest known cave entrance in the world is that of the Rakhiot Cave, Nan, Parbat, Kashmir at 21,860 feet.*

Chess

Origins The name chess is derived from the Persian word *shah* (a king or ruler). It is a descendant of the game *Chaturanga*. The earliest reference is from the Middle Persian Karnamak (*c.* A.D. 590–628), though there are grounds for believing its origins are from the 4th century in north west India. It reached Britain in *c.* 1255. The *Fédération Internationale des Échecs* was established in 1924. There were an estimated 5,000,000 competitive players in the U.S.S.R. in 1967.

World champions François André Danican, *alias* Philidor (1726–95), of France claimed the title of "world champion" from 1747 until his death. World champions have been generally recognized since 1843. The longest tenures were 28 years by Wilhelm Steinitz (1836–1900) of Austria, from 1866 to 1894, and 27 years by Dr. Emanuel Lasker (1868–1941) of Germany, from 1894 to 1921. The youngest was Paul Charles Morphy (1837–84) of New Orleans, Louisiana, U.S.A., who won the title in 1858, when aged 21, and held it until 1862. The women's world championship was won three times by Yelizaveta Bykova (U.S.S.R.) in 1953, 1958, and 1960. The world team championship (instituted 1927) has been won most often by the U.S.S.R.—8 times consecutively since 1952.

British titles Most British titles have been won by Dr. Jonathan Penrose (b. 1934) of East Finchley, London with 10 titles in 1958–63, 1966–68 and 1969. Mrs. Rowena M. Bruce (b. 1919) of Plymouth won 9 titles in 1950–51–54–55 (shared) –59–60–63–66.

Longest games The most protracted chess match on record was one drawn on the 191st move between H. Pilnik (Argentina) and Moshe Czerniak (Israel) at Mar del Plata, Argentina, in April 1950. The total playing time was 20 hours. A game of 21½ hours, but drawn on the 171st move (average over 7½ minutes per move), was played between Makagonov and Chekover at Baku, U.S.S.R., in 1945.

Marathon The longest recorded session is one of 101 hours between John P. Cameron and Jon Stevens at Ipswich Civic College, Suffolk, England, on 21–25 March 1970. The longest game at "lightning chess" (*i.e.* all moves completed by a player in five minutes) is 34 hours 8 min. by William Kerr (176½ games) and Anthony Tayler (78½ games) of Monash University, Clayton, Victoria, Australia, from noon on 6 March to 10.08 p.m. on 7 March 1968.

Slowest Lawrence Grant and Dr. Munro MacLennan, the latte now in Sydney, New South Wales, Australia, are sti playing a match begun at Glasgow University in 1927 They make one move every Christmas and expect result in about 1976.

Shortest game The shortest recorded game between masters was one of four moves when Lazard (Black) beat Gibaud in a Paris chess café in 1924. The moves were: 1. P–Q4 Kt–KB3; 2. Kt–Q2, P–K4; 3. PxP, Kt–Kt5; 4. P–KR3 Kt–K6. White then resigned because if he played 5. PxKt there would have followed Q–KR5 check and the loss of his Queen for a Knight by any other move.

Most opponents Records by chess masters for numbers of opponents tackled simultaneously depend very much on whether or not the opponents are replaced as defeated, are in relays, or whether they are taken on in a simultaneous start. The greatest number tackled on a replacement basis is 400 (379 defeated) by the Swedish master Gideon Ståhlberg (died 26 May 1967) in 36 hours of play in Buenos Aires, Argentina, in 1940. Georges Koltanowski (Belgium, now of U.S.A.) tackled 56 opponents "blindfold" and won 50, drew 6, lost 0 in 9¾ hours at Fairmont Hotel, San Fransicso, California, U.S.A., on 13 Dec. 1960.

Dr. Jonathan Penrose, ten times British chess champion

Sports, games and pastimes

Contract Bridge

Earliest references

Bridge (a corruption of Biritch) is of Levantine origin, having been played in Greece in the early 1880s. The game was known in London in 1886 under the title of "Biritch or Russian Whist".

Auction Bridge (highest bidder names trump) was introduced in 1904 but was swamped by the Contract game, which was devised by Harold S. Vanderbilt (U.S.A.) on a Caribbean voyage in November 1925. The new version became a world-wide craze after the U.S.A. v. Great Britain challenge match between Ely Culbertson (born in Romania, 1891) and Lt.-Col. Walter Buller at Almack's Club, London, on 15 Sept. 1930. The U.S.A. won the 54-hand match by 4,845 points.

World titles

The World Championship (Bermuda Bowl) has been won most often by Italy (1957–58–59, 1961–62–63, 1965–66–67, 1969), whose team also won the Olympiad in 1964 and 1968. Three of the Italian players, Massimo D'Alelio, Giorgio Belladonna and Pietro Forquet, were in 11 of these winning teams.

Perfect deals

The mathematical odds against dealing 13 cards of one suit are 158,753,389,899 to 1, while the odds against receiving a "perfect deal" consisting of all 13 spades are 635,013,559,599 to 1. The odds against each of the 4 players receiving a complete suit are 2,235,197,406,-895,366,368,301,559,999 to 1. Instances of this are reported frequently but the chances of it happening genuinely are extraordinarily remote—in fact if all the people in the world were grouped in bridge fours, and each four were dealt 120 hands a day, it would require 2×10^{12} years before one "perfect" deal should recur.

A "perfect" perfect deal with the dealer (South) with 13 clubs, round to East with 13 Spades was the subject of affidavits by Mrs. E. F. Gyde (dealer), Mrs. Hennion, David Rex-Taylor and Mrs. P. Dawson at Richmond Community Centre, Surrey, on 25 Aug. 1964. The deal, the second of the rubber, was with a pack *not* used for the first deal. In view of the fact that there should be 31,201,794 deals with two perfect hands for each deal with four perfect hands and that reports of the latter far outnumber the former, it can be safely assumed that most reported occurrences of perfect deals are bogus.

Longest session

The longest recorded session is one of 170 hours by Stuart McClelland, Michael Mikulin, Richard Taylor and Martin Webb at Inverness Court Hotel, Bayswater, London on 7–14 Nov. 1969.

Most master points

The player with the highest-lifetime total of master points is Barry Crane, a Hollywood television producer, with 11,357 points by May 1970. The most points scored in tournaments in one year is 1,434 by Paul Soloway of Los Angeles, California, U.S.A., in 1969.

At June 1970 the leading scorers of master points in the United Kingdom were the twin brothers Robert Sharples (2,025 points) and James (2,016).

Coursing

Origins

The sport of dogs chasing hares was probably of Egyptian origin in c. 3000 B.C. and brought to England by the Normans in 1067. The classic event is the annual Waterloo Cup, instituted at Altcar, near Liverpool, in 1836. A government bill to declare the sport illegal was "lost" owing to the dissolution of Parliament on 29 May 1970.

Most successful dog

The most successful Waterloo Cup dog recorded was Colonel North's *Fullerton*, sired by *Greentich*, who tied for first in 1889 and then won outright in 1890–91–92.

The only dogs to win the Victorian Waterloo Cup (instituted 1873) three times have been *Bulwark* in 1906–07–09, at which time it was known as the Australian Waterloo Cup, and *Byamee* in 1953–54–55.

Longest course

The longest authenticated course is one of 4 minutes 10 seconds, when Major C. Blundell's *Blackmore* beat *Boldon* in a Barbican Cup decider on 2 March 1934.

HIGHEST POSSIBLE SCORE

Opponents bid 7 of any suit or No Trumps doubled and redoubled and vulnerable

	Opponents make no trick	
Above Line	1st undertrick	400
	12 subsequent undertricks at 600 each	7,200
	All Honours	150
		7,750

Bid 1 No Trump, double and redouble, vulnerable

Below Line	1st trick (40×4)	160
Above Line	6 over tricks (400×6)	2,400
	2nd game of 2-Game Rubber	*350
All Honours	(4 aces)	
	Bonus for making redoubled contract	50
	(Highest Possible Positive Score)	3,110

In practice, the full bonus of 700 points is awarded after the completion of the second game rather than 350 after each game.

247

Sports, games and pastimes

Cricket

Earliest match The earliest evidence of the game of cricket is from a drawing depicting two men playing with a bat and ball dated *c.* 1250. The game was played in Guildford, Surrey, at least as early as 1550. The earliest major match of which the score survives was one in which a team representing England (40 and 70) was beaten by Kent (53 and 58 for 9) by one wicket at the Artillery Ground in Finsbury, London, on 18 June 1744. Cricket was played in Australia as early as 1803.

BATTING

Highest innings The highest recorded innings by any team was one of 1,107 runs by Victoria against New South Wales in an Australian inter-State match at Melbourne, Victoria, on 27–28 Dec. 1926.

England The highest innings made in England is 903 runs for 7 wickets declared, by England in the 5th Test against Australia at the Oval, London, on 20, 22 and 23 Aug. 1938. The highest innings in a county championship match is 887 by Yorkshire v. Warwickshire at Edgbaston on 7–8 May 1896.

Lowest The lowest recorded innings is 12 made by Oxford University v. the Marylebone Cricket Club (M.C.C.) at Oxford on 24 May 1877, and 12 by Northamptonshire v. Gloucestershire at Gloucester on 11 June 1907. On the occasion of the Oxford match, however, the University batted a man short. The lowest score in a Test match is 26 by New Zealand v. England in the 2nd Test at Auckland on 28 March 1955.

The lowest aggregate for two innings is 34 (16 in first and 18 in second) by Border v. Natal in the South African Currie Cup at East London on 19 and 21 Dec. 1959.

Greatest victory The greatest recorded margin of victory is an innings and 851 runs, when Pakistan Railways (910 for 6 wickets declared) beat Dera Ismail Khan (32 and 27) at Lahore on 2–4 Dec. 1964. The largest margin in England is one of an innings and 579 runs by England over Australia in the 5th Test at the Oval on 20–24 Aug. 1938 when Australia scored 201 and 123 with two men short in both innings. The most one-sided county match was when Surrey (698) defeated Sussex (114 and 99) by an innings and 485 runs at the Oval on 9–11 Aug. 1888.

FASTEST SCORING
The greatest number of runs scored in a day is 721 runs all out (10 wickets) in 6 hours by the Australians v. Essex at Southchurch Park, Southend-on-Sea on the first day on 15 May 1948.

The Test record for runs in a day is 588 at Old Trafford on 27 July 1936 when England put on 398 and India were 190 for 0 in their second innings by the close.

Innings of 200 or more The fastest recorded exhibition of hitting occurred in a Kent v. Gloucestershire match at Dover on 20 Aug. 1937, when Kent scored 219 runs for 2 wickets in 71 minutes, at the rate of 156 runs for each 100 balls bowled.

Fastest 50 The fastest 50 ever hit was completed in 8 minutes (1.22 to 1.30 p.m.) and in 11 scoring strokes by Clive C. Inman (born in Colombo, Ceylon, 29 Jan. 1936) in an innings of 57 not out for Leicestershire v. Nottinghamshire at Trent Bridge, Nottingham on 20 Aug. 1965.

Century The fastest century ever hit was completed in 35 minut by Percy George Herbert Fender (b. 22 Aug. 1892 when scoring 113 not out for Surrey v. Northampto shire at Northampton on 26 Aug. 1920. The mo prolific scorer of centuries in an hour or less wa Gilbert Laird Jessop (1874–1955), with 11 betwee 1897 and 1913. The fastest Test century was one of 7 minutes by Jack Morrison Gregory (b. 14 Aug. 189 of New South Wales, for Australia v. South Africa i the 2nd Test at Johannesburg on 12 Nov. 1921. Edwi Boaler Alletson (1884–1963) scored 189 runs in 9 minutes for Nottinghamshire v. Sussex at Hove o 20 May 1911.

Double century The fastest double century was completed in 12 minutes by Gilbert Jessop (1874–1955) (286) fc Gloucestershire v. Sussex at Hove on 1 June 1903.

Treble century The fastest treble century was completed in 18 minutes by Denis Charles Scott Compton (born 2 May 1918) of Middlesex, who scored 300 for th M.C.C. v. North-Eastern Transvaal at Benoni o 3–4 Dec. 1948.

1,000 in May The most recent example of scoring 1,000 runs *in Ma* was by Charles Hallows (Lancashire) (born 4 Apr 1895), who made precisely 1,000 between 5–31 May 1928. Both Donald George Bradman (Australia) anc William John Edrich (Middlesex) scored 1,000 run *before the end of May* (starting on 30 April) in 1938.

Slowest scoring The longest time a batsman has ever taken to open his scoring is 1 hour 37 minutes by Thomas Godfrey Evans (b. Finchley, 18 Aug. 1920) of Kent, who scored 10 not out for England v. Australia in the 4th Test at Adelaide on 5–6 Feb. 1947. Richard Gorton Barlow (1850–1919) utilized 2½ hours to score 5 not out for Lancashire v. Nottinghamshire at Nottingham on 8 July 1882. During his innings his score remained unchanged for 80 minutes.

The slowest century on record was by Derrick John (Jackie) McGlew (b. 11 March 1929) of South Africa in the Third Test v. Australia at Durban on 25 and 27 Jan. 1958. He required 9 hours 35 minutes for 105, reaching the 100 in 9 hours 5 minutes. The slowest double century recorded is one of 9½ hours by Sidney George Barnes (b. 5 June 1916) of New South Wales, during an innings of 234, lasting 10 hours 42 minutes, for Australia v. England in the 2nd Test at Sydney, New South Wales, on 14, 16 and 17 Dec. 1946.

Highest individual innings The highest individual innings recorded is 499 in 10 hours 40 minutes by Hanif Muhammad (born 21 Dec. 1934) for Karachi v. Bahawalpur at Karachi, Pakistan, on 8, 9 and 11 Jan. 1959. The record for a Test match is 365 not out in 10 hours 8 minutes by Garfield St. Aubrun Sobers (b. Barbados, 28 July 1936) playing for

Clive Inman, who scored 50 in 8 minutes in 1965

248

Sir Donald Bradman, whose test career average was 99·94 runs —just one 4 short of a century average

the West Indies in the Third Test against Pakistan at Sabina Park, Kingston, Jamaica, on 27 Feb.–1 March 1958. The England Test record is 364 by Sir Leonard Hutton (b. Fulneck, Pudsey, Yorkshire, 23 June 1916) *v.* Australia in the 5th Test at the Oval on 20, 22 and 23 Aug. 1938. The highest score in England is 424 in 7 hours 50 minutes by Archibald Campbell MacLaren (1871–1944) for Lancashire *v.* Somerset at Taunton on 15–16 July 1895.

Longest innings The longest innings on record is one of 16 hours 39 minutes for 337 runs by Hanif Muhammad (Pakistan) *v.* the West Indies in the 1st Test at Bridgetown, Barbados, on 20–23 Jan. 1958. The English record is 13 hours 17 minutes by Hutton (see above).

Least runs career S. Clarke, the Somerset wicket-keeper, played five matches for his county in 1930, scoring no runs in each of his innings.

Most runs in an over The first batsman to score the possible of 36 runs off a six-ball over was Garfield Sobers (Nottingham) off Malcolm Andrew Nash (Glamorgan) at Swansea on 31 Aug. 1968. The ball (recovered from the last hit from the road by a small boy) resides in Nottingham's Museum.

BIGGEST SCORERS

Season The greatest number of runs ever scored in a season is 3,816 in 50 innings (8 not out) by Denis Compton (Middlesex) in 1947. His batting average was 90·85.

Most runs a career The greatest aggregate of runs in a career is 61,237 in 1,315 innings (106 not out) between 1905 and 1934 by Sir John (Jack) Berry Hobbs (1882–1963) of Surrey and England. His career average was 50·65.

Test matches The greatest number of runs scored in Test matches is 7,249 in 140 innings (16 not out) by Walter Reginald Hammond (1903–65) of Gloucestershire, playing for England between 1927 and 1947. His average was 58·45.

CENTURIES

Season The record for the greatest number of centuries in a season is also held by Compton with eighteen in 1947. With their restricted fixture list the Australian record is eight by Sir Donald George Bradman (born 27 Aug. 1908) in only 12 innings in the 1947–48 season.

Career The most centuries in a career is 197 by Sir John Hobbs between 1905 and 1934. The Australian record is Sir Donald Bradman's 117 centuries between 1927 and 1949.

Test matches The greatest number of centuries scored in Test matches is 29 by Sir Donald Bradman (Australia) between 1928 and 1948. The English record is 22 by Walter Hammond (1903–65) of Gloucestershire, between 1927 and 1947.

Highest averages The highest recorded seasonal batting average in England is 115·66 for 26 innings (2,429 runs) by Don Bradman (Australia) in England in 1938. The English record is 96·96 by Herbert Sutcliffe (born 24 Nov. 1894) of Yorkshire, for 42 innings (3,006 runs) in 1931. The world record for a complete career is 95·14 for 338

innings (28,067 runs) by Bradman between 1927 and 1949. The record for Test matches is 99·94 in 80 innings (6,996 runs) by Bradman in 1928–48. The English career record is 56·37 for 500 innings (62 not out) by Kumar Shri Ranjitsinhji (1872–1933), later H.H. the Jam Saheb of Nawanagar, with 24,692 runs between 1893 and 1920.

Double centuries The only batsman to score double centuries in both innings is Arthur E. Fagg (born 18 June 1915), who made 244 and 202 not out for Kent *v.* Essex at Colchester on 13–15 July 1938.

Longest hit The longest measured drive is one of 175 yards by Walter (later the Rev.) Fellows (1834–1901) of Christ Church, Oxford University, in a practice on their ground, off Charles Rogers in 1856. J. E. C. Moore made a measured hit of 170 yards 1 foot 5 inches at Griffith, New South Wales, Australia, in February 1930. Peter Samuel Heine (b. 28 June 1929) of the Orange Free State is said to have driven a ball bowled by Hugh Joseph Tayfield (b. 30 Jan. 1929) of Natal for approximately 180 yards at Bloemfontein on 3 Jan. 1955.

Most sixes in an innings The highest number of sixes hit in an innings is 15 by John Richard Reid, O.B.E. (born 3 June 1928), in an innings of 296, lasting 3 hours 47 minutes, for Wellington *v.* Northern Districts in the Plunket Shield Tournament at Wellington, New Zealand, on 14–15 Jan. 1963. The Test record is 10 by Walter Hammond in an innings of 336 not out for England *v.* New Zealand at Auckland on 31 March and 1 April 1933.

Most sixes in a match The highest number of sixes in a match is 17 (10 in the first and 7 in the second innings) by William James Stewart (b. 31 Aug. 1934) for Warwickshire *v.* Lancashire at Blackpool on 29–31 July 1959. His two innings were of 155 and 125.

Most boundaries in an innings The highest number of boundaries in an innings was 68 (all in fours) by Percival Albert Perrin (1876–1945) in an innings of 343 not out for Essex *v.* Derbyshire at Chesterfield on 18–19 July 1904.

Most runs off a ball The most runs scored off a single hit is 10 by Samuel Hill Hill-Wood (1872–1949) off Cuthbert James Burnup (1875–1960) in the Derbyshire *v.* M.C.C. match at Lord's, London, on 26 May 1900.

GREATEST PARTNERSHIP

World The record stand for any partnership is the fourth wicket stand of 577 by Gul Muhammad (b. 15 Oct. 1921), who scored 319, and Vijay Samuel Hazare (b. 11 March 1915) (288) in the Baroda *v.* Holkar match at Baroda, India, on 8–10 March 1947.

England The highest stand in English cricket, and the world record for a first wicket partnership, is 555 by Percy Holmes (b. 25 Nov. 1886) (224 not out) and Herbert Sutcliffe (313) for Yorkshire *v.* Essex at Leyton on 15–16 June 1932.

Highest score by a No. 11 The highest score by a No. 11 batsman is 163 by Thomas Peter Bromly Smith (1908–67) for Essex *v.* Derbyshire at Chesterfield in August 1947.

Wally Hammond, who scored 7,249 runs for England between 1927 and 1947

249

BOWLING

Most wickets The largest number of wickets ever taken in a season is 304 by Alfred Percy ("Tich") Freeman (1888–1965) of Kent, in 1928. Freeman bowled 1,976·1 overs, of which 423 were maidens, with an average of 18·05 runs per wicket. The greatest wicket-taker in history is Wilfred Rhodes (born Kirkheaton, Yorkshire 29 Oct. 1877), who took 4,187 wickets for 69,993 runs (average 16·71 runs per wicket) between 1898 and 1930.

Tests The greatest number of wickets taken in Test matches is 307 for 6,625 runs (average 21·57) by Frederick Sewards Trueman (born Scotch Springs, Yorkshire, 6 Feb. 1931), in 67 Tests between June 1952 and June 1965. The lowest bowling average in a Test career (minimum 15 wickets) is 61 wickets for 775 runs (12·70 runs per wicket) by John James Ferris (1867–1900) in 9 Tests (8 for Australia and 1 for England) between 1886 and 1892.

Fastest The highest measured speed for a ball bowled by any bowler is 93 m.p.h. by Harold Larwood (born 14 Nov. 1904) of Nottinghamshire in 1933. The fastest bowler of all time is regarded by many as Charles Jesse Kortright (1871–1952), who played for Essex from 1889 to 1907. Albert Cotter (1883–1917) of New South Wales, Australia, is reputed to have broken a stump more than 20 times. Wesley Winfield Hall (b. 12 Sept. 1937) of Barbados was timed to bowl at 91 m.p.h. in practice in 1962–63, when playing for Queensland, Australia.

Most consecutive wickets No bowler in first class cricket has yet achieved five wickets with five consecutive balls. The nearest approach was that of Charles Warrington Leonard Parker (1884–1959) (Gloucestershire) in his own benefit match against Yorkshire at Bristol on 10 Aug. 1922, when he struck the stumps with five successive balls but the second was called as a no-ball. The only man to have taken 4 wickets with consecutive balls more than once is Robert James Crisp (b. 28 May 1911) for Western Province v. Griqualand West at Johannesburg on 23–24 Dec. 1931 and against Natal at Durban on 3 March 1934.

D. V. P. Wright, who achieved 7 hat tricks (1937-1949)

Most "hat tricks" The greatest number of "hat tricks" is seven by Douglas Vivian Parson Wright (born 21 Sept. 1914) on 3 and 29 July, 1937, 18 May 1938, 13 Jan. and 1 July 1939, 11 Aug. 1947 and 1 Aug. 1949. In his own benefit match at Lord's on 22 May 1907, Albert Edwin Trott (Middlesex) took four Somerset wickets with four consecutive balls and then later in the same innings achieved a "hat trick".

Most wickets in an innings The taking of all ten wickets by a single bowler has been recorded many times but only one bowler has achieved this feat on three occasions—Alfred Percy Freeman of Kent, against Lancashire at Maidstone on 24 July 1929, against Essex at Southend on 13–14 Aug. 1930 and against Lancashire at Old Trafford on 27 May 1931. The fewest runs scored off a bowler taking all 10 wickets is 10, when Hedley Verity (1905–43) of Yorkshire dismissed (8 caught, 1 l.b.w., 1 stumped) every Nottinghamshire batsman in 118 balls at Leeds on 12 July 1932. The only bowler to have "cleaned bowled" a whole side out was John Wisden (1826–84) of Sussex, playing for the North v. the South at Lord's in 1850.

Most wickets in a match James Charles Laker (born Bradford, Yorkshire, 9 Feb. 1922) of Surrey took 19 wickets for 90 runs (9–37 and 10–53) for England v. Australia in the 4th Test at Old Trafford on 26–31 July 1956. No other bowler has taken more than 17 wickets in a first class match. Henri Arkwright (1837–66) took 18 wickets for 96 runs in 12-a-side match, M.C.C. v. Gentlemen of Kent, a Canterbury on 14–17 Aug. 1861. Alfred Percy Freema (Kent) took ten or more wickets in a match on 14 occasions between 1914 and 1936.

Most wickets in a day The greatest number of wickets taken in a day's play i 17 by Colin Blythe (1879–1917) for 48 runs, for Ken against Northamptonshire at Northampton on 1 Jun 1907; by Hedley Verity for 91 runs, for Yorkshire Essex at Leyton on 14 July 1933; and by Thoma William John Goddard (1900–66) for 106 runs, fo Gloucestershire v. Kent at Bristol on 3 July 1939.

Most expensive bowling The greatest number of runs hit off one bowler in on innings is 362, scored off Arthur Alfred Mailey (bor 3 Jan. 1888) in the New South Wales v. Victoria inter State match at Melbourne on 24–28 Dec. 1926. Th greatest number of runs ever conceded by a bowler i one match is 428 by C. S. Nayudu in the Holkar v Bombay match at Bombay on 4–9 March 1945, whe he also made the record number of 917 deliveries.

Most maidens Hugh Joseph Tayfield bowled 16 consecutive 8-bal maiden overs (137 balls without conceding a run) fo South Africa v. England at Durban on 25–27 Jan. 1957 The greatest number of consecutive 6-ball maider overs bowled is 21 (130 balls) by Ragunath G. ("Bapu") Nadkarni (born 4 April 1932) for India v. England a Madras on 12 Jan. 1964. The English record is 17 overs (105 balls) by Horace L. Hazell (born 30 Sept. 1909) fo Somerset v. Gloucestershire at Taunton on 4 June 1949, and 17 (104 balls) by Graham Anthony (Tony) Richard Lock (born 5 July 1929) of Surrey, playing for the M.C.C. v. the Governor-General's XI at Karachi, Pakistan, on 31 Dec. 1955. Alfred Shaw (1842–1907) of Nottinghamshire bowled 23 consecutive 4-ball maiden overs (92 balls) for North v. the South at Nottingham in 1876.

Most balls The greatest number of balls sent down by any bowler in one season is 12,234 (651 maidens: 298 wickets) by Alfred Percy Freeman (Kent) in 1933. The most balls bowled in an innings is 588 (98 overs) by Sonny Ramadhin (born 1 May 1930) of Trinidad, playing for the West Indies in the First Test v. England at Birmingham on 30 May and 1, 3 and 4 June 1957. He took 2 for 179.

Best average The lowest recorded bowling average for a season is one of 8·61 runs per wicket (177 wickets for 1,525 runs) by Alfred Shaw of Nottinghamshire in 1880.

FIELDING

Most catches in an innings The greatest number of catches in an innings is seven, by Michael James Stewart (born 16 Sept. 1932) for Surrey v. Northamptonshire at Northampton on 7 June 1957, and by Anthony Stephen Brown (born 24 June 1936) for Gloucestershire v. Nottinghamshire at Trent Bridge on 26 July 1966.

In a match Walter Reginald Hammond (1903–65) held a record total of 10 catches (4 in the first innings, 6 in the second) for Gloucestershire v. Surrey at Cheltenham on 16–17 Aug. 1928. The record for a wicket-keeper is 11 (see page 251).

In a season and in a career The greatest number of catches in a season is 78 by Walter Hammond (Gloucestershire) in 1928, and 77 by Michael James Stewart (Surrey) in 1957. The most catches in a career is 913 by Frank Edward Woolley (born 27 May 1887) of Kent in 1906–1938. In his own book he claims 994. The Test record is 113 by Michael Colin Cowdrey (born 24 Dec. 1932) between 1954 and 1969.

Longest throw The longest recorded throw of a cricket ball (5½ oz.) is 140 yards 2 feet (422 feet) by R. Percival on Durham Sands Racecourse on Easter Monday, 14 April 1884.

WICKET-KEEPING

innings The most dismissals by a wicket-keeper in an innings is eight (all caught) by Arthur Theodore Wallace Grout (1927–68) for Queensland against Western Australia at Brisbane on 15 Feb. 1960. The Test record is six (all caught) by A. T. W. Grout (see above) for the 1st Australia v. South Africa Test at Johannesburg on 27–28 Dec. 1957.

match The greatest number of dismissals by a wicket-keeper in a match is 12 by Edward Pooley (1838–1907) (eight caught, four stumped) for Surrey v. Sussex at the Oval on 6–7 July 1868; nine caught, three stumped by Don Tallon (b. 17 Feb. 1916) of Australia for Queensland v. New South Wales at Sydney on 2–4 Jan. 1939; and also nine caught, three stumped by Hedley Brian Taber (b. 29 April 1940) of New South Wales against South Australia at Adelaide 17–19 Dec. 1968. The record for catches is 11 (seven in the first innings and four in the second) by Arnold Long (b. 18 Dec. 1940), for Surrey v. Sussex at Hove on 18 and 21 July 1964. The Test record for dismissals is 9 (eight caught, one stumped) by Gilbert Roche Andrews Langley of South Australia, playing for Australia v. England in the 2nd Test at Lords, London, on 22–26 June 1956.

season The record number of dismissals for any wicket-keeper in a season is 127 (79 caught, 48 stumped) by Leslie Ethelbert George Ames (born 3 Dec. 1905) of Kent in 1929. The record for the number stumped is 64 by Ames in 1932. The record for catches is 96 by James Graham Binks (born 5 Oct. 1935) of Yorkshire in 1960.

career The highest total of dismissals in a wicket-keeping career is 1,468 (a record 1,215 catches, plus 253 stumpings) by Herbert Strudwick (1880–1970) of Surrey between 1902 and 1927. The most stumpings in a career is 415 by Ames (1926–1951).

least byes The best wicket-keeping record for preventing byes is that of Archdale Palmer Wickham (1855–1935) when, keeping for Somerset v. Hampshire at Taunton on 20–22 July 1899, he did not concede a single bye in a total of 672 runs. The record for Test matches is no byes in 659 runs by Godfrey Evans for England in the 2nd Test v. Australia at Sydney, New South Wales, on 14, 16, 17 and 18 Dec. 1946.

most byes The records at the other extreme are those of Philip Harman Stewart-Brown (born 30 April 1904) of Harlequins, who let through 46 byes in an Oxford University innings of only 188 on 21–23 May 1927 and 58 byes let through by Anthony William Catt of Kent in a Northamptonshire total of 374 at Northampton on 20–22 Aug. 1955.

ENGLISH COUNTY CHAMPIONSHIP

The greatest number of victories has been secured by Yorkshire, with 29 outright wins up to 1968, and one shared with Middlesex in 1949. They have never been lower than twelfth (in 1953) on the table. The most "wooden spoons" have been won by Northamptonshire, with ten since 1923. They did not win a single match between May 1935 and May 1939. The record number of consecutive title wins is 7 by Surrey from 1952 to 1958. The greatest number of consecutive appearances for one county is 421 by Joe Vine (1875–1946) of Sussex.

oldest and youngest county cricketers The youngest player to represent his county was William Wade Fitzherbert Pullen (1866–1937), for Gloucestershire against Middlesex at Lord's on 5 June 1882, when aged 15 years 11 months. The oldest regular County players have been William George Quaife (1872–1951) of Sussex and Warwickshire, who played

his last match for Warwickshire against Hampshire at Portsmouth on 27–30 Aug. 1927, when aged 55, and John Herbert King (1871–1946) of Leicestershire, who played his last match for his county against Yorkshire at Leicester on 5–7 Aug. 1925, when aged 54.

Largest crowds The greatest recorded attendance at a cricket match is 350,534 (receipts £30,124) for the Third Test between Australia and England at Melbourne on 1–7 Jan. 1937. For the whole series the figure was a record 933,513 (receipts £87,963). The greatest recorded attendance at a cricket match on one day was 90,800 on the second day of the Fifth Test between Australia and the West Indies at Melbourne on 11 Feb. 1961, when the receipts were £A13,132 (£10,484 sterling). The English record is 159,000 for the Fourth Test between England and Australia at Headingley, Leeds, on 22–27 July 1948, and the record for one day probably a capacity of 46,000 for a match between Lancashire and Yorkshire at Old Trafford on 2 Aug. 1926. The English record for a Test series is 549,650 (receipts £200,428) for the series against Australia in 1953.

Greatest receipts The world record for receipts from a match is £72,882, from the paid attendance at the Second Test between England and Australia at Lord's, London, on 20–25 June 1968.

Highest benefit The highest "benefit" ever accorded a player is £14,000 for Cyril Washbrook (born 6 Dec. 1914) in the Lancashire v. Australians match at Old Trafford on 7–10 Aug. 1948.

Most Test appearances The record number of Test appearances is 104 by Michael Colin Cowdrey (England) between 1954 and 1969. The highest number of Test captaincies is 41, including 35 consecutive games, by Peter Barker Howard May of Cambridge University and Surrey, who captained England from 1955 to 1961 and played in a total of 66 Tests. The most innings batted in Test matches is 171 in 104 Tests by Cowdrey of Kent, playing for England between 1954 and 1969. Garfield Sobers (West Indies) holds the record for consecutive Tests, with 75 from 1955 to July 1969.

Longest match The lengthiest recorded cricket match was the "timeless" Test between England and South Africa at Durban on 3–14 March 1939. It was abandoned after 10 days (8th day rained off) because the boat taking the England team home was due to leave. The lengthiest in England was the 6-day 5th England v. Australia Test on 6–12 Aug. 1930, when rain prevented play on the fifth day.

MINOR CRICKET RECORDS
(where excelling those in First Class Cricket).

Bowling Stephen Fleming bowling for Marlborough College "A" XI, New Zealand v. Bohally Intermediate at Blenheim, New Zealand in Dec. 1967 took 9 wickets in 9 consecutive balls. In February 1931 in a schools match in South Africa Paul Hugo also took 9 wickets with 9 consecutive balls for Smithfield School v. Aliwal North.

Highest individual innings In a Junior House match between Clarke's House and North Town, at Clifton College, Bristol, in June 1899, A. E. J. Collins, aged 13, scored an unprecedented 628 not out in 6 hours 50 minutes, over five afternoons' batting, carrying his bat through the innings of 836. The scorer, E. W. Pegler, gave the score as "628—plus or minus 20, shall we say".

Fastest individual scoring S. K. Coen (South Africa) scored 50 runs (11 fours and 1 six) in 7 minutes for Gezira v. the R.A.F. in 1942, compared with the First Class record of 8 minutes. Cecil George Pepper hit a century in 24 minutes in a Services match in Palestine in 1943. Cedric Ivan James Smith hit 9 successive sixes for a Middlesex XI v. Harrow and District at Rayners' Lane, Harrow, in

Colin Cowdrey (England) record holder for Test appearances and innings

The earliest days
of cross-country
running c. 1864

Sports, games and pastimes

1935. This feat was repeated by Arthur Dudley Nourse, Jr. in a South African XI *v.* Military Police match at Cairo in 1942–43. Nourse's feat included six sixes in one over.

Highest scoring rate
In the match Royal Naval College, Dartmouth *v.* Seale Hayne Agricultural College in 1923, K. A. Sellar (now Cdr. "Monkey" Sellar, D.S.O., D.S.C., R.N.) and L. K. A. Block (now Judge Block, D.S.C.) were set to score 174 runs in 105 minutes but achieved this total in 33 minutes, so averaging 5·27 runs per minute.

Lowest score
There are at least 60 recorded instances of sides being dismissed for 0. A recent instance was on 11 March 1964, when Masterton Central Primary School, New Zealand, dismissed Masterton West School for no runs in 18 balls.

Greatest stand
T. Patten and N. Rippon made a third wicket stand of 641 for Buffalo *v.* Whorouly at Gapsted, Victoria, Australia, on 19 March 1914.

Wicket-keeping
In a Repton School match for Priory *v.* Mitre, H. W. P. Middleton caught one and stumped eight batsmen in one innings on 10 July 1930.

Croquet

Earliest references
Croquet, in its present-day form, originated as a country-house lawn game, possibly in Ireland in 1852.

Most championships
The greatest number of victories in the Open Croquet Championships (instituted at Evesham, Worcestershire, 1867) is ten by John William Solomon (born 1932) (1953, 1956, 1959, 1961, 1963 to 68). He has also won the Men's Championship on 8 occasions (1951, 1953, 1958 to 60, 1962, 1964–65), the Open Doubles (with E. Patrick C. Cotter) on 10 occasions (1954 to 55, 1958 to 59, 1961 to 65 and 1969) and the Mixed Doubles once (with Mrs. N. Oddie) in 1954, making a total of 29 titles. Solomon has also won the President's Cup on 8 occasions (1955, 1957 to 59, 1962 to 64 and 1968). He has also been Champion of Champions on all three occasions since this competition was instituted in 1967.

Miss Dorothy D. Steel, fifteen times winner of the Women's Championship (1919 to 39), won the Open Croquet Championship four times (1925, 1933, 1935–36). She had also five Doubles and seven Mixed Doubles titles making a total of 31 titles.

Lowest handicap
The lowest playing handicap has been that of Humphrey O. Hicks (Devon) with minus 5½. In 1964 the limit was fixed at minus 5, which handicap is held by J. W. Solomon, E. Patrick C. Cotter, H. O. Hicks, G. N. Aspinall, and K. F. Wylie.

Largest club
The largest number of courts at any one club is eleven, at the Sussex County (Brighton) Croquet and Lawn Tennis Club.

Cross-Country Running

International championships
The earliest recorded international cross-country ra[ce] took place over 9 miles 20 yards from Ville d'Avra[y] outside Paris, on 20 March 1898, between England a[nd] France (England won by 21 points to 69). The inaugur[al] International Cross-Country Championships too[k] place at the Hamilton Park Racecourse, Glasgow, [on] 28 March 1903. The greatest margin of victory [is] 56 seconds (representing 390 yards) by Jack Holden [at] Ayr Racecourse, Scotland, on 24 March 1934. Th[e] narrowest win was that of Jean-Claude Fayol[le] (France) at Ostend, Belgium, on 20 March 1965, whe[re] the timekeepers were unable to separate his time fro[m] that of Melvyn Richard Batty (England), who w[as] placed second.

The greatest team wins have been those of Englan[d] with a minimum of 21 points (the first six runners t[o] finish) on two occasions, at Gosforth Park, Newcast[le] upon Tyne, Northumberland, on 22 March 1924, an[d] at the Hippodrome de Stockel, Brussels, Belgium, o[n] 20 March 1932.

Most wins
The greatest number of victories in the Internation[al] Cross-Country Race is four by Jack Holden (Englan[d]) in 1933–34–35 and 1939, and four by Alain Mimoun-o[-] Kacha (France) in 1949, 1952, 1954 and 1956. Englan[d] have won 40 times to 1970.

Most appearances
The runners of participating countries with the larges[t] number of international championship appearance[s] are:—

Belgium	20	M. Van de Wattyne, 1946–65
Wales	14	D. Phillips, 1922, 1924, 1926–37
England	12	J. T. Holden, 1929–39, 1946
Spain	12	A. L. Amoros, 1951–62
Scotland	11	D. McL. Wright, 1920–30
	11	J. C. Flockhart, 1933–39, 1946–49
France	11	A. Mimoun-o-Kacha, 1949–50, 1952, 1954, 1956, 1958–62, 1964

English championship
The English Cross-Country Championship was in[-] augurated at Roehampton, South London, in 1877[.] The greatest number of individual titles achieved is fou[r] by P. H. Stenning (Thames Hare and Hounds) i[n] 1877–80 and Alfred Shrubb (South London Harriers) in 1901–04. The most successful club in the team rac[e] has been Birchfield Harriers from Birmingham with 27 wins and one tie between 1880 and 1953.

Largest field
The largest recorded field was one of 1,815 starter[s] (1,020 completed the course) at Gosforth Park[,] Newcastle upon Tyne in the summer of 1916. It wa[s] staged by the Northern Command of the Army and wa[s] won by Sapper G. Barber in 35 minutes 7·2 seconds, by a margin of over 40 yards.

Curling

Origins
An early form of the sport is believed to have originated in the Netherlands about 450 years ago. The first club was formed at Kilsyth, near Glasgow, in 1510. Organized administration began in 1838 with the formation of the Royal Caledonian Curling Club, the international legislative body based in Edinburgh. The first indoor ice rink to introduce curling was at Southport in 1879.

The U.S.A. won the first Gordon International Medal series of matches, between Canada and the U.S.A., at Montreal in 1884. The first Strathcona Cup match between Canada and Scotland was won by Canada in 1903. Although demonstrated at the Winter Olympics

Jacques Anquetil—
five times winner of
the *Tour de France*

of 1924, 1932 and 1964, curling is not yet included in the official Olympic programme.

titles The most Strathcona Cup wins is seven by Canada (1903–09–12–23–38–57–65) against Scotland. The record for international team matches for the Scotch Cup and Silver Broom (instituted 1959) is ten wins by Canada, in 1959–60–61–62–63–64–66–68–69–70.

athon The longest recorded curling match is one of 30 hours and 151 ends by two Rinks from the Glasgow Young Curlers Club skipped by D. Horton and B. Methuen on 7–8 March 1970.

argest rink The world's largest curling rink is the Big Four Curling Rink, Calgary, Alberta, Canada opened in 1959 at a cost of \$Can.2,250,000 (£867,050). Each of the two floors has 24 sheets of ice, accommodating 48 teams of 192 players.

Highest speed The highest speed ever achieved on a bicycle is 127·243 m.p.h. by Jose Meiffret (born April 1913) of France, using a 275-inch gear behind a windshield on a racing car at Freiburg, West Germany, on 19 July 1962. Antonio Maspes (Italy) recorded an unofficial unpaced 10·6 secs. for 200 metres (42·21 m.p.h.) at Milan on 28 Aug. 1962.

The greatest distance ever covered in one hour is 76 miles 604 yards by Leon Vanderstuyft (Belgium) on the Montlhéry Motor Circuit, France, on 30 Sept. 1928. This was achieved from a standing start paced by a motorcycle. The 24-hour record behind pace is 860 miles 367 yards by Hubert Opperman in Australia in 1932.

Most world titles The greatest number of world titles won since the institution of the amateur championships in 1893 and the professional championships in 1895 are:—

Amateur Sprint	4	William J. Bailey (U.K.)	1909–10–11, 1913
Amateur 100 kms. Paced	7	Leon Meredith (U.K.)	1904–05, 1907–09, 1911, 1913
Amateur Road Race	2	Giuseppe Martano (Italy)	1930, 1932
	2	Gustave Schur (East Germany)	1958–59
Professional Sprint	7	Jeff Scherens (Belgium)	1932–37, 1947
	7	Antonio Maspes (Italy)	1955–56, 1959–62, 1964
Professional 100 kms. Paced	6	Guillermo Timoner (Spain)	1955, 1959–60, 1962, 1964–65
Professional Road Race	3	Alfredo Binda (Italy)	1927, 1930, 1932
	3	Rik Van Steenbergen	1949, 1956–57

Cycling

Earliest race The earliest recorded bicycle race was a velocipede race over two kilometres (1·24 miles) at the Parc de St. Cloud, Paris, on 31 May 1868, won by James Moore (G.B.).

cycling Slow bicycling records came to a virtual end in 1965 when Tsugunobu Mitsuishi, aged 39, of Tōkyō, Japan stayed stationary for 5 hours 25 minutes.

Tour de France The greatest number of wins in the Tour de France (inaugurated 1903) is five by Jacques Anquetil (born 8 Jan. 1934) of France, who won in 1957, 1961, 1962, 1963 and 1964. The closest race ever was that of 1968 when after 2,898·7 miles over the 30 days (21 June–21 July) Jan Janssen (Netherlands) (b. 1940) beat Herman van Springel (Belgium) in Paris by 38 seconds. The longest course was 3,569 miles on 20 June–18 July 1926.

Most Olympic titles Cycling has been on the Olympic programme since the revival of the Games in 1896. The greatest number of gold medals ever won is four by Marcus Hurley (U.S.A.) over the $\frac{1}{4}$, $\frac{1}{3}$, $\frac{1}{2}$ and 1 mile in 1904.

WORLD RECORDS

OPEN AIR TRACKS

MEN

Professional unpaced standing start:

Distance	hrs.	mins.	secs.	Name and nationality	Place	Date	
1 km.		1	08·6	Reginald Hargreaves Harris (U.K.)	Milan	20 Oct.	1952
5 kms.		5	51·6	Ole Ritter (Denmark)	Mexico City	4 Oct.	1968
10 kms.		11	58·4	Ole Ritter (Denmark)	Mexico City	4 Oct.	1968
20 kms.		24	17·4	Ole Ritter (Denmark)	Mexico City	4 Oct.	1968
1 hour	30·225 miles			Ole Ritter (Denmark)	Mexico City	10 Oct.	1968

Professional unpaced flying start:

Distance	hrs.	mins.	secs.	Name and nationality	Place	Date	
200 metres			10·8	Antonio Maspes (Italy)	Rome	21 July	1960
500 metres			28·8	Marino Morettini (Italy)	Milan	29 Aug.	1955
1,000 metres		1	02·6	Marino Morettini (Italy)	Milan	26 July	1961

Professional motor-paced:

Distance	hrs.	mins.	secs.	Name and nationality	Place	Date	
100 kms.	1	03	40·0	Walter Lohmann (W. Germany)	Wuppertal	24 Oct.	1955
1 hour	58 miles 737 yards			Walter Lohmann (W. Germany)	Wuppertal	24 Oct.	1955

Amateur unpaced standing start:

Distance	hrs.	mins.	secs.	Name and nationality	Place	Date	
1 km.		1	03·91	Pierre Trentin (France)	Mexico City	17 Oct.	1968
4 kms.		4	37·54	Mogens Frey (Denmark)	Mexico City	17 Oct.	1968
5 kms.		6	01·6	Mogens Frey (Denmark)	Mexico City	5 Oct.	1969
10 kms.		12	23·8	Mogens Frey (Denmark)	Mexico City	5 Oct.	1969
20 kms.		25	00·5	Mogens Frey (Denmark)	Mexico City	5 Oct.	1969
100 kms.	2	19	00·16	Ole Ritter (Denmark)	Rome	19 Sept.	1965
1 hour	29 miles 921 yards			Mogens Frey (Denmark)	Mexico City	5 Oct.	1969

Amateur unpaced flying start:

Distance	hrs.	mins.	secs.	Name and nationality	Place	Date	
200 metres			10·61	Omari Phakadze (U.S.S.R.)	Mexico City	22 Oct.	1967
500 metres			27·85	P. Trentin (France)	Mexico City	21 Oct.	1967
1,000 metres		1	01·14	L. Borghetti (Italy)	Mexico City	21 Oct.	1967

Sports, games and pastimes

CYCLIN

WOMEN

Amateur unpaced standing start:

1 km.		1 15·1	Irena Kirichenko (U.S.S.R.)	Yerevan	8 Oct. 19
3 kms.		4 01·7	R. Obdovskaya (U.S.S.R.)	Brno	20 Aug. 19
5 kms.		7 03·3	N. Sadovaya (U.S.S.R.)	Irkutsk	2 July 19
10 kms.		14 27·0	Elsy Jacobs (Luxembourg)	Milan	9 Nov. 19
20 kms.		28 58·4	Mrs. Beryl Burton, O.B.E. (U.K.)	Milan	11 Oct. 19
100 kms.	2	44 57·0	Leena Turunen (Finland)	Helsinki	8 Sept. 19
1 hour	25 miles 1,218 yards		Elsy Jacobs (Luxembourg)	Milan	9 Nov. 19

Amateur unpaced flying start:

200 metres	12·3	Lyubov Razuvayeva (U.S.S.R.)	Irkutsk	17 July 19
500 metres	32·5	Irena Kirichenko (U.S.S.R.)	Irkutsk	19
1,000 metres	1 10·6	Irena Kirichenko (U.S.S.R.)	Irkutsk	19

COVERED TRACKS

MEN

Professional unpaced standing start:

1 km.		1 08·0	Reginald Hargreaves Harris (U.K.)	Zürich	19 July 19
5 kms.		6 05·6	Ferdinand Bracke (Belgium)	Brussels	5 Dec. 19
10 kms.		12 26·8	Roger Rivière (France)	Paris	19 Oct. 19
20 kms.		25 18·0	Siegfried Adler (W. Germany)	Zürich	2 Aug. 19
1 hour	29 miles 162 yards		Siegfried Adler (W. Germany)	Zürich	2 Aug. 19

Professional unpaced flying start:

200 metres	10·99	Oscar Plattner (Switzerland)	Zürich	1 Dec. 19
500 metres	28·6	Oscar Plattner (Switzerland)	Zürich	17 Aug. 19
1,000 metres	1 01·23	Patrick Sercu (Belgium)	Antwerp	3 Feb. 19

Professional motor-paced:

100 kms.	1 23 59·8	Guillermo Timoner (Spain)	San Sebastian	12 Sept. 19
1 hour	46 miles 669 yards	Guy Solente (France)	Paris	13 Feb. 19

Amateur unpaced standing start:

1 km.	1 06·76	Patrick Sercu (Belgium)	Brussels	12 Dec. 19
5 kms.	6 06·0	Xavier Kurmann (Switzerland)	Zürich	28 Nov. 19
10 kms.	12 26·2	Xavier Kurmann (Switzerland)	Zürich	1 Dec. 19
20 kms.	25 14·6	Ole Ritter (Denmark)	Zürich	30 Oct. 19
1 hour	28 miles 575 yards	Alfred Ruegg (Switzerland)	Zürich	16 Nov. 19

Amateur unpaced flying start:

200 metres	10·72	Daniel Morelon (France)	Zürich	4 Nov. 19
500 metres	28·89	Pierre Trentin (France)	Zürich	4 Nov. 19
1,000 metres	1 04·08	Pierre Trentin (France)	Zürich	4 Nov. 19

WOMEN

Amateur unpaced standing start:

1,000 metres	1 15·5	Elizabeth Eichholz (Germany)	Berlin	4 Mar. 19

Amateur unpaced flying start:

200 metres	13·2	Karla Günther (Germany)	Berlin	7 Mar. 19
500 metres	35·0	Karla Günther (Germany)	Berlin	7 Mar. 19

Most British titles The greatest number of National individual track cycling championships secured by any one rider is 12 by A. White (1920–25), ranging from the quarter mile to 25 miles. White also shared in three one-mile tandem championships.

ROAD CYCLING RECORDS
(British) as recognized by the Road Time Trials Council (out-and-home records).

MEN

Distance	hrs. mins. secs.	Name	Course area	Date
25 miles	51 0	Alf Engers	Northallerton	30 Aug. 196
30 miles	1 47 38	Dave Whitehouse	Wetherby	7 Sept. 196
50 miles	3 46 37	Anthony Taylor	Wetherby	31 Aug. 196
100 miles	3 51 41	Martyn Roach	Wetherby	21 July 196
12 hours	281·87 miles	John Watson	Blyth, Nottinghamshire	7 Sept. 196
24 hours	507·00 miles	Roy Cromack	Cheshire	26–27 July 196

WOMEN

10 miles	22 42	Beryl Burton, O.B.E.	Worcester	30 June 196
25 miles	56 7	Beryl Burton, O.B.E.	Southend Road	22 July 196
30 miles	1 12 30	Beryl Burton, O.B.E.	St. Neots	3 May 196
50 miles	1 55 4	Beryl Burton, O.B.E.	Catterick	21 Sept. 196
100 miles	3 55 5	Beryl Burton, O.B.E.	Essex	4 Aug. 1968
12 hours	277·25 miles	Beryl Burton, O.B.E.	Wetherby	17 Sept. 196
24 hours	427·86 miles	Christine Moody	Cheshire	26–27 July 1969

254

ROAD RECORDS ASSOCIATION'S STRAIGHT-OUT DISTANCE RECORDS

Distance	days	hrs.	mins.	secs.	Name	Date
50 miles		1	39	13	Peter Smith	7 Mar. 1970
100 miles		3	28	40	Ray Booty	28 Sept. 1956
1,000 miles	2	10	40	0	Reg Randall	19–21 Aug. 1960
12 hours		276½ miles			Harry Earnshaw	4 July 1939
24 hours		475¾ miles			Ken Joy	26–27 July 1954

PLACE TO PLACE RECORDS
(British) as recognized by the Road Records Association.

	days	hrs.	mins.	secs.	Name	Date
London to Edinburgh (380 miles)		18	50	0	Cliff Smith	2 Nov. 1965
London to Bath and back (210 miles)		9	36	23	Ken Joy	14 June 1953
London to York (197 miles)		8	23	0	Harry Earnshaw	4 July 1939
London to Brighton and back (104½ miles)		4	25	33	Ken Joy	28 May 1953
Land's End to London (287 miles)		12	34	0	Robert Maitland	17 Sept. 1954
Land's End to John o' Groats (879 miles)	1	23	46	0	Richard W. E. Poole	18 June 1965

The Land's End to John o' Groats (879 miles) feminine record is 2 days 11 hours 7 minutes (average speed 14·75 m.p.h.) by Mrs. Eileen Sheridan on 9–11 June 1954. She continued to complete 1,000 miles in 3 days 1 hour.

Roller cycling The greatest recorded distance registered in a 12-hour roller team cycling test is 508 miles 330 yards by Adrian Perkin, John Pugh, Bernard Trudgill and Lindsay Wigby of the Godric C.C. at Bungay, Suffolk on 23 March 1968.

Darts

Origins The origins of darts, date from the use by archers of heavily weighted ten-inch throwing arrows for self-defence in close quarters fighting. The "dartes" were used in Ireland in the 16th century and darts was played on the *Mayflower* by the Plymouth pilgrims in 1620. Today there are an estimated 6,000,000 dart players in the British Isles—a higher participation than in any other sporting pastime. No national or international controlling organization for the game has existed which has collated records and conditions of play. The throwing distances and boards vary considerably from one locality to another.

Lowest possible scores The lowest number of darts to achieve standard scores are: 201 four darts, 301 six darts, 501 nine darts, 1,001 seventeen darts. The four and six darts "possibles" have been many times achieved, the nine darts 501 occasionally but never the seventeen darts 1,001 which would require 15 treble 20's, a treble 17 and a 50. The lowest even number which cannot be scored with three darts (ending on a double) is 162. The lowest odd number which cannot be scored with three darts (ending on a double) is 159.

Fastest match The fastest time taken for a match of three games of 301 is 2½ minutes by Jim Pike (1903–1960) at Broadcasting House, Broad Street, Birmingham, in 1952.

Fastest "round the board" The record time for going round the board in "doubles" at arm's length is 14·5 seconds by Jim Pike at the Craven Club, Newmarket, in March 1944. His match record for this feat at the nine-feet throwing distance, retrieving his own darts, is 3 minutes 30 seconds at King John's Head, Blackfriars, London, in 1937.

Million and one up The shortest recorded time to score 1,000,001 up *on one board*, under the rules of darts, is 9 hours 48 minutes 31 seconds (scoring rate of 28·32 per second) by eight players from the Sergeant's Mess of the 13th/18th Royal Hussars (Q.M.O.) at Munster, West Germany on 15 March 1969.

Marathon record The most protracted recorded darts marathon was one of 66 hours 1 minute of continuous singles maintained by the four players David Kemp and Stephen Saltmer and Peter Eade and David McGregor at Scarborough Y.M.C.A., Yorkshire on 10–13 April 1970.

Greatest crowd The largest attendance at any darts match was the 17,000 at the Agricultural Hall, Islington, London, at the finals of the 1939 *News of the World* contest.

Most titles Re-instituted in 1947, the annual *News of the World* England and Wales individual Championships consist of the best of 3 legs 501 up, "straight" start and finish on a double with an 8-feet throwing distance. The only men to win twice are Tommy Gibbons (Ivanhoe Working Men's Club) of Conisbrough, Yorkshire, in 1952 and 1958; Tom Reddington (Derbyshire) in 1955 and 1960; and Tom M. Barrett (Odco Sports Club, London) in 1964 and 1965.

Equestrian Sports—Show Jumping

Origins Evidence of horse-riding dates from an Anatolian statuette dated *c.* 1400 B.C. Pignatelli's academy of horsemanship at Naples dates from the 16th century. The earliest show-jumping was in Paris in 1886. Equestrian events have been included in the Olympic Games since 1912.

Most Olympic medals The greatest number of Olympic gold medals is four by three horsemen:— Lt. C. Ferdinand Pahud de Mortanges (Netherlands), who won the individual three-day event in 1928 and 1932 and was in the

255

winning team in 1924 and 1928; by Major (later Col.) Henri St. Cyr (Sweden), who won the individual Grand Prix de dressage event in 1952 and 1956 and who was also in the winning teams; and by Hans Winkler (Germany), who won the Grand Prix jumping in 1956 and was in the winning team of 1956, 1960 and 1964. The most team wins in the Prix des Nations is four by Germany in 1936, 1956, 1960 and 1964. The lowest score obtained by a winner was no faults, by F. Ventura (Czechoslovakia) in 1928 and by Pierre Jonqueres d'Oriola (France), the only two-time winner (1952 and 1964), in 1952.

Jumping records The official *Fédération Equestre Internationale* high jump record is 8 feet 1¼ inches by *Huasó*, ridden by Capt. A. Larraguibel Morales (Chile) at Santiago, Chile, on 5 Feb. 1949, and 27 feet 2¾ inches for long jump over water by *Amado Mío* ridden by Col. Lopez del Hierro (Spain), at Barcelona, Spain on 12 Nov. 1951. *Heatherbloom*, ridden by Dick Donnelly was reputed to have covered 37 feet in clearing an 8 feet 3 inch *puissance* jump at Richmond, Virginia, U.S.A. in 1903. *Solid Gold* cleared 36 feet 3 inches over water at the Wagga Show, New South Wales, Australia in August 1936 for an Australian record.

At Cairns, Queensland, *Golden Meade* ridden by Jack Martin cleared an unofficially measured 8 feet 6 inches on 25 July 1946. *Ben Bolt* was credited with clearing 9 feet 6 inches at the 1938 Royal Horse Show, Sydney,

since that time. The foil was the practice weapon f the short court sword from the 17th century. The ép was established in the mid-19th century and the lig sabre was introduced by the Italians in the late 19 century.

Most Olympic titles The greatest number of individual Olympic go medals won is three by Nedo Nadi (Italy) in 1912 ar 1920 (2) and Ramon Fonst (Cuba) in 1900 and 1904 (2 Nadi also won three team gold medals in 1920 makir an unprecedented total of five gold medals at or celebration. Italy has won the épée team title six time France has won the foil team title five times. Hungar has won nine sabre team titles. Aladàr Gerevic (Hungary) was in the winning sabre team in 1932–3 1948–52–56–60. Allan Jay, M.B.E. (G.B.) compete in 5 Olympics (1952–68).

Most world titles The greatest number of individual world titles won four by Christian d'Oriola (France) with the foil i 1947–49–53–54. He also won the Olympic titles in 195 and 1956. Ellen Müller-Priess (Austria) won th women's foil in 1947 and 1949 and shared it in 195 She also won the Olympic title in 1932. Italy won th men's foil teams thirteen times; Hungary the ladie foil teams eleven times; Italy the épée teams ten time and Hungary the sabre teams thirteen times.

Most A.F.A. titles The greatest number of Amateur Fencing Associatio titles have been won as follows:—

Foil	(Instituted 1898)	7	J. Emrys Lloyd	1928, 1930–33, 1937–38
Épée	(Instituted 1904)	5	R. Montgomerie	1905, 1907, 1909, 1912, 19
Sabre	(Instituted 1898)	6	Dr. R. F. Tredgold	1937, 1939, 1947–49, 1955
Foil (Ladies)	(Instituted 1907)	10	Miss Gillian M. Sheen (now Mrs. R. G. Donaldson)	1949, 1951–58, 1960

Australia. The Australian record is 8 feet 4 inches by *Flyaway* (C. Russell) in 1939 and *Golden Meade* (A. L. Payne) in 1946. The world's unofficial best for a woman is 7 feet 5½ inches by Miss B. Perry (Australia) on *Plain Bill* at Cairns, Queensland, Australia in 1940. The greatest recorded height reached bareback is 6 feet 7 inches by *Silver Wood* at Heidelberg, Victoria, Australia, on 10 Dec. 1938.

The highest British performance is 7 feet 6¼ inches by the 16·2 hands bay gelding *Swank*, ridden by Donald Beard, at Olympia, London, on 25 June 1937. On the same day, the Lady Wright (*née* Margery Avis Bullows) set the best recorded height for a British equestrienne on her liver chestnut *Jimmy Brown* at 7 feet 4 inches. These records were over the now unused sloping poles. Harvey Smith on *O'Malley* cleared 7 feet 3 inches in Toronto, Canada in 1967.

Most titles The most B.S.J.A. championships won is four by Alan Oliver (1951–54–59–69). The only horses to have won twice are *Maguire* (Lt.-Col. Nathaniel Kindersley) in 1945 and 1947, *Sheila* (Hayes) in 1949–50 and *Red Admiral* (Oliver) in 1951 and 1954. The record for the Ladies' Championship is 8 by Miss Patricia Smythe (born 22 Nov. 1928), now Mrs. Samuel Koechlin, O.B.E. (1952–53–55–57–58–59–61–62). She was on Robert Hanson's *Flanagan* in 1955, 1958 and 1962— the only three time winner.

Marathon The longest continuous period spent in the saddle is 38 hours by Joseph Roberts of the Leicester School of Equitation in the Wimbledon Common-Putney Heath area, Greater London on 15–17 May 1968.

Fencing

Origins Fencing was practised as a sport in Egypt as early as the 12th century B.C. The first governing body for fencing in Britain was the Corporation of Masters of Defence founded by Henry VIII before 1540 and fencing was practised as sport, notably in prize fights,

Fives

ETON FIVES
A handball game against the buttress of Eton Colleg Chapel was recorded in 1825, but a court existed a Lord Weymouth's School, Warminster, as early as 177 and a handball game against the church wall a Babcary, Somerset, was recorded in June 1765. Nev courts were built at Eton in 1840, the rules wer codified in 1877, rewritten laws were introduced in 193 and the laws were last drawn up in 1950.

Most titles Only one pair have won the Amateur Championshi (Kinnaird Cup) five times—Anthony Hughes and Arthur James Gordon Campbell (1958 and 1965–68) Hughes also was in the winning pair in 1963 making six titles in all.

RUGBY FIVES
As now known, this game dates from *c.* 1850 with the first inter-public school matches recorded in the early 1870s. The Oxford *v.* Cambridge contest was in-augurated in 1925 and the Rugby Fives Association was founded in the home of Dr. Cyriax, in Welbeck Street, London, on 29 Oct. 1927. The dimensions of the Standard Rugby Fives court were approved by the Association in 1931.

Most titles The greatest number of Amateur Singles Champion-ships (instituted 1932) ever won is four by John Frederick Pretlove in 1953, 1955–56 and 1958, and by Eric Marsh in 1960–61–62–63. Pretlove also holds the record for the Amateur Doubles Championship (insti-tuted 1925), being co-champion in 1952, 1954, 1956–57–58–59 and 1961. The first person to have held all eight National and Provincial titles during his playing career is David E. Gardner. To 1970 he had won 10 Scottish titles (5 singles and 5 doubles), 12 North of England titles (4 singles and 8 doubles), 6 West of England titles (2 singles and 4 doubles), the Amateur Singles in 1964 and the Amateur Doubles in 1960, 1965, 1966 and 1970.

The record for individual goal-scoring in a British home international is 6 by Joe Bambrick for Ireland v. Wales at Belfast on 1 Feb. 1930.

Career The greatest total of goals scored in a career is 1,026 by Edson Arantes do Nascimento (born Baura, Brazil 28 June 1940), known as Pelé, the Brazilian inside right from 1957 to the World Cup final on 21 June 1970. His best year was 1958 with 139 and the *milesimo* (1,000th) came in a penalty for his club Santos in the Maracaña Stadium, Rio di Janeiro on 20 Nov. 1969 when playing in his 909th first-class match.

The best season League records are 60 goals in 39 League games by William Ralph ("Dixie") Dean (born 1906) for Everton (Division 1) in 1927–28 and 66 goals in 38 games by Jim Smith for Ayr United (Scottish Division 2) in the same season. With 3 more in Cup ties and 19 in representative matches Dean's total was 82.

The greatest number of goals scored in British first-class football is 550 (410 in League matches) by James McGrory of Glasgow Celtic (1922–38). The most scored in League matches is 434, for West Bromwich Albion, Fulham, Leicester City and Shrewsbury Town, by George Arthur Rowley (born 1926) between 1946 and April 1965. Rowley also scored 32 goals in the F.A. Cup and 1 for England "B".

Football

Origins A game with some similarities termed *Tsu-chin* was played in China in the 3rd and 4th centuries B.C. The earliest clear representation of the game is an Edinburgh print dated 1672–73. It became standardized with the formation of the Football Association in England on 26 Oct. 1863. A 26-a-side game, however, existed in Florence, Italy, as early as 1530, for which rules were codified in *Discorsa Calcio* in 1580. The oldest club is Sheffield F.C., formed on 24 Oct. 1857.

HIGHEST SCORES

Teams The highest score recorded in a British first-class match is 36. This occurred in the Scottish Cup match between Arbroath and Bon Accord on 5 Sept. 1885, when Arbroath won 36–0 on their home ground. The goals were not fitted with nets.

The highest margin recorded in an international match is 17. This occurred in the England v. Australia match at Sydney on 30 June 1951, when England won 17–0. The highest in the British Isles was when England beat Ireland 13–0 at Belfast on 18 Feb. 1882. The highest score in an F.A. Cup match is 26, when Preston North End beat Hyde 26–0 at Deepdale, Preston on 15 Oct. 1887. This is also the highest score between English clubs. The biggest victory in a final tie is 6 when Bury beat Derby County 6–0 at Crystal Palace on 18 April 1903, in which year Bury did not concede a single goal in the five Cup matches.

The highest score in a Football League (Division 1) match is 12 goals when West Bromwich Albion beat Darwen 12–0 at West Bromwich on 4 March 1892; when Nottingham Forest beat Leicester Fosse by the same score at Nottingham on 21 April 1909; and when Aston Villa beat Accrington 12–2 at Villa Park on 12 March 1892.

The highest aggregate in League Football was 17 goals when Tranmere Rovers beat Oldham Athletic 13–4 in a 3rd Division (North) match at Prenton Park, Birkenhead, on Boxing Day, 1935.

Individuals The most scored by one player in a first-class match is 16 by Stains for Racing Club de Lens v. Aubry-Asturies, in Lens, France, on 13 Dec. 1942. The record for any British first-class match is 13 by John Petrie in the Arbroath v. Bon Accord Scottish Cup match in 1885 (see above). The record in League Football is 10 by Joe Payne for Luton Town v. Bristol Rovers in a 3rd Division (South) match at Luton on 13 April 1936. The English 1st Division record is 7 goals by Ted Drake for Arsenal v. Aston Villa at Birmingham on 14 Dec. 1935, and James Ross for Preston North End v. Stoke at Preston on 6 Oct. 1888. The Scottish 1st Division record is 8 goals by James McGrory for Celtic v. Dunfermline Athletic at Celtic Park, Glasgow, on 14 Jan. 1928.

The greatest goal-scorer ever, Pelé (Brazil), with a thousand goals in 909 matches.

257

Sports, games and pastimes

Fastest goals The fastest goal on record was one variously claimed to be from 13 to 4 seconds after the kick-off by Jim Fryatt of Bradford in a Fourth Division match against Tranmere Rovers at Park Avenue, Bradford on 25 April 1964. John Scarth (Gillingham) scored 3 goals in 2 minutes against Leyton Orient at Priestfield Stadium, Gillingham on 1 Nov. 1952. John McIntyre (Blackburn Rovers) scored 4 goals in 5 minutes v. Everton at Ewood Park, Blackburn, on 16 Sept. 1922. W. G. ("Billy") Richardson (West Bromwich Albion) scored 4 goals in 5 minutes against West Ham United at Upton Park on 7 Nov. 1931.

The international record is 3 goals in 3½ minutes by Willie Hall (Tottenham Hotspur) for England against Ireland on 16 Nov. 1938 at Old Trafford, Manchester.

MOST APPEARANCES
The greatest total of full international appearances by a British footballer is 106 by Bobby Charlton, O.B.E. (born Ashington, Northumberland 1937) of Manchester United. His first was in 1958 and his 106th in the World Cup in Mexico City on 14 June 1970. Pelé (see p. 257) played his 106th international for Brazil in their unique third victorious World Cup final on 21 June 1970.

England The greatest number of appearances for England secured in the International Championship is 38 by Billy Wright, C.B.E. (1946–59).

Wales The record number of appearances for Wales in the International Championship is 48 by William (Billy) Meredith (Manchester City and United) in the longest

international span of 26 years (1895–1920). This a record for any of the four home countries. Iv Allchurch, M.B.E. (born 29 Dec. 1929) of Swanse Newcastle, Cardiff City and Worcester City played (times for Wales, including 37 times against the hon countries, between 15 Nov. 1950 and Feb. 1968.

Scotland The Scottish record for International Championshi matches is 30 by Alan Morton (Queen's Park an Glasgow Rangers) from 1920 to 1932. Morton also ha a single foreign international making a total of 31 cap George Young (Glasgow Rangers) has a record tot: of 53 appearances for Scotland, of which 29 were fo International Championship matches, between 194 and 1957.

Ireland The greatest number of appearances for Ireland is 56 t Billy Bingham (Sunderland, Luton, Everton and Po Vale) of which 34 were in the International Champior ship, between 1951 and 20 Nov. 1963.

Oldest cap The oldest cap has been William Henry (Billy) Meredit (1874–1958), who played outside right for Wales v England at Highbury, London, on 15 March 1920 whe aged 45 years 8 months 15 days.

Youngest caps The world's youngest international footballer has bee G. Dorval who played for Brazil v. Argentina in 195 while still 15.

The youngest cap in the British Isles has been N Kernoghan (Belfast United) who played for Ireland v Wales in 1936 aged 17 years 80 days. It is possible however that W. K. Gibson (Cliftonville) who playec for Ireland v. Wales in 1894 at 17 was slightly younger England's youngest international was Duncan Edward: (born 1 Oct. 1936, died 21 Feb. 1958, 15 days after the Munich air crash) the Manchester United left half against Scotland at Wembley on 2 April 1955, aged 18 years 6 months. The youngest Welsh cap was John Charles (born 19 Jan. 1932) the Leeds United centre half, against Ireland at Wrexham on 8 March 1950 aged 18 years 1 month. Scotland's youngest international has been Denis Law (born 24 Feb. 1940) o Huddersfield Town, who played against Wales on 18 Oct. 1958, aged 18 years 236 days.

Longest match The world duration record was set in the Western Hemisphere club championship in Santos, Brazil, on 2–3 Aug. 1962, when Santos drew 3–3 with Penarol F.C. of Montevideo, Uruguay. The game lasted 3½ hours, from 9.30 p.m. to 1.00 a.m.

The longest British match on record was one of 3 hours 23 minutes between Stockport County and Doncaster Rovers in the second leg of the 3rd Division (North) Cup at Edgeley Park, Stockport, on 30 March 1946.

Heaviest goalkeeper The biggest goalkeeper in representative football was the England international Willie J. Foulke (1874–1916), who stood 6 feet 3 inches and weighed 22 stone 3 lb. His last games were for Bradford, by which time he was 26 stone.

TRANSFER FEES
The world's highest reported transfer fee is more than £400,000 for the Varese centre forward Pietro Anastasi signed by Juventus, of Turin, Italy on 18 May 1968. The British cash record is £166,700 for the Leicester City striker Allan Clarke (born 1947) paid by Leeds United on 24 June 1969. The overall British record is £200,000 for the West Ham United player Martin Peters (born 1944) of which £125,000 was in cash and £75,000 for the reverse transfer of Jimmy Greaves from the buying club, Tottenham Hotspur on 16 March 1970.

The British aggregate record is held by the centre forward Tony Hateley (born 1942) who in five moves from 1963 to 21 Aug. 1969 was reportedly valued at £392,500.

The late Duncan Edwards,
England's youngest-ever international

ng fee On 26 May 1961, Luis Suarez, the Barcelona inside forward, was transferred to Internazionale (Milan) for £144,000, of which Suarez himself received a record £59,000. The British record is £10,000 for John Charles (Leeds United to Juventus, Turin on 19 April 1957), for Denis Law (Manchester City to Torino, Italy on 13 June 1961) and Martin Peters (see page 258).

CROWD AND GATES
The greatest recorded crowd at any football match was 199,854 for the Brazil v. Uruguay World Cup final in the Maracaña Municipal Stadium, Rio de Janeiro, Brazil, on 16 July 1950.

The British record paid attendance is 149,547 at the Scotland v. England international at Hampden Park, Glasgow, on 17 April 1937. It is, however, probable that this total was exceeded (estimated 160,000) on the occasion of the F.A. Cup Final between Bolton Wanderers and West Ham United at Wembley Stadium on 28 April 1923, when the crowd broke in on the pitch and the start was delayed 40 minutes until the pitch was cleared. The counted admissions were 126,047. The record gross F.A. Cup receipts at Wembley, Greater London, are a reported £128,000 (excluding radio and television fees) for the final between Manchester City and Leicester City on 26 April 1969, the same figure being reported for the Chelsea v. Leeds United final on 11 April 1970.

The Scottish Cup record attendance is 146,433 when Celtic played Aberdeen at Hampden Park on 24 April 1937. The record for a first-class match between British club teams is 143,570 at the Rangers v. Hibernian match at Hampden Park, Glasgow, on 27 March 1948. The highest attendance at a friendly match is 104,000 when Glasgow Rangers played Eintracht, Frankfurt at Hampden Park in 1961.

Smallest The smallest crowd at a full home international was 7,483 for the Scotland v. Northern Ireland match of 6 May 1969 at Hampden Park. The smallest crowd at a Football League fixture was for the Stockport County v. Leicester City Match at Old Trafford, Manchester, on 7 May 1921. Stockport's own ground was under suspension and the "crowd" numbered 13.

RECEIPTS
The greatest receipts at any match were £204,805, from an attendance of 96,924 at the World Cup final between England and West Germany at the Empire Stadium, Wembley, on 30 July 1966.

The record for a British international match is £105,000 for the England v. Scotland match at Wembley on 10 May 1969 (attendance 100,000). The receipts for the Manchester United v. Benfica match at Wembley on 29 May 1968 were £118,000 (attendance 100,000).

F.A. CHALLENGE CUP
Wins The greatest number of F.A. Cup wins is 7 by Aston Villa in 1887, 1895, 1897, 1905, 1913, 1920 and 1957 (nine final appearances). The 6-time winners Newcastle United have been in the final 10 times, as have 5-time winners West Bromwich Albion. The highest scores have been 6–1 in 1890, 6–0 in 1903 and 4–3 in 1953.

The greatest number of Scottish F.A. Cup wins is 20 by Celtic in 1892, 1899, 1900, 1904, 1907–8, 1911–12, 1914, 1923, 1925, 1927, 1931, 1933, 1937, 1951, 1954, 1965, 1967 and 1969.

Youngest The youngest player in a Cup Final was Howard
player Kendall (born 22 May 1946) of Preston North End, who played against West Ham United on 2 May 1964, 20 days before his 18th birthday.

Longest The most protracted F.A. Cup tie was that between
tie Stoke City and Bury in the 3rd round with Stoke winning 3–2 in the fifth meeting after 9 hours 22 minutes

of play in January 1955. The matches were at Bury (1–1) on 8 January; Stoke on 12 January (abandoned after 22 minutes of extra time with Stoke leading 1–0); Goodison Park (3–3) on 17 January; Anfield (2–2) on 19 January; and finally at Old Trafford on 24 January.

MOST LEAGUE CHAMPIONSHIPS
The greatest number of League Championships (Division 1) is 7, by Liverpool in 1901, 1906, 1922, 1923, 1947, 1964 and 1966; by Arsenal in 1931, 1933, 1934, 1935, 1938, 1948 and 1953; by Manchester United in 1908, 1911, 1952, 1956, 1957, 1965, 1967 and by Everton in 1891, 1915, 1928, 1932, 1939, 1963 and 1970. The record number of points is 67 by Leeds United in 1969. The only F.A. Cup and League Championship "doubles" are those of Preston North End in 1889, Aston Villa in 1897 and Tottenham Hotspur in 1961. Preston won the League without losing a match and the Cup without having a goal scored against them throughout the whole competition. Glasgow Rangers have won the Scottish League Championship 33 times between 1899 and 1964 and were joint champions on another occasion. Their 76 points in the Scottish 1st Division in 1921 represents a record in any division.

WORLD CUP
The *Fédération Internationale de Football* (F.I.F.A.) was founded in Paris on 21 May 1904 and instituted the World Cup Competition in 1930, two years after the four British Isles' associations had resigned.

The only country to win three times has been Brazil in 1958, 1962 and 1970. Brazil was also third in 1938

Howard Kendall,
the youngest-ever player
in a Cup Final

and second in 1950. Antonion Carbajal (born 1923) played for Mexico in goal in the competitions of 1950–54–58–62 and 1966. The record goal scorer has been Just Fontaine (France) with 13 goals in 6 games in the 1958 competition in Sweden. The most goals scored in a final is 3 by Geoffrey Hurst (born Ashton-under-Lyne, 1941) (West Ham United) for England v. West Germany on 30 July 1966.

EUROPEAN NATIONS CUP

The European F.A. started in 1958 a tournament to be staged every 4 years. Each tournament takes 2 years to run with the semi-finals and final on the same territory. The U.S.S.R. won the first when they beat Yugoslavia 2–1 in Paris on 10 July 1960 followed by Spain (1964) and Italy (1968).

EUROPEAN CHAMPIONS CUP

The European Cup for the League champions of the respective nations was approved by F.I.F.A. on 8 May 1955 and was run by the European F.A. which came into being in the previous year. Real Madrid defeated Rheims 4–3 in the first final in 1956 and went on to win the Cup in the next 4 seasons and in 1966. They took part in all competitions, either as holders or Spanish champions up to and including 1968–69.

Glasgow Celtic became the first British club to win the Cup when they beat Inter Milan 2–1 in the National Stadium, Lisbon, Portugal, on 25 May 1967. At the same time they established the record of being the only club to win the European Cup and the two senior domestic tournaments (League and Cup) in the same season.

EUROPEAN CUP WINNERS CUP

A tournament for the national Cup winners started in 1960–1 with 10 entries. Fiorentina beat Glasgow Rangers on 4–1 aggregate in a two-leg final in May 1961. Tottenham Hotspur were the first British club to win the trophy, beating Atletico Madrid 5–1 in Rotterdam on 15 May 1963 and were followed by West Ham United in 1965 and Manchester City on 29 April 1970.

FOOTBALL (Amateur)

Most Olympic wins The only countries to have won the Olympic football title twice are the United Kingdom (1908 and 1912); Uruguay (1924 and 1928) and Hungary (1952 and 1964). The United Kingdom also won the unofficial tournament in 1900. The highest Olympic score is Denmark 17 v. France "A" 1 in 1908.

Highest scores The highest score in a home Amateur International is 11 goals in the England v. Scotland match (8–3) at Dulwich on 11 March 1939. The foreign record was when England beat France 15–0 in Paris on 1 Nov. 1906.

The highest score in an F.A. Amateur Cup Final is 8, when Northern Nomads beat Stockton 7–1 at Sunderland in 1926, and when Dulwich Hamlet beat Marine (Liverpool) by the same score at Upton Park in 1932.

Individual The highest individual scores in amateur internationals are 6 by W. O. Jordan for England v. France (12–0) at Park Royal, London, on 23 March 1908; 6 by Vivian J. Woodward for England v. Holland (9–1) at Stamford Bridge, London, on 11 Dec. 1909; and 6 also by Harold A. Walden for Great Britain v. Hungary in Stockholm, Sweden, on 1 July 1912.

Most caps The record number of England amateur caps is 51 by Mike Pinner of Hendon, the former Pegasus goalkeeper who played for England between 1955 and 1963, when he became a professional with Leyton Orient.

F.A. Amateur Cup wins The greatest number of F.A. Amateur Cup (instituted 1893) wins is 10 by Bishop Auckland who won in 1896, 1900, 1914, 1921–22, 1935, 1939, 1955, 1956 and 1957.

Largest crowd The highest attendance at an amateur match is 100,00 at the Cup Final between Pegasus and Bishop Auckland at Wembley on 21 April 1951. The amateur gate record is £29,305 at the final between Bishop Auckland and Hendon on 16 April 1955.

Heading The highest recorded number of repetitions for heading a ball is 3,412 in 34 minutes 8 seconds by Colin Jones aged 15, at Queensferry, near Chester, on 8 March 1961.

Least successful goalkeeper The goalkeeper of the Victoria Boys' and Girls' Club Intermediate "B" team in the 1967–68 season in the Association for the Jewish Youth League Under 16 Division 2 in London, England, let through 252 goals in the 12 league matches, an average of better (or worse) than 21 per match.

Highest score In the match between Eastbourne United v. St. Mary's Youth Club in Sussex, England on 18 Jan. 1970 Eastbourne won 49–3 with one of their players scoring 10 goals and their goalkeeper contributing seven.

Most indisciplined In the local Cup match between Tongham Youth Club, Surrey and Hawley, Hampshire, England on 3 Nov. 1969 the referee booked all 22 players including one who went to hospital, and one of the linesmen. The match, won by Tongham 2–0, was described by a player as "A good, hard game".

Longest marathon games The longest recorded 11-a-side football match played under F.A. rules has been one of 15 hours with 10-minute breaks after each completed hours' play between Court Mercia (42 goals) and Tuffley Youth (39 goals) at Dowty Rotol Sports Ground, Gloucester, England on 9 May 1970. One substitute per side was permitted in the event of injury.

The longest recorded 5-a-side games recorded have been outdoors: 25 hours by two teams (no substitutes) from Nuneaton Boys' Club, Warwickshire on 2–3 May 1970. and indoors: 30 hours by two teams in the New University of Ulster gymnasium, Coleraine, Co. Londonderry, Northern Ireland on 28 April 1970.

Table football The most protracted game of 4-a-side table football on record was one of 157 hours maintained by 6 students from Acton Brunel reported in March 1970.

Football—Australian Rules

Origins The game evolved among the Irish diggers in the Ballarat goldfields in the 1840s and the rules were first formulated on 7 Aug. 1858 after a schools match in Melbourne umpired by Thomas W. Wills.

Most league premierships Since the Victorian Football League's inception in 1897 the greatest number of these league premierships has been won by Collingwood with 13 (1902–03–10–17–19–27–28–29–30–35–36–53 and 1958). Essendon won in 1897, 1901–11–12–23–24–42–46–49–50–62–65 and Melbourne in 1900–26–39–40–41–48–55–56–57–59–60–64. The record for successive league premierships is 10 by Fremantle in the West Australian League from 1887 to 1896.

Most Carnival wins Of the 16 triennial Carnival Matches played (instituted 1908) Victoria has won all but those in 1911, 1921 and 1961.

Highest team scores The highest recorded score occurred when Port Melbourne beat Sandringham 287 to 51, scoring 43 goals and 29 behinds against 7 goals and 9 behinds, in an Association match on 30 Aug. 1941.

Lowest The lowest score in senior competition occurred in August 1962, when Liverpool failed to score against St. George (122 points) at Rosedale Oval in the Sydney competition.

Highest Individual score The most goals scored in a match is 28 by Bill Wood of South Sydney against Sydney on 21 Aug. 1943. The record for a season is 188 goals by Ron Todd of Williamstown in 1945. W. Pearson of the Melbourne Amateur F.A. kicked 220 goals in 1934. Ken Farmer kicked 1,419 goals between 1929 and 1941 for a career record. In junior competition Kim Albiston, aged 15, kicked 40 goals and 8 behinds for Doncaster Youth Club against Vermont Under-15's in Melbourne on 13 May 1967. The score was 473 to nil.

Highest attendance The attendance record is 118,828 for the Grand Final between Carlton and Essendon at Melbourne Cricket Ground in 1968.

Brownlow Medal The Victorian League's Brownlow Medal (instituted 1924) has been won three times by three players—Haydn Bunton of Fitzroy (1931–32–35), R. "Dick" Reynolds (1934–37–38), who played a League record of 320 games for Essendon and Bob Skilton (1959–63–68).

Herald Trophy The Herald Trophy (instituted 1944) has been won three times by Bill Hutchinson (Essendon), in 1948 (shared), 1952 and 1953, and by R. Skilton (South Melbourne) in 1959, 1962 and 1963.

Kicking records

Place	107 yds. 2 ft. (practice)	A. Thurgood (Essendon) at East Melbourne, June 1899
	93 yds. (with wind)	D. McNamara at Melbourne, 19 May 1923
	91 yds. 1 ft.	F. Cooper at Fremantle, June 1895
Punt	91 yds. (with wind)	R. Kercheval (U.S.A.) at Chicago, Illinois, 1935
	87 yds.	S. Francis (U.S.A.) at Stanford, California, 30 Dec. 1936
Drop	84 yds.	P. Vinar (Geelong), 1965

Football—Gaelic

Earliest references The game developed from inter-parish "free for all" with no time-limit, no defined playing area nor specific rules. The formation of the Gaelic Athletic Association was in Thurles, Ireland, on 1 Nov. 1884.

Most titles The greatest number of All-Ireland Championships ever won by one team is 20 by Ciarraidhe (Kerry) between 1903 and 1962. The greatest number of successive wins is four by Wexford (1915–18) and four by Kerry (1929–32).

Highest scores The highest score in an All-Ireland final was when Cork (6 goals*, 6 points) beat Antrim (1 goal, 2 points) in 1911. The highest combined score was when Galway (2 goals, 13 points) beat Cork (3 goals, 7 points) in 1956.

Lowest scores In four All-Ireland finals the combined totals have been 7 points: 1893 Wexford (1 goal [till 1894 worth 5 points], 1 point) v. Cork (1 point); 1895 Tipperary (4 points) v. Meath (3 points); 1904 Kerry (5 points) v. Dublin (2 points); 1924 Kerry (4 points) v. Dublin (3 points).

Most appearances The most appearances in All-Ireland finals is ten by Dan O'Keeffe (Kerry) of which seven (a record) were on the winning side.

Individual score The highest recorded individual score in an All-Ireland final has been 2 goals, 5 points by Frank Stockwell (Galway) in the match against Cork in 1956.

Largest crowd The record crowd is 90,556 for the Down v. Offaly final at Croke Park, Dublin, in 1961.

Inter-provincials The province of Leinster has won most championships (Railway Cup) with 17 between 1928 and 1962. Kevin Heffernan (Dublin and Leinster) holds a record 7 medals (1952–1962).

A goal equals 3 points.

Football—Rugby League

Origins The Rugby League was formed originally in 1895 as "The Northern Rugby Football Union" by the secession of 22 clubs in Lancashire and Yorkshire from the parent Rugby Union. Though payment for loss of working time was a major cause of the breakaway the "Northern Union" did not itself embrace full professionalism until 1898. A reduction in the number of players per team from 15 to 13 took place in 1906 and the present title of "Rugby League" was adopted in 1922.

Most wins Under the one-league Championship system (1907–1962 and 1965–70) the club with the most wins was Wigan with nine (1909, 1922, 1926, 1934, 1946, 1947, 1950, 1952 and 1960).

In the Rugby League Challenge Cup (inaugurated 1896–97) the club with the most wins is Leeds with 8 in 1910–23–32–36, 1941–42 (wartime), 1957 and 1968. Oldham is the only club to appear in four consecutive Cup Finals (1924–27) and Bradford Northern is the only football club (Rugby League or Association) to have appeared at Wembley in three consecutive years (1947–48–49).

Only three clubs have won all four major Rugby League trophies (Challenge Cup, League Championship, County Cup and County League) in one season: Hunslet in 1907–08, Huddersfield in 1914–15 and Swinton in 1927–28.

In addition to the three "All Four Cup clubs", on only five other occasions has a club taken the Cup and League honours in one season: Broughton Rangers (1902); Halifax (1903); Huddersfield (1913); Warrington 1954); and St. Helens (1966).

Highest scores The highest aggregate scores in international Rugby League football are:

Match	Points	Score
Great Britain v. Australia (Test Matches)	62	Australia won 50–12 (Swinton, 9 Nov. 1963)
Great Britain v. New Zealand (Test Matches)	72	Great Britain won 52–20 (Wellington, 30 July 1910)
Great Britain v. France (Test Matches)	65	Great Britain won 50–15 (Leeds, 14 March 1959)
England v. Wales	63	England won 40–23 (Leeds, 18 Oct. 1969)
England v. France	55	France won 42–13 (Marseille, 25 Nov. 1951)
England v. Other Nationalities	61	England won 34–27 (Workington, 30 March 1933)
Wales v. France	50	France won 29–21 (Bordeaux, 23 Nov. 1947)
Wales v. Other Nationalities	48	Other Nationalities won 27–21 (Swansea, 31 March 1951)
Australia v. Great Britain	76	Australia won 63–13 (Paris, 31 Dec. 1933)
Australia v. Wales	70	Australia won 51–19 (Wembley, 30 Dec. 1933)
Australia v. France (Test Matches)	62	Australia won 56–6 (Brisbane, 2 July 1960)
Australia v. New Zealand (Test Matches)	74	New Zealand won 49–25 (Brisbane, 28 June 1952)
New Zealand v. France (Test Matches)	53	France won 31–22 (Lyon, 15 Jan. 1956)

Sports, games and pastimes

World Cup The record aggregate score in a World Cup match is 60 points, when Great Britain beat The Rest by 33 points to 27 at Bradford on 10 Oct. 1960.

There have been four World Cup Competitions. Great Britain were winners in 1954 and 1960, and Australia in 1957 and 1968.

Senior match The highest aggregate score in Cup or League football, in a game where a senior club has been concerned, was 121 points, when Huddersfield beat Swinton Park Rangers by 119 points (19 goals, 27 tries) to 2 points (one goal) in the first round of the Northern Union Cup on 28 Feb. 1914.

Cup Final The record aggregate in a Cup Final is 43 points, when Wigan beat Hull 30–13 at Wembley on 9 May 1959, and when Wakefield Trinity beat Hull 38–5 at Wembley on 14 May 1960.

The greatest winning margin was 34 points when Huddersfield beat St. Helens 37–3 at Oldham on 1 May 1915.

Touring teams The record score for a British team touring the Commonwealth is 101 points by England v. South Australia (nil) at Adelaide in May 1914.

The record for a Commonwealth touring team in Britain is 92 points (10 goals, 24 tries) by Australia against Bramley's 7 points (2 goals, one try) at the Barley Mow Ground, Bramley, near Leeds, on 9 Nov. 1921.

Record crowds and receipts The greatest attendance at any Rugby League match is 102,569 for the Warrington v. Halifax Cup Final replay at Odsal Stadium, Bradford, on 5 May 1954.

The highest receipts for a match in the United Kingdom have been £90,000 for the Castleford v. Wigan R.L. Cup Final at Wembley Stadium, Greater London on 9 May 1970.

Most international caps Test Matches between Great Britain and Australia are regarded as the highest distinction for a R.L. player in either hemisphere and Jim Sullivan, the Wigan full-back and captain, holds a Test record for a British player with 15 appearances in these games between 1924 an 1933, though Mick Sullivan (no kin) of Huddersfiel Wigan, St. Helens and York, played in 16 G.B. Australia games in 1954–1964, of which 13 were Tes and 3 World Cup matches.

In all Tests, including those against New Zealand an France, Mick Sullivan made the record number of 4 appearances and scored 43 tries.

Most Cup Finals Two players have appeared in seven Cup Finals: Ala Edwards (Salford, Dewsbury and Bradford Northern between 1938 and 1949, and Eric Batten (Leed Bradford Northern and Featherstone Rovers) betwee 1941 and 1952.

Eric Ashton, M.B.E., Wigan and Great Britain centr has the distinction of captaining Wigan at Wembley i six R.L. Cup Finals in nine years 1958–1966, taking th trophy three times (1958, 1959 and 1965).

The youngest player in a Cup Final was Reg Lloy (Keighley) who was 17 years 8 months when he playec at Wembley on 8 May 1937.

Most goals The record number of goals in a season is 224 b Bernard Ganley (Oldham) in the 1957–58 Season. Hi total was made up of 219 in League, Cup and repre sentative games and five in a "friendly" fixture.

MOST TRIES

Season Albert Aaron Rosenfeld (Huddersfield), an Australian born wing-threequarter, scored 80 tries in the 1913–14 Season.

Career Brian Bevan, an Australian-born wing-threequarter. scored 834 tries in League, Cup, representative or charity games in the 18 seasons (16 with Warrington. 2 with Blackpool Borough) from 1946 to 1964.

MOST POINTS

Cup C. H. ("Tich") West of Hull Kingston Rovers scored 53 points (10 goals and 11 tries) in a 1st Round Challenge Cup-tie v. Brookland Rovers on 4 March 1905.

League Lionel Cooper of Huddersfield scored 10 tries and kicked two goals against Keighley on 17 Nov. 1951.

Season B. Lewis Jones (Leeds) is the only player to have scored over 500 points in a season, with 505 (197 goals and 37 tries) in 1956–57. The record number of points in a single season by a team is 1,269 by Huddersfield (1914–15) and Wigan (1949–50).

Career Jim Sullivan (Wigan) scored 6,192 points (2,955 goals and 94 tries) in a senior Rugby League career extending from 1921 to 1946.

Record transfer fees The highest R.L. transfer fee is the reputed £15,000 deal which took Colin Dixon, the Halifax forward, to Salford on 19 Dec. 1968. Halifax were stated to have received £12,000 in cash and the winger M. Kelly, who was valued at £3,000.

Longest kick The longest recorded place kick was one of 80 yards by H. H. (Dally) Messenger for Australia v. Hull in Hull, Yorkshire in 1908.

Australian Premiership The St. George (Sydney) R.L. club won the Sydney Premiership (club championship) in September 1966 for the eleventh successive season.

Football—Rugby Union

The game is traditionally said to have originated from a breach of the rules of the football played in November 1823 at Rugby School by William Webb Ellis (later the Rev.) (c. 1807–72). This handling code of football

Jim Sullivan,
Rugby League's
top scorer

FOOTBALL—RUGBY UNION

evolved gradually but the Rugby Football Union was not founded until 1871.

MOST CAPPED PLAYERS
The totals below are limited to matches between the seven member countries of the "International Rugby Football Board" and France. Michel Crauste (born 7 July 1934) of France has appeared in 62 internationals of all kinds since 1958.

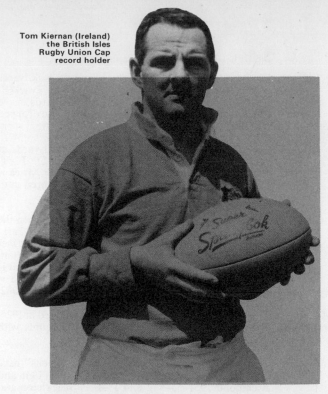

Tom Kiernan (Ireland)
the British Isles
Rugby Union Cap
record holder

Ireland	48	Thomas J. Kiernan	1960–70
Wales	44	Kenneth J. Jones, M.B.E.	1947–57
France	43	Michel Crauste, L.d'H.	1958–66
New Zealand	42	Colin E. Meads	1957–67
Scotland	40	Hugh F. McLeod, O.B.E.	1954–62
	40	David M. D. Rollo	1959–68
Australia	37	John E. Thornett, M.B.E.	To 1967
England	34	Derek Prior Rogers	1961–69
South Africa	33	John Gainsford	1960–67

HIGHEST SCORES
The highest aggregate for any match played under the auspices of the International Board since 1905, when modern scoring values came in, is 55 points when Wales beat England by 34 points to 21 at Cardiff in 1967. It has to be noted, however, that in 1881 England beat Wales by 7 goals, 1 drop goal and 6 tries to nil, which would amount in modern terms to a score of 56 points.

The highest score by any Overseas side in an international in the British Isles was when South Africa beat Scotland by 44 points to 0 at Murrayfield on 24 Nov. 1951.

The highest score in any full international was when France beat Romania by 59 points (7 goals, 6 tries and 2 penalty goals) to 3 in the Olympic Games at Colombes, Paris, on 24 May 1924. Fiji scored 113 points to 3 versus British Solomon Islands and 113 points to 13 versus New Caledonia at the 1969 South Pacific Games at Port Moresby.

The highest score in the "International Championship", in which France (which is not a member of the International Board) takes part, was when Wales beat France by 49 points to 14 at Swansea in 1910. The greatest winning margin in the "International Championship" was 42 points when Wales beat France by 47 points to 5 in Paris in 1909.

Ian S. Smith (Scotland) has scored most consecutive tries in international matches with 6; 3 in the second half of Scotland v. France in 1925 and 3 in the first half against Wales two weeks later.

Tour match The record score for any international tour match is 103–0 (17 goals, 5 tries and 1 penalty goal) when New Zealand beat Northern New South Wales at Quirindi, Australia, on 30 May 1962. Rod Heeps scored 8 tries (24 points) and Don B. Clarke kicked 10 conversions and the penalty goal (23 points).

George Nepia, the Maori full back, played in all 30 of New Zealand's (All Blacks) tour matches of 1924–25 in the British Isles.

Schools Scores of over 100 points have been recorded in club matches, for example Radford School beat Hills Court by 31 goals and 7 tries (in modern values 176 points) to nil on 20 Nov. 1886.

Individual The highest individual points score in any match between members of the International Board is 24 by Fergie McCormick—1 drop goal, 3 conversions and 5 penalty goals for New Zealand against Wales at Auckland on 14 June 1969.

In a match between Blundell's and Newton College at Tiverton, Devonshire on 17 Nov. 1900, P. J. Newby Vincent (died 11 April 1965) in a 146–0 win scored 6 tries and converted 25 (68 points).

SCORING RECORDS—AGGREGATE and MARGIN of VICTORY in the ten annual internationals in the "International Championship" (since modern scoring values came in in 1905).

Match	Pts.	Record aggregate	Pts.	Record margin
1. England v. Scotland	47	Scotland won 28–19 in 1931	19	England won by 19–0 in 1924 and 24–5 in 1947
2. England v. Wales	55	Wales won 34–21 in 1967	22	Wales won by 22–0 in 1907 and by 28–6 in 1922
3. England v. Ireland	50	England won 36–14 in 1938	22	England won by 36–14 in 1938 and Ireland by 22–0 in 1947
4. England v. France	54	England won 41–13 in 1907	37	England won by 37–0 in 1911
5. Scotland v. Wales	45	Scotland won 35–10 in 1924	25	Scotland won by 35–10 in 1924
6. Scotland v. Ireland	46	Scotland won 29–17 in 1913	21	Ireland won by 21–0 in 1950
7. Scotland v. France	34	Scotland won 31–3 in 1912	28	Scotland won by 31–3 in 1912
8. Wales v. Ireland	32	Wales won 28–4 in 1920	29	Wales won by 29–0 in 1907
9. Wales v. France	63	Wales won 49–14 in 1910	42	Wales won by 47–5 in 1909
10. Ireland v. France	33	France won 27–6 in 1964	24	Ireland won by 24–0 in 1913

Sports, games and pastimes

Longest kicks The longest recorded successful drop-goal is 90 yards by G. Brand for South Africa v. England at Twickenham, London, in 1932. This was taken 7 yards inside the England "half" 55 yards from the posts and dropped over the dead ball line.

The place kick record is reputed to be 100 yards at Richmond Athletic Ground, Surrey, by D. F. T. Morkell in an unsuccessful penalty for South Africa v. Surrey on 19 Dec. 1906. This was not measured until 1932.

Greatest crowd A crowd of 95,000 has twice been reported: when the British Lions beat South Africa 23–22 at Ellis Park, Johannesburg, on 6 Aug. 1955, and when France met Romania at Bucharest on 19 May 1957, as a curtain raiser for an Association match. The British record is over 76,000 for the Calcutta Cup match (England v. Scotland) at Murrayfield, Edinburgh, on 17 March 1962.

Middlesex Seven-a-Sides The Middlesex Seven-a-Sides were inaugurated in 1926. The most successful side has been Harlequins with 7 wins (1926–27–28–29–33–35–67).

The only players to be in five winning "sevens" have been N. M. Hall (St. Mary's Hospital 1944–1946 and Richmond 1951–53–55), and J. A. P. Shackleton and L. H. P. Laughland both of London Scottish (1960–61–62–63–65).

Fox Hunting

EARLIEST REFERENCES
Hunting the fox in Britain dates only from the middle of the 17th century. Prior to that time hunting was confined principally to the deer or the hare with the fox being hunted only by mistake. It is now estimated that huntsmen account for 10,000 of the 50,000 foxes killed each year.

OLDEST PACK
The oldest pack of foxhounds in existence in England is the Sinnington (1680), but the old Charlton Hunt in Sussex, now extinct, the Mid-Devon and the Duke of Buckingham in the Bilsdale country, Yorkshire, hunted foxes prior to that time.

LARGEST PACK
The pack with the greatest number of hounds has been the Duke of Beaufort's hounds maintained at Badminton, Gloucestershire, since c. 1780. At times hunting eight times a week, this pack had 120 couples.

LONGEST HUNTS
The longest recorded hunt was one led by Squire Sandys which ran from Holmbank, northern Lancashire, to Ulpha, Cumberland, a total of nearly 80 miles in reputedly only six hours, in January or February 1743. The longest hunt in Ireland is probably a run of 24 miles made by the Scarteen Hunt, County Limerick, from Pallas, to Knockoura in 1914. The longest duration hunt was one of 10 hours 5 minutes by the Charlton Hunt of Sussex, which ran from East Dean Wood at 7.45 a.m. to kill over 24½ miles away at 5.50 p.m. on 26 Jan. 1736.

LARGEST FOX
The largest fox ever killed by a hunt in England was a 23¾ lb. dog on Cross Fell, Cumberland, by an Ullswater Hunt in 1936. A fox weighing 28 lb. 2 oz. measuring 54 inches from nose to tail was shot on the Staffordshire-Worcestershire border on 11 March 1956.

BEAGLING
The oldest beagle hunt is the Royal Rock Beagle Hunt, Wirral, Cheshire, whose first outing was on 28 March 1845. The Newcastle and District Beagles claim their origin from the municipally-supported Newcastle Harriers existing in 1787. The Royal Agricultural College beagle pack killed 75½ brace of hares in the 1966–67 season.

Gambling

World's biggest lottery prize The world's biggest lottery is Spain's *Loteria de Navidad* (Christmas Lottery) drawn annually on 22 December. Ticket sales reach more than £60 million and the distribution of 85,000 prizes worth more than £25 million including *El Gordo* (the fat one) worth about £410,000 for a full £66 ticket.

BINGO
Origins Bingo is a lottery game which, as keno, was developed in the 1880s from lotto, whose origin is thought to be the 17th century Italian game *tumbule*. It has long been known in the British Army (called Housey-Housey) and the Royal Navy (called Tombola). The winner was the first to complete a random selection of numbers from 1–90. The U.S.A. version called Bingo differs in that the selection is from 1–75. With the introduction of the Betting and Gaming Act on 1 Jan. 1961, large scale Bingo sessions were introduced in Britain by Mecca Ltd., which played to more than 250,000 entrants in an average week during the summer of 1962.

Largest house The largest "house" in Bingo sessions was staged at the Empire Pool, Wembley, Greater London, on 25 April 1965 when 10,000 attended.

Largest prize Prizes have been controlled since 1 July 1970 by the Betting and Gaming Act 1968. Prior to limitation, prizes in linked games between more than 50 clubs reached £16,000. The largest in a single game was £5,000 won in the Mecca National Rally at the Empire Pool, Wembley on 29 March 1970.

Longest session A session of 60 hours (two callers) was held at St. Mark's Church Hall, London W.1 on 1–3 April 1970.

FOOTBALL POOLS
The winning dividend paid out by Littlewoods Pools Ltd. in their first week in February 1923 was £2 12s. 0d. In April 1937 a record £30,780 was paid to R. Levy of London on 4 away wins, and in April 1947 a record £64,450 for a 1d. points pool.

Progressive list of individual record winnings

Amount	Recipient	Date
£75,000	P. C. Frank H. Chivers, 54, Aldershot, Hampshire	6 April 1948
£91,832	George A. Borrett, Huyton, Lancashire	26 Sept. 1950
£94,335	Thomas A. Wood, 42, Carlisle	10 Oct. 1950
£104,990	Mrs. Evelyn Knowlson, 43, Manchester	7 Nov. 1950
£75,000 (limit)	(45 limit winners)	from 20 Nov. 1951 to 10 Sept. 1957
£205,235	Mrs. Nellie McGrail (now Mrs. Albert Cooper), 37, of Reddish, Cheshire	5 Nov. 1957
£206,028	W. John Brockwell, 29, Epsom, Surrey	18 Feb. 1958
£209,079	Tom Riley, 58, of Horden, Co. Durham	1 April 1958
£209,837	Ronald Smith of Liverpool	23 Dec. 1958
£260,104	John Dunn, 45, of Chelsea, London	27 Oct. 1959
£265,352	Arther Webb, 70, of Scarborough, Yorkshire	24 Nov. 1959
£301,739 9s.	Lawrence Freedman, 54, of Willesden, London	8 Dec. 1964
£338,356 16s.	Percy Harrison, 52, of East Stockwith, Lincolnshire	30 Aug. 1966

The odds for selecting 8 draws (if there are 8 draws) from 54 matches for an all-correct line are 1,040,465,789 to 1 against.

Shared winnings

The largest first dividend ever paid was one of £458,270, paid by Littlewoods and shared between 4,722 people on 1 March 1966. The most paid on one coupon for a first dividend is £331,196 received by Percy Harrison (see page 264).

HORSE RACING

Highest odds

The highest recorded odds secured by a backer were 30,319 to 1, taken at Ascot on 15 June 1951 by Mr. Pratley of Coventry, Warwickshire, on a 1s. stake each-way accumulator which built up to £3,032. His wins were on *Guerrier, Val d'Assa, Pun* and *Donore*. The highest odds in Irish tote history were £184 7s. 6d. on a 2s. 6d. stake, *viz.* 1,475 to 1 on *Hillhead VI* at Baldoyle on 31 Jan. 1970. The greatest odds payable on a fixed wager is the Tote Jackpot (6 winners) at over 250,000 to 1. The world record odds on a "double" are 24,741 to 1 secured by Mr. Montague Harry Parker of Windsor, England, for a £1 each-way "double" on *Ivernia* and *Golden Sparkle*.

Most complicated bet

The most complicated bet is the Harlequin, a compound wager on 4 horses with 2,028 possible ways of winning. It was invented by Monty H. Preston of London who is reputed to be the fastest settler of bets in the world. He once completed 3,000 bets in a 4½-hour test.

Largest bookmaker

The world's largest bookmaker is William Hill with an estimated annual turnover reaching £65,000,000. The largest chain of Betting Shops is Ladbroke's with 480 shops in the United Kingdom.

Topmost tipster

The only recorded instance of a racing correspondent forecasting 8 out of 8 winners on a race card was at Taunton, Somerset, on 15 April 1969 by Tom Cosgrove of the London *Evening News*.

The Casino at Monte Carlo, Monaco

ROULETTE

The longest run on an ungaffed (*i.e.* true) wheel recorded is 28 coups at Monte Carlo, Monaco for which the probability is 1 in 268,435,456. A run of 32 might be expected every 50 years from 1,000 true wheels spun 250 times a day.

Greatest pay out

The greatest pay out on a single bet is believed to be £62,500 by William Hill's to the Hon. Raymond Guest, U.S. Ambassador to Ireland, on 29 May 1968 for a £500 each-way bet at 100-1 placed on his Sir Ivor in September 1967 for the 1968 Derby.

Gliding

The earliest man-carrying glider was designed by Sir George Cayley (1773–1857) and carried his coachman (possibly John Appleby) about 500 yards across a valley near Brompton Hall, Yorkshire, in the summer of 1853. Gliders now attain speeds of 145 m.p.h. and the Jastrzab aerobatic sailplane is designed to withstand vertical dives at up to 280 m.p.h.

Highest

A Gold C with three diamonds (for goal flight, distance and height) is the highest standard in gliding. This has been gained by eleven British pilots up to August 1969.

Most titles

The British national championship (instituted 1939) has been won most often by Philip A. Wills (born 26 May 1907), in 1948–49–50 and 1955. The first woman to win this title was Mrs. Anne Burns of Farnham, Surrey on 30 May 1966.

Rear-Admiral H. C. N. Goodhart

SELECTED WORLD RECORDS

Distance	647·16 miles	A. H. Parker (U.S.A.) in a Sisu-1A, on 31 July 1964.
Declared Goal Flight	605 miles	W. A. Scott (U.S.A.) in an ASW-12 on 8 Aug. 1969
Absolute Altitude	46,266 feet	Paul F. Bikle, Jr. (U.S.A.) in a Schweizer SGS-123E, over Mojave, California (released at 3,963 feet) on 25 Feb. 1961 (also record altitude gain—42,303 feet)
Goal and Return	487 miles	Robert R. Clifford (South Africa) in a Libelle 15R on 1 Jan. 1969
Speed over Triangular Course		
100 km.	85·93 m.p.h.	H. M. Linke (Germany) in a Libelle in U.S.A. on 30 July 1967
300 km.	74·48 m.p.h.	A. Roehm (Germany) in a BS-1 on 4 June 1967
500 km.	85·25 m.p.h.	M. Jackson (South Africa) in a BJ-3 in South Africa on 28 Dec. 1967

BRITISH NATIONAL RECORDS[1]

Single-seater		
460·5 miles	P. D. Lane, in a Skylark 3F, Geilenkirchen to Hiersac, Germany on 1 June 1962	
360 miles	Rear-Ad. H. C. N. Goodhart, R.N., in a Skylark 3, Lasham, Hants. to Portmoak, Scotland on 10 May 1959	
37,050 feet	Rear-Ad. H. C. N. Goodhart, R.N., in a Schweizer 1-23, at Bishop, California, U.S.A. on 12 May 1955	
374 miles	Alfred H. Warminger, in a Standard Austria, South Africa on 13 Jan. 1966	
73·9 m.p.h.	Edward Pearson in a Cirrus in Rhodesia on 10 Oct. 1969	
62·0 m.p.h.[2]	Edward Pearson in a Cirrus in South Africa on 3 Jan. 1969	
64·20 m.p.h.[3]	Anne Burns, in a Standard Austria, at Kimberley, South Africa on 25 Dec. 1963	

[1] *British National records may be set up by British pilots in any part of the world.*
[2] *A speed of 69·09 m.p.h. by John Delafield in a Phoebus 17 in South Africa on 22 Dec. 1969 awaits ratification.*
[3] *Also women's world record. Mrs. Burns with Janie Oesch set a multi-seat altitude record of 31,600 feet from Colorado Springs, U.S.A. in a Schweizer 2-32 on 5 Jan. 1967.*

Sports, games and pastimes

Golf

Origins The earliest mention of golf occurs in a prohibiting law passed by the Scottish Parliament in March 1457. In February 1962 the Soviet newspaper *Izvestiya* claimed that the game was of 15th-century Danish origin. The earliest reference in England as "goffe" is dated 1658. Gutta percha balls succeeded feather balls in 1848 and were in turn succeeded in 1902 by rubber-cored balls, invented in 1899 by Haskell (U.S.A.). Steel shafts were authorized in 1929.

CLUBS
The oldest club of which there is written evidence is the Gentlemen Golfers (now the Honourable Company of Edinburgh Golfers) formed in March 1744—10 years prior to the institution of the Royal and Ancient Club at St. Andrews, Fife. The oldest existing club in North America is the Royal Montreal Club (1873) and the oldest in the U.S.A. is St. Andrew's, New York (1888).

Largest The only club in the world with 15 courses is the Eldorado Golf Club, California, U.S.A. The club with the highest membership in the world is the Wanderer's Club, Johannesburg, South Africa, with 9,120 members, of whom 850 are golfers. The club with the highest membership in the British Isles is the Royal and Ancient Golf Club at St. Andrews, Fife (1,750). The largest in England is Wentworth Club, Virginia Water, Surrey, with 1,702 members, and the largest in Ireland is Royal Portrush with 594 full gentlemen members.

COURSES
Highest The highest golf course in the world is the Tuctu Golf Club in Morococha, Peru, which is 14,335 feet above sea-level at its lowest point. Golf has, however, been played in Tibet at an altitude of over 16,000 feet.

The highest golf course in Great Britain is one of 9 holes at Leadhills, Lanarkshire, 1,500 feet above sea-level.

Lowest The lowest golf course in the world was that of the Sodom and Gomorrah Golfing Society at Kallia, on the north-eastern shores of the Dead Sea, 1,250 feet below sea-level. The clubhouse was burnt down in 1948 and it is now no longer in use.

Longest hole The longest hole in the world is the 17th hole (par 6) of 745 yards at the Black Mountain Golf Club, North Carolina, U.S.A. It was opened in 1964. In August 1927 the 6th hole at Prescott Country Club in Arkansas, U.S.A., measured 838 yards. The longest hole on a championship course in Great Britain is the sixth at Troon, Ayrshire, which stretches 580 yards. The 9th at Hillsborough Golf Course, Wadsley, Sheffield, Yorkshire is 654 yards.

Largest green Probably the largest green in the world is the 5th green at Runaway Brook G.C., Bolton, Massachusetts, U.S.A. with an area greater than 28,000 square feet.

Biggest bunker The world's biggest bunker (called a trap in the U.S.A.) is Hell's Half Acre on the seventh hole of the Pine Valley course, New Jersey, U.S.A., built in 1912 and generally regarded as the world's most trying course.

LOWEST SCORES
9 holes and 18 holes Men The lowest recorded score on any 18-hole course with a par score of 70 or more is 55 (15 under bogey) by A. E. Smith, the Woolacombe professional, on his home course on 1 Jan. 1936. The course measured 4,248 yards. The detail was 4, 2, 3, 4, 2, 4, 3, 4, 3 = 29 out, and 2, 3, 3, 3, 3, 2, 5, 4, 1 = 26 in. Nine holes in 25 (4, 3, 3, 2, 3, 3, 1, 4, 2) was recorded by A. J. "Bill" Burke in a round in 57 (32 + 25) on the 6,389-yard par 71 Normandie course, St. Louis, Missouri, U.S.A. on 20 May 1970. Homero Blancas also scored 55 (27 + 28) on a course of 5,002 yards (par 70) at the Premier Golf Course, Longview, Texas, U.S.A., on 19 Aug. 1962. The lowest recorded score on a long course (over 6,000 yards) is 58 by Harry Weetman (born 25 Oct. 1920), the British Ryder Cup golfer, for the 6,171-yard Croham Hurst Course, Croydon, on 30 Jan. 1956.

The United States P.G.A. tournament record for 18 holes is 60 by Al Brosch (30 + 30) in the Texas Open on 10 Feb. 1951; William Nary in the El Paso Open, Texas on 9 Feb. 1952; Ted Kroll (born August 1919) in the Texas Open on Feb. 20 1954; Wally Ulrich in the Virginia Beach Open on 11 June 1954; Tommy Bolt (born March 1918) in the Insurance City Open on 25 June 1954; Mike Souchak (born May 1927) in the Texas Open on 17 Feb. 1955 and Samuel Jackson Snead (born 27 May 1912) in the Dallas Open, Texas on 14 Sept. 1957. Snead went round in 59 in the 3rd round of the Sam Snead Festival, a non-P.G.A. tournament, at White Sulphur Springs, West Virginia, U.S.A., on 16 May 1959.

Harry Weetman holder of the record lowest score for a long course round

Women The lowest recorded score on an 18-hole course for a woman is 62 (30 + 32) by Mary (Mickey) Kathryn Wright (born May 1935) of Dallas, Texas, on the Hogan Park Course (6,286 yards) at Midland, Texas, U.S.A., in November 1964.

United Kingdom The British Tournament 9-hole record is 28 by John Panton (born 1917, Scotland) in the Swallow-Penfold Tournament at Harrogate, Yorkshire, in 1952; by Bernard John Hunt (born 2 Feb. 1930) of Hartsbourne in the Spalding Tournament at Worthing, Sussex, in August 1953; and by Lionel Platts (born 10 Oct. 1934 Yorkshire), of Wanstead in the Ulster Open at Shandon Park, Belfast, on 11 Sept. 1965. The lowest score recorded in a first class professional tournament on a course of more than 6,000 yards in Great Britain was set at 61 (29 + 32), by Thomas Bruce Haliburton (born in Scotland on 5 June 1915) of Wentworth G.C. in the Spalding Tournament at Worthing, Sussex, in June 1952. Peter Butler equalled the 18-hole record with 61 (32 + 29) in the Bowmaker Tournament on the Old Course at Sunningdale, Berkshire, on 4 July 1967.

36 holes The record for 36 holes is 122 (59+63) by Snead in the 1959 Sam Snead Festival (see page 266) on 16–17 May 1959.

72 holes The lowest recorded score on a first-class course is 257 (27 under par) by Mike Souchak (born May 1927) in the Texas Open at San Antonio in February 1955, made up of 60 (33 + 27), 68, 64, 65 (average 64·25 per round). The late Horton Smith (born 1908), a U.S. Masters Champion, scored 245 (63, 58, 61 and 63) for 72 holes on the 4,700-yard course (par 64) at Catalina Country Club, California, U.S.A., to win the Catalina Open on 21–23 Dec. 1928.

The lowest 72 holes in a national championship is 262 by Percy Alliss (born 8 Jan. 1897) of Britain, with 67, 66, 66 and 63 in the Italian Open Championship at San Remo in 1935. The lowest for four rounds in a British first-class tournament is 262 (66, 63, 66 and 67) by Bernard Hunt in the Piccadilly Stroke Play tournament on Wentworth East Course, Virginia Water, Surrey, on 4–5 Oct. 1966. Kel Nagle of Australia shot 260 (64, 65, 66, and 65) in the Irish Hospitals Golf Tournament at Woodbrook Golf Club, near Bray, Ireland, on 21–23 July 1961.

Eclectic record The lowest recorded eclectic (from the Greek *eklektikos* = choosing) score, *i.e.* the sum of a player's all-time personal low scores for each hole, for a course of more than 6,000 yards is 37 by William Stanley Shephard on a course of 6,585 yards (par 73) at Kooyonga Golf Club in Lockleys, South Australia. His previous record of 38 was made up of 3, 3, 2, 2, 2, 2, 1, 2, 2 = 19 (out) and 2, 2, 2, 2, 2, 2, 3, 2, 2 = 19 (in). The British record is 39 by John W. Ellmore at Elsham Golf Club, Lincolnshire (6,070 yards). This is made up of 2, 3, 2, 2, 2, 2, 2, 2, 3, 2 = 20 (out) and 3, 1, 2, 1, 2, 2, 3, 3, 2 = 19 (in).

Highest scores The highest score for a single hole in the British Open is 21 by a player in the inaugural meeting at Prestwick in 1860. Double figures have been recorded on the card of the winner only once, when Willie Fernie (1851–1924) scored a 10 at Musselburgh, Midlothian, in 1883. Ray Ainsley of Ojai, California, took 19 strokes for the par-4 16th hole during the second round of the U.S. Open at Cherry Hills Country Club, Denver, Colorado, on 10 June 1938. Most of the strokes were used in trying to extricate the ball from a brook. Hans Merrell of Mogadore, Ohio, took 19 strokes on the par-3 16th (222 yards) during the third round of the Bing Crosby National Tournament at Cypress Point Club, Del Monte, California, U.S.A., on 17 Jan. 1959. It is recorded that Chevalier von Cittern went round 18 holes in 316 at Biarritz, France, in 1888.

Most shots for one hole A woman player in the qualifying round of the Shawnee Invitational for Ladies at Shawnee-on-Delaware, Pennsylvania, U.S.A. in *c.* 1912, took 166 strokes for the

short 130-yard 16th hole. Her tee shot went into the Binniekill River and the ball floated. She put out in a boat with her exemplary, but statistically minded husband at the oars. She eventually beached the ball 1½ miles downstream but was not yet out of the wood. She had to play through one on the home run.

Fastest and slowest rounds With such variations in the lengths of courses, speed records, even for rounds under par, are of little comparative value. It is recorded that Ken Bousfield (born 2 Oct. 1919) completed the 18 holes at Burnham Beeches, Buckinghamshire, in 91 minutes on 20 Sept. 1938, scoring 69, one over the course record, to complete 6 rounds in 3 minutes outside a 12-hour target.

In 1939 a large team of players propelled a ball round the famous Tam O'Shanter Course at Niles, Illinois, U.S.A., in 17 minutes 20 seconds, hence maintaining an average of 57·8 seconds per hole. The record for holing out an 18-hole course is 14 minutes 33·2 seconds (95 strokes) by 46 members of Titirangi Golf Club, Auckland, New Zealand on 7 April 1968.

The slowest stroke play tournament round was one of 5 hours 15 minutes by Sam Snead and Ben W. Hogan (born 13 Aug. 1912) of the U.S.A. *v.* Stan Leonard and Al Balding (born April 1924) of Canada in the Canada Cup contest on the West Course, at Wentworth, Surrey, in 1956. This was a 4-ball medal round, everything holed out.

Most rounds in a day Col. Bill Farnham played 376 holes (20 rounds plus 16 holes) at his home course at Guilford Lakes, Connecticut, U.S.A., in 24 hours 10 minutes, from 2.40 p.m. on 11 Aug. to 2.50 p.m. on 12 Aug. 1934. Dean Cummings (U.S.A.) played 678 holes (37 rounds 12 holes) in 91½ hours in May 1962.

As a demonstration against slow players and the automatic 60-year retirement age for airline pilots Capt. Roland (Roger) Halford Ayers played 6 rounds on the par-70 6,271-yard Chigwell Golf Club course, Essex on 28 May 1970 in 9 hours 45 minutes. His sixth round in 79 (net 69) was achieved in 91 minutes.

Youngest and oldest champions The youngest winner of the British Open was Tom Morris, Jr. (born 1850, died 25 Dec. 1875) at Prestwick, Ayrshire, in 1868. The youngest winner of the British Amateur title was John Charles Beharrel (born 2 May 1938) at Troon, Ayrshire, on 2 June 1956, aged 18 years 1 month. The oldest winner of the British Amateur was the Hon. Michael Scott at Hoylake, Cheshire, in 1933, when 54. The oldest British Open Champion was Roberto de Vicenzo (born 14 April 1923, Buenos Aires, Argentina) aged 44 years and 93 days on 16 July 1967. The oldest United States Amateur Champion was Jack Westland (born 1905) at Seattle, Washington, in 1952.

Longest drives In long-driving contests 325 yards is rarely surpassed at sea level. The United States P.G.A. record is 341 yards by Jack William Nicklaus (born Columbus, Ohio, 21 Jan. 1940), weighing 14¾ stone, in July 1963. The Irish Professional Golfers Association record is however 392 yards by their amateur member William Thomas (Tommie) Campbell (Foxrock Golf Club) made at Dun Laoghaire, Co. Dublin, in July 1964. Under freak conditions of wind, slope, parched or frozen surfaces, or ricochet from a stone or flint, even greater distances are achieved. The greatest recorded drive is one of 445 yards by Edward C. Bliss (1863–1917), a 12 handicap player, at the 9th hole of the Old Course, Herne Bay, Kent, in August 1913. Bliss, 6 feet tall and over 13 stone, drove to the back of the green on the left-handed dog-leg. The drive was measured by a government surveyor, Capt. L. H. Lloyd, who also measured the drop from the tee to resting place as 57 feet.

Other freak drives include the driving of the 483-yard 13th at Westward Ho! by F. Lemarchand, backed by a gale; and to the edge of the 465-yard downhill 9th on the East Devon Course, Budleigh Salterton, by T. H. V. Haydon in September 1934. Neither drive was accurately measured.

Perhaps the longest recorded drive on level ground was one of an estimated 430 yards by Craig Ralph Wood (born 18 Nov. 1901) of the U.S.A. on the 530-yard fifth hole at the Old Course, St. Andrews, Fife, in the Open Championship in June 1933. The ground was parched and there was a strong following wind.

Tony Jacklin drove a ball from the roof of the Savoy Hotel (125 feet above the pavement) 353 yards to splash into the River Thames on 26 Nov. 1969. A drive of 2,640 yards (1½ miles) across ice was achieved by an Australian meteorologist named Nilstied at Mawson Base, Antarctica, in 1962. On the moon the energy expended on a mundane 300-yard drive would achieve, craters permitting, a distance of a mile.

British Amateur The lowest score for nine holes in the British Amateur Championship (inaugurated in 1885) is 29 by Richard Davol Chapman (born 23 March 1911) of the U.S.A. at Sandwich in 1948.

Michael Francis Bonallack (born 1935) shot a 61 (32 + 29) on the par-71 6,905-yard course at Ganton, Yorkshire, on 27 July 1968 for the English Amateur title.

U.S. Open The United States Open Championship was inaugurated in 1894. The lowest 72-hole aggregate is 275 (71, 67, 72 and 65) by Jack Nicklaus on the Lower Course (7,015 yards) at Baltusrol Country Club, Springfield, New Jersey, on 15–18 June 1967 and 275 (69, 68, 69 and 69) by Lee Trevino (born near Horizon City, Texas, 1940) at Oak Hill Country Club, Rochester, N.Y., on 13–16 June 1968. The lowest score for 18 holes is 64, achieved three times: by Lee Mackey, Jr., at Merion Country Club in Ardmore, Pennsylvania, on 8 June 1950; by Tommy Jacobs on the 7,053-yard course at the

Tony Jacklin (G.B.) attempting to drive a ball across the Thames

Longest hitter The golfer regarded as the longest consistent hitter the game has ever known is the 6 feet 5 inches tall, 17 st. 2 lb. George Bayer (U.S.A.), the 1957 Canadian Open Champion. His longest measured drive was one of 420 yards at the fourth in the Las Vegas Invitational, Nevada, in 1953. It was measured as a precaution against litigation since the ball struck a spectator. Bayer also drove a ball pin high on a 426-yard hole in Tucson, Arizona, U.S.A. Radar measurements show that an 87 m.p.h. impact velocity for a golf ball falls to 46 m.p.h. in 3·0 seconds.

The Open The Open Championship was inaugurated in 1860 at Prestwick, Ayrshire, Scotland. The lowest score for 9 holes is 29 by Tom Haliburton (Wentworth) and Peter W. Thomson, M.B.E. (Australia) in the first round of the Open on the Royal Lytham and St. Anne's course at Lytham St. Anne's, Lancashire, on 10 July 1963.

The lowest scoring round is 63 (all in qualifying rounds) by Frank Jowle (born 14 May 1912) at the New Course, St. Andrews (6,526 yards), on 4 July 1955; by Peter William Thomson, M.B.E. (born 23 Aug. 1929) of Melbourne, Australia at Royal Lytham and St. Anne's (6,635 yards) on 30 June 1958; and Maurice Bembridge (Little Aston) at Delamere Forest, Cheshire, on 7 July 1967. The best by an amateur is 65 by Ronnie David Bell Mitchell Shade, M.B.E. (born 15 Oct. 1938) in a qualifying round on the Eden Course (6,250 yards), St. Andrews, on 4 July 1964. The lowest rounds in The Open itself have been 65 by Christy O'Connor (born 1925) of Royal Dublin, Ireland at St. Anne's, Lancashire in the 2nd round on 10 July 1969 and 65 in the 2nd round by T. Henry Cotton, M.B.E. (born Holmes Chapel, Cheshire, 1906) at Royal St. George's, Sandwich, Kent, on 27 June 1934 to complete a 36-hole record of 132 (67 + 65). The lowest 72-hole aggregate is 276 (71, 69, 67, 69) by Arnold Daniel Palmer (born 10 Sept. 1929) of Latrobe, Pennsylvania, U.S.A., at Troon, Ayrshire, ending on 13 July 1962.

Congressional Country Club, Washington, D.C., on 19 June 1964; and by Rives McBee at the Olympic Country Club in San Francisco, California, on 17 June 1966.

U.S. Masters The lowest score in the U.S. Masters (instituted at Augusta National Golf Course, Georgia, in 1934) has been 271 by Jack Nicklaus in 1965. The lowest rounds have been 64 by Lloyd Mangrum (1st round, 1940) and Jack Nicklaus (3rd round, 1965).

Most internationals The greatest number of amateur international appearances to the end of 1969 is:

England	Michael Francis Bonallack (Thorpe Hall)	60 times	1957–1969
Ireland	Joseph B. Carr (Sutton)	81 times	1947–1969
Scotland	Ronnie David Bell Mitchell Shade, M.B.E. (Duddingston)	43 times	1957–1968
Wales	W. I. Tucker (Monmouth)	54 times	1949–1969

Richest prizes The greatest first place prize money is $60,000 (total

George Bayer (U.S.A.), regarded as the longest consistent hitter

J. B. Carr, holder of the British Isles Amateur International appearances record purse $300,000 [£125,000]) in the Dow Jones Open Invitational first played at Upper Montclair Country Club, Clifton, New Jersey on 27–30 Aug. 1970 and £25,000 ($60,000) in the John Player Classic at Notts. County, England on 6–8 Sept. 1970

Highest earnings The greatest amount ever won in official golf prizes is $1,121,000 (£467,080), by Arnold Palmer from 1954 to 27 Jan. 1970. During this period Palmer won 53 tournaments. The highest earnings in a season (all tournaments) are $267,000 by Jack Nicklaus in 1968, who reached the $1 million mark on 26 Jan. 1970.

Most tournament wins The record for winning tournaments in a single season is 19 (out of 31) by Byron Nelson (born 4 Feb. 1912) of Fort Worth, Texas, in 1945. Of these 11 were consecutive, including the P.G.A., Canadian P.G.A. and Canadian Open, from 16 March to 15 August. He was a money prize winner in 113 consecutive tournaments.

Steadiest player William Earl Casper (born 24 June 1931, San Diego, California) in the 11 years 1958–68 was only once (1963) outside the top 4 money winners on the U.S. professional circuit surpassing $1 million mark in January 1970. He has won the Vardon Trophy in 1960, 1963, 1965, 1966 and 1968.

Most club championships The British record for club championships is 20 consecutive wins (1937–39 and 1946–62) by R. W. H.

1902) between 20 June 1918 and 17 July 1965. In the year 1961 a lesser number of 12,888 "aces" were reported from the United States. Dr. Joseph O. Boydstone scored holes-in-one at the 3rd, 4th and 9th holes on the Bakersfield Public Golf Course, California, U.S.A., on 10 Oct. 1961. The holes measured 210, 132 and 135 yards.

Double albatross There is no recorded instance of a golfer performing three consecutive holes-in-one but there are at least twelve cases of "aces" being achieved in two consecutive holes of which the greatest was Norman L. Manley's unique "double albatross" on the par-4 330-yard 7th and par-4 290-yard 8th holes on the Del Valle Country Club course, Saugus, California, on 2 Sept. 1964.

Youngest and oldest The youngest golfer recorded to have shot a hole-in-one was Tommy Moore (6 years 1 month 7 days) of Hagerstown, Maryland on the 145-yard 4th at the Woodbrier Golf Course, Martinsville, West Virginia, on 8 March 1968. The oldest golfer to have performed the feat is T. S. South, aged 91, at the 17th (110 yards) at Highcliffe Castle Golf Club, Hampshire, in November 1952.

Shooting your age The record for scoring one's age in years over an 18-hole round is held by William Edmonds (born 7 March 1888) of Maritzburg Golf Club, Natal, South Africa, who has

MOST TITLES
The most titles won in the world's major championships are as follows:

The Open	Harry Vardon (1870–1937)	6	1896–98–99, 1903–11–14
British Amateur	John Ball (1861–1940)	8	1888–90–92–94–99, 1907–10–12
U.S. Open	W. Anderson	4	1901–03–04–05
	Robert Tyre Jones, Jr. (born 1902)	4	1923–26–29–30
	Ben William Hogan (born 1912)	4	1948–50–51–53
U.S. Amateur	R. T. Jones, Jr.	5	1924–25–27–28–30
P.G.A. Championship (U.S.A.)	Walter C. Hagen	5	1921–24–25–26–27
Masters Championship (U.S.A.)	Arnold D. Palmer	4	1958–60–62–64
U.S. Women's Open	Miss Elizabeth (Betsy) Earle-Rawls	4	1951–53–57–60
	Miss "Mickey" Wright	4	1958–59–61–64
U.S. Women's Amateur	Mrs. Glenna C. Vare (née Collett)	6	1922–25–28–29–30–35
British Women's	Miss Charlotte Cecilia Pitcairn Leitch	4	1914–20–21–26
	Miss Joyce Wethered (born 1901) (now Lady Heathcoat-Amory)	4	1922–24–25–29

Taylor at the Dyke Golf Club, Brighton, Sussex. He retired unbeaten in July 1963.

HOLES IN ONE
Longest The longest hole ever holed in one shot is the 10th hole (444 yards) at Miracle Hills Golf Club, Omaha, Nebraska, U.S.A. Robert Mitera achieved a hole-in-one there on 7 Oct. 1965. Mitera, aged 21, stands 5 feet 6 inches tall and weighs 165 lb. (11 st. 11 lb.). He is a two handicap player who can normally drive 245 yards. A 50 m.p.h. gust carried his shot over a 290-yard drop-off. The group in front testified to the remaining 154 yards. The feminine record is 393 yards by Marie Robie of Wollaston, Massachusetts, U.S.A., on the first hole at the Furnace Brook Golf Club, western Massachusetts, on 4 Sept. 1949.

The longest hole in one performed in the British Isles is the 5th (380 yards) on Tankersley Park course, near Sheffield, Yorkshire, by David Hulley in 1961.

Most The record total number of "aces" recorded in the United States in a year has been 18,319 (indicating more than 100 on some days) in 1969. The greatest number of holes-in-one in a career is 35 by Art Wall, Jr. (born November 1923) between 1936 and 1966. The British record is 30 by Charles T. Chevalier of Heaton Moor Golf Club, Stockport, Lancashire (born 22 July

won the Senior Golfers' Championship of South Africa and Rhodesia five times. On his 70th birthday, on 7 March 1958, he scored a 69. On 7 March 1964, aged 76, he went round a course of 6,565 yards at his club in 74. He had scored his age, or under his age, 202 times by 26 Feb. 1969. At 81 his handicap is 8.

The oldest player to score under his age is C. Arthur Thompson (born 1869) of Victoria, British Columbia, Canada, who scored 96 on the Uplands course of 6,215 yards on 3 Oct. 1966.

World Cup (formerly Canada Cup) The Canada Cup (instituted 1963) has been won most often by the U.S.A., with nine victories in 1955–56, 1960–61–62–63–64–66–67. The only man to have been on six winning teams has been Arnold Palmer (1960 to 1967). The lowest aggregate score for 144 holes is 548 by the U.S.A., with Palmer and Nicklaus, at the Yomiuri Country Club, Tōkyō, Japan, on 10–13 Nov. 1966, and the lowest scores by an individual winner have been 272 by Snead in Puerto Rico in 1961 and by George Knudson (Canada) with Hideyo Sugimoto (Japan) at Yomiuri Country Club, Tōkyō, Japan in 1966, which necessitated a play-off won by Knudson.

Throwing the golf ball The lowest recorded score for throwing a golf ball round 18 holes is 113 by David Hawkins at Sheerness Golf Club, Kent (5,895 yards) on 13 Sept. 1968.

269

Sports, games and pastimes
Greyhound Racing

Earliest meeting   Modern greyhound racing originated with the perfecting of the mechanical hare by Oliver P. Smith at Emeryville, California, U.S.A., in 1919. The earliest greyhound track race in the British Isles was at Belle Vue, Manchester, opened on 24 July 1926.

Derby   The only dog to have twice won the English Greyhound Derby (held since 1945 over 525 yards at the White City Stadium, London) was *Mick the Miller* (whelped in Ireland, June 1926 and died 1939) on 25 July 1929, when owned by Albert H. Williams, and on 28 June 1930 (owned by Mrs. Arundel H. Kempton). This dog won a record sequence of 19 consecutive races from 19 March to 20 Aug. 1930. The highest prize was £7,728 for *Faithful Hope* in 1966. The only dogs to win the English, Scottish and Welsh Derby "triple" are *Trev's Perfection*, owned by Fred Trevillion, in 1947, and *Mile Bush Pride*, owned by Noel W. Purvis, in 1959.

Grand National   The only dogs to have twice won the Greyhound Grand National (instituted 1927) over 525 yards and 4 flights are *Juvenile Classic* in 1938 and 1940 at the White City Stadium, London, and *Blossom of Annagura* on 21 May 1949 and 20 May 1950 (record time of 29·38 secs.). The latter also won the 1951 Irish Grand National.

The fastest *photo*-timing is 29·43 seconds by *Barrowside* in May 1955. *Barrowside* failed to secure the "double" by placing second in the Derby—27 inches behind the winner, but displaced the previous record of *Dangerous Prince*, who was second in both races in 1949.

Fastest dog   The highest speed at which any greyhound has been timed is 41·26 m.p.h. (345 yards in 17·1 secs.) by *Highland Dew* for a track record at Dapto, New South Wales, Australia. The highest speed recorded for a greyhound in Great Britain is 39·13 m.p.h. by *Beef Cutlet*, when covering a straight course of 500 yards in 26·13 seconds at Blackpool, Lancashire, on 13 May 1933. The highest speed on an oval course is 37·94 m.p.h. by *Yellow Printer*, the Derby record-holder at 28·44 secs., at White City, London on 3 June 1968 when he recorded 28·30 secs. for 525 yards.

Yellow Printer, the fastest-ever greyhound

Gymnastics

Earliest references   Gymnastics were widely practised in Greece during the period of the ancient Olympic Games (776 B.C. to A.D. 393), but they were not revived until c. 1780.

World Championships   The greatest number of individual titles won by a man in the World Championships is 10 by Boris Shakhlin (U.S.S.R.) between 1954 and 1964. He also won 3 team titles. The female record is 10 individual wins and 5 team titles by Larissa Semyonovna Latynina (born 1935, retired 1966) of the U.S.S.R., between 1956 and 1964.

Olympic Games   Italy has won most Olympic team titles with four victories in 1912, 1920, 1924 and 1932.

Nick Stewart, winner of the record number of British Championships

The only man to win six gold medals is Boris Shakhlin (U.S.S.R.), with one in 1956, four (two shared) in 1960 and one in 1964.

The most successful woman has been Vera Caslavska-Odlozil (Czechoslovakia), with 7 individual Gold Medals, three in 1964 and four (one shared) in 1968. She also won a team Silver Medal in 1960, 1964 and 1968 and an individual Silver Medal in 1968.

British Championship   The most times that the British Gymnastic Championship has been won is 9 by W. (Nick) Stuart, M.B.E.; the women's record is 5 wins by Miss Margaret Bell, 1965–69.

Rope climbing   The United States Amateur Athletic Union records are tantamount to world records: 20 feet (hands alone) 2·8 seconds, Don Perry (U.S.A.) at Champaign, Illinois, U.S.A., on 3 April 1954; 25 feet (hands alone), 4·7 seconds, Garvin S. Smith at Los Angeles, California, U.S.A., on 19 April 1947.

Chinning the bar   The greatest number of chin-ups (from a dead hang position) recorded is 106 by William D. Reed at the Weightman Hall, University of Pennsylvania, U.S.A. on 23 June 1969. The feminine record for one-handed chin-ups is 27 in Hermann's Gym, Philadelphia, Pennsylvania, U.S.A. in 1918 by Lillian Leitzel (Mrs. Alfredo Codona) (U.S.A.), who was killed in Copenhagen, Denmark, on 12 Feb. 1931. Her total would be unmatched by any male but it is doubtful if they were achieved from a "dead hang" position. It is believed that only one person in 100,000 can chin a bar one-handed. Francis Lewis (b. 1896) of Beatrice, Nebraska, U.S.A. in May 1914 achieved 7 consecutive chins using only the middle finger of his left hand. His bodyweight was 158 lb.

Press-ups   The greatest recorded number of consecutive press-ups is 6,006 in 3 hours 54 minutes by Chick Linster, aged 16, of Wilmette, Illinois, U.S.A., on 5 Oct. 1965. Masura Noma of Mihara, Japan did 1,227 press-ups in 37 minutes in January 1968.

Sit-ups   The greatest recorded number of consecutive sit-ups on a hard surface is 14,118 in 12 hours 3 minutes by Dale D. Cummings of Berry Academy, Rome, Georgia, U.S.A., from 11 p.m. on 29 Nov. to 11.03 a.m. on 30 Nov. 1965.

Greatest tumbler   The greatest tumbler of all time is Dick Browning (U.S.A.) who made a backward somersault over a 7-foot 3-inch bar at Santa Barbara, California, in April 1954. In his unique repertoire was a "round-off", backward handspring, backward somersault with half-twist, walk-out, tinsica tigna round-off, backward handspring, double backward somersault.

Hand-to-hand balancing   The longest horizontal dive achieved in any hand-to-hand balancing act is 22 feet by Harry Berry (top mounter) and the late Nelson Soule (understander) of the Bell-Thazer Brothers from Kentucky, U.S.A., who played at State fairs and vaudevilles from 1912 to 1918. Berry used a 10-foot tower and trampoline for impetus.

270

Sports, games and pastimes

Largest gymnasium The world's largest gymnasium is Yale University's Payne Whitney Gymnasium at New Haven, Connecticut, U.S.A., completed in 1932 and valued at $18,000,000 (£7,500,000). The building, known as the "Cathedral of Muscle", has nine storeys with wings of five storeys each. It is equipped with four basketball courts, three rowing tanks, 28 squash courts, 12 handball courts, a roof jogging track and a 25-yard by 42-foot swimming pool on the first floor and a 55-yard long pool on the third floor.

Handball

Handball is a game of ancient Celtic origin. In the early 19th century only a front wall was used but gradually side and back walls were added. The earliest international contest was in New York City, U.S.A. in 1887 between the champion of the U.S.A. and Ireland. The court is now a standardized 60 feet by 30 feet in Ireland and Australia, and 40 feet by 20 feet in Canada, Mexico and the U.S.A. The game is played with both a hard and a soft ball. The first international match was held in Copenhagen on 8 March 1935 when Sweden beat Denmark 18–12. In 1970 there were 41 countries affiliated to the International Handball Federation and an estimated 5,000,000 participants.

Championship World championships were inaugurated in New York in October 1964 with competitors from Australia, Canada, Ireland, Mexico and the U.S.A. James Jacobs (U.S.A.) was the individual winner and the U.S.A. beat Canada for the team title. In November 1967 Joe Maher (Canada, formerly Ireland) won the singles title and Canada and the U.S.A. shared the team title.

Most titles In Ireland the most titles (instituted 1925) have been won as follows:

Hardball
Singles John J. Gilmartin (Kilkerry)
10   1936–42, 1945–47
Doubles John Ryan and John Doyle (Wexford)
6   1952, 1954–58
Softball
Singles Paddy Perry (Roscommon)
8   1930–37
Doubles James O'Brien and Patrick Downey (Kerry)
7   1955–56, 1960–64

Hockey

ORIGINS
A representation of two hockey players apparently in an orthodox "bully" position was found in Tomb No. 16 at Beni Hasan, United Arab Republic (formerly Egypt) and has been dated to c. 2000 B.C. There is a British reference to the game in Lincolnshire in 1277. The oldest club is Blackheath, founded in 1861. The first country to form a national association was England (The Hockey Association) in 1886.

MEN
Earliest international The first international match was the Wales v. Ireland match at Rhyl on 26 Jan. 1895. Ireland won 3–0.

Highest international score The highest score in international hockey was when India defeated the United States 24–1 at Los Angeles, California, U.S.A., in the 1932 Olympic Games. The Indians were Olympic Champions from the re-inception of Olympic hockey in 1928 until 1960, when Pakistan beat them 1–0 at Rome. They had their seventh win in 1964. Three Indians have won 3 Olympic gold medals—Dhyan Chand and R. J. Allen (1928, 1932, 1936), Randhir Gentle (1948, 1952, 1956). The greatest number of goals in a home international match was when England defeated France 16–0 at Beckenham on 25 March 1922.

Longest game The longest international game on record was one of 145 minutes (into the sixth period of extra time), when Netherlands beat Spain 1–0 in the Olympic tournament at Mexico City on 25 Oct. 1968. After Moss Sports had played Symington's in the County mixed senior competition at Leicester on 22 March 1969 for 170 minutes without decision, a coin was tossed and Symington's won.

Most caps The most by a Briton is 89 by John W. Neill with 56 for Great Britain and 33 for England won from 1959 until the 1968 Olympic Games.

England 45, Denys John Carnill (Gloucestershire) (1950–60)
Wales 47, David J. Prosser (1961–70)
Scotland 52, Eric Douglas Watt (Aberdeen G.S.F.P.), 1950–65
    52, F. H. Scott (Hounslow) (up to 1969)
Ireland 51, Harold Cahill (1947–1970)
Great Britain 56, John W. Neill (England) (1959–1968)

Greatest scoring feat M. C. Marckx (Bowdon 2nd XI) scored 19 goals against Brooklands 2nd XI (score 23–0) on 31 Dec. 1910. He was selected for England in March 1912 but declined due to business.

WOMEN
Origins The earliest women's club was East Molesey in Surrey, England formed in c. 1887. The first national association was the Irish Ladies' Hockey Union founded in 1894. The All England Women's Hockey Association held its first formal meeting in Westminster Town Hall, London, on 23 Nov. 1895. The first international match was an England v. Ireland game in Dublin in 1896. Ireland won 2–0.

Highest international score The highest score in a women's international match occurred when England defeated France 23–0 at Merton, Surrey, on 3 Feb. 1923.

Most caps The England records are 53 caps by Miss Mildred Mary Knott (1923–39) and 17 seasons by Miss Mabel Bryant (1907–1929), who won 39 caps. The Irish record is 58 (46 full caps and 12 touring) by Mrs. Sean Kyle (born Maeve Esther Enid Shankey, 6 Oct. 1928) between November 1947 and 1966.

Highest attendance The highest attendance at a women's hockey match was 65,000 for the match between England and Wales at the Empire Stadium, Wembley, Greater London, on 8 March 1969.

Horse Racing

Origins Stone and bone carvings prove that horse racing is a sport at least thirty centuries old. The 23rd ancient Olympic Games of 624 B.C. in Greece featured horse racing. The earliest horse race recorded in England was one held in about A.D. 210 at Netherby, Yorkshire, among Arabians brought to Britain by Lucius Septimius Severus (A.D. 146–211), Emperor of Rome. The oldest race still being run annually is the Lanark Silver Bell, instituted in Scotland by William Lion (1165–1214).

The Jockey Club was formed in 1750–51 and the General Stud Book started in 1791. Racing colours (silks) became compulsory in 1889.

The Greeks included horse-racing in the Ancient Olympic Games

RACECOURSES

Largest The world's largest racecourse is the Newmarket course (founded 1636), on which the Beacon Course, the longest of the 19 courses, is 4 miles 397 yards long and the Rowley Mile is 167 feet wide. The border between Suffolk and Cambridgeshire runs through the Newmarket course. The world's largest grandstand is that opened in 1968 at Belmont Park, Nassau County, Long Island, N.Y., U.S.A. at a cost of $30,700,000 (£12·8 million). It is 110 feet tall, 440 yards long and contains 908 mutuel windows. The highest seating capacity at any racetrack is 40,000 at Atlantic City Audit, New Jersey, U.S.A.

Smallest The world's smallest racecourse is the Lebong racecourse, Darjeeling, West Bengal, India (altitude 7,000 feet), where the complete lap is 481 yards. It was laid out c. 1885 and used as a parade ground.

Greatest record The horse with the best recorded win-loss record and the only one on which it was safe to bet was *Kincsem,* a Hungarian mare foaled in 1874, who was unbeaten in 54 races (1877–1880), including the Goodwood Cup of 1878. The tallest horse ever to race was the bay colt *Ambergris,* who was foaled in 1873 and stood 18 hands.

Horses Highest price The highest price ever paid for a stallion is $4,800,000 paid after the 1967 season by a syndicate for *Buckpasser.* The syndicate comprises 32 shares of $150,000 (£62,500 each, of which 16 were taken by Mr. Ogden Phipps.

Greatest winnings The greatest amount ever won by a horse is $1,977,896 (then £706,391) by *Kelso* (foaled in 1957) in the U.S.A. between 1959 and his retirement on 10 March 1966. He is now the supreme status symbol of the hunt under Mrs. Richard C. du Pont. In 63 races he won 39, came second in 12 and third in 2. The most successful horse of all time has been *Buckpasser,* whose career winnings were $1,462,014 (£609,172) in 1965–66–67. He won 25 races out of 31. The most won by a mare is $783,674 (£279,883) by *Cicada.* In 42 races she won 23, came second in 8 and third in 6. The most won in a year is $817,941 (£340,808) by *Damascus* in 1967. His total reached $1,176,781.

Largest prizes The richest race ever held was the All-American Futurity, a race for quarter-horses over 400 yards at Ruidoso Downs, New Mexico, U.S.A., on 4 Sept. 1967. The prizes totalled $486,593 (then £173,783), including $228,300 (£81,535) for *Laico Bird,* the winner in 20·11 seconds. The largest single prize ever paid was 1,094,126

SPEED RECORDS

Distance	Time	m.p.h.	Name	Course	Date
¼ mile	20·8s.	43·26	*Big Racket* (U.S.A.)	Lomas de Sotelo, Mexico	5 Feb. 1945
⅓ mile (straight)	45·0s.	40·00	*Gloaming* (N.Z.)	Wellington, New Zealand	12 Jan. 1921
½ mile	45·0s.	40·00	*Beau Madison* (U.S.A.)	Phoenix, Arizona, U.S.A.	30 Mar. 1957
	45·0s.	40·00	*Another Nell* (U.S.A.)	Cicero, Ill., U.S.A.	8 May 1967
⅝ mile	53·6s.	41·98	*Indigenous* (G.B.)	Epsom, Surrey	2 June 1960
¾ mile	1m. 07·4s.	40·06	*Zip Pocket* (U.S.A.)	Phoenix, Arizona, U.S.A.	6 Dec. 1966
	1m. 06·2s.	40·78	*Broken Tindril* (G.B.)	*Brighton, Sussex	6 Aug. 1929
Mile	1m. 31·8s.	39·21	*Soueida* (G.B.)	*Brighton, Sussex	19 Sept. 1963
	1m. 31·8s.	39·21	*Loose Cover* (G.B.)	*Brighton, Sussex	9 June 1966
	1m. 32·2s.	39·04	*Dr. Fager* (U.S.A.)	Arlington, Ill., U.S.A.	24 Aug. 1968
1½ miles	2m. 26·0s.	36·98	*Meneleck* (G.B.)	Haydock Park	1 July 1961
2 miles	3m. 15·0s.	36·93	*Polazel* (G.B.)	Salisbury, Wiltshire	8 July 1924
3 miles	5m. 15·0s.	34·29	*Farragut* (Mexico)	Agua Caliente	9 Mar. 1941

* Course downhill for two-thirds of a mile.

Jockeys The most successful jockey has been John Eric Longden (U.S.A.), born at Wakefield, Yorkshire, on 10 Feb. 1907. He began riding in 1927, passed the record of Sir Gordon Richards at Del Mar on 3 Sept. 1956, rode his 5,000th winner on 28 Feb. 1957 and his 6,000th (from 31,965 races) on 17 Aug. 1965. He retired on 12 March 1966, after having ridden 6,032 winners. His career brought prizes totalling $24,665,800 (£10,277,416) to the owners of his mounts. The greatest number of wins in a season is 485 (from 1,683 mounts) by Willie Shoemaker (born weighing 2½ lb., 19 Aug. 1931) of the U.S.A. in 1953. Shoemaker's mounts won more than $41 million (£17,083,000) from 19 March 1949 to 1 Jan. 1970. He had ridden 5,855 winners (from 23,500 mounts) by this date.

The greatest amount ever won by any jockey in a year is $3,088,888 by Braulio Baeza (b. Panama) in the U.S.A. in 1967. The oldest jockey was Levi Barlingame (U.S.A.), who rode his last race at Stafford, Kansas, U.S.A., in 1932 aged 80. The youngest jockey was Frank Wootton (English Champion jockey 1909–12), who rode his first winner in South Africa aged 9 years 10 months. The lightest recorded jockey was Kitchener (died 1872), who won the Chester Cup on *Red Deer* in 1844 at 3 stone 7 lb. He was said to have weighed only 2 stone 12 lb. in 1840.

Trainers The greatest amount ever won by a trainer in one year is $2,456,250 (then £881,519) by Eddie A. Neloy (U.S.A.) in 1966 when his horses won 93 races.

francs, plus 78 per cent. of the entry fees, making 1,480,000 francs (then £107,000) to the owner of *Prince Royal II,* winner of the 43rd Prix de l'Arc de Triomphe at Longchamp, Paris, on 4 Oct. 1964.

Dead heats There is no recorded case in turf history of a quintuple dead heat. The nearest approach was in the Astley Stakes, at Lewes, England, in August 1880 when *Mazurka, Wandering Nun* and *Scobell* triple deadheated for first place, just ahead of *Cumberland* and *Thora,* who dead-heated for fourth place. Each of the five jockeys thought he had won. The only two known examples of a quadruple dead heat were between *The Defaulter, Squire of Malton, Reindeer* and *Pulcherrima* in the Omnibus Stakes at The Hoo, England, on 26 April 1851, and between *Overreach, Lady Go-Lightly, Gamester* and *The Unexpected* at the Houghton Meeting at Newmarket on 22 Oct. 1855. The earliest recorded photo-finish dead heat in Britain was between *Phantom Bridge* and *Resistance* in the 5-furlong Beechfield Handicap at Doncaster on 22 Oct. 1947.

Longest race The longest recorded horse race was one of 1,200 miles in Portugal, won by a horse *Emir* bred from Egyptianbred Blunt Arab stock. The holder of the world's record for long distance racing and speed is *Champion Crabbet,* who covered 300 miles in 52 hours 33 minutes, carrying 17½ stone, in 1920. In 1831 Squire George Osbaldeston (1787–1866), M.P. of East Retford, covered 200 miles in 8 hours 42 minutes at Newmarket, using 50 mounts, so averaging 22·99 m.p.h. In 1967 G. Steecher covered

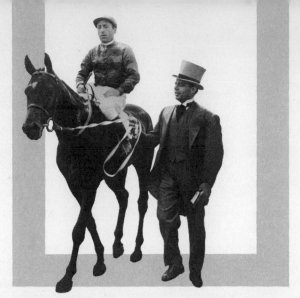

Most successful jockeys Sir Gordon Richards (born 5 May 1904) retired in 1954, having won 4,870 races from 21,834 mounts since his first win at Leicester on 21 March 1921. In 1953, after 27 attempts, he won the Derby, six days after being knighted. He set a record of 12 consecutive wins by winning the last race in which he rode at Nottingham on 3 Oct. 1933, all six at Chepstow on the 4th and the first five on the 5th. In 1947 he won a record 269 races. The most classic races won by a jockey is 27 by Frank Buckle (1766–1832), between 1792 and 1827.

Most runners The most horses in a race is 66 (a world record) in the Grand National of 22 March 1929. The record for the flat is 58 in the Lincolnshire Handicap on 13 March 1948. The most runners at a meeting were 214 (flat) in seven races at Newmarket on 15 June 1915 and 229 (National Hunt) in eight races at Worcester on 13 Jan. 1965.

THE DERBY
The greatest of England's five classic races, the Epsom Derby, was inaugurated on 4 May 1780 by the 12th Earl of Derby (1752–1834). It has been run over 1 mile 885 yards since 1784 (1½ miles since World War I) on Epsom Downs, Surrey, except for the two war periods, when it was run at Newmarket. Since 1884 the race has been for three-year-old colts carrying 9 stone and fillies carrying 8 stone 9 lb.

Highest prize The highest prize for winning any English race was £74,489 10s. for *Charlottown* in the Derby on 25 May 1966.

Most winning owners The only owner with five outright winners was the 3rd Earl of Egremont (1751–1837) with *Assassin* (1782), *Hannibal* (1804), *Cardinal Beaufort* (1805), *Election* (1807), and *Lapdog* (1826). H.H. Aga Khan III (1877–1957) had four winners in *Blenheim* (1930), *Bahram* (1935), *Mahmoud* (1936) and *Tulyar* (1952) and a half-share in *My Love* (1948).

Trainer The only two trainers with seven winners were John Porter with *Blue Gown* (1868), *Shotover* (1882), *St. Blaise* (1883), *Ormonde* (1886), *Sainfoin* (1890), *Common* (1891) and *Flying Fox* (1899), and Robert Robson with *Waxy* (1793), *Tyrant* (1802), *Pope* (1809), *Whalebone* (1810), *Whisker* (1815), *Azor* (1817), and *Emilius* (1823).

100 miles on a single horse in 11 hours 4 minutes in Victoria, Australia.

Shortest price The shortest odds ever quoted for any racehorse are 10,000 to 1 on for *Dragon Blood,* ridden by Lester Piggott (G.B.) in the Premio Naviglio in Milan, Italy on 1 June 1967. Odds of 100 to 1 on were quoted for the United States horse *Man o' War* (foaled 29 March 1917, died 1 Nov. 1947) on three separate occasions in 1920, and for the two British horses, *Ormonde* in the Champion Stakes on 14 Oct. 1886 (three runners), and *Sceptre* in the Limekiln Stakes on 27 Oct. 1903 (two runners).

BRITISH TURF RECORDS
Most expensive horses The highest price ever paid for a horse in the British Isles is £250,000, paid in February 1953 for *Tulyar* by the Irish National Stud to the Rt. Hon. Aga Sultan Sir Mohammed Shah, H.H. Aga Khan III, G.C.S.I., G.C.M.G., G.C.I.E., G.C.V.O. (1877–1957) of Iran (Persia). *Sir Ivor* commands a covering fee of £8,000. A sum of £250,000 was also paid for *Ballymoss* by a syndicate in September 1958. The French horse *Charlottesville* was bought by a syndicate for £336,000 from H.H. Shah Karim, Aga Khan IV (born 13 Dec. 1936), in November 1960. The record payment for a horse in training is 136,000 guineas (£142,800) for *Vaguely Noble* at Park Paddocks, Newmarket auction sale by Dr. Robert A. Franklyn (U.S.) on 7 Dec. 1967.

Most successful horses No horse has yet won all five classics. The nearest approach was in 1902, when *Sceptre* won the 1,000 Guineas, 2,000 Guineas, Oaks and St. Leger. In 1868 *Formosa* won the same four but dead-heated in the 2,000 Guineas. The most races won in a season is 23 by *Fisherman* in 1856. *Catherina* won 79 out of 174 races between 1833 and 1841. The only horse to win the same race in seven successive years was *Dr. Syntax*, who won the Preston Gold Cup from 1815 to 1821. The most successful sire was *Stockwell,* whose progeny won 1,153 races (1858–76) and in 1866 set a record of 132 races won.

The greatest amount of prize money ever won by an English horse on English racecourses is £163,949 15s. by *Royal Palace* in 1966–67–68.

Most successful owners The greatest amount of stake money won is £1,025,592 from 784 races by H.H. Aga Khan III (1877–1957) from 1922 until his death. These included 35 classics, of which 17 were English classics. The record for a season was set by Mr. H. J. Joel, who surpassed the previous record of £100,668 by winning £120,924 in 1967. The most wins in a season is 105 (*not* 111) in 1873 by Mr. C. J. Lefevre. The most English classics won is 20 by the 4th Duke of Grafton, K.G. (1760–1844), from 1813 to 1831.

Most successful trainers Captain Sir Cecil Charles Boyd-Rochfort, K.C.V.O. (b. 16 April 1887) has earned more than £1,500,000 for his patrons. The record for a season is £256,899 by Charles Francis Noel Murless (born 1910) in 1967. The most classics won by a trainer is 40 or 41 by John Scott, including 16 St. Leger winners between 1827 and 1862.

Tattenham Corner, the Derby's most famous landmark

Fred Darling had seven winners, including two in the war-time meetings at Newmarket (1940–41).

Jockey The most successful jockey was Jem Robinson, who won six times in 1817, 1824–25, 1827–28 and 1836. Steve Donoghue (1884–1945) rode six winners in 1915, 1917, 1921–23 and 1925, but the first two were war-time races not on the Epsom Course.

Record time The record time for the Derby is 2 minutes 33·8 seconds (average speed 35·06 m.p.h.) by *Mahmoud,* ridden by Charlie Smirke, owned by H.H. Aga Khan III, trained by Frank Butters (1878–1957), winning at 100 to 8 by three lengths from a field of 22 in 1936. The fastest time recorded over the Derby course is, however, 2 minutes 33·0 seconds by the four-year-old *Apelle* in winning the 1928 Coronation Cup.

Dead heats The two instances of dead heats were in 1828, when *Cadland* beat *The Colonel* in the run off, and in 1884 between *Harvester* and *St. Gatien* (stakes divided).

Disqualifications The two disqualifications were of *Running Rein* (race awarded to *Orlando*) in 1844 and of *Craganour* (race awarded to *Aboyeur*) in the "Suffragette Derby" on 4 June 1913, when Miss Emily Davison killed herself by impeding King George V's horse *Anmer.*

Other records The only greys to have won were *Gustavus* (1821), *Tagalie* (1912), *Mahmoud* (1936) and *Airborne* (1946). Only two black horses have ever won—*Smolensko* (1813) and *Grand Parade* (1919). The longest odds quoted on a placed Derby horse were 200–1 against for *Black Tommy,* second to *Blink Bonny* in 1857. The shortest priced winner was *Ladas* (1894) at 9–2 on and the highest priced winners were *Jeddah* (1898), *Signorinetta* (1908) and *Aboyeur* (1913), all at 100 to 1 against. The smallest field was four in 1794 and the largest 34 in 1862. The smallest winner was *Little Wonder* (14 hands 3½ inches) in 1840.

GRAND NATIONAL

Most wins Horse The first official Grand National Steeplechase may be regarded as the Grand Liverpool Steeplechase of 26 Feb. 1839 though the race was not so named until some years later. The first winner of the Grand Liverpool Steeplechase was Mr. Pott's *The Duke* in 1837. The race is for six-year-olds and over (since 1930) and is run over a course of 4 miles 856 yards, with 30 jumps, at Aintree, near Liverpool. No horse has won three times but six share the record of two wins:

Peter Simple	1849 and 1853	The Colonel	1869 and 1870
Abd-el-Kader	1850 and 1851	Manifesto	1897 and 1899
The Lamb	1868 and 1871	Reynoldstown	1935 and 1936

Manifesto was entered eight times (1895–1904) and won twice, came third three times and fourth once. *Poethlyn* won in 1919 having won the war-time Gatwick race in 1918.

Jockey The only jockey to ride five winners was G. Stevens on *Free Trader* (1856), *Emblem* (1863), *Emblematic* (1864) and *The Colonel* (1869–70).

Owner The only owners with three winners, since the race became a handicap in 1843, are Captain Machell with *Disturbance* (1873), *Reughy* (1874) and *Regal* (1876) and Sir Charles Assheton-Smith with *Cloister* (1893) *Jerry M* (1912) and *Covertcoat* (1913).

Trainer The only trainer with four winners was the Hon. Aubrey Hastings with *Ascetic's Silver* (1906), *Ally Sloper* (1915), *Ballymacad* (1917, Gatwick) and *Master Robert* (1924).

Highest prize The highest prize was £22,334 5s. won by *Anglo* on 26 March 1966.

Fastest time Times before the 1939–45 War were not officially returned. In 1935 the eight-year-old *Reynoldstown* ridden by Mr. F. Furlong won by 3 lengths from a field of 27 in times variously reported as 9 minutes 21·6 seconds or 9 minutes 20·2 seconds. *Golden Miller,* a seven-year-old ridden by G. Wilson, carrying 12 stone 2 lb., and owned by the Hon. Miss Dorothy Paget, won by 5 lengths from a field of 30 in 9 minutes 20·4 seconds (28·82 m.p.h.) in 1934.

Highest jump The 15th jump, known as the "Open Ditch", is 5 feet 2 inches high and 3 feet 9 inches thick. The ditch on the take-off side is 6 feet wide, and the guard rail in front of the ditch is 1 foot 6 inches in height.

National Hunt record The greatest number of winners saddled in a National Hunt season is 86 by Arthur Stephenson of Bishop Auckland, in 1966–67. In that season Ryan Price won £41,232 with 73 winners.

Hurling

Earliest reference A game of very ancient origin, hurling only became standardized with the formation of the Gaelic Athletic Association in Thurles, Ireland, on 1 Nov. 1884.

Most titles The greatest number of All-Ireland Championships won by one team is 21 by Tipperary in 1887, 1895–96, 1898–99–1900, 1906, 1908, 1916, 1925, 1930, 1937, 1945, 1949–50–51, 1958, 1961–62 and 1964–65. The greatest number of successive wins is four by Cork (1941–44).

Highest score The highest score* in an All-Ireland final was in 1896 when Tipperary (8 goals, 14 points) beat Dublin (no goals, 4 points). The record aggregate score was when Kilkenny (4 goals, 17 points) beat Waterford (6 goals, 8 points) in 1963. *A goal equals 3 points.

Lowest score The lowest score in an All-Ireland final was when Tipperary (1 goal, 1 point) beat Galway (nil) in the first championship at Birr in 1887.

Most The most appearances in All-Ireland finals is ten shared by Christy Ring (Cork) and John Doyle (Tipperary). They also share the record of All-Ireland medals won with 8 each. Ring's appearances on the winning side were in 1941–42–43–44, 1946 and 1952–53–54, while Doyle's were in 1949–50–51, 1958, 1961–62 and 1964–65.

Individual score The highest recorded individual score was by Nick Rackard (Wexford), who scored 7 goals and 7 points against Antrim in the 1954 All-Ireland semi-final.

Largest crowd The largest crowd was 84,856 for the final between Cork and Wexford at Croke Park, Dublin, in 1954.

Inter-provincials Munster holds the greatest number of inter-provincial (Railway Cup) championships with 28 (1928–1963). Christy Ring (Cork and Munster) played in a record 22 finals (1942–1963) and was on the winning side 18 times.

Longest stroke The greatest distance for a "lift and stroke" is one of 129 yards credited to Tom Murphy of Three Castles,

Kilkenny, in a "long puck" contest in 1906. The record for the annual *An Poc Fada* (Long Puck) contest (instituted 1961) in the ravines of the Cooley Hills, north of Dundalk, County Louth, is 65 pucks (drives) plus 87 yards over the course of 3 miles 320 yards by Fionnbar O'Neill (Cork) in 1966. This represents an average of 84·8 yards per drive.

Ice Hockey

Origins The game probably originated in 1860 at Kingston, Ontario, Canada, but Montreal and Halifax also lay claims as the originators.

Olympic Games Canada has won the Olympic title six times (1920–24–28–32–48–52) and the world title 19 times, the last being at Geneva in 1961. The longest Olympic career is that of Richard Torriani (Switzerland) from 1928 to 1948. The most gold medals won by any player is two, this was achieved by nine U.S.S.R. players in the 1968 Games, who had been in the 1964 gold medal team.

Stanley Cup The Stanley Cup, presented by the Governor-General Lord Stanley (original cost $48·67), became emblematic of world professional team supremacy several years after the first contest at Montreal in 1893. It has been won most often by the Montreal Canadiens [*sic*], with 16 wins in 1916, 1924, 1930, 1931, 1944, 1946, 1953, 1956 (winning a record 45 games), 1957, 1958, 1959, 1960, 1965, 1966, 1968 and 1969.

Longest match The longest match was 2 hours 56 minutes 30 seconds when Detroit Red Wings eventually beat Montreal Maroons 1–0 in the sixth period of overtime at the Forum, Montreal, at 2.25 a.m. on 25 March 1936.

Most goals Ottawa defeated Dawson City 23–2 at Ottawa on 16 Jan. 1905.

Most cup goals in a season: Robert (Bobby) Marvin Hull Jr. (born Ontario, Canada, 3 Jan. 1939) (Chicago Black Hawks) scored 54 goals in 1965–66. The most points in a season is 97 (54 goals, 43 assists) by Hull in 1965–66 and by Stan Mikita (Chicago) with 35 goals

Sports, games and pastimes

and 62 assists in 1966–67. The North American career record for goals is 743 (678 in regular season, 65 in playoffs) by Gordie Howe (Detroit Red Wings) to February 1968. He has also collected 500 stitches in his face. Two players have scored 1,000 goals in Great Britain—Chick Zamick (Nottingham Panthers and Wembley Lions) and George Beach (Wembley Monarchs and later Wembley Lions).

Fastest scoring Toronto scored 8 goals against the New York Americans in 4 minutes 52 seconds on 19 March 1938. Bill Mosienko (Chicago) scored three goals in 21 seconds against New York Rangers on 23 March 1952.

Fastest player The highest speed measured for any player is 29·7 m.p.h. for Bobby Hull (Chicago Black Hawks). The highest puck speed is also attributed to Hull, whose left-handed slap shot has been measured at 118·3 m.p.h.

BRITISH LEAGUE
The highest score on record was when Streatham beat Racing Club de Paris 23–3 in 1949–50. Bud McEachern shot seven goals for Streatham.

Most wins The British League championship (instituted 1934 but not still running) has been won most often by the Wembley Lions with four victories in 1936–37, 1952 and 1957.

Ice Skating

Origins The earliest reference to ice skating is that of a Danish writer dated 1134. The earliest English account of 1180

Valeriy Muratov (U.S.S.R.), the world 1,000 metre record holder

WORLD SPEED SKATING RECORDS

	Distance	mins. secs.	Name and Nationality	Place	Date
MEN	500 metres	38·46*†	Hasse Bjoerjes (Sweden)	Inzell, West Germany	8 Mar. 1970
	1,000 metres	1:19·25*	Valery Muratov (U.S.S.R.)	Medeo, U.S.S.R.	25 Jan. 1970
	1,500 metres	2:01·90*	Cornelis Verkerk (Netherlands)	Inzell, West Germany	8 Mar. 1970
	3,000 metres	4:16·40	Jan Bols (Netherlands)	Cortina, Italy	27 Jan. 1970
	5,000 metres	7:13·20	Cornelis Verkerk (Netherlands)	Inzell, West Germany	1 Mar. 1969
	10,000 metres	15:03·60	Cornelis Verkerk (Netherlands)	Inzell, West Germany	26 Jan. 1969
WOMEN	500 metres	43·22*	Tatyana Sidorova (U.S.S.R.)	Medeo, U.S.S.R.	17 Jan. 1970
	1,000 metres	1:29·10	L. Fechnina (U.S.S.R.)	Medeo, U.S.S.R.	17 Jan. 1970
	1,500 metres	2:17·82*	Nina Statkevich (U.S.S.R.)	Medeo, U.S.S.R.	17 Jan. 1970
	3,000 metres	4:50·30	Ans Schut (Netherlands)	Inzell, West Germany	23 Feb. 1969
	5,000 metres	9:01·60	Rimma Zhukova (U.S.S.R.)	Medeo, U.S.S.R.	24 Jan. 1953

BRITISH OUTDOOR RECORDS

	Distance	mins. secs.	Name	Place	Date
MEN	500 metres	40·90	A. John Tipper	Cortina d'Ampezzo, Italy	28 Jan. 1970
	1,000 metres	1:24·00	A. John Tipper	Cortina d'Ampezzo, Italy	27 Jan. 1970
	1,500 metres	2:08·40	A. John Tipper	Cortina d'Ampezzo, Italy	28 Jan. 1970
	3,000 metres	4:34·70	John B. Blewitt	Cortina d'Ampezzo, Italy	16 Jan. 1968
	5,000 metres	7:57·10	Terence A. Malkin	Oslo, Norway	12 Feb. 1964
	10,000 metres	16:30·10	Terence A. Malkin	Oslo, Norway	19 Jan. 1964
WOMEN	500 metres	51·90	Patricia K. Tipper	Cortina d'Ampezzo, Italy	16 Jan. 1968
	1,000 metres	1:44·20	Patricia K. Tipper	Inzell, West Germany	7 Jan. 1968
	1,500 metres	2:42·80	Patricia K. Tipper	Cortina d'Ampezzo, Italy	17 Dec. 1967
	3,000 metres	5:39·40	Patricia K. Tipper	Cortina d'Ampezzo, Italy	16 Dec. 1967

* *Subject to ratification by the International Skating Union.*
† *This represents a speed of 29·08 m.p.h.*

refers to skates made of bone. Metal blades date from probably *c*. 1600. The earliest skating club was the Edinburgh Skating Club formed in 1742. The earliest artificial ice rink in the world was the "Glaciarium" in Chelsea, London, in 1876.

Longest race The longest race regularly held is the "Elfstedentocht" ("Tour of the Eleven Towns") in the Netherlands. It covers 200 kilometres (124 miles 483 yards) and the fastest time is 7 hours 35 minutes by Jeen van den Berg (born 8 Jan. 1928) on 3 Feb. 1954.

Largest rink The world's largest indoor ice rink is the Tōkyō Ice Rink, completed in 1960, which has an ice area of 43,000 sq. ft. (or 0·99 of an acre). The largest artificial outdoor rink is the Fujikyu Highland Promenade Rink, Japan opened at a cost of £335,000 in 1967 and with an area of 165,750 square feet (3·8 acres). The largest in the U.K. is the Crossmyloof Ice Rink, Glasgow, with an ice area of 225 feet by 97 feet.

SPEED SKATING

Most titles World The greatest number of world speed skating titles (instituted 1893) won by any skater is five by Oscar Mathisen (Norway) in 1908–09 and 1912–14, and Clas Thunberg (born 5 April 1893) of Finland, in 1923, 1925, 1928–29 and 1931. The most titles won by a woman is four by Mrs. Inga Voronina, *née* Artomonova (1936–66) of Moscow, U.S.S.R., in 1957, 1958, 1962 and 1965.

Olympic The most Olympic gold medals won in speed skating is six by Lidia Skoblikova (born 8 March 1939) of Chelyaminsk, U.S.S.R., in 1960 (2) and 1964 (4).

FIGURE SKATING

World The greatest number of world men's figure skating titles (instituted 1896) is ten by Ulrich Salchow (born 7 Aug. 1877) of Sweden, in 1901–05 and 1907–11. The women's record (instituted 1906) is ten titles by Frk. Sonja Henie (born 8 April 1912) of Norway, between 1927 and 1936.

Cecilia Colledge, winner of the record number of British Women's Figure Skating Championships

276

Olympic The most Olympic gold medals won by a figure skat is three by Gillis Graftström (born 7 June 1893) Sweden in 1920, 1924 and 1928 (also silver medal 1932); and by Sonja Henie (see above) in 1928, 19: and 1936.

British The record number of British titles is 11 by Jack Pa: (Manchester S.C.) in 1922–31 and 1933, and six t Miss Cecilia Colledge (Park Lane F.S.C., London) : 1935–36–37(2)–38 and 1946.

Ice Yachting

Origin The sport originated in the Netherlands from the yea 1600 (earliest patent granted) and along the Balt coast. The earliest authentic record is Dutch, datin from 1768. The largest known ice yacht was *Icicle,* bui for Commodore John E. Roosevelt for racing on th Hudson River, New York, in *c.* 1870. It was 68 fee 11 inches long and carried 1,070 square feet of canvas The highest speed officially recorded is 143 m.p.h. b John D. Buckstaff in a Class A stern-steerer on Lak Winnebago, Wisconsin, U.S.A., in 1938. Such a spee is possible in a wind of 72 m.p.h.

Judo (Jiu-jitsu)

Origins Judo is a modern combat sport which developed out o an amalgam of several old Japanese fighting arts, th most popular of which was ju-jitsu (jiu-jitsu), which i thought to be of pre-Christian Chinese origin. Judo ha been greatly developed by the Japanese since 1882 when it was first devised by *Shihan* Dr. Jigoro Kano World championships were inaugurated in 1956. Grea Britain has won most consecutive European champion ships (instituted in 1951) with 3 victories (1957–58–59) France won in 1951–52, 1954–55 and 1962.

Highest grade The efficiency grades in Judo are divided into pupi (*kyu*) and master (*dan*) grades. The highest awarded i: the extremely rare red belt *Judan* (*10th dan*), given only to seven men. The Judo protocol provides for an *11th dan* (*Juichidan*) who also would wear a red belt anc even a *12th dan* who would wear a white belt twice a: wide as an ordinary belt, but these have never been bestowed. The highest British native held grade i: *6th dan* by Trevor P. Leggett.

Heaviest champion The heaviest world champion was Antonius (Anton) J. Geesink (born 6 April 1934) of the Netherlands, who won the 1964 Olympic open title in Tōkyō at a weight of 17 stone. He was 19 stone in 1965 and stands 6 feet 6 inches tall.

Karate

Origins Originally *karate* (empty hand) is known to have been developed by the unarmed populace as a method of attack on, and defence against, armed oppressors in Okinawa, in the Ryukyu Islands, in the 17th century. It is accepted that it may have been of Chinese origin. It was introduced into Japan in 1916. The four major schools of *Karate* in Japan are *Shotokan, Wado-ryu, Goju-ryu* and *Shito-ryu*. Military *Karate* for killing, as used by Korean troops, is *tae kwan do*.

Top exponents The only winner of two All-Japanese titles was Hirokazu Kanazawa (*6th dan*) in 1957 and 1958. He won his first title with a broken arm. The highest *dan* among *karatekas* is Yamaguchi Gogen (born 1907) a *10th dan* of the Gojuryu Karate Do.

The leading exponents in the United Kingdom are Tatsuo Suzuki (*7th dan, Wado-ryu*), chief instructor to the All-Britain Karate-Do Association; Kanazawa (*5th dan, Shotokan*), resident instructor to the K.U.G.B. (Karate Union of Great Britain); and Steve Arneil (born in South Africa), who is a *5th dan*.

eatest force The force needed to break a brick with the abductor digiti quinti muscle of the hand is normally 130–140 lb. The highest measured impact is 196 lb.

Lacrosse

Origin The game is of American Indian origin, derived from the inter-tribal game *baggataway*, and was played before 1492 by Iroquois Indians in lower Ontario, Canada and upper New York State, U.S.A. It was introduced into Great Britain in 1867. The English Lacrosse Union was formed in 1892. The Oxford *v.* Cambridge match was instituted in 1903 and the game was included in the Olympic Games of 1908 and featured as an exhibition sport in the 1928 and 1948 Games.

World ionship The first World Tournament was held at Toronto, Canada in 1967 and the U.S.A. won.

ongest throw The longest recorded throw is 162·86 yards by Barney Quin of Ottawa in 1892.

t titles The English Club Championship (Iroquois Cup), instituted in 1890, has been won most often by Stockport with 15 wins between 1897 and 1934.

Highest score The highest score in any international match was England's 18–2 win over Wales at Cardiff in 1907.

Most ationals The record number of international representations for England is 13 by G. A. MacDonald of Mellor, Cheshire to 1967. (No internationals were played in 1968.)

Lawn Tennis

Origins The modern game is generally agreed to have evolved as an outdoor form of Tennis (see separate entry) and to have first become organized with the court and equipment devised, and patented in February 1874, by Major Walter Clopton Wingfield, M.V.O. (1833–1912). This was introduced as "sphairistike" but the game soon became known as lawn tennis. Open lawn tennis was introduced in 1968.

ALL TIME RECORDS

GREATEST DOMINATION

The earliest occasion upon which any player secured all four of the world's major titles was in 1935 when Frederick John Perry (U.K.) won the French title having won Wimbledon (1934), the United States title (1933–34) and the Australian title (1934).

The earliest example of a man holding all four titles at the same time was J. Donald Budge (U.S.A.) who won the championships of Wimbledon (1937), the U.S.A. (1937), Australia (1938), France (1938). He subsequently retained Wimbledon (1938) and the U.S.A. (1938). Rodney George Laver (Australia) repeated the grand slam of the four major championships in 1962 and again, when the events were open, in 1969.

The only example of a woman player holding all four titles at the same time was Miss Maureen Catherine Connolly (1935–1969) (U.S.A.). She won the United States title in 1951, Wimbledon in 1952, retained the U.S. title in 1952, won the Australian in 1953, the French in 1953 and Wimbledon again in 1953. She won her third U.S. title in 1953, her second French title in 1954, and her third Wimbledon title in 1954. Miss Connolly

(later Mrs. Norman Brinker) was seriously injured in a riding accident shortly before the 1954 U.S. championships and died in June 1969 aged only 34.

In the course of her playing career (from 1960) Miss Margaret Jean Smith (later Mrs. Barry Court, M.B.E.) (Australia) won the singles, the women's doubles and the mixed doubles titles in all four of the leading championships, those of Australia, France, Wimbledon and the U.S. She won a total of 46 titles in all at these meetings.

Fred Perry (G.B.), the first man to win all four of the world's major championships

Singles match The greatest number of games ever played in a singles match is 126. Roger Taylor (U.K.) beat Wieslaw Gasiorek (Poland) 27–29, 31–29, 6–4 on an indoor court in Warsaw, Poland, on 5 Nov, 1966, in a King's Cup tie. The match lasted 4 hours 35 minutes.

Doubles match The greatest number of games ever played in a doubles match is 147. Dick Leach and Dick Dell of Michigan University beat Tommy Mozur and Lenny Schloss 3–6, 49–47, 22–20 at Newport, Rhode Island, U.S.A. on 18–19 Aug. 1967.

Longest match Mark Cox and Robert K. Wilson (G.B.) beat Charles M. Pasarell and Ron E. Holmberg (U.S.A.) 26–24, 17–19, 30–28 in a match lasting 6 hours 23 minutes at the U.S. Indoor Championships at Salisbury, Maryland on 16 Feb. 1968.

Fastest service The fastest service ever *measured* was one of 154 m.p.h. by Michael J. Sangster (U.K.) in June 1963. Crossing the net the ball was travelling at 108 m.p.h. Some players consider the service of Robert Falkenberg (U.S.A.) the 1948 Wimbledon Champion as the fastest ever used.

Greatest crowd The greatest crowd at a tennis match was 25,578 at the first day of the Davis Cup Challenge Round between Australia and the United States at the White City, Sydney, New South Wales, Australia, on 27 Dec. 1954.

WIMBLEDON RECORDS
(The first Championship was in June 1877. Professionals first played in 1968.)

MOST GAMES
Singles The most games in a singles match at Wimbledon was 112 when Ricardo Alonzo Gonzalez (United States) beat Charles M. Pasarell (United States) 22–24, 1–6, 16–14, 6–3, 11–9 in the first round on 24–25 June 1969. The match, which was interrupted by nightfall, lasted a Wimbledon record total of 5 hours and 12 minutes.

Doubles The most games in a doubles match at Wimbledon was 98 when Eugene L. Scott (U.S.A.) and Nicola Pilic (Yugoslavia) beat G. Cliff Richey (U.S.A.) and Torben Ulrich (Denmark) by 19–21, 12–10, 6–4, 4–6, 9–7 in the first round of the men's doubles on 22 June 1966.

Set The most games in a set at Wimbledon was 62 when Pancho Segura (Ecuador) and Alex Olmedo (Peru) beat Abe A. Segal and Gordon L. Forbes (South Africa) 32–30 in a second round match in 1968.

Dennis Ralston (U.S.A.), the youngest-ever winner of the Men's Wimbledon Championship

MOST GAMES IN FINALS
The most games in a Wimbledon men's singles final wa[s] 58 when Jaroslav Drobny (then Egypt) beat Kennet[h] R. Rosewall (Australia) 13–11, 4–6, 6–2, 9–7 in 1954.

The most games in a Wimbledon ladies' singles fin[al] was 46 when Mrs. Barry M. Court, M.B.E., 27, be[at] Mrs. L. W. King (U.S.A.) by 14–12, 11–9 on 3 July 197[0] in a match lasting 2 hours 25 minutes.

The most games in a Wimbledon men's doubles fin[al] was 70 when John D. Newcombe and Anthony [D.] Roche (Australia) beat Kenneth R. Rosewall an[d] Frederick S. Stolle (Australia) 3–6, 8–6, 5–7, 14–1[2,] 6–3 in 1968.

The most games in a Wimbledon ladies' doubles fin[al] was 38, on two occasions. Mme. Simone Mathie[u] (France) and Miss Elizabeth ("Bunny") Ryan (U.S.A.) beat Miss Freda James (now Mrs. S. H. Hammersley) and Miss Adeline Maud Yorke (now Mrs. D. E. [C.] Eyres) (both U.K.) by 6–2, 9–11, 6–4 in 1933, and Mis[s] Rosemary Casals and Mrs. Billie Jean King (U.S.A.) beat Miss Maria Bueno (Brazil) and Miss Nancy Riche[y] (U.S.A.) 9–11, 6–4, 6–2 in 1967.

The most games in a Wimbledon mixed doubles fin[al] was 48 when Eric W. Sturgess and Mrs. Sheila Summer[s] (South Africa) beat John E. Bromwich (Australia) an[d] Miss A. Louise Brough (U.S.A.) 9–7, 9–11, 7–5 in 194[9.]

Longest match The longest Wimbledon match was the 5 hours 1[2] minutes required by the Gonzalez v. Pasarell matc[h] (*see* Most games, singles, left).

Youngest champions The youngest ever champion at Wimbledon was Mis[s] Charlotte Dod (1871–1960), who was 15 years [8] months when she won in 1887.

The youngest male singles champion was Wilfre[d] Baddeley (born 11 Jan. 1872) who won the Wimbledo[n] title in 1891 at the age of 19.

Richard Dennis Ralston (born 27 July 1942) of Bakersfield, California, U.S.A. was 25 days short of his 18th birthday when he won the men's doubles with Rafael H. Osuna (1938–1969) of Mexico in 1960.

Most appearances Arthur W. Gore (1868–1928) of the U.K. made 36 appearances between 1888 and 1927, and was in 1909 at 41 years the oldest ever singles winner. In 1964, Jean Borotra (born 13 Aug. 1898) of France made his 35th appearance since 1922.

Most wins Miss Elizabeth Ryan (U.S.A.) won her first title in 1914 and her nineteenth in 1934 (12 women's doubles with 5 different partners and 7 mixed doubles with 5 different partners).

The greatest number of wins by a man at Wimbledon has been 14 by William C. Renshaw (G.B.) who won 7 singles titles (1881–2–3–4–5–6–9) and 7 doubles (1880–1–4–5–6–8–9), partnered by his twin brother Ernest. Hugh Lawrence Doherty (1875–1919) won 5 singles (1902–3–4–5–6), 8 men's doubles (1897–8–9–1900–01 and 1903–4–5), partnered by his brother Reginald F. Doherty (1872–1911), and two mixed doubles (then unofficial) in 1901–02, partnered by Mrs. A. Sterry.

The greatest number of singles wins was eight by Mrs. F. S. Moody (*née* Helen N. Wills), now Mrs. Aiden Roark, of the U.S.A., who won in 1927, 1928, 1929, 1930, 1932, 1933, 1935 and 1938.

The greatest number of singles wins by a man was seven by William C. Renshaw (G.B.), as quoted above.

The greatest number of doubles wins by men was 8 by

the brothers R. F. and H. L. Doherty (G.B.). They won each year from 1897 to 1905 except for 1902.

The most wins in women's doubles were 12 by Miss Elizabeth Ryan (U.S.A.) between 1914 and 1934, as mentioned on page 278.

The most wins in mixed doubles was 7 by Miss Elizabeth Ryan (U.S.A.) between 1919 and 1932. The male record is four wins shared by Elias Victor Seixas (U.S.A.) in 1953–54–55–56 and Kenneth N. Fletcher (Australia) in 1963–65–66–68.

ssional tennis The professional game became established in 1934 with William Tatem Tilden II (1893–1953) and H. Ellsworth Vines (both U.S.A.). The longest domination was achieved by Ricardo Anzalo ("Pancho") Gonzalez (born 9 May 1928) of the U.S.A., who was ranked No. 1 for 8 years, from 1954 to 1961.

n tennis athons The longest recorded non-stop lawn tennis doubles game is one of 19 hours by John Rice, Graham Oxley, John Long and Geoffrey King from Walton-on-the-Naze, Essex on 23–24 Aug. 1969. The duration record for the maintenance of continuous singles by 4 players is 40 hours at The Rumney Youth Centre, Cardiff, South Wales on 3–5 May 1968. They played 802 games.

DAVIS CUP

Most ictories The greatest number of wins in the Davis Cup (instituted 1900) has been (inclusive of 1969) Australia and Australasia 22 times and U.S.A. 21 times. The British Isles/Great Britain have won 9 times, in 1903–04–05–06, 1912, 1933–34–35–36.

dividual rmance Nicola Pietrangeli (Italy) played 159 rubbers, 1954 to 1969, winning 116. He played 108 singles (winning 76) and 51 doubles (winning 40). He took part in 62 ties.

Greatest mber of games In a tie the greatest number of games played was 281 in Perth in 1960 when in the Inter-Zone final Italy beat the U.S.A. 3–2.

In a match the greatest number of games played was 95 when at Edgbaston, Birmingham in 1969 in the quarter-final of the European Zone Wilhelm Bungert and Christian Kuhnke (Germany) beat Mark Cox and Peter Curtis (Great Britain) 10–8, 17–19, 13–11, 3–6, 6–2.

In a singles match the greatest number of games played was 82 when at Cleveland, Ohio, in the Inter-Zone semi-final Arthur Ashe (U.S.) beat Manuel Santana (Spain) 11–13, 7–5, 6–3, 13–15, 6–3.

Sports, games and pastimes
Modern Pentathlon

The Modern Pentathlon (Riding, Fencing, Shooting, Swimming and Running) was inaugurated into the Olympic Games at Stockholm in 1912. The Modern Pentathlon Association of Great Britain was formed in 1922.

MOST TITLES

World The record number of world titles won is 5 by András Balczo (Hungary) in 1963, 1965, 1966, 1967 and 1969.

British The pentathlete with most British titles is Sgt. Jeremy Robert Fox, R.E.M.E. with 6 (1963, 1965, 1966, 1967, 1968 and 1970).

Sergeant J. R. Fox, winner of most British Championships

The highest world and British scores in the five events in Olympic Games or world championship competition are:

	World				British			
Riding	1,237	S. Escobedo (Mexico), Rome	26 Aug.	1960	1,152	C.S.M.I. George R. Norman, Budapest	10 Oct.	1954
Fencing (Epée)	1,140	I. Novikov (U.S.S.R.), Stockholm	25 Oct.	1957	930	Sgt. Donald Cobley, Stockholm	25 Oct.	1957
Shooting	1,066	P. Macken (Australia) and R. Phelps (U.K.), Leipzig	21 Sept.	1965	1,066	R. Phelps, Leipzig	21 Sept.	1965
	1,066	I. Mona (Hungary), Jönköping	11 Sept.	1967	1,042	L/Cpl. B. Lillywhite, Melbourne	Oct.	1966
Swimming	1,144	K-H. Kutschke (E. Germany), Jönköping	12 Sept.	1967				
Cross-Country	1,312	A. Balczo (Hungary), Bern	26 Sept.	1963	1,255	Sgt. Donald Cobley, Melbourne	27 Nov.	1956
Overall	5,302	A. Balczo (Hungary), Leipzig	19–23 Sept.	1965	4,818	Sgt. J. R. Fox, Melbourne	Oct.	1966

Note: The highest known total in any competition is 5,530 points by Sgt. J. R. Fox in the R.A.F. Championships at Halton, Buckinghamshire in July 1966.

Earliest races The first motorcycle race was one from Paris to Dieppe, France, in 1897. The oldest motorcycle races in the world are the Auto-Cycle Union Tourist Trophy (T.T.) series, first held on the 15¾-mile "Peel" ("St. John's") course in the Isle of Man in 1907, and still run in the island, on the "Mountain" circuit (37·73 miles) and, until 1959, on the Clypse circuit of 10·79 miles.

FASTEST CIRCUITS

World The highest average lap speed attained on any closed circuit is 157·343 m.p.h. by Gene Romero (U.S.A.) when he lapped the 2·50-mile Daytona International Speedway, Daytona Beach, Florida, U.S.A., which is banked at 31 degrees, in 57·20 seconds on a 741 c.c. three-cylinder Triumph Trident, in practice, on 12 March 1970.

The fastest road circuit is the Francorchamps circuit near Spa, Belgium. It is 14·10 kilometres (8 miles 1,340 yards) in length and was lapped in 4 minutes 1·4 seconds (average speed of 130·658 m.p.h.) by Giacomo Agostini (born Lovere, Italy, 16 June 1942)

Mike Hailwood, the most successful-ever rider in the Isle of Man T.T. races

on a 500 c.c. three-cylinder M.V.-Agusta on lap 7 of th 500 c.c. Belgian Grand Prix on 6 July 1969.

United Kingdom The fastest circuit in the United Kingdom is th 10·637-mile Portstewart-Coleraine-Portrush circuit i Londonderry, Northern Ireland. The race lap record 5 minutes 50·6 seconds (average speed 109·222 m.p.h by Ralph Bryans (born Belfast, Northern Ireland, March 1942) on a 250 c.c. six-cylinder Honda, durin the North-West 200, on 18 May 1968. Rodney Alfre Gould (born Banbury, Oxfordshire, 10 March 1943 lapped in 5 minutes 47·6 seconds (110·165 m.p.h.) on 350 c.c. parallel twin TR2 Yamaha, in practice, o 22 May 1969.

The record for the outer circuit lap (2·767 miles) at th Brooklands Motor Course near Weybridge, Surre (open between 1907 and 1939) was 80·0 second (average speed 124·51 m.p.h.) by Noel Baddow "Bill" Pope (later Major) (born Liverpool 1910) on a Brough Superior powered by a supercharged 996 c.c. V-twin "8–80" J.A.P. engine developing 110 b.h.p., on 4 Jul 1939.

FASTEST RACES

World The fastest race in the world was held over 10 laps of th A.V.U.S. track, Berlin, East Germany (5 miles 27: yards lap). It was won by H. Reginald Armstrong o Dublin in 24 minutes 23·3 seconds (average spee 126·882 m.p.h.) on a 493 c.c. four-cylinder Gilera, o 16 September 1956.

The fastest road race is the 500 c.c. Belgian Grand Prix held on the Francorchamps circuit (8 miles 1,340 yards) near Spa, Belgium. The record for this 13-lap (113·898 miles) race is 54 minutes 18·1 seconds (average speed 125·850 m.p.h.) by Giacomo Agostini, on a 500 c.c. three-cylinder M.V.-Agusta, on 6 July 1969.

United Kingdom The fastest race in the United Kingdom is the 350 c.c. event of the North-West 200 held on the Londonderry circuit (see above). The record for this 7-lap (74·459 miles) race is 41 minutes 25·0 seconds (average speed 107·868 m.p.h.) by Rodney Gould on a 350 c.c. parallel twin TR2 Yamaha on 24 May 1969.

Longest race The longest race is the Barcelona 24 hours held on the Montjuich Park circuit, Barcelona, Spain (2 miles 625 yards). The greatest distance ever covered is 1,611·09 miles (average speed 67·129 m.p.h.) by Salvador Carellas and Carlos Rocamora (both of Spain) on a 360 c.c. single-cylinder Bultaco on 5–6 July 1969.

Longest circuit The 37·73-mile "Mountain" circuit, over which the two main T.T. races have been run since 1911, has 264 curves and corners and is the longest used for any motorcycle race.

MOST SUCCESSFUL RIDERS
The record number of victories in the Isle of Man T.T. races is 12 by Stanley Michael Bailey Hailwood, M.B.E. (born Oxford, 2 April 1940), now of Durban, South Africa, between 1961 and 1967. The first man to win three consecutive T.T. titles in two events was James A. Redman (Rhodesia) (born in Hampstead, London, 8 Nov. 1931). He won the 250 c.c. and 350 c.c. events in 1963–64–65. Mike Hailwood is the only man to win three events in one year, in 1961 and 1967.

World championships Most world championship titles (instituted by the *Fédération Internationale Motorcycliste* in 1949) won are:

9 Carlo Ubbiali (born Bergamo, Italy, 1929)
   125 c.c. 1951, 55, 56, 58, 59, 60;
   250 c.c. 1956, 59, 60.
9 Mike Hailwood (G.B.)
   500 c.c. 1962, 63, 64, 65;
   350 c.c. 1966, 67;
   250 c.c. 1961, 66, 67.

John Surtees, M.B.E. (born Tatsfield, Surrey, 11 Feb. 1934) is the only man to win two world championships in three consecutive years (350 and 500 c.c. titles in 1958–59–60).

Mike Hailwood won 76 races in the world championship series between 1959 and 1967, including a record 19 in 1966.

Trials Sammy H. Miller (born Belfast, Northern Ireland, 1935), won eleven A.-C.U. Solo Trials Drivers' Stars in 1959–60–61–62–63–64–65–66–67–68–69.

ambles Jeffrey Vincent Smith, M.B.E. (born Colne, Lancashire, 14 October 1934) won nine A.-C.U. 500 c.c. Scrambles Stars in 1955–56, 1960–61–62–63–64–65 and 1967.

Torsten Hallman (born Uppsala, Sweden, 1940) has won four 250 c.c. Moto-Cross World Championships (1962–63–66–67).

Most cessful achines Italian M.V.-Agusta machines won 30 World Championships between 1952 and 1969 and 199 World Championship races between 1952 and 1969. Japanese Honda machines won 29 World Championship races and five World Championships in 1966.

SPEED RECORDS
The official world speed record (average speed for two runs over a 1 kilometre course) is 224·569 m.p.h. (average time 9·961 seconds) by Bill A. Johnson, aged 38, of Garden Grove, Los Angeles, California, U.S.A., riding an unsupercharged Triumph Bonneville T120 "Streamliner" with a 667·25 c.c. parallel twin-cylinder engine running on methanol and nitro-methane and developing 75 to 80 b.h.p. at Bonneville Salt Flats, Tooele County, Utah, U.S.A., on 5 Sept. 1962. His machine was 17 feet long and weighed 400 lb. His first run was made in 9·847 seconds (227·169 m.p.h.).

Robert Leppan, 28, of Detroit, recorded higher speeds over the measured mile, without F.I.M. observers, at Bonneville on 25 Aug. 1966 riding his 17 feet 9 inches long, 1,298·6 c.c. "Gyronaut X-1" streamliner powered by two unsupercharged parallel twin-cylinder Triumph "Trophy" engines developing a total of 140 b.h.p. when running on methanol. In the first run he covered the mile in 14·78 seconds (243·572 m.p.h.). In the second run his time was 14·53 seconds (247·763 m.p.h.). The average time for the two runs was 14·655 seconds (average speed 245·650 m.p.h.).

The world record for the two runs over 1 kilometre (1093·6 yards) from a standing start is 116·903 m.p.h. (19·135 seconds) by Alfred Joseph Hagon (born Ilford, Essex, 3 Oct. 1931) on his supercharged 1,260 c.c. Hagon-J.A.P. vee-twin, at Elvington Airfield, Yorkshire on 16 Oct. 1966. The faster run was made in 18·964 seconds.

The world record for two runs over 440 yards from a standing start is 91·696 m.p.h. (9·815 seconds) by Dave Lecoq on the supercharged 1,287 c.c. Drag-Waye powered by a flat four Volkswagen engine, at Elvington Airfield, Yorkshire on 11 Oct. 1969. The faster run was made in 9·75 seconds.

The fastest time for a single run over 440 yards from a standing start is 8·68 seconds by E. J. Potter of Ithaca, Michigan, U.S.A., on his 5,359 c.c. Chevrolet Corvette V8 Special at Castlereagh Airstrip near Sydney, Australia on 26 Jan. 1970.

Motor Racing

Earliest races The first automobile trial was one of 20 miles from Paris to Versailles and back on 20 April 1887, won by Georges Bouton's steam quadricycle in 74 minutes, at an average of 16·22 m.p.h. The first "real" race was

Pedro Rodriguez in his Porsche 917 lapping the Spa Circuit at over 160 m.p.h.— 8 m.p.h. faster than any F1 car

from Paris to Bordeaux and back (732 miles) on 11–13 June 1895. The winner was Emile Levassor (France) driving a Panhard-Levassor two-seater, with a 1·2 litre Daimler engine developing 4 horse-power. His time was 48 hours 47 minutes (average speed 15·01 m.p.h.).

The oldest motor race in the world, still being regularly run, is the R.A.C. Tourist Trophy (35th race held in 1970), first staged on 14 Sept. 1905 in the Isle of Man. The oldest continental races are the Targa Florio (54th in 1970), in Sicily, first held on 9 May 1906, and the French Grand Prix (48th in 1970), first held on 26–27 June 1906.

FASTEST CIRCUITS
World The highest average lap speed attained on any closed circuit is 200·447 m.p.h. by Buddy Baker of Charlotte, North Carolina, driving a 1970 Dodge Daytona, powered by a 600 b.h.p., 426 cubic inch V8 engine, at the Alabama International Motor Speedway, Talladega, Alabama, U.S.A., in March 1970. The race lap average for this 2·66 mile, 33 degree banked tri-oval is also a record. On 14 Sept. 1969 it was lapped at over 195 m.p.h. during a 500-mile race by Richard Brickhouse driving a 1969 Dodge Daytona.

The fastest road circuit is the Francorchamps circuit near Spa, Belgium. It is 14·10 kilometres (8 miles 1,340 yards) in length and was lapped in 3 minutes 16·5 seconds (average speed of 160·513 m.p.h.) during the Francorchamps 1,000 kilometre sports car race on 17 May 1970, by Pedro Rodriguez (born Mexico City,

281

Sports, games and pastimes

Mexico, 18 Jan. 1940) driving a 4,907 c.c. flat 12 Porsche 917 Group 5 sports car.

United Kingdom The fastest circuit in the United Kingdom is the ex-aerodrome course of 2·927 miles at Silverstone, Northamptonshire (opened 1948). The race lap record is 1 minute 21·3 seconds (129·609 m.p.h.) by John Young "Jackie" Stewart (born Dumbuck, Dunbartonshire, 11 June 1939) driving a 2,993 c.c. Matra MS80–Cosworth V8 on laps 57 and 60 of the 22nd British Grand Prix on 19 July 1969. He set the record practice lap the day before with 1 minute 20·6 seconds (130·734 m.p.h.).

The record for the outer circuit lap (2·767 miles) at the Brooklands Motor Course near Weybridge, Surrey (open between 1907 and 1939) was 1 minute 9·44 seconds (average speed 143·44 m.p.h.) by John Rhodes Cobb (1899–1952) in his 3-ton 23,856 c.c. Napier-Railton, with a Napier "Lion" 12-cylinder aero-engine developing 450 b.h.p., on 7 Oct. 1935. His average speed over a kilometre was 151·97 m.p.h. (14·72 seconds). The race lap record at Brooklands was 1 minute 9·6 seconds (average speed 143·12 m.p.h.) by Oliver Henry Julius Bertram (born Kensington, London, 26 Feb. 1910), driving a 7,963 c.c. Barnato-Hassan Special, during the 7-lap "Dunlop Jubilee Cup" handicap race on 24 Sept. 1938.

The Motor Industry Research Association (MIRA) High Speed Circuit (2·82 miles lap with 33 degree banking on the bends) at Lindley, Warwickshire, was

lapped in 1 minute 2·8 seconds (average speed 161·6 m.p.h.) by Norman Dewis (born 20 Aug. 1920) drivi a Jaguar development car on an officially undisclos date prior to 1967.

FASTEST RACES

World The fastest race in the world was the 50-mile event the NASCAR Grand National meeting at Dayto International Speedway on 8 Feb. 1964. It was wo by Richard Petty (born 2 July 1937) of Randlema North Carolina in 17 minutes 27 seconds (average spee 171·920 m.p.h.), driving a 405 b.h.p. 1964 Plymouth V

The fastest road race is the Belgian Grand Prix held o the Francorchamps circuit (8 miles 1,340 yards) nea Spa, Belgium. The record time for this 28-lap (245·31 miles) race is 1 hour 38 minutes 9·9 seconds (averag speed 149·942 m.p.h.) by Pedro Rodriguez, driving 2,999 c.c. B.R.M. P153 V12, in the 28th race on 7 Jun 1970.

United Kingdom The fastest race in the United Kingdom is the Britis Grand Prix. The record for this 84-lap (245·868 miles race is 1 hour 55 minutes 55·6 seconds (average spee 127·254 m.p.h.) by Jackie Stewart driving a 2,993 c.c Matra MS80–Cosworth V8, at Silverstone (see left) in the 22nd race, on 19th July 1969.

The fastest race at Brooklands was won at an averag of 133·58 m.p.h. by Oliver Bertram, driving a 7,963 c.c Barnato-Hassan Special, over 50 miles (22 minutes 27·50 seconds) on 17 Sept. 1938.

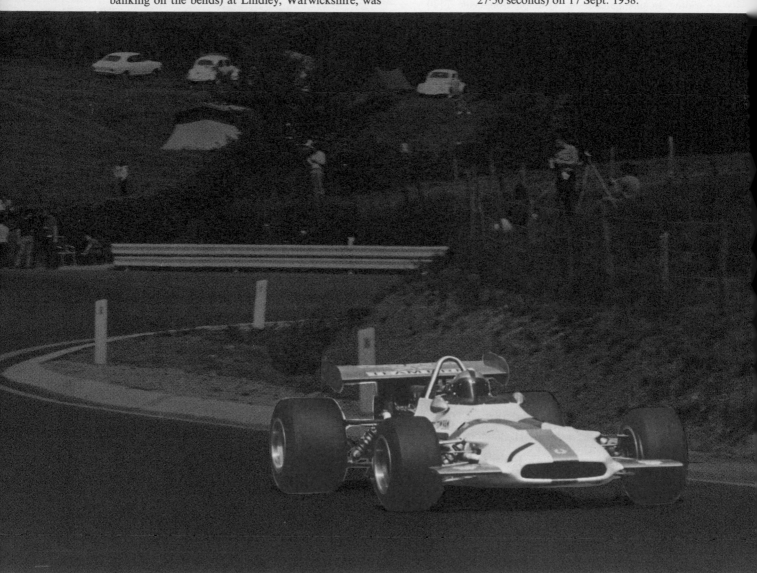

Pedro Rodriguez in his BRM on his way to winning the 1970 Belgian Grand Prix, the fastest road race ever

TOUGHEST CIRCUITS

The Targa Florio (first run 1906) is widely acknowledged to be the most arduous race. Held on the Piccolo Madonie Circuit in Sicily, it now covers eleven laps (492·126 miles) and involves the negotiation of 9,350 corners, over severe mountain gradients, and narrow rough roads. The record time is 6 hours 35 minutes 30·0 seconds (average speed 74·659 m.p.h.) by Joseph Siffert (born Fribourg, Switzerland, 7 July 1936) and Brian Herman Thomas Redman (born Burnley, Lancashire, 9 March 1937) driving a 2,997 c.c. flat 8 Porsche 908/3 Spyder Group 6 prototype sports car in the 54th race on 3 May 1970. The lap record is 33 minutes 36·0 seconds (average speed 79·890 m.p.h.) by Leo Kinnunen (born Finland 1943) on lap 11 of this race in a similar Porsche.

The most difficult Grand Prix circuit is generally regarded to be that for the Monaco Grand Prix (first run 1929), run round the streets and the harbour of Monte Carlo. It is 3,145 metres (1 mile 1,679 yards) in length and has ten pronounced corners and several sharp changes of gradient. The race is run over 80 laps (156·337 miles) and involves on average more than 2,000 gear changes. The record for the race is 1 hour 54 minutes 36·6 seconds (average speed 81·845 m.p.h.) by Karl Jochen Rindt (born Mainz, Germany, 18 April 1942), now a naturalised Austrian, driving a 2,993 c.c. Lotus 49C—Cosworth V8, on 10 May 1970. The lap record is 1 minute 23·2 seconds (average speed 84·557 m.p.h.) by Rindt on lap 80 of the above race.

LE MANS

The world's most important race for sports cars is the 24-hour *Grand Prix d'Endurance* (first held 1923) on the Sarthe circuit at Le Mans, France. The greatest distance ever covered is 3,251·573 miles (average speed 135·481 m.p.h.) by A. J. (Anthony Joseph) Foyt, Jr. (born Houston, Texas 1935) and Daniel Sexton Gurney (born Port Jefferson, Long Island, New York, U.S.A., 13 May 1931) of Santa Ana, California, driving an American Ford Mk. IV powered by a 6,980 c.c. V8 engine, on 10–11 June 1967. The race lap record (8 miles 650 yards lap) is 3 minutes 21·0 seconds (average speed 149·896 m.p.h.) by Victor Henry Elford (born Peckham, London, 10 June 1935) driving a 4,907 c.c. flat 12 Porsche 917 Group 5 sports car on 13 June 1970. On 11 June 1970 he set a record practice lap with 3 minutes 19·8 seconds (average speed 150·797 m.p.h.). The pre-war record average speed was 86·85 m.p.h. by a 3·3 litre Bugatti in 1939.

Most wins   The race has been won by Ferrari cars nine times, in 1949, 1954, 1958 and 1960–61–62–63–64–65. The most wins by one man is four by Olivier Gendebien (born 1924) (Belgium), who won in 1958 and 1960–61–62.

British wins   The race has been won 12 times by British cars, thus: Bentley in 1924 and 1927–28–29–30, once by Lagonda in 1935, five times by Jaguar in 1951, 1953 and 1955–56–57 and once by Aston Martin in 1959.

INDIANAPOLIS 500

The Indianapolis 500-mile race (200 laps) was inaugurated in the U.S.A. in 1911. The most successful drivers have been Wilbur Shaw (killed in plane crash in 1954), who won in 1937, 1939 and 1940, Louis Meyer, who won in 1928, 1933 and 1936, and A. J. Foyt, Jr., who won in 1961, 1964 and 1967. Mauri Rose won in 1947 and 1948 and was the co-driver of Floyd Davis in 1941. The record time is 3 hours 11 minutes 14·71 seconds (average speed 156·867 m.p.h.) by Mario Gabriele Andretti (born Trieste, Italy, 1939) now of Nazareth, Pennsylvania, U.S.A., driving a 2·65 litre 700 b.h.p. turbocharged STP Oil Treatment-Brawner-Hawk-Ford Special on 30 May 1969. Al Unser (born Albuquerque, New Mexico, U.S.A., 30 May 1939) received a record $271,697·72 from a record prize fund of $1,000,002·22 for winning the 54th race on 30 May 1970. The race lap record is 53·36 seconds (average speed 168·666 m.p.h.) by Lloyd Ruby (born 1927) of

The Porsche team left to right: Kinnunen, Rodriguez, Redman and Siffert

Wichita Falls, Texas, driving a 2·75 litre 625 b.h.p. turbocharged Mongoose Offenhauser Gene White Company Special, on lap 94, on 30 May 1968. The lap record is 52·06 seconds (average speed 172·877 m.p.h.) by Joe Leonard (born San Jose, California, 1935), driving an STP Oil Treatment-Paxton-Lotus 56 Special powered by a Pratt and Whitney gas turbine developing 510 b.h.p. during practice in May 1968.

Fastest pit stop The Wood brothers of Salem, Virginia, U.S.A. took 19·8 seconds over Jim Clark's first fuel stop during the Indianapolis 500 on 31 May 1965. During this time they loaded 50 gallons of fuel without pressure.

Duration record The greatest distance ever covered in one year is 400,000 kilometres (248,548·5 miles) by François Lecot (1879–1949), an innkeeper from Rochetaillée, near Lyon, France, in an 11 c.v. Citroën (1,900 c.c., 66 b.h.p.),

mainly between Paris and Monte Carlo, from 22 Jul 1935 to 26 July 1936. He drove on 363 of the 370 days

The world's duration record is 185,353 miles 1,74 yards in 133 days 17 hours 37 minutes 38·64 second (average speed 58·07 m.p.h.) by Marchand, Presalé an six others in a Citroën on the Montlhéry track nea Paris, France, during March–July 1933.

MOST SUCCESSFUL DRIVERS
Based on the World Drivers' Championships, inaugu rated in 1950, the most successful driver is Juan-Manue Fangio y Cia (born Balcarce, Argentina, 24 June 1911 who won five times in 1951–54–55–56–57. He retired i 1958, after having won 24 Grand Prix races (2 shared) The most successful driver in terms of race wins i Stirling Craufurd Moss, O.B.E. (born London, 17 Sept 1929), with 167 (11 shared) races won, including 16

The late Jim Clark, the winner of the greatest number of Grand Prix races with 25 between 1962 and 1968

Grand Prix victories (1 shared), from 18 Sept. 1948 to 11 Feb. 1962. Moss was awarded the annual Gold Star of the British Racing Drivers' Club in 1950–51–52, 1954–55–56–57–58–59 and 1961, a record total of ten awards.

The most Grand Prix victories is 25 by Jim Clark, O.B.E. (1936–1968) of Scotland between 17 June 1962 and 1 January 1968. Clark also holds the record of Grand Prix victories in one year with 7 in 1963. He won a record 61 Formula One and Formula Libre races between 1959 and 1968.

st and ungest inners The youngest Grand Prix winner was Bruce Leslie McLaren (1937–1970) of New Zealand, who won the United States Grand Prix at Sebring, Florida, U.S.A. on 12 December 1959 aged 22 years 104 days. The oldest Grand Prix winner was Louis Alexandre Chiron (born Monaco, August 1899), who won the Grand Prix de France for Formula One cars at Reims, France on 17 July 1949 aged 49 years 11 months. Tazio G. Nuvolari (1892–1953) of Italy drove in this race at Reims on 18 July 1948 aged 55 years 245 days.

Peak race The Pike's Peak Auto Hill Climb, Colorado, Nevada (instituted 1916) has been won by Bobby Unser (born Colorado Springs, Colorado, U.S.A., 1934) 11 times between 1956 and 1969 (9 championship, 1 stock and 1 sports car title). On 30 June 1968 in the 46th race, he set a record of 11 minutes 54·9 seconds in his 336 cubic inch Chevrolet for the 12·42-mile course rising from 9,402 feet to 14,110 feet through 230 curves.

Hill imbing The British National Hill Climb Championship inaugurated in 1947 has been won six times by Anthony Ernest Marsh (born Stourbridge, Worcestershire, 20 July 1913), 1955–56–57, 1965–66–67. Raymond Mays (born Bourne, Lincolnshire, 1 Aug. 1899) won the Shelsey Walsh hill climb, near Worcester, 19 times between 1923 and 1950.

RALLIES

Earliest The earliest long rally was promoted by the Parisian daily Le Matin in 1907 from Peking, China, to Paris over a route of about 7,500 miles. Five cars left Peking on 10 June. The winner, Prince Scipione Borghesi, arrived in Paris on 10 Aug. 1907 in his 40 h.p. Itala.

Longest The world's longest ever rally was the £10,000 Daily Mirror World Cup Rally run over 16,243 miles starting from Wembley, London on 19 April 1970 to Mexico City via Sofia, Bulgaria and Buenos Aires, Argentina passing through 25 countries. It was won on 27 May 1970 by Hannu Mikkola (born Finland, 1942) and Gunnar Palm (born Sweden, 1937) in a 1,900 c.c. Ford Escort. The longest held annually is the East African Safari (first run 1953), run through Kenya and Uganda, which is up to 3,200 miles long, as in March 1970. The smallest car to win the Monte Carlo Rally (founded 1911) was an 841 c.c. Saab driven by Erik Carlsson (born Sweden, 1929) and Gunnar Haggbom of Sweden on 25 Jan. 1962, and by Carlsson and Gunnar Palm (Sweden) on 24 Jan. 1963.

DRAGGING

Piston engined The highest terminal velocity recorded by a piston-engined dragster is 240·00 m.p.h. by Donald Glenn "Big Daddy" Garlits (born 1932) of Tampa, Florida driving his 426-cubic inch supercharged V8 Dodge "Swamp Rat" in the United States on 13 July 1968. The lowest elapsed time is 6·437 seconds by the Beebe and Mulligan Chrysler AA/FD dragster driven by John "Zoo Keeper" Mulligan of Garden Grove, Los Angeles, California, U.S.A. (fatally burnt on 1 Sept. 1969) during the National Hot Rod Association's 15th Annual Nationals at Indianapolis Raceway Park, Indiana, U.S.A. on 30 Aug. 1969.

Rocket or t-engined The highest terminal velocity recorded by any dragster is 273·555 m.p.h. (elapsed time 6·14 seconds) by Arthur

Eugene Arfons (born Akron, Ohio, 3 Feb. 1926) driving "Cyclops", powered by a General Electric J79 GE-2 jet engine developing 17,500 lb. s.t., at Rockingham, North Carolina, U.S.A. on 25 Sept. 1969. The lowest elapsed time by any dragster is 5·41 seconds (terminal velocity 229 m.p.h.) by the Reaction Dynamics X-1 "Rislone Rocket" powered by a hydrogen peroxide rocket motor developing 2,500 lb. static thrust, driven by Chuck Suba (U.S.A.) in the U.S.A. early in 1968.

Terminal velocity is the speed attained at the end of a 440-yard run made from a standing start and elapsed time is the time taken for the run.

LAND SPEED RECORDS
The highest speed ever recorded by a mechanically-propelled wheeled vehicle was achieved by Norman Craig Breedlove (born 23 March 1938) of Los Angeles, California, at Bonneville Salt Flats, Utah, U.S.A., on 15 Nov. 1965. He drove the Spirit of America—Sonic I, weighing 9,000 lb. and measuring 34 feet 7 inches long and 7 feet 1 inch wide. This car cost $200,000 to build and was powered by a General Electric J79 GE-3 turbo-jet engine which, with its afterburner, could develop 15,000 lb. static thrust at sea-level. On his first run, at 8.10 a.m. (local time), he covered the flying kilometre in 3·746 seconds (average speed 597·152 m.p.h.) and the mile in 6·069 seconds (593·178 m.p.h.). On the second run, at 8.51 a.m., his times were 3·699 seconds for the kilometre (604·740 m.p.h.) and 5·919 seconds for the mile (608·211 m.p.h.); so the intervening distance (666·386 yards) was covered in 2·220 seconds (average speed 613·995 m.p.h.). The average times for the two runs were 3·7225 seconds for the kilometre (600·922 m.p.h.) and 5·994 seconds for the mile (600·601 m.p.h.).

The most successful land speed record breaker was Major Sir Malcolm Campbell (1885–1948) of the United Kingdom. He broke the official record nine times between 25 Sept. 1924, with 146·157 m.p.h. in a Sunbeam, and 3 Sept. 1935, when he achieved 301·129 m.p.h. in the Rolls-Royce engined Bluebird.

The world speed record for compression ignition engined cars is 169·3 m.p.h. (average for 2 runs over 1 kilometre) by Dana Fuller, Jr., in the 6,974 c.c. Fuller Diesel 6/71 at Bonneville Salt Flats, Utah, U.S.A., on 11 Sept. 1953.

Go-kart Circum-navigation The only recorded instance of a go-kart being driven round the world was a circumnavigation by Stan Mott, of New York (U.S.A.), who drove a Lambretta-engined 175 c.c. "Italkart" with a ground clearance of two inches, 23,300 land miles through 28 countries from 15 Feb. 1961 to 5 June 1964, beginning and finishing in New York (U.S.A.).

Orienteering

Origins Orienteering was invented by Major Ernst Killander in Sweden in 1918. World championships were inaugurated in 1966 and are held biennially. Annual British championships were instituted in 1967.

Most titles World Sweden won the world men's relay titles in 1966 and 1968 and the women's relay in 1966 with Ulla Lindkvist (Sweden) winning the individual titles in both 1966 and 1968.

Britain The most successful British team has been Southern Navigators, who won both the men's and women's titles in 1967 and retained the latter in 1968. Gordon Pirie won the men's individual title in 1967 and 1968 and Carol McNeill won the women's title in 1967 and 1969.

Sports, games and pastimes
Mountaineering

Origins   Although bronze-age artifacts have been found on the summit of the Riffelhorn, mountaineering, as a sport, has a continuous history dating back only to 1854. Isolated instances of climbing for its own sake exist back to the 14th century. The Atacamenans built sacrificial platforms near the summit of Llullaillaco (22,058 feet) in late pre-Columbian times *c.* 1490. The earliest recorded rock climb in the British Isles was of Stacna Biorrach, St. Kilda by Sir Robert Moray in 1698.

Mount Everest   Mount Everest (29,028 feet) was first climbed at 11.30 a.m. on 29 May 1953, when the summit was reached by Edmund Percival Hillary (born 20 July 1919), created K.B.E., of New Zealand, and the Sherpa, Tenzing Norkhay (born, as Namgyal Wangdi, in Nepal in 1914, formerly called Tenzing Khumjung Bhutia), who was awarded the G.M. The successful expedition was led by Col. (later Hon. Brigadier) Henry Cecil John Hunt, C.B.E., D.S.O. (born 22 June 1910), who was created a Knight Bachelor in 1953 and a life peer on 11 June 1966.

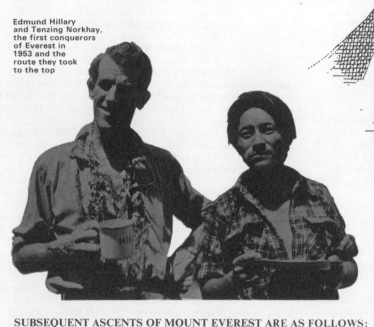

Edmund Hillary
and Tenzing Norkhay,
the first conquerors
of Everest in
1953 and the
route they took
to the top

SUBSEQUENT ASCENTS OF MOUNT EVEREST ARE AS FOLLOWS:

Climbers	Date		Climbers	Date	
Ernst Schmidt, Jürg Marmet	23 May	1956	Dr. William F. Unsoeld, Dr. Thomas F. Hornbein	22 May	196
Hans Rudolf von Gunten, Adolf Reist	24 May	1956	Capt. A. S. Cheema, Sherpa Nawang Gombu	20 May	196
*Wang Fu-chou, Chu Yin-hua, Konbu	25 May	1960	Sonam Gyaltso, Sonam Wangyal	22 May	196
James Warren Whittaker, Sherpa Nawang Gombu	1 May	1963	C. P. Vohra, Sherpa Ang Kami	24 May	196
Barry C. Bishop, Luther G. Jerstad	22 May	1963	Capt. H. P. S. Ahluwalia, H. C. S. Rawat, Phu Dorji	29 May	196
Not internationally accepted as authentic.			Naomi Uemura, Tero Matsuura (Japan)	13 May	197

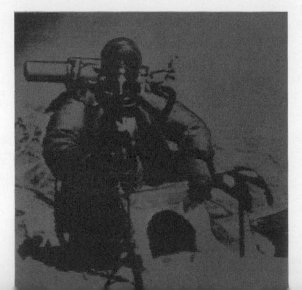

Tero Matsuura
(Japan) the latest
conqueror of Everest

MOUNTAIN RACING

The record time for the race from Fort William to the summit of Ben Nevis and return is 1 hour 38 minutes 50 seconds by Peter Hall (Barrow A.C.) on 5 Sept. 1964. The feminine record is 1 hour 51 minutes for the ascent only, by Elizabeth Wilson-Smith on 14 Sept. 1909, and 3 hours 2 minutes for the ascent and return by Kathleen Connachie, aged 16, on 3 Sept. 1965. The full course by the bridle path is about 14 miles but distance can be saved by crossing the open hillside. The mountain was first climbed in about 1720 and the earliest race was in 1895.

The Lake District 51 peaks record is 22 hours 13 minutes by Kenneth Heaton, aged 35, on 24–25 June 1961, covering 82 miles and 31,000 feet of ascents. The

Yorkshire three peak record is 2 hours 40 minutes 34 seconds by Michael P. Davies (Reading A.C.) in 1968.

The "Three Thousander" record over the 14 Welsh peaks of over 3,000 feet is 5 hours 13 minutes by Eric Beard (Leeds A.C.) on 17 June 1965.

e Peak record The Three Peaks record from sea level at Fort William, Inverness-shire, to sea-level at Caernarvon, *via* the summits of Ben Nevis, Scafell Pike and Snowdon, is a little under 11 hours by Peter Hall (Barrow A.C.), aged 22, with Frank Davies as driver for the 480 miles on the road, from 10 p.m. on 1 July to just before 9 a.m. on 2 July 1964.

running Bill Teasdale won the Guides' Race at the Grasmere Sports, Westmorland, for the eleventh time in 1965. It involves running to the summit of Butter Crag (1,500 feet) and back, a distance of more than 2 miles.

Greatest fall The greatest recorded fall survived by a mountaineer was when Christopher Timms (Christchurch University) slid 7,500 feet down an ice face into a crevasse on Mt. Elie de Beaumont (10,200 feet), New Zealand on 7 Dec. 1966. His companion was killed but he survived with concussion, bruises and a hand injury.

Netball

Origins The game was invented in the U.S.A. in 1891 and introduced into England in 1895 by Dr. Toles. The All England Women's Netball Association was formed in 1926.

orld title The inaugural world title was won by Australia in August 1963. The present world champions are New Zealand.

Highest scores England has never been beaten in a home international. England's record score is 94 goals to 12 *v.* Wales in 1970. The highest international score recorded was when New Zealand beat Northern Ireland 112–4 at Eastbourne, Sussex on 2 Aug. 1963.

Most nationals The record number of internationals is 36 by Annette Cairncross in 1954–63.

Marathon A record marathon match lasting 36¼ hours was played by Newport Athletic Club Netball team in April 1969.

Olympic Games

Note: *The Guinness Book of Olympic Records* (2nd Edition Bantam, New York, 1967) contains a complete roll of all the medal winners in currently contested events and their performances from 1896 to 1964. A 3rd edition is being published in 1971.

Origins The earliest celebration of the ancient Olympic Games of which there is a certain record is that of July 776 B.C., when Koroibos, a cook from Elis, won a foot race, though their origin probably dates from *c.* 1370 B.C. The ancient Games were terminated by an order issued in Milan in A.D. 393 by Theodosius I, "the Great" (*c.* 346–395), Emperor of Rome. At the instigation of Pierre de Fredi, Baron de Coubertin (1863–1937), the Olympic Games of the modern era were inaugurated in Athens on 6 April 1896.

Largest crowd The largest crowd at any Olympic site was 150,000 at the 1952 ski-jumping at the Holmenkollen, outside Oslo, Norway. Estimates of the number of spectators of the marathon race through Tōkyō, Japan on 21 Oct. 1964 have ranged from 500,000 to 1,500,000.

MOST GOLD MEDALS

Individual In the ancient Olympic Games victors were given a chaplet of olive leaves. Milo (Milon of Krotōn) won 6 titles at *palaisma* (wrestling) 540–516 B.C. The most individual gold medals won by a male competitor in the modern Games is eight by Ray C. Ewry (U.S.A.) (see Athletics). The female record is seven by Vera Caslavska-Odlozil (see Gymnastics). The most won by a British competitor is four by Paul Radmilovic (1886–1968) in Water Polo in 1908, 1912 and 1920 and in the 800 metres team swimming event in 1908. The sculler and oarsman Jack Beresford won three gold and two silver medals in the five Olympics from 1920 to 1936.

National The United States has won most medals in all Olympic events (summer and winter) with (gold, silver, bronze) 574–415–363=1,352, with U.S.S.R. (formerly Russia) (did not compete 1920 to 1948 inclusive) second with 191–176–172=539, and the United Kingdom third with 143–193–158=494.

Oldest and youngest competitors The oldest recorded competitor was Oscar G. Swahn (Sweden), who won a silver medal for shooting running deer in 1920, when aged 73. The youngest-ever female gold medal winners are Miss Marjorie Gestring (U.S.A.), aged 13, in the 1936 women's springboard event and Miss Aileen Riggin (U.S.A.), aged 13, in the same event in 1920. Bernard Malivoire, aged 12, coxed the winning French pairs in 1952.

287

Longest span
The longest competitive span of any Olympic competitor is 40 years by Dr. Ivan Osiier (Denmark), who competed as a fencer in 1908, 1912 (silver medal), 1920, 1924, 1928, 1932 and 1948, totalling seven celebrations. He refused to compete in the 1936 Games on the grounds that they were Nazi-dominated. The longest feminine span is 24 years (1932–1956) by the Austrian fencer Ellen Müller-Preiss. The longest span of any British competitor is 20 years by George Mackenzie who wrestled in the Games of 1908, 1912, 1920, 1924 and 1928, and by Mrs. Dorothy J. B. Tyler (née Odam), who high-jumped in 1936–48–52 and 56. The only Olympian to win 4 consecutive titles in athletics has been Alfred A. Oerter (b. 19 Sept. 1936, Astoria, N.Y.) of the U.S.A. who won the discus title in 1956–60–64–68.

Celebrations have been allocated as follows:—

I	Athens	6–15 April 1896
II	Paris	2–22 July 1900
III	St. Louis	29 Aug.–7 Sept. 1904
†	Athens	22 April–2 May 1906
IV	London	13–25 July 1908
V	Stockholm	6–15 July 1912
VI	*Berlin	1916
VII	Antwerp	14–29 Aug. 1920
VIII	Paris	5–27 July 1924
IX	Amsterdam	28 July–12 Aug. 1928
X	Los Angeles	30 July–14 Aug. 1932
XI	Berlin	1–16 Aug. 1936
XII	*Tōkyō, then Helsinki	1940
XIII	*London	1944
XIV	London	29 July–14 Aug. 1948
XV	Helsinki	19 July–3 Aug. 1952
XVI	Melbourne	22 Nov.–8 Dec. 1956
XVII	Rome	25 Aug.–11 Sept. 1960
XVIII	Tōkyō	10–24 Oct. 1964
XIX	Mexico City	12–27 Oct. 1968
XX	Munich	26 Aug.–10 Sept. 1972
XXI	Montreal	17 July–1 Aug. 1976

* *Cancelled due to World Wars.*
† *Intercalated Celebration.*

The Winter Olympics were inaugurated in 1924 and have been allocated as follows:—

I	Chamonix, France	25 Jan.–4 Feb. 1924
II	St. Moritz, Switzerland	11–19 Feb. 1928
III	Lake Placid, U.S.A.	4–13 Feb. 1932
IV	Garmisch-Partenkirchen, Germany	6–16 Feb. 1936
V	St. Moritz, Switzerland	30 Jan.–8 Feb. 1948
VI	Oslo, Norway	14–25 Feb. 1952
VII	Cortina d'Ampezzo, Italy	26 Jan.–5 Feb. 1956
VIII	Squaw Valley, California	18–28 Feb. 1960
IX	Innsbruck, Austria	29 Jan.–9 Feb. 1964
X	Grenoble, France	6–18 Feb. 1968
XI	Sapparo, Japan	3–13 Feb. 1972
XII	Denver, Colorado	20–29 Feb. 1976

Pelota Vasca (Jai-alai)

Origins
The game, which originated in Italy as *longue paum* and was introduced into France in the 13th century, said to be the fastest of all ball games with speeds up to 160 m.p.h. Gloves were introduced *c.* 1840 and the *chisterak* was invented *c.* 1860 by Gantchi Dithurbide of Sainte Pée. The long *chistera* wa invented by Melchior Curuchage of Buenos Aire Argentina in 1888. The world's largest *fronton* (th playing court) is that built for $4,500,000 (no £1,875,000) at Miami, Florida, U.S.A.

Games played in a *fronton* are *Frontenis, pelote* an *paleta* with both leather and rubber balls. The sport i governed by the International Federation of Basqu Pelote.

Making chistera, which make Pelota the fastest of ball games

Pigeon Racing

Earliest references Pigeon Racing was the natural development of the use of homing pigeons for the carrying of messages—a quality utilized in the ancient Olympic Games (776 B.C.–A.D. 393). The sport originated in Belgium and came to Britain c. 1820. The earliest major long-distance race was from Crystal Palace, South London, in 1871. The earliest recorded occasion on which 500 miles was flown in a day was by "Motor" (owned by G. P. Pointer of Alexander Park Racing Club) which was released from Thurso, Scotland, on 30 June 1896 and covered 501 miles at an average speed of 1,454 yards per minute (49½ m.p.h.).

Longest flights The greatest recorded homing flight by a pigeon was made by one owned by the 1st Duke of Wellington (1769–1852). Released from a sailing ship off the Ichabo Islands, West Africa, on 8 April, it dropped dead a mile from its loft at Nine Elms, London, on 1 June 1845, 55 days later, having flown an airline route of 5,400 miles, but an actual distance of possibly 7,000 miles to avoid the Sahara Desert. The official British duration record (into Great Britain) is 1,141 miles by A. Bruce of Fraserburgh's winner of the 1960 Barcelona Race which was liberated on 9 July and homed on 5 August.

Highest speeds In level flight in windless condition it is very doubtful if any pigeon can exceed 60 m.p.h.

The 500 miles record is 2,095 yards per minute (71·42 m.p.h.) by W. Reed's winner of the Thurso Race in 1948. The world's longest reputed distance in 24 hours is 803 miles (velocity 1,525 yards per minute) by E. S. Peterson's winner of the 1941 San Antonio R.C. event, Texas, U.S.A.

The best 24-hour performance into the United Kingdom is 686 miles by A. R. Hill's winner of the 1952 race from Hanover, Germany to St. Just, Cornwall—average speed 28·58 m.p.h.

Polo

Earliest games The earliest polo club was the Kachar Club (founded in 1859) in Assam, India. The game was introduced into England from India in 1869 by the 10th Hussars at Aldershot, Hampshire and the earliest match was one between the 9th Lancers and the 10th Hussars on Hounslow Heath, west of London, in July 1871. The first All-Ireland Cup match was at Phoenix Park, Dublin, in 1878. The earliest international match between England and the U.S.A. was in 1886.

The game is played on the largest pitch of any ball game in the world. A ground measures 300 yards long by 160 yards wide with side boards or, as in India, 200 yards wide without boards.

Highest handicap The highest handicap based on eight 7½-minute "chukkas" is 10 goals introduced in the United Kingdom and in Argentina in 1910. The only active player with a handicap of 10 is Juan C. Harriot (Argentina). The highest handicap of any active player in the British Commonweath is one of 9 by Sinclair Hill (Australia).

The highest handicap of any of the United Kingdom's 300 players is 7, achieved in the Argentine in October 1966 by Paul Withers and John Lucas. H.R.H. the Prince Philip, the Duke of Edinburgh (born 10 June 1921) has a handicap of 5 at back and thus ranks among the highest handicapped players in the United Kingdom.

Highest score The highest aggregate number of goals scored in an international match is 30, when Argentina beat the U.S.A. 21–9 at Meadow Brook, Long Island, New York, U.S.A., in September 1936.

Most internationals The greatest number of times any player has represented England is four in the case of Frederick M. Freake in 1900, 1902, 1909 and 1913. Thomas Hitchcock, Jr. (1900–44) played five times for the U.S.A. v. England (1921–24–27–30–39) and twice v. Argentina (1928–36).

Most expensive pony The highest price ever paid for a polo pony was $22,000 (now £7,857), paid by Stephen Sanford for Lewis Lacey's *Jupiter* after the U.S.A. v. Argentina international in 1928.

Largest trophy The world's largest trophy for a particular sport is the Bangalore Limited Handicap Polo Tournament Trophy. This massive cup standing on its plinth is 6 feet tall and was presented in 1936 by the Raja of Kolanke.

Powerboat Racing

Origins The earliest application of the petrol engine to a boat was Gottlieb Daimler's experimental power boat on the River Seine, Paris, France, in 1887. The sport was given impetus by the presentation of an international championship cup by Sir Alfred Harmsworth In 1903, which was also the year of the first off-shore race from Calais to Dover.

Harmsworth Cup Of the 25 contests from 1903 to 1961, the United States has won 16, the United Kingdom 5, Canada 3 and France 1.

The greatest number of wins has been achieved by Garfield A. Wood with 8 (1920–21, 1926, 1928–29–30, 1932–33). The only boat to win three times is *Miss Supertest III,* owned by James G. Thompson (Canada), in 1959–60–61. This boat also achieved the record speed of 115·972 m.p.h. at Picton, Ontario, Canada in 1960.

Gold Cup The Gold Cup (instituted 1903) has been won four times by Garfield A. Wood (1917, 1919–20–21) and by Bill Muncey (1956–57, 1961–62). The record speed is 120·356 m.p.h. for a 3-mile lap by Rolls-Royce-engined *Miss Exide,* owned by Milo Stoen, driven by Bill Brow at Seattle, Washington, U.S.A. on 4 Aug. 1965.

Highest off-shore speeds The highest race speed attained is 73·1 m.p.h. by Don Aronow (U.S.A.) in his 32-foot *The Cigarette,* powered by two 475 h.p. Mercruiser engines over 214 miles at Viarreggio, Italy on 20 July 1969. The highest average race speed off British shores has been 69·5 m.p.h. by Vincenzo Balastrieri (Italy) and D. Pruett in *Red Tornado* of 184·24 miles from Southsea Pier, Hampshire to Weymouth, Dorset to Hillhead Buoy, south of the

Isle of Wight in the Wills International Race on 14 June 1969.

Longest race The longest race is the *Daily Telegraph and B.P.* Round Britain event inaugurated on 26 July 1969 at Portsmouth with 1,403 miles in 10 stages west-about England, Wales and across Northern Scotland *via* the Caledonian Canal. The 1969 race (26 July to 7 August) was won by *Avenger Too* (Timo Makinen and Pascoe Watson) in 39 hours 9 minutes 37·7 seconds. Of the 42 starters 24 finished.

Cowes-Torquay race The record average for the *Daily Express* International Off-Shore Race (instituted 1961) is 66·47 m.p.h. by *The Cigarette* (Don Aronow) (see above) over the 236-mile Cowes, Isle of Wight to Torquay, Devon and back in 3 hours 33 minutes.

Rackets

Earliest world champion The first world rackets champion was Robert Mackay, who claimed the title in London in 1820. The first closed court champion was Francis Erwood at Woolwich in 1860. The first new court built in Great Britain since 1914 was the Second Court opened at Harrow School in 1965.

Longest reign Of the 18 world champions since 1820 the longest reign is held by British-born U.S. resident Geoffrey W. T. Atkins, who has held the title since beating the professional James Dear in 1954 and completed a fourth successful defence of it in April 1970.

Most amateur titles Since the Amateur singles championship was instituted in 1888 the most titles won by an individual is nine by Edgar M. Baerlein between 1903 and 1923. Since the institution of the Amateur doubles championship in 1890 the most shares in titles has been eleven by David Sumner Milford, between 1938 and 1959. He also has seven Amateur singles titles (1930–52), an open title (1936) and held the world title from 1937 to 1947.

Rodeo

Origins Rodeo came into being with the early days of the North American cattle industry. The earliest references to the sport are from Sante Fe, New Mexico, U.S.A., in 1847. Steer wrestling came in with Bill Pickett (Oklahoma) in 1903. The other events are calf roping, bull riding, saddle and bare-back bronc riding.

Geoffrey Atkins, world rackets champion since 1954

A scene from the Calgary Stampede the largest rodeo in the world

The largest rodeo in the world is the Calgary Exhibition and Stampede at Calgary, Alberta, Canada. The record attendance has been 853,620 on 9–18 July 1969. The record for one day is 127,043 on 15 July 1967.

Most world titles The record number of all-round titles is five by Jim Shoulders (U.S.A.), in 1949 and 1956–57–58–59. The record figure for prize money in a single season is $57,726 (£24,052) in the three riding events by Larry Mahan, aged 25, of Brooks, Oregon, U.S.A. in 1969.

Time records Records for timed events, such as calf-roping and steer wrestling, are meaningless, because of the widely varying conditions due to the size of arenas and amount of start given the stock. The fastest time recorded for roping a calf is 7·5 seconds by Junior Garrison of Marlow, Oklahoma, at Evergreen, Colorado, U.S.A. in 1967, and the fastest time for overcoming a steer was 2·4 seconds by James Bynum of Waxahachie, Texas, at Marietta, Oklahoma, in 1955.

The standard required time to stay on in bareback events is 8 seconds and in saddle bronc riding 10 seconds. In the now obsolete ride-to-a-finish events, rodeo riders have been recorded to have survived 90+ minutes, until the horse had not a buck left in it.

Champion bull The Brahma-Hereford crossbreed *Aught*, owned by Joe Kelsey of Tonasket, Washington State, U.S.A., had the reputation of being the most impossible rodeo mount. He unseated 476 of his 482 mounts in under 8 seconds, missing only on days when he felt colicky. He loved children and died in 1964. *Tornado*, another Brahma-Hereford cross, was unridden from 1961 to 1966, was finally conquered at the 1967 National Finals Rodeo in Oklahoma City by Freckles Brown, aged 46, of Soper, Oklahoma.

Champion bronc The greatest bucking bronco of all time was *Midnight*, owned by Verne Elliott of Platteville, Colorado. In seven years (1923–1930) he was ridden by only four riders once each, and of these only Frank Studnick (at Pendleton, Oregon, in 1929) was not subsequently thrown because he did not mount him again.

Roller Skating

Origin The first roller skate was devised by Joseph Merlin of Huy, Belgium, in 1760. Several "improved" versions appeared during the next century, but a really satisfactory roller skate did not materialize before 1866, when James L. Plimpton of New York produced the present four-wheeled type, patented it, and opened the first public rink in the world at Newport, Rhode Island, that year. The great boom periods were 1870–75, 1908–12 and 1948–54, each originating in the United States.

Largest rink The largest indoor rink ever to operate was located in the Grand Hall, Olympia, London. It had an actual skating area of 68,000 square feet. It first opened in 1890, for one season, then again from 1909 to 1912.

Roller hockey Roller hockey (previously known as Rink Hockey in Europe) was first introduced in this country as Rink Polo, at the old Lava rink, Denmark Hill, London, in the late 1870s. The Amateur Rink Hockey Association was formed in 1905, and in 1913 became the National Rink Hockey (now Roller Hockey) Association. Britain was undefeated in all international championships from 1925 to 1939.

Most titles Leslie E. Woodley of Birmingham won 12 British national individual titles over the three regulation distances (880 yards, one mile and five miles) between 1957 and 1964. Chloe Ronaldson of London won 16 ladies' titles over 440 yards and 880 yards since 1958.

Records The fastest speed put up in an official world's record is 25·78 m.p.h. when Giuseppe Cantarella (Italy) recorded 34·9 seconds for 440 yards on a road at Catania, Italy on 28 Sept. 1963. The world mile record on a rink is 2 minutes 25·1 seconds by Johnny Ferriti (Italy). The greatest distance skated in one hour on a rink by a woman is 20 miles 1,355 yards by C. Patricia Barnett (G.B.) at Brixton, London on 24 June 1962. The men's record on a closed road circuit is 22 miles 465·9 yards (35 km. 831 m.) by Alberto Civolani (Italy) at Bologna, Italy on 15 Oct. 1967.

Marathon record The longest recorded continuous roller skating marathon was performed by Professor Eckard with 108 hours at Rockhampton, Queensland, Australia in 1913. The longest reported skate was by Clinton Shaw from Victoria, British Columbia to St. John's, Newfoundland (4,900 miles) on the Trans-Canadian Highway *via* Montreal from 1 April to 11 Nov. 1967.

Rowing

Oldest race The earliest established sculling race is the Doggett's Coat and Badge, which was rowed on 1 Aug. 1716 over 5 miles from London Bridge to Chelsea and is still being rowed every year over the same course, under the administration of the Fishmongers' Company. The first English regatta probably took place on the Thames by the Ranelagh Gardens, near Putney in 1775. Boating began at Eton in 1793, 72 years before the "song". The Leander Club was formed in *c.* 1818.

BOAT RACE
The earliest University Boat Race, which Oxford won, was from Hambleden Lock to Henley Bridge on 10 June 1829. In the 116 races to 1970, Cambridge won 64 times, Oxford 51 times and there was a dead heat on 24 March 1877.

Record time The race record time for the course of 4 miles 374 yards (Putney to Mortlake) is 17 minutes 50 seconds by Cambridge in 1948. Oxford returned 17 minutes 37 seconds in practice on 19 March 1967. The smallest winning margin was Oxford's win by a canvas in 1952. The greatest margin (apart from sinking) was Cambridge's win by 20 lengths in 1900. The record for the distance (rowed on the ebb from Mortlake to Putney) is 17 minutes 24 seconds by the Tideway Scullers School in the Head of the River Race on 21 March 1964.

HENLEY ROYAL REGATTA
The annual regatta at Henley-on-Thames, Oxfordshire, was inaugurated on 26 March 1839.

Since 1839 the course, except in 1923, has been about 1 mile 550 yards, varying slightly according to the length of boat. In 1967 the shorter craft were "drawn up" so all bows start level. Prior to 1922 there were two slight angles. Classic Records (year in brackets indicates the date instituted):

Larry Mahan, winner of the record rodeo prize money

			mins. secs.	
Grand Challenge Cup (1839)	8 oars	Ratzeburger Ruderclub (West Germany)	6:16	3 July 1965
Ladies' Challenge Plate (1846)	8 oars	Lady Margaret	6:43	1949
Thames Challenge Cup (1868)	8 oars	Isis	6:35	3 July 1965
Princess Elizabeth Challenge Cup (1946)	8 oars	Emmanuel School	6:44	1 July 1965
		Tabor Academy, U.S.A. (twice)	6:44	3 July 1965
Stewards' Challenge Cup (1841)	4 oars	Quintin	6:55	3 July 1965
Visitors' Challenge Cup (1847)	4 oars	St. Edmund Hall, Oxford	7:13	3 July 1965
Wyfold Challenge Cup (1855)	4 oars	Derby R.C.	7:06	3 July 1965
Prince Philip Cup (1963)	4 oars	Leander	7:03	3 July 1965
Britannia Challenge Cup	4 oars	Thame R.C. (coxed)	7:26	6 July 1968
Silver Goblets and Nickall's Cup (1895)	Pair oar	Peter Gorny and Gunther Bergau (ASK Vorwaerts Rostock, East Germany)	7:35	1 July 1965
Double Sculls Challenge Cup (1939)	Sculls	Melch Buergin and Martin Studach (Grasshoppers Club, Zürich)	7:01	3 July 1965
Diamond Challenge Sculls (1844)	Sculls	Donald M. Spero (New York A.C., U.S.A.)	7:42	3 July 1965

Intermediate times The record to the Mile Post is 3 minutes 47 seconds (Oxford 1960 and 25 March 1967); Hammersmith Bridge 6 minutes 42 seconds (Oxford 25 March 1967); Chiswick Steps 10 minutes 45 seconds (Oxford 1965, in practice) and Barnes Bridge 14 minutes 39 seconds (Oxford 19 March 1967, in practice).

Oarsman Heaviest The heaviest man ever to row in a University boat has been David L. Cruttenden (b. Hartlepools, 1947) the No. 4 in the 1969 Cambridge boat at 15 st. 10 lb. The 1969 Cambridge crew averaged a record 13 st. 9⅜ lb.

Lightest The lightest oarsman was the 1882 Oxford Stroke, A. H. Higgins, at 9 stone 6½ lb. The lightest cox was F. H. Archer (Oxford) in 1862 at 5 stone 2 lb.

OLYMPIC GAMES

Since 1900 there have been 93 Olympic finals, of which the U.S.A. have won 27, Germany 16 and the United Kingdom 14. Three oarsmen have won 3 gold medals: John B. Kelly (U.S.A.), father of Princess Grace of Monaco, in the sculls (1920) and double sculls (1920 and 1924); Paul V. Costello (U.S.A.) in the double sculls (1920, 1924 and 1928), and Jack Beresford, Jr. (G.B.) in the sculls (1924), coxless fours (1932) and double sculls (1936).

Sculling The record number of wins in the Wingfield Sculls (instituted 1830) is seven by Jack Beresford, Jr. (see Olympics), from 1920 to 1926. The record number of world professional sculling titles (instituted 1831) won

Jack Beresford (G.B.) winner of three Olympic gold medals

is seven by W. Beach (Australia) between 1884 an· 1887. Stuart A. Mackenzie (Great Britain and Australi· performed the unique feat of winning the Diamon· Sculls at Henley for the sixth consecutive occasion o· 7 July 1962. In 1960 and 1962 he was in Leander colour·

Highest speed Speeds in tidal or flowing water are of no comparativ· value. The highest recorded speed for 2,000 metres b· an eight in the World Championships is 5 minute· 50·83 seconds (12·75 m.p.h.) by Germany in 1962 an· in the Olympic Games 5 minutes 54·02 seconds (12·6· m.p.h.) also by Germany at Toda, Japan in 1964.

BUMP RACES

In the Oxford Eights Brasenose College has been mos· often Head of the River with 18 times and Trinit· longest consecutively with 6 races running, 1938–3· and 1946–47–48–49. In the Cambridge May Race· Trinity has been Head 50 times (as 1st Trinity [27· 2nd Trinity [2], 3rd Trinity [14] and 1st and 3rd Trinit· [5] and as "Trinity" [twice]). Jesus has been longes· Head with 11 years running, 1875–85. In 1934 St· Edmund Hall, Oxford made 14 bumps with two crews·

Loch Ness Loch Ness, the longest stretch of inland water in Grea· Britain (22·7 miles), was rowed by a coxed four jolly· boat from Eastern Amatern Rowing Club of Portobell· in 11 Oct. 1969 in 4 hours 11 minutes.

Shooting

Olympic Games The record number of gold medals won is five by Morris· Fisher (U.S.A.) with three in 1920 and two in 1924.

Record heads The world's finest head is the 23-pointer stag head in the Maritzburg collection, Germany. The outside span is 75½ inches, the length 47½ inches and the weight 41½ lb. The greatest number of points is probably 33 (plus 29) on the stag shot in 1696 by Frederick III (1657–1713), the Elector of Brandenburg, later King Frederick I of Prussia.

The record head for a British Red Deer is a 47-pointer (length 33½ inches) from the Great Warnham Deer Park, Sussex, in 1892. The record for a semi-feral stag is a 20-pointer with an antler length of 45⅜ inches from Endsleigh Wood, Devon, found in December 1950 and owned by G. Kenneth Whitehead.

WORLD RECORDS

		Possible—Score			
Free Pistol	50m. 6 × 10 shot series	600—570	A. Yegrishchin (U.S.S.R.)	Lahti	1968
Free Rifle	300 m. 3 × 40 shot series	1,200—1,157	G. L. Anderson (U.S.A.)	Mexico City	23 Oct. 1968
Small Bore Rifle	50 m. 3 × 40 shot series	1,200—1,164	L. W. Wigger, Jr. (U.S.A.)	Tōkyō	20 Oct. 1964
		1,200—1,164	G. L. Anderson (U.S.A.)	Johannesburg	1969
Small Bore Rifle	50 m. 60 shots prone	600—598	D. Boyd (U.S.A.)	Wiesbaden	1966
		598	A. Mayer (Canáda)	Winnipeg	1967
		598	J. Kurka (Czechoslovakia)	Mexico City	19 Oct. 1968
		598	L. Hammerl (Hungary)	Mexico City	19 Oct. 1968
Centre-Fire Pistol	25 m. 60 shots	600—597	T. D. Smith (U.S.A.)	São Paulo	1963
Rapid Fire Pistol	25 m. silhouettes 60 shots	600—596	V. Antanasiu (Romania)	Wiesbaden	1966
Running Target	50 m. 40 shots	—171	M. Nordfors (Sweden)	Pistoia, Italy	1967
Trap	300 birds	300—297	K. Jones (U.S.A.)	Wiesbaden	1966
Skeet	200 birds	200—200	N. Durnev (U.S.S.R.)	Cairo	1962

Bench Rest Open Rifle: five shots put through a hole 0·0630 of an inch in diameter at 100 yards by Zeiser (U.S.A.) on 30 Aug. 1958.

LARGEST BRITISH BAGS

Woodpigeon	550	1 gun	Major A. J. Coates, near Winchester	10 Jan.	1962
Snipe	1,108	2 guns	Tiree, Inner Hebrides	25 Oct.–3 Nov.	1906
Hares	1,215	11 guns	Holkham, Norfolk	19 Dec.	1877
Woodcock	228	6 guns	Ashford, County Galway	28 Jan.	1910
Grouse	2,929	8 guns	Littledale and Abbeystead, Lancashire	12 Aug.	1915
Grouse	1,070	1 gun	Lord Walsingham in Yorkshire	30 Aug.	1888
Geese (Brent)	704*	32 punt-guns	Colonel Russell i/c, River Blackwater, Essex	c. 1860	
Rabbits	6,943	5 guns	Blenheim, Oxfordshire	17 Oct.	1898
Partridges	2,015†	6 guns	Rothwell, Lincolnshire	12 Oct.	1952
Pheasants	3,937	7 guns	Hall Barn, Beaconsfield, Buckinghamshire	18 Dec.	1913

*Plus about 250 later picked up.   †Plus 104 later picked up.

argest houlder guns The largest bore shoulder guns made were 2 bores. Less than a dozen of these were made by two English wildfowl gunmakers in *c.* 1885. Normally the largest guns are made double-barrelled 4-bore weighing up to 26 lb., which can be handled only by men of exceptional physique. Larger smooth-bore guns have been made, but these are for use as punt-guns.

Highest muzzle velocity The highest muzzle velocity of any rifle bullet is 7,100 feet per second (4,840 m.p.h.) by a 1937 0·30 calibre M 1903 Standard U.S. Army Ordnance Department rifle.

pigeon The record number of clay birds shot in an hour is 1,308 by Joseph Nother (formerly Wheater) (born 1918) of Kingston-upon-Hull, Yorkshire, at Bedford on 21 Sept. 1957. Using 5 guns and 7 loaders he shot 1,000 in 42 minutes 22·5 seconds.

BISLEY
The National Rifle Association was instituted in 1859. The Queen's (King's) Prize has been shot since 1860 and has only once been won by a woman—Miss Marjorie Elaine Foster, M.B.E. (score 280) in 1930. Only Arthur G. Fulton, M.B.E. has won 3 times (1912, 1926, 1931). The highest score (possible 300) is 292 by Capt. C. H. Vernon, with 146 in both the 2nd and 3rd stages, on 15–16 July 1927. The record for the Silver Medal, shot at 300, 500 and 600 yards, is 148 (possible 150) by four marksmen in 1927, C. A. Sutherland on 19 July 1935, Warrant Officer Norman L. Beckett (Canada) on 21 July 1961 and Keith M. Pilcher on 19 July 1963.

tossing Using a pair of auto-loading Remington Nylon 66 ·22 calibre guns, Tom Frye (U.S.A.) tossed 100,000 blocks (2½-inch pine cubes) and hit 99,994—his longest run was 32,860—on 5–17 Oct. 1959.

est bag The largest animal ever shot by any big game hunter was a bull African elephant (*Loxodonta africana*) shot by J. J. Fénykövi (Hungary), 48 miles north-northwest of Macusso, Angola, on 13 Nov. 1955. It required 16 heavy calibre bullets from an 0·416 Rigby and weighed an estimated 24,000 lb. (10·7 tons), standing 13 feet 2 inches at the shoulders. In November 1965 Simon Fletcher, 28, a Kenyan farmer, claimed to have killed two elephants with one 0·458 bullet.

The greatest recorded lifetime bag is 556,000 birds, including 241,000 pheasants, by the 2nd Marquess of Ripon (1867–1923). He himself dropped dead on a grouse moor after shooting his 52nd bird on the morning of 22 Sept. 1923.

Revolver shooting The greatest rapid fire feat was that of Ed. McGivern (U.S.A.), who twice fired from 15 feet 5 shots which could be covered by a silver half-dollar piece (diameter 1·1875 inches) in 0·45 seconds at the Lead Club Range, South Dakota, U.S.A., on 20 Aug. 1932.

Quickest draw There are 10 categories of fast drawing records recognized in the U.S.A. Al Brian of California has featured in six of them. The fastest category is "Self Start at 8 feet", firing at 4-inch diameter balloons. In May 1966 Brian held the single shot at 0·060 of a second, the 3 shot average at 0·066 of a second and the 5 shot average at 0·071 of a second. Jerry Shafer of Kentucky, U.S.A. (born 1934) claimed to have drawn and fired in 0·04 of a second and hit a 3-inch target at 25 yards. The feminine single shot record is 0·270 of a second by Becky Munden (California).

Ski-ing

Origins The earliest dated skis found in Fenno-Scandian bogs have been dated to *c.* 2500 B.C. A rock carving of a skier at Rødøy, Tjøtta, North Norway, dates from 2000 B.C. The earliest recorded military competition was an

Miss Marjorie Foster the only woman to win the Queen's Prize at Bisley

isolated one in Oslo, Norway, in 1767. Ski-ing did not develop into a sport until 1843 at Tromsø. Ski-ing was known in California by 1856, having been introduced by "Snowshoe" Thompson from Norway. The Kiandra Snow Shoe Club (founded 1878), Australia, claims it is the world's oldest. Ski-ing was not introduced into the Alps until 1883, though there is some evidence of earlier use in the Carniola district. The first Slalom event was run at Mürren, Switzerland, on 21 Jan. 1922. The Winter Olympics were inaugurated in 1924. The Ski Club of Great Britain was founded on 6 May 1903.

Most Olympic wins The most Olympic gold medals won by an individual for ski-ing is four (including one for a relay) by Sixten Jernberg (born 6 Feb. 1929) of Sweden, in 1956–60–64. In addition, Jernberg has won three silver and two bronze medals. The only woman to win three gold medals is Klavdiya Boyarskikh (U.S.S.R.), who won the 5 kilometres and 10 kilometres, and was a member of the winning 3 × 5 kilometres Nordic relay team, at Innsbruck, Austria, in 1964.

Most world titles The world alpine championships were inaugurated at Mürren, Switzerland, in 1931. The greatest number of titles won is 12 by Christel Cranz (born 1 July 1914) of Germany, with four Slalom (1934–37–38–39), three Downhill (1935–37–39) and five Combined (1934–35–37–38–39). She also won the gold medal for the Combined in the 1936 Olympics. The most titles won by a man is seven by Anton ("Toni") Sailer (born 17 Nov. 1935) of Austria, who won all four in 1956 (Giant Slalom, Slalom, Downhill and the non-Olympic Alpine Combination) and the Downhill, Giant Slalom and Combined in 1958.

Anton Sailer (Austria) (right) the only man to win seven world Alpine championships

In the Nordic events Johan Gröttumsbraaten (born 24 Feb. 1899) of Norway won six titles (two at 18 kilometres and four Combined) in 1931–32. The record for a jumper is five by Birger Ruud (born 23 Aug. 1911) of Norway, in 1931–32 and 1935–36–37.

The World Cup, instituted in 1967, has been twice won by Jean-Claude Killy (France) (b. 30 Aug. 1943) in 1967 and 1968 and by Karl Schranz (Austria) in 1969 and 1970. The women's cup has been twice won by Miss Nancy Greene (Canada) in 1967 and 1968.

Most British titles The greatest number of British Ski-running titles won is three by Leonard Dobbs (1921, 1923–24), William R. Bracken (1929–31) and Jeremy Palmer-Tomkinson (1965–66–68). The most Ladies Titles is four by Miss Isobel M. Roe (1938–39, 1948–49) and Miss Gina Hathorn (1966–68–69–70). The most wins in the British Ski-jumping Championship (discontinued 1936) is three, by Colin Wyatt (1931, 1934, 1936).

Highest speed The highest speed claimed for any skier is 109·14 m.p.h. by Ralph Miller (U.S.A.) on the 62 degree slopes of the Garganta *Schuss* at Portillo, Chile, on 25 Aug. 1955. Since the timing was only manual by two time-keepers standing half a kilometre back from a marked 50-metre section of *piste*, this claim cannot be regarded as reliable. Some error is further indicated by the fact that to achieve such a speed 50 metres would have to be covered in 1·0248 seconds—an accuracy quite impossible on a stopwatch. The highest speed recorded in Europe is 108·589 m.p.h. over a flying 100 metres by Luigi de Marco (Italy) on a 62·8 degree gradient on the Rosa plateau above Cervinia, Italy, on 18 July 1964. The average race speeds by the 1968 Olympic downhill champion on the Chamrousse course, Grenoble, France were Jean-Claude Killy (France) (53·93 m.p.h.) and Olga Pall (Austria) (47·90 m.p.h.).

Duration The longest non-stop ski-ing marathon was one lasting 48 hours by Onni Savi, aged 35, of Padasjoki, Finland, who covered 305·9 kilometres (190·1 miles) between noon on 19 April and noon on 21 April 1966.

Largest entry The world's greatest Nordic ski race is the "Vasa Lopp", which commemorates an event of 1521 when Gustav Vasa (1496–1560), later King Gustavus Eriksson, skied 85 kilometres (52·8) miles from Mora to Sälen, Sweden. The re-enactment of this journey in reverse direction is now an annual event, with 7,887 starters on 3 March 1968. The record time is 4 hours 39 minutes 49 seconds by Janne Stefansson in 1968.

Longest jump The longest ski-jump ever recorded is one of 165 metres (541·3 feet) by Manfred Wolf (East Germany) at Planica, Jugoslavia on 23 March 1969.

The British record is 61 metres (200·1 feet) by Guy Nixon at Davos on 24 Feb. 1931. The record at Hampstead, London, on artificial snow is 28 metres (90·8 feet) by Reidar Andersen (born 20 April 1911) of Norway on 24 March 1950.

Longest run The longest all-downhill ski run in the world is the Weissfluhjoch-Küblis Parsenn course (9 miles long), near Davos, Switzerland. The run from the Aiguille du Midi top of the Chamonix lift (vertical lift 8,176 feet) across the Vallée Blanche is 13 miles.

Longest lift The longest chair lift in the world is the Alpine Way to Kosciusko Châlet lift above Thredbo, near the Snowy Mountains, New South Wales, Australia. It takes from 45 to 75 minutes to ascend the 3·5 miles, according to the weather. The highest is at Chactaltaya, Bolivia, rising to 16,500 feet.

SKIJORING

The record speed reached in aircraft skijoring (being towed by an aircraft) is 109·23 m.p.h. by Reto Pitsch on the Silsersee, St. Moritz, Switzerland, in 1956.

SKI-BOB

The ski-bob was invented by Mr. Stevens of Hartford, Connecticut, U.S.A., and patented (No. 47334) on 19 April 1892 as a "bicycle with ski-runners". The Fédération Internationale de Skibob was founded on 14 Jan. 1961 in Innsbruck, Austria. The Ski-Bob Association of Great Britain was registered on 23 Aug. 1967. The highest speed attained is 103·4 m.p.h. by Erich Brenter (Austria) at Cervinia, N. Italy, in 1964.

Ove Fundin (Sweden) the only five-time winner of the World Speedway Championship

SNOWMOBILE

Ky Michaelson, in the snowmobile *Sonic Challenger*, was timed at 114·5 m.p.h. over 440 yards at Mallet's Bay, Vermont, U.S.A. on 15 Feb. 1970.

Snooker

Earliest mention Research shows that snooker was originated by Lt.-Gen. Sir Neville Chamberlain (1820–1902) as a variation of "black pool", in the Ootacamund Club, Nilgiris, South India in 1875. It did not reach England until 1885.

Highest breaks It is possible if an opponent commits a foul with 15 reds on the table that his opponent can exercise an option of nominating a colour as a red and then pots this free ball and then goes on to pot the black with 15 reds still on the table, he can score 155. The official world record break is the maximum possible (excluding handicaps or penalties) of 147 by Joe Davis, O.B.E. (born 15 April 1901) against Willie Smith at Leicester Square Hall, London, on 22 Jan. 1955 and by Rex Williams (G.B.) against Manuel Francisco at Cape Town, South Africa, on 22 Dec. 1965. Horace Lindrum "cleared the table" with an unofficial 147 in Sydney in 1941. The highest officially recognized break by an amateur is one of 122 by Ratan Badar (India) in 1964. On 11 Jan. 1970 Eric Baxter, 45, scored 136 at Wombwell Reform Club, Yorkshire which score is being submitted for ratification.

Most centuries Joe Davis secured his 500th century on 18 Feb. 1953, at which time the game's next most prolific scorer was his brother, Fred, with 144 centuries. His record of centuries made in public exhibitions reached 687 before he retired in 1965. The highest total of centuries logged in public and private is over 2,000 by Norman Squire (Australia). Rex Williams recorded 682 centuries to March 1967.

Marathon The official snooker endurance record is 72 hours (271 frames) by David Turiccki, Michael Cox and Steve Lay at the Embassy Billiards Club, Wellingborough, Northamptonshire on 21–23 Dec. 1968. A game with 3 players John C. Jackson, Jeremy P. Scaife and Kenneth H. Charlton, maintained continuous play for 215 frames and 20,970 points for 120 hours at Rose Street Snooker Centre, Aberdeen, Scotland on 20–25 April 1970.

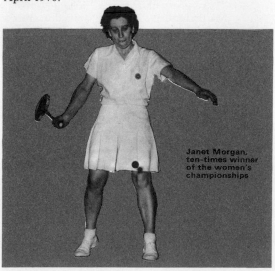

Janet Morgan, ten-times winner of the women's championships

Speedway

Origins The first organized races were at the Maitland (New South Wales, Australia) Agricultural Show of 1925. The sport was introduced to Great Britain at High Beech, Essex, on 19 Feb. 1928. After three seasons of competition in southern and northern leagues, the National League was instituted in 1932. The best record is that of the Wembley Lions who won in 1932, 1946–47, 1949–53, making a record total of eight victories. Since the National Trophy knock-out competition was instituted in 1931, Belle Vue (Manchester) have been most successful with nine victories in 1933–34–35–36–37, 1946–47, 1949 and 1958. In 1965 the League was replaced by the British League.

Most world titles The world speedway championship was inaugurated in 1936. The only five-time winner has been Ove Fundin (b. Tranås, 1933) (Sweden), who won in 1956, 1960, 1961, 1963 and 1967. In addition he was second in 1957–58–59 and third in 1962, 1964 and 1965.

Lap speed The only First Division speedway track record (time over 4 laps) in Britain with an average above 50 m.p.h. is Peter Craven's (Belle Vue) 50·40 m.p.h. in 1959 on the 425 yard circuit at Norwich, Norfolk.

Squash Rackets

(Note: "1968", for example, refers to the 1968–69 season.)

Earliest champion Although rackets (U.S. spelling, racquets) with a soft ball was evolved in *c.* 1850 at Harrow School (England), there was no recognized champion of any country until J. A. Miskey of Philadelphia won the American Amateur Singles Championship in 1906.

World title The inaugural international (world) championships were staged in Australia in August 1967 when Australia won the team title in Sydney and Geoffrey B. Hunt (Victoria) took the individual title, both titles being retained at the second championships played in London (individual) and Birmingham (team), England in February 1969.

MOST WINS

Open Championship The most wins in the Open Championship (amateur or professional), held annually in Britain, is seven by Hashim Khan (Pakistan) in 1950–51–52–53–54–55 and 1957.

Amateur Championship The most wins in the Amateur Championship is six by Abdel Fattah Amr Bey (Egypt, now the United Arab Republic), later appointed Ambassador in London, who won in 1931–32–33 and 1935–36–37. Norman F. Borrett of England won in 1946–47–48–49–50.

Professional Championship The most wins in the Professional Championship is five by J. P. Dear (Great Britain) in 1935–36–37–38 and 1949, and Hashim Khan (Pakistan) in 1950–51–52–53–54.

Most international selections The record for international selections is held by O. L. Balfour (Scotland) with 45 between 1954 and 1968. The record for England is 43 by G. J. A. Lyon from 1956 to 1968; for Ireland 36 jointly by B. Kilcoyne from 1956 to 1969 and D. M. Pratt from 1956 to 1969 and for Wales 44 by L. J. Verney between 1949 and 1965.

Longest span of internationals P. Harding-Edgar first played for Scotland in 1938 and last played 21 years later in 1959.

Longest championship match The longest recorded championship match was one of 2 hours 13 minutes in the final of the Open Championship of the British Isles at the Edgbaston-Priory Club, Birmingham in December 1969 when Jonah P. Barrington (Ireland) beat Geoffrey B. Hunt (Australia) 9–7, 3–9, 3–9, 9–4, 9–4 with the last game lasting 37 minutes.

Most wins in the women's championship The most wins in the Women's Squash Rackets Championship is ten by Miss Janet R. M. Morgan (now Mrs. Shardlow) of England in 1949–50–51–52–53–54–

55–56–57–58. Miss Morgan won all three of the world's major titles, the Australian, British and U.S. championships in 1954.

Marathon record The longest recorded squash singles marathons have been those of 32 hours 15 minutes at the University of Otago, New Zealand on 5–7 May 1969 between John Hornal and Graham Leigh and between Bill Crane and John Thurlow.

Surfing

Origins The traditional Polynesian sport of surfing in a canoe (*ehorooe*) was first recorded by Captain James Cook, R.N., F.R.S. (1728–79) on his third voyage at Tahiti in December 1771. Surfing on a board (*Amo Amo iluna ka lau oka nalu*) was first described ("most perilous and extraordinary... altogether astonishing, and is scarcely to be credited") by Lt. (later Capt.) James King, R.N., F.R.S. in March 1779 at Kealakekua Bay, Hawaii Island. A surfer was first depicted by this voyage's official artist John Webber.

The sport was revived at Waikiki by 1900. Australia's first club, the Bondi Surf Bathers Lifesaving Club, was formed in February 1906. Australia's most successful champion has been Bob Newbiggin, who won the senior title in 1939–40–45–46–47 and the senior Belt Race in 1940. Hollow boards came in in 1929.

Highest waves ridden Makaha Beach, Hawaii provides the reputedly highest consistently high waves often reaching the rideable limit of 30–35 feet. The highest wave ever ridden was the *tsunami* of "perhaps 50 feet", which struck Minole, Hawaii on 3 April 1868, and was ridden to save his life by a Hawaiian named Holua.

Longest ride On 1 June 1936 Tom Blake rode a wave from First Break South Castle north and east of Waikiki Beach, Oahu, Hawaiian Islands, an estimated distance of 4,500 feet.

Swimming

Earliest references It is recorded that inter-school swimming contests in Japan were ordered by Imperial edict of Emperor Go-Yoozei as early as 1603. In Great Britain competitive swimming originated in London *c.* 1837, at which time there were five or more pools.

Largest pools The largest swimming pool in the world is the sea-water Orthlieb Pool in Casablanca, Morocco. It is 480 metres (1,547 feet) long and 75 metres (246 feet) wide, and has an area of 3·6 hectares (8·9 acres). The largest land-locked swimming pool with heated water is the Fleishhacker Pool on Sloat Boulevard, near Great Highway, San Francisco, California, U.S.A. It measures 1,000 feet by 150 feet (3·44 acres) and up to 14 feet deep, and contains 7,500,000 gallons of heated water. The world's largest competition pool is that at Osaka, Japan, which accommodates 25,000 spectators. The largest in the United Kingdom is the Empire Pool, Cardiff, completed in 1958.

Fastest swimmer Excluding relay stages with their anticipatory starts, the highest speed reached by a swimmer is 4·89 m.p.h. by Stephen Edward Clark (U.S.A.), who recorded 20·9 seconds for a heat of 50 yards in a 25-yard pool at Yale University, New Haven, Connecticut, U.S.A., on 26 March 1964. Wenden's 100 metre record of 52·2 seconds required an average of 4·285 m.p.h.

Most world records Men, 31, Arne Borg (Sweden), 1921–1929.
Women, 43, Ragnhild Hveger (Denmark), 1936–1942.

Most Olympic titles The greatest number of individual Olympic gold medals ever won is five by John Weissmuller (U.S.A.), who won 3 individual and 2 relay medals in 1924 and 1928. The most gold medals won at one Games is four by Donald Arthur Schollander (U.S.A.), who won the individual 100 metres and 400 metres free style races, and swam on the last stage in the 4×100 metres and 4×200 metres free style relays, in Tōkyō, Japan, in 1964. Dawn Fraser, M.B.E. (born Sydney, Australia, 1937) now Mrs. Gary Ware, won the 100 metres free style in 1956, 1960 and 1964 and a fourth gold medal in the 4×100 metres free style relay in 1956. Mrs. Patricia McCormick (U.S.A.) won four gold medals in the highboard and springboard diving contests in 1952 and 1956. The greatest number by a British swimmer is three by John A. Jarvis, who won the 100 metres, 1,000 and 4,000 metres in Paris in 1900.

Most difficult dives Those with the highest tariff (degree of difficulty 2·9) are the "1½ forward somersaults with triple twist"; the "2½ forward somersaults with double twist" and the "1½ reverse with 2½ twists". Joaquin Capilla of Mexico has performed a 4½ somersaults dive from a 10-metre board, but this is not on the international tariff.

WORLD RECORDS—MEN (at distances recognized by the *Fédération Internationalede Natation Amateur*)

Those marked with an asterisk are awaiting ratification.   †=salt water   ††=fresh and salt water mixed.
Only performances set up in 50 metres or 55 yards baths are recognized as World Records.
F.I.N.A. no longer recognize any records made for distances over non-metric distances.

Distance	Time mins. secs.	Name and Nationality	Place	Date
FREE STYLE				
100 metres	52·2	Michael Wenden (Australia)	Mexico City, Mexico	19 Oct. 1968
200 metres	1:54·3	Donald Arthur Schollander (U.S.A.)	Long Beach, California, U.S.A.	30 Aug. 1968
	1:54·3	Mark Spitz (U.S.A.)	Santa Clara, California, U.S.A.	12 July 1969
400 metres	4:04·0	Hans Fassnacht (West Germany)	Louisville, Kentucky, U.S.A.	14 Aug. 1969
800 metres	8:28·8	Michael J. Burton (U.S.A.)	Louisville, Kentucky, U.S.A.	17 Aug. 1969
1,500 metres	16:04·5	Michael J. Burton (U.S.A.)	Louisville, Kentucky, U.S.A.	17 Aug. 1969
BREASTSTROKE				
100 metres	1:05·8	Nikolai Pankin (U.S.S.R.)	Magdeburg, East Germany	20 April 1969
200 metres	2:25·4	Nikolai Pankin (U.S.S.R.)	Magdeburg, East Germany	19 April 1969
BUTTERFLY STROKE				
100 metres	55·6	Mark Spitz (U.S.A.)	Long Beach, California, U.S.A.	30 Aug. 1968
	55·6	Mark Spitz (U.S.A.)	Santa Clara, California, U.S.A.	11 July 1969
200 metres	2:05·7	Mark Spitz (U.S.A.)	West Berlin	8 Oct. 1967
BACKSTROKE				
100 metres	57·8	Roland Matthes (East Germany)	Würzburg, West Germany	23 Aug. 1969
	57·8*	Roland Matthes (East Germany)	Novosibirsk, U.S.S.R.	15 April 1970
200 metres	2:06·4	Roland Matthes (East Germany)	Berlin, East Germany	29 Aug. 1969
INDIVIDUAL MEDLEY				
200 metres	2:09·6	Gary Hall (U.S.A.)	Louisville, Kentucky, U.S.A.	17 Aug. 1969
400 metres	4:33·9	Gary Hall (U.S.A.)	Louisville, Kentucky, U.S.A.	15 Aug. 1969
FREE STYLE RELAYS				
4 × 100 metres	3:31·7	United States Olympic Team (Zachery Zorn, Stephen Reyrch, Mark Spitz, Kenneth Walsh)	Mexico City, Mexico	17 Oct. 1968
4 × 200 metres	7:52·1	United States Olympic Team (Stephen Edward Clark, Roy Allen Saari, Gary Steven Ilman, Donald Arthur Schollander)	Tōkyō, Japan	18 Oct. 1964
	7:52·1	Santa Clara Team, U.S.A. (Gary Steven Ilman, Michael Wall, Mark Spitz, Donald Arthur Schollander)	Oak Park, Illinois, U.S.A.	21 Aug. 1967
MEDLEY RELAYS				
4 × 100 metres	3:54·9	United States Olympic Team (Charles Hickcox, Donald McKenzie, Douglas A. Russell, Kenneth Walsh)	Mexico City, Mexico	26 Oct. 1968

WORLD RECORDS—WOMEN

Distance	Time mins. secs.	Name and Nationality	Place	Date
FREE STYLE				
100 metres	58·9	Dawn Fraser (now Ware), M.B.E. (Australia)	North Sydney††	29 Feb. 1964
200 metres	2:06·7	Deborah Meyer (U.S.A.)	Los Angeles, California, U.S.A.	24 Aug. 1968
400 metres	4:24·5	Deborah Meyer (U.S.A.)	Los Angeles, California, U.S.A.	25 Aug. 1968
800 metres	9:10·4	Deborah Meyer (U.S.A.)	Los Angeles, California, U.S.A.	28 Aug. 1968
	9:09·1*	Karen Moras (Australia)	Sydney, Australia	1 Mar. 1970
1,500 metres	17:19·9	Deborah Meyer (U.S.A.)	Louisville, Kentucky, U.S.A.	17 Aug. 1969
BREASTSTROKE				
100 metres	1:14·2	Catharine Ball (U.S.A.)	Los Angeles, California, U.S.A.	25 Aug. 1968
200 metres	2:38·5	Catharine Ball (U.S.A.)	Los Angeles, California, U.S.A.	26 Aug. 1968

BUTTERFLY STROKE

| 100 metres | 1:04·5 | Ada Kok (Netherlands) | Budapest, Hungary | 14 Aug. 19 |
| 200 metres | 2:21·0 | Ada Kok (Netherlands) | Blackpool, England† | 25 Aug. 19 |

BACKSTROKE

| 100 metres | 1:05·6 | Karen Yvette Muir (South Africa) | Utrecht, Netherlands | 6 July 19 |
| 200 metres | 2:21·5 | Susan Atwood (U.S.A.) | Louisville, Kentucky, U.S.A. | 14 Aug. 19 |

INDIVIDUAL MEDLEY

| 200 metres | 2:23·5 | Claudia Anne Kolb (U.S.A.) | Los Angeles, California, U.S.A. | 25 Aug. 19 |
| 400 metres | 5:04·7 | Claudia Anne Kolb (U.S.A.) | Los Angeles, California, U.S.A. | 24 Aug. 19 |

FREE STYLE RELAYS

| 4 × 100 metres | 4:01·0 | Santa Clara S.C. (Linda Gustavson, Lillian Debra Watson, Pamela Carpinelli, Jan Margo Henne) | Santa Clara, California, U.S.A. | 6 July 19 |

MEDLEY RELAYS

| 4 × 100 metres | 4:28·1 | U.S. Team (Kaye Hall, Catharine Ball, Ellie Daniel, Sue Pedersen) | Air Force Academy, Colorado, U.S.A. | 14 Sept. 196 |

LONG DISTANCE SWIMMING

A unique achievement in long distance swimming was established in 1966 by the cross-Channel swimmer Mihir Sen of Calcutta, India. These were the Palk Strait from India to Ceylon (in 25 hours 36 minutes on 5–6 April); the Straits of Gibraltar (Europe to Africa in 8 hours 1 minute on 24 August); the Dardanelles (Gallipoli, Europe to Sedulbahir, Asia Minor in 13 hours 55 minutes on 12 September) and the entire length of the Panama Canal in 34 hours 15 minutes on 29–31 October. He had earlier swum the English Channel in 14 hours 45 minutes on 27 Sept. 1958.

CHANNEL SWIMMING

Earliest Man The first man to swim across the English Channel (without a life jacket) was the Merchant Navy captain Matthew Webb (1848–83) (G.B.), who swam breaststroke from Dover, England, to Cap Gris-Nez, France, in 21 hours 45 minutes from 12.56 p.m. to 10.41 a.m., 24–25 Aug. 1875. He swam an estimated 38 miles to make the 21-mile crossing. Paul Boyton (U.S.A.) had swum from Cap Gris-Nez to the South Foreland in his patent life-saving suit in 23 hours 30 minutes on 28–29 May 1875. There is good evidence that Jean-Marie Saletti, a French soldier, escaped from a British prison hulk off Dover by swimming to Boulogne in July or August 1815. The first crossing from France to England was made by Enrique Tiraboschi, a wealthy Italian living in Argentina, who crossed in 16 hours 33 minutes on 11 Aug. 1923, to win the *Daily Sketch* prize of £1,000.

Woman The first woman to succeed was Gertrude Ederle (U.S.A.) who swam from Cap Gris-Nez, France to Dover, England on 6 Aug. 1926, in the then record time of 14 hours 39 minutes. The first woman to swim from England to France was Florence Chadwick of California, U.S.A., in 16 hours 19 minutes on 11 Sept. 1951. She repeated this on 4 Sept. 1953 and 12 Oct. 1955.

Fastest The fastest swim is one of 9 hours 35 minutes by Barry Watson, aged 25, of Bingley, Yorkshire, who left Cap Gris-Nez, France, at 2 a.m. and arrived at St. Margaret's Bay, near Dover, at 11.35 a.m. on 16 Aug. 1964. The record for an England-France crossing (recognized by *The English Channel Association*) is 10 hours 21 minutes by Nitindra Naryan Roy (born Calcutta, India, 1940) from Dover to Cap Gris-Nez on 11–12 Sept. 1967. The record recognized by the *Channel Swimming Association*, founded in 1927, is, however, 10 hours 23 minutes by Helge Jensen (Canada) on 31 Aug. 1960. The feminine record is 9 hours 59 minutes 57 seconds by Linda McGill, M.B.E., 21, of Sydney, Australia who left Cap Gris-Nez at 4 a.m. on 29 Sept. 1967 and landed

Ada Kok (Netherlands)
holder of the world women's
100 metres butterfly record

at St. Margaret's Bay. The feminine record for an England to France crossing is 13 hours 40 minutes by Greta Andersen (born Denmark, now of Los Alamitos, California, U.S.A.) from Dover to Cap Gris-Nez on 29–30 Sept. 1964. The fastest crossing by a relay team is one of 9 hours 29 minutes by Radcliffe Swimming Club of Lancashire, from Cap Gris-Nez to Walmer on 13 June 1966.

Slowest The slowest crossing was the third ever made, when Henry Sullivan (U.S.A.) swam from England to France in 26 hours 50 minutes on 5–6 Aug. 1923. The slowest from France to England and the slowest ever by a Briton was one of 23 hours 48 minutes by Philip Mickman (born Ossett, Yorkshire, 1931) on 23–24 Aug. 1949.

Earliest and latest The earliest time in the year on which the Channel has been swum is 6 June by Dorothy Perkins (England), aged 19, in 1961, and the latest is 14 October by Ivy Gill (England) in 1927. Both swims were from France to England.

Youngest The youngest conqueror is Leonore Modell of Sacramento, California, U.S.A., who swam from Cap Gris-Nez to near Dover in 15 hours 33 minutes on 3 Sept. 1964, when aged 14 years 3 months. The youngest relay team to cross are the *Swim Kids* of Stoke-on-Trent from France to England in 12 hours 33 minutes on 1 Aug. 1967 with an average age of 13 years and 2 months.

Double crossing First Antonio Abertondo (born Buenos Aires, Argentina), aged 42, swam from England to France in 18 hours 50 minutes (8.35 a.m. on 20 Sept. to 3.25 a.m. on 21 Sept. 1961) and after about 4 minutes rest returned to England in 24 hours 16 minutes, landing at St. Margaret's Bay at 3.45 a.m. on 22 Sept. 1961, to complete the first "double crossing" in 43 hours 10 minutes. The first swimmer to achieve a crossing both ways was Edward H. Temme (born 1904) on 5 Aug. 1927 and 19 Aug. 1934.

Fastest The fastest double crossing, and only the second ever achieved, was one of 30 hours 3 minutes by Edward (Ted) Erikson, aged 37, a physiochemist from Chicago, Illinois, U.S.A. He left St. Margaret's Bay, near Dover, at 8.20 p.m. on 19 Sept. 1965 and landed at a beach about a mile west of Calais, after a swim of 14 hours

15 minutes. After a rest of about 10 minutes he returned and landed at South Foreland Point, east of Dover, at 2.23 a.m. on 21 Sept. 1965.

Most conquests Brojan Das (Pakistan) attempted a Channel crossing six times in 1958–61, succeeding on each occasion. Greta Andersen (U.S.A.) has swum the Channel four times (1957–65).

Underwater The first underwater cross-Channel swim was achieved by Fred Baldasare (U.S.A.), aged 38, a frogman, who completed the distance from France to England in 18 hours 1 minute on 11 July 1962. The fastest underwater swim was by Simon Paterson, aged 20, a frogman from Egham, Surrey, who swam from France to England in 14 hours 50 minutes on 28 July 1962.

Loch Ness The first person to swim the length of Great Britain's longest lake, the 22¾-mile-long Loch Ness was Brenda Sherratt of West Bollington, Cheshire, aged 18 in 31 hours 27 minutes on 26–27 July 1966.

Treading water The duration record for treading water (vertical posture without touching the lane markers) is 17½ hours by Peter Strawson of Lawford, Essex on 25–26 July 1967.

Ice swimming Wilhelm Simons (born 1899) of Berlin, Germany, swam 30 metres in 43·7 seconds in the Riessersee, near Garmisch-Partenkirchen, West Germany on 3 Feb. 1968. The ice had to be broken and the water temperature was 2°C. (35·6°F.).

24-hour relay The longest recorded mileage in a 24-hour swim relay (team of 5) is 63 miles 487 yards by a relay team from the Paarl Amateur Swimming Club, South Africa, on 5–6 Jan. 1970.

Underground swimming The longest recorded underground swim is one of 3,402 yards in 87 minutes by David Stanley Gale through the Dudley Old Canal Tunnel, Worcestershire, in August 1967.

Sponsored swimming The greatest amount of money raised in a sponsored swim is £1,507 7s. 6d. at the Quarry Pool, Shrewsbury, England, on 28 June 1969 by 111 swimmers of the Shrewsbury Amateur Swimming Club who covered 212¼ miles.

Table Tennis

Earliest reference The earliest evidence relating to a game resembling table tennis has been found in the catalogues of London sports goods manufacturers in the 1880s. The old Ping Pong Association was formed in 1902 but the game proved only a temporary craze until resuscitated in 1921. The English Table Tennis Association was formed on 24 April 1927.

Barry Watson, the fastest ever Channel swimmer

MOST WINS IN WORLD CHAMPIONSHIPS (Instituted 1926–27)

Event	Name and Nationality	Times	Years
Men's Singles (St. Bride's Vase)	G. Viktor Barna (Hungary)	5	1930, 1932–33–34–35
Women's Singles (G. Geist Prize)	Angelica Rozeanu (Romania)	6	1950–51–52–53–54–55
Men's Doubles	G. Viktor Barna (Hungary) with two different partners	8	1929–35, 1939
Women's Doubles	Maria Mednyanszky (Hungary) with three different partners	7	1928, 1930–31–32–33–34–35
Mixed Doubles (Men)	Ferenc Sido (Hungary) with two different partners	4	1949–50, 1952–53
(Women)	Maria Mednyanszky (Hungary) with three different partners	6	1927–28, 1930–31, 1933–34

G. Viktor Barna gained a personal total of 15 world titles, while 18 have been won by Miss Maria Mednyanszky.

MOST TEAM TITLES

Event	Team	Times	Years
Men's Team (Swaythling Cup)	Hungary	11	1927–31, 1933–35, 1938, 1949, 1952
Women's Team (Marcel Corbillon Cup)	Japan	7	1952, 1954, 1957, 1959, 1961, 1963, 1967

MOST WINS IN ENGLISH OPEN CHAMPIONSHIPS (Instituted 1921)

Event	Name and Nationality	Times	Years
Men's Singles	Richard Bergmann (Austria then G.B.)	6	1939–40, 1948, 1950, 1952, 1954
Women's Singles	Miss K. M. Berry (G.B.)	3	1923–24–25
	Miss G. Farkas (Hungary)	3	1947–48, 1956
Men's Doubles	G. Viktor Barna (Hungary, then G.B.) with five different partners	7	1931, 1933–34–35, 1938–39, 1949
Women's Doubles	Miss Diane Rowe (G.B.) with four different partners	12	1950–56, 1960, 1962–65
Mixed Doubles (Men)	G. Viktor Barna (Hungary, then G.B.) with four different partners	8	1933–36, 1938, 1940, 1951, 1953
(Women)	Miss Margaret Osborne (G.B.) with one partner	4	1935–36, 1938, 1940
	Miss Diane Rowe (G.B.) with two different partners	4	1952, 1954, 1956, 1960

The highest total of English men's titles is 20 by G. Viktor Barna. The women's record is 17 by Diane Rowe (born 14 April 1933), now Mrs. Eberhard Scholer. Her twin Rosalind (now Mrs. Cornett) has won 9 (two in singles).

Youngest international The youngest ever international (probably in any sport) was Joy Foster, aged 8, the 1958 Jamaican singles and mixed doubles champion.

Marathon records In the Swaythling Cup final match between Austria and Romania in Prague, Czechoslovakia, in 1936, the play lasted for 25 or 26 hours, spread over three nights.

The longest recorded marathon by 4 players maintaining continuous singles is 384 hours (16 days) by Gary Coles, 16; David Nation, 16; David Gardner, 15 and David Copeland, 15 at Castle Secondary School, Taunton on 20 July–5 Aug. 1969. A total of 3,402 games was played using up 120 balls.

Highest speed No conclusive measurements have been published, but Chuang Tse-tung (China) the world champion of 1961–63–65, has probably smashed at a speed of more than 60 m.p.h.

Tennis—Real or Royal

Origins The game originated in French monasteries *c.* 1050.

Oldest court The oldest of the 16 surviving Tennis Courts in the British Isles is the Royal Tennis Court at Hampton Court Palace, which was built by order of King Henry VIII in 1529–30 and rebuilt by order of Charles II in 1660. The oldest court in the world is one built in Paris in 1496. In 1969 there were 3,000 players and 27 courts in the world.

World titles The first recorded World Tennis Champion was Clerge (France) in *c.* 1740. Pierre Etchebaster won the title at Prince's, Paris, in May 1928, last defended it in New York (winning 7–1) in December 1949 and retired undefeated in 1955, after 27 years. Etchebaster also holds the record for the greatest number of successful defences of his title, with six.

Tiddlywinks

Accuracy The lowest number of shots taken to pot 12 winks from 3 feet is 23, achieved by M. Brogden (Hull University) on 18 Oct. 1962. This record was equalled by A. Cooper (Altrincham Grammar School) in December 1963 and by J. King (Ealing Grammar School) on 2 May 1965.

Speed The record for potting 24 winks from 18 inches is 21·8 seconds by Stephen Williams (Altrincham Grammar School) in May 1966.

Marathon Allen R. Astles (University of Wales) potted 10,000 winks in 3 hours 51 minutes 46 seconds at Aberystwyth,

Cardiganshire in February 1966. The most protracted game on record is one of 120 hours 2 minutes staged by eight students from Lane Technical High School, Chicago, Illinois, U.S.A. from 27 April to 2 May 1970 at the offices of Sun and Snow Inc., Westmont, Illinois, U.S.A.

Trampolining

Origins The sport of trampolining (from the Spanish word *trampolin,* a springboard) dates from 1936, when the prototype "T" model trampoline was developed by George Nissen (U.S.A.). Trampolines were used in show business at least as early as "The Walloons" of the period 1910–12.

Most difficult manoeuvre The two most difficult manoeuvres yet achieved are the triple twisting double back somersault, known as a Miller after the only trampolinist able to achieve it— Wayne Miller (born 1947) of the U.S.A., and the women's Wills ($5\frac{1}{2}$ twisting back somersault), named after the five-time world champion Judy Wills (born 1948) of the U.S.A.

Plan of the location of
the 430-year-old Royal tennis court
at Hampton Court, London

Judy Wills (left) winner of every world's women's championships

Highest price The highest price paid for a trotter is $3,000,000 (£1,250,000) for *Nevele Pride* by the Stoner Creek Stud of Lexington, Kentucky from Louis Resnick and Nevele Acres in the autumn of 1969. The highest price ever paid for a pacer is $2,000,000 (now £833,333) for *Bret Hanover* in August 1966.

Greatest winnings The greatest amount won by a trotting horse is $956,161 (£398,400) by *Roquepine*, a French mare, from 1963 to 1969. The record for a pacing horse is $1,000,837 (£417,015) by the New Zealand-bred *Cardigan Bay* from 1959 to his retirement in September 1968. In 134 starts he had 66 wins and 24 seconds.

Volleyball

Origin The game was invented as Minnonette in 1895 by William G. Morgan at the Y.M.C.A. gymnasium at Springfield, Massachusetts, U.S.A. The International Volleyball Association was formed in Paris in April 1947. The Amateur Volleyball Association of Great Britain was formed in May 1955. The ball travels at a speed of up to 70 m.p.h. when smashed over the net, which measures 2·43 metres (7 feet 11·6 inches).

World titles World Championships were instituted in 1949. The U.S.S.R. has won six men's titles (1949, 1952, 1960, 1962, 1964 and 1968) in the seven meetings held. Czechoslovakia won in 1956. The U.S.S.R. won the women's championship in 1952, 1956, 1960 and 1968. The record crowd is 60,000 for the 1952 world title matches in Moscow, U.S.S.R.

Marathon The longest recorded volleyball marathon is one of 72 hours by four sets of 6-a-side teams from the Cardinal Wiseman R.C. School, Coventry, England on 24–27 Oct. 1969.

Walking

Trans-Continental The record for walking across the United States from San Francisco, California, to New York is 66 days by Flt. Sgt. P. Maloney and Staff Sgt. M. Evans, ending on 17 June 1960. The feminine record for the 3,207-mile route is 86 days by Dr. Barbara Moore (born, Varvara Belayeva, in Kalouga, Russia, 22 Dec. 1903), ending on 6 July 1960.

End to end The record for walking from John o' Groats to Land's End (route varies between 876 and 891 miles) is 11 days 23 hours 45 minutes achieved by Malcolm Taylor of Milnsbridge, Huddersfield, Yorkshire on 18–30 July 1969. The feminine record is 17 days 7 hours by Miss Wendy Lewis ending on 14 March 1960. On 18 Dec. 1966 Frederick E. Westcott, aged 31, completed a unique End to end and back walk of 1,760 miles. David Ryder, 21, a polio victim from Chigwell, Essex, arrived at Land's End from John o' Groats on 18 Aug. 1969 having completed the entire course on crutches.

London to Brighton The record time for the London to Brighton walk is 7 hours 35 minutes 12 seconds by Donald James Thompson (born 20 Jan. 1933) on 14 Sept. 1957. The record time for London to Brighton and back is 18 hours 5 minutes 51 seconds by William Frederick Baker (born 5 April 1889) of Queen's Park Harriers, London, on 18–19 June 1926.

Marathon record The longest recorded trampoline bouncing marathon is one of 442 hours, set by a team of 5 girls and 10 boys led by Jim Larkin at Graylands Hostel Youth Club, Western Australia between 23 Aug. and 10 Sept. 1969.

Most titles The only man to retain a world title (instituted 1964) is Dave Jacobs (U.S.) the 1967–68 champion. Judy Wills has won every women's title (1964–65–66–67–68). Three United Kingdom titles have been won by David Curtis (1966–67–68); while Miss Jackie Allen (1960–61), Mary Hunkin (*née* Chamberlaine) (1963–64) and Lynda Ball (1965–66) have each won twice. The first European titles were won in Paris in June 1969 by Paul Luxon (G.B.) and Ute Czech (West Germany). After 1969 World and European championships have alternated annually.

Trotting and Pacing

The trotting gait (the simultaneous use of the diagonally opposite legs) was first recorded in England in *c.* 1750. The sulky first appeared in harness-racing in 1829. Pacers thrust out their fore and hind legs simultaneously on one side.

Records against time	Trotting			Pacing		
World (mile track)	1:54·8	Nevele Pride (U.S.A.), Indianapolis, Indiana	31 Aug. 1969	1:53·6	Bret Hanover (U.S.A.) Lexington, Kentucky	7 Oct. 1966
Australia	2:01·8	Gramel, Harold Park, Sydney	1964	1:57·3	Halwes, Harold Park, Sydney	1968
New Zealand	2:02·4	Control, Addington, Christchurch	1964	1:56·2	Cardigan Bay, Wellington	1963

OFFICIAL WORLD RECORDS (Track Walking)

(As recognized by the International Amateur Athletic Federation) (*Awaiting ratification)

Distance	Time Hrs.	mins.	secs.	Name and Nationality	Place	Date
20,000 metres	1	26	45·8	Gennadiy Agapov (U.S.S.R.)	Simfyeropol, U.S.S.R.	6 April 196
30,000 metres	2	17	16·8	Anatoliy I. Yegorov (U.S.S.R.)	Leningrad, U.S.S.R.	15 July 195
20 miles	2	31	33·0	Anatoliy S. Vedyakov (U.S.S.R.)	Moscow, U.S.S.R.	23 Aug. 195
30 miles	4	00	06·4*	Christoph Höhne (East Germany)	Berlin, East Germany	18 Oct. 196
50,000 metres	4	08	05·0*	Christoph Höhne (East Germany)	Berlin, East Germany	18 Oct. 196
2 hours	26,657 metres (16 miles 991 yards)*			Boris Khrolovich (U.S.S.R.)	Minsk, U.S.S.R.	30 Sept. 196

UNOFFICIAL WORLD BEST PERFORMANCES (Track Walking)

(Best valid performances over distances or times for which records are no longer recognized by the I.A.A.F.)

Distance	Time			Name and Nationality	Place	Date
5 miles		34	21·2	Kenneth Joseph Matthews (U.K.)	London	28 Sept. 195
10 miles	1	09	40·6	Kenneth Joseph Matthews (U.K.)	Walton-on-Thames	6 June 196
50,000 metres (road)	3	55	36·0	Gennadiy Agapov (U.S.S.R.)	Alma Ata, U.S.S.R.	17 Oct. 196
1 hour	8 miles 1,294 yards			Grigoriy Panichkin (U.S.S.R.)	Stalinabad, U.S.S.R.	1 Nov. 195
24 hours	133 miles 21 yards			Huw D. M. N. Neilson (U.K.)	Walton-on-Thames	14–15 Oct. 196

Ken Matthews (U.K.) world's fastest walker over 5 and 10 miles

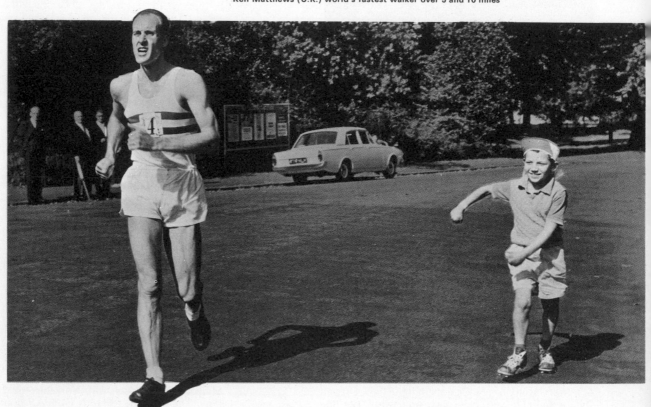

Water Polo

Origins Water Polo was developed in England as "Water Soccer" in 1869 and was first included in the Olympic Games in Paris in 1900.

Olympic Games Hungary has won the Olympic tournament five times, in 1932, 1936, 1952, 1956 and 1964. Great Britain won in 1900, 1908, 1912 and 1920.

A.S.A. championships The club with the greatest number of Amateur Swimming Association titles is Plaistow United Swimming Club of Greater London, with eleven from 1928 to 1954.

Most goals The greatest number of goals scored by an individual in a home international is eleven by Terry C. Miller (Plaistow United), when England defeated Wales 13–3 at Newport, Monmouthshire, in 1951.

Most caps The greatest number of internationals is 151 by Gyorgy Karparti of Hungary to 1966.

Water Ski-ing

Origins The origins of water ski-ing lie in plank gliding or aquaplaning. A photograph exists of a "plank-riding" contest in a regatta won by a Mr. S. Storry at Scarborough, Yorkshire on 15 July 1914. Competitors were towed on a *single* plank by a motor launch. The present day sport of water ski-ing was pioneered by Ralph W. Samuelson on Lake Pepin, Minnesota, U.S.A., on two curved pine boards in the summer of 1922, though claims have been made for the birth of the sport on Lake Annecy (Haute Savoie), France, in 1920. The British Water Ski Federation was founded in London in 1954.

Longest jumps The first recorded jump on water skis was by Dick Pope, Sr. at Miami Beach, Florida, U.S.A. in 1928. The longest jumps ever recorded are ones of 162 feet by Mike Suyderhoud (U.S.A.) at Callaway Gardens, Pine Mountain, Georgia on 15 July 1969 and at Berkeley Aquatic Park, California on 7 Sept. 1969. The official

WATER SKI-ING

women's record is 106 feet by Elizabeth Allen (born 1951) of Florida, U.S.A., at Callaway Gardens, Pine Mountain, Georgia, U.S.A., on 17 July 1966.

The British record is 146 feet 11 inches by Charlie Brown (Scotland) at Bedfont, Middlesex in September 1969. The women's record is 106 feet $3\frac{1}{2}$ inches by Jeannette Stewart-Wood (born 1946) at Ruislip, Greater London on 11 June 1967. This could not be ratified as a world record because a minimum improvement of 8 inches is required.

oys and tricks The world record for slalom is 53 buoys (final five on a 33-foot rope) by Bruce Martin (U.S.A.) at Berkeley Aquatic Park, California on 22 Aug. 1969. The record for tricks is 5,600 points by Suyderhoud. The British records are 32 buoys by Ian Walker (two on a 13-metre rope) in 1969 and 3,765 points by Paul Adlington in 1969.

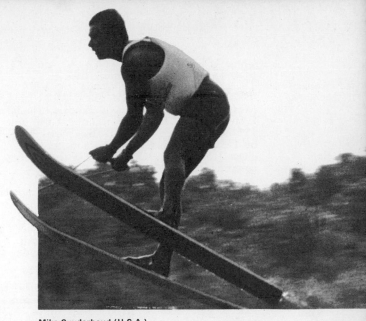

Mike Suyderhoud (U.S.A.) holder of the world's water ski jumping record

Ian Walker holder of the British slalom record

Longest run The greatest distance travelled non-stop is 818·2 miles by Marvin G. Shackleford round McKellar Lake, Memphis, Tennessee, U.S.A. in 35 hours 15 minutes in September 1960. The British record is 470·67 miles (in 15 hours 1 minute 53·2 seconds) by Charles Phipps, 30, on Lake Windermere from 4.4 a.m. to 7.5 p.m. on 4 Oct. 1959. The chief driver was George Price and the co-ordinator Charles Hulme.

Highest speed The water ski-ing speed record is 122·11 m.p.h. by Chuck Stearns of Bellflower, California, U.S.A., at the Marine Stadium, Long Beach, California, U.S.A., on 11 Jan. 1969 towed by the nitromethane alcohol burner *Panic Mouse*. He survived a fall at *c.* 125 m.p.h. Sally Younger, 15, set a feminine record the same day with 92·68 m.p.h.

Most titles World overall championships (instituted 1949) have been won twice by Alfredo Mendoza (U.S.A.) in 1953–55 and Mike Suyderhoud (U.S.A.) in 1967–69 and three times by Mrs. Willa McGuire (*née* Worthington) of the U.S.A., in 1949–50 and 1955. Mendoza won five championship events and McGuire and Elizabeth Allen (U.S.A.) seven each. The most British overall titles (instituted 1953) ever won by a man is four by Lance Callingham in 1959–60 and 1962–63, and the most by a woman is three by Maureen Lynn-Taylor in 1959–60–61 and by Jeanette Stewart-Wood in 1963–66–67.

Barefoot The barefoot duration record is 67 minutes over about 36 miles by Stephen Z. Northrup (U.S.A.) in 1969. The backwards barefoot record is 33 minutes 19 seconds by Paul McManus (Australia) in 1969.

Water ski flying The altitude record is 2,890 feet by Bill Moyes of Sydney, Australia over Lake Ellesmere, New Zealand on 4 Feb. 1969. The endurance record surpasse[d] 24 hours in 1969.

Weightlifting

Origins Amateur weightlifting is of comparatively moder[n] origin, and the first world championship was staged a[t] the Café Monico, Piccadilly, London, on 28 March 1891. Prior to that time, weightlifting consisted o[f] professional exhibitions in which some of the advertised poundages were open to doubt. The first 400 lb. clean and jerk is, however, attributed to Charles Rigoulo[t] (1903–62), a French professional, in Paris, with 402½ lb. on 1 Feb. 1929.

Greatest lift The greatest weight ever raised by a human being is 6,270 lb. (2·80 tons) in a back lift (weight raised off trestles) by the 26-stone Paul Anderson (U.S.A.) (born 1933), the 1956 Olympic heavyweight champion, at Toccoa, Georgia, U.S.A., on 12 June 1957. The heaviest Rolls-Royce, the Phantom V, weighs 5,600 lb. (2½ tons). The greatest lift by a woman is 3,564 lb. with a hip and harness lift by Mrs. Josephine Blatt *née* Schauer (1869–1923) at the Bijou Theatre, Hoboken, New Jersey, U.S.A., on 15 April 1895.

The greatest overhead lift ever made by a woman, also professional, is 286 lb. in a continental clean and jerk by Katie Sandwina, *née* Brummbach (Germany) (born 21 Jan. 1884 died as Mrs. Max Heymann in New York City, U.S.A., in 1952) in *c.* 1926. This is equivalent to seven 40-pound office typewriters. She stood 6 feet 1 inch tall, weighed 220 lb. (15 stone 10 lb.) and is reputed to have unofficially lifted 312½ lb. and to have once shouldered a 1,200 lb. cannon.

Vasiliy Alexeysev
the world's
super heavyweight
record holder

WEIGHTLIFTING

ver lifts Paul Anderson, as a professional, has bench-pressed 627 lb. and has achieved 1,200 lb. in a squat so aggregating, with an 820 lb. dead lift, a career total of 2,647 lb. The A.A.U. of America record for a single contest is an aggregate of 2,040 lb. by Bob Weaver set in 1967.

The highest recorded two-handed dead lift is 820 lb. by Paul Anderson. Hermann Gorner (Germany) performed a one-handed dead lift of 727½ lb. in Leipzig on 8 Oct. 1920. Peter B. Cortese (U.S.A.) achieved a one-armed dead lift of 22 lb. over triple his bodyweight with 370 lb. at York, Pennsylvania on 4 Sept. 1954. Gorner (see above) raised 24 men weighing 4,123 lb. on a plank on the soles of his feet in London on 12 Oct. 1927 and also carried on his back a 1,444 lb. piano for a distance of 52½ feet on 3 June 1921.

It was reported that an hysterical 8 stone 11 lb. woman, Mrs. Maxwell Rogers, lifted one end of a 3,600 lb. (1·60 ton) station wagon which, after the collapse of a jack, had fallen on top of her son at Tampa, Florida, U.S.A., on 24 April 1960. She cracked some vertebrae.

levering The only man ever to have levered six 16 oz. billiard cues simultaneously by their tips through 90 degrees to the horizontal, is W. J. (Bill) Hunt of Darwen, Lancashire at the Unity Club, Great Harewood, Lancashire on 25 June 1954.

Sports, games and pastimes

Paul Anderson (U.S.A.), the greatest ever power lifter

Olympic Games The U.S.S.R. has won 18, the U.S.A. 14 and France 9 of the 68 titles at stake. Eight lifters have so far succeeded in winning Olympic titles in successive Games. Three lifters have won 2 gold and 1 silver medal:—

Louis Hostin (France) Light-heavy: Silver 1928; Gold 1932 and 1936.
Tommy Kono (Hawaii/U.S.A.) Lightweight: Gold 1952; Light-heavy: Gold 1956; Middleweight: Silver 1960.
Yoshinobu Miyake (Japan) Bantam: Silver 1960; Featherweight: Gold 1964, 1968.

OFFICIAL WORLD RECORDS

Bodyweight Class	Lift	Lifted (lb.)	Name and Nationality	Place	Date	
Flyweight (Less than 56 kg.–123·46 lb.)	Press	250	Vladislav Krishishin (U.S.S.R.)	Lvov, U.S.S.R.	16 Dec.	1969
	Snatch	220¼	Koji Miki (Japan)	Yufuin, Japan	19 Aug.	1966
	Jerk	286½	Vladislav Krishishin (U.S.S.R.)	Szombathely, Hungary	20 June	1970
	Total	749¼	Vladislav Krishishin (U.S.S.R.)	Szombathely, Hungary	20 June	1970
Bantamweight (56 kg.–123·46 lb.)	Press	275½	Imre Földi (Hungary)	Budapest, Hungary	21 June	1969
	Snatch	250	Koji Miki (Japan)	Osaka, Japan	15 Nov.	1968
	Jerk	330½	Mohamed Nassiri (Iran)	Mexico City, Mexico	13 Oct.	1968
	Total	820¾	Imre Földi (Hungary)	Szombathely, Hungary	21 June	1970
Featherweight (60 kg.–132·28 lb.)	Press	293	Mladen Kuchev (Bulgaria)	Szombathely, Hungary	22 June	1970
	Snatch	276½	Yoshinobu Miyake (Japan)	Matsuura, Japan	28 Oct.	1969
	Jerk	337¼	Yoshinobu Miyake (Japan)	Matsuura, Japan	28 Oct.	1969
	Total	881½	Yoshinobu Miyake (Japan)	Matsuura, Japan	28 Oct.	1969
Lightweight (67·5 kg.–148·81 lb.)	Press	320¾	Yevgeniy Katsura (U.S.S.R.)	Ordzhonikidze, U.S.S.R.	28 July	1966
	Snatch	299¾	Waldemar Baszanowski (Poland)	Warsaw, Poland	23 Sept.	1969
	Jerk	375¾	Waldemar Baszanowski (Poland)	Warsaw, Poland	23 Sept.	1969
	Total	980¾	Waldemar Baszanowski (Poland)	Warsaw, Poland	23 Sept.	1969
Middleweight (75 kg.–165·35 lb.)	Press	356	Viktor Kurentsov (U.S.S.R.)	Rostov-on-Don, U.S.S.R.	16 May	1969
	Snatch	319½	Masashi Ohuchi (Japan)	Yufuin, Japan	18 June	1967
	Jerk	413¼	Viktor Kurentsov (U.S.S.R.)	Mexico City, Mexico	16 Oct.	1968
	Total	1,063¼	Viktor Kurentsov (U.S.S.R.)	Dubna, U.S.S.R.	31 Aug.	1968
Light-heavyweight (82·5 kg.–181·77 lb.)	Press	386¾	Hans Bettembourg (Sweden)	Söderhamn, Sweden	10 May	1970
	Snatch	336	Masashi Ohuchi (Japan)	Warsaw, Poland	25 Sept.	1969
	Jerk	422	Gennadi Ivanchenko (U.S.S.R.)	Lvov, U.S.S.R.	18 Dec.	1969
	Total	1,102	Gennadi Ivanchenko (U.S.S.R.)	Vilnius, U.S.S.R.	24 April	1970
Middle-heavyweight (90 kg.–198·42 lb.)	Press	401	Sergei Poltoratskiy (U.S.S.R.)	Vilnius, U.S.S.R.	25 April	1970
	Snatch	354¾	Kaarlo Kangasniemi (Finland)	Kiruna, Sweden	15 Nov.	1969
	Jerk	443	Vasiliy Kolotov (U.S.S.R.)	Szombathely, Hungary	26 June	1970
	Total	1,173½	Vasiliy Kolotov (U.S.S.R.)	Vilnius, U.S.S.R.	25 April	1970
Heavyweight (100 kg.–242·51 lb.)	Press	429¾	Valeriy Yakubovsky (U.S.S.R.)	Vilnius, U.S.S.R.	25 April	1970
	Snatch	363¾	Karl Utsar (U.S.S.R.)	Vilnius, U.S.S.R.	25 April	1970
	Jerk	473¼	Yan Talts (U.S.S.R.)	Szombathely, Hungary	27 June	1970
	Total	1,239½	Yan Talts (U.S.S.R.)	Szombathely, Hungary	27 June	1970
Super-heavyweight (Above 100 kg.–242·51 lb.)	Press	483¾	Vasily Alexeyev (U.S.S.R.)	Szombathely, Hungary	28 June	1970
	Snatch	388	Leonid Zhabotinsky (U.S.S.R.)	Leningrad, U.S.S.R.	25 June	1968
	Jerk	497	Vasily Alexeyev (U.S.S.R.)	Szombathely, Hungary	28 June	1970
	Total	1,350¼	Vasily Alexeyev (U.S.S.R.)	Szombathely, Hungary	28 June	1970

(As supplied by Mr. Oscar State, General Secretary of the Fédération Internationale Haltérophile)

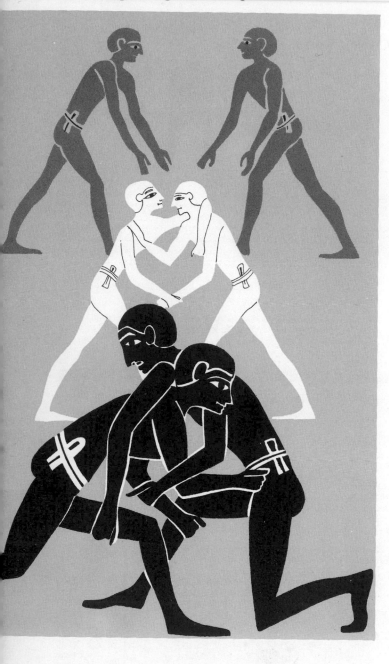

weight event in the 1964 Olympic Games. This was h 186th successive win and he had never been defeate The flyweight Ali Aliyer (U.S.S.R.) won 3 worl freestyle titles (1959, 1961, 1962).

Longest bout The longest recorded bout was one of nearly 11 hou between Max Klein (Russia) and Alfred Asikaine (Finland) in the Graeco-Roman middleweight "A event in the 1912 Olympic Games in Stockholm Sweden.

Great Britain Most titles

Heavyweight	10	Ken Richmond, 1949–60
Middleweight	7	Thomas Albert Baldwin (born 27 Sept. 1905), 1942, 1944–46, 1948, 1951–52 (also Welterweight in 1941)
Welterweight	9	Joe Feeney, 1957–60, 1962, 1964–66, 1968
Lightweight	8	Arthur Thompson, 1933–40
Featherweight	8	H. Hall, 1952–57, 1961, 1963 and Lightweight 1958–59
Bantamweight	6	Joe Reid, 1930–35

Longest span The longest span for B.A.W.A. titles is 24 years by G. Mackenzie, who won his first title in 1909 and his last in 1933. Mackenzie also jointly holds (see Fencing) the record of having represented Great Britain in five successive Olympiads from 1908 to 1928.

Heaviest heavyweight The heaviest heavyweight champion in British wrestling history was A. Dudgeon (Scotland), who won the 1936 and 1937 B.A.W.A. heavyweight titles, scaling 22 stone.

Professional wrestling Professional wrestling dates from *c.* 1875 in the United States. Georges Karl Julius Hackenschmidt (1877–1968) made no submissions in the period 1898–1908. The highest paid professional wrestler ever is Antonio ("Tony") Rocca of Puerto Rico, with $180,000 (£75,000) in 1958. The heaviest ever wrestler has been William J. Cobb of Macon, Georgia, U.S.A. (born 1926), who was billed in 1962 as the 802 lb. (57 st. 4 lb.) "Happy" Humphrey. What he lacked in mobility he possessed in suffocating powers. By July 1965 he had reduced to a more modest 232 lb. (16 st. 8 lb.).

Sumo wrestling The sport's legendary origins in Japan were 2,000 years ago. The heaviest ever performer was probably Dewagatake, a wrestler of the 1920s who was 6 feet 5 inches tall and weighed up to 30 stone. Weight is amassed by over alimentation with a high protein sea food stew called *chanko-rigori.* The tallest was probably Ozora, an early 19th century performer, who stood 7 feet 3 inches tall. The most successful wrestler has been Koki Naya (born 1940), *alias* Taiho ("Great Bird"), who won his 26th Emperor's Cup on 10–24 Sept. 1967. He was first a *Yokozuna* (Grand Champion) in 1967. The highest *dan* is Makuuchi.

Yachting

Origin Yachting in England dates from the £100 stake race between Charles II and his brother James, Duke of York, on the Thames on 1 Sept. 1661 over 23 miles, from Greenwich to Gravesend. The earliest club is the Royal Cork Yacht Club (formerly the Cork Harbour Water Club), established in Ireland in 1720.

Highest speed A speed of 30 knots was attained in September 1966 by *Lady Helmsman,* the 25-foot C class catamaran built by Reg. White (b. 1936) of Brightlingsea, Essex. The aerodynamic mast accounts for a third of the 300 square feet of sail area permitted. She won the Little America's Cup in 1966–67–68.

Most successful The most successful racing yacht in history was the Royal Yacht *Britannia* (1893–1935), owned by King George V, which won 231 races in 625 starts.

America's Cup The America's Cup races, open to challenge by any nation's yachts, began on 8 Aug. 1870 with the unsuccessful attempt by J. Ashbury's *Cambria* (G.B.) to capture the trophy from the *Magic,* owned by F. Osgood (U.S.A.). Since then the Cup has been challenged by

Wrestling

Earliest references Wrestling holds and falls, depicted on the walls of the Egyptian tombs of Beni Hasan, prove that wrestling dates from 3000 B.C. or earlier. It was introduced into the ancient Olympic Games in the 18th Olympiad in *c.* 704 B.C. The Graeco-Roman style is of French origin and arose about 1860.

Most Olympic titles Two wrestlers have won three Olympic titles. They are:

Carl Westergran (Sweden)

Graeco-Roman Middleweight A	1920
Graeco-Roman Middleweight B	1924
Graeco-Roman Heavyweight	1932

Ivar Johansson (Sweden)

Freestyle Middleweight	1932
Graeco-Roman Welterweight	1932
Graeco-Roman Middleweight	1936

Best record Osamu Watanabe (Japan) won the freestyle feather-

Great Britain in 15 contests, by Canada in two contests, and by Australia twice, but the United States holders have never been defeated. The closest race ever was the fourth race of the 1962 series, when the 12-metre sloop *Weatherly* beat her Australian challenger *Gretel* by about 3½ lengths (75 yards), a margin of only 26 seconds, on 22 Sept. 1962. The fastest time ever recorded by a 12-metre boat for the triangular course of 24 miles is 2 hours 46 minutes 58 seconds by *Gretel* in 1962.

Little America's Cup

The catamaran counterpart to the America's Cup was instituted in 1961. The British club entry has won on each annual occasion to 1968 *v.* the U.S.A. (1961–66 and 1968) and *v.* Australia in 1967.

Largest yacht

The largest private yacht ever built was Mrs. Emily Roebling Cadwalader's *Savarona* of 4,600 gross tons, completed in Hamburg, Germany, in Oct. 1931, at a cost of $4,000,000 (now £1·66 million). She (the yacht), with a 53-foot beam and measuring 407 feet 10 inches overall, was sold to the Turkish government in March 1938. Operating expenses for a full crew of 107 men approached $500,000 (now £208,000) per annum.

The largest private sailing yacht ever built was the full-rigged 350-foot auxiliary barque *Sea Cloud* (formerly *Hussar*), owned by the oft-married Mrs. Marjorie Merriweather Post-Close-Hutton-Davies-May (born 1888), one-time wife of the U.S. Ambassador in the U.S.S.R. Her four masts carried 30 sails with the total canvas area of 36,000 square feet.

Largest sail

The largest sail ever made was a parachute spinnaker with an area of 18,000 square feet (more than two-fifths of an acre) for Vanderbilt's *Ranger* in 1937.

Olympic Games

The first sportsman ever to win individual gold medals in four successive Olympic Games was Paul B. Elvstrom of Denmark in the Firefly class in 1948 and the Finn class in 1952, 1956 and 1960. He has also won 8 other world titles in a total of 6 classes. The lowest number of penalty points by the winner of any class in an Olympic regatta is 3 points (6 wins [1 disqualified] and 1 second in 7 starts) by *Super-docius* of the Flying Dutchman class (Lt. Rodney Pattison, M.B.E., R.N. and Ian Macdonald-Smith, M.B.E.) at Acapulco, Mexico in October 1968.

"Lady Helmsman" (left) multiple winner of the Little America's Cup for catamarans

stop stop
press press

CHAPTER 1—THE HUMAN BEING

Dimensions
Page 16
Armitage attained 40 stone 1 lb. (561 lb.) on 15 Feb. 1970.

Reproductivity
Page 21
Quadruplets reputedly survived birth near Devil's Bridge, Cardiganshire, Wales in 1856 only to die of cholera later in the same year.

Chest measurements
Page 22
Re-assessments would indicate figures of 104 inches (Hughes) and 65 inches (MacAskill) are more supportable. George MacAree (b. 1923) of Newham, London has Britain's record chest measurement of 71½ inches.

Surgical instruments
Page 26
Some bronchoscopic forceps measure 60 cms. (23½ inches) overall. Abbey Surgical of Chingford, Essex make robot-tractors for thoracic surgery which weigh 15 lb.

Heart transplant
Father Damien Boulogne (France) died in Paris on 18 Oct. 1969 having survived a record 524 days.

I.Q.
Herbert de Crote of Baja California, Mexico has been attested to have extracted the 7th root of a 63-digit number by exclusively mental process in 20 minutes in a test in Chicago, Illinois on 16 Oct. 1969. His answer was 858,312,524. No comparable feat has been recorded.

Lowest detectable sound
Sensitivity depends on the frequency (pitch) of the sound. The optimum is higher than the standard reference frequency of 1,000 Hz at *c.* 2,750 Hz, where sounds can be heard nearly 10 dB below the threshold of audition at the standard frequency.

CHAPTER 2—ANIMAL AND PLANT KINGDOMS

Rarest British mammal and rarest bat
Page 30
The pine marten is the rarest British *land* mammal since the mouse-eared bat (*Myotis myotis*) must qualify as the rarest British mammal of any kind. Its wing-span of up to 450 mm. (17·7 inches) and weight of 45 grammes (1·58 oz.) also qualify it as the largest bat seen in Great Britain.

Most valuable furs
Page 34
A "Kojah" fur coat costing $125,000 (£52,083) was sold by Neiman & Marcus of Dallas, Texas to Richard Burton for his wife in May 1970.

Heaviest dog
Page 34–35
"Schwarzwald Hot Duke" weighed 21 stone 1 lb. (295 lb.) on 2 May 1969 and died in August 1969 aged 4 years 10 months. "Montmorency of Hollesley," known as "Monty", owned by Mr. R. Simon of Wilmington, Sussex whelped on 1 May 1962 was estimated to weigh 19 stone (266 lb.) in April 1970.

Most prolific
Page 35
Mrs. Amhurst reported the death of *Low Pressure* at Waltham Cross, Essex on 27 Nov. 1969 by when his registered total of offspring was 2,414 with at least 600 others unregistered.

Heaviest cat
Page 35
Gigi, a tabby cat in Cumberland, England was weighed at 42 lb. and measured to have a girth of 24 inches.

Most abundant birds
Page 37
Latest published estimates indicate that the most abundant wild bird in Great Britain is the blackbird (*Turdus merula*) with just more than 10,000,000 or 8·3 per cent. of the total. The fowl stock was estimated at 90,000,000 in 1965, producing nearly 200,000,000 chicks each year.

The country with the most varied ovifauna is Colombia with 1,700 species recorded to 1963 (cf. 775 for U.S.A.-Canada).

Longest frog jump
Page 40
The 1970 Jubilee winner, the swamp-bred *Corrosion,* owned by Leonard Hall, leaped 36 times his own length to reach 18 ft. 0½ in. on 18 May 1968.

Viruses
Page 48
The trachoma and psittacosis organisms are not now classified as viruses. The largest true viruses are the brick-shaped pox viruses (e.g. smallpox, vaccinia, orf etc.) measuring *c.* 250×300 millimicrons. Viruses measuring 20 millimicrons in diameter from the pico-dna group include the adenovirus associated viruses and the Kilham rat virus. SF having now been cultured has been re-allocated to its former status of an ultravirus.

Gigi, Britain's new claimant to the title of the world's heaviest cat

Soyuz 9 which established a manned space duration record in July 1970

Stop press

...TER 3—THE NATURAL WORLD

Longest river
Page 60
A new source to mouth survey of the River Amazon by the National Geographic Society indicates a total length of c. 4,190 miles.

Highest ...erature
Page 63
Note: Amos and Mammoth Tank, California are one and the same place. The San Lais (Sonora *not* Potosi) reading of 1933 is now regarded in the same category as that of 1953.

...ometric ...ressure
Page 64
1083·8 mb (32·00 inches) was recorded at Agata, Siberia, U.S.S.R. (altitude 862 feet) on 31 Dec. 1968.

...der-days (...note [11])
38 thunder-days were recorded at Huddersfield, Yorkshire in 1967.

...inimum sunshine
During the same month (December 1890) the figure recorded at Westminster was "0·0 hours".

...aximum sunshine
78·3 per cent. (382 hours) was recorded at Pendennis Castle, Falmouth, Cornwall in June 1925.

Intense rainfall
Page 65
2·21 inches in 15 minutes was recorded at Bolton, Lancashire on 18 July 1964.

...PTER 4—THE UNIVERSE AND SPACE

...st distant object
Page 69
It was announced in May 1970 from Kitt Peak National Observatory, Arizona, U.S.A., that a fairly bright quasar 4C 05·34 was exhibiting a red-shift of 2·877 and thus qualified as the fastest moving and most distant object yet discovered.

Space duration
Page 72
Soyuz 9, carrying Col. Andrian Nikolayev and Flight Engineer Vitaliy Sevastyanov, broke the space duration record landing near Vorkuta, U.S.S.R. after 17 days 16 hours 59 minutes on 18 June 1970. U.S. *Explorer 1*, launched 31 Jan. 1958 flamed out over the Pacific on 31 March 1970 after a record 58,376 orbits.

...APTER 5—THE SCIENTIFIC WORLD

Strongest beer
Page 76
Revised data on draught Thomas Hardy ale shows that this qualifies as the strongest beer in the world with 10·15 per cent. alcohol by weight and 12·58 per cent. by volume.

Strongest magnetic field
Page 82
The strongest steady magnetic field yet achieved is one of 220,000 gauss in a cylindrical bore of 1·25 inches, requiring 10 megawatts of power, called the "1J" magnet which has been in operation at the Massachusetts Institute of Technology since 1964.

Largest computers
Page 83
Precision Instrument Co., Palo Alto, announced in June 1970 a contract to supply a "trillion bit" ($1·0 \times 10^{12}$) Unicorn memory storage unit system for *Illiac IV* at the University of Illinois, U.S.A. Unicorn is the acronym for the uni-density coherent light recording computer laser mass memory system.

...IAPTER 6—THE ARTS AND ENTERTAINMENTS

Highest priced painting
Page 84
The highest price paid for an item of Pop Art is $60,000 (£25,000) for "Soup Can" the 72 × 54 inch "masterpiece" by Andy Warhol sold at Parke-Bernet Galleries, New York in May 1970.

Last Manx speaker
Page 87
Ned Maddrell celebrated his 92nd birthday on 20 Aug. 1969.

Best sellers
Page 93
It has been reported by *Publisher's Weekly* that the sales of the novel *Valley of the Dolls* by Jacqueline Susann had surpassed 10,000,000 copies.

Largest print order
Page 94
The run on the 46th edition of the A.A. Handbook (1970–71) was 5,130,000 copies bringing its total to 53,510,000.

Longest symphonies
Page 98
Recordings by the London Symphony Orchestra, conducted by Georg Solti of Bruckner's eighth and Mahler's ninth show the latter to be more than three minutes longer.

CHAPTER 7—THE WORLD'S STRUCTURES

Tallest buildings
Page 108
The 365-foot antenna tower atop the World Trade Center will bring the total height to 1,715 feet. It will be superseded by The Sears Tower which will be 1,451 feet in height with 109 storeys. It will cost more than $100 million and will be completed in 1974.

North Sea drilling
Page 124
The off-shore records are now 19,171 feet in the U.K. fields and 17,500 feet in the Netherlands fields.

CHAPTER 8—THE MECHANICAL WORLD

L tests
Page 133
Mrs. Hargrave triumphed at her 40th attempt on 3 Aug. 1970.

Pedal car
Page 134
Six apprentices from Broom & Wade Ltd., High Wycombe, Bucks., with the assistance of two maintenance men, two cooks, a photographer and a team manager (also 2 service vehicles) pedalled from Marble Arch, London starting at 1·00 hours 19 May 1970 arriving 27 hours 57 minutes later at the Arc de Triomphe. Excluding the Channel crossing an average speed of 10 m.p.h. was maintained.

Longest platform
Page 136
Kharagpur is in Bihar, N.E. India.

World's most powerful crane
Page 146
A 32-wheel hydraulic gantry hoist with a span of 95 feet and a capacity of 2,000 short tons (1,785 long tons) is being designed for lifting the 600,000 kW generator parts in the Grand Coulee Third Powerplant project, Washington, U.S.A.

CHAPTER 9—THE BUSINESS WORLD

Hotel chain
Page 150
The 1969 revenue of Holiday Inns Inc. was reported as $541,301,234 (£225,542,180).

Silver Most expensive
Page 157
The highest price paid at auction for a single piece of silver is £78,000 at Christies of London on 1 July 1970 for a unique silver Charles I ink stand hallmarked for 1639 weighing 172 oz. It had been sold also at Christies on 5 June 1893 for £446.

CHAPTER 10—HUMAN ACHIEVEMENTS

Earliest east to west crossing
Page 163
Sidney Genders, 51, rowed from Sennen Cove, Cornwall, England to Miami, Florida, U.S.A. via the Canary Islands and Antigua in 166 days from 11 Jan. to 27 June 1970.

Singing marathon
Page 172
The longest recorded singing marathon was one of 26 hours 3 minutes by John Holdridge, 19, on 4–5 July 1970, at the Coach and Horses Inn, Horns Cross, Bideford, Devon. He sang 241 songs.

Train spotting
Page 174
D. B. Tillotson completed the spotting of every locomotive (over 15,000) on British Rail after 13½ years in May 1970.

The World Trade Center which will, after 40 years, depose the Empire State Building as the skyscraper champion

ATHLETICS (Track and Field) World Records—Men   Page 231

Page 231

Event	Record	Name and Nationality	Event	Date	
100 yards	9·1*	Willie McGee (U.S.A.)	Houston, Texas, U.S.A.	8 May	197
120 yards hurdles	13·2*	Thomas Hill (U.S.A.)	Wichita, U.S.A.	13 June	197
3,000 metres steeplechase	8:22·0*	Kerry O'Brien (Australia)	West Berlin, Germany	4 July	197

(*=awaiting ratification)

Page 232

Event	Record	Name and Nationality	Event	Date	
Pole Vault	17 ft. 10½ ins.*	Wolfgang Nordwig (E. Germany)	East Berlin, Germany	17 June	197
Marathon		The best British time is 2 hours 09 minutes 28·0 seconds by Dr. Ronald Hill of Bolton United Harriers at Edinburgh		23 July	197

Women   Page 233

Event	Record	Name and Nationality	Event	Date	
100 yards	10·0*	Chi Cheng (Formosa)	Portland, Oregon, U.S.A.	13 June	197
100 metres	11·0*	Chi Cheng (Formosa)	Vienna, Austria	18 July	197
200 metres	22·4*	Chi Cheng (Formosa)	Munich, West Germany	12 July	197
220 yards	22·7*	Chi Cheng (Formosa)	Portland, Oregon, U.S.A.	13 June	197
400 metres	51·0*	Marilyn Neufville (Jamaica)	Edinburgh, Scotland	22 July	197

Page 234

Event	Record	Name and Nationality	Event	Date	
100 metres	11·0*	Renate Meissner (East Germany)	East Berlin, Germany	2 Aug.	197
200 metres	23·2*	Margaret Critchley	East Berlin, Germany	2 Aug.	197
100 metres hurdles	12·8*	Chi Cheng (Formosa)	Münich, West Germany	12 July	197
	13·4*	Christine Bell (*née* Perera)	East Berlin, Germany	2 Aug.	197
200 metres hurdles	25·8*	Annelie Jahns (East Germany)	Erfurt. East Germany	4 July	197
4 × 440 yards relay	3:41·3*	Atoms Track Club of Brooklyn, U.S.A. (Michele McMillan, Shelley Marshall, Gail Fitzgerald, Cheryl Toussaint)	Los Angeles, California, U.S.A.	4 July	197C
4 × 800 metres relay	8:27·0*	Great Britain (Rosemary Stirling, Mrs. Sheila Carey, Patricia Lowe, Lillian Board)	Edinburgh, Scotland	13 June	197C

U.K. National Records—Men   Page 235

Event	Record	Name and Nationality	Event	Date	
5,000 metres	13:22·8*	Ian Stewart	Edinburgh, Scotland	25 July	1970
100 metres hurdles	13·6*	Alan Pascoe	Zurich, Switzerland	3 July	1970
Pole Vault	16 ft. 8¾ ins.*	Michael Bull	Edinburgh, Scotland	23 July	1970
Hammer Throw	225 ft. 9 ins.*	Arthur Howard Payne	London (White City)	11 July	1970
Javelin Throw	273 ft. 8 ins.*	David Howard Travis	Zurich, Switzerland	2 Aug.	1970
Decathlon	7,486 pts.*	Barry King	Los Angeles, California, U.S.A.	31 May–	

WOMEN   Page 236

Event	Record	Name and Nationality	Event	Date	
400 metres	51·0*	Marilyn Neufville	Edinburgh, Scotland	22 July	1970
1,500 metres	4:15·4*	Rita Ridley (*née* Lincoln)	London (Crystal Palace)	20 July	1970
High Jump	5 ft. 10½ ins.*	Barbara Inkpen	London (White City)	11 July	1970
Pentathlon	5,148 pts.*	Mary Elizabeth Peters	Edinburgh, Scotland	21–22 July	1970

Chi Cheng (Formosa), the first girl to run the hundred yards in even time

---

Yo-yo   Page 174
The world's endurance record was raised to 8 hours 7 minutes 13 seconds by David Rose, at Chadds Department Store, Hereford on 23 May 1970.

Most expensive decoration   Page 178
The highest price paid for any U.K. decoration is £2,000 at Sotheby's salerooms, London on 24 June 1970 for the Victoria Cross awarded on 10 April 1921 to Sepoy (later Captain) Ishar Singh.

CHAPTER 11—THE HUMAN WORLD

Population   Page 184
The mid-1970 population of the Commonwealth can be estimated at 960 million.

Electorates   Page 190
The largest electorate for any seat on the register in force until February 1971 is 143,544 in Antrim South. The largest electorate in Great Britain is Billericay, Essex with 123,121.

The smallest electorate for any seat on the current register is Ladywood, Birmingham with 18,734.

Majorities   The smallest majority of any current Member is that of E. D. D. Money who was elected the Member for Ipswich by a majority of 13 votes, 27,704 compared with 27,691 for Sir Dingle Foot, Q.C. (Labour) on 18–19 June 1970. The largest majority is 41,433 held by James Kilfedder (Ulster Unionist) in Down North. The largest in Great Britain is 30,474 by Alan Beany (Labour) in Hemsworth, Yorkshire. The largest Conservative majority is 27,376 of Henry Kerby in Arundel and Shoreham, Sussex.

Recounts   The record number of recounts is seven at Peterborough on 31 March to 1 April 1970.

Highest poll   Page 190
The highest figure in the 1970 General Election was 92·18 per cent. at Fermanagh and South Tyrone. The highest figure in Great Britain was North Cornwall with 85·11 per cent.

Oldest M.P.   The oldest Member sitting after the 1970 election was Stephen Owen Davis (Ind. Lab.) who was born in November 1886, the Member of Parliament for Merthyr Tydfil.

Explosion   Page 196
Detonation on 7 June 1917 not 17 June 1917.

Traffic density   Page 215
As at 31 May 1970 the number of motor vehicles (excluding motor or motorized cycles) in Hong Kong was 122,274 on 600 miles of serviceable roads thus giving a density of 8·64 yards per vehicle.

Briefest offence   Page 216
Mr. Arthur Randall of Hildenborough, Kent in May 1970 unwittingly parked on a clearway to visit a baker's shop. On emerging after 60 seconds his car was gone. At the pound the ticket showed an offence between 9.00 a.m. and 9.01 a.m. and the cost of recovery was £6.10.0 or 2s. 2d. per second.

Largest university   Page 217
The 1968–69 enrolment figure for Calcutta University was 196,257.

CHAPTER 12—SPORTS, GAMES AND PASTIMES

Athletics   Page 237
London-Edinburgh Road Relay (8 runners, Captain Don Taylor) from Hillingdon Youth Service. 410 miles in 47 hours 29 minutes on 12–14 July 1970 to average 8·56 m.p.h.

Badminton   Page 238
The most titles won, including doubles, by women is 17 shared by Miss M. Lucas and Mrs. G. C. K. Hashman (U.S.A.) from 1954 to 1967.

The longest recorded game was one of 174 hours 28 minutes by Alistair Gibson, Mike Spence, Colin Gourley, David Penman and Henry Chapell from Edinburgh 29 May to 6 June 1970.

Basketball   Page 240
The longest recorded basketball maratnon was of 100 hours by 24 boys of Hutton Grammar School, Preston, England from 11.00 7 July to 3.00 11 July 1970.

Skittles   Page 241
The highest score in 24 hours is 45,143 by eight members of the Cwmbran Christian Youth Council at Cwmbran, Monmouthshire on 10–11 July 1970.

E. D. D. Money, M.P. (Con.) who has the lowest Parliamentary majority—13

Karen Moras, holder of the world 400 and 800 metre freestyle records

Page 245
noeing The record for Eskimo rolls is 225 in 12 minutes 58·8 seconds by Captain Darrald Jones (R.A.F.) at R.A.F. Halton, Bucks., on 15 June 1970.

Page 247
ontract bridge Include in the highest possible positive score of 3,110 the score for all honours (4 aces), *i.e.* 150 points.

Page 249
Cricket The greatest number of runs scored in Test matches is 7,292 by Colin Cowdrey, playing for England, by the close of play on 6 July 1970.

Page 267
Golf The greatest number of holes completed in under 24 hours is 257 by Peter Chambers, 23, of Scarborough South Cliff Golf Club on 19–20 June 1970. The course is 5,827 yards and he walked an estimated 59·65 miles (14 rounds, 5 holes ending with the fifth on the sixth green).

Page 268
Neil C. Coles set a new record for the Open with 65 on 8 July 1970 at St. Andrews.

Page 278
Tennis The most games in a Wimbledon ladies' singles final was 46 when Mrs. Barry M. Court (*née* Margaret Smith) of Australia beat Mrs. L. W. King (*née* Billie-Jean Moffitt) of the United States by 14–12, 11–9 on 2 July 1970. The match took 2 hours 27 minutes.

Page 279
Lawn Tennis The longest recorded non-stop lawn tennis doubles game is one of 19 hours 5 minutes by 1 girl and 3 boys from the Bourne Hereward Youth Club, Bourne, Lincolnshire from 3.25 a.m. to 10.30 p.m. on Saturday 4 July 1970, with 369 games completed.

Page 297
Swimming Men's world records
4 × 200 metres freestyle 7:50·8* by Australia (Gregory Rogers, William C. Devenish, Graham White and Michael V. Wenden), Edinburgh 24 July 1970.
Women's world records
800 m. freestyle 9:02·4* by Karen L. Moras (Australia), Edinburgh 18 July 1970.

Page 298
200 m. butterfly 2:20·6* by Karen Moe (U.S.A.), Santa Clara, California, U.S.A. 11 July 1970.

Page 301
Trampolining Six boys and three girls from the Sighthill Community Centre, Edinburgh set a non-stop trampolining record of 300 hours from 30 May to 11 June 1970.

Page 302
Walking World record 20 kms. 1 H. 26:45·8 by Peter Frankel (East Germany) Erfurt, East Germany 4 July 1970.

Page 303
Water Ski-ing Longest jump British record 156 feet 1½ inches by Ian Walker at Halstead, Essex on 18 July 1970.

index index

A BOMB, see Bomb
ABBREVIATION, longest 89
ABEYANCE, of peerage, longest 181
ACCELERATOR, most powerful 82
ACCENTS, word with most 89
ACCIDENTS AND DISASTERS, worst world, U.K. 182, sports 226
ACE, air 179
ACID, strongest 75
ACROBATICS, greatest feats 175
ACTOR, highest earnings 105
ADDRESS, longest legal 197, highest numbering postal 217–218
ADHESIVE, most powerful 82
ADVERTISING, highest rate, expenditure 96, largest agents 148, sign: greatest ever, largest, highest 123
ADVERTISER, biggest 148
AERIALIST, acrobatic feats 175
AEROPLANE, see Aircraft
AGRICULTURE, 158–160
AIR ACE, top scoring, world, U.K., top jet, top woman 179
AIR FORCE, earliest, greatest 195
AIR SPEED RECORDS, world 140, 161
AIRCRAFT, Mach scale, earliest world, British Isles 137, cross-channel, trans-Atlantic, first non-stop, solo, trans-Atlantic, New York—London, earliest, fastest circumnavigation 138, jet-engined, supersonic flights, largest, heaviest, largest wing span, most powerful, lightest, smallest, heaviest bomber, fastest bomber, airliner: largest world 139, U.K. 139–140, fastest world, Britain, longest scheduled flight, speed records, fastest jet, biplane, piston-engined, propeller-driven, largest propeller, greatest altitude, flight duration record 140, largest, fastest, highest helicopter, fastest, highest flying-boat, record payload, largest airship, earliest licence 141, earliest human-powered 141–142, earliest hovercraft, model aircraft records 142
AIRCRAFT CARRIER, largest world, Britain, most deck landings 128
AIRCRAFT DISASTER, worst world, U.K. 182
AIRCRAFT MANUFACTURER, largest 148

AIRLINE, largest commercial: oldest, most passengers, greatest mileage of routes 149, country with busiest system 214
AIRLINER, largest world 139, heaviest U.K. 139–140, heaviest, fastest 140
AIRPORT, largest world, U.K., busiest, highest, lowest, longest runway in world, U.K. 141
AIRSHIP, largest rigid, non-rigid 141
ALBATROSS, largest wing span 36, longest incubation 38
ALCOHOL, strongest, most expensive drink, beer, wine, liqueurs 76, spirits 77
ALIMONY, highest awards 198
ALKALI, 75
ALPHABET, oldest, longest and shortest 87
ALPHORN, longest 97
ALTITUDE RECORDS, mammal (dog) 35, (bird) 37–38, rocket 72, aircraft 140, 141, 142, man, woman, balloon 161, kite 170, parachute 170–171, gliding 265
ALUMINIUM, largest producer, largest smelter 149
AMBER, largest piece 78
AMBERGRIS, heaviest 34
AMPHIBIANS, largest, highest, most poisonous, longest frog jump, largest British, smallest world, British 40, longest lived 40–41, most southerly, earliest 47
AMPHIBIOUS VEHICLE, first Channel crossing 133
AMPHITHEATRE, earliest 100, largest 101
AMPUTATION, fastest 26
AMUSEMENT RESORT, largest 111
ANAGRAM, longest 89
ANCHORAGE, deepest 130
ANCIENT MONUMENT, youngest 120
ANGLING, 226–229
ANIMAL, kingdom 28–48, tallest, smallest, rarest, longest 28, largest, heaviest 28–29, largest on land 29, fastest land, heaviest brain 30, fastest flying, speeds (air, land, water) 37, longest lived 39, largest marine, shortest, lightest vertebrates, fastest water, shortest lived vertebrates, deepest, most eggs, largest egg 41, most electric 41–42, most acute sense of smell, most legs 44, extinct-largest 45–47, most brainless 46, earliest, smallest organism, most densely

existing 47, highest, most primitive 48, most valuable 53, earliest husbandry, order of domestication 158
ANNUAL GENERAL MEETING, largest 147
ANT, largest, smallest 43
ANTARCTIC CONTINENT, first sighting, landing 163, conquest South Pole 163–164, first crossing, longest sledge journey 164
ANTELOPE, fastest 32, largest, smallest, rarest 33
ANTHEM, National, oldest, longest, shortest, longest rendition 98
ANTIQUE, largest sold 155
ANTLERS, largest span 33
APE, earliest 47
APOSTLE SPOONS, record price 158
APPEAL, most successful TV 106
APPENDICECTOMY, earliest 26
APPLAUSE, greatest 169
APPLE PICKING, record 167
AQUAMARINE, largest 77
AQUARIUM, largest, record attendances 53
AQUEDUCT, greatest, longest in world, U.K. 115
ARACHNIDS, 42, largest extinct, earliest 47
ARCH, longest natural bridge 63
ARCH BRIDGE, longest, largest steel 115
ARCHERY, 230
ARCHIPELAGO, greatest 58
ARCTIC CROSSING, first 163
AREA, smallest unit 81
ARIA, longest 99
ARMED FORCES, largest 192
ARMOUR, most expensive 155
ARMY, largest, smallest, oldest 193, oldest old soldiers, oldest British regiment 194
ARREST, greatest mass 204
ART, painting 84–86, greatest robbery 205
ART GALLERY, largest 85–86
ARTESIAN WELL, deepest Britain 124
ARTIFICIAL MOUND, largest prehistoric 120
ARTIFICIAL PLANETS, extremes 72
ARTIFICIAL SATELLITES, first, escape velocities, earliest successful manned, first woman in space 71, extremes, first admitted fatality, first walk in space, longest space flight, longest lunar mission, longest stay on Moon, most expensive project, accuracy record 72
ARTILLERY, see Guns, Cannon
ASPIDISTRA, largest 52
ASSETS, business, greatest 147–148
ASSIZES, bloodiest 203
ASSOCIATION, largest 212
ASSOCIATION FOOTBALL, 257–260
ASTEROIDS, largest, only visible, closest 69
ASTRONAUT, see Cosmonaut
ASYLUM, see Mental Hospital
ATHLETICS (Track and Field), 230–237
ATLANTIC CROSSING, first, fastest 126, fastest submerged 127, first air, non-stop, solo, fastest 138, smallest boat, first rowing, fastest solo sail, record solo Britain–U.S.A. 163
ATOLL, largest, largest land area 58
ATOMIC BOMB, worst 195–196, 182, largest arsenal 196
ATOM SMASHER, see Accelerator
ATOMIC PLANT, largest 108
ATOMIC POWER STATION, largest 142
ATOMIC REACTOR, largest 143
AUCTION, greatest 154

AUDIENCE, greatest concert, pop festival 98, television 106
AUDITORIUM, largest 111
AURORA (Borealis and Australis), most frequent, highest, lowest, southernmost, greatest displays 67
AUSTRALIAN RULES FOOTBALL, 260–261
AUTHOR, see Writer
AUTOGRAPH, earliest, most expensive 94, largest collection 167
AUTOMOBILE, see Car
AVALANCHE, largest 62, worst world, U.K. 182
AVES, see Birds
AWARDS, see Medals
AXEMANSHIP, records 174

BABIES, most by one mother in world, Britain 19–20, multiple births 20–21, largest world, U.K., Ireland, smallest 22
BABY-SITTING SERVICE, largest 187
BACTERIA, largest, highest, longest lived, toughest 48
BADMINTON, 238
BAGPIPES, longest duration record 167
BAIL, highest 197
BAKED BEANS, eating record 178
BALANCE, finest 82
BALL PUNCHING, duration record 167
BALLET DANCING, records 169
BALLOON, distance record, largest 141, human powered flight 141–142, highest manned, unmanned 161
BALLROOM, largest 111
BALLROOM DANCING, record 169
BAMBOO, tallest, fastest growing 50
BANANA, eating record 178
BAND, longest playing 169
BANK, largest, largest building, largest vault 155
BANK-NOTE, earliest, oldest surviving, largest, smallest, highest 209, lowest denominations, most expensive, highest circulation 210
BANK RATE, lowest, highest 209
BANK ROBBERY, greatest 205
BANK VAULT, largest 155
BANQUET, largest 152
BAR, longest 112
BARBITURATE, quickest poison 75
BARLEY, record yield 159
BARN, longest tithe Britain 122
BAROMETRIC PRESSURE, highest, lowest 64
BARONET, oldest, most and least creations 181
BARREL-JUMPING, greatest number 167
BARROW, largest, largest long 120
BASEBALL, 239
BASIN, largest river 60–61
BASKETBALL, 239
BATH, most dwellings with 187
BATS, largest, smallest, fastest, rarest 32
BATTLE, Britain, last pitched land, clan 191, last in Britain 191–192, worst, worst in Britain 192, greatest naval 193
BATTLESHIP, largest world, Britain, largest guns, thickest armour 128
BAY, largest world, Great Britain 56
BEACH, pleasure, largest 111
BEAGLING, oldest hunt 264
BEAR, largest 31
BEARD, longest 23
BED, largest 155

BED OF NAILS, *duration record on 167*
BED-PUSHING, *record push 167*
BEECH, *tallest hedge 52*
BEER, *strongest, weakest, most expensive 76, largest exporter 149–150, drinking records 178, biggest consumers 213*
BEETLES, *largest, longest, heaviest, smallest, longest lived 43*
BELL, *heaviest, oldest, largest, heaviest carillon 99*
BELL-RINGING, *most changes rung 99–100*
BEQUEST, *greatest 177*
BEST DRESSED WOMEN, *177*
BEST MAN, *most often 167*
BEST SELLER, *world, non-fiction, fiction, post card 93, gramophone records 102–103*
BIBLE, *earliest printed, most valuable 91, highest price manuscript 91–92, oldest, earliest printed English, longest and shortest books, longest, shortest psalm, verse, total letters, words, longest name, reading record 92, print figures 93*
BICYCLE, *earliest, penny-farthing, longest tandem, most capacious, largest tricycle, tallest unicycle 134*
BICYCLE FACTORY, *largest 149*
BIG WHEEL, *largest 112, riding endurance record 168*
BIGAMIST, *greatest 206*
BILLIARDS, *240*
BILLIONAIRES, *176*
BINGO, *264*
BIPLANE, *fastest 140*
BIRD, *largest, heaviest, largest wing-span, greatest wing area 36, smallest 36–37, most abundant, smallest sea-bird, rarest, longest lived, fastest flying, fastest running, fastest wingbeats, fastest swimmer, longest flights 37, highest flying 37–38, most acute vision, largest, smallest eggs, shortest and longest incubation, longest, most feathers, earliest and latest cuckoo, largest turkey; domesticated birds: largest caged bird, longest lived, most talkative 38; largest extinct 46, earliest 47*
BIRTHS, *multiple 20–21, latest post mortem delivery 24*
BIRTH RATE, *highest, lowest 186*
BISHOP, *oldest Church of England, Roman Catholic, youngest 223*
BISHOPRIC, *longest tenure 223–224*
BITTEREST SUBSTANCE, *75*
BLACK-OUT, *biggest 142*
BLADES, *penknife with greatest number 157*
BLANKET-MAKING, *record 168*
BLAST FURNACE, *largest 144*
BLENDING VAT, *largest 112*
BLINDNESS, Colour, *highest and lowest rate 27, 100 yards record 237*
BLOOD DONOR, *champion 24*
BLOOD GROUP, *commonest, rarest 24*
BLOOD TEMPERATURE, *highest and lowest mammalian 34*
BLOOM, *largest, largest inflorescence, largest blossoming plant 50*
BOAT, *see Ship*
BOBSLEIGH, *240–241*
BOILER, *largest 143*
BOILING POINT, *lowest and highest for gases 73, metals 74*
BOMB, *defusing record 168, worst disaster world, U.K. 182, heaviest conventional 195, most powerful atom 195–196*
BOMB-DEFUSING, *record number 168*
BOMBER, *heaviest, most powerful, fastest 139*
BOMBING, *worst in world, U.K. 182*
BOND SIGNING, *greatest feat 168*
BONE, *oldest fragment 17–18, longest, smallest human 22*
BOOK, *oldest mechanically printed, largest, largest art, smallest hand-written, smallest printed, most valuable, highest priced 20th century, longest novel, encyclopaedia: most comprehensive, largest; top-selling: largest dictionary 91, Bible 92, 93; best-sellers: world, non-fiction, fiction 93, most overdue 95, largest shop, largest single display in one room 149*
BOOK SHOP, *largest 149*
BOOMERANG, *greatest throws 168*
BORES, River, *greatest 61*
BORING, *deepest world, U.K. 124*
BOTTLE, *largest, smallest (spirit) 76, fastest bottling line 153, message in 170*
BOUNDARY, *see Frontier*
BOWLING (Ten Pin), *241*
BOWLS, *241*
BOXING, *241–244*
BOX-OFFICE, *biggest theatre 101, film 105*
BRAIN (human), *largest, smallest 22, (animal), heaviest 30, least 46*
BRASS INSTRUMENT, *largest 97*
BREACH OF CONTRACT, *highest damages 197–198*
BREACH OF PROMISE, *highest damages 198*
BREAD, *longest loaf 157*
BREAKWATER, *longest, U.K. 121*
BREEDER, *fastest 30*
BREWERY, *largest 149*
BRIBE, *largest 206*
BRICK-CARRYING, *record for man, woman 168*
BRICK-THROWING, *greatest distance 168*
BRICKLAYING, *world record 168*
BRICKWORKS, *largest 150*
BRIDGE, *longest natural 63, oldest world, British, progressive records, longest suspension world, U.K. 114, longest cantilever, longest steel arch, largest, longest floating, railway, longest spans (by type), highest*

suspension, railway, widest 115
BRIDGE (Contract), *247*
BRIDGE-TUNNEL, *longest 119*
BROADCAST (Radio), *first advertised, trans-Atlantic, longest 105, (television) first 106*
BROADCASTER, *fastest 26–27*
BROADCASTING, *see Radio*
BROADMOOR, *longest detention, longest escape 204*
BUBBLE CHAMBER, *largest world 82*
BUDGERIGAR, *longest lived, most talkative 38*
BUDGET, *largest, greatest surplus, deficit 207*
BUILDING (see also Structure), *largest theatre 100, largest cinema 104, earliest world, U.K. 107, 109, largest manufacturing, scientific, administrative, commercial 107, office 107–108, tallest, maximum sway, stair climbing record, most storeys, highest, northernmost, southernmost 108, wooden 109, for living 109–111, entertainment 111–112, tallest (progressive records) 113, largest university 218, largest religious 220, oldest religious 221*
BUILDING CONTRACTOR, *largest 150*
BUILDING SOCIETY, *largest, oldest 150*
BULB, *most powerful light 83*
BULL, *heaviest England 159, highest price 160*
BULLFIGHTING, *244–245*
BULLDOZER, *largest 133*
BURIAL ALIVE, *record 168*
BUS, *largest 132*
BUSINESS, *oldest, greatest assets 147–148, sales, profits, losses 148*
BUTTER FAT, *record lifetime, one lactation, day yields 160*
BUTTERFLY, *slowest wing beat 43, largest, smallest, rarest 44*

CABER TOSS, *greatest 237*
CABLE (Telephone), *longest submarine 216*
CABLE CARS, *largest 145*
CABLE SHIP, *largest 129*
CACTUS, *largest 52*
CADENZA, *longest 99*
CAKE, *largest 213*
CALF, *highest birthweight, most at one birth 159*
CALORIES, *most and least calorific fruit 50, highest, lowest consumption, largest available total 212*
CAMERA, *earliest, largest, smallest, fastest cine, most expensive 80*
CAMP, *concentration, largest penal 206*
CANAL, *earliest, longest, longest big ship, inland waterway U.K., irrigation 116, largest cut 117, longest tunnel world, U.K. 118*
CANNON, *largest 195*
CANNON BALL, Human, *record distance 170*
CANOEING, *245*
CANTILEVER BRIDGE, *longest world 114–115, U.K. 115*
CANYON, *deepest, deepest submarine 62*
CAPE HORN, *earliest rounding 163*
CAPITAL CITY, *most populous 184–185, largest, highest, oldest, northernmost, southernmost 185, most and least expensive 187*
CAPITAL PUNISHMENT, *see Execution*
CAR, *largest ferry 129, earliest, earliest mechanically-propelled, earliest petrol driven, first, oldest internal-combustion, earliest registration, fastest jet driven, wheel driven, piston engine, fastest production, largest, longest 131, most expensive world, most expensive standard, U.K., vintage, cheapest, longest in production, largest engines, petrol consumption 132, longest skid marks 133, largest manufacturer 151–152, largest single plant 152, greatest T-bone dive 173*
CAR CRAMMING, *greatest number of people in car 168*
CAR FERRY, *largest 129*
CAR MANUFACTURER, *largest 151–152, largest single plant 152*
CAR PARKING, *briefest offence 216*
CAR PARKING METERS, *earliest 216*
CARAVAN, *towing record 133*
CARD HOUSES, *largest number of storeys 170*
CARDINAL, *oldest, youngest 223*
CARGO VESSEL, *largest 129*
CARILLON, *largest, heaviest 99*
CARNIVORE, *largest land, smallest 31, largest 41*
CARPET, *earliest, largest, most expensive, most finely woven 155*
CARRIER, *typhoid, most notorious 23*
CARTOON, *largest, longest lived strip, most read 96*
CASH, *most found and returned 177*
CASTING, *sport 226–227*
CASTLE, *earliest world, British Isles, Irish, largest world 109, U.K. and Ireland 110*
CAT, *largest 31–32, heaviest 35, oldest 35–36, largest litter, most prolific, greatest fall, most lives, richest, most valuable, rarest breed, ratting, biggest show 36*
CATALYST CRACKER, *largest 144*
CATHEDRAL, *tallest (progressive records) 113, largest 220–221, smallest, longest, longest nave 221, tallest spire 222*
CATTLE, *longest horns 34, heaviest, highest birthweight, prolificacy record 159, record prices 160*
CATTLE STATION, *largest 159*
CAVE, *largest, most extensive system 62, deepest by countries, longest systems by countries 63, progressive depth 245, deepest,*

duration 246
CAVERN, *largest 62*
CAVING, *245–246*
CELLAR, *wine, largest 112*
CEMETERY, *largest world, U.K. 124*
CENTENARIAN, *oldest 18–19*
CENTI-MILLIONAIRES, *176*
CENTIPEDE, *longest, most legs, shortest, least legs 44*
CENTRIFUGE, *fastest 81*
CEREAL, *biggest consumers 212*
CHAIN STORE, *largest grocery, department 150*
CHAMBER, *largest underground 62*
CHAMPIONS (sports), *youngest and oldest, longest reign 226*
CHANCELLORSHIP, *longest, shortest tenure, most appointments 191*
CHANNEL CROSSING, *see Cross-Channel*
CHAPEL, *smallest U.K. 221*
CHARLESTON, *duration record 169*
CHEESE, *heaviest eaters, biggest producer, oldest, varieties, most expensive, largest 160, eating record 178*
CHELONIANS, *largest, longest lived, slowest moving 39, largest prehistoric 46–47*
CHEMICAL COMPANY, *largest 150*
CHEMICAL NAME, *longest 88*
CHEQUE, *most bad 206, largest, oldest surviving 210*
CHESS, *246*
CHEST MEASUREMENT, *largest 23*
CHESTNUT, *greatest girth 49*
CHICKEN, *eating record 178*
CHILDREN'S HOSPITAL, *largest U.K. 187*
CHIMNEYS, *tallest world, U.K. 108*
CHINNING THE BAR, *270*
CHOCOLATE, *largest factory 150*
CHORUS LINE, *longest 102*
CHRISTMAS, "white", *most recent 65*
CHURCH, *tallest (progressive records) 113, longest Gothic, largest, smallest, oldest 221, tallest spire 222*
CIGAR, *largest, most expensive, peak smoking 155*
CIGARETTE, *consumption, most expensive 155, most popular 155–156, longest and shortest, largest collection; packets (cartons): largest collection, earliest, largest; cards: earliest and most valuable, earliest abstention 156*
CINEMA, *earliest, highest film production, most attendances, most per population, largest, oldest, biggest screen, most expensive film 104, longest film 104–105, highest box office gross, highest earning actor, most Óscars, most durable newsreel commentator 105*
CIRCUIT TRAINING, *most protracted 168*
CIRCULAR STORM, *worst in world, U.K. 182*
CIRCULATION, *highest newspaper, periodical 96*
CIRCUMNAVIGATION, *first orbital 71, air: earliest, first solo, fastest 138; sea: earliest, first solo with one stop, non-stop, fastest solo, longest voyage, submarine 162*
CIRCUS, *acrobatic feats, largest 175*
CITY, *longest name 89, most populous 184–185, largest, highest, oldest, smallest, northernmost, southernmost capitals, furthest from sea 185*
CIVIL WAR, *bloodiest 192*
CLAPPING, *longest continuous 168*
CLERGY, *largest 220*
CLIFFS, *highest 63*
CLOCK, *oldest 145, largest world, U.K., tallest public, most accurate, most expensive 146*
CLOTH, *finest 156*
CLOUDS, *highest, lowest, greatest vertical range 65*
COACHING, *131*
COAL CARRYING, *record time 167*
COAL SHOVELLING, *record 168*
COASTLINES, *U.K. Counties longest 184*
COFFEE, *greatest drinkers 213–214*
COIN, *swallowing 25, largest robbery 205, oldest, heaviest, smallest, highest, lowest denomination 210, rarest, most expensive, legal tender: oldest, largest, heaviest, highest current denomination, lightest, smallest, greatest collection, largest treasure trove, largest mint, greatest hoarders, largest pile of pennies 211*
COLDEST PLACE, *world, U.K., Ireland, annual mean, coldest inhabited 64*
COLLEGE, *oldest, largest university 218*
COLLIERY TIP, *largest U.K. 125*
COLONY, *smallest 183*
COLOUR BLINDNESS, *highest, lowest rate 27*
COLOUR SENSITIVITY, *23, 25*
COLUMN, *tallest monumental 120, tallest, tallest stone 121*
COMA, *longest 24*
COMET, *earliest, speed, closest, largest, shortest, longest period 68*
COMIC STRIP (Newspaper), *most durable 94*
COMMENTATOR, *most durable 105*
COMMERCE, *147–158*
COMMON, *largest U.K. 53*
COMMUNICATIONS, *214–218*
COMMUNIST PARTY, *largest 189*
COMMUTER, *most durable 168*
COMPANY, *oldest, greatest assets world 147, U.K. 147–148, sales, profit, loss, most efficient, biggest work force 148, largest manufacturing 151–152, number of companies registered, most directorships, largest investment 154*

COMPENSATION (legal), *greatest 197*
COMPETITIONS, *champion winner, largest single prize 168*
COMPOSER, *most prolific, most rapid 98*
COMPOSITION, *longest piano 98–99, longest silence 99*
COMPUTER, *most powerful world, largest U.K. 83*
CONCENTRATION CAMP, *worst 206*
CONCERT, *greatest attendance classical, pop festival 98*
CONDIMENT, *rarest 213*
CONSONANTS, *language with most, least 88*
CONSTELLATION, *largest, smallest 70*
CONSTRUCTION JOB, *most massive 122*
CONSUMPTIONS, *food and drink 212–214*
CONTINENT, *largest, smallest 57, area 183*
CONTRACT, *biggest TV 106*
CONTRACT, Breach of, *highest damages 197–198*
CONTRACT BRIDGE, *247*
CONURBATION, *largest 184–185*
CONVEYOR BELT, *longest 145*
COOLING TOWERS, *largest U.K. 108*
COPPER MINE, *most productive, largest underground, largest excavation 125*
CORK, *density 50, champagne distance record 77*
CORPORATIONS, *greatest sales profit and loss 148*
CORRESPONDENCE, *shortest 94*
COSMONAUT, *earliest, first woman 71, altitude, maximum speed 161*
COST OF LIVING, *greatest increase 187, worst inflation 210*
COSTS, *highest legal 198*
COUNTRY, *total number of, largest, smallest, most frontiers, longest frontiers 183, population 183–184, largest, smallest, densest, sparsest 184*
COUNTY, *highest points U.K. and Ireland 58–59, oldest name, youngest U.K. 90, U.K. largest and smallest areas and populations, longest and shortest coastlines 184*
COURSING, *247*
COURT, *largest judicial building 206*
COW, *prolificacy record, record milk yield 159, butterfat yields, record price 160*
COW SHED, *largest 160*
CRAB, *largest 42, smallest U.K., most abyssal 43*
CRANE, *largest and highest lifting capacity, most powerful, highest, greatest weight lifted, largest floating 146*
CRATER, *largest (volcano) 55, (meteoric) 66, largest and deepest lunar 67*
CREATURE, *largest flying (extinct) 46, most southerly, earliest four-legged 47*
CREMATION, *first legal 124*
CREMATORIUM, *oldest U.K., first legal cremation, largest Europe 124*
CRESTA RUN, *records 240*
CRICKET, *248–252*
CRIME AND PUNISHMENT, *199–207*
CRIMINAL ORGANISATION, *largest 200*
CRISPS, *potato, eating record 178*
CROCODILE, *largest and heaviest 38, largest extinct 46, worst disaster 182*
CROP YIELD, *record wheat, barley 159*
CROQUET, *252*
CROSS-CHANNEL, *first amphibious vehicle 133, earliest flight 138, record trip 162, swimming 298–299*
CROSS-COUNTRY RUNNING, *252*
CROSSWORD, *first 94, largest 94–95, slowest 95*
CROWD, *largest 224, sports, Olympic Games 287*
CRUISER, *most powerful 128*
CRUSTACEANS, *largest 42, smallest, oldest, most abyssal 43, earliest 47*
CRYPT, *church, largest 221*
CRYSTAL, *largest 78*
CUCKOO, *earliest, latest 38*
CURLING, *252–253*
CURRENT, *greatest, strongest 56, most powerful electric 82*
CURTAIN, *largest 156*
CUT, *finest 83, largest canal 117*
CUTLER, *oldest firm 157*
CYCLING, *duration 166, sport 253–255*

DAM, *earliest, most massive, largest concrete, highest, longest river, sea, world; most massive, highest and longest, U.K. 117, progressive records 118*
DAM DISASTER, *worst world, U.K. 182*
DAMAGES, *loss of life 197, highest breach of contract 197–198, personal injury, breach of promise, defamation, divorce, greatest patent infringement 198*
DANCE, *largest 168*
DANCE BAND, *longest playing 169*
DANCE COURSE, *most expensive 169*
DANCING, *marathon 168, ballet: most turns, most curtain calls; ballroom, Charleston, flamenco, go-go, jiving, limbo, twist records, most expensive course, modern marathon 169*
DARTS, *255*
DEATH RATE, *highest, lowest 186*
DEBT, *largest National 208–209*
DECATHLON, *world record 232, U.K. 235*
DECORATIONS, *see Medals*
DEEP SEA DIVING, *record depth, progressive records 165*
DEER, *fastest 30, largest, largest antler span, smallest, rarest 33*
DEFAMATION, *highest damages 198*
DEFENCE, *world expenditure, greatest, smallest 193*
DEGREES, *most honorary 181*

ELTA, largest 61
EMONSTRATION, largest 224
ENTISTS, most 187
EPARTMENT STORE, largest chain, rgest U.K., most profitable 150
EPRESSIONS, deepest ocean 60
ERRICKS, most powerful 130
ESCENDANTS, most 20
ESCENT, greatest ocean 164, progressive ocean records 165
ESERT, largest 62
ESPATCHES, most mentions 179
ESTROYER, fastest 128
EVALUATION, 210
IAMOND, hardest, largest, rarest coloured, rice, highest auction price 77, deepest open it 125
ICTIONARY, largest 91
INNER SERVICE, highest price 156
INOSAUR, largest 45
IRECTORSHIPS, most 154
ISASTERS AND ACCIDENTS, worst world, U.K. 182, sports 226
ISC, earliest slipped 24
ISC-JOCKEY, marathon 169
ISEASE, commonest, rarest, most and east infectious 23
ISENROLMENT, greatest 219
ISH, largest 213
ISTILLERY, largest 150
IVE, highest 170, most difficult 297
IVING (Deep Sea), record depth 164, progressive records 165
IVORCE, most 166–167, longest case 197, highest damages, settlements 198
OCK, largest dry 121, floating 122
OCTORS, highest percentage 187
OCUMENT, earliest vellum 91
OG, largest 34–35, tallest, smallest, oldest, rarest, largest litter, most prolific, most popular, most expensive, record altitude, highest and longest jump, strongest, ratting record, tracking feat record 35
OME, largest world, U.K. 121
OMESTICATED ANIMALS, 34–36
OMESTICATED BIRDS, largest caged population, longest lived, most talkative 38
OMESTICATION, Animal 34–36, time sequence 158
ONKEY, lowest price 160
OOR, largest world, U.K., oldest U.K. 122
OUBLE-BASS, largest 97
OW JONES AVERAGE, peak 154
OWRY, biggest 176
RACONE, largest 130
RAGLINE, largest world, U.K. 144
RAGONFLY, largest, smallest 43, largest extinct 47
RAWING, highest price 85
REDGER, largest 130
RESSAGE, see Equestrian Sports
RIEST PLACE, world, U.K., Ireland, annual mean 64
RILLING, deepest in world, U.K. 124
RINK, most alcoholic, most expensive, beer, wine, liqueurs 76, spirits 77, top-selling brand (spirits) 150, (soft) 153
RINKER, hardest 24
RINKING, records 178
RIVER (car), worst 216
RIVING TESTS, most failures 133
ROUGHT, longest 64
RUG, most powerful, most expensive, addicts 75–76
RUM, largest 97
RUMMER, most highly paid 99
RUMMING, duration record 169
RY DOCK, largest 121
UNES, highest sand 60
UODENAL ULCER, earliest 24
UST, finest aluminium 75
WARF, shortest 15, lightest 17
WELLING UNITS, largest number, largest number with piped water, baths, electricity 187

EARNINGS, see Income
EARTH, largest diameter, greatest circumference, area, axial rotation, weight, density, volume, most abundant element 54, sea area, depth, weight and volume 55, land surface 56, age 57, orbital speed around sun 67, land area 183 (see also Structure and Dimensions 57–63)
EARTH–MOON SATELLITES, extremes 72
EARTHQUAKE, greatest, worst world, U.K., Ireland 54–55, highest tidal wave or tsunami 56, worst world, U.K. 182
EARTH SATELLITES, extremes 72
EARTHWORK, most massive 117, most extensive 120
EARTHWORM, longest in world, U.K. 44
EATING, records 178
EATING OUT, world champion 167
ECLIPSES, earliest, most recent in U.K., longest, most and least frequent 68
ECONOMICS, 207–218
EDITORSHIP, longest 96
EDUCATION, 218–219
EGG, largest, smallest bird 38, most, largest 41, largest extinct 46, largest extinct reptilian 47, laying records, largest hen's 159, longest distance thrown 169, eating records 178
EGG AND SPOON RACE, marathon 169
ELECTION, largest, closest, most one-sided, highest personal majority 189, fewest votes, quickest change of fortune, biggest swing, highest poll 190
ELECTORATES, largest, smallest 190
ELECTRIC CURRENT, most powerful 82
ELECTRIC GENERATOR, largest 143
ELECTRIC MOTOR, largest, smallest 143

ELECTRIC RAILWAY, first, fastest train, regular run 134, longest line 135, underground 137
ELECTRICITY, most dwellings with 187
ELECTRON MICROSCOPE, most powerful 82
ELECTRONIC BRAIN, see Computer
ELEMENTS, 73–75, number, sub-nuclear particles, gases, commonest, metals 73, highest melting point, rarest, most and least magnetic, newest, most expensive 74, most and least isotopes, longest and shortest half-lives, hardest, finest powder 75
ELEPHANT, largest 29, longest lived, gestation period 30, longest tusks 33, heaviest tusks 33–34, 46 (extinct), tallest extinct mammoth 46
ELEVATOR, see Lift
ELEVATOR, grain, largest, largest collection 109, lock, highest 116
EMBASSY, largest 108
EMBEZZLEMENT, greatest 205
EMERALD, largest 77
EMIGRATION, most from U.K. 185
EMPEROR, longest dynasty 188
EMPLOYMENT, highest 212
ENCYCLOPAEDIA, most comprehensive, largest, top-selling 91
ENERGY, world average, highest, lowest consumption 214
ENGAGEMENT, longest 167
ENGINE, Car, largest 132
ENGINE, Jet, see Jet Engine
ENGINE, Military, largest 195
ENGINE, Railway, first, fastest electric, steam, most powerful 134, progressive speed records 136, model 137
ENGINE, Ship, earliest steam 126
ENGINEERING, 144–146
ENGLISH CHANNEL, (first crossing) amphibious vehicle 133, aircraft 138, swimming 298
EPONYMOUS RECORD, largest object named after human 178
EQUESTRIAN SPORTS, 255–256
ERUPTION, greatest volcanic 55
ESCALATOR, fastest U.K., longest world 145
ESCAPE, longest prison, asylum 204, greatest gaol break 205
ESCAPE-VELOCITY, terrestrial, solar 71
E.S.P., best performer 27
ESPIONAGE, greatest industrial 205
ESTUARY, longest 61
ETON FIVES, 257
EVACUATION, greatest military 193
EXAMINATIONS, most 'O' and 'A' levels passed 219
EXCAVATION, greatest earth-moving job, world's largest (coppermine) 125
EXCAVATOR, largest 144
EXECUTION, greatest number in Communist China 199, Nazi Germany 199–200, most 201, last public hanging, last from yard-arm, youngest, oldest, last public guillotining, most attempts, slowest 202
EXECUTIONER, longest in office 202–203
EXHIBITION, largest international 112
EXPECTATION OF LIFE, highest and lowest at birth, at 60 years 186
EXPLOSION, greatest volcanic 55, worst world, U.K. 182, largest "conventional" 196
EXPOSITION, largest international 112
EXTINCT ANIMALS, largest land, heaviest 45, largest predator, longest, heaviest tusks, longest horns, most brainless, largest mammal, bird, southernmost, largest flying creature, marine reptile, crocodile 46, chelonians 46–47, longest snake, largest reptile eggs, largest fish, Arachnid, insect, shelled mollusc, most southerly, earliest of their type 47
EXTRA-SENSORY PERCEPTION, see E.S.P.
EYE, smallest visible object, colour sensitivity, colour blindness 25

FABRIC, most expensive 156
FACE SLAPPING, duration record 169
FACTORY, largest underground 108, largest whale ship 129, earliest motorcycle 133, largest bicycle 149, largest chocolate 150
FAIR, largest, largest international, big wheel, fastest switchback 112
FALL, greatest altitude without parachute 171
FAMILY, richest, most millionaires 176
FAMINE, worst world, U.K. 182
FANGS, longest (snake) 40
FARM, earliest site, largest, largest arable 158, largest mushroom, largest turkey 159
FAST, longest 27
FATTEST, man, woman 16–17
FEATHERS, longest, most 38
FELINE, largest 31
FELL RUNNING, 287
FENCE, longest 122
FENCING, 256
FERMENTATION VESSEL, largest 123
FERN, largest, smallest 52
FERRIS WHEEL, largest 112, endurance record 168
FERRY, largest car 129
FIELD, largest wheat 158, hop 158–159
FIELD GUN, competition 169
FIGURE SKATING, most titles 276
FILIBUSTER, longest 189
FILLING STATION, largest 109
FILM, earliest, highest production, most expensive 104, longest 104–105, longest run, longest title, highest box office gross, most Oscar awards 105
FINE, heaviest, smallest 207
FINGER NAILS, longest 23

FINGERS, most 23
FIRE, greatest oil 124, worst world, U.K. 182
FIRE-EATER, most voracious 27
FIRE ESCAPE, tallest in world 123
FIREWORK, largest 156, worst disaster 182
FISH, largest sea, carnivorous, freshwater, smallest sea, freshwater, fastest, longest lived, shortest lived, most abyssal, most, largest eggs, most venomous 41, most electric 41–42, largest extinct, earliest 47, largest catch, world, U.K., Irish records 227–229
FISHERIES, highest recorded catch, highest proportion of the world catch 153
FISHING, see Angling
FISHMONGER, largest 153
FIVES, 257
FIXED BARS, acrobatic feats 175
FJORDS, longest 61
FLAG, oldest, largest 156
FLAGSTAFF, tallest world, U.K. 120
FLAMENCO, fastest dancer 169
FLARE, oil, greatest 124
FLATS, largest, tallest block 110
FLEA, smallest water, oldest, longest and highest jumps, varieties 43
FLIGHT, longest (bird) 37, aircraft: earliest 137, cross-Channel, trans-Atlantic, round the world 138, jet, supersonic 139, longest scheduled 140
FLOAT, largest 156
FLOATING BRIDGE, longest 115
FLOATING CRANE, largest world 146
FLOATING DOCK, largest 122
FLOOD, worst world, U.K. 182
FLOWER, earliest, commonest flowering plant 48, largest bloom, largest blossoming plant, smallest, slowest flowering plant 50, largest orchid 51
FLYING-BOAT, largest aircraft 139, fastest, highest, record payload 141
FLYING CREATURE, largest extinct 46
FLYING HOURS, most 162
FLYING TRAPEZE, greatest artistes 175
FOG, longest 64
FOOD CONSUMPTION, highest, lowest calorie consumers, highest, lowest protein consumers, biggest cereal, potato 212, sugar, meat, beer, spirit consumers, sweets, tea, coffee (most expensive) 213, freshwater, energy 214
FOOT-AND-MOUTH DISEASE, worst outbreak 160
FOOTBALL, Association 257–260, Australian rules 260–261, Gaelic 261, Rugby League 261–262, Rugby Union 262–264, Seven-a-side 264
FOOTBALL POOLS, 264–265
FOOTWAY, longest moving 145
FORCED LABOUR, 200
FOREIGN AID, total given by U.S. 207–208
FOREST, largest world, U.K. 48
FORGERY, greatest 206
FORGING, largest 144
FOSSIL, oldest plant 48, oldest human 17–18, oldest animal 47
FOUNDATIONS, deepest of any structure 115
FOUNTAIN, tallest world, U.K. 123–124
FOX, fastest 30, largest 264
FOX HUNTING, 264
FRAUD, largest 206
FREE FALLING, see Parachuting
FREEDOMS, most conferred 181
FREEZE, longest 65
FREIGHT RATE, most expensive 137
FREIGHT TRAIN, longest, heaviest 136–137
FRESHWATER LAKE, largest 61
FRICTION, lowest 82
FROG, largest, most poisonous, longest jump, smallest 40
FROGMAN, longest submergence, farthest underwater 173
FRONTIERS, country with most, longest continuous 183
FROST FAIR, last recorded 65
FROSTS, earliest U.K. 63
FRUIT, most and least nutritive 50, record dimensions and weights, U.K. 51
FRUIT MACHINE, continuous play 169
FUEL, most powerful 75
FUEL ECONOMY, world car record 132
FUNGUS, largest 51–52, most poisonous 52
FUNICULAR, longest, largest car 145
FUR, most valuable 34
FURNACE (blast), largest 144
FURNITURE, most expensive, oldest U.K. 156

G FORCE, highest sustained, momentary 27
GAELIC FOOTBALL, 261
GALAXIES, number of, Milky Way, remotest objects 70
GALLERY, largest art 85–86
GAMBLING, 264–265
GAMES MANUFACTURER, largest company 150
GAOL, see Prison
GARAGE, largest, largest underground, largest private 109
GAS, lightest, heaviest, lowest and highest melting and boiling points, commonest, rarest 73, nerve gas, most powerful 75
GAS FLARE, greatest 124
GAS PIPELINE, longest 144
GAS WORKS, largest 143–144
GASHOLDER, largest world, U.K. 123
GASTRONOMIC RECORDS, 177–178
GAUGE, widest railway track, highest standard 134
GEMS, most precious, largest, rarest, hardest, densest, diamond, highest auction price, emeralds, sapphires 77, rubies, pearl, opal,

crystal, topaz 78
GENERATING PLANT, see Power Station
GENERATOR, electric, largest 143
GESTATION PERIOD, mammalian, longest and shortest 30
GEYSER, tallest 55
GHERKINS, eating record 178
GIANT, tallest 13–14
GIANTESS, tallest 14–15
GIRAFFE, tallest 28
GLACIER, longest 62
GLASS, largest sheet 122
GLASSHOUSE, largest U.K. 109
GLIDING, 265
GOATS, record milk yield 159–160
GO-GO, duration record 169
GO-KART, record 285
GOLD, largest nugget 78, greatest reserves, accumulation 209
GOLD MEDALS (Olympic), most 287
GOLD MINE, largest world, U.K., richest 125
GOLD PLATE, highest auction price 156
GOLD RESERVES, greatest 209
GOLDEN DISC, earliest 102, most awarded 102–103, youngest age 103
GOLDEN HANDSHAKE, most 177
GOLDFISH, eating record 178
GOLF, 266–269
GORGE, largest, deepest 62
GRADIENT, steepest railway 135
GRAIN, earliest cultivated 158
GRAIN ELEVATOR, largest, largest collection 109
GRAMOPHONE, 102–104, invention, greatest number 102
GRAMOPHONE RECORD, peak sales, oldest, largest library, most successful artist, platinum disc award, earliest jazz 102, golden disc award 102–103, fastest sales, most recorded song, greatest seller, best selling charts, most recordings, biggest sale chart monopolists 103, long players 103–104, fastest seller, greatest advance sales, highest fee 104, longest running radio programme 106
GRANDPARENTS, most greats 20
GRAPES, eating record 178
GRASS, commonest 48, longest, shortest 52
GRASSHOPPER, largest 43
GRAVE DIGGING, record 169
GREAT GRANDPARENTS, multiple 20
GREENHOUSE, largest 109
GREYHOUND RACING, 270
GROCERY STORE, largest chain 150
GROSS NATIONAL PRODUCT, largest 209
GUILLOTINING, last public 202
GULF, largest 56
GUN, earliest, largest, greatest range 194, largest Naval 128, largest shoulder 293
GUN RUN, competition record 169
GUSHER, oil, most prolific 124
GYMNASIUM, largest 271
GYMNASTICS, 270–271

H BOMB, see Bomb
HABITATION, greatest altitude, northernmost, southernmost 108
HAGGIS, eating record 178
HAIL DISASTER, worst 182
HAILSTONES, largest 64
HAIR, longest 23
HAIRDRESSING, world record 169
HALF-LIFE (Isotopes), longest and shortest 75
HAMBURGER, eating record 178
HANDBALL, 271
HANDBUCKING, see Sawing
HANDSHAKING, world records 169
HANDWRITING, smallest 90
HANGAR, largest world, group, U.K. 109
HANGING, see Execution
HARBOUR, biggest artificial 214
HARDEST SUBSTANCE, 75
HARMONIUM, marathon record 97
HARNESS RACING, 301
HAT, most expensive 156
HEADMASTER, youngest 219
HEART, heaviest whale 29
HEART STOPPAGE, longest 24
HEART TRANSPLANTS, first 26
HEAVENLY BODIES 66–70
HEDGE, tallest 52
HELICOPTER, largest, fastest, highest 141
HERB, largest, slowest flowering 50
HERD (Animals), largest 30
HIBERNATION, longest 30–31
HICCOUGHING, longest attack 24–25
HIGH DIVING, highest 170
HIGH WIRE, highest act 173, most on a 175
HIGHEST POINTS, Counties of U.K., Republic of Ireland 58–59
HIGHWAY, most lanes 215
HIKE, longest 166
HILL, longest name 89, steepest 215
HILL FIGURE, largest, oldest, ground 121
HILL-FORT, largest Celtic 120
HITCH-HIKING, British record 170
HOARDERS, greatest 211
HOCKEY, 271, Ice, 275
HOISTING TACKLE, greatest weight lifted 146
HOLE, deepest in world, U.K. 124
HOLES IN ONE (Golf), longest, most 269
HOLY BIBLE, see Bible
HONORARY DEGREES, most 181
HONOURS, DECORATIONS AND AWARDS, 178–181
HOOP ROLLING, world record 170
HOP FIELD, largest 158–159
HOPSCOTCH, most protracted game 170
HORNS, longest 34, extinct 46
HORSE, oldest, largest, heaviest draught 34,

313

highest price 160, jumping 256, racing 271–274
HORSEBACK RIDING, greatest feats 175, 271–274
HORSEPOWER (Car), highest 132
HORSERACING, 271–274
HOSPITAL, largest world, U.K., mental, maternity, children's 187
HOTEL, largest in world, U.K., largest room, tallest, highest rooms, most expensive 110
HOTEL CHAIN, largest 150–151
HOTELIER, largest company 150–151
HOTTEST PLACE, world, U.K., Ireland, annual mean 64
HOUSE, highest rent 154, earliest 107, largest world 110–111, U.K., smallest, most expensive 111
HOUSE OF COMMONS, see Parliament
HOUSE OF LORDS, see Parliament
HOUSING, see Dwelling Units
HOUSING ESTATE, largest U.K. 110
HOVERCRAFT, inventor, earliest patent, first flight, public service, largest, longest non-stop trip 142
HUMAN BEING (see also Man) 13–27
HUMAN CANNON BALL, record distance 170
HUMAN JUGGLING, acrobatic feats 175
HUMAN MEMORY, most retentive 26
HUMIDITY AND DISCOMFORT, 65
HUNGER STRIKE, longest 27
HURLING, 274–275
HYDRO-ELECTRIC PLANT, largest world, U.K. 142
HYDRO-ELECTRIC STATION, largest world, U.K., progressive list 142
HYDRO-ELECTRIC TUNNEL, longest world, U.K. 119
HYDROFOIL, fastest patrol boats 128, largest 129
HYDROPLANE, fastest 162
HYMN, earliest, longest, shortest, most prolific writer, longest hymn-in 100
HYPNOSIS, first from the air 142
HYPOCHONDRIAC, greatest 26

I.Q., highest 26
ICE, thickest 60
ICEBERG, largest, most southerly Arctic, most northerly Antarctic 56
ICEBREAKER, northernmost, southernmost 127, most powerful, largest 130
ICE CAVES, largest 63
ICE CREAM SUNDAE, largest 156
ICE HOCKEY, 275
ICE RINK, largest 276
ICE SKATING, 275–276
ICE YACHTING, progressive human speed records 276
ILLITERACY, extent of 218
ILLNESS, commonest, rarest 23
IMMIGRATION, most to U.S. 185
IMPEACHMENT, longest 197
INCOME, highest average for a country 186–187, highest individual, highest in one year, lowest 177, sport 226
INCOME TAX, highest informer's reward 198, see also Taxation
INCUBATION, shortest, longest 38
INCUMBENCY, longest 224
INDUSTRIAL DISPUTE, longest, most serious 212
INDUSTRIAL ESPIONAGE, greatest robbery 205
INDUSTRY, oldest 147
INFANT MORTALITY, lowest, highest 186
INFLATION, worst 210
INFLORESCENCE, largest 50
INFLUENZA, earliest 24
INFORMER, highest reward 198
INJURY, personal, highest damages 198
INLAND SEAS, largest 61
INLAND WATERWAY, longest U.K. 116, country with greatest, greatest navigable length 218,
INSECT, largest, longest, heaviest U.K., smallest, smallest eggs, fastest flying, longest lived, loudest, southernmost, largest swarm, fastest, slowest wing beat, largest ant, grasshopper, dragonfly, oldest flea, longest flea jump 43, largest extinct, earliest 47
INSECTIVORES, largest, smallest 33
INSTRUMENTS, musical, 97–98, oldest, largest and loudest, greatest man-power required 97, highest and lowest notes 98
INSTRUMENT, surgical, largest, smallest 26
INSURANCE COMPANY, largest in world, U.K., largest life policy, marine insurance 151
INTELLIGENCE QUOTIENT, highest 26
INTERNATIONAL (sports), youngest and oldest 226
INVASION, greatest, seaborne, airborne, most recent British 192
INVERTEBRATE, heaviest 44–45
INVESTMENT COMPANY, largest 154
IRON MINE, largest, greatest reserves 125
IRRIGATION CANAL, longest 116
ISLAND, largest, largest off-shore U.K., largest freshwater, largest inland, remotest, remotest inhabited 57, newest, greatest archipelago, northernmost, largest atoll 58
ISOLATION, longest period 27
ISOTOPES (Elements), gaseous: heaviest, rarest 73. Metallic: lightest, heaviest 73, rarest 74, most and least, longest and shortest half-lives 75

JADE, largest piece 78, highest price 156
JAI-ALAI, 288
JAIL, see prison
JAZZ RECORD, earliest 102

JELLY FISH, longest 45
JET ACE, most kills 179
JET AIRCRAFT, first 138, fastest airliner, fastest 140, fastest flying boat 141
JET ENGINE, earliest, first flight 139, fastest 140, most powerful 144
JET STREAM, fastest 65
JETTY, longest 121
JEWELS, record theft 205
JEWS, world total 220
JIG-SAW, largest 156–157
JIU JITSU, see Judo
JIVING, duration record 169
JOCKEY, lightest, most successful 272
JUDGE, oldest, youngest 198
JUDICIAL BUILDING, largest 206
JUDICIAL CODE, earliest 196
JUDO (Jiu Jitsu), 276
JUGGLER, greatest 170
JUGGLING, human, greatest feat 175
JUMP, highest and longest kangaroo 34, dog 35, frog 40, flea 43
JUMPING (Horse), 225–226
JUNCTION, railway, busiest 135
JUNK, largest 130

KANGAROO, largest, highest and longest jump 34
KARATE, 276–277
KEEP, most massive, largest Norman in U.K. 110
KIDNAPPING, highest ransom 205–206
KIDNEY STONE, largest 24
KILLINGS, greatest mass 199–200
KING, longest, shortest reign, longest, shortest British reign, longest lived, youngest, most children, most married, longest absence 188, tallest and shortest 188–189
KINGDOM, richest 175
KITE FLYING, record altitude 170
KNIGHT, youngest 181
KNITTING, duration record 170
KNOCKOUTS (Boxing), fastest, most 242–243
KNOT-TYING, marathon 170

LABELS, oldest matchbox, longest and dullest set 157
LABORATORY, world's deepest 73, world's highest 108
LABOUR CAMPS, total number 200
LABOUR DISPUTES, see Strike
LACROSSE, 277
LADDER, tallest fire brigade 123
LAKE, largest, largest U.K., largest freshwater, lake in a lake 61, largest Ireland, deepest, highest 62
LAMB, highest birthweight, prolificacy record 159
LAMP, most powerful 83
LAND, remotest spot from 55, Earth's land surface 56, remotest from the sea 57, northernmost 58, largest owner 153–154, longest tenure, highest, lowest values 154, area 197
LAND SPEED RECORDS, 131, 162, 285
LAND'S END TO JOHN O' GROATS, hitch-hiking 170, cycling 255, walking 301
LANDSLIDE, worst world, U.K. 182
LANGUAGE, earliest, oldest English words, commonest, most complex, rarest and commonest sounds, most and least regular verbs, vocabulary, oldest, longest, shortest alphabet 87, most and least vowels and consonants, largest letter, greatest linguist, longest chemical name, longest words, various languages and world 88, English, longest palindromes, most frequently used letters, most accents, worst tongue twisters, longest abbreviation, anagram, shortest holo-alphabetic sentence, longest sentence 89
LASER, highest note 82, brightest light, first illumination of moon 83
LATHE, largest 144
LAVA FLOWS, longest 55
LAW, 196–207
LAW CASE, longest 196–197
LAWN BOWLS, 241
LAWN MOWER, fastest 134
LAWN TENNIS, 277–279
LAWYER, highest paid 199
LEAD, largest mine 125
LEAF, largest 50
LEGAL COSTS, highest English 198
LEGISLATORS, highest paid, longest span 189
LEGISLATURE, see Parliament
LEGS, creatures with most 44
LENGTH, shortest unit 81
LENS, earliest use, largest astronomical 78
LEPIDOPTERA, largest, smallest butterflies and moths, most acute sense of smell 44
LETTERS, most (alphabet) 87, largest 88, most frequently used in English 89, longest, longest to an Editor, shortest correspondence, highest price 94, most sent 216
LEVEES, largest 117
LIBRARY, largest world, U.K., oldest Scotland, most overdue book 95, largest gramophone 102
LICENCES, sound-broadcasting 105, television, U.S., U.K. 106, earliest airship pilot's 141
LIEN, largest 198
LIFE, most basic, earliest 48
LIFE EXPECTATION, highest and lowest at birth, at 60 years 186
LIFE POLICY, largest 151
LIFT, fastest passenger world, longest U.K. 145
LIGHT, brightest artificial 83, greatest visible range 165
LIGHT BULB, most durable 83

LIGHT-YEAR, 66
LIGHTHOUSE, most powerful world, brightest English, tallest, remotest 122
LIGHTNING, greatest length, speed, temperature 65
LIMBO DANCING, lowest bar 169
LINER, passenger, largest, fastest, longest, progressive list 127
LINGUIST, greatest 88
LION, heaviest African 31–32
LION-TAMING, most lions mastered 170
LIQUEUR, most expensive 76–77
LIQUOR, most alcoholic, smallest bottle 76
LITIGATION, most protracted 196–197
LITTER, largest 30, puppies 35, kittens 36
LIVESTOCK RECORDS, 160
LIVING STANDARD, greatest cost increase 187
LIZARD, smallest U.K. 38, fastest 38–39, largest, oldest 39, largest extinct 45
LOAD, heaviest draught 34, heaviest and largest, tallest (overland) 133, heaviest (railway) 134, greatest air 139, parachute 171
LOAF, longest 157
LOBSTER, largest 42
LOCH, longest sea 61, largest inland U.K. 61–62, longest, deepest, highest 62
LOCK, largest, deepest, highest lock elevator, longest flight 116
LOCOMOTIVE, see Engine, Railway
LOCUSTS, largest swarm 43
LOG ROLLING, longest contest 170
LONGEVITY, 18–19
LORRY, largest 132
LOUGH, largest 61–62
LOW WIRE ACT, acrobatic feats 175
LUGEING, 240–241
LUNAR CONQUEST, 161
LYNCHING, worst, last in U.K. 204

MACH NUMBER, highest attained with air 83, scale for aircraft speeds 137
MACHINE TOOL, largest 144
MACHINERY, oldest 144
MAGAZINE, largest circulation, highest advertising rates 96
MAGNET, strongest and heaviest 82
MAGNETIC FIELD, strongest 82–83
MAGNITUDE, Stellar 66, 69
MAIL, greatest robbery 205
MAJORITY: Electoral see Elections; Parliamentary see Parliament
MAMMALS, 28–36, largest, tallest 28, smallest, rarest, fastest, longest lived, largest herd, gestation periods, largest litter, fastest breeders 30, largest toothed 31, highest and lowest blood temperatures 34, largest prehistoric 46, earliest 47
MAMMOTH, heaviest tusks, tallest 46
MAN, tallest 13–14, shortest 15–16, most variable stature 15, heaviest in world, U.K. 16, thinnest, lightest, greatest slimming feat, greatest weight gain 17, earliest 17–18, oldest 18–19, largest chest 22, most fingers, longest finger nails, longest hair, beard, moustache 23, most alcoholic, highest, lowest temperature 24, first space flight 71, greatest altitude, fastest 161, most travelled 162, most married 166–167, longest engaged, married 167, richest in world 175–176, richest in U.K., highest salary in world 176, U.K., highest, lowest income 177, most statues 180, most bemedalled 179
MANUFACTURING COMPANY, largest 151–152
MANUSCRIPT, highest price: Bible 91–92, at auction, literary, by living author, personal papers 92
MAP, oldest 95
MARATHON, fastest 232 (see also separate activities)
MARBLE, largest slab 78
MARCH (Military), longest, fastest 195
MARINE DISASTER, worst world, U.K. 181
MARQUEE, largest 123
MARRIAGE, lowest, highest average ages 186, most 166–167, 206, longest 167
MARSUPIALS, largest, smallest, rarest, longest jump 34
MASER, first illumination of moon 83
MASS ARREST, greatest 204
MASS KILLINGS, greatest 199–200
MASSACRES, greatest 199–200
MASTS, Radio and T.V. 113
MATADOR, greatest 244–245
MATCHBOX LABELS, oldest, longest and dullest set 157
MATERNITY HOSPITAL, largest world, U.K. 187
MATTER, rarest form 74
MEASURE OF WEIGHT, earliest 81
MEASUREMENT, smallest particle 81
MEAT, eating record 178, biggest consumers 213
MEAT PIES, eating record 178
MECHANISM, slowest moving designed 195
MEDALS, highest auction price 156, oldest, rarest, commonest, most expensive 178, V.C.—most bars, oldest, youngest, longest lived, most frequently decorated man, U.K., most mentions in despatches, highest decorations, U.S.S.R., U.S.A., most bemedalled man 179
MEDICAL CENTRE, largest 187
MELTING POINT, lowest and highest for gases 73, metals 74
MEMBER OF PARLIAMENT, largest, smallest majority, narrowest personal, fewest votes, most rapid change of fortune, greatest swing, highest poll, youngest, oldest 190,

longest span of service 190–191, earlie women M.P.s, longest speech 191
MEMORIAL, tallest (progressive record 113, tallest 120–121
MEMORY (human), most retentive 26
MENTAL HOSPITAL, largest 187, longe sentence in Broadmoor 203, longest escap 204
MENU, longest 157
MERCHANDISING FIRM, largest 150
MERCHANT SHIPPING, world tota largest fleet 214
METAL, lightest, densest 73, lowest an highest melting and boiling points, highe and lowest expansion, highest ductility highest tensile strength, rarest, commones most non-magnetic, newest 74, purest 75
METEOR, greatest shower 66
METEORITE, largest world, U.K., Irelan largest craters 66
METEOROIDS, 66
METROPOLITAN CENSUS AREA, larg est world 184–185
MICROBE, Bacteria: largest, highest, long est lived, toughest. **Viruses:** largest, smalles most primitive 48
MICROSCOPE, most powerful, electron 8.
MIDGET, shortest 15, lightest 17
MILESTONE, oldest 216
MILITARY ENGINE, largest 195
MILK, drinking record 178
MILK YIELD, cows, lifetime, one lactation day; goats 159
MILKING, hand milking record 160
MILLION AND ONE (Darts), 255
MILLIONAIRES, richest, most in one family 176
MILLIONAIRESSES, world, U.K., youngest, earliest 176
MILLIPEDE, most legs 44
MINARET, tallest 222
MINE, earliest 124, deepest world, U.K., largest, largest gold, richest gold, largest iron, copper, silver, lead and zinc, spoil heap, largest open pit, deepest open pit, diamonds, copper 125, winding cage speed 145, greatest depth, shaft sinking record 166
MINERALS, see Gems
MINERAL WATER, largest firm 151
MINING, winding cage speed 145, greatest depth, shaft sinking record 166, worst disaster world, U.K. 182
MINING DISASTER, worst world, U.K. 182
MINK, highest price 34
MINT, largest 211
MIRROR, largest (solar furnace) 143
MOATS, world's largest 110
MOBILE, largest, heaviest 86
MODEL AIRCRAFT, altitude, speed, duration record 142
MODEL RAILWAY, record run 137
MODERN PENTATHLON, 279
MOLLUSC, largest squid 44–45, octopus, most ancient, largest, smallest, rarest, longest lived, shells, snail: largest, speed 45, largest shelled extinct 47
MONARCH, longest descent 187–188, longest, shortest reign, British: longest, shortest reign, longest lived, youngest, most children, most married, longest absence 188, tallest and shortest 188–189
MONETARY VOTE, largest Parliamentary 181
MONEY, 209–211
MONKEY, largest, smallest, rarest, longest lived 33
MONOCYCLE, tallest 134, duration record 166, distance record 134
MONOPOLY music, greatest of sales charts 103, **game** most protracted 150
MONORAIL, highest speed 137
MONUMENT, tallest, largest prehistoric, youngest ancient, largest 120, most 180
MOON, distance extremes, diameter, earliest radar echo, speed, first direct hit, first photographs hidden side, first soft landing, blue moon, largest and deepest craters, brightest spot, highest mountains, temperature extremes, oldest rocks 67, eclipses: earliest, longest, most, least frequent 68, longest lunar mission, duration record on 70, first man on 161
MORBIDITY, highest 23
MORSE, highest speed 170
MORTALITY, infant, lowest, highest 186
MORTAR, largest 194
MOSAIC, largest 86
MOSQUE, largest 222
MOSS, smallest, longest 51
MOTH, largest, smallest, rarest, most acute sense of smell 44
MOTHER, most prolific in world 19, U.K. 19–20, oldest in world, U.K., Ireland 20
MOTIONLESSNESS, longest 26
MOTOR CAR, see Car
MOTORCYCLE, earliest, earliest factory, fastest road machine, track machines, largest, most expensive 133, greatest body jump 168
MOTORCYCLING, 280–281
MOTOR RACING, 281–285
MOTOR RALLY, earliest, longest 285
MOTOR ROAD, highest 215
MOTOR VEHICLE, see Car
MOUND, largest artificial 120
MOUNTAIN, highest submarine 56, highest, highest insular, remotest from Earth's centre 58, highest U.K. and Ireland 58–60, highest unclimbed, largest, greatest ranges 60, highest lunar 67, racing 286
MOUNTAINEERING, conquest of Everest, highest summit by woman 164, worst disaster world, U.K. 182, sport 286–287

OUNTAINEERING DISASTER, worst ld, U.K. 182
OUSE, smallest 33
OUSTACHE, longest 23
ULTIPLE BIRTHS, 20–21
ULTIPLE GREAT GRANDPARENTS,
URAL, earliest, largest 86
URDER, longest, shortest, best attended al 197, highest rate, lowest 200, most olific murderers, world 200–201, U.K., st gang murders 201
URDERESS, most prolific 201
USCLE, largest, smallest 22, fastest ovement 24, 43
USEUM, oldest, largest world, U.K. 87
USHROOM, largest farm 159
USIC, 97–100, longest silence 99
USICAL FILM, best-selling record 103, ost expensive, highest price rights 104, ghest box office gross 105
USICAL INSTRUMENTS, 97–98, old- l, largest and loudest, greatest man-power quired 97, highest and lowest notes 98
USICAL NOTATION, oldest 97
USICAL NOTE, generated by "laser" eam 82, highest and lowest orchestral 98
USICAL SHOW, longest runs, most ostly, shortest run 101
USICIANS, most for one instrument 97, ghest paid 99
MUZZLE VELOCITY, highest 225, 292

NAILS (finger), longest 23
NAME, longest chemical 88, place: longest 9–90, shortest, earliest, commonest, per- onal: earliest, longest, shortest, commonest, ost contrived 90, longest Biblical 92
NARCOTICS, greatest haul 206
NATION, richest 207, 209, largest 183
NATIONAL ANTHEM, oldest, longest, shortest, longest rendition 98
NATIONAL DEBT, largest 208–209
NATIONAL INCOMES, highest 186–187
NATIONAL PRODUCT, largest 209
NATIONAL SAVINGS, highest total 209
NATIONAL WEALTH, total 209
NATURAL BRIDGE, longest 63
NATURAL INCREASE (population), high- est, lowest rates 186
NATURE RESERVE, smallest, world 53
NATURISTS, first and largest camps 122
NAVAL BATTLE, greatest 193
NAVE, longest world, U.K. 221
NAVY, largest, greatest battle 193
NEBULAE, farthest visible 70
NECK, longest 23
NEEDLE THREADING, record strands 170
NERVE GAS, most powerful 75
NETBALL, 287
NEWSPAPER, comic strip: most durable, most read; first crossword 94, greatest number, oldest, most expensive, largest 95, largest page 95–96, smallest, heaviest circu- lation, "earliest", most read, most smoked 96
NEWSREELS, most durable commentator 105
NEWT, largest, smallest world, U.K. 40
NIGHT CLUB, oldest, largest, highest, lowest 111
NOBEL PRIZE, highest cash value, most awards by country, individual, oldest prize- man, youngest 180
NONUPLETS, 20
NOISE, loudest 82
NORTH POLE, conquest 163
NORTHERN LIGHTS, 67
NOTE, highest and lowest attained by human voice 25, highest generated by "laser" beam 82, highest and lowest orchestral 98
NOUNS, most cases 87
NOVEL, longest 91, highest sales 93
NOVELIST, most prolific, fastest, top- selling 92, youngest 92–93
NUCLEAR EXPLOSION, greatest 195– 196
NUDIST CAMP, first, largest 122
NUGGET, largest gold, silver 78
NUMEROLOGY, expression of large num- bers 80
NUMBER, highest named, lowest and high- est prime, lowest and highest perfect, most primitive 80, most decimal places 80–81
NUMBER PLATE (Car), earliest, most expensive 131
NUT (Engineering), largest 145
NYLON, sheerest 157

OAK, largest U.K. 49
OARS, earliest 126
OBELISK, oldest, largest 120
OBITUARY, longest 181
OBJECT, smallest visible to human eye 25, farthest visible, remotest (universe) 70, largest named after human 178
OBSERVATORY, highest 79
OCEAN (see also Sea), largest (area, depth, weight, volume), most southerly, remotest spot from land, temperature 55, greatest descent 164, progressive descent records·165
OCEANARIUM, earliest, largest 53
OCTOPUS, largest 45
OCTUPLETS, 20
ODDS (Gambling), longest, shortest 264– 265
OFFICE BUILDING, administrative, com- mercial world's largest, 107, tallest in U.K. 108
OIL COMPANY, largest 152
OIL FIELD, largest world, greatest gusher, greatest fire 124
OIL FIRE, greatest 124

OIL GUSHER, most prolific 124
OIL PIPELINE, longest world, U.K. 144
OIL POLLUTION, greatest 130
OIL REFINERY, largest 152
OIL RIG, largest 130
OIL WELL, deepest world, U.K. 124
OLD SCHOOL TIE, oldest 219
OLD SOLDIERS, oldest 194
OLYMPIC GAMES, 287–288
OMELETTE, greatest number 170
ONAGER, largest 195
ONIONS, pickled, eating record 178
OPAL, largest 78
OPERA, longest, longest aria, cadenza 99
OPERA HOUSE, largest, most tiers 99
OPERATION, longest, oldest subjects, heart transplants, earliest appendicectomy, anaes- thesia, fastest amputation 26
ORCHESTRA, most 97, largest 97–98, highest paid, largest attendance, highest and lowest notes 98
ORCHID, rarest U.K. 48, largest, tallest, smallest, highest priced 51, smallest seed 52
ORDERS AND MEDALS, 178–179
ORDER OF MERIT, longest lived holder, oldest recipient, oldest holder, youngest recipient 181
ORGAN, largest, largest church, loudest stop, marathon 97, highest and lowest notes 98
ORGANISM, smallest 47, largest, most basic, earliest 48
ORIENTEERING, 285
OSCARS, most 105
OSTRICH, largest, running speed 36, largest egg 38
OWL, rarest 37, most acute vision 38
OX, heaviest England 159, eating record 178
OYSTERS, eating record 178

PACIFIC CROSSING, fastest 126
PACING, 301
PAGODA, tallest 222
PAINTER, most prolific 85
PAINTING, earliest, largest world, U.K., most valuable, highest price Old Master 84, auction records, world, U.K., by British artist, highest price modern, living artist 85, young- est exhibitor at R.A., upside-down record, earliest, largest mural, highest priced (pro- gressive records) 86
PALACE, largest world, U.K., longest ever 110
PALINDROME, longest 89
PANCAKE RACE, fastest 237
PANDA, most valuable 53
PANDEMIC, worst world, U.K. 182
PANIC, worst world, U.K. 182
PAPER, most expensive writing 158
PAPER MILL, largest 152
PAPER MONEY, 209–210
PAPERWEIGHT, highest auction price 157
PARACHUTING, earliest demonstration, earliest descent, longest delayed drop, man 170, group, woman, highest escape, heaviest load, most descents, longest fall without, highest landing, most northerly 171
PARISH, largest, smallest, longest incum- bency 224
PARISH REGISTER, oldest 224
PARK, largest, smallest 53
PARKING, briefest offence 216
PARKING METERS, earliest 216
PARLIAMENT, world: oldest, largest, smallest quorum, highest paid legislators, longest membership, filibusters, greatest peti- tion, largest elections, closest, most one- sided elections, highest personal majority; U.K.: longest, shortest 189, longest sittings, most divisions, party majorities, largest personal, narrowest, fewest votes, most rapid change of fortune, greatest swing, highest poll, M.P.s, youngest, oldest 190, longest span 190–191, earliest women M.P.s, House of Lords, longest speech, Premiership, long- est and shortest terms, most times, oldest, youngest Chancellorship, longest and shortest tenures, most appointments, Speakership, longest 191
PARTICLE, number, lightest and heaviest sub-nuclear, fastest 73
PARTICLE ACCELERATOR, most power- ful 82
PARTIES, largest communist, country with most 189
PARTY GIVING, most expensive 167
PASS, highest 215
PASSENGER LIFT, fastest world, longest U.K. 145
PASSENGER LINER, largest, longest, progressive list 127
PATENT, earliest radio 105, television 106, earliest H-Bomb, earliest English, most applications 196, greatest infringement dam- ages 198
PEARL, largest 78
PEDAL CAR, longest distance propelled 134
PEER, oldest created, most aged, highest succession number, most prolific 180–181
PEERAGE, most ancient, oldest creation 180, oldest, longest, shortest, highest num- bering, most creations, longest abeyance, most prolific 181
PEERESS, most prolific 181
PELOTA VASCA, 288
PENAL CAMPS, largest 206
PENAL SETTLEMENT, largest French 206
PENINSULA, largest 57
PENKNIFE, most blades 157
PENNY, largest pile 211
PENSION, longest retirement 167
PENTATHLON, MODERN, 279

PERFECT DEALS (Bridge), 247
PERFECT NUMBERS, lowest, highest 80
PERFORMER, highest paid T.V. 106
PERFUME, most expensive 75
PERIODICAL, largest circulation, highest advertising rates, longest editorship 96
PERMAFROST, deepest 65
PERMANENT WAY, longest, longest straight, electric, widest gauge, highest, low- est, steepest gradients 135
PERSONAL INJURY, highest damages 198
PERSONAL NAMES, earliest, longest, shortest, commonest, most contrived 90
PETITION, greatest parliamentary 189
PHILANTHROPY, greatest 177
PHONOGRAPH, see Gramophone
PHOTOGRAPHY, expenditure U.S.A., U.K., earliest, earliest aerial, largest print, largest colour transparency, highest 80
PHYSICAL EXTREMES, 81–83
PHYSICIANS, most, highest, lowest pro- portion 187
PI, most accurate version 80–81
PIANIST, highest paid 99
PIANO, earliest 97, highest and lowest notes 98
PIANO COMPOSITION, longest 98–99
PIANO PLAYING, world, U.K., woman's record 171
PIANO SMASHING, record 171
PICTURE GALLERY, largest 85–86
PIER, longest pleasure 111, longest 121
PIG, heaviest, prolificacy record 159, highest price 160
PIGEON RACING, 289
PIGGERY, largest 160
PILL-TAKER, greatest 24
PILLAR BOX, oldest 218
PILLAR BOX STANDING, record number of people 171
PILOT, most travelled 162, most deck landings 128
PINNIPEDS, largest, smallest, fastest, deep- est dive, longest lived, rarest 32
PIPE, most expensive, longest 157
PIPE SMOKING, duration record 171
PIPED WATER, most dwellings with 187
PIPELINE, gas: longest natural, oil: long- est world, U.K. 144
PISTOLS, most expensive 157
PIT, deepest, largest 125
PITCH, highest detectable 28, highest 82
PLACE-NAMES, longest 89–90, shortest, earliest, commonest in U.K., most widely used British 90
PLAGUE, most infectious disease 23
PLANET, largest, smallest, shortest "day", highest orbital speed, hottest, coldest, nearest 68, brightest and faintest, longest "day", conjunctions: most dramatic, next 69
PLANETARIUM, first, largest, earliest U.K. 79
PLANT KINGDOM, 48–52, earliest life, oldest fossil, rarest, commonest, northern- most, southernmost, deepest roots 48, largest blossoming, largest leaves, smallest flower- ing, slowest flowering 50, smallest proto- phyte 47
PLATE SPINNING, greatest number spun 171
PLATFORM, Railway, longest, largest number of U.K. 136
PLATINUM DISC, unique award 102
PLAY, longest runs, longest 101, Shake- speare, longest title 102
PLEASURE BEACH, biggest 111
PLEASURE PIER, longest 111
PLOUGHING, world championship, fastest 160
POEM, longest, shortest 93
POET LAUREATE, earliest, youngest, oldest 93
POISON, quickest, most potent 75, most active venom (frog) 40 (also most poisonous snake 40, most venomous fish 41, most poisonous spider 42, most poisonous toad- stool 52)
POLAR CONQUESTS, first North 163, South 163–164
POLAR LIGHTS, see Aurora
POLDER, largest 117
POLE SQUATTING, records 171
POLICY (life insurance), largest 151
POLITICAL DIVISION, largest 183
POLITICAL PARTIES, country with most 189
POLITICAL SPEECH, longest on record 173
POLL, highest (general election) 191
POLO, 289
POP FESTIVAL, greatest attendance 98
POP GROUP, non-stop playing 171
POPE, longest, shortest reign, oldest 222, youngest 222–223, last non-Italian, last ex- Cardinalate, English, last married, quickest and slowest election 223
POPULATION, world 183–184, progres- sive mid-year estimates, largest, smallest, densest, sparsest, British Isles 184, increase 186
PORCELAIN, highest price 157
PORT, largest, busiest 214
POST CARD, best selling 93
POST OFFICE, northernmost U.K. and southernmost 218
POSTAGE STAMPS, see Stamp
POSTAL SERVICE, largest and highest average letter mail 217, highest numbered address 217–218, northernmost and southern- most post office, oldest pillarboxes, most telegrams, largest telegraph company 218
POTATO, biggest consumers 212
POTATO CRISPS, eating record 178

POWDER, finest 75
POWER BOAT RACING, 289
POWER FAILURE, greatest 142
POWER PRODUCERS, 142–144
POWER STATION, largest world, non- hydro-electric, largest U.K. 142, atomic, tidal, solar 143
PRAM PUSHING, record distance 171
PREDATOR, largest 46
PREFIXES, most 87
PREHISTORIC ANIMALS, see Extinct Animals
PREHISTORIC MONUMENT, largest 119–120
PREMIER, see Prime Minister
PREMIUM (Insurance), largest 151
PRESS-UPS, most 270
PRESSURE, highest, lowest Barometric 64, laboratory 81
PRIMATE, earliest 17, 47, largest, heaviest 32, smallest, longest lived, most and least intelligent 33
PRIME MINISTER, oldest, longest term of office 189, U.K. records: oldest, youngest, longest term of office, shortest, most times 191
PRIME NUMBER, lowest, highest 80
PRINTER, largest 94, fastest 145
PRINTING, earliest; earliest, largest, small- est, most valuable books 91, largest job, print order 94
PRISON, longest sentences: world, U.K. 203, Broadmoor 203–204, longest escapes, longest escape from Broadmoor 204, greatest break 205, largest, smallest, highest popula- tion, most secure 206
PRIZE, largest T.V. 106, competition 168, Bingo 264
PROFESSOR, youngest, most durable 218
PROFIT AND LOSS, greatest 148
PROMISE, Breach of, highest damages 198
PROPELLER, largest ship 130, largest aircraft 140
PROPER MOTION, 66
PROPERTY, most valuable 154
PROSECUTION, rarest 207
PROTEIN, most and least proteinous fruit 50, highest, lowest consumption 212
PROTISTA, largest, smallest, fastest mov- ing, fastest reproduction, densest 47
PROTOPHYTE, smallest 47
PROTOZOAN, largest, smallest, fastest moving, fastest reproduction, densest 47
PRUNES, eating record 178
PSALM, longest, shortest 92
PSYCHIATRIST, fastest 172, most 187
PUBLICATION, largest 91
PUBLIC HOUSE, largest world, U.K., smallest, highest, oldest, longest named, shortest named, longest bars 112, pub- crawling 172
PUBLIC RELATIONS, largest firm 152
PUBLISHER, largest 94
PUBLISHING, most active country 93, fastest 94, largest enterprise 152
PULL-UPS, most 270
"PULSARS", first, fastest 70
PUMP-TURBINE, largest 143
PURGE, greatest 199
PYGMIES, smallest 15–16
PYRAMID, tallest (progressive records) 113, largest 119, oldest 120

Q.C., see Queen's Counsel
QUADRUPLETS, heaviest, earliest U.K., Ireland 21
QUARRY, deepest, largest world, U.K. 125
QUASARS, 70
QUAY, longest 121
QUEEN, longest, shortest British reign, longest lived, youngest, most children, most married 188, shortest 189
QUEEN'S COUNSEL, youngest 198
QUIETEST PLACE, 82
QUINTUPLETS, 20–21
QUIZ, largest T.V. prize 106, league, largest and oldest 170
QUORUM, smallest parliamentary 189

RABBITS, largest, smallest breed, heaviest specimen 36
RACE (Ethnology), tallest 15, smallest, shortest 15–16, poorest 177
RACKETS, 290
RADAR, largest installations 146
RADIO, most transmitters, total number of sets, origins, earliest patent, earliest broad- cast, earliest trans-Atlantic, longest broad- casts 105, most durable programmes 106, tallest masts 113
RADIO TELESCOPE, first fully steerable, largest 79
RAFT, longest survival alone, longest voyage 166
RAILWAY, longest, highest bridge, viaduct 115, tunnel, progressive records 118, earliest, speed records, longest non-stop, most power- ful engine 134, longest permanent way, straight, electric line, widest gauge, highest, lowest, steepest gradients, busiest junction 135, largest stations, world, U.K., oldest U.K., highest, largest waiting rooms, longest platform, progressive records 136, freight train 136–137, greatest load, greatest mileage, most expensive freight rate, underground, model, monorail 137, disasters 182, country with greatest length, greatest density 214, furthest place from in U.K., number of journeys 215
RAILWAY DISASTER, worst world, U.K. 182
RAILWAY ENGINE, see Engine, Railway
RAINFALL, greatest, least 64, most intense 65

315

RAINY DAYS, *most in year 64*
RALLY (motor), *earliest, longest 285*
RANSOM, *highest 205–206*
RAPIDS, *fastest 61*
RATTING, *record by dog 35, by cat 36*
RAVIOLI, *eating record 178*
REACTOR, *largest single atomic 143*
REAL ESTATE, *most valuable 154*
REAL TENNIS 300
RECEPTION, *Ticker-tape, greatest 180*
RECIPE, *oldest 214*
RECORD, Gramophone, *see Gramophone Record*
RECORD PLAYERS, *most 102*
RECORDING ARTIST, *most successful, earliest golden disc 102, most golden discs 102–103, youngest, fastest sales, best-selling charts, most recordings, greatest monopoly 103, greatest advance sales, highest fee 104*
REDWOOD, *tallest 48–49*
REED, *tallest 52*
REEF, *longest 58*
REFINERY (Oil), *largest 152*
REFLECTING TELESCOPE, *largest and most powerful 78–79*
REFLEXES, *fastest 24*
REFRACTING TELESCOPE, *prototype, largest 78*
REGIMENT, *British: oldest, senior 194*
REGISTRATION PLATE, *earliest, most expensive 131*
REIGN, *longest, shortest, longest British, shortest British 188*
RELIGION, *largest Christian, largest non-Christian, smallest, largest clergy, total world jewry 220*
RENT, *highest house 154*
REPTILE, *largest, heaviest, smallest 38, fastest 38–39, lizards: largest and oldest; chelonians: largest, longest lived, slowest; snakes: longest, heaviest, shortest, oldest 39, fastest 39–40, most poisonous 40; largest extinct, winged, marine 46, largest extinct egg, earliest 47*
REPUBLIC, *smallest 183*
RESERVOIR, *largest world, U.K., deepest Europe 117*
RESTAURATEURS, *largest 152*
RETIREMENT, *longest pension 167*
RHODODENDRON, *largest 52*
RIBBON WORMS, *longest 45*
RICHEST, *ruler, private citizen 175, family 176*
RINK, *largest ice 276, roller 291*
RIOT, *greatest 204*
RISLEY, *acrobatic feats 175*
RIVER, *longest world, Ireland, U.K., greatest flow 60, greatest basin, longest tributary 60–61, sub-tributary, submarine, subterranean, longest estuary, largest delta, greatest bores, fastest rapids 61, longest dam 117, longest navigable 218*
RIVETING, *world record 172*
ROAD, *driving tests, most failures 133, greatest length, vehicle density, busiest, widest, narrowest, longest straight road, longest world, U.K., longest street, longest hill, highest world 215, U.K. 215–216, longest viaduct, worst jams, first traffic lights, parking meters, briefest offence, worst driver, oldest milestone 216*
ROAD DISASTER, *worst world, U.K. 182*
ROAD TRANSPORTER, *largest 133*
ROAD TUNNEL, *progressive records 118, longest world 118–119, sub-aqueous, longest world, U.K., largest diameter 119*
ROAD VEHICLE (*see also individual road vehicles*), *greatest density per mile 215, worst traffic jams 216, longest 132, largest road transporter 132–133, heaviest, tallest load, amphibious, most driving test failures 133*
ROBBERY, *greatest, greatest embezzlement, bank, mail-train, art, jewels, coins 205*
ROCK, *oldest, largest 57, oldest known lunar 67*
ROCKET, *earliest, longest ranges 70, most powerful world, U.K., least powerful, ion, altitude records 71*
ROCKING-CHAIR, *duration record 172*
RODENT, *largest, smallest, rarest 33*
RODEO, *290*
ROLLER SKATING, *291*
ROLLING PIN, *woman's greatest throw 172*
ROOTS, *deepest 48*
ROPE, *largest 157, longest wire 145*
ROPE CLIMBING, *270*
ROPEWAY, *highest, longest, longest single span, largest cable cars 145*
ROSE TREE, *largest 52*
ROTARY SPEED, *highest man-made 81*
ROTATING-WING AIRCRAFT, *fastest 141*
ROWING, *Atlantic crossing 163, sport 291–292*
ROYAL TENNIS, *300*
ROYALTY, *oldest ruling house 187, longest, shortest reign, British monarchs: longest, shortest reign, longest lived, oldest members of Royal Family, youngest, most children, most often married, longest absence 188, tallest and shortest 188–189*
RUBY, *value 77, largest 78*
RUGBY FIVES, *256*
RUGBY LEAGUE, *261–262*
RUGBY UNION, *262–264*
RULER, *richest 175–176, most durable 188*
RUMINANT, *largest 30*
RUNNING, *endurance records, longest race 166, (see also Athletics), progressive human speed records (see front end paper)*
RUNWAY, *longest world, U.K. 141*

SAFARI, *longest 172*
SAIL, *largest 130*
SAILING, *see Yachting*
SAILING SHIP, *earliest vessel 126, largest, slowest voyage, largest junks, longest day's run, highest recorded speed, largest sails 130*
SAINT, *most and least rapidly canonized 222*
ST. SWITHIN'S DAY, *falsest 65*
SALAMANDER, *largest, smallest, longest lived 40*
SALARY, *highest world 176, U.K. 177*
SALES, *Corporation, greatest 148*
SALVAGING, *record observation chamber depth, deepest operation, record recovery, largest vessel 164, most expensive, highest award 166*
SAND DUNES, *highest 60*
SAPPHIRE, *largest 77*
SATELLITE, ARTIFICIAL, *first, escape velocities, earliest successful manned, first woman in space 71, extremes, first admitted fatality, first walk in space, longest space flight, longest lunar mission, duration record on Moon, most expensive project, accuracy record 72*
SATELLITE, NATURAL, *most, least, largest and smallest 69*
SAUSAGE, *longest 160, eating record 178*
SAVINGS, National, *highest total 209*
SAWING, *world record 174*
SCALE OF TIME, *18*
SCALES, *most accurate 82*
SCENIC RAILWAY, *see Switchback*
SCHOOL, *largest world, U.K., oldest U.K., oldest old school tie, most expensive, greatest disenrolment, most 'O' and 'A' level exams, youngest headmaster 219*
SCRAMBLING (Motorcycling), *281*
SCROLLS, *earliest 91, longest 92*
SCULLING, *see Rowing*
SCULPTURE, *largest, uncompleted, most expensive 121*
SEA (*see also Ocean*), *remotest spot from land, temperature 55, largest, highest wave 56*
SEA CLIFFS, *highest 63*
SEA DAM, *longest 117*
SEA LOCH, *longest 61*
SEA-LION, *see Pinnipeds*
SEAL, *see Pinnipeds*
SEAMOUNT, *highest 56*
SEARCHLIGHT, *most powerful 83*
SEAWAY, *longest artificial 116*
SEAWEED, *longest 51*
SEE-SAW, *duration record 172*
SEED, *largest, smallest, most viable, resistance to heat 52*
SEGMENTED WORMS, *longest 44*
SEISMIC SEA WAVE, *highest, fastest 56*
SENIOR WRANGLER, *order of 218–219*
SENSITIVITY, *of touch 23, colour 25*
SENTENCE, *shortest holo-alphabetic, longest (classical literature) 89, longest Bible 92, longest prison, world 203, U.K. 203–204*
SEPTUPLETS, *20*
SERMON, *longest 172*
SETTLEMENT, *highest legal 198, largest French penal 206*
SEVEN WONDERS OF THE WORLD, *119*
SEWAGE WORKS, *largest world, U.K. 109*
SEWING MACHINES, *fastest 172*
SEX RATIO, *largest woman surplus, shortage 186*
SEXTUPLETS, *20*
SHAFT, *deepest 124, longest vertical, sub-incline, world, deepest U.K. 125, sinking record 166*
SHARES, *see Stock Exchanges*
SHAVING, *fastest barber 172*
SHEAF TOSSING, *best performance 172*
SHEEP, *longest horns 34, largest station, move, highest birthweight, prolificacy record 159, highest price, auction, shearing record 160*
SHEET MUSIC, *top-selling 100*
SHELL, *largest, smallest, rarest, longest lived 45*
SHIP, *earliest, earliest power, earliest turbine, fastest Atlantic crossing, Pacific crossing 126, fastest submerged crossing, northernmost, southernmost, largest warship, largest passenger liner, progressive list 127, largest battleships, guns, thickest armour, largest aircraft carrier, most landings, most powerful cruiser, fastest destroyer, fastest warship 128, largest, fastest, deepest submarine, largest submarine fleet, tanker, cargo vessel, fastest built, cable ship, largest whale factory, most powerful tug, largest car ferry, largest hydrofoil 129, most powerful icebreaker, largest dredger, heaviest wooden, largest sailing, largest junks, longest day's run, slowest voyage, largest sails, largest propeller, Dracones, deepest anchorage, most powerful derricks, largest oil rig, largest wreck 130*
SHIP-BUILDING, *annual launching, leading firm, largest shipyard 152*
SHIP CANAL, *longest 116*
SHIPPING, *largest merchant fleet 152, 214*
SHIPPING LINE, *largest 153*
SHOE, *most expensive 157*
SHOE SHOP, *largest 153*
SHOOTING, *292–293*
SHOP, *largest book 149, most profitable department store 150, most expensive, largest shoe, largest store, largest toy 153*
SHOPPING CENTRE, *largest 153*
SHORTHAND, *speed records 172*
SHOUTING, *greatest number of wins 172*
SHOW (Theatre), *longest run, shortest run, most costly 101*
SHOW JUMPING, *255–256*
SHOWERING, *most prolonged bath 172*

SHREW, *smallest 30, 33*
SIAMESE TWINS, *original 21*
SIEGE, *longest 192*
SIGN (Advertising), *greatest ever, largest, highest 123*
SIGNALLING, *Morse, record receiving 170*
SIGNATURE, *see Autograph*
SILK, *see Queen's Counsel*
SILVER, *largest nugget 78, most expensive piece 157–158*
SILVER, LEAD & ZINC MINE, *largest 125*
SINGER, *greatest earnings, finest middle register 99*
SINGING, *longest marathon 172*
SIT-UPS, *most 270*
SKATING (Ice), *275–276*
SKATING (Roller), *291*
SKID MARKS, *longest 133*
SKI-BOB, *294*
SKI-ING, *speed records 293–294*
SKI-ING (Water), *302–304*
SKI JUMPING, *293–294*
SKIJORING, *294*
SKIPPING, *records 172*
SKITTLES, *marathon 241*
SKULL, *oldest 17–18*
SKYSCRAPERS, *tallest 108*
SKY-WRITING, *largest letters, earliest 88*
SLAG HEAP, *largest 125*
SLEDGE JOURNEY, *longest 163, longest Antarctic 164*
SLEDGING, *progressive human speed records, see front end paper*
SLEEPLESSNESS, *longest period 26*
SLIMMING, *greatest feat 17*
SLINGING, *greatest distance 172*
SLIPPED DISC, *earliest 24*
SMELL, *most acute sense of 44, strongest 75*
"SMELLING OUT", *greatest 201*
SMELTER, *largest aluminium 149*
SMOKESTACK, *tallest 108*
SMOKING, *heaviest 155*
SNAIL, *most ancient, largest, fastest, slowest 45*
SNAKE, *longest and heaviest, shortest, oldest 39, fastest 39–40, most poisonous, longest fangs 40, longest extinct 47*
SNEEZING, *longest fit, highest speed 25*
SNOOKER, *295*
SNORING, *loudest 25*
SNOW AVALANCHE, *greatest 62, worst in world, U.K. 182*
SNOWFALL, *greatest 64*
SNUFF, *most expensive 158*
SNUFF BOX, *record price 158*
SOCCER, *see Football*
SOCIAL INSECT, *earliest 47*
SOLAR FURNACE, *largest world 143*
SOLAR POWER PLANT, *largest 143*
SOLAR PROMINENCE, *largest 68*
SOLAR SATELLITES, *extremes 72*
SOLAR TELESCOPE, *largest 79*
SOLDIER, *oldest old 194*
SOLITARY CONFINEMENT, *longest period 27*
SONG, *oldest, most frequently sung, top-selling, most monotonous, most successful writers 100, most recorded 103*
SOUND, *lowest, highest pitch 26, rarest and commonest (speech) 87*
SOUNDING, *deepest 55*
SOUTH POLE, *first crossing, sighting, landing, conquest 163–164*
SPA, *largest, highest 110*
SPACE FLIGHT, *earliest successful manned, first woman 71, extremes, first admitted fatality, first space "walk", longest, longest lunar mission, duration record on Moon, most expensive project, accuracy record 72, worst disaster 182*
SPAGHETTI, *eating record 178*
SPAN, Bridge, *longest 114–115, Parliamentary, longest service 190–191*
SPEAKER, *most boring of the year 167; House of Commons, longest in office 191*
SPEECH, *fastest 27, earliest 87, longest filibuster 189, longest parliamentary 191, longest political 173*
SPEED RECORDS, *car 131, 285, motorcycle 133, 281, railway 134, progressive speed records 136, monorail 137, bomber 139, aircraft 141, fastest man, woman, space 161, land, water 162*
SPEEDWAY, *295*
SPICE, *most expensive, hottest 213*
SPIDERS, *most southerly, largest, heaviest, smallest, largest web, most poisonous, rarest, fastest, longest lived 42, earliest 47*
SPINNING (balance wheel), *duration record 172*
SPIRE, *tallest cathedral, church 222*
SPIRIT, *highest strength 76, most expensive 77, top-selling brands 150, freest drinkers, most abstemious 213*
SPITTING, *greatest distance 173*
SPONGE, *largest, smallest, rarest colour, deepest 45*
SPOONS (apostle), *record price 158*
SPORT, *from 225 (see also individual sports)*
SPORTS DISASTER, *worst in world, U.K. 226*
SPRING BOARD, *acrobatic feats 175*
SPUTNIK, *see Satellite*
SQUASH RACKETS, *295–296*
SQUATTING, Pole-, *records 171*
SQUID, *heaviest 44, longest 45*
STADIUM, *largest, largest football, covered, indoor, roofed 111*
STAG, *heaviest 30*
STAGE-TOWER, *largest 120*
STAINED GLASS (window), *oldest, largest 224*

STAIRS, *climbing record 108, 114, longe[st] 123*
STALACTITE, *longest 63*
STALAGMITE, *tallest 63*
STAMPS, Postage, *earliest adhesive, larg[est], smallest, highest and lowest denomin[a]tions 216, highest price world 216–217, U.K. most valuable, unique and rarest Britis[h] commonest British stamp, greatest collectio[n] 217*
STANDARDS OF LIVING, *186–187, 20*
STANDING HIGH JUMP, *237*
STAR, *magnitude 66, 69, largest, mos[t] massive, smallest, lightest, oldest, farthes[t] nearest, brightest, most and least luminou[s] coolest, densest, brightest supernovae 69 constellations, stellar planets 70*
STARFISH, *largest, smallest 42*
STATE, *see Country*
STATELY HOME, *most visited 111*
STATION, Railway, *busiest, largest world U.K., oldest, highest 136*
STATUE, *tallest 121, most 180*
STATURE, *most variable 15*
STATUTE, *oldest, longest U.K., shortest, most 196*
STEAM LOCOMOTIVE, *fastest, most powerful 134*
STEAMER, *oldest 126*
STEEL, *largest company, works 153*
STEEL ARCH BRIDGE, *longest, largest 115*
STEELWORKS, *largest 153*
STEER, *heaviest 159*
STELLAR MAGNITUDE, *66, 69*
STELLAR PLANETS, *70*
STILTS, *highest mastered 173*
STOCK EXCHANGE, *oldest, world total, most markings, greatest overall daily movement, highest share index figure, highest, lowest par values, U.S. records, largest issue, greatest appreciation, largest investment house 154*
STONE, *largest columns 120–121, mined slab 125*
STONE, human, *largest 24*
STORE, *see Shop*
STORM, *Circular, worst world, U.K. 182*
STRAITS, *longest, broadest, narrowest 56*
STRATOSPHERE, *earliest penetration— see back end papers, lowest temperature 65*
STREET, *widest, narrowest, longest 215, commonest name (London) 215*
STRETCHER-BEARING, *longest carry 173*
STRIKE, *longest hunger 27, most serious, biggest annual total, longest 212*
STRINGED INSTRUMENT, *largest 97*
STRUCTURE (*see also Buildings*), *earliest known human 107, 109, tallest world 112, U.K., tallest-progressive records, T.V. and radio masts by countries 113, towers 113–114, deepest foundations 115, largest concrete 117, oldest religious 221*
SUB-ATOMIC PARTICLES, *number and pattern 73*
SUBMARINE, *fastest Atlantic crossing 127, largest, fastest, deepest, largest fleet 129, first circumnavigation 163, most anti-submarine kills 179, most successful captain 180, worst disasters 182*
SUBMARINE DISASTER, *worst world, U.K. 182*
SUBMERGENCE, *record human, greatest descent, deep sea diving 164, progressive records (Oceandescents), progressive records (deep diving) 165, longest by frogman 173*
SUB-NUCLEAR PARTICLES, *lightest and heaviest 73*
SUBSTANCES, *strongest, most expensive 74, smelliest, sweetest, bitterest, most poisonous 75, hardest 75, 77*
SUB-TRIBUTARY, *longest 61*
SUBWAY, *busiest 137, longest tunnel 118*
SUGAR, *biggest consumers 213*
SUICIDE, *highest, lowest rate 201*
SUIT, *fastest made 173*
SUMMER, *earliest hot 63, best and worst British 65*
SUMO WRESTLING, *306*
SUN, *distance extremes, temperature, core pressure, luminosity, density, diameter, mass 67, eclipses: earliest, most recent total, next U.K., longest, most and least frequent 68, sun-spot: largest 67, most frequent 68*
SUN-SPOT, *largest 67, most frequent 68*
SUNSHINE, *maximum, minimum 64*
SUPER-NOVA, *brightest 69*
SUPERMARKET, *largest U.K. 153*
SUPERSONIC FLIGHT, *Mach scale 137, first, bomber 139, airliner, speed records, jet 140*
SURFING, *296*
SURGICAL INSTRUMENTS, *largest, smallest 26*
SURNAME, *longest, shortest, commonest, most contrived 90*
SURTAX, *highest 208*
SUSPENSION BRIDGE, *longest world 114–115, longest U.K., highest 114*
SWALLOWING, *compulsive swallowing, coin, sword swallowing 25*
SWARM, *largest (insects) 43*
SWEETEST SUBSTANCE, *75*
SWEETS, *biggest consumers 213*
SWIMMING, *greatest distance, longest duration swim by man, woman 166, sport 296–299*
SWIMMING POOL, *largest 296*
SWINDLE, *greatest 206*
SWING, *biggest (general election) 190*
SWITCHBACK, *fastest 112, longest ride 173*
SWORD, *highest price 158*

ORD SWALLOWING, longest 25
MPHONY, longest 98
NAGOGUE, largest world, U.K. 222

BLE TENNIS, 299–300
LORING, fastest made suit 173
LKING, fastest 26–27, longest non-stop

NDEM BICYCLE, longest 134
NK (military), earliest, heaviest 194
NK (water), largest 53
NKER, largest world, U.K., largest
ck 129
PESTRY, earliest, largest, longest, most
ensive 158
RTAN, earliest 158
TTOOS, most 24
XATION, most, highest surtax, least
ed country, highest, lowest rates in U.K.
8
AXI FLEET, largest 133
BONE DIVE, greatest 173
A, most expensive, largest firm 213
A PARTY, largest 152
A POT, highest auction price 156
ETER BOARD, acrobatic feats 175
ETH, earliest, most 25
ETH-PULLING, greatest weight pulled
3
EKTITE, largest 67
ELEGRAM, most sent 218
ELEGRAPH COMPANY, largest 218
ELEPHERIQUE, highest, longest, longest
ngle span, largest cable cars 145
ELEPHONE, world total, country without,
untry with most, least per head, highest
roportion city, town, most calls, fewest calls,
ngest submarine cable, longest call 216
ELESCOPE, earliest, largest refracting 78,
flecting 78–79, largest radio, solar 79
ELEVISION, earliest, first public service,
ost sets, first trans-Atlantic transmission,
reatest audience, largest prizes, most suc-
essful appeal, biggest contracts, highest
aid performer, longest telecast, most flexible programme 106, tallest mast, tallest
progressive records) transmitting tower,
allest masts by countries 113
EMPERATURE, progressive extremes 63,
most equable 63–65, highest shade, lowest
creen 64, greatest ranges, atmospheric
owest 65, Sun 67, lowest stellar 69, man-
made: highest, lowest 81
EMPERATURE, animal, highest, lowest
4, bird 28
EMPERATURE, human, highest, lowest
4, highest endured 27
TEMPERATURE, sea 55
TEMPLE, largest 220, oldest 221, tallest
Chinese 222
TEN-PIN BOWLING, 241
TENNIS (Lawn), 277–279
TENNIS (Real or Royal), 300
TENSILE STRENGTH, highest 74, 81
8
TENT, largest 123
TEXT, oldest written 90–91, printed, largest
book, publication, smallest, most valuable,
20th century, longest novel 91
THEATRE, earliest, oldest world, U.K. 100,
largest world 100–101, largest U.K., smallest
U.K., largest amphitheatre, longest runs,
biggest box-office, shortest runs, longest play
101, longest by Shakespeare, longest title,
longest chorus line 102
THREE-LEGGED RACE, fastest 237
THUG, worst 201
THUNDER-DAYS, most 64
TICKER-TAPE RECEPTION, greatest 180
TIDAL POWER STATION, world's first
143
"TIDAL" WAVE, highest, fastest 56
TIDDLYWINKS, 300
TIDE, greatest world, U.K., Ireland 56
TIE, oldest old school 219
TIERS, most in opera-house 99
TIGER, largest 31
TIGRESS, man-eating, worst 182
TIGHTROPE WALKING, greatest walker,
endurance record, longest rope, highest high
wire act 173, most on high wire 175
TIME, scale of 18, longest, shortest measure
81, most accurate measure 146
TIME (Magazine), youngest, oldest cover
subject, most frequent subject 181
TIME MEASURER, most accurate 146
TIN MINE, deepest Cornish 125
TINNED FOOD, oldest 214
TITHE BARN, longest Britain 122
TITLE, longest play 102, longest film 105,
most titled person 178
TOAD, largest, highest, smallest world,
U.K., longest lived 40
TOADSTOOL, most poisonous 52
TOASTMASTERS, most durable, most
boring speaker 167
TOBACCO, largest company 153, most
expensive snuff 158, heaviest smokers 155
TOBOGGANING, see Bobsleigh
TOES, most 23
TOMATO, largest plant 51
TOMB, largest 120
TONGUE, heaviest and longest whale 29
TONGUE TWISTERS, worst 89
TOOTH, see Teeth
TOPAZ, largest 78
TORNADO, highest speed 64, worst world,
U.K. 182
TORTOISE, heaviest, longest lived, slowest
39, largest extinct 47
TOSSING THE CABER, 237
TOTEM POLE, tallest 120
TOUCH, sensitivity 23
TOUR DE FRANCE (Cycling), 253

TOURISTS, most, highest spending 185–186
TOWER, tallest structure 112, tallest world
113, U.K. 114
TOWN, highest, earliest walled, largest,
northernmost, most remote from sea 185
TOWN CRIER, most title wins 172
TOXIN, most deadly 75
TOY MANUFACTURER, largest 153
TOY SHOP, biggest 153
TRACK AND FIELD ATHLETICS, 230–
237
TRACKING, greatest feat 35
TRACTOR, most powerful 133
TRADE UNION, longest name, largest
211–212, smallest 212
TRAFFIC, highest density 215, worst jams,
lights—first in U.K. 216
TRAIN, see Railway
TRAMPOLINING, 300–301
TRANS-ATLANTIC CROSSING, see
Atlantic Crossing
TRANSFER FEES, Association Football
258–259, Rugby League 262
TRANSFORMER, largest 145
TRANSMISSION LINE, longest, highest
world, U.K., highest voltages 145
TRANSMISSIONS, earliest radio broad-
casts, earliest trans-Atlantic wireless 105,
television: earliest, earliest trans-Atlantic,
earliest satellite 106
TRANSMITTERS, greatest number radio,
earliest 105, television 106
TRANSPORTER, longest road 132
TRAPEZE, greatest artistes 175
TRAVELLED (person), most on land, in air,
in space, on cruise 162
TRAVOLATOR, largest 145
TREASURE TROVE, largest 211
TREE, largest 48, tallest world 48–49,
Britain, Ireland, greatest girth, greatest oaks
Britain, oldest living, Britain, earliest, tallest
in Britain by species 49, fastest growing 49–
50, slowest growing, most spreading 50,
largest rose 52
TREE-CLIMBING, fastest 174
TREE-SITTING, duration record 174
TRENCHERMAN, greatest 178
TRIAL, longest, longest murder, shortest,
best attended 197
TRIBUTARY, longest 60–61
TRICYCLE, largest 134
TRIPLETS, heaviest 21
TROLLEY BUS, largest 132
TROPHY (Sporting), largest 226
TROTTING AND PACING, 301
TSUNAMI, highest, fastest 56
TUBA, largest 97
TUBING, smallest 146
TUG, first power-driven vessel 126, most
powerful 129
TUG OF WAR, 237
TUMBLER, greatest 270
TUNNEL, largest, most powerful wind 83,
progressive records, longest water supply
world, U.K., longest passenger, railway,
world, U.K., subway, main line U.K. 118,
longest road—world 118–119, U.K., largest
diameter, sub-aqueous, longest hydroelectric
—world, U.K., longest bridge, longest canal
119
TUNNEL OF FIRE, longest 174
TURBINE, first ship 126, largest single-
shaft, gas, reversible pump 143
TURKEY, largest 38, largest farm 159,
record price 160
TURTLE, fastest, largest, heaviest, longest
lived 39, largest extinct 46–47
TUSKS, longest 33, 46 (extinct animals),
heaviest 33–34, 46 (extinct animals)
TWINS, heaviest 17, most pairs 19, heaviest,
lightest, oldest, Siamese 21
TWIST, duration record 169
TYPEWRITER, most travelled 174
TYPEWRITING, fastest, slowest, longest
174
TYPHOID CARRIER, most notorious 23
TYPING, see Typewriting
TYRES, largest 133

ULCER, Duodenal, earliest 24
UNCONSCIOUSNESS, longest 24
UNDERGROUND CHAMBER, largest 62
UNDERGROUND FACTORY, largest 108
UNDERGROUND RAILWAY, most ex-
tensive, oldest, passenger records, greatest
depth, tour record, busiest subway, record
travelling 137
UNDERWATER, longest stay 27
UNEMPLOYMENT, highest, lowest, U.K.
212
UNICYCLE, tallest 134
UNION, Trade, largest world, longest name
211, largest, smallest U.K. 212
UNIT OF LENGTH, earliest 81
UNITS, shortest length, smallest area 81
UNIVERSE, 70, farthest visible object,
quasars, "pulsars", remotest object, brightest
object 70
UNIVERSITY, oldest, oldest colleges U.K.,
greatest enrolment, largest building, richest,
youngest, most durable professor 218, senior
wranglers 218–219, boat race 291

V.C., see Victoria Cross
VACUUM, highest 81
VASE, most expensive 158
VAT, largest blending 112, largest 123
VAULT, Bank, largest 155
VEGETABLES, record dimensions and
weights, U.K. 51
VEHICLE, most massive 132, longest 133,
Road, see Road Vehicle
VEIN, largest human 24

VELOCIPEDE, see Bicycle
VENOM, most active (frog) 40
VERBS, most forms, most and least regular
87
VERSE, longest, shortest Bible 92
VERTEBRATE, shortest, lightest, shortest
lived 41, earliest 47
VESSEL, largest fermentation 123
VIADUCT, road: longest in world 115,
Europe 216, rail: longest in world 115
VICTORIA CROSS, highest priced 178,
most bars, oldest, youngest person awarded,
longest lived 179
VILLAGE, shortest name 90, highest, oldest,
northernmost, southernmost 185
VINE, largest 52
VIOLIN, most valuable, smallest 97
VIOLINIST, highest paid 99
VIRUS, largest, smallest, most primitive 48
VISCOSITY, lowest 82
VISION, most acute (bird) 38
VOCABULARY, richest 87
VOICE, highest, lowest 25, longest ranged 26
VOLCANO, total number, greatest erup-
tion, greatest explosion, highest extinct,
highest dormant, highest active, northern-
most, southernmost, largest crater 55
VOLLEYBALL, 301
VOTE, largest parliamentary monetary 181,
fewest received by Parliamentary candidate
190
VOWELS, language with most, least 88
VOYAGE, longest by sailing boat 162

WAIST, smallest 22
WAITING ROOM, railway, largest 136
WALKING, in space 72, endurance records
166, on stilts 173, on hands 174, track records
301–302
WALL, longest world, Britain 122
WALRUS, see Pinnipeds
WAR, longest 191, shortest, bloodiest, worst
battle, most costly, bloodiest battle on British
soil, greatest invasions, largest armed forces
192, greatest naval battle, evacuation 193
WAREHOUSES, largest world, U.K. 109
WARSHIP, largest 127, fastest 128
WASP, smallest, smallest eggs 43
WATCH, oldest, most expensive, smallest
146
WATER, Fresh, biggest consumers 214
WATER POLO, 302
WATER SKI-ING, 302–304
WATER SPEED RECORDS, 162
WATER WELL, deepest world, Britain 124
WATERFALL, highest, greatest, widest,
tallest U.K., Ireland 61
WATERSPOUT, highest world, Britain 65
WATERWAY (inland), longest U.K., arti-
ficial seaway, irrigation canal 116, country
with greatest navigable length, longest navig-
able river 218
WATERWHEEL, largest in British Isles 122
WAVE, highest, highest and fastest seismic
56
WEALTH, individual 175–177, National 209
WEATHER, records 63–65
WEB, largest 42
WEED, worst 52
WEIGHT GAIN AND LOSS, greatest 17
WEIGHTLIFTING, 304–305
WEIGHT-MEASURE, earliest 81
WELL, deepest oil, world, British, deepest
water 124
WETTEST PLACE, world, U.K., Ireland,
annual mean 64
WHALE, largest, heaviest 28–29, greatest
recorded depth 29, longest lived, heaviest
brain 30
WHALE FACTORY SHIP, largest 129
WHEAT, largest field 158, record yield 159
WHELKS, eating record 178
WHIP, longest cracked 174

"WHITE" CHRISTMAS, most recent 65
WHITE HORSE, oldest in Britain 121
WHO'S WHO, youngest entrant, longest
entry 181
WIG, largest 158
WILL, shortest, longest 198, greatest in
U.K., Ireland 176–177
WIND-SPEED, highest surface 64
WIND-TUNNEL, largest, most powerful 83
WINDIEST PLACE, 64
WINDMILL, earliest recorded, oldest still
complete, largest in England 122
WINDOW, largest 122, stained glass: oldest,
largest 224
WINE, most expensive, largest bottles 76
WINE CELLAR, largest 112
WING AREA, greatest (bird) 36
WING BEAT, fastest (bird) 37, fastest,
slowest (insect) 43
WING-SPAN, longest (bird) 36, (Airplane)
139
WINTER, earliest severe, worst in Britain 63
WIRE, high and low, acrobatic feats 175
WIRE-JUGGLING, acrobatic feats 175
WIRE ROPE, longest 145
WIRELESS, see Radio
WOMAN, tallest 14–15, shortest 15, heaviest 16, oldest 18–19, reproductivity 19–22,
smallest waists 22, longest necks 23, longest
coma, lowest temperature, latest post mortem
delivery 24, first cosmonaut 71, greatest altitude 161, fastest 161–162, highest climb 164,
longest swim 166, longest delayed parachute
drop, piano playing record 171, submergence
and underwater distance record 173, richest,
best dressed 176, most titles 178, leading air
ace 179, greatest surplus, shortage 186,
earliest M.P.s 191
WONDERS OF THE WORLD, Seven 119
WOOD, heaviest, lightest 50
WOOD-CUTTING, world record, sawing
174
WOODEN SHIP, largest 130
WOOL, highest price 160
WORD, oldest English 87, longest world and
other languages 88, longest English, longest
palindrome, commonest, most accents, most
unpronounceable, longest anagram 89
WORKING CAREER, longest 167
WORKING WEEK, longest 167
WORLD CUP (Football), records 259–260
WORLD RECORD BREAKER (SPORT),
youngest 226
WORM, longest earthworm 44, longest
ribbon 45
WRANGLER, Senior, order of 218–219
WRECK, largest ship 130
WRESTLING, 306
WRIST WATCH, earliest, most expensive
146
WRITER, most prolific, short stories, fastest
novelist, highest paid, top-selling 92, young-
est 92–93
WRITING, smallest hand 90
WRITING PAPER, most expensive 158

X-RAY, largest 80

YACHT, largest ice 276, largest 307
YACHTING, Atlantic crossing 163
YARD-ARM, last execution 202
YAWNING, most persistent 25
YEW, oldest, tallest 49, tallest hedge 52
YO-YO, most difficult trick, endurance
record, group marathon 174

ZINC, largest mine, smelter 125
ZIGGURAT, largest 120
ZOO, largest, largest collection, oldest,
oldest privately owned, most comprehensive
in U.K., greatest attendances, most valuable
animal 53

Photograph Credits

The numbers refer to pages on which the photographs appear

PROGRESSIVE HUMAN ALTITUDE RECORDS

Metres	Feet	Pilot	Vehicle	Place	Date
25	84	Jean François Pilâtre de Rozier (France)	Hot Air Balloon (tethered)	Fauxbourg, Paris	15 & 17 Oct. 1783
64	210	J. F. Pilâtre de Rozier (France)	Hot Air Balloon (tethered)	Fauxbourg, Paris	19 Oct. 1783
80	262	J. F. Pilâtre de Rozier (France)	Hot Air Balloon (tethered)	Fauxbourg, Paris	19 Oct. 1783
98·75	324	de Rozier and Girand de Villette (France)	Hot Air Balloon (tethered)	Fauxbourg, Paris	19 Oct. 1783
c. 100	c. 330	de Rozier and the Marquis François-Laurent d'Arlandes (1742–1809) (France)	Hot Air Balloon (free flight)	La Muette, Paris	21 Nov. 1783
c. 600	c. 2,000	Dr. Jâcques-Alexandre-César Charles (1746–1823) and Ainé Robert (France)	Charlière Hydrogen Balloon	Tuileries, Paris	1 Dec. 1783
c. 2 750	c. 9,000	J. A. C. Charles (France)	Hydrogen Balloon	Nesles, France	1 Dec. 1783
c. 4 000	c. 13,000	James Sadler (G.B.)	Hydrogen Balloon	Manchester	May 1785
c. 6 100	c. 20,000	E. G. R. Robertson (U.K.) and Loest (Germany)	Hydrogen Balloon	Hamburg, Germany	18 July 1803
7 000	22,965	Joseph Louis Gay-Lussac (France)	Hydrogen Balloon	Paris	15 Sept. 1804
c. 7 620	c. 25,000	Charles Green, Edward Spencer (G.B.)	Coal Gas Balloon *Nassau*	Vauxhall, London	24 July 1837
7 740	25,400[1]	James Glaisher (U.K.)	Hydrogen Balloon	Wolverhampton	17 July 1862
8 520	27,950	H. T. Sivel, J. E. Crocé-Spinelli, Gaston Tissandier (only survivor)	Coal Gas Balloon *Zénith*	La Villette, Paris	15 April 1875
9 615	31,500	Prof. A. Berson (Germany)	Hydrogen Balloon *Phoenix*	Strasbourg, France	4 Dec. 1894
10 800	35,433	Prof. Berson and Dr. R. J. Süring (Germany)	Hydrogen Balloon *Preussen*	Berlin, Germany	30 June 1901
11 145	36,565	Sadi Lecointe (France)	Nieuport Aircraft	Issy-les-Moulineaux, France	30 Oct. 1923
12 945	42,470[2]	Capt. Hawthorne C. Gray (U.S.A.)	Hydrogen Balloon	Scott Field, Illinois	4 May 1927
12 945	42,470	Capt. Hawthorne C. Gray (U.S.A.)	Hydrogen Balloon	Scott Field, Illinois	4 Nov. 1927
13 157	43,166	Lt. Appollo Soucek (U.S.A.)	U.S. Navy Wright *Apache*	Washington, D.C.	4 June 1930
15 837	51,961	Prof. Auguste Piccard (Switzerland) and Paul Kipfer	*F.N.R.S. I* Balloon	Augsburg	27 May 1931
16 196	53,139	Piccard & Dr. Max Cosyns (Belgium)	*F.N.R.S. I* Balloon	Dübendorf, nr. Zürich	18 Aug. 1932
18 500	60,695[3]	G. Profkoviev, F. N. Birnbaum and K. D. Godunov (U.S.S.R.)	Army Balloon *U.S.S.R.*	Moscow, U.S.S.R.	30 Sept. 1933
18 665	61,237	Lt.-Col. T. G. W. Settle, U.S.N. and Major Chester L. Fordney, U.S.M.C.	Hydrogen Balloon *Century of Progress*	Akron, Ohio	20 & 21 Nov. 1933
22 000	72,178[4]	Raul F. Fedoseyenko, A. B. Vasienko and E. D. Ususkin (U.S.S.R.)	*Osaviakhim* Balloon	Moscow, U.S.S.R.	30 Jan. 1934
22 060	72,377	Capts. Orvill A. Anderson and Albert W. Stevens (U.S. Army)	U.S. *Explorer II* Helium Balloon	Rapid City, South Dakota, U.S.A.	11 Nov. 1935
24 230	79,494	William B. Bridgeman (U.S.A.)	U.S. Douglas D558-II *Skyrocket*	California, U.S.A.	15 Aug. 1951
25 370	83,235	Lt.-Col. Marion E. Carl, U.S.M.C.	U.S. Douglas D558-II *Skyrocket*	California, U.S.A.	21 Aug. 1953
c. 28 350	c. 93,000	Major Arthur Murray (U.S.A.F.)	U.S. *Bell X-1A* Rocket 'plane	California, U.S.A.	4 June 1954
38 465	126,200	Capt. Iven C. Kincheloe, Jnr. (U.S.A.F.)	U.S. *Bell X-2* Rocket 'plane	California, U.S.A.	7 Sept. 1956
41 605	136,500	Major Robert M. White (U.S.A.F.)	U.S. *X-15* Rocket 'plane	California, U.S.A.	12 Aug. 1960
51 694	169,600	Joseph A. Walker (U.S.A.)	U.S. *X-15* Rocket 'plane	California, U.S.A.	30 Mar. 1961